DATE DUE

DEMCO 38-296

MODERN COMMERCIAL PAPER:
the new law of negotiable instruments (and related commercial paper)

Steve H. Nickles
Roger F. Noreen Chair in Law
University of Minnesota Law School

John H. Matheson
Professor of Law
University of Minnesota Law School

Edward S. Adams
Associate Professor
University of Minnesota Law School

American Casebook Series

West Publishing Company
ST. PAUL, MINN., 1994

PRINTED ON 10% POST CONSUMER RECYCLED PAPER

With Much Affection And Gratitude,
Dedicated To

———————

*My Teachers, Milton Copeland, Robert A. Leflar
and Albert M. Witte*

S.H.N.

My Wife, Judy

J.H.M..

*My Parents, Ed and June Adams, and to
Aunt Dorothy and Uncle Bud*

E.S.A.

Acknowledgements

We thank the authors and publishers who have permitted us to reproduce portions of the following copyrighted works.

The American Law Institute and the National Conference of Commissioners on Uniform State Laws: Restatement (Second) of Contracts (1981); Restatement of Restitution (1937); Restatement of Security (1941); Uniform Consumer Credit Code, 1974 Official Text; Uniform Commercial Code, 1990 Official Text; Uniform Commercial Code, 1989 Official Text; Uniform Commercial Code, 1952 Official Text.

William E. Britton, HANDBOOK OF THE LAW OF BILLS AND NOTES (2d ed., West Publishing 1961).

Barkley Clark, THE LAW OF BANK DEPOSITS, COLLECTIONS AND CREDIT CARDS (3d ed., Warren, Gorham & Lamont 1991).

Milton Copeland, *A Statutory Primer: Revised Article 3 of the U.C.C.--Negotiable Instruments*, 1992 ARKANSAS LAW NOTES 65.

John F. Dolan, *Standby Letters of Credit and Fraud (Is the Standby Only Another Invention of the Goldsmiths in Lombard Street?)*, 7 CARDOZO LAW REVIEW 1 (1985).

Grant Gilmore, *The Commercial Doctrine of Good Faith Purchase*, 63 YALE LAW JOURNAL 1057 (1954).

Grant Gilmore, *The Good Faith Purchase Idea and the Uniform Commercial Code: Confessions of a Repentant Draftsman*, 15 GEORGIA LAW REVIEW 605 (1981).

Robert A. Hillman, Julian B. McDonnell & Steve H. Nickles, COMMON LAW AND EQUITY UNDER THE UNIFORM COMMERCIAL CODE (Warren, Gorham & Lamont 1985).

Linda Rusch, Possible Issues to be Addressed in Revision of U.C.C. Article 7, memorandum prepared for the ABA Article 7 Task Force (1993).

Stanley V. Kinyon, *Actions on Commercial Paper: Holder's Procedural Advantages under Article 3*, 65 MICHIGAN LAW REVIEW 1441 (1967).

Note, *Payees as Holders in Due Course of Negotiable Instruments*, 7 FORDHAM LAW REVIEW 90 (1938).

Reade H. Ryan, BANKER'S ACCEPTANCES IN PLI COMMERCIAL LAW AND PRACTICE COURSE HANDBOOK ON LETTERS OF CREDIT AND BANKERS' ACCEPTANCES (Practicing Law Institute 1988).

Stephen L. Sepinuck, *Classifying Credit Card Receivables Under the U.C.C.: Playing With Instruments?*, 32 ARIZONA LAW REVIEW 789 (1990).

J. S. Waterman, *The Promissory Note as a Substitute for Money*, 14 MINNESOTA LAW REVIEW 313 (1930).

R. David Whitaker, *Electronic Documentary Credits*, 46 THE BUSINESS LAWYER 1781 (August 1991).

Preface

The law is largely new. Articles 3 and 4 have been substantially revised. Recognizing this, our book seeks to familiarize and instruct both professors and students alike on the changes in these important provisions. In studying these, and related areas, the text adopts a somewhat different, mildly innovative approach--blending a discussion of the requisite background black-letter law (in the "story" section) with cases (the "law") and problems ("practice"). Much consideration has been given to integrating the three sections in a manner that is eminently logical and easy to teach. The chapters, we believe, can teach the basics by themselves in some places and thereby free class time for wider or more difficult matters. Equally importantly, however, the chapters have not been formulated in a way so as to impair individual instructor preferences. Professors can teach 'a given area using all three sections, only two sections, or even one section. Finally, to encourage the further exploration of topics of interest to students and instructor alike, we have added an annex of supplemental materials in certain selected areas. These materials can be selectively assigned by the professor as he or she chooses.

As one might expect, because of the very recent revision of Articles 3 and 4, the cases are pre-revision decisions. We are very sensitive to the difficulties that might be created by including such decisions (often the only cases in many of the covered areas). Therefore, we have carefully chosen cases under pre-revision law which contain principles sanctioned by the new law.

In the last analysis, our goal throughout this book is a simple one: to achieve a high level of accessibility and clarity in an area which many students find very difficult. We believe that our different format goes a long way toward reaching that goal, and we sincerely hope that you find the materials as enjoyable to use as we did to prepare.

Several of our students helped us, and we thank them very much: Terri Georgin, Claire Taylor-Sherman, Elizabeth Cumming, and Tom Osteraas. They were already good lawyers when they worked with us. Their contributions improved the book itself and our teaching of the subject.

Two very good practicing lawyers also contributed: Susan Barnes of Norwest Bank and Kathleen Wooden Flanagan of First Bank Systems. They are experts on credit card law and advised us on several matters pertaining to the area.

STEVE H. NICKLES
JOHN H. MATHESON
EDWARD S. ADAMS

Summary of Contents

Table of Contents

———

Table of Cases

The principal cases are in bold type. Cases cited or discussed in the text are roman type. References are to pages. Cases cited in principal cases and within other quoted materials are not included.

A

B

D

E

Vaughn v. United States National Bank, 598

W

X

Y

Table of Statutes and Regulations

UNITED STATES CODE ANNOTATED

12 U.S.C.A.-Banks and Banking

STATUTES AT LARGE

POPULAR NAME ACTS

CARRIAGE OF GOODS BY SEA ACT

CONSUMER CREDIT PROTECTION ACT

STATE STATUTES

MINNESOTA STATUTES ANNOTATED

UNIFORM COMMERCIAL CODE (cont'd)

UNIFORM COMMERCIAL CODE (cont'd)

UNIFORM COMMERCIAL CODE (cont'd)

UNIFORM COMMERCIAL CODE (cont'd)

UNIFORM COMMERCIAL CODE (cont'd)

UNIFORM COMMERCIAL CODE (cont'd)

UNIFORM COMMERCIAL CODE (cont'd)

UNIFORM COMMERCIAL CODE (cont'd)

UNIFORM COMMERCIAL CODE (cont'd)

Table of Disposition

TABLE OF DISPOSITION OF SECTIONS IN FORMER ARTICLE 3

The reference to a section in Revised Article 3 is to the section that refers to the issue addressed by the section in Former Article 3. If there is no comparable section in Revised Article 3 to a section in Former Article 3, that fact is indicated by the word "Omitted."

Former Article 3 Section	Revised Article 3 or 4 Section
3-101	3-101
3-102(1)(a)	3-105(a)
3-102(1)(b)	3-103(a)(6)
3-102(1)(c)	3-103(a)(9)
3-102(1)(d)	Omitted See Comment 2 to 3-414
3-102(1)(e)	3-104(b)
3-102(2)	3-103(b)
3-102(3)	3-103(c)
3-102(4)	3-103(d)
3-103(1)	3-102(a)
3-103(2)	3-102(b)
3-104(1)	3-104(a)
3-104(2)(a)	3-104(e)
3-104(2)(b)	3-104(f)
3-104(2)(c)	3-104(j)
3-104(2)(d)	3-104(e)
3-104(3)	Omitted
3-105(1)(a)	3-106(a)
3-105(1)(b)	Omitted See Comment 1 to 3-106
3-105(1)(c)	Omitted See Comment 1 to 3-106
3-105(1)(d)	Omitted See Comment 1 to 3-106
3-105(1)(e)	Omitted See Comment 1 to 3-106
3-105(1)(f)	3-106(b)(ii)
3-105(1)(g)	3-106(b)(ii)
3-105(1)(h)	3-106(b)(ii)
3-105(2)(a)	3-106(a)(ii)
3-105(2)(b)	3-106(b)(ii)
3-106(1)	3-104(a)

Former Article 3 Section	Revised Article 3 or 4 Section
3-106(2)	Omitted
3-107(1)	Omitted See Comment to 3-107
3-107(2)	3-107
3-108	3-108(a)
3-109(1)	3-108(b)
3-109(2)	Omitted
3-110(1)	3-109(b)
3-110(1)(a)	Omitted
3-110(1)(b)	Omitted
3-110(1)(c)	Omitted
3-110(1)(d)	3-110(d)
3-110(1)(e)	3-110(c)(2)(i)
3-110(1)(f)	3-110(c)(2)(iv)
3-110(1)(g)	Omitted
3-110(2)	Omitted
3-110(3)	3-109(b)
3-111(a)	3-109(a)(1)
3-111(b)	3-109(a)(1)
3-111(c)	3-109(a)(3) and 3-205(b)
3-112(1)(a)	Omitted
3-112(1)(b)	3-104(a)(3)(i)
3-112(1)(c)	3-104(a)(3)(i)
3-112(1)(d)	3-104(a)(3)(ii)
3-112(1)(e)	3-104(a)(3)(iii)
3-112(1)(f)	3-311
3-112(1)(g)	Omitted
3-112(2)	Omitted
3-113	Omitted
3-114(1)	Omitted See Comment to 3-113
3-114(2)	3-113(a)
3-114(3)	Omitted See Comment to 3-113
3-115	3-115
3-116(a)	3-110(d)
3-116(b)	3-110(d)
3-117(a)	3-110(c)(2)(ii)
3-117(b)	3-110(c)(2)(i)
3-117(c)	Omitted
3-118(a)	3-104(e) and 3-103(a)(6)
3-118(b)	3-114
3-118(c)	3-114
3-118(d)	3-112
3-118(e)	3-116(a)
3-118(f)	Omitted
3-119	3-117 and 3-106(a) and (b)

Former Article 3 Section	Revised Article 3 or 4 Section
3-304(4)(d)	Omitted
3-304(4)(e)	3-307
3-304(4)(f)	3-304(c)
3-304(5)	3-302(b)
3-304(6)	Omitted
3-305(1)	3-306
3-305(2)(a)	3-305(a)(1)(i)
3-305(2)(b)	3-305(a)(1)(ii)
3-305(2)(c)	3-305(a)(1)(iii)
3-305(2)(d)	3-305(a)(1)(iv)
3-305(2)(e)	3-601(b)
3-306(a)	3-306
3-306(b)	3-305(a)(2)
3-306(c)	3-305(a)(2); 3-303(b); 3-105(b)
3-306(d)	3-305(c)
3-307(1)(a)	3-308(a)
3-307(1)(b)	3-308(a)
3-307(2)	3-308(b)
3-307(3)	3-308(b)
3-401(1)	3-401(a)
3-401(2)	3-401(b)
3-402	3-204(a)
3-403(1)	3-402(a)
3-403(2)(a)	3-402(b)(2)
3-403(2)(b)	3-402(b)(2)
3-403(3)	3-402(b)(1)
3-404(1)	3-403(a)
3-404(2)	3-403(a)
3-405(1)(a)	3-404(a)
3-405(1)(b)	3-404(b)(i)
3-405(1)(c)	3-405
3-405(2)	3-403(c)
3-406	3-406
3-407(1)(a)	3-407(a)(i)
3-407(1)(b)	3-407(a)(ii)
3-407(1)(c)	3-407(a)(i)
3-407(2)(a)	3-407(b)
3-407(2)(b)	3-407(b)
3-407(3)	3-407(c)
3-408	3-303(b)
3-409(1)	3-408
3-409(2)	Omitted See Comment 1 to 3-408
3-410(1)	3-409(a)
3-410(2)	3-409(b)

Former Article 3 Section	Revised Article 3 or 4 Section
3-410(3)	3-409(c)
3-411(1)	3-409(d); 3-414(c); 3-415(d)
3-411(2)	3-409(d)
3-411(3)	Omitted
3-412(1)	3-410(a)
3-412(2)	3-410(b)
3-412(3)	3-410(c)
3-413(1)	3-412; 3-413(a)
3-413(2)	3-414(b) and (e)
3-413(3)	Omitted
3-414(1)	3-415(a) and (b)
3-414(2)	Omitted
3-415(1)	3-419(a)
3-415(2)	3-419(b)
3-415(3)	Omitted See 3-605(h)
3-415(4)	3-419(c)
3-415(5)	3-419(e)
3-416(1)	Omitted
3-416(2)	3-419(d)
3-416(3)	Omitted
3-416(4)	3-419(c)
3-416(5)	Omitted
3-416(6)	Omitted
3-417(1)	3-417
3-417(2)	3-416
3-417(3)	Omitted
3-417(4)	Omitted
3-418	3-418
3-419(1)	3-420(a)
3-419(2)	3-420(b)
3-419(3)	3-420(c)
3-419(4)	3-206(c)(4) and (d)
3-501(1)(a)	3-414(b); 3-502(b)(3) and (4)
3-501(1)(b)	3-415(a); 3-502(a)(1) and (2); 3-502(b),(c),(d),(e)
3-501(1)(c)	3-414(f); 3-415(e)
3-501(2)(a)	3-503(a)
3-501(2)(b)	Omitted See Comment 2 to 3-414
3-501(3)	Omitted See Comment to 3-505
3-501(4)	Omitted
3-502(1)(a)	3-415(e)
3-502(1)(b)	3-414(f)
3-502(2)	Omitted See Comment to 3-505
3-503	Omitted See Comment to 3-502
3-504(1)	3-501(a)

Former Article 3 Section	Revised Article 3 or 4 Section
3-504(2)(a)	3-501(b)(1)
3-504(2)(b)	3-501(b)(1)
3-504(2)(c)	3-501(b)(1); 3-111
3-504(3)(a)	3-501(b)(1)
3-504(3)(b)	Omitted
3-504(4)	3-501(b)(1)
3-504(5)	Omitted
3-505(1)(a)	3-501(b)(2)(i)
3-505(1)(b)	3-501(b)(2)(ii)
3-505(1)(c)	Omitted
3-505(1)(d)	3-501(b)(2)(iii)
3-505(2)	Omitted
3-506(1)	Omitted
3-506(2)	Omitted
3-507(1)	3-502
3-507(2)	Omitted
3-507(3)	3-501(b)(3)(i)
3-507(4)	Omitted
3-508(1)	3-503(b)
3-508(2)	3-503(c)
3-508(3)	3-503(b)
3-508(4)	Omitted
3-508(5)	Omitted
3-508(6)	Omitted
3-508(7)	Omitted
3-508(8)	3-503(b)
3-509(1)	3-505(b)
3-509(2)	3-505(b)
3-509(3)	3-505(b)
3-509(4)	Omitted
3-509(5)	Omitted
3-510(a)	3-505(a)(1)
3-510(b)	3-505(a)(2)
3-510(c)	3-505(a)(3)
3-511(1)	Omitted
3-511(2)(a)	3-504(a)(iv)
3-511(2)(b)	3-504(a)(ii), (iv) and (v); 3-504(b)
3-511(2)(c)	3-504(a)(i)
3-511(3)(a)	3-504(a)(ii)
3-511(3)(b)	3-504(a)(ii)
3-511(4)	3-502(f)
3-511(5)	Omitted
3-511(6)	Omitted
3-601(1)	3-601(a)

Former Article 3 Section	Revised Article 3 or 4 Section
3-601(2)	3-601(a)
3-601(3)	Omitted
3-602	3-601(b)
3-603(1)	3-602(a) and (b)
3-603(1)(a)	3-602(b)(2)
3-603(1)(b)	Omitted See 3-206(c)(3)
3-603(2)	Omitted
3-604(1)	3-603(c)
3-604(2)	3-603(b)
3-604(3)	3-603(c)
3-605(1)(a)	3-604(a)(i)
3-605(1)(b)	3-604(a)(ii)
3-605(2)	3-604(b)
3-606(1)(a)	3-605(b) and (c)
3-606(1)(b)	3-605(e)
3-606(2)	Omitted
3-701(1)	Omitted
3-701(2)	Omitted
3-701(3)	Omitted
3-801(1)	Omitted
3-801(2)	Omitted
3-801(3)	Omitted
3-801(4)	Omitted
3-802(1)(a)	3-310(a) and (c)
3-802(1)(b)	3-310(b) and (c)
3-802(2)	Omitted
3-803	3-119
3-804	3-309
3-805	Omitted See Comment 2 to 3-104

MODERN COMMERCIAL PAPER:
the new law of negotiable instruments

Chapter 1. Introduction And Overview: Instruments And Their Negotiability

Within the meaning of Uniform Commercial Code Article 3, a *negotiable instrument* is a signed writing that, in a prescribed form, promises or orders the payment of money. An instrument is a *note* if it promises payment and is a *draft* if it orders payment.

Example 1

a. Debtor borrows money from Bank. Common-law contract obligates her to repay the loan. No writing of any kind is required to establish this obligation or make it enforceable. Nevertheless, Bank will require Debtor to sign a *note* in which Debtor promises to pay Bank, or its order, the total of principal and interest.

b. Debtor owes money to Seller because of a sale of goods. Other Person owes money to Debtor. Debtor orders Other Person to pay Seller or order the amount that Other Person owes Debtor. This order is a *draft* if it is in writing and meets the other requirements of form for an instrument. The draft is a *check* if Other Person is a bank and the order is to pay upon demand. Other Person is not liable on the draft or otherwise to Seller. Debtor, however, is liable on the draft if the instrument is not paid by Other Person. This liability is different from Debtor's obligation under sales law to pay Seller the price of the goods.

In more general and very basic terms, a negotiable instrument is a contract that, because of its form, is governed by special rules of liability. An instrument is also a type of property and is governed by special rules of property which define transfer and the rights of transferees.

These special rules of contract and property are not entirely the same everywhere because the source of law for them is not the same everywhere. The principal law is Uniform Commercial Code (U.C.C. or the Code) Article 3 to which every state subscribes. A new, official uniform version of the statute was approved in 1990 by the National Conference of Commissioners on Uniform State Laws and the American Law Institute (NCCUSL and ALI). At the same time, these organizations approved numerous changes in the official version of Article 4, which contains specialized rules about checking accounts and the collection of checks. The new uniform statutes are known as the 1990 Revised Articles 3 and 4. The states quickly began to enact this new law, but years will pass before it is universally adopted. Moreover, whether a state is quick or slow to enact the 1990 version, the state's old law will continue to govern transactions that predate the effectiveness of the new law.

The two sets of laws are fundamentally alike. They share the same scope and most of the same basic principles of liability and transfer. The new Article 3 mostly clarifies, refines and modernizes the old to make the statute easier to understand and apply. The new Article 4 does the same and, additionally, conforms state law to federal rules about checks.

Substance is affected mainly in two ways, but only piecemeal and not radically. First, in upgrading the law, the new Articles 3 and 4 choose between competing views of how the old statutes handle and decide a variety of issues. Second, but only in a very few places, the new law outright changes the old because of shifts and reversals in underlying policies. Most significant is how the new Article 3 reallocates the risks of employee check fraud between employers and banks. The reallocation favors the banks, as do other changes in the substance of check law.

In form, the new Articles 3 and 4 contain about the same number of sections but the order in which subjects are covered is somewhat different and some matters are consolidated or divided. Thus, the section numbers do not exactly correspond between the old and new statutes. They are close, but not quite the same.

This book targets the new law, the Revised 1990 Article 3. Most of the cases, however, are based on the old law. Using these cases causes no problem of substance because most of them illustrate indelible principles that have not changed. There is a problem of form because the cases speak the language (including the section numbers) of the past. To help you translate, a conversion table is included in the front of the book (Table of Disposition). It lists each section of the old law and reports which provisions of the new law are comparable.

story

Instrument as a kind of contract

Broadly defined, a **contract** is any enforceable promissory obligation, that is, any promise for the breach of which the law gives a remedy. Restatement (Second) of Contracts § 1 (1979). In this sense, every negotiable instrument is a contract. Every instrument embodies either an explicit or implicit promise to pay money according to the terms expressed in the instrument itself and other terms implied by Article 3 and other law. Anyone who signs an instrument thereby makes this promise, and the promise is enforceable solely by force of, and to the extent provided by, Article 3. A common-law basis of validation, such as consideration or reliance, is unnecessary to prima facie liability. In sum, anybody who signs an Article 3 instrument thereby makes, and becomes liable on, a contract to pay the instrument; and the only reason for this liability (or a sufficient reason) is that the writing is in the form of an Article 3 instrument.

In commercial paper law the term **contract liability** is commonly used in referring to the liability that Article 3 imposes on a person for having signed an Article 3 instrument. The nature of this liability varies depending on (1) the kind of instrument that is signed and (2) the capacity in which the person signs it. Article 3 explains this liability and codifies a host of rules that describe, limit, condition, extinguish and otherwise regulate it. You will study the most important of these rules in Chapter 3. An overview of the most fundamental rules appears later in this chapter.

For now, you need only know that there are two basic kinds of instruments -- the **note** and the **draft** -- and four capacities or roles in which a person can sign an instrument -- **maker, drawer, indorser** or **acceptor**. A **note** is an instrument that contains an explicit promise to pay. 3-104(e). The person who creates a note, and makes this promise, is the **maker**, 3-103(a)(5), who ordinarily signs a note in the lower, right-hand corner of the instrument. Not surprisingly, the contract liability of a maker is to pay the note according to its terms. 3-412 & 3-105(c). The maker's promise is ordinarily directed to a specific person(s) named in the instrument, i.e., the **payee**, who is not liable on the instrument unless and until she signs it.

A **draft** is an instrument that orders someone else to pay the payee. 3-104(e). The order is given by the **drawer**, 3-103(a)(3), who issues the draft usually by signing it in the lower-right corner. The person ordered to pay is the **drawee**, 3-103(a)(2), who is usually named in the lower, left-hand corner of the instrument. The drawer implicitly promises to pay the draft, but only if the drawee refuses to do so. See 3-414(b). The drawee is not a signer of the instrument and thus is not liable on it in the role of drawee. If the drawee does sign the draft, she assumes the role of **acceptor**, 3-103(a)(1), and implicitly promises to pay the instrument. 3-413(a). The traditional place for an acceptor's signature is across the face of the instrument. An acceptor's liability, like that of a maker, is not conditioned on someone else refusing to pay the instrument.

An **indorser** on a note or draft promises to pay the instrument only if the maker or drawee-acceptor refuses to do so. 3-415(a). An indorser usually signs an instrument on the back, or in the left or right margin on the face of the instrument. Usually, the only indorser on an instrument is the payee who signs not because the law requires her signature, but because it is demanded by the bank or other person paying or taking the instrument from her.

A **check** is a draft on which the drawee is a bank that is ordered to pay on demand. 3-104(f). The law recognizes two subforms of the check: **cashier's check**, 3-104(g), and **teller's check**, 3-104(h). The law also recognizes the **traveler's check**, 3-104(i), which is always a draft but not always a check.

A **certificate of deposit** is essentially a specialized form of note issued by a bank that is both a receipt for a deposit of money and a promise to repay same. 3-104(j).

Instrument as a form of property

The promise or contract made by a person who signs an instrument is **re-ified** or embodied in the instrument itself. Buried there, too, along with the promisor's obligation to pay money, is a corresponding right to receive the money. This right, in the form of an Article 3 instrument, is valuable property which is freely assignable.

An assignment of the right is ordinarily accomplished by transferring the instrument itself. Usually, the transferor will sign the instrument and in doing so will herself incur contract liability on the instrument for the very reason that she signed it. Moreover, through the transfer process itself, the transferor (whether this person is the original promisee or an assignee) makes certain warranties with respect to the right to payment and the instrument itself. See 3-416 & 3-417. These warranties are implied by Article 3 just as other law implies warranties when other forms of property are transferred, such as the Article 2 warranties that are implied in sales of goods. See 2-312, 2-314 and 2-315. U.C.C. Article 4 provides a very similar, essentially duplicate set of warranties that applies when checks and other items are transferred to and among banks for collection. See 4-207 & 4-208.

This warranty liability is in addition to the contract liability on an instrument that a person incurs by signing it. Warranty liability, however, is not dependent on the transferor having signed the instrument, although the scope of her warranties is affected somewhat by whether or not she signed. Warranty liability is the major means of allocating risks and losses associated with instruments. These risks and losses are explored in Chapter 4, which covers warranties.

A transferee of an instrument can enforce the embodied right to payment against any person(s) who signed it (no matter when or why she signed it) so long as the transferee is entitled to enforce the right. Generally speaking, the law presumes that a transferee is so entitled if she is a **holder** of it. **Holder** is a very important Article 3 concept. In non-technical terms, holder describes a person who is in possession of an instrument showing, on its face, that the person is entitled to payment. The technicalities of holder status are investigated in Chapter 4 as part of a larger discussion about the mechanics of transferring and negotiating instruments. **Negotiation** is a special form of transfer through which a person becomes a holder.

According to the general principle of derivative title, which usually governs the transfer of any kind of property, a transferee acquires only the rights of her transferor. So, by force of this principle, any transferee of an instrument, including a holder, steps into the shoes of the transferor. That is, the transferee cannot enforce the instrument to any greater extent than the transferor. Thus, any third-party claims to the instrument, and any defenses of the promisor(s) to payment, that could be asserted against the transferor can also be asserted against the transferee.

The central doctrine of Article 3, the **holder-in-due-course doctrine**, is a major exception to the general principle of derivative title. The doctrine applies to Article 3 instruments and provides that certain transferees of instruments acquire them (acquire the right to enforce them) free of all claims and most defenses that could have been asserted against the assignor or other prior parties. As a result, Article 3 instruments can be less risky and thus more desirable rights to the payment of money than ordinary contract rights. The transferees who benefit from the holder-in-due-course doctrine are known, not surprisingly, as **holders in due course**. In general terms, a **holder in due course** is a holder of an instrument who took it for value, in good faith and without notice of claims or defenses to the instrument. Most of Chapter 5 is devoted exclusively to the holder-in-due-course doctrine, but the special rights of holders in due course are so important and pervasive that they are mentioned throughout this book.

Types of instruments and how and why they are used

When credit is extended, as when a bank makes a loan or a merchant finances a sale of goods, the creditor earns a right to the payment of money from the debtor. The right exists despite the lack of a writing. Nonetheless, the creditor for evidentiary purposes will want a written memorial of this right, and a statute of frauds may condition the enforceability of the right on the execution of a writing of some kind. See, e.g., 2-201 (statute of frauds for sales of goods). Moreover, a writing facilitates a transfer of the right and also reduces transaction costs. This right is an asset that the creditor may wish to sell for its present value or to use as security for credit extended to her.

If the writing takes a certain form prescribed by Article 3, i.e., if it satisfies Article 3's **requisites of negotiability**, an instrument is thereby created. The person who signs the instrument is liable on the instrument itself simply because she signed it. By transferring the writing, the creditor thereby transfers her right to receive payment of the instrument from the debtor. It is sometimes said, therefore, that in creating an instrument, the process of **reification** occurs, which means that a right is embodied in a writing. In this case, the right is a right to the payment of money.

This liability on the instrument does not necessarily take the place of the debtor's liability, based on other law, for the underlying transaction or obligation between her and the creditor. For example, if the debtor borrowed money from the creditor, the common law obligates the debtor to repay the loan. If the debtor purchased goods on credit, Article 2 obligates her to pay the price when it is due. This common-law or Article 2 obligation persists despite the debtor's execution and delivery of an instrument to the creditor. In other words, taking an instrument for an underlying obligation does not usually discharge the underlying obligation. Rather, the underlying obligation is suspended, 3-310(b), and the instrument gives the creditor another right against the debtor.

You will learn about important connections between liability on an instrument and liability on an obligation that underlies the instrument (e.g., a loan or a credit sale of property or services). Most importantly, discharge of a person's liability on an instrument ordinarily discharges her liability on the underlying transaction. Yet, you must keep in mind that, generally speaking, liability on an instrument is distinct and independent, resting on its own bottom. Indeed, a person who signs an instrument is liable thereon even though no underlying obligation exists, as when a person executes and delivers an instrument as a gift.

Transfer of a right to the payment of money does not require reifying the right in an instrument. Intangible property that exists only in the air is nonetheless transferable by common-law assignment. Yet, when a right to payment of money is represented by an instrument, an assignee is better protected by Article 3, more than the common law protects her, against the risk that the debtor will pay the assignor instead of her; and she is also better protected against the risk that the assignor will make a successive assignment of the right to someone else who may collect the right from the debtor. By the rules of Article 3, no one can safely address a right embodied in an instrument without dealing with the person who holds the instrument.

Reification of a right to payment in an instrument is also attractive because it simplifies collection of the debt. For example, when a credit seller of goods is forced to sue on an intangible right to payment, the creditor must plead and prove all the elements of the debtor's liability under U.C.C. Article 2 and the common law of contracts. The procedure is much easier if the debtor has signed and delivered an instrument to the creditor because, in so doing, the debtor has become liable on the instrument itself. Thus, instead of suing to enforce the debtor's contractual obligation to pay the price, the creditor can enforce the debtor's liability on the instrument, which is established prima facie simply by the holder producing the instrument in court. 3-308(b). In short, reification reduces transaction costs associated with common, ordinary business deals.

All kinds of instruments share basic characteristics, i.e., the 3-104(a) requisites of negotiability, but there are subsets of instruments that differ in use and form. The two basic types of instruments are the **note** and the **draft**. A **note** is most often used as the means of capturing a seller's or lender's right against a debtor when credit is extended. The distinguishing feature of a note is that it contains an explicit promise to pay. 3-104(e). The form of a note can be as simple as this illustration:

> # I promise to pay to Paul Payee, or to his order, the sum of $1,000,000.00.
>
> *Martha M. Maker*

By executing and delivering a note to her creditor, the debtor is said to have "issued" the instrument, 3-105(a), and is referred to as its maker because she is the person who makes the promise expressed in the instrument. The maker's promise or, in old Article 3 terms, her "engagement" is to "pay the instrument according to its tenor [i.e., its terms] at the time of his engagement [i.e., at the time he signed the note]." 3-413(1) (1989 Official Text). In modern terms, the maker is obliged to pay the instrument according to its terms at the time it was issued. 3-412. Because the maker's promise is not conditioned on anyone else refusing to pay the instrument, her contract liability is commonly characterized as **primary**.

The maker's promise initially runs to the **payee** of the note. The payee can easily transfer the note, which normally involves signing the instrument herself as indorser and delivering it to a transferee. By her indorsement, the payee becomes liable on the note, which means that the instrument now embodies two rights, i.e., a right against the maker, 3-412, and a separate right against the indorser. 3-415(a). An indorser's liability on a note or other instrument formalizes her implicit promise to pay the instrument if the maker or other payor refuses to do so. Because an indorser's promise is conditioned on someone else not paying the instrument, her contract liability is commonly characterized as **secondary**.

Example 2

Suppose that M gets a $10,000 loan from P. M agrees to repay the money in one year. By force of the common law of contracts, M is obligated to repay the loan. An instrument is not necessary to make M's obligation to P enforceable. Suppose, however, that P nevertheless requires M to sign an instrument in the form of a note that is payable to P or her order.

a. **M is the maker, and P is the payee. Upon taking possession of the note, P is also its holder. See 1-201(20).**

b. **By signing the note as maker, M becomes obliged to pay the instrument according to its terms at the time she issued it. 3-412. The terms of the note naturally reflect the terms of the loan agreement. So, the note will require M to pay P $10,000 in one year.**

c.   This liability on the note is technically separate from M's liability on the underlying contractual obligation to repay the loan. Yet, until the instrument is due, the underlying obligation is suspended. 3-310(b).

A year later the note becomes due, i.e., matures. M pays the instrument to P, who has kept the note.

d.   By paying the instrument to P, who is the holder of the note, M's liability thereon is discharged, 3-602(a), and for this reason her liability on the underlying obligation is also discharged. 3-310(b)(2).

e.   If M had failed to pay the note, P could have sued M on the instrument and made a prima facie case simply by producing the instrument in court. 3-308(b). Alternatively, P could have sued M on the underlying obligation, which would have been resurrected by M's failure to pay the note. 3-310(b)(3).

Example 3

Suppose that during the one-year term of the note, P finds herself in need of cash. She cannot force M to pay the note earlier because M's obligation on the instrument is defined by its terms, which specify payment in a year. P therefore sells the note to H, or uses it as collateral for a loan to her by H. In the process, P indorses the note and delivers it to H who is now the holder of the instrument and can enforce it against M.

a.   If M fails to pay the note at maturity, H can sue P as the indorser. By signing the instrument as indorser, P becomes obliged to pay the amount of the instrument according to the terms of the instrument at the time it was indorsed. 3-415(a). Dishonor, which is a condition of an indorser's liability, would result from M refusing to pay the note upon presentment, i.e., upon H's demand for payment from M. See 3-502 & 3-501(a). Upon P satisfying the note, her liability thereon would be discharged, and so too her liability on any underlying obligation to H. 3-310(b)(2).

b.   Upon paying H, P would reacquire the note and would once again become the holder of it. M remains liable thereon, and P could enforce the note against M as the maker. Moreover, since M dishonored the instrument, her liability to P on the underlying transaction between the two of them is no longer suspended. So P could chose to sue M on the underlying obligation rather than on the instrument. 3-310(b)(3).

The payee of a note could conceivably use the instrument as a means of paying a debt of her own by transferring the note to her creditor who would collect it from the maker. Usually, however, a draft is used when a person wishes to satisfy her own obligations by having debts owed her, whether or not these debts are reified in instruments, paid to a third person. A draft and a note share the same essential characteristics, and each of them carries a right against the person who issued it. The distinguishing feature of a draft, which sometimes goes by its original name, bill of exchange, is that it expresses an order to pay instead of a promise to pay. 3-104(e). The terminology differs, too: She who issues a draft is said to draw the instrument and thus is labeled the drawer. 3-103(a)(3). The drawee is the person to whom the order in a draft is directed. 3-103(a)(2). This order commands the drawee, who is ordinarily obligated to the debtor, to pay the payee of the instrument, either immediately or at some future time, part or all of the sum that the drawee owes the drawer. Implicit in a draft is the drawer's promise to pay the instrument if the drawee fails to pay as ordered. The drawer's contract liability on the instrument, like that of an indorser, is secondary because her promise to pay is conditioned on someone else not paying the instrument.

Example 4

Suppose that B wishes to buy S's expertly prepared canned briefs of commercial paper cases. B, however, is short of cash. D owes B money, but B has been unable to find D for several days. S volunteers that she has an afternoon class with D and sees D daily. B then reasons that she can pay S for the briefs by having D pay S the sum that D owes B. So B draws a draft ordering D to pay the sum of $15.00, which is the exact price of the briefs and the amount D owes B. B then hands the draft to S.

a. **B is the drawer of the draft, which is a negotiable instrument. Consequently, B has agreed that upon dishonor of the draft, she will pay the amount of the instrument according to its terms at the time it was issued. 3-414(b).**

b. **S is the payee and holder of the draft. D is the drawee, but she is not liable on the instrument because she has not signed it.**

c. **S's taking the draft in exchange for the briefs does not relieve B of B's Article 2 obligation to pay the price of the goods. Rather, this obligation is suspended. 3-310(b).**

In the afternoon, S shows D the draft and asks for payment, as ordered by B. This amounts to presentment of the draft. 3-501(a). Suppose that D refuses to pay the draft.

d. **This refusal amounts to dishonor of the draft. 3-502.**

e. **D is not liable to S on the draft or otherwise. 3-401(a) & 3-408.**

f. **S is not out of luck, however. B is liable on the instrument as drawer, and is still liable on the underlying obligation (Article 2 liability for the price), which sprang back to life when D dishonored the draft.**

Suppose D obeys B's order and pays the draft.

g. **The effect is to discharge B's liability on the instrument and also on the underlying obligation.**

h. **Furthermore, though for reasons beyond Article 3, D's debt to B is eliminated.**

The most common form of the draft is a check, which is an instrument ordering a bank to pay money upon demand. 3-104(f). Here is the familiar form of a typical personal check:

```
                                                              3162
   Darlene Drawer
   Minneapolis, MN                           9/28      19  93

   Pay to the
   order of      University Bookstore                  $  107.00

   One hundred seven & no/100   ------------------------------

   First Drawee Bank
   St. Paul, MN
     For    law books                  Darlene Drawer
```

The relationship between a bank and a depositor is that of debtor and creditor. The bank owes the depositor the balance in her deposit account. When a depositor draws a check against her account, she is ordering the drawee-bank to pay to the person named in the instrument, or in accordance with that person's instructions, part or all of what the bank owes her. If the bank complies with the order, its debt to the depositor is reduced accordingly. If the bank refuses to follow the order, the check is not fully expended because embodied therein is a right against the drawer, 3-414(b), who implicitly promised to pay the instrument herself, personally, if the drawee-bank failed to pay it.

Example 5

B wishes to buy S's expertly annotated copy of the U.C.C. The price is $50.00. B is short of cash, but S agrees to take a check. B draws a check against her checking account at State Bank, and gives the instrument to S in exchange for the U.C.C.

a. **Once again, B is the drawer of the instrument.**

b. **S is the payee and holder. This time, however, State Bank is the drawee.**

State Bank has agreed, by contract with B, to pay checks drawn on her account so long as there are sufficient funds in the account. As it happens, the balance of B's account has dropped to $1.50. So, when S takes the check to State Bank and asks for payment (which is presentment), the Bank refuses to pay, i.e., dishonors the check, due to insufficient funds in the drawer's account.

c. **S can now sue B on the check or on B's Article 2 obligation to pay the price of the goods.**

d. **S cannot sue State Bank which is not liable on the dishonored check , or otherwise, to S.**

Suppose State Bank paid the check, either because B made a quick deposit or because the Bank decided to create an overdraft in B's account.

e. **B's liability on the check and the underlying obligation to S is discharged.**

f. **The amount of the check will be debited against B's account, thereby reducing State Bank's debt to B as represented by the account.**

g. **To the extent that State Bank's payment of the check exceeds the customer's account, an overdraft is created; and the customer is liable, by statute and contract law, for the amount of the overdraft. See 4-401(a).**

A check is a sight or demand instrument, meaning that the drawee is ordered to pay whenever the check is presented to her. A draft, however, can order the drawee to pay at some definite time in the future. In this case, if the instrument is presented before payment is due, the drawee need not pay it to avoid dishonoring the instrument, but can sign the draft and thereby acknowledge her willingness to pay it at maturity. In this fashion a drawee accepts a draft and thus becomes, and has the liability of, an acceptor of the instrument. She thereby becomes obligated on the instrument itself and, like a maker with primary contract liability, must pay the instrument according to its terms at the time of her acceptance. 3-413(a). Customarily, a drawee accepts by signing vertically across the face of the instrument, but a signature anywhere on the instrument -- even on the back of it -- is sufficient as an acceptance. 3-409 comment 2.

Before acceptance, there is no right on the instrument against the drawee. 3-408. Moreover, nothing in Article 3 imposes a duty on a drawee to accept a draft drawn against her. Usually, a drawee accepts a draft because she is committed to do so by an independent agreement between her and the drawer to whom the drawee owes some debt.

Example 6

S agrees to sell goods on a regular basis to B. B will be unable to pay cash for the goods, but S is unwilling to extend credit to B alone. Luckily, B's bank, State Bank, is willing to finance B's purchases from S. So B and State Bank agree that the Bank will accept 60-day drafts drawn against it by B to S's order. The parties use this arrangement, instead of the Bank agreeing to pay drafts or simply making a loan for the purchases, so that the Bank will not actually commit funds before B has had the opportunity to fully inspect the goods.

When S makes a delivery of goods, B will draw a draft to S's order for the price of the shipment. The terms of the draft require payment "60 days after sight," which essentially means 60 days after the draft is presented for acceptance to the drawee, State Bank. S will then present the draft to State Bank, and State Bank -- because of its agreement with B -- will accept the instrument through an officer signing on the face of the draft on behalf of the Bank. (In practice, the draft would be referred to as a banker's acceptance.) S will then hold an instrument on which State Bank is liable as acceptor, and B is liable as drawer.

a.   State Bank's engagement, as acceptor, is to pay the draft when the draft matures, that is, 60 days after the date of acceptance. 3-413(a).

b.   B's obligation is to pay the draft if the instrument is dishonored, i.e., not paid by State Bank at maturity.

c.   If State Bank refuses to accept a draft, the Bank has no liability on the instrument to anyone. Such a refusal, however, will violate the Bank's contract with B, and State Bank will therefore become liable, under contract law, for damages that the breach causes B.

d.   A refusal to accept, or a refusal to pay a draft that has been accepted, would result in dishonor of the instrument. In this event, S could enforce B's liability as drawer of the draft.

e.   When State Bank pays a draft that it has accepted, the Bank is discharged on the instrument and so too is B, who thereby is also discharged on her underlying obligation to S for the goods.

Because a check is a demand instrument, the drawee-bank does not accept the item and thus does not become liable thereon. Consequently, a bank that fails for whatever reason to pay a check as ordered by the drawer has no liability on the instrument to anyone. The bank for other reasons may be liable, however, such as for having violated a duty to the drawer or another person that is imposed by contract or by the law governing the collection of checks. The principal source of check collection law is Uniform Commercial Code Article 4, which is the principal subject of Chapter 6.

Example 7

Refer back to Example 5, and suppose that B had a balance of $500 in her account with State Bank when S presented the check for payment.

a.   In this event, State Bank's refusal to pay the check would have been a breach of its contract with B, and the Bank would have been liable to B. Indeed, Article 4 gives B a statutory cause of action in such a case for wrongful dishonor. See 4-402.

b. Yet, despite this wrong, State Bank incurred no liability to S. The Bank, as drawee, was not liable on the instrument, and in this kind of case no law apart from Article 3 creates liability in favor of the holder of the check.

A draft, like a note, is transferable. The payee of a draft thus can use the instrument as a means of satisfying or securing a debt of her own by transferring the draft, usually with her indorsement, to her creditor. The creditor would acquire the right against the drawer which is embodied in the instrument, 3-414(b), and also would become the beneficiary of the drawer's order that the drawee pay the instrument according to its terms. Moreover, the creditor's right against the payee would be added to the draft as a result of the payee's indorsement. 3-415(a). This entire bundle of rights, in turn, could be transferred again and again by successive transferees. Each of them would acquire an ever lengthening chain of obligors, any one of whom could be forced, as an indorser, to make good on the instrument should the drawee refuse to pay it as ordered by the drawer.

If, as is more likely, the drawee complies with the order and pays the draft to a person properly entitled to payment, all of the rights embodied therein are satisfied in seriatim; the liability of each party on the instrument concomitantly is discharged; and the instrument expires. 3-602(a). The same result follows when a note with a string of indorsements is paid to a proper party by its maker. Moreover, discharge from liability on an instrument ordinarily extinguishes the person's correlative liability on the underlying obligation. 3-310(b).

Example 8

Refer back to Example 6. Suppose that S cannot afford to hold the drafts for 60-day periods. She needs money sooner for the goods she has sold B. S can sell the drafts or use them as collateral for a loan, just as P in Example 3 could similarly use the note she took in loaning money to M. The process for S to transfer the drafts would be the same as P followed in transferring the note. So S might sell or pledge the drafts to National Bank by indorsing and delivering the instruments to National Bank.

a. The drafts are backed by the liabilities of B as drawer, State Bank as acceptor, and S as indorser.

b. State Bank's liability is primary.

c. In their roles, B and S are secondarily liable. The engagement of each is to pay the instrument if State Bank dishonors it upon maturity.

d. When State Bank pays a draft to National Bank, the effects are to discharge State Bank, B and S on the instrument and to discharge their underlying obligations.

The least common instrument is a certificate of deposit (CD). It is unlike a check or other draft and is rather a form of note. A CD that satisfies Article 3's requisites of negotiability is an instrument containing neither a promise nor an order. Rather, it contains a bank's acknowledgment of receipt of a sum of money and a promise to repay the money. 3-104(j). In practice, a CD represents a special form of a deposit account. The depositor cannot reach the account by check, and can usually recover the account only after a specified period of time rather than upon demand. Functionally, therefore, a CD is like the bank's note to its depositor in which the bank implicitly promises to pay the amount of the CD when the instrument becomes due.

Little is said about CDs in this book because, in real life, negotiable CDs i.e., CDs that are Article 3 instruments, are very rare. More common are CDs in nonnegotiable form. Increasingly, CDs are maintained as electronic, book-entry accounts that are uncertificated. Even when a certificate is issued, its terms commonly declare that the writing is "NON-NEGOTIABLE." Such a declaration violates Article 3's requisites of negotiability (see 3-104(a)) and thereby precludes negotiability under Article 3. So, even if the writing carries the legend "Certificate of Deposit," it is not an Article 3 instrument.

The significance of instruments -- especially negotiability

Drafts (a/k/a bills of exchange) and notes are not recent inventions. Both kinds of instruments were developed hundreds of years ago to satisfy the needs of trade. To serve those needs in England, instruments were forced to struggle for freedom from the conventions of ordinary contracts.

CHITTY ON BILLS OF EXCHANGE AND PROMISSORY NOTES 1-7
(11th ed. J. Russell 1878)

History, Properties, and Classification of Bills. The origins of bills of exchange, as of many other inventions in daily use, and of great practical value, are so involved in obscurity, that we have nothing better than the conjectures of distinguished writers, as to the age or the country to which we are indebted for this instrument of commerce. Pothier finds no trace of it among the ancient Romans, and adduces the language of Papinian in connection with the law *de nautico foenore*, as positive evidence that it was at that time unknown in the empire. Montesquieu, and others who have followed him, attribute the invention to the Jews, as an expedient which they used when driven from France by Philip II., and again by Philip V., to recover the effects which they had left behind them; but the author of the Commentaries disputes this opinion, on grounds which appear to him to be satisfactory. And in a recent case it was said, that bills of exchange were first brought into use, so far as is at present known, by the Florentines in the twelfth, and by the Venentians in the thirteenth century.

We have the evidence in our own Statute Book, that bills were in use with the English merchant about the middle of the fourteenth century; but of the precise time at which this species of contract was first introduced into this country, we have no record. There is, however, no doubt that it originated in this, as in other countries, from the necessities of foreign trade. It derived its form and properties entirely from the custom on merchants; and although, as early as the reign of Richard II., there is mention of bills of exchange on the Rolls of Parliament, yet it is not till the time of James I., that we have any mention of them in the regular Reports. For many years after this time, they were still viewed by our courts as restricted to the purposes of foreign commerce; and bills drawn by and upon persons resident in England, or what we now call inland bills, came for the first time before the courts at Westminster within the memory of Lord Holt, *i.e.*, not much earlier than the reign of Charles II. Even then, however, the introduction of inland bills was regarded by the judicial bench as so great an innovation, that the pleader was obliged to allege a special custom between the towns, or in the town where the drawer and drawee resided, in order to justify such a transaction, as one resident Englishman drawing a bill upon another; whilst a further restriction confined the privilege of being parties to inland bills, to such only as were merchants. But these restraints gradually yielded to the wants and convenience of society: and now any one capable of making a contract, is competent in this country to be a party to a bill of exchange.

Much of the distrust with which inland bills of exchange were regarded in our Courts, is attributable to certain properties peculiar to those instruments, which were derived from the custom of merchants, and were alien to the spirit and opposed to the rules of the common law. We refer chiefly to the assignable quality of a bill of exchange, and to the presumption which the law makes in its favour, that it is founded on a good consideration.

1st. That which distinguishes a bill of exchange, in respect of its assignable quality, is, that though it be a *chose in action*, it may yet be assigned so as to vest the interest therein, legal as well as equitable, in the indorsee or assignee, and to entitle him to sue thereon in his own name. This peculiar property, now so familiar to every one, was in direct opposition to the rule of the common law, which refused to sanction the assignment of a *chose in action*, that is, of any mere right of suit with regard to property, real or personal.

And although this doctrine was not adopted by the Courts of equity, and even the Courts of law so far sanctioned such assignments, that they took notice of the equitable interest of the assignee, still they steadily adhered to the formal objection, that the assignee of a *chose in action* must sue thereon, not in his own name, but in the name of the assignor. Notwithstanding this rule, however, the assignable quality of bills of exchange, which had already been established by the custom of merchants, came, with the gradual adoption into the common law of the law-merchant, to be recognized by our Courts. And it is now settled law, that any one who, by a genuine indorsement, or, when it is payable to bearer, by delivery, becomes holder of a bill or note, may sue thereon in his own name.

2nd. The other property which distinguishes bills of exchange is, that, although they are contracts not under seal, they are always presumed to have been made upon a good consideration, until the contrary is shown.

Contracts, as known to the law of England, are of three kinds: contracts of record; contracts under seal, or specialties; and simple contracts, or contracts not under seal: and, considered in relation to our present subject, they may be briefly thus described. Contracts or obligations of record, such as judgments or recognizances, are, as the name implies, of record in a Court of Record, and are therefore of the highest authority and force; a consideration is not necessary to render them binding; and they cannot be impeached, even for error apparent on the face of them, in any action which is founded upon them. So, contracts under seal have always been held, on account of the deliberation with which they are supposed to be made and executed, to bind the parties executing them, although they were not founded on any consideration; whilst simple contracts, whether reduced to writing or not, must be founded on a good, *i.e.*, on a *valuable* consideration; and if there be no such consideration, there is no binding contract, but a mere *nudum pactum*, which cannot be enforced at law or in equity.

In this respect, however, bills and notes are distinguished from all other simple contracts. For it is a presumption of law, that they are founded on good consideration; and it is only when a contrary presumption is raised by evidence of fraud or illegality, that the plaintiff can be called on to prove, that he gave consideration for the bill or note on which he sues.

3rd. But although a bill or note is a *chose in action*, still it falls for some purposes within the designation of "goods and chattels." Thus the gift of a bill or note, payable to order, is good as a *donatio mortis causa*, although it be not indorsed by the donor. * * * So, a bill or note may be taken under an extent, or in execution. * * *"

By the law of England bills of exchange are distinguished into two classes, namely, foreign [or outland] and inland [or domestic]; and there is this chief difference made with regard to them in this country, that a protest for dishonour is indispensable in the case of a foreign bill, but in the case of an inland bill it is unnecessary.

1st. Foreign [or outland] bills are those which are drawn by a person abroad, upon a person in England, or *vice versa*, or where both the drawer and drawee are resident in a foreign country.

2nd. The geographical limits within which bills are regarded as inland [or domestic], have been extended by modern statutes. Before the passing of the statutes referred to, a bill was deemed to be an inland bill, when both the drawer and the drawee were resident in England, or in that part of the United Kingdom where the bill was drawn and payable. So that a bill drawn in Ireland upon England, was not an inland but a foreign bill.

But by the statutes for assimilating the mercantile laws of the United Kingdom, it was enacted, that "Every bill of exchange or promissory note, drawn or made in any part of the United Kingdom of Great Britain and Ireland, the Islands of Man, Guernsey, Jersey, Alderney, and Sark, and the islands adjacent to any of them, being part of the dominions of Her Majesty, and made payable or drawn upon any person resident in any part of the said United Kingdom or Islands, shall be deemed to be an inland bill."

J. STORY, COMMENTARIES ON THE LAW OF PROMISSORY NOTES §§ 5 & 6
(7th ed. J. Thorndike 1878)

Origin of Notes. The origin of promissory notes is quite as obscure as that of bills of exchange. There is no doubt that promissory notes in writing (*chirographa*) were well known and in use among the Romans. * * * But this instrument never seems to have been known as a negotiable instrument among the Romans, or as a general medium used in purchases and sales, with that superadded quality; but its negotiability seems to be exclusively the invention of modern times. Probably the origin of promissory notes is somewhat later than that of bills of exchange, and grew out of the same general causes as the later, viz., to facilitate the operations of commerce, and to extend the negotiability of debts. Mr. Kyd's remarks on this subject seem at once well founded and satisfactory, at least as conjectures. "As commerce," he says, "advanced in its progress, the multiplicity of its concerns required, in many instances, a less complicated mode of payment than by bills of exchange. A trader, whose situation and circumstances rendered credit from the merchant or manufacturer, who supplied him with goods, absolutely necessary, might have so limited a connection with the commercial world at large that he could not easily furnish his creditor with a bill of exchange on another man. But his own responsibility might be such, that his simple promise of payment, reduced to writing for the purpose of evidence, might be accepted with equal confidence as a bill on another trader. Hence, it may reasonably be conjectured, promissory notes were at first introduced."

Undoubtedly, negotiable promissory notes were well known upon the continent of Europe, long before their introduction into England. They were, probably, first brought into use in England about the middle of the 17th century, although Lord Holt has been thought to assign to them a somewhat later origin. They seem at first to have been called bills of debt, or bills of credit, indifferently. Indeed, as Lord Mansfield has observed, there seems much confusion in the reports in the times of King William and Queen Anne, so that it is difficult, without consulting the records, to ascertain whether the action arose upon a bill or note, as the words "bill" and "note" were used promiscuously. There was a long struggle in Westminster Hall, as to the question whether promissory notes were negotiable or not at the common law; for there could be no doubt that they were by the law merchant, at least as recognized upon the continent of Europe. Lord Holt most strenuously, and with a pride of opinion not altogether reconcilable with his sound sense and generally comprehensive views, maintained the negative. The controversy was finally ended by the statute of 3 & 4 Anne, c. 9 (1705), which * * * proceeded to enact, "That all notes in writing * * * that shall be made and signed by any person or persons * * * whereby such person or persons * * * doth or shall promise to pay to any other person or persons * * * or their order, or unto bearer, any sum of money mentioned in such note * * * shall be assignable or indorsable over, in the same manner as inland bills of exchange are or may be, according to the custom of merchants; and that the person or persons * * * to whom such sum of money is or shall be by such note made payable, shall and may maintain an action for the same, in such manner as he, she, or they might do upon any inland bill of exchange, made or drawn according to the custom of merchants, against the person or persons * * *." In most of the states of America, this statute has been either expressly adopted by statute, or recognized as part of their common law.

□□□□□

Today, the principal advantages of an instrument spring from its negotiability, which is an exceptional concept of great importance in the law generally. In the law of commercial paper, negotiability refers to

a concept designating a group of legal characteristics of certain commercial instruments, such as assignability, which confers on the assignee the power to sue upon the instrument in his own name, the immunity of certain holders of such instruments from claims of ownership, the immunity of certain holders from equities of defense of prior parties on their contractual liability, and a presumption of consideration.

J. S. Waterman, *The Promissory Note as a Substitute for Money*, 14 MINN. L. REV. 313, 318 (1930). In effect, negotiability makes it possible for a transferee of property to acquire rights therein that are better or greater than the rights of the transferor.

Property is not generally negotiable in the sense that a transferee's rights exceed those of the transferor. Rather, the general rule, that applies throughout the law to every kind of property, is that title is derivative, which means that a transferor of property can ordinarily convey nothing more or better than her own rights in the property. Even the most innocent of bona fide purchasers for value acquires nothing more.

An expression of this very basic general rule, which pervades the whole of English and American property law, is the first sentence of 2-403(1): "A purchaser of goods acquires all title which his transferor had or had power to transfer * * *," and acquires nothing more. The Code codifies this rule of derivative title not only in Article 2, but also in Article 2A concerning leases of goods (2A-304(1) & 2A-305(1)), Article 7 on documents of title (7-504(1)), Article 8 governing investment securities (8-301(1)), and Article 9 governing secured transactions (9-201, 9-306(2) & 9-318(1)).

The principle of derivative title generally applies not only to transfers of tangible property, but also to assignments of intangibles of all types. When applied to contract rights, the principle is commonly restated as this familiar maxim: An assignee steps into the shoes of the assignor. For this reason, an assignee is subject to whatever claims and defenses the obligor has against the assignor. 9-318(1); Restatement (Second) of Contracts §336 (1979).

The derivative title rule generally applies as well to transfers of intangible rights that have been reified in Article 3 instruments. Uniform Commercial Code Article 3 declares that a transferee of an instrument gets only her transferor's rights. 3-203(b). Article 3 also confirms that, in most respects, a mere transferee of an instrument stands in the shoes of the transferor. 3-305(a) & 3-306.

The rule of derivative title is an essential attribute of an economic-legal-social system such as ours which recognizes, protects and even sanctifies private ownership of property. Yet, our society is mercantilistic, as well as capitalistic; and a rule which fails to protect innocent purchasers does little, if anything, to promote society's interests in fostering trade and commerce. Imagine the effects on business if, in order to guarantee good title, buyers of goods and other personal property from merchants were required to investigate the chain of ownership as they do when purchasing real estate; and imagine a marketplace where merchants cannot assume that they receive good title to money paid by buyers of their products. Competing policy goals thus sometimes override the desire to protect property rights. For example, the heart of Article 9 are its priority rules that describe circumstances when third parties' claims can beat a prior security interest which, ordinarily, would be superior because of derivative title.

Similarly, the very heart of Article 3 is a most important exception to the rule of derivative title known as the holder-in-due-course doctrine. "Holder in due course" is the name Article 3 gives a holder of a negotiable instrument who takes the instrument for value, in good faith, and without knowledge of any claim or defense to it. See 3-302(a). Such a person acquires the instrument free from all adverse claims and free also from virtually all defenses to its enforcement, including claims and defenses that could have been asserted against the holder's transferor. See 3-305(b) & 3-306. It is a balancing of policies:

> It is, of course, true that the maker of a negotiable instrument may suffer hardship because he is unable to assert against a holder in due course valid

defenses he might have against the payee or any subsequent holder not a holder in due course. The possibility of that consequence should be envisaged by one who executes negotiable paper. It is a consequence he may suffer, however, whether or not he anticipates it; for the law regards the security of negotiable instruments in the hands of holders who took for value before maturity without notice of infirmities or defects as of far greater importance than the preservation of the defenses of those who executed them.

Tucker v. Meredith, 232 F.2d 347, 350-51 (D. D.C. 1956).

Near the bottom of the modern law supporting the holder-in-due-course doctrine are two ancient cases: *Miller v. Race,* 97 Eng.Rep. 398 (K.B.1758) and *Peacock v. Rhodes,* 99 Eng.Rep. 402 (K.B.1781). Through these cases the common law conferred negotiability on notes and drafts in order to accommodate business and economic needs. A question you should consider throughout this part of the book is how far the reasoning of these cases continues to sustain modern applications of the principle. In the *Miller* case, Lord Mansfield imputed negotiability to Bank of England notes because they were treated as cash and so that "their currency should be established and secured." Protecting the currency of drafts was the only stated basis of the result in *Peacock.* Is protecting the currency of notes and drafts as important today as it was in the 18th century? Is any kind of modern instrument likely to be transferred as many times among as many strangers as was the draft in *Peacock,* which had circulated among a small crowd before being stolen from the holder. It ended up finally in the hands of a person who did not know the payors but who successfully enforced the instrument against them.

A personal check, which is a variant of the draft, is certainly not so well traveled. Moreover, hardly anyone treats personal checks as cash in the sense of relying on them as indisputable and undeniable obligations of the issuer. Trade and commerce seem not to suffer from the public's mistrust of personal checks.

Furthermore, with respect to cutting off defenses to the payment of instruments, the situation of the eighteenth century taker of commercial paper is very different from that of the modern financing assignee, such as the bank in the foregoing problem that purchased the farmer's note for the price of a tractor. Consider this:

In the late eighteenth century, mercantile bills of exchange and bank notes, a sort of unofficial currency which the merchants and bankers had invented, served as an indispensable supplement to the official currencies, which were in short supply. Without these bills and notes, the primitive banking system could not possibly have coped with the enormously increased number of transactions that followed the industrial revolution. This commercial paper typically passed from hand to hand in a long series of transfers, ending up in the hands of strangers who knew nothing about the original transaction or about earlier transfers of the bill or note and had no way of finding out about them. The need to protect the strangers who bought the paper in the market, even at the cost of doing harm to the obligors and earlier holders, was the compelling reason that led the courts to elaborate the good faith purchaser, or holder in due course, idea in negotiable instruments law.

> [T]he twentieth-century financing assignee [is] not in the least like the stranger who, one hundred and fifty years earlier, had bought goods, commercial paper, and other property in an open market without being able to find out about the prior history of whatever he bought. The financing assignee, who serves a useful function in providing working-capital loans, is not an ignorant stranger. He is in a position to find out -- and, before putting up his money, does find out -- all there is to know about the operations of his borrowers. He has a close and continuing relationship with them. He can, if he chooses, require the strictest accounting from them. He does not need to be insulated, as a matter of law, from the risks of the transactions in which they engage. Because he can investigate, supervise, and control, he should be encouraged to do so and penalized if he has not done so.

Grant Gilmore, *The Good Faith Purchase Idea and the Uniform Commercial Code: Confessions of a Repentant Draftsman*, 15 GA. L. REV. 605, 612-13, 626-27 (1981).

Some people argue that the negotiability of instruments is a concept that has outlived widespread usefulness. Indeed, the law has decided rather recently that the goal of consumer protection outweighs the need for negotiability of consumer credit instruments. See the section in Chapter 5, infra, that deals with restrictions on holder-in-due-course rights. On the other hand, instruments are fully negotiable in commercial transactions. Moreover, in all settings -- both commercial and consumer -- instruments continue to serve as major tools for creating and transferring credit that involve a great many important incidents other than negotiability. In fact, the simple check, used repeatedly and routinely every day by consumers and businesses alike, is still a much more common means of payment than electronic banking or credit cards. Thus, there is ample justification for studying Articles 3 and 4.

RESTATEMENT (SECOND) OF CONTRACTS
Chapter 15
Assignment and Delegation

Introductory Note: The subject matter of this Chapter is part of the larger subject of the transfer of intangible property. The historic rule in the common-law courts of England was that a "chose in action" could not be assigned. The scope of that rule was progressively narrowed by the reception into the common law of doctrines developed in the law merchant and in the courts of equity and by statute. Little remains of it today, but modern rules, both decisional and statutory, must often be read in the light of the development.

The law merchant. The law merchant is a tradition with an international and maritime flavor. It was followed in special merchant tribunals in England; during the seventeenth century it became part of the common law of England. Under its influence mercantile instruments such as the bill of exchange were held transferable by delivery, or by indorsement and delivery, and similar rules have been extended in modern times, by decision and by statute, to documents of title and to investment securities. See Uniform Commercial Code Articles 3, 7, 8. The rules governing such instruments are beyond the scope of this Restatement. * * *

Law and equity. Also during the seventeenth century, it was established that an assignment could take effect in the common-law courts as a power of attorney enabling the assignee to sue in the assignor's name, and that courts of equity would protect the assignee in cases of death or bankruptcy of the assignor or revocation by him. During the eighteenth century the common-law courts began to give effect to the equitable rights of the assignee. In the United States[,] statutes generally require actions to be brought in the name of the real party in interest, and the assignee of a contract right can sue in his own name without regard to the distinction between actions at law and suits in equity. * * *

Topic 1. What Can Be Assigned Or Delegated

§ 317. Assignment of a Right

(1) An assignment of a right is a manifestation of the assignor's intention to transfer it by virtue of which the assignor's right to performance by the obligor is extinguished in whole or in part and the assignee acquires a right to such performance. * * *

Topic 2. Mode Of Assignment Or Delegation

§ 324. Mode of Assignment in General

It is essential to an assignment of a right that the obligee manifest an intention to transfer the right to another person without further action or manifestation of intention by the obligee. The manifestation may be made to the other or to a third person on his behalf and, except as provided by statute or by contract, may be made either orally or by a writing.

§ 325. Order as Assignment

(1) A written order drawn upon an obligor and signed and delivered to another person by the obligee is an assignment if it is conditional on the existence of a duty of the drawee to the drawer to comply with the order and the drawer manifests an intention that a person other than the drawer is to retain the performance.

(2) An order which directs the drawee to render a performance without reference to any duty of the drawee is not of itself an assignment, even though the drawee is under a duty to the drawer to comply with the order and even though the order indicates a particular account to be debited or any other fund or source from which reimbursement is expected.

Topic 4. Effect On The Obligor's Duty

§ 336. Defenses Against an Assignee

(1) By an assignment the assignee acquires a right against the obligor only to the extent that the obligor is under a duty to the assignor; and if the right of the assignor would be voidable by the obligor or unenforceable against him if no assignment had been made, the right of the assignee is subject to the infirmity.

(2) The right of an assignee is subject to any defense or claim of the obligor which accrues before the obligor receives notification of the assignment, but not to defenses or claims which accrue thereafter except as stated in this Section or as provided by statute.

(3) Where the right of an assignor is subject to discharge or modification in whole or in part by impracticability, public policy, nonoccurrence of a condition, or present or prospective failure of performance by an obligee, the right of the assignee is to that extent subject to discharge or modification even after the obligor receives notification of the assignment.

(4) An assignee's right against the obligor is subject to any defense or claim arising from his conduct or to which he was subject as a party or a prior assignee because he had notice.

§ 338. Discharge of an Obligor After Assignment

(1) Except as stated in this Section, notwithstanding an assignment, the assignor retains his power to discharge or modify the duty of the obligor to the extent that the obligor performs or otherwise gives value until but not after the obligor receives notification that the right has been assigned and that performance is to be rendered to the assignee. * * *

(4) Where there is a writing of a type customarily accepted as a symbol or as evidence of the right assigned, a discharge or modification is not effective

(a) against the owner or an assignor having a power of avoidance, unless given by him or by a person in possession of the writing with his consent and any necessary indorsement or assignment;

(b) against a subsequent assignee who takes possession of the writing and gives value in good faith and without knowledge or reason to know of the discharge or modification.

IN RE TWO (2) BOSE SPEAKERS
Kansas Court of Appeals, 1992
17 Kan. App.2d 179, 835 P.2d 1385

Gernon, Judge. This is an appeal from a court order to return property, which was pawned but was later seized as evidence, to its original owner.

Jerry King, d/b/a King's Pawn Shop, the appellant, took the property from a thief in exchange for a loan of $90. The pawn ticket indicates that King took the property from L.J. L.J. was never charged with any crime involving the theft of or possession of the property involved. The property was owned by Barbara Garnes, who reported it stolen. A police investigation found the property listed on King's pawn slip, where it was seized by the authorities after King signed a consent to search and a release for the property. * * *

King argues that he was a "purchaser in good faith" and has a possessory interest against the rest of the world, although he admits that "a purchaser under defective title might not hold against the true owner." We agree with King on both counts. The important concept here is that the owner, not the rest of the world, was making the claim against the property.

Even though King is a good faith purchaser for value, he acquired possession from a thief who had void title, not voidable title, and who had no power to divest the original owner of the property.

The regulations governing pawnbrokers also support the conclusion that a pawnbroker cannot acquire title through a thief. The Code of the City of Wichita, Charter Ordinance No. 134, §18 (1991), provides: "When converted or stolen property has been pawned or purchased by a pawnbroker, secondhand dealer, or precious metal dealer and the pawnbroker, secondhand dealer, or precious metal dealer refuses to redeliver such property to the rightful owner upon demand and presentation of a bill of sale or other proper indicia of ownership by the owner, and legal action by the rightful owner to recover the property becomes necessary, the court may assess the pawnbroker, if the court finds that the pawnbroker or secondhand dealer wrongfully withheld the converted or stolen property." Section 11 requires pawnbrokers to keep detailed records of each transaction and provide a daily report listing all property received to the police department. Code of the City of Wichita, Charter Ordinance 134, §11 (1991).

Because the pawnbroker is the one who deals with the thief, he or she should bear the risk of accepting stolen property. The pawnbroker's remedy in this case is to find the thief and recover against the thief for breach of the warranty of title in K.S.A. 84-2-312.

King argues that his rights are superior to Garnes' rights in the property because Garnes has been compensated by her insurance company and has signed a release. There is no evidence in the record, other than King's accusation, to support a conclusion that Garnes assigned her interest in the property to her insurer. The relationship between Garnes and her insurance company is a matter of contract. Therefore, any interest the insurer may have in the property is governed by the contract of insurance. King, who is neither a party to that contract nor an intended third-party beneficiary, cannot enforce the insurer's rights.

If the insurer is entitled to subrogation because it has paid Garnes' claim, it is entitled to stand in the shoes of its insured, and assert Garnes' superior rights in the property in question. It is clear that King's right to possess the property is inferior to that of either Garnes or her insurer, regardless of which party has the ability to assert those rights against King. After the property is returned to Garnes, her insurer will have the opportunity to assert its subrogation rights against her.

Affirmed.

MILLER V. RACE
97 Eng. Rep. 398 (K.B. 1758)

It was an action of trover against the defendant, upon a bank note, for the payment of twenty-one pounds ten shillings to one William Finney or bearer, on demand.

The cause came on to be tried before Lord Mansfield at the sittings in Trinity term last at Guildhall, London: and upon the trial it appeared that William Finney, being possessed of this bank note on the 11th of December 1756, sent it by the general post, under cover, directed to one Bernard Odenharty, at Chipping Norton in Oxfordshire; that on the same night the mail was robbed, and the bank note in question (amongst other notes) taken and carried away by the robber; that this bank note, on the 12th of the same December, came into the hands and possession of the plaintiff, for a full and valuable consideration, and in the usual course and way of his business, and without any notice or knowledge of this bank note being taken out of the mail.

It was admitted and agreed, that, in the common and known course of trade, bank notes are paid by and received of the holder or possessor of them, as cash; and that in the usual way of negotiating bank notes, they pass from one person to another as cash, by delivery only and without any further inquiry or evidence of title, than what arises from the possession. It appeared that Mr. Finney, having notice of this robbery, on the 13th December, applied to the Bank of England, "to stop the payment of this note:" which was ordered accordingly, upon Mr. Finney's entering into proper security "to indemnify the bank."

Some little time after this, the plaintiff applied to the bank for the payment of this note; and for that purpose delivered the note to the defendant, who is a clerk in the bank: but the defendant refused either to pay the note, or to re-deliver it to the plaintiff. Upon which this action was brought against the defendant.

The jury found a verdict for the plaintiff, and the sum of 21L. 10s. damages, subject nevertheless to the opinion of this Court upon this question -- "Whether under the circumstances of this case, the plaintiff had a sufficient property in this bank note, to entitle him to recover in the present action?"

Sir Richard Lloyd, for the defendant.

Now this note, or these goods (as I may call it,) was the property of Mr. Finney, who paid in the money: he is the real owner. It is like a medal which might entitle a man to payment of money, or to any other advantage. And it is by Mr. Finney's authority and request that Mr. Race detained it.

It may be objected, that this note is to be considered as cash "in the usual course of trade." But still, the course of trade is not at all affected by the present question, about the right to the note. A different species of action must be brought for the note, from what must be brought against the bank for the money. And this man has elected to bring trover for the note itself, as owner of the note; and not to bring his action against the bank for the money. In which action of trover, property can not be proved in the plaintiff: for a special proprietor can have no right against the true owner.

This note is just like any other piece of property until passed away in the course of trade. And here the defendant acted as agent to the true owner.

Mr. Williams contra for the plaintiff.

The holder of this bank note, upon a valuable consideration has a right to it, even against the true owner.

1st, the circulation of these notes vests a property in the holder, who comes to the possession of it, upon a valuable consideration.

2dly, this is of vast consequence to trade and commerce; and they would be greatly incommoded if it were otherwise.

3dly, this falls within the reason of a sale in market-overt; and ought to be determined upon the same principle.

But it is objected by Sir Richard, "that there is a substantial difference between a right to the note, and a right to the money." But I say the right to the money will attract to it a right to the paper. Our right is not by assignment, but by law, by the usage and custom of trade. I do not contend that the robber, or even the finder of a note, has a right to the note: but after circulation, the holder upon a valuable consideration has a right.

Sir Richard Lloyd in reply --

I agree that the holder of the note has a special property: but it does not follow that he can maintain trover for it, against the true owner.

This is not only without, but against the consent of the owner.

Supposing this note to be a sort of mercantile cash; yet it has an ear-mark by which it may be distinguished; therefore trover will lie for it. And so is the case of *Ford v. Hopkins*.

And you may recover a thing stolen from a merchant, as well as a thing stolen from another man. And this note is a mere piece of paper; it may be as well stopped, as any other sort of mercantile cash, (as, for instance, a policy which has been stolen). And this has not been passed away in trade; but remains in the hands of the true owner. And therefore it does not signify in what manner they are passed away, when they are passed away: for this was not passed away. Here the true owner, or his servant (which is the same thing) detains it. And, surely, robbery does not devest the property.

This is not like goods sold in market overt; nor does it pass in the way of a market overt; nor is it within the reason of a market overt. Suppose it was a watch stolen: the owner may seize it, (though he finds it in a market overt,) before it sold there. But there is no market overt for bank notes.

I deny the holder's (merely as holder) having a right to the note, against the true owner; and I deny that the possession gives a right to the note.

Lord Mansfield now delivered the resolution of the Court.

After stating the case at large, he declared that at the trial, he had no sort of doubt, but this action was well brought, and would lie against the defendant in the present case; upon the general course of business, and from the consequences to trade and commerce: which would be much incommoded by a contrary determination.

It has been very ingeniously argued by Sir Richard Lloyd for the defendant. But the whole fallacy of the argument turns upon comparing bank notes to what they do not resemble, and what they ought not to be compared to, viz. to goods, or to securities, or documents for debts.

Now they are not goods, not securities, nor documents for debts, nor are so esteemed: but are treated as money, as cash, in the ordinary course and transaction of business, by the general consent of mankind; which gives them the credit and currency of money, to all intents and purposes. They are as much money, as guineas themselves are; or any other current coin, that is used in common payments, as money or cash.

They pass by a will, which bequeaths all the testator's money or cash; and are never considered as securities for money, but as money itself. Upon Ld. Ailesbury's will, 900L in bank-notes was considered as cash. On payment of them, whenever a receipt is required, the receipts are always given as for money; not as for securities or notes.

So on bankruptcies, they cannot be followed as identical and distinguishable from money: but are always considered as money or cash.

It is a pity that reporters sometimes catch at quaint expressions that may happen to be dropped at the Bar or Bench; and mistake their meaning. It has been quaintly said, "that the reason why money can not be followed is, because it has no ear-mark:" but this is not true. The true reason is, upon account of the currency of it: it can not be recovered after it has passed in currency. So, in case of money stolen, the true owner can not recover it, after it has been paid away fairly and honestly upon a valuable and bona fide consideration: but before money has passed in currency, an action may be brought for the money itself. There was a case in 1 G. 1, at the sittings, *Thomas v. Whip*, before Ld. Macclesfield: which was an action upon assumpsit, by an administrator against the defendant, for money had and received to his use. The defendant was nurse to the intestate during his sickness; and, being alone, conveyed away the money. And Ld. Macclesfield held that the action lay. Now this must be esteemed a finding at least.

Apply this to the case of a bank-note. An action may lie against the finder, it is true; (and it is not at all denied:) but not after it has been paid away in currency. And this point has been determined, even in the infancy of bank-notes; for 1 Salk. 126, M. 10 W. 3, at Nisi Prius, is in point. And Ld. Ch. J. Holt there says that it is "by reason of the course of trade;

which creates a property in the assignee or bearer." (And "the bearer" is a more proper expression than assignee.)

Here, an inn-keeper took it, bona fide, in his business from a person who made an appearance of a gentleman. Here is no pretence or suspicion of collusion with the robber: for this matter was strictly inquired and examined into at the trial; and is so stated in the case, "that he took it for a full and valuable consideration, in the usual course of business." Indeed if there had been any collusion, or any circumstances of unfair dealing; the case had been much otherwise. If it had been a note for 1000L. it might have been suspicious: but this was a small note for 21L.10s. only: and money given in exchange for it.

Another case cited was a loose note in 1 Ld. Raym. 738, ruled by Ld. Ch. J. Holt at Guildhall, in 1698; which proves nothing for the defendant's side of the question: but it is exactly agreeable to what is laid down by my Ld. Ch. J. Holt, in the case I have just mentioned. The action did not lie against the assignee of the bank-bill; because he had it for valuable consideration.

In that case, he had it from the person who found it: but the action did not lie against him, because he took it in the course of currency; and therefore it could not be followed in his hands. It never shall be followed into the hands of a person who bona fide took it in the course of currency, and in the way of his business.

The case of *Ford v. Hopkins*, was also cited: which was in Hil. 12 W. 3, coram Holt Ch. J. at Nisi Prius, at Guildhall; and was an action of trover for million-lottery tickets. But this must be a very incorrect report of that case: it is impossible that it can be a true representation of what Ld. Ch. J. Holt said. It represents him as speaking of bank-notes, Exchequer-notes, and million lottery tickets, as like to each other. Now no two things can be more unlike to each other, than a lottery-ticket, and a bank-note. Lottery tickets are identical and specific: specific actions lie for them. They may prove extremely unequal in value: one may be a prize; another, a blank. Land is not more specific, than lottery-tickets are. It is there said, "that the delivery of the plaintiff's tickets to the defendant, as that case was, was no change of property." And most clearly it was no change of the property; so far, the case is right. But it is here urged as a proof "that the true owner may follow a stolen bank-note, into what hands soever it shall come."

Now the whole of that case turns upon the throwing in bank-notes, as being like to lottery tickets.

But Ld. Ch. J. Holt could never say "that an action would lie against the person who, for a valuable consideration, had received a bank note which had been stolen or lost, and bona fide paid to him:" even though the action was brought by the true owner: because he had determined otherwise, but two years before; and because bank notes are not like lottery-tickets, but money.

The person who took down this case, certainly misunderstood Lord Ch. J. Holt, or mistook his reasons. For this reasoning would prove, (if it was true, as the reporter represents it,) that if a man paid to a goldsmith 500L. in bank notes, the goldsmith could never pay them away.

A bank-note is constantly and universally, both at home and abroad, treated as money, as cash; and paid and received, as cash; and it is necessary, for the purposes of commerce, that their currency should be established and secured.

There was a case in the Court of Chancery, on some of Mr. Child's notes, payable to the person to whom they were given, or bearer. The notes had been lost or destroyed many years. Mr. Child was ready to pay them to the widow and administratrix of the person to whom they were made payable; upon her giving bond, with two responsible sureties, (as is the custom in such cases,) to indemnify him against the bearer, if the notes should ever be demanded. The administratrix brought a bill; which was dismissed because she either could not or would not give the security required. No dispute ought to be made with the bearer of a cash-note; in regard to commerce, and for the sake of the credit of these notes; though it may be both reasonable and customary, to stay the payment, till inquiry can be made, whether the bearer of the note came by it fairly, or not.

Lord Mansfield declared that the Court were all of the same opinion, for the plaintiff; and that Mr. Just. Wilmot concurred. * * *

PEACOCK V. RHODES
99 Eng.Rep. 402 (K.B. 1781)

In an action upon an inland bill of exchange, which was tried before Willes, Justice, at the last Spring Assizes for Yorkshire, a verdict, by consent, was found for the plaintiff, subject to the opinion of the Court on a special case, stating the following facts:

"The bill was drawn at Halifax, on the 9th of August, 1780, by the defendants, upon Smith, Payne, & Smith, payable to William Ingham, or order, 31 days after date, for value received. It was indorsed by William Ingham, and was presented by the plaintiff for acceptance and payment, but both were refused, of which due notice was given by the plaintiffs to the defendants, and the money demanded of the defendants. The plaintiff, who was a mercer at Scarborough, received the bill from a man not known, who called himself William Brown, and, by that name, indorsed the bill to the plaintiff, of whom he bought cloth, and other articles in the way of the plaintiff's trade as a mercer, in his shop at Scarborough, and paid him that bill, the value whereof the plaintiff gave to the buyer in cloth and other articles, and cash, and small bills. The plaintiff did not know the defendants, but had before, in his shop, received bills drawn by them, which were duly paid. William Ingham, to whom the bill was payable, indorsed it; John Daltry received it from him, and indorsed it; Joseph Fisher received it from John Daltry; and it was stolen from Joseph Fisher, at York, (without any indorsement or transfer thereof by him,) along with other bills in his pocket-book, whereof his pocket was picked, before the plaintiff took it in payment as aforesaid. The plaintiff declared as indorsee of Ingham."

Wood, for the plaintiff, argued, that the bill was taken, by Peacock, in the ordinary course of business, and there was no pretence that he had notice that it had been obtained unfairly. If he had, he admitted that he could not recover. A bill indorsed by the payee, is to be considered to all intents as cash, unless he chooses to restrain its currency, which he may do by a special indorsement, as "Pay the contents to William Fisher". The very object in view, in making negotiable securities, is, that they may serve the purposes of cash. The case of *Miller v. Race*, although the question there arose upon a bank-note, establishes the principle just stated. *** The argument on the part of the present defendants *** would stop the currency of bills of exchange, because it would render it necessary for every indorsee to insist upon proof of all the circumstances, and the manner in which the bill came to the indorser.

Fearnly, for the defendants. -- The cases on this subject are all modern, but all of them establish a distinction between bank notes, or banker's cash notes payable to bearer, and indorseable bills or notes. The two first sorts only are considered as cash. No case that I have found is exactly in point to that before the Court. * * * The arguments from inconvenience are in favour of the defendants. No man is obliged to take a bill of exchange in payment. A trader should not, in prudence, take a bill, unless he know the person from whom he receives it. But if the law were as contended for on the part of the plaintiff, the temptations to theft would be increased.

Lord Mansfield told Wood, he need not reply, and delivered the opinion of the Court, as follows:

Lord Mansfield. -- I am glad this question was saved, not for any difficulty there is in the case, but because it is important that general commercial points should be publicly decided. The holder of a bill of exchange, or promissory note, is not to be considered in the light of an assignee of the payee. An assignee must take the thing assigned, subject to all the equity to which the original party was subject. If this rule applied to bills and promissory notes, it would stop their currency. The law is settled, that a holder, coming fairly by a bill or note, has nothing to do with the transaction between the original parties; unless, perhaps, in the single case, (which is a hard one, but has been determined,) of a note for money won at play. I see no difference between a note indorsed blank, and one payable to bearer. They both go by delivery, and possession proves property in both cases. The question of mala fides was for the consideration of the jury. The circumstances, that the buyer and also the drawers were strangers to the plaintiff, and that he took the bill for goods on which he had a profit, were grounds of suspicion, very fit for their consideration. But they have considered them, and have found it was received in the course of trade, and, therefore, the case is clear, and within the principle of all those Mr. Wood has cited, from that of *Miller v. Race*, downwards ***.

The postea to be delivered to the plaintiff.

UNBANK CO. V. DOLPHIN TEMPORARY HELP SERVICES, INC.
Minnesota Court of Appeals, 1992
485 N.W.2d 332

The Unbank Company appeals from a judgment for respondent Dolphin Temporary Help Services, Inc. Unbank claims it is a holder in due course of a check Dolphin issued to Ricky D. Smith. We agree and reverse.

The parties stipulated to the following facts. Unbank operates a number of check cashing facilities in the metropolitan area. Dolphin operates a temporary employment business for casual laborers.

On December 5, 1991, Dolphin issued a payroll check to Ricky D. Smith. Smith reported the check as lost. Dolphin stopped payment on the check and issued a replacement check. Someone, believed by both parties to be Smith, brought the "lost" check to Unbank to have it cashed on December 15, 1991. Unbank checked the individual's signature against its account card and cashed the check. Unbank learned Dolphin had stopped payment when the check was dishonored by Dolphin's bank.

Unbank sued Dolphin for payment on the check. The trial court concluded Unbank was not a holder in due course and was, therefore, not entitled to payment from Dolphin. Unbank appeals.

* * *

A holder in due course is a holder who takes an instrument: (a) for value; and (b) in good faith; and (c) without notice that it is overdue or has been dishonored or of any defense against or claim to it on the part of any person. Minn.Stat. §336.3-302(1) (1990).

Value

It is undisputed that Unbank paid Smith cash for the check. A party that pays cash for a check takes the instrument for value.

Good Faith

" 'Good faith' means honesty in fact in the conduct or transaction concerned." Minn.Stat. §336.1-201(19) (1990). "Good faith" is a subjective rather than an objective determination.

The issue is honesty of intent rather than diligence or negligence. Good faith is simply the honest belief that one's conduct is rightful.

Unbank cashed the check without knowing that a stop payment order had been issued on it. Unbank followed standard procedure in cashing the check. Before cashing the check, Unbank compared the signature of the person who presented the check for payment to Smith's signature on his Unbank account card. There was nothing even remotely suspicious about the transaction. There are no facts that would support a finding that Unbank lacked good faith.

Notice

A person has notice of a fact when that person

    (a) has actual knowledge of it; or

    (b) has received a notice or notification of it; or

    (c) from all the facts and circumstances known to the person at the time in question, has reason to know that it exists.

Minn.Stat. §336.1-201(25) (1990). There is no evidence Unbank had actual knowledge or had received notice of the stop payment order on the check Dolphin issued to Smith. The only issue is whether Unbank had reason to know about the stop payment order.

Failure to inquire about an unknown fact is not "notice" of what a person might discover. Where an instrument is regular on its face and there are no suspicious circumstances that show a deliberate desire to evade knowledge, the law does not impose a duty on the holder to inquire about possible defenses to the instrument.

A bank has no higher duty of inquiry than does any other holder. There is nothing about using a check cashing service instead of a bank that would lead to a rule imposing different standards on the two types of institutions. Moreover, there is nothing in the Uniform Commercial Code to support a distinction on that basis.

Unbank followed standard procedure in cashing the check Dolphin issued to Smith. There was nothing about the face of the check or the transaction to even create a suspicion that anything was wrong. There are no facts that would support a finding that Unbank had reason to know about the stop payment order or any defense to payment of the check.

The trial court found that either Smith or a thief cashed the check. Unbank argues the finding should be amended to state that Smith cashed the check. We disagree. The stipulated facts left open the question of who cashed the check.

The issue of whether Smith or a thief cashed the check does not affect Unbank's right to payment from Dolphin. A holder in due course takes an instrument free from any defenses except those listed in Minn.Stat. §336.3-305 (1990). Theft is not a defense against a holder in due course.

Because there was no evidence to show Smith's signature on the check was forged, we do not consider the issue of whether the unauthorized signature defense would have been available to Dolphin had the endorsement been forged.

Unbank took the check for value, in good faith, and without notice of any defense against it. Unbank is a holder in due course entitled to payment from Dolphin.

Reversed.

BANK OF NEW YORK v. ASATI, INC.
Supreme Court, New York County, July 8, 1991
1991 WL 322989

Carol E. Huff, Justice. Plaintiff, The Bank of New York ("BNY") moves for an order pursuant to CPLR 3212 granting summary judgment against CWM Chemical Services, Inc.,

("CWM"). Defendant, CWM cross-moves for summary judgment pursuant to CPLR 3212 dismissing the complaint.

On March 31, 1989, Asati, Inc., ("Asati") opened a business checking account at BNY's Harrison, New York branch. When it opened the account, Asati submitted a corporate resolution indicating that it then had three officers: Donato M. Fraoli, President; Theodore E. Weiner, Executive Vice President; and Chiam Silber, Vice President.

At or about the time it opened its account, Asati received from BNY a pamphlet explaining its funds availability policy. The pamphlet explained that BNY generally made items available to its customers no later than the second business day after deposit.

For nine months, BNY had a satisfactory and normal business relationship with Asati, and no problems had arisen with reference to Asati's account.

On December 29, 1989 Asati endorsed and deposited into its account a check drawn by CWM (the "CWM Check") on First Union payable to the order of Asati in the amount of $610,205.

The CWM Check was regular in every respect. There were no extraordinary notations or interlineations on it, nor was there any language on it indicating it represented conditional payment. Accordingly, BNY provisionally credited Asati's account and promptly forwarded the CWM Check via the Federal Reserve to First Union for payment.

BNY made the funds from the CWM Check available to Asati on Wednesday, January 3, 1990, two business days after Asati had deposited it with BNY in accordance with its funds availability policy. (Monday, January 1, 1990 was a bank holiday).

At approximately 3:00 p.m., defendant Silber, came into BNY's Harrison branch and requested that BNY issue three certified checks of $200,000 each, payable to the order of Faioli, Weiner and himself. The teller checked the status of Asati's account, determined that it possessed available funds sufficient to cover the checks and placed a hold on $600,000 of those funds after determining that Asati possessed available funds. The teller then brought this information to Richard E. Stout, Harrison Branch Manager, who approved the request. BNY then issued three certified checks to Silber at approximately 3:15 p.m. and put the certified check request form through the computer.

Later that day, at approximately 3:32 p.m., BNY's Domestic Wire Transfer Department located in Utica, N.Y. received from First Union via Fedwire an advance notification indicating that First Union had dishonored the CWM Check on the basis of a stop payment order from CWM. On Tuesday, January 2, 1990, an air supported structure erected by Asati the consideration for which the CWM Check was partial payment, collapsed. As the back of the CWM Check reveals that First Union received the CWM Checks on January 2, First Union's January 3 notice of dishonor was timely sent before the expiration of its midnight deadline.

By letter dated January 3, First Union returned the CWM Check via the Federal Reserve to BNY. BNY received the CWM Check on January 8. When the received item was entered into BNY's system it created an overdraft of $571,495.44 in Asati's account. Neither Asati nor CWM has made payment to BNY.

BNY commenced this action in January against Asati, its officers and CWM. It now seeks summary judgment against CWM, asserting its alleged status as a holder in due course and requests that CWM pay $571,495.44, the amount of the CWM Check less the amount of monies remaining in Asati's account with BNY.

CWM opposes the motion and cross-moves to dismiss the complaint as against it asserting that BNY is not a holder in due course because it failed to take the CWM Check for value since BNY only provisionally credited the Asati account, and later reversed it, claiming a chargeback against Asati. In addition, it argues that BNY had notice of a defense or remained willfully ignorant of the alleged defense of failure of consideration (i.e., the collapse of the air-supported structure) at the time it issued the checks to Asati and is therefore not a holder in due course. CWM's attorney speculates that the request forms were stamped prior to issuing the checks and that it might have "took more than 17 minutes for Mr. Silber to get physical possession of the three checks after the 'Request Forms' were stamped at 3:15 p.m. and 3:16 p.m." and thus at 3:32 BNY knew of the dishonor. Alternatively, CWM argues BNY "remained wilfully ignorant" of CWM's alleged defense by not inquiring into why Asati had received the CWM Check from CWM. The sole basis for CWM imposing this duty on BNY is that Asati's request to draw three certified checks on its account was the first request for certification Asati had made.

It is well-settled that when drawer CWM made its check payable to Asati, CWM engaged that, upon dishonor (by stop payment or otherwise) of the check and any notice of dishonor, it would pay the amount of the check to any holder (see, UCC 3-413[2]). Accordingly, if BNY is a "holder" of the CWM Check, CWM Is obligated to make payment on its check to BNY.

Under section 1-201(20) of the Uniform Commercial Code, BNY is a "holder" if it is in possession of the CWM Check and the check was drawn, issued or endorsed to it or to its order or to bearer or in blank. It is undisputed that BNY is in possession of the CWM Check and that Asati endoresed [sic] the CWM Check for deposit into its acount [sic]. Thus, BNY is a holder of the CWM Check.

The lone exception to CWM's liability to BNY under section 3-413 is if CWM "establishes a defense" to its payment on the check (see, UCC §3-307[2]). Here, CWM's "defense" is that Asati, the payee of the CWM Check, "had breached the agreement for which the CWM Check was given" (CWM's Amended Answer). Even assuming CWM can raise a factual issue as to the existence of that "defense" CWM is nonetheless obligated to make payment to BNY if BNY can establish that it is a holder in due course of the CWM Check. (See, UCC §3-307[3]).

To establish "holder in due course status", BNY must show that it took the CWM Check for value, in good faith and without notice that the instrument had been dishonored or of any defense against or claim to it on the part of any person (see, UCC §3-302[1]).

Once BNY allowed Asati to withdraw the proceeds of the CWM Check, BNY obtained a security interest in the CWM Check (see, UCC §4-208[1]). To the extent that BNY obtained a security interest in the CWM Check, BNY has given value for the CWM Check for purposes of determining its holder in due course status (see, UCC §4-209; see also, Marine Midland Bank v. Graybar Elec., 41 NY2d 703, 711; Pazol v. Citizens Nat'l Bank, 112 ? [sic] App. 161, 144 S.E.2d 117, 2 UCC Rep 330).

> "[A] bank which accepts a check from the payee for deposit and permits him to withdraw the proceeds of such check prior to notice of its dishonor has given value for the check to the extent that it has a security interest in the item and thereupon becomes a holder in due course of the check".

To avoid the result in Pazol, which was summary judgment in favor of the depositary bank, and to circumvent the language of section 4-208, CWM claims that "more recent case law" has changed this principle of law. However, neither of the two cases CWM cites, Marine Midland Bank v. Graybar Electric Co., 41 NY2d 703 and In re Stemnon, 73 B.R. 905 (W.D.Wisc.1987), supports its contention or alters the rule of law in Pazol and its progeny.

   * * *

As to BNY's taking the CWM Check in good faith and without notice of CWM's defenses, UCC 1-201(19) defines "good faith" as "honesty in fact in the conduct or transaction concerned". A bank's permitting its customers to draw against uncollected funds does not negate its good faith.

In Mellon the Court held that "[p]ayment by the collecting bank might be imprudent and is certainly a risk assumed by the depositary-collecting bank as to the drawee but it does not affect plaintiff's rights against defendant who by drawing the instrument and placing it in the stream of commerce has engaged to pay it to any holder". * * *

Where a depositary bank provides value for a subsequently dishonored check without any knowledge of the nature of the underlying transaction between its customer and the drawer of the check, the depositary bank is deemed to have taken the check without notice of any claim to or defense against it (Western Bank v. RaDec Construction Co., 382 N.W.2d 406, 42 UCC Rep.Serv. 1340, the fact that immediate credit was given to its customer who had an existing overdraft did not evidence that the bank had notice of a defense; Frantz v. First Nat'l Bank of Anchorage, 584 P.2d 1125, 25 UCC Rep.Serv. 240, awareness of an overdraft or other financial problems does not impart notice of a defense; Mercantil De Sao Paulo S.A. v. Nara, 120 Misc2d 517, where the court held that plaintiff's protests that defendants "should have known" that the checks were forgeries where the checks were not endorsed and were purchased on the black market were insufficient as a matter of law to negate the defendant's holder in due cause status as actual knowledge was not shown).

BNY has alleged and demonstrated that when it provided value to Asati for the CWM Check, it did so in good faith and with no knowledge that CWM had any defense against its issuance of the CWM Check. CWM's opposition papers do not disprove these facts. CWM attorney's suspicions as to the possibility of BNY's actual knowledge of the stop payment order prior to BNY's delivery of three certified checks to Silber without more are contrary to the evidence and all that moer [sic] are insufficient to defeat a summary judgment motion. Genuine issues of material fact and not possibilities are necessary to defeat summary judgment.

Moreover, CWM's argument that BNY "remained wilfully ignorant" of CWM's defense is also unavailing as the aforementioned cases demonstrate that a request for immediate credit, or a request to draw three certified checks does not impart a notice of a defense or a duty to inquire.

In the final analysis, CWM has offered nothing to deny BNY holder in due course status. Once it attains that status, BNY, as CWM readily admits, takes the CWM Check free and clear of alleged breach of contract (see, UCC §3-302).

Accordingly, BNY is entitled to summary judgment against the drawe[r], CWM. CWM's cross-motion is denied.

practice

Case 1

A promised to pay B $1,000, but A breached the promise and B sued to enforce it.

a.   Do these allegations state a claim for relief?

b.   Is a claim for relief stated if the complaint also alleges that A issued to B a negotiable promissory note for $1,000 that is due and has not been paid?

Yes

c.   Is a claim stated if the complaint only alleges the overdue note and not the underlying promise?

Case 2

B extended credit to A either by making a loan or selling property or services on credit. The law that governs the loan or the sale obligates A to pay B.

a.   Does the enforceability of A's obligation to B depend on the execution of an instrument or other legally sufficient writing signed by A payable to B?

No

b.   How will B enforce the obligation if A fails to pay it?

c.   Suppose that A issues a negotiable promissory note to B in the amount of the obligation.

  i.   Does this instrument take the place of the obligation? 3-310(b).

No

  ii.   How will B enforce the instrument if A fails to pay it? 3-412; 3-308

  iii. What is the effect on the obligation if the instrument is paid? 3-310(b)(2).

Case 3

B extended credit to A by either making a loan to A or selling property or services to her on credit. The law that governs the loan or the sale obligates A to repay B. There is no instrument. C agrees with B to buy B's right to payment from A.

a.   B refuses to close her deal with C. What law governs the enforceability of their agreement? See 9-203(1); Restatement (Second) of Contracts §§317 & 324.

b.   Is the agreement enforceable against A in the absence of A's consent? 2--210(2); 9-318(4).

Yes

c.   Can A safely pay B in the absence of a prior demand that A pay C? Restatement (Second) of Contracts § 338; 9-318(3).

Yes

Case 4

B extended credit to A. The law that governs the loan or sale transaction between them obligates A to pay B. Also, there is a negotiable promissory note that A issued to B. C bought the note from B. B indorsed the note and delivered to C.

a.   How is A obligated to C? 3-412.

Yes
    b.   Does A remain obligated on the underlying loan or sale transaction? 3-310(b)(2) & (4)(first sentence).

Discharge
    c.   What is the effect on A's liabilities if she pays the note to C? 3-602(a); 3-310(b).

Holder
    d.   The effects on A's liabilities are not the same if she pays B. What is missing to prevent the same rules from working the same outcome?

e.   How are the parties' liabilities affected if A paid B before C bought the note? 3-602(a); 3-601; 3-302(a) & (b).

Case 5

B extended credit to A by selling property or services to A on credit. The law that governs the loan or the sale obligates A to pay B. C buys B's right to payment from A. A refuses to pay C because B's performance under the contract with A was non-conforming.

Yes
    a.   Is B's breach of contract a defense that A can assert against C? 9-318(1)(a); Restatement (Second) of Contracts §336(1) & (2).

b.   Suppose that B breached an unrelated contract between her and A. Can A assert this breach of contract claim against C? Restatement (Second) of Contracts § 336(2); 9-318(1)(b).

Case 6

B sold property or services to A.

a.   A paid in cash and is thereby freed from liability to A with respect to this transaction. Why?

Suspension
    b.   A gave B a check for the price. Explain in legal rules and terms why A is not thereby freed from liability to B with respect to this transaction.   3-310(b)(2).

Discharge
    c.   What is the effect if A "pays" with a cashier's check? 3-310(a).

Case 7

B sold property or services to A who gave B a check for the price. B indorsed the check and C cashed it. (In effect, C bought the check.) C thereafter presented the check to A's bank for payment. The check was not paid. Rather it was dishonored and bounced back to C.

No
    a.   Is A's bank liable to C? 3-408; Restatement (Second) of Contracts §325.

b. A is liable to C *on* the check. Can A nevertheless defend against enforcement by C on the basis that B breached the underlying transaction between A and B? 3-414(b); 3-305(a)(2) & (b); *Bank of New York v. Asati, Inc.,* supra.

Probably not

c. How is B liable to C? See 3-415(a); 3-416(a)(4).

Case 8

B sold property or services to A. B drew a draft ordering A to pay C. B sold the draft to C. A refused to pay the draft when C presented it for payment.

a. Is A liable to C? 3-408.

No

b. Is B liable to C? 3-414(b).

Yes

c. How is A liable to B?

d. Are the answers different if A had signed the draft -- "accepted" it -- and thereby had become an acceptor of the instrument? 3-413(a); 3-414(d).

Case 9

B sold property or services to A. A gave B a check for the price drawn on C Bank. The check was not paid.

a. What are the parties' liabilities if the instrument was a check drawn by A against her account at C Bank? 3-310(b)(1); 3-408; 3-414(b).

   i. Is C Bank liable to anyone *on* the check? 3-408.

   No

   ii. Is C Bank liable to A or B for any reason? 4-402(a) & (b).

   Maybe to A

   iii. Suppose that C Bank paid the check. How does C Bank recover? 4-401(a).

b. What are the liabilities if the instrument was a cashier's check that A, as remitter, had purchased from C Bank? 3-412; 3-310(a).

c. What are the liabilities if the instrument was a check drawn by A against C Bank that C Bank had accepted ("certified")? 3-409(d); 3-413; 3-414(c); 3-310(a).

Chapter 2. The Meaning Of "Negotiable Instrument"

Article 3 applies only to "negotiable instruments." 3-102(a). This term therefore establishes the scope of the statute. Only a negotiable instrument triggers its peculiar rules of contract liability and property law.

Generally speaking, "the term 'negotiable instrument' is limited to a signed writing that orders or promises payment of money." 3-104 comment 1. More precisely, the writing must satisfy the requirements of section 3-104(a), which are amplified by other provisions of Chapter 1 of Article 3. These requirements are referred to as the *requisites of negotiability*, which go to matters of form exclusively rather than the manner in which a writing is used or the kind of transaction out of which it arose.

> "[N]egotiable instrument" means an unconditional promise or order to pay a fixed amount of money, with or without interest or other charges described in the promise or order, if it:
>
> (1) is payable to bearer or to order at the time it is issued or first comes into possession of a holder;
>
> (2) is payable on demand or at a definite time; and
>
> (3) does not state any other undertaking or instruction by the person promising or ordering payment to do any act in addition to the payment of money, but the promise or order may contain (i) an undertaking or power to give, maintain, or protect collateral to secure payment, (ii) an authorization or power to the holder to confess judgment or realize on or dispose of collateral, or (iii) a waiver of the benefit of any law intended for the advantage or protection of an obligor.

3-104(a). A further, built-in requirement is that the promise or order is in writing. Promise and order are defined as a *written* instruction or undertaking. 3-103(a)(6) & (9).

Why have any requisites of negotiability? Article 3 is an extraordinary set of rules that is justified, at core, by consent. It applies only when a person agrees, in a special manner, to be bound by the statute. The special manner of agreement that triggers Article 3 is signing a writing that satisfies the 3-104 requisites of negotiability. Because Article 3's rules are extraordinary, consent to them should be *clear*. Because the means of consent is satisfying the 3-104 requisites, any writing to be negotiable should *clearly* satisfy them.

Why these particular requisites? Why not trigger Article 3 whenever a promise to pay money is signed in red ink or whenever a smiley face is added to the signature? For the most part the answer is custom and tradition that has been modified by the needs and interests of contemporary business and trade.

story

GRANT GILMORE, THE COMMERCIAL DOCTRINE OF GOOD FAITH PURCHASE
63 Yale L.J. 1057, 1068-72 (1954)

The Formal Requisites

Few generalizations have been more often repeated, or by generations of lawyers more devoutly believed, than this: negotiability is a matter rather of form than substance. It is bred in the bone of every lawyer that an instrument to be negotiable must be "a courier without luggage." It must conform to a set of admirably abstract specifications which, for our generation, have been codified in Section 1 of the Negotiable Instruments Law and spelled out in the nine following sections. [These specifications with a few changes were recodified in Article 3 of the U.C.C, first in section 3-104(1) (1989 Official Text) and thereafter in Revised Article 3 section 3-104(a).] These rules are fixed, eternal and immutable. No other branch of law is so clear, so logical, so inherently satisfying as the law of formal requisites of negotiability. To determine the negotiability of any instrument, all that need be done is to lay it against the yardstick of NIL sections 1-10: if it is an exact fit it is negotiable; a hair's breadth over or under and it is not.

Few generalizations, legal or otherwise, have ever been less true; the truth is, in this as in every other field of commercial law, substance has always prevailed over form. "The law" has always been in a constant state of flux as it struggles to adjust itself to changing methods of business practice; what purport to be formal rules of abstract logic are merely *ad hoc* responses to particular situations.

Nevertheless, the cherished belief in the sacrosanct nature of formal requisites serves, as do most legal principles, a useful function. The problem is what types of paper shall be declared negotiable so that purchasers may put on the nearly invincible armor of the holder in due course. The policy in favor of protecting the good faith purchaser does not run beyond the frontiers of commercial usage. Beyond those confines every reason of policy dictates the opposite approach. The formal requisites are the professional rules with which professionals are or ought to be familiar. As to instruments which are amateur productions outside any concept of the ordinary course of business, or new types which are just coming into professional use, it is wiser to err by being unduly restrictive than by being over liberal. The formal requisites serve as a useful exclusionary device and as a brake on a too rapid acceptance of emerging trends.

Under NIL Section 1 [as under U.C.C. 3-104(a)] an instrument to be negotiable must be: (1) a signed writing which is (2) an unconditional promise or order (3) to pay a sum certain in money (4) on demand or at a fixed determinable future time (5) to bearer or to the order * * *.

The above statement was an apt description of the types of commercial paper which were actually in use during the 17th and 18th centuries when the law of negotiability was taking shape. It is still valid for the mercantile bill of exchange and the check. But even at the time the NIL was drafted, it had ceased to be an adequate description of what the promissory note had become.

Historically, the promissory note was a much later invention than the bill of exchange. The common law courts, which had worked out the elements of negotiability in connection with the bill as early as the beginning of the 17th century, were still denying them to notes a hundred years later. The denial was based on the essentially sound reason (if true) that notes were "not within the custom of merchants," and it took an act of Parliament to put notes on the same footing with bills. In this country, until well after the Revolution, notes seem to have been regarded as distinctly less "commercial" than bills. In a group of commercially important jurisdictions the indorser of a note was held to have assumed a lesser degree of liability toward subsequent transferees than did the indorser of a bill. Despite, or because of, the fact that the rules relating to the note were relatively fluid, it became the vehicle for the 19th century transformation of the American economy both from a cash to a credit basis and from an unsecured to a secured basis. In the process the skeletonic note of 1800 put on a great deal of weight.

The NIL furnishes an authoritative statement of how far the law of promissory notes had departed from the courier without luggage theory by the end of the 19th century. Despite the apparently restrictive approach of Sections 1 and 5 [which approach is continued in U.C.C. 3-104(a)] the statute affirmatively authorizes the presence on the face of the note of many clauses which might seem fatal to negotiability. The note may be made payable in installments, and may further provide that on default in payment of any installment or of interest the whole shall become due. The note may bind the obligor to pay costs of collection or an attorney's fee in case payment is not made at maturity. It may contain a waiver of the benefit of any law intended for the advantage or protection of the obligor, and may authorize a confession of judgment if the instrument is not paid at maturity. Since it may authorize the sale of collateral security on default, impliedly the note may call for the deposit of collateral in the first place. And since the note may give the holder an election to require something to be done in lieu of payment of money, he apparently may, among other things, call for the posting of additional collateral.

The NIL's generous listing of what notes may "give," "authorize" or "provide for" reflects two key developments in patterns of short-term lending. One is the emergence of the consumer loan, where the borrower is looked on as sub-marginal and more likely than not to default. What sort of person the new borrower was is revealed by the provisions for amortization of the loan by installment payments, for the borrower's promise to pay collection costs and an attorney's fee, for his waiver of rights under debtor-protective legislation, and for his agreement in advance to confess judgment. The second development is the omnipresence of security. Under the NIL any lender may -- and most banks do -- write a comprehensive collateral pledge agreement into the note.

Grant that it is the function of a codifying statute to reflect going patterns of business behavior and the conclusion follows that the NIL achieved a remarkably skillful adjustment of rigid theory to flexible fact. Aside from the special problem of the negotiable note or bond tied to a separate security agreement, there has been under the NIL relatively little formal-requisites litigation of a type which a better drafting of the statute could have avoided. As long as the law distinguishes between commercial and noncommercial property on the basis of form, there will have to be borderline or fringe litigation. On the whole a continuing trickle of such litigation is not obnoxious; it produces a clearer state of the law than does the law of sales where the doctrines say one thing and mean another, a situation not productive of certainty and predictability.

Theoretically it would have been possible to draft the NIL without reference to formal requisites. The courts could have determined what instruments were entitled to the benefits of the NIL on a case by case basis. That approach commended itself neither to the draftsmen of the NIL nor to those of the Commercial Paper Article of the Uniform Commercial Code. In both codifications an apparently rigid statement of formal requisites is followed by a series of sections authorizing all the clauses generally in use. The only difference between the NIL and the Code is that the Code, being fifty years later, carries a longer list of permissible clauses. There may well be merit in an approach which has now been twice [and again in 1990] adopted by successive generations of draftsmen. There is little virtue in revolutionizing the law merely to achieve jurisprudential elegance or an impeccably logical form of statement. If traditional vocabulary and categories work well enough, it is the part of wisdom to leave them undisturbed.

⊏⊐⊐⊐⊐

Whether or not a writing satisfies 3-104(a), i.e., whether or not the writing is negotiable, is determined solely by its contents. Negotiability "is a question of law to be determined solely from the face of the instrument, without reference to the intent of the parties," *Cooperative Centrale Raiffeisen-Boerenleenbank v. Bailey*, 710 F. Supp. 737, 738 (C.D. Cal. 1989), "from the face, the four corners * * * without reference to extrinsic facts." *Western Bank v. RaDec Const. Co., Inc.*, 382 N.W.2d 406, 409 (S.D. 1986).

The provisions that 3-104(a) requires must appear in the writing, and the provisions that 3-104(a) prohibits must not appear there. On the other hand, if a writing satisfies 3-104(a) and thus by its terms is negotiable, the presence of a separate agreement (oral or written) does not affect negotiability, not even when the terms of the agreement would prevent negotiability if they were part of the writing itself. See 3-117 (by implication). Thus, it is usually possible to determine very quickly if a writing is negotiable simply by having the writing in hand and 3-104(a) in mind, except that 3-104(a) is amplified and supplemented by the balance of the provisions in Part 1 of Article 3. In effect, these provisions define the 3-104(a) requisites of negotiability, and these definitions are often more generous, tolerant and lenient than the plain language of 3-104(a) itself. Any decision about negotiability, especially that a writing is not negotiable, is not complete without checking these supplemental provisions.

Example 1

Martha got a loan from Paul. To evidence the deal she gave him this very simple writing which satisfies 3-104(a) and is a negotiable promissory note:

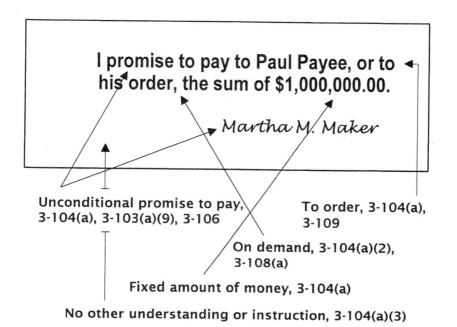

Example 2

First State Bank made a $50,000 loan to Acme Corp. which signed this very common, standard-form, negotiable note (it is only slightly more complex than the writing Martha gave Paul):

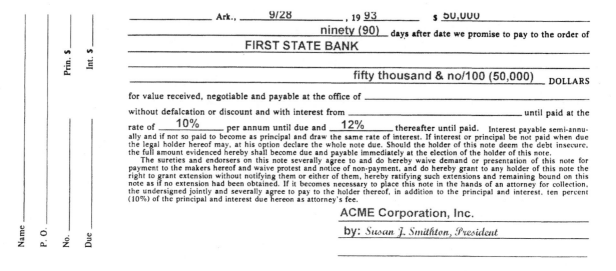

a. The note is a "promise," see 3-103(a)(9), because:

    i.   it is "written," 1-201(46);

    ii.   "undertakes" to pay by expressing a promise to pay B Bank; and

    iii.   promises the payment of "money." 1-201(24).

b. No other undertaking or instruction is promised except for certain additional matters that Article 3 expressly allows, including:

    i.   the provision for interest and other charges, such as costs of collection and an attorney's fees, 3-104(a);

    ii.   the acceleration clause triggered by default or insecurity;

    iii.   the waiver of certain rights by sureties and indorsers;

    iv.   the place where the note was executed and the place where it is payable.

c. The amount of money promised is "fixed." The absence of a stated total or maximum amount of interest or other charges does not affect negotiability because the "fixed amount" requirement applies only to principal. 3-112 comment 1.

d. The promise is "unconditional." A promise is conditional only if an express condition is stated, or the instrument expressly subjects itself to the terms of another writing or expressly refers to another writing for rights or obligations with respect to the promise. 3-106(a).

e. The note is payable at a "definite time" because it is payable at a fixed date, 3-108(b), i.e., 90 days after the note's date of September 28, 1993. The holder's right to extend the time of payment makes no difference. Id. & comment.

f. The note is payable "to order" because it is payable to the order of an identified person, "to the order of B Bank." 3-109(b).

Example 3

Darlene purchased goods from the University Bookstore and paid for them with an ordinary, negotiable check in this familiar form:

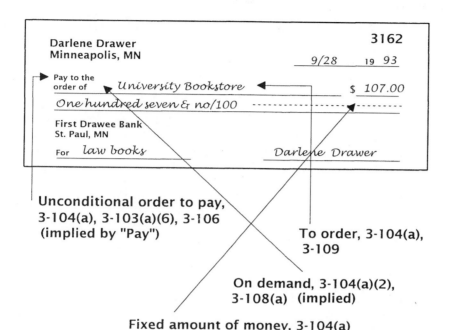

Unconditional order to pay,
3-104(a), 3-103(a)(6), 3-106
(implied by "Pay")

To order, 3-104(a),
3-109

On demand, 3-104(a)(2),
3-108(a) (implied)

Fixed amount of money, 3-104(a)

No other understanding or instruction, 3-104(a)(3)

---

a.　The check "orders" the payment of a fixed amount of money. The order is not expressed. It is not in the words "to the order of." Rather, the order, i.e., the written instruction to pay, 3-103(a)(6), is implied by the imperative "Pay."

b.　The check is payable "to order" because it is payable to the order of an identified person, P.

c.　Because the check does not state any time of payment, it is "payable on demand." 3-108(a).

Typically, checks and other drafts are standard forms that are not modified when put to use. The parties fill in the blanks and add nothing beyond the information that is called for. Issues of negotiability are uncommon.

Notes are a different story. Parties often make their own notes from scratch or materially add to (or change) standard forms. The usual reasons for doing so are to link the note to the parties' underlying transaction and to insure that the former reflects the latter. This customization often creates doubts about negotiability. Anything unusual -- any provision or language that does not perfectly fit prescribed and common form -- creates uncertainty.

The nine requisites of negotiability

1. Writing

The core requirement of a negotiable instrument is a promise or order to pay money; and a promise or order, by its own definition, must be written. Commercial paper is usually executed on printed, paper forms, but this kind of writing is not necessary for negotiability. "*Written*" or "*writing*" includes any "intentional reduction to tangible form." 1-201(46). Therefore, the requirement of a writing can be met by engraving, stamping, lithographing, photographing, typing, or longhand writing in pencil or ink on anything tangible, or by any similar process or any combination of them. There are stories of instruments painted on cows and coconuts.

2. Signed By Maker Or Drawer

The order or promise that negotiability requires means a written instruction or undertaking that is *signed* by the person who instructs or undertakes to pay. The meaning of "signed" is very broad, including "any symbol executed or adopted by a party with present intention to authenticate a writing." 1-201(39). Normally, this requirement is met by a person using a pen to write her name in longhand. It may also be met by the person using a symbol that she affixes to the instrument by hand, machine or in any other manner. A smiley face drawn or stamped on a writing can be a signature as well as a rubber stamped signature or a name or number that a computer prints on paper.

> Authentication may be printed, stamped or written; it may be by initials or by thumbprint. It may be on any part of the document and in appropriate cases may be found in a billhead or letterhead.

1-201 comment 39. It may be a symbol the party adds to the writing or a symbol that is already there. Thus, a computer-produced check with a facsimile signature is a signed instrument; and a person can be found to have signed a writing because she wrote on paper preprinted with her name. In short, the decisive issue is never the kind or nature of graphic mark or how it got on the writing. Any symbol however done will do. The decisive issue "always is whether the symbol was executed or adopted by the party with present intention to authenticate the writing." Id.

No symbol is a signature that lacks the purpose of authentication. Not even a person's name on a writing is, by itself, a signature. This explains why name and signature are not synonymous terms. A name is not a signature unless it is executed or adopted with the present intention to authenticate a writing. On the other hand, a person's signing a writing using someone else's name is a signature so long as the signer does so with the requisite intent to authenticate. The other person's name is as good a symbol as a smiley face or a thumbprint.

A further, different issue is whether or not a person who signs an instrument, or whose name is signed, is liable on it. This issue is considered in Chapter 3 infra.

3. Promise Or Order

Fundamentally, an instrument is a signed writing that, on its face, orders or promises the payment of money. At the core is the requirement of a promise or order. Either of them will satisfy negotiability, but the choice determines the nature of the instrument. An instrument that promises payment is a *note*. An instrument that orders payment is a *draft*. By force of law, a draft obligates the drawer to pay if the drawee refuses to do so, but this obligation -- which is often described as an implied promise -- is irrelevant in determining the nature of the instrument. A note requires language of promise that is missing from a draft which, on its face, orders payment instead of promising it. For the purpose of characterizing the instrument, the drawer's legally implied promise in a draft is ignored.

The promise that satisfies negotiability "means a written *undertaking* to pay money signed by the person undertaking to pay." 3-103(a)(9) (emphasis added). Typically, a note contains the very word "promise," providing "I or we promise to pay to the order of * * * ." It is not necessary, however, to use the word "promise." Other, equivalent language that expresses a promise will suffice.

Mere acknowledgment of a debt, however, is not a promise for purposes of Article 3 negotiability. 3-103(a)(9) (second sentence). Therefore, "an I.O.U. or other written acknowledgment of indebtedness is not a note unless there is also an undertaking to pay the obligation." 3-103 comment 3. Accordingly, such statements as "I.O.U. $100" and "Borrowed $100" by themselves, are not promises; but it has been held that the requirement of a promise is met by adding such words as "to be paid on demand" or "due on demand."

An order that marks a draft is "a written *instruction* to pay money signed by the person giving the instruction." 3-103(a)(6) (emphasis added). It is not sufficient that a person named in the writing is authorized to pay: the writing must also instruct her to pay. Id. The usual way of expressing the order is to use the imperative form of the verb "Pay." "Pay to the order of Steve" is clearly an order. The reason is not the use of the word "order," which satisfies the altogether different requirement that the writing is payable to order or bearer. The order to pay is inferred from the instruction that the drawee "Pay." Thus, the requirement or an order is met if the writing provides "Pay Bearer."

An instruction may be an order even though it is couched in courteous form such as "please pay" or "kindly pay." On the other hand, there must be more than an authorization or request to pay. Such uncertain language as "I wish you would pay" is not an order.

We emphasize once again that, although the drawer does not expressly promise to pay the instrument, the law obligates her to pay the draft upon certain conditions. 3-414(b). In short, the drawer of a draft that is dishonored by the drawee is liable on the instrument even though the draft itself contains no express promise to pay. This liability is discussed in Chapter 3 infra.

4. Unconditional

Two major functions of commercial paper are to serve as a substitute for money and as a reliable basis for credit. If commercial paper is to perform either function effectively, business people must be assured that there are no strings attached to payment. Therefore, negotiability requires a promise or order that is unconditional. It must be expressed in absolute terms which are not subject to contingencies, provisos, qualifications, or reservations that undermine or impair the obligation to pay. It must be a "courier without luggage." *Overton v. Tyler*, 3 Pa. 346, 347 (1846).

Generally, a promise or order is unconditional unless the writing states:

* an express condition to payment,
* that the promise or order is subject to or governed by another writing, or
* that rights or obligations with respect to the promise or order are stated in another writing.

3-106(a). In other words, if the writing contains none of these provisions, the order or promise is unconditional. On the other hand, if the writing contains even one of the three kinds of provisions that 3-106(a) describes, the promise or order is conditional, negotiability is impossible, and the writing is not an instrument.

Terms of Instrument Determine Presence of Condition

As far as negotiability is concerned, determining if a promise or order is conditional requires an examination of the writing itself -- the putative instrument -- and nothing else. Its express provisions are the only statements that matter in applying the tests of 3-106(a). No matter what anyone has said about the instrument, for the purpose of determining negotiability the promise or order it contains is unconditional unless something in the instrument itself is to the contrary. For example, assume that M hands P a note that provides, "I promise to pay $1,000 to the order of P on demand. (Signed) M." In doing so M says, "This money will not be paid unless a bond is delivered to me." The note is negotiable because the promise contained in the note itself is unconditional and all other requirements for negotiability are satisfied. The same is true if the condition is stated in a separate writing prepared before, after, or contemporaneously with the note. 3-117. Other agreements, oral or written, are themselves irrelevant in deciding negotiability. In contrast, if the note itself provides that payment is to be made only if the bond is delivered, the note is not negotiable.

Effect of Another Agreement

Negotiable instruments are rarely issued in isolation. Usually, they are issued pursuant to or as part of some underlying transaction and agreement between the parties. For example, a check may be delivered to pay for property sold pursuant to a sales contract, or a note may be issued to evidence a loan agreement that is probably secured by collateral. The security aspect of the loan transaction will itself involve typically elaborate agreements about the creditor's rights.

When determining the respective rights and duties of the original parties to transactions of this kind, the Code follows the common-law rule that writings executed as part of the same transaction are to be read and enforced together as a single, integrated agreement. In terms of Article 3, "the obligation of a party to an instrument to pay the instrument may be modified, supplemented, or nullified by a separate agreement of the obligor and a person entitled to enforce the instrument, if the instrument is issued * * * as part of the same transaction giving rise to the agreement." 3-117. The supplemental agreement is a defense to payment of the instrument. Id.

Example 4

"Suppose X requested credit from Creditor who is willing to give the credit only if an acceptable accommodation party will sign the note of X as co-maker. Y agrees to sign as co-maker on the condition that Creditor also obtain the signature of Z as co-maker. Creditor agrees and Y signs as co-maker with X. Creditor fails to obtain the signature of Z on the note. Y is obliged to pay the note, but Section 3-117 applies. In this case, the agreement modifies the terms of the note by stating a condition to the obligation of Y to pay the note. * * * Section 3-117, in treating the agreement as a defense, allows Y to assert the agreement against Creditor ." 3-117 comment 1.

On the other hand, the separate agreement -- whether oral or written -- does not affect negotiability. Regardless of the provisions any outside writing may provide, it does not destroy the negotiability of an instrument which otherwise meets the requisites of negotiability. Thus, if the note in the example meets the requisites of negotiability, it is an instrument despite the agreement between Creditor and Y; and the rights and liabilities on the note are governed by Article 3, including 3-117.

The only problem for Y in relying on 3-117 is that its rule that honors separate agreements is subject to applicable non-Code "law regarding exclusion of proof of contemporaneous or previous agreements." 3-117. So, if the parol evidence rule applies, Y is barred from proving the separate agreement despite 3-117. The parol evidence rule overrides 3-117.

Referring to Another Agreement

The *existence* of another agreement does not affect negotiability. That an instrument makes *express reference* to an outside agreement or other writing can, however, affect negotiability depending on the nature of the reference.

A statement is inoffensive that simply mentions the outside writing or reports that the instrument arises out of or in connection with the writing. Negotiability is denied, however, if the statement ties the instrument to the writing by providing either that the instrument is subject to or governed by the outside writing, or that the latter defines rights or obligations with respect to the former. 3-106(a)(ii-iii). The fact that the terms of payment cannot be determined by looking at the instrument itself, that it is necessary to look to an outside agreement, is contrary to the concept of negotiability. This is so even though the outside agreement, which governs or defines rights in the instrument, contains no conditions or other provisions that are contrary to the requirements of negotiability. "It is not relevant whether any condition to payment is or is not stated in the writing to which reference is made." 3-106 comment 1.

Example 5

a.   A ordered a swimming pool from B and gave B a check for the price which included the memorandum, "for pool kit to be delivered." The check is negotiable. *Strickland v. Kafko Manuf., Inc*, 512 So.2d 714 (Ala. 1987).

b.   A drew a $33,000 check payable to B's order on which A noted, "Just to hold for the security of future business." The check is negotiable. *Carador v. Sana Travel Service, Ltd*, 700 F. Supp. 787 (S.D. N.Y. 1988), aff'd, 876 F.2d 890 (2d Cir. 1989).

c.   Limited partners issued notes to their partnership. The notes declared they were "subject to" the terms of a Partnership Debt Assumption Agreement *** which is incorporated herein." This agreement conditioned payment of the notes and restricted alienabilty. The notes are not negotiable. *Growth Equities Corp. v. Freed*, 277 Cal. Rptr. 848 (Cal. App. 1991).

d.   Credit Corporation and Farmer refinanced two installment sales contracts covering certain farm equipment. Subsequently, they refinanced. "[T]he refinancing agreement states:

> I understand and agree that the execution and delivery of this agreement shall not rescind or revoke the refinanced Contract(s) or affect in any way the rights and obligations thereunder except as expressly amended or revised herein.

"By its own language, the agreement requires reference to the combine and tractor installment contracts. These contracts contain provisions as to legal use of the property and restrictions on the debtor removing the property from outside the county of the debtor's residence. Such references to other contracts defeat the purpose of a negotiable instrument, to-wit: permitting a holder to tell from the face on an instrument whether that person is able to take the instrument as a holder in due course. SDCL 57A-3-105(2) provides, in pertinent part, that an order to pay is made conditional by such subjugating language: (2) A promise or order is not unconditional if the instrument (a) States that it is subject to or governed by any other agreement[.] Here, the language of the refinancing agreement went beyond mere reference to underlying agreement; it required reference to the contracts to determine terms of the agreement and spelled out the refinancing agreement's subservience to the contracts if the terms were not addressed in the refinancing agreement. Therefore, the refinancing agreement contained a promise subjecting it to another agreement, thereby making it conditional. SDCL 57A-3-105. * * * Thus, the refinancing statement cannot qualify as a negotiable instrument under SDCL 57A-3-104." *Massey Ferguson Credit Corp. v. Bice*, 450 N.W.2d 435, 442-43 (S.D. 1990).

There is a very important exception, however, to the rule against expressly subordinating an instrument to the terms of the underlying deal or an extrinsic agreement. Notes that are secured by collateral often refer to the mortgage or other security agreement for rights with respect to collateral, prepayment, or acceleration. This kind of reference is expressly excepted from the rule of 3-106 that would otherwise deny negotiability. 3-106(b)(i). "For example, a note would not be made conditional by the following statement: 'This note is secured by a security interest in collateral described in a security agreement dated April 1, 1990 between the payee and maker of this note. Rights and obligations with respect to the collateral are [stated in] [governed by] the security agreement.'" 3-106 comment 1. The reason for this exception is mostly business convenience and practice. Also, the obligation of an instrument is not diluted and can only be enhanced by rights with respect to collateral, prepayment or acceleration. Thus, a reference to such rights existing beyond the instrument should not impede its transfer or, therefore, its negotiability.

Example 6

Lender financed a subdivision project in exchange for the assignment of notes signed by lot purchasers. Each of the notes contained this clause:

> Should any default be made in payment of any installment of this note or in the performance of any of the covenants or conditions of the deed of trust, ... the entire unpaid amount hereof shall become due and payable forthwith at the election of the holder of this note and without notice.

"In *Salomonsky v. Kelly*, 232 Va. 261, 349 S.E.2d 358 (1986), the promissory notes there in question contained a provision saying they were 'payable as set forth in that certain agreement dated March 15, 1976, an executed copy of which is attached hereto and made a part hereof by this reference.' Citing Code §§ 8-3.104(1)(b) and -105(2)(a), we said '[t]his reference to another document for the payment terms of the notes makes the notes nonnegotiable.' Id. at 263, 349 S.E.2d at 359. In *Taylor v. Roeder*, 234 Va. 99, 360 S.E.2d 191 (1987), the promissory notes considered there provided for interest at 3% over Chase Manhattan Bank's prime rate, to be adjusted monthly. Citing *Salomonsky*, we said the notes were nonnegotiable because they suffered from 'the disadvantage that the amount required to satisfy the debt cannot be ascertained without reference to an extrinsic source.' Id. at 104, 360 S.E.2d at 194. The present case differs substantially from both *Salomonsky* and *Taylor*. The face of each note involved here shows with exactness the amount payable, including interest, the number of installments required, and the amount of each installment. Reference to no other document is required to ascertain 'the payment terms of the notes,' *Salomonsky*, or 'the amount required to satisfy the debt,' *Taylor*. Accordingly, we do not think that either Code §3.3-104(1)(b) or §3.3-105(2)(a) is implicated in this case. Rather, we think that the clause in question is merely an acceleration clause and, therefore, that Code §8.3-105(1)(c) controls [and allows the clause]." *Marriott v. Harris*, 368 S.E.2d 225, 238 (Va. 1988).

Implied Conditions Not Recognized, Only Express

Because the breach of a separate agreement can be a defense to an instrument, 3-117, it might be argued that a mere reference to an underlying executory contract between the parties, or even the existence of it, impliedly conditions the instrument on due performance of the contract and thereby denies negotiability to the instrument. This argument fails. Commercial paper often refers to contractual arrangements still to be performed. Usually such recitals are intended as statements of consideration without implications of any kind. If the maker or drawer intends to condition her liability, the Code requires her to do more than leave it to inference.

The rule is that an order or promise is conditional only if it states "an *express* condition to payment," 3-106(a)(i) (emphasis added), which is not true when the statement simply reports that the instrument is given for an executory promise. For example:

> [S]uppose a promise states, "In consideration of John Doe's promise to convey title to Blackacre I promise to pay $100,000 to the order of John Doe." That promise can be an instrument if Section 3-104 is otherwise satisfied. Although the recital of the executory promise of Doe to convey Blackacre might be read as an implied condition that the promise be performed, the condition is not an express condition as required by Section 3-106(a)(i).

3-106 comment 1.

Similarly, if an instrument otherwise negotiable provides that it is given in accordance with or "as per" some collateral contract, the possible inference that payment is conditioned on performance of the other contract is not permitted to destroy negotiability. Rather it is treated merely as a recital of the origin of the instrument or as an informational reference to another contract. In like vein, a statement in a draft that it is drawn under a letter of credit does not state a condition but merely identifies the occasion for the issuance of the instrument.

Express Conditions That Are Permitted

There are a couple of very narrow exceptions to the general rule against express conditions. First, the requirement of a countersignature in a traveler's check does not affect negotiability. 3-106(c). Although this requirement "is a condition to the obligation to pay, traveler's checks are treated in the commercial world as money substitutes and therefore should be governed by Article 3." 3-106 comment 2.

Second, an instrument can contain a statement, that is required by other law, preserving the issuer's claims and defenses against the payee. 3-106(d). For example, federal law requires including the following notice in a consumer credit contract for the sale of goods or services, including a contract in the form of an instrument:

> ANY HOLDER OF THIS CONSUMER CREDIT CONTRACT IS SUBJECT
> TO ALL CLAIMS AND DEFENSES WHICH THE DEBTOR COULD
> ASSERT AGAINST THE SELLER OF GOODS OR SERVICES OBTAINED
> PURSUANT HERETO OR WITH THE PROCEEDS HEREOF.

16 C.F.R. 433.2(a). This notice does not prevent negotiability, even though the effect is to subject the note to the underlying transaction. This kind of notice nevertheless accomplishes its purpose because there cannot be a holder in due course of the instrument. 3-106(d). Thus, any transferee takes subject to the claims and defenses that the issuer could assert against the original payee. Thus, if a consumer buys goods and signs a note for the price and the seller-payee fails to perform, the buyer can assert the breach as a defense or counterclaim against any third party who took the note and sues the buyer on it.

Reference to Account or Fund

The fact that an instrument indicates a particular account to be debited or any fund or source from which reimbursement is expected does not render a promise or order conditional. For example, the drawer of a bill may direct the drawee to pay the money to the order of the payee and "charge the same to the amount of the drawer" or to the "merchandise account" or the like. Such directions are for accounting purposes, and the drawer's obligation is in no way contingent upon a credit balance in the account. Negotiability is unaffected.

The result would be different under former law if the instrument states that payment is to be made only from a particular fund or source. In this case, former law denied negotiability because the obligation to pay is necessarily contingent on the sufficiency of the fund. It was thought that to be unconditional, an order or promise must carry the general credit of the maker or drawer.

The law changed its mind on this issue when Article 3 was amended in 1990. The rule now is that "[a] promise or order is not made conditional * * * because payment is limited to resort to a particular fund or source." 3-106(b). The explanation is this:

> There is no cogent reason why the general credit of a legal entity must be pledged to have a negotiable instrument. Market forces determine the marketability of instruments of this kind. If potential buyers don't want promises or orders that are payable only from a particular source or fund, they won't take them, but Article 3 should apply.

3-106 comment 1. This reasoning would justify eliminating every requirement of negotiability. A truer explanation, probably, is further relaxation and compromise in negotiability that reflect changes in business customs, practices, or expectations.

5. Money

The unconditional promise or order that negotiability requires is a promise or order to pay *money*. An instrument is payable in money if it is stated as payable in "a medium of exchange authorized or adopted by a domestic or foreign government and includes a monetary unit of account established by an intergovernmental organization or by agreement between two or more nations." 1-201(24). Money, therefore, is not limited to United States dollars. If the instrument is payable in foreign money, the amount "may be paid in the foreign money or in an equivalent amount in dollars calculated by using the current bank-offered spot rate at the place of payment for the purchase of dollars on the day on which the instrument is paid." 3-107.

Example 7

"On October 11, 1979, defendants Gary and Joan Doerhoff signed a Bill of Sale transferring their cabinet business, known as Ozark Cabinet and Millwork Shop, to defendant, Nancy Clardy. As part of the sale, the Doerhoffs received a note dated October 12, 1979, in the amount of $31,000, purportedly signed by Nancy Clardy. The note stated that $5000 was to be paid on October 25, 1979. The balance of the note was to be paid in monthly installments of $1250 'to be paid in cabinets figured at the prevailing builders price for Jefferson City ... until October 12, 1981, at which time the entire balance thereof is due and payable in cash.' Subsequently, on July 18, 1980, plaintiffs sold a four-plex to Gary and Joan Doerhoff in exchange for 6.81 acres of land and the Nancy Clardy note. The Doerhoffs did not endorse the note but merely delivered it, along with the Bill of Sale to which the note was attached, to plaintiffs. * * * Although the note was delivered to plaintiffs, the Doerhoffs continued to receive the cabinets which were delivered as payments on the note. Under the contract between plaintiffs and the Doerhoffs, the Doerhoffs were to pay plaintiffs the cash value of any cabinets received under the note. The contract stated: 'Buyer [Doerhoffs] agree to buy cabinets from Ozark Cabinet Shop per agreement stated in the Note from Nancy Clardy as long as Ozark Cabinet Shop will furnish said cabinets until October 12, 1981. Buyer also agrees to get a statement of value of the cabinets from Ozark Cabinet shop and pay the sellers [plaintiffs] the amount of said statement in cash within 15 days after delivery of each set of cabinets.' * * * From July 18, 1980 until the spring of 1981, plaintiffs received only two payments totaling $800 from the Doerhoffs. Then in the spring of 1981, plaintiffs were informed by Bruce Clardy that the cabinet shop was 'going under.' Plaintiff Means said that he told Mr. Clardy that he would expect Mrs. Clardy to pay the note in full on October 12, 1981." *Means v. Clardy*, 735 S.W.2d 6 (Mo. Ct. App. 1987). The note is not negotiable.

6. Fixed Amount

The money payable must be a *fixed amount*. The law formerly expressed this requirement as a "sum certain." The meaning is fundamentally the same: a total which the holder can determine from the instrument by any necessary computation at the time the instrument is payable, without reference to any outside source. There is, however, a big difference in present law: the requirement of a fixed amount applies only to the principal. 3-112 comment 1. It does not apply to interest or, presumably, to other charges that are less commonly included in an instrument -- such as collection costs and attorneys fees which are notoriously uncertain in amount.

Example 8

a.   "In March 1976, J. Monte Williamson, the owner of a 16.65% interest in Lake Manor Associates, a partnership, agreed to sell his partnership interest, 50% to H. Louis Salomonsky and 50% to Tiffany H. Armstrong. In return, Salomonsky and Armstrong each agreed to give Williamson 400 shares of a certain stock valued at $15.00 a share with a total worth of $6,000 and a noninterest bearing note in the amount of $4,000 for the balance. The notes were executed on March 15, 1976. On that same date, the parties executed an agreement which was incorporated in the notes by reference and which itself referred to the notes. The agreement set forth various conditions which had to be satisfied before the debt evidenced by the notes became due and payable. The evidence established that these conditions were met in October 1981. In early 1982, Williamson made an oral demand for payment upon Salomonsky. Later, by letter dated May 18, 1982, Williamson demanded payment from both Salomonsky and Armstrong. On June 7, 1982, when no payments were forthcoming, Williamson filed two separate suits on the separate notes and related agreement. In the trial court, Salomonsky and Armstrong defended on the grounds that the March 15, 1976 notes were negotiable instruments under the UCC; that the notes were demand instruments; that a five-year statute of limitations applied to the notes; that the statute of limitations began to run on March 15, 1976; and that the suits, filed on June 7, 1982, were untimely. * * * The Armstrong note and the Salomonsky note both contained the following language:

> FOR VALUE RECEIVED, the undersigned promises to pay to the order of J. MONTE WILLIAMSON, ... the principal sum of Four Thousand Dollars ($4,000.00), payable as set forth in that certain agreement dated March 15, 1976, an executed copy of which is attached hereto and made a part hereof by this reference.

"This reference to another document for the payment terms of the notes makes the notes nonnegotiable." *Salomonsky v. Kelly,* 349 S.E.2d 358, 359 (Va. 1986).

b. "Stewart owned the Astro Motel in Cedar City, Utah. Defendant Roland Vance, a real estate agent for defendant C.J. Realty, approached Stewart about listing the motel for sale with C.J. Realty. The listing agreement was entered into, and Vance subsequently obtained a potential buyer for the motel. On September 24, 1979, Stewart and the potential buyer entered into a lease agreement and option to purchase. The agreement provided that the lessees could exercise an option to purchase the motel on or before May 1, 1980. Also on September 24, 1979, Stewart executed a promissory note for $15,900 payable to C.J. Realty to secure the real estate commission to which C.J. Realty would be entitled if the lessees exercised their option to purchase. The promissory note provided that it would be payable as follows:

> Total due in full upon final closing between D.C. Stewart Co., Seller, and Wendell James Downward and Connie Downward, husband and wife, Buyers, which shall be on or before May 1, 1980, when Buyers exercise their option to purchase the Astro Motel in Cedar City, Utah.

"On September 27, 1979, the promissory note was sold by Vance, acting on behalf of C.J. Realty, to the plaintiff Calfo for $12,720. The lessees never exercised their option to purchase the Astro Motel. However, after May 1, 1980, Calfo made demand upon all of the defendants for payment of the note. When payment was not forthcoming, suit was brought on the note against Stewart, and against Vance as guarantor of the note. Stewart then cross-claimed against his co-defendants for indemnity. On January 5, 1982, the trial court heard Calfo's motion for summary judgment. Calfo argued that the promissory note was a negotiable instrument on its face, that it was past due, and that he was a holder in due course. On that same date, the court also heard Stewart's motion for a summary judgment. Stewart asserted that the note was not a negotiable instrument and that Calfo was not a holder in due course. * * * On these facts, we find the note to be both conditional and indefinite on its face." *Calfo v. D.C. Stewart Co.,* 717 P.2d 697, 698-70 (Utah 1986).

c.   **A issued a note to B for the price of goods. The note provided that interest**

> shall accrue on the unpaid principal of this note (the Note) from time to time outstanding from the date hereof, at a rate per annum equal to the lesser of (i) 2-1/2 per cent per annum above the London InterBank Offered Rate (LIBOR) or (ii) the highest rate of interest permitted under applicable law until the principal balance of this note is paid in full.

The note is negotiable even though computing the interest from the face of the note is impossible and the interest rate varies depending on an extrinsic index.

d.   **In the case *National Union Fire Ins. Co. v. Krasner,* 7 U.C.C. Rep. Serv.2d 1524 (N.Y. Sup. Ct. 1989), the note called for interest at "1.25% over the prime rate to be adjusted automatically on and as of the effective date of any change in the prime rate." The term "prime rate" is defined in the note as "the prime commercial rate of a major bank with assets in excess of $5 billion in effect from time to time as publicly announced by the bank." The court concluded that "even if the provision for a variable rate based on a prime rate did not itself render the note nonnegotiable, the fact that the note does not refer to a named financial institution or some recognized index in order to ascertain the interest rate renders it nonnegotiable for failure to provide for the payment of a sum certain." Id. at 1526.**

An instrument is not payable with interest unless it so provides. 3-112(a). Negotiability is unaffected whether or not the instrument provides for interest, and is also unaffected by providing for interest without describing the rate. In the latter event, "interest is payable at the judgment rate in effect at the place of payment of the instrument and at the time interest first accrues." 3-112(b). Therefore, "if an instrument calls for interest, the amount of interest will always be determinable." 3-112 comment 1.

The typical note provides for interest and describes an amount or contract rate. Article 3 is very tolerant with respect to these provisions. "Interest may be stated * * * as a fixed or variable amount of money or it may be expressed as a fixed or variable rate or rates." 3-112(b). Also, "[t]he amount or rate of interest may be stated or described in the instrument in any manner" and, most significantly, "*may require reference to information not contained in the instrument.*" Id. (emphasis added). The emphasized language specifically addresses a dispute among the courts under prior law. They disagreed on whether or not negotiability is denied when an instrument calculated interest by reference to an extrinsic formula or index, such as a bank's prime rate or an economic indicator published by the government or a market. The law is now clear, because of the specific language of 3-112(b), that negotiability is unaffected. This result would seem to flow from the general principle that the requirement of "fixed amount" applies only to principal, not to interest or other charges.

Presumably, however, negotiability is denied if the principal itself is tied to an extrinsic index. The reason is not that the amount is subject to change after issue. The reason is that the total principal cannot be calculated, at the time payable, from the face of the instrument. An exception is implied for a conversion rate in the event that an instrument stated in foreign money is paid in dollars. 3-107. It is also implied that fluctuations in such a rate do not render the amount unfixed.

As long as the principal can be determined when payable from information within the instrument, it is not always necessary for the instrument to state an indelible total. Mathematical calculation using the information is permitted, so that the amount is fixed if the instrument promises or orders 12 payments of $1,000 each. It is uncertain whether or not Article 3 continues the former law of tolerating a fixed discount or increase if the instrument is paid before or after a stated time for payment. The argument for tolerance is that the minimum amount is calculable. The possibility that an extra sum might be paid (icing on the cake) will not affect marketability or retard circulation and could even enhance it.

7. Payable On Demand Or At A Definite Time

Negotiability requires that an instrument "is payable on demand or at a definite time." 3-104(a)(2). An instrument is "payable on demand" if it:

- states that it is payable on demand or at sight,
- otherwise indicates that it is payable at the will of the holder, or
- does not state any time of payment.

3-108(a). Most instruments that are payable on demand, including virtually all checks, are so payable for the last reason: they make no express provision for time of payment.

An instrument is payable at a definite time if it is payable:

- at a fixed date or dates,
- on elapse of a definite period of time after sight or acceptance, or
- at a time or times readily ascertainable at the time the instrument is issued,

even if it is subject to prepayment, acceleration, or certain extensions. 3-108(b). This description largely follows and even restates the former law. For example, an instrument would be payable at a definite time if it were payable "on July 1, 1992," "thirty days after date" (assuming, of course, that the instrument is dated), or "on or before March 1, 1992." Although "on or before" may suggest indefiniteness, there is no reason to deny such instruments negotiability because there is no more uncertainty involved than in an instrument payable on demand. Similarly, when an instrument is payable at a fixed period after sight, the holder controls the matter and may have maturity promptly determined by presenting the instrument for acceptance.

Section 3-108(b) differs from former law by broadening definite time to include payable "at a time or times readily ascertainable at the time the promise or order is issued." 3-108(b). This language presumably allows, for example, tying payment to a scheduled event certain to happen, such as "payable on the 150th anniversary of Northwestern University Law School" or "the day of Super Bowl XXXVI." It would not allow tying payment to an event certain to occur but at an uncertain time, such as the death of a particular person. It is nevertheless possible to accomplish the usual purpose of such a provision without offending negotiability by specifying a far distant definite time for payment subject to acceleration by the person's death.

Acceleration Clauses

If the time for payment is otherwise definite, the fact that the instrument provides for accelerating payment does not render the time indefinite. 3-108(b)(ii). This is so whether the acceleration is automatic upon the occurrence of some event (certain to occur or not) or is at the option of one of the parties. For example, it is permissible that a term note accelerates the time for payment if the maker sells collateral securing the note, or permits the holder to demand earlier payment if she is insecure about the maker's financial condition. See 1-208. The instrument can also permit the maker to accelerate by allowing prepayment, 3-108(b)(i), but she may pay a penalty for doing so or remain liable for the unaccrued interest.

Extension Clauses

The requirement of payable at a definite time is not violated by making the time for payment subject to:

- an extension at the option of the holder,
- an extension to a further definite time at the option of the maker or acceptor, or
- an extension to a further definite time automatically upon or after a specified act or event.

3-108(b)(iii)-(iv). A provision for extension by the holder need not specify a time limit for the extension. It can be open-ended because, even without the clause, the holder is naturally free to forebear for as long as she wishes. The holder cannot use this right to create additional interest charges over the obligor's objection. The obligor can tender payment on the due date and thereby escape liability for additional interest that she has not agreed to pay. 3-603(c) ("If tender of payment of an amount due on an instrument is made to a person entitled to enforce the instrument, the obligation of the obligor to pay interest after the due date on the amount tendered is discharged.")

A provision allowing the maker or acceptor to extend the time for payment, or automatically extending such time if an act or event occurs, must specify a definite time limit on the period of extension. So done, negotiability is unaffected by the provision because "the effect upon certainty of time of payment is the same as if the instrument were made payable at the ultimate date with a term providing for acceleration." 3-108 comment. Not done, negotiability is lacking because the unlimited right to extend negates the definite time for payment. No limit is ever implied by law, as sometimes happened under former law, to cure this violation of negotiability.

At a Definite Time and On Demand

It is possible that an instrument may be payable *both* at a definite time *and also* on demand. Negotiability is not offended. The instrument is deemed payable "on demand until the fixed date and, if demand for payment is not made before that date, becomes payable at a definite time on the fixed date." 3-108(c).

8. Payable To Order or To Bearer (Words of Negotiability)

Negotiability requires that the instrument is "payable *to bearer* or *to order* at the time it [the instrument] is issued or first comes into possession of a holder." 3-104(a)(1). Words that satisfy this requirement are called *words of negotiability*. These words are the most common earmarks of negotiability. They most clearly indicate the intention of the maker or drawer to issue an instrument that is negotiable and subject to all the incidents attaching to this form of contract and property. They alert the prospective purchaser, more certainly than anything else, of the possibility that if the instrument is negotiated to a holder in due course, the effect is to cut off any claims and defenses of the maker or drawer against the payee. Also, requiring these words of negotiability

> provides a simple device to clearly exclude a writing that does not fit the pattern of typical negotiable instruments and which is not intended to be a negotiable instrument. If a writing could be an instrument despite the absence of "to order" or "to bearer" language and a dispute arises with respect to the writing, it might be argued that the writing is a negotiable instrument because the other requirements of [3-104(a)] are somehow met. Even if the argument is eventually found to be without merit it can be used as a litigation ploy. * * * [By requiring words of negotiability for an instrument] [a]bsence of the words precludes any argument that such contracts might be negotiable instruments.

3-104 comment 2.

"To order" or "to bearer" are alternative forms of the words of negotiability. In determining if a writing is a negotiable instrument, it makes no difference whether it is payable to order or to bearer so long as it is payable to one or the other. The difference is important in deciding how the instrument is negotiated so that the transferee becomes a holder and is entitled to the rights of that status, which can include the rights of a holder in due course. An instrument that is payable to order (a/k/a *order paper*) is negotiated by transfer of possession and indorsement; *bearer paper* is negotiated by transfer of possession alone. 3-201(b).

Payable to Order

Typically, an instrument is payable to order, which means it is not payable to bearer and is payable:

- to the order of an identified person, or
- to an identified person or order.

3-109(b). This meaning covers the most common form of the words of negotiability: "Pay to the order of Jane Doe." It also covers the typical variation, "Pay Jane Doe or order." (Significantly, an instrument that uses this form is payable to order even if Doe is fictitious. 3-109 comment 2.) Other language is sufficient that is the clear equivalent of the statutory language. *Cooperatieve Centrale Raiffeisen-Boerenleenbank v. Bailey*, 710 F. Supp. 737, 738-39 (C.D. Cal. 1989) ("pay to the order to" is equivalent).

The word "order" (or, perhaps, a very close equivalent) is essential. It makes clear that the maker or drawer intends payment to transferees as well as the identified person. It empowers this person, through the process of negotiation, to redirect the obligation that runs to her, as payee, to someone else she designates or to anyone who holds the instrument. Former law expressly tolerated using the word "assigns" as a synonym for "order" or designating the instrument as "exchange" or the like. These substitutes equally signal transferability by the named payee.

An instrument is not payable to order that provides only "Pay Jane Doe," because the magic "order" word is missing. Neither is it payable to bearer. The writing therefore lacks words of negotiability and is not a negotiable instrument. See *Tompkins Printing Equipment Co. v. Almik, Inc.*, 725 F. Supp. 918, 920-21 (E.D. Mich. 1989) (note that promises "to pay American Typesetting" is not negotiable); *Spidell v. Jenkins*, 727 P.2d 1285, 1287 (Idaho Ct. App. 1986) (note payable to specific persons, rather than to order or bearer, is nonnegotiable); *Sunrizon Homes, Inc. v. American Guaranty Investment Corp.*, 782 P.2d 103, 106 (Okla. 1988); *Turner v. Bank of Commerce*, 768 S.W.2d 683, 685 (Tenn. Ct. App. 1988). Furthermore, contrary to former law, the writing is entirely beyond Article 3.

The single exception is the 3-104(c) check. It is an order to pay that satisfies all of the requisites of negotiability, and that otherwise falls within the definition of "check," except that it lacks words of negotiability. Section 3-104(c) deems that such a check, despite its missing words, is a negotiable instrument and a check. Therefore, a check payable "Pay Jane Doe" is fully negotiable, is covered by Article 3, and a transferee of it can become a holder in due course, even though the check lacks words of negotiability. Here is the reason:

> [I]t is good policy to treat checks, which are payment instruments, as negotiable instruments whether or not they contain the words "to the order of." These words are almost always pre-printed on the check form. Occasionally the drawer of a check may strike out these words before issuing the check. In the past some credit unions used check forms that did not contain the quoted words. Such check forms may still be in use but they are no longer common. Absence of the quoted words can easily be overlooked and should not affect the rights of holders who may pay money or give credit for a check without being aware that it is not in the conventional form.

3-104 comment 2.

This exception for the 3-104(c) check is very narrow. Any other draft that is payable only to an identified person, and not also her order, is not negotiable. This order language is not supplied by the "order to pay" that distinguishes the draft from a note and that is implied by the direction "Pay." The "order to pay" in a draft satisfies a requirement of negotiability that is different from the requirement of words of negotiability. The former identifies the nature and purpose of the instrument and the issuer's undertaking. The latter signals transferability. A negotiable draft requires both an order to pay that, additionally, is payable to order or bearer, except for the 3-104(c) check.

An instrument may be made payable to the order of anyone, whether a natural person or legal or commercial entity, including the maker, drawer, or drawee. It may be made payable to the order of two or more persons together as "A, B and C," or in the alternative as "A, B or C." 3-110(d).

A person to whom an instrument is payable may be identified in any way, including by name, identifying number, office, or account number. 3-110(c). The test to determine who the instrument identifies is the intent of the person signing as, or in the name or behalf of, the issuer, whether or not the person signing is authorized to do so. 3-110(a). "If X signs a check as drawer of a check on X's account, the intent of X controls. If X, as President of Corporation, signs a check as President on behalf of Corporation as drawer, the intent of X controls. If X forges Y's signature as drawer of a check, the intent of X also controls." 3-110 comment 1. In case the signer is not human, as with a computer or checkwriting machine, the relevant intent is that of the person who supplied the payee's name. 3-110(b).

The issue of whom the instrument names as payee usually translates into the issue of who can properly indorse the instrument. It concerns the process of negotiation, which is covered in Chapter 4 infra. The discussion there includes a few more rules about determining to whom an instrument is payable, i.e., who can properly deal with it as holder.

Payable to Bearer

An instrument that is not payable to order is not, automatically, payable to bearer. The two forms of the words of negotiability -- order and bearer -- are alternatives of the same requirement and either of them can be used in creating a negotiable instrument, but each of them has its own peculiar meaning. Failing one does not satisfy the other by default; and if the instrument does not use one form or the other, as Article 3 defines them, the instrument lacks the words of negotiability that 3-104(a) requires.

"Payable to bearer" means that a promise or order:

- states that it is payable to bearer or to the order of bearer or otherwise indicates that the person in possession of the promise or order is entitled to payment;
- does not state a payee; or
- states that it is payable to or to the order of cash or otherwise indicates that it is not payable to an identified person.

3-109(a). The unofficial essence of payable to bearer is that anyone who possesses or holds the instrument can enforce it, which negatively implies that payment is not limited to a particular person or people. The issuer intends payment to anybody with the instrument. Thus, an instrument that expresses this intent in so many words is, officially, payable to bearer. 3-109(a)(1). The most common expressions of this intent, which meet the test of "payable to bearer," are:

"Pay to Bearer,"
"Pay to the order of Bearer"
"Pay to Cash," or
"Pay to Cash, or Order,"

as long as "Bearer" or "Cash" is not used to identify a person.

Naming a fictitious person who cannot be paid is different and does not qualify as "payable to bearer." In such a case the instrument indicates that it is payable to an identified person whether or not, in fact, the person exists. If the fictitious person's name is coupled with order language, the instrument is payable to order; otherwise, it is not negotiable. See 3-109 comment 2.

If the instrument is payable to bearer and also to an identified person, the instrument is payable to bearer whether or not it is also payable to the person's order. Thus an instrument is payable to bearer that reads "Pay to Jane Doe or bearer" or "Pay to the order of Jane Doe or bearer." In the former case, the bearer language supplies words of negotiability that otherwise would be entirely lacking because "Pay to Jane Doe" is not payable to order. In the latter case, the order language itself constitutes words of negotiability, but the additional bearer language overrides the order language. In the first case the bearer language is necessary for negotiability; in the second case the bearer language is not needed for negotiability and does not deny negotiability, but puts the instrument in bearer form and determines how, initially, it can be negotiated.

An instrument that does not state a payee is also payable to bearer, 3-109(a)(2), as in "Pay to ____ " or "Pay to the order of ___." By leaving the space blank, the issuer might have intended that the instrument was payable to anybody. More likely, she intended to fill in someone's name and forgot, or she planned that someone else would fill in the name. In any event, the instrument is "payable to bearer" even if it is also an incomplete instrument. 3-109 comment 2.

When The Instrument Must Be So Payable

Negotiability requires that the instrument is payable to bearer or to order at *the time it is issued or first comes into possession of a holder.* The term *"issue"* means "the first delivery of an instrument by the maker or drawer, whether to a holder or nonholder, for the purpose of giving rights on the instrument to any person." 3-105(a). Basically, therefore, the instrument must contain the words of negotiability when the maker or drawer gives it to the payee. It is not an instrument if it lacks these words and the payee adds them. Thus, a note in which M promises to "Pay P" is not an instrument and does not become an instrument, as to M, by P later adding order language.

Suppose, however, that P nevertheless transferred the nonnegotiable note, which would be governed by law other than Article 3. In so doing, P followed the conventions of Article 3 despite the statute's inapplicability. Thus, P indorsed the note to T, "Pay to the order of T." These are words of negotiability. It could be argued that at this point, from P forward, the note becomes a negotiable instrument if it then satisfies the other requirements of negotiability. With a tug of the bootstraps, T would be a holder because the note contained words of negotiability when it first came into her possession.

The opposite case is a fully negotiable note payable to P's order that P indorses, "Pay T." The note remains negotiable because, at the time of issue, it contained words of negotiability.

Absence Of Words Of Negotiability

Former law gave special treatment to an instrument that satisfies all of the requirements of negotiability except that it lacks words of negotiability, i.e., it is not payable to either order or bearer. Such an instrument was governed in all respects by Article 3, except no one could be a holder in due course of the instrument.

The new Article 3 changes this law. Such an order or promise, whether in the form of a draft or note, is not negotiable and is entirely beyond the scope of Article 3, unless it is a check. A check that lacks words of negotiability but is otherwise negotiable is fully a negotiable instrument, 3-104(c), and is fully governed by

Article 3, including the holder-in-due-course doctrine. A person can become a holder in due course of such a check according to the usual rules that Article 3 prescribes for such status.

9. No Other Undertaking Or Instruction

The final requirement of negotiability is that beyond the maker's order or promise to pay money, the instrument itself must not contain "any other undertaking or instruction" by the maker or drawer "to do any act in addition to the payment of money," with a few exceptions that Article 3 describes. For example, an instrument is not negotiable that also contains a promise or order to render services or to sell or lease property. An Article 9 security agreement or some other subsidiary understanding can live within a contract for the sale of goods or lease of real estate, but a negotiable instrument cannot reside there. A negotiable instrument can freely exist along with a separate sales contract or other undertaking or instruction that supplements or even modifies the instrument, 3-117; but the latter must not be included within the former. It is their integration that precludes negotiability.

The principal exceptions are incorporated into 3-104(a) itself. Negotiability is not affected if the writing also contains:

- an undertaking or power to give, maintain, or protect collateral to secure payment,
- an authorization or power to the holder to confess judgment or realize on or dispose of collateral, or
- a waiver of the benefit of any law intended for the advantage or protection of an obligor.

3-104(a)(3)(i-iii). It is therefore possible to put an Article 9 security agreement in a note; and it is common for notes to include language whereby indorsers, sureties, and other parties waive requirements of notice and also waive other rights under Article 3 and rights to collateral and other protections under Article 9. Each of these exceptions is intended to strengthen the promise or order to pay money and has no independent value of its own.

Example 9

The Supreme Court of South Dakota decided that a refinancing agreement was "not a negotiable instrument because it contains 'other promises' made by the drawer. These include the following: (1) the purchase of property damage insurance; (2) the purchase of credit life insurance; (3) provision for late payment fees; (4) a provision for rebate of unearned finance charge; and (5) an agreement to pay all taxes levied against the property. Other courts examining this same issue have repeatedly held that provisions such as the ones in question rendered an instrument non-negotiable. *Insurance Agency Managers v. Gonzales*, 578 S.W.2d 803 (Tex.Civ.App.1979) (retail

> installment contract included other promises including purchase of property insurance); *Chrysler Credit Corp. v. Friendly Ford, Inc*, 535 S.W.2d 110 (Mo.App.1976) (tractor contract required purchase of insurance); *All Lease Co., Inc. v. Bowen*, 20 UCC Rep.Serv. 790 (Cir.Ct.Md.1975) (provision for late payments and to insure goods); *Allen-Parker Company v. Lollis*, 257 S.C. 266, 185 S.E.2d 739 (1971) (required to keep free of taxes); *Geiger Finance Company v. Graham*, 123 Ga.App. 771, 182 S.E.2d 521 (1971) (application for insurance)." *Massey Ferguson Credit Corp. v. Bice*, 450 N.W.2d 435, 443 (S.D. 1990).

There are other terms that can be included in an instrument (and often are) without affecting negotiability. Good examples are the place where the instrument is issued or payable, see 3-111 (place of payment), and the date of issue. See 3-113(b) (date of instrument). These and other terms are benign and permissible so long as they are not additional instructions or undertakings that negotiability forbids, and so long as the terms do not compromise any other provision of the instrument that is essential in satisfying another requirement of negotiability.

Relatedly, negotiability is unaffected by not including terms that are commonly included in instruments, except for terms that are essential for negotiability. Negotiability is exclusively defined by the requirements of 3-104(a). An instrument is created by any writing that meets them. Really, these requirements are very few and slim, so that very short and skimpy instruments are possible, not uncommon, and even encouraged by the narrowness and usual intolerance of 3-104(a) for anything beyond its plain letter.

Negotiable instrument (or not) by declaration

After tediously examining the requirements for negotiability, one might ask whether the parties can shortcut the matter by simply declaring on the writing that it is "intended to be negotiable" or by stamping it "NEGOTIABLE." Does such a declaration by the maker or drawer, by itself, establish a writing as a negotiable instrument under Article 3? No. "[A] writing cannot be made a negotiable instrument within Article 3 by contract or conduct of its parties." 3-104 comment 2, not even by the parties' stipulation in court. *Tompkins Printing Equipment Co. v. Almik, Inc.*, 725 F. Supp. 918, 920-21 (E.D. Mich. 1989). The only way that a writing becomes an Article 3 instrument is to satisfy the 3-104 requisites of negotiability. Thus, for example, if a writing were payable in other than money or contained a conditional promise, a statement that "This Note is Negotiable" would not be effective to qualify the writing as an instrument.

On the other hand, if an otherwise negotiable note lacks the exact, magic words "payable to order" but declares on its face that it is "NEGOTIABLE," the declaration might itself satisfy the requirement of words of negotiability if it is intended as a substitute for the magic words, is a close equivalent, and does not undercut the commercial justifications for the concept of negotiability. The new Article 3, however, is less clear than former law that equivalent language is sufficient.

The opposite issue is whether or not the parties can use a form that is a negotiable instrument and avoid negotiability by declaring, on the instrument, that it is *not* negotiable. The answer is yes, except for a check.

> A promise or order *other than a check* is not an instrument if, at the time it is issued or first comes into possession of a holder, it contains a *conspicuous* statement, however expressed, to the effect that the promise or order is not negotiable or is not an instrument governed by this Article.

3-104(d) (emphasis added). The effect is the same as eliminating the words of negotiability.

> For example, a promissory note can be stamped with the legend NOT NEGOTIABLE. The effect * * * is not only to negate the possibility of a holder in due course, but to prevent the writing from being a negotiable instrument for any purpose.

3-104 comment 3.

A declaration on a check that it is not negotiable is ineffective. The explanation is probably the same reason that a check without words of negotiability is fully negotiable. See 3-104(c). Such a declaration, like the absence of order or bearer language, is uncommon in checks and unexpected, and so could "easily be overlooked and should not affect the rights of holders who may pay money or give credit for a check without being aware that it is not in the conventional form." 3-104 comment 2.

Negotiability by agreement or other conduct

Although a promise or order that fails the requisites of negotiability cannot become a negotiable instrument by any conduct of the parties, the equivalent effects of negotiability can attach to the promise or order because of other law that is triggered by certain conduct by the parties. According to the official explanation:

> An order or promise that is excluded from Article 3 because of the requirements of Section 3-104(a) may nevertheless be similar to a negotiable instrument in many respects. Although such a writing cannot be made a negotiable instrument within Article 3 by contract or conduct of its parties, nothing in Section 3-104 or in Section 3-102 is intended to mean that in a particular case involving such a writing a court could not arrive at a result

similar to the result that would follow if the writing were a negotiable instrument. For example, a court might find that the obligor with respect to a promise that does not fall within Section 3-104(a) is precluded from asserting a defense against a bona fide purchaser. The preclusion could be based on estoppel or ordinary principles of contract. It does not depend upon the law of negotiable instruments.

Moreover, consistent with the principle stated in Section 1-102(2)(b), the immediate parties to an order or promise that is not an instrument may provide by agreement that one or more of the provisions of Article 3 determine their rights and obligations under the writing. Upholding the parties' choice is not inconsistent with Article 3. Such an agreement may bind a transferee of the writing if the transferee has notice of it or the agreement arises from usage of trade and the agreement does not violate other law or public policy. An example of such an agreement is a provision that a transferee of the writing has the rights of a holder in due course stated in Article 3 if the transferee took rights under the writing in good faith, for value, and without notice of a claim or defense.

Even without an agreement of the parties to an order or promise that is not an instrument, it may be appropriate, consistent with the principles stated in Section 1-102(2), for a court to apply one or more provisions of Article 3 to the writing by analogy, taking into account the expectations of the parties and the differences between the writing and an instrument governed by Article 3. Whether such application is appropriate depends upon the facts of each case.

3-104 comment 2. In these cases the parties' conduct does *not* create a negotiable instrument, and the law that directly applies is *not* Article 3. Rather, their conduct triggers other law that gives Article 3-like effects to the parties' transaction. It is virtual, rather than actual, negotiability. There is more about this "virtual negotiability" in Chapter 5 infra.

law

The following cases were decided under the old Article 3 but, for the most part, they remain good law and are helpful guides in understanding the requisites of negotiability under Revised Article 3. In each case, however, you should carefully check to insure that the decision about negotiability would be the same under the new law. Equally important, in each case you should also consider why the issue of negotiability is important. What difference does it make whether or not a negotiable instrument is involved and whether or not Article 3 applies? The cases illustrate the important lesson that differences in contract liability and property rights can sometimes greatly vary (and sometimes not) depending on the source of governing law.

Mauricio v. Mendez

Texas Court of Appeals, San Antonio, 1987
723 S.W.2d 296

Cadena, Chief Justice. Plaintiff, Paul Mauricio, appeals from a judgment in a case tried to the court, denying him recovery in his suit to collect from defendant, Jose Mendez, on a lease agreement and what plaintiff described in his pleadings as a "note." The trial court rendered judgment at the conclusion of plaintiff's evidence, holding that plaintiff had failed to prove a cause of action against defendant. We reverse and remand. Plaintiff, who operated a bar and restaurant on premises owned by him in San Antonio, by written agreement sold the restaurant and bar equipment, furniture and supplies to defendant and his wife on October 9, 1984, for $9,373.00, with defendant making a down payment of $1,000.00. As part of this transaction, defendant, who planned to operate the bar and restaurant on the premises owned by plaintiff, orally agreed to pay $600.00 per month as rent for the premises and to reimburse plaintiff for utility charges incurred by defendant in the operation of the bar and restaurant. The written agreement relating to the sale of the bar and restaurant equipment read as follows:

10-9-84

To Whom it may Concern
Equipment sold to Jose Mendez or Carolina S. Mendez From Paul Mauricio

Amount	9373.00
down payment	1000.00
Balance due--	8373.00

There will be no interest [sic] charged until 10-9-85. Interest will be at the rate of 12% per year
Mr. & Mrs. Mendez will pay as much as possible per month
Minimum amount will be $500.00 per. month

Seller /s/ Paul Mauricio
Buyer /s/ Jose Mendez S.

After defendant made payments of $500.00 each on November 10 and December 10, 1984, there was a fire on the premises and defendant made no further payments. Plaintiff then brought this suit to recover the $7,373.00 due on the written agreement which was alleged to be a note. Plaintiff also sought to recover $1,103.78 as reimbursement for the amounts paid by him for utilities used by defendant in the operation of the bar and restaurant.

Plaintiff first argues that the October 9, 1984, written agreement is a promissory note as alleged in his petition. Defendant contends that the instrument is not a promissory note, relying, as does plaintiff, on § 3.104 of the Texas Uniform Commercial Code (UCC).

Subsection (a) of § 3.104 provides that, to be a negotiable instrument, a writing must (1) be signed by the maker; (2) contain an unconditional promise to pay a sum certain in money; (3) be payable on demand or at a definite time; and (4) be payable to order or to bearer.

According to § 3.104(b), a writing which complies with the requirements of § 3.104(a) is a "note" if it is a promise other than a certificate of deposit. "Promise" is defined by § 3.102(a)(3) as an undertaking to pay which must be more than the acknowledgment of an obligation.

The written agreement is not a negotiable instrument since it is not payable to bearer or order.

But this does not mean that the writing is not a promissory note. It is possible to have a nonnegotiable note. See § 3.104(c). Whether the instrument is negotiable or not is irrelevant, since the suit here is between the original parties to the instrument. The written agreement contains an unconditional promise to pay plaintiff at least a certain sum of money each month. It is, therefore, in the form of a note.

Defendant's liability on the instrument is not governed by the law of negotiable instruments, but by the law of contracts. The evidence established the existence of the agreement, performance by plaintiff, defendant's breach and plaintiff's right to recover for the breach of the agreement.

The trial court erred in rendering judgment against plaintiff as to the $7,373.00, representing payments for the restaurant and bar equipment, at the close of plaintiff's testimony, since plaintiff made out a prima facie case. Since defendant has had no opportunity to present evidence, we cannot render judgment for plaintiff here.

* * *

That portion of the judgment denying plaintiff recovery on the written agreement relating to the sale of the bar and restaurant equipment is reversed and the cause is remanded to the trial court for further proceedings.

Ramirez v. Bureau of State Lottery
Court of Appeals of Michigan, 1990
186 Mich.App. 275, 463 N.W.2d 245

J.H. Gillis, P.J. [Lottery player who allegedly lost winning lottery ticket brought action against Bureau of State Lotteries seeking to obtain prize.] Defendant further noted tickets *** contained the following language on the back:

TO CLAIM YOUR PRIZE
Present this ticket to any "Daily/Lotto Game" lottery agent for prize payment or receipt of claim. All prizes must be claimed within one (1) year of end date on ticket face.
THIS TICKET IS A BEARER INSTRUMENT SO TREAT IT AS IF IT WERE CASH.

The Lottery recommends signing this ticket immediately after purchasing it.

Noting that contract principles applied to Lotto transactions, defendant argued that presentment of the winning ticket was required before proceeds could be paid. Because plaintiff had not presented the winning ticket, defendant argued that he had failed to state a claim upon which relief could be granted. * * *

Plaintiff * * * claims that M.C.L. § 440.3804; M.S.A. § 19.3804 should apply [which allows the owner of an instrument to enforce it even though the instrument has been lost, stolen, or destroyed]. Plaintiff notes that the ticket states on its back that it is a bearer instrument; therefore, plaintiff argues that a Lotto ticket is a negotiable instrument * * * to which M.C.L. § 440.3804; M.S.A. §19.3804 applies. In response, defendant argues that the lottery act, M.C.L. § 432.1 et seq.; M.S.A. § 18.969(1) et seq., is a specific statute which is complete in itself and applies even though the Uniform Commercial Code, M.C.L. §440.1101 et seq.; M.S.A. § 19.1101 et seq., applies to commercial transactions in general. We agree with defendant.

In any event, defendant also argues that a Lotto ticket does not fall within the definition of a negotiable instrument because it is not signed by the maker or drawer, it does not contain an unconditional promise or order to pay a sum certain in money, and is not payable on demand or at a definite time. M.C.L. § 440.3104(1)(a)-(c); M.S.A. § 19.3104(1)(a)-(c). Assuming, arguendo, that a Lotto ticket is a negotiable instrument as defined in M.C.L. §440.3104(1); M.S.A. §19.3104(1), we note that M.C.L. §440.1102(3); M.S.A. §19.1102(3) allows the parties to vary the provisions of the Uniform Commercial Code by agreement. As noted above, plaintiff agreed to present the ticket before payment would be required.

First National Bank v. Fulk
Court of Appeals of Ohio, 1989
566 N.E.2d 1270

Evans, Judge. * * * On July 30, 1979, Donald married Maudie Harrell. During the marriage Maudie used Donald's Visa charge card on at least three different occasions. Evidence was produced at trial to show that on March 23, 1981, Maudie's signature appeared on a charge slip to Kar Gard in the amount of $145.48; on December 24, 1981, to Thomas Jeweler in the amount of $103.16; on June 4, 1982, to Bryant's Shoes in the amount of $57.23 and a second purchase in the amount of $16.80. Copies of these charge slips were the evidence introduced at trial which proved that Maudie used Donald's Visa charge card. However, purchases totaling $703.75 were charged to the account. This amount due was not paid by either Donald or Maudie. On July 13, 1984, Donald and Maudie were divorced.

Several attempts were made by the bank to collect the past due amount from Donald. However, no attempt was made to collect the amount due from Maudie. After several unsuccessful collection attempts, the bank filed a cause of action against Donald and Maudie, claiming that they were jointly and severally liable for the amount due on the Visa charge card. A trial was held before the bench on February 24, 1986, after which the municipal judge ruled in favor of the bank, finding that the defendants were jointly and severally liable to the bank for $703.75 plus ten percent interest and costs. Judgment was granted in favor of the plaintiff accordingly. It is this decision that Maudie Harrell, the defendant-appellant, appeals.
* * *
There is no dispute that Maudie was not a cardholder since the Visa credit card was in Donald's name only. However, the bank argues that Maudie was an authorized user and is liable for the amount due on the account pursuant to R.C. 1303.39(B), which states in pertinent part:

"An authorized representative who signs his own name to an instrument:
"(1) is personally obligated if the instrument neither names the person represented nor shows that the representative signed in a representative capacity;
"(2) except as otherwise established between the immediate parties, is personally obligated if the instrument names the person represented but does not show that the representative signed in a representative capacity * * *."

First, if we were to accept the bank's argument we would note that the only evidence presented at trial that showed what purchases Maudie made on Donald's Visa charge card were copies of four charge slips totaling $322.67. Therefore, according to this section of the Revised Code, Maudie could be held liable for only those purchases for which she signed, or purchases totaling $322.67. However, we do not believe this section of the code applies to the case at bar. R.C. 1303.39(B) refers to an "instrument" signed by an authorized representative. The term "instrument" is defined in R.C. 1303.01(A)(5) as a "negotiable instrument." A writing is negotiable only if it is a draft, a check, a certificate of deposit or a note that is payable in money "to order" or "to bearer" or contains words of negotiability. The charge slips signed by Maudie were not checks, drafts or certificates of deposit. While they may be considered to be notes they do not contain words of negotiability; therefore, they are not negotiable instruments. Since the charge slips are not negotiable instruments, and R.C. 1303.39(B) pertains only to negotiable instruments, we find that this section of the Ohio Revised Code is not applicable to the case at bar. Thus, Maudie cannot be held liable under R.C. 1303.39(B).

Dann v. Team Bank
Court of Appeals of Texas, Dallas, 1990
788 S.W.2d 182

Rowe, Justice. Cathy Towns Dann appeals from a summary judgment entered in favor of Team Bank, f/k/a Deposit Guaranty Bank, on a guaranty. In two points of error, Dann contends that the trial court erred in granting the Bank's motion for summary judgment and in denying her motion for summary judgment. We overrule both points of error and affirm the judgment of the trial court.

Cetcon Corporation executed a deed of trust in the principal amount of $550,000 payable to the Bank of Dallas. At the same time, Dann signed a guaranty in the amount of $550,000, together with interest, penalty fees, and expenses, including attorney fees.

* * *

The thrust of Dann's appeal is that she is not liable in her individual capacity under the guaranty. We disagree.

* * *

Dann * * * contends that she signed in her representative capacity based on section 3.403 of the Texas Business and Commerce Code, which [deals with the personal liability of agents who sign negotiable instruments]. The Business and Commerce Code * * * provides that, when used therein, the term "instrument" means a negotiable instrument. TEX.BUS. & COM.CODE ANN. § 3.102(a)(5) (Tex. UCC) (Vernon 1968). To be a negotiable instrument under the Code, a writing must (1) be signed by the maker or drawer; (2) contain an unconditional promise or order to pay a sum certain in money and no other promise, order, obligation, or power given by the maker or drawer except if authorized by chapter 3 of the Code; (3) be payable on demand or at a definite time; and (4) be payable to order or to bearer. TEX.BUS. & COM.CODE ANN. § 3.104(a) (Tex. UCC) (Vernon 1968).

According to Dann, section 3.403 codifies the general rule which should apply to nonnegotiable guaranties. We disagree. This guaranty is not a negotiable instrument. The guaranty in question here does not specify the amount of the liability to be paid as required in section 3.104. Instead, it provides a ceiling on the amount of the guarantor's obligation. In addition, the guaranty is not payable upon demand or at a definite time as required in section 3.104. Instead, the guarantor's duty of performance is not triggered until the default of the borrower. Furthermore, the guaranty is not payable to order or bearer. See Branch, 269 S.E.2d at 122 (the guaranty did not contain any provision that it is "payable to order or bearer").

* * *

Accordingly, we * * * affirm the judgment of the trial court.

P & K Marble, Inc. v. La Paglia

New York Supreme Court, Appellate Division, Third Department, 1989
147 A.D.2d 804, 537 N.Y.S.2d 682

Mahoney, Presiding Justice. Appeal from a judgment of the Supreme Court (Klein, J.), entered August 4, 1988 in Ulster County, which, in a proceeding pursuant to CPLR article 78, granted respondent's motion to dismiss the petition for failure to state a cause of action.

Petitioner obtained a $36,392 judgment against Arthur Pearce, who simultaneously held a $124,500 combination note and mortgage under which petitioner was the mortgagor. Petitioner docketed its judgment with the Ulster County Clerk on February 5, 1987 and thereafter delivered a property execution directing respondent to levy by seizure of the note and mortgage pursuant to CPLR 5232(b) and sell it at public auction. Respondent refused, apparently because the note and mortgage was considered a nonnegotiable instrument under UCC 3-104(1)(b) and, therefore, not capable of delivery so that the levy could only be by service of the execution pursuant to CPLR 5232(a). Petitioner commenced this CPLR article 78 proceeding to compel respondent to levy by seizure of the note and mortgage and sell it at public auction. Respondent moved to dismiss the petition for failure to state a cause of action. Supreme Court granted the motion, and this appeal by petitioner ensued.

Since both parties agree that a money judgment may be enforced against any property which is capable of being assigned or transferred (CPLR 5201[b]), and, further, that Pearce's note and mortgage is assignable and, therefore, property against which a money judgment may be enforced, the dispositive issue is whether CPLR 5232(a) or (b) provides the proper means for respondent to levy upon the note and mortgage.

In the case at bar, petitioner seeks to levy by seizure upon an intangible property interest represented by a note and mortgage. However, a note given in connection with a mortgage in a real estate transaction generally is not a negotiable instrument. Indeed, the subject note and mortgage does not fulfill at least one of the requirements of a negotiable instrument as contained in UCC 3-104(1)(b) in that it fails to contain an unconditional promise or order to pay a sum certain in money and no other promise except as authorized by UCC article 3. The note and mortgage contains [sic] numerous promises, such as to keep the mortgaged property insured, which are not authorized by UCC article 3. Since the property is represented by a nonnegotiable instrument, it is property not capable of delivery (CPLR 5201[c][4]). Therefore, pursuant to CPLR 5232(a), it can be levied upon only by service of a copy of the execution. "Seizure of a non-negotiable instrument * * * will not operate as a levy upon the debt it represents" (6 Weinstein-Korn-Miller, N.Y.Civ.Prac. ¶5201.11). Since petitioner refused respondent's offer to enforce the money judgment through levy by service of the execution pursuant to CPLR 5232(a), it therefore follows that the judgment must be affirmed.

Judgment affirmed, with costs.

First Federal Savings & Loan Ass'n of Salt Lake City v. Gump & Ayers Real Estate, Inc.

Court of Appeals of Utah. April 4, 1989
771 P.2d 1096

Billings, Judge: First Federal Savings & Loan Association of Salt Lake City ("First Federal") brought suit against Air Terminal Gifts, Inc. ("Air Terminal") on a promissory note executed by Air Terminal and payable to Sunayers Limited Partnership ("Sunayers"). The Air

Terminal note had been assigned to First Federal by Gump & Ayers Real Estate, Inc. ("Gump & Ayers"), the general partner of Sunayers. After an evidentiary hearing, the trial court found the note was not negotiable and First Federal was not a holder in due course. First Federal takes exception to both rulings, claiming it is entitled to enforce the note notwithstanding any claims or defenses of Air Terminal. We agree, and reverse and remand this case for further proceedings consistent with our opinion.

The facts are not in dispute. Sunayers was developing a condominium project in St. George, Utah called Sunflower. On June 5, 1984, Air Terminal invested $200,000 in the Sunayers Limited Partnership by paying $75,000 in cash and executing a $125,000 promissory note ("the Air Terminal note") secured by a Purchase and Security Agreement. The note provides: "This Note is secured by that certain Purchase and Security Agreement date June ----, 1984. Reference is made to the Purchase and Security Agreement for additional rights of the holder hereof."

On June 27, 1984, Gump & Ayers, the general partner of Sunayers, executed a promissory note in the amount of $100,000 ("the Gump & Ayers note") payable to First Federal. Gump & Ayers assigned the Air Terminal note as further security for the loan to Sunayers. The proceeds from the Gump & Ayers note were to be used by Sunayers for debts incurred in developing the Sunflower project, one of which was described as the "Morse Shortfall." Morse was the contractor on the Sunflower project, and part of the Morse Shortfall was an $18,500 debt due Gump & Ayers.

Air Terminal claims the language in its note referring to the Purchase and Security Agreement for "additional rights of the holder hereof" makes the note non-negotiable. Air Terminal further claims that even if the note is negotiable, First Federal is not a holder in due course because it took the note with notice of claims made by and defenses of Air Terminal. Specifically, Air Terminal claims First Federal knew a portion of the proceeds from the loan would be used to pay Gump & Ayers as part of the Morse Shortfall. According to the Purchase and Security Agreement, Air Terminal was to be indemnified by Sunayers and Gump & Ayers from any obligations arising from the Morse Shortfall.

There are two issues on appeal. First, is the Air Terminal note a negotiable instrument? Second, is First Federal a holder in due course of the Air Terminal note?

Since our task is to interpret the language of the Air Terminal note to determine if it is negotiable, and on undisputed facts, determine if First Federal is a holder in due course, we accord the trial court's conclusions no deference but review for a correction of error.

The trial court held the Air Terminal note was not a negotiable instrument because the note referenced "additional rights" provided for in the Purchase and Security Agreement thereby creating additional powers and promises outside those provided in the note itself. We must decide whether the "reference" in the Air Terminal note to the Purchase and Security Agreement "for additional rights" creates an additional "promise" or "power" under controlling statutory language which renders the note non-negotiable.

When determining negotiability, only the instrument in question should be examined. In order for a writing to be a negotiable instrument, it must "contain an unconditional promise or order to pay a sum certain in money and *no other promise*, order, obligation or *power given by the maker* or drawer except as authorized by this chapter." Utah Code Ann. § 70A-3-104(1)(a) (1988) (emphasis added). A promise or order, otherwise unconditional, does not become conditional simply because the instrument *"refers* to or states that it *arises out* of a separate agreement or refers to a separate agreement for rights as to prepayment or acceleration...." Utah Code Ann. § 70A-3-105(1)(c) (1988). In contrast, a promise or order is conditional if the instrument "states that it is *subject to or governed by* any other agreement." Utah Code Ann. § 70A-3- 105(2)(a) (1988). Negotiability is not, however, affected by "a statement that collateral has been given to secure obligations either on the instrument or otherwise of an obligor on the instrument or that in the case of default on those obligations the holder may realize on or dispose of the collateral...." Utah Code Ann. § 70A-3-112(1)(b) (1988).

Thus, the issue is whether the Air Terminal note simply refers to or is governed by the Purchase and Security Agreement. The language of the relevant clause, providing that "reference is made to the Purchase and Security Agreement" persuades us that the note is negotiable under § 70A-3-105(1)(c).

Cases from other jurisdictions interpreting similar provisions support our conclusion. See, e.g., *Third Nat'l Bank in Nashville v. Hardi-Gardens Supply of Illinois*, 380 F.Supp. 930, 938 (M.D.Tenn.1974) (an obligation is not made conditional because the instrument refers to or states that it arises out of a separate agreement); *Federal Factors, Inc. v. Wellbanke*, 241 Ark. 44, 406 S.W.2d 712, 713 (1966) ("The mere reference to the transaction giving rise to the instruments does not affect negotiability."); and 5 R. Anderson, Uniform Commercial Code § 3-105:12 at 236 (3d ed. 1984) ("The fact that a reference to collateral security for commercial paper may be ineptly worded does not impair negotiability when the sense of the provision is that something is added rather than subtracted from the obligation of the commercial paper.") (citing *First Nat'l City Bank v. Valentine*, 62 Misc.2d 719, 309 N.Y.S.2d 563 (1970)).

Based on the foregoing, we conclude the Air Terminal note is a negotiable instrument.
    * * *

We hold that the Air Terminal note is a negotiable instrument and First Federal is a holder in due course. The judgment of the trial court is, therefore, reversed, and the case is remanded for proceedings consistent with this opinion.

International Minerals & Chemical Corp. v. Matthews
Court of Appeals of North Carolina. Nov. 6, 1984
71 N.C.App. 209, 321 S.E.2d 545

By a verified complaint plaintiff sued defendant for $155,737.20, together with interest and attorney's fees, allegedly due under the terms of a note dated August 28, 1980. A copy of the note, attached as an exhibit to the complaint, showed that it was in the principal sum of $188,850.04, was payable upon demand, and was executed by defendant, her husband, and Benson Agri Supply, Inc. The note also contained the following statement: "This note is given to secure the account of Benson Agri Supply, Inc., and is secured by a security agreement and deed of trust on the corporate maker's property and deed of trust on individual maker's real estate which is a lien upon the property therein described. The provisions of all security instruments securing this note are incorporated herein by reference." In an unverified answer, defendant admitted that she executed the note and had refused to pay the sum demanded, but she denied the debt, asserting as an affirmative defense that the note was without consideration in that it was given to secure a preexisting debt. Contending that no genuine issue of fact is involved in the case, plaintiff moved for summary judgment under the authority of Rule 56, N.C. Rules of Civil Procedure. Plaintiff's motion was supported by the affidavit of its account executive to the effect that defendant executed the note to secure a debt that Benson Agri Supply, Inc. already owed plaintiff. Defendant filed no response or counter-affidavit. The trial judge granted the motion and entered an order establishing defendant's indebtedness to plaintiff in the amount of principal, interest and attorney's fees stated in the complaint and note.

Phillips, Judge. If the note involved in this case is a negotiable instrument, governed by the Uniform Commercial Code, the order of summary judgment was correctly entered and the defendant's appeal is without merit. This is because execution, demand and nonpayment are admitted and the only defense raised, that the note was for a pre-existing debt and without consideration, has been rendered nugatory by G.S. 25-3-408. This statute, in pertinent part, provides as follows:

> Want or failure of consideration is a defense as against any person not having the rights of a holder in due course (§25-3-305), except that no consideration is necessary for an instrument or obligation thereon given in payment of or as security for an antecedent obligation of any kind.

Defendant contends that this statutory provision does not apply to this case, because she did not owe the pre-existing debt, Benson Agri Supply did, and signed the note only as an accommodation. But the statute contains no such exception, and we see no basis for inserting one by interpretation. The statute is not ambiguous. Even though accommodation makers and obligors alike in great numbers sign instruments given in payment of or as security for antecedent obligations of various kinds, the statute states without limitation or reservation that consideration is not required for such instruments. It seems obvious to us, therefore, and we so hold, that both the intent and effect of this enactment was to deprive all signers of such instruments of the common law defense of no consideration that defendant now relies upon. Nevertheless, defendant's position is not entirely without judicial support. In *Capital City Bank v. Baker*, 59 Tenn.Ct.App. 477, 442 S.W.2d 259 (1969), which involved circumstances similar to those recorded here, the Tennessee Court of Appeals held that that state's identical enactment applies only to obligors and that the accommodation co-maker's plea of no consideration was sound. But, so far as our research discloses, all other courts that have considered this question have construed the provision as we do * * *.

The defendant further contends, however, that the note involved is not governed by the Uniform Commercial Code because it is not a negotiable instrument within the terms of G.S. 25-3-104. In pertinent part, this statute provides:

> (1) Any writing to be a negotiable instrument within this article must
>   (a) be signed by the maker or drawer; and
>   (b) contain an unconditional promise or order to pay a sum certain in money and no other promise, order, obligation or power given by the maker or drawer except as authorized by this article; and
>   (c) be payable on demand or at a definite time; and
>   (d) be payable to order or bearer.

As a writing signed by the several makers that is payable to the holder on demand, the note clearly meets the requirements of subparagraphs (a), (c) and (d) above, and defendant does not contend otherwise. Defendant does contend, however, that the note does not contain the unconditional promise to pay required by subparagraph (b) because of the two deeds of trust and security agreement that are incorporated into the note by reference. Certainly, as defendant argues and the statute provides, a promise is not unconditional if the instrument containing it states that it is *subject to* or *governed by* any other agreement or writing. G.S. 25-3-105(2)(a). But referring to a mortgage or other collateral does not impair negotiability. G.S. 25-3- 105(1)(e); G.S. 25-3-112(1)(b). Nor, in our opinion, does incorporating into a note the liens that secure its payment, as was done here. The deeds of trust and security agreement given to secure the debt or promise to pay could not have rendered defendant's promise to pay uncertain or conditional. The decision most relied upon by defendant, *Booker v. Everhart*, 294 N.C. 146, 240 S.E.2d 360 (1978), is not in point. In that case the note lost its negotiability because the instruments incorporated into it were a deed of separation and property settlement agreement, which from their nature could contain offsetting obligations that would eliminate or reduce the obligation to pay the note as promised. But mere liens securing payment of a debt cannot affect the obligation to pay it.

Affirmed.

practice

Case 1

To evidence a $10,000 loan from Pauline (P) to Mike (M), the parties filled in a standard form that they bought at a local office supply store:

```
                                                          09/28/93              , 19
   I. O. U.              30    days after date, I, we, or either of us, promise to pay to the order of
                              ---- PAULINE PAYEE ----

                      Ten thousand & no/100 ($10,000)
                                                                            DOLLARS,
for value received, negotiable and payable at the office of    the payee          without defalcation or discount,

and with interest from             now              until paid at the rate of ten per cent per annum until due and ten per cent thereafter
until paid. Interest payable semi-annually and if not so paid to become as principal and draw the same rate of interest with costs of collection
or an attorney's fee in case payment shall not be made at maturity. If interest be not paid when due the legal holder hereof may, at his
option declare the whole note due.
     The sureties and endorsers on this note severally agree to and do hereby waive demand or presentation of this note for payment to the
makers hereof and waive protest and notice of non-payment, and do hereby grant to any holder of this note the right to grant extension
without notifying them or either of them, hereby ratifying such extensions and remaining bound on this note as if no extension had been
obtained.
                                        Mike Maker          No.              INTEREST PAID
ADDRESS                                                     Due
                                                           Ex. to

2000—BENNETT'S—DALLAS
```

They also labeled the form -- "I.O.U" -- in big, dark letters. M indorsed and sold the I.O.U. to T. After the I.O.U. became due and was not paid, T sued M on the theory that M was liable to T under 3-412. M made a motion to dismiss the action. M's argument is that the I.O.U. is an I.O.U., not a negotiable instrument. M cites cases holding that a sales contract, a guaranty, a lottery ticket, and a mortgage are what they purport to be and are not negotiable instruments.

a. **M's argument is flawed. Why?**

b. **Is it therefore safe to say that I.O.U.s are negotiable instruments?**   *No*

Case 2

Is the I.O.U. (which is a note in its present form) a negotiable instrument if its terms are changed so that:

It's okay

a. instead of providing "I or we promise to pay," the note provides "I or we undertake to pay." See 3-103(a)(9). (Think about the typical check. It's a negotiable instrument. Where is the necessary "order or promise" required by 3-104(a)?)

b. although the note provides "I or we promise to pay," a further provision reserves to the maker the right to divert payment to a person other than the payee. See *Illinois State Bank v. Yates,* 678 S.W.2d 819 (Mo. Ct. App.1984) (such a reservation renders the promise conditional).

It's okay

c. the interest rate is variable depending on changes in the consumer price index. See 3-112(b).

It's okay

d. principal and interest are payable in Italian lire. 1-201(24). (Could such a note which by its terms is payable in lire be paid nevertheless in dollars? 3-107; see generally Krahmer, *Foreign Currency Instruments under the Uniform Commercial Code,* 86 COM.L.J. 9 (1981).)

It's maybe not okay

e. the instrument provides that it is payable " 30 days after date" but no date is supplied. See 3-108; 3-113; 3-115.

f. the instrument is dated and provides that it is payable " _____ days after date" and the blank is not filled in.

g. the time for payment is "30 days after presentment or sight." See 3-108(b).

It's okay

h. the instrument is due "upon the death of the maker but in no event later than January 7, 1991."

It's not okay

i. the instrument matures "upon the death of the maker." *Matter of Estate of Balkus,* 128 Wis.2d 246, 381 N.W.2d 593 (1985) (deposit slips "payable on death" were not negotiable instruments).

j. the maker is empowered to extend the time for payment for "a further reasonable time." 3-108(b)(iii).

k. the note provides that it is "VOID AFTER NINETY (90) DAYS."

Case 3

Source or fund?

Suppose that M adds this language to the note when she signs it: "Payable from the earnings of my business." Is negotiability defeated? See 3-106(b).

Case 4

M agrees to provide collateral for the loan by giving P a mortgage on real estate or a security agreement covering personal property. M therefore executes a security document at the same time she signs the note.

a.   Suppose that nothing is added to the note itself. Does the contemporaneous execution of a separate agreement affect the negotiability of the note? See 3-117; *Northwestern Bank v. Neal,* 271 S.C. 544, 248 S.E.2d 585 (1978).

No

b.   Would negotiability be defeated by a clause reciting that the note:

   i.   is secured? See 3-104(a)(3); 3-106(a)&(b).

   Okay

   ii.   is secured by a mortgage or other security agreement executed contemporaneously with the note?

   Okay

   iii.   is further secured by the maker's obligations to maintain and protect the collateral and to give additional collateral in the event that the sums due under the note at any time exceed the value of the original security?

   Okay

   iv.   is further secured by the right of the payee or any transferee to realize and dispose of the collateral as permitted by law and the terms of the accompanying mortgage?

   Okay

   v.   is subject to acceleration for breach of any terms of the mortgage which secures the note?

   Okay

   vi.   is secured by a mortgage or other security agreement executed even date herewith, the terms of which are by reference made a part hereof. Compare *Holly Hill Acres, Ltd. v. Charter Bank,* 314 So.2d 209 (Fla.App.1975) (such a clause renders note non-negotiable) with *International Minerals & Chemical Corp. v. Matthews,* 71 N.C.App. 209, 321 S.E.2d 545 (1984) (negotiability unaffected). On the issue of whether language mentioning a separate security agreement is merely a reference or an incorporation, see Carl Doozan, *Incorporating Collateral Security -- Effect on Negotiability,* 13 NOTRE DAME LAW. 133 (1938). Should the answer depend on whether any of the provisions in the separate agreement would offend any aspect of 3-104(a)? See generally 3-106 comment 1; *Enoch v. Brandon,* 249 N.Y. 263, 266, 164 N.E. 45, 46 (1928).

Suppose that the parties included the mortgage or security agreement within the note itself. For example, suppose they used the following form which was filled in and signed by M and which described the collateral as "all of M's equipment, inventory, and receivables, present and after-acquired." **(Please see form on next page.)**

Interest @_____   Amount $_____

Elkins, Arkansas,_____19_____   Maker_____

_____Months   Extended to_____Number_____Due_____
_____Days after date, for value received, I, We or either of us, jointly and severally, promise to pay to the order of

BANK OF ELKINS, Elkins, Arkansas

_____DOLLARS

in_____monthly installments of $_____ each, and one installment of $_____, the first installment to become due and

payable on or before the_____day of_____19_____, and one installment to become due and payable on or

before the_____day of each succeeding month until the whole indebtedness is paid, with interest from_____or any

unpaid sum until paid, at the rate of_____per cent per annum. If default be made at anytime in the payment of any of said installments all
the remaining installments shall, at the option of the holder, become immediately due and payable. Having deposited herewith, as collateral security for payment of this or any other liabilities of maker or makers to said Bank due or to become due, or which he hereafter contracted,

the following property, viz.:_____

which the undersigned authorize(s) the holder of this note to sell at public or private sale, without demanding payment of this note or debt due thereon and without
further notice by advertising or otherwise, and apply proceeds, or as much thereof as may be necessary, to the payment of this note, and all expense and charges,
together with 10 per cent commission on all sales, holding myself responsible for any deficiency, and further agrees to pay costs and a fee not to exceed 10% of
principal and accrued interest as attorney's fee, should this note be placed in the hands of an attorney for collection. Shall there be any depreciation in value of said
security prior to the maturity of this note, such an amount of additional security shall be furnished as will be satisfactory to said Bank of Elkins, and if additional
security is not furnished within two days after the demand is made, either in person or by written notice put in Post Office, said Bank may proceed at once to
sell security as above specified. The makers and endorsers of this note hereby severally waive presentment for payment, notice of non-payment, protest and notice of
protest, and consent that the time of payment may be extended without notice thereof.

Postoffice Address_____

Cr. Life_____

Yes

c. This form, when properly completed, would be an Article 9 security agreement. See 9-203(1)(a). Would it also be an Article 3 negotiable instrument?

Probably not

d. Is negotiability defeated by including language in a note that creates a real estate mortgage?

e. Is negotiability more certain if, instead of adding a mortgage to a note, a note is included in a mortgage by:

   i. segregating the note at the bottom of the first page?

   ii. segregating the note there and also separating it by a perforated line from the mortgage?

   iii. putting the note, by itself, on the back?

Case 5

In signing the note M crossed out the words "to the order of" so that M promised "to pay ~~to the order of~~ P."

a. Is it "legal" to strike this language?

Yes

b. Does striking out the language affect negotiability? See 3-104(a)(1).

Suppose that in paying her debt to P, M drew a check on her account at Drawee Bank but struck the order language. It is payable "to P" rather than "to the order of P." P indorsed this item and cashed it at Collecting Bank. The check bounced and Collecting Bank sued P on her indorsement, 3-415. P has moved to dismiss, arguing that the item is not a negotiable instrument.

c. Should the court grant or deny the motion?   *Deny*

d. Is there an additional or alternative theory on which Collecting Bank can recover from P? See 4-214(a).

e. Suppose that instead of striking the language, M simply stamped the note or check "NONNEGOTIABLE." Same answers? See 3-104(d).   *Yes and no*

Case 6

Suppose that M and P drafted the I.O.U. themselves instead of using a standard form. Their custom form provided simply:

I. O.U.

The undersigned, Mike Maker, owes Pauline Payee $10,000 and agrees to pay the money on demand. Maker also agrees that if the debt is assigned, he will pay it -- absolutely and irrevocably -- regardless of any complaint that he has or may have against Payee.

/s/ Mike Maker

P borrowed money from Bank and gave Bank a security interest in all of P's rights to payment, including the $10,000 I.O.U that M owed P.

a. Is this I.O.U. a negotiable instrument?   *Probably not*

b. Can Bank collect the I.O.U. from M even if M has a personal defense to enforcement of the debt by P?   *Probably*

Chapter 3. Contract Liability On Negotiable Instruments

§ 1. Basis of Liability: Signature

"Obligation on an instrument depends on a signature that is binding on the obligor." 3-401 comment 1. This principle is two-sided. It means that no person is liable on an instrument unless she signed it, either personally or through someone else whose signature binds her. See 3-401(a). Conversely, a person who signs an instrument, or is bound by someone else's signature, is prima facie liable because of the signature. The rule is that, in an action with respect to an instrument on which the signatures are valid and binding, the plaintiff is entitled to recover simply by producing the instrument, unless the defendant establishes a defense. 3-308(b). The plaintiff's prima facie case depends on nothing else. It is the signature on the instrument that creates the defendant's liability.

story

Mechanics of signature

To sign a writing means to execute or adopt "any symbol * * * with present intention to authenticate a writing." 1-201(39). A signature may take any form, including a pseudonym or a mark of any kind. Yet, no mark, name, or other symbol on an instrument is effective as a signature unless the symbol is used with the present intention to authenticate the writing.

In lay terms, to authenticate means "to prove the genuineness or truth of." NEW LEXICON WEBSTER'S DICTIONARY 64 (1989). In legal terms "[a]uthentication is merely the process of showing that a document is genuine and that it is what its proponent claims it to be." *Owens v. Commonwealth*, 10 Va.App. 309, 311, 391 S.E.2d 605, 607 (1990). It is more than mere process, however, and implies a particular purpose. It is the same purpose that is behind the requirement of a signature to satisfy a statute of fraud, which is "to show the intention of the party to admit his liability upon the contract. The mere insertion of his name in the body of an instrument, where it is applicable to a particular purpose, will not constitute a signature within the meaning of the statute."

Clinton Paper Co. v. Mills Paper Co., Inc., 83 N.Y.S.2d 875, 877 (N.Y. Sup. Ct. 1948) (quoting Browne on the Statute of Frauds § 357 (5th ed.)).

Formality, however, is not required. On the contrary,

"[t]he inclusion of authentication in the definition of 'signed' is to make clear that as the term is used in this Act a complete signature is not necessary. Authentication may be printed, stamped or written; it may be by initials or by thumbprint. It may be on any part of the document and in appropriate cases may be found in a billhead or letterhead. No catalog of possible authentications can be complete and the court must use common sense and commercial experience in passing upon these matters. The question always is whether the symbol was executed or adopted by the party with present intention to authenticate the writing." UCC § 1-201, Comment 39, 1962 Official Text. In conformity with the spirit behind the broad definition of "signed," the courts have looked to the writing as well as to the attendant circumstances to determine whether the symbol was executed or adopted by the party with present intention to authenticate, and in the great majority of cases the requisite intent has been found notwithstanding the fact that irregularities appeared on the writings or the niceties and formalities of manual signatures were lacking.

Kohlmeyer v. Bowen, 129 Ga. App. 700, 192 S.E.2d 400, 404 (1972).

Example 1

a.   A borrowed $50,000 from B and typed a "Note" on her letterhead stationery which promised to repay the same amount to B's order. B gave the "Note to A but did not write her name on it. The "Note" may nevertheless have been signed by B. In *Rural American Bank of Greenwald* 485 N.W.2d 702, 706 (Minn. 1992), the court decided that the Bank signed a loan agreement that was drafted and typed by an officer of the Bank on the Bank's letterhead stationery, even though no one representing the Bank thereafter wrote her name or made any other mark on the agreement.

> The letterhead included the names of the Bank officers; two of whom were present at the May 1, 1986 loan execution. The Loan Agreement referred to other documents that were executed in conjunction with the Loan Agreement. Its terms were presented to the Loan Committee and were part of the Herickhoff loan file. If the Bank did not have the intent to authenticate the writing, they would not have drafted the Loan Agreement in the first place, would not have typed it on Bank letterhead, would not have presented it to the Loan Committee, nor retained it in the file. "Common sense and

commercial experience" compel the conclusion that the Bank intended to be bound by the provisions of the Loan Agreement.

Id. at 706.

b. "In some cases it may not be clear whether a signature was meant to be that of an indorser, a party to the instrument in some other capacity such as drawer, maker or acceptor, or a person who was not signing as a party. The general rule is that a signature is an indorsement if the instrument does not indicate an unambiguous intent of the signer not to sign as an indorser. Intent may be determined by words accompanying the signature, the place of signature, or other circumstances. For example, suppose a depositary bank gives cash for a check properly indorsed by the payee. The bank requires the payee's employee to sign the back of the check as evidence that the employee received the cash. If the signature consists only of the initials of the employee it is not reasonable to assume that it was meant to be an indorsement. If there was a full signature but accompanying words indicated that it was meant as a receipt for the cash given for the check, it is not an indorsement. If the signature is not qualified in any way and appears in the place normally used for indorsements, it may be an indorsement even though the signer intended the signature to be a receipt. To take another example, suppose the drawee of a draft signs the draft on the back in the space usually used for indorsements. No words accompany the signature. Since the drawee has no reason to sign a draft unless the intent is to accept the draft, the signature is effective as an acceptance. Custom and usage may be used to determine intent. For example, by long-established custom and usage, a signature in the lower right hand corner of an instrument indicates an intent to sign as the maker of a note or the drawer of a draft. Any similar clear indication of an intent to sign in some other capacity or for some other purpose may establish that a signature is not an indorsement. For example, if the owner of a traveler's check countersigns the check in the process of negotiating it, the countersignature is not an indorsement. The countersignature is a condition to the issuer's obligation to pay and its purpose is to provide a means of verifying the identity of the person negotiating the traveler's check by allowing comparison of the specimen signature and the countersignature. The countersignature is not necessary for negotiation and the signer does not incur indorser's liability. See Comment 2 to Section 3-106. " 3-204 comment 1.

Means of signature: by an agent or representative

The signature that obligates a person on an instrument can be put there by the person herself, or it can be the signature of an agent or representative. In the latter case, there are two basic requirements to obligate the person represented (i.e., the principal). First, the representative must herself sign the instrument.

3-401(a). Article 3 requires no special form, and nothing in Article 3 turns on whether she uses her name or the principal's name.

Second, the representative's signature must be binding on the principal. Id. This turns on other law, usually ordinary agency law. The rule is that "the represented person is bound by the signature to the same extent the represented person would be bound [by agency law] if the signature were on a simple contract." 3-402(a). The effect is that to this extent, "the signature [of the representative] is the authorized signature of the represented person." 3-402 comment 1; see also 3-402(a). Whether or not the principal is named in the instrument is unimportant, as far as Article 3 is concerned, to the principal's own liability on the instrument. Therefore, even an undisclosed principal can be liable on an instrument that only her agent signed if, under the same or similar circumstances, agency law would obligate the principal on a simple contract.

Agent's liability

Even when an authorized representative is acting for someone else, her signature on the instrument may appear to be solely for her own benefit and can mislead third parties who know nothing different. Therefore, when an authorized representative signs her name to an instrument, even while acting for the principal and with the principal's specific authority, *the representative is herself prima facie liable* unless:

- the form of the signature shows unambiguously that the signature is made on behalf of the represented person, and
- the represented person is identified in the instrument.

3-402(b)(1). By this rule the representative is freely and entirely safe only if both conditions are met, as by signing "P, by A, Treasurer." 3-402 comment 2. In this case she avoids liability as a matter of law.

If the form of the representative's signature fails *either* of these conditions or both of them, she is liable on the instrument unless she "proves that the original parties did not intend the representative to be liable on the instrument." 3-402(b)(2). In effect, it is a defense to liability that the representative acted for someone else and that her signature was not intended to be personally binding. She can assert this defense against anyone, except a holder in due course who "took the instrument without notice that the representative was not intended to be liable on the instrument." Id. It makes no difference to the availability or applicability of the defense that the instrument shows nothing but the representative's signature in her own name and is entirely silent as to both the principal's identity and the representative's capacity. Even in this case, except as against the innocent holder in due course, the representative is free to prove the defense that the original parties did not intend to bind her on the instrument.

Example 2

Jane Doe is the authorized agent of Rachel Roe. Jane signs a note on behalf of Rachel. In each of the following cases the original parties to the instrument intend that Rachel is liable on the note but Jane is not liable. In each case, however, Jane is liable on the note to a holder in due course without notice that Jane was not intended to be liable.

a. Jane signs "Jane Doe" without indicating in the note that she is signing as agent. The note does not identify Rachel as the represented person.

b. Jane signs "Jane Doe, Agent" but the note does not identify Rachel as the represented person.

c. The name "Rachel Roe" is written on the note and immediately below that name Jane signs "Jane Doe" without indicating that Jane signed as agent. 3-402 comment 2.

An exceptional rule that better protects the agent applies to checks. By law, the authorized agent is not liable to anyone on a check that she draws on the principal's account, *even if the agent neglects to indicate her agency status*, so long as the check identifies the principal. 3-402(c). The reason is that such a check effectively identifies somebody else as the owner of the account and thus the true obligor. Therefore, "nobody is deceived into thinking that the person signing the check is meant to be liable." 3-402 comment 3.

Effect Of Unauthorized Signature

The general rule is that an unauthorized signature binds no one and is entirely ineffective. Most significantly, it is ineffective to bind the person whose name is signed. 3-403(a). An *unauthorized signature* includes both an outright forgery and also the signature of an agent which does not bind the principal under the law of agency. 1-201(43). Therefore, an agent's unauthorized signature of a principal does not bind the principal, even if the signer represents a principal for other purposes, and even if the principal's name is used by the unauthorized signer. Similarly, an outright forgery by a thief who steals a checkbook does not create liability for the owner of the checking account even though the forger uses the owner's name and the owner's personal checks. In both cases, the only person liable on the instrument is the unauthorized signer. Id.

In two situations, however, exceptional rules apply to bind the person whose name is signed even though she did not authorize the signature and the signature was a complete forgery. The exceptions are, first, that an unauthorized signature binds the unauthorized signer herself by operating as her signature "in favor of a person who in good faith pays the instrument or takes it for value." 3-403(a). This is true even if the unauthorized signer uses someone else's name, such as the name of the person she purports to represent. It makes no difference whether or not the signer believes, when she signs, that she is acting for and with the authority of someone else. An innocent and a forger are themselves equally bound by their unauthorized signatures.

Second, because of extraordinary rules that reach even cases of outright forgery, a person's unauthorized signature can sometimes bind her for reasons of ratification and culpability or fault.

1. Ratification

A person's unauthorized or forged signature binds her if she ratifies the signature. 3-403(a).

> Ratification is a retroactive adoption of the unauthorized signature by the person whose name is signed and may be found from conduct as well as from express statements. For example, it may be found from the retention of benefits received in the transaction with knowledge of the unauthorized signature. Although the forger is not an agent, ratification is governed by the rules and principles applicable to ratification of unauthorized acts of an agent.

3-403 comment 3.

2. Culpability or Fault

More important, a person is bound even by her forged signature if she is responsible or culpable or at fault with respect to the making of the signature. This statement of principle is a broad generalization that is not itself law but summarizes particular expressions of the principle that are law. For example, there is the possibility of common-law estoppel against the person who name is signed, "as where he expressly or tacitly represents to an innocent purchaser that the signature is genuine * * * ." 3-404 comment 4 (1989 Official Text).

A much wider example is the rule that a person cannot complain of a forged signature that results from her own negligence. This rule is codified in 3-406, which provides:

> A person whose failure to exercise ordinary care substantially contributes to an alteration of an instrument or to the making of a forged signature on an instrument is precluded from asserting the alteration or the forgery against a person who, in good faith, pays the instrument or takes it for value or for collection.

3-406(a). For example, a person who is in the habit of using a signature stamp or an automatic signing device might substantially contribute to a forgery by negligently allowing outsiders to have access to it. Absent the negligence and 3-406, the person would escape liability because her signature would be missing from the instrument. Because of the negligence and 3-406, she is precluded or stopped or prevented from using the forgery as a defense or as an offense. She is stuck with the signature, as if she had made it herself.

The rule can also work to stop a person from complaining about the forgery of someone else's signature that legally harms her. For example, a drawee bank cannot properly charge a drawer's account with a check on which there is a forged indorsement. (See Chapter 6 infra.) The drawer-customer can require the bank to recredit her account, but not if the drawer's negligence is responsible for the forged indorsement within the terms of 3-406. This use of 3-406 is not common, however. It is much more often applied to the negligent person's own signature for the simple reason that the forgery of someone's else signature is more difficult for her to cause.

Section 3-406 extends not only to cases where negligence substantially contributes to a forged signature but also to cases where negligence substantially contributes to an alteration. Suppose, for example, that the amount payable on an instrument has been raised from $500 to $5,000. The holder recovers only $500 in the absence of negligence; but, under 3-406, she is entitled to recover the full $5,000 if the negligence of the defendant substantially contributed to the alteration.

Absent her negligence, a person's liability on an instrument is usually discharged by a fraudulent alteration, 3-407(b), except that it can be enforced according to its original terms by a person who takes the instrument for value, in good faith, and without notice of the alteration. 3-407(c). Also, the drawee bank can charge the drawer's account for the original amount, but no more. 3-407(c), 4-401(d)(1). It is a different case, however, if the instrument is left incomplete as to amount and is filled in for a greater sum than authorized. Then, an innocent taker for value or the bank can enforce the instrument or charge the drawer's account according to the terms of the instrument as completed. 3-407(c), 4-401(d)(2).

Section 3-406 does not protect or work in favor of everybody. It is, in effect, a defense that is only available to a person who, in good faith, pays the instrument or takes it for value or for collection. Moreover, under former law, even a person whom 3-406 was designed to protect would lose her protection if she herself had acted unreasonably in dealing with the instrument -- failed to follow the usual commercial standards and practices of her business. Now, under the 1990 Article 3, this negligence is considered only comparatively and is not a contributory, absolute bar. The rule is *comparative* negligence:

> Under [3-406(a)], if the person asserting the preclusion fails to exercise ordinary care in paying or taking the instrument and that failure substantially contributes to loss, the loss is allocated between the person precluded and the person asserting the preclusion according to the extent to which the failure of each to exercise ordinary care contributed to the loss.

3-406(b).

Wider culpability than negligence is behind two other rules that give effect to unauthorized signatures, 3-404 and 3-405, but they deal *only* with indorsements. They give effect to unauthorized indorsements when the maker or drawer is fooled by an impostor, does not intend the payee to have any interest in the instrument, or issues the instrument to a fictitious payee, and also when the indorser is an employee whom the employer entrusted with responsibility with respect to the instrument. These sections apply to instruments generally, but normally the instruments are checks. For this reason we cover 3-404 and 3-405 in Chapter 6 which is devoted exclusively to checks. Section 3-406 is revisited there too.

Proving authenticity of a signature or authority to sign

The 1990 Article 3 did not change the basic rules on proving signatures. Only the section number is different. It changed from 3-307(1) to 3-308(a). The court explained this law in *First Nat'l Bank v. Blackhurst*, 176 W. Va. 472, 345 S.E.2d 567 (W. Va. 1986), in which the defendant Blackhurst contested the genuineness of his signature on several notes. This section

governs who has the burden of establishing signatures on commercial paper. If the plaintiff can establish the effectiveness of the obligor's signature, produces the instrument, and proves that he is the holder in due course, he has established a prima facie case for recovery. *The signature is presumed to be genuine.*

The Code's presumption of regularity requires that the trier of fact find the signature on a negotiable instrument to be genuine unless and until the defendant-obligor has introduced sufficient evidence to support a finding that the signature is not genuine. The evidence need not be sufficient to require entry of summary judgment in the defendant's favor, 'but it must be enough to support his denial by permitting a finding in his favor.' Once sufficient evidence is introduced, the presumption completely disappears. Although a mere denial of the signature's genuineness is insufficient, a denial along with a sample of his true signature will rebut the presumption of genuineness. In the present case, Mr. Blackhurst denied the genuineness of his signature and introduced a financial statement bearing his signature into evidence. Accordingly, this evidence was substantial enough to remove the presumption in favor of the bank.

But this only means that the bank bore the burden of establishing that it was more probable than not that the signature was genuine. Again, both sides introduced witnesses and evidence, the jury believed the bank, and we will not second guess the jury's verdict.

345 S.E.2d at 572.

The same rules apply to proof of a representative's authority to sign an instrument and thereby bind the represented person. In *Bowers v. Winitzki*, 83 Or. App. 169, 730 P.2d 1253 (1986), plaintiffs sought to recover on two promissory notes signed by defendant Sletten for himself and as the purported attorney in fact for defendants Winitzki and Mercer. The only evidence plaintiffs produced to show that Sletten had authority to sign the notes for defendants were the signed notes themselves. Defendants rested without putting on evidence and moved for a directed verdict on the ground that plaintiffs had not proved Sletten's authority. The trial court granted the motion, and plaintiffs appealed from the resulting judgment. The appeals court reversed. This decision is probably correct under 3-308(a), and would equally govern if the principal were undisclosed.

3-403. Signature by Authorized Representative
(1989 Official Text) (withdrawn 1990)

(1) A signature may be made by an agent or other representative, and his authority to make it may be established as in other cases of representation. No particular form of appointment is necessary to establish such authority.

(2) An authorized representative who signs his own name to an instrument:

    (a) is personally obligated if the instrument neither names the person represented nor shows that the representative signed in a representative capacity;

    (b) except as otherwise established between the immediate parties, is personally obligated if the instrument names the person represented but does not show that the representative signed in a representative capacity, or if the instrument does not name the person represented but does show that the representative signed in a representative capacity.

(3) Except as otherwise established the name of an organization preceded or followed by the name and office of an authorized individual is a signature made in a representative capacity.

First Safety Fund Nat'l Bank v. Friel
Appeals Court of Massachusetts, 1987
23 Mass.App.Ct. 583, 504 N.E.2d 664

Kass, Justice. On two separate occasions, Janet M. Friel, the defendant, signed promissory notes on behalf of New England Office Products Co., Inc., of which she was president. On each note Friel signed twice: once, directly under the typed name of the corporate borrower, she wrote "Janet M. Friel, President"; upon the line below that signature she wrote, without qualification, "Janet M. Friel." The question presented is whether the second signatures rendered Friel personally liable on the notes. We conclude that they did and reverse the court below.

The appeal is from a divided opinion of the Appellate Division of the District Court for the Western District. That tribunal dismissed a report, claimed by the First Safety Fund National Bank (bank), from a judgment entered by the trial judge in favor of Friel. Dismissal of the report had the effect of affirming the trial court judgment.

We take our facts from those found by the trial judge and for which there was a basis in the evidence summarized in the report to the Appellate Division. Friel became the president of the New England Office Products Co., Inc. (company), in 1981 upon the death of her husband, who had founded the company in 1972. Her presidency was substantially titular. General management of daily operations devolved upon Friel's brother-in-law, David Friel, but Mrs. Friel kept her hand in by keeping the checkbook and signing all corporate checks.

The loans in question were made on May 13, 1982, and March 30, 1983, in the amounts of $10,000 and $30,000, respectively. In connection with the later and larger loan, the bank took a security interest in "[a]ll of the [company's] inventory, present and future accounts and contracts receivable." Mrs. Friel signed the security agreement which memorialized that loan only once, expressly as president of the company. Early in 1984, the company ceased to do business, and it is implicit that at the time of its demise the company was insolvent, hence the bank's pursuit of Mrs. Friel.

* * *

To be sure, when the name of a corporation is followed by the name and office of an authorized individual, that signature is made in a representative capacity. G.L. c. 106, § 3-403(3). Mrs. Friel's difficulty is that one signature fits in the 403(3) category, i.e., representative capacity; the second fits in the 403(2) category; i.e., it denotes personal obligation. Indeed, were there not some such purpose, signing a second time without a modifier as to representative status would be a peculiarly empty gesture. Dual obligations on the parts of a corporate borrower and its principal officers or stockholders are not unusual when small, closely held corporations borrow money. Reaching by lenders for the additional credit is the norm. Although the dual signature point has not arisen in the Massachusetts cases, other jurisdictions have held a corporate officer personally liable when he or she has signed twice, once in a representative capacity and once without any representative indicia.

That does not, however, end the inquiry. The person who signs a note in an apparent individual capacity may escape personal liability by establishing that the immediate parties to the note -- here the bank, the company, and Mrs. Friel -- had established that personal obligation was not to attach. G.L. c. 106, §3-403(2)(b). The burden of affirmatively showing the parties had "otherwise established" that personal liability would not attach to an apparently unqualified signature on a note falls upon the signer.

In the instant case the Appellate Division concluded on the basis of the report and the trial judge's findings of fact that the bank and Mrs. Friel had established she would not be personally liable. We, therefore, recite additional elements of the facts. It was David Friel who applied for the loans on behalf of the company and conducted whatever negotiations were involved. He arranged to accompany Mrs. Friel to the bank, where, after small talk, a bank officer presented prepared loan documents and instructed Mrs. Friel to sign her name and title, then pointed to the next line and told her to sign only her name. Mrs. Friel asked no questions about why she was asked to sign twice. She glanced over but did not read the papers -- at least not in any comprehending fashion. Reading the instruments carefully would not have done her much good, as Mrs. Friel was without experience in business, banking, or corporate finance. There were no words such as "co-maker" or "guarantor" next to the defendant's signature, nor was there anything in the text of the notes which would have alerted an unsophisticated bank customer that a second signature without a title indicating representative capacity would create personal liability.

The address of the promisor on the notes was that of the company. Loan proceeds were for company purposes. Mrs. Friel did not intend that her signatures create personal liability on the notes. For its part, the bank at neither of the signing ceremonies warned Mrs. Friel that her second signatures created personal obligations.

What follows from the facts found by the trial judge was that the bank and Mrs. Friel had not arrived at common ground. That is the antithesis of the immediate parties to the instrument having "established" limits of liability, a word that implies an agreement. We may accept as a fact Mrs. Friel's subjective understanding that she was signing for a purely corporate loan but, in order for her to prevail, the bank must either (1) have given her to understand that it was not looking to her credit or (2) it must appear that the bank's intent was not to look beyond the company's assets. Neither proposition finds support in the facts found or the compendium of the evidence contained in the report.

From those sources we know that Mrs. Friel did not negotiate the terms of the loans, she asked no questions, and the bank said nothing one way or the other about requiring her to become personally obligated on the loans. All that falls well short of an affirmative showing that the parties had agreed that the corporation was to be solely liable. * * * [W]e know something about the borrower's intent, but there is no manifestation of intention on behalf of the bank. An undisclosed intention by a maker to sign only in a representative capacity does not establish the understanding required by G.L. c. 106, §3-403(2)(b).

In its opinion, the majority of the Appellate Division appears to have relieved the defendant of liability on the basis of defenses of mutual mistake and fraud. There was, however, no finding -- nor would evidence have supported it -- that the bank was mistaken about Mrs. Friel's personal obligation. That the bank asked for her indorsement on two separate occasions, a year apart, and did not seek a second signature on the security agreement (on which it would have been of no effect) bespeaks a conscious policy. Mrs. Friel may have been mistaken as to the consequence of her second signatures but the mistake of one party to the transaction is not sufficient to invoke the principle of mutual mistake; the mistake must be shared by both parties. There are limited circumstances in which a party may avoid a contract on the basis of a unilateral mistake: "if he does not bear the risk of mistake ..., and (a) the effect of the mistake is such that enforcement of the contract would be unconscionable, or (b) the other party had reason to know of the mistake or his fault caused the mistake." Restatement (Second) of Contracts §153. A contract is unconscionable if "the sum total of its provisions drives too hard a bargain for a court of conscience to assist." Restatement (Second) of Contracts §208 comment b. As we have seen, a note of a close corporation indorsed by a principal officer is a commercial commonplace, hence scarcely unconscionable. The record does not suggest that the bank knew or had reason to know about Mrs. Friel's ignorance of the consequences of her second signature. Section 3-402 of the Uniform Commercial Code, discussed above, places the risk of mistake on the signer of an instrument. See Restatement (Second) of Contracts §154. See also Allen v. Plymouth, 313 Mass. 356, 362-363, 47 N.E.2d 284 (1943), stating the general rule that relief is not granted for a mistake about what the law is if a person is ignorant of the law or mistaken about what it prescribes.

As to fraud, it requires a material misrepresentation or, through words or conduct, the conveyance of half truths which deceive. The failure of the bank to explain to Mrs. Friel the consequences of her second signature did not rise to fraud. There were no preliminary dealings between Mrs. Friel and the bank by which she might have been misled. On neither signing occasion did the parties discuss the legal significance of the instruments and the signatures required of Mrs. Friel. This is not a case, as the defendant argues, where silence would reasonably lead a party to a particular conclusion.

One might wish that a conscientious loan officer would explain the consequences of documents and signatures to a borrower not represented by counsel, but the law, in a commercial transaction context, imposes no duty so to do. In the instant case, it should be remarked, the record does not permit us to suppose that the bank officer was aware of the defendant's commercial naiveté. The bank officer may well have felt no call to discourse on what he would have thought a quite routine transaction.

Our conclusions are consistent with the policy expressed in the comment to G.L. c. 106, §3-402, to give consistent meaning to what appears on the face of commercial paper.

When reviewing decisions of the Appellate Division, we can make such order as the Appellate Division ought to have made. The judgment entered in the trial court is reversed. Judgment is to enter for the plaintiff for the unpaid principal amounts of the two notes, together with accrued interest, plus reasonable attorney's fees (for which the notes provided) incurred by the plaintiff.

So ordered.

Federal Deposit Insurance Corp. v. Tennessee Wildcat Services, Inc.

United States Court of Appeals, Sixth Circuit, 1988
839 F.2d 251

LIVELY, Chief Judge. The question to be answered in these consolidated appeals is whether signers of promissory notes, who claim to have signed as corporate agents, sufficiently complied with legal requirements for avoiding personal liability. Holding that the signers had so complied, the district court, in separate orders, granted summary judgment in their favor. The Federal Deposit Insurance Corporation (FDIC), holder of the notes in its corporate capacity by virtue of purchase and assumption transactions, appeals, and we affirm.

* * *

In each case the district court concluded that under the law of Tennessee, use of the word "by" preceding a signature is legally sufficient to establish that the signature is made in a representative capacity when the principal is fully disclosed.

As it did in the district court, FDIC argues that the signers were required to show the capacity in which they signed the notes in addition to the use of "by." It supports this argument by pointing out that the district court relied on a Tennessee case that was decided prior to adoption of the Uniform Commercial Code (UCC) and contending that mere use of "by" is not sufficient under the UCC. As an alternative argument, FDIC asserts that use of the word "by" preceding a signature at most creates an ambiguity. This ambiguity cannot be resolved by parol evidence in this case, according to FDIC, because such evidence is admissible to rebut the presumption of a signer's personal liability only in actions between the immediate parties to an instrument.

The appellees maintain that the district court correctly applied Tennessee law and reached the proper result under the UCC and case law. They argue that the corporations were shown as the makers of the notes and the signers' representative capacities were clearly shown by use of the word "by." No holder of the notes, they contend, could reasonably believe that the signers personally obligated themselves under these facts.

* * *

National uniformity is necessary in dealing with commercial transactions involving the United States. This rule has been applied in cases where FDIC seeks to recover on promissory notes in its corporate capacity. The required uniformity is achieved, however, by adopting relevant portions of the UCC as the federal rule. Although the parties discuss the question of whether state or federal law controls, this does not present a real problem in the present case because Tennessee has adopted the UCC.

Both FDIC and the signers rely on §3-403 of the Model Uniform Commercial Code .
* * *

Although the district court decided these cases under Tennessee case law, we believe the decisions are correct under the UCC. Nowhere in §3-403 is there a requirement that an agent designate the precise capacity in which he signs. A comment to this section does suggest that the best way to avoid personal liability is to show the principal's identity, use the word "by" before the signer's signature, and follow the signature with a designation of the signer's capacity. Under §3-403(3), as a matter of law, a person who signs in this manner is not individually liable. However, other provisions of §3-403 permit variations. A signer is personally obligated under §3-403(2)(a) "if the instrument *neither* names the person represented *nor* shows that the representative signed in a representative capacity." (emphasis added) In each of the cases under review, however, the name of the principal was shown on the face of the note as the maker and the signature on the note was preceded by the word "by," indicating that it was signed in some representative capacity. Thus §3-403(2)(a) is inapplicable as well.

Section 3-403(2)(b) would have come into play if either the names of the principals had been shown but there had been no indication that the signers acted in a representative capacity, or if the names of the principals had not been shown, but the notes had shown that the signers acted as representatives. In either of these circumstances, as between the immediate parties to the notes, parol evidence would be admitted to supply the missing information -- either the identity of the principal or the fact of the signer's agency. However, as between a holder of the note other than the original lender and the signer, such parol evidence is not admissible and the signer is personally liable because he cannot supply the missing ingredient. When the principal is named on the face of a note or other negotiable instrument and the word "by" precedes the signature, while the signer is not exonerated from personal liability as a matter of law under §3-403(3), neither is there an ambiguity requiring the application of §3-403(2)(b). Such a situation falls between §§3-403(2)(a) and 3-403(2)(b), and the court should determine from the entire instrument whether the signer is personally liable.

A reading of §3-403 as a whole supports our conclusion that while §3- 403(3) may identify the clearest way to establish that a signer acts in a representative capacity, it is not the only way. A leading treatise, J. White and R. Summers, Uniform Commercial Code (2d Ed. 1980), states at page 494, "section 3-403(3) does not purport to be an exclusive statement of symbols that show representative capacity." (Footnote omitted). The test should be whether a person who takes the note would reasonably believe, on the basis of what appears on its face, that the signer was personally responsible for payment. Where the principal is identified and shown on the face of the note as the maker and the word "by" precedes the signature of the signer, there is no ambiguity and the signer is not personally liable, absent some showing of fraud or other circumstance that requires a court to look beyond the face of the note.
* * *

CONCLUSION

If the manner of naming the maker or the manner of signing is such as to cause a person dealing with the instrument reasonably to believe that the signer is personally liable, he will be held personally liable unless the original parties are involved and the signer is permitted to establish agency by parol evidence. However, where the principal is clearly identified on the face of the instrument, use of the word "by" before the signature is sufficient to establish that the signer did so in a representative capacity.

The judgment of the district court is affirmed.

M & M Welding, Inc. v. Pavlicek

Supreme Court of Wyoming, 1986
713 P.2d 236

BROWN, Justice. M & M, an oilfield fabrication business, was started in 1974 by Edward Mudge, his wife Edna F. Mudge, Robert Mudge, and his wife Sybil Mudge. On July 31, 1981, the Mudges entered into an agreement to sell M & M to Larry Redding for one million dollars. Under this agreement, Redding was to make a down payment of $175,000, and pay the balance over a period of years. Redding made his down payment under the agreement on September 2, 1981, and was placed in control of the business.

After acquiring control of the business, Redding elected himself president and director of M & M. To conduct business Redding approached the bank to obtain a $100,000 line of credit in the form of a revolving credit note. Before approving the loan, the bank required Redding to submit financial statements, asset lists, and a list of accounts receivable. The bank also required Redding to submit a certified copy of the corporate resolution authorizing Redding to borrow money on behalf of M & M. Such was provided and the loan was approved. On September 25, 1981, Mr. Redding executed the note on behalf of M & M.

Redding failed to make his payments to the Mudges under the sales agreement, and the Mudges repossessed M & M. The note executed by Redding subsequently went into default. The bank instituted action to collect on the loan. The trial court rendered judgment in favor of the bank finding M & M liable for the note executed by Redding.

I

In its first issue, appellant claims Redding had no authority to borrow money on behalf of M & M. In its decision letter the trial court found that Redding had actual authority to incur the note in question, thereby obligating M & M: "I find that actual authority existed, by implication if not necessarily expressly, and that clearly there was apparent authority, to bind the defendant corporation to the bank. * * * "*

We think the facts attendant in the case amply support such conclusion by the court. A special meeting of M & M's board of directors was held on August 18, 1981, wherein Redding was elected chairman and president. The minutes of the meeting reflect that the board authorized any officer to borrow up to $200,000 * * *.

* * *

[T]here is ample evidence which supports the trial court's conclusion that Redding was clothed with express authority to borrow money on behalf of M & M.

II

The note in question was signed as follows: "M & M Welding, Inc., Larry L. Redding." In its second issue, appellant contends that the note was improperly executed and was therefore invalid on its face * * *.

* * *

---

* See comment, "Inherent Authority of a Corporate President in Wyoming", 5 Wyo. Law Journal 93 (1950): "Inherent authority has been defined as, 'An authority possessed without it being derived from another.' The authority of the corporate president is conventionally divided into four classes which are as follows: (1) Express authority; (2) Implied authority; (3) Apparent authority; (4) Inherent authority. Express authority is that which is conferred by the by-laws and resolutions of the board of directors. Implied authority is that which is inferred from the express authority. Apparent authority is that which arises from the conduct of the corporation or that which the corporation allows the officer to assume without objection. Inherent authority is that which arises merely by virtue of his office."

Section 34-21-340(a) * * * states that the authority of an agent or representative "may be established as in other cases of representation." This statute is identical to Uniform Commercial Code (U.L.A.) §3-403. The official comment to §3-403 states in part: "The power to sign for another may be an express authority, or it may be implied in law or in fact, or it may rest merely upon apparent authority. It may be established as in other cases of representation, and when relevant parol evidence is admissible to prove or deny it."

The law is clear that when a signing is ambiguous, parol evidence is admissible to prove the intent of the parties to establish the character of the signing. When one signs his name after a corporate name, the signing is deemed ambiguous. Anderson, Uniform Commercial Code, § 3-403:35. That is precisely how the note at issue here was signed.

Indeed the trial court in its decision letter stated, " * * * In at least one instance (the note) there was sufficient ambiguity to warrant parol [evidence] which clearly tied the bank both to money obligation and to the commitment of its security. * * *" We think the trial court was correct in its conclusion. Parol evidence then clearly established, as set forth infra, that Redding was acting in a representative capacity for M & M.

Having found no reversible error, the judgment of the trial court is affirmed in all respects.

Affirmed

Hendrix v. First Bank
Court of Appeals of Georgia, 1990
195 Ga.App. 510, 394 S.E.2d 134

Sognier, Judge. Thomas L. Hendrix brought suit against the First Bank of Savannah, alleging that the bank had converted his funds when it accepted for deposit to his attorney's escrow account a check payable to Hendrix bearing an allegedly forged endorsement. The trial court granted the bank's motion for summary judgment and Hendrix appeals.

The record reveals that after his wife died, appellant retained the services of attorney William Braziel, an old family friend, to assist in collecting funds due him as a result of his wife's death, including paychecks, insurance proceeds, and other benefits. No specific written or oral authorization to endorse the checks was given Braziel by appellant at that time, but it is uncontroverted that Braziel had represented appellant several times previously, and on those occasions was given such authority and, in fact, did endorse and deposit checks without complaint from appellant. The check in question was issued in October 1987 by Mutual Benefit Insurance Company for payment of the proceeds of a life insurance policy issued to appellant's deceased wife as a fringe benefit of her employment at a local hospital and on which appellant was the designated beneficiary.

[A]n instrument is converted when it is paid on a forged endorsement. The trial court granted appellee's motion for summary judgment [on the alternative basis] * * * that even if the endorsement was unauthorized, * * * appellant had both by his subsequent actions and his inaction ratified the alleged forgery.

Appellant asserts several alternate bases for his contention that the trial court erred by granting appellee's motion for summary judgment, and we address the last of these first, because even if jury issues remain regarding whether appellee acted in accordance with commercially reasonable standards, it is apparent that there was nothing irregular or suspicious about the endorsement on its face which would estop appellee from asserting the defense of ratification, which was uncontroverted. Thus, if appellant, by his own conduct, ratified Braziel's unauthorized signature on the check, he is precluded from recovering on a claim for conversion against appellee, and summary judgment for appellee was proper.

Ratification, the confirmation by one of an act performed by another without authority, is an affirmative defense, and the burden of proving it is on the party asserting it. The ratification must be made by the principal with knowledge of the material facts, and "may be express or implied from the acts or silence of the principal." "[I]f the principal, with full knowledge of all the material facts, accepts and retains the benefits of the unauthorized act, he thereby ratifies the act." In this case, appellant admitted that he discovered the alleged forgery in February 1987. The record reveals, however, that he failed to notify appellee of this alleged forgery until the filing of this action in October 1987, nor did he take any action against Braziel at the time of his discovery of the alleged forgery. Rather, appellant continued to retain Braziel as his attorney to collect similar benefit checks until July 1987. Further, although the deposition testimony of Braziel and appellant conflicts as to when the decision was made to treat Braziel's deposit of the check in question as a loan and as to whether a note was ever executed for the amount of that check, it is undisputed that either before the check was deposited or when appellant discovered the alleged forgery in February 1987, an agreement *was* reached to treat the deposited check as a loan, and that Braziel made payments to appellant of both principal and interest.

Moreover, subsequent to appellant's discovery of the alleged forgery, he made further loans to Braziel, and on April 13, 1987 Braziel executed a security deed covering the total amount lent to him by appellant, $293,584.48, this amount exactly equalling the sum of the subject check plus three other undisputed loans, and pledged as collateral four parcels of property owned by Braziel. By appellant's own admission, in July 1987 he lent Braziel another $10,000 without a note. In September 1987 appellant, through his new attorney, notified Braziel that the notes were in default, but no accusations of forgery or conversion were made. In October 1987 Braziel instituted bankruptcy proceedings, and the schedules filed reflected $228,584 owed to appellant, which included all loans made including the approximately $83,000 from the insurance proceeds check in question here, less $75,000 paid toward the principal by Braziel.

> "[T]he acts of a principal are to be liberally construed in favor of an adoption of the acts of the agent, and when the unauthorized act of the agent is done in the execution of power conferred, but in excess or misuse thereof, a presumption of ratification readily arises from slight acts of confirmation, or from mere silence or acquiescence, or where the principal receives and holds the fruits of the agent's act. [Cit.]"

Kelley v. Carolina Life Ins. Co., 48 Ga.App. 106, 107(3), 171 S.E. 847 (1933). In the case sub judice, not only does appellant admit that he failed to notify appellee or take action against the alleged forger for eight months after discovery, a silence from which ratification ordinarily may be presumed, the evidence establishes that he also chose to treat the alleged forgery as though it were a loan, thereby reaping benefit in the form of security, as well as interest and principal payments, and thereby indicating ratification as well.

* * *

Judgment affirmed.

Thompson Maple Products, Inc. v. Citizens Nat'l Bank

Superior Court of Pennsylvania, 1967
211 Pa.Super. 42, 234 A.2d 32

Hoffman, Judge: In this assumpsit action, the plaintiff, Thompson Maple Products, Inc., seeks to recover more than $100,000 paid out on a series of its checks by defendant bank, as drawee. The payee's signature on each of the checks was forged by one Emery Albers, who then cashed the checks or deposited them to his account with the defendant.

The case was tried to the court below sitting without a jury. That court entered judgment in favor of the plaintiff in the amount of $1258.51, the face amount of three checks which the defendant had paid without any endorsement whatever. It dismissed the remainder of the claim, and this appeal followed.

The plaintiff is a small, closely-held corporation, principally engaged in the manufacture of bowling pin "blanks" from maple logs. Some knowledge of its operations from 1959 to 1962 is essential to an understanding of this litigation.

The plaintiff purchased logs from timber owners in the vicinity of its mill. Since these timber owners rarely had facilities for hauling logs, such transportation was furnished by a few local truckers, including Emery Albers.

At the mill site, newly delivered logs were "scaled" by mill personnel, to determine their quantity and grade. The employee on duty noted this information, together with the name of the owner of the logs, as furnished by the hauler, on duplicate "scaling slips."

In theory, the copy of the scaling slip was to be given to the hauler, and the original was to be retained by the mill employee until transmitted by him directly to the company's bookkeeper. This ideal procedure, however, was rarely followed. Instead, in a great many instances, the mill employee simply gave both slips to the hauler for delivery to the company office. Office personnel then prepared checks in payment for the logs, naming as payee the owner indicated on the scaling slips. Blank sets of slips were readily accessible on the company premises.

Sometime prior to February, 1959, Emery Albers conceived the scheme which led to the forgeries at issue here. Albers was an independent log hauler who for many years had transported logs to the company mill. For a brief period in 1952, he had been employed by the plaintiff, and he was a trusted friend of the Thompson family. After procuring blank sets of scaling slips, Albers filled them in to show substantial, wholly fictitious deliveries of logs, together with the names of local timber owners as suppliers. He then delivered the slips to the company bookkeeper, who prepared checks payable to the purported owners. Finally, he volunteered to deliver the checks to the owners. The bookkeeper customarily entrusted the checks to him for that purpose.

Albers then forged the payee's signature and either cashed the checks or deposited them to his account at the defendant bank, where he was well known. Although he pursued this scheme for an undetermined period of time, only checks paid out over a three-year period prior to this litigation are here in controversy. See Uniform Commercial Code, Act of April 6, 1953, P.L. 3, as amended, §4--406, 12A P.S. §4--406.

In 1963, when the forgeries were uncovered, Albers confessed and was imprisoned. The plaintiff then instituted this suit against the drawee bank, asserting that the bank had breached its contract of deposit by paying the checks over forged endorsements. See U.C.C. §3--404, 12A P.S. §3--404.

The trial court determined that the plaintiff's own negligent activities had materially contributed to the unauthorized endorsements, and it therefore dismissed the substantial part of plaintiff's claim. We affirm the action of the trial court.

Both parties agree that, as between the payor bank and its customer, ordinarily the bank must bear the loss occasioned by the forgery of a payee's endorsement. Philadelphia Title Insurance Company v. Fidelity-Philadelphia Trust Company, 419 Pa. 78, 212 A.2d 222 (1965); U.C.C. §3--404, 12A P.S. §3--404.

The trial court concluded, however, that the plaintiff-drawer, by virtue of its conduct, could not avail itself of that rule, citing §3--406 of the Code: "Any person who by his negligence substantially contributes to * * * the making of an unauthorized signature is precluded from asserting the * * * lack of authority against * * * a drawee or other payor who pays the instrument in good faith and in accordance with the reasonable commercial standards of the drawee's or payor's business." 12A P.S. §3--406.

Before this Court, the plaintiff Company argues strenuously that this language is a mere restatement of pre-Code law in Pennsylvania. Under those earlier cases, it is argued, the term "precluded" is equivalent to "estopped," and negligence which will work an estoppel is only such as "directly and proximately affects the conduct of the bank in passing the forgery ***." The plaintiff further asserts that those decisions hold that "negligence in the conduct of the drawer's business," such as appears on this record, cannot serve to work an estoppel.

Even if that was the law in this Commonwealth prior to the passage of the Commercial Code, it is not the law today. The language of the new Act is determinative in all cases arising after its passage. This controversy must be decided, therefore, by construction of the statute and application of the negligence doctrine as it appears in §3--406 of the Code.

Had the legislature intended simply to continue the strict estoppel doctrine of the pre-Code cases, it could have employed the term "precluded," without qualification, as in §23 of the old Negotiable Instruments Law, 56 P.S. §28 (repealed). However, it chose to modify that doctrine in §3--406, by specifying that negligence which "*substantially contributes to * * * the making of an unauthorized signature * * *.*" will preclude the drawer from asserting a forgery. (emphasis supplied). The Code has thus abandoned the language of the older cases (negligence which "directly and proximately affects the conduct of the bank in passing the forgery") and shortened the chain of causation which the defendant bank must establish. "(N)o attempt is made," according to the Official Comment to §3--406, "to specify what is negligence, and the question is one for the court or jury on the facts of the particular case."

In the instant case, the trial court could readily have concluded that plaintiff's business affairs were conducted in so negligent a fashion as to have "substantially contributed" to the Albers forgeries, within the meaning of §3--406.

Thus, the record shows that pads of plaintiff's blank logging slips were left in areas near the mill which were readily accessible to any of the haulers. Moreover, on at least two occasions, Albers was given whole pads of these blank logging slips to use as he chose. Mrs. Vinora Curtis, an employee of the plaintiff, testified:

"Q. Did you ever give any of these logging slips to Mr. Albers or any pads of these slips to Mr. Albers?

"A. Yes.

"Q. What was the reason for giving [a pad of the slips] to him, Mrs. Curtis?

"A. Well, he came up and said he needed it for [scaling] the logs, so I gave it to him."

Mrs. Amy Thompson, who also served as a bookkeeper for the plaintiff, testified:

"Q. As a matter of fact, you gave Mr. Albers the pack of your logging slips, did you not?

"A. Yes, I did once.

"Q. Do you remember what you gave them to him for?

"A. I don't right offhand, but it seems to me he said he was going out to look for some logs or timber or something and he needed them to mark some figures on * * *.

"Q. Well, if he was going to use them for scratch pads, why didn't you give him a scratch pad that you had in the office?

"A. That's what I should have done."

In addition, the plaintiff's printed scaling slips were not consecutively numbered Unauthorized use of the slips, therefore, could easily go undetected. Thus, Mr. Nelson Thompson testified:

"Q. Mr. Thompson, were your slips you gave these haulers numbered?

"A. No, they were not.

"Q. They are now, aren't they?

"A. Yes.

"Q. Had you used numbered logging slips, this would have prevented anybody getting logging slips out of the ordinary channel of business and using it to defraud you?

"A. Yes."

Moreover, in 1960, when the company became concerned about the possible unauthorized use of its scaling slips, it required its own personnel to initial the slips when a new shipment of logs was scaled. However, this protective measure was largely ignored in practice. Mrs. Amy Thompson testified:

"Q. And later on in the course of your business, if you remember Mr. Thompson said he wanted the logging slips initialed by one of the so-called authorized people?

"A. Yes.

"Q. (D)idn't you really not pay too much attention to them at all?

"A. Well, I know we didn't send them back to be sure they were initialed. We might have noticed it but we didn't send them back to the mill.

"Q. In other words, if they came to you uninitialed, you might have noticed it but didn't do anything about it.

"A. Didn't do anything about it."

The principal default of the plaintiff, however, was its failure to use reasonable diligence in insuring honesty from its log haulers including Emery Albers. For many years, the haulers were permitted to deliver both the original and the duplicate of the scaling slip to the company office, and the company tolerated this practice. These slips supplied the bookkeeper with the payees' names of the checks she was to draw in payment for log deliveries. Only by having the company at all times retain possession of the original slip could the plaintiff have assured that no disbursements were made except for logs received, and that the proper amounts were paid to the proper persons. The practice tolerated by the plaintiff effectively removed the only immediate safeguard in the entire procedure against dishonesty on the part of the haulers.*

Finally, of course, the company regularly entrusted the completed checks to the haulers for delivery to the named payees, without any explicit authorization from the latter to do so.

While none of these practices, in isolation, might be sufficient to charge the plaintiff with negligence within the meaning of §3--406, the company's course of conduct, viewed in its entirety, is surely sufficient to support the trial judge's determination that it substantially contributed to the making of the unauthorized signatures. In his words, that conduct was "no different than had the plaintiff simply given Albers a series of checks signed in blank for his unlimited, unrestricted use."

---

* We note that this procedure placed Albers in a position comparable to that of a trusted agent or employee, whose similar activities would have precluded his principal from asserting the forgeries, under § 3--405(1)(c). That section provides: '(1) An endorsement by any person in the name of a named payee is effective if * * * (c) an agent or employee of the drawer has supplied him with the name of the payee intending the latter to have no such interest.' The trial court's opinion characterizes Albers as an 'agent' of the plaintiff, but makes no findings with reference to this section. We decline the invitation to do so now, since the decision must be affirmed on other grounds.

Finally, the plaintiff argues that the defendant bank cannot rely on §3--406 because it did not pay the checks in accordance with "reasonable commercial standards" as required by that section. All the checks were regular on their face and bore the purported endorsement of the named payee. It is asserted, however, that the defendant bank was required, as a matter of law, to obtain the second endorsement of Albers before accepting the checks for deposit to his account.

The short answer to that contention is that the trial court did not find, nor does the record show, that obtaining such a second endorsement is a reasonable, or even a general, commercial practice, where the depositor is well-known to the bank and where his identity can later be ascertained from code markings on the check itself.

Furthermore, under the Code, the bank did not have an unqualified right to a second endorsement. A check endorsed in blank is bearer paper. It is negotiable by delivery alone, without further endorsement. See U.C.C. §§ 3--201, 3--204, 12A P.S. §§ 3--201, 3--204.

To the extent that banks do obtain such endorsements, they apparently do so for their own protection, over and above that provided by the warranties arising on presentment and transfer. Cf. U.C.C. §3--414, 12A P.S. §3--414 (Contract of Indorser), with U.C.C. §3--417, 12A P.S. §3--417 (Warranties). In short, the practice is not designed for the protection of the drawer. We are reluctant to hold that the plaintiff may shift the loss to the defendant bank, in this case, merely because the bank failed to exercise an excess of caution on its own behalf.

Judgment affirmed.

practice

Case 1

Immediately after Ed Adams finished a fabulous bar review lecture on law and economics, he was swarmed by students who wanted his autograph. Using a rubber stamp, he put his name -- "*Eddie Adams*" -- on anything they put in front of him. Unbeknownst to Professor Adams, he autographed -- in the place reserved for maker -- a form promissory note in the amount of one million dollars.

a. Is Professor Adams prima facie liable on the note, i.e., did he sign it? 1-201(39); 3-401(b).

b. How might it matter if the stamp read, "*The Official Autograph of Eddie Adams*"?

Case 2

A is the president of XYZ, Inc. On behalf of XYZ and with authority given her by the company, A procured a $100,000 loan from B and issued a note to B on which A wrote her own name in the place reserved for maker. B knew that the loan was intended for XYZ and understood that A was not intended to be liable on the note. B, however, negotiated the note to C who became a holder in due course without any notice that A intended no liability on the instrument.

a.   Is A personally liable to C if

    i.   A's signature was bare? See 3-402(b)(2).

    ii.   A had signed the note, "XYZ, Inc., by A, President of XYZ, Inc."?
       3-402(b)(1).

    iii.   A signed her own name and added below this signature, "XYZ, Inc." or
       "President" or "President of XYZ, Inc."?   3-402(b)(1) or (2).

    iv.   A signed, "XYZ Co. by A"? 3-402(b)(1) or (2); see *Federal Deposit
       Insurance Corp. v. Tennessee Wildcat Serv., Inc.*, 839 F.2d 251 (6th
       Cir. 1988) (use of the word "by" preceding a signature is legally
       sufficient to establish that the signature on note is made in a
       representative capacity when the principal is fully disclosed);
       Wyandot, Inc. v. Gracey Street Popcorn Co., Inc., 208 Conn. 248, 544
       A.2d 180 (1988) (check sufficiently named corporate principal even
       though the corporate name printed on the face of the check was
       "Gracey Street Popcorn, Inc." and the correct corporate name, i.e.,
       that registered with the secretary of state, was "Gracey Street
       Popcorn Company, Inc.").

b.   In which of the above circumstances is A liable to B if (1) C enforced the note
against B as indorser and B then sued A as maker or (2) B sued A on the
note without ever having sold it? (Before 1990, Article 3 barred parol
evidence even between the immediate parties if A's signature was bare. A
was liable as a matter of law. See, e.g., *Bradley v. Romeo*, 716 P.2d 227 (Nev.
1986). Moreover, in such a case the agent could not rely on parol evidence
to avoid personal liability under the equitable remedy of reformation.
Thomas v. McNeill, 448 N.W.2d 231 (S.D. 1989).)

c.   In which of the above circumstances is XYZ liable on the note? 3-402(a).

d.   Suppose that in getting the loan and signing the note, A said nothing about
acting for XYZ. Is A personally liable to B?

e.   Suppose that A signed the note, "XYZ, Inc., by A, President of XYZ, Inc." but B
can prove that when A signed the note, A agreed that she would be
personally liable on the note. Is A liable to B?

Case 3

A is the president of XYZ, Inc. On behalf of XYZ and with authority the
company gave her, A bought widgets from B for $100,000 and issued a check
to B for the price. A wrote her own name in the place reserved for drawer.
This signature was bare; but the check was drawn against XYZ's account.
XYZ's name and account number were printed on the check, and B knew that A
was not intended to be liable on the check. B, however, negotiated the check
to C who became a holder in due course without notice that A intended no
liability on the instrument. The check bounced because XYZ is insolvent.

    a.   Is A personally liable on the check? See 3-402(c). (Before the 1990 law there was plenty of authority that a corporate name imprinted on a check was not sufficient in itself to give notice that the individual who drew the check had signed it in a representative capacity. *Carador v. Sana Travel Service, Ltd,* 700 F. Supp. 787, 791 (S.D. N.Y. 1988); *Provecasa v. Gemini Associated Corp.,* 532 So.2d 1106 (Fla. App. 1988).)

    b.   Suppose that XYZ's name was not printed on the check. Only its account number appeared there. Is A liable to C in this case?

Case 4

A is Z's agent. Both of them are natural persons. A acted for Z in negotiating a loan from B and in issuing a note to B's order. In signing the note, A signed the note using Z's name. B sold the note to C who became a holder in due course without notice that A did not intend liability.

No   a.   Is A liable on the note? 3-402(b).

Yes   b.   Is Z liable? (Be careful!) 3-402(a).

Case 5

A is an officer of XYZ, Inc.. Purporting to act for XYZ *but without any kind of authority from the company,* A procured a $100,000 loan from B and issued a note to B on which A wrote her own name in the place reserved for maker. Below her name she wrote, "as secretary for XYZ." A kept the money for herself.

Yes   a.   XYZ is not liable on the note. Is A liable on it? See 3-403(a).

Yes, on the note   b.   Suppose that instead of keeping the money for herself, the money was given to XYZ and used by the company for its own purposes. Is XYZ liable on the note or otherwise? See 3-403 comment 3.

    c.   Suppose that A used the money for her own purposes but, despite her wrongdoing, XYZ pardoned A and continued to employ her. Does this conduct amount to ratification that obligates XYZ on the note?

Case 6

B issued a check in payment of goods purchased from S. Instead of signing the check by hand, B impressed her name on the instrument using an inked, rubber stamp that bears her facsimile signature. S presented the check to B's bank for payment. The bank dishonored the instrument. S then sued B on the instrument.

Yes   a.   Is B liable on the check? 3-413(b).

b. Through no fault of B, one of her employees misappropriated the signature stamp and several of B's blank check forms. Without any authority whatsoever from B, the employee completed the check forms by making them payable to various suppliers of goods who believed that B had ordered them. Immediately after the goods had been delivered, the dishonest employee disposed of a large part of them, pocketed the proceeds, and disappeared. Upon discovering what had happened, B notified her bank which refused to pay the checks when the suppliers presented the items for payment. The suppliers sued B on the checks. What result?

    i. The suppliers' pretrial discovery reveals that B had failed to take any steps to safeguard the rubber stamp and her blank check forms which were easily accessible to everyone who worked in B's office and to anyone who might wander through. Does this fact argue that B is liable to the suppliers on the checks? See 3-406 & comment 3 (*Case #1*).

    ii. One of the suppliers, X, was a company that had been reluctant in the past to accept checks bearing B's facsimile signature. To allay the supplier's fears, B had in writing assured X that it could accept such checks "without further inquiry" and that it would be "fully protected" in accepting checks drawn over B's facsimile signature. Is X more likely than the other suppliers to recover against B on checks issued by the dishonest employee? See 1-103.

c. What if B's signature was preprinted on her checks, and a thief misappropriated and misused some of them?

§ 2. Nature Of Liability

A person's signature on an instrument subjects her to prima facie liability on the instrument, but the nature of this liability is not the same for every signer. Article 3 imposes conditions on liability which vary with the capacity in which the person signed the instrument. *Capacity* refers to the role the signer plays with respect to the instrument itself, i.e., maker, drawer, acceptor, or indorser. The signature creates liability. The person's capacity defines and limits this liability. So defined, a person's liability on an instrument that results from her signature is known as her "*contract of liability*."

story

Determining capacity in which a person signed

Normally it is clear that the person who signs on the face of an instrument in the lower right-hand corner is either the maker or the drawer, depending on whether the instrument is a note or draft. A *maker* is "a person who signs or is identified in a note as a person undertaking to pay." 3-103(5). A *drawer* "signs or is identified in a draft as a person ordering payment." 3-103(3).

It usually is equally certain that the person named in the lower left-hand corner of a draft is the *drawee*, but the drawee is not liable unless and until she *accepts* the instrument. 3-408. The drawee accepts by signing the draft for the purpose or intent of agreeing to pay it, and she usually does so by signing vertically across the face of the instrument. This signature is an *acceptance* which obligates the drawee as an *acceptor*. The term acceptance also includes the act of the drawee accepting the draft. A bank's acceptance of a check has a special name, *certification*. A check that a bank certifies is, amazingly, a *certified check*.

When a person signs an instrument but not as maker, drawer or acceptor, her signature is an *indorsement* if it is

> a signature, other than that of a signer as maker, drawer, or accep-
> tor, that alone or accompanied by other words is made on an instru-
> ment for the purpose of
> ✓ negotiating the instrument,
> ✓ restricting payment of the instrument, or
> ✓ incurring indorser's liability on the instrument.

3-204(a). An indorsement is usually in the margin or on the reverse side of the instrument but can appear anywhere. It is the purpose of the signature, not its placement, that determines indorsement. Yet, as is true of every signature, its placement on the instrument helps to define the purpose.

When the capacity of the person signing is ambiguous, the law generally deems that her signature is an indorsement. Indorser is the catchall capacity by force of section 3-204(a), which provides:

> regardless of the intent of the signer, a signature and its accompanying
> words is an indorsement unless the accompanying words, terms of the
> instrument, place of the signature, or other circumstances unambiguously
> indicate that the signature was made for a purpose other than indorsement.

In other words, "[t]he general rule is that a signature is an indorsement if the instrument does not indicate an unambiguous intent of the signer not to sign as an indorser." 3-204 comment 1.

Sometimes a person whose signature appears on an instrument is not liable in any capacity because it is clear that she signed for a benign purpose. For example, a person normally would not be liable on the instrument if she placed "witness" after her name. Nor would she be liable if she signed below the words "payment received" because these words show a purpose to give a receipt, not to indorse or otherwise incur liability on the instrument. They unambiguously indicate that the signature was for a purpose that carries no liability.

Capacity and contract of liability

A person's capacity in signing an instrument -- maker, drawer, acceptor, or indorser -- defines the terms and conditions of her liability -- her *contract of liability* on the instrument. In general, the liability of makers and acceptors is described as *primary*, while the liability of drawers and indorsers is *secondary*.

For this purpose, *secondary liability* does not mean that somebody else is more or earlier *liable* on the instrument. Consider, for example, an ordinary draft or check that has not been accepted. The only person *liable* on the instrument is the drawer. A drawee is named but is not *liable* on the draft because she has not signed it. On the other hand, the draft itself directs the holder to seek payment from the drawee, and everyone expects the drawee to pay. They also expect that the drawer will not be required to pay unless the drawee dishonors. It is in this sense that a drawer and indorser's liability is secondary: both parties' liability is conditioned on someone else not paying the instrument who (party or not) was expected to do so. *Primary liability,*by contrast, means that the maker or acceptor is obligated to pay without initial resort to anyone else.

In detail, however, the liabilities of makers and acceptors are not exactly alike; and the differences in the liabilities of drawers and indorsers are even greater in some respects, especially under the new Article 3. Most noticeably, an indorser's liability requires giving her notice of dishonor that former law also required for a drawer. Under the new law, this notice is not generally a condition on a drawer's liability. This change in the terms of a drawer's liability is reported to mean that a drawer's liability is now primary rather than secondary. See 3-414 comment 2. This overstates the effect of the change because now, as before, a drawer is generally not liable unless the drawee dishonors. In this sense, a drawer's liability, now as before, is secondary.

In truth, Article 3 does not use the terms *primary* and *secondary* to describe liability or parties. The terms are not themselves part of the law; rather, they are mainly organizing concepts that serve to explain the law. Article 3 prefers to separate and distinguish the different capacities in which a person can sign an instrument, and to describe separately the terms and conditions of each capacity.

1. Maker

Basically, the maker of a note "is obliged to pay the instrument according to its terms at the time it was issued" or, if the maker signed an incomplete note, "according to its terms when completed * * *." 3-412. This obligation runs "to a person entitled to enforce the instrument or to an indorser who paid the instrument." Id. It is primary liability. The maker must pay the note at maturity absent discharge or some other defense that is effective against the person who wants payment. Nobody else must first fail to pay the note; and, normally, nobody else is liable to the maker on the instrument after she pays it. The instrument is then finished or expended, so long as the maker reacquires it and does not reissue it.

2. Drawer

Unlike the maker of a note, the drawer of a draft does not expressly promise to pay the instrument. She does not even expect to pay it personally. Instead, the drawer orders someone else, the drawee, to pay the draft. 3-103(a)(3). It is only if the drawee refuses or fails to pay the instrument that the drawer expects to honor it herself.

Consider the ordinary check. The drawer in effect says to the bank, "Pay the amount of this check to the holder when she presents it and charge my account." In effect, she says to the payee, "Take this check to the bank and ask for payment and if it does not pay, come back to me and I will." This conditional promise is not stated in the draft she signs, which contains no promise but only an order expressed by the word "Pay" addressed to the drawee. Rather, the drawer's promise is implied in the draft because of the contract of liability that a drawer makes by force of Article 3:

> *If an unaccepted draft is dishonored, the drawer is obliged to pay the draft (i) according to its terms* at the time it was issued or, if not issued, at the time it first came into possession of a holder, or (ii) if the drawer signed an incomplete instrument, according to its terms when completed, to the extent stated in Sections 3-115 and 3-407.

3-414(b) (emphasis added). In the unusual case in which the drawer is also the drawee, the contract is different. The liability is primary like the maker of a note. 3-414(a), 3-412. In every case, the drawer's obligation runs to a person entitled to enforce the instrument or to an indorser who paid it. 3-412; 3-414(b).

What constitutes *dishonor* that fixes or triggers the drawer's liability in the ordinary case is discussed later. It basically involves nothing more than the holder or her agent presenting the draft to the drawee who fails to pay or accept it. As a general rule, a drawer may avoid contract liability on an *ordinary draft* by ading words to her drawer's signature that disclaim liability to pay the draft. The most commonly-used disclaimer are the words "without recourse." For example:

Suppose, in a documentary sale, Seller draws a draft on Buyer for the price of goods shipped to Buyer. The draft is payable upon delivery to the drawee of an order bill of lading covering the goods. Seller delivers the draft with the bill of lading to Finance Company that is named as payee of the draft. If Seller draws without recourse Finance Company takes the risk that Buyer will dishonor. If Buyer dishonors, Finance Company has no recourse against Seller but it can obtain reimbursement by selling the goods which it controls through the bill of lading.

3-414 comment 5.

A drawer of a *check*, however, is not permitted to disclaim her liability. "There is no legitimate purpose served by issuing a check on which nobody is liable." Id.

3. Drawee

A drawee is the person who is ordered to pay a draft. 3-103(a)(2). A drawee who is not also the drawer is not liable on a draft until she *accepts* it, 3-408, which means signing the draft for the purpose of agreeing to pay it as presented. See 3-409(a). Therefore, so long as the drawee refrains from signing the draft, she incurs no liability to the holder *on the instrument* as the result of refusing to pay or accept it. If the drawee accepts the draft, she becomes liable but in the role of acceptor rather than drawee.

Sometimes, when a drawee refuses to pay, it is argued that the instrument assigns, to the payee and any later holder, the drawer's rights against the drawee. This argument typically fails. The reason is that a check or other draft does not *of itself* operate as an assignment of any money or credit, not even of funds in the hands of the drawee that are held and available for the draft's payment. 3-408. This is so even though the drawee holds sufficient funds of the drawer to pay the draft and has made a binding contract with the drawer to honor the draft upon presentment. The payee or other holder cannot herself sue the drawee for breaching this contract because she is normally only an incidental beneficiary of the contract, which means that the contract gives the holder no rights whatsoever against anyone. Of course, a drawee who fails to honor a proper demand for payment might be held liable to the drawer if the failure violates a duty owed to the drawer on the basis of a deposit agreement or otherwise.

In an extraordinary case, however, other facts may establish that the parties intended the draft to operate as an assignment. In this event, the instrument will be treated as a device for carrying out an assignment so that the drawee is liable to the holder as assignee.

Also, a drawee may become liable for conversion if, having had a draft presented to her for acceptance or for payment, she not only refuses to pay or accept but also refuses to return the instrument despite a demand for its return. 3-420(a). Although such a refusal does not constitute an acceptance, the result is possibly the same because damages for conversion can equal the face amount of the draft. 3-420(b). Depending on the circumstances, a person named as drawee might become liable to a holder on other bases such as the law of Article 5 on letters of credit. In a very extraordinary case, liability is also possible based on supplemental principles of common law and equity such as fraud, breach of trust, and various contract theories including ordinary contract, promissory estoppel, and the theory that the holder is an intended, third-party creditor beneficiary of the contract between the drawer and drawee. 1-103. The cases are very rare, however, that involve the unusual facts necessary to trigger these supplemental principles and theories.

A most common source of liability for a drawee of a check is U.C.C. Article 4, which governs bank deposits and collections. Article 4 imposes certain duties on a drawee-bank in the check collection and payment process. Violation of these duties can subject the bank to liability *with respect to* an item even though the bank, as drawee, has no liability *on* the instrument. This liability is covered in Chapter 6 infra.

4. Acceptor

An acceptor is the drawee of a draft who has accepted the instrument by signing it for the purpose of agreeing to pay it as presented to her. 3-409(a). A bank's acceptance of a check is called *certification* and the instrument is then referred to as a *certified check*. 3-409(d). Under earlier negotiable instruments law, it was possible to accept by signing the instrument *or* a separate paper such as a telegram or a letter. Because these *extrinsic acceptances* caused a degree of uncertainty inconsistent with the free transferability of commercial paper, the Code now provides that the acceptance "must be written on the draft" itself. 3-409(a).

Nothing in Article 3 or in other commercial paper law obligates a drawee to accept a draft or a bank to certify a check. 3-409(d). Acceptance results because the drawer and drawee have so arranged under other law and have done so because of business needs and reasons of convenience. It also can result from mistake. If the arrangement legally obligates the drawee to accept, the obligation is because of the other law, not because of Article 3. Moreover, the existence of the obligation or its breach means nothing for purposes of Article 3. What matters to Article 3 is only that acceptance occurs, not why .

The acceptance "may consist of the drawee's signature alone." 3-409(a). It is customary for an acceptor to sign vertically across the face of the draft, but a drawee's signature anywhere on the draft normally is sufficient because usually the only possible reason for signing it is to accept. 3-409 comment 2. The acceptor may, and usually does, insert the word "accepted" above her signature. She may add the date, which is important information if the draft is payable a stated period "after sight." If the acceptor fails to insert the date of her acceptance, the holder may supply the date in good faith and the inserted date will bind the acceptor. 3-409(c). Also, the acceptor may indicate the place where the draft is payable.

3-410(b). None of this extra information is necessary, but none of it affects negotiability or undermines the acceptance, which is the signature alone.

The acceptor's liability on the draft, like a maker's liability on a note, is primary. If the instrument is complete when she accepts it, the acceptor engages that she will pay the draft according to its terms as of the time of acceptance. 3-413(a).

An acceptance not only creates a contract of liability for the acceptor, it also dilutes or discharges the liability of other parties. Always, the effect of acceptance is to convert the drawer's liability to that of an indorser. 3-414(d). The transactional reality is that, in the beginning, the drawer is the principal debtor on the draft because no one else is liable on it. Upon acceptance, the acceptor is typically considered the principal debtor and is primarily liable, like the maker of a note. The drawer remains liable but is considered more like a surety. The law harmonizes with this custom and practice by transforming the drawer's liability to that of an indorser when the drawee accepts.

The effect is even greater when the acceptor is a bank. In this case, because of the usually assured solvency of the bank, the reality is that holders rely only on the bank's obligation and not on the liability of other parties to the instrument. For this reason, acceptance of a draft by a bank, including certification of a check, discharges the liability of the drawer and any indorser. 3-414(c), 3-415(d). It makes no difference when acceptance was obtained or who procured it. 3-414 comment 3. Former law is changed that provided for discharge only if the holder obtained acceptance.

5. Indorser

An indorser is someone who is not a maker, drawer, or acceptor and who signs an instrument (whether a note or draft) in order to negotiate it, restrict payment, or just to incur liability on the instrument. 3-204(a). Her signature is known as an *indorsement*. Id. An instrument is most commonly indorsed for the purpose of negotiating an order instrument so that the transferee becomes a holder. See Chapter 4 infra.

An indorser's liability is secondary. Her liability, like a drawer's, is conditioned on *dishonor* of the instrument. 3-415(a). Also, unlike a drawer, an indorser is generally entitled to *notice of dishonor*. Her contract is conditioned on notice, 3-503(a), and lack of notice is a defense to liability. 3-415(c). An indorser does not say, "I will pay." Rather she says, "I will pay if the instrument is dishonored and any necessary notice of dishonor is given." Assuming that these conditions are satisfied, she agrees to be liable according to the terms of the instrument at the time of her indorsement. 3-415(a). This obligation "is owed to a person entitled to enforce the instrument or to a subsequent indorser who paid the instrument * * * ." Id.

An indorser's liability is conditioned on dishonor even when the instrument is a note. In this case, to trigger the indorser's liability, the instrument must be presented to the maker for payment. It is the maker's dishonor that triggers the indorser's liability on the note. In the case of a draft, the drawee's dishonor is the trigger.

Several people may indorse the same instrument. Upon dishonor and with proper notice, the person entitled to enforce the instrument may immediately proceed against any one of the indorsers without proceeding against the others. It can therefore become important to determine if the indorser who is required to pay has any rights against the other indorsers or anyone else. Generally, indorsers are liable to one another in the order in which they indorse, that is, each indorser is liable to every subsequent indorser. Thus, an indorser who pays can recover from people who indorsed before her, and any indorser can recover directly from the maker or drawer.

An indorser can disclaim her contract of liability on the instrument by *qualifying* her indorsement, which means adding to her signature words such as "without recourse" or the like. 3-415(b). These words usually precede, but may follow, the signature. Although a *qualified indorser* incurs no contract liability on the instrument, she incurs liability on warranties as do unqualified indorsers and persons who transfer an instrument without any indorsement. See Chapter 8 infra.

An indorsement that is not qualified is unqualified. Every indorsement is either qualified or unqualified. Typically, it is unqualified. Someone who gives value for an instrument is entitled to the transferor's unqualified indorsement. 3-203(c).

Conditions of secondary liability

The contract liability of drawers and indorsers is conditioned on *dishonor* of the instrument, which usually involves *presentment* of it. An indorser's liability is further conditioned on *notice of dishonor*. These three events -- presentment, dishonor, and notice of dishonor -- are the conditions of secondary liability. If any of them that is required for liability on an instrument is not satisfied or excused, the liability is not enforceable. Absent excuse of the condition, enforcement must await satisfaction of the condition. The explanation is that secondary parties -- drawers and indorsers -- normally are not expected to pay unless someone else (the maker or drawee or acceptor) fails to do so. The conditions of secondary liability -- presentment, dishonor, notice of dishonor -- are the tools for asking the expected payor to pay. Thus, until the conditions have been met, the payor has not been properly asked to pay and secondary parties cannot be required to do so.

1. Dishonor

Dishonor is the core or prime condition of secondary liability. It is the fundamental key to this liability and is served by the other conditions of presentment and notice of dishonor. They are defined in terms of dishonor. Essentially, dishonor is the failure of a drawee or primary party (maker or acceptor) to pay or accept an instrument, usually upon proper presentment which is a demand for payment or acceptance. How dishonor occurs in a particular case depends on the nature and terms of the instrument. The legally significant combinations produce about a dozen separate descriptions or prescriptions for dishonor. See 3-502(a-d). Considered here are the basics, i.e., dishonor of typical instruments in simple, common cases.

Notes

A demand note is dishonored if "presentment [for payment] is duly made to the maker and the note is not paid on the day of presentment." 3-502(a)(1). Presentment is not required to dishonor a term note. Dishonor occurs when, and solely because, the note is not paid on the day it becomes payable. 3-502(a)(3). In other words, "[i]f the note is not paid on its due date it is dishonored." 3-502 comment 3. A different rule applies, however, if the term note is domiciled or the note itself provides for presentment. In this case, "the note is dishonored if presentment is duly made and the note is not paid on the day it becomes payable or the day of presentment, whichever is later." 3-502(a)(2).

In truth, dishonor of notes is practically unimportant, a moot issue. The reason is that a typical note includes a waiver of dishonor which, expressly or implicitly, includes a waiver of presentment and notice. Indorsers on the note contractually abandon the conditions on their liability and become, in effect, primary parties. Such waivers are valid and enforceable (3-504, 3-502(e)) and do not affect negotiability. 3-104(a)(3)(iii).

Drafts

Drafts are a different story. They rarely contain any waiver; and, therefore, the usual conditions on secondary liability are fully effective and meaningful, especially including conditions on the liability of secondary parties to checks. Another difference from notes is that, unfortunately, the meaning of dishonor for drafts is more complicated.

Begin with an ordinary draft. The complication here is that dishonor can occur upon presentment for payment *or* acceptance, depending on when the instrument is payable and when it is presented. The applicable rules are mostly collected in 3-502(b) and (c). These rules reflect what the usual parties to drafts ordinarily expect of the drawee with regard to payment and acceptance. Dishonor results whenever the drawee violates these rules. There is no dishonor, however, if the drawee is asked to pay or accept extraordinarily, beyond the normal expectations that are reflected in the 3-502 rules.

If the draft is payable on demand, "the draft is dishonored if presentment *for payment* is duly made to the drawee and the draft is not paid on the day of presentment." 3-502(b)(2) (emphasis added). Presentment for acceptance can be made, but the drawee's refusal to accept is not dishonor. It is only dishonor if there is presentment for payment that is refused. Nevertheless, if presentment for acceptance is made, the drawee may accept. Still, however, for dishonor to occur, the accepted draft must be presented for payment, and the acceptor must fail to pay it on that day.

If the draft is payable on elapse of a period of time after sight or acceptance, the time for payment is tied to acceptance. Therefore, it is expected and necessary that the draft is first presented *for acceptance*. Dishonor occurs if the drawee fails to accept on the day of that presentment. 3-502(b)(4). There is no dishonor if the drawee refuses to pay the draft before she has accepted it.

If the drawee properly accepts, there is a second chance for dishonor by non-payment. The accepted draft is dishonored "if presentment *for payment* is duly made to the acceptor and payment is not made on the day it becomes payable or the day of presentment, whichever is later." 3-502(d)(2) (emphasis added). In either event, whether it is the acceptance or payment that is refused, there is dishonor that triggers a secondary party's liability. The dishonor of a due presentment for acceptance is sufficient alone. The holder need not also make a further demand for payment, then or later.

In the case of a draft payable on a stated date, presentment for acceptance is not required. Dishonor occurs if the draft is presented *for payment*, and the payment is not made on or after the due date. 3-502(b)(3). Here, too, however, there is more than one chance for dishonor. Although presentment for acceptance is not necessary, it is permitted "to establish whether the drawee is willing to assume liability by accepting," 3-502 comment 4; and if the holder so presents the draft *before the due date of the instrument,* dishonor occurs if the drawee refuses to accept. Id. & 3-502(b)(3)(ii). It is not dishonor to refuse to accept if presentment for acceptance is made on or after the date of maturity. Even then, however, the drawee remains free to accept, even though not doing so would not amount to dishonor. If and whenever the drawee accepts, the rule applies that governs dishonor of an accepted draft payable at a definite time, i.e., "the draft is dishonored if presentment *for payment* is duly made to the acceptor and payment is not made on the day it becomes payable or the day of presentment, whichever is later." 3-502(d)(2) (emphasis added).

Checks

A check is a draft that is drawn on a bank and is payable on demand. 3-104(f). When a check is presented over the counter to the drawee-bank for immediate payment, dishonor is governed by the same rule that explains dishonor of an ordinary draft payable on demand. Dishonor is possible only upon presentment for payment, and occurs if this presentment is duly made to the drawee and the check is not paid on the day of presentment. 3-502(b)(2).

Very few checks, however, are presented over the counter for immediate payment. Such presentment implies, in its purest form, that the holder walks into the drawee-bank during public hours and personally asks a teller to exchange the check for cash money or its equivalent.

Most checks are not presented this way, and their dishonor is governed by a very different, entirely peculiar meaning of dishonor that never applies to ordinary drafts. Here is the rule:

> If a check is duly presented for payment to the payor bank otherwise than for immediate payment over the counter, the check is dishonored if the payor bank makes timely return of the check or sends timely notice of dishonor or nonpayment under Section 4-301 or 4-302, or becomes accountable for the amount of the check under Section 4-302.

3-502(b)(1). This rule defines dishonor in terms of Article 4. The basic meaning is that dishonor occurs if the drawee bank *provisionally* paid the check but returned it without having made *final* payment under 4-215(a) and 4-301(a) or, whether or not the check is returned, the bank has become accountable for it under 4-302.

The Article 4 process of paying checks is somewhat complicated the first time through. Drawee banks are encouraged to settle quickly for checks. A drawee bank becomes accountable, i.e., liable, for a check that it retains beyond midnight of the banking day of receipt without settling, i.e., provisionally paying for the check. If the bank settles on this day, it can still dishonor the check and get back the settlement if the bank returns the check, as 4-301 prescribes, before midnight of the next banking day following the day of receipt. If this second deadline is missed, the check is deemed finally paid even if the bank actually returns it. In this event, despite the actual return, there is no dishonor. Payment has occurred and the bank is responsible. More is said about this process in Chapter 6 infra.

2. Presentment

Secondary liability fundamentally requires dishonor of the instrument. Dishonor usually requires, as a necessary prerequisite, due or proper presentment which satisfies the procedural and other requirements of Article 3. When presentment is required, there is no dishonor without it, not even if the facts prove an actual refusal to pay or accept the instrument; and, in terms of Article 3, there is no presentment absent compliance with Article 3's rules of presentment.

Officially, "presentment" means:

a demand made by or on behalf of a person entitled to enforce an instrument
√ (i) to *pay* the instrument made to the drawee or a party obliged to pay the instrument or, in the case of a note or accepted draft payable at a bank, to the bank, or
√ (ii) to *accept* a draft made to the drawee.

3-501(a) (emphasis added). Generally speaking, dishonor occurs if the demand is refused, so long as two conditions are met, one of substance and the other of procedure.

First, the substance or nature of the presentment must be appropriate. The kind of presentment made, either for payment or acceptance, must have been a kind that, if refused, triggers dishonor in the circumstances of the particular case. The maker of a note refusing presentment for acceptance is never dishonor. The kind of presentment that is appropriate in the circumstances -- the nature or substance of it -- is determined by the rules of dishonor, which are described above. They define dishonor in terms of the kind of presentment that must be refused for dishonor to occur. It generally turns on the nature of the instrument, when it is payable, and when the presentment is made. Thus, to judge if dishonor has occurred, the right approach is to decide first, under the rules of dishonor, if the person's refusal to pay or accept, whichever happened, is a defining event of dishonor.

Second, if the kind or substance of the presentment is appropriate, the presentment must comply with the procedural rules that Article 3 details. See 3-501.

There are two different issues with respect to time of presentment. The first issue is when presentment can be made so that a refusal is dishonor. For example, a payor does not dishonor by refusing a presentment for payment made before the date for payment. It is really the question of how soon presentment can be made. When presentment is appropriate, in this sense, is defined in terms of dishonor and its rules which are explained earlier in this chapter.

The other issue is when presentment must be made in the sense that delay dilutes the holder's rights by reducing or releasing a secondary party's liability. It is really the question of how late presentment can be made. The answer is found in the contract of liability that a person incurs when she signs as drawer or indorser. Generally, there is no time limit in this sense, except as may result from a statute of limitations or be required by good faith.

Exceptional rules apply to checks. An indorser on a check is discharged unless the check is presented for payment or given to a depositary bank for collection within 30 days after the day the indorsement was made. 3-415(e). In a rare case, the drawer of a check may be discharged if the same action is not taken within 30 days after the date of the instrument. 3-414(f). For more on these consequences, see Chapter 4 supra and the earlier discussion in this chapter about the effects of failing to satisfy the conditions of secondary liability.

3. Notice of Dishonor

Notice of dishonor is always a condition to the liability of an indorser, and is a condition to a drawer's liability if a nonbank accepts the draft because, in this event, the drawer's liability is transformed into the liability of an indorser. 3-503(a), 3-414(d), 3-415(c). If due notice of dishonor is not timely given, the indorser or drawer who is entitled to notice is discharged. Due notice requires compliance with the rules of Article 3 that define and govern notice of dishonor.

With respect to timing, "notice of dishonor must [generally] be given within 30 days following the day on which dishonor occurs." 3-503(c). Exceptional rules apply with respect to checks and other instruments that a collecting bank takes for collection:

- The bank itself must give notice before midnight of the next banking day following the banking day on which the bank received notice of dishonor.
- Anybody else must give notice within 30 days following the day on which she herself received notice.

Id. Suppose, for example, that the payor bank dishonors a check by returning it to the depositary-collecting bank that had presented the check for payment. This bank now wishes to sue an indorser on the check. It must have notified the indorser by the midnight deadline. Suppose that the bank had done so and the indorser paid the bank. This indorser now wishes to recover over, in turn, from a prior indorser who must be given notice of dishonor. The subsequent indorser gets 30 days to do so from the time she herself received notice.

Suppose the bank, in the first instance, delays giving notice of dishonor to the subsequent indorser. The effect is clearly to discharge her liability. It is less explicit under the new Article 3 that, technically, the prior indorser is concomitantly discharged, but she need not worry. The bank cannot sue the prior indorser because the bank will have equally missed its midnight deadline for notice of dishonor as to her. The subsequent indorser, because she was discharged by the bank's delay in notice to her, will have no reason to recover over against the prior party.

4. Effect of Failing to Satisfy the Conditions

Postponement of secondary liability is the usual consequence of not meeting these conditions. Sometimes, however, failure or delay in presentment or notice of dishonor can entirely discharge the liability of an indorser or a drawer. The further effect is to discharge, pro tanto, the person's obligation on the transaction underlying the instrument.

Indorsers

An indorser is liable on an instrument because she signed it, but her liability is normally unenforceable unless and until:

- the instrument is presented to the person expected to pay (the maker, drawee or acceptor);
- this person dishonors by not paying or accepting; and,
- the indorser is duly notified of the dishonor.

It is a defense to liability that these events have not occurred. Enforcement must await them. Further, an indorser's liability is completely and forever discharged by an unexcused delay in notice of dishonor of any instrument, 3-415(c), 3-503(a); and, her liability on checks is discharged by a delay in presentment. 3-415(e).

Drawers

Presentment and dishonor are conditions of a drawer's liability but, with one exception, notice of dishonor is not required to charge a drawer. A drawer will or should know of dishonor on her own because of her relationship with the drawee.

> There is no reason why drawers should be discharged on instruments they draw until payment or acceptance. They are entitled to have the instrument presented to the drawee and dishonored before they are liable to pay, but no notice of dishonor need be made to them as a condition of liability.

3-503 comment 1. The exception is a draft accepted by a nonbank. In this event, the drawer is treated as an indorser and, like an indorser, she is entitled to timely notice of dishonor. 3-414(d), 3-503(a).

In the case of checks, a drawer's liability, like an indorser's, is tied not only to presentment but to *prompt* presentment. An undue delay can result in discharge. In the case of a drawer, the rule requires presenting the check to the drawee for payment, or giving it to a depositary bank for collection, within 30 days after the date of the instrument. 3-414(f). On the other hand, while delay in presenting a check discharges an indorser, the delay only rarely discharges a drawer and even then the discharge is not complete or automatic. A discharge is possible for the drawer only if:

- the drawee suspends payments after expiration of the 30-day period without paying the check, and
- because of the suspension of payments, the drawer is deprived of funds maintained with the drawee to cover payment of the check.

3-414(f). In this event, the drawer gets a discharge but only to the extent she is deprived of funds and only then upon assigning to the person entitled to enforce the check the drawer's rights against the drawee with respect to the funds. This discharge is even smaller than it looks because the drawer is not deprived of funds that are covered by state or federal bank deposit insurance. 3-414 comment 6.

It is only in this very limited case of bank failure that delay in presentment discharges a drawer, and delay in notice of dishonor will almost never discharge a drawer because notice is very rarely a condition to her liability. This scheme prevents unjust enrichment of a drawer, who normally has received consideration for the issue of the instrument. At the same time, it insures the drawer against the major risk that she is made to bear because of delay in presentment, which is the failure of a drawee on a check.

5. Excuse of Conditions or Delay

In some cases, making proper presentment or giving due notice of dishonor would be an empty formality contributing nothing to the persons intended to benefit by them. In other cases, whatever advantage might accrue from complying with these requirements is more than outweighed by the disadvantage to the person of whom compliance normally is required. Consequently, the law makes allowance in appropriate circumstances, relaxing the conditions of secondary liability.

Presentment for payment or acceptance is entirely excused if:

- the person entitled to present the instrument cannot with reasonable diligence make presentment,
- the maker or acceptor has repudiated an obligation to pay the instrument or is dead or in insolvency proceedings,
- by the terms of the instrument presentment is not necessary to enforce the obligation of indorsers or the drawer,
- the drawer or indorser whose obligation is being enforced has waived presentment or otherwise has no reason to expect or right to require that the instrument be paid or accepted, or
- the drawer instructed the drawee not to pay or accept the draft or the drawee was not obligated to the drawer to pay the draft.

3-504(a). Where dishonor is predicated on presentment that is excused for any of these reasons, the dishonor is deemed to occur "without presentment if the instrument is not duly accepted or paid." 3-502(e). There is no comparable express provision that deems notice of dishonor to be given if the instrument is not thereafter duly accepted or paid. It would therefore appear that any necessary notice is still required despite the fictional dishonor, unless notice is otherwise excused.

Notice is expressly excused, entirely, in only two situations:

- by the terms of the instrument notice of dishonor is not necessary to enforce the obligation of a party to pay the instrument, or
- the party whose obligation is being enforced waived notice of dishonor or presentment.

3-504(b). "Delay in giving notice of dishonor is excused if the delay was caused by circumstances beyond the control of the person giving the notice and the person giving the notice exercised reasonable diligence after the cause of the delay ceased to operate." 3-504(c).

An excuse may extend to one or more conditions and may affect the liability of one or more parties. Regardless of which conditions and whose liabilities are affected, the legal effect of excusing a condition or delay is that the law regards the condition as having been properly met within the time normally allowed.

Greer v. White Oak State Bank
Court of Appeals of Texas, Texarkana, 1984
673 S.W.2d 326

Cornelius, Chief Justice. This is an appeal from a district court judgment in favor of the White Oak State Bank against the payee and two indorsers of a check paid by the bank before it was dishonored by the drawee bank. We reverse the judgment against the two indorsers because they were discharged from liability by the bank's failure to give timely notice of dishonor. We reform and affirm the judgment against the payee for a reduced recovery on the basis of unjust enrichment.

Jack Greer and Donald Biesel owned a bowling alley in Marshall. George Ford and Bowling and Billiard Supply of Dallas, Inc. (B & B), held outstanding liens on the alley and they, along with the owners, were named as beneficiaries of an insurance policy on the facility. The bowling complex burned and on July 15, 1981, the insurance company issued a check for $490,000.00 to Greer, Biesel, Ford and B & B. On July 24, 1981, Greer and Biesel indorsed the check and had Ford and B & B indorse it. Greer then wrote Ford a check for $99,561.25 and B & B a check for $327,727.54 in payment of their liens, and deposited the insurance check in his account at the White Oak State Bank. The bank gave Greer immediate credit rather than handling the check as a collection item. It developed that the insurance company was insolvent and the drawee bank dishonored the check. On August 3, 1981, the White Oak State Bank was notified by a telephone call from its clearing house, First National Bank in Dallas, that they were returning the check. The telephone message gave the amount of the check, the date it passed through the White Oak State Bank, and the names of two of the indorsers: Greer and Biesel. The bank did not receive written notice of dishonor until August 13, 1981, and did not notify the indorsers until August 14. The bank paid out $68,849.26 after August 3, 1981, from Greer's account, based on the credit to his account of the $490,000.00 represented by the insurance check. On March 18, 1982, the bank debited Greer's account $27,488.59 as a commercial offset.

White Oak State Bank brought suit against Greer, Biesel, Ford and B & B as payees and indorsers of the check. Biesel failed to file an answer and was not represented by counsel. No judgment was entered against him. Greer, Ford and B & B denied liability as indorsers because of the bank's failure to promptly notify them of the dishonor. Seventeen of the eighteen special issues were answered in favor of Greer, Ford, Biesel and B & B, but Greer was found to have been unjustly enriched by payment of the check. The trial court disregarded the jury answers to four special issues and entered judgment against Greer, Ford and B & B for $363,464.84, together with interest, costs and attorney's fees.

Tex.Bus. & Com.Code Ann. §§ 3.501, 3.508, 3.502 (Vernon 1968), respectively, provide that unless excused, notice of dishonor is necessary to charge any indorser of an item; notice must be given by a bank before its midnight deadline (the next banking day after the banking day it received the item) [Tex.Bus. & Com.Code Ann. §4-104(a)(8) (Vernon 1968); and that any unexcused delay in giving notice of dishonor discharges any indorser. The bank argues that these code provisions do not apply to Greer, Ford and B & B because (1) oral notice of dishonor is not effective and the indorsers were promptly notified after the bank received written notice of the check's dishonor on August 14, 1981, and (2) the telephone notice from the bank in Dallas did not specify that Ford and B & B were indorsers, so in any event it did not receive notice of dishonor *as to them* until August 13, 1981. We cannot agree with either of these propositions.

Section 3.508 expressly provides that notice of dishonor may be oral. The bank contends that Section 4.202(a) of Tex.Bus. & Com.Code Ann. (Vernon 1968), [which in part requires a collecting bank to exercise ordinary care in sending notice of dishonor and in returning a dishonored item], supersedes Section 3.508 with respect to notice from a collecting bank, and because that section refers to "sending" notice of dishonor, only a written notice is contemplated. We disagree. The adequacy of oral notice is confirmed by Section 4.104(c) which specifically makes the notice of dishonor provisions of Section 3.508 applicable to transactions under Chapter 4. Moreover, the jury found upon sufficient evidence that White Oak State Bank and the First National Bank in Dallas had agreed prior to August 3, 1981, that notice of returned items could be sent by telephone. The requirements of Chapter 4 may be modified by agreement. Tex.Bus. & Com.Code Ann. §4.103(a).

The failure of the telephone notice to name Ford and B & B as indorsers did not render the notice ineffective as to them. Section 3.502(a)(1) provides that if notice of dishonor is not given when due, *any* indorser is discharged. Delay in giving notice may be excused when a party does not know it is due or when the delay is caused by circumstances beyond his control. Tex.Bus. & Com.Code Ann. §3.511(a) (Vernon 1968). But there was no jury finding here that any circumstance existed which would excuse the Bank from notifying Ford and B & B. In fact, the employee who received the telephone notice testified that the information she received was sufficient to enable her to identify the check and all parties to it.

As indicated, Greer, Ford and B & B were all discharged, *as indorsers*, from any obligation on the check. Greer, however, was also a *customer* of the bank, and a recovery against him on a cause of action for money had and received, or unjust enrichment, was proper under the jury findings.

Atlantic Cement Co., Inc. v. South Shore Bank

United States District Court, D. Massachusetts, 1983,
36 U.C.C. Rep. Serv. 890, aff'd,
United States Court of Appeals, First Circuit, 1984
730 F.2d 831

Skinner, District Judge. Plaintiff Atlantic Cement Co., Inc. brings this action for breach of contract and violation of Mass GL c 93A against defendant South Shore Bank ("Bank") ***.

The undisputed facts are as follows. In March, 1982, plaintiff sold and delivered cement to Marshfield Sand and Gravel, Inc. ("Marshfield") and was paid by checks drawn on Marshfield's account with the Bank. Each check bore the legend "Payable at South Shore Multi-bank, Quincy, Ma". In early April, 1982, plaintiff received a check for $44,166.75 as full payment for the March delivery to Marshfield. The check was deposited but returned, marked "insufficient funds". Plaintiff received Marshfield's assurances that sufficient funds existed to cover the check but was unable to verify this statement with the bank. Plaintiff redeposited the check which was again returned. Plaintiff then spoke with an officer of the Bank and was told that Marshfield had sufficient funds but the Bank would not pay plaintiff due to an agreement among all of Marshfield's creditors. Although plaintiff claimed not to be a party to the alleged agreement, the Bank refused to honor the check. Plaintiff subsequently made futile demands for immediate payment on Marshfield and the Bank. Marshfield ceased doing business in early May and on May 26, 1982 was forced into involuntary bankruptcy.

Plaintiff claims that it was harmed by the Bank's refusal to honor the check drawn on Marshfield's account and it therefore has a cause of action against the Bank for the face value of the check. The rights of plaintiff against the Bank are governed exclusively by Mass GL c 106, §3-409(1) which states:

> A check or other draft does not of itself operate as an assignment of any funds in the hands of the drawee available for its payment, and the drawee is not liable on the instrument until he accepts it.

This section restricts plaintiff's rights in two ways. First, since the check is not an assignment of funds, it does not of itself invest rights in the fund to plaintiff. Second, the Bank does not become liable to plaintiff until it accepts the check. The printed legend on the check does not constitute an acceptance according to Mass GL c 106, §3-410(1) which defines acceptance as "drawee's signed engagement to honor the draft as presented *** (that) must be written on the draft and may consist of his signature alone".

Because under the statute plaintiff is not an assignee of the fund, it has rights only against Marshfield. The Bank has incurred no obligation to plaintiff. The agreement between Marshfield and the Bank involved a promise by the Bank to pay Marshfield's debts out of a specified fund, but that implies no contractual duty to plaintiff as distinguished from Marshfield, to see that the check was paid to the payee.

Plaintiff's assertion that its claim is "on the agreement" but "off the instrument" and not governed by Mass GL c 106 is without merit since the whole claim revolves around the payment of a check, exclusively governed by Mass GL c 106.

Plaintiff alleges that as an intended beneficiary of the contract between Marshfield and the Bank, it has the right to sue for breach of that contract. Plaintiff cites modern Massachusetts cases which recognize the rights of a third party beneficiary, but none deal with a similar factual situation as the case before me. This case law cannot be read so as to alter the liability of the parties and disrupt the established statutory scheme set forth in Mass GL c 106, §3-409. This statute excludes plaintiff from intended beneficiary status by repudiating the Bank's liability to plaintiff. When there is a statute on point, case law proposing conflicting theories is "not meant to be a vehicle to disrupt the symmetry of the relevant provision *** or create new levels of risk not contemplated by (the statute) or bargained for by the parties".

Plaintiff's second claim is based on Mass GL c 93A which provides that unlawful or deceptive acts or practices in the conduct of trade or commerce are unlawful. It is settled that c 93A applies to the conduct of banks. Chapter 93A, §11 entitled only persons who suffer loss due to the unfair practices defined by c 93A, §2 to bring actions under the statute. Plaintiff suffered no loss or damage due to any action of the Bank. The cement had been delivered to Marshfield before plaintiff had any contact with the Bank. Plaintiff did not make cement deliveries on reliance of any statements by the Bank. Under Mass GL c 106, §3-409(1), the Bank had no duty to honor the checks presented for payment by plaintiff. The Bank's conduct was consistent with commercial law and not a violation of c 93A.

Accordingly, defendant's motion to dismiss the complaint is allowed.

W.B. Farms v. Fremont Nat'l Bank

United States Court of Appeals, Eighth Circuit, 1985
756 F.2d 663

Arnold, Circuit Judge. W.B. Farms brought this action for breach of an oral agreement it says it made with Fremont National Bank & Trust Co. It contends that Fremont National Bank agreed to pay a check made payable to W.B. Farms whenever sufficient funds came into the account of the drawer. Jurisdiction is based on diversity of citizenship, and Nebraska law governs. Fremont appeals from a judgment entered on a jury verdict against it. * * *

This case arises out of a sale of cattle by W.B. Farms to Keith Mumma. In payment for the cattle, Mumma issued to W.B. Farms a check for $31,358.50 drawn on the Fremont National Bank & Trust Co. of Fremont, Nebraska, in which Mumma had an account. W.B. Farms entrusted the check to the Farmers State Bank of Brush, Colorado, for collection. The head teller of the Farmers State Bank telephoned the head teller of Fremont, and, according to the teller of the Farmers State Bank, secured an agreement that Fremont would pay the check whenever sufficient funds came into Mumma's account. The Farmers State Bank then sent the check to Fremont. On November 15, 1979, there was enough money in Mumma's account to pay the check, but Fremont did not pay it. The account was later exhausted by other charges, and Mumma went bankrupt. The plaintiff W.B. Farms now looks to Fremont for payment of the check, claiming the bank's failure to pay the check violated the oral agreement it made with W.B. Farms through the Farmers State Bank.

* * *

A check is a bill of exchange, drawn on a bank, and payable on demand. Checks represent three-cornered transactions. The person who signs the check, then delivering it to someone else in payment for goods or services, is known as the drawer, here Keith Mumma. The drawee of the check is the bank to which it is directed, in which, presumably, the drawer has an account. The third party to the transaction is the payee, the person to whose order the check is made payable, here W.B. Farms. Checks are not instant assignments of the drawer's funds to the payee. In fact, drawers have no money in banks. Only bankers have money in banks. Drawers have choses in action against banks. A bank's failure to pay a check, therefore, may be a breach of its contract of deposit with the drawer, but it is neither a breach of contract nor a tort actionable at the instance of the payee. To put it another way, drawee banks are generally not liable to payees on checks. To this rule there is an exception, as one might expect: under Neb.Rev.Stat. (U.C.C.) §3-409(1) & §3-410(1) (Reissue 1980), a drawee is liable on a check if it accepts the check in writing. (It can also be liable if the check is certified, but that has nothing to do with this case.) Here, it is undisputed that the Fremont National Bank & Trust Co. never agreed in writing to accept the check that Mumma delivered to W.B. Farms. The plaintiff claims, however, that an agent of Fremont (about whose authority no question is raised) made an oral agreement to pay the check, and that the oral agreement is valid and enforceable.

The validity of this agreement is a question of Nebraska law. Although courts strive for uniformity in the interpretation of the Uniform Commercial Code, the Code still represents the act of the legislatures of the various states that have adopted it, and we have no general license to federalize the U.C.C. by interpreting it according to our own lights. As with other questions of state law, we normally defer to the knowledge and experience of a district judge sitting in the state whose law is involved. His or her judgment as to the content of state law is usually accepted unless it is "deficient in analysis or otherwise lacking in reasoned authority." *Ancom, Inc. v. E.R. Squibb & Sons, Inc.*, 658 F.2d 650, 654 (8th Cir.1981). Here, there is no opinion of the Supreme Court of Nebraska rejecting the District Court's holding that an oral agreement to accept a check is valid as a matter of Nebraska law.

We accept this holding. In principle, we see no reason why a bank cannot make any contract it wishes, so long as no provision of positive law purports to take away its right to do so. No such provision in the Uniform Commercial Code is suggested, and, as a matter of fact, §4-103(1) of the Code specifically provides that provisions of Article 4 may be varied by contract. Fremont argues that this provision of the Code is not meant to include agreements concerning the drawee bank's obligation to pay checks since the conditions for such agreements are already covered in the U.C.C. provisions for acceptance, guaranty, assignment, and certification. If such agreements were effective, the argument runs, then the U.C.C. provisions governing certification, guaranty, assignment, and acceptance would be undercut. In support of this proposition, Fremont cites the case of *Sabin Meyer Regional Sales Corp. v. Citizens Bank*, 502 F.Supp. 557 (N.D.Ga.1980). In *Sabin*, bank officers assured the plaintiff that the drawer's account contained and would contain sufficient funds to cover the checks when they were presented. This "agreement" is akin to an oral acceptance or certification of the checks, and its enforcement would arguably encroach upon the U.C.C. provisions requiring written acceptance or certification. In contrast, the agreement here is much less like an acceptance or certification. Fremont, unlike the bank in *Sabin*, did not unconditionally agree to pay the check, but rather agreed to pay it only if and when there were sufficient funds in the drawer's account. Thus, Fremont had no duty to pay the check unless sufficient funds came into the account during the time that it agreed to hold the check.

Concededly, there are several policies which favor the exclusion of conditional agreements to pay, such as the prevention of fraudulent claims against banks and the promotion of efficient banking practice. But on the other hand, the policies of contractual freedom and the protection of reasonable expectation would support allowing such agreements. In the absence of any controlling Nebraska law on this matter or any compelling reasons for disallowing such agreements, we shall defer to the District Court's interpretation of state law. We, therefore, hold that the oral agreement alleged here is valid and enforceable under Nebraska law.

practice

Case 1

A issued a demand note to B who indorsed and delivered it to C. Months passed without anyone stepping forward to pay it. C decides to take action to collect the instrument.

a. Presentment is necessary.

B

    i.   To charge A or B or both of them? 3-415(a) (requires "dishonor"); 3-502(a)(1) (dishonor requires "presentment").

    ii.   How will presentment be accomplished? 3-501(a).

A

    iii.   To whom is presentment made? 3-501(a); 3-502(a)(1).

iv. How soon must it be done?

b. Suppose that A is in bankruptcy or the terms of the instrument waive the requirement of presentment.

    i. Presentment is not necessary. Why not? 3-504(a)(ii), (iii), (iv).

    ii. Is notice of dishonor unnecessary too? 3-504(b) (second sentence).

    iii. Does a waiver of presentment affect the negotiability of the note? 3-104(a)(3)(iii).

No

c. Suppose that the note is due on July 1. Presentment is not necessary to establish B's liability, but notice of dishonor is required unless excused.

    i. How is the latter accomplished without the former? See 3-502(a)(3).

    ii. When must the notice be given? 3-503(c); 3-415(c).

30 days

d. What difference does it make if the note is *domiciled* at First State Bank, i.e., is due and payable on July 1 at First State Bank? See 3-502(a)(2).

e. Would there be any difference if B indorsed "without recourse"? See 3-415(b).

Case 2

A issued a note to B who indorsed and delivered it to C. The note was not paid on the due date of July 1.

a. How soon must C notify B of dishonor? 3-503(c).

30 days

b. What is the consequence of delay in notifying B? 3-415(c).

Discharge

c. Suppose that C waited six months before notifying B of dishonor, but B had learned from A on July 7 that A had failed to pay the note. See 3-503(b).

d. Would it matter if C's delay in notification was due to postal and communication strikes that were beyond C's control?

Case 3

A paid B for goods with a check drawn on PB Bank.

a. Suppose that B waited several months before depositing the check with her bank, also PB Bank. So what? 3-414(f).

b. Suppose that B immediately indorsed the check to C, and it was C who sat on the check for several months. So what? 3-415(e).

c. Suppose that B immediately indorsed the check to C, and C just as quickly indorsed and deposited the check with DB Bank for collection. The drawee, PB Bank, dishonored the check and timely returned it to DB. So what? 3-414(b); 3-415(a); 3-502(b)(1); 4-214(a).

C immediately deposited the check with her bank, DB Bank. DB then presented the check for payment to PB Bank. PB dishonored the check and returned it to DB, which sent the check to C.

d. What happens if DB immediately sent the check to C, and C waited several weeks to notify B about dishonor? 3-503(a) & (c)(ii).

e. What happens if DB waited several weeks to send the check to C, and C immediately notified B of dishonor? 3-503(a) & (c)(i).

f. What happens if PB waited several banking days before returning the check to DB? 4-302(a)(2); 4-301(a); 4-215.

Case 4

"Ford provides blank, preprinted drafts *** to approved dealers of Ford Motor Company. The drafts are among the numerous documents used in the system by which Ford finances automobile sales to consumers. The customer who wants to buy a car on credit from a Ford Motor Company dealer enters into a retail installment sales agreement with the dealer, promising to pay the amount financed and giving the dealer a security interest in the automobile. Since dealers do not typically want to finance the sale themselves, Ford's system provides a means by which Ford assumes responsibility for financing the consumer's purchase and the dealer receives the amount financed. To use this system, a dealer does two things. First, after the consumer signs the retail installment sales agreement, the dealer assigns the agreement to Ford and sends the agreement and related documents to Ford for approval. Second, the dealer completes one of the preprinted drafts (by paying itself or its bank the amount financed) and presents the draft for payment through the commercial banking system. Assuming that the documents are in order and that Ford agrees to finance the transaction, Ford transfers the amount financed to the dealer by honoring the sight draft. *** [S]ight drafts are commonly used in the automobile industry. Their purpose is to facilitate and expedite payment to the dealer.

"The *** sight drafts also contain the language 'payable through *** The First National Bank, Colorado Springs, Colorado,' which is printed in the lower left-hand side of each draft. To understand how the drafts were used, this provision must be explained. Ford employed The First National Bank of Colorado Springs as its 'collecting bank.' *** After a collecting bank such as the First National Bank of Colorado Springs receives a sight draft from a depositary bank, it contacts Ford to ask Ford if it is prepared to pay the draft. If Ford disapproves the transaction, it instructs its collecting bank to dishonor the sight draft. If it wants to pay the draft, Ford instructs the collecting bank to pay the draft and mails the collecting bank a Ford check in the amount of the draft. The collecting bank, in turn, pays depositary banks, such as First

National Bank in Alamosa, the amount of the sight draft, by means of interbank credits provided through the Federal Reserve system.

"Dealers often execute and deposit the preprinted Ford sight draft with their local bank as soon as the consumer sale is made. This can create problems. If the sight draft reaches Ford's collecting bank through the bank collection system before the retail installment sales agreement reaches Ford through the mails, Ford will instruct its bank not to honor the dealer's sight draft. More importantly, Ford will not honor a sight draft if the agreement and related documents are not in order, or if the dealer has failed to pay Ford the wholesale price for the car which the dealer has sold and proposes to finance through Ford." *First Nat'l Bank v. Ford Motor Credit Co.*, 748 F. Supp. 1464 (D. Colo. 1990).

a. Ford dishonored nine of these drafts that First National Bank in Alamosa had treated as cash items -- that is, it credited Alamosa Motors' account and permitted Alamosa Motors to have immediate use of the funds represented by that credit, as had been its practice when Alamosa Motors deposited similar drafts on prior occasions. Unfortunately, the principals of Alamosa Motors left town, literally in the middle of the night, around March 12, 1986. By the time the sight drafts (1) had been presented through the interbank collection system, (2) were dishonored, and (3) came back to the Bank, Alamosa Motors' account at the Bank was overdrawn by $64,543.28. Unable to recover from Alamosa Motors, the Bank sued Ford on three theories. First, the Bank asserted that Ford was liable on the drafts themselves. Second, the Bank alleged that Ford was negligent in introducing "confusing and misleading negotiable instruments" into the commercial banking system. Third, the Bank asserted a promissory estoppel claim. Both sides moved for summary judgment. What result if you were the judge?

The real judge sided with Ford.

b. Additionally or alternatively, can Bank recover from the car buyers?

No

Case 5

S sold goods to B and drew a draft against B payable to T, to whom S was indebted. The draft was payable 30 days sight. It was delivered to T.

a. T presented the draft for payment and B refused to pay it.

i. Is B liable to T?

No

ii. Is S liable?

No

b. T presented the draft for acceptance and B refused to accept it. T sued S. What result?

i. Is B liable to T?

No

ii. Is S liable?

Yes

    c.   T presented the draft and B accepted it.

        i.   What is B's liability? 3-413(a).

        ii.   What is S's liability after B's acceptance? 3-414(d).

        iii.   What if B was a bank? 3-414(c).

    d.   What if B refused to accept the draft after having promised S that she would accept and pay it?

    e.   What if B had made the promise to T?

Case 6

A paid B for goods with a check drawn on PB Bank. Before taking the check, B called PB and talked with a bank officer about the check and A's account. Thereafter, B deposited the check with her bank, DB Bank. DB then presented the check for payment to PB Bank. PB dishonored the check because of insufficient funds and timely returned it to DB, which immediately sent the check to B. A is bankrupt. Is PB liable to B on the check or otherwise if

a.   PB promised B that the check would be paid?

b.   PB reported that "the check will clear"?

c.   In the past PB had customarily paid A's overdrafts?

d.   PB misreported that the current balance would cover the check?

e.   PB kept the check for two weeks before returning it?

§ 3. Payment And Discharge Of Contract Liability

"Discharge" means that an obligor is released from contract liability on the instrument for reasons of Article 3 or by contract law. It happens in a variety of ways for different reasons. The purpose is sometimes to protect an obligor whose rights or obligations with respect to the instrument have been offended, as by:

- modification of the principal obligor's liability that causes loss to a surety, 3-605;
- impairment of collateral, 3-605;

- unexcused delay in presentment or notice of dishonor with respect to a check, 3-414(f), 3-415(e);
- acceptance varying draft, 3-410; or,
- alteration, 3-407.

A different purpose is served by discharging the drawer's liability when a draft is accepted by a bank. 3-414(c). It adjusts liability on the instrument to match the realities of the transaction and reflect normally implied expectations. Discharge most often occurs, however, because the instrument is paid or because the parties expressly, deliberately intended to release the obligor, as by cancellation or renunciation or by contract.

Discharge by payment of the instrument

A person who signs an instrument becomes liable to pay it. It is natural, therefore, that her payment of the instrument should end her liability on it. The law confirms and reaches this outcome by way of discharge, by providing that "[t]o the extent of the payment, the obligation of the party obliged to pay the instrument is discharged." 3-602(a). Also, by separate rule, payment of the instrument usually discharges the underlying obligation. 3-310(b-c).

Three very important limits are built into the rule that payment of an instrument discharges liability on it. First, the discharge is pro tanto only, "to the extent" of payment. Second, the actual payment must match the statutory definition of "payment" that applies here, which requires that payment is made:

- by or on behalf of a party obliged to pay the instrument, and
- to a person entitled to enforce the instrument.

3-602(a)(i-ii). Whenever someone other than a party gives value for the instrument, it is a purchase rather than "payment" and there is no discharge by this rule unless she acts for a party to the instrument. There is also no payment and no discharge if a right person pays the wrong person. The rule requires payment to a person entitled to enforce, who is usually the holder of the instrument. See 3-301.

Interestingly, the mechanics of "payment" are not described. The medium obviously is money; but other aspects are less clear, including the means of payment and the point at which payment is accomplished. These matters are important because they affect how and when the risks shift with respect to the funds.

The third and final limit of 3-602(a) is that the discharge only affects the liability of the party who pays the instrument. For this reason, payment alone does not extinguish the whole instrument or discharge any other party's liability on it. Former law agreed but also applied a supplemental rule that discharged everybody on the instrument when any party was discharged who herself had no right of recourse on the instrument. 3-601(3)(b) (1989 Official Text). Thus, if the maker of a note paid it, an indorser was discharged. The 1990 Article 3 lacks this rule, but the result is the same. An indorser's liability is conditioned on dishonor. 3-415(a). Because of the maker's payment, the indorser's liability never will mature.

1. Distinguishing Payment of the Underlying Obligation

It is important to understand that the discharge of 3-602 is based on payment of the instrument, not payment of the underlying obligation. They are not the same. Paying the instrument also results, by separate rule, in discharge of the underlying obligation. See 3-310. The converse is not true. *Paying the underlying obligation, technically, does not discharge liability on the instrument.* By most accounts, this lack or absence of discharge is important.

Suppose, for example, that S takes B's note for the price of goods and immediately negotiates the instrument to T. B pays S. T sues B on the note. B does not have the 3-602(a) defense of discharge by payment. B paid S, but S was not then a person entitled to enforce the instrument. This right already had passed to T. The common understanding is that B must pay T even if T lacks the rights of a holder in due course. The reasoning is that when a negotiable instrument is assigned, the risk of paying the right person is on the obligor. The risk is on her even though she has not been notified of the assignment, which is different from the common-law and Article 9 rule that applies in the case of an ordinary contract right. See 9-318(3). The reasoning is that in the case of an instrument, "the right [to payment] is regarded as intimately connected with the writing and performance rendered to a party that does not produce the writing is rendered at the obligor's peril, regardless of the lack of notification." E. Farnsworth, CONTRACTS §11.7 at 806 (1990).

Possibly, however, this analysis is technically flawed and B should win. It is true that B's payment did not discharge her on the instrument. The payment nevertheless satisfied her underlying obligation to S. Satisfying this debt would have been a defense for her if S sued on the sales contract. T's rights on the instrument, if she is not a holder in due course, are subject to "a defense of the obligor *** that would be available if the person entitled to enforce the instrument were enforcing a right to payment under a simple contract." 3-305(a)(2). On this basis, B could argue that her payment of the sales contract is a defense good against T, and that her lack of discharge on the instrument is unimportant. This argument appears sound, but opposes commonly accepted doctrine. In any event, the argument rightly fails and B flatly loses if T is a holder in due course.

2. Tender of Payment

If the obligor on a negotiable instrument makes a proper tender of full payment to the holder at or after maturity, but the holder improperly refuses to accept the payment, the obligation of the party making the tender is *not* discharged. Her obligation continues, but the holder's refusal of a proper tender completely discharges any indorser or accommodation party having a right of recourse with respect to the obligation to which the tender relates. 3-603(b). Furthermore, the party making the tender is discharged to the extent of her subsequent obligation to pay interest after the due date on the amount tendered. 3-603(c).

The underlying reason for discharging a person who has a right of recourse against the person whose tender is refused is that if the tender had been accepted, the party having the right of recourse would have been completely discharged from liability. It would be unjust to continue her liability and her risks solely because the holder chooses to refuse payment.

An instrument sometimes is made or accepted to be payable at a particular place -- typically the place of business of the maker or acceptor or a bank. Unless the instrument is payable on demand, tender is deemed to have been made on the due date if the maker or acceptor is then able and ready to pay at every place of payment stated in the instrument. Id.

Cancellation or renunciation

The holder of an instrument may discharge any party's obligation on an instrument by *cancellation* or *renunciation*. 3-604(a). The former is "an intentional voluntary act, such as surrender of the instrument to the party, destruction, mutilation, or cancellation of the instrument, cancellation or striking out of the party's signature, or the addition of words to the instrument indicating discharge." Id. Renunciation occurs differently, "by agreeing not to sue or otherwise renouncing rights against the party by a signed writing." Id. Neither cancellation nor renunciation requires consideration, id., but they must be (1) by a person entitled to enforce the instrument and (2) intentional. This means, for example, that surrender or mutilation of an instrument by mistake or because of fraud is not an effective cancellation. No discharge results.

Although canceling an indorsement discharges the indorser's liability on the instrument, it does not "affect the status and rights of a party derived from the indorsement." 3-604(b). The cancellation does not negate a negotiation of the instrument that depended on the indorsement. It does not create a missing necessary indorsement that, *nunc pro tunc*, undermines holder status.

Discharge by agreement or other act

The reasons for discharge that Article 3 describes are geared to the character of a negotiable instrument as a special form of contract. Fundamentally, an instrument is and remains a contract; and the common-law rules of discharge that govern simple contracts apply equally to instruments. 3-601(a). Thus, an agreement to discharge liability on an instrument is enforceable under Article 3 to the extent that contract law would enforce it, even in the absence of renunciation, cancellation, payment, or any other discharge provided by Article 3 itself.

Discharge by fraudulent alteration

"Alteration" of an instrument has two meanings. The expected meaning is any "unauthorized change in an instrument that purports to modify in any respect the obligation of a party." 3-407(a). Another meaning is any "unauthorized addition of words or numbers or other change to an incomplete instrument relating to the obligation of a party." Id. Any *fraudulent* alteration, in either sense, results in discharging a party whose liability is thereby affected. 3-407(b).

1. Changing An Instrument

The general rule of 3-407 is that an alteration of an instrument discharges completely any party whose contract is thereby changed if the alteration is fraudulent. 3-407(b) & comment 1. Basically, any change is an alteration. 3-407(a). "Fraudulent" is not defined. Courts commonly define the term to require " 'a dishonest and deceitful purpose to acquire more than one was entitled to under the [instrument as executed].'" *Citizens Nat'l Bank v. Taylor*, 368 N.W.2d 913, 917 (Minn.1985); *Logan v. Central Bank*, 397 So.2d 151, 153 (1981); *Bank of Ripley v. Sadler*, 671 S.W.2d 454, 459 (Tenn.1984); *Thomas v. Osborn*, 13 Wash.App. 371, 377, 536 P.2d 8, 13 (1975). In any event, no discharge results under 3-407 from an alteration made with a benevolent purpose. 3-407 comment 1. On the other hand, if the purpose is fraudulent, discharge results even if the alteration is favorable to the obligor. Id.

Discharge because of a material and fraudulent alteration by a holder cannot be raised successfully by an obligor who assented to the alteration (either before or after the fact) or who is precluded from asserting the alteration. See 3-406. Nor can the defense be raised successfully by a person whose liability was unaffected by the alteration, such as a person who became an obligor on the instrument after it was changed. Moreover, even in the absence of assent and preclusion, discharge under 3-407 cannot be asserted against "[a] payor bank or drawee paying a fraudulently altered instrument or a person taking it for value, in good faith and without notice of the alteration." 3-407(c). (Discharge of any kind is a personal "defense" of which a holder in due course takes free. 3-601(b).) Such a drawee or taker can enforce an altered instrument according to its original terms, i.e., the terms before the alteration. 3-407(c).

2. Completing An Incomplete Instrument

"*Incomplete instrument*" is a term of art with a special, limited meaning and special rules, mainly about the effect of completion by someone other than the issuer. An incomplete instrument is **not** any order or promise that for any reason fails any of the requisites of negotiability. It does not include, for example, a draft ordering "Pay to B." Rather, an "incomplete instrument" is "a signed writing, whether or not issued by the signer, the contents of which show at the time of signing that it is incomplete but that the signer intended it to be completed by the addition of words or numbers." 3-115(a). It includes a true instrument that, though incomplete, satisfies the requisites of negotiability, and also a writing that fails these requisites but is intended to satisfy them and be an instrument when complete. In both cases the test is "whether the contents show that it is incomplete and that the signer intended that additional words or numbers be added." 3-115 comment 1.

An "incomplete instrument" that is not truly an instrument will nevertheless become an instrument, and be treated as such in every respect under Article 3, if the requirements of negotiability are met when it is completed. 3-115(b).

> An example is a check with the amount not filled in. The check cannot be enforced until the amount is filled in. If the payee fills in an amount authorized by the drawer the check meets the requirements of 3-104 and is enforceable as completed. If the payee fills in an unauthorized amount there is an alteration of the check and Section 3-407 applies.

3-115 comment 3. Significantly, 3-407 handles alterations of instruments and does not say that the check is not an instrument if filled in with an unauthorized amount; rather, the effect is that the drawer gets a defense to payment. Article 3 governs in any event. In contrast, a note that the maker deliberately issues "Pay P" does not become an instrument by P adding words of negotiability. The rules of 3-115 would not apply as in the example of the check lacking an amount. In this case, the note was not an incomplete instrument. The maker intended the "Pay P" form, and hence to create a nonnegotiable instrument. She did not intend that anybody would add order language.

The rules of 3-407 generally apply to incomplete instruments that are completed otherwise than as authorized. 3-115(c); 3-407(a). There is a major difference, however, in the treatment between instruments that are changed and incomplete instruments completed otherwise than as authorized. In the case of the former, a drawee or holder in due course gets immunity from the discharge of 3-407 only to a limited extent. She can enforce the instrument despite a fraudulent and material alteration by a prior holder but only to the extent of its original tenor. She can enforce the instrument as altered only if the obligor assented to the alteration or is precluded from asserting the alteration. In the case of an incomplete instrument that has been completed otherwise than as authorized, the drawee or taker for value enjoys complete immunity from the discharge. She can enforce the instrument fully as completed in every case even in the absence of assent or preclusion. 3-407(c).

Discharge as a defense against holder in due course

Normally, notice of a defense to an instrument prevents a person from becoming a holder in due course of it. 3-302(a)(2)(vi). Notice of an Article 3 discharge of liability on an instrument does not have this effect. Discharge is not a "defense" for purposes of 3-302. On the other hand, any party's "[d]ischarge is effective against a holder in due course * * * if the holder had notice of the discharge when holder in due course status was acquired." 3-601 comment. Subject to this person's defense, the holder in due course can enforce the instrument against any other party and in doing so is immune to personal defenses, including any party's discharge of which the holder was unaware. "Discharge of the obligation of a party is not effective against a person acquiring rights of a holder in due course of the instrument without notice of the discharge." 3-601(b).

law

McGrew v. Mix

Appellate Court of Illnois, Fifth District, 1983
67 Ill. Dec. 738, 112 Ill. App.3d 14, 445 N.E.2d 30

Karns, Justice: Plaintiff, William F. McGrew, commenced this action in the circuit court of Clay County to recover $20,545.18 plus 7% interest on a promissory note executed by defendants, Larry Mix, Sandra Mix and Grace Mix. The trial court, sitting without a jury, entered judgment for plaintiff and against Larry and Sandra Mix in the amount of $27,598.11, and entered judgment in favor of Grace Mix and against plaintiff. Defendants' post trial motion to vacate judgment, or in the alternative, to modify the judgment was denied, and defendants, Larry Mix and Sandra Mix, now appeal. Plaintiff's cross-appeal against defendant, Grace Mix, has been abandoned.

The material facts of this case are uncontroverted. On March 28, 1973, Larry and Sandra Mix, husband and wife, executed a promissory note payable to the First National Bank of Flora, Illinois. The note was in the amount of $26,200 and was payable in installments of

$651.84 per month. Interest on the note was set at 8%. The note was payable on demand, or if not demanded, it was to be paid on March 29, 1977.

Grace Mix, mother of Larry Mix, signed as an accommodation party at his request because the collateral offered as security was insufficient. Subsequent to the execution of the note, plaintiff married Grace Mix on November 11, 1973. After the marriage, Grace Mix informed plaintiff that she had co-signed the note.

In March of 1975, defendant, Grace Mix, then Grace McGrew, received a letter from Roger Wells, president of the First National Bank, which advised her that payments on the note were in arrears. The letter suggested that she come in with the other co-makers to discuss the arrearage. From March 18, 1975, the arrearage increased from $5,220.40 to $6,775. Sometime during this period, plaintiff saw the letter sent by Mr. Wells to his wife.

Plaintiff discussed the note with Larry Mix, his stepson, but did not tell him or the other defendants that he intended to pay the note. On June 9, 1975, plaintiff went to the bank and paid $20,313.68 in principal and $213.22 in interest. Roger Wells, president of the bank, marked the note "paid, June 9, 1975, R.W.", and gave the note to plaintiff. Plaintiff took the note home and placed it in a dresser drawer.

On June 26, 1975, defendant, Larry Mix, stated to plaintiff that he learned at the bank that plaintiff had paid the note, and inquired about what arrangements would be made for his payment of the note. Defendant wrote out a check to plaintiff for $300 as a payment on the note. Sometime thereafter, the note was delivered by either plaintiff or his wife to Larry and Sandra Mix. Plaintiff testified that this was done so that they would have the note for bookkeeping purposes.

Defendants, Larry and Sandra Mix, made payments on the note on October 30, 1975--$281.57; December 17, 1975--$513.33; January 27, 1976--$513.33, and February 9, 1976--$1,000. Plaintiff and defendant, Grace Mix, were separated on December 29, 1976, and were divorced on April 23, 1979. After plaintiff and Grace Mix were separated in December of 1976, defendant Larry Mix stopped making payments on the note. Plaintiff asked defendant, Larry Mix, for payment of the note and when none was forthcoming, brought this suit.

On appeal, defendants, Larry and Sandra Mix, challenge plaintiff's right to recover on the note under the several theories set forth in the complaint. The primary issue for review, we believe, is whether the plaintiff's payment and receipt of the promissory note entitled him to recover on the note from defendants under the Uniform Commercial Code. This case appears to be one of first impression in this state.

At the outset, we note that the trial court's decision implicitly rests upon the finding that plaintiff's payment of the note did not constitute a gift. This conclusion is well-founded upon the record which discloses that plaintiff and defendant, Larry Mix, discussed the note and that defendant testified that he knew that plaintiff expected him to pay on it. Plaintiff's adjustment of the interest on the note from 8% to 7% and defendants' several payments on the note lend additional support to the court's finding of fact.

The evidence further establishes that on June 9, 1975, plaintiff went to the First National Bank and paid the promissory note which defendants had executed. After receiving this payment, Roger Wells, the bank president, stamped the note "paid," put his initials and the date on it and handed it to plaintiff. On the basis of these facts, plaintiff contends that he acquired the bank's rights in the note including the right to demand payment.

In support of his position, plaintiff cites section 3-603(2) of the Uniform Commercial Code (Ill.Rev.Stat.1981, ch. 26, par. 3-603(2)) which provides: "Payment or satisfaction may be made with the consent of the holder by any person including a stranger to the instrument. Surrender of the instrument to such a person gives him the rights of a transferee. (3-201.) The rights of a transferee are discussed in Ill.Rev.Stat.1981, ch. 26, par. 3-201: "Transfer of an instrument vests in the transferee such rights as the transferor has therein * * *."

Section 3-603(2) of the Uniform Commercial Code represents a marked departure in the law as it previously had been under the Negotiable Instrument Law. The official comments to that section state that the original sections 171-177 of the Negotiable Instrument Law (Ill.Rev.Stat.1961, ch. 98, pars. 192-198) provided for payment of a draft "for honor" after protest. (Ill.Ann.Stat., ch. 26, par. 3-603(2), Uniform Commercial Code Comment at 398 (Smith-Hurd 1976).) It provided a method by which a third party might intervene to protect the credit of the drawer and at the same time protect his own rights. Under the prior law, a payment for honor in order to operate as such and not as a mere voluntary payment was required to be attested by a notarial act of honor. The drafters of the Restatement of Restitution recognized this rule stating in section 117(2): "(2) A person who pays a negotiable bill of exchange which has been protested for nonpayment, declaring that he does so for the honor of a party thereto whom he names and having this attested by a notarial act of honor, is entitled to restitution from the person for whose honor he made payment." Restatement of Restitution, §117(2) (1957).

With the elimination of "payment for honor", section 3-603(2) provides that any person may pay with the consent of the holder. In addition, subsection 2 states that the surrender of the instrument to such person gives him the rights of a transferee. Plaintiff contends that the promissory note was surrendered to him when the bank handed the note to him. Defendants challenge this contention and maintains that surrender did not occur because the note was not endorsed by the bank.

"Surrender" as used in section 3-603(2) is not defined in the code nor in Illinois case law. In the absence of such definition, defendant concludes that the most logical approach is to assign "surrender" the same meaning as "transfer," a term which is discussed in section 3-201. Section 3-201(3) provides: "Unless otherwise agreed any transfer for value of an instrument not then payable to bearer gives the transferee the specifically enforceable right to have the unqualified indorsement of the transferor. Negotiation takes effect only when the indorsement is made and until that time there is no presumption that the transferee is the owner." (Ill.Rev.Stat.1981, ch. 26, par. 201(3).) Defendants contend that plaintiff cannot be presumed to be the owner of the note because it lacked the indorsement of the bank as required by section 3-201(3). Furthermore, defendants contend that plaintiff's failure to secure the bank's indorsement is evidence that he lacked the authority to do so. We find both propositions to be without merit.

We believe the word "surrender" should be read in the context of section 3-603. This section permits any person with the consent of the holder to make payment of a negotiable instrument. Upon payment and surrender of the paper, the payor succeeds to the rights of the holder, subject to the limitation found in section 3-201 that one who has himself been a party to any fraud or illegality affecting the instrument or who as a prior holder had notice of a defense or claim against it cannot improve his position by taking from a later holder in due course. (Ill.Ann.Stat., ch. 26, par. 3-603, Uniform Commercial Code Comments at 399 (Smith-Hurd 1976.) Defendants have not set forth any persuasive authority which suggests that the word "surrender" be given a technical meaning which would place an additional limitation upon section 3-603. Consequently, we find that plaintiff acquired the rights of a transferee including the right to demand payment on the note from its makers.

Defendants further argue that plaintiff should not be allowed to recover on the promissory note because the note was cancelled and the makers discharged under 3-605. Section 3-605 which governs discharge states in pertinent part: "The holder of an instrument may even without consideration discharge any party (1) in any manner apparent on the face of the instrument or indorsement * * *." (Ill.Rev.Stat.1981, ch. 26, par. 3-605.) Defendants maintain that the fact that the bank president wrote "paid" on the face of the note and placed his initials, "R.W.," together with the date of payment is evidence that the promissory note was cancelled.

We believe that the bank president's act of marking the note "paid" merely acknowledged receipt of payment from plaintiff and did not extinguish the underlying obligation. Section 3-603(2) would be rendered meaningless if the original payee were permitted to unilaterally discharge the maker upon payment by a third party. The party paying on the note essentially would become a transferee without one of the principal rights of a transferee, that is the authority to enforce the note according to its original tenor. Accordingly, we find that defendants were not discharged by the bank, and defendants, as makers, remain obligated on the note.

* * *

For the foregoing reasons, the judgment of the trial court is affirmed.
AFFIRMED.

Firstier Bank v. Triplett
Supreme Court of Nebraska, 1993
242 Neb. 614, 497 N.W.2d 339

Fahrnbruch, Justice. After finding that Richard L. and Coralea J. Triplett had not fully paid a promissory note they had given for money they borrowed from FirsTier Bank, N.A., the district court for Washington County entered a $7,231.55 judgment in favor of FirsTier and against the Tripletts.

At trial and in this appeal, the Tripletts, who are husband and wife, contend that their debt was satisfied when their note was marked "paid" and mailed to them by FirsTier. The trial court found that the note was unintentionally marked "paid" and mailed to the Tripletts as a result of clerical error and without the bank's authority.

Restated, the sole issue on appeal is whether the district court erred in granting a money judgment on a promissory note that had been marked "paid" and returned to the maker. * * *

FACTS

At trial, two original promissory notes the Tripletts gave to FirsTier were referred to as exhibits 7 and 8. Exhibit 7, dated April 17, 1986, was for $14,000. It was secured by a 1985 Toyota pickup and a 1979 Lincoln automobile and was originally due April 20, 1990. By subsequent agreement, the due date was extended to June 20, 1990. Exhibit 8, dated June 16, 1987, was for $3,500. The note was secured by a 1979 Ford van.

The Tripletts sold the Toyota, and on July 6, 1987, Richard Triplett tendered a check for $7,200 as payment on the notes to FirsTier's branch at Blair, Nebraska. At the time the check was tendered, the balances were $10,498.79 on exhibit 7 and $2,418.73 on exhibit 8.

In late July 1987, the Tripletts received a letter from FirsTier containing an original "Note and Security Agreement," exhibit 7, which was stamped "PAID ... FirsTier Bank, N.A. Omaha, Nebraska." The stamp was signed by a clerk and hand dated "7-7-87." In November 1987, exhibit 8 was returned to the Tripletts. It also was stamped "PAID ... FirsTier Bank, N.A. Omaha, Nebraska," and hand dated "7-7-87," but was signed by another clerk.

At trial, a bank officer testified that when a note has been paid in full, it is FirsTier's practice to send a computer-generated form letter over the original loan officer's name, thanking the customer for his or her business. He testified that the loan officer never sees or signs these letters, which he believed were signed by a clerk.

Richard Triplett testified that more than a year after receiving the last note, he received notice from FirsTier that the Tripletts still owed money on one of the notes. When FirsTier demanded payment of the note, Richard Triplett indicated to FirsTier that "the loan was paid up."

In May 1989, FirsTier sued the Tripletts for payment of the balance remaining on exhibit 7, for reformation and reinstatement of the erroneously canceled note, and for reinstatement of FirsTier's security interest.

At trial, Leonard Olson, FirsTier's vice president and manager of loan operations, testified that exhibit 7 had never been paid in full, although regular payments had been made until one large payment of $4,781.27 was made on July 6, 1987. At the time of trial, exhibit 7 had an outstanding balance of $7,231.55, representing $5,717.52 in principal plus accrued interest, which continued to accrue at a rate of 10 percent, or $1.57 per day. Olson also testified that with the payment of $2,418.73 on July 6, 1987, exhibit 8 was paid in full.

Olson testified that through clerical error, the file for exhibit 7 was pulled instead of the file for exhibit 8 and that a clerk erroneously marked exhibit 7 "paid." Olson testified that the employee who marked exhibit 7 "paid" was a loan service clerk, one step above an entry-level position. According to Olson, the loan service clerk did not have authority to release a note which had not been paid in full, and FirsTier never intended to discharge exhibit 7 without payment in full. Both Olson and Lloyd Sheve, vice president and manager of FirsTier's Blair branch, testified that only the bank's collection department could authorize the release of an unpaid note, and they testified that neither of them had ever received authorization to settle and release exhibit 7.

In spite of Richard Triplett's initial representation to FirsTier that "the loan was paid up," the Tripletts do not dispute the fact that exhibit 7 has never been paid in full. Both of the Tripletts testified that they knew the $7,200 check was insufficient to pay off the balances of both notes. Richard Triplett testified that he had made no representations to FirsTier that he was paying off both notes. He testified that he did not know whether FirsTier had made an error in releasing exhibit 7.

Instead, the Tripletts alleged that exhibit 7 was discharged pursuant to §3-605 (Reissue 1980) by (1) intentional cancellation of the note which was not a result of a mutual mistake or a unilateral mistake caused by the Tripletts' fraud or inequitable conduct and (2) surrender of the note.

The district court made specific factual findings that at the time of the $7,200.00 payment by the Defendants [Tripletts] to the Plaintiff [FirsTier], the Defendants specifically acknowledged and knew that said $7,200.00 was insufficient to make payment in full on both promissory notes.... [T]here was no intent on the part of FirsTier Bank to release promissory note [exhibit 7] for less than payment in full thereof, there was no agreement nor consideration to support same that promissory note [exhibit 7] would be released without payment in full, the stamping of [exhibit 7] as paid in full and the return thereof to the Defendants was as a result of a clerical error, allowing said release of promissory note [exhibit 7] would result in unjust enrichment to the [Tripletts], and the individual in the clerical position stamping promissory notes for return to bank customers did not have the authority or power to authorize the release of promissory notes without payment in full thereof.

The court entered a $7,231.44 judgment, plus interest and costs, in favor of FirsTier on its first cause of action and granted no relief on the second and third causes of action. The Tripletts appealed. FirsTier did not cross-appeal.

ANALYSIS

The Tripletts claim that their debt on exhibit 7 was discharged as a matter of law under §3-605(1) (Reissue 1980) because FirsTier marked exhibit 7 "paid" and returned it to them.

FirsTier counters that a promissory note is not discharged when it is canceled as the result of clerical error by a party who has no authority to release a loan. The bank's position is that such an action does not constitute intent to cancel the maker's indebtedness and that therefore there was no discharge of the note.

Section 3-605 governed the discharge of negotiable instruments through cancellation or renunciation at all times material to this case. That statute provided in part: (1) The holder of an instrument may even without consideration discharge any party (a) in any manner apparent on the face of the instrument or the indorsement, *as by intentionally cancelling the instrument* or the party's signature by destruction or mutilation, or by striking out the party's signature; or (b) by renouncing his rights by a writing signed and delivered or *by surrender of the instrument to the party to be discharged.* (Emphasis supplied.)

Whether a promissory note is discharged pursuant to the Uniform Commercial Code when it is marked "paid" and surrendered to the maker is a question of first impression in Nebraska. Other jurisdictions have considered the question, and their opinions are persuasive in deciding this case.

Because FirsTier both stamped exhibit 7 "paid" and surrendered it to the Tripletts by mailing it back to them, we must consider whether either of these actions by FirsTier had the effect of discharging the Tripletts' indebtedness under the note.

Subsection (a) of §3-605(1) clearly stated that cancellation must be done "intentionally." Courts that have considered discharge of a promissory note under their states' counterparts to subsection (a) have held that cancellation must be accompanied by an *intent to discharge the maker.* Such intent is not the equivalent of a clerk's stamping the note "paid" when, in fact, it has not been paid. The Tripletts' assertion that the physical act of intentionally stamping exhibit 7 "paid" discharges the note as a matter of law is plainly incorrect in the absence of FirsTier's intent to discharge the Tripletts' indebtedness.

Although subsection (b) of §3-605(1) did not specifically state that *surrender* of an instrument must be intentional in order to effect a discharge, "[t]he courts have glossed this section by requiring that surrender of the instrument be accompanied by an intent to discharge the party." This is consistent with the Legislature's latest revision of Nebraska's Uniform Commercial Code. Discharge by cancellation or renunciation is now governed by Neb.U.C.C. §3-604 (Reissue 1992), which replaced §3-605 (Reissue 1980). Section 3-604(a) provides that "[a] person entitled to enforce an instrument ... may discharge the obligation of a party to pay the instrument (i) by an intentional voluntary act, such as surrender of the instrument to the party ... or cancellation of the instrument ...." (Emphasis supplied.) This language requires that discharge be intentional, whether by cancellation or surrender.

All jurisdictions that have considered the issue have concluded that clerical error does not have the legal effect of canceling an existing debt or discharging an instrument. This is simply an application of the general rule that cancellation or surrender of an instrument has no effect when done by a person without authority from the holder of the instrument. A bank may recover even when its agents or officers have acted negligently, to prevent the maker of a note from retaining a gratuitous benefit to which he or she is not entitled.

Although the Tripletts, citing *J.J. Schaefer Livestock Hauling v. Gretna St. Bank*, 229 Neb. 580, 428 N.W.2d 185 (1988), and *Peterson v. Crown Financial Corp.*, 661 F.2d 287 (3d Cir.1981), argue that subjective intent of the holder is irrelevant, both of these cases are distinguishable from the case at bar on their facts.

In *J.J. Schaefer Livestock Hauling*, the president and vice president of a bank satisfied promissory notes which the bank was holding by exercising the bank's right of setoff against the maker's account, to the detriment of third parties who were entitled to the funds in the account. The notes were canceled and returned to the maker. Only after the bank was compelled by legal process to reimburse the third parties did the bank attempt reformation of the notes in what was essentially a claim for indemnity against the maker. This court held that surrender of the notes discharged the obligations as a matter of law. The court adopted the rationale of *Peterson* that " 'parties ... which deal regularly in negotiable instruments, "ought to be held, as a matter of law, to an understanding of the implications which normal business practice assigns to 'intentionally cancelling [an] instrument'...." [Citation omitted.] [S]ubjective intent not to discharge was irrelevant; mere intent to cancel was sufficient.'" *J.J. Schaefer Livestock Hauling v. Gretna St. Bank*, 229 Neb. at 588, 428 N.W.2d at 190, quoting *Peterson v. Crown Financial Corp.*, supra.

In *Peterson*, a lender incorrectly advised a maker, Peterson, that $499,658.85 in interest was due on his note, instead of the $860,837.57 which was actually due. Peterson paid $500,000 in interest, and a vice president of the lending institution sent him a letter thanking him for his payment and advising him that this payment represented the interest due at that time. Peterson executed a new note to replace the previous note. The lender stamped the first note "canceled" and returned it to Peterson. When the second note became due 3 years later, the lender attempted to collect the deficiency in interest from the previous note.

Construing Pennsylvania law, the U.S. Court of Appeals for the Third Circuit held that the first note was discharged as a matter of law. However, the court made it clear that this was a very narrow holding: In such a situation ... the lending institution is deemed as a matter of law not to have intended that the old indebtedness survive. Subjective intent *under these circumstances* is irrelevant; *in the absence of clerical error or other mistake -- neither of which is claimed here* -- the lender cannot, consistent with the dictates of §3-605, remain free to insist upon the terms of a cancelled note simply because it did not subjectively intend to alter its terms. (Emphasis supplied.) *Peterson v. Crown Financial Corp.*, 661 F.2d at 292. The court explicitly stated that an underlying obligation would not be discharged by unintentional or mistaken cancellation.

Thus, both *J.J. Schaefer Livestock Hauling* and *Peterson* are distinguishable from the present case. In *J.J. Schaefer Livestock Hauling*, the notes were intentionally canceled and surrendered by bank officers who had the authority of the holder to discharge the indebtedness. They also had actual knowledge of the transactions and their legal ramifications. No clerical error was involved in *J.J. Schaefer Livestock Hauling*. In *Peterson*, there also was no claim of clerical error. In the case at bar, FirsTier had no intention to cancel the Tripletts' indebtedness. The claimed discharge was through clerical error by an individual who had no authority to do so.

Therefore, the issue before the court is whether FirsTier possessed the requisite intent to discharge the Tripletts' indebtedness, as evidenced by exhibit 7, by either cancellation or surrender of the note. Intent is a question of fact. As previously noted, a trial court's factual findings have the effect of a verdict and will not be set aside unless clearly erroneous.

That exhibit 7 has never been fully paid is undisputed. Two of FirsTier's vice presidents testified that FirsTier had no intention to discharge exhibit 7 without payment in full, that no one with authority to discharge exhibit 7 had done so, and that the cancellation and surrender of the note was done through clerical error. The Tripletts offered no evidence to refute this testimony.

CONCLUSION

The district court's factual finding that the note, exhibit 7, was unintentionally released through clerical error is not clearly erroneous. We hold that the unintentional cancellation and surrender of a promissory note through clerical error do not discharge the maker of the note. The district court's judgment is affirmed.

AFFIRMED.

Grant, Justice, dissenting.

I respectfully dissent. When the promissory notes in question were made, and when payment of the notes was sought by litigation, Neb.U.C.C. §3-605 (Reissue 1980) provided, in part: "(1) The holder of an instrument may even without consideration discharge any party ... (b) by renouncing his rights by a writing signed and delivered or by surrender of the instrument to the party to be discharged."

The evidence shows that plaintiff renounced its rights against defendants "by a writing signed and delivered" in a letter to defendants, which letter enclosed defendants' note stamped "paid." The instrument in question was surrendered to defendants.

The majority recognizes that subsection (b) of §3-605 did not specifically state that surrender of an instrument must be intentional in order to effect a discharge. The majority, however, adopts the view of commentators and other courts that "'courts have glossed this section by requiring that surrender of the instrument be accompanied by an intent to discharge the party.'" When language in a statute is clear, I do not believe that courts should "gloss" legislative language to reach a goal which courts guess that the Legislature desired.

By adopting Neb.U.C.C. §3-604 (Reissue 1992) to replace §3-605 (Reissue 1980), the Legislature recognized that the earlier act did not give lending institutions the protection that the court has afforded such institutions in this case. Section 3-605, prior to adoption of §3-604 (Reissue 1992), provided (without glossing) that the holder of a note could discharge the maker of the note in various ways that did not require intent. Plaintiff, the holder of the note in question, so acted, without any fraud or inducement by defendants.

To permit a bank to prevail in this litigation removes much certainty in banking transactions. The resulting uncertainty is bad for lenders and borrowers. All parties to promissory notes must now wonder if a bank means that a note is paid just because the bank says that it is paid.

I would reverse the judgment, but if the judgment must be affirmed, I also question the amount of the judgment. At the time of trial, apparently, plaintiff contended that the principal sum of $5,717.52 was due. Most of any delay in repayment was caused specifically by plaintiff's actions in telling defendants that the note was paid. Under those circumstances, when the trial court did not reform or reinstate the note in question as plaintiff requested, I do not see how plaintiff is entitled to any interest as set out in the note. If judgment must be entered, it should be in the amount of $5,717.52. Granting interest on that judgment, of course, is different from, in effect, granting plaintiff prejudgment interest.

Caporale, Justice, dissenting.

I join in that portion of Judge Grant's dissent which declares that we ought not read into Neb.U.C.C. §3-605 (Reissue 1980) an intent requirement which is absent from the statutory language. Indeed, we have piously pronounced that courts may not add language to the plain terms of a statute so as to either restrict or extend its meaning. See Wittler v. Baumgartner, 180 Neb. 446, 144 N.W.2d 62 (1966). The fact that courts of other jurisdictions saw fit to engage in acts of judicial legislation does not license us to do the same.

practice

Case 1

Maybe T

B buys goods on credit from S and signs a note for the price. Before the note was due, B paid S the price but failed to retrieve the note she signed. S sold the note to T. When the note matured, B refused to pay it. T sues on the note. Who wins? See 3-412; 3-305(a) or (b); *National Credit Union Admin. Bd. v. Metzler*, 625 F.Supp. 1551 (E.D.Mo.1986) (maker of note pays a party without possession at the maker's risk).

Case 2

S sells goods to B on credit. B signs a note for the price and eventually defaults. S and B settle this account and other charges between them by a workout agreement that purports to release B from all contract and tort liabilities to S.

B wins.

a.   S later sues B on the note. What result? 3-601(a); 3-604(a).

No

b.   Is it necessary for discharge in this case that the note be surrendered?

c.   Is surrender -- alone -- sufficient for discharge, or must it be backed by

    i.   an agreement of discharge?

    ii.   an intent to discharge?

d.   Defendants, for value, executed a note payable to Oregon Bank. Luther G. Jerstad signed the note as accommodation at the bank's request. The bank made demand upon Jerstad for payment of the note. LJA, Inc., of which Jerstad was principal owner, paid the bank the balance due on the note ($3,256.11). Bank thereupon delivered the note to LJA, and LJA then sued defendants on the note. *Jerstad v. Warren,* 73 Or.App. 387, 698 P.2d 1033 (1985). Bank prevails. Why doesn't 3-602(a) or 3-604(a) discharge defendants?

Case 3

B gives S a check for the price of goods. S alters the instrument before presenting it for payment by raising the amount the drawee is ordered to pay.

Depends

a.   Suppose that upon presentment of the check, the drawee dishonors the instrument because of a suspicion that the instrument has been altered. S sues B on the check. Who wins?   See 3-407(b).

b. Suppose that S cashed the altered check at DB Bank. After the check was dishonored, it was bounced back to DB Bank which sued B as drawer. What result? 3-407(c).

c. Suppose that the drawee bank pays the check. Can the bank charge the amount of the item against B's account? 3-407(c); 4-401(d)(1).

Original tenor

Case 4

B sends S a blank check and instructs S to complete the check by filling in the price of goods that B has purchased from S. The price is actually $100 but S fraudulently fills in $1,000.

a. Does S's fraudulent completion affect B's liability? According to the general rule of 3-407(b), the drawer's liability is discharged. She has no liability whatsoever on the completed check unless she assents to the unauthorized completion (as by ratification) or is precluded from asserting it. (Does preclusion result as a matter of law under 3-406 in any case when a drawer signs a blank check? See generally *E. Bierhaus & Sons, Inc. v. Bowling* 486 N.E.2d 598 (Ind.Ct.App.1985) (signing and delivering a blank check is negligence which can expose drawer to liability to a person who is not contributorily culpable).) This result is standard fare under 3-407: the unauthorized completion is treated just as though the check was drawn originally by the drawer for $100 and raised by the payee to the higher amount.

b. Suppose that DB Bank cashes the check or the drawee bank pays it as completed. Can DB Bank enforce the check against B, or can the drawee charge the check against B's account? 3-407(c); 4-401(d)(2).

§ 4. Relationship Between Liability On The Instrument and Liability On The Underlying Transaction

In the typical case, the maker or drawer issues an instrument because of an underlying transaction, specifically to evidence or effect payment of an obligation that the transaction creates. ("Issue" is the "first delivery of an instrument by the maker or drawer * * * for the purpose of giving rights on the instrument to any person." 3-105(a).) An obligee, however, is not ordinarily required, by law, to take an instrument that is issued for an underlying obligation; but the parties commonly agree on the use of an instrument and, for this reason, the payee takes the instrument that is issued to her. The overall effect between the parties, especially on the underlying obligation, is important to understand.

story

Stanley V. Kinyon, *Actions On Commercial Paper: Holder's Procedural Advantages Under Article 3*
65 Mich.L.Rev. 1441, 1443-47 (1967)

A negotiable note, check, or draft is usually issued or transferred either in connection with a concurrent contractual transaction between the signer and the holder or to evidence, secure, pay, or collect a pre-existing debt or other monetary obligation. These instruments were invented and developed by merchants and bankers to facilitate the transfer, collection, and payment of the monetary obligations which arose from commercial loans, deposits, or purchases of goods or services. Even though at present such paper is widely used by non-merchants, it still almost always represents underlying debts or other monetary obligations of the signers which result from contractual or other legal commitments. Of course, an occasional note is issued for accommodation or to evidence a charitable subscription or other promise of gift, and checks are often issued as Christmas, birthday, or wedding presents, but these are insignificant in number in comparison with the millions of instruments issued every day in connection with the creation, extension, transfer, or payment of legally binding obligations.

Checks, drafts, and promissory notes, however, are not and do not purport to be simply written evidence of transactions or mere acknowledgments of monetary obligations like I.O.U.'s or non-promissory certificates of deposit. Rather, they are distinct and self-contained monetary commitments or directives, serving separate and distinct commercial purposes. By expressing an unqualified promise or order to pay a specified sum, on demand or at a prescribed time, either to the bearer or to the order of a named person, they make the right to receive such payment expressly transferable, that is, "negotiable." Thus, the usual purpose of a negotiable *promissory note* or *promissory certificate of deposit* is not only to make explicit and definite the monetary commitment but also to split it off, in a sense, from the transaction or occasion that gave rise to it, and to put the commitment in such a form as to be readily and completely transferable by way of sale, discount, pledge, or collection. Similarly, the usual purpose of a negotiable *check* or *bank draft* is to use one underlying obligation -- the bank deposit debt owed to the drawer -- to pay another underlying obligation owed by the drawer-depositor to the payee by means of a payment directive by the drawer to the bank drawee, and to put this directive in transferable form in order to facilitate its cashing, its collection, or the making of a further payment through its indorsement and transfer by the payee. Finally, the purpose of a *seller's* negotiable *draft* on the *buyer* is not only to facilitate bank collection of payment for the goods sold but also, in many cases, to make possible the financing of the seller through discount of the draft.

All of these instruments thus have financing or payment functions distinct from the objectives of the underlying obligations and transactions in which they arise or on which they are based. In many cases, moreover, these functions could not readily be achieved by mere assignment of the underlying monetary claim, even if such claims had always been legally assignable. Therefore, ever since the days of the ancient law merchant, our law, as eventually codified in the NIL and in Article Three of the Code, has recognized that such instruments embody separate obligations and that the holder -- simply by virtue of his holdership and of the form and terms of the instrument -- has a legal right to receive payment and to discharge the obligations, as well as a right to enforce the obligations by an action in his own name. Moreover, that law has prescribed, in considerable detail, the nature and extent of the primary or secondary payment obligations of the maker, drawer, acceptor, and indorser to the holder in the event that the instrument is not paid when due or is dishonored; and has also established rules governing transfer and negotiation, the requirements for being a holder in due course, and the special rights of such a holder.

That these instruments embody rights and obligations distinct from those involved in the underlying obligation or transaction is clear when the holder is a subsequent transferee who is not a party to the issuance, or to a prior transfer, of the instrument and has not received an express assignment of the underlying claim. Yet even between the immediate parties -- between the maker or drawer and the payee, or between an indorser and his immediate indorsee -- the instrument constitutes a *separate basis* for claim and action since the instrument does not normally merge or replace the underlying obligation but rather creates a sort of alter-ego obligation that co-exists until one or the other is finally paid or satisfied. This has been clarified by [section 3-310] in the Code[.]

    * * *

In some instances, of course, commercial paper will be taken as an immediate satisfaction and discharge of the underlying obligation between the parties, as when an obligor obtains a cashier's check or a bank draft which is payable directly to his obligee and delivers it as a remitter without indorsing it. Immediate discharge may also occur when, in settlement of a *disputed* claim, the claimant agrees to take the other party's note for a specified amount as an accord and satisfaction. In most instances, however, the giving of the obligor's note for a debt, the issuance of his check in payment, or the indorsement and delivery of third-party paper by the obligor, as security for or in payment of the obligation, merely "suspends" the obligation until the instrument is due or presented. In such cases, the instrument is regarded either as *representing* or *securing* the obligation or as a *conditional payment* of it, and not as itself being a final payment or satisfaction. If the instrument is paid or the signer is otherwise discharged, his underlying obligation is also discharged pro tanto because the claim on the instrument is based upon and represents that obligation. If, however, the instrument is not paid at maturity or is dishonored, the underlying obligation remains unsatisfied and the obligee may either disregard the instrument and sue the obligor to enforce the original obligation, or as holder, sue on the instrument to enforce the obligor's liability as signer. When he chooses the latter course, the obligee has the procedural advantages [of Code section 3-308], since these advantages are for the benefit of any holder, or person having the rights of a holder under section [3-203(b)] of the Code, regardless of whether he is a remote holder or the party with whom the signer dealt and to whom the underlying obligation is directly owed. Unlike most of the special privileges incident to the holdership of negotiable paper, the procedural advantages in suing on such paper are not restricted to that "most favored plaintiff in the law," the holder in due course.

Underlying obligation usually suspended

To begin, by getting possession of the instrument, the payee to whom the instrument is issued becomes a "holder," 1-201(20). She thereby acquires rights with respect to the instrument, most significantly including the right to enforce it against the issuer, 3-301, but normally does not lose rights against the issuer on their underlying deal. The issuer's liability on the instrument does not ordinarily replace her underlying obligation. This obligation usually continues; but the holder-payee-obligee gets no windfall, no possibility of double recovery.

The explanation is that the usual effect of taking the instrument is to *suspend* the underlying obligation pro tanto, i.e., "to the same extent the obligation would be discharged if an amount of money equal to the amount of the instrument were taken." 3-310(b). In the case of an ordinary note or uncertified check, the suspension continues until the instrument is paid or dishonored. 3-310(b)(1-2). Payment of the instrument serves a double purpose. It discharges the maker or drawer's liability on instrument itself, 3-602(a), and also on underlying obligation. 3-310(b)(1-2).

If the instrument is dishonored, the underlying obligation is revived. Then, the payee-obligee "may enforce *either* the instrument or the obligation." 3-310(b)(3) (emphasis added). She is likely to choose enforcing the instrument because doing so is procedurally easier than suing on the underlying obligation. See 3-308. Principally, she makes her case on the instrument by producing it. The prima facie case requires nothing more.

If the obligee loses the instrument, or it is stolen or destroyed, she is not free to pursue the underlying obligation. Rather, "the obligation may not be enforced to the extent of the amount payable on the instrument, and to that extent the obligee's rights against the obligor are limited to enforcement of the instrument." 3-310(b)(4) (second sentence). Special rules govern the enforcement of a lost, destroyed, or stolen instrument that aim to protect the obligor against a claim to the instrument that may appear at some later time. See 3-309.

Enforcing an instrument obligates the holder to observe Article 3's statute of limitations, 3-118, and to meet any applicable requirements of presentment, dishonor, and notice that Part 5 of Article 3 imposes. Also, enforcement of the instrument is generally subject to defenses and counterclaims that are produced by the underlying transaction. 3-305(a)(2). Enforcement is even subject to a claim in recoupment of the obligor against the original obligee that arose from the same transaction as the instrument. 3-305(a)(3). In short, the payee-obligee is generally in the same position as if she had sued on the underlying obligation. In sum, as between the immediate parties, there is not much substantive advantage in suing on the instrument.

Of course, defenses and the like of the underlying transaction are rooted in the terms of the parties' underlying contract. If the instrument controls as the exclusive source of rights and duties, there is a fundamental advantage in suing on the instrument, which is to suppress the terms of the wider contract that could provide a defense. In truth, however, the instrument blends with other writings of the parties' transaction that are not barred by the parol evidence rule. The instrument is construed with the other writings, not apart from them, in determining the rights, duties, and defenses to the underlying contract and the instrument itself.

When the person entitled to enforce the instrument is not the original obligee

Suppose that M makes a note to P that P indorses over to T. In both cases the instrument is taken for an underlying obligation. The effects on the relationship between M and P are already known, and the effects between P and T are essentially identical. The underlying obligation of P to T is suspended until paid or dishonored by M. 3-310(b)(2). In the latter case, T can sue P as indorser or on the underlying obligation P owes T, which will have been revived by the dishonor. 3-310(b)(3). T could also sue M as maker, but not on M's underlying debt to P. T is neither a party to this debt nor an assignee of it. She thus has no rights with respect to the debt.

M's payment of the note would discharge her liability on the instrument and, pro tanto, her underlying obligation to P. The payment by M would have the same effects for P, but confirming these effects for P is not so neatly done as under former law. Here is how it worked under the old Article 3:

1. M's payment discharged her on the instrument. 3-603(1) (1989 Official Text).
2. Because M, as maker, had no right of action herself on the instrument, her discharge freed P from liability on the instrument because of the separate rule that "[t]he liability of all parties is discharged when any party who has himself no right of action or recourse on the instrument * * * is discharged * * *." 3-601(3)(b) (1989 Official Text).
3. Then, because P is discharged on the instrument, she is also discharged on her underlying obligation. 3-802(1)(b) (1989 Official Text).

The new Article 3 is clear in discharging M on the instrument, and also in discharging P on her underlying obligation when P is discharged on the instrument. 3-310(b)(3). The problem is finding a rule that discharges P on the instrument when M pays it and is discharged. The old 3-601(3)(b) was omitted from the new Article 3.

The answer is not that the same rule that discharged M on the instrument because of her payment also discharged P on the instrument. This rule provides that:

> an instrument is paid to the extent payment is made (i) by or on behalf of *a party* obliged to pay the instrument, and (ii) to a person entitled to enforce the instrument. To the extent of the payment, the obligation of *the party* obliged to pay the instrument is discharged.

3-602(a) (emphasis added). P, as an indorser, is obliged "to pay the amount due on the instrument"; indeed, the statute that defines an indorser's contract of liability uses these exact words. 3-415(a). The problem is that 3-602(a) discharges only the party who pays, not everyone who is obliged to pay. Thus, M's payment discharges her but not P.

An unsatisfactory, jerrybuilt answer is found in 3-310(b)(2). It provides that when a note is taken for an underlying obligation, "[p]ayment of the note results in discharge of the obligation." Here, the discharge is not so explicitly limited to the person who makes payment. Therefore, by literally applying this rule, M's payment to T would directly discharge P's underlying obligation to T. P would not get a discharge on the instrument. Her freedom from liability on the instrument would depend, practically, on the functional death of the instrument and, technically, on the absence of dishonor.

This answer is weak for two reasons. First, the instrument may have been dishonored even though it was later paid by M. Second, applying 3-310(b)(2) by its plain meaning is probably wrong. It can lead to unexpected and unnatural results in other cases. For example, applying 3-310(b)(2) literally would mean that indorser P's payment of the instrument to holder T would discharge maker M's underlying obligation to P.

This silly result under 3-310(b)(2) is avoided by limiting the rule's discharge to the obligation of the person who makes payment, via 3-602(a). Alternatively, the result is avoided by defining "payment" narrowly to mean payment by the maker, who is the expected payor. This approach is in line with former law that normally defined payment as conduct limited to a maker, drawee, and acceptor. In technical terms of former law, these people were the only people who paid or made payment of instruments. Either construction of 3-310(b)(2) would mean, however, that it does not discharge P's underlying obligation to T if M pays the note.

A better basis for discharging P when M pays is 3-603. It provides:

> If tender of payment of an obligation to pay an instrument is made to a person entitled to enforce the instrument and the tender is refused, there is discharge, to the extent of the amount of the tender, of the obligation of an indorser or accommodation party having a right of recourse with respect to the obligation to which the tender relates.

3-603(b). It is commonsensical that if M's *tender* of payment would discharge P, M's *actual* payment should have the same effect. Still, however, this basis for P's discharge is imperfect because 3-603 literally applies only to tender, not payment itself.

The best answer to this riddle is the practical answer that M's payment precludes dishonor so that this condition to P's liability on the instrument is never met. The technical effect is only to bar enforcement of liability rather than erase the liability that is created by P's signature on the instrument. There is no discharge of liability on the instrument and therefore nothing that triggers the rule that such a discharge also discharges the underlying obligation. Nevertheless, because dishonor is necessary to trigger liability on the instrument and to resurrect liability on the underlying obligation, payment preventing dishonor is as good as discharging these liabilities.

It is a different and easier case to explain if, instead of M paying the note to T, M dishonored the note. Suppose, then, that T notified P of the dishonor. P satisfied her indorser liability to T, "paying" and then reacquiring the instrument from T. The effects of P's payment would be to discharge P on the instrument, 3-602(a), and also discharge P, pro tanto, on her underlying debt to T. 3-310(b)(3) (second sentence). P could then recoup by suing M as maker of the note, or by suing M on M's underlying debt to P. Id. (first sentence).

When taking an instrument discharges the obligation

In two exceptional situations, taking an instrument for an underlying obligation discharges the obligation instead of only suspending it.

1. Agreement

Taking an instrument discharges the underlying debt when the parties to the deal agree to this effect. 3-310(b) ("Unless otherwise agreed * * *"). Such an agreement, which is very rare, is effective to discharge the underlying obligation regardless of the nature or kind of instrument that is taken, even if it is an ordinary note or check of the person who is the issuer of the instrument and the underlying obligor.

2. Bank Instruments

The other situation in which taking an instrument discharges the underlying debt is much more common. It is when the instrument is a certified check, cashier's check, or teller's check, or any other instrument on which a bank is liable as maker or acceptor. 3-310(a). This rule follows the common business understanding that such an instrument is the equivalent of cash. The obligor who remits the instrument thus satisfies the underlying debt and is freed of liability for it. Also, she ordinarily lacks any liability on the instrument itself. Thus, in the unlikely event the bank does not pay the instrument, the obligee cannot look to the obligor on any basis or theory.

There are exceptions to this exception. Even though a bank instrument is used, the parties can keep alive the underlying debt by agreeing to do so. Id. ("Unless otherwise agreed * * *"). Also, even if they make no such agreement so that the debt is discharged, the obligor may indorse the instrument and thereby become secondarily liability on it behind the primary liability of the bank as "drawer-maker" (3-412) or acceptor.

law

General Motors Acceptance Corp. v. Abington Casualty Ins. Co.

Supreme Judicial Court of Massachusetts, 1992
413 Mass. 583, 602 N.E.2d 1085

Nolan, Justice. On April 13, 1990, General Motors Acceptance Corporation (GMAC), filed a complaint against Abington Casualty Insurance Company (Abington), alleging breach of contract and conversion. In response, Abington moved to dismiss the complaint for failure to state a claim on which relief can be granted. After a hearing, the trial judge granted Abington's motion to dismiss, and reported his decision to the Appellate Division of the District Courts which dismissed the report. GMAC filed a timely claim of appeal on July 18, 1991. We transferred the case to this court on our own motion. We conclude that GMAC has presented a claim on which relief can be granted, and, therefore, we reverse the order of the Appellate Division dismissing the report.

* * *

In its complaint, GMAC alleges the following facts. Abington issued a physical damage insurance policy covering a 1984 Jeep motor vehicle to Robert A. Azevedo. GMAC, the holder of a security interest in the vehicle, was the loss payee beneficiary of that policy. In 1988 the vehicle sustained damage. Abington appraised the loss and issued a check on November 14, 1988, payable jointly "to the order of Robert A. Azevedo and G.M.A.C." The check was delivered to Azevedo who then presented it to the drawee bank without GMAC's endorsement. The check was drawn on an account with sufficient funds, and Azevedo received full payment. To date, GMAC has received none of the proceeds issued by Abington.

GMAC now seeks recovery of the insurance proceeds from neither the drawee bank, which mistakenly accepted the check without the necessary endorsements, nor Azevedo, who is subject to GMAC's lien, but instead from Abington, the drawer of the check. GMAC claims that in these circumstances, the payment on a check to only one of two joint payees does not discharge the underlying obligation of the payor to the remaining payee. This claim presents two novel issues to this court: (1) whether the delivery of a negotiable instrument to one joint payee operates as delivery to all joint payees, and (2) whether a drawer's underlying obligation to joint payees, who are not in an agency relationship, is discharged when one joint payee cashes a check without the endorsement of the other.

Although the issue has never been addressed in Massachusetts, other States have held that the delivery of a negotiable instrument to one joint payee constitutes delivery to all joint payees. The Uniform Commercial Code (U.C.C.), G.L. c. 106 (1990 ed.), expressly provides for instruments payable to two or more persons, see G.L. c. 106, §3-116, and when, as in this case, the instrument is payable not in the alternative, it may be negotiated, discharged, or enforced only by consent of all the payees. §3-116(b). To obtain the rights of a holder who may discharge or demand payment of the instrument pursuant to §3-301, one must take the instrument by negotiation. §3-202. Negotiation of an instrument payable to order entails delivery of the instrument with all the necessary endorsements. §3-202(1). Thus, since under Massachusetts law a person must seek the endorsements of every payee to negotiate, transfer, or discharge a negotiable instrument, delivery of the instrument to one payee does not jeopardize the rights of other payees. We hold, therefore, that Abington's delivery of the check to only one joint payee, Azevedo, nevertheless constitutes delivery to the remaining joint payee, GMAC.

Obligations on a negotiable instrument, however, do not end with delivery to a payee. To discharge its liability, a party to an instrument must make payment or satisfaction to the holder. §3-603. Once payment discharges the instrument, the underlying obligation is also discharged. §3-802(1)(b). When a check is involved, final payment is made when it is accepted by the drawee bank. §§ 3-410, 3-418. If a check is dishonored, then the drawer becomes obligated to pay the amount of the check, §3-413, or satisfy the underlying obligation, §3-802(1) (b).*

In this case, the drawee bank accepted the check, and payment was made to a payee. Ordinarily, an underlying debt is discharged when the check is " 'drawn on an account with sufficient funds to cover [it] at a solvent bank' and is delivered to the payee." *First Nat'l Ins. Co. v. Commonwealth*, 391 Mass. 321, 326-327, 461 N.E.2d 789 (1984), quoting *Terry v. Kemper Ins. Co.*, 390 Mass. 450, 455, 456 N.E.2d 465 (1983). Even delivery of a check to the payee's authorized agent who then cashes it, discharges the drawer's liability. However, in this case, where there are copayees who are not in an agency relationship, a negotiable instrument cannot be discharged by the actions of only one payee. Section 3-116(b) expressly prohibits the discharge of an instrument except by *all* the payees. "[T]he rights of one [payee] are not discharged without his consent by the act of the other." Uniform laws comment to G.L. c. 106, §3-116 at 581 (Law.Co-op.1984). Without this rule, there would be no assurance that all the joint payees would receive payment and that the drawer's underlying obligation would be fully discharged.

Prior to the adoption of §3-116, the common law rule that any joint obligee has power to discharge the promisor by receipt of the promised performance, Restatement of Contracts §130(a) (1932), had created particular incongruities when applied to negotiable instruments. The unpaid copayee could not collect from the *drawer* because the instrument was deemed discharged; on the other hand, the unpaid copayee could sue the *drawee* on a conversion of funds theory. Id. Section 3-116 settles the issue by requiring the endorsements of every joint payee before an instrument can be discharged. The Restatement of Contracts (Second) expressly recognizes this exception to the common law rule.

---

* Contract liability on a check falls primarily on the drawee and only secondarily on the drawer because the check is taken as conditional payment of the underlying obligation. See §3-802. The drawer's primary contractual liability is revived only when the check is dishonored. §3- 413.

Prohibiting the discharge of a check without all the necessary endorsements also accords with §3-603, which discharges a party's liability on an instrument only if payment or satisfaction is made to a holder. Lacking GMAC's endorsement, Azevedo could not have taken the check by negotiation and thereby become a holder. §3-202. Without payment to a holder, the liabilities of the parties to the check are not discharged. §3-603. This holding also comports with §3-419(1)(c), which provides that payment over a forged endorsement results in liability for conversion rather than acceptance and discharge. Further, to hold that an instrument is discharged when payment is made to one copayee without the endorsement of the other would effectively convert a "payable to A *and* B" instrument into one "payable to A *or* B." Thus, to protect the rights of all joint payees as well as the integrity of the commercial paper itself, we hold that payment of a check to one copayee without the endorsement of the other copayee does not discharge the drawer of either his liability on the instrument or the underlying obligation.

Because Abington's obligation to GMAC as a joint payee is not discharged, GMAC has two legal claims against Abington. First, as a loss payee beneficiary, GMAC may sue on the underlying contract claim. Second, as the owner of a lost instrument, GMAC may assert a claim under §3-804. A suit under §3-804 in this case is not blocked by payment to the holder pursuant to §3-603 because, as stated above, Azevedo was never a holder of the check. GMAC does not have a conversion claim against the drawer under §3-419(1)(c) because Abington never paid on the missing endorsement.

* * *

For these reasons, we reverse the order of the Appellate Division dismissing the report and remand the case to the District Court.

So ordered.

practice

Case 1

B purchased goods on credit from S. To evidence her obligation to pay the price, B signed a promissory note due in one year.

Suspension a. Six months later, S sued B for the price of the goods under U.C.C. Article 2. What result? 3-310(b).

b. Suppose S waits a year. The note is not paid. What causes of action does S have against B? 3-310(b)(3).

Case 2

The sale between S and B was a "cash" deal. B paid by check.

a. The check bounced (i.e., the drawee dishonored it). What causes of action does S have against B? 3-310(b)(3).

b.   What are S's causes of action if the check for the purchase price had been a cashier's check that was dishonored?   3-310(a); 3-412.

c.   Suppose that B tendered a personal check for the price and S refused it, insisting that the check be certified. B got the drawee's certification, and S then took the certified check as payment of the price.

    i.   Is B still liable to S? 3-310(a); 3-414(c).

                                     No

    ii.   Would B be liable to S if B refused to have the check certified and, instead, called off the deal? See 2-511(2).

Case 3

B bought goods from S and executed a promissory note as evidence of her obligation to pay the price. B paid the note to S when the instrument matured. S thereafter sued B for the price of the goods under U.C.C. 2-709(1). What result? 3-602(a); 3-310(b)(2).

B wins.

Case 4

B buys goods on credit from S. The price of the goods is charged to an account. S assigns the account to A. B pays S the price of the goods purchased. A sues B to collect the account.

a.   Can B raise her payment to S as a defense to A's action? See 9-318(1) & (3).   *Yes*

b.   Suppose that B had executed a promissory note in the amount of the price of the property. Before the note was due, B paid S the price but failed to retrieve the note she signed. S sold the note to A. When the note matured, B refused to pay it. A sues on the note. Can B raise her payment to S as a defense? See 3-305(b); *National Credit Union Admin. Bd. v. Metzler,* 625 F.Supp. 1551 (E.D.Mo.1986) (maker of note pays a party without possession at the maker's risk).

Maybe not

Case 5

S takes a personal check from B in payment for the price of goods sold by S to B. S cashes the check at the drawee bank. S later sues B for the price of the goods under U.C.C. 2-709(1).

a.   What is B's best defense? See *Siegel v. New England Merchants Nat'l Bank,* 386 Mass. 672, 437 N.E.2d 218 (1982) (even when a check is not properly payable, the drawee's payment may discharge a legal obligation of the drawer); *Bankers Trust v. South Carolina Nat'l Bank,* 284 S.C. 238, 325 S.E.2d 81 (App.1985) (payment of a check by a drawee discharges all parties to the instrument).

Discharge

b. Suppose that S cashes the check at her bank rather than at the drawee bank. S's bank, acting as a collecting bank on behalf of S, presents the check to the drawee for payment. The drawee pays the item.

No

    i. Can S now sue B for the price of the goods under Article 2? See *Miske v. Stirling*, 199 Mont. 32, 647 P.2d 841 (1982) (payment to a collecting bank is the equivalent of payment to its principal).

Yes

    ii. Is the result different if the drawee bank dishonors the check?

Instead of cashing the check, S indorsed it to T in exchange for widgets.

c. Can S sue B for the price? 3-310(b)(4).

d. In due course T presented the item to the drawee which paid it.

    i. Can S successfully sue B? See 3-602(a); 3-310(b).

    ii. Why can't T sue B? 3-602(a).

    Iii. Why can't T sue S for the price of the widgets? (Be careful!)

e. What if the drawee dishonored the check?

Case 6

S takes a personal check from B in payment for the price of goods sold by S to B. S indorsed the check by signing her name (and saying nothing else) on the back of the instrument. Through no fault of S, a stranger, T, took the check and got the drawee to pay the instrument.

a. S sues B for the price of the goods under U.C.C. 2-709(1). What result? 1-201(20); 3-602(a); 3-310(b)(1); 3-301.

b. Is the outcome different if S never signed the check and T forged S's indorsement? (Hint: As you will learn in Chapter 4, the stranger is not a "holder" or other person entitled to enforce the instrument, so there was no discharge under 3-602 or 3-310.)

Chapter 4. Instruments As Property

Instruments are, first, contracts. They embody enforceable promises to pay money. Accordingly, this book focuses first on the contract liability of parties to instruments. Instruments are also property. Their ownership is assignable, and enforceability is transferable. Significantly, ownership of an instrument and the right to enforce it are not the same or inseparable. They often coincide, but they can split so that someone other than the owner of an instrument can enforce it, sometimes even when the instrument was stolen from the owner.

Typically, the right to enforce an instrument is deliberately transferred rather than stolen. *Transferring an instrument* vests in the transferee, derivatively, any right of the transferor to enforce the instrument. Normally, the transfer is part of a larger process of *negotiating* the instrument, which gives the transferee a fresh and independent right of enforcement. She enforces in her own name rather than through the transferor.

A transfer also involves duties because the law normally implies *warranties* that bind transferors of property, including negotiable instruments. *Warranty liability* is different from contract liability on an instrument. Warranty liability usually is in addition to contract liability, but the former is not dependent on the latter and can exist without contract liability. Even a person who has not signed an instrument may incur warranty liability if she transfers the instrument or presents it for payment.

In effect, transferors guarantee certain qualities about the instruments they convey and back this guarantee with their personal liability. So do the people who present instruments for payment. The transfer warranties differ somewhat from the presentment warranties, but both sets are alike in assuring a right to enforce the instrument.

A right to enforce, however, is not payment. Between the two are the risks that the obligor will be insolvent or can assert defenses that reduce or eliminate her obligation to pay the instrument. There is also the risk that a third party will intervene and assert an overriding claim of ownership. The transferee of an instrument -- even if she is a holder -- is generally subject to a fundamental principle of property law, *derivative title*. As applied to contract rights, it is normally expressed as the familiar rule that an assignee stands in the shoes of the assignor. It means that an assignee of a contract right or a transferee of an instrument is subject to the same claims and defenses that would prevent collection by the assignor or transferor.

Article 3 creates a very important exception that protects a *holder in due course* of an instrument. She takes free of most defenses to liability on the instrument that arose from an occurrence with a third party, and also takes free from a third party's claim to the instrument. Article 3 gives other favors to a holder in due course, but none so important as this immunity from claims and defenses. It is Article 3's most important property principle.

§ 1. Persons Entitled To Enforce

The contract liabilities of maker, drawer, indorser, and acceptor are alike in a most important respect: each of them is obligated to:

- "a *person entitled to enforce the instrument * * *,*" or
- an *indorser* who pays the instrument, except that indorsers themselves are liable inter se only to subsequent indorsers.

3-412, 3-413(a), 3-414(b), 3-415(a).
   "Person entitled to enforce" means

- the holder of the instrument,
- a nonholder in possession of the instrument who has the rights of a holder, or
- a person not in possession of the instrument who is entitled to enforce the instrument pursuant to Section 3-309 or 3-418(d), which concern instruments that are lost, were stolen, or paid by mistake.

3-301. Any person who fits any of these categories is entitled to enforce the instrument "even though the person is not the owner of the instrument or is in wrongful possession of the instrument." Id. This last point can be confusing until you understand the relationship between title to an instrument and the right to enforce it. For this understanding you must know about the transfer and negotiation of instruments and holder status.

story

An instrument is property. It is a reified a right to the payment of money. 3-203 comment 1. Someone always owns the instrument in the sense of having title to it. Yet, an instrument is like other property that sometimes can be used or enjoyed by another person without the owner's permission, and that in exceptional circumstances can even be conveyed by the other person free of the owner's claim. Always, it is a matter of balancing the importance of protecting the owner's claim against the need to insure the property's currency to the rest of the world.

Who owns an instrument -- who has title -- is determined by principles of property law apart from Article 3. 3-203 comment 1. Who can use and enjoy an instrument -- who can enforce it and exercise its other rights -- is determined by Article 3.

Generally, any "holder" of an instrument can enforce it, and enforcement is normally restricted to a holder or someone with a holder's rights. 3-301. Holder does not mean owner, although typically the holder of an instrument owns it. Holder generally means someone in possession of an instrument that is payable to bearer or to her, meaning that she is identified on the instrument as the person to whom it is payable. 1-201(20). Why is such a person entitled to enforce an instrument?

> It is inherent in the character of negotiable instruments that any person in possession of an instrument which by its terms is payable to that person or to bearer * * * may be dealt with by anyone as a holder [that is, as someone entitled to enforce the instrument].

3-202 comment 2. It is inherent because of tradition and common understanding and also because the order or promise -- by its very terms -- extends to such a person.

The first holder of an instrument usually gets possession because the instrument is *issued* to her. "'*Issue*' means the first delivery of an instrument by the maker or drawer, whether to a holder or nonholder, for the purpose of giving rights on the instrument to any person." 3-105(a). "Delivery" means "voluntary transfer of possession." 1-201(14).

Example

Buyer gives Seller a check or note payable to Seller's order. Buyer thereby *issues* the instrument. Seller takes it, gets possession, and is thereby a holder.

The possibility of issuance to a nonholder covers the case in which a cashier's check is bought by a person who is the remitter only.

Example

Buyer purchases a cashier's check from Bank for delivery to Seller. Bank issues the check to Buyer that is payable to Seller. Buyer is the remitter only and is not herself a holder. Buyer delivers the check to Seller who then becomes a holder because Seller is in possession of an instrument payable to her. Issuance occurs only when Bank issues the check to Buyer. Buyer's delivery to

Seller is not issue. It is negotiation, which is another means of transferring an instrument so that the transferee becomes a holder. (Negotiation is discussed later.)

As holder of the note or check, Seller is a person entitled to enforce the instrument. She can convey this right of enforcement by *transferring the instrument*. This transfer is more than merely changing possession of the instrument. Transferring the instrument means delivery of the instrument "by a person other than its issuer for the purpose of giving to the person receiving delivery the right to enforce the instrument." 3-203(a).

Example

Seller, the payee of Buyer's note or check, sells the instrument to Bank or uses it as collateral or deposits it for collection. Seller thereby transfers it to Bank. Transfer gives the transferee any right of the transferor to enforce the instrument. 3-203(b). Because Seller was a holder, Seller had the right to enforce the instrument. 3-301. Because of the transfer by Seller, Bank gets Seller's right of enforcement.

On the other hand, a transfer does not give the Bank or any transferee a self-evident right of enforcement, only a derivative right that must be proved. Only when the plaintiff is herself a holder is she entitled to enforce an instrument on the basis of her status alone. A nonholder is entitled to enforce only by establishing that she claims through a holder. 3-301(ii). She must prove that the instrument was transferred to her by a holder or by someone who had the rights of a holder or that she acquired these rights by subrogation or succession. 3-308 comment 2.

A person becomes a holder of an instrument, post-issuance, only by the process of *negotiation*. 3-201(a). A voluntary transfer is normally part of negotiation, 3-201 comment 1, but is not always necessary for negotiation. Basically, an instrument is *negotiated* to a person when (1) she gets possession of an instrument (2) payable to bearer or to her that has been indorsed by everyone to whom previously it has been payable. No indorsements are necessary in the case of a bearer instrument that has never been payable to any identified person.

Always, however, even in the case of a bearer instrument, holder status is never decided by possession alone. The nature or state of the instrument is an equal concern. A person in possession of a bearer instrument is not a holder solely because she is in possession of an instrument. She is a holder because of her possession of an instrument payable to bearer.

In the hypothetical case, Bank would become the holder of Buyer's note or check to Seller by taking possession of the instrument that Seller had indorsed. How Bank acquired possession of the instrument would not matter so long as the instrument carried Seller's indorsement. Typically, virtually always, possession changes by *delivery*, which is a voluntary transfer of possession. 3-203(a), 1-201(14). Seller intentionally and deliberately passes the instrument to Bank.

Yet, the possession requirement of holder status would be met if Bank stole the instrument from Seller. All that matters to Bank's holder status is possession, however obtained, of the instrument indorsed by Seller.

Stealing the instrument would be wrong in every sense, and Bank would not own the instrument. Seller could retrieve it from Bank, and could stop an action by Bank to enforce the instrument. 3-305(c). On the other hand, so long as Bank kept possession of the instrument and thereby its holder status, Buyer could discharge her liability on the instrument by voluntarily paying the Bank, even if Buyer knew of Seller's claim to the instrument, 3-602(a); also, a subsequent holder who took in due course from the Bank (or from a mediate transferee) could even enforce the instrument in a court action that Seller could not stop despite her status as true owner. The holder in due course would take free of -- cut off -- Seller's claim. 3-305(b).

The Seller or any payee can avoid these consequences by not indorsing the instrument until the time she intends to transfer it. No one can become holder of an instrument, post-issuance, without the indorsement of a named payee; and the unindorsed instrument cannot be rightfully collected or enforced (in or out of court) by any person (immediate or remote), and cannot be freely paid, without proof that the payee voluntarily transferred her right to enforce.

Here, in the end, is the connection between property principles of ownership and Article 3 rules of transfer, negotiation, and enforcement. While title to an instrument and the right to enforce it are so far legally separate and distinct that neither establishes the other, the rules that determine the latter are a means of protecting the former. To insure this protection, owners respect Article 3's rules of transfer and negotiation so that, in practice, title and the right to enforce an instrument normally coincide throughout the instrument's life.

Holder

A holder is a person in possession of an instrument that is "payable to bearer or, in the case of an instrument payable to an identified person, if the identified person is in possession." 1-201(20). A person becomes a holder either by issuance or negotiation.

1. By Issuance

In the typical case the immediate parties to the instrument are the maker or drawer and the payee who are also the immediate parties to an underlying transaction involving the provision (sale or use) of property (real or personal, including money) or services. The instrument represents the buyer's obligation to pay for the property or services. The buyer creates the instrument and liability by signing it; and, rather than keeping it, she surrenders possession of the instrument by deliberately giving it to the supplier who is the payee. By getting possession, the payee is now a person who can enforce the instrument against the maker or drawer who is liable on the instrument for having signed it in her particular capacity.

This conduct of the maker or drawer in giving possession of the instrument and rights to the payee is known as "issue." It officially means "the first delivery of an instrument by the maker or drawer, whether to a holder or nonholder, for the purpose of giving rights on the instrument to any person." 3-105(a). In this role a maker or drawer is known as the "issuer." 3-105(c). The "delivery" that is required means "voluntary transfer of possession." 1-201(14). By this "issue" the payee becomes a "holder," 1-201(20), and is therefore a person entitled to enforce the instrument. 3-301.

It is possible, but relatively rare, that the first holder acquires the instrument other than by issuance. It happens in two exceptional cases. The more common case is the issuance of an order instrument to a remitter who then delivers it to the payee. The other case is the original payee of an order instrument getting possession from the maker or drawer other than by delivery of it to her; or anyone getting possession of a bearer instrument from its maker or drawer without delivery. In both exceptional cases, the person becomes a holder but not by issuance. It happens by negotiation in both cases, except when the payee of an order instrument takes it from the maker or drawer without delivery. In this very rare case, the payee fits the definition of holder but her possession results from neither issue nor negotiation.

2. By Negotiation

"'Negotiation' means a transfer of possession, whether voluntary or involuntary, of an instrument by a person other than the issuer to a person who thereby becomes its holder." 3-201(a) (emphasis added). It most commonly explains how a person -- any person -- becomes a subsequent holder, either immediately or remotely, after the first holder who normally will have acquired the instrument by issue to her. Only by negotiation can "the status of holder * * * arise * * * after issuance." 3-201 comment 1.

Negotiation is both a noun and a verb, an end and the means for accomplishing it. The purpose of 3-201(a) is only to label the process and explain the result of negotiation, which is that the transferee becomes a holder. The process itself -- the conduct necessary for this result -- is the verb form of negotiation and is explained in 3-201(b). It depends on how the instrument is payable:

- If an instrument is *payable to an identified person*, negotiation requires
  - ✓ transfer of possession of the instrument, *and*
  - ✓ its *indorsement* by the holder.
- If an instrument is *payable to bearer*, it may be negotiated by transfer of possession alone.

3-201(b). To engage in this conduct is to negotiate the instrument. Doing so is a negotiation of the instrument, and the result of this negotiation is that the transferee of possession becomes a holder. Her situation thereupon matches the Article 1 definition of "holder." See 1-201(20).

The Common Requirement: "Transfer of Possession"

Whether the instrument is payable to bearer or an identified person, a *"transfer of possession"* is necessary. "Negotiation always requires a change in possession of the instrument because nobody can be a holder without possessing the instrument, either directly or through an agent." 3-201 comment 1. *It is very important to understand that "transfer of possession" for purposes of 3-201 is not the same as the transfer of an instrument [when "[a]n instrument is transferred"] for purposes of 3-203.* The latter requires and is limited to a voluntary transfer. The former includes an involuntary transfer and any other change of possession. Indeed, how possession is acquired is unimportant, both as to means and motive. It is a transfer of possession when a thief steals an instrument. In sum, the clearer and more accurate meaning of negotiation is becoming a holder by *getting or taking possession in any manner,* even without a voluntary or involuntary transfer by the person who thereby loses possession.

Indorsements

Whether or not an indorsement is necessary to negotiate an instrument depends on how the instrument is payable. Indorsement is necessary only if the instrument is payable to an identified person. If it is payable to bearer, getting possession of the instrument is alone sufficient for the process of negotiation, 3-201(b); and whoever gets possession is a holder because of the negotiation. 3-201(a). *There is more here than meets the eye because how an instrument is presently payable can turn on how it was formerly payable.*

As originally drawn or made, an instrument is payable either to order or to bearer. See 3-104(a)(1). If the instrument is payable to bearer, as defined in 3-109(a), it is equally payable to bearer for purposes of 3-201(b) and negotiation. The instrument "may be negotiated by transfer of possession alone." 3-201(b). For this purpose, "transfer of possession" means any change of possession. Negotiation occurs when anybody gets possession in any way. Anybody in possession is a holder.

Example

Suppose Buyer issued a check or note payable to cash or otherwise to bearer. Thief stole the instrument before Seller indorsed. Thief is a holder. Seller's indorsement was unnecessary for negotiation.

An instrument originally drawn or made payable to order is -- by definition -- payable to an identified person. 3-109(b). Negotiation of the instrument requires the payee's indorsement, which means her signature on the instrument. She or her authorized representative must sign it. Nobody else's signature is her signature; therefore, nobody else's signature is her indorsement; thus, nobody can become a holder without her signature.

Example

Suppose Buyer's instrument was payable to Seller's order. Thief stole the instrument before Seller indorsed. Thief indorsed the instrument using Seller's name. Thief is not a holder. The result is the same if an unauthorized representative of Seller indorsed rather than Thief.

Whether an instrument originally was payable to order or to bearer, it is payable to an identified person if it is *specially indorsed*. A "*special indorsement*" is "an indorsement * * * made by the holder of an instrument, whether payable to an identified person or payable to bearer," that "identifies a person to whom it makes the instrument payable." 3-205(a). It usually consists of a simple instruction to pay an identified person, such as "Pay Jane Smith" or "Pay Named Bank," that is followed by the holder's signature. It need not contain the "order" language of 3-109(b), and can identify the person to pay in any manner that is permitted by 3-110, which contains rules for identifying the original payee.

A special indorsement changes an instrument from payable to bearer to payable to an identified person (the person whom the indorser named). The special indorsement would not be required for negotiation of a bearer instrument but would insure against enforcement by anyone except the identified person (or someone with her rights). Any further negotiation would require this person's indorsement. No one else could become a holder without it.

Example

Suppose Buyer issued a bearer instrument to Seller. Negotiation would occur by anyone getting possession of the instrument. Anyone who got possession would become a holder entitled to enforce even without Seller's consent. To guard against this happening, Seller could specially indorse to herself or another identified person whom Seller intends to become a holder.
Negotiation would require the indorsement of whomever she named. No one could become a holder without the person's consent.

An indorsement by a holder that is not special is a "*blank indorsement*," which means that the holder indorses without identifying a person to whom the instrument is payable. A blank indorsement changes an instrument that is payable to the holder, as an identified person, to an instrument that is payable to bearer. 3-205(b). Thereafter, it "may be negotiated by transfer of possession alone until specially indorsed," id., just as if it had been issued originally as a bearer instrument. This was recognized by Lord Mansfield in 1781 in deciding *Peacock v. Rhodes*, 2 Doug. 633, 99 Eng.Rep. 402, wherein he said, "I see no difference between a note indorsed blank and one payable to bearer. They both go by delivery, and possession proves property in both cases."

Example

> Suppose Buyer's instrument is payable to Seller's order, which is typical. Therefore, Seller's indorsement is required to negotiate the instrument to Bank. How the instrument is thereafter negotiated is determined by how Seller indorses when she transfers the instrument to Bank. If Seller specially indorses to Bank, the Bank's indorsement is required for negotiation. If Seller indorses in blank, negotiation occurs whenever anybody gets possession. Anyone in possession is a holder. To prevent this from happening, Bank could specially indorse, or it could convert the blank indorsement to special merely by inserting "Pay" followed by its name directly above the blank indorsement.

Every indorsement is either special or blank, in addition to being either qualified or unqualified. See Chapter 3 supra. Special or blank and qualified or unqualified describe different, entirely separate qualities of the indorsement. The typical indorsement is blank and unqualified.

In the end, the whole process of negotiation can be encapsulated and summarized in two grand rules:

- An instrument cannot be negotiated that is missing the indorsement of any former or present holder to whom, as an identified person, the instrument was or is payable. Except for her, nobody is or can become a holder until she indorses.
- An instrument is negotiated whenever any person gets possession of an instrument that is indorsed by every former holder to whom, as identified persons, the instrument was payable. Anybody in possession is a holder.

Everything else about negotiation really serves to explain and support these rules, but they cannot be understood or even stated without knowing everything else.

Identifying the Identified Person (3-110)

Suppose an instrument is made payable to Jane Smith or John Jones or (in Minnesota) Jon Olsen. There are lots of people with this name. Which one of them is *the* payee whose indorsement is necessary and sufficient for purposes of negotiation? The answer is in 3-110 which provides rules for determining the identity of the particular person to whom an instrument is initially payable if it is payable to an identified person.

The general rule is that this identity "is determined by the intent of the person, whether or not authorized, signing as, or in the name or behalf of, the issuer of the instrument." 3-110(a). The right Smith or Jones or Olsen is the Smith, Jones or Olsen intended by the individual who actually signed the draft or note. If this person is a representative, it is her intent that controls rather than the intent of her principal. If the signer is a forger, it is her intent that controls rather than that of the person whose name she used. The person that the signer has in mind is *the* payee "even if that person is identified in the instrument by a name or other identification that is not that of the intended person." Id.

Suppose a computer prints the check. It is not the computer's intent that controls. Rather, it is the intent of the person who caused the instrument to be printed, 3-110(b), whether this person is an employee of the issuer or a thief engaging in fraud. 3-110(b) & comment 1; 3-404 comment 2 (Case # 4). Just think of the checkwriting machine or computer as a kind of pen.

Multiple Payees

An instrument payable to order may name several payees either in the alternative, as "A, B, or C," or together as "A, B and C." A special indorsement may do the same. Negotiability is unaffected, but there are special rules about how to negotiate such an instrument.

- If the instrument is payable to two or more payees in the alternative, it is payable to any one of them and it may be negotiated, discharged or enforced by any one of them who has possession of it. To negotiate such an instrument, the indorsement of only one of them is required.
- If the instrument is payable to several payees together, it may be negotiated, discharged, or enforced only by all of them acting together. To negotiate an instrument that names several payees together, it must be indorsed by all of them.
- If an instrument payable to two or more people is ambiguous as to whether it is payable to the persons alternatively, the instrument is payable to the persons alternatively.

3-110(d).

The naming of several payees together is often a convenient device for a person who owes one obligation to several persons. If all such named payees indorse an instrument to negotiate it or if all sign a receipt for payment, the distribution of the proceeds need not concern the party issuing the instrument. But everybody is concerned when less than all of the payees transfer the instrument or obtain payment for themselves alone.

An example is *Cincinnati Ins. Co. v. First Nat'l Bank of Akron*, 63 Ohio St.2d 220, 407 N.E.2d 519 (1980). The court held that a drawee bank breached the contract of deposit with the drawer when it paid a check payable to joint payees without obtaining the proper indorsement of both. And if the drawee pays A without obtaining the indorsement of B, a joint payee, the drawee will be liable to B for conversion. 3-420(a). *Trust Co. v. Refrigeration Supplies, Inc.*, 241 Ga. 406, 246 S.E.2d 282 (1978).

3. By Law (Constructive Negotiation)

Checks Deposited For Collection

Occasionally, through oversight or otherwise, a payee deposits a check or other item in a bank for collection without indorsing it. If ordinary principles applied, the bank could not become a holder without getting the depositor's indorsement. For the bank to return the item for indorsement in this situation, however, delays collection with little advantage to the drawer and none to the depositor or bank. This explains why 4-205(1) provides:

> If a customer delivers an item to a depositary bank for collection * * * the depositary bank becomes a holder of the item at the time it receives the item for collection if the customer at the time of delivery was a holder of the item, whether or not the customer indorses the item, and, if the bank satisfies the other requirements * * * is a holder in due course."

Under this section a depositary bank that receives an item for collection without the depositor's indorsement is automatically a holder if the depositor was a holder. The depositor's indorsement is not necessary to the bank's holder status even if the instrument identifies the depositor as the person to whom the instrument is payable. Further, if the bank otherwise qualifies, it becomes a holder in due course. Also, if a drawee bank pays such an item, it is entitled to charge the drawer's account. The check is properly payable and chargeable to the drawer's account despite the missing indorsement of the depositor.

On the other hand, federal regulatory law requires a depositary bank to indorse all checks that it handles for collection. Indeed, the regulation requires that any "bank (other than a paying bank) that handles a check during forward collection or a returned check shall legibly indorse the check" in accordance with a standard that the regulation itself describes. 12 CFR 229.35(a). The slack in this rule is tiny. A depositary bank may arrange for another bank to add the depositary bank's indorsement, id. 229.35(d), as when the other bank handles collections for the depositary bank.

This federal rule requiring banks to indorse is part of a large regulatory scheme, Regulation CC, designed to expedite the collection and return of checks so that deposited funds are sooner available for withdrawal. Inconsistent state law is preempted but only to the extent of the inconsistency. Id. 229.41. Therefore, 4-205(1) is preempted to the extent it fails to require a depositary bank to indorse, but is probably not preempted in giving holder status to a bank that fails to indorse. Holder status without an indorsement is not inconsistent with the letter or purpose of Regulation CC.

Overriding Policies

It is by withholding her indorsement from an instrument that an identified payee protects and insures her ownership of the instrument and her right to enforce it. The maker or other payor cannot safely pay anybody else; and any third person who messes with the instrument without the payee's permission risks liability for conversion. See 3-420. The law has decided, however, that in some circumstances, the rights of an identified payee will not be preserved by the lack of the payee's indorsement. Overiding policy reasons favor the payor or third persons who otherwise would have been accountable to the payee for having paid or dealt with the instrument in an offensive way. You already know that a person can be precluded by ratification, estoppel or her negligence from denying that she signed an instrument. See 1-103; 3-403(a); & 3-406(a). These reasons can work equally well to stop a person from complaining about the absence of a payee's indorsement.

The effect is the same when certain risks occur that the law believes are better borne by the payee, such as the risk of theft by an employee responsible for instruments. When this risks occurs, as outlined by 3-405, the law deems that an indorsement by anybody -- including a wrongdoer -- is effective in determining the rights of a person who, in good faith, pays the instrument or takes it for value. The law believes that the drawer can more easily protect herself or "that the employer is in a far better position to avoid the loss by care in choosing employees, in supervising them, and in adopting other measures to prevent forged indorsements." 3-405 comment 1. Similar overriding policies are behind 3-404 which makes any indorsement effective in cases of impostors and fictitious payees. Although these sections apply to instruments generally, normally the instruments are checks. Therefore, 3-404 and 3-405 are covered in Chapter 6 which is devoted to checks.

Nonholder in possession with holder's rights

A nonholder is entitled to enforce an instrument in her possession if she "has the rights of a holder." 3-301(ii). A nonholder having a holder's rights occasionally happens by subrogation or succession, and most commonly when a holder *transfers the instrument* to a person who does not herself become (i.e., qualify as or meet the requirements of) a holder. For example, Payee sells the instrument to Bank or pledges it as collateral for a loan and fails to indorse. A transfer occurred but not negotiation. Payee was a holder. Bank is not a holder. Nevertheless, as a result of the *transfer*, 3-203(a), the transferee acquires the right of the transferor, as a holder, to enforce the instrument. 3-203(b). The transferee therefore becomes a person entitled to enforce it within the meaning of 3-301, even though she is a nonholder. In sum, because a holder enjoys the right to enforce an instrument, so does her transferee even if the transferee is not herself a holder.

The same holds true for a remote transferee of a holder if the mediate conveyances between them were all transfers of the instrument, i.e., deliveries of the instrument intended to give each transferee the right to enforce the instrument. The right to enforce an instrument, which originates with any holder, will slide undiluted through an infinite number of transfers and can be asserted by the ultimate transferee as if she had taken the instrument directly from the holder. The transferee's only problem is proving that she claims through a holder and inherits the holder's right to enforce.

This derivative right of enforcement flows from the basic principle of property law that title is derivative. A transferee gets only the interest in the property that belonged to her transferor and nothing more. All of the limits that applied to the transferor apply equally to the transferee. (A large exception is the holder-in-due-course doctrine which is not relevant at this point but is terribly important later in this chapter and in Chapter 5 infra.)

The up side of derivative title, which applies here, is the rule that whatever interest the transferor could and did convey, it fully passes to the transferee with any accompanying benefits. This up side is known as the "*shelter principle*." It means that whatever rights a transferor could have enjoyed, these rights belong to her transferee who can freely assert them even though she does not personally and directly qualify for the rights. Because the transferor could have exercised the rights had she kept them, her transferee can use them in the transferor's stead. In doing so, the transferee does not act for the transferor as agent for principal; rather, the transferee acts for her own account, instead or in place of the transferor who likewise could have enforced the rights. The purpose of the "shelter principle" is to insure the widest market for property interests and rights and thereby enlarge their value.

This shelter principle works with any property rights, not just a holder's right to enforce. Most significantly, it works equally well to give a transferee the protections of a holder in due course that her transferor enjoyed, even though the transferee does not qualify for the status herself. The next chapter says more on this point.

Nonholder without possession in exceptional cases

Ordinarily, to enforce an instrument, a nonholder must not only have the rights of a holder, she must have possession of the instrument itself. 3-301(ii). The same is true for a holder because her very status requires possession. It is an element of the definition of "holder." 1-201(20). In sum, possession is essential for almost every person's right to enforce an instrument. Only in two very narrow, exceptional cases is a person entitled to enforce an instrument not in her possession.

1. Lost, Destroyed or Stolen Instruments

The easier exception to understand is the case in which the person would be entitled to enforce the instrument if she had possession of it, but the instrument was *lost, destroyed, or stolen.* Enforcement is possible in this case but only if these conditions are met:

- the person was in possession of the instrument and entitled to enforce it when loss of possession occurred,
- the loss of possession was not the result of a transfer by the person or a lawful seizure,
- the person cannot reasonably obtain possession of the instrument because the instrument was destroyed, its whereabouts cannot be determined, or it is in the wrongful possession of an unknown person or a person that cannot be found or is not amenable to service of process, and
- the person seeking enforcement proves the terms of the instrument and the person's right to enforce the instrument.

3-309(a-b). There is room here for harmful mischief or costly mistake. The instrument could be found or set free and end up in the hands of a holder in due course. This person would be entitled to payment even though the instrument had already been enforced through 3-309. For this reason, 3-309, provides for insurance: the court may not enter judgment in favor of the person seeking enforcement unless it finds that the person required to pay the instrument is adequately protected against loss that might occur by reason of a claim by another person to enforce the instrument. Adequate protection may be provided by any reasonable means. 3-309(b).

In many states a different statutory rule applies to cashier's, teller's, and certified checks. A person who claims to own such a check that is lost, destroyed or stolen can notify the bank of her claim; and, if a certain time period has passed and the check has not been presented for payment, she is entitled to payment from the bank without providing security. The bank is discharged of all liability with respect to the check. See Chapter 4, supra, for more about this special rule.

2. Instruments Paid by Mistake

In the other case in which a person can enforce an instrument not in her possession, a payor has paid the instrument by mistake and recovered the money. The person from whom payment is recovered should be free to collect from the right person; but the person who mistakenly paid the instrument probably got possession at that time and may be unable to return it in actionable form. In this case, the person from whom payment is recovered "has rights as a person entitled to enforce the * * * instrument." 3-418(d). Significantly, any discharge that resulted from the mistaken payment is effectively expunged because, upon recovery of the payment, the instrument is deemed dishonored. 3-418(d).

Suppose, for example, that Buyer gives Seller a check as prepayment for goods that Seller promised to deliver. Bank pays the check, but payment is a mistake because Buyer's account is empty. The Bank gets restitution from Seller. Seller can sue Buyer on the check, even if Bank inadvertently had returned the check to Buyer. Also, Buyer cannot defend on the basis of discharge by payment. When the Bank recovered the payment, the check was deemed dishonored.

Indorsers

The contract liability of parties to instruments runs not only to a "person entitled to enforce" the instrument, whom 3-301 defines. It also runs to an indorser who pays the instrument and to a drawer-turned-indoser in the case of an acceptor's liability. The reason is that an indorser is really a surety to any other party, except subsequent indorsers; and, as between a surety and the principal obligor, the latter should ultimately bear the responsibility of payment. Technically, however, an indorser is empowered to sue on an instrument only when and because she fits 3-301, not because a party's contract of liability is owed to her. Yet, in describing the persons entitled to enforce an instrument, 3-301 does not expressly include an indorser who paid the instrument and to whom, therefore, the maker, drawer, or acceptor is obligated.

The paradox is avoided because the indorser, by other names, will usually fit both of the main categories in 3-301 of people entitled to enforce. When an indorser pays an instrument, her liability is discharged but not the liability of persons liable to her. The instrument remains viable, and the indorser gets possession of it because, when she pays in full, the instrument is "surrendered" to her. 3-501(b)(2)(ii). If the instrument is then payable to bearer, the indorser becomes a holder and thus a person entitled to enforce.

More likely, the instrument is payable to the person whom the indorser paid. This person will not indorse the instrument herself when she surrenders it, and her indorsement cannot be compelled. Almost surely, the rule that a transferee for value is entitled to the transferor's unqualified indorsement (3-203(c)) does not apply. Surrendering an instrument upon payment is not a transfer. The *purpose* of the surrender, apart from its effect, is not the purpose required for transfer, which is to give the indorser the right to enforce the instrument. 3-203(a). As Professor Britton wrote:

> Instruments are "negotiated" to purchasers. Instruments are not usually negotiated to principal debtors and other payors but are "delivered up", or "surrendered", to the payor.

W. Britton, BILLS AND NOTES §265 (2d ed. 1961).

On these facts, without the indorsement of the person who was paid, the indorser is not a holder. She is in possession of the instrument, but it is not payable to her or to bearer. It remains payable to the person whom the indorser paid. The problem would be easily solved if the surrender were a transfer, because a transfer -- whether or not a negotiation -- gives the transferee any right to enforce the instrument. Since the person who was paid had a right to enforce, the indorser would inherit the same right. Because surrender is not transfer, there is no such inheritance.

Nevertheless, by different means the problem is easily solved if the indorser *formerly* was a holder. In this case, her again getting possession of the instrument is called *reacquisition*. She can cancel or strike out her indorsement and any subsequent indorsement, including the indorsement that made the instrument payable to the person whom she paid. 3-207. By striking these indorsements, the instrument becomes payable to her or to bearer. By her own hand, she magically becomes a holder. Yes, it's legal! Id.

It is possible and not uncommon that an indorser who pays the instrument is not a former holder. It happens when the instrument was never negotiated to her; rather, she signed *only* as a surety, probably to lend her name and credit to the maker or drawer when the instrument was issued. In this case, her indorsement is out of the chain of transfer and is referred to as an "*anomalous indorsement*," 3-205(d), that is signed for *accommodation*. 3-419(a). She is an *accommodation party*, which is Article 3's name for a surety on a negotiable instrument. The magic of reacquisition, which allows striking indorsements, is not certainly available to her because, in terms of 3-207, she is not a "former holder." Prior law spoke in terms of reacquisition by a prior "party," 3-208 (1989 Official Text), N.I.L. 50, 121, and it was possible that reacquisition alone entitled an accommodation indorser to sue parties before her on the instrument. W. Britton, BILLS AND NOTES §297 (2d ed. 1961). In a different way, the 1990 Article 3 provides in a limited way for the accommodation indorser. Because she is an accommodation party, and whether or not she is a holder, the indorser in this case who pays the instrument is, by special provision, a person "entitled to enforce the instrument against the *accommodated party*." 3-419(e (emphasis added)). More is said later about sureties and accommodation parties.

Summerlin v. National Service Industries, Inc.
Court of Appeals of North Carolina, 1985
72 N.C.App. 476, 325 S.E.2d 12

Becton, Judge. In this action filed 14 May 1982 by plaintiff, Gerald F. Summerlin, to recover pension funds which had accumulated during his fourteen years of employment with the defendant, National Service Industries, Inc., the trial court granted directed verdict for defendant. On appeal, the plaintiff contends that the trial court erred in denying his motion for summary judgment, or at the very least, erred when it denied his motion for directed verdict and granted defendant's motion for directed verdict. Believing that this case should have been submitted to the jury, we reverse.

I

In August of 1978, plaintiff terminated his employment with defendant, left his wife and home in Florida, and moved to North Carolina. According to plaintiff's wife, plaintiff left a note saying, among other things, that she would soon be receiving a check for approximately $4,000. The plaintiff denies indicating that a check in any amount would be coming to his wife.

The terms of the pension plan provided that, at the termination of his employment with defendant, plaintiff would have the option of either receiving a lump sum cash refund consisting of the value of his personal contributions to the plan immediately and a deferred monthly benefit or of receiving a larger monthly benefit starting the first day of the month following his sixty-fifth (65th) birthday. On 27 October 1978, plaintiff's wife opened a letter addressed to him at his Florida address, advising plaintiff of his election under the corporate pension plan. According to Mrs. Summerlin, when she could not locate her husband, she signed the document for her husband, electing a cash refund. Thereafter, defendant mailed a check in the amount of $3,361.38 made payable to the order of Gerald F. Summerlin to plaintiff's Florida address. Mrs. Summerlin indorsed the check "Gerald F. Summerlin," deposited it in the Summerlin's joint checking account, and paid some of the plaintiff's outstanding liabilities and some of the "outstanding joint liabilities" of the parties. According to plaintiff, he did not find out about the status of his pension fund until 1981, when the Internal Revenue Service assessed him for failing to include it on his 1978 tax return.

Defendant contends it satisfied its contractual obligations to plaintiff by mailing the check to his last known address; that plaintiff had constructively received the sum in controversy since his wife cashed the check and paid his obligations; and that, in any event, since the bank honored the signature on the check, defendant was no longer liable. We cannot agree with defendant.

Since the check issued to plaintiff constitutes a "negotiable instrument" under N.C.Gen.Stat. Sec. 25-3-104 (1965), defendant's ongoing liability on the check and on the underlying obligation is governed by the commercial paper provisions of the Uniform Commercial Code (the Code), codified at N.C.Gen.Stat. Sec. 25-3-101 et seq. (1965). A party is discharged from liability on a negotiable instrument "to the extent of (its) payment or satisfaction to the *holder*." N.C.Gen.Stat. Sec. 25-3-603(1) (1965) (emphasis added.). Discharge of the party on the instrument also discharges him on the underlying obligation to the extent of his discharge on the instrument. N.C.Gen.Stat. Sec. 25-3-802(b) (Supp.1983).

The key issue becomes whether payment or satisfaction has been made to the "holder" in the case *sub judice*, thus discharging the defendant's liability on the instrument and the underlying obligation.

We begin with the definition of a "holder" as "a person who is in possession of *** an instrument *** issued or indorsed to him or to his order or to bearer or in blank." N.C.Gen.Stat. Sec. 25-1-201(20) (1965). From the record, it is clear that plaintiff's wife was in possession of a check which was neither "issued or indorsed to [her] or to [her] order or to bearer or in blank." Id. She therefore does not qualify as a "holder."

However, the parties have stipulated in the record that the check *** was "made payable to the order of Gerald F. Summerlin." See N.C.Gen.Stat. Sec. 25-3-110 (1965) ("Payable to order"). Under N.C.Gen.Stat. Sec. 25-3-202 (1965) a "payable to order" instrument may be "negotiated by delivery with any necessary indorsement *** written by or on behalf of the holder." Consequently, an indorsement by an authorized agent of the "holder" is sufficient to validate the transaction. This interpretation is substantiated by N.C.Gen.Stat. Sec. 25-1-201(43) (1965): an " '(u)nauthorized' signature or indorsement means one made without actual, implied or apparent authority. *** " Since an indorsement by an authorized agent of the "holder" is sufficient to negotiate an instrument, payment or satisfaction to an authorized agent of the "holder" is sufficient to discharge the defendant's liability on the instrument and on the underlying obligation.

Alternately, the defendant's liability on the instrument and the underlying obligation may be discharged, if the plaintiff has ratified the allegedly unauthorized indorsement or if the plaintiff is precluded from denying that the indorsement is unauthorized. N.C.Gen.Stat. Sec. 25-3-404 (1965) (unauthorized signatures and endorsements).

Therefore, if the plaintiff's wife had the actual, implied or apparent authority to indorse plaintiff's check, the check was negotiated and the defendant's liability on the check and on the underlying obligation was discharged. Similarly, if the plaintiff ratified his wife's unauthorized indorsement or if he is precluded from denying it, defendant's liability on the check and on the underlying obligation is discharged.

Significantly, we find no agency relationship between the plaintiff and his wife, nor any ratification by the plaintiff or facts precluding him from denying that the indorsement is unauthorized, as a matter of law. Although we summarily reject the plaintiff's argument that he was entitled to summary judgment, we nevertheless believe that the case should have been submitted to the jury.

Because factual issues must be resolved by the jury, the trial court erred in entering a directed verdict for the defendant.

* * *

The evidence creates a factual dispute with regard to whether plaintiff mentioned in his handwritten note that his wife would be receiving a check for approximately four thousand dollars. And the fact that plaintiff left Florida without leaving a forwarding address and that the funds, when received by plaintiff's wife, were deposited in a joint account are not conclusive to show an agency relationship. For example, plaintiff's wife's testimony that she attempted to locate plaintiff before signing his name on the form requesting a cash payment and again before she indorsed the check made payable to him, seem incongruous with defendant's implicit argument that plaintiff's wife had authority to do what she wanted to with the money by virtue of the note plaintiff left her. Further, in resolving the credibility issue, the jury may also deem it significant that the plaintiff was unaware that the pension fund was paid until he was notified of that fact by the Internal Revenue Service. In this regard, a stipulation by the parties that the husband had the option of withdrawing his funds at the termination of employment or leaving them in the pension plan until he reached the age of sixty-five, becomes important, especially since the plaintiff was fifty-seven at the time he terminated his employment with defendant.

In short, since marriage alone does not create an agency relationship, and since the evidence does not so clearly establish the facts in issue that no reasonable inference to the contrary can be drawn, a directed verdict was inappropriate as credibility remained an issue.

For the foregoing reasons, this matter is

Reversed and remanded.

Perry & Greer, Inc. v. Manning

Supreme Court of Oregon, 1978
282 Or. 25, 576 P.2d 791

Richardson, J. pro tem. Plaintiff Perry & Greer, Inc. brought an action against defendants seeking damages for breach of contract. In the same complaint plaintiffs Greer and Hoyt, as the sole shareholders of plaintiff corporation, alleged two causes of action against defendants. The first cause was for breach of the contract and the second for collection of a dishonored check. The validity and terms of the contract were in dispute and are discussed more fully later in the opinion. Following trial to the court judgment was entered against both defendants on the cause of action respecting the dishonored check and for attorney fees.

Prior to trial defendants moved to have plaintiffs elect whether they would proceed as individuals or as a corporation and whether they would proceed on the cause of action respecting the dishonored check or the underlying agreement. The court delayed ruling on the motion until plaintiffs had completed presentation of their case. Plaintiffs, at that time, elected to proceed as individuals on the dishonored check. Defendants then moved for a nonsuit, which was denied whereupon defendants rested, without putting on any evidence, and moved for a directed verdict on the grounds that the underlying agreement was vague and unenforceable and that plaintiffs did not have standing to sue on the dishonored check because the individual plaintiffs were not the holder or owner of the instrument. The motion for directed verdict was denied.

* * *

We develop the facts of this controversy from admissions in the pleadings and the evidence presented on behalf of plaintiffs. As indicated, defendants presented no evidence. Plaintiffs, either as individuals or as a corporation, entered into an agreement with defendants for the purchase and sale of the business assets, accounts and stock of plaintiff corporation. Although the validity of the contract is in conflict it in essence provided for a sale of the complete business to defendants. The agreed price was a $6,000 lump sum payment and the assumption by defendants of past due bills of the corporation. On April 17, 1974, defendants made the lump sum payment by the $6,000 check which is now in issue. The check was made out to both individual plaintiffs and signed by B.J. Manning as the maker. His signature was directly under the printed notation "POOL SIDE GRAINOLA." The check was postdated to April 26, 1974, and plaintiffs were told it would not be covered until that date, the reason being they were waiting for receipt of money from a third party in California.

Prior to April 26, 1974, defendants contacted plaintiffs to inform them that the money would not be there by the 26th. Plaintiffs made several subsequent inquiries about the money and each time were told the money, although forthcoming, had not arrived. Finally, in the latter part of June 1974, plaintiffs were informed the check would not be honored.

Plaintiffs then transferred the check to Bay Area Crane Hoist, Co., Inc. (Bay Area) with the following endorsement: "Ginny Hoyt, David Greer to Bay Area Crane Hoist Co., for funds advanced." David Greer's father was the principal owner of Bay Area. He had assisted in financing the business carried on by plaintiff Perry & Greer, Inc. Bay Area was told by plaintiffs the check would probably not be paid.

Bay Area sent the check for collection to Security Pacific National Bank (Bank) of Oakland, California, with the endorsement "Pay to the order of Security Pacific National Bank" and "For Deposit Only." The Bank endorsed and sent the check for collection and upon dishonor canceled its endorsement and physically returned the check to Bay Area without endorsement. Bay Area, as admitted in defendants' answer, physically returned the check to plaintiffs and assigned to plaintiffs all of Bay Area's right, title and interest in the check. Bay Area made no further endorsements on the check when it was given to plaintiffs and plaintiffs did not cancel any endorsements. Plaintiffs made written demand for payment of the check on defendant B.J. Manning.

Defendants argue that plaintiffs do not have standing to sue on the check because they are not holders or transferees for value of the instrument. Defendants contend that while Bay Area was a holder prior to negotiation of the check to the Bank it lost this status upon transfer to the Bank by negotiation. When the check was dishonored and returned to Bay Area there was no endorsement to Bay Area and no value given for the transfer and it was therefore not a holder, defendants contend. Since Bay Area was not a holder, the argument continues, it could not confer holder status on plaintiffs by transfer. Additionally, defendants argue that even if Bay Area reacquired status of a holder of the instrument the transfer to plaintiffs was without value and plaintiffs cannot collect the obligation. We disagree.

When Bay Area, as holder and owner of the check, transferred it to the Bank for collection the Bank became Bay Area's agent, ORS 74.2010(1). That section provides: "Unless a contrary intent clearly appears *** " the collecting bank acts as an agent of the owner of the instrument." This provision conferring prima facie agency status applies regardless of the form of the endorsement. There is nothing in this record to counter the prima facie principal-agency relationship between Bay Area and the Bank.

When the Bank returned the check to Bay Area following dishonor it was a return of the instrument by an agent to the principal and endorsement by the Bank was unnecessary. By this transfer, Bay Area, having physical possession, reacquired its status as a holder of the check.

Defendants admitted in their answer that the check was transferred from Bay Area to plaintiffs. ORS 73.2010(1) provides: "Transfer of an instrument vests in the transferee such rights as the transferor has therein." Since Bay Area was a holder the rights encompassed in this status passed to plaintiffs by the transfer. In *Scheid v. Shields*, 269 Or. 236, 524 P.2d 1209 (1974), we held a transferee, even though not a holder, could maintain an action on the instrument in his own name under the Uniform Commercial Code. It would follow that plaintiffs, who were transferees from a holder, can maintain an action to enforce payment of the obligation the same as the holder-transferor.

The principle of *Scheid v. Shields*, supra, defendants contend, should be restricted to transferees for value. Since the transfer to plaintiffs was not for value, it is urged, they cannot maintain the action on the check.

The transfers specified in ORS 73.2010 are not limited to transfers for value. An instrument may be transferred by gift and the donee acquires whatever rights the donor had. See Legislative Counsel Committee pamphlet on Oregon's Uniform Commercial Code with Comments, at 139 (1962). Transfer for value invokes the status of a holder in due course, ORS 73.3020. As such, a holder in due course can defeat certain defenses which may be raised to enforcement of the obligation, ORS 73.3050.

A transferee need not be a holder in due course to have the rights of a transferee. A transfer of an instrument may be by endorsement making the transferee a holder; by transfer for value, making the transferee a holder in due course; or by transfer without value or endorsement giving the transferee those rights possessed by the transferor. It is thus not necessary for the status of transferee that the transfer be for value. To follow defendants' line of reasoning would mean a donative transferee could never enforce payment of the instrument; a result we think the Uniform Commercial Code does not intend.

Defendants further argue that plaintiffs, not being holders, i.e., possession and transfer by endorsement, ORS 73.2020, or owners of the check, cannot recover under the provisions of ORS 73.3070(2). This section provides:

When signatures are admitted or established, production of the instrument entitles a holder to recover on it unless the defendant establishes a defense.

We quote from the official comments to ORS 73.2010:

"8. The final clause of subsection (3) of ORS 73.2010 *** is intended to make it clear that the transferee without indorsement of an order instrument is not a holder and so is not aided by the presumption that he is entitled to recover on the instrument provided in subsection (2) of ORS 73.3070. The terms of the obligation do not run to him, and he must account for his possession of the unindorsed paper by proving the transaction through which he acquired it. Proof of a transfer to him by a holder is proof that he has acquired the rights of a holder and that he is entitled to the presumption." Legislative Counsel Committee pamphlet on Oregon's Uniform Commercial Code at 140.

Plaintiffs acquired the check from Bay Area, which was a holder of the instrument, and thus are entitled to the presumption set out in ORS 73.3070(2). Defendants elected not to establish any of the defenses pleaded and it is thus unnecessary for plaintiffs to establish they were holders in due course, ORS 73.3070(3). We hold plaintiffs were entitled to recover on the check and the motion for directed verdict was properly denied.

* * *

Affirmed.

Resolution Trust Corp. v. Juergens
United States Court of Appeals, Seventh Circuit, 1992
965 F.2d 149

Shadur, District Judge. * * * On May 31, 1984 Peter Juergens ("Juergens") executed and delivered to limited partnership National Select Placement XV ("National") a promissory note (the "Juergens Note") in the principal amount of $134,200--the purchase price for 20 "Interests" in the partnership. On June 29, 1984 National borrowed money from Community Savings & Loan Association ("Community"), evidenced by a note in the principal amount of $2,331,300 (the "National Note"). National indorsed the Juergens Note to Community as partial collateral for the National Note.

At some unknown date Community indorsed the Juergens Note to Admiral Insurance Company ("Admiral"). At some later but also unknown date before this case began, Admiral allegedly transferred the Juergens Note back to Community, though without an indorsement.

Each of Juergens, National and Community appears to have suffered some financial calamity since entering into the transactions relevant to this case. National defaulted on the National Note, and it remains in default to the tune of $77,951.15 plus interest. Juergens has defaulted on the Juergens Note, owing $52,400 plus interest. And on February 17, 1989 Federal Savings & Loan Insurance Corporation ("FSLIC") declared Community insolvent and became conservator of its assets.

RTC came into existence as the result of the August 9, 1989 enactment of the Financial Institutions Reform, Recovery & Enforcement Act of 1989, and it then succeeded to the rights of FSLIC as conservator. Community went into receivership on February 9, 1990, and RTC was then appointed receiver. As receiver RTC succeeded to "all rights, titles, powers and privileges of [Community]" (Section 1821(d)(2)(A)(i)), including the power to "collect all obligations and money due [Community]" (Section 1821(d)(2)(B)(ii)).

* * *

When RTC acquired Community's rights in the Juergens Note, the chain of written indorsements ran from Juergens to National to Community to Admiral. Community had then gotten the note back without an indorsement back to Community. Section 403.208 renders the lack of such an indorsement irrelevant: Where an instrument is returned to or reacquired by a prior party he may cancel any indorsement which is not necessary to his title and reissue or further negotiate the instrument, but any intervening party is discharged as against the reacquiring party and subsequent holders not in due course and if his indorsement has been canceled is discharged as against subsequent holders in due course as well.

In terms of that statute Community "reacquired" the Juergens Note when Admiral returned it. Under the UCC, as at common law, a reacquirer needs only to possess the note -- it need not be the last indorsee in order to exercise its rights to cancel prior indorsements (either before or after bringing suit, incidentally) and to demand payment. That conclusion emerges clearly from the decisions of non-Wisconsin courts construing their own states' versions of UCC § 3-208).

Intervening indorsements simply vanish from the chain of title when cancelled by a reacquirer. That concept is the obvious product of the principle that permits the current holder of a negotiable instrument to sue its predecessor in the indorsement chain, in which event that party can in turn look to its own predecessor. If those lawsuits up the chain would ultimately lead back to the current holder, that pointless circular process is best avoided by the cancellation of the intervening indorsements and the discharge of those intermediate parties from liability (as Section 403.208 specifies).

It follows that a reacquiring party does not simply reacquire the note. Along with the note comes the bundle of rights that the reacquiring party had when it last possessed the note. Thus when it came into possession of the Juergens Note, RTC -- which at that point became entitled to cancel the indorsement from Community to Admiral -- acquired the same rights as a holder that its predecessor Community had possessed when it earlier held the Juergens Note.

In this instance Juergens unquestionably did not default until after Community had acquired the Juergens Note from National. That being so, nothing in the record casts a cloud on Community's original holder-in-due-course status. And because that same status attaches to Community's reacquisition (and hence to RTC, which stands in Community's shoes for that purpose), we need not reach Juergens' argument that his later default somehow makes it impossible for RTC to be a holder in due course.

* * *

[T]he decision of the district court granting RTC * * * judgment is AFFIRMED.

practice

Case 1

D draws a check payable to the order of P Corp. and delivers the instrument to the company.

a. Is P Corp. a holder? 1-201(20); 3-105(a).

Yes

b. How must the company transfer the check so that the transferee becomes a holder? 1-201(20); 3-201; 3-204.

Suppose that P Corp.'s representative delivers the instrument to the transferee along with a separate signed writing purporting to assign to the transferee all the rights of P Corp. to the check. The representative does not sign the check itself, however.

c. Does the transferee become owner of the instrument?

Probably

d. Is the transferee a holder?

No

Case 2

D draws a check payable to the order of P Corp. and delivers the instrument to the company. An employee of P Corp. takes the check, indorses the instrument without authority, and cashes it at a grocery store.

a. Was the employee a holder?

No

b. Is the grocery store a holder?

No

c. Can any subsequent taker become a holder? See Douglas J. Whaley, *Forged Indorsements and the UCC's "Holder"*, 6 IND.L.REV. 45 (1972) (no one can qualify as a holder following the forgery of an indorsement necessary to the chain of title)

Case 3

D draws a check payable to cash and delivers it to P Corp.

a. How must the company transfer the check so that the transferee becomes a holder? 1-201(20); 3-201; 3-109.

Suppose that an employee of P Corp., acting without authority, takes and cashes the check at a grocery store.

b. Was the employee a holder?

Yes

Yes   c.   Is the employee's transferee a holder? Cf. *Miller v. Race*, 97 Eng.Rep. 398 (K.B. 1758).

Case 4

D draws a check payable to the order of P Corp. and delivers the check to the company. The company indorses the instrument through an authorized representative who signs her name, indicates her representative capacity, and discloses the principal. The check is taken by an employee who cashes it without authority.

a.   **Is the employee's transferee a holder? See *Santos v. First Nat'l State Bank*, 186 N.J.Super. 52, 451 A.2d 401, 35 U.C.C. Rep.Serv. 518 (1982) ("thief can negotiate bearer paper by delivery to a holder in due course who will be protected against the rightful owner").**

Suppose that when the check is indorsed for the corporation, the representative adds the words, "Pay to the order of Sally Rodgers." The employee who takes the check signs Sally's name upon cashing the instrument.

No   b.   **Is the employee's transferee a holder? 3-205(a).**

c.   **Suppose the check is properly delivered to Sally Rodgers.**

Yes   i.   Does she becomes the holder?

Yes   ii.   Can anyone thereafter become a holder? How?

Yes   iii.   Can Sally or anyone after her become a holder if the special indorsement read, "Pay to Sally Rodgers"?

Case 5

A draws a check to B's order. B's employee takes the check and, using B's name without authority, indorses the instrument specially to C. C thereafter indorses the check in blank to D who delivers it to E.

No   a.   Was D a holder?

No   b.   Is E?

Case 6

D issues a check to A and B jointly. A cashes the check at a grocery store after signing her name and, without authority, B's name.

a.   **Is the grocery store a holder? 3-110(d).**

b. Suppose B sues D on the underlying obligation for which the instrument was issued. Who wins the lawsuit? 3-602(a); 3-310(b).

B

c. Suppose the debt owed to B was D's obligation to B under a settlement agreement reached by the parties after an automobile accident caused by D's negligence. A was B's lawyer. "It is, of course, clear that the mere existence of the attorney-client relationship does not alone create an implied authority for counsel to endorse his client's name on a negotiable instrument. * * * The legal question * * * is therefore the * * * narrower one of whether an attorney, specifically authorized to compromise a claim and collect the proceeds, may endorse the client's name on a check or draft tendered to effect the settlement. The decisions on this question are in clear and irreconcilable conflict. We believe that the better, and clearly the majority rule is that no such authority exists." *Florida Bar v. Allstate Ins. Co.,* 391 So.2d 238, 240 (Fla. App. 1981); but see, e.g., *Terry v. Kemper Ins. Co.,* 390 Mass. 450, 456 N.E.2d 465 (1983) (applying common-law rule of agency law that if an agent who is authorized to receive a check payable to principal as conditional payment forges the principal's indorsement to the check, the drawer is relieved of any and all liability to the principal if the drawee bank pays the check and charges the amount to the drawer's account); *Hutzler v. Hertz Corp.,* 39 N.Y.2d 209, 383 N.Y.S.2d 266, 347 N.E.2d 627 (1976) (essentially the same); compare *Navrides v. Zurich Ins. Co,* 5 Cal.3d 698, 488 P.2d 637, 97 Cal. Rptr. 309 (1971) (attorney is not authorized to forge client's indorsement, but client ratifies forgery by suing drawer and ratification discharges the drawer on underlying deal; suit against collecting bank nevertheless remains for conversion).

d. Suppose A was not authorized to indorse the instrument for B. Can D nevertheless avoid liability altogether to B if the underlying obligation was a debt owed to A and B jointly?

Consider this universally applied rule of the common law:

> A note payable to two creditors jointly, may be paid by paying either, and when paid to either, a mortgage to secure its payment is extinguished. *** The general principle is that a payment to one of two joint creditors does extinguish the joint debt. This principle seems to be based upon the idea that such joint creditors are mutual agents of each other, in the nature of partners pro hac vice -- mutual agents about that debt.

Long v. Cash, 54 Ga.App. 764, 189 S.E. 73, 74 (1936); see also, e.g., *Cober v. Connolly,* 20 Cal.2d 741, 128 P.2d 519 (1942); *Mathews v. De Foor,* 173 Ga. 318, 158 S.E. 7 (1931); *Delaney v. Fritz,* 221 Minn. 190, 21 N.W.2d 479 (1946); *Hamrick v. Lasky,* 107 S.W.2d 201 (Mo.App.1937); *Hill v. Breeden,* 53 Wyo. 125, 79 P.2d 482 (1938); but cf. *Quintana v. Allstate Ins. Co,* 378 N.W.2d 40 (Minn.Ct.App.1985). In the *Quintana* case, Allstate issued two insurance settlement drafts drawn on itself payable jointly to Rudolph and Loretta Quintana. The instruments represented payment of claims for the destruction by fire of the couple's mobile home and its contents. Ms. Quintana's indorsements of the drafts were forged, and she received none of the proceeds. Thus, she sued Allstate for her share on the theory that Allstate was guilty of conversion for having paid checks bearing forged indorsements. Ms. Quintana prevailed at trial, and the appellate court affirmed. On appeal, Allstate argued "that a general principle of contract law provides that payment of an entire obligation to one of several joint obligees discharges the obligation." Id. at 44. The argument was rejected:

> Although preexisting principles of law and equity may supplement the Uniform Commercial Code, they cannot displace particular provisions of the Code. Minn.Stat. §336.1-103 (1984). Furthermore, the basic purposes of the Code are "to simplify, clarify and modernize the law governing commercial transactions" and "to make uniform the law governing the various jurisdictions." Minn.Stat. §336.1-102 (1984). Thus, we will not resort to pre-Code law in order to circumvent the purpose and effect of the Code in this case.

Id. at 44-45; accord *General Motors Acceptance Corp. v. Abington Casualty Ins. Co.*, 413 Mass. 583, 602 N.E.2d 1085 (1992), which is reprinted in Chapter 3 supra.

e. **Assume that A was not authorized to indorse for B and that the underlying obligation was not a joint debt owed to A and B. Can B recover the full amount of the instrument from D, or is B's recovery limited to the amount of the proceeds to which she was entitled?**

Case 7

M executed a note payable to P. Upon selling the note to T, P delivered the instrument but neglected to sign it. The note matured, M dishonored it, and T sued M to enforce the instrument.

No   a. **Is T a holder? 1-201(20); 3-201; 3-204; 3-203(c).**

Yes   b. **Is T a person entitled to enforce the instrument? 3-301(ii); 3-203(b).**

Case 8

D issues check to A's order. A cashes the check at her bank but fails to indorse it. The check is dishonored and bounced back to A's bank. A's account is empty, and the bank sues D on the instrument. D's defense is A's breach of the underlying transaction between the two of them. Is the bank subject to this defense? 3-305(b). (The answers partly depends on whether or not the bank is a holder.) See 4-205.

Case 9

P purchased a certificate of deposit from State Bank. Upon borrowing money from National Bank, P pledged the certificate as security for the loan but neglected to indorse it. P defaulted on the loan and National Bank demanded that the proceeds of the certificate be paid to it. State Bank refused because it had already paid the proceeds to P.

a.   **Is National Bank subject to this defense?**   *Yes*

b.   **Suppose P indorsed the CD by signing her name and adding, "I hereby give a security interest to Bank." 3-204(c).**

Case 10

B gave S a note for the price of goods. S pledged the note to Bank with a special indorsement and for the "purpose of security." The note matured but was not paid by B. Bank notified S and collected the note from her. Bank then returned the note to S but without Bank's indorsement. S wants to sue B.

a.   **Is S a person entitled to enforce the note?   3-203(b).**

b.   **Is she a holder?   3-301; 3-207.**

c.   **Suppose B has a defense to payment that could not have been raised against Bank because Bank was a holder in due course. Can B raise the defense against S?**

§ 2. Defenses

Ultimately, the value of an instrument is determined by whether or not the obligor must pay the instrument and, if so, whether or not she is financially able to do so. The latter issue is beyond this book and mostly beyond the law. The former issue is discussed here and in the next chapter. It largely depends on whether or not a defense to payment or an adverse claim to the instrument is proved and, if so, whether or not the plaintiff is subject or immune to the claim or defense. Usually, immunity depends on the plaintiff having the rights of a holder in due course, which means she takes free of most claims and defenses that arose before the instrument was negotiated to her.

True defenses to negotiable instruments are commonly grouped into two classes: *real* and *personal* or *ordinary*. The "*real defenses*" are distinguished because they are good against *every person* entitled to enforce the instrument, *including a holder in due course*. They include such serious sins as gun-to-the-head duress, fraud in the factum, and nullifying illegality. In truth, the real defenses are relatively few, very narrow and rarely proved.

All other defenses are called "*ordinary*" or "*personal defenses*." They are much wider and much more common, but a holder in due course takes free of them. Ordinary defenses have two sources. Article 3 itself creates a few of them, but they mostly come from the law that governs the underlying contract. In the language of section 3-305(a)(2), the right to enforce an instrument is subject not only to "a defense of the obligor stated in another section of this Article" but also to "a defense of the obligor that would be available if the person entitled to enforce the instrument were enforcing a right to payment under a simple contract." In other words, if the law applicable to the underlying transaction provides a defense to the contract, the defense can also be asserted to avoid liability on the instrument.

The same provision subjects enforcement of an instrument to a *claim in recoupment*, 3-305(a)(3), which refers to a related counterclaim for damages. Recoupment is an offsetting cause of action which dilutes liability rather than a defense which avoids liability. Nevertheless, recoupment is typically grouped with ordinary defenses for two reasons. First, the bottom-line effect on liability is the same. Second, a holder in due course of an instrument takes free of claims of recoupment as well as ordinary defenses. 3-305(b).

Different from defenses to payment and claims in recoupment are *claims to an instrument*. These claims are property interests and possessory rights in instruments that follow them everywhere and into the hands of every person, except holders in due course. Just as holders in due course take free of personal defenses, they also take free of all prior claims to instruments. 3-306. A claim in recoupment is different because it is a cause of action that acts as a defense to payment of the instrument and is not a property interest or right to the instrument.

story

Real defenses

The *real defenses* are few, narrow and mostly depend on outside law. Article 3 collects some of them in 3-305(a)(1):

- *infancy* of the obligor to the extent that infancy is a defense to a simple contract;
- *duress, lack of legal capacity, or illegality* of the transaction which, under other law, nullifies the obligation of the obligor;
- *fraud* that induced the obligor to sign the instrument with neither knowledge nor reasonable opportunity to learn of its character or its essential terms; and
- *discharge of the obligor in insolvency* proceedings.

Beyond these "real defenses" are several other reasons for not paying that may be asserted against any person entitled to enforce an instrument, including a holder in due course. The most important are these:

Forgery. A person is not liable on an instrument unless she signed it or an authorized representative signed for her. 3-401(a). This freedom from liability is effective against the world, including a holder in due course.

Alteration. No one can enforce an altered instrument beyond its original terms. 3-407(b-c). To the extent of the alteration, the obligor is immune to liability even when the person entitled to enforce the instrument is a holder in due course.

Discharge Of Which There Is Notice. An Article 3 discharge of a party's liability on an instrument is a personal defense, 3-601(b); but even a holder in due course takes subject to a party's discharge of which the holder has notice when she takes the instrument. The notice does not have the greater effect of preventing due-course status, and the holder who takes in due course can enforce the instrument against other parties free of their personal defenses.

Subsequent Claims and Defenses. A holder in due course takes free of *prior* claims and defenses only, not any arising *when or after* she becomes a holder in due course. The need for good faith and the other requirements for becoming a holder in due course minimize the likelihood of a defense arising from the transaction of negotiation to a holder in due course. Occasionally, however, a defense arises at that time. For example, as part of the transaction of transfer, the holder in due course may agree to cancel her transferor's obligation by striking out her signature; or unknown to the holder in due course, a transaction may be voidable on the ground of illegality; or the parties may be acting on the basis of a mutual material mistake.

Also, defenses may arise after she acquires an instrument. For example, an obligor might pay the holder in due course; the latter might renounce her rights in a separate writing without giving up the instrument; the transferor or a prior party might obtain a discharge in bankruptcy; or a secondary party might be discharged by the holder's failure to make a proper presentment or to give due notice of dishonor. Another possibility is the holder impairing collateral for the instrument and thereby creating a defense for an obligor. Regardless of the nature of the defense arising when she receives the instrument or later, a holder in due course is subject to the defense just as if she were not a holder in due course.

Claims and Defenses Chargeable to the Holder. A holder in due course is not immune to liability or other accountability for her own conduct that creates a defense or claim for relief. She is liable for her own contracts, accountable for her own actions under Article 3 that create defenses or claims, and is liable for the breach of any duty imposed on her by other law that gives the obligor an offsetting defense or counterclaim in a suit on the instrument. It makes no difference when this liability arose, either before or after the holder became a holder in due course; and it makes no difference that the liability would be a personal claim or defense not enforceable against her if a prior party were responsible for it. Taking an instrument in due course will not permit a holder to escape responsibility for her own conduct, or for the conduct of others, when the law charges the holder directly and not merely derivatively through the transfer of the instrument.

Ordinary defenses

Ordinary or *personal defenses* are reasons of the law that allow an obligor to avoid or reduce liability on an instrument except as against a holder in due course. The rule is:

> Except as stated in subsection (b), the right to enforce the obligation of a party to pay an instrument is subject to * * * a defense of the obligor stated in another section of this Article or a defense of the obligor that would be available if the person entitled to enforce the instrument were enforcing a right to payment under a simple contract * * *.

3-305(a)(2). Except for a holder in due course, these defenses are good against every person entitled to enforce the instrument, including the original payee and any transferee. A holder in due course takes free of the personal defenses that are attributable to prior parties, which means that the defenses cannot be asserted against a holder in due course or someone claiming through her. 3-305(b). The personal defenses are found in Article 3 itself and also in the contract law that surrounds and governs the underlying transaction that produced the instrument.

1. Article 3 Defenses

The ordinary defenses created by Article 3 itself are spread throughout the statute, but they are conveniently listed in a comment to 3-305:

- nonissuance of the instrument, conditional issuance, and issuance for a special purpose (3-105(b));
- failure to countersign a traveler's check (3-106(c));
- modification of the obligation by a separate agreement (3-117);
- payment that violates a restrictive indorsement (3-206(f));
- instruments issued without consideration or for which promised performance has not been given (3- 303(b)); and
- breach of warranty when a draft is accepted (3-417(b)).

3-305 comment 2. Most of these defenses are tiny and tied to a very specific situation or context discussed elsewhere. The most important defense on this list concerns the "consideration" for the instrument. Really, this defense is rooted in the contract law of the underlying transaction. Article 3 recognizes and regulates the defense but does not create it. It better fits under the heading of defenses based on contract law.

Oddly, the most important reason that Article 3 gives for not paying an instrument is not on the list of Aricle 3 defenses. It is "discharge," which means that an obligor is released from liability on the instrument for reasons of Article 3 or contract law. Discharge is not thought of, technically, as a defense and therefore is not included in the ordinary defenses of 3-305(a)(2). See 3-302 comment 3. For the same reason, discharge is not discussed here. It occupies its own place in Chapter 3 which concerns contract liability on instruments. Nevertheless, "[d]ischarge is effective against anybody except a person having rights of a holder in due course who took the instrument without notice of the discharge." Id.; see also 3-601(b). It is, functionally, a complete defense. The only distinction is that notice of discharge does not prevent holder in due course status as does notice of a defense. 3-302(a)(2)(vi). Notice of discharge merely subjects the holder to the discharge despite her due-course status. In sum, therefore, discharge is not a defense only for purposes of 3-302(a).

2. Defenses Of Contract Law

In addition to the Article 3 defenses specifically stated in Article 3, the personal defenses to an instrument also include defenses "of the obligor that would be available if the person entitled to enforce the instrument were enforcing a right to payment under a simple contract." 3-305(a)(2). These defenses derive from the underlying obligation and are based on the contract law that governs it. *This law includes the common law and any applicable statutory law*, such as U.C.C. Article 2 when a sale of goods is involved.

Range of Defenses, Especially Including Problems of Consideration

The contract defenses cover a wide range. At one end are broad common-law defenses concerned with fairness in the very beginning of the contract when it was formed, such as fraud, misrepresentation, and mistake. At the other end is breach of contract which turns on precise, very narrow issues of contract interpretation and on events that often occurred at the end of the contractual relationship. There is everything in between that would be available to the obligor if contract law governed the enforceability of her promise to pay, including the age-old defense of no consideration. It is an Article 3 defense that the instrument was issued or taken without consideration, 3-303(b); but, for the most part, it is contract law that defines consideration and it is the underlying transaction that is the source of any consideration. Really, therefore, lack of consideration is a contract defense.

Consideration is not an element of the plaintiff's prima facie case in a suit on an instrument, as it is when a person sues for breach of common-law contract. Nevertheless, "[t]he drawer or maker of an instrument has a defense if the instrument is issued without consideration." 3-303(b). Moreover, the issuer has a defense to the extent that she was promised performance that has not been duly performed. Id.

It is a different issue whether or not the holder of an instrument gave "value" to qualify as holder in due course. See 3-302(a)(2), 3-303(a). The lack of value for that purpose is not itself a defense to payment of an instrument. The issue, in terms of defense to payment, is whether or not the drawer or maker got "consideration" in exchange for issuing the instrument. If not, she has a defense.

Not only are the issues different, the key terms are defined differently. "Consideration" basically keeps its common-law meaning, 3-303(b), but Article 3 gives a meaning to "value" that is both broader and more narrow than common-law consideration. See 3-303(a). Value is broader because it includes a preexisting debt, 3-303(a)(3), and more narrow because a bare executory promise is not "value." 3-303(a)(1) (by negative implication). Significantly, Article 3 enlarges the definition of "consideration" to include anything that is "value." Therefore, by statute, consideration -- like value -- includes preexisting debt. Because of the common-law meaning, consideration -- unlike value -- also includes an executory promise.

Nevertheless, if an obligor issues an instrument in exchange for consideration that is an executory promise, she gets a pro tanto defense to the extent that the promise is due and unperformed. 3-303(b). Correspondingly, for purposes of holder in due course, "value" includes an executory promise to the extent the promise has been performed, 3-303(a)(1), but this point is relevant here solely to complete the comparison between value and consideration.

To illustrate, suppose that R gave P a $500 check as a birthday gift. The drawee dishonored the check because R stopped payment. P will not recover on the check because R has the defense of lack of consideration. 3-303(b). It is possible, however, that P can prove a local substitute for consideration that supports recovery under the common law if not on the instrument.

Suppose R gave P the check as prepayment for goods that P promised, by contract, to deliver later. R stops payment. P sues. The defense of lack of consideration is not available to R. P's executory promise itself was consideration. On the other hand, R has a defense to the extent that P's promise is due and unperformed. R has no defense if the time for P's performance has not yet arrived, and R loses the defense altogether if a holder in due course takes the instrument.

Significantly, 3-303(b) does not extend the defense of no consideration to an acceptor or indorser. A probable reason is the reality that acceptors and indorsers rarely act gratuitously. Even an anomalous indorser or other surety, known as an "accommodation party," 3-419(a), typically gets consideration in the value that is given to the principal debtor. It is so common that by express provision, consideration is unnecessary to bind an accommodation party. 3-419(b). Practically, it is always there, so having to prove it is wasted effort.

Caveat: Defense Must be Chargeable to Plaintiff

The contract defenses that the obligor can raise are the defenses that applicable law gives to her, not the defenses of someone else. 3-305(a)(2) ("of the obligor"). Another limitation is that the defenses must be chargeable to the plaintiff against whom they are asserted. In other words, the plaintiff must be subject to the defenses by law or agreement. Suppose, for example, that A and B signed a note to Bank that evidenced a loan. Unbeknownst to Bank, A was induced to sign the note only because of B's fraud that amounted to a personal defense. A got nothing from the loan. If B paid the instrument and sued A for contribution, A would have a good defense against B. On the other hand, if Bank sued A on the note, B's fraud would not be a good defense against Bank. *Standard Finance Co. v. Ellis*, 657 P.2d 1056 (Haw. 1983). Whether Bank is a holder in due course is irrelevant. A's obligation runs directly to Bank. The Bank's rights against A because of this obligation are not affected by the conduct of someone else that is not attributable to Bank.

The result is different if B's fraud resulted in A issuing a note payable to B that B transferred to Bank. In this case, if Bank sued A on the note, B's fraud would be a good defense for A, unless Bank was a holder in due course. The difference is that, in this case, Bank's rights derive from B and are therefore subject to any defenses good against B. As a holder in due course, however, Bank's rights would be greater and Bank would take free of fraud that amounted to only a personal defense.

Even if Bank is a holder in due course, the result is different in both cases if B's fraud or other conduct amounts to a real defense. Real defenses are good against the world. It would make no difference that Bank took the instrument directly from A because to the extent that a real defense exists, the law effectively deems that the obligor never became liable to anyone on the instrument

Recoupment

Strictly speaking, *recoupment* is not a defense but accomplishes as much. A defense is a reason why *liability* is reduced, eliminated or never arises because of the plaintiff's conduct in the transaction that gives rise to her cause of action. A *claim in recoupment* is similarly related to the plaintiff's cause but reduces or eliminates *damages* by way of offset. Basically, recoupment is a related cause of action that is asserted only so far as is possible and necessary to reduce the amount of liability, only to wipe out or cut down the plaintiff's demand. In this respect recoupment differs from a counterclaim which, when it exceeds the amount of liability, is asserted both to offset damages for liability and also to produce a net recovery against the plaintiff. In sum, recoupment is essentially a counterclaim that is asserted defensively only.

Example

Because of a seller's breach of warranty, the buyer of goods may reject them and cancel the sales contract. If she is sued for the contract price, her cancellation of the contract is a defense. If the buyer accepted the goods, she is liable for the price but can assert the breach of contract as a claim in recoupment or a counterclaim. Defenses and counterclaims often go together. The buyer who defends against liability by virtue of cancellation can also counterclaim for damages because of the seller's breach of warranty.

When a person lacks the rights of a holder in due course, her right to enforce the instrument is subject to "a claim in recoupment of the obligor against the original payee of the instrument if the claim arose from the transaction that gave rise to the instrument." 3-305(a)(3). The claim, however, can be asserted against a transferee only for purposes of recoupment, "only to reduce the amount owing on the instrument at the time the action is brought." Id. In short, it cannot be asserted as a counterclaim. If the person enforcing the instrument is the original payee, this limitation does not apply. The claim can be asserted fully, as a counterclaim, to permit an affirmative, net recovery for the obligor.

A holder in due course takes free of all rights of action against prior parties, whether asserted as claims in recoupment or as counterclaims, except such claims that are against the holder personally.

Example

Suppose that the seller took the buyer's note for the price. A payee can be a holder in due course by meeting the usual requirements. Yet, even if the seller is such a holder, which is possible but highly unlikely, the buyer can assert any claim for breach of warranty, and she can assert it fully as a counterclaim and not only to reduce the amount of her liability. If the seller negotiates the note, the buyer can assert her claim against the third-party holder only in recoupment, to reduce the amount owed on the note; and the buyer cannot assert the claim to any extent if the holder is a holder in due course. The third party's knowledge of the claim when she took the instrument would prevent her from becoming a holder in due course. 3-302(a)(2)(vi).

It is explicitly stated that being a holder in due course does not protect the original payee from the obligor's claims:

[t]he right of a holder in due course to enforce the obligation of a party to pay the instrument is subject to * * * claims in recoupment * * * against a person *other than the holder*."

3-305(b) (emphasis added). This vulnerability would exist even without this explicit statement. First, a holder-payee who takes the instrument in a transaction that produces a claim against her is very unlikely to be a holder in due course. Second, the immunity of a holder in due course has always been limited to claims and defenses against prior parties. The immunity does not protect the holder from her own sins and the responsibilities that she herself owes the obligor. Former law said so by an express caveat providing that a holder in due course took free of defenses (including claims in recoupment) of a party "with whom the holder has *not* dealt." 3-305(2) (1989 Official Text) (emphasis added). The holder-in-due-course doctrine was thus inapplicable when the holder sued an obligor with whom she had dealt. The Revised Article 3 omitted this caveat because of the belief that it was unnecessary, not because it was wrong. The new statute continues to believe that "the holder-in-due-course doctrine is irrelevant" between parties who have dealt together, as in the case of a seller who takes the buyer's instrument for the price of the property. 3-302 comment 4.

Both of these reasons also explain why a holder in due course is subject to defenses for which she personally is responsible, even though 3-305(b) does not expressly say so as it does with respect to claims in recoupment. To make a holder in due course accountable for her own conduct, the caveat with respect to recoupment is superfluous and a corresponding caveat for defenses is unnecessary.

Different from recoupment is *setoff*. It concerns *un*related debts and claims. The rule on setoff as applied to instruments is that a transferee, whether or not a holder in due course, is not subject to the obligor's setoffs against a *prior party*. Yet, in line with local procedure, the obligor should be allowed to assert any setoff she has against the transferee personally, just as it should be appropriate for her to setoff against the original payee if this person sued to enforce the instrument. The reason for protecting a transferee from a prior-party setoff is that "it is not reasonable to require the transferee to bear the risk that wholly unrelated claims may also be asserted [as well as claims arising from the transaction that produced the instrument]." 3-305 comment 3. This reason does not apply to setoff against the plaintiff herself, whether she is the original payee or a transferee and whether or not she is a holder in due course.

law

Federal Savings & Loan Ins. Corp. v. Gordy
United States Court of Appeals, Eleventh Circuit, 1991
928 F.2d 1558 , 1565

Fraud in the factum has been described as "the sort of fraud that procures a party's signature to an instrument without knowledge of its true nature or contents, as fraud which occurs "within the instrument itself," and as fraud arising "when a party signs a document without full knowledge of the character or essential terms of the instrument."   * * *   Fraud in the inducement, which does not go to the very essence of the agreement but rather merely induces the party to enter the agreement, would not have the same effect because it would render the instrument merely voidable and thus capable of transfer.

New Jersey Mortgage And Investment Co. v. Dorsey
Superior Court of New Jersey, Appellate Division, 1960
60 N.J.Super. 299, 158 A.2d 712, 714

At common law, such fraud in the procurement of the execution of a note or bill as results in the signer's being ignorant of the nature of the instrument he is signing, sometimes designated as fraud in the *factum*, was held to be a real defense, i.e., invocable even against a holder in due course, provided the maker or drawee was not negligent in failing to discover the actual character of the instrument. Such fraud was distinguished from "fraud in the inducement," where the signer was led by deception to execute what he knew to be a negotiable instrument, this being only a personal defense, not available against a holder in due course.

Curtis v. Curtis
Supreme Court of New Mexico, 1952
56 N.M. 695, 248 P.2d 683, 688-89

It is frequently declared that the effect of fraud in the factum, or as sometimes called, fraud in the procurement, is to render the instrument so executed void ab initio, while fraud in the inducement renders the instrument merely voidable. * * * The commonest form of fraud in the factum exists where an instrument in writing is drawn up and signed by one party under a false belief as to its contents, due to the fraud of the adversary party. In such case the contract is generally held to be void. Hence such a contract need not be rescinded, and the party seeking to avoid liability need not return what he has received thereunder. Thus substituting a quitclaim deed for a mortgage, or a deed for a power to collect rents, omission to read to mortgagor a clause assuming a mortgage, or inserting without the knowledge of the adversary party a clause making a certain pledge collateral security for all debts owing, instead of for the debt in question, a false statement as to the covenants in a written lease, or the amount of goods specified in a written order, or the manner of payment, each makes such instruments void. * * * Fraud in the inducement exists where the defrauded party understands the identity of the adversary party, the consideration, the subject-matter, and the terms of the contract, and he is willing to enter into the contract in question; but his willingness so to enter is caused by a fraudulent misrepresentation of the adversary party as to a material fact. * * * As affecting the validity of the contract, fraud in the inducement renders the contract voidable, not void.

Standard Finance Co. v. Ellis

Intermediate Court of Appeals of Hawaii, 1983
3 Haw.App. 614, 657 P.2d 1056 (1983)

Tanaka, Judge. In an action on a promissory note, defendant Betty Ellis, now known as Betty Orlans, appeals from the summary judgment in favor of plaintiff Standard Finance Company, Limited.

The only issue is whether the granting of summary judgment was proper. We hold that it was and affirm.

The record shows that on September 30, 1976, defendant and her then husband, W.G. Ellis (hereinafter "Ellis"), executed and delivered to plaintiff a promissory note in the amount of $2,800.

Nothing having been paid on the note, plaintiff filed a collection suit on May 15, 1980. On January 15, 1981, the trial court entered its order granting plaintiff's motion for summary judgment. On March 9, 1981, judgment in the amount of $5,413.35 was filed. Defendant's timely appeal followed.

* * *

The dispositive question *** is whether a genuine issue of fact existed as to any of defendant's alleged defenses.

II. Misrepresentation

In Defendant's Answers to Second Set of Interrogatories filed on October 21, 1980, she indicates that "(s)hortly before" defendant executed the note, Ellis gave her "(c)onstant assurances" that her "signature was a formality and that he (Ellis) alone was liable and that the debt would be repaid without any participation by her." (Record at 35.) Thereafter, defendant accompanied Ellis to plaintiff's office and executed the note.

Defendant argues that Ellis' misrepresentation induced her to sign the note and since such misrepresentation dealt with its essential terms, her execution of the note was not a manifestation of her assent. Consequently, the note was *void ab initio* and unenforceable as to her.

The principles of law as to when misrepresentation prevents the formation of a contract and when it makes a contract voidable are set forth in Restatement (Second) of Contracts §§163 and 164(1) (1981). Section 163 (hereinafter "§ 163") states:

§ 163. When a Misrepresentation Prevents Formation of a Contract

If a misrepresentation as to the character or essential terms of a proposed contract induces conduct that appears to be a manifestation of assent by one who neither knows nor has reasonable opportunity to know of the character or essential terms of the proposed contract, his conduct is not effective as a manifestation of assent.

Comment a to §163 provides in part as follows:

This Section involves an application of that principle where a misrepresentation goes to what is sometimes called the "factum" or the "execution" rather than merely the "inducement." If, because of a misrepresentation as to the character or essential terms of a proposed contract, a party does not know or have reasonable opportunity to know of its character or essential terms, then he neither knows nor has reason to know that the other party may infer from his conduct that he assents to that contract. In such a case there is no effective manifestation of assent and no contract at all.

Section 164(1) (hereinafter "§ 164(1)") reads:

§ 164. When a Misrepresentation Makes a Contract Voidable

(1) If a party's manifestation of assent is induced by either a fraudulent or a material misrepresentation by the other party upon which the recipient is justified in relying, the contract is voidable by the recipient.

A.

Based on the facts in the record, we hold as a matter of law that the misrepresentation by Ellis was not a §163 "fraud in the factum" or "fraud in the execution" to render the note void at its inception.

A common illustration of "fraud in the factum" is that of the "maker who is tricked into signing a note in the belief that it is merely a receipt or some other document." Comment 7 to §3-305. *Gonsalves v. Ikei*, 47 Haw. 145, 384 P.2d 300 (1963) is an example of that type of fraud. See also, *Atkinson v. Englewood State Bank*, 141 Colo. 436, 348 P.2d 702 (1960) (defendant was induced to sign a note in blank on the representation that it was a contract).

In the instant case, no representation was made to defendant that the note was anything other than a note. In fact, as indicated above, it is uncontradicted that Ron Higa explained the "terms and conditions of the note" to defendant and Ellis prior to their execution of the note.

Comment 7 to §3-305 further states that the defense of "fraud in the factum" is that of "excusable ignorance of the contents of the writing signed" and the party claiming such fraud "must also have had no reasonable opportunity to obtain knowledge." *Page v. Krekey*, 137 N.Y. 307, 33 N.E. 311 (1893), and *First National Bank of Odessa v. Fazzari*, 10 N.Y.2d 394, 223 N.Y.S.2d 483, 179 N.E.2d 493 (1961), both cited by defendant, are examples in this category of "fraud in the factum." In *Page*, an intoxicated, illiterate defendant, who could not read nor write, was induced to sign a guaranty on a false representation that it was an application for a license. In *Fazzari*, defendant who was unable to read or write English was induced to sign a note upon the misrepresentation that it was a statement of wages earned.

The record in this case fails to show any fact constituting "excusable ignorance" of the contents of the paper signed or "no reasonable opportunity to obtain knowledge" on the part of defendant. In fact, in his affidavit, Ron Higa states:

6. At no time prior to or contemporaneously with the execution of the note did Defendant Ellis state that she did not understand the terms and conditions of said note as explained to her by Affiant.

7. After Affiant explained the terms and conditions of the note to Defendant Ellis, she made no request to read said note and was not prevented at anytime from reading said note. (Record at 46.)

Under the foregoing uncontradicted facts, the words of the court in *Bancredit, Inc. v. Bethea*, 68 N.J.Super. 62, 172 A.2d 10 (1961) are appropriate. There, the court stated:

The signer must in such a situation exercise the caution of a reasonable prudent man to determine the character of the paper upon which he has purposefully placed his signature. The rationale of such a requirement may be found in the desirability of preserving general confidence in commercial paper, as well as in the equitable principle that where one of two innocent persons must suffer by the wrongful act of a third party, he who enabled the third party to perpetrate the wrong must sustain the loss.

Id. at 66, 172 A.2d at 12.

B.

As a matter of law, the facts in the record, viewed in the light most favorable to defendant, do not justify defendant's voiding of the note under §164(1).

Plaintiff did not induce defendant by any misrepresentation. As set forth above, Ellis' misrepresentation to defendant occurred before they appeared at plaintiff's office to sign the note. Ron Higa says in his affidavit:

> 5. At no time prior to or contemporaneously with the execution of the note did Defendant Ellis inform affiant that she would not repay the note or that she was executing said note on the condition that only her ex-husband was to be solely liable for the repayment of said note. (Record at 46.)

III. Duress

In her answers to interrogatories, defendant states that she was "forced" to sign the note under duress. (Record at 13.) "(P)hysical beatings" of and "psychological pressure" on her by Ellis "(f)or at least the 3 yrs. prior to signing of note" constituted the duress. (Record at 33-34.) She argues that her execution of the note which was compelled by duress was not a manifestation of her assent. Thus, the note is void and unenforceable.

The law concerning duress resulting in void or voidable contracts is discussed in Restatement (Second) of Contracts §§174 and 175(1) (1981). Section 174 (hereinafter "§ 174") reads:

§ 174. When Duress by Physical Compulsion Prevents Formation of a Contract

> If conduct that appears to be a manifestation of assent by a party who does not intend to engage in that conduct is physically compelled by duress, the conduct is not effective as a manifestation of assent.

Comment a to §174 provides in part:

> This Section involves an application of that principle to those relatively *rare situations in which actual physical force has been used* to compel a party to appear to assent to a contract. *** The essence of this type of duress is that a party is compelled by physical force to do an act that he has no intention of doing. He is, it is sometimes said, "a mere mechanical instrument." The result is that there is no contract at all, or a "void contract" as distinguished from a voidable one. (Emphasis added.)

Section 175(1) (hereinafter "§ 175(1)") states:

§ 175. When Duress by Threat Makes a Contract Voidable

> (1) If a party's manifestation of assent is induced by an improper threat by the other party that leaves the victim no reasonable alternative, the contract is voidable by the victim.

A.

We hold that as a matter of law the facts in the record do not constitute the type of duress which renders the note void under §174. Such duress involves the use of actual physical force to compel a person to sign a document. It may include the example given in Comment 6 to §3-305 of an "instrument signed at the point of a gun" being void.

Here, the only evidence of duress is "physical beatings" and "psychological pressure" by Ellis on defendant over a course of three years prior to defendant's signing of the note. Without more, such evidence does not constitute §174 duress resulting in the voiding of the note. From such evidence it cannot reasonably be inferred that the physical beatings by Ellis directly resulted in defendant signing the note in question.

B.

As a matter of law, based on the facts in the record, the note was not voidable by defendant under §175(1).

Defendant relies heavily on *Furnish v. Commissioner of Internal Revenue*, 262 F.2d 727 (9th Cir.1958). In *Furnish*, a wife had signed blank income tax forms at the request of her husband. The court of appeals reversed the judgment imposing a deficiency against the wife and remanded the case for a determination of duress stating that it is "harshly inequitable for the wife to be forced to pay a penalty for fraud arising out of nothing she had done, save signing a blank return required of her by a dominating husband." Id. at 733.

Furnish is distinguishable from this case. There duress was discussed in regards to its validity as a defense to a tax liability created by 26 U.S.C. §51(b) (1939). Here, under the Uniform Commercial Code, comment 6 to §3-305 states in part, "They (duress and illegality) are primarily a matter of local concern and local policy. All such matters are therefore left to the local law." Hawaii has adopted the Restatement's definition of duress that "where a party's manifestation of assent is induced by an improper threat that leaves him no reasonable alternative, the contract is voidable by that party." *Penn v. Transportation Lease Hawaii, Ltd.*, 2 Haw.App. 272, 275, 630 P.2d 646, 649 (1981).

Plaintiff did not threaten defendant. In his affidavit, Ron Higa makes the following uncontradicted statement:

> 8. At no time prior to or contemporaneously with the execution of said note did Defendant Ellis state or indicate in any manner that she was acting under coercion or duress in the execution of said note. (Record at 46.)

IV. Consideration

Finally, defendant claims that the entire amount of the loan of $2,800 went to Ellis and she received no part of it. Thus, there was lack or failure of consideration and summary judgment was improper. We cannot agree.

Exhibit "B" attached to plaintiff's motion for summary judgment is a copy of plaintiff's check for $2,800 made payable to "W.G. Ellis and Betty Ellis." The reverse side of the check bears the endorsement of "Betty Ellis." This was sufficient evidence of consideration for the transaction involved.

However, defendant states that she "(n)ever got the money or the use of it" and "(i)t all went to my ex-husband and this was understood by the Plaintiff." (Record at 24.) This fact does not constitute lack or failure of consideration. It is fundamental that consideration received by a co-maker on a note from the payee is sufficient consideration to bind the other co-maker. *Territorial Collectors v. Harrison*, 43 Haw. 98 (1959), aff'd, 278 F.2d 539 (9th Cir.1960).

Thus, contrary to defendant's contention, no genuine issue of material fact existed. The facts and their inferences viewed in the light most favorable to defendant do not constitute valid defenses to the action, and summary judgment was properly granted.

Affirmed.

OLSEN-FRANKMAN LIVESTOCK MARKETING SERV. v. CITIZENS NAT'L BANK, 605 F.2d 1082, 1084-87 (8th Cir.1979). [Plaintiff, Olsen-Frankman, drew two checks payable to Keim. Keim transferred the instruments to the defendant, Citizens National Bank, which was not a holder in due course. The principal issue in the case was whether plaintiff could defend against the defendant's enforcement of the checks by asserting a setoff arising out of an unrelated debt Keim owed plaintiff.] Focusing on *** [U.C.C. §3-306(b)] ***, the appellee Bank asserts that the phrase "all defenses of any party which would be available in an action on a simple contract" does not contemplate a defense by way of setoff arising from an independent transaction extrinsic to the instrument. To the contrary, appellant urges that specific provisions of *** Minnesota *** law authorize a drawer of a check to set off against a mere holder the obligations owed to the drawer by the payee. The Minnesota statute which appellant cites reads as follows:

> If a thing in action be assigned, an action thereon by the assignee shall be without prejudice to any set-off or defense existing at the time or before notice of the assignment; but this section does not apply to negotiable paper, transferred in good faith and upon good consideration before due. (Minn.Stat. §540.03 (1974).)

***

The *United Overseas Bank [v. Veneers, Inc.*, 375 F. Supp. 596 (D. Md. 1974)] opinion held that under U.C.C. §3-306(b) the right of a drawer to assert a setoff against a transferee (not a holder in due course) rested upon the drawer's rights according to state law existing before the enactment of the N.I.L. As already noted, U.C.C. §3-306(b) intended no substantive change in N.I.L. section 58, and Minnesota allowed setoffs both prior and subsequent to its adoption of the N.I.L.

* * *

In summary, the history of the Minnesota setoff statute and negotiable instrument law, the U.C.C. Comment and the views of legal scholars indicate that the obligor on a negotiable instrument may set off against a holder not in due course an existing obligation owed by the obligee on the instrument. Under the setoff statute, the transfer of a negotiable instrument to one not a holder in due course occurs" *** without prejudice to any set-off or defense existing at the time or before notice of the assignment(.)" Minn.Stat. §540.03 (1974). Thus, in the present case the Bank took these checks subject to any existing setoff rights of Olsen-Frankman.

practice

Case 1

B buys goods from S and issues to S a note for the purchase price. S sells and delivers the note to Bank without indorsing it. B dishonors the note because of a latent defect in the goods which amounts to a breach of warranty under the sales contract between the parties. Bank sues B on the note.

a.   **Bank is subject to B's defense arising from the underlying transaction. Why? See 3-305(a).**

B buys goods from S and pays for them with proceeds of a loan from Bank. The loan is evidenced by a note issued by B to Bank. Bank is otherwise unconnected to the sales transaction and S. The note matures, and B dishonors the note because the goods she purchased from S are defective.

b.   **Bank is not subject to this defense. Why not?**

B and C get a loan from Bank. The loan is evidenced by a note that B and C sign as makers. The note matures, and Bank sues C on the note. C proves that she got nothing from the loan and signed the note because B had a gun pointed at her.

c.   **Bank is subject to this defense. Why?**

Case 2

Estepp sought a loan from Bank which was unwilling to lend Estepp money without a co-signer who owned property in the county. Estepp approached Schaeffer, whom Estepp supervised at work, and explained that he needed someone to attest to his good character. Estepp displayed a paper which he said contained a statement that he, Estepp, was of good character and could be depended on to repay a loan. Schaeffer signed the paper which, in fact, was a promissory note payable to Bank. Schaeffer is a man of limited intelligence, little education, and virtually no ability to read English. He did not know the true nature of the paper he signed. Bank sues Schaeffer on the note and moves for summary judgment. *Schaeffer v. United Bank & Trust Co*, 32 Md.App. 339, 360 A.2d 461 (1976), *aff'd*, 280 Md. 10, 370 A.2d 1138 (1977).

a.   **How should the court rule?**

b.   **Suppose Schaeffer also moves for summary judgment. If the court denies the Bank's motion, should it grant Schaeffer's?**

c.   **Suppose that Estepp explained to Schaeffer that the paper was a note but represented that Schaeffer's signature was a mere formality and that Schaeffer never could be held liable on the instrument. Or suppose that Estepp misrepresented the amount of the note. Does the real defense of fraud in the factum include misrepresentations as to the nature of one's liability on the instrument? Compare *Leasing Serv. Corp. v. River City Constr., Inc*, 743 F.2d 871 (11th Cir.1984) with *Standard Finance Co. v. Ellis* 3 Haw. App. 614, 657 P.2d 1056 (1983).**

Case 3

B buys goods from S and issues to S a note for the purchase price. S sells the note to Bank without indorsement. B dishonors the note upon maturity because of a defect in the goods giving B a breach of warranty claim under the sales contract between the parties. Bank sues B on the note, after first getting S's indorsement.

a.   Can B assert the breach of warranty claim against Bank? 3-305(a).   *Yes*

b.   Can B set off an unrelated debt that S owes B? 3-305(a)(3) & comment 2.

No

c.   Suppose that S repurchases the note

   i.   How far can B assert the breach of warranty claim?

   ii.   Can B offset the unrelated debt?

§ 3.   Claims (Property Interests)

   "The right to enforce an instrument and ownership of the instrument are two different concepts." 3-203 comment 1. A person can own a property interest in an instrument even though somebody else holds the instrument and is the person entitled to enforce it. On the other hand, everybody except a holder in due course takes an instrument "subject to a claim of a property or possessory right in the instrument or its proceeds, including a claim to rescind a negotiation and to recover the instrument or its proceeds." 3-306.

story

For purposes of section 3-306, the term "*claim*" is very broad. It includes:

   not only claims to ownership but also any other claim of a property or possessory right. It includes the claim to a lien or the claim of a person in rightful possession of an instrument who was wrongfully deprived of possession. Also included is a claim * * * for rescission of a negotiation of the instrument by the claimant.

3-306 comment. (It does not include a claim in recoupment which is a counter-claim used as a defense to payment rather than a property right or interest.)
   There are several remedies for a person with a claim to an instrument.

   ♦   recover the instrument by replevin or otherwise;
   ♦   impound it or enjoin its enforcement, collection, or negotiation;
   ♦   recover its proceeds from the holder; or
   ♦   intervene in any action brought by the holder against the obligor. 3-202 comment 2.

Replevin (sue for the instrument)

A person with a superior claim to an instrument can sue to replevy it or use other appropriate means to recover the instrument from another person holding it who lacks the rights of a holder in due course.

> Replevin *** [is] [t]he statutory remedy *** which provides *** [for] an action to recover the possession of personal property. Judgment for the plaintiff may be for the possession, or for the recovery of possession, or the value thereof in case a delivery cannot be had, and of damages for the detention. *** [R]eplevin tests the right to possess the disputed personal property. The [law] has recognized replevin as an appropriate form of action to recover a promissory note, and a certificate of deposit [which] is essentially a promissory note.

Farha v. Federal Deposit Ins. Corp., 963 F.2d 283 (10th Cir. 1992) (applying Oklahoma law). It is clear too that a check "is an item of property and a chattel which is properly the subject of replevin." *Whitman v. Kovacs*, 89 N.Y.S.2d 21, 22 (Sup. Ct. 1949).

Conversion (sue for damages)

A conversion action is a common way of vindicating rights to chattels when there is interference by someone with an inferior claim to the property. Conversion equally protects rights to instruments.

> The law applicable to conversion of personal property applies to instruments. An instrument is also converted if it is taken by transfer, other than a negotiation, from a person not entitled to enforce the instrument, or a bank makes or obtains payment with respect to the instrument for a person not entitled to enforce the instrument or receive payment.

3-420(a). Generally, the measure of damages is "presumed to be the amount payable on the instrument, but recovery may not exceed the amount of the plaintiff's interest in the instrument." 3-420(b).

Intervention (collect from the obligor)

Because ownership of an instrument can separate from the right to enforce the instrument, a situation may arise in which the instrument is in the hands of a holder who wants payment but a third person objects, claiming that she owns the instrument or part of it or that she owns a better interest or superior possessory right than the holder. Paying the claimant is risky even if her claim is true. A holder in due course would take free of the claim and not be subject to the obligor's defense of having honored it.

On the other hand, because of 3-602, the obligor would be safe in paying the holder. Discharge by payment requires payment *to the holder* or other person entitled to enforce the instrument. 3-602(a). The rule does not require this person to be the exclusive owner. The rule does not even require her to have any interest whatsoever beyond having a right to enforce under the rules of Article 3. The obligor's knowledge of the third person's claim, in itself, does not jeopardize the discharge that 3-602(a) would give her if she paid the holder. The discharge applies "even though payment is made with knowledge of a claim to the instrument * * * by another person." 3-602(a). The third person's remedy is a court order blocking payment and giving her possession of the instrument.

Discharge is denied if payment is made in the face of certain other circumstances that are beyond bare knowledge of a third person's claim. Specifically, the discharge is denied if:

- ◆ (1) a claim to the instrument under Section 3-306 is enforceable against the party receiving payment and
  - ✓ (i) payment is made with knowledge by the payor that payment is prohibited by injunction or similar process of a court of competent jurisdiction, or
  - ✓ (ii) in the case of an instrument other than a cashier's check, teller's check, or certified check, the party making payment accepted, from the person having a claim to the instrument, indemnity against loss resulting from refusal to pay the person entitled to enforce the instrument; or
- ◆ (2) the person making payment knows that the instrument is a stolen instrument and pays a person it knows is in wrongful possession of the instrument.

3-602(b)(1-2). The knowledge that (b)(2) covers is much more than merely knowing of a third person's claim; in truth, it is knowing that the third person has no claim, which is true of any thief or anyone who holds through a thief. The exclusion in (b)(1)(ii) for bank checks is part of a scheme to encourage payment of these instruments, or to discourage dishonor of them. See also 3-411. The bank's payment to a holder effects a discharge even though the claimant has provided indemnification, but the bank is liable to the claimant for breaching any agreement not to pay the instrument. With respect to both (b)(1)(i) and (ii), they apply to deny the discharge only if the third person's claim is good against the person who is paid, which will not be true if this person is a holder in due course who took free of the claim. The obligor who pays in this case nevertheless faces liability apart from the instrument if the injunction ran personally against her, or if her payment to the holder violated an indemnity agreement with the claimant.

Because of the uncertainties, the person obliged to pay an instrument may withhold payment so the holder is forced to sue to enforce the instrument. The issue then is whether or not the obligor can defend against liability on the basis of the third-party claim. (This is sometimes referred to as the defense of *jus tertii*, meaning right of a third party.) The answer is no unless the third person "is joined in the action and personally asserts the claim against the person entitled to enforce the instrument." 3-305(c). The only exception is when the plaintiff lacks the rights of a holder in due course "and the obligor proves that the instrument is a lost or stolen instrument." Id.

In no event can the obligor avoid payment of an instrument, or can anyone else enforce a prior claim to it, if the instrument was taken by a holder in due course and is not held by her or someone claiming through this person. "A person having rights of a holder in due course takes free of the claim to the instrument." 3-306.

law

Farmers State Bank v. National Bank
Appellate Court of Illinois, Third District, 1992
172 Ill.Dec. 894, 230 Ill.App.3d 881, 596 N.E.2d 173

Justice Slater delivered the opinion of the court: Plaintiff, Farmers State Bank of Somonauk, initiated an action against defendant, First State Bank of Earlville, for conversion of a certain check, alleging that it represented proceeds of collateral in which plaintiff had a perfected security interest. The trial court granted defendant's motion for summary judgment. Plaintiff appeals and we affirm.

In November, 1986, plaintiff entered into two loan and security agreements with a local farmer, Harry Erickson, pursuant to which plaintiff lent Erickson $239,275.70. As collateral, Plaintiff was assigned a blanket security interest which included the 1986 crops grown and stored on the Erickson farm. Plaintiff perfected its security interest by filing a financing statement with the recorder of deeds of La Salle County.

In January of 1987, Erickson sold a quantity of soybeans from his 1986 crop to Bakers Feed & Grain. Bakers issued a check payable to Erickson in the amount of $26,104.54. On January 20, 1987, Erickson negotiated that same check to defendant in partial payment of an unsecured promissory note which Erickson owed to defendant Bank. Negotiation of the check to defendant by Erickson was without the knowledge or consent of the plaintiff, and defendant had no knowledge of plaintiff's security interest. Plaintiff made a written demand on the defendant for the grain proceeds which was refused.

Plaintiff's amended complaint alleged that defendant unlawfully converted the check to its own use by failing to tender it to plaintiff on demand. Plaintiff alleged that it was entitled to possession of the check under section 9-306 of the Uniform Commercial Code (the Code)

(Ill.Rev.Stat.1989, ch. 26, par. 9-306) because the check constituted identifiable cash proceeds of collateral. Both parties moved for summary judgment. The trial judge granted summary judgment for defendant, finding that defendant was a holder in due course and therefore took the check free of plaintiff's security interest. This appeal followed.

   * * *

  A holder in due course is defined in section 3-302 of the Code as follows: "A holder in due course is a holder who takes the instrument (a) for value; and (b) in good faith; and (c) without notice that it is overdue or has been dishonored or of any defense against or claim to it on the part of any person." (Ill.Rev.Stat.1989, ch. 26, par. 3-302(1).) In the case at bar, defendant took the check in partial payment of an outstanding promissory note. Section 3-303 of the Code states that a holder takes an instrument for value "when he takes the instrument in payment of * * * an antecedent claim against any person whether or not the claim is due." (Ill.Rev.Stat. (1989), ch. 26, par. 3-303(b).) There is no allegation that defendant did not act in good faith or that defendant had notice of plaintiff's security interest. Defendant was a holder in due course of the check in question. Section 3-305 of the Code states that a holder in due course takes the instrument free from "all claims to it on the part of any person." Ill.Rev.Stat. (1989), ch. 26, par. 3-305(1).

  Plaintiff argues that even if defendant is a holder in due course, it is entitled to possession of the check under section 9-306 of the Code because the check constitutes proceeds of collateral in which plaintiff has a properly perfected security interest. Section 9-306 provides in relevant part as follows:

> "(1) 'Proceeds' includes whatever is received upon the sale, exchange, collection or other disposition of collateral or proceeds. * * * Money, checks, deposit accounts and the like are 'cash proceeds'. All other proceeds are 'non-cash proceeds'. (2) Except where this Article otherwise provides, a security interest continues in collateral notwithstanding sale, exchange or other disposition thereof unless the disposition was authorized by the secured party in the security agreement or otherwise, and also continues in any identifiable proceeds including collections received by the debtor." (Ill.Rev.Stat. (1989), ch. 26, par. 9-306.)

  Plaintiff contends that this provision in Article 9 takes priority over the holder in due course provisions of Article 3. We disagree. Section 9-306(2) states that a security interest continues in collateral notwithstanding sale, "*[e]xcept where this Article otherwise provides.*" Article 9 does in fact "otherwise provide" in section 9-309:

> "Nothing in this Article limits the rights of a holder in due course of a negotiable instrument (Section 3-302) or a holder to whom a negotiable document of title has been duly negotiated (Section 7-501) or a bona fide purchaser of a security (Section 8-302) and *such holders or purchasers take priority over an earlier security interest even though perfected.* Filing under this Article does not constitute notice of the security interest to such holders or purchasers. (Emphasis added.) (Ill.Rev.Stat. (1989), ch. 26, par. 9-309.)

Section 9-309 establishes that defendant, as a holder in due course, takes priority over plaintiff's earlier perfected security interest. A leading commentator has explained how section 9-309 operates under the factual situation of this case: "[A] problem is presented when a prior lender claims a proceeds (9-306) interest in negotiable instruments that arise on the sale of his collateral, and the debtor transfers the instrument to a holder in due course. By virtue of 9-309 and Article three, the holder in due course will be victorious in such a case."

* * *

Plaintiff's reliance on *Bank of the West v. Commercial Credit Financial Services, Inc.* (N.D.Cal.1987), 655 F.Supp. 807, is misplaced. In that case the plaintiff initiated an action for conversion of certain accounts receivable of a debtor which were subject to plaintiff's security interest. Defendant, a junior secured creditor of the same accounts, argued that it was a holder in due course of certain checks negotiated to it by account debtors. The court rejected defendant's argument and in doing so noted that plaintiff's conversion claim was not based on an interest in the checks negotiated to defendant. Rather, the claim was to the value of the accounts which the defendant had converted by accepting the checks as payment. Because the claim was not based on an interest in the checks, the court held that the holder in due course rule did not apply. (*Bank of the West*, 655 F.Supp. at 820.) In the instant case, plaintiff's conversion claim *is* based on an interest in the check negotiated to defendant by Erickson.

* * *

In summary, defendant is a holder in due course and holds the check in question free of plaintiff's perfected security interest by virtue of section 9-309 of the Code. The order of circuit court granting summary judgment in favor of defendant is affirmed.

Affirmed.

Capital Investors Co. v. Executors of the Estate of Morrison

United States Court of Appeals, Fourth Circuit, 1973
484 F.2d 1157

Donald Russell, Circuit Judge: * * * In May, 1963, Morrison, the husband, acting in conjunction with the defendant James T. Benn, deeded his Florida property to Capital Investors Co. (hereinafter described as Capital) which was a corporate "shell", owned and controlled completely by Benn, and which may be considered legally as identical with Benn. Capital promptly sold the property in June, 1963, to Do- Mor, Inc., a Florida corporation, which in payment executed four promissory notes of even date with the purchase, naming Capital as original payee. The notes were secured by a mortgage over the real estate sold. The controversy between the parties relates to only two of these notes, one in the principal amount of $100,000 payable in two equal installments on June 21, 1964, and June 21, 1965, and the second in the sum of $225,000, payable within sixty days, or August 21, 1963. After delivery, the notes were shifted about by Benn among three corporations, which represented his *alter egos* and were completely under his control and ownership. * * * In March, 1965, however, when both notes were in default and after maturity, Benn, through one of his "shell" corporations endorsed the two notes in question to the defendant Frost, who initially had the notes endorsed over to a nominee, Peters and Company, a real estate brokerage firm headed by Frost's son-in-law, and later in favor of the defendant Dreisen, as nominee. Dreisen, however, later acquired from Frost a half-interest in his purchase.

* * *

After a full hearing in March, 1971, pursuant to the notice, the Court issued its opinion, dated May 4, 1971 in which it found specifically that Capital had not "paid any consideration for the Florida properties" and that Capital "held the assets described, transferred and conveyed as a constructive or resulting trustee. All of the properties were owned by Mr. Morrison. No consideration was paid by Capital. Mr. Morrison is entitled to have all of the property returned to him, or the proceeds therefrom, subject to the right of any bona fide transferee." In this opinion, it described the notes as "subject to a pledge", thereby indicating uncertainty of the nature of any claim of Frost and Dreisen, who were not at the time parties to the action, in and to the notes. This finding was confirmed in the judgment of the Court dated June 21, 1971.

Thereafter, the present controversy over the ownership of the two notes in question quickly developed between the estate of Morrison, relying on the judgment giving it beneficial equitable ownership of the Florida property "or the proceeds therefrom," and Frost and Dreisen claiming as endorsees and transferees for value without notice of the claims of Morrison. After a hearing on the respective claims, the District Court filed its decree "in equity" concluding, on the basis of its balancing of the equities of the parties, that the rights of Frost as a purchaser for value without notice were superior to those of the estate, even though the estate be deemed to have a constructive trust in and to the notes. Predicated on those findings, it sustained the claim of the defendants Frost and Dreisen to the notes. In so ruling, the Court gave no consideration in its opinion to the Uniform Commercial Code and its applicability to the issues between the parties. The estate has appealed. We reverse.

The notes in dispute are negotiable instruments and the transferability of such notes, as well as the rights flowing from such transfers, are to be determined by the legal principles unique to negotiable instruments. This is so, though the notes are secured by a real estate mortgage. In ascertaining what the rights attaching to a negotiation of a negotiable instrument are, the Courts are to apply the law, not of the place of payment, but of the place where the negotiation occurred. The transfer of the notes in question to Frost occurred in the City of Washington. At the time of that transfer, the applicable law was represented by the Uniform Commercial Code, earlier adopted in that jurisdiction. All of this the defendants Frost and Dreisen conceded on oral argument. Nor could they have taken any other position in view of the clarity of the law. The District Court, in its decision from which this appeal is taken, however, gave no consideration to the provisions of the Uniform Commercial Code and erroneously applied general equitable principles applicable to the transfers of non-negotiable instruments in resolving the rights of the parties.

Broadly speaking, the Uniform Commercial Code divides the purchasers of negotiable paper into two categories; and, following the ancient maxim, *nomen est numen*, it fixes the rights of a purchaser by his classification within those categories. The two categories are "holder in due course" and one not a "holder in due course." And the Code provides a simple test for ascertaining within which category a purchaser of a negotiable paper falls. To be a "holder in due course," one must have acquired the negotiable instrument before maturity and before default. It is conceded that Frost acquired the notes in this case after maturity and with knowledge of default. It follows necessarily, then, that he was not a "holder in due course." The Uniform Commercial Code plainly provides that one not a "holder in due course," such as was Frost, takes the notes "subject to (a) all valid claims to it on the part of any person; * * *." And the breadth of the phrase in the Code of "all valid claims * * * on the part of any person" is stated in the Official Comment on the section to include "not only claims of legal title, but all liens, equities or other claims of right against the instrument or its proceeds. It includes claims to rescind a prior negotiation and to recover the instrument or its proceeds." The Official Comment goes further and states that this provision "includes all claims for rescission of a negotiation, whether based in incapacity, fraud, duress, mistake, illegality, breach of trust or duty or any other reason. * * * It includes claims of legal title, lien, constructive trust or other equity against the instrument or its proceeds." The Comment, also, makes clear that the provision applies to and limits the rights of "a bona fide purchaser" for value, provided he took "with notice that the instrument is overdue." Since Frost took the notes with actual notice they were overdue and in default, he acquired only the right of his transferor, Benn, in and to the notes or their proceeds and his right to the notes was specifically subject to any constructive trust in and to the notes or their proceeds in favor of the estate and all references in the District Court's opinion to the rights of a "bona fide purchaser" for value were irrelevant. In short, the controversy between the parties resolved itself into the clear-cut question whether the estate had established its right to claim the notes as the beneficiary of a constructive trust in the notes or their proceeds. If it had, Section 3-306 was applicable and controlling.

* * *

Even if this controversy were not controlled by the clear provisions of the Uniform Commercial Code, we are not certain that the decree below could be sustained. Frost's standing as a *bona fide* purchaser for value without notice is open to serious question. His relationship with Benn was not casual. It was conceded that Benn frequented Frost's office, received mail there, and apparently gave Frost's office as the address for at least one of his "shell" corporations. Indeed, the very notes involved in this litigation had Frost's offices listed as the address of the payee Capital. Frost testified that this holding out of his offices by Benn was not with his approval and he said, when he heard of it, he ordered Benn to discontinue. But Benn was doing more than merely frequenting at odd times Frost's office; he had business dealings with Frost. Frost acted as attorney on behalf of several corporations connected in some way with Benn, with his fee guaranteed by Benn individually. He explained, however, that, while Benn was to pay his fee, Benn was not his client; in fact, he went further and stated that conflicts of interest would have prevented him from representing Benn in the litigation. Yet, conflict of interest or not, his fee was paid by Benn in the form of a credit of $50,000 against the purchase price of the very notes in litigation. Normally, he who pays one's fee is his client. Moreover, Frost concedes that Benn's operations were "unethical," though he testified that he did not discover this until a few weeks after he had purchased the notes. And, for some largely unaccountable reason, Frost would not take an assignment of the notes in his own name because he did not wish his name associated with the notes. And he purchased the notes at a considerable discount, a fact which, of itself, would not impugn the good faith of the assignment, but is a fact that can properly be considered in connection with all the other facts in the case, including the unique form in which payment was made by Frost to Benn. It must be borne in mind that the notes, in default as they were, carried "suspicion" on their face. It is of interest that the assignment to Frost's nominee came after the District Court had begun its consideration of the ownership of the Florida property and after Morrison had given notice, by his motion for leave to file a counterclaim, of his claim to the property or its proceeds. We are by no means as certain as apparently the District Court was that Frost could, even under the normal rules applicable to non-negotiable instruments, have qualified as a bona fide purchaser for value without notice. This is, of course, aside from the real issues in the case, which turn on the proper application of the Uniform Commercial Code for resolution.

Reversed and remanded with directions.

Louis Falcigno Enterprises, Inc. v. Massachusetts Bank & Trust Co.

Appeals Court of Massachusetts, Plymouth, 1982
14 Mass.App.Ct. 92, 436 N.E.2d 993

Dreben, Justice. The question before us is whether a bank which has issued a treasurer's or cashier's check may, when sued by the payee, assert as defenses claims of its customer arising out of the underlying transaction for which the treasurer's check was delivered by the bank's customer to the payee. We hold that in the circumstances of this case the bank may not assert such defenses and that summary judgment was properly entered for the plaintiff, the payee of the cashier's check.

An affidavit of the bank's customer filed by the defendant indicates that the dispute between the customer and the plaintiff relates to a license given by the plaintiff to the customer to exhibit a championship boxing match on closed circuit television. Prior to the telecast, the plaintiff demanded payment in the form of a bank check for expenses amounting to $47,305. When the customer claimed the expenses were not then due, the plaintiff indicated that it would not transmit the necessary signals for the telecast unless the bank check was delivered. As a result of the plaintiff's threat, and because it had already incurred substantial expenses, the customer delivered the check as demanded. After the telecast, the customer prevailed upon the bank to dishonor the check.

The customer's affidavit also alleges that, despite its repeated protests, the plaintiff refused to make adjustments. Because of the plaintiff's "misrepresentations", the customer sustained losses in excess of $50,000. The alleged misrepresentations related to receipts of prior matches, to the availability of certain facilities, and to the number of spectators who would buy tickets on the evening of the match.

The defendant also filed an affidavit of its president appending a letter of the customer, the body of which is set forth in the margin. The affidavit refers to the letter as a "written indemnification agreement."[*]

These affidavits establish that *** the defense asserted is not that of the bank but is a defense of the customer. Moreover, the defense relates to the underlying transaction and is not a "claim *** to the instrument."

No cases have been cited to us and we have found none which allow this kind of contract defense of its customer to be asserted by a bank where the bank is the sole obligor on the instrument. Compare *Leo Syntax Auto Sales, Inc. v. Peoples Bank & Sav. Co.*, 6 Ohio Misc. 226, 215 N.E.2d 68 (Ct.C.P.1965), the only case found allowing the bank to raise such defenses; in that case the purchaser as endorser of the check was also liable on the instrument. To the contrary, the authorities seem in accord in holding that a bank may not raise such a contract defense on a cashier's check. They reach this result, however, by different routes, as the Uniform Commercial Code (Code) does not deal specifically with defenses to cashier's checks. See generally Lawrence, Making Cashier's Checks and Other Bank Checks Cost-Effective: A Plea for Revision of Articles 3 and 4 of the Uniform Commercial Code, 64 Minn.L.Rev. 275 (1980).

Some cases hold flatly that a cashier's check may not be dishonored. One rationale given for these cases is that the check is drawn by the bank on itself and is accepted by the mere act of issuance.

Other cases treat cashier's checks like ordinary negotiable instruments under the Code. They point out that while some defenses of a third party may be available, both under the Code and prior law, only claims to the instrument and not defenses to the underlying transaction may be asserted by the bank. This is true even where the third party defends the lawsuit. Some authorities would apply the full scope of G.L. c. 106, §3-306(d), to cashier's checks and would, therefore, permit as a defense claims on account of the underlying

---

[*] "Please stop payment on your treasurers check No. 032615 in the amount of $47,305.00 to Lou Falcigno Enterprises, Inc., issued Wednesday, October 1, 1980.

"The reason for this stop payment is that the goods and services ordered and agreed upon were not delivered as agreed upon.

"I agree to hold this bank harmless and also agree to indemnify this bank against any loss arising from the stop payment."

transaction which are serious enough to give rise to the right of rescission. See G.L. c. 106, §3-306, U.C.C. comment 5.*

We think it plain that the policy in favor of reliability of bank checks requires a rule that the bank be precluded from raising the contract defenses claimed here on behalf of its customer. Thus, even if we were to accept the defendant's invitation and reject an absolute rule against dishonor of cashier's checks where claims of a remitter are involved, we would, in any event, not permit defenses broader than those permitted under G.L. c. 106, §3-306(d).** Since the customer's claims do not fall within that section or §3-603, the plaintiff must prevail.

Judgment affirmed.

United Home Life Ins. Co. v. Bellbrook Community Bank

Court of Appeals of Ohio, Greene County, 1988
50 Ohio App.3d 53, 552 N.E.2d 954

Syllabus by the Court

1. An endorsement of a check by an agent of the payee who expressly lacks authority to endorse checks is a forged endorsement, and payment on the endorsement is a conversion of the check.

2. A bank which pays a check on a forged endorsement is liable for conversion regardless of whether the bank is a depositary bank or the payor bank.

3. The payee of a check may recover for conversion of the check even though it was never delivered to the payee, so long as the drawer intended to make the check an enforceable obligation by surrendering control over it and placing it under the power of the payee or of some third person for the payee's use.

Wolff, Judge.   United Home Life Insurance Company, Inc. ("UHL") was granted judgment, after a bench trial, against Bellbrook Community Bank in the amount of $1,200, and costs.

The bank appeals. We affirm.

* * *

The uncontroverted facts in this case establish that Ben R. Grinnell was a general agent of UHL. By the terms of his contract with UHL, he was an independent contractor with "no authority * * * to endorse checks payable to [UHL]." On November 3, 1983, Grinnell established a sole proprietorship account at the bank under the name "Ben R. Grinnell-Insurance Agency." Into this account, he deposited a $1,200 check, payable to UHL

---

*   Another rule for cashier's checks has been suggested by one commentator, namely, "the finality of payment" rule of the Code. G.L. c. 106, §3-418. We note that the uncontroverted allegation in the plaintiff's affidavit as to its expenditures based on the issuance of the bank check brings the plaintiff within the final payment rule * * *.

** The defendant concedes that if the plaintiff is a holder in due course, the bank may not assert the customer's contract defenses. It argues, however, that there is a question of material fact as to whether the plaintiff is a holder in due course. We need not consider that question since we hold that even if the plaintiff is not a holder in due course so that c. 106, §3-306, and not c. 106, §3-305, is applicable, the defenses claimed do not fall within §3-306(d). Different views have been expressed as to whether a payee who receives a bank check from a remitter who claims failure of consideration is a holder in due course.

and representing a premium, drawn by Florence Dietrich on the Peoples Banking Company of Lewisburg, Ohio. He endorsed the check:

"United Home Life Ins. Co.
"Ben R. Grinnell Ins. Agcy.
"Ben R. Grinnell"

Grinnell apparently appropriated the $1,200 to his own use because UHL, by its counsel's letter to the bank of January 13, 1984, demanded $1,200 from the bank.

Grinnell was no kinder to the bank. His account was overdrawn by $605.20 as of November 30, 1983 and by $273.39 as of December 20, 1983, and the bank has not recovered the deficit.

In March 1984, UHL sent its check for $1,200, representing a premium refund, to George Dietrich, Florence Dietrich's husband.

R.C. 1303.55(A)(3) and (C) provide in pertinent part:

> (A) an instrument is converted when:
> (3) it is paid on a forged indorsement.
> (C) * * * [A] representative, including a depositary or collecting bank, who has in good faith and in accordance with the reasonable commercial standards applicable to the business of such representative dealt with an instrument or its proceeds on behalf of one who was not the true owner is not liable in conversion or otherwise to the true owner beyond the amount of any proceeds remaining in his hands.

The trial court determined that the bank had not acted in accordance with reasonable commercial standards and, accordingly, granted judgment to UHL against the bank for $1,200.

Before addressing the bank's arguments, we note that both parties have referred us to Annotation, Payee's Right of Recovery, in Conversion Under UCC §3-419(1)(c), For Money Paid on Unauthorized Indorsement (1983), 23 A.L.R.4th 855. Footnote 8 at 858 states:

> "In apparently no reported case has a claim been successfully asserted that an indorsement which was unauthorized was not a 'forged indorsement' within the meaning of UCC §3-419(1)(c)."

R.C. 1303.55(A)(3) is the Ohio counterpart to UCC 3-419(1)(c).

A

The bank first argues that the judgment is not supported by the law or facts.

The gist of this contention is that UHL failed to establish that the bank did not act in accordance with reasonable commercial standards.

The problem with this contention is the bank's failure to recognize that it was the bank's burden to establish that it acted in accordance with reasonable commercial standards.

The bank's evidence as to reasonable commercial standards was presented by its cashier, Kathleen Long. We have reviewed this testimony and are satisfied that the trial court could have reasonably accorded it no weight. After testifying on cross-examination in UHL's case that the standard practice of the bank would not permit the occurrence of what happened in this case, she contradicted this testimony upon direct examination in the bank's case. Her attempt to harmonize her testimony upon further cross-examination by UHL was, to say the least, unsatisfactory.

In view of the trial court's proper determination that the bank failed to act in accordance with reasonable commercial standards, it is of no consequence that there were no monies remaining in Grinnell's account.

The bank also contends that UHL was "negligent in its handling of this affair." The bank does not elaborate upon this contention, and the record fails to support it.

B

The bank next states that it was a depositary bank and not the payor bank.

While this is an accurate statement, the bank gives us no insight into its significance and we glean none from the language of R.C. 1303.55.

Under this statement, the bank argues that UHL failed to show an unauthorized endorsement.

The bank contends that the evidence established that Grinnell had sent money to UHL by check. The bank argues that UHL thereby gave Grinnell "implied, if not expressed, authority to endorse the check."

We have previously noted that UHL's contract with Grinnell expressly stated he had no authority to *endorse checks* payable to UHL and nothing in the evidence suggests UHL deviated from this provision. UHL's agency director, Fred Schoettle, testified that UHL received checks from Grinnell and suggested that those checks represented cash payments made by UHL customers to Grinnell.

3 Ohio Jurisprudence 3d (1978) 84-85, Agency, Section 52, states:

> "It is a well-recognized principle that where power is conferred upon an agent, he has by implication such incidental authority as is necessary to carry his power into effect and complete the business he is authorized to do. * * *
> " * * *
> " * * * However, an agent's implied authority generally embraces nothing except the powers necessary to carry into effect the purposes of the agency * * *." (Footnotes omitted.)

While Grinnell may have implied authority to deposit cash payments in his personal account to ensure safe transmittal by check of monies owed to UHL, this implied authority did not reasonably extend to endorsing and depositing checks payable to UHL, because the concern for safety of transmittal is not present where the original payment by the UHL customer is by check rather than cash.

C

The bank next argues that it could not be liable for conversion in the absence of delivery of the check to UHL. 23 A.L.R.4th 855, supra, digests cases on both sides of the issue of whether delivery of the check to the payee is a prerequisite to recovery under UCC 3-419(1)(c) and (3), of which R.C. 1303.55(A)(3) and (C) are the Ohio versions. Id. at 861-862, Section 3.

The cases holding delivery to be a prerequisite, including *City Natl. Bank of Miami v. Wernick* (Fla.App.1979), 368 So.2d 934, certiorari denied. (Fla.1979), 378 So.2d 350, cited by the bank, involve unusual facts, the likes of which are not present here. Indeed, the court in *Wernick* acknowledged the viability of recovery based on "constructive delivery" where the drawer evinces an intention to make the check an enforceable obligation by surrendering control over it and intentionally placing it under the power of the payee or of some third person for the payee's use. Although the facts in *Wernick* did not demonstrate an intention to pass title or give effect to the instrument, the facts in this case do.

Closer to the facts here are those in *Thornton & Co., Inc. v. Gwinnett Bank & Trust Co.* (1979), 151 Ga.App. 641, 260 S.E.2d 765, where actual delivery to the payee did not occur. In *Thornton*, the payee's, i.e., Thornton's, agent fraudulently induced the drawer to issue a draft, then forged the payee's signature. The court held that on these facts the bank honoring the check could be liable in an action for conversion. The court held that recovery for conversion required title, possession, or a right to possession, and that the drawer's designating a party as payee gives that party a right to possession. Here, Mrs. Dietrich's designation of UHL as payee gave UHL a right to possession, and to recover against the bank for conversion.

D

We also reject the bank's argument that UHL failed to establish damages.

Grinnell deposited the Dietrich check to UHL for $1,200, representing a premium, and appropriated the money to his own use. UHL eventually refunded the $1,200 to the Dietrichs. The evidence supports the award of $1,200, and we have difficulty understanding the bank's contention to the contrary. As stated in Thornton, supra, at 646, 260 S.E.2d at 769:

> " * * * [T]he measure of the Bank's liability for the conversion is presumed to be the face amount of the instrument. * * * [UCC 3-419(2) (R.C. 1303.55[B].)] This means that the Bank is liable for this amount unless and until evidence is introduced which would support a finding to the contrary. * * * [UCC 1-201(31) (R.C. 1301.01(EE).]"

Judgment affirmed.

practice

Case 1

B gave S a note for the price of goods. S used the note as collateral for a loan from Bank but Bank neglected to get possession of the note. Possession, however, is not essential to Bank's Article 9 security interest. S sold, indorsed, and delivered the note to C who became a holder in due course. Who has the better claim to the note, Bank or C? See 3-306.

C

Case 2

B gave S a note for the price of goods. S indorsed the note in blank and then lost it. The note was found by C who sold and delivered it to D.

a. Who is the holder of the note?

D

b. Who is the owner of the note?

Arguably S

c. Who wins if S sues to replevy the note from D?

D

No   d.   Could S instead sue D for conversion?

Yes; No   e.   Additionally or alternatively, could S sue C for conversion? Does it depend on whether or not S can recover from D?

f.   Additionally or alternatively, could S sue B on the instrument? On the underlying transaction between them? See 3-309; 3-310.

Case 3

Suppose that S and D both demand payment from B.

a.   What is the basis of D's claim to payment?

a.   What is the basis of S's claim to payment?

c.   Whom should B pay? Whom can B pay? 3-306; 3-309; 3-602.

Case 4

B gave S a check for the price of goods. C stole the check and cashed it at DB Bank. The drawee, PB Bank, "paid" the check and charged it to B's account.

a.   Identify the means whereby S can recover from

i.   C. 3-420.

ii.   DB Bank.

iii. PB Bank .

iv.   B. 3-309; 3-310.

b.   From whom could S recover if C had stolen the check from B before it was sent to S?

c.   Could B recover from anyone in either case? 4-401(a).

Case 5

B bought a cashier's check from PB Bank and gave it to S for the price of goods. It turns out that S had hoodwinked B. PB Bank refunded B's money and stopped payment on the cashier's check. S sued PB Bank on the cashier's check.

No   a.   Is there a defense to payment?

b.   Does it matter whether or not B participates in the action? See 3-305(c), but be careful!

Case 6

B bought a cashier's check from PB Bank payable to S's order. Shortly thereafter B tells PB Bank that she lost the check and asks for a refund. What advice would you give PB Bank? See 3-312.

§ 4. Warranty and Restitution

A person incurs contract liability on an instrument because she signs it. A person incurs warranty liability with respect to an instrument because she transfers the instrument and also because the instrument is presented for payment or acceptance. Warranty liability is a property concept. It is not dependent on promise and contract. Therefore, warranty liability attaches whether or not the warrantor indorsed the instrument. In case she indorsed, her contract liability is in addition to the warranty liability.

Warranty liability is personal liability that the law imposes on a person because of a breach of the warranties that Articles 3 and 4 and federal law impose with respect to the transfer and presentment of instruments. The purpose of transfer warranties, like warranties in the sale of goods or other property, is to insure the instrument's "title" and basic "quality." They assure or guarantee a right to enforce the instrument and against the existence of certain defenses and claims to the instrument that would dilute the instrument's value. The main purpose of presentment warranties is to assure the payor or acceptor that the person presenting the instrument for payment or acceptance is entitled to it.

Presentment warranties are not insurance that payment or acceptance was proper by the terms of the contract or other relationship that provides the underlying reason for the payment or acceptance. There is no warranty against payment or acceptance beyond these terms, by mistake. Avoiding mistake is within the personal control of the payor or acceptor and, for reasons of finality, the law is slow to provide any remedy for mistake. On the other hand, the common law of restitution permits recovering mistaken payments in limited circumstances. This law has always supplemented Articles 3 and 4, and the 1990 Article 3 codifies a restitution recovery for some mistakes. Restitution from any source is always very limited, however, because the remedy generally cannot reach innocent persons who gave value or who detrimentally relied on the mistaken payment or acceptance.

In largest effect, warranties and restitution serve the same purpose. They are the law's principal means for distributing risks (and thereby losses) in dealing with commercial paper; and the distribution is complete because the risks that are not covered by warranties or restitution are necessarily assigned and left to the transferee, payor, or acceptor who suffers the loss. What is not covered is therefore equally important to what is covered.

Article 3 is the general source of warranty law for all instruments. Section 3-416 creates the transfer warranties and 3-417 the presentment warranties. Article 4 provides its own warranties, 4-207 for transfer and 4-208 for presentment. Also, 4-209 adds encoding and retention warranties that are peculiar to electronic check collection and truncation. Article 4's warranty provisions override Article 3 whenever Article 4 is applicable. It applies to the collection and payment of checks and other "items" by banks. An "item" is "an instrument or a promise or order to pay money handled by a bank for collection or payment." 4-104(a)(9). Because the scope of "item" and Article 4 reach beyond negotiable instruments, the Article 4 warranties are applied more widely than Article 3's. More significant, the Article 4 warranties will apply to checks and other Article 3 negotiable instruments that are transferred and presented as part of the bank collection process. This is not a big deal, however, because the warranty provisions of the two articles are basically the same, and the warranties themselves are substantively identical.

In turn, Article 4's warranties are preempted to the extent that federal law provides different and additional warranties for items in the bank collection process. Regulation J describes warranties that are made to and by a Federal Reserve Bank. 12 CFR 210.5(a), 210.6(b). They are fewer than the Code's warranties but not very different and, in any event, apply only to a Reserve Bank. Regulation CC applies more broadly to all banks in the collection process; but, with an important exception, it mostly describes warranties that accompany the return of checks upon dishonor rather than forward-collection transfer and presentment warranties. 12 CFR 229.34. The exception is a warranty-like rule by which any bank that handles a check for forward collection or return is liable to any subsequent bank that does not receive payment for the check for any reason. Id. § 229.35(b). Article 4 includes essentially the same rule. 4-207(b).

In sum, the federal preemption of Article 4 warranties is small, and these warranties are mostly the same as the warranties of Article 3. Thus, nothing significantly reduces Article 3's role as the general source of warranty law for instruments, which explains why this chapter mainly speaks in terms of Article 3 warranties.

story

Transfer warranties

When Article 3 applies and in the absence of an effective disclaimer, any person who transfers an instrument and receives consideration gives five separate implied warranties:

      (1) the warrantor is a person entitled to enforce the instrument;

      (2) all signatures on the instrument are authentic and authorized;

      (3) the instrument has not been altered;

      (4) the instrument is not subject to a defense or claim in recoupment of any party which can be asserted against the warrantor; and

      (5) the warrantor has no knowledge of any insolvency proceeding commenced with respect to the maker or acceptor or, in the case of an unaccepted draft, the drawer.

3-416(a). These warranties arise with or without negotiation, with or without indorsement, and whether or not an indorsement is qualified or unqualified. They are triggered by a simple transfer for consideration. "Transfer" implies voluntary transfer of possession of the instrument. 3-203(a), 1-201(14). Consideration keeps its common-law meaning and is not entirely synonymous with any of the Code's definitions of "value." Whether or not the transferor indorses is important in only one respect. It determines to whom the warranties run. A transferor without indorsement warrants only to her immediate transferee. An indorser warrants to her immediate transferee *and every subsequent transferee.* Her warranties therefore run with the instrument.

Confusion is sometimes caused by the similarities between the five transfer warranties and the three presentment warranties, which are discussed later under their own heading. Although, as will become clear, there are several important differences between the two classes of warranties, it is sufficient here to mention only the basic difference: presentment warranties run only to those who pay or accept whereas transfer warranties run only to the transferor's immediate transferee and, with indorsement, all later transferees. At least in this context, a person who pays or accepts is not a transferee.

Transfer warranties are potentially important when a person who is expected to pay or accept the instrument dishonors, or she pays or accepts the instrument and later recovers payment or escapes the acceptance. If the reason is covered by a warranty, the person who is unpaid or, who loses payment or acceptance, can recoup from the warrantor because of warranty liability, apart from any contract liability the warrantor may have on the instrument. It is no defense for the warrantor that she was a holder in due course of the instrument or that initially the instrument was finally paid.

In truth, contract liability on the instrument normally furnishes a sufficient basis for recovering from a transferee when the party expected to pay or accept fails to do so. Transfer warranties are therefore most important in the exceptional cases where actionable indorsement liability is lacking because, for example:

- the instrument was transferred without an indorsement;
- the indorsement was qualified;
- the secondary liability of an unqualified indorser was discharged, as by untimely presentment of a check; or

- the instrument was paid or accepted but the payor or acceptor recovers for a reason covered by the transfer warranties.

Even when there is an actionable indorsement, a breach of warranty claim may be preferable because the right to sue for breach of warranty arises as soon as the claimant has reason to know of the breach, 3-416(d), even though the time for payment and possible dishonor of the instrument has not arrived. Also, in cases where the aggrieved party is entitled to sue on an underlying obligation, she may sometimes prefer to proceed on the basis of breach of warranty because this claim is easier to prove.

The transfer warranties can be disclaimed, except with respect to checks. 3-416(c). "Between the immediate parties disclaimer may be made by agreement. In the case of an indorser, disclaimer * * * must appear in the indorsement with words such as 'without warranties' or some other specific reference to warranties." 3-416 comment 5. Qualifying an indorsement with words such as "without recourse" does not disclaim warranty liability, only contract liability. Disclaimer is outlawed with respect to checks because the banking system relies on warranties and its automated processing systems cannot detect disclaimers.

Payment, finality, and the limits of restitution law -- the need for presentment warranties

In a perfect world, the right decision would always be made whether to pay, accept, or dishonor. In this world, the wrong decision is often made. Instruments are paid or accepted that should have been dishonored. The usual reason is that the payors or acceptors are not fully aware of all the relevant circumstances at the time of presentment. Thereafter, upon learning of this "mistake," they want to undo it. The acceptor denies liability, and the payor sues to recover her payment.

There is a very large, fundamental obstacle to undoing payment or acceptance. It is the *doctrine of finality of payment* that is deeply embedded in the common law and supplements Article 3. Payment by mistake normally cannot be recovered except by the somewhat strict, narrow rules of restitution law. These rules generally protect against unjust enrichment by any means but specifically include cases of mistake in conferring a benefit.

The mistake may be one of law or fact; it may be as to the existence of an agreement or as to the existence of elements necessary for a contract; it may be as to what is transferred or what is received, as to the existence of a duty or of ownership, or as to circumstances causing the conferring of a gratuity. The mistake may be the result of the fraud or innocent inducement of the other party or of a third person, or it may have resulted wholly from the inattention or lack of intelligence of the mistaken party.

Restatement of Restitution Ch. 2 Introductory Note 26 (1937). There are even special rules for cases in which money is paid by mistake for negotiable instruments. The tight brake on common-law restitution is that recovery is never allowed from a person who, having paid value in good faith for the instrument, receives the payment without reason to know of the mistake.

Article 3 expressly allows restitutionary recovery under the common law. The statute provides, as a general principle, that:

> [I]f an instrument has been paid or accepted by mistake * * * the person paying or accepting may, to the extent permitted by the law governing mistake and restitution, (i) recover the payment from the person to whom or for whose benefit payment was made or (ii) in the case of acceptance, may revoke the acceptance.

3-418(b). Also, restitutionary recovery is codified for a drawee who mistakenly pays or accepts a draft on which the drawer's signature is unauthorized, or who mistakenly pays a draft for which the drawer has issued a stop order countermanding payment. 3-418(a). Neither common-law nor statutory restitution is barred by the rules of Article 4 or other law that determine when an instrument is paid provisionally or finally. 3-418 comment 4. Restitution is an exception to finality of payment, so much so that

> [I]f an instrument is paid or accepted by mistake and the payor or acceptor recovers payment or revokes acceptance under [restitution law], the instrument is deemed not to have been paid or accepted and is treated as dishonored, and the person from whom payment is recovered has rights as a person entitled to enforce the dishonored instrument.

3-418(d).

Nevertheless, both the common-law recovery that Article 3 recognizes and the codified remedy it creates are limited by the usual immunity from restitution that the law affords good faith purchasers for value. They and people who rely are expressly protected by the following statutory defense:

> The remedies [of restitution] provided by [3-418(a)] or [3-418(b)] may not be asserted against a person who took the instrument in good faith and for value or who in good faith changed position in reliance on the payment or acceptance.

3-418(c). This defense effectively eliminates restitution except in rare cases because, almost always, the person who obtains payment or acceptance took the instrument in good faith from her transferor and paid value for it. In sum, therefore, mistaken payment or acceptance is rarely undone on the basis of restitution law.

Significantly, there is a large exception to the doctrine of finality and the good-faith purchaser defense of restitution law. Mistaken payment always can be recovered from a person who assumed the risk of the mistake, including a person who assumes the risk by operation of law. Therefore, when the law implies warranties that are breached upon presentment for payment or acceptance, the payor or acceptor can recover the payment or revoke the acceptance on the basis of warranty alone, despite the doctrine of finality and apart from restitution law and its defenses.

Article 3 implies presentment warranties which insure against certain risks that the payor or acceptor could not avoid without undue cost and delay. The mixed goal is to achieve fairness and efficiency in the allocation of risks between persons who pay or accept and persons who obtain payment or acceptance. Without warranties that remove some risks, which restitution law rarely does and only for mistake, payors and acceptors could not be expected to act as quickly and responsively as is necessary to accommodate business and commerce.

Presentment warranties

A person who pays or accepts an instrument may worry that she is doing so rightly, for the right person, and in the right amount. *Presentment warranties* provide some insurance against these risks. They are described in 3-417, which provides different warranty coverage for different payors. *Drawees of unaccepted drafts* are covered by 3-417(a). *All other payors* are covered by 3-417(d). In the case of the *drawee of an unaccepted draft*, including an uncertified check, the person who obtains payment or acceptance and prior transferors warrant to the drawee making payment or accepting the draft in good faith that:

> (1) the warrantor is, or was, at the time the warrantor transferred the draft, a person entitled to enforce the draft or authorized to obtain payment or acceptance of the draft on behalf of a person entitled to enforce the draft;
> (2) the draft has not been altered; and
> (3) the warrantor has no knowledge that the signature of the drawer of the draft is unauthorized.

3-417(a). In *all other cases*, there is only one warranty and it is the same as (a)(1):

> If (i) a dishonored draft is presented for payment to the drawer or an indorser or (ii) or any other instrument is presented for payment to a party obliged to pay the instrument, and (iii) payment is received, * * * [t]he person obtaining payment and a prior transferor of the instrument warrant to the person making payment in good faith that the warrantor is, or was, at the time the warrantor transferred the instrument, a person entitled to

enforce the instrument or authorized to obtain payment on behalf of a person entitled to enforce the instrument.

3-417(d)(1). The two provisions differ in the range of risks against which they provide insurance, but they agree that recovery for breach of warranty is apart from restitution law and not limited by it or the doctrine of finality of payment. Specifically, recovery for breach of warranty:

- does not depend on a mistake by the payor or acceptor,
- cannot be defended on the basis that the warrantor was a holder in due course or other good faith purchaser for value, 3-418(c), and,
- is not precluded by final payment under Article 4 or other law.

In sum, liability for presentment warranties is strict liability that is generally determined by the terms of the warranty provisions themselves without resort or deference to other Code rules or collateral law.

The reason for the different coverage between 3-417(a) and (d) is that the risks, and therefore the warranty insurance, are greater for a drawee of an unaccepted draft (including the common, uncertified check) than for anyone else. Typically, the drawee was not present when the instrument was issued and cannot know first hand if the draft is genuine and unaltered. If the drawer's signature is forged or unauthorized, the drawee acts gratuitously if she pays or accepts the draft. She cannot charge or recoup from the person whose name appears as drawer. The accounts between them will not be affected. If the amount of the instrument has been raised, which is the usual alteration, the drawee may get credit against the drawer only for the original amount. The drawee can avoid these risks by verifying the draft and its terms with the drawer, but doing so is costly in time, money, and transactional effects. The presentment warranties address these risks but provide only limited insurance for the risk of a bogus drawer's signature.

A drawee of an unaccepted draft also gambles that she is paying a person entitled to enforce the instrument. If she pays anyone else, she cannot charge anything to the drawer. Again, the accounts between them would be unaffected. It is even more costly to verify that the person making presentment is a person entitled to enforce. Practically, it is impossible.

The risk of paying the right person -- a person entitled to enforce -- is also faced by parties who pay other kinds of instruments, namely: makers of notes, acceptors and drawers of drafts, and indorsers. These people, however, can hardly complain about the risks to them that the instrument is not genuine or altered. Makers and drawers should know their own signatures, and should remember the terms of the instruments they signed.

The same is true for acceptors who pay. An acceptor, however, cannot be sure that the drawer's signature is valid or that the terms of the instrument were not altered before she accepted. On the other hand, warranties as to these matters were made to her as drawee when the instrument was presented for acceptance. 3-417(a)(1-2). A breach of these warranties to her as drawee "is a defense to the obligation of the drawee as acceptor to pay the draft." 3-417 comment 4. Moreover, "[i]f the drawee pays the accepted draft * * * [she] may recover the payment from any warrantor who was in breach of warranty when the draft was accepted." Id.

Indorsers are equally capable of detecting alterations made after they signed. Also, the transfer warranties protect indorsers against prior alterations and insure them that all of the earlier signatures on the instrument are authentic and authorized.

In sum, all that these other payors really need and deserve is a single warranty, that the person they pay is a person entitled to enforce the instrument and is therefore entitled to payment. The only person who needs wider warranty protection is the drawee of an unaccepted draft who pays or accepts the instrument. She gets wider (though incomplete) protection in the three warranties of 3-417(a). In every other case the payor gets the only warranty of 3-417(d), that the warrantor is entitled to enforce the instrument.

Although the warranty coverage is different between drawees of unaccepted drafts and payors in all other cases, the people who make the warranties are the same in every case for every payor or acceptor. The warrantors always are the person who obtains payment or acceptance *and also* every previous transferor, except that each transferor's warranties are limited to the condition of the instrument at the time of her transfer. She is not responsible for later defects. Similarly, the person who obtains payment or acceptance is not responsible for earlier defects that are corrected before she makes presentment, but such defects rarely (if ever) cause loss.

Nobody is liable for presentment warranties that she disclaims in the same way that transfer warranties are disclaimed, as discussed earlier. A general disclaimer that is not limited to either transfer or presentment warranties would seem to disclaim all of them, at least in favor of the person who makes the disclaimer. As is true with transfer warranties, however, presentment warranties cannot be disclaimed, either generally or specifically, with respect to checks. The warranties are too important to the banking industry's check-collection system.

law

Restatement Of Restitution (1937)
Chapter 2 (Mistake, Including Fraud)

Introductory Note. This Chapter states the conditions under which there is a right to restitution because of a mistake in the conferring of a benefit. The mistake may be one of law or fact; it may be as to the existence of an agreement or as to the existence of elements necessary for a contract; it may be as to what is transferred or what is received, as to the existence of a duty or of ownership, or as to the circumstances causing the conferring of a gratuity. The mistake may be the result of the fraud or innocent inducement of the other party or of a third person, or it may have resulted wholly from the inattention or lack of intelligence of the mistaken party.

There is no universal principle that one who makes a mistake in the conferring of a benefit is entitled to restitution. Nevertheless, if a benefit is conferred because of a serious mistake of fact by the transferor and he has not agreed to assume the risk of mistake, he is entitled to restitution unless the transferee or beneficiary is protected by virtue of the fact that he is a contracting party or a bona fide purchaser, or unless there is some other reason which makes it inequitable or inexpedient for restitution to be granted.

Topic 2 (Mistake Of Fact)
Title A. Money Paid by Mistake: In General

23. *Mistaken Belief That Third Party Owes Duty to Payee*

(1) A person is entitled to restitution from another to whom he had paid his own money because of the erroneous belief induced by a mistake of fact,

(a) that he was thereby performing the terms of a contract between a third person and the payee, which contract never existed, or had been avoided or otherwise discharged, or

(b) that he was performing a noncontractual duty owed by a third person to the payee, which duty was not owed ***.

Title B. Special Rules for Bills and Notes

29. *In General*

A person, who because of a mistake, has paid money to another in the payment or the purchase of a bill of exchange or promissory note, is entitled to restitution in accordance with the rules stated in §§6-28, except as modified by the rules stated in §§30-38.

33. *Mistaken Belief by Drawee as to Duty to Drawer*

The holder of a check or other bill of exchange who, having paid value in good faith therefor, receives payment from the drawee without reason to know that the drawee is mistaken, is under no duty of restitution to him although the drawee pays because of a mistaken belief that he has sufficient funds or that he is otherwise under a duty to pay.

34. *Duties of Good Faith and Care Owed by Holder of Instrument*

The holder of a bill or exchange or promissory note, who, under the rules stated in §§30-33, otherwise would be entitled to retain the amount received in payment thereof, is under a duty of restitution to the payor who paid because of a mistake of fact, if

(a) he made a misrepresentation causing the mistake, or

(b) at the time of payment he suspected or had reason to know of the mistake of the payor, except where before such time he acquired a contractual right to receive payment, or

(c) having received payment, he learned facts from which he had reason to know of the payor's mistake, and failed to use care to notify the payor, to the extent that the payor has been thereby prevented from obtaining restitution from a third person.

Price v. Neal

King's Bench, 1762
97 Eng. Rep. 871

This was a special case reserved at the sittings at Guildhall after Trinity term 1762, before Lord Mansfield.

It was an action upon the case brought by Price against Neal; wherein Price declares that the defendant Edward Neal was indebted to him in 80l. for money had and received to his the plaintiff's use; and damages were laid to 100l. The general issue was pleaded; and issue joined thereon.

It was proved at the trial, that a bill was drawn as follows -- "Leicester, 22d November 1760. Sir, six weeks after date pay Mr. Rogers Ruding or order forty pounds, value received for Mr. Thomas Ploughfor; as advised by, sir, your humble servant Benjamin Sutton. To Mr. John Price in Bush-Lane Cannon-Street, London;" indorsed "R. Ruding, Anthony Topham, Hammond and Laroche. Received the contents, James Watson and Son: witness Edward Neale."

That this bill was indorsed to the defendant for a valuable consideration; and notice of the bill left at the plaintiff's house, on the day it became due. Whereupon the plaintiff sent his servant to call on the defendant, to pay him the said sum of 40l. and take up the said bill: which was done accordingly.

That another bill was drawn as follows -- "Leicester, 1st February 1761. Sir, six weeks after date pay Mr. Rogers Ruding or order forty pounds, value received for Mr. Thomas Ploughfor; as advised by, sir, your humble servant, Benjamin Sutton. To Mr. John Price in Bush-Lane, Cannon-Street, London." That this bill was indorsed, "R. Ruding, Thomas Watson and Son. Witness for Smith, Right and Co." That the plaintiff accepted this bill, by writing on it, "Accepted John Price:" and that the plaintiff wrote on the back of it -- "Messieurs Freame and Barclay, pray forty pounds for John Price."

That this bill being so accepted was indorsed to the defendant for a valuable consideration, and left at his bankers for payment; and was paid by order of the plaintiff, and taken up.

Both these bills were forged by one Lee, who has been since hanged for forgery.

The defendant Neale acted innocently and bona fide, without the least privity or suspicion of the said forgeries or of either of them; and paid the whole value of the bills.

The jury found a verdict for the plaintiff; and assessed damages 80l. and costs 40s. subject to the opinion of the Court upon this question--

"Whether the plaintiff, under the circumstances of the case, can recover back, from the defendant, the money he paid on the said bills, or either of them."

Mr. Stowe, for the plaintiff, argued that he ought to recover back the money, in this action; as it was paid by him by mistake only, on supposition "that these were true genuine bills;" and as he could never recover it against the drawer, because in fact no drawer exists; nor against the forger, because he is hanged.

He owned that in a case at Guild-Hall, of *Jenys v. Fawler*, (an action by an indorsee of a bill of exchange brought against the acceptor,) Lord Raymond would not admit the defendants to prove it a forged bill, by calling persons acquainted with the hand of the drawer, to swear "that they believed it not to be so:" and he even strongly inclined, "that actual proof of forgery would not excuse the defendants against their own acceptance, which had given the bill a credit to the indorsee."

But he urged, that in the case now before the Court, the forgery of the bill does not rest in belief and opinion only; but has been actually proved, and the forger executed for it.

Thus it stands even upon the accepted bill. But the plaintiff's case is much stronger upon the other bill which was not accepted. It is not stated "that that bill was accepted before it was negotiated;" on the contrary, the consideration for it was paid by the defendant, before the plaintiff had seen it. So that the defendant took it upon the credit of the indorsers, not upon the credit of the plaintiff; and therefore the reason, upon which Lord Raymond grounds his inclination to be of the opinion "that actual proof of forgery would be no excuse," will not hold here.

Mr. Yates, for the defendant, argued that the plaintiff was not entitled to recover back this money from the defendant.

He denied it to be a payment by mistake: and insisted that it was rather owing to the negligence of the plaintiff; who should have inquired and satisfied himself "whether the bill was really drawn upon him by Sutton, or not." Here is no fraud in the defendant; who is stated "to have acted innocently and bona fide, without the least privity or suspicion of the forgery; and to have paid the whole value for the bills."

Lord Mansfield stopt him from going on; saying that this was one of those cases that could never be made plainer by argument.

It is an action upon the case, for money had and received to the plaintiff's use. In which action, the plaintiff can not recover the money, unless it be against conscience in the defendant, to retain it: and great liberality is always allowed, in this sort of action.

But it can never be thought unconscientious in the defendant, to retain this money, when he has once received it upon a bill of exchange indorsed to him for a fair and valuable consideration, which he had bona fide paid, without the least privity or suspicion of any forgery.

Here was no fraud: no wrong. It was incumbent upon the plaintiff, to be satisfied "that the bill drawn upon him was the drawer's hand," before he accepted or paid it: but it was not incumbent upon the defendant, to inquire into it. Here was notice given by the defendant to the plaintiff of a bill drawn upon him: and he sends his servant to pay it and take it up. The other bill, he actually accepts; after which acceptance, the defendant innocently and bona fide discounts it. The plaintiff lies by, for a considerable time after he has paid these bills; and then found out "that they were forged:" and the forger comes to be hanged. He made no objection to them, at the time of paying them. Whatever neglect there was, was on his side. The defendant had actual encouragement from the plaintiff himself, for negotiating the second bill, from the plaintiff's having without any scruple or hesitation paid the first: and he paid the whole value, bona fide. It is misfortune which has happened without the defendant's fault or neglect. If there was no neglect in the plaintiff, yet there is no reason to throw off the loss from one innocent man upon another innocent man: but, in this case, if there was any fault or negligence in any one, it certainly was in the plaintiff, and not in the defendant.

Per Cur'. Rule -- That the postea be delivered to the defendant.

Payroll Check Cashing v. New Palestine Bank
Court of Appeals of Indiana, First District, 1980
401 N.E.2d 752

Neal, Judge. *** The undisputed facts relevant to our review are as follows: A man purporting to be R.E. Merriman tendered three checks at PCC's [Payroll Check Cashing's] place of business. Each check was drawn on the account of Allied Construction Company (Allied) in the amount of $298.84, was payable to the order of R.E. Merriman, and bore the signature of Steve Snider. PCC had previously cashed checks drawn on Allied's account and was in possession of a credit rating from NPB [New Palestine Bank] which reflected Allied's average monthly balance and the length of time the account had been maintained. PCC cashed the checks, then indorsed and deposited them in a People's Bank and Trust Company (People's). Thence, the checks went through the banking cycle and were presented to NPB for payment. At NPB, the checks were inspected and paid. The cancelled checks were sent to Allied in its monthly statement. Allied notified NPB that the three checks bore forged signatures and forwarded affidavits of forgery. NPB returned the checks to People's, but they were refused due to untimely notice. NPB commenced the present action against PCC, and received a judgment for the amount claimed. PCC appeals.

* * *

Essentially, the issue is this: As between NPB, the drawee-payor bank which made payment on checks bearing forged drawer's signatures, and PCC, which cashed the checks, who should bear the loss?

* * *

The obstacle NPB must clear if it is to succeed in recovering against PCC is the final payment rule which has its roots in the 18th century case of *Price v. Neal*, (1762) 3 Burr. 1354, 97 Eng.Rep. 871. That case held that a drawee who pays an instrument bearing a forged drawer's signature is bound on his acceptance and cannot recover back his payment. Indiana has long followed this rule. In the pre-Uniform Commercial Code case of *Commercial and Savings Bank Company v. Citizens National Bank*, (1918) 68 Ind.App. 417, 424, 120 N.E. 670, 672, it was held that "(w)here a check purporting to have been drawn by one of *** (the drawee bank's) depositors is presented to the bank by a bona fide holder thereof for value, and is paid by the bank, the latter cannot compel such holder to whom payment has been so made to repay the amount to it, if it subsequently discovers the check to have been forged." An exception was recognized where the party accepting payment was negligent in failing to ascertain the identity of the person from whom it took the instrument.

The rule of *Price v. Neal*, supra, is maintained in the Code at Ind. Code 26-1-3-418. *** Ind. Code 26-1-4-213 defines the points at which final payment by a payor bank is effected as follows, in relevant part: [The court quoted U.C.C. §4-213(1)(c).] *** Unless the drawee can recover upon a warranty as prescribed by Ind. Code 26-1-4-207 or Ind. Code 26-1-3-417, its payment is final in favor of a holder in due course or a person who has in good faith changed his position in reliance on the payment.

The warranties made by a customer who obtains payment of an item are found at Ind. Code 26-1-4-207. PCC is a "customer" within the meaning of the Code. "Customer" is defined as "any person having an account with a bank or for whom a bank has agreed to collect items and includes a bank carrying an account with another bank." Ind. Code 26-1-4-104(1)(e).

The warranties extended by the parties in the bank collection process with which we are here concerned are found at Ind. Code 26-1-4-207(1) and (2).

The warranties of Ind. Code 26-1-4-207(2) do not run to payor banks. If the warranty of Ind. Code 26-1-4-207(2)(b), i.e., that all signatures are "genuine or authorized," were to run to payors, the doctrine of *Price v. Neal*, alive in the Code, would be obliterated. Further, the language "to his transferee and any subsequent collecting bank" would not include a payor, as a "collecting bank" does not include a payor bank. Ind. Code 26-1-4-105(d). *See also,* UCC §4-207, Official Comment (4). Thus, the drawee bank making payment receives only the warranties of Ind. Code 26-1-4-207(1). The warranty against material alterations, Ind. Code 26-1-4-207(1)(c), is not applicable in the instant case.

Ind. Code 26-1-4-207(1)(a) provides the warranty of good title to an item, and this warranty is not broken upon the transfer of a check bearing a forged drawer's signature. "A warranty of title is nothing more than an assurance that no one has better title to the check than the warrantor, and therefore, that no one is in a position to claim title as against the warrantee, as the payee or other owner of a genuine check could do if his indorsement were forged." *Aetna Life and Casualty Co. v. Hampton State Bank*, (Tex.Civ.App.1973), 497 S.W.2d 80, 84. The warranty of good title generally means that the item bears no forged indorsements. White and Summers, supra, 510. Thus the only party who could possibly claim title as against the warrantee NPB would be the ostensible payee Merriman, and this the latter has not done. We have already determined that this case is to be properly treated as a forged check case rather than a forged indorsement case. There being no evidence whatsoever that Merriman's indorsement was forged, we find that the warranty of good title to the checks was not broken.

This leaves the Ind. Code 26-1-4-207(2)(b) warranty against knowledge of the unauthorized signatures.

* * *

The trial court did not enter any findings to enlighten us as to its reasons for entering judgment for NPB. In applying our standard of review to this case, we are obliged to determine whether any theory exists to support the judgment below, and next to determine whether sufficient evidence is in the record to support such a theory.

As our discussion above reveals, payment of an item is final in favor of a holder in due course or a person who has in good faith changed his position in reliance on the payment, unless a warranty of Ind. Code 26-1-4-207(1) has been broken. Ind. Code 26-1-3-418. There is no evidence that PCC changed its position in reliance on the payment, and that was not an issue at trial.

Under these facts, two possibilities arise that could support the trial court's judgment: (1) The trial court found PCC lacked holder in due course status and was thereby ineligible for the finality protection accorded such holders by Ind. Code 26-1-3-418; or (2) PCC was a holder in due course of the checks but acted in bad faith to NPB, breaching the warranty of Ind. Code 26-1-4-207(1)(b) against knowledge of the unauthorized signatures.

* * *

The liability of a drawee bank paying an instrument bearing the unauthorized signature of its depositor-drawer is fixed. NPB presented as its only witness its president, Dale Fout. His testimony showed substantially the following relevant facts: The checks were presented to NPB for payment; NPB's employee inspected the checks; the checks were paid; Allied notified NPB that the signatures were unauthorized and forwarded to NPB affidavits to that effect; and NPB attempted to return the checks to PCC's depository bank without success. Physical evidence included only the checks and Allied's affidavits of forgery.

We believe that the foregoing facts are insufficient to establish a prima facie case of PCC's liability on the checks. NPB had the further burden of proof of bringing itself within the exceptions of *Price v. Neal*. NPB offered no evidence whatsoever tending to show that PCC failed as a holder in due course, that it transferred the checks with any knowledge of the unauthorized signatures, or that PCC acted in bad faith to NPB in any respect. If we consider the testimony of PCC's witness, Earl Schiesz, the most that we could infer is that PCC was possibly negligent in ascertaining the identity of R.E. Merriman, and as was recognized above, such negligence is no longer a viable exception to the rule of *Price v. Neal*. There is thus no showing that PCC is liable on the checks, and we cannot uphold the judgment of the trial court as a matter of law.

For the foregoing reasons, the judgment of the trial court is reversed. This cause is remanded with instructions to the trial court to enter judgment for Payroll Check Cashing, Division of Lou's Liquors.

Reversed and remanded with instructions.

Morgan Guaranty Trust Co. of New York v. American Savings and Loan Ass'n

United States Court of Appeals, Ninth Circuit, 1986
804 F.2d 1487

Fletcher, Circuit Judge. Morgan Guaranty Trust Company of New York appeals from the district court's grant of summary judgment in favor of American Savings & Loan Association and Chase Manhattan Bank on Morgan's claims for unjust enrichment, money had and received, and conversion. This appeal centers around a question of first impression: whether a holder-in-due-course is entitled to retain funds mistakenly paid to it on notes presented after the holder has knowledge that the maker of the notes has filed a petition for bankruptcy. We hold that it is not so entitled, and reverse in part.

BACKGROUND

The material facts of the case are undisputed. On July 8, 1982, American purchased two Manville Corporation bearer notes due and payable September 2, 1982, at Morgan, each with a face value of $5 million. The notes were held for American by Chase until maturity.

On August 26, 1982, Manville filed a Chapter 11 petition in bankruptcy. In response to the filing, Morgan, which held several Manville accounts, instituted special procedures to process Manville notes and checks. American, aware of the bankruptcy, did not anticipate payment of the notes on September 2.

On September 2, Chase, acting without instructions from American, presented the notes to Morgan through the New York Clearing House 2:00 a.m. exchange. [At that time, there was less than $2 million in available funds in Manville's accounts at Morgan.] Morgan effected a provisional settlement of $10 million for the notes at 10:00 a.m. that day. Under Clearing House rules, once the provisional settlement was made, Morgan could revoke it only by taking action before 3:00 p.m. the same day.

Morgan processed the notes in accordance with its special procedures for dealing with Manville paper. Unfortunately, the employees in the special channels were unfamiliar with Clearing House procedures. By the time bankruptcy counsel had been consulted and the decision to dishonor the notes was conveyed, it was 4:00 p.m., too late to revoke the settlement.

The next day, Chase transferred $10 million credit to American. Morgan demanded repayment of the money, first from Chase, then from American. American refused to return the money.

Morgan filed this action against American. American filed a third-party complaint against Chase seeking indemnity if American should be found liable on a promise by Chase, acting as its agent, to return the money to Morgan. American and Morgan filed cross-motions for summary judgment and Chase filed a motion to dismiss for failure to state a claim. American then moved for partial summary judgment on the issues raised in Chase's motion. All motions were presented and heard together.

The district court granted American's motion for summary judgment. *Morgan Guaranty Trust Co. v. American Savings & Loan Assoc.*, 605 F.Supp. 1086 (C.D.Cal.1985). The court found Morgan's claims for unjust enrichment, and money had and received, barred by section 3-418 of the New York Uniform Commercial Code. 605 F.Supp. at 1090-93. It found that the action for conversion would not lie because Morgan had not established any legal or equitable right to the money and because there was no specific, identifiable fund capable of being converted. Id. at 1094. Morgan timely appeals.
* * *

II. *Restitution Under New York Common Law*

Morgan argues that even if presentment of the Manville notes was proper, it has an equitable right to return of the money. American counters that equity does not provide a remedy for Morgan's careless payment and, even if there is a remedy, it has been displaced by the Uniform Commercial Code. We first address the availability of equitable remedies.

New York allows actions for unjust enrichment or money had and received to recover money paid by mistake where it would be inequitable for the payee to retain the money.

New York courts have allowed restitutionary actions for payments "by mistake" in a wide variety of circumstances, some of which appear to involve simple carelessness. * * * It appears that any unintentional result can be categorized as a "mistake".

The case that best demonstrates the breadth that New York courts give the mistaken payment theory of recovery is *Valley Bank of Nevada v. Bank of Commerce*, 74 Misc.2d 195, 343 N.Y.S.2d 191 (N.Y.City Civ.Ct.1973). In *Valley Bank*, a forged check drawn on the defendant was deposited with the plaintiff's predecessor-in-interest, the Bank of Las Vegas. After paying the check, the defendant discovered the forgery, and requested repayment from the Bank of Las Vegas. Although the court found that under the U.C.C. the defendant had no right to the money, Bank of Las Vegas paid. When its depositor refused to reimburse it, Bank of Las Vegas realized its mistake and sued defendant to recover the money. The court held that Bank of Las Vegas could recover whether its error was characterized as a mistake of fact (it may have believed its depositor would not object to being charged with funds to cover the forged check) or a mistake of law (it may have believed defendant had a valid claim). The court stated that because Bank of Las Vegas paid a claim on the basis of a mistake of fact or law and the payee "received a windfall which in fairness it should not be allowed to retain," the court would grant restitution. We believe that *Valley Bank* demonstrates that if a bank makes a payment, however carelessly, and the payee has no right to the money, New York courts will order return of the mistaken payment unless the payee has changed its position.

Applying New York's unjust enrichment analysis to the case before us, we have no trouble concluding that Morgan has an equitable right to restitution. It is "self-evident" that Morgan made some sort of mistake when it failed timely to dishonor the notes. Whether this error is characterized as mistake of fact or law is irrelevant under New York law. Once Manville filed its petition in bankruptcy, American had no right to receive payment on the notes until the proper disposition of Manville's estate was determined. Because American had no right to the money, Morgan is entitled to restitution unless American changed its position in reliance on the mistaken payment. American has made no showing of changed position, and we do not think it could. It had no reasonable expectation of receiving the money and Morgan notified it of the mistake immediately. We conclude that a New York court would not allow American to retain the $10 million windfall and would provide restitution to Morgan absent a statutory bar.

American argues that because Morgan's payment was voluntary, Morgan cannot get equitable relief. We disagree. A voluntary payment is one made "by design or intentionally or purposefully or of one's own accord or by the free exercise of the will." Morgan's failure to dishonor, which came about through careless failure to educate its employees as to deadlines, hardly fits this definition. The payment made in *Valley Bank* was more nearly "voluntary" than that made by Morgan, yet the New York court awarded restitution.

American argues, however, that Morgan should be treated as a volunteer because its mistake was the result of "conscious ignorance." Under the conscious ignorance doctrine, parties that have entered a contract or made payments knowing that they were uncertain of material facts are barred from claiming resulting mistakes as a basis for equitable relief. For example, a pipe manufacturer that funded repairs on leaky pipes conscious of the fact that it did not know who was responsible for the leaks cannot claim mistake as grounds for restitution when it later discovers the installer was at fault.

The conscious ignorance doctrine encourages parties to investigate before they act. Equity will not aid someone who deliberately forgoes an opportunity to discover material facts. However, American asks us to bar recovery because Morgan became aware, as the deadline flew by, that it did not know what the deadline was. Morgan never made a conscious decision to proceed in the face of insufficient information. We find the conscious ignorance doctrine inapplicable to this case. Because we find that Morgan would have an equitable remedy under New York law, we must determine whether that remedy has been displaced by the U.C.C.

III. *Displacement and the Uniform Commercial Code*

We begin our analysis of the effect of the U.C.C. on Morgan's right to restitution with section 1-103, which the leading commentators on the Code have called its most important provision. J. White & R. Summers, *Handbook of the Law Under the Uniform Commercial Code* 19 (2d ed. 1980) ("Handbook"). Section 1-103 provides:

> Unless displaced by the particular provisions of this Act, the principles of law and equity, including the law merchant and the law relative to capacity to contract, principal and agent, estoppel, fraud, misrepresentation, duress, coercion, mistake, bankruptcy, or other validating or invalidating cause shall supplement its provisions.

The drafters specifically intended that courts would use equitable principles and section 1-103 to create exceptions to U.C.C. provisions. Judges have a duty to consider the equities of a case unless equitable principles have been displaced, and "nothing short of an express code provision limiting plaintiff's remedy" demonstrates displacement.

American contends, and the district court held, that section 3-418 explicitly displaces Morgan's restitutionary remedy. Section 3-418 provides:

> Except for recovery of bank payments as provided in the Article on Bank Deposits and Collections (Article 4) and except for liability for breach of warranty on presentment under the preceding section, payment or acceptance of any instrument is final in favor of a holder in due course, or a person who has in good faith changed his position in reliance on the payment.

Morgan does not contend that American breached a warranty or that any provision of Article 4 gives it a right to restitution. It also concedes that American is a holder in due course. Consequently, our inquiry is whether 3-418 was intended to bar a restitutionary remedy to a payor bank against a holder in due course that had knowledge of the bankruptcy of the maker at the time the instrument was presented. We find nothing in the comments to the section or the case law to suggest that the question was ever considered by the drafters.

Section 3-418 was intended to codify the rule of *Price v. Neal*, 3 Burr. 1354, 97 Eng. Reprint 871 (1762), under which a drawee that accepts or pays an instrument on which the signature of the drawer is forged cannot recover from an innocent payee. Section 3-418, comment 1. The bank was said to be responsible for knowing the authentic signatures of its customers and having the means to compare them with the signature on the instrument. Id. Another rationale for the rule is to promote finality of transactions: "it is highly desirable to end the transaction on an instrument when it is paid rather than reopen and upset a series of commercial transactions at a later date when the forgery is discovered." Section 3-418, comment 1.

The provision has been applied in forgery cases, as well as in cases where instruments were paid despite insufficient funds or stop payment orders. Extension to the latter situations was contemplated by the drafters, and is justified by the same rationales as the Price v. Neal rule: the transactions should be final and the bank should be responsible for knowing the condition of its customers' accounts. See Section 3-418, comment 2. There are two major differences between the case before us and the cases contemplated by the drafters of 3-418. First, American had notice of the problem with the instrument. Second, the problem was bankruptcy of the maker, not forgery, insufficient funds or a stop order.

Section 3-418, by imposing liability on the party who best can avoid loss, makes perfect sense as a rule to determine which of two innocent parties should bear the loss. However, if both parties to a transaction know that the payee is not entitled to payment on an instrument, the rationales behind 3-418 are inapplicable. The payee who receives payment aware that he is not entitled to it does not have the same expectation of finality as an innocent payee and the payor bank in this circumstance does not have superior knowledge. A party who accepts payment on an instrument knowing that the payor was entitled to dishonor it justifiably receives less favorable treatment by a court of equity than a payee ignorant of any problem. American points to no cases applying section 3-418 to bar recovery from a payee who had notice that the payor had reason to dishonor the instrument. But see section 3-417, comment 4 (suggesting that, in absence of bad faith, a holder in due course that knowingly presents a forged instrument is entitled to keep money mistakenly paid on it).

The second distinguishing factor about this case is that the maker filed a petition in bankruptcy. The district court characterized this as an insufficient funds case. We disagree. Unlike defendants in insufficient funds cases, who generally have rights against the maker or drawer of the instrument, American had no right to any recovery from Manville until the proper distribution of Manville's estate was determined. The absence of such rights also distinguishes this case from stop payment and forgery cases. The payee of a check subject to a stop order often has a present right to recover against the drawer. If it does not have such a right, the payor bank can assert the drawer's rights and recover the mistaken payment. See section 4-407. Forgery cases generally arise between an innocent collecting bank and an innocent payor bank, both of whom have a present right to recover from the forger.

The fact that the holder of a note of a bankrupt maker has no present right of recovery makes the equitable balance different from that in other section 3-418 cases. A payee with no present right to payment is differently situated than a party who is entitled to money but cannot receive it because of the state of the drawer's account or the unavailability of a culpable forger.

In addition, one of the primary goals of the bankruptcy laws is to provide for equality of treatment among creditors. Allowing American to retain its windfall, derived solely from Morgan's mistake, puts it in a better position than similarly situated creditors. Although there is no provision of the bankruptcy laws that prohibits American from keeping the money, we would further the goal of equality of treatment by allowing restitution. Our point is not as the dissent would have it, that "This result is required by operation of federal bankruptcy law," but that bankruptcy policy is an additional equitable consideration favoring Morgan's position.

We conclude that 3-418 does not displace a restitutionary action by a payor bank for recovery of a mistaken payment to a payee with knowledge of the bankruptcy of the maker of the instrument in question. *Met Frozen Food v. Nat'l Bank of America*, 89 Misc.2d 1033, 393 N.Y.S.2d 643 (1977), * * * is not inconsistent with our holding. In Met, there were no allegations either that plaintiff was not entitled to receive payment at the time the bank attempted to dishonor the checks or that plaintiff knew that the checks should be dishonored. Moreover, the bank's reason for dishonoring the checks was *not* the bankruptcy of the depositor; the bankruptcy took place *after* the bank attempted to dishonor the checks. Nor is there any indication in the case that the bank knew of the impending bankruptcy when it attempted to dishonor. The fact that American is a holder in due course adds to the equitable balance on its side, but, on balance, does not overcome the equities in Morgan's favor.

In cases closely analogous to the one at bar, defendants have been allowed recovery of mistaken payments. When a payee discovers before presenting an instrument that its maker has died, he becomes a general creditor of the estate of the deceased and has no right to payment until the proper disposition of assets has been determined. The only case applying 3-418 in the context of the death of the maker found that 3-418 did not bar recovery of a mistaken payment from a payee with knowledge. Similarly, holders of cashier's checks drawn on an insolvent bank become creditors of the bank and can receive payment only in compliance with the National Bank Act. When an insolvent bank's receiver mistakenly honored cashier's checks, the Tenth Circuit held 3-418 inapplicable and ordered restitution. Id. Though these cases are not controlling, they support our conclusion that 3-418 does not bar restitution when the payee has actual knowledge that it has no present right to receive payment.

American argues that the warranty provisions of section 3-417 demonstrate that the drafters of the code explicitly displaced a restitutionary remedy against a payee with knowledge of bankruptcy. The 3-417 warranties are a major exception to the final payment rule of 3-418. Under 3-417(2)(e), when a party transfers an instrument for value, it warrants that it has no knowledge of insolvency proceedings instituted with respect to the maker. By contrast, the presentor of an instrument makes no such warranty. *See* section 3-417(1). American concludes from section 3-417 that the drafters, by not requiring a payee to warrant lack of knowledge of insolvency proceedings to a payor bank, made a deliberate decision to place the risk of loss from payments mistakenly made despite insolvency on the payor bank. Thus, it argues, a payee's knowledge of insolvency proceedings cannot form the basis of an equitable action. We read section 3-417 differently. Section 3-511(3)(a) provides that a payee with knowledge of the insolvency of the maker of an instrument *need not* present the instrument to preserve the rights that ordinarily are lost if timely presentment is not made. Section 3-511(3)(a) and comment 6. If the payee has knowledge of the bankruptcy, normally it will not present the instrument. The drafters had no reason to anticipate that the situation in this case would arise. On the other hand, there is no reason for the holder of a note of an insolvent maker not to transfer the instrument. For the protection of the transferee, the holder, who generally is in a better position to know of any insolvency proceedings, must warrant that it is not aware of them when it transfers the note. See section 3-417 comment 10. We conclude that the different treatment accorded to payor banks and transferees by section 3-417 was designed to protect transferees, not to assign the risk of loss in a situation the drafters had no reason to anticipate. Consequently, we remain unconvinced that the drafters specifically considered the effect of 3-418 on a payee with knowledge of bankruptcy.

American also contends that carving out "judicial exceptions" to the final payment rule of section 3-418 will "have a chilling effect upon the transferability and fluidity of commercial paper." This argument ignores section 1-103, which mandates equitable exceptions to the Code, and fails to recognize the narrowness of our holding. The case we decide today apparently has not arisen before and we think it unlikely that it will recur often enough to undermine seriously the operation of the nation's financial markets. The dissent similarly argues that our opinion will undermine the finality of commercial transactions. Contrary to the dissent's views, courts could not engage in this kind of analysis in every case to reach results they find "equitable". The vast majority of cases that implicate section 3-418 involve forgeries, insufficient funds or stop payment orders. They understandably are governed by the final payment rule. We believe that individual consideration under section

1-103 of the rare cases that involve situations apparently not contemplated by the drafters is merited and will not undermine the basic operation of section 3-418 or render "the Rules of the New York Clearing House mere verbiage."

* * *

We conclude that sections 3-418, 4-108 and 4-213 do not displace Morgan's equitable remedy for payment by mistake. We reverse the district court's grant of summary judgment for American and remand to allow the court to enter judgment for Morgan on its claims for unjust enrichment and money had and received.

* * *

Cynthia Holcomb Hall, Circuit Judge, wrote a [convincing] dissenting opinion.

Valley Bank & Trust Co. v. Zions First National Bank
Supreme Court of Utah, 1982
656 P.2d 425

Oaks, Justice: Defendant Zions Bank presented two cashier's checks for $12,500 to plaintiff Valley Bank and received payment. These cashier's checks, on which Valley Bank was drawer and drawee, were payable to "Peck & Shaw Fine Cars" and to an individual joint payee, Steven J. Gibbs on one check and Jeffrey Olson on the other. When paid by Valley Bank, each check was endorsed with the name of both joint payees and also bore Zions Bank's notation, "PEG" (prior endorsements guaranteed). After Valley Bank learned that the Peck & Shaw endorsements were forgeries, it brought this action against Zions Bank to recover on Zions' guarantee of endorsements or for breach of Zions' warranty of good title, as provided in U.C.A., 1953, §70A-3-417(1) and §70A-4-207(1). The question in this appeal is whether the district court correctly granted summary judgment to Zions Bank on the basis that the manner in which these cashier's checks were obtained excused Zions Bank (the collecting bank) from its normal liability to Valley Bank (the payor bank) for obtaining payment on a forged endorsement.

A cashier's check is a bill of exchange on which the payor bank is both the drawer and drawee. Rights with respect to cashier's checks are governed by Chapters 3 and 4 of the Uniform Commercial Code, as enacted in U.C.A., 1953, tit. 70A.

It is settled beyond argument that a collecting bank obtaining payment on a cashier's check bearing a forged endorsement is liable upon its warranty of good title and its guarantee of endorsements to the payor bank. This statutory liability under U.C.C. sections 3-417(1) and 4-207(1) duplicates the liability incurred by the guarantee of prior endorsements, which Zions Bank entered upon these cashier's checks.

Zions Bank has * * * arguments to avoid the effect of the normal rule of liability. On the basis of one or more of these arguments, it prevailed by summary judgment.

First, Zions Bank argues that Valley Bank cannot recover damages sustained in respect to cashier's checks for which it previously received payment. Specifically, Zions cites the fact that Gibbs and Olson each obtained his cashier's check by executing a note and security agreement promising to pay Valley Bank $12,500 plus finance charges and granting Valley Bank a security interest in a new automobile (serial number noted in the agreement) he intended to purchase from Peck & Shaw with the proceeds. Zions argues that Gibbs and Olson each used his loan proceeds to pay for his cashier's check, in consequence of which Valley has previously received payment and cannot recover a second time on Zions' guarantees and warranties. * * * [T]his previous-payment argument is without merit.

Even if a cashier's check were originally purchased with cash, its subsequent payment on a forged endorsement would subject the collecting bank to the statutory liability to the payor bank. In that event, the payor bank would not be recovering an amount beyond its payouts and liabilities. Its statutory recovery from the collecting bank would merely make the payor bank whole for the amount it had paid to the collecting bank on a check with a forged endorsement. The payor bank would remain liable to pay the cashier's check, properly endorsed, and would even be liable to the owner of the cashier's check for any damages he sustained from the conversion involved in the payor bank's paying that check on a forged endorsement. Similarly, in this case Valley Bank remains liable as drawer and drawee to the owner of the cashier's checks for their face amount. The previous payments it received in the form of the Gibbs and Olson promissory notes and purported security agreements were payments for its liability on the cashier's checks, not payments that can be used to forestall the statutory liability a collecting bank incurs to a payor bank that makes payment on forged endorsements.

Second, Zions Bank argues that Valley Bank is barred from recovery by the rule precluding a party from pursuing inconsistent remedies. This argument asserts that Valley Bank's actions against Gibbs and Olson on their defaulted promissory notes and for fraudulently procuring the loans constituted such an election. But the remedies are not inconsistent, as explained above. In respect to each of these cashier's checks, Valley Bank has made a payout to the collecting bank and has a continuing liability to the owner of the check. Valley Bank is entitled to pursue different remedies to attempt to make itself whole in respect to both transactions.

* * *

The summary judgment for Zions Bank being contrary to law, the judgment of the district court is reversed, and the case is remanded for further proceedings consistent with this opinion. Costs to appellant.

practice

Case 1

A drew a draft payable to herself forging B's signature as drawer. The draft was drawn on C, whom A knew owed money to B. A indorsed the draft, and sold the instrument to D. D presented the draft to C, and C paid it.

a. B eventually demanded the money that C owed her. C's defense is that the credit was satisfied by her paying the draft presented by D. Is this a good defense?

No

b. If C is liable to B, can C recover against D for breach of warranty upon presentment? See 3-417(a).

c. Can C recover under the law of restitution? See 3-418(c).

d.   Suppose that C is a bank where B maintains her checking account, and D is another bank that cashed the check for A. Are the answers the same?   *Essentially*

Case 2

B was indebted to S for the price of goods. S knew that B was insolvent but continued to demand payment. Finally, B gave S a check just to get S off her case. S did not expect the check to clear. Sure enough, B's account was empty, but -- surprise! surprise! -- the drawee "mistakenly" paid the check. Can the drawee recover the money from S? 3-418(c); *Morgan Guaranty,* supra.

Case 3

"Al Debtor signed and delivered to Mary Truebleu, the longtime and trusted secretary of Debtor's creditor Bob Trust, the following written instrument:

I promise to pay on demand to Bob Trust, or order, the sum of $250, with interest thereon at the annual rate of six per centum (6%) from the date hereof.

Witness my hand this 15th day of July, 1977.

(signed) Al Debtor

"On delivering the instrument to Mary Truebleu, Al received assurance that she would deliver it to Bob Trust on his return to his office the following week. However, on July 18th Mary cleverly forged Bob Trust's name to an endorsement in blank on the back of the instrument, and the following day sold it, purportedly on Bob Trust's behalf, to Don Holder who paid Mary Truebleu in cash the sum of $245 in good faith, believing the endorsement to be that of Bob Trust. On August 19, 1977, Don Holder presented the instrument to Al Debtor who, not knowing Bob Trust's endorsement had been forged, paid Don Holder the face amount of $250 plus accumulated interest. A few days later Al Debtor learned of the forgery committed by Mary Truebleu, and asks whether you believe he has a right of action to recover from Don Holder the $250 and interest he has paid him. What advice would you give Al Debtor on this question? State and discuss legal reasons for your opinion? Arkansas Bar Examination Question 1 (July, 1978).

a.   Why would Al want to recover from Don?

b.   Can Al recover from Don under the law of restitution? 3-418.

c.   Can Al otherwise recover from Don? 3-417(a)(1).

d.   On what theory could Don recover from Mary? 3-416(a).

Case 4

B gave S a check for the price of goods. T stole the check and cashed it at DB Bank. The drawee, PB Bank, "paid" the check and charged B's account.

a. How is it possible that the loss, which first visits S, could ultimately be shifted to PB Bank? 3-309; 4-401.

b. Could PB Bank recover from DB Bank? 3-417(a); 4-208(a).

Chapter 5. Holder In Due Course And Like Rights

A holder in due course is Article 3's most favored person. It gives her advantages with respect to an instrument that no one else enjoys. These advantages are scattered throughout Article 3 and are explored throughout this book. Most important, a holder in due course is immune to the personal defenses of prior parties, and takes free of all property claims to the instrument. In this respect, holder in due course is an exception to the general rule of derivative title which provides that a transferee of property gets no greater rights than her transferor.

What explains this affection for the holder in due course of a negotiable instrument? Part of the answer may be historical. At common law, the bona fide purchaser of tangible personal property took free of equities and defenses while the purchaser of a chose in action did not. Once it was decided that the underlying contract right merged with the instrument upon issue, it was but a short step to the conclusion that the good faith purchasers of this form of tangible personal property also "took free." A more complete answer, however, must take into account perceived commercial needs for a protected market in which drafts and notes can be freely and safely traded. The chief hallmarks of Article 3 are economic advantages of free and easy transferability, requirements of form on the face of the writing and in the process of negotiation, and protection of purchasers "in due course" who rely on this form in the various credit markets; and all of these hallmarks reflect a body of law intended to facilitate trade in instruments.

§ 1. Requirements of Due-Course Status

To earn the special protections of a holder in due course, the holder of an instrument must meet certain requirements. First and second, she must be the *holder* of an *instrument*. These basic requirements are covered elsewhere. This chapter focuses on the additional, peculiar requirements commonly known as the *due-course requirements*. They require the holder to take the instrument:

- for value;
- without notice --
  - ✓ that the instrument is overdue or has been dishonored or that there is an uncured default with respect to payment of another instrument issued as part of the same series,
  - ✓ that the instrument contains an unauthorized signature or has been altered,
  - ✓ of any claim to the instrument, and
  - ✓ that any party has a defense or claim in recoupment described in subsection 3-305(a);
- without reason to question the authenticity of the instrument;
- in good faith; and
- apart from certain unusual circumstances.

3-302(a).

story

For value

1. Article 3's Definition -- 3-303

The Code contains two overlapping but clearly different definitions of "value." A general definition in Article 1 defines value broadly as including, among other things, "any consideration sufficient to support a simple contract." 1-201(44)(d). Article 3 defines value much more narrowly, 3-303(a), and this definition controls the meaning of value for purposes of Article 3. Throughout this discussion, therefore, value is used only in the narrower sense of 3-303.

Fundamentally important is the distinction between "value" and "consideration." First, their major roles under Article 3 are quite different. The primary legal significance of value is as a requirement for holder in due course. 3-302(a)(2)(i). Value is an essential element in establishing this status. The primary legal significance of consideration is that a defect in consideration for the instrument (lack of, nonperformance, failure) is a defense to payment against a person who lacks the rights of a holder in due course. 3-303(b), 3-305(a)(2).

Second, the meanings of value and consideration are not the same, but to some extent the key to the meaning of value is consideration. Consideration means the same in Article 3 as in the law of simple contracts. 3-303(b). A reasonably workable definition is that consideration consists of doing or promising to do what one is not already legally bound to do, or refraining or promising to refrain from doing what one has a legal right to do, in return for a promise. Value is defined by 3-303(a), which provides that an instrument is issued or transferred for value if:

- the instrument is issued or transferred for a promise of performance, to the extent the promise has been performed;
- the transferee acquires a security interest or other lien in the instrument other than a lien obtained by judicial proceeding;
- the instrument is issued or transferred as payment of, or as security for, an antecedent claim against any person, whether or not the claim is due;
- the instrument is issued or transferred in exchange for a negotiable instrument; or
- the instrument is issued or transferred in exchange for the incurring of an irrevocable obligation to a third party by the person taking the instrument.

Thus, value is both broader and more narrow than consideration: broader because it includes preexisting debt and more narrow because it excludes an executory promise.

2. Bank Credit As Value -- 4-210 & 4-211

Very often, it is important to decide if and when a depositary bank gave credit for a check deposited by its customer. It is important in the event the check is dishonored; the depositary bank cannot recoup the credit from the depositor's account; the bank decides to enforce the instrument against the drawer or an indorser; and this person has personal defenses to payment of the instrument. Under these circumstances the outcome is determined by the extent to which the bank is a holder in due course. Usually, the only issue is how much value the bank gave the depositor before the bank learned of the defense. For this situation there is a special definition of value in Article 4 which is basically consistent with 3-303. It refines 3-303 for application in this particular context.

The Article 4 definition is in two parts, 4-210 and 4-211. The easier analysis begins with 4-211 which basically provides that, for purposes of holder in due course, the depositary bank has given value to the extent that the bank has a security interest in the check. If and when the bank acquired a security interest in the check (a/k/a "item") is explained by 4-210(a):

> A collecting bank has a security interest in an item and any accompanying documents or the proceeds of either:
> (1) in case of an item deposited in an account, to the extent to which credit given for the item has been withdrawn or applied;
> (2) in case of an item for which it has given credit available for withdrawal as of right, to the extent of the credit given, whether or not the credit is drawn upon or there is a right of charge-back; or
> (3) if it makes an advance on or against the item.

Here's what 4-210(a) means and how it usually works. In the typical case in which a bank receives one or more negotiable instruments for deposit in a customer's account, the bank immediately credits the customer's account, but the depositor acquires no right to draw against the items -- and the bank need not permit her to do so -- until the item is collected, subject to a contrary agreement between the parties and subject also to federal law on funds availability. This law limits how long a depositary bank can withhold credit to a customer's account that was given for a deposited check. It determines when, by federal right, the funds must be made available to the customer if the check has not been sooner dishonored. See Chapter 6 infra.

As might be expected, the bank does not become a holder for value merely by crediting the depositor's account. The bank is safe without due-course protection because the bank can take back the credit from the customer's account if the check is dishonored. 4-214(a).

If, however, the depositor is permitted to draw against a deposited item before it is collected, the bank immediately becomes a holder for value concerning that item to the extent of the withdrawal. 4-211; 4-210(a)(1). Consequently, if it becomes necessary for the bank to sue on the item, the bank normally enjoys the status of holder in due course to the amount of the credit withdrawn or applied before the bank learned of a defense or claim. This is true even though the deposit is made under a restrictive indorsement such as "for deposit only" and the deposit slip expressly states that the bank is acting only as agent for collection. It is reasoned that the provision is for the protection of the bank and that the bank may waive the protection.

When a bank credits a depositor with a series of deposits and permits a number of withdrawals over a period of time, it is not always easy to determine whether the depositor has been permitted to withdraw funds credited on the basis of a particular item before the bank learns of a claim or defense on the item. In tracing the deposits to withdrawals, the Code applies the rule of "first in, first out" or "fifo" as it is sometimes called: "credits first given are first withdrawn." 4-210(b).

In an exceptional case, the depositor may have a right to draw against the check that imposes on the bank a corresponding duty to allow withdrawals before the drawee has paid the check. Whether this right and the corresponding duty arise from an express contract between the parties or from federal or state law governing the collection process, the bank is considered as having given value immediately when the right arises and before any withdrawal against the item has been made. 4-210(a)(2). If the depositor's contract with the bank entitles her to withdraw immediately any credit given for a check that she deposits, the bank has given value in the amount of the check as soon as the check is deposited, "whether or not the credit is drawn upon or there is a right of charge-back." 4-210(a)(2).

Sometimes, a bank takes an instrument for collection that is not a check of its customer. For example, the customer may transfer an ordinary draft to the bank that is drawn on a buyer of goods who bought them from the seller and owes the price. The draft orders the buyer to pay the seller a sum that equals the price. The bank will forward the draft through banking channels for the purpose of having it presented to the buyer-drawee for payment or acceptance. The draft is not deposited, and there are no withdrawals against it in the usual sense. Yet, the bank may buy the draft from the customer, loan against the draft, or otherwise make advances on or against it. To this extent, the bank gives value. 4-210(a)(3).

Without notice

A further requirement of holder in due course is taking the instrument "without notice" --

- that the instrument is overdue or has been dishonored or that there is an uncured default with respect to payment of another instrument issued as part of the same series,
- that the instrument contains an unauthorized signature or has been altered,
- of any claim to the instrument, or
- that any party has a defense or claim in recoupment described in subsection 3-305(a).

3-302(a)(2). Notice of any of these facts should serve as a danger signal to a person who is contemplating taking an instrument for value. It should warn her that she may be buying a lawsuit and that she should not expect to occupy the favored position of holder in due course.

Of course, a person should be barred from being a holder in due course by *actual* knowledge of any of these facts. If she sees the danger signal but chooses to disregard it, she must take the consequences. But actual knowledge is not essential to "notice" of a fact, which is established by any of three alternative tests:

(a) he has *actual knowledge* of it; or
(b) he has *received* a notice or notification of it; *or*
(c) from all the facts or circumstances known to him at the time in question he *has reason to know* that it exists.

1-201(25) (emphasis added).

Receiving notice of a fact, which itself amounts to notice, does not require actually seeing or even getting in hand a writing that describes the fact: "A person 'receives' a notice or notification when (a) it comes to his attention; *or* (b) *it is duly delivered * * * at any * * * place held out by him as the place for receipt of such communications.*" 1-201(26) (emphasis added).

"*Reason to know*" of a fact also establishes notice even though the person herself, actually, is completely unaware of the fact and has never received a notification of it. Notice by this test is sometimes referred to as *inferable knowledge*. A person is charged with knowledge of information that a reasonable person would infer from the facts and circumstances actually known to her. This test does not require a person to investigate, not even if a reasonable person would do so; but the test does require a person to open her eyes to everything she already knows. She is charged with notice of facts that others would see or discern from her own knowledge, even if she herself was subjectively blind to these facts.

Constructive notice does not count. For example, a public filing or recording of a property interest often works to protect the interest against subsequent lienors or purchasers of the property. Such a recording, however, "does not of itself constitute notice of a defense, claim in recoupment, or claim to the instrument" that would bar a person from becoming a holder in due course of it. 3-302(b).

To bar a purchaser from becoming a holder in due course, any kind of notice must be received at such time and in such manner as to give a reasonable opportunity to act on it. 3-302(f). If notice is given to an organization, it is effective when it is brought to the attention of the person conducting the transaction or when it would have been brought to her attention with the exercise of due diligence, whichever is sooner. 1-201(27). For example, a notice received by a bank president a minute before a teller cashes a check is not likely to be effective to bar it from being a holder in due course. But if the president acts swiftly and succeeds in bringing the notice to the teller's attention before she cashes the check, the bank is charged with notice and cannot be a holder in due course of the check.

Suppose that notice was received so long ago that the fact is forgotten by the time the instrument is purchased. Can the purchaser be a holder in due course? Prior to the Code, courts were divided. See *Graham v. White-Phillips Co.*, 296 U.S. 27, 56 S.Ct. 21, 80 L.Ed. 20 (1935). The Code avoids taking sides by providing that "[t]he time and circumstances under which a notice or notification may cease to be effective are not determined by this Act." 1-201(25).

Authenticity of the instrument

Former law provided that a person has notice of a defense or claim if "the instrument is so incomplete, bears such visible evidence of forgery or alteration, or is otherwise so irregular as to call into question its validity, terms or ownership or to create an ambiguity as to the party to pay." 3-304(1)(a) (1989 Official Text). *The 1990 Article 3 makes the condition of the instrument a wholly separate requirement of holder in due course*, requiring that "the instrument when issued or negotiated to the holder does not bear such apparent evidence of forgery or alteration or is not otherwise so irregular or incomplete as to call into question its authenticity." 3-302(a)(1). The word "'authenticity' is used to make clear that the irregularity or incompleteness must indicate that the instrument may not be what it purports to be." 3-302 comment 1. It makes no difference, at least not under the new law, that the obligor's claim or defense is unrelated to the irregularity or incompleteness of the instrument. It also makes no difference, technically, that the taker is without notice of the irregularity or incompleteness; but the problem must be "apparent" and in this event the taker ordinarily would have reason to know of the problem and thus would have notice of it. The statute imposes a test of "crude alteration" that would "excite suspicion." *J.M. Heinike Associates, Inc. v. Liberty Nat'l Bank*, 560 N.Y.S.2d 720 (S.D. 1990) (Obliteration of restrictive "for deposit" indorsement did not meet the test because it is not uncommon for a payee initially to decide to deposit a check and then decide to cash it.).

Most cases are clear, such as bungled forgery or an obvious alteration raising the amount of the instrument. But an irregularity also might be a change of date, of the payee's name, or of some other material term. Also, a person who purchases a negotiable instrument is expected to examine the reverse side as well as the face. Consequently, she is charged with notice of any irregularities that appear there, including irregular or telling indorsements. Hence, a person who receives an instrument which has been indorsed on the reverse side, "In payment for poker losses (Signed) J. Smith" would be charged with knowing of a defense in most states even though she did not read the indorsement or know that gambling transactions are illegal. But the fact that an indorsement is qualified, or for accommodation or restrictive, or contains words of guarantee or assignment, is not sufficient of itself to charge a person with notice of a defense or claim.

It is entirely possible, of course, for an instrument to have been altered or forged without any apparent evidence of the wrongdoing. Notice of the alteration or forgery from extrinsic facts and circumstances nevertheless bars due-course status. 3-302(a)(2)(iv).

Good faith

Even though a holder acquires an apparently perfect instrument for value and without prohibited notice, she does not qualify as a holder in due course unless she also takes the instrument in "*good faith*." Because the requirement of good faith is so often confused with the requirement of taking without notice, perhaps it should be emphasized that these are two separate requirements. No degree of good faith makes it possible for one who fails to meet the notice requirement to qualify as a holder in due course, and good faith is not established by showing that a person received an instrument without notice. Of course, these two requirements are closely related so that the conclusion that a holder has failed to satisfy one of these requirements is often bolstered by evidence that she failed to meet the other; but doing so is overkill. Failing either requirement is sufficient by itself to deny due-course status.

Since at least as early as *Miller v. Race*, 1 Burr. 452, 97 Eng.Rep. 398 (1758), the courts, and more recently, the legislatures, have been trying to develop a definition of good faith that is satisfactory to all concerned. That they have not been wholly successful is attributable mainly to disagreement over the extent to which the test of good faith should be *subjective*, depending only on what is found to be the state of the holder's mind, or *objective*, depending on other facts. As seen above, the requirement that a holder give value is totally objective, having nothing to do with the holder's state of mind when she takes the instrument. In contrast, the requirement of taking without notice sometimes depends on the holder's state of mind and sometimes on extrinsic circumstances; thus it is both subjective and objective.

The 1952 Edition of the Code required "good faith," "including observance of reasonable commercial standards of any business in which the holder may be engaged." 3-302 (1952 Official Text). This latter requirement was deleted from later editions because it seemed to imply an objective rather than a subjective test of good faith. The test of good faith as it is existed through 1989 was entirely subjective, meaning "honesty in fact in the conduct or transaction concerned." 1-201(19) (1989 Official Text). Taken literally, this test does not require either diligence or prudence. See *Riley v. First State Bank*, 469 S.W.2d 812 (Tex.Civ.App.1971). A gullible person might be found to have acted in good faith in circumstances where a shrewd person would not. It protects the person with the "pure" heart and the "empty" head.

Under the subjective test, a holder is not necessarily barred from being a holder in due course merely because she receives the instrument from a total stranger or for substantially less than its face value, or because in some way she has failed to observe reasonable standards of the business community. It is said that the subjective test promotes the policy of encouraging the free transferability of commercial paper. In some cases, however, it has appeared to run counter to the general policy of protecting consumers from unfair or deceptive practices; and some courts and legislatures have reacted against it.

The reaction grew so that the 1990 Article 3 changed the test of good faith. ***Now, it is both subjective and objective.*** It means "honesty in fact *and the observance of reasonable commercial standards of fair dealing*," 3-103(a)(4) (emphasis added), which is "concerned with the fairness of conduct rather than the care with which an act is performed." 3-103 comment 4. History explains that when this objective test is added to the subjective, "a business man engaging in a commercial transaction is not entitled to claim the peculiar advantages which the law accords to the * * * holder in due course * * * on a bar showing of 'honesty in fact' when his actions fail to meet the generally accepted standards current in his business, trade, or profession." 3-302 comment 1 (1952 Official Text).

The most important issue of the objective test is whether or not it imposes an obligation to investigate the circumstances of an instrument before purchasing it. A purely subjective test requires no investigation, unless the failure to inquire indicates a deliberate desire to evade knowledge because of a belief that further investigation would disclose an actual claim or defense. The objective test, however, has roots that extend to *Gill v. Cubitt* (1824) 107 Eng.Rep. 806. This case was commonly regarded as standing for a duty to inquire into merely suspicious circumstances, and many American courts followed *Gill* until about the end of the nineteenth century when the Negotiable Instruments Law (NIL) rejected it.

Arguably, *Gill* was revived and codified by the objective test of good faith of the 1952 Article 3, and it is this test -- or something very close to it -- that the 1990 Article 3 resurrects. If *Gill* is again good law, a duty to investigate may now be an element of good faith and thus may be a necessary step in becoming a holder in due course whenever commercially reasonable fairness would require inquiry. If and when such a duty exists and is not obeyed, the holder will be charged with facts that a reasonable inquiry would have uncovered.

It is uncertain, however, that the 1952 Article 3 was intended to revive *Gill*. Robert Braucher, *The Legislative History of the Uniform Commercial Code*, 58 Co-LUM. L. REV. 798, 813 (1958) (the sponsors of the Code in New York argued that the objective test of good faith for holder in due course did not incorporate *Gill* but merely made reasonable commercial standards relevant on the issue of good faith). It is even less certain that *Gill* is behind the 1990 objective test of good faith. Moreover, because accepted business practice will seldom require investigation and because the law strongly favors the free flow of negotiable instruments, it is likely that only the most compelling circumstances would trigger any duty to inquire that might be part of the new objective test of good faith. For one reason or another, therefore, the objective and subjective tests of good faith probably will not be very different in terms of requiring investigation.

Apart from certain unusual circumstances

Even though she satisfies the usual requirements previously described, a person does not acquire the rights of a holder in due course of an instrument taken:

- by legal process or by purchase in an execution, bankruptcy, or creditor's sale or similar proceeding,
- by purchase as part of a bulk transaction not in the ordinary course of business of the transferor, or
- as a successor in interest to an estate or other organization.

3-302(c). In these situations the transferee merely is acquiring the rights of the prior holder and there is no substantial interest in facilitating commercial transactions, which is the underlying reason for giving holders in due course their special advantages. Thus, there is no holder in due course when:

- an instrument is purchased in an execution sale or sale in bankruptcy or is acquired by other legal process;
- a representative, such as an executor, administrator, receiver or assignee for the benefit of creditors takes the instrument as part of an estate;
- a bank purchases a substantial part of the paper held by another bank which is threatened with insolvency and seeks to liquidate its assets;

- a new partnership takes over for value all of the assets of an old one after a new member has entered the firm;
- a reorganized or consolidated corporation takes over the assets of a predecessor; or
- a state bank commissioner sells the assets of an insolvent bank.

3-302 comment 5.

Of course, federal law can preempt and often gives protection like that of a holder in due course to federal insurers of financial institutions which take over insolvent banks. Also, in accordance with the shelter principle discussed later, the transferee in any of these situations acquires the due-course rights of any prior holder who was a holder in due course.

Citizens Nat'l Bank v. Fort Lee Sav. & Loan Ass'n
Superior Court of New Jersey, Law Division, 1965
89 N.J.Super. 43, 213 A.2d 315

Botter, J.S.C. Citizens National Bank of Englewood has moved for summary judgment to recover monies advanced against a check which was deposited with the bank for collection but was later dishonored. The issue is whether the bank should be protected for advances made to its depositor before the check cleared. The summary judgment is sought against the drawer and payee-indorser who stopped payment on the check.

On August 27, 1963, George P. Winter agreed to sell a house in Fort Lee, New Jersey to defendant Jean Amoroso and her husband. On the same day Amoroso requested her bank, Fort Lee Savings and Loan Association (Fort Lee Savings), to issue the bank's check to her order for $3,100 to be used as a deposit on the contract for sale. Fort Lee Savings complied by drawing the check against its account with the Fort Lee Trust Company. Later that day Amoroso indorsed and delivered the check to Winter, and he deposited the check in his account at the plaintiff bank. At that time he had a balance of $225.33. After the $3,100 check was deposited the bank cashed a $1,000 check for him against his account. In addition, on August 27 or August 28, the bank cleared and charged Winter's account with four other checks totaling $291.76.

The next day Amoroso discovered that Winter had previously sold the property to a third party by agreement which had been recorded in the Bergen County Clerk's Office. Amoroso immediately asked Winter to return her money. She claims that he admitted the fraud and agreed to return the deposit. But when Mrs. Amoroso and her husband reached Winter's office they learned that he had attempted suicide. He died shortly thereafter.

Upon making this discovery, in the afternoon of August 28, the Amorosos went to Fort Lee Savings to advise it of the fraud and request it to stop payment on the check. The bank issued a written stop payment order which was received by the Fort Lee Trust Company, the drawee, on the following day, August 29. In the meantime the $3,100 check was sent by plaintiff through the Bergen County Clearing House to the Fort Lee Trust Company. By then the stop payment order had been received. Notice of nonpayment was thereafter transmitted to plaintiff.

Plaintiff contends that, under the Uniform Commercial Code, N.J.S. 12A:1-101 et seq., N.J.S.A., it is a holder in due course to the extent of the advances made on Winter's account and is entitled to recover these moneys from the drawer and payee-indorser of the check. Plaintiff's claim against the drawee, Fort Lee Trust Company, was voluntarily dismissed by plaintiff at the pretrial conference.

The central issue is whether plaintiff bank is a holder in due course, since a holder in due course will prevail against those liable on the instrument in the absence of a real defense. Of course, it must first be determined that plaintiff is a "holder" if plaintiff is to be declared a holder in due course. Amoroso contends that plaintiff bank does not own the check because it is only an agent of its depositor Winter for collection purposes and, consequently, plaintiff is not a "holder." It is true that a collecting bank is presumed to be an agent of the owner of the item unless a contrary intention appears, or until final settlement. N.J.S. 12A:4-201(1), N.J.S.A. Assuming that the bank was at all times an agent in this case, it does not follow that the bank cannot also be a holder. On the contrary, a collecting bank may be a holder whether or not it owns the item. N.J.S. 12A:4-201(1) and 12A:3-301, N.J.S.A. The definition of "holder" includes a person who is in possession of an instrument indorsed to his order or in blank. N.J.S. 12A:1-201(20), N.J.S.A. It is clear that the bank is a holder of the check notwithstanding that it may have taken the check solely for collection and with the right to charge back against the depositor's account in the event the check is later dishonored.

To be a holder in due course one must take a negotiable instrument for value, in good faith and without notice of any defect or defense. N.J.S. 12A:3-302(1), N.J.S.A. Amoroso contends that plaintiff did not act in good faith or is chargeable with notice because it allowed Winter to draw against uncollected funds at a time when his account was either very low or overdrawn. Winter's account was low in funds. However, this fact, or the fact that Winter's account was overdrawn, currently or in the past, if true, would not constitute notice to the collecting bank of an infirmity in the underlying transaction or instrument and is not evidence of bad faith chargeable to the bank at the time it allowed withdrawal against the deposited check. N.J.S. 12A:1-201(19) and (25); N.J.S. 12A:3-304, N.J.S.A.

* * *

[A] depositary bank may properly charge an account by honoring a check drawn by a depositor even though it creates an overdraft. N.J.S. 12A:4-401(1), N.J.S.A. It would be anomalous for a bank to lose its status as a holder in due course merely because it has notice that the account of its depositor is overdrawn.

Lacking bad faith or notice of a defect or defense, plaintiff will be deemed a holder in due course if one additional element is satisfied, namely, the giving of value for the instrument. Prior to the adoption of the Uniform Commercial Code the general rule was that a bank does give value and is a holder in due course to the extent that it allows a depositor to draw against a check given for collection notwithstanding that the check is later dishonored. ***

This result is continued by provisions of the Uniform Commercial Code which give plaintiff a security interest in the check and the monies represented by the check to the extent that credit given for the check has been withdrawn or applied. N.J.S. 12A:4-208 and 209, N.J.S.A. See also N.J.S. 12A:4-201, N.J.S.A. and U.C.C. Comment 5 thereunder. ***

The New Jersey Study Comment under N.J.S. 12A:4-209, N.J.S.A., includes the following:

> Because the bank is a holder of the item in most cases, it is possible for it to be a holder in due course if it otherwise qualifies by its good faith taking, prior to maturity,

for value. See, U.C.C. sec. 3-302; N.I.L. sec. 52 (N.J.S.A. 7:2-52). It is important for a bank to be a holder in due course when the depositor fails, for this status enables it to prevail over the obligor (drawer or maker) of the instrument even though the obligor has some personal defense against the payee (depositor).

It would hinder commercial transactions if depositary banks refused to permit withdrawal prior to clearance of checks. Apparently banking practice is to the contrary. It is clear that the Uniform Commercial Code was intended to permit the continuation of this practice and to protect banks who have given credit on deposited items prior to notice of a stop payment order or other notice of dishonor. N.J.S. 12A:4-208 and 209, N.J.S.A., supra[.] ***

It is also contended that liability on the check is excused because N.J.S. 12A:4-403, N.J.S.A. gives Fort Lee Savings the right to order Fort Lee Trust Company to stop payment on the check. However, U.C.C. comment 8 under this section makes it clear that the stop payment order cannot avoid liability to a holder in due course. "The payment can be stopped but the drawer remains liable on the instrument to the holder in due course ***."

Finally, Amoroso attempts to raise the fraud perpetrated by Winter against Amoroso as a defense to plaintiff's claim. Plaintiff's status as a holder in due course insulates it from all personal defenses of any party to the instrument with whom it has not dealt, although real defenses may still be asserted. N.J.S. 12A:3-305, N.J.S.A. The defense raised here is fraud in inducing Amoroso to enter into the contract. There is no suggestion that either defendant signed the check without knowledge of "its character or its essential terms." N.J.S. 12A:3-305(2)(c), N.J.S.A. Therefore the fraud is a personal defense available only against Winter and cannot be asserted against plaintiff.

Accordingly both Fort Lee Savings as drawer and Amoroso as indorser of the check are liable to plaintiff. N.J.S. 12A:3-413(2) and 12A:3-414(1), N.J.S.A., defining the liability of a drawer and indorser of a negotiable instrument to a holder in due course.

The motion for summary judgment will be granted in the sum of $1,066.43, plus interest. The amount of the judgment represents advances made on Winter's account before notice of dishonor, $1,291.76, less the existing balance of $225.33 in Winter's account. This opinion will not deal with the disposition of claims between Amoroso and Fort Lee Savings. By reason of the stop payment order Fort Lee Savings has on hand sufficient funds which were charged against Amoroso's account to meet plaintiff's judgment, and part of these funds, representing the difference between the potential judgment and the $3,100 retained, has been refunded to Amoroso pursuant to the pretrial order.

MARINE MIDLAND BANK v. GRAYBAR ELECTRIC CO., 41 N.Y.2d 703, 395 N.Y.S.2d 403, 363 N.E.2d 1139 (1977). [Dynamics Corporation was obligated to Marine Midland Bank on a $4 million note. The note matured on July 28, but Dynamics could not pay it. On the same day, a $138,000 check drawn by Graybar to Dynamics was deposited in, and credited to, Dynamics' account at Marine Midland upon Marine Midland's indorsement. Later in the day, Marine Midland unilaterally set off all the funds in the account against the note. The Graybar check was dishonored and returned to Marine Midland because the drawer had issued a stop payment order. Marine Midland thereafter reversed so much of the credit given against the note that was based on the Graybar check. Dynamics filed bankruptcy. Marine Midland sued Graybar on the check. The Bank's recovery depended on whether it was a holder in due course of the instrument. The Bank was a holder in due course if it had given value for the check. The trial court dismissed the Bank's complaint. The Appellate Division affirmed, as did the Court of Appeals on the following reasoning.]

Cooke, Judge. *** The proper resolution of this matter turns on the nature of the fund against which the bank seeks a setoff. This is not like the usual situation where a bank sets off funds that are already on deposit in an account, although here such funds were set off. The disputed fund is an additional amount represented by a check which was indorsed and deposited by the bank in the account against which, and on the same day that, the bank set off its loan against that account. Since *** the bank [was authorized by agreement with Dynamics] to indorse checks for deposit in the account, under this arrangement the bank appears to have acquired the status of a "holder" of the check (see Uniform Commercial Code, §1-201, subd. (20); §4-205, subd. (1); §3-202, subd. (1).

* * *

A bank, of course, gives value to the extent that a credit given for an item is withdrawn by the party whose account was credited (Uniform Commercial Code, §4-208, subd. (1), par. (a). Value is also given by a holder when it takes a check in payment of, or as security for, an antecedent debt (§ 3-303, subd. (b). Long before the enactment of the Uniform Commercial Code, however, the entry of a credit on a bank's books was held not to be parting with value under circumstances manifesting that the pre-existing debt or a part thereof was not, in fact, extinguished in consideration for the item for which the credit was given . The basis for that decision was that the bookkeeping entry of the credit was not a parting with value.

These events present somewhat of a hybrid situation in that the bank first gave Dynamics a credit for the Graybar check and then applied this credit, by way of setoff, to Dynamics' indebtedness to it. A literal reading of the Uniform Commercial Code suggests that under section 4-208 (subd. (1), par. (a)) and subdivision (b) of section 3-303 the net result of the credit followed by the setoff is that the bank had taken the check for value. The difficulty with this analysis is, however, that the credit given to Dynamics' account was provisional because the bank could and did reverse the credit after notice of the stop payment order, thereby reinstating that portion of the loan against which the credit was set off.

Considering first the credit given to Dynamics' account for the Graybar check, it is established that the giving of a provisional credit is not a parting with value under the Uniform Commercial Code. In discussing the notion that it is not necessary to give holder in due course status to one who has not actually paid value, the Official Commentary to the Uniform Commercial Code cites as an illustration "the bank credit not drawn upon, which can be and is revoked when a claim or defense appears".

An exception to the proposition that the mere crediting of an account for a deposited check is not a giving of value is when the credit, though not drawn upon, is available for "withdrawal as of right" (Uniform Commercial Code, §4-208, subd. (1), par. (b)). A credit is available for "withdrawal as of right" within a reasonable time after the bank learns of a final settlement in the collection process of the check for which the credit is given (see §4-213, subd. (4), par. (a)). Until such final settlement, in the absence of any agreement between the bank and the depositor, the bank should not be viewed as having given value until there is a final payment of the credited check. In this respect, the bank suggests that because there is a dispute over whether it permitted Dynamics to draw on credits for uncollected checks, a question of fact is raised, the resolution of which requires an evidentiary hearing. The record does not, however, reveal any agreement permitting withdrawal by the bank, and the mere conclusory statements of the bank officers are insufficient to raise a question of fact. The short of the matter is that the credit given here was not available to Dynamics.

Turning then to the argument that by applying the credit by way of setoff to Dynamics' indebtedness the bank gave value, the following is relevant. The clearest instance of giving value in this sort of case is where a bank actually extinguishes a debt by, for example, parting with a note in exchange for a check and then seeking to collect on the check. With respect to subdivision (1) of section 4-208, however, one text has suggested that its purpose was to give "the bank protection in any case in which it is not clear that the bank purchased the item outright, but in which it is clear that the bank has done something, of advantage to the depositor, more than giving the depositor a mere credit on the bank's books." Here, the bank argues that by applying the credit to Dynamics' indebtedness it was giving value as contemplated under section 4-208.

This argument should be rejected. To say that the bank was doing something of advantage to Dynamics by applying the credit to that depositor's indebtedness is to ignore what actually occurred. The bank was merely seeking to protect itself and not giving value, in any traditional sense, or under the Uniform Commercial Code. Since the credit given to the Dynamics account was not, as noted, available to Dynamics, there is no reason for allowing the bank to benefit from this credit, particularly since the bank reinstated that portion of the debt against which the credit was applied upon learning that payment was not to be forthcoming on the check. Under this analysis the bank is in no worse position than any other creditor, and the bank's unilateral agreement to take the credit for the indebtedness, conditioned on payment of the check for which the credit was given, is recognized for what it was -- an attempt to recoup its losses.

This is not to diminish the bank's right of setoff of mutual debts in a bankruptcy situation. Nor is this holding intended to suggest that the setoff was impermissible simply because the check was uncollected at the time of the setoff. Rather, this determination is based on the conclusion that what the bank did was merely give a provisional credit for the Graybar check. That the bank unilaterally agreed to apply this provisional credit to Dynamics' indebtedness should not elevate the transaction to the level of those instances where value is considered to be given under the Uniform Commercial Code. Therefore, since the bank did not give value, it is not a holder in due course and cannot recover on the check.

Bowling Green, Inc. v. State Street Bank & Trust Co.,

United States Court of Appeals, First Circuit, 1970
425 F.2d 81

Coffin, Circuit Judge. On September 26, 1966, plaintiff Bowling Green, Inc., the operator of a bowling alley, negotiated a United States government check for $15,306 to Bowl-Mor, Inc., a manufacturer of bowling alley equipment. The check, which plaintiff had acquired through a Small Business Administration loan, represented the first installment on a conditional sales contract for the purchase of candlepin setting machines. On the following day, September 27, a representative of Bowl-Mor deposited the check in defendant State Street Bank and Trust Co. The Bank immediately credited $5,024.85 of the check against an overdraft in Bowl-Mor's account. Later that day, when the Bank learned that Bowl-Mor had filed a petition for reorganization under Chapter X of the Bankruptcy Act, it transferred $233.61 of Bowl-Mor's funds to another account and applied the remaining $10,047.54 against debts which Bowl-Mor owed the Bank. Shortly thereafter, Bowl-Mor's petition for reorganization was dismissed and the firm was adjudicated a bankrupt. Plaintiff has never received the pin-setting machines for which it contracted. Its part payment remains in the hands of defendant Bank.

Plaintiff brought this diversity action to recover its payment from defendant Bank on the grounds that the Bank is constructive trustee of the funds deposited by Bowl-Mor. In the court below, plaintiff argued that Bowl-Mor knew it could not perform at the time it accepted payment, that the Bank was aware of this fraudulent conduct, and that the Bank therefore received Bowl-Mor's deposit impressed with a constructive trust in plaintiff's favor. The district court rejected plaintiff's view of the evidence, concluding instead that the Bank was a holder in due course within the meaning of Mass.Gen.Laws Ann. c. 106 §4-209 and §3-302, and was therefore entitled to take the item in question free of all personal defenses.

Plaintiff's appeal challenges the conclusion of the district court in three respects. First, plaintiff maintains that the Bank has not met its burden of establishing that it was a "holder" of the item within the meaning of Mass.Gen.Laws Ann. c. 106 §1-201(20), and thus cannot be a "holder in due course" within the meaning of §4-209 and §3-302. Second, plaintiff argues that the Bank's close working relation with Bowl-Mor prevented it from becoming a holder in good faith. Finally, plaintiff denies that defendant gave value within the meaning of §4-209 for the $10,047.54 which it set off against Bowl-Mor's loan account.

* * *

This brings us to plaintiff's final argument, that the Bank gave value only to the extent of the $5,024.85 overdraft, and thus cannot be a holder in due course with respect to the remaining $10,047.54 which the Bank credited against Bowl-Mor's loan account. Our consideration of this argument is confined by the narrow scope of the district court's findings. The Bank may well have given value under §4-208(1)(a) when it credited the balance of Bowl-Mor's checking account against its outstanding indebtedness. But by that time the Bank knew of Bowl-Mor's petition for reorganization, additional information which the district court did not consider in finding that the Bank acted in good faith and without notice at the time it received the item. We must therefore decide whether the Bank gave value for the additional $10,047.54 at the time the item was deposited.

Resolution of this issue depends on the proper interpretation of §4-209, which provides that a collecting bank has given value to the extent that it has acquired a "security interest" in an item. In plaintiff's view, a collecting bank can satisfy §4-209 only by extending credit against an item in compliance with §4-208(1). The district court, on the other hand, adopted the view that a security interest is a security interest, however acquired. The court then found that defendant and Bowl-Mor had entered a security agreement which gave defendant a floating lien on Bowl-Mor's chattel paper. Since the item in question was part of the proceeds of a Bowl-Mor contract, the court concluded that defendant had given value for the full $15,306.00 at the time it received the deposit.

With this conclusion we agree. Section 1-201(37) defines "security interest" as an interest in personal property which secures payment or performance of an obligation. There is no indication in §4-209 that the term is used in a more narrow or specialized sense. Moreover, as the official comment to §4-209 observes, this provision is in accord with prior law and with §3-303, both of which provide that a holder gives value when he accepts an instrument as security for an antecedent debt. Finally, we note that if one of the Bank's prior loans to Bowl-Mor had been made in the expectation that this particular instrument would be deposited, the terms of §4-208(1)(c) would have been literally satisfied. We do not think the case is significantly different when the Bank advances credit on the strength of a continuing flow of items of this kind. We therefore conclude that the Bank gave value for the full $15,306.00 at the time it accepted the deposit.

We see no discrepancy between this result and the realities of commercial life. Each party, of course, chose to do business with an eventually irresponsible third party. The Bank, though perhaps unwise in prolonging its hopes for a prospering customer, nevertheless protected itself through security arrangements as far as possible without hobbling each deposit and withdrawal. Plaintiff, on the other hand, not only placed its initial faith in Bowl-Mor, but later became aware that Bowl-Mor was having difficulties in meeting its payroll. It seems not too unjust that this vestige of caveat emptor survives.

Affirmed.

Eldon's Super Fresh Stores, Inc. v. Merrill Lynch, Pierce, Fenner & Smith, Inc.

Supreme Court of Minnesota, 1973
296 Minn. 130, 207 N.W.2d 282

O. Russell Olson, Justice. Plaintiff, drawer of a check payable to defendant Merrill Lynch, Pierce, Fenner & Smith, Inc., appeals from a summary judgment entered in favor of defendant. The appeal raises the issue of whether the payee was, as a matter of law, a holder in due course and thus not subject to the drawer's claim that the check, possession of which it gave to its agent, was wrongfully delivered to defendant-payee in payment of the agent's own personal obligation to defendant rather than for the benefit of plaintiff-drawer.

Eldon's Super Fresh Stores, Inc. (hereafter Eldon's) is a closely held corporation headquartered in Faribault, Minnesota, and engaged in the retail grocery business. Merrill Lynch, Pierce, Fenner & Smith, Inc. (hereafter Merrill Lynch) is a national stock brokerage firm with offices in St. Paul, Minnesota. William E. Drexler was the attorney for and corporate secretary of Eldon's and the personal attorney of Eldon Prinzing, the corporation's president and sole shareholder.

The relevant facts are not in dispute. From January 1968 through January 1970, Drexler maintained a trading account in his name with Merrill Lynch by which he purchased and sold stock at various times. Eldon's, on the other hand, maintained no trading account with Merrill Lynch at any time relevant herein. On August 12, 1969, Drexler purchased 100 shares of Clark Oil & Refining Company stock through his stockbroker at Merrill Lynch for $41.50 per share. A confirmation statement was mailed to Drexler by the stockbroker, and Drexler then mailed the $4,150 check here involved, together with the confirmation statement, to Merrill Lynch in payment for the stock purchase. The check was drawn by the corporation, Eldon's Super Fresh Stores, Inc., on the Security National Bank and Trust Company of Faribault, Minnesota, and contained corporate identification as follows:

"ELDON'S SUPER FRESH STORES,
INC.
FAMOUS FOR
FRESH FRUITS & VEGETABLES
DBA PRINZING'S MARKETS
[PHONE AND AREA CODE NUMBERS]FARIBAULT, MINNESOTA"

The check, in the exact amount of the purchase price of the 100 shares of stock (not including commission charge of $39.75) and payable to Merrill Lynch, was dated August 12, 1969, and signed for the corporation by E.C. Prinzing, its president. The check contained no other designation or directive as to its use. On August 15, 1969, Merrill Lynch accepted the check in payment of Drexler's stock purchase, treating Drexler as the remitter. Pursuant to its customary practice with Drexler, Merrill Lynch retained custody of the Clark Oil & Refining Company stock certificate together with five other stock certificates previously purchased for him embodying shares in various other corporations. Five of the six stock certificates were ultimately delivered to Drexler in November 1969. There was no communication between Drexler and Merrill Lynch except the stock purchase order for Drexler's personal account on August 12, the mailing of the confirmation statement of Drexler, and the receipt by Merrill Lynch on August 15 of the check and confirmation statement. Drexler sold the stock to his brother in December 1970. Drexler was in 1969 an attorney duly licensed to practice law in Minnesota although he has since that date been disbarred. There was no communication between Eldon's and Merrill Lynch until November 1970, 15 months after the issuance of the check, at which time Eldon's inquired of Merrill Lynch relative to the stock certificate and asserted a claim to its ownership.

Additional facts bearing on the claim of Eldon's, but not material to the determination of whether Merrill Lynch was a holder in due course, reveal a dispute between Eldon's and Drexler as to whether the check was delivered to Drexler in payment of legal services or whether it was delivered by Eldon Prinzing to Drexler as agent of Eldon's to purchase the corporate stock for Eldon's. The resolution of that issue is not before the court on this appeal. The record establishes that Merrill Lynch had no knowledge of that dispute and assumed that Drexler had received the check as remitter to use for his own purpose in paying for stock. If he did not have such right, then Merrill Lynch is subject to plaintiff's claim unless it took as a holder in due course.

The narrow issue, therefore, is whether under the recited factual circumstances Merrill Lynch, as payee of the check, was a holder in due course. Since defendant, as payee, took as a holder and obviously took for full value, decision turns on whether the payee, which received the check from the drawer's agent who in turn had received possession with the drawer's consent, took it "without notice *** of any defense against or claim to it on the part of any person," Minn.St. 336.3-302(1)(c), and thus became a holder in due course free of any claim of the drawer that the delivery to the payee was wrongful.

The trial court succinctly characterized Eldon's claims as follows:

> The thrust of Plaintiff's argument is that the third-party check itself was "notice" to Merrill Lynch; that Merrill Lynch should have contacted Plaintiff upon receipt of the check and made a full inquiry as to the agreements or understandings between Plaintiff and Drexler, and that Merrill Lynch had no right to assume that Drexler was acting properly.

* * *

Minn.St. 336.3-302 sets out the requirements for being a HDC of negotiable instruments as follows:

> (1) A holder in due course is a holder who takes the instrument
>
> a) for value; and
>
> (b) in good faith; and
>
> (c) *without notice* that it is overdue or has been dishonored or *of any defense against or claim to it on the part of any person.*
>
> (2) A payee may be a holder in due course. (Italics supplied.)

* * *

It is the third and critical requirement -- taking "without notice *** of any defense against or claim to it on the part of any person" -- with which we must deal.

The holder of an instrument has the burden of proving that he is a HDC when defenses or claims are shown. Minn.St. 336.3-307(3). See, also, Chamberlin v. Twin Ports Development Co., 195 Minn. 58, 261 N.W. 577 (1935).

"Notice" is defined in §336.1-201(25) as follows:

> A person has "notice" of a fact when
>
> (a) he has *actual knowledge* of it; or
>
> (b) he has received a notice or notification of it; or
>
> (c) from all the facts and circumstances known to him at the time in question he has *reason to know* that it exists.

A person "knows" or has "knowledge" of a fact when he has actual knowledge of it. (Italics supplied.)

The Minnesota Code Comment to Minn.St. 336.1-201(25), 21A M.S.A. 76, points out that "notice" (as with "notice" in other recited uniform acts) is restricted-

to actual knowledge of the fact, receipt of notification of it, or knowledge of facts from which the fact in question is inferable; and they all exclude the situation in which a person does not have actual or inferable knowledge but merely *could discover* the fact by reasonable investigation. In the latter situation it is sometimes said that when a person has a duty to another to investigate a matter he has "notice" of what he could have discovered, but the U.C.C. does not employ "notice" in that sense under this definition except in the case covered by paragraph (b) where one has *received notification* but may not have read or understood it.

The knowledge which a person has that constitutes "notice" according to §336.1-201(25) could, then, be termed "inferable" knowledge.

In addition to Minn.St. 336.1-201(25), §336.3-304 describes circumstances which do and do not constitute notice for the purpose of being a HDC. * * * The comments to paragraphs (2) and (4)(e) make clear that the test of "notice" is the existence of actual knowledge of a fact or of facts from which one can infer the fact in question. Under the "notice" test, the question then becomes: (a) Did Merrill Lynch have actual knowledge of Eldon's claim, or (b) did Merrill Lynch have "inferable knowledge" of the claim, i.e., did Merrill Lynch have actual knowledge of facts from which it could reasonably infer the probable existence of the drawer's claim?

Facts or circumstances from which a purchaser could infer that a claim exists on the part of any person are referred to in Minnesota as "danger signals" and knowledge of such facts is the "red light" test. Sometimes the cases speak in terms of "good faith," but they concern "notice" and they are applicable to the "notice" question under the U.C.C. rather than "good faith." We have in Minnesota several cases applying this test to facts similar to the case at hand. In applying the test, this court has rather consistently held that having notice by way of the "inferable knowledge" test is something more than failure to make inquiry about an unknown fact. Failure to make such inquiry may be negligence and lack of diligence, but it is not "notice" of what he might discover.

* * *

Applying the "inferable knowledge" test to the instant case, this court concludes that Merrill Lynch did not have "notice of any claim of the drawer, Eldon's, simply by virtue of its receipt of the check and confirmation notice from Drexler. The fact that Merrill Lynch was the named payee on the check drawn by Eldon's did not in and of itself constitute "notice" that Drexler was using the check improperly. Significantly, there were no other identification or designation marks on the check to indicate or give notice that it was drawn in payment for stock for Eldon's. Furthermore, and equally as significant, Eldon's had no account with Merrill Lynch. The designation on the check that the corporate maker was doing business as Prinzing's Markets is not by itself sufficient to constitute such "notice." Merrill Lynch was entitled to conclude that Drexler, known to be an attorney, had lawfully obtained and was delivering the instrument to discharge the debt incurred by his own stock purchase. Merrill Lynch was not required to surmise that the check, rather than being a payment for Drexler's legal services, was being misused.

There is a case in Minnesota which may appear contrary to the decision in the instant case. In Bjorgo v. First Nat. Bank of Emmons, 127 Minn. 105, 149 N.W. 3 (1914), reheard under the same name after a second trial in 132 Minn. 273, 156 N.W. 277 (1916), a land developer, Haugan, presented for payment to the Emmons bank a bank draft drawn by an Iowa bank on a Chicago bank; the Emmons bank was the payee of the draft. The holding as stated by the court was that the fact the draft was payable to the bank rather than to the individual claiming ownership "was so out of the ordinary mode of doing business" as to place a duty on the bank to inquire. 127 Minn. 109, 149 N.W. 5. The bank, however, extrinsically had knowledge of representations by Haugan that the monies would be deposited in the bank pending the exercise of certain land options by Haugan. The holding as stated in the case is actually overbroad since the recited extrinsic circumstance constitutes a basis for application of the inferable knowledge test.

Courts are often confronted with the obligation of applying rules to determine which of two relatively innocent persons must suffer a loss due to misconduct of a third person. The instant case is such a situation. The Minnesota cases dealing with situations such as the one at bar have indicated that the loss must fall on the drawer rather than upon the payee (or other holder) because it was the drawer who created the situation and opportunity for defalcation by its agents. Eldon's did intend in fact to have the check delivered to Merrill Lynch.

Under the circumstance of this case, namely, where (1) a bank check was delivered to the payee by the drawer's agent with the drawer's consent and knowledge, (2) the check itself contained no restrictions or designations as to its use, and (3) the payee, a stock brokerage firm, had no trading account with, or indebtedness to, the drawer, we hold that the payee took the check without notice of the drawer's claims. Thus, the payee became a holder in due course of the instrument.

This court is not deciding in this case whether, as between Drexler and Eldon's, Drexler was authorized to deliver the check to Merrill Lynch in payment of his personal stock purchase.

Lastly, plaintiff claims a cause of action against the holder, Merrill Lynch, on the basis of common-law negligence. There is no basis for such an action. Minn.St. 336.3-305 provides in part:

> To the extent that a holder is a holder in due course he takes the instrument free from
> (1) all claims to it on the part of any person.

The statute provides an exclusive remedy.

Affirmed.

Gill v. Cubitt
l07 Eng. Rep. (1824)

Where a bill of exchange was stolen during the night, and taken to the office of a discount broker early in the following morning by a person whose features were known, but whose name was unknown to the broker, and the latter being satisfied with the name of the acceptor, discounted the bill, according to his usual practice, without making any enquiry of the person who brought it: Held that, in an action on the bill by the broker against the acceptor, the jury were properly directed to find a verdict for the defendant if they thought that the plaintiff had taken the bill under circumstances which ought to have excited the suspicion of a prudent and careful man; and they having found for the defendant, the Court refused to disturb the verdict.

Declaration by the plaintiff as indorsee of a bill of exchange, bearing date the 19th Of August 1823, drawn by one R. Evered and accepted by the defendants. Plea, general issue. At the trial before Abbott C.J., at the London sittings after Hilary term 1824, the plaintiff proved the handwriting of the acceptors, and indorser. The defendant then proved, that on the 20th of August a letter containing the bill in question and two others, was inclosed in a parcel and delivered at the Green Man and Still coach-office, and booked for Birmingham. The parcel arrived at Birmingham by the coach, but the letter containing the bills had been opened, and the bills taken out of it. On the following day the drawer advertised the loss of the bills in two newspapers. The plaintiff, who was a bill broker in London, then proved by bis nephew who assisted him in his business, that the bill was brought to his office between the hours of nine and ten on the morning of the 21st of August, by a person having a respectable appearance, and whose features were familiar to the witness, but whose name was unknown to him. He desired that the bill might be discounted for him, but the witness at first declined so to do, because the acceptors were not known to him. The person who brought the bill then said, that a few days before he had brought other bills to the office, and that if enquiry was made, it would be found that the parties whose names were on this bill were highly respectable. He then quitted the office and left the bill, and upon enquiry the witness was satisfied with the names of the acceptors. The stranger returned after a lapse of two hours and indorsed the bill in the name of Charles Taylor, and received the full value for it, the usual discount and a commission of two shillings being deducted. The witness did not enquire the name of the person who brought the bill, or his address, or whether he brought it on his own account or otherwise, or how he came by the bill. It was the practice in the plaintiff's office not to make any enquiries about the drawer or other parties to a bill, provided the acceptor was good. Upon this evidence the Lord Chief Justice told the jury, that there were two questions for their consideration; first, whether the plaintiff had given value for the bill, of which there could be no doubt; and, secondly, whether he took it under circumstances which ought to have excited the suspicion of a prudent and careful man. If they thought that he had taken the bill under such circumstances, then, notwithstanding he had given the full value for it, they ought to find a verdict for the defendant. Then the Lord Chief Justice, after stating the evidence and commenting upon the practice in the plaintiff's office of discounting bills for any persons whose features were known to him, but whose names and abode were unknown, without asking any questions; asked the jury what they would think if a board were affixed over an office with this notice, "Bills discounted for persons whose features are known, and no questions asked." The jury having found a verdict for the defendants, a rule nisi for a new trial was obtained in Easter term last, upon the ground that the plaintiff having paid a valuable consideration for the bill, was entitled to recover its value; and, secondly, that the case had been put too strongly to the jury, when it was compared to the case of a public notice given by a broker that he would discount all bills without asking questions.

Scarlett and Parke now shewed cause. Where a bill or note has been acquired by theft, and afterwards comes to the possession of a holder for valuable consideration, it is incumbent upon him when he brings an action, not only to shew that he paid that consideration, but also that he used due diligence to ascertain, before he took the bill or note, whether the party bringing it to him came by it honestly. Unless he does this he cannot be said to have taken it bona fide, although he may have paid the full value for it. It is true, that *in Lawson v. Weston (4 Esp.* 56), Lord Kenyon was of opinion, that it was sufficient for a person who discounted such a bill, to shew that he paid value for it, but the propriety of that decision has always been doubted. If it is to be laid down as a rule, that a party in possession of a stolen bill or note may obtain the value of it without being subject to any enquiry, it will give a great facility to the disposal of property so acquired, and operate as an encouragement to fraud and theft. It is desirable that the rule laid down should have the effect of preventing parties, who are either guilty or cognizant of such fraud, from profiting by it. Then if that be the correct rule upon the subject, the Lord Chief Justice was well warranted in the observations he made to the jury, and their verdict is supported by the evidence. The plaintiff took the bill from a person whose features were known to him, but of whom he knew nothing else, and made no inquiry as to how he came by the bill; and it was in evidence that he always conducted his business in this mode. Surely that is like the case of a person giving a public notice, "Bills discounted for persons whose features are known, and no questions asked."

Guruey and F. Pollock, contra. A party who has paid the full value for a bill which has been lost or stolen, is entitled to recover the amount from the acceptor. The circulation of negotiable paper would be greatly impeded if it were laid down as a rule, that a party discounting a bill was bound to investigate the title of the person from whom he receives it. In the case of *Lawson v. Weston (4* Esp. 56), the plaintiffs, who were bankers, had discounted the bill in the usual course of their business for a person who brought it to their shop, but who was unknown to them. It was contended by the defendant, that although a person might pay a bill, to which he was a party, to one who had come dishonestly by it, by reason of the personal liability attached to his name on the bill, a banker or any other should not discount a bill for a person unknown without using due diligence to enquire into the circumstances, as well respecting the bill as of the person who offered to discount it. But Lord Kenyon said, that to adopt the principle of the defence to the full extent stated, would be at once to paralize the circulation of all the paper in the country, and with it all its commerce. The circumstance of the bill having been lost, might have been material if they could bring knowledge of that fact home to the plaintiffs. They might or might not have seen the advertisement and it would be going great length to say, that a banker was bound to make enquiry concerning every bill brought to him to discount, it would apply as well to a bill for 101. as for 10,0001. In that case, there fore, the very point now raised was made and overruled by Lord Kenyon, and although the bill was of the amount of 5001., the parties acquiesced in that decision. The principle acted upon in that case had been previously adopted in *Miller v. Race* (1 Burr. 452), Grant v. *Vaughan* (3 Burr. 1516), and *Peacock v. Rhodes* (Doug. 611). At all events, the case was put too strongly to the jury by my Lord Chief Justice. It was not like the case of a public notice, that all bills would be discounted for persons whose features were known, and no questions would be asked. That mode of putting it excited an undue prejudice against the plaintiff, and the case ought to be submitted to a second jury.

Abbott C.J. If we thought that, upon reconsideration of the evidence, another jury ought to come to a different conclusion, we would send the case down to another trial. But being of opinion, that the proper conclusion has been drawn from the evidence, we think that this rule ought to be discharged. I agree with the counsel for the plaintiff, that this case is hardly distinguishable from *Lawson v. Weston. If* there is any distinction it is, that in this case the plaintiff's clerk said it was not usual with the plaintiff to ask any questions, or to make any enquiry if bills were brought to them by persons whose features they supposed themselves to be acquainted with, provided they were satisfied with the names of the acceptors. I cannot help thinking, that if Lord Kenyon had anticipated the consequences which have followed from the rule laid down by him in Lawson v. *Weston,* he would have paused before he pronounced that decision. Since the decision of that case, the practice of robbing stagecoaches and other conveyances of securities of this kind, has been very considerable. I cannot forbear thinking, that that practice has received encouragement by the rule laid down in *Lawson v. Weston,* by which a facility has been given to the disposal of stolen property of this description. I should be sorry if I were to say any thing, sitting in the seat of judgment, that either might have the effect, or reasonably be supposed to have the effect of impeding the commerce of the country by preventing the due and easy circulation of paper. But I am decidedly of opinion, that no injury will be done to the interests of commerce, by a decision that the plaintiff cannot recover in this action. It appears to me to be for the interest of commerce, that no person should take a security of this kind from another without using reasonable caution. If he take such security from a person whom he knows, and whom he can find out, no complaint can be made of him. In that case he has done all any person could do. But if it is to be laid down as the law of the land, that a person may take a security of this kind from a man of whom he knows nothing, and of whom he makes no enquiry at all, it appears to me that such a decision would be more injurious to commerce than convenient for it, by reason of the encouragement it would afford to the purloining, stealing, and defrauding persons of securities of this sort. The interest of commerce requires that bona fide and real holders of bills, known to be such by those with whom they are dealing, should have no difficulties thrown in their way in parting with them. But it is not for the interest of commerce that any individual should be enabled to dispose of bills or notes without being subject to enquiry. I think the sooner it is known that the case of Lawson v. *Weston* is doubted, at least by this Court, the better. I wish doubts had been cast OD that case at an earlier time. If that had been done, this plaintiff probably would not have suffered. Coming to the facts of this case, they are these, that the young man, acting according to the course which the plaintiff when he was present followed, gave money for this bill to a person of whom, though he supposed he knew him, he really knew nothing. This is done at a very early hour, between nine and ten in the morning on the day after the bill was lost. I cannot help saying that that practice, in the plaintiff' business of a bill broker, is a practice inconvenient for the reasons I have already given. It seems to me, that it is a great encouragement to fraud, and it is the duty of the Court to lay down such rules as will tend to prevent fraud and robbery, and not give encouragement to them. For these reasons, notwithstanding all the unfeigned reverence I feel for every thing that fell from Lord Kenyon, by whom *Lawson v. Weston* was decided, I cannot think the view taken by that learned lord at that time was a correct one; and that being so, I am of opinion that this rule ought to be discharged.

Bayley J. I agree that the way in which my Lord Chief Justice put this case for the consideration of the jury, by asking what would be the case if a man were to put over his shop, "Bills discounted for strangers, if they have good names on them, without any questions being asked," was a very strong way of putting the case for their consideration. But I think it was no more than the facts of this case warranted, and that he was putting a9 a general proposition, that which exactly squared with the particular facts of this case. If a man commonly dealt in that way, (and it appeared to be the plaintiff's habit as a broker,) it would warrant such an advertisement as that which was described. If in general that was not the plaintiff's course and habit, then in this particular instance he deviated from his general course. In this case a party goes to a shop between nine and tell in the morning to get a bill discounted, the clerk does not know his name; he thinks he knows his features; he does not know where he lives; he knows nothing at all about him. The bill is left for two hours, and at the expiration of that time the party comes back again; and the clerk then has the opportunity of asking names, and whether he came on his own account, or from any and what house. No question of that description is put to him. Under these circumstances, I think it was the duty of my Lord Chief Justice to put it to the consideration of the jury whether there was due caution used by that party in that particular instance. If there was not due caution used, the plaintiff has not discounted this hill in the usual and ordinary course of business, or in that way in which business properly and rightly conducted would have required. But it is said that the question usually submitted for the consideration of the jury in cases of this description, up to the period of time at which my Lord Chief Justice's direction was given, has been whether the bill was taken bona fide, and whether a valuable consideration was given for it. I admit that has been generally the case; but I consider it was parcel of the bona fides whether the plaintiff had asked all those questions which, in the ordinary and proper manner in which trade is conducted, a party ought to ask. I think from the manner in which my Lord Chief Justice presented this case to the consideration of the jury, he put it as being part and parcel of the bona fides; and it has been so put in former cases. In the case of *Miller v. Race,* 1 Burr., Lord Mansfield says: "Here an innkeeper took the note bona fide in his business from the person who made the appearance of a gentlemen. Here is no pretence or suspicion of collusion with the robber. For this matter was strictly inquired and examined into at the trial; and is so stated in the case that he took it for a full and valuable consideration in the usual course of business. Indeed if there had been any collusion, or any circumstance of unfair dealing, the case had been much otherwise." Now, the question which my Lord Chief Justice has put to the consideration of the jury, whether a party uses due caution or not, is, in other words, putting to them, whether be took it in the usual course of business; for the course of business must require, in the usual and ordinary manner of conducting it, a proper and reasonable degree of caution necessary to preserve the interest of trade. The next case, in order of time, is *Grant v. Vaughan.* Mr. Justice Wilmott there says: "The note appears to have been taken by him fairly and bona fide in the course of trade, and even with the greatest caution. He made inquiry about it, and then gave the change for it; and there is not the least imputation or pretence of suspicion that be had any notice of its being a lost note." That learned Judge did not consider the question of bona fides to be merely whether the note was taken by a party without having any real suspicion in his own mind, but whether he had taken it in the usual course of trade, and with caution. In *Peacock v. Rhodes,* a shopkeeper at Scarborough took from a perfect stranger a bill of exchange. The latter bought certain goods in the way of the plaintiff's trade. Lord Mansfield says: "The question of mala fides was for the consideration of the jury. The circumstance that the buyers and the drawers were strangers to the plaintiff, and that be took the bill for goods on which he had a profit, were grounds of suspicion very fit for their consideration. But they have considered them, and have found it was received in the course of trade, and therefore the case is clear." Then if in that case those were questions fit for the consideration of a jury, as part and parcel of the question of bona fides, is it not also a fit and proper question for their consideration, (when the point to be decided is whether a man has acted bona fide or not,) whether he has inquired with that degree of caution which, in the ordinary course of trade, a prudent trader ought to use. That was the question propounded by my Lord Chief Justice in his direction to the jury; and they have exercised their judgment on it. I think the question was a fit question for their decision, and I think their decision was one with which we are not at liberty to quarrel. On the contrary, it appears to me to be material for the interests of trade, to lay down as a rule that a party cannot in law be considered to act bona fide, or with due caution and due diligence, if he takes a bill of exchange from a person whose features alone he knows, without knowing what his name is, where he lives, or whether he i9 a person with whom he has been in the habit of trading. If we were to say that in this instance there had been due caution, it would certainly be giving a great facility to the disposal of bills of exchange which have been lost or stolen, by persons who have found or dishonestly obtained them. For these reasons it appears to me that my Lord Chief Justice took the right view of this case; that it was consistent with the doctrine laid down in former cases; and that the decision of the jury was warranted by the evidence.

Holroyd J. I think the rule was correctly laid down to the jury by my Lord Chief Justice, and that there is no ground for granting a new trial. A party who discounts a bill which has been stolen is bound to shew, not only that a good consideration was really and bona fide given for the bill (although that of itself would tend to the establishing of the other point requisite for him to shew), but he must also make it appear to the satisfaction of a jury that he actually took it bona fide. If he takes it with a view to profit arising from interest or commission, under circumstances affording reasonable ground of suspicion, without inquiring whether the party of whom he takes it came by it honestly or not, or if he takes it merely because it is drawn upon a good acceptor, then be takes it at a risk (or what ought, in the contemplation of a reasonable man, to be a risk), whether the bill be stolen or not: he takes it at his peril. I cannot agree with the doctrine laid down in *Lawson* v. *Weston*. The question whether a bill or note has been taken bona fide involves in it the question whether it has been taken with due caution. It is a question of fact for the jury, under all the circumstances of the case, whether a bill has been taken bona fide or not; and whether due and reasonable caution has been used by the person taking it. And if a bill be drawn upon parties of respectability capable of answering it, and another person discounts it merely because the acceptance is good, without using due caution, and without inquiring how the holder came by it, I think that the law will not, under such circumstances, assist the parties so taking the bill, in recovering the money. If the bill be taken without using due means to ascertain that it has been honestly come by, the party, so taking on himself the risk for gain, must take the consequence if it should turn out that it was not honestly acquired by the person of whom he received it. Here the person in possession of the bill was a perfect stranger to the plaintiff, and he discounted it, and made no inquiry of whom the bill had been obtained, or to whom he was to apply if the bill should not be taken up by the acceptor. I think those circumstances tend strongly to shew that the party who discounted the bill did not choose to make inquiry, but supposing the questions might not be satisfactorily answered, rather than refuse to take the bill, took the risk in order to get the profit arising from commission and interest. I am therefore of opinion that the direction of my Lord Chief Justice to the jury was correct in point of law, that they have drawn the proper conclusion, and that there is no ground for granting a new trial.

Rule discharged.

In re Joe Morgan, Inc.
United States Court of Appeals, Eleventh Circuit, 1993
985 F.2d 1554

Carnes, Circuit Judge: Appellant Sunburst Bank ("Sunburst") appeals the district court's affirmance of an order of the bankruptcy court holding that: (i) Appellee Utility Contractors Financial Services ("UCON") was a holder in due course with respect to any checks received from account debtors of Joe Morgan, Inc. ("JMI") prior to July 17, 1989 and, therefore, had priority over Sunburst's prior perfected security interest in JMI's accounts receivable; and (ii) Sunburst was estopped from asserting its security interest in the proceeds of JMI's accounts receivable for the period beginning on July 17, 1989. We affirm the estoppel determination but reverse the holding that UCON was a holder in due course of the pre-July 17, 1989 checks.

I. STATEMENT OF FACTS

JMI was a corporation engaged in the telephone utility contracting business. In September 1988, JMI and Sunburst agreed in principle to enter into certain financing arrangements including a $1 million revolving line of credit. While the documentation for this financing was being prepared, Sunburst extended credit to JMI in the form of two "bridge" loans. These loans were secured by all of JMI's equipment, general intangibles, and accounts receivable. Although these loans were made in October 1988, Sunburst did not file a financing statement with the Secretary of State of Alabama--and thereby perfect its security interest--until March 15, 1989. Sunburst placed no restrictions on JMI's use of the receivable accounts except to require that they be used in the "ordinary, normal course of business."

Sunburst became concerned about the JMI loans in December 1988, and was aware that JMI was searching for alternative financing sources. Sunburst consolidated the two bridge loans (the "Consolidated Loan"), but simultaneously downgraded this loan into a status which indicated a substandard performance trend. Sunburst subsequently learned that another financial institution had denied JMI's request for a line of credit and that AmSouth Bank had declined to renew its existing loan to JMI.

During March and April 1989, Sunburst made clear to Joe Morgan, President of JMI, that it wanted to terminate its banking relationship with JMI and urged Morgan to find other sources of financing. According to its officers, Sunburst "anticipated [JMI's] bankruptcy unless JMI could find working capital and all of their creditors cooperate[d] in harmony."

Enter UCON, a newly-formed Nevada corporation engaged in the business of purchasing receivable accounts from telephone utility contractors. Under its program, UCON purchased (or "factored") a customer's receivables at a 5% discount of the face value of the account. UCON would then collect the account from the account debtor. The bankruptcy court found that UCON's factoring of JMI receivables began in March or April of 1989, and further found that JMI's account debtors always paid UCON by check. The bankruptcy court also found that Sunburst did not learn of this factoring until July 17, 1989.

Robert Watters, a principal of UCON, testified that when UCON began operations, he had not engaged previously in the factoring business and was unaware of the need to file or check for prior Uniform Commercial Code filings in connection with the factoring enterprise. Although UCON occasionally ran credit checks on its customers, it did not do so with JMI. Watters and UCON did not know of Sunburst's interests in JMI's receivables because, as the bankruptcy court found, "JMI did not inform UCON of Sunburst's prior security interest in JMI's accounts receivable."

Temporarily reinvigorated by the working capital obtained through the UCON factoring, JMI was able to "renew" its Consolidated Loan with Sunburst (the "Renewal Loan") under terms permitting a longer period of repayment. JMI subsequently made two payments on the Renewal Loan. Douglas McCrory, a senior vice president of Sunburst and the credit officer charged with oversight of the JMI loans, testified that he "assume[d JMI was] getting the capital from conversion of accounts receivable."

At a chance meeting of Watters and McCrory on July 17, 1989, UCON and Sunburst "discovered" each other's involvement with JMI. During this meeting and a subsequent meeting on July 20, Watters and McCrory discussed various issues relating to their respective relationships with JMI. Thus, as of July 17, 1989, UCON's Watters had actual notice of Sunburst's prior security interest in JMI's receivables. Watters confirmed Sunburst's interest with a visit to the Alabama Secretary of State's office on July 19, 1989.

The parties' characterizations of the July 1989 meetings vary significantly. According to Sunburst, UCON principal Watters stated to Sunburst official McCrory that UCON was viewed as merely "a short term fix" for JMI. Sunburst claims that Watters misrepresented that JMI had $1.8 million in good receivables which would satisfy both AmSouth's and Sunburst's claims. In reality, the receivables were in the neighborhood of $1.4 million. The difference, Sunburst asserts, approximates the amount of JMI's indebtedness to Sunburst. Sunburst also complains that it was misled into believing that JMI was generating new receivables in an amount at least equal to the amount being factored.

UCON, on the other hand, contends that its principal, Watters, merely "estimated" the level of receivables as $1.8 million. UCON also contends that Watters indicated that UCON was unwilling to continue its factoring of JMI receivables beyond August 1, 1989. UCON claims that at the July meetings Sunburst raised no objection to UCON's continued factoring of JMI's receivables. UCON's Watters testified that Sunburst officials encouraged UCON to remain involved until August 1st because "everyone there ... understood ... [that] you can't sell a company that's in bankruptcy or that's being liquidated." Watters further testified that there was no threat of suit or other reservation of rights made by Sunburst during these meetings.

The bankruptcy court found that the upshot of the July meetings was that Sunburst permitted UCON to "continue to factor JMI's accounts receivable until August 1, 1989 on the following conditions: 1) the funds received by JMI would be used to cover payroll; and 2) JMI would generate new receivables in an amount greater than the amount being factored." McCrory of Sunburst conceded in his testimony that there was no dispute that each of these terms was met.

UCON continued to factor JMI receivables until August 31, 1989. Throughout this period, Sunburst and UCON had "almost daily" contact regarding UCON's factoring activities. Their relationship after the July meetings was characterized by UCON's Watters as one of cooperation regarding the transfer of funds to meet JMI's ongoing capital requirements. Watters testified that when a potential overdraft situation arose, someone from JMI or Sunburst (including McCrory) would call Watters and instruct him to purchase sufficient receivables to yield a certain dollar amount to be wire transferred to JMI's payroll account.

The bankruptcy court found that UCON factored a total of $2,511,481.01 in JMI's accounts receivable and collected $2,099,209.56. UCON factored $837,195.42 of the total from July 20, 1989 to August 31, 1989. The amount of the receivables factored but uncollected by UCON was $412,271.45.

JMI filed a Chapter 11 petition on September 13, 1989. At the time of the petition, JMI owed Sunburst $399,910.00 in principal and $15,613.44 in interest.

On September 26, 1989, UCON filed an adversary proceeding against AmSouth, Sunburst, and JMI to determine the priority of its claim. Sunburst counterclaimed seeking relief that included a declaration that Sunburst's prior perfected security interest was superior to UCON's interests, and an order compelling UCON to pay over to Sunburst all proceeds of accounts receivable of JMI which UCON received.

After a bench trial, the bankruptcy court held that UCON was a holder in due course ("HDC") of the pre-July 17, 1989 checks it had received and, therefore, had priority over Sunburst's prior security interest. The court further found that Sunburst was estopped from asserting its claims to the checks for accounts factored by UCON after the July 17, 1989 meeting. The district court affirmed the judgment of the bankruptcy court.

II. DISCUSSION

A. ISSUES ON APPEAL

We address two questions in this appeal. The first one concerns UCON's status as an HDC with respect to checks received from JMI's account debtors for the accounts factored prior to the first meeting between UCON and Sunburst officials in July of 1989. As the district court correctly observed, "[t]he holder in due course issue is relevant only with regard to the accounts factored prior to July 17, 1989. It is undisputed by the parties that UCON had notice of the existence of Sunburst's security interest in the accounts factored after July 17, 1989." March 9, 1992 Order at 4 n. 1. As to the accounts factored before that meeting, we must initially decide if UCON is entitled to HDC status. If it is, then we must decide whether, pursuant to Ala.Code §7-9-309, UCON, as an HDC, has a priority interest in checks it received in payment on accounts receivable which were purchased from JMI, notwithstanding Sunburst's senior, perfected security interest in those receivable accounts.

* * *

C. THE HOLDER IN DUE COURSE ISSUE

Both the bankruptcy court and the district court concluded that UCON was an HDC under Ala.Code §7-3-302 with respect to the checks sent to UCON from JMI's account debtors. The district court analyzed this issue in some detail and rejected Sunburst's attack on each of the three elements of the HDC test. March 9, 1992 Order at 4-6. Sunburst again argues that "UCON fails to meet all of the requirements for holder in due course status as to checks it received from account debtors of JMI."

Ala.Code §7-3-302 provides in material part: (1) A holder in due course is a holder who takes the instrument: (a) For value; and (b) In good faith; and (c) Without notice that it is overdue or has been dishonored or of any defense against or claim to it on the part of any person. (2) A payee may be a holder in due course. "Holder," in turn, is defined as "a person who is in possession of a document of title or an instrument or an investment security drawn, issued or indorsed to him or to his order or to bearer or in blank." Ala.Code §7-1- 201(20). There is no dispute that UCON was a holder of the checks it received, so we examine each of the other three requirements for HDC status.

1. The "For Value" Requirement

Alabama's Uniform Commercial Code ("UCC"), explains the "for value" requirement as follows:

> A holder takes the instrument for value: (a) To the extent that the agreed consideration has been performed or that he acquires a security interest in or a lien on the instrument otherwise than by legal process; or (b) When he takes the instrument in payment of or as security for an antecedent claim against any person whether or not the claim is due; or (c) When he gives a negotiable instrument for it or makes an irrevocable commitment to a third person.

Ala.Code §7-3-303. The breadth of this provision was recognized by one commentator who observed that: "A holder takes for value when he takes the instrument in payment of any antecedent claim of any person, regardless of the circumstances from which the claim arose. The antecedent debt may be the obligation of any person and is not restricted to the maker of the note given in payment of or as security for value."

The district court found that: "UCON paid value for each account assigned to it by JMI. UCON paid 95% of the face value of the uncollected accounts receivable. JMI received value because it obtained capital more quickly than it would have if it had attempted to collect the debts itself." March 9, 1992 Order at 5. In other words, UCON gave JMI 95 cents on the dollar *and* the time-value of those 95 cents. Obviously, JMI made the judgment that 95 cents today was of greater value than the prospect of $1.00 in 30 days.

The difficult part of the analysis is in deciding between two characterizations of what happened when UCON received the checks from the account debtors. Either the account debtors were paying UCON's "antecedent claim" against JMI when they paid UCON or, as the district court concluded, "[t]he checks were negotiated to UCON in payment of antecedent debts owed by the makers to JMI, a third party." March 9, 1992 Order at 5. If UCON purchased the accounts without recourse against JMI, UCON was really purchasing a chance at collecting $1.00 on a 95 cent investment. Under this scenario, claims of or against JMI were extinguished. Thus, Sunburst could legitimately argue that there was no "payment ... for an antecedent claim" as is required for HDC status.

The better approach focuses on the antecedent claims of UCON against the account debtors. As it did before the district court, in this Court Sunburst attempts to engraft onto §7-3-303 the requirement that UCON "give value to the account debtors that wrote checks." Sunburst was properly criticized by the district court for failing to cite any "direct authority for this proposition." March 9, 1992 Order at 5. Not only is Sunburst's view without precedential support, it also interjects the irrelevant concept of consideration. Under

Sunburst's approach, an assignee of rights in accounts receivable would never be able to enforce those rights because consideration did not flow from the assignee to the account debtor. UCON purchased from JMI an antecedent claim JMI had against each account debtor. UCON then took checks in payment of those antecedent claims which had been assigned to it by JMI. The bankruptcy and district courts were correct in concluding that the checks were taken by UCON for value.

2. The "Good Faith" Requirement

The UCC defines "good faith" as "honesty in fact in the conduct or transaction concerned." Ala.Code §7-1-201(19). The majority rule, recognized by courts and commentators alike, holds that this definition creates a subjective test for good faith:

> [T]he existence of good faith is determined by looking to the mind of the particular holder. It is sufficient that the holder honestly believed that there was nothing wrong, and the fact that there was reason to know that something was wrong is immaterial.

Anderson on the UCC, §3-302:15, at 499. See also 1 James J. White & Robert S. Summers, Uniform Commercial Code, §14-6, at 709 (3d ed. 1988) [hereinafter 1 White & Summers] ("At the conclusion of the scrimmaging among the Code drafters and the various proponents of different positions, it was clear that the draftsmen intended to adopt a subjective standard for the good faith test in Article Three"). This majority rule was illustrated in the case of Dallas Bank & Trust Co. v. Frigiking, Inc., 692 S.W.2d 163 (Tex.Ct.App.1985) in which the court found that "[i]t is not sufficient that [the holder] had knowledge that would put a reasonable person on inquiry which would lead to discovery. There must be actual knowledge of facts and circumstances which amounted to bad faith." Id. at 166; see also Farmers & Merchants State Bank, 841 F.2d at 1443 ("In applying this definition [of "good faith" under UCC §1-201(19)], '[t]he appropriate standard is a subjective one.' ").

The district court clearly applied the majority rule subjective test in reaching the following conclusions: Knowledge which would lead a reasonable person to inquire about and discover facts of another's claim is not bad faith; instead, the holder must subjectively act in good faith, no matter how negligent he may be in overlooking important facts. There are no facts establishing that UCON acted in bad faith when it factored JMI's accounts. The facts are also insufficient to show that UCON had actual notice of Sunburst's security interest. March 9, 1992 Order at 6 (citation omitted).

The problem for UCON is that Alabama does not follow the majority rule which is the subjective test. Rather, Alabama has embraced a test that is composed of both a subjective component and an objective component. Two Alabama Supreme Court cases support the proposition that failure under either component of the test will deny a holder HDC status:

> It is our conclusion that under the totality of the facts presented ... the Chancellor was justified in concluding that [the holder] had knowledge, or was possessed of facts, sufficient to impute such knowledge, that [the holder's] action in purchasing the Bell mortgage was questionable as to good faith.

United States Fin. Co. v. Page, 285 Ala. 645, 235 So.2d 791, 794 (1970); see also United States Fin. Co. v. Jones, 285 Ala. 105, 229 So.2d 495, 498 (1969) (holding to the same effect). The foregoing holding appears to have been applied more recently by the Alabama Supreme Court in Strickland v. Kafko Mfg., Inc., 512 So.2d 714 (Ala.1987) where the court stated that: "[B]ecause [the holder] gave full value for the check, the only question is whether [the holder] took it in good faith. There was no evidence of any actual knowledge on [the holder's] part that the Strickland's pool had not been delivered. *Neither* is there any evidence of constructive knowledge that would justify a finding of lack of good faith." Id. at 717 (emphasis added).

While UCON does meet the subjective good faith component, we hold that it has failed to satisfy the objective component. The record, including the following illustrative facts, adequately supports our conclusion that UCON was "possessed of facts, sufficient to impute" knowledge to UCON that another lender had a prior security interest in the accounts.

> (i) UCON's principal, Watters, learned shortly after UCON began factoring JMI receivables that AmSouth claimed a security interest in those receivables, but failed to notify AmSouth of the factoring, and failed to take steps to determine if there were other security interests in JMI's receivables;
>
> (ii) Watters testified that he knew two to three months before the July 17, 1989 meeting that financing statements had to be filed in the secretary of state's office. Nevertheless, UCON failed to conduct UCC searches of the filing records; and
>
> (iii) UCON was aware of JMI's "desperate" financial condition when it began factoring the receivables, yet UCON failed to take any of its normal precautions it had used previously with other companies, such as reviewing UCC filing reports and credit analyses.

Reviewing the matter de novo, we disagree with the district court's conclusion that "[t]here is nothing [in] the facts listed by Sunburst above which would have led a reasonable third party such as UCON to believe that another party had a prior perfected security interest in JMI's accounts." March 9, 1992 Order at 6. In light of the facts known to UCON and reflected in the record, a "reasonable" receivables factoring company would have investigated the state filing records before undertaking to factor the receivables of a company in JMI's financial condition. We concur with the bankruptcy court's and the district court's conclusions that the record reflects that UCON acted with subjective good faith, i.e., "an empty head, but a white heart." Unfortunately for UCON, Alabama law incorporates the objective good faith requirement which does not countenance turning a blind eye, however empty the head and white the heart.

3. The "Without Notice" Requirement

Both the bankruptcy and the district courts appear to have skirted around the notice prong of the HDC analysis. However, to achieve such status, UCON must have been found to have taken each check "*[w]ithout notice* that it is overdue or has been dishonored or of any defense against or *claim to it on the part of any person*." Ala.Code §7-3-302(1)(c) (emphasis added). Sunburst clearly had a claim to these checks under Ala.Code §7-9-306(2). The question thus becomes whether UCON had "notice" of that claim.

Under the UCC, "[a] person has 'notice' of a fact when: (a) He has actual knowledge of it; or (b) He has received a notice or notification of it; or (c) *From all the facts and circumstances known to him at the time in question he has reason to know that it exists*." Ala.Code §7-1-201(25) (emphasis added). Professors White and Summers have observed that this definition of "notice" "introduces at least the flavor of the objective-subjective fight. It is a short step from that definition to say that one 'knows' what a reasonably prudent man in his circumstances 'knows.'" 1 White & Summers, §14-6, at 711. The Alabama Supreme Court applied §7-1-201(25) in *Jones* to conclude that an endorsee of a negotiable promissory note is an HDC "unless ... [he] was possessed of facts sufficient to impute knowledge, or unless he had 'knowledge of such facts that his action in taking the instrument amounted to bad faith.'"

Jones, 229 So.2d at 498 (quoting *Tri-D Acceptance Corp. v. Scruggs*, 284 Ala. 153, 223 So.2d 273, 276 (1969)).

Because Alabama has included an objective component in its Article 3 "good faith" standard, the "good faith" and "notice" elements of the HDC test will frequently merge so that the answer to one inquiry is the answer to the other. See, e.g., *In re Legel Braswell Gov't Sec. Corp.*, 695 F.2d 506, 512 (11th Cir.1983) (because, under New York's UCC Article 8, "'actual knowledge or disregard of suspicious circumstances may constitute evidence of bad faith' ... the concepts of notice and good faith are interrelated in the assessment of bona fide purchaser status") (citations omitted). Whether or not this is what the UCC drafters intended, it is the law in Alabama. Thus, the facts recited by Sunburst and reflected in the record will also support a finding that UCON had reason to know of claims of other parties to the checks. At a minimum, it must be true that when UCON's Watters learned of AmSouth's perfected security interest in JMI's receivables, UCON had "notice" of a "claim to [the account debtor's checks] on the part of any person," namely AmSouth.

Because UCON does not meet the good faith and without notice requirements, it is not entitled to holder in due course status and, therefore, it has no shield against Sunburst's prior, perfected security interest in JMI's accounts receivable factored before July 17, 1989. Because we conclude that UCON was not an HDC, we do not reach the issue of whether, under Ala.Code §7-9-309, the interest of an HDC in checks received from account debtors trumps the interest of a third party with a senior, perfected security interest in those accounts receivable.

* * *

III. CONCLUSION

Alabama has adopted a test for the "good faith" of a holder in due course that includes both an objective and a subjective component. From all the facts and circumstances known to UCON at the time in question, UCON had reason to know that a claim to the checks existed; therefore, UCON fails the objective good faith component, as well as the notice requirement, and thus was not an HDC. The judgment of the district court that UCON was entitled to the proceeds of JMI's accounts receivable during the period before July 17, 1989 is REVERSED.

* * *

This case is AFFIRMED in part as modified, REVERSED in part, and REMANDED for further proceedings consistent with this opinion.

Northwestern Nat'l Ins. Co. v. Maggio,
United States Court of Appeals, Seventh Circuit, 1992
976 F.2d 320

Posner, Circuit Judge. This diversity suit on a promissory note was brought by Northwestern National Insurance Company against the note's maker, Anthony Maggio. The district court, holding that Northwestern was a holder in due course and had therefore taken the note free of any defenses Maggio might have had to a suit by the promisee, gave judgment for Northwestern on the latter's motion for summary judgment.

In 1981 Maggio had purchased a limited partnership in a new venture created by a former astronaut to develop an optoelectronic scanner designed to provide perimeter security for sprawling properties such as airfields, oil fields, and pipelines. As consideration for his partnership interest Maggio gave the partnership a noninterest-bearing note for $55,000 maturing October 31, 1990. The partnership negotiated the note to a venture-capital company that in turn negotiated it to Goldman Sachs which in 1988 negotiated it to Northwestern, along with other notes of the limited partners, at a 50 percent discount. When the note matured on October 31, 1990, Northwestern demanded payment from Maggio of the full face amount. He refused.

Maggio claims that he was induced to purchase the limited partnership by fraud. If so he has of course a claim against the partnership itself and perhaps the general partner and others, but he has no claim against Northwestern if the latter is a holder in due course. It is not if (so far as relevant here) it either did not take the note "in good faith" or "purchas[ed] it as part of a bulk transaction not in the regular course of business of the transferor." UCC §§3-302(1)(b), (3)(c) (1987); Ariz.Rev.Stat. §§47- 3302(A)(2), (C)(3). We take up these questions in reverse order, and ignore Maggio's frivolous argument of judicial estoppel. The note recites, and the parties agree, that disputes concerning it are to be resolved under the law of Arizona, where the partnership was formed.

The rarely litigated bulk-transfer exception identifies a narrow class of transactions where the purchaser of the (otherwise) negotiable instrument ought to be suspicious that the seller may be trying to thwart promisors' defenses and prefer one creditor over others, or committing outright fraud (the transferee might be a successor of the transferor), perhaps en route to bankruptcy. The existence of those defenses makes the promisors creditors; the wholesale transfer of their notes to a "holder in due course" would extinguish the promisors' claims; and the fact that the transfer is not in the ordinary course of business reinforces the inference that the transfer is an attempt to extinguish creditors' claims. There is no indication that the sale by Goldman Sachs of the limited partners' notes to Northwestern was of this character. Bulk transfer it was, but there is no evidence that Goldman Sachs, a large investment bank, was acting outside the ordinary course of its business in making such a transfer.

The more substantial issue is whether the 50 percent discount at which Northwestern bought the note should have made Northwestern inquire into the possible existence of defenses. Maggio does not argue that the discount itself established bad faith--only that it was a sufficiently suspicious circumstance to make Northwestern guilty of ostrich conduct, or more precisely to raise a jury issue and thus forestall summary judgment. Bad faith is a conscious state but it includes the deliberate avoidance of inquiry by one who fears what inquiry would bring to light.

Northwestern reminds us that a noninterest-bearing note at fixed maturity *must* sell at a discount. No one will pay $1,000 today for the right to receive $1,000 in two years, and Northwestern bought Maggio's note from Goldman Sachs two years before it was to mature. But a 50 percent discount on a note bought two years before maturity implies an interest rate of about 40 percent a year, and Maggio asks us to infer that no one would compensate the buyer of a note at such a rate unless the promisor had defenses (we do not know whether Goldman Sachs was a holder in due course). But this overlooks an obvious reason for the discount besides compensation for the time value of Northwestern's money--the risk that Maggio, even if he had no defenses to a suit for collection brought by the original promisee, would raise some anyway, as he has done, or wouldn't have the assets to pay the note when it matured. A bird in the hand is said to be worth two in the bush. Goldman Sachs got the bird in the hand; Northwestern got the two birds in the bush.

The fact that a note is sold at a discount is thus not in itself a suspicious circumstance that triggers a duty of inquiry by the buyer. This would hardly be worth saying but for a sentence in an opinion by the Supreme Court of Arizona that, because this case is governed by Arizona law, we must take with more than ordinary seriousness: "That fact alone [that the note was purchased at a 33 percent discount] is sufficient to alert a prospective purchaser to a possible defense." *Stewart v. Thornton*, 116 Ariz. 107, 110, 568 P.2d 414, 417 (1977). Well, but as in other cases in which such dicta appear, such as *Winter & Hirsch, Inc. v. Passarelli,*

122 Ill.App.2d 372, 377-79, 259 N.E.2d 312, 315-16 (1970), and *Financial Credit Corp. v. Williams*, 246 Md. 575, 584, 229 A.2d 712, 716 (1967) (where the discount was 80 percent), that fact didn't stand alone. The note had been sold (at the discount) within the 48-hour period in which the buyer of the property in exchange for which the note was issued was entitled under Arizona law to rescind the purchase. The court held that the buyer of the note was charged with knowing the law and therefore would be assumed to have known when it bought the note that the maker had a defense against the note's seller (the promisee). The discount merely reinforced the inference of knowledge. In our case, the discount stands alone.

"[A]lone ..." It is *conceivable* that by use of this word the Supreme Court of Arizona intended to revolutionize the law of negotiable instruments, bore a large hole in negotiability, and thereby raise transaction costs in financial markets. But nothing in the opinion besides that one word suggests any such perverse ambition. Judicial opinions are frequently drafted in haste, with imperfect foresight, and without due regard for the possibility that words or phrases or sentences may be taken out of context and treated as doctrines. We shouldn't like this done to our opinions and are therefore reluctant to do it to the opinions of other courts. No court, even a federal court in a diversity suit, is obliged to treat a dictum of another court (or, for that matter, its own dicta) as binding precedent. The dictum in *Stewart* does not persuade us that the courts of Arizona would hold that the purchase of a promissory note at a discount is alone enough to defeat negotiability by requiring the buyer to determine whether, were he the original promisee, the promisor would have a defense to a suit for collection. We add that no court in Arizona (or for that matter anywhere else) has ever cited *Stewart* for that proposition, though the case is now fifteen years old.

Affirmed.

Fred Brunoli & Sons, Inc. v. United Bank & Trust Co.

Connecticut Superior Court, Judicial District of Hartford-New Britain, 1991
1991 WL 162187

Aurigemma, Judge. The defendant United Bank & Trust Company (United Bank) has moved for summary judgment based on its claim that the material facts are undisputed and it is entitled to judgment as a matter of law.

The court finds the following facts. An employee of the plaintiff forged the signature of the maker on one of the plaintiff's checks which was drawn on the co-defendant, Bank of Boston Connecticut (Bank of Boston). The check was in the amount of $3,387.77 and the name of the payee was left blank. The plaintiff's employee presented the check for payment to United Bank. United Bank provisionally credited her account and presented the check for payment to Bank of Boston for collection. Bank of Boston paid the check, charging the plaintiff's account. Two months later the plaintiff discovered the forgery and demanded payment of both defendants.

United Bank claims that it is not liable to the plaintiff under the so-called final payment rule, which has been codified in §42a-3-418(1) of the Connecticut General Statutes, which states:

[e]xcept for recovery of the bank payments as provided in article 4 and except for liability for breach of warranty on presentment under the preceding section, payment or acceptance of any instrument is final in favor of a holder in due course, or a person who has in good faith changed his position in reliance on the payment.

The foregoing provision of the Uniform Commercial Code is a codification of the rule set forth in the case of Price v. Neal, 3 Burr. 354 (1762) under which a drawee bank who accepts or pays an instrument on which the signature of the drawer is forged is bound on his acceptance and cannot recover back his payment. A comment to Uniform Commercial Code Section 42a-3-418 sets forth the rationale of this rule as follows:

> The traditional justification for the result is that the drawee is in a superior position to detect a forgery because he had the maker's signature and is expected to know and compare it; a less fictional rationalization is that it is highly desirable to end the transaction on an instrument when it is paid rather than reopen and upset a series of commercial transactions at a later date when the forgery is discovered.

United Bank relies on Fireman's Fund Insurance Co. v. Security Pacific National Bank, 85 Cal.App.3d 797, 149 Cal.Rptr. 883 (1978) in which the Court held that the final payment rule of Section [42a]-3-418 barred the drawer from recovering from the depository/collecting bank, which relied in good faith on the drawee bank's final payment, even though the collecting bank acted negligently when it took the check for deposit by the malefactor.

In Fireman's Fund the identity of the payee was, arguably, ambiguous. The plaintiff argued that the collecting bank was negligent in taking the check with the ambiguous payee. The court pointed out that Comment 4 to Uniform Commercial Code §3-418 indicates that that section "rejects decisions under the original Act permitting recovery on the basis of mere negligence of the holder in taking the instrument" unless such negligence amounts to a lack of good faith as defined by §1-201 or notice under §3-304. Comment 4, §42a-3- 418.

The Court in Fireman's Fund found that the collecting bank acted in good faith and that the claimed irregularity in the identity of the payee was not sufficient to constitute notice of a claim or defense under Section 3-304. That section (42a-3-304) provides that a purchaser has notice of a claim or defense if "(a) the instrument is so incomplete, bears such visible evidence of forgery or alteration, or is otherwise so irregular as to call into question its validity, terms or ownership or to create an ambiguity as to the party to pay."

In this case the check in question was sufficiently incomplete as to create not only ambiguity, but complete uncertainty, as to the party to pay: the payee portion of the check was left blank. Therefore, United Bank may well have had sufficient notice of a claim or defense to fall outside the protection of the final payment rule. Moreover, under Section 42a-3-104(1)(d), in order to constitute a negotiable instrument a check must "be payable to order or to bearer." An "order" is a direction to pay and "must identify the person to pay with reasonable certainty." Section 42a-3-102(1)(b). Since the check in question seemingly did not satisfy the foregoing requirements for a negotiable instrument, its payment by United Bank, arguably, is not covered by §42a-3-418 since that section applies only to the payment of negotiable instruments. See §42a-3-102(1)(e).

For the foregoing reasons it does not appear that United Bank is entitled to judgment as a matter of law and its motion for summary judgment is, therefore, denied.

St. Paul Fire & Marine Ins. Co. v. State Bank
Court of Appeals of Indiana, First District, 1980
412 N.E.2d 103

NEAL, Judge. This action was brought by the State Bank of Salem (Bank) against the drawer of a check, Aubrey, Inc. (Aubrey), and the Bank's insurer, St. Paul Fire and Marine

Insurance Company (St. Paul), under a bankers blanket bond. Following a trial to the court without intervention of a jury, judgment was entered in favor of the Bank and against Aubrey and St. Paul. Judgment was also entered in favor of St. Paul on its cross claim against Aubrey. Aubrey and St. Paul appeal the award in favor of the Bank; Aubrey appeals the judgment in favor of St. Paul on its cross claim.

We affirm in part and reverse and remand in part.

The facts most favorable to the judgment and relevant to our consideration of this appeal are largely undisputed and reveal the following.

On November 26, 1975, Stephens, a farmer, delivered and sold 184 bushels of corn to Aubrey for $478.23. Aubrey was engaged at the time in the sale and distribution of feed and grain in Louisville, Kentucky, under the name of Aubrey Feed Mills, Inc. The following day, Aubrey prepared its check payable to Stephens in payment for the corn and mailed it to Stephens. The check was prepared in the following fashion: the amount "478.23" was typewritten upon the line customarily used to express the amount of the check in numbers, abutting the printed dollar sign. On the line customarily used to express the amount in words there appeared "The sum of $100478 and 23 cts," which was imprinted in red by a checkwriting machine; the line ended with the printed word "Dollars."

On December 9, 1975, Stephens appeared at the Bank's branch in Hardinsburg, Indiana, and presented the Aubrey check and two other items totalling $5,604.51 to the branch manager Charles Anderson. Stephens told Anderson that he wished to apply these funds to the amount of his indebtedness to the Bank, to withdraw $2,000.00 in cash, and to deposit the balance in his checking account. During the interval between November 27, 1975, and December 9, 1975, someone had typed on the check the figures "100" immediately before the typed figures "478.23." This was rather crudely done, and involved typing the "100" in an uneven line; the second "0" was typed directly over the printed dollar sign on the check.

Anderson questioned Stephens about the Aubrey check since Stephens's prior dealings with the Bank had not involved transactions in the amount represented by the Aubrey check. Anderson also knew that Stephens had filed a voluntary petition in bankruptcy several months prior, but had subsequently reaffirmed his obligations to the Bank. Stephens explained that he had purchased a large quantity of corn in northern Indiana and had sold it in Kentucky at a higher price. Evidently satisfied with his explanation, Anderson stamped nine promissory notes, of which Stephens was maker, "paid" and returned them to Stephens. Anderson then directed a teller at the Bank to fill out a deposit slip for the transaction. At that point, neither Anderson nor the teller noticed the typewritten modification on the check. The transaction consisted of applying the funds represented by the three items in the deposit ($106,082.74) to Stephens's debt represented by the nine promissory notes ($31,851.81), an installment payment, of which Stephens was a joint obligor, of $27,559.27, accrued interest owed the Bank by Stephens in the amount of $5,265.65, and the $2,000 cash given to Stephens. The balance was credited to Stephens's account. Stephens then left the Bank.

Later that afternoon, Anderson began thinking about the transaction and examined the items in the deposit. He noted that Aubrey's check bore signs of possible tampering and contacted Aubrey's office in Louisville to inquire about the validity of the check. An Aubrey representative told Anderson that a check in that amount was suspicious, and Anderson then "froze" the transaction. The next day, Aubrey stopped payment on the check.

Thereafter, the Bank attempted to recover possession of the nine promissory notes from Stephens but was unsuccessful. Stephens subsequently left Hardinsburg and his present whereabouts are unknown.

After freezing Stephens's account, the Bank reversed the December 9, 1979, transaction by applying the $5,604.51 then on deposit in Stephens's account (said sum representing the amount of the two checks deposited on December 9, 1979 with Aubrey's check) against the

$2,000 paid to Stephens in cash on December 9, 1979, and crediting the remaining $3,604.51 against the aggregate principal balance of the nine promissory notes delivered to Stephens on that date. As a result, the Bank claimed a loss of $28,193.91 and made demand therefor upon Aubrey and upon St. Paul. Such demands were refused, and this action followed.

    * * *

We think the only issue dispositive of Aubrey's appeal is whether the trial court could rightfully have found on the evidence that the Bank was a holder in due course of the Aubrey check under the Uniform Commercial Code (U.C.C.) as adopted in Indiana. Hereinafter all references to U.C.C. sections will be designated by the appropriate chapter number followed by the section number, as found in Title 26, Article 1 of the Indiana Code. Thus, for example, §3-302 refers to Ind. Code 26-1-3-302.

The Bank's right to recover on the check is conditioned upon its status as a holder in due course of the check. Section 3-305 states in part: "To the extent that a holder is a holder in due course he takes the instrument free from (1) all claims to it on the part of any person; and (2) all defenses of any party to the instrument with whom the holder has not dealt except ...."

Assuming, without presently deciding, that Aubrey showed the existence of a defense, the burden was on the Bank to prove by a preponderance of the evidence that it was in all respects a holder in due course of the check. §3-307(3).

Section 3-302(1) defines a holder in due course as a holder who takes an instrument "(a) for value; and (b) in good faith; and (c) without notice that it is overdue or has been dishonored or of any defense against or claim to it on the part of any person."

There is no contention on appeal, and there was none at trial, that the Bank did not take the Aubrey check in good faith, which means honesty in fact in the transaction concerned. §1-201(19). There is also no question that the Bank was a holder of the instrument, as it was in possession of the check indorsed by the payee Stephens in blank. See §1-201(20).

(1) We initially consider whether the Bank took the Aubrey check for value. The Bank contends that it gave value for the check to the extent that it (a) acquired a security interest in the instrument under §§3-303(a), 4-208, and 4- 209; and *** (b) took the check in payment of an antecedent claim under §3-303(b). Aubrey contends that the Bank did not take the check for value since it immediately froze Stephens's account upon apprisal that the validity of the check was suspect and cancelled the amounts it had credited against Stephens's debt. Aubrey considers that the Bank's action in crediting Stephens's debt on the notes merely constituted a bookkeeping procedure and the Bank did not change its position by doing so, particularly since the Bank could still maintain an action against Stephens on the notes. Finally, Aubrey maintains that general principles of law and equity render the U.C.C provisions relied on by the Bank inapplicable.

We are of the opinion that the Bank took the check for value. The issue is most readily resolved by §3-303(b) which states in part: "A holder takes the instrument for value (b) when he takes the instrument in payment of or as security for an antecedent claim against any person whether or not the claim is due; ..." The statute plainly states that value is given for an instrument when the instrument is taken in payment for an antecedent debt not yet due. The statute contains no provision precluding application of the rule when fraud is exercised by the presenter of the instrument, as Aubrey would have us find.

While this section has not been construed in Indiana, an examination of authorities from other jurisdictions lends support to the Bank's position that the application of funds made available by the Aubrey check to Stephens's indebtedness and the surrender of the notes constituted taking the instrument for value.

In *Citizens Bank, Booneville, Arkansas v. National Bank of Commerce, Tulsa, Oklahoma*, (10th Cir. 1964) 334 F.2d 257, an Arkansas bank accepted from its debtor, in payment of a note, a check payable to the debtor drawn on an Oklahoma bank. The bank delivered the debtor's note to him. The Arkansas bank presented the check to the Oklahoma-drawee bank, which accepted the check and issued its cashier's check in payment. Later that day, the Oklahoma bank discovered that the check presented by the Arkansas bank bore a forged drawer's signature and dishonored the cashier's check. The Arkansas bank then brought an action against the Oklahoma bank on the cashier's check. The Oklahoma bank argued, as Aubrey does here, that since the Arkansas bank had recourse against its depositor, notwithstanding discharge of the debt, it could not recover from the Oklahoma drawee bank on the cashier's check. Reversing the trial court, the Court of Appeals held that the Arkansas bank was a holder in due course, stating, "Undoubtedly, credit was given for the forged check by the discharge of the pre-existing debt," 334 F.2d at 261, and recognizing the prevailing rule, "if the negotiated instrument is taken in satisfaction of an antecedent debt, the taker is a holder for value and in due course." Id.

Further, we believe that the Bank gave value for the check under §§4-208(1) and 4-209, in that it acquired a security interest in the check to the extent funds represented thereby were applied to Stephens's debt. Section 4-208(1)(a) states in part: "(1) A bank has a security interest in an item and any accompanying documents or the proceeds of either (a) in case of an item deposited in an account to the extent to which credit given for the item has been withdrawn or applied; ..." Section 4-209 provides: "For purposes of determining its status as a holder in due course, the bank has given value to the extent that it has a security interest in an item provided that the bank otherwise complies with the requirements of section 3- 302 on what constitutes a holder in due course."

In *Waltham Citizens National Bank v. Flett*, (1968) 353 Mass. 696, 234 N.E.2d 739, a depositary bank allowed its depositor, at the time he deposited a check upon which payment was later stopped, to draw a check against those funds in satisfaction of a note which the bank returned to the depositor. The court found the bank to have given value for the former check, apparently considering the bank to have "applied" credit against the deposited check under §4-208(1)(a). One commentary has suggested that the bank's delivery of the note to the depositor may have been determinative of the value issue.

We find no support for Aubrey's argument that the Bank did not give value since it did not change its position vis-a-vis Stephens and made a bookkeeping entry only of the credit given Stephens. Aubrey appears to liken the transaction under review to the situation arising when a bank provisionally credits a depositor's account pending final settlement of a deposited item. It is true that the giving of provisional credit, which has not ripened into credit available for withdrawal as a matter of right, and nothing more, does not constitute the giving of value for deposited item. §4-208(1)(a); *Universal C.I.T. Credit Corporation v. Guaranty Bank and Trust Company*, (D.Mass.1958) 161 F.Supp. 790. Official Comment 3 to §3-303 states that it is not necessary to give holder in due course status to one who has not actually paid value, and cites as illustration "the bank credit not drawn upon, which can be and is revoked when a claim or defense appears." West's AIC 26-1-3-303. When the credit is drawn upon, however, value is given to that extent. §4- 208(1)(a). Further, if the depositor's account is overdrawn at the time the check is taken, and funds represented thereby are applied to the overdrawal by way of set-off, value is given to that extent if the check is later dishonored.

We have been directed to two cases in which appellate courts have held that value was not given. Aubrey relies on *Coconut Grove Bank v. M. R. Harrison Construction Corporation*, (Fla.App.1969) 226 So.2d 120. In that case, the depositor deposited a check drawn to his order in his account at the bank. The bank allowed the depositor to withdraw some funds against the check. Further, the depositor drew two checks payable to the bank to be applied to a loan not then due, and the bank applied that amount on its books to the depositor's loan account. The drawer of the check stopped payment thereon, and upon notice thereof, the bank reversed its bookkeeping entry and destroyed the credit given toward the debt. The bank prevailed as to the former amount, but was denied recovery on the latter. The court did not consider whether §3-303(b), the section stating that taking an instrument in payment for an antecedent claim is value, applied in the case. Further, the opinion does not state whether the note evidencing the debt was returned to the depositor. We do not consider this case to be controlling on the issue.

In *Marine Midland Bank-New York v. Graybar Electric Company, Inc.*, (1977) 41 N.Y.2d 703, 395 N.Y.S.2d 403, 363 N.E.2d 1139, the bank was held not to have given value for a check deposited by its depositor. The bank had provisionally set off the amount of that check against its depositor's indebtedness. The court noted that the note had not been returned to the depositor and indicated in dicta that had the note been returned, a different result might have been obtained. The case, then, is clearly distinguishable.

We hold that the Bank in the instant case gave value for the Aubrey check to the extent that funds represented thereby were applied to Stephens's note.

We find no support for Aubrey's contention that the fraud exercised by Stephens vitiates the application of the U.C.C. sections that are controlling here. Aubrey set this mischief afoot by its own carelessness in preparing the check, using the checkwriting machine, for the higher amount and placing it into circulation. Our finding is in accord with the purposes of the U.C.C. provisions under consideration, which have been characterized as preventing "the hinderance to commercial transactions which would result if depository banks refused to permit withdrawal prior to clearance of checks." Our task is to construe the provisions of the U.C.C. liberally and apply them to promote the underlying purposes and policies of the Code, which include "to simplify, clarify, and modernize the law governing commercial transactions." Sections 1-201(1) and (2).

Aubrey vigorously contends the Bank was not a holder in due course of the check because, under the objective standard imposed upon the Bank by §3-304(1), the Bank took the check with notice of a defense to the check on the part of Aubrey. Aubrey argues the evidence of alteration on the face of the check and the irregular circumstances attending the transaction were such as to put a reasonably prudent banker, exercising normal commercial standards, on notice. The circumstances alleged to have imparted notice to Bank include the small size of Stephens's farming operations, Stephens's banking history including frequent indebtedness and overdrawals, the Bank's knowledge of Stephens's petition in bankruptcy, the size of the Aubrey check in relation to typical transactions undertaken by the Bank, and the implausibility of Stephens's explanation to Anderson, himself familiar with farming, of the transaction underlying Stephens's receipt of the check. The Bank concedes the U.C.C. imposed an objective standard of conduct upon it in the transaction. The essence of the Bank's contention is that the matter of the Bank's notice is a question of fact, and the trial court's implicit finding that the Bank took the check without notice of Aubrey's defense was not erroneous.

The general notice provision of the U.C.C. is stated in §1-201(25), which provides in part: "A person has 'notice' of a fact when (a) he has actual knowledge of it; or (b) he has received a notice or notification of it; or (c) from all the facts and circumstances known to him at the time in question he has reason to know that it exists." Section 3-304, titled "Notice to Purchasers," states in part: "(1) The purchaser has notice of a claim or defense if (a) the instrument is so incomplete, bears such visible evidence of forgery or alteration, or is otherwise so irregular as to call into question its validity, terms or ownership or to create an ambiguity as to the party to pay; ..." The Bank is a "purchaser" within the meaning of §3-304. See seriatim §§1-201(33), 1-201(32), 3-202, 1-201(20), 3-102(1)(e).

Section 1-201(25) imposes subjective and quasi-objective standards; §3-304 imposes an objective standard. An irregularity on the face of an instrument is sufficient to impart notice under §3-304(1)(a) where, "A reasonably prudent person exercising normal commercial standards would immediately be put on notice that there was something very irregular about the terms of the (instrument.)"

The gist of Aubrey's argument is that the alleged "alteration" on the face of the check, i.e. the typed figure "100," was "such visible evidence" of alteration as to call into question its validity or terms.

We do not think that the trial court erred as a matter of law in finding that the Bank took the Aubrey check without notice of a defense.

The Bank's branch manager, Anderson, with whom Stephens dealt in the transaction, admitted that he took the check without comparing the amount expressed by the checkwriting machine with the amount expressed in typewritten figures; indeed, he testified that he did not even look at the figures. He relied, instead, upon the amount expressed by the checkwriter that was entered upon the line generally used to express the amount of a check in words.

Section 3-118, captioned "Ambiguous terms and rules of construction," states in part: "The following rules apply to every instrument: *** (b) Handwritten terms control typewritten and printed terms, and typewritten control printed. (c) Words control figures except that if the words are ambiguous figures control." Official Comment 1 to §3-118 states: "The purpose of this section is to protect holders and to encourage the free circulation of negotiable paper by stating rules of law which will preclude a resort to parol evidence for any purpose except reformation of the instrument. Except as to such reformation, these rules cannot be varied by any proof that any party intended the contrary." West's AIC §26-1-3-118. The holder is thus able to take an instrument confident that he will be able to enforce the instrument according to the written terms without having to bring in the original parties to the instrument to ascertain the intended amount.

As the section makes clear, in the event of an ambiguity between printed terms and typewritten terms, the latter would control. We do not consider the impressions made by the check imprinter to be "printed" terms under this section.

A conflict between the two amounts on a check would be resolved by §3-118(c) which states that words control figures. Arguably, the amount imprinted by the checkwriting machine upon the line customarily expressing the amount in words, is expressed in figures. (Recall that the entry reads: "The sum of $100478 and 23 cts.") We think, however, that the purposes of the U.C.C. are best served by considering an amount imprinted by a checkwriting machine as "words" for the purpose of resolving an ambiguity between that amount and an amount entered upon the line usually used to express the amount in figures.

Two purposes behind the rule that words control figures have been expressed which support the proposition expressed here, i. e. that impressions made by checkwriting machines upon the "words" line control typed or written figures. In United States Fidelity and Guaranty Company v. First National Bank of South Carolina of Columbia, supra, it is stated: "A prime purpose, as we see it, of making a sum payable when expressed in words controlling over the sum payable expressed in figures is the very fact that words are much more difficult to alter. The perforated imprinting by a checkwriting machine, while expressing the sum payable in figures, is even more difficult to successfully alter than a sum payable in written words." 137 S.E.2d at 589. Earlier, in Payne v. Commercial National Bank of Los Angeles, (1917) 177 Cal. 68, 169 P. 1007 at 1008, the court said: "The theory is that a man is more apt to commit an error with his pen in writing a figure than in writing a word, and that the words ought to be deemed the better and more solemn statement, and therefore should govern." 169 P. at 1008.

In United States Fidelity & Guaranty Company, supra, a pre-U.C.C. case, a bank was presented with several checks upon which the amount in figures on the line generally used for figures had been "changed, altered, or corrected" to conform to the amount imprinted by a checkwriting machine on the line generally used for words. The former amount was handwritten in pen and ink. A question on appeal concerned the issue of the bank's negligence in accepting the checks in that condition. The court looked to the Negotiable Instruments Law which provided that upon a discrepancy between words and figures, the words control. The court found that the bank's action in relying on the amount as imprinted by the checkwriter did not conclusively amount to negligence.

We cannot say as a matter of law that the bank acted unreasonably in relying upon the amount expressed by the checkwriting machine. Aubrey presented no evidence that customary banking standards require a bank to closely examine and compare the two amounts on the check, and it was Aubrey's burden to prove the existence of such custom. *Western State Bank of South Bend*, supra. The issue of the Bank's constructive knowledge of any defense Aubrey may have had to the check, based on the alleged irregularity on the face of the check, was a question of fact for the trial court to determine. It was not error for the court to have determined that the Bank acted reasonably in relying on the amount imprinted by the checkwriting machine and took the check without notice, actual or constructive, of a defense thereto.

Aubrey further argues that the circumstances surrounding the transaction were so irregular as to put a reasonably prudent banker on notice of a defense to Aubrey's check. Aubrey directs us to no cases in which a holder was denied holder in due course status because of its knowledge of the questionable general financial position of the presenter of the instrument. Our research reveals that such knowledge is not sufficient in itself to defeat holder in due course status. See, e. g., *St. Cloud National Bank & Trust Company v. Sobania Construction Company, Inc.*, (1974) 302 Minn. 71, 224 N.W.2d 746 (knowledge that payee-depositor had a bad financial record, had overdrawn his account, or was otherwise a "bad risk" not sufficient to deny holder in due course status to depositary bank in suit against drawer of check who had stopped payment thereon). In *Texico State Bank v. E. U. Hullinger*, (1966) 75 Ill.App.2d 212, 220 N.E.2d 248, the court considered that the fact a bank knew that the payee's credit was such that his own checks "bounced with regularity all over the place" was not germane to the issue of whether the bank took a particular check with notice of an infirmity in that check. The court said, "Whatever may have been (the payee's) financial record, it had nothing to do with the integrity of (the drawer's) checks or with any notice express or implied that the (drawer) could not or would not honor his commercial paper or that any person had a defense against or claim to any part of them." 220 N.E.2d at 250. The only knowledge the Bank had concerning the transaction underlying the issue of the Aubrey check to Stephens, and thus the only knowledge relevant to the issue of Bank's notice of a possible defense to the check, grew out of Stephens's explanation to Anderson of how the check came into his hands. This was not sufficient to call into question the integrity of the Aubrey check.

We therefore hold that the evidence supports the trial court's determination that the Bank was a holder in due course of the Aubrey check. Since Aubrey has not shown a "real defense" under §3-305(2) the Bank may enforce the check against Aubrey to the extent it gave value therefor, and we shall not disturb the trial court's award of that amount.

* * *

Affirmed in part; reversed and remanded in part.

practice

Case 1

Payee negotiated a $1,000 note to Holder who agreed to pay $900 for it. The note was not paid when due and Payee sued Maker. Maker raised a personal defense that would entirely eliminate her liability on the instrument. To what extent is this defense good against Holder? 3-305; 3-302; 3-303(a).

Completely   a. **Holder has paid nothing of the $900 she promised Payee for the note.**

b. **Holder has paid $500 to Payee. 3-302(d).**

Not at all   c. **Holder has paid the full $900.**

Case 2

Payee negotiated a $1,000 note to Bank as security for a $500 loan. The note was not paid when due and Bank sued Maker.

$1,000; $500   a. **Maker is defenseless. How much can Bank collect? How much can Bank keep? 3-302(e).**

$500   b. **Maker raised a personal defense that would entirely eliminate her liability on the instrument. How much can Bank collect if Bank is a holder in due course?**

$1,000; $500   c. **Suppose Payee had sold and negotiated the note to T, a holder in due course. T was the pledgor of the note to Bank to secure a $500 loan to T. How much can Bank collect and keep if Maker has a complete defense to payment? See 3-302 comment 6 (*Case # 6*).**

Case 3

S sold goods to B who paid for them by check in the amount of the purchase price, which was $1,000. S deposited the check in her account at State Bank.

a. **S's balance at the time was zero. State Bank presented the check to B's bank, National Bank, for payment. National Bank dishonored the item because B had stopped payment upon discovering that the goods were defective. The check is bounced back to State Bank. Is it a holder in due course? 4-211; 4-210.**

b. **Suppose that before the check bounced, S deposited an additional $10,000 in her account and had withdrawn a total of $1,000. When the check was returned to State Bank, S's balance was $10,000. State Bank could have** charged the $1,000 dishonored item to S's account. 4-214(a). Instead, State Bank sued B as drawer of the instrument. Who prevails?

State Bank

c. Start again. There was no withdrawal or additional deposit. Immediately after S deposited the check, State Bank set off the deposit against S's overdue loan balance. When the check bounced, State Bank sued B. Who prevails?

d. Is the answer different or more certain if the debt against which State Bank applied the deposit was an overdraft S had drawn against the account? *Tokai Bank v. First Pacific Bank*, 186 Cal.App.3d 1664, 231 Cal.Rptr. 503 (Cal. App. 1986) (bank gave value when it applied cashier's check against checks drawn on insufficient funds in the depositor's account). What if the loan balance or overdraft was secured by an Article 9 security interest in all of S's goods, present and after-acquired, including the goods that were sold to B?

Case 4

P negotiated an instrument to T. From all the facts and circumstances surrounding the negotiation of which T was aware, a reasonable person in T's position would have known of a claim or defense to the instrument. T swears that she was unaware of any claim or defense.

a. Did T take the instrument with notice? 3-302(a); 1-201(25).

Yes

b. Suppose that the facts actually known to T would not have tipped off a reasonable person. Yet, the circumstances surrounding T's taking of the instrument were such that a reasonable person easily would have discovered a claim or defense to the instrument had the person investigated the history of the instrument. T swears that she knew nothing. Did T take with notice?

No

c. Suppose that a reasonable person would have investigated the history of the instrument. T did not investigate. Is T a holder in due course if an investigation would have led to facts that precluded due-course status?

i. It is a question of good faith rather than notice. It seems right that a holder lacks good faith if, in failing to investigate, the holder did so "as part of a deliberate desire on its part to evade knowledge because of a belief or fear that investigation would disclose a defense arising from the transaction," *Joint Venture Asset Acquisition v. Zellner*, 808 F. Supp. 289, 299 (S.D. N.Y. 1992); "for the purpose of remaining ignorant of facts which he believes would disclose a defect in the transaction," *Corn Exchange Bank v. Tri-State Livestock Auction Co., Inc.*, 368 N.W.2d 596, 600 (S.D.1985); "closed its eyes and in bad faith simply did not seek the truth in order to get its money", *E. Bierhaus & Sons, Inc. v. Bowling*, 486 N.E.2d 598, 605 (Ind.Ct.App.1985); and so is "guilty of a reckless or intentional avoidance of knowledge." *United States v. Mark Twain Bank*, 771 F.2d 361, 365 (8th Cir.1985). Yet, the principal case *Eldon's*, reprinted earlier in this chapter, also seems right that under a purely subjective test, failing to investigate, when a reasonable person would inquire, does not in itself amount to a lack of good faith. See, e.g., *National Union Fire Ins. Co. v. Woodhead*, 917 F.2d 752, 756 (2d Cir. 1990) (there is no duty to investigate underlying transaction absent knowledge of some fact that would prevent a commercially honest individual from taking up the instrument); *Schwegmann Bank & Tr. Co. v. Simmons*, 880 F.2d 838, 842 (5th Cir. 1989) (a duty of inquiry is implied only if the circumstances reveal a deliberate desire by the holder to evade knowledge of a claim by the maker); *Bankers Trust Co. v. Crawford*, 781 F.2d 39 (3d Cir.1986) (same); *J&B Schoenfeld Fur Merchants, Inc. v. Kilbourne & Donohue, Inc.*, 704 F. Supp. 466, 472 (S.D. N.Y. 1989) (no duty of inquiry absent wilful ignorance); *Mox v. Jordan*, 463 N.W.2d 114 (Mich. Ct. App. 1990) (no duty to make an inquiry as to the validity of the underlying transaction if the negotiable instrument is valid on its face); *Dallas Bank & Trust Co. v. Frigiking, Inc.*, 692 S.W.2d 163 (Tex.Ct.App.1985). Moreover, "[f]ailure to make such inquiry may be negligence and lack of diligence, but it is not 'notice' of what he might discover." *Eldon's Super Fresh Stores, Inc. v. Merrill Lynch, Pierce, Fenner & Smith, Inc.*, 296 Minn. 130, 138, 207 N.W.2d 282, 288 (1973).

    ii.   The hard question is whether or not an objective test of good faith requires an investigation whenever a reasonable person would inquire. 3-103(a)(4).

  d. Suppose that Maker issued the note to invest in P's enterprise. When T bought the note from P, T knew that

    i.   P was experiencing financing difficulties at the time she got Maker involved in the enterprise (*Schwegmann Bank & Tr. Co. v. Simmons*, 880 F.2d 838, 843 (5th Cir. 1989) (mere knowledge of poor financial health provides no notice of defense);

    ii.   P had a "bad reputation" (*J&B Schoenfeld Fur Merchants, Inc. v. Kilbourne & Donohue, Inc.*, 704 F. Supp. 466 (S.D. N.Y. 1989) (bad reputation or suspicious circumstances do not amount to notice); *Sundsvallsbanken v. Fondmetal, Inc.*, 624 F. Supp. 811 (S.D. N.Y. 1985) (mere existence of suspicious circumstances not sufficient); *Lawton v. Walker*, 343 S.E.2d 335 (Va. 1986) (the fact that the purchaser may have acted negligently or may have been affected with notice of suspicious circumstances is not sufficient to deny her due-course status);

    iii.   allegations of fraudulent business practices by P had been broadcast to the general public by the news media. See *Thomas v. State Mortg., Inc.*, 439 N.W.2d 299, 303 (Mich. App. 1989) (court opines that it could be persuaded that knowledge of these allegations would amount to notice that denied due-course status) (dicta); or,

iv. she was getting an extraordinarily "good deal" in buying the note from P -- an unusually high rate of return on her investment. Compare *In re Nusor*, 123 B.R. 55 (Bankr 9th Cir. 1991) (the extraordinarily favorable terms of the note indicated that this was an unusual type of commercial transaction, and higher than usual interest rate affects good faith) with *Northwestern Nat'l Ins. Co. v. Maggio*, 976 F.2d 320 (7th Cir. 1992) which is reprinted earlier in this chapter.

Does this knowledge prevent T from being a holder in due course? (It may not be notice, but do the facts affect "good faith" under the new, objective test?)

e. **Suppose that unbeknownst to T, the rate of interest provided by the note is legally usurious. T is not a lawyer and was actually ignorant of the usury laws. She did not have a clue or any suspicion that the rate was illegal. Is she a holder in due course? *Paul v. U.S. Mut. Fin. Corp*, 389 N.W.2d 487, 493 (Mich. App. 1986) (a note which is usurious on its face gives actual notice of the usury defense thereby precluding HDC status)**

f. **Suppose that the evidence that a holder took in good faith and without notice is equal in persuasive value to the evidence that she did not. Should the holder be allowed to enforce the instrument free from a defendant's personal defenses?**

The burden of establishing that the requirements for becoming a holder in due course have been satisfied is on the person claiming the rights of such a person. This person must persuade the trier of fact that she, or someone through whom she claims, took the instrument for value, in good faith, and without notice of any claim or defense. Nevertheless, this burden is not unduly heavy. According to the New York Court of Appeals:

> Since the requirement that a holder show that it did not have knowledge of a defense or claim to the instrument involves proof of a negative fact, we have held that its burden of proof is a slight one. In *Chemical Bank of Rochester v. Haskell*, 51 N.Y.2d 85, 93, 432 N.Y.S.2d 478, 411 N.E.2d 1339, we held that the testimony of the holder that it had no knowledge of a defense to the note in issue was sufficient to sustain its burden on that point and to require the defendant to come forward with evidence to directly controvert the holder's testimony. Implicit in that decision is the recognition that rarely, if ever, will the holder have documentary evidence showing its lack of knowledge. In this situation, evidence, if any, that the holder had knowledge of defenses will ordinarily be in the hands of the defendant. It is appropriate, therefore, to require the defendant in such cases to proffer such evidence to rebut the holder's statement of no knowledge.

First Int'l Bank v. L. Blankstein & Son, Inc, 59 N.Y.2d 436, 444, 465 N.Y.S.2d 888, 892, 452 N.E.2d 1216, 1220 (1983). In the *First International* case, the decisive issue was whether the plaintiff bank, which was suing to enforce two notes, was a holder in due course. The defendant maker proffered extrinsic evidence to establish the plaintiff's awareness upon taking the notes that the defendant's obligation on the notes was voidable, which knowledge would have prevented the plaintiff from becoming a holder in due course. The appellate division reasoned that the evidence was inconsistent with the terms of the notes, under which defendant was unconditionally liable, and held that the parol evidence rule thus barred use of the evidence in determining if plaintiff was a holder in due course. The New York Court of Appeals disagreed. It decided that the rule preventing reliance on extrinsic evidence to vary the terms of a writing did not bar the use of such evidence in deciding the holder-in-due-course issue.

> Subdivision (1) of section 3302 of the Uniform Commercial Code specifically provides, in conjunction with sections 3102 (subd. (1), par. (e)) and 3104, that a holder of a note which is unconditional on its face is not a holder in due course if he has not taken the note for value, in good faith and without notice of claims or defenses to it. Consequently, the introduction of evidence for the purpose of showing that a holder has not satisfied one or more of these three requirements is contemplated by the code. This is so even though the terms of the written instrument are, by definition, clear on its face. The Appellate Division's error was in failing to recognize that evidence offered to show that a holder did not take the instrument for value, in good faith or without notice of claims or defenses, is not introduced to vary the terms of the note, but, rather, to show that the bank was not a holder in due course. Parol evidence is clearly admissible for those purposes. Indeed, in *Ehrlich v. American Moninger Greenhouse Mfg. Corp*, 26 N.Y.2d 255, 258, 309 N.Y.S.2d 341, 257 N.E.2d 890, we stated that parol evidence is admissible to rebut the recital of "value received" on the note.

Id. at 446, 465 N.Y.S.2d at 893, 452 N.E.2d at 1221. For other cases recognizing that parol evidence is admissible to show that a person seeking to enforce an instrument is not a holder in due course, see *Barclays Discount Bank Ltd. v. Bogharian Bros., Inc*, 568 F.Supp. 1116 (C.D.Cal.1983), reversed on other grounds, 743 F.2d 722 (9th Cir.1984); *Israel Discount Bank Ltd. v. Rosen*, 59 N.Y.2d 428, 465 N.Y.S.2d 885, 452 N.E.2d 1213 (1983).

Case 5

"On October 25, 1983, in payment for cattle sold at auction, Fort Pierre issued check number 19074 for $31,730.23 to its customer, Gene Hunt, naming as additional payees Cheyenne River Sioux Tribe Superior Court and PCA. Later Fort Pierre discovered it had miscounted the cattle and so it issued check 19331 dated October 31, 1983, for $36,343.95 to Hunt and the other payees. This check was meant to replace check 19074, but no notation to that effect was written on it. Fort Pierre did not ask Hunt to return check 19074, but attempted to issue a stop payment order. Its bank has no record of such order. Neither check emerged for a year. Then on October 26, 1984, a PCA representative met with Hunt to arrange repayment of a huge delinquen t loan.

At this meeting Hunt agreed, among other things, to give PCA checks 19074 and 19331 in exchange for the forgiveness of his remaining debt. PCA did not know one check replaced the other or that Fort Pierre attempted to stop payment on check 19074." *American State Bank v. Northwest South Dakota Production Cr. Ass'n,* 404 N.W.2d 517 (S.D. 1987). Is the PCA a HDC?

Case 6

D drew a check to P. P indorsed the check in blank and cashed it at State Bank the next morning. In the afternoon of the same day, State Bank learned that D had a defense to the instrument. State Bank nevertheless allowed P to withdraw almost all funds from her account and forwarded the check to the drawee for payment. Payment was refused. State Bank sued D on the check.

a. Is State Bank a holder in due course? See, e.g., *Bricks Unlimited, Inc. v. Agee,* 672 F.2d 1255 (5th Cir.1982) ("knowledge learned subsequent to the time of negotiation of an instrument does not impair holder in due course status"); *Allison-Kesley Ag Ctr., Inc. v. Hildebrand,* 485 N.W.2d 841, 844 (Iowa 1992) (proper time for determining whether the recipient of an instrument has notice of a claim or defense is the time of negotiation of the instrument to the holder); *Morgan v. Depositors Trust Co.,* 33 U.C.C.Rep.Serv. 1473 (Me.1982); *Thomas v. State Mortg., Inc.,* 439 N.W.2d 299, 303 (Mich. Ct.App. 1989); *Chase Manhattan Bank v. Coleman,* 496 A.2d 935 (R.I. 1985).

b. Same facts except that the president of State Bank learned of the defense 15 minutes before the check was cashed by a bank teller. Is State Bank a holder in due course if the teller himself learned of the defense only after having cashed the check? 1-201(27); 3-302(f).

c. Same facts except that the president of State Bank, whose office was at the main banking house, learned of the defense an hour before the check was cashed by a teller at a branch office of the bank. Is State Bank a holder in due course if the teller himself learned of the defense only after having cashed the check? Is 4-107 relevant to this question?

Case 7

Payee cashed a check at DB Bank knowing that there were insufficient funds in Drawer's account and even though payee had agreed that delivery of the check was conditional. The check bounced. DB Bank sued Drawer whose defense is the conditional delivery. It is a good defense against a person who lacks the rights of a holder in due course. It turns out that the payee is a majority stockholder and director of DB Bank. Is DB Bank an HDC? *Vail Nat'l Bank v. Finkelman,* 800 P.2d 1342 (Colo. Ct. App. 1990) (payee's knowledge not imputer to bank because payee was not acting within scope of his authority as bank's agent but rather in his individual capacity).

Case 8

D borrowed money from Bank and secured the loan by executing a written assignment of a certificate of deposit which was in possession of D's insurance company. The insurance company was holding the CD as collateral for a separate loan it had made to D. Bank advanced all the loan proceeds to D except for a portion paid to the insurance company to satisfy D's debt to it. The insurance company then delivered the CD, which had been indorsed in blank, to Bank. After having advanced the loan proceeds but before getting possession of the CD, Bank learned that the issuer of the CD had already paid the proceeds of the instrument to D.

No   **a.   Is Bank a holder in due course of the CD?**

b.   Suppose that Bank did not learn of the issuer's payment of the CD until after the instrument had been delivered to Bank. Upon delivery, however, Bank learned that the maturity date of the CD was three months earlier. Is Bank a holder in due course? See 3-304; but see *Yahn & McDonnell, Inc. v. Farmers Bank,* 708 F.2d 104 (3d Cir.1983) (unlike other instruments, a CD is not necessarily due upon maturity and trial court erred in holding that plaintiff was not a holder in due course simply because it came into possession of the CD more than 20 months after its maturity date).

Case 9

In July, 1984, S sold land to B who signed a promissory note for the purchase price. The note was payable in five installments, the first of which was due in 1986. The note was secured by a mortgage on the land. Shortly after the deal had been formally closed, B discovered that S had defrauded her. B filed suit to rescind. Everyone in town knew of this action, including the officers of State Bank. Talk of the squabble soon died down and the lawsuit lay dormant. A year later, in July, 1985, S sold the note to State Bank which acted through an officer who had joined the bank only five months earlier. This officer knew nothing of the rift between S and B. Is State Bank a holder in due course? See 1-201(25) (last sentence); *McCook County Nat'l Bank v. Compton,* 558 F.2d 871, 875-76 (8th Cir.1977) (discussion of the doctrine of forgotten notice); William E. Britton, HANDBOOK OF THE LAW OF BILLS AND NOTES §107 (1961) (effect of forgotten notice); see also *American State Bank v. Northwest South Dakota Prod. Cr. Ass'n,* 404 N.W.2d 517, 518 (S.D. 1987) (a holder with notice should not be able to undo that notice except in the most extraordinary circumstances).

Case 10

Bank had a security interest in D's inventory of trucks and proceeds of the property. Bank had perfected its security interest by filing with the secretary of state. D made a cash sale of a truck to B who paid with a check. D indorsed this check to C, a general creditor, in satisfaction of an unsecured debt owed by D to C. There is no doubt that Bank had a perfected security interest in the check. See 9-306(1), (2) & (3). C will take free of Bank's interest, however, if C is a holder in due course. See 3-306; 9-309. Is C a holder in due course? Did Bank's filing give C notice of Bank's interest? 3-302(b).

Case 11

Should a person take subject to a claim or defense that is totally unrelated to the reason the person is not a holder in due course? For example, assume that M executes a note to P. After the note matures, P transfers it to T. T is not a holder in due course. See, e.g., *United States v. Gray*, 552 F.Supp. 943 (N.D.Ill.1982) (in purchasing defaulted notes from lender, government was not holder in due course inasmuch as notes were overdue). Does this mean that T is subject to any and every *defense* that M has against P whether or not the defense is connected to the fact that the note was overdue when T bought it? Is there a stronger argument for allowing a purchaser of an overdue instrument who is a holder to take free of adverse *claims*? Zechariah Chafee, Jr., *Rights In Overdue Paper*, 31 Harv.L.Rev. 1104 (1918).

Case 12

B drew a check to S in payment for goods, but B neglected to fill in the name of a payee. S transferred the check at a six percent discount to Ace Check Guarantee Co., which filled in its name as payee of the instrument. The check was dishonored by the drawee. Ace sued B who raised a personal defense. Is Ace subject to the defense? See *Gray v. American Express Co.*, 34 N.C.App. 714, 239 S.E.2d 621 (1977) (person to whom draft issued with payee left blank had authority to complete the instrument and bind the drawer) (dictum); cf. *United States v. Second Nat'l Bank*, 502 F.2d 535 (5th Cir.1974) (United States was holder in due course of money orders bank delivered to government even though the government supplied name of IRS as payee of instruments after delivery).

Case 13

G is C's guardian. In payment of a debt to C, D drew a check payable to the order of "G, Guardian of the Property of C" and delivered the instrument to G. G indorsed the check, deposited it in her own personal account at DB Bank, and misappropriated the proceeds. C's successor guardian brought suit against DB Bank. Is the bank a holder in due course? See 3-307; *Matter of Knox*, 64 N.Y.2d 434, 488 N.Y.S.2d 146, 477 N.E.2d 448 (1985) (a bank which allows a fiduciary to cash a check payable to him as fiduciary, and to deposit some of the proceeds in his own personal account, without first establishing his authorization to do so is not, without more, liable to the beneficiary when the fiduciary exceeds his powers in dealing with the check); *Soloff v. Dollahite*, 779 S.W.2d 57 (Tenn. Ct. App. 1989) (putting cash into the hands of a fiduciary in exchange for an instrument payable to the corporation will not affect due-course status without actual knowledge that the fiduciary is committing a breach of duty); but see *Smith v. Olympic Bank*, 103 Wash.2d 418, 693 P.2d 92 (1985) (a bank is not a holder in due course where it allows a check that is made payable to a guardian to be deposited in a guardian's personal account because the bank has notice that the guardian is breaching its fiduciary duty).

Case 14

No

M made a note to P who indorsed the instrument to T. T later discharged P's liability on the check by cancelling P's indorsement. T then sold the instrument to S. M dishonored the note when it matured, and S sued M who raised a personal defense. Is S subject to the defense? 3-302(b).

Case 15

Siegman and Blankstein made a contract for the sale of diamonds by the former to the latter. The terms of the contract provided that Siegman would deliver the stones within 30 days, and that Blankstein would immediately execute a note for the price of the diamonds, which note was payable in 90 days. Siegman's duty to deliver and Blankstein's promise to pay were absolute and unconditional under the terms of their binding contract. Blankstein issued the note and Siegman immediately sold the instrument to Bank. The Bank knew upon taking the note that the instrument was given by Blankstein in exchange for Siegman's executory promise to deliver diamonds at a later date.

a. **Siegman breached her contract with Blankstein by failing to deliver the diamonds. Blankstein thus refused to pay the note upon maturity. Bank sued Blankstein on the instrument. Is Bank a holder in due course?**

Yes

b   **Suppose that both Siegman and Blankstein considered their agreement nonbinding in the sense that Siegman could refuse to deliver the diamonds or, if delivered, Blankstein could return the diamonds without further obligation and receive full credit. The parties fully understood that if either of them chose not to perform, the agreement of sale and the note would be considered of no force or effect. Bank knew of this understanding. Is Bank a holder in due course?**

No

Under Article 3 before 1990:

> The distinction between executory promises and voidable obligations is an important one in the law of commercial paper as set out in article 3 of the Uniform Commercial Code. An executory contract is one in which a party binds itself to perform at some time in the future. The usual method by which a party can avoid an executory obligation is to prove a breach by the other party. A holder who takes a note merely with knowledge that the note is referable to an executory contract is not charged with notice of a defense or claim which has not yet arisen in conjunction with the executory obligation. Of course, where a defense has arisen to the executory obligation, the obligation becomes voidable at that point and the purchaser of the instrument who has notice of said defense at the time he accepts the instrument is precluded from asserting holder in due course status. Similarly, an agreement which is rescindable at will is also a voidable obligation. A holder who takes a note with notice of the maker's absolute right to rescind is properly chargeable with the ramifications of this knowledge. As where the holder has knowledge that a defense has arisen to the performance of an underlying executory obligation, knowledge that an agreement is rescindable at will similarly provides the holder with notice

that a defense to the performance of the agreement has arisen and such notice precludes the holder from asserting that he is a holder in due course. Therefore, the disposition of these appeals necessarily tu rns on whether the subject notes are referable to a binding executory agreement or are merely voidable obligations, and if they are voidable obligations, the extent of the bank's knowledge with respect thereto.

First Int'l Bank v. L. Blankstein & Son, Inc., 59 N.Y.2d 436, 443-44, 465 N.Y.S.2d 888, 891, 452 N.E.2d 1216, 1219 (1983). This distinction surely survives under Article 3 after 1990. Notice that an obligation is voidable is notice of a defense.

c.   D issued a note to S who sold and negotiated it to T. When T took the note she was aware that the note arose out of a sale of goods by S to B and that B -- who had accepted the goods, could not revoke her acceptance, and was liable for the price -- was nevertheless suing S for damages under 2-714(1). It is a counterclaim rather than a defense. Is T a holder in due course?

d.   Can a person become a holder in due course of an instrument if she knows about claims -- such as reasons for setoff -- against the obligee-payee that have nothing to do with the instrument and do not amount to claims or defenses to it? See, e.g., *Ecoban Capital Ltd. v. Ratkowski,* 712 F. Supp. 1120 (S.D. N.Y. 1989) (due-course status is not denied because of knowledge of possible fraud claims that had nothing to do with the note); *Sundsvallsbanken v. Fondmetal, Inc,* 624 F. Supp. 811 (S.D. N.Y. 1985) (notice of a defense rather than setoff or counterclaim affects due-course status.).

§ 2. Payee As Holder In Due Course

The holder in due course doctrine is irrelevant to cases in which only two parties are involved. "Its essence is that the holder in due course does not have to suffer the consequences of a defense of the obligor on the instrument that arose from an occurrence with a third party." 3-305 comment 2. Typically, therefore, the doctrine is irrelevant when defenses are being asserted against the payee of an instrument because, typically, only one other person -- the maker or drawer -- is involved. So, "[i]f Buyer issues an instrument to Seller and Buyer has a defense against Seller, that defense can obviously be asserted. Buyer and Seller are the only people involved. The holder-in-due-course doctrine has no relevance." Id. In terms of the statute itself, a holder in due course takes free of "defenses of the obligor * * * [and] claims in recoupment * * * against a person *other than the holder.*" 3-305(b) (emphasis added). The holder is subject to defenses and claims against herself.

In a few common situations, however, the payee of an instrument can be involved in a three-sided deal in which the holder in due course doctrine becomes relevant to shield the payee from the obligor's claims and defenses against the third person. In these cases the payee is a holder in due course and is immune to the claims and defenses if she meets the usual requirements of 3-302. More often, the payee's due-course status is irrelevant in three-sided deals either because (1) the payee is not subject to the defense to begin with and thus needs no protection from it or (2) the defense is a real defense that is effective even against a holder in due course.

story

Payees As Holders In Due Course Of Negotiable Instruments

7 FORDHAM L.REV. 90, 92-94 (1938)

It was the well settled and generally accepted rule at common law that the right of a payee to be a holder in due course was co-extensive with that of any other holder of a negotiable instrument. The cases wherein this rule was established were, for the most part, those in which an intermediate party, in the regular and customary course of business, came into possession of paper by taking it from the maker, and then transferred it to the payee, who subsequently brought suit. This occurred, for example, when a debtor bought a bill payable to his creditor, intending to turn it over to the payee in satisfaction of a debt which he owed the latter; or a debtor, at his creditor's request, drew a note naming as payee the bank where the creditor expected to pledge the instrument, which was turned over to him for that purpose; or, as often happened, an accommodation maker drew paper payable to the bank where it was to be discounted to the accommodated party to whom it was entrusted. Had it been held under the common law that a payee who took from an intermediate party was subject to personal defenses existing between the latter and the maker, these useful three-way transactions would have become valueless to the commercial world. Apparently desirous of averting that unfavorable result, the early courts gave immunity from personal defenses to one, whether named payee or not, who had taken from such an intermediary for value and without notice. Indeed, the great majority of courts went even further and extended similar protection where the intermediate party was an agent or bailee of the maker, or a wrongdoer in possession of the paper, provided always that, in selling the same to the payee, he had feigned the appearance of a rightful owner.

There are also classes of cases where no third party handles the document during its transfer from the maker to the payee and in which the present problem arises most interestingly. For example, a maker fraudulently obtains the signature of an accommodator and then transfers the paper to an innocent payee; or, obtaining the signature honestly but subject to a condition, he transfers the bill or note free of the condition to a payee unaware thereof. It was well settled at common law that even in these situations the payee could claim the favored status of a purchaser for value without notice.

ⵑⵑⵑⵑⵑ

Despite the well-accepted view under the common law that in the classes of cases described above a payee took free of a maker's or drawer's defenses, there was a technical problem in perpetuating this view under the Negotiable Instruments Law (N.I.L.). A very close reading of various provisions of the N.I.L. supported the argument that a payee could never be a holder, which meant that a payee could never be a holder in due course and thus could never take free of the defenses of a maker or drawer. A majority of courts refused to read the N.I.L. so closely and held that a payee could be a holder in due course under the same circumstances that a payee could take free of a maker's or drawer's defenses under the common law. A minority of courts, however, applied the statute strictly without regard to the common law. For detailed discussions on the problem of a payee as a holder in due course under the N.I.L., see, e.g., Ralph W. Aigler, *Payees as Holders in Due Course*, 36 YALE L.J. 608 (1926-27); William E. Britton, *The Payee as a Holder in Due Course*, 1 U.CHI.L.REV. 728 (1933-34); Lester W. Feezer, *May the Payee of a Negotiable Instrument Be A Holder in Due Course?* 9 MINN.L.REV. 101 (1924-25).

Article 3 agrees with the majority reading of the N.I.L., that a payee can be a holder in due course. Before 1990, this proposition was explicitly stated in 3-302(2) (1989 Official Text). Through this provision the drafters of Article 3 intended to restate the common-law rule that the right of a payee to be a holder in due course is co-extensive with that of any other bona fide purchaser for value. Indeed, the examples illustrating the provision just as well illustrate the range of cases in which a payee took free of a maker's or drawer's defenses under the common law:

a. A remitter, purchasing goods from P, obtains a bank draft payable to P and forwards it to P, who takes it for value, in good faith and without notice as required by this section.

b. The remitter buys the bank draft payable to P, but it is forwarded by the bank directly to P, who takes it in good faith and without notice in payment of the remitter's obligation to him.

c. A and B sign a note as comakers. A induces B to sign by fraud, and without authority from B delivers the note to P, who takes it for value, in good faith and without notice.

d. A defrauds the maker into signing an instrument payable to P. P pays A for it in good faith and without notice, and the maker delivers the instrument directly to P.

e. D draws a check payable to P and gives it to his agent to be delivered to P in payment of D's debt. The agent delivers it to P, who takes it in good faith and without notice in payment of the agent's debt to P. But as to this case see Section 3-304(2), which may apply.

f. D draws a check payable to P but blank as to the amount, and gives it to his agent to be delivered to P. The agent fills in the check with an excessive amount, and P takes it for value, in good faith, and without notice.

g. D draws a check blank as to the name of the payee, and gives it to his agent to be filled in with the name of A and delivered to A. The agent fills in the name of P, and P takes the check in good faith, for value and without notice.

3-302 comment 2 (1989 Official Text) (withdrawn 1990).

The Revised Article 3 dropped 3-302(2) as unnecessary. "Former Section 3-302(2) has been omitted in revised Article 3 because it is surplusage and may be misleading." 3-302 comment 4. It remains just as true, however, that "[t]he payee of an instrument can be a holder in due course." It is also true, now and before, that "use of the holder-in-due-course doctrine by the payee of an instrument is not the normal situation." Id.

law

Graves v. Porterfield
Louisiana Court of Appeals, First Circuit, 1989
555 So.2d 595

Watkins, Judge. This is a suit on a promissory note. Plaintiff James R. Graves, as Liquidator of Performance Motor Sport Service, Inc. (PMSS), payee of the note, brought suit against defendant, John W. Porterfield, maker of the note. Mr. Porterfield answered the suit alleging failure of consideration and asserting the exception of no right of action. It is undisputed that Mr. Porterfield executed the note on September 29, 1983, for the sum of $2,702.73, payable on demand to payee, PMSS. The note also provides for 10% interest and attorney's fees in the amount of 25%. After trial on the merits the trial court found defendant liable on the note as well as for interest and attorney's fees. Mr. Porterfield has appealed that judgment. We reverse.

Plaintiff contends that the note represents a debt owed for repairs which payee performed on a 1976 Jensen GT vehicle on behalf of Mr. Porterfield and his client, Automobile Construction and Testing Inc. (ACT). On the contrary, Mr. Porterfield contends that he signed the note as security that he would return the vehicle to PMSS after he showed it to Mr. Eddie Anderson, the vehicle owner's attorney. Apparently Mr. Porterfield and Mr. Anderson were attempting to determine a price for which the vehicle could be sold. During these negotiations Mr. Anderson requested to see the vehicle. Pursuant to this request Mr. Porterfield arranged for Mr. Anderson to meet him at Mr. Porterfield's home on September 29, 1983, to view the vehicle. When Mr. Porterfield went to pick up the vehicle from payee's premises, he was required to sign a note to secure the return of the vehicle. He returned the vehicle the same day and requested that the note be destroyed.

* * *

The defense of failure of consideration may not be asserted against a holder in due course.

* * *

Although a payee may be a holder in due course, this status is not automatic. When a payee has dealt directly with the maker he will usually have notice of defenses and claims by the maker which will preclude status as a holder in due course. In the present case, the payee, PMSS, through its agent, was an immediate party to the transaction and was aware of the maker's defense of failure of consideration. Thus, payee is not a holder in due course.

    * * *

[W]e reverse the trial court and dismiss plaintiff's claims against defendant, John Porterfield. Costs to be paid by plaintiff-appellee.

Eldon's Super Fresh Stores, Inc. v. Merrill Lynch, Pierce, Fenner & Smith, Inc.
Minnesota Supreme Court, 1973
296 Minn. 130, 207 N.W.2d 282

[The opinion in this case is reprinted earlier in this chapter at pages 246-49 supra.]

First National Bank v. Creston Livestock Auction, Inc.
Iowa Supreme Court, 1989
447 N.W.2d 132

Harris, Justice. * * * Jerry Parker, a Union County farmer, had dealings with two banks. He first obtained a loan from the First National Bank in Lenox, Iowa (Lenox Bank). Lenox Bank took a security interest in all of Parker's livestock and livestock proceeds. Parker later obtained another loan from the First National Bank in Creston (Creston Bank) and that bank also took a security interest in Parker's livestock and livestock proceeds.

Sometime later Parker sold steers to Creston Livestock Auction, Inc. (Creston Livestock). There is no dispute that Lenox Bank held a perfected security interest in the steers at the time and had mailed notice of this fact to Creston Livestock.

Creston Livestock nevertheless paid for the steers by delivering to Parker a check made payable to Parker and Creston Bank. * * *

Lenox Bank brought a conversion action against Creston Livestock, claiming it was entitled to the funds received by Creston Bank. Creston Livestock paid the amount of the check to Lenox Bank in settlement, then brought this cross- petition against Creston Bank for contribution.

The trial court determined that Creston Bank was a holder in due course * * *.

This determination is controlling of the question in the case because, if Creston Bank was the holder in due course, it held the check free and clear of the claims of Lenox Bank. Iowa Code §554.3305 (1987). If Creston Bank was not a holder in due course it held the check subject to all claims and defenses. See Iowa Code §554.3306.

    * * *

It is somewhat rare but entirely possible for a payee to be a holder in due course. Iowa Code §554.3302(2). It is somewhat unusual because a payee ordinarily has been involved in the transaction which gave rise to the check and hence will most often have actual knowledge of claims or defects in it. But "[i]t is participation in the transaction out of which the instrument arose, rather than the taking of the instrument, which precludes holder-in-due-course status." Creston Bank did not participate in the sale of the steers at the livestock auction. Its status as copayee does not prevent it from being a holder in due course.

* * *

The parties stipulated that when Creston Bank took the check it had "no actual knowledge of the Lenox Bank's security interest in Parker's livestock or the proceeds thereof." The record is devoid of any hint that Creston Bank considered the transaction as anything other than the routine collection of an honest debt.

We conclude that Creston Bank was a holder in due course. This being true, its rights do not yield to those of Lenox Bank's earlier perfected security interest. Iowa Code §554.9309 (holders in due course "take priority over earlier security interest even though perfected"). Creston Bank took the check free of the claims of Lenox Bank.

DECISION OF COURT OF APPEALS VACATED; DISTRICT COURT JUDGMENT AFFIRMED.

John Deere Co. v. Broomfield

United States Court of Appeals, Eighth Circuit, 1986
803 F.2d 408

Ross, Circuit Judge.   John Deere Company (Deere) brought suit against F.L. Broomfield on a promissory note. The note was signed by Broomfield in connection with a deal for a tractor between Broomfield and Eddie Blackmon, d/b/a Blackmon Machinery Company (Blackmon), a John Deere dealer. A jury in the district court found [for the defendant]. * * * The trial judge denied Deere's motion for directed verdict and alternative motion for judgment notwithstanding the verdict and entered judgment based on the jury's findings. We reverse.

In March 1983, Blackmon approached Broomfield, a farmer, about an arrangement whereby Broomfield could obtain a tractor. Blackmon allegedly told Broomfield that if Broomfield would sign a note for the tractor, Broomfield could use the tractor without cost, and Blackmon would make the payments on the note. In connection with their agreement, Broomfield signed a loan contract and promissory note to Deere. The note was for the purchase of a new tractor, and reflected a downpayment of $18,000 and a principal balance due of $20,000. No downpayment was actually made. Broomfield admitted at trial that he signed the note although he knew that the transaction was not a "proper deal." Broomfield understood that the note would be sent to Deere, and if accepted, Deere would pay $20,000 to Blackmon. Further, Broomfield understood that the note obligated him to pay Deere on the note.

Blackmon never delivered the tractor to Broomfield. Further, Blackmon made no payments on the note, and went into receivership two months after the note was signed. At some point Broomfield had received a letter from Blackmon which stated that Blackmon was in possession of the tractor and that Blackmon was responsible for paying the note. A Deere representative, investigating Blackmon's activities, went to Broomfield's farm and discovered that Broomfield did not have the tractor. Broomfield gave the Deere representative the letter from Blackmon. Deere subsequently brought suit against Broomfield for default, two months before the first payment was due on the contract, because Deere deemed that its security was unsafe.

On appeal, Deere alleges that the district court erred in failing to grant Deere's motion for a directed verdict because Broomfield failed to contradict Deere's prima facie evidence for recovery on the note, namely that Deere was the owner and holder of the note which

Broomfield had signed, Deere had given consideration for the note, and Broomfield had defaulted. Further, Deere asserts that Broomfield had contractually waived any of its affirmative defenses against Deere, and that Blackmon was not Deere's agent. In the alternative, Deere asserts that there was insufficient evidence to support the jury's findings.

Broomfield argues, and the jury found, that Deere should not recover on the note because there was a failure of consideration. Broomfield contends that his bargained-for consideration was the tractor, which he never received. We disagree. Consideration is either a benefit to the person making the promise or a detriment to the person to whom the promise is made. Consideration need not move from the person promising, but may move to a third person. Payment made to a third person at the promisor's request constitutes consideration. In the present case, the $20,000 loan proceeds which Deere paid to Blackmon at Broomfield's request served as consideration for Broomfield's promise to pay on the note. Likewise, Deere took the note for value.

Deere also contends it took the note in good faith and without notice of any claims or defenses to the note by Broomfield. Although the dealership agreement between Blackmon and Deere gave Deere access to Blackmon's records, there was no evidence presented that Deere knew that Blackmon was experiencing financial problems. Further, although the fact that Blackmon hand delivered the note to Deere for approval may have indicated that he was in a hurry to get the money, there was evidence that Blackmon previously had hand delivered notes for Deere's approval. Moreover, "suspicious circumstances surrounding a transaction are not sufficient to defeat good faith." *United States v. Mark Twain Bank--Kansas City*, 771 F.2d 361, 365 (8th Cir.1985) (citations omitted) (applying Missouri law). Additionally, Deere had no knowledge that Broomfield had not taken delivery of the tractor when it received the note. Therefore, Deere took the note in good faith and without notice of any claims by Broomfield.

* * *

Therefore, we determine that the evidence was conclusive that Deere was entitled to recover on the note. The judgment of the district court is reversed, and remanded for a computation of damages.

practice

Case 1

B, purchasing goods from P, obtains a bank draft payable to P and forwards it to P, who takes it for value, in good faith and without notice.

a. **B, the remitter, obtained the bank draft by fraud. P can be a holder in due course and take free of Bank's defense of fraud. Right?**

Right

b. **Suppose B buys the bank draft payable to P, but it is forwarded by the bank directly to P, who takes it in good faith and without notice in payment of the remitter's obligation to her. Does P take free of the fraud defense?**

Yes

    c.   Suppose B buys the draft payable to herself and winds up keeping it and suing on the draft to enforce payment against the issuer whom B defrauded.

Case 2

A and B sign a note as comakers. A induces B to sign by fraud and, without authority from B, A delivers the note to P, who takes it for value, in good faith and without notice.

Yes   a.   Is P immune from the fraud?

    b.   Is the result different if P did not give value for the note or the note is not negotiable?

Case 3

D draws a check payable to P and gives it to his agent to be delivered to P in payment of D's debt. The agent delivers it to P, who takes it in good faith and without notice.

    a.   The problem is that the agent gives the check to P in payment of the agent's own debt to P. In this event D will assert a claim to the proceeds of the check. Did P take free of any such claim? (But as to this case, see 3-307 which may apply.)

    b.   Suppose that D draws the check payable to P but blank as to the amount, and gives it to his agent to be delivered to P. The agent fills in the check with an excessive amount, and P takes it for value, in good faith, and without notice. 3-115; 3-407.

Case 4

B bought goods from S and signed a note for the price. Unbeknownst to S, the goods were defective. The defect was latent and nobody could have discovered it. Nevertheless, the defect amounts to a breach of warranty that entitles B to cancel the contract and/or recover damages.

    a.   Is S a holder in due course?

Yes   b.   Is S subject to the defense even if she is such a holder?

Probably   c.   Suppose that B had paid with a cashier's check issued by Bank to S's order. Can S enforce the check against Bank despite the breach of warranty?

§ 3. Equivalent Rights To Holder In Due Course

Being a holder in due course is only a means to the end of enforcing a right to the payment of money free from adverse claims and the obligor's defenses against a third person. There are other ways to reach this end without requiring the plaintiff herself to satisfy 3-302 and even without the obligor signing a negotiable instrument.

story

Taking *through* (not *as*) a holder in due course -- shelter principle

"Transfer of an instrument, whether or not the transfer is a negotiation, vests in the transferee any right of the transferor to enforce the instrument, *including any right as a holder in due course.* 3-203(b) (emphasis added). Because of this rule "a holder in due course that transfers an instrument transfers those rights as a holder in due course to the purchaser." 3-203 comment 2.

Actually, this rule is only a specific application of a general, widely applicable principle of property law. It is the upside of derivative title, that is, a transferee gets her transferor's rights and accompanying immunities to defenses. Therefore, whenever any rule of law permits a person to enforce a right to the payment of money free from the obligor's defenses, this same immunity is available via the shelter principle to her transferee. See, e.g., *Federal Sav. & Loan Ins. Corp. v. Cribbs*, 918 F.2d 557 (5th Cir. 1990) (federal immunity is passed to a bank that purchased note from FSLIC); *NCNB Texas Nat'l Bank v. Campsie*, 788 S.W.2d 115 (Tex. Ct. App. 1990) (FDIC immunity passed to transferee bank).

There is an exception to the rule of 3-203(b), which is that a "transferee cannot acquire rights of a holder in due course by a transfer, directly or indirectly, from a holder in due course if the transferee engaged in fraud or illegality affecting the instrument." 3-203(b). The purpose is to prevent "[a] person who is a party to fraud or illegality affecting the instrument [from washing] * * * the instrument clean by passing it into the hands of a holder in due course and then repurchasing it." 3-203 comment 2. Before 1990 the exception was triggered by lesser culpability, i.e., by the transferee either having himself been a party to any fraud or illegality affecting the instrument *or as a prior holder having had notice of a defense or claim against the instrument.* 3-201(1) (1989 Official Text). Prior notice as a nonholder was not important. See, e.g., *National Union Fire Ins. Co. v. Woodhead*, 917 F.2d 752 (2d Cir. 1990); *National Union Fire Ins. v. Fremont*, 760 F. Supp. 334 (S.D. N.Y. 1991).

Estoppel

"An order or promise that is excluded from Article 3 because of the requirements of Section 3-104(a) may nevertheless be similar to a negotiable instrument in many respects. Although such a writing cannot be made a negotiable instrument within Article 3 by contract or conduct of its parties, nothing in Section 3-104 or in Section 3-102 is intended to mean that in a particular case involving such a writing a court could not arrive at a result similar to the result that would follow if the writing were a negotiable instrument. For example, a court might find that the obligor with respect to a promise that does not fall within Section 3-104(a) is precluded from asserting a defense against a bona fide purchaser. The preclusion could be based on estoppel or ordinary principles of contract. It does not depend upon the law of negotiable instruments." 3-104 comment 2.

Contractual waiver of claims and defenses

"Moreover, consistent with the principle stated in Section 1-102(2)(b), the immediate parties to an order or promise that is not an instrument may provide by agreement that one or more of the provisions of Article 3 determine their rights and obligations under the writing. Upholding the parties' choice is not inconsistent with Article 3. Such an agreement may bind a transferee of the writing if the transferee has notice of it or the agreement arises from usage of trade and the agreement does not violate other law or public policy. An example of such an agreement is a provision that a transferee of the writing has the rights of a holder in due course stated in Article 3 if the transferee took rights under the writing in good faith, for value, and without notice of a claim or defense." 3-104 comment 2.

Direct financing

A person is always free to borrow cash from a lender -- a bank, credit union, small loan company -- and use that cash to pay for goods or services that the person wants. In this event she has executed two contracts: a sales contract with the merchant and a promissory note with the lender or other contract to repay the loan. The two transactions are separate. If the lender sues the consumer on the note or other credit contract, the borrower will not be able to assert any defenses based on her transaction with the merchant. In other words, without the ability or need to invoke the holder-in-due-course doctrine or use of a waiver-of-defense clause, the lender escapes the borrower's claims against the seller.

It is not uncommon for a merchant-seller to develop a working arrangement with a lender whereby customers desiring credit are referred to a particular lender -- or lenders, if the customer needs to borrow the down-payment separately from the balance -- for cash loans which are paid directly to the merchant-seller. The "interlock" between seller and lender can take many forms: common ownership, formal agreement, long course of dealing, the lender providing loan applications to the seller who assists customers in procuring the loan, free transportation from the seller's place of business to the lender, and so on. In such a case,

> [t]he note is a direct obligation of [the borrower-maker] payable to plaintiff finance company as payee. As such it is a separate and distinct legal transaction from the sale of the [goods]. Therefore, the bad faith or fraudulent conduct practiced by the vendor, if any, in the sale of the [goods] to the defendant, has no bearing whatever on plaintiff's loan to [the borrower-maker], nor can it affect the rights of the payee under the instrument. Only these equities and defenses arising in connection with the confection of the instrument and the consideration for its negotiation can be interposed by the maker in bar of the plaintiff's right to recover thereon.

Beneficial Finance Co. v. Bienemy, 244 So.2d 275, 279 (La.Ct. App. 1971).

Federal immunity

Federal law can give immunity from adverse claims and defenses to holders of contracts that are not instruments; and it can give the same immunity to transferees of instruments who are not holders in due course. The most important example is the *D'Oench* doctrine. In the controversial case, *D'Oench, Duhme & Co. v. FDIC*, 315 U.S. 447, 62 S.Ct. 676, 86 L.Ed. 956 (1942), the Supreme Court held that one who has dealt with a failed financial institution that is insured by the Federal Deposit Insurance Corporation may not assert a claim or defense against the FDIC that depends on some understanding that is not reflected in the insolvent bank's records. A federal statute, 12 U.S.C.A. 1823(e), codifies *D'Oench, Duhme* and its progeny and specifically directs that agreements with failed banks are unenforceable against federal insurers, including the FDIC and Resolution Trust Corporation (RTC), unless the agreements meet four formal non-secrecy requirements. This statute provides:

> No agreement which tends to diminish or defeat the interest of the Corporation in any asset acquired by it under this section or section 1821 of this title, either as security for a loan or by purchase or as receiver of any insured depository institution, shall be valid against the Corporation unless such agreement-- (1) is in writing, (2) was executed by the depository

institution and any person claiming an adverse interest thereunder, including the obligor, contemporaneously with the acquisition of the asset by the depository institution, (3) was approved by the board of directors of the depository institution or its loan committee, which approval shall be reflected in the minutes of said board or committee, and (4) has been, continuously, from the time of its execution, an official record of the depository institution.

12 U.S.C.A. 1823(e). The statutory and common-law *D'Oench, Duhme* doctrines bar essentially the same claims and defenses. They are virtually interchangeable. Together, the doctrines protect the FDIC in its several capacities, including receiver, and also protects bridge banks and successors of any protected entity.

As explained in *Texas Refrigeration Supply, Inc. v. Federal Deposit Ins. Corp.*, 953 F.2d 975 (5th Cir. 1992), at least two articulated policies support this broad, and, at times, arguably harsh rule:

> *D'Oench, Duhme* favors the interests of depositors and creditors of federally insured banks (who cannot protect themselves from unwritten accords) over the interests of borrowers, to whom such agreements are presumably accessible. Ease of understanding a bank's financial health is an equally important reason. We have recognized that *D'Oench, Duhme* "ensure[s] that FDIC examiners can accurately assess the condition of a bank based on its books." Simply put, oversight agencies should not bear too great a burden in getting their information. Because of the doctrine, the government need not research and compile extensive parol evidence, including inherently unreliable oral histories, to determine a bank's unrecorded liabilities.

953 F.2d at 979.

Another benefit of the *D'Oench* doctrine is that the notes and other contracts that a bank owns are more valuable to someone who purchases the assets or to the insurer if it sues to enforce them. They are more valuable because most unrecorded defenses of the obligors are cut off, as if the FDIC or its assignee were a holder in due course of a negotiable instrument. Even when actual Article 3 instruments are involved, actual holder-in-due-course status is not possible because the instruments were acquired under extraordinary circumstances in which Article 3 denies such status. 3-302(c).

For example, in *Oliver v. Resolution Trust Corp.*, 955 F.2d 583 (8th Cir. 1992), the Olivers entered into two financial agreements with Sooner Federal Savings and Loan Association (Sooner) and Sooner's wholly-owned subsidiary, Tandem. In the first agreement, the Olivers gave Sooner a mortgage on their home to secure the refinancing of loans Sooner had made to several limited partnerships in which Luther Oliver was a general partner. In the second agreement, the Olivers guaranteed loans Tandem made to two corporations Luther Oliver owned as sole shareholder. Based on these agreements, Sooner threatened to foreclose on the Olivers' home and Tandem sought repayment of the funds Tandem had advanced. The Olivers brought this action against Sooner and Tandem contending both financial agreements were accompanied by separate side agreements protecting the Olivers from personal liability and guaranteeing Sooner would not foreclose on the Olivers' home. After Sooner fell into financial difficulties, the RTC was appointed receiver for Sooner and was substituted as a party in this action. On the RTC and Tandem's motion, the action was dismissed because *D'Oench, Duhme* and its statutory counterpart, 12 U.S.C.A. 1823(e), precluded oral side agreements from serving as the basis for the Olivers' claims.

Significantly, the courts broadly define the "agreements" that are affected by *D'Oench*. In the landmark case of *Langley v. FDIC*, 484 U.S. 86, 108 S.Ct. 396, 98 L.Ed.2d 340 (1987), the Supreme Court read the term "agreement" expansively to include fraudulent misrepresentations since such statements are, in effect, fraudulent warranties. Later cases have further expanded the *Langley* broad definition of "agreement" to include the nondisclosure of material information. For example, in *McCullough v. FDIC*, 1992 WL 72825 (D.Mass. April 10, 1992), the plaintiffs sued the FDIC in its capacity as receiver of the failed Bank of New England ("BNE"). The plaintiffs alleged that BNE was the financier and co-developer of an industrial condominium project in which the plaintiffs bought four units. The plaintiffs funded this purchase with a promissory note from the BNE in the amount of $350,000 secured by a mortgage on the units. Plaintiffs alleged that at the time of this sale BNE was aware that the property was subject to a Notice of Responsibility, issued by the Massachusetts Department of Environmental Quality Engineering ("DEQE"), requiring the removal of hazardous waste located on the property and that BNE failed to inform plaintiffs of this fact. Based in part upon BNE's failure to disclose this material information, the plaintiffs sued for misrepresentation and violation of other state law. The action was dismissed because the claims made by the plaintiffs were grounded in undocumented agreements and were thus barred under the *D'Oench, Duhme* doctrine.

The bottom line is that "[t]he *D'Oench* doctrine extends broadly to cover any secret agreement [-- broadly defined, really any secret defense --] adversely affecting the value of a financial interest that has come within the [federal insurer's] control as receiver of a failed financial institution." *Oliver v. Resolution Trust Corp.*, 955 F.2d 583, 585 (8th Cir. 1992). It makes no difference that the insurer or its successor is not a holder in due course under Article 3 because the *D'Oench* doctrine rests on preemptive federal law that defines for itself the terms of immunity from claims and defenses.

law

Weast v. Arnold
Court of Appeals of Maryland, 1984
299 Md. 540, 474 A.2d 904

Rodowsky, Judge. This is a suit against the makers of promissory notes which the payee pledged as collateral for a loan. The delinquent balance on that loan has been paid by the pledgor's surety who thereby acquired the notes and who now sues on them. Contrary to the trial court's conclusion we shall hold that the plaintiff enjoys holder in due course status, as transferee of the lender's rights in the notes, but only to the extent of the lender's security interest in the notes. The excess of the plaintiff's claim is subject to a breach of contract defense on which the defending makers proved entitlement to no more than nominal damages as a setoff.

On September 26, 1972 George E. Weast, Jr. (George), then the husband of the plaintiff, Ruth W. Weast (Ruth), borrowed $140,000 from State National Bank of Maryland (SNB). Ruth had "co-signed for (her) husband" in connection with this indebtedness. Although the documents evidencing this loan are not in evidence, the premise on which the parties presented the instant case was that, as between Ruth and George, George was the principal obligor and Ruth was an accommodation party. We shall call this obligation and its later modifications the "Weast debt." By November of 1973 the Weast debt was in default and an agreement was reached with SNB modifying the terms. As part of this modification the notes on which the instant suit is based were made part of SNB's security. The notes came about in the following manner.

On November 23, 1973 George sold to Francis A. Arnold (Francis), one of the defendants, and to Randall Printing Company, Inc., a District of Columbia corporation (Randall Co.), common stock in Randall Co. Consideration moving to George in this transaction included three promissory notes in the combined original principal amount of $100,000, consisting of respective face amounts of $41,364, $38,636 and $20,000. Francis and his wife, Josephine Arnold (Josephine), the other defendant herein, signed each of the notes as makers. Randall Co. also signed the $38,636 note as a maker. We shall call these three notes the "Arnold notes." Francis and Randall Co. each pledged the Randall Co. stock respectively purchased by them as security and cross-security for the payment, inter alia, of the Arnold notes. Subsequently Randall Co. failed so that neither it nor its stock are involved in the case before us.

As part of the restructuring of the Weast debt to SNB, George on November 27, 1973 executed a security agreement in favor of SNB and indorsed the Arnold notes to the order of SNB. The security agreement recited that "as collateral security for the payment of any and all indebtedness" of George the Arnold notes and the pledges of Randall Co. stock had been "deposited with" and "pledged" to SNB. SNB was "also given a lien upon the title or interest of (George) in all property and securities now in *** the custody or possession of the Bank ***." The Arnolds were notified to make payments on their notes to SNB. Further to secure SNB, George and Ruth placed a second deed of trust on their residence in favor of SNB.

George petitioned for voluntary bankruptcy on July 1, 1975 in the District of Maryland. He listed SNB as a secured creditor and stated the principal balance due SNB, without accumulated interest, to be $104,235.12. His petition referred to the second lien on the residence and the Arnold notes as SNB's security. On April 5, 1977 George received a discharge in bankruptcy. The trustee of George's bankruptcy estate reported there to be no assets and the bankruptcy judge, also on April 5, 1977, approved that report and ordered the estate closed.

Payments to SNB on the Arnold notes ceased in the summer of 1976. At the times of the defaults on those notes the principal balances due totaled $67,844.22. SNB never sued on the Arnold notes.

About December 23, 1975 George and Ruth entered into a voluntary separation, support and property settlement agreement under which George was required to assign to Ruth all of George's interest in the Arnold notes. The Weasts were divorced June 10, 1976. By a writing dated June 3, 1976 George assigned "all rights and interests" in the Arnold notes to Ruth. This assignment was made after George had been adjudicated a bankrupt but before his discharge and the closing of his bankruptcy estate. The Arnold notes were then in the possession of SNB and were not, and never have been, indorsed by George to Ruth.

The record in this case leaves us uninformed as to whether there were any credits against the Weast debt, once payment on the Arnold notes ceased, until 1979. In order to avoid foreclosure of the deed of trust held by SNB on the residence, Ruth, on June 5, 1979, agreed with SNB to sell the property and, from the proceeds, to pay all principal and accrued interest on the Weast debt. Ruth also agreed to the release of $10,000 to SNB from the principal of an escrow account, together with the interest earned thereon, all of which was applied to the Weast debt, including counsel fees to SNB's attorneys. The total paid by Ruth in 1979 in order to satisfy the Weast debt to SNB appears to have been approximately $58,400.

One aspect of the settlement between Ruth and SNB was that SNB on July 13, 1979 indorsed to the order of Ruth each of the Arnold notes. At the same time Ruth assigned to SNB "all or such part of her interest in any proceeds collected thereon to the extent of the then unpaid balance of her obligations" to SNB, pursuant to the settlement agreement.

Ruth brought the present action on December 21, 1979 against Arnold and Josephine. Ruth's position at trial was that she acquired her interest in the Arnold notes by indorsement from SNB to her. She measured her claim by the total unpaid principal balance of the Arnold notes, together with 8% per annum interest thereon, as specified in the notes. Computed to February 1, 1982, the day of trial, the claim totaled $97,615.21. The Arnolds' principal contention was that Ruth was subject to a defense based on breach by George of the agreement for sale of Randall Co. stock which gave rise to the Arnold notes. The agreement provided that George, the original pledgee, would release part of the stock from pledge as increments of the stock purchase price were paid. One of these payment levels had been reached in 1974 but SNB, George's pledgee, would not release any of the stock. Ruth's reply was that this defense was not available against her because she enjoyed the rights of a holder in due course. Ruth based that status on her being a transferee of SNB which, she said, had acquired the Arnold notes in that capacity. Another issue raised by the Arnolds was that Ruth had acquired from SNB no more than SNB's security interest in the notes.

The trial court, in a written opinion, first considered Ruth's possible entitlement to the notes as assignee of George in June of 1976. It concluded that the assignment from George to Ruth was invalid because he was then in bankruptcy. We express no views on that holding because it is not before us. Ruth has not challenged that holding in her brief, presumably because she does not desire to trace her interest via assignment from George and thereby, arguably, be subject to defenses, if any, arising out of the alleged breach of the terms of the stock sale transaction between George and Francis. In this Court Ruth stands exclusively on her position that she acquired the same rights as SNB had, and that they are those of a holder in due course.

The trial court next reasoned that Ruth had become the owner of the Arnold notes by what amounted to a sale to Ruth by SNB of the collateral following default on the Weast debt. George's bankruptcy was pointed to as the event of default. In concluding that SNB had transferred to Ruth full title to the Arnold notes, the court relied on Md.Code (1975), §9-504(4) of the Commercial Law Article (CL). However, in the view of the circuit court, Ruth was not a holder in due course of the Arnold notes inasmuch as they were in default at the time she acquired them from SNB. Then, because Ruth was an assignee and had not presented any rebuttal to testimony suggesting that the failure of Randall Co. was attributable to the breach of the pledge agreement, it was held that there was "no choice other than to enter judgment in favor of the defendants," Francis and Josephine.

Certiorari was issued on our own motion prior to consideration of Ruth's appeal by the Court of Special Appeals. We shall reverse and remand.

(1)

SNB was a holder in due course. Under the test of §3-302(1) it took the Arnold notes for value, in good faith and without notice that any instrument was overdue or had been dishonored, or that any person asserted a defense against or claim to the instrument. See 5 R. Anderson, Uniform Commercial Code §§3-302:13 to 3-302:34 (3d ed. 1984); J. White and R. Summers, Uniform Commercial Code §§14-1 to 14-10 (2d ed. 1980). A holder takes an instrument for value "(t)o the extent that *** he acquires a security interest in *** the instrument otherwise than by legal process," or "(w)hen he takes the instrument *** as security for an antecedent claim against any person whether or not the claim is due." Sec. 3-303(a) and (b). See Anderson, supra, §3-303:12-17, §3-201:14, and §3-302:35; 2 Bender's Uniform Commercial Code Service, F. Hart and W. Willier, Commercial Paper Under the Uniform Commercial Code §§11.03(3)-(4) (1972, 1984 Supp.); Annot., 97 A.L.R.3d 1114, at §11 (1980, 1983 Supp.). There is no evidence that SNB took the Arnold notes other than in good faith. The notes were then only four days old. Express evidence that no default or dispute existed at that time is uncontradicted. Rights as a holder in due course can be acquired by a lender who takes as security notes of third parties payable to the borrower.

However, SNB's acquisition of the Arnold notes as a holder in due course does not per se give SNB full title to and ownership of the notes. CL §3-302(4) provides that "(a) purchaser of a limited interest can be a holder in due course only to the extent of the interest purchased." Hart & Willier, supra, §12.02(3) at 12-14-15, explain the concept more fully.

Being a holder of is not synonymous with having title to an instrument. "Title" in an ownership sense consists of a number of different kinds of interests. *** Article 3 honors this distinction by providing: (1) A transferee can be a transferee of a "security interest," something less than ownership. (2) A lien on or security in a negotiable instrument to secure an antecedent debt constitutes "value." (3) "Value" is measured by what is actually given for an instrument as opposed to what is promised, or by the extent of the lien or security interest of the holder. (4) A holder may have a limited interest and be a holder in due course only to the extent of that interest. (5) A holder in due course has rights "to the extent he is a holder in due course," implying that he may not have all rights of such a holder. The result is that a holder or transferee may not have or succeed to *all* rights of a holder or may have *all* such rights but be entitled to limited enforcement.

Article 9 provides that a security interest in any personal property, including negotiable instruments, may be created by a security agreement signed by the debtor. However, such an interest can be protected against the interest of third persons who may acquire conflicting interests only by the secured party's taking physical possession of the instruments. Thus, only when a secured party in fact takes possession *can* he be a holder under Article 3 and be protected under Article 9. While the secured party must give value to create a security interest, what he is acquiring is governed by Article 9. He is not a buyer of the instrument as such. Article 9 governs the sale of accounts, contract rights, and chattel paper, but not negotiable instruments alone. Article 3 governs their sale. (Emphasis in original; footnotes omitted.)

Because SNB acquired only a security interest in the Arnold notes, its rights as a holder in due course extended only to that security interest. The result is recognized in Comment 4 to §3-302. ***

The next question is whether Ruth acquired SNB's holder in due course status as Ruth contends she did.

(2)

In deciding that Ruth was not a holder in due course the trial court applied §3-302(1) to Ruth as of the time SNB indorsed the notes to Ruth. However Ruth's argument that she achieved holder in due course status rests on the "shelter" provision of §3-201. That section reads in relevant part: *** Ruth is not a prior holder of the Arnold notes. Nor has it been suggested that she was party to any fraud or illegality affecting those instruments. Thus, under §3-201(1) SNB, as a holder in due course, transferred its rights as such a holder to Ruth. This result is explained in Official Comment 3 to §3-201:

A holder in due course may transfer his rights as such. The "shelter" provision of the last sentence of the original Section 58 is merely one illustration of the rule that anyone may transfer what he has. Its policy is to assure the holder in due course a free market for the paper, and that policy is continued in this section.

The comment is followed by illustrations of which example (a) is particularly pertinent here.

A induces M by fraud to make an instrument payable to A, A negotiates it to B, who takes as a holder in due course. After the instrument is overdue B gives it to C, who has notice of the fraud. C succeeds to B's rights as a holder in due course, cutting off the defense.

In the instant case, even though the Arnold notes were overdue, and even if Ruth knew when SNB indorsed to her that the Arnolds asserted a breach of contract defense, Ruth nevertheless succeeded to SNB's status as a holder in due course. ***

Here SNB's status as a holder in due course extended only to its security interest. Accordingly, as SNB's transferee, Ruth's holder in due course status extends only to the security interest. The result is explicit in §3-201, dealing with the rights of transferees of instruments, which provides in subsection (2) that "(a) transfer of a security interest in an instrument vests (such rights as the transferor has therein) in the transferee to the extent of the interest transferred." See Official Comment 5 to §3-201; (citations omitted).

(3)

The foregoing conclusion necessarily means we do not agree with the circuit court's analysis of Ruth's acquisition of the notes. Basically that court said that the following steps had occurred:

    1. The security agreement between George and SNB relative to the Arnold notes provided that George's bankruptcy could be a default.

    2. George defaulted by petitioning for bankruptcy.

    3. SNB took possession of the collateral under §9-503(1).

    4. SNB sold the Arnold notes pursuant to §9-504(4), dealing with the disposition of collateral by a secured party after default.

The fact of the matter is that SNB did not take possession of the collateral as a consequence of default. SNB had been in possession of the Arnold notes which were indorsed by George to the order of SNB. Nor did default on the Weast debt, whether by George's bankruptcy or by failure to pay, result in a sale of the Arnold notes. SNB simply ignored its security interest in the Arnold notes and pressed Ruth based on her obligation for the Weast debt. When Ruth paid SNB in 1979 she discharged her obligation to SNB on the Weast debt.

Even though Ruth was obligated to SNB, as between her and George, George was the principal debtor and Ruth was simply an accommodation party. The relation between George, Ruth and SNB was one of suretyship, as defined in Restatement of Security §82 (1941), reading:

> Suretyship is the relation which exists where one person has undertaken an obligation and another person is also under an obligation or other duty to the obligee, who is entitled to but one performance, and as between the two who are bound, one rather than the other should perform.

It is well-settled that a surety who pays the debt for the principal obligor becomes subrogated to the rights of the creditor, including rights in the security. We said in *Finance Co. v. United States Fidelity & Guaranty Co.*, 277 Md. 177, 182, 353 A.2d 249, 252 (1976) that "(s)ubrogation is a long-standing equitable doctrine in Maryland whereby one who is secondarily liable for a debt, and has paid it, stands in the place of the creditor *** and is entitled to the benefit of all the securities and remedies which could have been resorted to for the payment of the debt." (Citations omitted.)

A good statement of the rule is found in *Reimann v. Hybertsen*, 275 Or. 235, 550 P.2d 436, modified, 276 Or. 95, 553 P.2d 1064 (1976). There an accommodation comaker paid the debt evidenced by notes. The principal obligor had secured the notes by mortgages. Having satisfied the principal debt the accommodation party sued to require the creditor to assign to the plaintiff the mortgages posted as collateral for the principal obligation. In affirming a grant of that relief the court quoted from *Simpson on Suretyship* §47 at 206-207, the following statement (id. at 239, 550 P.2d at 437-38):

> It is universally recognized that the surety upon paying the creditor is entitled to be substituted to the creditor's position. This right is known as the right of subrogation. It amounts to equitable assignment, in that equity will treat the surety as though he were an assignee of the creditor, *standing in his shoes to enforce* the debt against the debtor together with *any collateral held as security for the debt*, entitled to all priorities and immunities enjoyed by the creditor. Against the creditor, the right is strictly equitable, and is simply *a right that the creditor assign to the surety* his claim against the principal as well as any security held by him. It amounts in reality to specific performance, differing only in the respect that the duty of the creditor, which the court enforces, does not arise from contract, but is imposed upon him by equity, to increase the probability of the surety's obtaining reimbursement. The creditor, of course, has no basis upon which

he can object to assigning his claim and his security to the surety. ***. (Emphasis ours; footnotes omitted.)

In the instant matter, SNB indorsed the Arnold notes to Ruth. Absent such indorsement Ruth had an equitable right to compel SNB legally to transfer the security to her.

Ruth's rights to the security as a paying surety were not lost as a result of George's discharge in bankruptcy. George's bankruptcy was administered under the Bankruptcy Act of 1898, as amended, former 11 U.S.C. §1 et seq. (the Act). George's discharge gave him the defense of discharge to SNB's claim against him on the Weast debt and on any instrument evidencing that debt. The discharge was also defensive to a claim by Ruth, as a paying surety, against George as the principal obligor, for reimbursement or indemnity. See *Williams v. United States Fidelity & Guaranty Co.*, 236 U.S. 549, 35 S.Ct. 289, 59 L.Ed. 713 (1915); Maryland Casualty Co. v. Jones, 140 Md. 395, 117 A. 765 (1922). However, discharge of the principal obligor does not discharge the surety. See §16 of the Act, former 11 U.S.C. §34. Under the circumstances of the instant matter, which are uncomplicated by questions of preference, fraudulent conveyance or the like, SNB, following default on the Weast debt, could have proceeded against the security unaffected by George's discharge. ***

The common law principles under which a paying surety is subrogated to the rights of the creditor, including rights in the collateral, are recognized by the U.C.C. CL §3-415(5) provides that "(a)n accommodation party is not liable to the party accommodated, and if he pays the instrument has a right of recourse on the instrument against such party." Further, subsection (5) of §9-504, the subsection immediately following the one relied upon by the trial court in its analysis of Ruth's acquisition of the Arnold notes, reads:

> A person who is liable to a secured party under a guaranty, indorsement, repurchase agreement or the like and who receives a transfer of collateral from the secured party or is subrogated to his rights has thereafter the rights and duties of the secured party. Such a transfer of collateral is not a sale or disposition of the collateral under this title.

Thus, from the standpoint of Article 9, Ruth obtained the same rights in the collateral which SNB had. (Citations omitted.) There was no sale of the collateral to Ruth when Ruth, a party liable to SNB, received a transfer of the Arnold notes upon paying the Weast debt. ***

However, because in this case the collateral consists of instruments, which were transferred to Ruth by indorsement, there is a further wrinkle. It is a wrinkle which we must consider because of a combination of factors. First, Ruth asks that judgment be entered in her favor for the entire principal balance due on the Arnold notes, together with all accumulated interest at the contract rate specified in the notes. Next, Ruth has not proved that, as surety, she paid any part of the Weast debt other than her payments in 1979. Finally it appears that the amount which Ruth claims on the Arnold notes exceeds the balance on the Weast debt at the time Ruth satisfied that balance. In other words, for Ruth to obtain judgment in the full amount requested, she must predicate that part of her claim which exceeds the balance of the Weast debt on some legal theory other than her being subrogated to SNB's security interest.

(4)

SNB's indorsement of the Arnold notes to Ruth makes Ruth a holder under §1-201(20). The rights of a holder are set forth in §3-301 which in relevant part provides that "(t)he holder of an instrument whether or not he is the owner may ... enforce payment in his own name." The result is that a non-owner holder suing on an instrument can be both a holder and a holder in due course as to different interests in the instrument at the same time. Illustrative is

Schranz v. I.L. Grossman, Inc., supra, 45 Ill.Dec. 654, 412 N.E.2d 1378. In settlement of litigation X Co. executed its promissory note for $60,000 to the plaintiffs. X Co. secured its note to the plaintiffs by a $135,000 note payable to the order of X Co., made by A and guaranteed by B. Both X Co. and A defaulted. In the plaintiffs' suit against A and B the trial court gave judgment for approximately $49,000, the balance due on the $60,000 note, which was treated as limiting the plaintiffs' claim. This was reversed. It was held that the plaintiffs could enforce payment of the $135,000 note. However, the plaintiffs were holders in due course of the $135,000 note only to the extent of their security interest and as to the excess, they were holders who were subject to defenses good against an assignee.

In sum, Ruth is a holder in due course to the extent of SNB's security interest in the Arnold notes. Ruth acquired that security interest by subrogation when she paid the balance due on the Weast debt. Ruth is also a holder of the Arnold notes as to any excess of the balance due on the Arnold notes over SNB's interest in the security acquired by Ruth by subrogation. Because the trial court denied Ruth any holder in due course status in the Arnold notes, and entered judgment for the defendants, we reverse. Whether a remand is required and, if so, the scope of the issues on remand, will turn on the disposition of Ruth's argument that the Arnolds' evidence on the contract defense was insufficient.

(5)

Alternatively Ruth argues that there was no legally sufficient evidence to support the contract defense raised by the Arnolds so that, even if Ruth is not a holder in due course, Ruth was entitled to judgment as a matter of law. These arguments take us into evidentiary detail.

* * *

(6)

* * *

Appellees also assert that Ruth cannot sue in her own name as holder of the Arnold notes because, after indorsement by SNB to Ruth, Ruth by a writing separate from the instruments assigned the proceeds of the instruments to SNB. This assignment, however, was for security purposes in the period following the formation of the settlement agreement between SNB and Ruth up to Ruth's full performance of that agreement by payment to SNB out of the proceeds from the sale of the residence. Any secondary security interest, which might have been created by that assignment from Ruth to SNB, was extinguished by Ruth's payment of the balance of the Weast debt. That interim assignment does not affect Ruth's status as a holder of the Arnold notes.

Because there was no sale by SNB of the security for the Weast debt, as explained supra, there was no need for SNB to notify George's trustee in bankruptcy of a sale, as the Arnolds contend.

Nor is there merit in the argument that, in applying the shelter doctrine, SNB's status as a holder in due course should be determined as of the time of its transfer to Ruth, so that, even if SNB took as a holder in due course, it no longer had that status when it indorsed to Ruth. Section 3-302(1) specifies the time of taking the instrument as the time for determining holder in due course status. * * * To hold otherwise would greatly weaken the market for notes taken as a holder in due course which thereafter become due and would undermine the policy of the shelter doctrine.

(7)

Because of our conclusion that the Arnolds are entitled only to nominal damages on the breach of the partial release provision, proceedings on remand in this case will be limited to computing the amount of judgment to be entered in favor of Ruth against Francis and Josephine. Judgment should be entered in the amount of the principal unpaid balance on the

Arnold notes, together with interest at the rate specified in those notes to the date of judgment, less $1.00, the nominal damages setoff.

JUDGMENT OF THE CIRCUIT COURT FOR HOWARD COUNTY REVERSED AND CASE REMANDED FOR THE ENTRY OF JUDGMENT IN FAVOR OF RUTH W. WEAST IN ACCORDANCE WITH THIS OPINION.

COSTS TO BE PAID BY FRANCIS A. ARNOLD AND JOSEPHINE ARNOLD.

In re Joe Morgan, Inc.
United States Court of Appeals, Eleventh Circuit, 1993
985 F.2d 1554

[*The facts of this case and first of two issues on appeal are reported earlier in this chapter at pages 254-60 supra.*] The second question we must address [on this appeal] is whether Sunburst was equitably estopped from asserting its claims to the checks received by UCON from JMI's account debtors based on Sunburst's acquiescence in and encouragement of UCON's factoring activities after July 20, 1989.

* * *

D. THE EQUITABLE ESTOPPEL ISSUE

UCON does not contend that it was an HDC as to JMI's accounts receivable factored after July 17, 1989, which is when UCON gained actual knowledge of Sunburst's prior security interest. Nonetheless, UCON argues, and the bankruptcy and district courts found, that Sunburst was equitably estopped from asserting its prior security interest insofar as accounts factored after July 17, 1989 are concerned.

We have previously articulated the scope of appellate review of a finding of estoppel: Whether the established facts give rise to an estoppel is a question of law reviewable on appeal. However, the constituent elements of estoppel constitute questions of fact, and the district court's findings on these matters must be upheld unless clearly erroneous. *Keefe v. Bahama Cruise Line, Inc.*, 867 F.2d 1318, 1323 (11th Cir.1989) (citations omitted). Under Alabama law, the constituent elements of equitable estoppel are: 1) the actor, who usually must have knowledge of the facts, communicates something in a misleading way, either by words or conduct, or silence; 2) another relies upon that communication; and 3) the other party would be harmed materially if the actor is later permitted to assert any claim inconsistent with his earlier conduct. *Ex parte Baker*, 432 So.2d 1281, 1285 (Ala.1983).

The bankruptcy court found that Sunburst and UCON agreed on July 20, 1989 that UCON should continue to factor JMI's receivable accounts provided that the funds generated by the factoring would be used for JMI's payroll and that JMI would continue to generate new receivables in excess of the amount being factored. Sunburst has acknowledged that these conditions were met. Based on its review of the record, the district court found: "At the July 20, 1989 meeting, Sunburst was fully apprised of UCON's activities. Nevertheless, Sunburst chose to allow UCON to continue factoring the collateral because it kept JMI solvent.... The court finds that there is no evidence of misrepresentation on the part of UCON in the record." March 9, 1992 Order at 8-9. We review this conclusion de novo.

At the July 20, 1989 meeting, and thereafter, Sunburst clearly communicated to UCON that it acquiesced in UCON's continuing factoring of JMI accounts subject to two conditions, both of which were met. UCON clearly relied upon that communication and would be materially harmed if Sunburst were permitted to assert its claim that UCON should not have continued factoring JMI's accounts. We agree with the bankruptcy court and the district court that UCON has established all the elements of estoppel. We have only one minor disagreement with the holding of the bankruptcy court and the district court concerning estoppel. Those courts held that equitable estoppel applied as to accounts factored after July 17, 1989. This is three days too early, because it was not until the July 20, 1989 meeting that Sunburst agreed to permit UCON to continue factoring JMI's accounts receivable. UCON could not have relied on that communication from Sunburst before it was made.

* * *

Because the record amply demonstrates that UCON and Sunburst agreed that UCON should continue to factor JMI's accounts after July 20, 1989 as a means of keeping JMI afloat, and because UCON's statements during the July 1989 meetings did not rise to the level of misrepresentations, the judgment of the district court that Sunburst was equitably estopped from asserting claims that are inconsistent with the UCON-Sunburst agreement is AFFIRMED, insofar as it applies to accounts factored after July 20, 1989.

First State Bank v. Clark
Supreme Court of New Mexico, 1977
91 N.M. 117, 570 P.2d 1144

Easley, Justice. First State Bank of Gallup (First State), Plaintiff-Appellee sued M.S. Horne (Horne), Defendant-Appellant on a promissory note. The trial court granted summary judgment against defendant and we affirm.

FACTS

Horne had executed a $100,000 note in favor of R.C. Clark which contained a restriction that the note could not be transferred, pledged or assigned without the written consent of Horne. As part of the transaction between Horne and Clark, Horne gave Clark a separate letter authorizing Clark to pledge the note as collateral for a loan of $50,000 which Clark anticipated making with First State. Clark did make the loan and pledged the note, which was accompanied by Horne's letter authorizing the note to be used as collateral. First State also called Horne to verify that he was in agreement that his note could be accepted as collateral. First State attempted to collect from Horne on Horne's note to Clark which had been pledged as collateral. Horne refused to pay and this suit resulted.

ISSUES

The issues raised on appeal include (1) whether the note was a negotiable instrument for purposes of Article 3 of the Uniform Commercial Code (U.C.C.) [§ 50A-3-101 et seq.; N.M.S.A.1953] (this issue is a matter of first impression under New Mexico law); (2) if it is, whether First State qualifies as a holder in due course under the U.C.C.; (3) whether, if Article 3 does not apply to the instrument, the note was nevertheless negotiable as between the parties under ordinary contract principles; and (4) whether, under ordinary contract law, Horne is estopped to deny the note's validity.

NEGOTIABLE INSTRUMENTS UNDER ARTICLE 3 OF THE U.C.C.

Article 3 of the U.C.C. defines a certain type of readily transferable instrument and lays down certain rules for the treatment of that instrument and rules concerning the rights, remedies and defenses of persons dealing with it.

In order to be a "negotiable instrument" for Article 3 purposes the paper must precisely meet the definition set out in §3-104, since §3-104 itself states that, to be a negotiable instrument, a writing "must" meet the definition therein set out. Moreover, it is clear that in order to determine whether an instrument meets that definition *only the instrument itself* may be looked to, *not* other documents, even when other documents are referred to in the instrument. As Hart & Willier, 2 Bender's U.C.C. Service, Commercial Paper, §2.03(1) points out in its text and in footnote 3:

> The applicability of Article 3 must be determined from the instrument itself, without reference to other documents or oral agreements. The "four-corners test" is still applicable: the determination of negotiability under Article 3 must be made by inspecting only the instrument itself. ***

> This is clear from the mandatory language of U.C.C. §3-104, and from the following language from the Official Comment to U.C.C. §3-105 found under the heading "Purposes of Changes": "The section is intended to make it clear that, so far as negotiability is affected, the conditional or unconditional character of the promise or order is to be determined by what is expressed in the instrument itself. ***"

We recognize the Official Comments to the U.C.C. as persuasive, though they are not controlling authority.

Section 3-104 thus requires that, in order to be a negotiable instrument for Article 3 purposes, one must be able to ascertain without reference to other documents that the instrument:

> (a) [is] signed by the maker or drawer; and (b) contain[s] an unconditional promise or order to pay a sum certain in money and no other promise, order, obligation or power given by the maker or drawer except as authorized by [Article 3]; and (c) [is] payable on demand or at a definite time; and (d) [is] payable to order or to bearer.

Carper, supra, *Walls*, supra.

The note in question here failed to meet the requirements of §3-104, since the promise to pay contained in the note was not unconditional. Moreover, the note was expressly drafted to be non-negotiable since it stated:

> This note may not be transferred, pledged, or otherwise assigned without the written consent of M.S. Horne.

These words, even though they appeared on the back of the note, effectively cancelled any implication of negotiability provided by the words "Pay to the order of" on the face of the note. Notations and terms on the back of a note, made contemporaneously with the execution of the note and intended to be part of the note's contract of payment, constitute as much a part of the note as if they were incorporated on its face.

Counsel argue that §3-119 applies and allows incorporating other documents to remove the defects on the face of the instrument. They argue that Horne's separate letter to Clark authorizing the pledging of the note to First State removed the conditions in the note and the express prohibition therein against its negotiability and rendered the note negotiable for Article 3 purposes. This is incorrect. An instrument which in and of itself does not meet the requirements of §3-104 cannot be made negotiable for Article 3 purposes by reference to another document which purports to cure the defects in the note's negotiability.

Section 3-119 and the Official Comments thereto go only to clarifying what the effect is of referring to other documents which may affect negotiability where such reference is on the face of *an otherwise negotiable instrument.* See U.C.C. §3-119, Official Comment, Purposes. Neither §3-119 nor any other U.C.C. section applies to allow the use of other documents to correct defects in otherwise *non-negotiable* instruments.

The whole purpose of the concept of a negotiable instrument under Article 3 is to declare that transferees in the ordinary course of business are only to be held liable for information appearing in the instrument itself and will not be expected to know of any limitations on negotiability or changes in terms, etc., contained in any separate documents. The whole idea of the facilitation of easy transfer of notes and instruments requires that a transferee be able to trust what the instrument says, and be able to determine the validity of the note and its negotiability from the language in the note itself. 2 Bender's U.C.C. Service supra, §2.03(1). See *Carlos v. Fancourt,* 5 Term Rep. 482 (1794). Section 3-119 and comments thereunder serve to clarify that a holder of an instrument which refers to another document need not inform himself of conditions in that document unless he has notice of the particular limitation contained therein. Thus, as the comment clarifies, a holder can remain a holder in due course in spite of a reference to another document on the face of an *otherwise negotiable* instrument. Section 3-119 in no way implies or states, and neither do any comments thereunder, that an instrument non-negotiable on its face can be cured by reference to a document removing the defect which renders the instrument non-negotiable.

Since the note in question is not negotiable for Article 3 purposes, First State cannot be a holder in due course under Article 3, *Carper,* supra, and we need not discuss that issue.

NEGOTIABLE INSTRUMENTS UNDER ORDINARY CONTRACT LAW

Even though a note or instrument is not a "negotiable instrument" for Article 3 purposes, it may nevertheless be negotiable between the parties involved under ordinary contract law. The Official Comments to §3-119 which counsel have cited recognize this principle. E.g., U.C.C. §3-119, Official Comment 3. The comments assert that even where an instrument *is* negotiable for Article 3 purposes the parties in any transaction are always bound by the totality of documents which are intended to form a contract between them, not just the terms set forth in one which happens to be a negotiable instrument. The same is true when the instrument does not meet Article 3 requirements.

As between Clark and Horne, Clark had a contract right to pledge Horne's note to Clark as security. Clark had a contract right to negotiate the note. Thus the note was negotiable for Clark's limited purposes even though it was not an Article 3 negotiable instrument. Before accepting Clark's pledge, First State verified by direct conversation with Horne that Clark had Horne's authority to pledge the note as the letter permitted. Horne in no way suggested that he had any offsetting defense to the validity of the note. Horne failed to notify First State that Clark had given him an offsetting note which was intended to nullify the effect of Horne's note to Clark should Clark default on his loan obligation secured by that note.

U.C.C. §3-104, Official Comment 2 states in part:

> While a writing cannot be made a negotiable instrument within this Article by contract or by conduct, nothing in this section is intended to mean that in a particular case a court may not arrive at a result similar to that of negotiability by finding that the obligor is estopped by his conduct from asserting a defense against a bona fide purchaser. Such an estoppel rests upon ordinary principles of the law of simple contract.

We have long recognized the possibility of estoppel in appropriate cases. These cases clarify that equitable estoppel results from a course of conduct which precludes one from asserting rights he otherwise might assert against one who has in good faith relied upon such conduct to his detriment.

In the instant case the evidence clearly indicates that First State relied on the validity of Horne's note to Clark as a pledge to secure Clark's obligation to First State. First State not only required the pledge before loaning Clark the money, but was concerned enough to solicit verbal assurances from Horne prior to making the loan that the note was valid. Horne knew he had an offsetting note from Clark which would in effect invalidate or cancel his obligation under the pledged note, but he failed to tell First State the true state of affairs. First State relied in good faith on Horne's conduct -- his failure to reveal material facts -- to First State's detriment. As a matter of law Horne cannot assert any defenses he has against First State arising from the material facts he failed to reveal. Thus as a matter of law he cannot defend against the prima facie case made by First State and since there is no genuine issue as to any material fact regarding the genuineness of Horne's note and letter, summary judgment for First State against Horne was proper.

The summary judgment of the district court is hereby affirmed for the stated reasons, although we reject the trial court's conclusion that the note in question was a negotiable instrument as contemplated by Article 3.

It is so ordered.

Norstar Bank v. Corrigan
Supreme Court, Oneida County, 1987
136 Misc.2d 920, 519 N.Y.S.2d 447

John R. Tenney, Justice. In this action to recover for default in payment on a computer lease, the plaintiff assignee has moved for summary judgment. Defendant concedes the default in payment but alleges, inter alia, that the equipment has never worked, that the lessor has breached a variety of express and implied warranties, and that the contract is void because of the lessor's fraudulent inducement. The issue before this court is whether these substantial defenses are available against the assignee. It should also be noted that since the lessor is apparently bankrupt or otherwise unavailable, impleader is an impractical solution.

Paragraph 10 of the lease states that the "Lessors may assign ... this Lease and ... the assignee shall have all of the rights and remedies of Lessor hereunder, and shall hold this Lease free of any counterclaim, offset, defense or cross-complaint as against such assignee, Lessee reserving such remedies hereunder solely against the Lessor." Whether the underlying transaction is a true lease (as plaintiff contends) or an installment sale (as defendant contends), the provisions of Uniform Commercial Code Section 9-206 apply. That Section provides, in part,

"(1) Subject to any statute or decision which establishes a different rule for buyers or lessees of consumer goods, an agreement by a buyer or lessee that he will not assert against an assignee any claim or defense which he may have against the seller of lessor is enforceable by an assignee who takes his assignment for value, in good faith and without notice of a claim or defense, except as to defenses of a type which may be asserted against a holder in due course of a negotiable instrument."

Although defendant raises two possible defenses which would survive Section 9-206, neither is available on the facts of this case. Defendant first alleges fraud in the inducement. While fraud in the factum (relating to the instrument itself) can be a defense against a holder in due course, Chemical Bank v. Haskell, 51 N.Y.2d 85, 432 N.Y.S.2d 478, 411 N.E.2d 1339, the "overwhelming weight of recent authority stands for the proposition that fraud in the inducement is not an available defense". Chase Manhattan Bank v. Finger Lakes Motors, Inc., 102 Misc.2d 48, 52, 423 N.Y.S.2d 128.

Defendant also alleges either bad faith or notice of a claim or defense. He essentially argues that as the financing agency for Lessor, plaintiff knew or should have known that the Lessor had defective equipment and would be subject to defenses in any direct action to enforce the lease. Such conclusory allegations are insufficient and would impose an intolerable burden on banks and financing agencies. Under Section 1-201(19) of the Code, good faith requires "honesty in fact in the conduct or transaction". There are no evidentiary facts to the contrary here.

While the result in this case may seem harsh in light of the Lessor's insolvency, it is consistent with the intention of the Code's draftsmen:

> "The Code's conclusion, except for consumer goods, harmonizes with the Code's regular thrust toward the abolition of formal differences. Obviously, if a bank made a loan with which the borrower bought goods, the borrower could not defend against his loan on the ground that he was not happy with the goods. The use of credit sales by sellers, with the banks almost immediately stepping into the sellers' position as to the credit obligations, is simply another legal mechanism which reaches the same ultimate result. Thus, there is little reason for the bank to end up in a more exposed position when it obtains the credit obligation through the seller." Kripke, Practice Commentaries, UCC §9- 206, McKinney's Cons.Laws of N.Y. at 416-417.

Plaintiff's motion must, therefore, be granted.

Beneficial Finance Co. v. Bienemy
Court of Appeals of Louisiana, Fourth Circuit, 1971
244 So.2d 275

Stoulig, Judge. The Beneficial Finance Co. of New Orleans filed suit against Shalin S. Bienemy and his wife, Geraldine, to enforce the collection of the balance due of $294.45 on a promissory note, in the principal sum of $300, executed by the defendants and dated October 2, 1968. The note was made pursuant to the Small Loan Act and was secured by a chattel mortgage on a 1961 Chrysler sedan.

In their responsive pleadings the defendants admitted signing the note and chattel mortgage. They acknowledged the balance due as being correct, but urged in bar of plaintiff's right to recover that it was not a holder in due course because of a pre-existing legal relationship, express or implied, between the finance company and the vendors of the automobile. More specifically, the defendants contend they were induced by the sellers to borrow the remainder of the purchase price from the plaintiff and were actually escorted to the loan office for this purpose. In consideration of procuring business for the plaintiff, the vendors were paid a 5% commission. As such, it is urged the sellers were acting as agents for the loan company, and their fraudulent conduct and bad faith involved in the sale of the car is imputable to their principal, thereby destroying the presumption of plaintiff's good faith and rendering the obligation it held vulnerable to attacks of fraud or the want or failure of consideration.

* * *

The uncontradicted evidence reflects that the defendant Shalin S. Bienemy, on September 18, 1968, agreed to purchase a 1961 Chrysler sedan from Used Car Brokers, Inc., for $600. All of the negotiations leading up to and including the sale were with D. Daniel Bragg and Jeff Collette, the owner and salesman, respectively, of the above-named used automobile dealership.

Having no funds with which to pay the purchase price, Mr. Bienemy was taken by Mr. Collette to the Prudent Credit Corporation, where a loan of $300 was made. Lacking the balance of the sales price, the physical possession of the car was retained by the sellers. On October 2, 1968, upon the suggestion of the vendor, the defendant was driven to the plaintiff's office where he applied for a $300 loan to cover the balance of the sales price. In connection with the loan transaction, the defendants executed an installment note payable to the order of the finance company, which was secured by a chattel mortgage on the automobile they had just acquired.

* * *

It is at this point in the sequence of events that contradictions in the testimony arise. Mr. Bienemy stated when they returned to the lot he was given possession of the car, and in starting the motor noticed it was missing. Upon being assured by the vendor that a minor motor tune-up would remedy this condition, he drove it from the lot. While on his way home, the motor became overheated requiring him to stop at a service station for assistance. He immediately notified the seller of his difficulties, and was instructed to return the car so it could be checked by a mechanic. This he did some two days later.

* * *

The mechanic determined that $190 would be required to repair the engine which had a blown head gasket and also required valve work. Mr. Bienemy was unable to make the deposit of $50 required by the mechanic, and left his automobile on the lot which adjoined the repair shop. How and when the owner regained possession of his car is not known by any of the third party defendants.

The trial court rendered judgment for $294.45 plus interest, attorney's fees and costs in favor of the plaintiff in the principal action * * *.

Defendant's contention, that the plaintiff is not a holder in due course because of a preexisting principal-agent relationship between the finance company and his vendor, is not germane to the issues presented in the original demand. Admittedly plaintiff is not a holder in due course as defined by LSA-R.S. 7:52, but, in fact, is the payee named in the instrument which was negotiated to it by the maker.

Under the definition expressed in LSA-R.S. 7:52, a holder in due course is one who accepts an instrument from a prior holder without actual knowledge or knowledge of such facts as would make the act of accepting the instrument amount to bad faith. In the instant matter the plaintiff accepted the instrument from the maker and not a holder; therefore, plaintiff is the initial holder, having been the designated payee in the obligation.

The instrument was executed by the defendant as evidence of his indebtedness to the plaintiff for a $300 cash loan, the proceeds of which were paid to the maker. It is not a vendor's lien note representing a part of the credit portion of the sales price negotiated to the used car dealer, who subsequently transferred it to the present holder.

The note is a direct obligation of Mr. Bienemy payable to plaintiff finance company as payee. As such it is a separate and distinct legal transaction from the sale of the car. Therefore, the bad faith or fraudulent conduct practiced by the vendor, if any, in the sale of the car to the defendant, has no bearing whatever on plaintiff's loan to Mr. Bienemy, nor can it affect the rights of the payee under the instrument. Only these equities and defenses arising in connection with the confection of the instrument and the consideration for its negotiation can be interposed by the maker in bar of the plaintiff's right to recover thereon. None was presented and the plaintiff is therefore entitled to judgment for the unpaid balance due on the note, together with interest, cost and attorney's fees, in accordance with the tenor of the instrument.

* * *

Amended and affirmed.

Redmann, Judge [concurring as to the main demand, dissenting as to the third party demand].

* * *

Plaintiff sues on an obligation given in connection with the purchase of a car, from a person who was, in addition to being the seller, an agent of the plaintiff lender.

Plaintiff paid the seller a commission on this loan, as it had on loans for "10 or 15 cars a month, you know, 8 or 9 cars a month at least" during the previous four or five years.

Still, the seller did not *sell* for the lender; his function as agent of the lender was to procure borrowers. But it is true that this particular agent's method of procuring borrowers was the selling of cars (not, however, *solely* for the loan commission).

These circumstances trouble me in respect to the lender's entitlement to recover where its agent (but not exclusively as such) has sold a *** defective car, which was the buyer-borrower's ultimate principal motive for undertaking the obligation to the lender.

(Yet, if a loan is made as an entirely separated contract, even though the lender knows the purpose is to buy a car, the mere knowledge of ultimate purpose cannot defeat the claim of a lender for return of money loaned in accordance with the loan contract.)

It seems to me that the real question in a suit of this kind to enforce an an obligation remains whether the cause for which the obligation was given makes the obligation enforceable, or whether for some defect of cause the obligation is unenforceable.

In the case of a note issued to the seller and by him negotiated to a third party, *if* the third party is not a holder in due course the defense of *** defects would be good against him. But the theory is that the obligation sued on had the car as its cause, and since the car is so defective the buyer cannot be obliged to pay the credit portion of the price. There is no cause, no consideration, for the buyer's note: he didn't get what he bargained for.

Here (unless the seller's commission on the loan affects the theory) the note was not issued for the car, but for the lender's discharge of the buyer's obligation to pay the balance of the price of the car, the sale having been perfected by agreement several days earlier. (The lender shows a paper transaction, a check issued by lender to buyer and, in effect, seller jointly, and endorsed by both but deposited into the *lender's* own account). While it might technically be argued that the discharged obligation itself had no cause, the discharging of the obligation did cost the lender $294.

Thus the defendant did get from the lender what he bargained for in exchange for his note. So whatever we might say about the payment to the seller of a commission on the loan, the lender is not subject to the typical *** defense, which is lack of cause or consideration.

There is a substantial similarity between the seller-payee case, where the lender *buys* the seller's claim against the purchaser, and our case, where the lender "buys" the purchaser from the seller (paying him a commission) in order to obtain the purchaser's note in exchange for which the lender *pays* the seller's claim against the purchaser.

But there is also a substantial dissimilarity between the two situations, as noted above.

Unable to convert my doubt about the circumstances into an express and reasonable differentiation from the simple promise-for-good-cause case, I agree with the majority that the judgment for plaintiff on the main demand must be affirmed.

Courtesy Financial Services, Inc. v. Hughes
Court of Appeals of Louisiana, First Circuit, 1982
424 So.2d 1172

Shortess, Judge. Courtesy Financial Services, Inc. (plaintiff) filed suit against John A. Hughes and Teresa Hughes (defendants) for $1,025.43, the unpaid balance due on a promissory note executed for the purchase price of a used car. Finding that plaintiff was not a holder in due course, and that defendants established a failure of consideration in that the car was defective, the trial judge dismissed plaintiff's suit.

On October 13, 1978, defendants purchased a used 1976 Plymouth Fury Station Wagon from Security Motors. Paul A. Crumrin, Jr., handled the transaction both as salesman for Security Motors and as loan officer for plaintiff. One month after the sale, defendants experienced problems with the brakes and replaced them. During the two years that defendants drove the car, numerous other problems arose: the ceiling liner inside the car fell out and emitted a musty smell; the gas tank rusted and leaked; the water pump went out; the radiator overheated; the electrical system shorted and the brake lights ceased to function; the heater, air conditioner and power steering went out, etc. As the various problems arose, defendants attempted to repair the car themselves. However, they finally "gave up the ghost" in June of 1980. Since that time, the car has been sitting in defendants' front driveway.

Defendants' last payment was made on July 1, 1980. Payments stopped because breakdowns were causing defendants to be late for work, and because defendants felt that they were "getting further and further in the hole trying to keep the car running." Prior to July 1, 1980, defendants continued to make payments even though they were both out of work. Defendants paid approximately $2,502.06, the difference between the amount financed ($3,527.49) and the amount sued upon ($1,025.43) before they ceased making payments. When payments were made, defendants informed plaintiff that they were having problems with the car. In fact, defendants asked plaintiff for a loan of $600.00 so they could get repair work done. In response to plaintiff's suit, defendants raised the affirmative defense of failure of consideration, asserting that the car was defective, rendering it totally unfit for normal use.

Plaintiff says that: (1) the trial judge erred in entering judgment based on the defense of failure of consideration, and (2) the trial judge erred in finding that the plaintiff was not a holder in due course.

In a suit on a promissory note by a payee against the maker, the plaintiff will be given the presumption that the instrument was given for value received unless the maker casts doubt upon the consideration. Once the maker has cast doubt upon the issue of consideration, the burden shifts to the payee to prove consideration by a preponderance of the evidence.

Defendants testified as to the various malfunctions in the car and cast doubt on the issue of consideration. Plaintiff did not offer any evidence to rebut the testimony of defendants or to establish that consideration was given. Whether defendants' testimony alone was sufficient to cast doubt on the issue of consideration was a question of fact which the trial judge, by judging the credibility of the witnesses, was most competent to determine. The trial judge found that:

> Defendants have presented evidence, largely uncontradicted, of an impressive array of defects and malfunctions for even a two-year old used automobile. This court is persuaded that, taken as a whole, they manifest a failure of consideration.

We agree with the conclusion of the trial court that a failure of consideration existed.

Although the original payee on the note, plaintiff claims the status of holder in due course, and thus an exemption from the defense of failure of consideration.

After it is shown that a defense exists a person claiming the rights of a holder in due course has the burden of establishing that he or some person under whom he claims is in all respects a holder in due course. La.R.S. 10:3-307(3)

Plaintiff says that La.R.S. 10:3-302(2) gives a payee the status of a holder in due course. However, said provision only states that a "payee *may* be a holder in due course." La.R.S. 10:3-302(2); (emphasis added). Although a payee may be a holder in due course, said status is not automatic. When the payee deals with the maker through an intermediary (remitter) and does not have notice of defenses, such an isolated payee may take as a holder in due course. In most instances, however, a payee will not be a holder in due course because said payee will usually have notice of defenses and claims by virtue of the fact that he has dealt directly with the maker. In order for a payee to be a holder in due course, all of the basic requirements must be met. A holder in due course is a holder who takes the instrument (1) for value, (2) in good faith, and (3) without notice that the instrument is overdue or has been dishonored or of any defense or claim affecting the instrument. La.R.S. 10:3-302. Thus, a payee who is an immediate party to the transaction is not automatically entitled to holder in due course status.

In this case, Security Motors, the vendor, and plaintiff were owned by the same person and occupied the same building. Paul A. Crumrin, Jr., the branch manager for plaintiff, testified that he handled the sale both as salesman for Security Motors and also as loan officer for plaintiff, as he was employed by both corporations. The trial court correctly found that plaintiff, a payee who was an immediate party to the transaction, was not entitled to holder in due course status. Thus, defendants may properly assert the defense of failure of consideration.

Failure of consideration is a defense to an action by one who does not have the rights of a holder in due course. La.R.S. 10:3-306(c), La.R.S. 10:3-408. Since defendants cast doubt upon the issue of consideration, and plaintiff did not meet its burden of proving consideration by a preponderance of the evidence, the trial judge correctly dismissed plaintiff's claim. Because plaintiff is not entitled to the rights of a holder in due course, the personal defense of failure of consideration can be used to defeat plaintiff's claim. La.R.S. 10:3-306(c); La.R.S. 10:3-408.

Accordingly, this appeal is affirmed at plaintiff's costs.

Affirmed.

practice

Case 1

Bank 1 and Bank 2 merged. The latter survived and acquired, as part of a bulk transfer of assets from Bank 1, Maker's note that had been sold and negotiated to Bank. With respect to this instrument Bank 1 was a holder in due course.

a.   Is Bank 2 a holder in due course?   *No*

b.   Is Bank 2 subject to Maker's personal defenses? See *Fidelity Bank v. Avrutick*, 740 F. Supp. 222 (S.D. N.Y. 1990) (Bulk transfer restriction on due-course status does not prevent operation of shelter principle.).   *No*

Case 2

Maker invested in a limited partnership by issuing a note that the partnership sold and negotiated to MHT. Surety issued a financial guarantee bond in favor of MHT that obligated Surety to make payment in the event of Maker's default. Maker defaulted. Surety paid and was subrogated to the rights of MHT against Maker.

a.   Is Surety a holder in due course?

b.   Does the shelter principle protect Surety if MHT was a holder in due course and

   i.   Surety learned after it had paid the note that Maker had been fraudulently induced into making the note?   *Yes*

   ii.   Surety knew of the fraud before it paid the note?   *Yes*

   iii.   Surety participated in the fraud?   *No*

   iv.   Surety was aware of the fraud at the time the fraud was committed? See 3-203(b) & comment 2.

Case 3

A federal agency, as government receiver, took over a failed savings and loan (S&L) association. In this role the agency acquired an overdue note that the agency sold to Bank. Maker complained that the S&L fraudulently induced her into signing the note.

a.   Is Bank a holder in due course?   *No*

b.   Is Maker's defense good against Bank? See *Federal Sav. & Loan Ins. Corp. v. Cribbs*, 918 F.2d 557 (5th Cir. 1990) (federal immunity is passed to a bank that purchased note from FSLIC); *NCNB Texas Nat'l Bank v. Campsie*, 788 S.W.2d 115 (Tex. Ct. App. 1990) (FDIC immunity passed to transferee bank).   *No*

Case 4

"On or about June 18, 1990, a representative from Tift County Tractor Co., Inc. ('Tift County Tractor') contacted a representative of plaintiff Ford Motor Credit Co. concerning the possible financing of a purchase agreement between Tift County Tractor and defendant Branch. Under the agreement, Branch was to purchase heavy construction equipment from Tift County Tractor for approximately $75,000. After studying the transaction, Ford Motor agreed to finance the purchase for the sum of $67,382.72.

"On or about June 20, 1990, defendant Branch signed a contract for the purchase of construction equipment ('Contract') from Tift County Tractor. Prior to signing the Contract, Branch had been contacted by defendant Goodman of Tift County Tractor concerning the purchase of the equipment. Goodman told Branch that if Branch purchased the equipment, then Goodman would lease the equipment on Branch's behalf.

"Goodman brought the Contract documents to Branch's office on or about June 20, 1990, for Branch's signature. Ford Motor supplied standard forms for the Contract. However, when Branch signed the Contract, the forms were completely blank except for the preprinted portions. At the time he signed the Contract, Branch knew that he was signing a retail installment contract for the purchase of construction equipment. He also knew that the transaction would be financed by Ford Motor. He did not know the cost of the equipment, and he never attempted to verify any part of the transaction. He relied upon Goodman to take care of the details of the transaction. The entire transaction took place in approximately two minutes. [The Contract contains a waiver provision as required in the statute: 'You will not assert against any assignee or subsequent holder of this contract any claims, defenses, or set-offs which you may have against the seller or manufacturer of the property.']

"Ford Motor received a copy of the contract on June 22, 1990, and mailed a check for $64,078.38 to Tift County Tractor in exchange for the assignment of the Contract. When Ford Motor accepted the assignment, it had no knowledge of any defenses that Branch had against Tift County Tractor on the Contract.

"Between July 28, 1990, and July 12, 1991, Branch made nine payments to Ford Motor on the Contract. The checks for these payments were drawn upon Branch's accounts. According to Branch, he delivered the coupon book for monthly payments on the Contract to Goodman. Each month Goodman sent Branch a check for the monthly payment accompanied by a monthly coupon. Branch deposited the check into his account and paid Ford Motor with a check from his own account. During this time, Branch assumed that Goodman was collecting rents from the lease of the equipment and remitting the payment to Branch.

"After July 12, Branch stopped making payments, and Ford Motor declared all sums due and payable. Ford Motor attempted to recover the construction equipment through a Writ of Possession action in the Superior Court of Tift County; however, Ford Motor was unable to locate the equipment.

"Branch never saw or received the construction equipment he purchased in the Contract. Furthermore, no person or entity has any knowledge of the whereabouts of the equipment. Shortly after obtaining the assignment of the Contract from Tift County Tractor, Ford Motor received a bill of sale for the equipment which indicated that Tift County Tractor had purchased the equipment from L.A. Womack. However, L.A. Womack claims that the bill of sale is a forgery." *Ford Motor Credit Co. v. Branch*, 805 F. Supp. 42, 43-44

(M.D. Ga. 1992). Ford Motor sued Branch and moved for summary judgment. Branch's defenses are failure of consideration and various kinds of fraud. How should the trial judge have ruled on Ford's motion?

Case 5

IMB Company purchased a piece of equipment on credit from S. IMB's obligation to pay the price was evidenced by a sales contract containing a waiver of defenses clause. S assigned the contract to A in exchange for A's promise to undertake some performance in the future. A notified IMB of the assignment and instructed IMB that contract payments should be made to A, not S. Shortly thereafter, IMB refused to make any further payments under the contract because the equipment purchased from S was defective. A argues that this defense is not effective against it because of the waiver of defenses clause in the contract IMB signed. Is the clause effective to cut off IMB's defense against A? Incidentally, A has not yet performed the promise it made to S. 9-206; 1-201(44).

Case 6

"In late 1983, Lawson State Community College and Energy Recovery for Industry and Commerce, Inc., began negotiating the sale of a heating, ventilating, and air conditioning system to be installed at the College. In broad outline, this proposed sale was to the effect that Energy Recovery was to act as a dealer-consultant to the College--Energy Recovery was to select, install, and maintain the system to be used by the College. Importantly, as part of its service, Energy Recovery guaranteed the College that Energy Recovery's efforts would result in substantial energy savings.

"The purchase price for the proposed equipment and services was $120,000. Instead of ordering this transaction in the form of an outright sale, however, the parties decided to finance the transaction by way of an equipment lease. Under the terms of this arrangement, Energy Recovery was given a lump-sum payment in full for the equipment and its services. Payment was made to Energy Recovery, however, not by the College, but by a financing lessor, First Continental Leasing Corporation, which took title to the equipment from Energy Recovery. First Continental then leased the equipment to the College. Under the terms of this lease, which is styled an 'Equipment Lease-Purchase Agreement,' the College was required to pay $2,618.68 per month for 60 months for equipment rentals. At the end of the 60-month payment period, the College had the right to purchase the equipment outright for a 'concluding payment' of $1.00.

"The lease agreement was subject to two subsequent assignments. In the first assignment, First Continental assigned the lease to Christopher Capital Corporation, which held its interest for less than three weeks. Christopher Capital subsequently reassigned the lease to First Westside Bank. First Westside still holds its interest in the lease.

"All did not go well as to the underlying contract between the College and

Energy Recovery. The College soon found itself dissatisfied, not only with the quality of the equipment itself, which, it is alleged, is defective, but also with the energy savings the College has achieved by hiring Energy Recovery and installing the equipment. The College consequently sued Energy Recovery for breach of warranty as to the quality of the equipment itself and also for fraud for allegedly overstating the energy savings to be gained from Energy Recovery's program for the College.

"We are not, however, concerned * * * with the claims against Energy Recovery, which are still pending in the trial court. Rather, we are asked to determine whether similar claims for breach of warranty and fraud can also be asserted against the financing lessor, First Continental, and its subsequent assignees, Christopher Capital and First Westside Bank. * * *

"The College alleges that First Continental has breached various warranties regarding the equipment and has committed a fraud upon the College. These theories depend upon the contention that First Continental was a manufacturer of or dealer in the equipment installed at the College, and upon the contention that First Continental's relationship with Energy Recovery was such that it was a knowing facilitator of and therefore a participant in Energy Recovery's alleged overstatement of the energy savings to be derived from the installation of the equipment." *Lawson State Community College v. First Continental Leasing Corp.*, 529 So.2d 926, 927, 933-34 (Ala. 1988). What do you think? Is the Bank accountable to the College?

Chapter 6. Special Concerns About Checks

§ 1. Check Collection

U.C.C. "Article 4 defines rights between parties with respect to bank deposits and collections." 4-101 comment 3. Bank collections refer, principally, to the ways and means of collecting checks -- getting them paid by the banks on which they are drawn.   Article 4 is "a uniform statement of the principal rules of the bank [check] collection process." 4-101 comment 1. Bank deposits refer, principally, to checking accounts. Article 4 governs the relationship between banks and their customers with respect to these accounts. It addresses such issues as when the bank must pay checks drawn on the accounts, when the bank can or must dishonor such instruments, and the bank's accountability for wrongfully dishonoring or paying checks. Article 4 also provides rules for distributing risks and losses associated with check fraud.

These matters also are affected by federal law. A principal reason is that the Federal Reserve System, an institution of the United States government, is a regular player in the check collection system. Indeed, the twelve Federal Reserve Banks and their several branches and service centers, which are spread throughout the country, form the principal structure for interbank check collection. Half or more of the checks drawn in this country are collected through the Federal Reserve, even when the collecting and payor banks are located in the same city; and, when a Federal Reserve entity is involved in the collection of a check, the application of Regulation J (12 CFR part 210) is triggered.

Also, Congress has empowered the Federal Reserve "to impose on or allocate among depository institutions the risks of loss and liability in connection with any aspect of the payment system, including the receipt, payment, collection, or clearing of checks, and any related function of the payment system with respect to checks." 12 U.S.C.A. 4010(f). This statute is a general delegation of power for the Federal Reserve to regulate any aspect of bank deposits and collections. It even empowers complete and comprehensive regulation of deposits and collections, totally preempting state law. The first product of this wide regulatory power is Regulation CC (12 CFR part 229) which mainly deals with funds availability in depositors' accounts and also with the return process for checks that are dishonored.

For the most part, however, Regulations CC and J and other federal laws on bank deposits and check collection are supplemental rather than preemptive. They respect and treat Article 4 as the general law and add to it with respect to issues on which state law is thin or altogether lacking. So, in this book and probably in your classroom, bank deposits and check collection are covered mainly in terms of Article 4. Federal law is covered at the places where it significantly embellishes -- or overrides -- the structure and rules of state law.

story

Proposed Rule to Require Paying Bank to Provide Same-Day Settlement
Federal Reserve System, Docket No. R-0723, Wednesday, February 6, 1991
56 FR 4743-01

Supplementary Information: As a result of concerns related to the practice of delayed availability--the holds that some depository institutions place on the proceeds of checks deposited into their customers' accounts before the funds may be withdrawn--Congress passed the Expedited Funds Availability Act ("Act") (12 U.S.C. 4001-4010). The Act specifies maximum time limits on the holds that depository institutions may place on funds deposited into transaction accounts.

Prior to enactment of the Act, some depository institutions had argued that their availability schedules reflected the time needed for the collection and return of checks that were not paid and provided a measure of protection against the risk that the depository institution could not recover funds from the depositor if those funds had already been withdrawn from the depositor's account. In part to reduce the risk to depository institutions from the Act's requirements that funds be made available within a certain period of time, Congress granted the Board broad regulatory authority to make improvements to the check collection and return system. Section 609(c) of the Act (12 U.S.C. 4008(c)) provides that the Board, in order to carry out the provisions of the Act, has the responsibility to regulate "any aspect of the payment system, including the receipt, payment, collection, or clearing of checks; and any related function of the payment system with respect to checks." In addition, section 609(b) of the Act (12 U.S.C. 4008(b)) directs the Board to consider proposals to improve the check processing system.

The Board's Regulation CC (12 CFR part 229), which implements the Act, includes a number of provisions designed to accelerate the check return system. In addition to an improved check return process, the Board believes it is also possible to make improvements to the forward collection process in order to lower the costs to collect checks and to improve availability, thus further reducing risk in the check system. Specifically, the Board believes that the forward collection process can be improved by eliminating barriers to presentment that many paying banks[*] impose on private-sector collecting banks. The Board believes that

---

[*] Regulation CC defines bank to include all depository institutions, including commercial banks, savings institutions, and credit unions. A depositary bank is defined as the first bank to which a check is transferred. A paying bank is a bank by, at, or through which a check is payable and to which it is sent

these barriers to presentment have resulted in some inefficient intermediation in the check collection process, to the extent that collecting banks use intermediary collecting banks because the intermediary collecting banks can present checks to paying banks on terms more advantageous than those available to the collecting bank itself.

Therefore, the Board is proposing amendments to Regulation CC that would require paying banks to settle for checks presented by private-sector presenting banks on the day of presentment without the imposition of presentment fees,* if specified conditions are met. The proposal provides an 8 a.m. (local time of the paying bank) presentment deadline for same-day settlement for checks presented by private-sector presenting banks. The Board believes that providing for more balanced bargaining power between presenting banks and paying banks should lead to faster settlement for checks and a more efficient payments system, consistent with the objectives of the Expedited Funds Availability Act.

* * *

Background on the Check Collection System

The check collection process involves the movement of checks from the depositary bank to the paying bank and the corresponding movement of the funds represented by the check from the paying bank to the depositary bank. The check collection system, which is composed of depositary banks, intermediary collecting banks (including correspondent banks and Federal Reserve Banks), and paying banks, makes use of automated equipment to sort checks, extensive ground and air transportation to move checks, and bank accounting systems.

Approximately 56 billion checks are written annually in the United States. As estimated 30 percent of these checks are deposited in the bank on which they are drawn, and thus are not sent through the check collection system. Of the remaining 70 percent, or 39 billion checks, it is estimated that more than 85 percent are collected on an overnight basis.

The check collection process begins at the depositary bank where checks are deposited by the bank's customers. At the end of each day, the depositary bank posts deposits to its customers' accounts and begins the process of collecting the funds represented by the checks. The depositary bank outsorts the checks drawn on itself (on-us checks) and then sends the remaining checks through the check collection system to the appropriate paying bank.

The depositary bank has several options available for clearing the checks it receives. The check collection paths chosen by each depositary bank are influenced by many factors, including the cost and speed of collection alternatives, the location of the paying bank, the dollar amount of the check, the size and check processing capability of the depositary bank, and the correspondent relationships the bank has established. Depositary banks generally seek to collect checks as quickly as possible to maximize the availability of funds, and larger depositary banks frequently use more than one collection path.

A depositary bank may send a check directly to the paying bank, either by direct presentment or through a clearinghouse arrangement. A clearinghouse is a group of banks, usually in a city or metropolitan area, that has agreed to exchange checks among themselves. The depositary bank may also use an intermediary collecting bank, either a correspondent bank or a Federal Reserve Bank, to complete the check collection process.

A portion of the checks that correspondent banks receive from depositary banks are payable by the correspondent bank. Correspondent banks may also present a portion of the

---

for collection. The Uniform Commercial Code defines collecting bank as a bank, other than the paying bank, that handles a check for collection. An intermediary bank is a bank to which a check is transferred in the course of collection, except the depositary bank or the paying bank. A presenting bank is a bank, other than the paying bank, that presents a check.

* Presentment fees are charges that certain paying banks charge private-sector presenting banks when presentment is made. The Federal Reserve Act prohibits Reserve Banks from paying presentment fees

checks received from depositary banks through local clearinghouses. Correspondent banks typically send checks that are not drawn on themselves or that cannot be presented at clearinghouses to which they belong to other correspondent banks or to Federal Reserve Banks for collection or directly to the paying bank, generally pursuant to an agreement with that bank.

Generally, settlement for checks that are presented directly by a private- sector collecting bank will occur by a credit to the account of the collecting bank on the books of the paying bank, or the settlement may occur through the accounts of the collecting and paying banks on the books of the Federal Reserve Banks. Settlement for presentments made through clearinghouse arrangements typically occurs on a net basis through accounts of the participating banks maintained at the Federal Reserve. With respect to checks collected through the Federal Reserve, the Federal Reserve credits the account of the collecting bank on the books of the Reserve Bank; the paying bank's account held at the Reserve Bank is debited in accordance with an automatic-charge agreement.

The Federal Reserve Banks collected about 18.5 billion checks in 1990. Approximately 64 percent of the checks they handle are received from local depositors--banks located in the region served by the particular Federal Reserve office. Nearly ten percent of the checks received by Federal Reserve offices were previously processed by another Federal Reserve office. Another five percent of the checks were deposited initially at another Federal Reserve office under the "consolidated" deposit program.* The remaining approximately 21 percent of the checks received by a Federal Reserve office are deposited directly by nonlocal banks without being handled by the depositor's local Federal Reserve office--"direct send" checks.

About 25 percent of all checks handled by the Federal Reserve are deposited in "fine-sort" packages.** Approximately 26 percent of the fine-sorted checks are drawn on city banks, 70 percent on regional banks, and 4 percent on country banks.

The Federal Reserve maintains an Interdistrict Transportation System (ITS) that utilizes contracted air and ground transportation to transport checks among Federal Reserve check processing offices. All Federal Reserve offices are interconnected through a "hub and spoke" transportation network that provides each Federal Reserve office a convenient and reliable means to transport checks nationwide. In addition, each Federal Reserve office has a local transportation network to deliver checks from the Federal Reserve office to the paying bank.

Payments System Objectives

An analysis of the potential impact of a proposed same-day settlement rule on payments system participants must consider the effects on public policy objectives for the payments system. Several payments system objectives that were established to provide a framework for the Board's consideration of proposed modifications to the Federal Reserve's payments system risk-control program are also pertinent to this analysis. The objectives are: (1) Lower risk; (2) rapid final payment; (3) lower operating expense of making payments; and (4) equitable treatment of all service providers and users in the payments system.

The risk reduction objective addressed both direct financial risks incurred by the Federal Reserve and private-sector and systemic risk. Systemic risk in the payments system is the risk

---

* Checks deposited under the consolidated deposit program are not processed by the automated sorting equipment at the depositing bank's Federal Reserve office, because the checks are deposited in cash letters sorted by availability zone of the receiving Federal Reserve office or by paying bank.

** A fine-sort package includes checks that are to be presented to a particular paying bank. In the case of fine-sort packages, the Federal Reserve office would not use automated equipment to process the individual checks, but would instead sort and deliver the package of checks to the appropriate paying bank.

that the failure of one bank to settle its payments obligations on time and in full will lead to the inability of other banks to meet their payment or other obligations. The risk of settlement failure thus imposes financial risks on other economic agents, in particular payors and payees with unsettled payments and the general creditors of banks, which could, in turn, be unable to meet their obligations.

The second objective relates to improving the speed of final payment. Rapid final payment is desirable because it promotes the efficient exchange of goods, services, and financial instruments, and facilitates the financing of such transactions by minimizing the need for short-term working capital, including intraday credit. This objective also embodies the legal notion that those economic agents who are entitled to funds should receive payment and final settlement in a timely manner.

The objective of lower operating expense addresses the real resource costs associated with handling payments. Such costs are incurred as a result of handling checks and, all other things equal, increases as the number of intermediaries in the collection process increases, because certain operating steps must be repeated each time an additional party handles a check.

Equitable treatment of all service providers and users promotes competition in the payments system. The Board believes that competition is an important means of promoting the efficiency of the payments system. Generally, a competitive environment provides incentives for payment service providers to increase the quality of their services, while minimizing their costs, and thus serves to promote efficiency in the payments system.

Current Inefficiencies in the Check Collection Process

It is possible that the current set of legal and institutional arrangements introduces inefficiencies in the check collection process. There are differences between the abilities of Federal Reserve Banks and private-sector collecting banks to present checks to paying banks for same-day settlement. Today, Federal Reserve Banks generally receive same-day settlement for checks presented to paying banks prior to 2 p.m. by debiting the paying bank's account or the account of a correspondent settlement agent held at a Federal Reserve Bank. The General Accounting Office found that private-sector banks, such as correspondent banks, frequently are unable to obtain settlement terms as favorable as those available to the Federal Reserve.[*] Some paying banks impose barriers to presentment, including presentment fees and requirements to maintain balances at the paying bank or settlement by remittance draft, which itself requires collection, that slow the speed or increase the cost of the forward collection of checks. Banks impose these barriers to obtain an additional source of revenue, to facilitate the provision of controlled disbursement services to their corporate customers,[**] to delay the presentment of checks, and/or to govern the timing of check presentments so as to maximize the efficient use of processing resources.

Presentment of and settlement for checks between banks is governed generally by Articles 3 and 4 of the Uniform Commercial Code (UCC). While the UCC does not explicitly sanction the use of barriers to same-day settlement, neither does it explicitly prohibit them. Thus, delayed settlement for checks between banks or the payment of presentment fees to obtain same-day settlement has become a common business practice despite the fact that most checks are payable on demand.

---

[*]   United States General Accounting Office, "Check Collection: Competitive Fairness is an Elusive Goal", May 1989.

[**] Banks offering controlled disbursement services notify their corporate customer early in the day of the amount of the corporation's check payments that have been presented that day.

In order to obtain same-day settlement, private-sector presenting banks commonly pay presentment fees when they present checks to certain paying banks. Proponents of presentment fees maintain that the fees either discourage presentments after locally established clearinghouse deadlines, thus allowing paying banks to operate more efficiently by controlling the timing of the work flow in their check operations, or offset the cost of processing checks that are presented after the deadlines. Presentment fees, however, often do not reflect a service rendered to the collecting bank by the paying bank, and may discourage the most economically efficient presentment of checks by encouraging greater intermediation to avoid the imposition of presentment fees and related balance requirements.

If a collecting bank attempts to present checks directly rather than use intermediation channels that increase real resource costs, it may incur other costs, in addition to presentment fees, that are imposed by the paying bank. Some paying banks impose other barriers to presentment that increase the collection costs of presenting banks and that may result in increased revenue for themselves.

For example, when presenting banks present checks to paying banks without having established account relationships, paying banks may settle in the form of a remittance draft drawn on another bank. This form of settlement can further delay the availability of funds to the presenting banks for a day or more because the remittance draft is subject to the same type of collection process as the original checks. This type of settlement results in an opportunity cost to the presenting bank because these funds could have been used for investment purposes.

To avoid receiving settlement for checks by remittance draft, a presenting bank may need to establish an account relationship with a paying bank. The presenting bank would present checks to the paying bank and receive settlement for the checks through credit to its account. Under the terms of the UCC, the paying bank must settle by midnight of the day of deposit in order to be able to return the checks the following day. Through terms of its agreement with the presenting bank, however, the paying bank may delay the presenting bank's use of those funds and may charge account maintenance fees to the presenting bank. The delay in availability of these funds represents an opportunity cost to the presenting bank and the account maintenance fees increase the presenting bank's costs to collect checks.

Barriers to presentment may result in inefficient intermediation in the check collection process. The Board believes that the differences in presentment abilities among collecting banks have resulted in some inefficient intermediation in the check collection process because more checks are collected through the Federal Reserve Banks, and to a lesser extent, through correspondent banks, than would be the case if private-sector collecting banks could obtain settlement for checks on the day of presentment without being subject to presentment fees and other barriers to presentment. If all collecting banks had equal presentment abilities, banks would choose to use intermediary banks due primarily to the economies of scale with respect to processing, transportation, and/or settlement that the intermediaries could pass on to their collecting bank customers. For example, intermediary banks handle large numbers of checks from a diversity of sources and thereby can optimize the use of fixed cost resources, such as transportation. Spreading these fixed costs across a larger number of checks allows intermediary banks to offer check collection services at a lower cost per check.

The decision to use an intermediary collecting bank and the choice of which intermediary bank to use is influenced in many cases, however, by the intermediary collecting bank's ability to present checks to paying banks on terms more advantageous than those available to the collecting bank itself. For example, a bank may collect some checks through the Federal Reserve because of the Federal Reserve's ability to obtain same-day settlement from the paying bank without the imposition of presentment fees. Similarly, a bank may collect certain checks through a correspondent bank because that correspondent bank receives same-day settlement from some paying banks through clearinghouse arrangements or through individual agreements, although the agreements may be conditioned on the payment of presentment fees and the maintenance of balances by the correspondent bank at the paying bank.

The Board believes that the use of intermediary collecting banks because of the economies of scale that those banks bring to the check collection process generally enhances the efficiency of the payments system. To the extent that intermediary collecting banks system inefficiencies may result.

In addition to the inefficiencies described above, further payments system inefficiencies may result from the use of checks, rather than electronic payments, as the dominant noncash method of payment. Checks can take longer to clear than electronic payments and are generally more costly to process. However, the choice of payment method generally rests with the originator of the payment and the inherent inefficiencies of check payments (e.g., float, particularly the time between issuance of a check and deposit of the check in the banking system) provides incentives for continued reliance on the check mechanism by the drawer of the check.

Role of collecting banks

Any bank handling a check or other item for collection, except the payor bank, is a *collecting bank*. 4-105(5). This term includes the *depositary bank* (4-105(2)) and any *intermediary bank* (4-105(4)), but not the payor bank. The collecting bank that actually presents the check to the payor bank for payment is also known as the *presenting bank* (4-105(6)). None of these collecting banks pays a check that it takes for collection. Only a payor bank, the drawee, which is not a collecting bank, pays a check. The role of a collecting bank is rather to assist the owner of the check in getting payment from the payor bank by forwarding the item for presentment for payment and, if the item is dishonored, to assist in returning it to the owner if the item is returned through the collecting bank.

In their role of helping the owner of a check get payment from the payor bank, collecting banks ordinarily serve as agents of the owner. Actually, the depositary bank is the agent, and intermediary banks are sub-agents. 4-201(a); 12 CFR 229.36(d) Commentary. Because collecting banks are agents or sub-agents of the owner of the item, the banks are responsible to her for their collection conduct. In general, they owe the owner a duty of good faith, 1-203, and they must also act reasonably, according to a standard of ordinary care, in carrying out tasks with respect to both forward collection and return of items. 4-202(a).

Settlements

As a check is deposited and moves from bank to bank in the collection process, everybody usually gets an almost immediate credit or settlement for the item. Article 4 provides that these settlements in the forward collection process generally are provisional -- between the depositor and depositary bank and also between banks involved in the collection process. 4-201(a), 4-214(a)&(c) & 4-301. They become final upon final payment by the payor bank. If the payor bank dishonors the item instead of paying it, the item is returned by the same path that took it to the payor bank. Each transferee in the return process takes back (revokes) the provisional credit the transferee gave for the item. It is by this revocation of settlements that a bank returning a check gets paid for the return.

Overriding federal law declares that settlements between banks for the forward collection of a check are final when made. 12 CFR 229.36(d). Yet, "[s]ettlement by a paying bank is not considered to be final payment for the purposes of [Article 4], because a paying bank has the right to recover settlement from a returning or depositary bank to which it returns a check under this subpart [C of Regulation CC]." Id. Commentary. Correspondingly, a returning bank can recover from the bank to which it returns the item, and the depositary bank can recover from the depositor. More is said later on this right of recovery. The immediate point is that making recovery independent and unrelated to forward collection settlements eliminates any reason for these settlements to be provisional.

Principal duties of payor banks in the return process

Article 4 deals thoroughly with the forward collection process -- getting the check from the depositary bank to the payor bank and presenting it for payment. The statute says less about the return process -- getting a dishonored check from the payor to the depositary bank and, ultimately, to the depositor. Together, Articles 3 and 4 define dishonor of a check in terms of the payor bank seasonably returning a dishonored check in order to avoid accountability for the item or finally paying it. These state statutes are very sketchy, however, on the details and duties of this return process, especially after the item leaves the payor banks. Federal law fills the gaps, principally with Regulation CC which requires and explains "expeditious return" of dishonored checks. Regulation CC also requires special, quick notice when a large-dollar item is dishonored.

This combination of Articles 3 and 4 and Regulation CC produces three main responsibilities of payor banks with respect to the return of checks for nonpayment: (1) pay or dishonor by returning by the Article 4 midnight deadline; (2) return expeditiously; and (3) quickly notify the depositary bank when a large-dollar item is dishonored. The main rights and duties of returning and depositary banks with respect to returned checks are separately discussed later in this chapter.

1. Article 4 Return -- Mainly, The *Midnight Deadline* Rule(s)

A payor bank cannot indefinitely retain a check that has been presented for payment. The check usually belongs to the depositor who expects payment, and federal law will require the depositary bank to make funds available for the check in fairly short order unless the check is sooner dishonored. 12 U.S.C.A. 4001-4010. By rule of 4-302 the payor bank becomes accountable for the item -- liable for it -- unless it returns the check by the **midnight deadline** with respect to the item -- **midnight of the next banking day following the banking day on which the item is received**, 4-301(a)(1); and a payor bank that is not the depositary bank can retain the item this long only if the bank settles for the item -- gives credit for it -- by midnight of the banking day of receipt. Id. If the item is presented through a Federal Reserve Bank, accountability results at the end of the banking day unless the payor bank settles by then. 12 CFR 210.9(a).

In practice, a payor bank almost always settles for an item on the day the item is received and often settles immediately upon receiving it, even when the payor bank is also the depositary bank. Accountability under 4-302 is thus avoided.

Settlement is an accounting. Until the midnight deadline, however, this settlement can be recovered by a return that is timely under 4-301 and in compliance with other provisions of state law and federal Regulation CC. Failure to make such a timely return results in the settlement becoming final -- final payment occurs. A final settlement cannot be lawfully recovered. Unlawfully recovering the settlement results in liability for converting the funds.

For the most part, federal law does not disturb the Article 4 midnight deadline rules, except to provide a very limited extension for *expedited delivery*. Specifically, the 4-301 midnight deadline "is extended if a paying bank, in an effort to expedite delivery of a returned check to a bank, uses a means of delivery that would ordinarily result in the returned check being received by the bank to which it is sent on or before the receiving bank's next banking day following the otherwise applicable deadline; this deadline is extended further if a paying bank uses a highly expeditious means of transportation, even if this means of transportation would ordinarily result in delivery after the receiving bank's next banking day." 12 CFR 229.30(c).

2. Large-Dollar Notice

Even when a payor bank makes a timely and otherwise proper return under 4-301, the bank is also bound to give quick, special notice if the item is for $2,500 or more. This special notice is required by a rule of Regulation CC, commonly called the large-dollar notice requirement:

> If a paying bank determines not to pay a check in the amount of $2,500 or more, it shall provide notice of nonpayment such that the notice is received by the depositary bank by 4:00 p.m. (local time) on the second business day following the banking day on which the check was presented to the paying bank.

12 CFR 229.33(a). The notice carries no value, and is no substitute for returning the check in compliance with Regulation CC (the expeditious return rule) and U.C.C. Article 4-301 (the midnight deadline rule). To reiterate, this large-dollar notice requirement is in addition to the rule of Article 4 requiring a timely, proper 4-301 return in order to recover a settlement. Satisfying the large-dollar notice requirement does not satisfy 4-301. On the other hand, the large-dollar notice requirement is not part of 4-301, so that failing to meet the requirement does not bar a payor bank from recovering a settlement if 4-301 is met. The consequence of violating the large-dollar notice requirement is liability for damages under Regulation CC.

To be effective, the notice must be unequivocal. "To qualify, the notice of dishonoring must be specific, precise, unequivocal, and certain, and it must be delivered to a responsible person at the depositary bank." *Federal Deposit Ins. Corp. v. Lake Country Nat'l Bank*, 873 F.2d 79 (5th Cir. 1989). Here's what happened in this case:

> On June 24, 1986, LANB received for deposit a $17,565 check from one of its customers, Bruce H. Evans. The check was drawn by Lakes Area Motor Company on its account at Lake Country National Bank. LANB placed the check on a five-day hold to prevent payment or crediting before June 30, 1986, and routed it for collection through the San Antonio Branch of the Federal Reserve Bank of Dallas.
> Lake Country received the check for collection on June 25, 1986. Under Regulation J, 12 C.F.R. §210.12, Lake Country's deadline for notifying LANB that it was returning the check unpaid was midnight, June 30, 1986. On June 25 at 9:32 a.m. and June 26 at 9:45 a.m., an LANB employee called Lake Country to inquire about the check. During each of these telephone conversations LANB was told that there were not then sufficient funds in the account of Lakes Area Motor Company for payment of the check. On the afternoon of June 26 Lake Country refused to pay the check and returned it to LANB through the San Antonio Branch of the Federal Reserve Bank of Dallas. LANB received the dishonored check on July 2, 1986.
> In the interim, on June 30 Evans withdrew $300 from his account at LANB. On July 1, after the five-day hold had expired and prior to LANB's receipt of the returned check, LANB credited Evans' account and allowed him to withdraw $16,240. Evans withdrew another $100 from his account on July 2.
> On May 21, 1987 LANB was closed due to insolvency and the FDIC was appointed receiver. Thereafter, in its corporate capacity the FDIC filed suit claiming damages because Lake Country had failed to notify LANB, as required by 12 C.F.R. §210.12(c), that it was returning the subject check

unpaid. After trial, the district court found that the telephone calls between LANB and Lake Country constituted sufficient notice that the check would not be paid, and it rejected the FDIC's claims. The FDIC timely appealed, contending that the district court erred in its factual findings and legal conclusion that Lake Country notified LANB that the $17,565 check would be returned unpaid.

Id. at 80. The Fifth Circuit agreed. Here's the court's analysis:

> [N]otice of rejection had to be given to LANB before midnight June 30, 1986. The required notice may be given by various means, including the return of the cash item to the depositary bank, telephone or telegraph communication to the depositary bank, or by request that the Federal Reserve Bank provide notice.
>
> Regardless of the means used to effect notification, we perceive that Regulation J contemplates an unqualified notice from the paying bank that it will not pay the item. The primary purpose of requiring timely notification of nonpayment is to alert the depositary bank so that it may protect itself from potential loss. To this end, the notification must identify the instrument and state in sufficiently specific terms that it will not be honored.
>
> In the case at bar, Lake Country did not telephone or telegraph LANB, it did not request that the Federal Reserve Bank provide notice, nor did LANB receive the returned check before midnight June 30. The only communications between the two banks were the two telephone calls placed by LANB employees inquiring as to whether the check would be paid.
>
> The testimony of the Lake Country bookkeeper, Peggy Birkelback, reflects that as of the second telephone call on June 26 Lake Country had not yet decided whether to honor or dishonor the check. She testified as follows about that June 26 telephone conversation: Q: Who was that call from, if you know? A: It was from Lake Austin Bank. Q: What did you tell them? What did they ask you during that inquiry? A: They wanted to know was the check going to clear. Q: And what did you tell them? A: That it wasn't as of that morning. Q: Okay. What did you mean by that? Or what did you tell them in that regard? A: Okay. I told them that our cutoff time for our checks was 3:00 o'clock in the afternoon and they could call back and make sure that it--if it was going to clear or not.
>
>   * * *
>
> Q: When you spoke to the Lake Austin person that morning, did you--do you recall if you said, please call back, or you can call back in the afternoon, or--or did you insist that they call back in the afternoon? A: No, I told them that they could call back. Q: That they could call back in the afternoon? A: That's right. It is clear that LANB was informed only that there were insufficient funds "as of that morning" to pay the check and it was invited to call again later in the day for an update.
>
> We do not view that scenario as within the intendment of the notice requirement of Regulation J. After deciding to return the check unpaid, Lake Country made no effort whatever to notify LANB of its decision, other than to put in motion the return of the check. Unfortunately, the returned

check was not received by LANB until after the notification cutoff, and after the LANB five-day hold on the check had expired and the check was credited to Evans' account.

We hold that the equivocal responses by the Lake Country employee to the telephone inquiries by the LANB employee were insufficient to comply with the notice requirement of 12 C.F.R. §210.12(c).

* * *

LANB acted prudently in placing a hold on Evans' check to prevent withdrawal of the funds prior to the deadline for notification of nonpayment. Had Lake Country exercised ordinary care in giving notice of nonpayment, LANB could have declined the $16,340 of withdrawals from Evans' account on July 1 and July 2. Under section 210.12(c)(6), Lake Country is liable to the FDIC for that amount.

The decision of the district court is REVERSED, judgment is RENDERED in favor of the FDIC, and this case is REMANDED for entry of judgment in the principle amount of $16,340, plus applicable interest, and for determination and assessment of reasonable attorneys' fees and court costs.

Id. at 81-82.

3. Expeditious Return

Banks returning checks must also abide by Regulation CC's requirement of *expeditious return*. 12 CFR 229.30(a). This requirement is imposed not only on the payor bank that returns an item, but also on intermediary banks involved in the return process (known as returning banks). As applied to payor banks, the expeditious return rule is separate from and in addition to the large-dollar notice requirement and is also in addition to the midnight deadline rules of Article 4. A check must be timely returned under Article 4 and must also be expeditiously returned under Regulation CC. The midnight deadline and expeditious return rules are closely related but different. It is possible to meet one rule and not the other, and the consequences of violating the rules are different. A way to view the relationship between the two requirements is that a return must begin by the midnight deadline of state law and must be accomplished expeditiously under federal law.

Alternative Tests

There are two alternative tests for expeditious return:

Two-Day/Four-Day Test. A check is considered expeditiously returned if the check is returned such that it would normally be received by the depositary bank by 4:00 p.m. (local time of the depositary bank) two business days after the banking day of presentment in the case of a local check, or by 4:00 p.m. four business days after presentment in the case of a nonlocal check. 12 CFR 229.30(a)(1).

    Forward Collection Test. A check is nonetheless considered returned expeditiously if the paying bank uses transportation methods and routes for return comparable to those used for forward collection checks, even if the check is not received by the depositary bank within the two-day or four-day period. 12 CFR 229.30(a)(2). Essentially, to satisfy the forward collection test, the bank must use means of routing and transporting a returned check that are as efficient as the means a similarly situated bank uses for forward collection of a similar item deposited with the bank by noon on the banking day following the bank day of presentment of the returned check. **In effect, the paying bank should treat a returned check as if the check were drawn on the depositary bank and deposited with the paying bank by noon on the banking day following the bank day of presentment of the returned check.**

    The reference to a "similarly situated bank" indicates a general community standard. In the case of a paying bank, a similarly situated bank is a bank of similar asset size, in the same community, and with similar check handling activity as the paying bank. A paying bank has similar check handling activity to other banks that handle similar volumes of checks for collection. 12 CFR 229.30(a) Commentary.

Relation To Article 4's Midnight-Deadline Rule

    Nothing in or about the expeditious return rule relieves the payor bank from the state-law midnight deadline rule. Regulation CC is explicit on this issue, providing that the rule of expeditious return "does not affect a paying bank's responsibility to return a check within the deadlines required by the U.C.C." 12 CFR 229.30(a)(2); see also 12 CFR 229.30(b) Commentary ("A paying bank's return under [Regulation CC's rules of expeditious return] is also subject to its midnight deadline under U.C.C. § 4-301."). Thus, satisfying the rule of expeditious return does not prevent a payor bank's liability for accountability or final payment of a check that it bounces in violation of Article 4. On the other hand, the consequences of violating the expeditious return rule are described by Regulation CC, not by Article 4. The violation can result in damages but not accountability or final payment. In the event the payor bank violates both the midnight deadline rule of Article 4 and the Regulation CC rule of expeditious return, the bank is liable under the former or the latter, *but not both.* 12 CFR 229.38(b).

Returning banks in the return process

    A returning bank is a bank (other than a paying or depositary bank) handling a returned check or notice in lieu of return. 12 CFR 229.2(cc). A paying bank is authorized to return a dishonored check through a returning bank rather than directly to the depositary bank. In any event, a returning bank is required to return a returned check expeditiously, that is, according to standards that are similar to the tests of expeditious return established for paying banks.

A returning bank shall settle with a bank sending a returned check to it for return by the same means that it settles or would settle with the sending bank for a check received for forward collection from the sending bank. 12 CFR 229.31(c). This is true even if the returning bank handled the check during forward collection. Id. Commentary. The settlement becomes final when made. 12 CFR 229.31(c).

Any bank that handles a check for forward collection or return is liable to any bank that subsequently handles the check to the extent that the subsequent bank does not receive payment for the check because of suspension of payments by another bank or otherwise, whether or not the prior bank so handling the check has indorsed it. 12 CFR 229.35(b). For example, if a returning bank returned a check to an insolvent depositary bank, and did not receive the full amount of the check from the failed bank, the returning bank could obtain the unrecovered amount of the check from any bank prior to it in the collection and return chain, including the payor bank. Because each bank in the collection and return chain could recover from a prior bank, any loss would fall on the first collecting bank that received the check from the depositary bank. To avoid circuity of actions, the returning bank could recover directly from the first collecting bank. 12 CFR 229.35(b) Commentary.

Under the U.C.C., the first collecting bank might ultimately recover from the depositary bank's customer or from the other parties on the check. (A bank has the rights of a holder with respect to each check it handles. 12 CFR 229.35(b) (last sentence)). Alternatively, the returning bank has a preferred claim against the failed depositary bank. 12 CFR 229.39(b). If the returning bank elects to recover from a prior bank, then this prior bank is subrogated to the returning bank's preferred claim against the insolvent depositary bank. 12 CFR. 229.39(b) Commentary.

Regulation CC imposes the duties of a returning bank that are described here. Thus, the bank's liability for breaching them is prescribed by CC, and is the same liability that a payor bank suffers for violating CC. Basically, it is liability for negligence in failing to comply with CC that causes damages measured by the actual loss suffered, up to the amount of the check and reduced by the amount of the loss that would have been incurred even if the bank had exercised ordinary care. Consequential damages are recoverable only if the bank fails to act in good faith. 12 CFR 229.38(a).

Article 4 echoes CC by separately requiring a collecting bank to act reasonably in returning a check. 4-202(a)(2). Damages under this rule are "the amount of the item reduced by an amount that could not have been realized by the exercise of ordinary care. If there is also bad faith it includes any other damages the party suffered as a proximate consequence." 4-103(e).

Depositary banks' rights and duties upon return of checks

1. Paying For Returns

"A depositary bank shall pay the returning or paying bank returning the check to it for the amount of the check prior to the close of business on the banking day on which it received the check ('payment date') by

- Debit to an account of the depositary bank on the books of the returning or paying bank;
- Cash;
- Wire transfer; or
- Any other form of payment acceptable to the returning or paying bank; ***.

These payments are final when made." 12 CFR 229.32(b).

2. Main Rights Against Customer And Others When Returned Check Has Been Dishonored

Charging Back Against Customer's Account

Probably the longest sentence in the U.C.C., perhaps in the whole of recorded law, is the rambling first sentence of 4-214(a). It allows a depositary bank, that is not the payor bank, to recover the amount of credit it gave its customer for a check if the check is dishonored or for some other reason the depositary bank is not paid for the check. It is self-help recovery. The bank simply debits the customer's account for the amount of the check even though the specific credit attributable to the check has been withdrawn or applied. If the account is insufficient to cover the charge back, the bank can sue to "obtain refund from its customer." 4-214(a). The customer is personally liable for the refund.

A depositary bank that is also the payor bank enjoys rights of charge back and refund against its customer, 4-214(c), but for this bank the rights are governed by 4-301(a). See 4-301(b). In effect, when the depositary bank is the payor bank, charging back equates with returning and dishonoring the item, so that the limits of the 4-301 midnight deadline rule and sooner final payment apply. Most significantly, if the bank credits the depositor's account and fails to return the check by its midnight deadline, final payment has occurred and the rights of charge back and refund are lost. Also, if the bank cashes the item, the effect is final payment of the item then and there. There is no right to return, charge back or seek refund even if the bank bounces the check, notifies the customer, or takes other action prior to the midnight deadline.

Suing On The Check

The payor bank's dishonor of the check triggers the secondary liability of the drawer and any indorser. Thus, the depositary bank can sue them on the check. With respect to the bank's status, the depositary bank will be a holder even if the customer-depositor neglected to indorse the check so long as the customer herself was a holder. In this case the bank's holder status results not from the shelter principle but by declaration of law. 4-205(1). The depositary bank typically will also satisfy the other requirements for holder in due course. This status most commonly is important in suing the drawer of the check. It allows the bank to take free of the drawer's defenses against the payee, who typically is the bank's customer. Usually, the only issue that presents any difficulty is whether or not the bank gave value. See 4-211 & 4-210.

3. Rights When Returned Check Is Not Dishonored and Is Unlawfully Returned In Violation of Midnight Deadline

No Right of Charge Back or Refund – Payor Bank's Final Payment Terminates Depositary Bank's Right of Charge Back

The third sentence of 4-214(a) provides: "These rights to revoke, charge back, and obtain refund terminate if and when a settlement for the item received by the [depositary or other collecting] bank is or becomes final." In terms of Article 4, a settlement given or received by a depositary bank becomes final when the payor bank finally pays the item. See 4-215(a) & (c). So, when the payor bank finally pays an item, as described in 4-215(a)(3) and 4-301(a), a depositary bank loses the 4-214(a) rights of charge back and refund and thus cannot recover the credit the bank gave its customer for the item.

No Actions On The Check

The liability of the drawer or any indorser of the check is conditioned on dishonor of the instrument. Thus, if the payor bank violates 4-301 and thereby finally pays an item, the depositary bank cannot sue anybody on the check. There was payment rather than the dishonor that is necessary to charge the drawer or an indorser. Moreover, the payment discharged liability on the instrument.

Warranties

In the end, therefore, the depositary bank is left with a returned check for which it paid and for which it cannot lawfully recover. The answer is to look for recovery in the other direction -- back up the collection stream toward the payor bank which wrongfully returned the item despite final payment. The best theory is federal warranty law:

> Each paying bank or returning bank that transfers a returned check and receives a settlement or other consideration for it warrants to the transferee returning bank, to any subsequent returning bank, to the depositary bank, and to the owner of the check, that

- *The paying bank timely returned the check within its deadline under the UCC*, Regulation J and Regulation CC (regarding expeditious return);
- It is authorized to return the check;
- The returned check has not been materially altered; and
- In the case of a notice in lieu of return, the original check has not and will not be returned.

12 CFR 229.34(a) (emphasis added). "Damages for breach of these warranties shall not exceed the consideration received by the paying or returning bank, plus finance charges and expenses related to the returned check, if any." Id. 229.34(c). In truth, however, the depositary bank is very likely to charge the item back against the customer's account even though the bank lacks the right to do so.

How "Return" Is Even Possible After Final Payment

Some people might think that a payor bank that has finally paid an item cannot return it (see 4-301(a)), and thus they will wonder why a collecting bank would have reason to sue on the check or charge the item back against its customer. While it is true that final payment takes away the payor bank's right of return, the bank nevertheless retains the raw power to return an item that it has finally paid; and, when this power is exercised, a ripple of wrongful recoveries for the returned item results: between the payor bank and the returning bank; between returning banks; between a returning bank and the depositary bank; and, finally, between the depositary bank and its customer. The bank to which the payor bank returns the item could prevent the ripple effect by contesting the payor bank's return, arguing that payor bank lost any right of return because of final payment bank. This argument is sound. Yet, banks seldom try to stop a wrongful return because they often are unaware that it has been returned wrongfully. They routinely send it back through usual banking channels for returns and it is charged back to the depositor's account as though proper dishonor had occurred.

Customer's Predicament And Rights When She Is Charged With Wrongful Return

Consider the position of the depositary bank's customer in the event of a wrongful return in violation of 4-301. The customer's account will be debited for the amount of the item, yet there is no one to whom she can pass the loss. Because the payor bank finally paid the item, the drawer of the check is discharged, and there is no dishonor that is necessary to charge the drawer or indorsers.

The customer's rights are against the banks: The customer can force the depositary bank to recredit her account for the item because the bank's charge back to her account was wrongful. Moreover, upon final payment by the payor bank, the settlement between the customer and the depositary bank became final. 4-215(d). The depositary bank could then shift the loss back to any returning bank or directly to the payor bank because the bank breached the federal warranty that the check was timely returned under the U.C.C., Regulations J and CC. 12 CFR 229.34(a). The customer could sue directly any returning bank or the payor bank because the federal warranty runs to the customer herself. Id.

The analysis is slightly different if the payor bank never settled for the item but became accountable for it under 4-302(a) as a result of not returning the item by the deadlines of that section. In this case of late return, the customer has no claim against the depositary bank. Dishonor occurred, 3-502(b)(1), so that the depositary bank's 4-214(a) charge back was rightful. On the other hand, the dishonor triggered the liability of the drawer and prior indorsers. The customer can sue them on the check. Also, even though the item was not finally paid, the payor bank is accountable -- liable for the item -- to the customer.

Final payment

Final payment is the point beyond which payor banks cannot dishonor checks that have been presented for payment and cannot lawfully return the checks and take payment for them from the depositary bank or a returning bank. In short, a payor bank that finally pays a check is usually stuck with it as against persons upstream in the collection process, even if the drawer's account is empty or the check cannot properly be charged against the account. Usually, the payor bank's only lawful remedy is to charge the drawer's account, and this remedy is possible only if the item is properly payable. If there are not sufficient funds in the drawer's account to cover the check, the customer is liable for the amount of the overdraft because of common-law contract. (The bank's payment discharged the drawer on the check itself.) If the customer is insolvent, the bank takes the loss.

It is very important to understand that this liability of the payor bank is strict liability rather than negligence liability for which a collecting bank is responsible.

> [A] payor bank is strictly liable for its failure to return an item before expiration of the applicable midnight deadline. The Supreme Court of New Mexico stated in *Engine Parts v. Citizens Bank of Clovis* (1978) 92 N.M. 37, 582 P.2d 809, that the liability created by that state's version of section 4302 (§50A-4-302) is "independent from negligence and is an absolute or strict liability for the full amount of the items which it fails to return." (Id., 582 P.2d at p. 815; see, also, *Morgan Guar. Trust Co. v. American Sav. and Loan* (9th Cir.1986) 804 F.2d 1487, 1499; *State and Sav. Bank of Monticello v. Meeker* (Ind.App. 1 Dist.1984) 469 N.E.2d 55, 57-58.) In *Reynolds-Wilson Lumber v. Peoples Nat. Bank* (Okla.1985) 699 P.2d 146, the Supreme Court of Oklahoma held pursuant to its version of section 4302 that the word "'[a]ccountable' has been uniformly construed to mean strict liability for the full amount of the draft, *with no requirement that there be proof of actual damage.* [Citations.]" (Id., at p. 152, emphasis added.)
>
> In *First State Bank v. Twin City Bank* (1986) 290 Ark. 399, 720 S.W.2d 295, the defendant urged that because the plaintiff depositary/collecting bank had failed to use ordinary care in granting immediate credit to a customer who later was discovered to be operating a check-kiting scheme, the defendant should not be liable for its omission to return the depositary drafts before the midnight deadline imposed by section 85-4-302 (that state's version of §4302). The court, rejecting this argument, stated: "Even if the evidence reflects that [the plaintiff] was negligent, this argument would fail because the liability created by §85-4-302(b) is a statutory liability and is independent of liability based upon negligence. [Citations.]" (Id., 720 S.W.2d at p. 296.)
>
> In *Toronto-Dominion Bank v. Cent. Nat. Bank & Trust* (8th Cir.1985) 753 F.2d 66, the plaintiff depositary bank brought an action to recover the face amount of checks which the defendant payor bank had dishonored and failed to return by the midnight deadline. The defendant asserted in defense that one of the plaintiff's employees had participated in a check-kiting scheme with the perpetrator of the fraud and therefore the plaintiff had acted in bad faith. The court ruled that unless the activities of the plaintiff's employee induced the defendant to return the checks after expiration of its deadline and thereby breach its obligation pursuant to section 554.4302 (the State of Iowa's version of §4302), the defendant could not assert this as an affirmative defense. (Id., at p. 70.)
>
> These cases support our conclusion that respondent [the payor bank in this case] may be held strictly liable for its failure to return the checks by the applicable deadlines, regardless whether appellant demonstrated it suffered actual damage solely as a result of respondent's omission. As respondent suggests, section 1103 provides that general principles of law, which would include the defense that a party's own negligence caused its loss, may apply where not displaced by specific provisions of the Commercial Code. As the above cases indicate, however, the rule of strict liability afforded by section 4302 does displace the defense that appellant's own

negligence caused its loss. In order to further the statutory objectives of certainty and finality, a bank that fails to return a check by the midnight deadline is deemed to have paid it and thus is held accountable.

In connection with a discussion of the duty of a collecting bank pursuant to New York Uniform Commercial Code section 4-202 to use ordinary care in forwarding checks for collection and in returning checks deemed uncollectible, where the plaintiff also is shown to be negligent, the court in *United States Fid. & Guar. v. Federal Reserve Bank* (S.D.N.Y.1985) 620 F.Supp. 361 discussed certain differences in the respective goals of tort law and of the Uniform Commercial Code. It noted that tort law "is designed primarily to apportion loss" and that the guiding principle in such an apportionment is fairness. "In tort law courts have equated fairness with fault. The rule of comparative negligence is a perfect expression of this principle.

The UCC, however, was designed to facilitate commerce primarily by guiding and making predictable the consequences of behavior," and its loss apportionment function is secondary to this primary function. (*Id.*, at p. 370; *Town & Country State Bank v. First State Bank* (Minn.1984) 358 N.W.2d 387, 395.)

Although, for example, tort law ordinarily would distribute loss caused by a forged signature or endorsement on a negotiable instrument on the basis of fault, "[t]he UCC, however, for the most part does not look at actual fault. [Fn. omitted.] Instead, it places responsibility on the party which ordinarily would be in the best position to prevent the loss. [Fn. omitted; citations.] Such a result accomplishes two purposes: first, it increases the efficiency and fraud-resistance of the banking system by placing upon those best able to guard against it the responsibility for preventing fraud [fn. omitted], and, second, it speeds the resolution of disputes by establishing clear rules of liability which do not depend heavily upon the specific facts of individual instances of fraud. [Citation.]" (*United States Fid. & Guar. v. Federal Reserve Bank*, supra, 620 F.Supp. at p. 370.) The check clearance chain among banks appropriately has been described as "a high stakes game of hot potato." (*United States Fid. v. Fed. Reserve Bank* (S.D.N.Y.1984) 590 F.Supp. 486, 499.)

Los Angeles Nat'l Bank v. Bank of Canton, 229 Cal. App.3d 1267, 1277-79, 280 Cal. Rptr. 831, 837-38 (Cal. Ct. App. 1991), followed in *Chicago Title Ins. Co. v. California Candian Bank*, 1 Cal. App.4th 798, 2 Cal. Rptr.2d 422 (1992).

Final payment under Article 4 also has consequences under Article 3 because it gives meaning to the term "payment" as used in important provisions 3-602 (discharge through payment to a holder) and 3-418 (payment is final in favor of certain classes).

1. How Final Payment Is Made

Article 4 describes three different, alternative means of finally paying an item. 4-215(a). Each of them is discussed below in an order that varies from the statutory listing of them. Remember that each method of final payment is an alternative to the others, and that final payment occurs as soon as the payor bank has first done any of them.

Paid In Cash

A check is finally paid when the payor bank pays the item in cash. 4-215(a)(1). Cash is money. The term also includes instruments issued by the payor bank that are generally regarded as money equivalents, such as a cashier's check, which is a draft drawn by the bank on itself.

Cash payment usually occurs only when the check is presented "over the counter" for immediate payment, which might be done by the payee or other owner of a check but is rarely done by collecting banks acting for a customer. Payor banks rarely settle in cash with collecting banks. The typical case of final payment by payment in cash involves the owner of an item personally presenting a check to the payor bank and asking for payment in money. Upon the teller complying with this request, the payor bank thereby makes final payment. This is the consequence whether the owner of the item maintains her own account at the payor bank or is a stranger who banks elsewhere. Though straightforward and easily understood and applied in the great bulk of cases, final payment by payment in cash raises a couple of important issues.

Settled Without Right to Revoke

A check is finally paid if the payor bank settles for it without having a right to revoke the settlement under statute, clearinghouse rule, or agreement. 4-215(a)(2). In terms of state law, final payment by this means almost never occurs because, by state law and usual practice, settlements are almost always provisional. Regulation CC provides the overriding rule that settlements between banks in the forward collection process are final when made. Putting this rule together with 4-215(a)(2) would seem to mean that anytime a collecting bank presents a check for payment, the payor bank's usually immediate settlement would be final rather than provisional, final payment would therefore occur, and the payor bank therefore would not have a right to return under 4-301 because final payment had occurred. This analysis cannot be true for practical reasons even if it is technically, literally correct, and the comments to Regulation CC obligingly reject it:

> [Even though 12 CFR 229.36(d)] makes settlement between banks during forward collection final when made * * *[s]ettlement by a paying bank is not considered to be final payment for the purposes of U.C.C. [4-215(a)(2) or (3)], because a paying bank has the right to recover settlement from a returning or depositary bank to which it returns a check under [Regulation CC].

12 CFR 229.36(d) Commentary. Regulation CC elsewhere provides that a payor bank that returns a check by the 4-301 midnight deadline has a federal right to recover the amount of the check from the bank to which the check is returned -- whether this bank is the depositary or an intermediary returning bank. This right of recovery is discussed below, under the heading of where returns are sent and how they are paid for. In the end, therefore, what was said in the beginning still applies -- final payment by means of 4-215(a)(2) will almost never happen and only in extraordinary cases.

Failed Properly To Recover Provisional Settlement

A payor bank finally pays a check by making a provisional settlement for the item and failing to revoke the settlement in the time and manner permitted by statute, clearing-house rule, or agreement. 4-215(a)(3). Of course, 4-301 is such a statute, so that failing to make a return by the midnight deadline is final payment and is the way in which final payment usually occurs. There is more, however, to 4-215(a)(3).

The 4-301 right to return can be varied by agreement (e.g., a clearinghouse arrangement) or preempted by federal law. In this event, the limits of the payor bank's right to revoke, including the time and manner of exercising the right, are set by the agreement or law that overrides 4-301. If the time limit for return is sooner than the midnight deadline, failing to meet this earlier limit is final payment and cuts off the 4-301 right of return even if the midnight deadline has not expired.

"It is very common for clearing-house rules to provide that items exchanged and settled for in a clearing, (e.g., before 10:00 a.m. on Monday) may be returned and the settlements revoked up to but not later than 2:00 p.m. on the same day (Monday) or under deferred posting at some hour on the next business day (e.g., 2:00 p.m. Tuesday). Under this type of rule the Monday morning settlement [can be recovered but only in line with law and the clearing house rules]." 4-215 comment 4. "[I]f the time limit for the return of items received in the Monday morning clearing is 2:00 p.m. on Tuesday and the provisional settlement has not been revoked at that time in a manner permitted by the clearing-house rules, the * * * settlement made on Monday morning becomes final at 2:00 p.m. on Tuesday." Id. comment 7. The item cannot be returned or the settlement recovered. This is true even though, under 4-301(a), the right to return extended until midnight on Tuesday because the clearinghouse rules, as a form of agreement among the parties, override 4-301(a).

When a payor bank receives an item directly or indirectly from a Federal Reserve Bank, Regulation J governs the bank's right to return the item. In this respect, Regulation J defers to Article 4. The federal right is as follows:

> A paying bank that receives a cash item directly or indirectly from a Reserve Bank, other than for immediate payment over the counter, *and that pays for*

the item as provided in §210.9(a) of this subpart, may, before it has finally paid the item, return the item in accordance with Subpart C of Part 229 [Regulation CC], the Uniform Commercial Code, and its Reserve Bank's operating circular. The rules or practices of a clearinghouse through which the item was presented, or a special collection agreement under which the item was presented, may not extend these return times, but may provide for a shorter return time.

12 CFR 210.12(a) (emphasis added). The emphasized language is important because the effect of incorporating 210.9(a) is to limit the federal right to return to items for which the payor bank has settled by *close of the banking day* on which the items were received. In contrast, the 4-301(a) right is available with respect to settlements made by *midnight* of the day of receipt.

2. Liabilities That Are Excepted From Final Payment (and 4-302 Accountability)

A payor bank can sometimes, in effect, avoid (by end run) the finality of final payment. Even though a settlement has become final under the rules of Article 4, the bank can recover damages on collateral theories and thereby effectively recoup the payment made, even when the payment was made in cash. With respect to an item that has been finally paid, the principal bases of recoupment are: breach of warranty of presentment (4-208), restitution for mistaken payment (3-418), and subrogation to rights of the drawer.

Warranty and restitution were introduced in Chapter 4, supra. The only stranger here is subrogation. Sometimes, a drawee bank finally pays a check that cannot be charged to the drawer's account because the check is not properly payable, which basically means that the customer who owns the account has a good reason for objecting to her payment of the check. It happens, for example, when a payor bank ignores an effective stop payment order. In this event, the bank is subrogated to the rights of the drawer against the payee or any other holder of the item with respect to the transaction out of which the item arose. 4-407(3). The bank can assert these rights despite having made final payment of the check; and 3-418(c), which is a defense to a payor's restitution action, does not apply.

More is said about subrogation in § 2, infra, of this chapter. There, too, are a few more words about restitution, and warranty comes up again in § 3.

law

Availability Of Funds And
Collection Of Checks
12 CFR part 229

SECTION 229.30 -- Paying Bank's Responsibility For Return Of Checks

(a) *Return of checks.* If a paying bank determines not to pay a check, it shall return the check in an expeditious manner as provided in either paragraphs (a)(1) or (a)(2) of this section.

(1) *Two-day/four-day test.* A paying bank returns a check in an expeditious manner if it sends the returned check in a manner such that the check would normally be received by the depositary bank not later than 4:00 p.m. (local time of the depositary bank) of--

(i) The second business day following the banking day on which the check was presented to the paying bank, if the paying bank is located in the same check processing region as the depositary bank; or

(ii) The fourth business day following the banking day on which the check was presented to the paying bank, if the paying bank is not located in the same check processing region as the depositary bank.

If the last business day on which the paying bank may deliver a returned check to the depositary bank is not a banking day for the depositary bank, the paying bank meets the two-day/four-day test if the returned check is received by the depositary bank on or before the depositary bank's next banking day.

(2) *Forward collection test.* A paying bank also returns a check in an expeditious manner if it sends the returned check in a manner that a similarly situated bank would normally handle a check--

(i) Of similar amount as the returned check;

(ii) Drawn on the depositary bank; and

(iii) Deposited for forward collection in the similarly situated bank by noon on the banking day following the banking day on which the check was presented to the paying bank.

Subject to the requirement for expeditious return, a paying bank may send a returned check to the depositary bank, or to any other bank agreeing to handle the returned check expeditiously under §229.31(a). A paying bank may convert a check to a qualified returned check. A qualified returned check must be encoded in magnetic ink with the routing number of the depositary bank, the amount of the returned check, and a "2" in position 44 of the MICR line as a return identifier, in accordance with the American National Standard Specifications for Placement and Location of MICR Printing, X9.13 (Sept. 1983). This paragraph does not affect a paying bank's responsibility to return a check within the deadlines required by the U.C.C., Regulation J (12 CFR Part 210), or §229.30(c).

(b) *Unidentifiable depositary bank.* A paying bank that is unable to identify the depositary bank with respect to a check may send the returned check to any bank that handled the check for forward collection even if that bank does not agree to handle the check expeditiously under §229.31(a). A paying bank sending a returned check under this paragraph to a bank that handled the check for forward collection must advise the bank to which the check is sent that the paying bank is unable to identify the depositary bank. The expeditious return requirements in §229.30(a) do not apply to the paying bank's return of a check under this paragraph.

(c) *Extension of deadline.* The deadline for return or notice of nonpayment under the UCC, Regulation J (12 CFR part 210), or § 229.36(f)(2) of this part is extended:

(1) If a paying bank, in an effort to expedite delivery of a returned check to a bank, uses a means of delivery that would ordinarily result in the returned check being received by the bank to which it is sent on or before the receiving bank's next banking day following the otherwise applicable deadline; this deadline is extended further if a paying bank uses a highly expeditious means of transportation, even if this means of transportation would ordinarily result in delivery after the receiving bank's next banking day; or

(2) If the deadline falls on a Saturday that is a banking day, as defined in the applicable UCC, for the paying bank, and the paying bank uses a means of delivery that would ordinarily result in the returned check being received by the bank to which it is sent prior to the cut-off hour for the next processing cycle, in the case of a returning bank, or on the next banking day, in the case of a depositary bank, after midnight Saturday night.

(d) *Identification of returned check.* A paying bank returning a check shall clearly indicate on the face of the check that it is a returned check and the reason for return.

(e) *Depositary bank without accounts.* The expeditious return requirements of paragraph (a) of this section do not apply to checks deposited in a depositary bank that does not maintain accounts.

(f) *Notice in lieu of return.* If a check is unavailable for return, the paying bank may send in its place a copy of the front and back of the returned check, or, if no such copy is available, a written notice of nonpayment containing the information specified in §229.33(b). The copy or notice shall clearly state that it constitutes a notice in lieu of return. A notice in lieu of return is considered a returned check subject to the expeditious return requirements of this section and to the other requirements of this subpart.

(g) *Reliance on routing number.* A paying bank may return a returned check based on any routing number designating the depositary bank appearing on the returned check in the depositary bank's indorsement.

SECTION 229.33 Notice Of Nonpayment

(a) *Requirement.* If a paying bank determines not to pay a check in the amount of $2,500 or more, it shall provide notice of nonpayment such that the notice is received by the depositary bank by 4:00 p.m. (local time) on the second business day following the banking day on which the check was presented to the paying bank. If the day the paying bank is required to provide notice is not a banking day for the depositary bank, receipt of notice on the depositary bank's next banking day constitutes timely notice. Notice may be provided by any reasonable means, including the returned check, a writing (including a copy of the check), telephone, Fedwire, telex, or other form of telegraph.

(b) *Content of notice.* Notice must include the--

(1) Name and routing number of the paying bank;

(2) Name of the payee(s);

(3) Amount;

(4) Date of the indorsement of the depositary bank;

(5) Account number of the customer(s) of the depositary bank;

(6) Branch name or number of the depositary bank from its indorsement;

(7) Trace number associated with the indorsement of the depositary bank; and

(8) Reason for nonpayment.

The notice may include other information from the check that may be useful in identifying the check being returned and the customer, and, in the case of a written notice, must include the name and routing number of the depositary bank from its indorsement. If the paying bank is not sure of an item of information, it shall include the information required by this paragraph to the extent possible, and identify any item of information for which the bank is not sure of the accuracy with question marks.

(c) *Acceptance of notice.* The depositary bank shall accept notices during its banking day--

(1) Either at the telephone or telegraph number of its return check unit indicated in the indorsement, or, if no such number appears in the indorsement or if the number is illegible, at the general purpose telephone or telegraph number of its head office or the branch indicated in the indorsement; and

(2) At any other number held out by the bank for receipt of notice of nonpayment, and, in the case of written notice, as specified in §229.32(a).

(d) Notification to customer. If the depositary bank receives a returned check or notice of nonpayment, it shall send notice to its customer of the facts by midnight of the banking day following the banking day on which it received the returned check or notice, or within a longer reasonable time.

(e) *Depositary bank without accounts.* The requirements of this section do not apply to checks deposited in a depositary bank that does not maintain accounts.

SECTION 229.34 -- Warranties By Paying Bank And Returning Bank

(a) *Warranties.* Each paying bank or returning bank that transfers a returned check and receives a settlement or other consideration for it warrants to the transferee returning bank, to any subsequent returning bank, to the depositary bank, and to the owner of the check, that--

(1) The paying bank, or in the case of a check payable by a bank and payable through another bank, the bank by which the check is payable, returned the check within its deadline under the U.C.C., Regulation J (12 CFR Part 210), or §229.30(c) of this part;

(2) It is authorized to return the check;

(3) The check has not been materially altered; and

(4) In the case of a notice in lieu of return, the original check has not and will not be returned.

These warranties are not made with respect to checks drawn on the Treasury of the United States, U.S. Postal Service money orders, or checks drawn on a state or a unit of general local government that are not payable through or at a bank.

(b) *Warranty of notice of nonpayment.* Each paying bank that gives a notice of nonpayment warrants to the transferee bank, to any subsequent transferee bank, to the depositary bank, and to the owner of the check that--

(1) The paying bank, or in the case of a check payable by a bank and payable through another bank, the bank by which the check is payable, returned or will return the check within its deadline under the U.C.C., Regulation J (12 CFR Part 210), or §229.30(c) of this part;

(2) It is authorized to send the notice; and

(3) The check has not been materially altered.

These warranties are not made with respect to checks drawn on a state or a unit of general local government that are not payable through or at a bank.

(c) *Warranty of settlement amount, encoding, and offset.* (1) Each bank that presents one or more checks to a paying bank and in return receives a settlement or other consideration warrants to the paying bank that the total amount of the checks presented is equal to the total amount of the settlement demanded by the presenting bank from the paying bank.

(2) Each bank that transfers one or more checks or returned checks to a collecting, returning, or depositary bank and in return receives a settlement or other consideration warrants to the transferee bank that the accompanying information, if any, accurately indicates the total amount of the checks or returned checks transferred.

(3) Each bank that presents or transfers a check or returned check warrants to any bank that subsequently handles it that, at the time of presentment or transfer, the information encoded after issue in magnetic ink on the check or returned check is correct.

(4) A paying bank may set off the amount by which the settlement paid to a presenting bank exceeds the total amount of the checks presented against subsequent settlements for checks presented by that presenting bank.

(d) *Damages.* Damages for breach of these warranties shall not exceed the consideration received by the bank that presents or transfers a check or returned check, plus interest compensation and expenses related to the check or returned check, if any.

(e) *Tender of defense.* If a bank is sued for breach of a warranty under this section, it may give a prior bank in the collection or return chain written notice of the litigation, and the bank notified may then give similar notice to any other prior bank. If the notice states that the bank notified may come in and defend and that failure to do so will bind the bank notified in an action later brought by the bank giving the notice as to any determination of fact common to the two litigations, the bank notified is so bound unless after seasonable receipt of the notice the bank notified does come in and defend.

SECTION 229.35 -- Indorsements

(b) *Liability of bank handling check.* A bank that handles a check for forward collection or return is liable to any bank that subsequently handles the check to the extent that the subsequent bank does not receive payment for the check because of suspension of payments by another bank or otherwise. This paragraph applies whether or not a bank has placed its indorsement on the check. This liability is not affected by the failure of any bank to exercise ordinary care, but any bank failing to do so remains liable. A bank seeking recovery against a prior bank shall send notice to that prior bank reasonably promptly after it learns the facts entitling it to recover. A bank may recover from the bank with which it settled for the check by revoking the settlement, charging back any credit given to an account, or obtaining a refund. A bank may have the rights of a holder with respect to each check it handles.

SECTION 229.36 -- Presentment And Issuance Of Checks

(f) *Same-day settlement.* (1) A check is considered presented, and a paying bank must settle for or return the check pursuant to paragraph (f)(2) of this section, if a presenting bank delivers the check in accordance with reasonable delivery requirements established by the paying bank and demands payment under this paragraph (f)--

(i) At a location designated by the paying bank for receipt of checks under this paragraph (f) that is in the check processing region consistent with the routing number encoded in magnetic ink on the check and at which the paying bank would be considered to have received the check under paragraph (b) of this section or, if no location is designated, at any location described in paragraph (b) of this section; and

(ii) By 8 a.m. on a business day (local time of the location described in paragraph (f)(1)(i) of this section).

A paying bank may require that checks presented for settlement pursuant to this paragraph (f)(1) be separated from other forward-collection checks or returned checks.

(2) If presentment of a check meets the requirements of paragraph (f)(1) of this section, the paying bank is accountable to the presenting bank for the amount of the check unless, by the close of Fedwire on the business day it receives the check, it either:

(i) Settles with the presenting bank for the amount of the check by credit to an account at a Federal Reserve Bank designated by the presenting bank; or

(ii) Returns the check.

(3) Notwithstanding paragraph (f)(2) of this section, if a paying bank closes on a business day and receives presentment of a check on that day in accordance with paragraph (f)(1) of this section, the paying bank is accountable to the presenting bank for the amount of the check unless, by the close of Fedwire on its next banking day, it either:

(i) Settles with the presenting bank for the amount of the check by credit to an account at a Federal Reserve Bank designated by the presenting bank; or

(ii) Returns the check.

If the closing is voluntary, unless the paying bank settles for or returns the check in accordance with paragraph (f)(2) of this section, it shall pay interest compensation to the presenting bank for each day after the business day on which the check was presented until the paying bank settles for the check, including the day of settlement.

SECTION 229.38 -- Liability

(a) *Standard of care; liability; measure of damages.* A bank shall exercise ordinary care and act in good faith in complying with the requirements of this subpart. A bank that fails to exercise ordinary care or act in good faith under this subpart may be liable to the depositary bank, the depositary bank's customer, the owner of a check, or another party to the check. The measure of damages for failure to exercise ordinary care is the amount of the loss incurred, up to the amount of the check, reduced by the amount of the loss that party would have incurred even if the bank had exercised ordinary care. A bank that fails to act in good faith under this subpart may be liable for other damages, if any, suffered by the party as a proximate consequence. Subject to a bank's duty to exercise ordinary care or act in good faith in choosing the means of return or notice of nonpayment, the bank is not liable for the insolvency, neglect, misconduct, mistake, or default of another bank or person, or for loss or destruction of a check or notice of nonpayment in transit or in the possession of others. This section does not affect a paying bank's liability to its customer under the U.C.C. or other law.

(b) *Paying bank's failure to make timely return.* If a paying bank fails both to comply with §229.30(a) and to comply with the deadline for return under the U.C.C., Regulation J (12 CFR Part 210), or §229.30(c) in connection with a single nonpayment of a check, the paying bank shall be liable under either §229.30(a) or such other provision, but not both.

(c) *Comparative negligence.* If a person, including a bank, fails to exercise ordinary care or act in good faith under this subpart in indorsing a check (§229.35), accepting a returned check or notice of nonpayment (§§229.32(a) and 229.33(c)), or otherwise, the damages incurred by that person under §229.38(a) shall be diminished in proportion to the amount of negligence or bad faith attributable to that person.

(d) *Responsibility for certain aspects of checks.* (1) A paying bank, or in the case of a check payable through the paying bank and payable by another bank, the bank by which to check is payable, is responsible for damages under paragraph (a) of this section to the extent that the condition of the check when issued by it or its customer adversely affects the ability of a bank to indorse the check legibly in accordance with §229.35. A depositary bank is responsible for damages under paragraph (a) of this section to the extent that the condition of the back of a check arising after the issuance of the check and prior to acceptance of the check by it adversely affects the ability of a bank to indorse the check legibly in accordance with §229.35. Responsibility under this paragraph shall be treated as negligence of the paying or depositary bank for purposes of paragraph (c) of this section.

(2) Responsibility for payable through checks. In the case of a check that is payable by a bank and payable through a paying bank located in a different check processing region than the bank by which the check is payable, the bank by which the check is payable is responsible for damages under paragraph (a) of this section, to the extent that the check is not returned to the depositary bank through the payable through bank as quickly as the check would have been required to be returned under §229.30(a) had the bank by which the check is payable--

(i) Received the check as paying bank on the day the payable through bank received the check; and

(ii) Returned the check as paying bank in accordance with §229.30(a)(1).

Responsibility under this paragraph shall be treated as negligence of the bank by which the check is payable for purposes of paragraph (c) of this section.

(e) *Timeliness of action.* If a bank is delayed in acting beyond the time limits set forth in this subpart because of interruption of communication or computer facilities, suspension of payments by a bank, war, emergency conditions, failure of equipment, or other circumstances beyond its control, its time for acting is extended for the time necessary to complete the action, if it exercises such diligence as the circumstances require.

(f) *Exclusion.* Section 229.21 of this part and §611 (a), (b), and (c) of the Act (12 U.S.C. 4010 (a), (b), and (c)) do not apply to this subpart.

(g) *Jurisdiction.* Any action under this subpart may be brought in any United States district court, or in any other court of competent jurisdiction, and shall be brought within one year after the date of the occurrence of the violation involved.

(h) *Reliance on Board rulings.* No provision of this subpart imposing any liability shall apply to any act done or omitted in good faith in conformity with any rule, regulation, or interpretation thereof by the Board, regardless of whether the rule, regulation, or interpretation is amended, rescinded, or determined by judicial or other authority to be invalid for any reason after the act or omission has occurred.

SECTION 229.39 Insolvency Of Bank

(a) *Duty of receiver.* A check or returned check in, or coming into, the possession of a paying, collecting, depositary, or returning bank that suspends payment, and which is not paid, shall be returned by the receiver, trustee, or agent in charge of the closed bank to the bank or customer that transferred the check to the closed bank.

(b) *Preference against paying or depositary bank.* If a paying or depositary bank finally pays a check or returned check and suspends payment without making a settlement for the check with the prior bank which is or becomes final, the prior bank has a preferred claim against the paying or depositary bank.

(c) *Preference against collecting, paying, or returning bank.* If a collecting, paying, or returning bank receives settlement from a subsequent bank for a check or returned check, which settlement is or becomes final, and suspends payments without making a settlement for the check with the prior bank, which is or becomes final, the prior bank has a preferred claim against the collecting or returning bank.

(d) *Preference against presenting bank.* If a paying bank settles with a presenting bank for one or more checks, and if the presenting bank breaches a warranty specified in § 229.34(c)(1) or (3) with respect to those checks and suspends payments before satisfying the paying bank's warranty claim, the paying bank has a preferred claim against the presenting bank for the amount of the waranty claim.

(e) *Finality of settlement.* If a paying or depositary bank gives, or a collecting, paying, or returning bank gives or receives, a settlement for a check or returned check and thereafter suspends payment, the suspension does not prevent or interfere with the settlement becoming final if such finality occurs automatically upon the lapse of a certain time or the happening of certain events.

Azalea City Motels, Inc. v. First Alabama Bank

Supreme Court of Alabama, 1989
551 So.2d 967

Shores, Justice.

I. The Facts

Azalea City Motels, Inc. (hereinafter "Azalea City"), is a corporation primarily engaged in the business of buying, managing, and selling hotel and motel properties. The corporation was, during the majority of the period relevant to this litigation, exclusively owned and operated by W.C. Greene and Paul M. Jackson. Azalea City maintained at least one checking account at FAB (formerly the Merchants National Bank of Mobile) under the name "Azalea City Motels, Inc." In 1984, Mr. Greene and Mr. Jackson opened an additional account at FAB under the name "Azalea Management Company" (hereinafter "Azalea Management"). Although Greene and Jackson argue that this account was a trade account for Azalea City, the account's signature card indicates that Greene and Jackson owned the account individually, that they were both authorized signatories for the account, and that the account was listed neither as a corporate account nor as a partnership account.

On October 23, 1984, William Hannah, an associate of Greene and Jackson, issued a check for $100,000 drawn on a trust account at the First National Bank of Livingston, Tennessee (FNBL). The check was made payable to Azalea City Motels, Inc., but was not indorsed by Azalea City. Instead, the check bore the indorsement of Azalea Management Company and was deposited to the Azalea Management Company account at FAB on October 24, 1984. A day later, an FAB employee incorrectly encoded the check to reflect a $10,000 item rather than a $100,000 item. Consequently, the Azalea Management Company account was provisionally credited $10,000 instead of $100,000.

FAB then sent the check to the New Orleans branch of the Federal Reserve Bank of Atlanta for collection through the normal check collection process. Relying upon the misencoded information on the check, the New Orleans branch provisionally credited FAB with $10,000 and forwarded the check to the Nashville Federal Reserve branch so that it could present the check to FNBL. Both the Nashville Federal Reserve Bank and FNBL processed the check as a $10,000 item. FNBL received the check on October 26, 1984, paid the item as if it were a $10,000 draft, and deducted a corresponding $10,000 from Hannah's account. On the same day, Hannah issued a stop payment order on the check in the amount of the original instrument. Despite the stop payment order, the check went through the normal sorting and filing procedures at FNBL. Without correcting the encoding error or honoring the stop payment order, FNBL returned the original $100,000 check to Hannah with his statement on October 30, 1984. The evidence fails to indicate whether Hannah entered the stop payment order before or after the Federal Reserve presented the check to FNBL for payment.

Sometime prior to November 5, 1984, the defendants became aware that FAB had miscredited their account. On that date, FAB provisionally credited the Azalea Management account for $90,000, the difference between the original check and the misencoded item. On November 6, 1984, FAB presented a $90,000 adjustment and a photocopy of the check to the Federal Reserve Branch in New Orleans. On November 7, 1984, the Federal Reserve Branch in New Orleans submitted the adjustment to the Federal Reserve Branch in Nashville. The Federal Reserve Branch in Nashville received the adjustment on November 8, 1984. While awaiting final payment of the adjustment, FAB allowed Greene and Jackson to withdraw funds against the $100,000 provisional credit. By November 19, 1984, Greene and Jackson had withdrawn virtually all of the funds from the Azalea Management account.

Meanwhile, the Federal Reserve Branch in Nashville allowed almost 30 days to elapse before it presented the adjustment to FNBL. FNBL received the entry of adjustment on December 4, 1984, and, at that time, informed FAB that it was charging back (debiting FAB) the $100,000 item. The same day, FAB notified the defendants that FNBL had dishonored the item, 41 days after the initial deposit. FAB put a hold on the Azalea Management account on December 5, 1984, but released the hold on December 7, 1984. During the interim, FAB neither returned nor dishonored any items presented for payment against the Azalea Management account.

In March 1985, FAB sued Hannah, individually and d/b/a Southern Properties; Southern Properties, Inc.; Azalea City Motels, Inc.; Azalea City d/b/a Azalea Management; and W.C. Greene. Jackson was not named in the original complaint. In December 1985, FAB obtained a default judgment against Hannah, but was unable to enforce the judgment because the whereabouts of Hannah were unknown. After a lengthy period of relative inactivity in the Azalea Management account, Jackson procured new signature cards on February 14, 1986, and his wife, Barbara, replaced Greene as an owner of and signatory on the account. In April 1986, after the Jacksons had deposited a substantial amount of money to the account, FAB seized the assets and offset them against the $100,000 check from Hannah. In May, FAB amended its complaint, adding Paul Jackson as a defendant in this action. Jackson counterclaimed, alleging that FAB had wrongfully frozen his account and had wrongfully set off assets in the account against the $100,000 check.

Following a nonjury trial on the merits, the trial court, without articulating any findings of fact or conclusions of law, entered a judgment in favor of FAB in the amount of $73,419.46, which sum represents the $100,000 check, less $26,580.54 seized from the Azalea Management account. In addition, the court entered judgment for FAB on Jackson's counterclaim. Azalea City Motels, Inc., W.C. Greene, and Paul M. Jackson appealed.

* * *

FAB alleges in its complaint two principal causes of action: indorsement liability under Alabama's version of the Uniform Commercial Code (hereinafter "UCC"), and the common law claim of money had and received. Although not alleged in its complaint, FAB also argues, concomitant to its theory of indorsement liability, that the defendants, as customers, are liable to it based upon their UCC engagement to honor checks deposited to their account. We address the UCC claims together.

II. Indorsement Liability and Engagement to Honor

The first claim alleged by FAB upon which the trial court may have found the defendants liable is based upon Code 1975, §7-3-414. Section 7-3-414, entitled "Contract of indorser; order of liability," provides:

"(1) Unless the indorsement otherwise specifies (as by such words as 'without recourse') every indorser engages that upon dishonor and any necessary notice of dishonor and protest he will pay the instrument according to its tenor at the time of his indorsement to the holder or to any subsequent indorser who takes it up, even though the indorser who takes it up was not obligated to do so.

"(2) Unless they otherwise agree indorsers are liable to one another in the order in which they indorse, which is presumed to be the order in which their signatures appear on the instrument."

* * *

Although we conclude that the Azalea Management indorsement served as both an authorized signature of Azalea City and as indorsements of Greene and Jackson, proving the existence of an indorsement is not the only prerequisite to a finding of indorsement liability. The UCC makes it clear that indorsers of checks or other drafts are only secondarily liable to the maker of the note. §7-3-102(1)(d). "Secondary liability means that the holder may not sue the drawer or indorsers on a check or other draft until certain procedural conditions--presentment, dishonor and notice of dishonor-- have been met." Barkley Clark, *The Law of Bank Deposits, Collections, and Credit Cards*, §1.3 (rev. ed. 1981). See, §7-3-501(1)(b), (1)(c), (2)(a), and (2)(b). The appellants argue that neither dishonor nor timely notice of dishonor is present under the facts of this case. Thus, before we may affirm the trial court's judgment in favor of FAB upon these grounds, we must determine whether the prerequisites to indorsement liability exist.

While appellants concede that the threshold requirement of presentment was established at trial, they take issue with the trial court's apparent finding that the second prerequisite was met. Contrary to what the trial court must have found, appellants argue that the check was never dishonored. They suggest, instead, that the partial payment of the check by FNBL constituted final payment under the UCC, and that final payment precludes any later attempt by FNBL to dishonor the check. Alternatively, appellants argue that even if partial payment of the check by FNBL did not constitute final payment, then FNBL's retention of the check beyond its midnight deadline did constitute final payment. In either instance, they reason, the necessary prerequisite of dishonor never occurred, and, thus, the trial court erred in its judgment if its holding was based upon a theory of indorsement liability.

* * * We quote at length from Professor Barkley Clark's discussion of this case as he addressed it within the context of the underencoding conundrum:

"Suppose that there is an underencoding situation in which the buyer draws a $500 check in payment for goods; the seller deposits the check; the depositary bank encodes the item for $50; and the item is ultimately paid in the amount of $50 by the drawee bank. The buyer in this case may not be so quick to report this underencoding error. However, when it is discovered, the drawee bank is clearly authorized by the UCC to debit the buyer's account for the extra $450.

"If the depositary bank has correctly credited the seller in the amount of $500 and received only $50 in remittance proceeds, the drawee bank could be forced to remit the excess $450 on a restitution theory under Section 1-103. Even more clearly, the depositary bank could recover the excess from the drawee on the theory that the drawee became accountable for the true amount of the item ($500) upon paying it.

"However, if the buyer absconds before the drawee bank has the opportunity to charge his account for the extra $450, can the depositary bank still recover from the drawee? Since the depositary bank's encoding error was the negligent act that made the loss possible, and since the drawee bank is in no way unjustly enriched, the loss would presumably fall on the depositary bank. Although Article 4 does not cover this case specifically, Section 1-103, with its importation into the UCC of common-law negligence theory to fill holes left by the drafters, would seem to be directly in point. In addition, liability for negligent collection under Section 4-202 would lead to the same result.

"In summary, although specific amendments to Article 4 would help to clear up the problem of loss allocation due to encoding errors, the Article as presently drafted dictates no unfair or incongruous results, except perhaps with respect to wrongful dishonor, at least when the Article is used in conjunction with Section 1-103.

"A good underencoding case is *Georgia Railroad Bank & Trust Co. v. First Nat'l Bank & Trust Co. of Augusta*, where A drew a check to the order of B in the amount of $25,000. B deposited the check in the depositary bank, which mistakenly encoded it as a $2,500 item. The [depositary] bank's electronic equipment read the check according to its magnetic encoding, credited B's account for $2,500, and forwarded the item to the drawee bank, which debited A's account in the amount of $2,500. When B informed the depositary bank of the error, B's account was immediately credited with $22,500. The depositary bank then requested reimbursement from the drawee bank, which refused after being instructed by A not to 'bother' the account. The depositary bank sued the drawee bank for the $22,500 discrepancy and prevailed.

"The court, in line with the analysis set forth above, concluded that the item had been finally paid within the meaning of Section 4-213(3), so that the drawee bank was accountable for the full, proper amount of the item. The court also cited Section 4-302, since the payor bank had retained the item beyond its midnight deadline. A's contention that payment on the item had been stopped was properly rejected, since the countermand clearly came too late. In the case at hand, the court emphasized that A's account had sufficient funds to shift the loss from the shoulders of the drawee bank. It left open the possibility that it might reach a different result where the drawee bank could not recover from the drawer because of insufficient funds in the account. In such a case, the court suggested, the drawee bank would have a defense or counterclaim which could be asserted against the collecting bank that had [underencoded] the check."

Barkley Clark, *The Law Of Bank Deposits, Collections And Credit Cards*, §10.5[3] (rev. ed. 1981).

* * *

To support its contention that FNBL's failure to dishonor Hannah's check is irrelevant to the controversy between FAB (a collecting bank) and the defendants (its customers), FAB cites two cases: *Yoder v. Cromwell State Bank*, 478 N.E.2d 131 (Ind.Ct.App.1985), and *Mercantile Bank & Trust Co. v. Hunter*, 31 Colo.App. 200, 501 P.2d 486 (1972). In *Yoder*, a husband and wife appealed from a summary judgment granted in favor of Cromwell State Bank (hereinafter "CSB") in CSB's suit to recover on three checks. Mr. Yoder had presented the three checks to CSB for deposit into his and his wife's joint account and CSB provisionally credited the account with the amount represented by the checks. Blue Mound Dairy, the maker of the checks, stopped payment, and the payor bank, the State Bank of Worthington, returned the checks to CSB without making payment. CSB subsequently set off funds found in the Yoders' account against the total amount of the returned checks and brought an action to recover the balance. In affirming the trial court's summary judgment, the Indiana Court of Appeals rejected the Yoders' argument that the payor bank's actions precluded CSB's exercise of its right of charge back:

"The Yoders insist that factual questions concerning the processing, posting and dishonor procedures followed by the payor bank ... give rise to the inference that CSB's right of charge-back had terminated. We recall that the provision of Section 4-212(1) which states that a collecting bank's rights to revoke, charge-back and obtain refund terminate if and when settlement for the item received by the bank is or becomes final. The Yoders' argument based on this provision proceeds as follows: if the payor bank, SBW, had completed its process of posting (4-109) before receiving the stop payment orders on the three checks, then the stop-payment orders were too late because the final payment is deemed to have already occurred. (4-213). If final payment had occurred when CSB's right to charge-back terminated (4-212(1)) and the Yoders were no longer liable for the amount of the dishonored checks [sic]. [We assume that what the Indiana court meant to say was: 'If final payment had occurred, then CSB's right to charge-back terminated....'] This line of argument misses the point. The State Bank of Worthington is not a party to this action; whether it followed proper procedures in deciding to dishonor the checks should not be the focus of inquiry in determining the propriety of CSB's claim against the Yoders. The operative facts are that CSB received notice that the items were dishonored by the payor bank and in turn notified the Yoders."

Yoder v. Cromwell State Bank, 478 N.E.2d 131, 134 (Ind.Ct.App.1985). The *Yoder* court cites *Hunter* in support of its reasoning.

In *Hunter*, the defendant, James M. Hunter, appealed a summary judgment in favor of the plaintiff, Mercantile Bank & Trust Company, in an action to recover $37,500 from Hunter on a check payable to and indorsed by Hunter, deposited with Mercantile, and subsequently dishonored by the payor bank. Hunter argued on appeal that summary judgment should not have been entered because it precluded him from pleading the defense of final settlement, which would have required a factual determination as to when the check was presented to the payor bank for payment. Under this theory, Hunter argued that the provisional settlement between himself and Mercantile became final because the payor bank failed to timely dishonor the check, and that, therefore, Mercantile lost its right of refund against Hunter. The Colorado Court of Appeals found Hunter's final settlement argument inadequate as a matter of law. That court acknowledged that UCC §4-302 does provide, as Hunter contended, that if a payor bank retains a demand item beyond its midnight deadline without settling it, it is accountable for the amount of the item. The court stated, however, that the rule that a payor bank is "accountable" for an item does not mean that there has been a final settlement that would preclude a depositary bank from charging the amount of the item back to its depositor. Section 4-213, the court found, sets forth the circumstances under which a provisional settlement becomes final, and there is no provision that mere accountability of a payor bank for a check is a final settlement, unless the check is actually paid by the payor bank. Since nothing occurred here to cause the provisional settlement to become a final settlement under §4-213, the court concluded, Mercantile still had a right of refund under §4-212.

It appears to us that, despite FAB's argument to the contrary, the courts in *Yoder* and *Hunter* are not in accord with one another. On the one hand, FAB argues, the *Yoder* court would, in an action by a depositary bank against its customer, find that the prerequisite of dishonor had been met whether or not final payment had occurred. The rationale offered by that court for such a finding is that, "[g]iven the volume and speed of check processing it would be unrealistic to require the collecting bank to inquire and ascertain the grounds for and propriety of every item which is dishonored." *Yoder*, 478 N.E.2d at 135. On the other hand, the *Hunter* court recognizes, under similar facts, that actual payment of an item by the payor bank will constitute final payment, see UCC §4-213(1); that final payment will preclude dishonor, see §3-507(1), (2); and implicitly that final failure to dishonor will discharge indorsers' liability, see §3-502(2).

We distinguish *Yoder* from *Hunter* by noting that the UCC recognizes four instances in which an item is finally paid: when the payor bank pays the item in cash; when the payor bank settles for the item without reserving the right to revoke the settlement; when the payor bank completes the process of posting the item to the account of the maker; and when the payor bank makes provisional settlement for an item and fails to revoke that settlement before midnight of the next banking day following the banking day on which it received the relevant item. Code 1975, §§7-4-213(1), 7-4-104(1)(h), and 7-4-302(a). However, only two of these instances are reflected in §7-3-507(1)(a), namely: when an instrument is presented to a payor bank and either acceptance or payment is refused, or, since we are dealing here with collecting banks, when the instrument is seasonally returned by the midnight deadline. That is to say, while, as a practical matter, we generally recognize the concepts of final payment and dishonor as mutually exclusive principles, a technical reading of these two Code sections suggests that final payment and dishonor are mutually exclusive only when a payor bank pays the item in cash or when the payor retains the item beyond its midnight deadline. Because final payment precludes dishonor in only these two of the four instances in which final payment may potentially occur under §7-4-213(1), it is technically conceivable that dishonor may occur after final payment occurs as a result of the payor bank's settling for the item without reserving a right to revoke the settlement, or where final payment occurs as a result of the payor bank's completing the process of posting the item to the maker's account. *Yoder*, therefore, is clearly distinguishable from *Hunter* and from the case presently before the Court, because the Indiana court, in *Yoder*, based its decision upon the Yoders' argument that the posting of checks before stop-payment orders were entered constituted final payment and that final payment terminated CSB's right to charge-back. Thus, technically, in *Yoder*, dishonor could have occurred after final payment, while in *Hunter*, and in this case, payment of the item constituted final payment, and final payment precluded the later possibility of dishonor.

We hold, therefore, that under the express provisions of the UCC, FAB has failed to establish and prove a claim of indorsement liability, because it has failed to prove an essential element of that claim: dishonor of the check involved.

By arguing that this Court should adopt the rationale of *Yoder* and apply it to the facts of the present case, FAB would have this Court hold banking customers strictly liable for any item that they deposit, regardless of whether the banks handling the items are negligent and regardless of whether final payment has occurred (thus precluding proof of dishonor of the item, a necessary element of a claim for indorsement liability). The customers in this case did what all banking customers do: they accepted a check from its maker; they indorsed the check; they deposited the check to their account. From that point, there occurred a series of events, all of which were outside the control of the customers: FAB misencoded the item; the collecting banks failed to identify FAB's mistake; FNBL failed to compare the encoded amount with the actual amount of the check; FNBL returned the draft to its maker; and when the mistake was found and the adjustment entered, the Federal Reserve delayed almost 30 days before presenting the adjustment to FNBL.

When we apply Professor Clark's reasoning, the common law, and the Code to the present case, it becomes apparent that the defendants may not be held liable under a theory of indorsement liability. The UCC provides that every indorser engages that upon dishonor he will pay the instrument according to its tenor at the time of his indorsement to any subsequent indorser who takes it up. Code 1975, §7-3-414. FAB took up and indorsed an instrument previously indorsed by Azalea Management on its own behalf, its owners Jackson and Greene, and Azalea City. The Code provides further that an instrument is dishonored when presentment is made and either acceptance or payment is refused or cannot be obtained within the prescribed time, or, in the case of bank collections, when the instrument is not seasonably returned by the midnight deadline. §7-3-507(1)(a). Here, FAB transferred the instrument to collecting banks, which in turn presented the instrument to FNBL. FNBL made payment on the instrument within the prescribed time and retained the instrument beyond its midnight deadline. Therefore dishonor, as specifically defined in the UCC, did not occur.

The UCC provides that the payor bank becomes accountable for an item upon paying the item. §7-4-213(1). Like our sister state of Georgia, we hold that the partial payment of the item by FNBL constituted final payment within the meaning of §7-4-213(3), so that the drawee bank was rendered accountable for the full and proper amount of the item. Moreover, even if the partial payment of the $100,000 check did not constitute final payment, FNBL's retention of the item beyond its midnight deadline discharged the appellants' indorsement liability. §§7-4-302, 7-3-507(1)(a).

* * * [W]e make no determination as to the proper allocation of loss between FNBL, the Federal Reserve, and FAB.

Concomitant with its argument of indorsement liability, FAB argues here, for the first time, that the defendants are also liable for breach of their §7-4-207(2) engagement to honor. Section 7-4-207(2) provides:

"In addition each customer and collecting bank so transferring an item and receiving a settlement or other consideration engages that upon dishonor and any necessary notice of dishonor and protest he will take up the item."

Relying upon this section, FAB contends that, as customers who transferred an item to a collecting bank and received consideration, Jackson and Greene fall squarely within the scope of this provision. As such, FAB maintains that formal notice of dishonor is not necessary to charge a customer under this provision and that final settlement for an item does not affect the collecting bank's right to recover under this section. While we make no determination as to whether formal notice of dishonor is a necessary prerequisite to a recovery under §7-4-207(2), we can say unequivocally that final settlement does and must affect a collecting bank's right to recover.

Dishonor is a clear requirement under §7-4-207. Section 7-3-507(1)(a) enumerates the instances when dishonor occurs:

"An instrument is dishonored when a necessary or optional presentment is duly made and due acceptance or payment is refused or cannot be obtained within the prescribed time or in case of bank collections the instrument is seasonably returned by the midnight deadline."

FNBL made payment on the instrument within the prescribed time and retained the instrument beyond its midnight deadline. Both acts render payment final, and both acts preclude any subsequent dishonor of the instrument.

Because the $100,000 instrument was never dishonored by FNBL, neither indorsement liability under §7-3-414, nor the defendants' engagement to honor the check under §7-4-207(2), was implicated. For this reason, the trial court's judgment cannot be affirmed based upon a theory of indorsement liability or engagement to honor.

III. Money Had and Received

The second theory of liability under which the trial court may have found the defendants liable in this case arises under the common law claim of money had and received.

Appellants argue that the UCC's statutory scheme for bank deposits and collections precludes FAB's recovery against its customers under a common law cause of action for money had and received, restitution, or unjust enrichment. While the appellants cite several cases that ostensibly support this position, we recognize that a split of authority exists among the states. We are persuaded by the reasoning of the Texas District Court of Appeals in the case of *Greer v. White Oak State Bank*, [673 S.W.2d 326 (Tex.Dist.Ct.App.1984)]. In *Greer*, the court held that while a collecting bank could not recover against its customer as an indorser because it failed to give the indorser timely notice of dishonor, the collecting bank was not precluded from proceeding against him on a cause of action for money had and received:

> "As indicated Greer [and others] were all discharged, as *indorsers*, from any obligation on the check. Greer, however, was also a *customer* of the bank, and a recovery against him on a cause of action for money had and received, or unjust enrichment, was proper under the jury findings.
>
> "When a bank provisionally settles with its customer, and by reason of a dishonor of the item fails to receive the funds, it may revoke its settlement and charge the item back or obtain a refund from its customer. [Citations omitted.] *Greer contends this remedy is exclusive and prohibits a recovery against him on equitable principles. But [UCC §4-212(5)] provides that a failure to charge back or claim a refund does not affect other rights of the bank against the customer, and [UCC §1-103] provides that unless displaced by other provisions of the code the principles of law and equity shall supplement its provisions.* [Emphasis added.] Hence the equitable right of restitution is still available unless it conflicts with code provisions. [Citations omitted]. We find no provision of the code which conflicts with or abrogates the equitable right of a bank to proceed against its *customer* for restitution of funds which rightfully belong to the bank."

Id., at 329. Similarly, in *Great Western Bank & Trust v. Nahat*, 138 Ariz. 260, 674 P.2d 323 (Ariz.Ct.App.1983), the court held that a collecting bank's right to charge back a dishonored check was lost by its failure to notify its customer of the dishonor within the required time, but that this did not preclude recovery from the customer on a theory of restitution:

> "[The collecting bank] concedes that it is not entitled to a chargeback because it failed to notify [the customer] of the check's dishonor within the required time. [Citations omitted.] It argues that this does not preclude recovery under a theory of restitution. "
>
> ....
>
> "Since restitution was adequately pled, we must next determine whether chargeback pursuant to [UCC §4-212(1)] is an exclusive cause of action. We begin by recognizing that common law principles are incorporated into the commercial law of Arizona by [UCC §1-103] unless displaced by a particular statutory provision.
>
> "[The collecting bank] cites [UCC §4-212(5)] to support its position that the remedy of restitution should be recognized. That statute provides:
>
> > "'A failure to charge back or claim refund does not affect other rights of the bank against the customer or any other party.'

"By its terms [UCC §4-212(5)] expressly recognizes that the right to charge-back is not an exclusive remedy.

> "Other jurisdictions have held that UCC §4-212(1) ... is not the sole remedy.
>
> ....

"... [W]e hold that the common law remedy of restitution was available to the bank." *Id.*, 674 P.2d at 326-27.

By the authority of *Greer* and *Nahat*, and the express provisions of §§7-4-212(5) and 7-1-103, we find that FAB is not precluded by the UCC from asserting and proving a right of recovery under the principles of money had and received. Thus, we next look to determine whether FAB adduced the necessary evidence to prove the elements of its case so that the trial court may have justifiably granted a recovery to FAB based upon this common law theory.

The cause of action for money had and received "is based upon the theory that one person shall not be unjustly enriched at the expense of the other, and is equitable in nature. That is to say, the action lies wherever one has received and holds money which in good conscience belongs to another, or where one wrongfully converts the property of another the tort may be waived and an action brought for the proceeds arising from such conversion." *Christie v. Durden*, 205 Ala. 571, 572, 88 So. 667, 668 (1921). Thus, the question that this Court must answer by weighing the facts is whether the appellants received and held money that rightly belonged to FAB.

After a careful review of the record, we find that the evidence clearly indicates that the appellants paid good and valuable consideration in exchange for the $100,000 check issued them by Hannah. When we further consider FAB's failure to encode the instrument properly, the collecting banks' failure to remedy the error, FNBL's failure to compare the encoded amount of the draft against the true tenor of the check, FNBL's return of the instrument to Hannah, and the 41-day delay in notifying the appellants of the purported dishonor of the check, we can reach but one conclusion: the appellants were not unjustly enriched. If anyone, under these facts, could be found to have unjustly benefited from these turns of events, we would have to say it was Hannah. After all, it was he who received consideration for the $100,000 check, it was he who had but a tenth of what he truly owed debited from his account, and it was he who had the instrument upon which his obligation was based returned to him by FNBL. We note, also, that FAB currently holds a judgment against Hannah for the full amount of the $100,000 check.

The appellants, in contrast, were severely prejudiced by the actions of the banks. Forty-one days elapsed between the date of deposit and the date on which they were finally given notice of dishonor. It was during that period of time that Hannah apparently absconded with whatever funds remained in his account. Had FAB properly encoded the check, one of two things is certain. When the full and proper amount of the instrument was presented for payment to FNBL, either the full amount of the check would have been paid, or Hannah's stop payment order would have prevented payment and the check would have been dishonored and returned to the appellants. Obviously, in the first instance, no one would have been injured. In the second instance, however, the appellants would have been placed in a significantly better position to pursue Hannah, either to recover their consideration or to sue upon the instrument.

Because the appellants were not unjustly enriched, the judgment of the trial court cannot be affirmed based upon a theory of money had and received.

IV. Seizure and Set Off

In Alabama, a bank has the right of set-off to a customer's account when the bank and the customer are in a debtor-creditor relationship and there is mutuality of demands. The debtor-creditor relationship is created when a customer deposits money into a bank account, thus transforming the deposit into a debt owed by the bank to the customer. Under Code 1975, §7-4-212, FAB has a right of charge back for any credit given to the Azalea

Management checking account if the item of credit was a provisional settlement that was later dishonored. "These rights to revoke, charge back and obtain refund terminate if and when a settlement for the item received by the bank is or becomes final (subsection (3) of section 7-4-211 and subsections (2) and (3) of section 7-4-213)." Code 1975, §7-4-212(1). Because the $100,000 check credited to the Azalea Management account became final within the meaning of the UCC, and because FAB failed to prove any right of restitution for the $100,000 credit to the Azalea Management account, FAB possessed no right of set-off against Azalea Management's account.

For the foregoing reasons, the judgment of the trial court must be reversed and the cause remanded. REVERSED AND REMANDED.

Blake v. Woodford Bank And Trust Co.
Kentucky Court of Appeals, 1977
555 S.W.2d 589

Park, Judge. This case involves the liability of the appellee and cross-appellant, Woodford Bank and Trust Company, on two checks drawn on the Woodford Bank and Trust Company and payable to the order of the appellant and cross-appellee, Wayne Blake. Following a trial without a jury, the Woodford Circuit Court found that the bank was excused from meeting its "midnight deadline" with respect to the two checks. Blake appeals from the judgment of the circuit court dismissing his complaint. The bank cross-appeals from that portion of the circuit court's opinion relating to the extent of the bank's liability on the two checks if it should be determined that the bank was not excused from meeting its midnight deadline.

Basic Facts

The basic facts are not in dispute. On December 6, 1973, Blake deposited a check in the amount of $16,449.84 to his account at the Morristown Bank, of Morristown, Ohio. This check was payable to Blake's order and was drawn on the K & K Farm Account at the Woodford Bank and Trust Company. The check was dated December 3, 1973.

On December 19, 1973, Blake deposited a second check in the amount of $11,200.00 to his account in the Morristown Bank. The second check was also drawn on the K & K Farm Account at the Woodford Bank and Trust Company and made payable to Blake's order. The second check was dated December 17, 1973.

When Blake deposited the second check on December 19, he was informed by the Morristown Bank that the first check had been dishonored and returned because of insufficient funds. Blake instructed the Morristown Bank to re-present the first check along with the second check. Blake was a cattle trader, and the two checks represented the purchase price for cattle sold by Blake to James Knight who maintained the K & K Farm Account. Blake testified that he had been doing business with Knight for several years. On other occasions, checks had been returned for insufficient funds but had been paid when re-presented.

The two checks were forwarded for collection through the Cincinnati Branch of the Federal Reserve Bank of Cleveland. From the Federal Reserve Bank, the two checks were delivered to the Woodford Bank and Trust Company by means of the Purolator Courier Corp. The checks arrived at the Woodford Bank and Trust Company on Monday, December 24, 1973, shortly before the opening of the bank for business. The next day, Christmas, was not a banking day. The two checks were returned by the Woodford Bank and Trust Company to the Cincinnati Branch of the Federal Reserve Bank by means of Purolator on Thursday, December 27, 1973.

The two checks were received by the bank on Monday, December 24. The next banking day was Wednesday, December 26. Thus, the bank's "midnight deadline" was midnight on Wednesday, December 26. KRS 355.4-104(1)(h). As the bank retained the two checks beyond its midnight deadline, Blake asserts that the bank is "accountable" for the amount of the two checks under KRS 355.4-302(1)(a)

* * *

Excuse for Failing to Meet Midnight Deadline

* * *

The circuit court found that the bank's failure to return the two checks by its midnight deadline was excused under the provisions of UCC §4-108[2].

* * *

The basic facts found by the circuit court can be summarized as follows: a) the bank had no intention of holding the checks beyond the midnight deadline in order to accommodate its customer; b) there was an increased volume of checks to be handled by reason of the Christmas Holiday; c) two posting machines were broken down for a period of time on December 26; d) one regular bookkeeper was absent because of illness. Standing alone, the bank's intention not to favor its customer by retaining an item beyond the midnight deadline would not justify the application of §4-108(2). The application of the exemption statute necessarily will turn upon the findings relating to heavy volume, machine breakdown, and absence of a bookkeeper.

The bank's president testified that 4,200 to 4,600 checks were processed on a normal day. Because the bank was closed for Christmas on Tuesday, the bank was required to process 6,995 checks on December 26. The bank had four posting machines. On the morning of December 26, two of the machines were temporarily inoperable. One of the machines required two and one half hours to repair. The second machine was repaired in one and one half hours. As the bank had four bookkeepers, the machine breakdown required the bookkeepers to take turns using the posting machines for a time in the morning. One of the four bookkeepers who regularly operated the posting machines was absent because of illness on December 26. This bookkeeper was replaced by the head bookkeeper who had experience on the posting machines, although he was not as proficient as a regular posting machine operator.

Because of the cumulative effect of the heavy volume, machine breakdown and absence of a regular bookkeeper, the bank claims it was unable to process the two checks in time to deliver them to the courier from Purolator for return to the Federal Reserve Bank on December 26. ***

The increased volume of items to be processed the day after Christmas was clearly foreseeable. The breakdown of the posting machines was not an unusual occurrence, although it was unusual to have two machines broken down at the same time. In any event, it should have been foreseeable to the responsible officers of the bank that the bookkeepers would be delayed in completing posting of the checks on December 26. Nevertheless, the undisputed evidence establishes that no arrangements of any kind were made for return of "bad" items which might be discovered by the bookkeepers after the departure of the Purolator courier. The two checks in question were in fact determined by Mrs. Stratton to be "bad" on December 26. The checks were not returned because the regular employee responsible for handling "bad" checks had left for the day, and Mrs. Stratton had no instructions to cover the situation.

Even though the bank missed returning the two checks by the Purolator courier, it was still possible for the bank to have returned the checks by its midnight deadline. Under UCC

§4-301(4)(b) an item is returned when it is "sent" to the bank's transferor, in this case the Federal Reserve Bank. Under UCC §1-201(38) an item is "sent" when it is deposited in the mail. 1 R. Anderson, *Uniform Commercial Code* §1-201 pp. 118-119 (2d ed. 1970). Thus, the bank could have returned the two checks before the midnight deadline by the simple procedure of depositing the two checks in the mail, properly addressed to the Cincinnati branch of the Federal Reserve Bank.

This court concludes that circumstances beyond the control of the bank did not prevent it from returning the two checks in question before its midnight deadline on December 26. The circumstances causing delay in the bookkeeping department were foreseeable. On December 26, the bank actually discovered that the checks were "bad," but the responsible employees and officers had left the bank without leaving any instructions to the bookkeepers. The circuit court erred in holding that the bank was excused under §4-108 from meeting its midnight deadline. The facts found by the circuit court do not support its conclusion that the circumstances in the case were beyond the control of the bank.

Re-Presentment of Check Previously Dishonored by Nonpayment

On its cross-appeal, the bank argues that the circuit court erred in holding that there was no difference in the status of the two checks. The bank makes the argument that it is not liable on the first check which had previously been dishonored by nonpayment. Blake received notice of dishonor when the first check was returned because of insufficient funds. The bank claims that it was under no further duty to meet the midnight deadline when the check was re-presented for payment.

The bank relies upon the decision of the Kansas Supreme Court in *Leaderbrand v. Central State Bank*, 202 Kan. 450, 450 P.2d 1, 6 UCC Rep. 172 (1969). A check drawn on the Central State Bank was presented for payment on two occasions over the counter. On both occasions, the holder of the check was advised orally that there were not sufficient funds in the account to honor the check. Later, the holder deposited the check in his own account at the First State Bank. The First State Bank did not send the check through regular bank collection channels, but rather mailed the check directly to the Central State Bank for purposes of collection. The check arrived at the Central State Bank on March 21 or March 22, and the check was not returned by the Central State Bank to the First State Bank until April 5. The Kansas Supreme Court held that there was no liability under §4-302 of UCC for a check which had previously been dishonored when presented for payment.

Relying on the provisions of UCC §3-511(4), the Kansas Supreme Court held that "any notice of dishonor" was excused when a check had been "dishonored by nonacceptance" and was later re-presented for payment. The Kansas Supreme Court specifically held that §3-511(4) applied to a check which was dishonored when presented for payment, stating:

> While the language of 84-3-511(4), supra -- "Where a draft has been dishonored by nonacceptance" -- does not refer to a dishonor by nonpayment, we think reference to the dishonor of a "draft" "by nonacceptance" would, a fortiori, include the dishonor of a check by nonpayment.

* * *

The decision of the Kansas Supreme Court in the *Leaderbrand* case has been criticized. As UCC §3-511(4) applies by its terms to a "draft" which has been "dishonored by nonacceptance," most of the criticism has been directed to the Kansas court's application of §3-511(4) to a check which had been dishonored by nonpayment. [The court also notes that two courts have rejected the decision on the basis that §3-511(4) is inapplicable inasmuch as acceptance applies only to time items and has nothing to do with demand items.]

* * *

However, there are more fundamental reasons why the *Leaderbrand* decision is unsound and should not be followed in Kentucky.

The *Leaderbrand* decision is based upon the assumption that the sanctions of §4-302 are applied to a failure to give timely notice of dishonor. This assumption may appear reasonable from an initial reading of UCC §4-302(1)(a). Under that section, a payor bank is accountable for a check if it "does not pay or return the item or send notice of dishonor until after its midnight deadline." If a payor bank were excused from giving notice of dishonor, it would be plausible to argue that it was not accountable under §4-302. However, this reasoning ignores the primary purpose of notice of dishonor, and it completely ignores the language of UCC §4-301.

Prior to the time that he received the first check, Blake had a contractual claim for the purchase price of the cattle. When Blake took the first check, his claim for the purchase price of the cattle was not discharged, but that claim was "suspended pro tanto" until Blake presented the check for payment. See UCC §3-802(1)(b). Furthermore, at the moment he took the check, Blake had no claim against Knight on the check itself. As drawer of the check, Knight was a "secondary party." UCC §3-102(1)(d). As a secondary party, Knight was not liable on the first check until Blake had presented the check for payment and notice of dishonor had been given. See UCC §3-501(1)(c) and (2)(b). The first check was dishonored when it was returned in a timely manner for insufficient funds. See UCC §3-507(1)(a). As soon as the first check was dishonored, Blake had a right to maintain an action on the check itself or on the underlying contract for the cattle. See UCC §3-802(1)(b). When Blake re-presented the check for payment, there was no need for a further notice of dishonor in order to revive the underlying contract or to make Knight liable on the check.

Even if it was unnecessary to give further notice of dishonor when the check was re-presented for payment in order to make Knight liable on the check and to revive the underlying contract, it does not follow that the bank was relieved of its obligation to meet the midnight deadline. Most opinions and commentaries have focused on UCC §4-302 which only defines the extent of the payor bank's liability for failure to meet its midnight deadline. Whether a payor bank has met its midnight deadline for return of an item is determined by UCC §4-301, not §4-302. Under §4-301(1), a payor bank may "revoke" a provisional settlement if, before its midnight deadline, the payor bank complies with the following requirements:

> (a) returns the item; or
> (b) sends written notice of dishonor or nonpayment if the item is held for protest or
> is otherwise unavailable for return.

Written notice of dishonor is a permitted method of revoking a provisional settlement *only* if the check is unavailable for return or it is being held for protest. Otherwise, the check itself must be returned.

* * *

In the present case, both checks were available to the bank for return. Neither check was being held for protest. Consequently, the only way the bank could revoke its provisional settlement for the check was by returning the check before its midnight deadline. As notice of dishonor was not available as a means of revoking the provisional settlement, the provisions of §3-511(4) excusing notice of dishonor could have no application to the case.

A practical reason also exists for rejecting the *Leaderbrand* decision. In 1972, approximately 25 billion checks passed through the bank collection process. The Federal Reserve Banks handled 8 billion checks that year. *Community Bank v. Federal Reserve Bank of San Francisco*, 500 F.2d 282, (9th Cir.1974) modified, 525 F.2d 690 (9th Cir.1975), cert. denied 419 U.S. 1089, 95 S.Ct. 680, 42 L.Ed.2d 681. An earlier study indicated that only one half of one percent of all checks were dishonored when first presented for payment. Of those initially dishonored, approximately one half were paid upon re-presentment. F. Leary, Check Handling Under Article Four of the Uniform Commercial Code, 49 *Marq.L.Rev.* 331, 333, n. 7 (1965). A significant number of previously dishonored checks are paid upon re-presentment in the regular course of the check collection process. Such checks are often presented through intermediate collecting banks, such as the Federal Reserve Bank in this case. Each collecting bank will have made a provisional settlement with its transferor, and, in turn, received a provisional settlement from the bank to which it forwarded the check. In this way, a series of provisional settlements are made as the check proceeds through the bank collection process.

Under UCC §4-213(2), final payment of a check "firms up" all of the provisional settlements made in the collection process. Under subsection (1)(d) of UCC §4-213, a payor bank makes final payment of a check when it fails to revoke a provisional settlement "in the time and manner permitted by statute, clearing house rule or agreement." As to items not presented over the counter or by local clearing house, this means that a payor bank is deemed to have made final payment of a check when it fails to revoke a provisional settlement by its midnight deadline. See UCC §4-213, Official Code Comment 6. In his article on check handling, Leary has described §4-213 as the "zinger" section: "when provisional credit given by the payor bank becomes firm then -- 'zing' -- all prior provisional credits are instantaneously made firm." Leary, op.cit., at 361. If a payor bank was not required to meet its midnight deadline with respect to previously dishonored items, then none of the other banks involved in the collection process could safely assume that the check had been paid. Consider the problems of the depository bank. It must permit its customer to withdraw the amount of the credit given for the check when provisional settlements have become final by payment and the bank has had "a reasonable time" to learn that the settlement is final. See UCC §4-213(4)(a). The depository bank will rarely receive notice that an item has been paid. In actual practice, the depository bank will utilize availability schedules to compute when it should receive the check if it is to be returned unpaid. Leary, op.cit., at 345-346. If a payor bank is not bound by its midnight deadline as to previously dishonored items, then there is no way for the depository bank to know whether a previously dishonored item has been paid upon re-presentment except by direct communication with the payor bank. Such a procedure would impose an unnecessary burden upon the check collection process.

This court concludes that the circuit court was correct in holding that there was no difference in the status of the two checks.

Measure of Liability

The bank contends that its liability should be determined under subsection (5) of UCC §4-103. The general measure of damages for failure to exercise ordinary care in handling a check in the collection process is the face amount of the check less any sum which could not have been realized even by the exercise of ordinary care. As there was never more than $1,853.32 in the K & K Farm Account at any time after December 11, 1973, the bank claims that Blake can show no actual damage resulting from the one day delay in returning the two checks. This argument ignores the fact that a payor bank is liable for the face amount of the check under UCC §4-302 when it delays returning a check beyond its midnight deadline.

Farmers Cooperative Livestock Market v. Second National Bank, supra; *Rock Island Auction Sales v. Empire Packing Company,* 32 Ill.2d 269, 204 N.E.2d 721, 18 A.L.R.3d 1368 (1965). The bank's liability for the face amount of the check is not based upon its failure to exercise ordinary care. By delaying return of the check beyond its midnight deadline, the bank is deemed to have paid the check. Having paid the check, it is therefore accountable for the face amount of the check. See UCC §4-213(1). Damages have no relevance to the concept of accountability.

There is a rational basis for imposing a different liability on payor banks than is imposed upon collecting banks. The payor bank is the only bank in the collection process in a position to know the actual state of the drawer's account, and it is the only bank in the collection process that can actually pay the check.

Deferred posting was authorized by the Bank Collection Article of the Uniform Commercial Code, and by its predecessor, the Model Deferred Posting Statute, in order to grant payor banks additional time within which to determine whether to pay a check presented for collection. If banks are no longer able to meet their midnight deadline because of new banking conditions, then the remedy of the banks is to be found in the legislature. The present statute is intended to provide a mechanical standard of easy application for determining the time of payment of checks and the liability of payor banks. Having in mind the need for prompt settlement of items in the collection process, this court is not at liberty to tinker with the present statute by judicial amendment.

First American Savings v. M & I Bank
United States Court of Appeals, Third Circuit, 1989
865 F.2d 561

Stapleton, Circuit Judge: In this appeal we must determine the relationship between a paying bank's liability for failure to notify a depositary bank of a check's dishonor as required by Federal Reserve Regulation J, 12 C.F.R. §210:1 et seq. ("Regulation J"), and a depositary bank's liability for breach warranty under the Uniform Commercial Code, 13 Pa.C.S.A. §4207(a)(1) ("UCC"), and Regulation J, 12 C.F.R. §210.5(a)(2). The district court held that the paying bank's warranty claim defeated the depositary bank's notification claim. 685 F.Supp. 473. We will reverse.

I.

On January 2, 1987, the appellant, First American Savings ("First American"), received a check for deposit by its customer, Martha Bonanni, drawn on the appellee, M & I Bank of Menomonee Falls ("M & I"). The check, in the amount of $18,800.00, was made payable to Henry Skorr and contained the purported endorsement of Henry Skorr, followed by the endorsement of Martha Bonanni. First American provisionally credited Mrs. Bonanni's account with $18,800.00, and then forwarded the check through the federal reserve system for presentment to M & I.

On January 5, 1987, M & I was presented with the check, and on the next day, January 6, it dishonored it because the account on which it had been drawn was closed. M & I, however, did not notify First American that it dishonored the check although required to do so under Regulation J which provides as follows:

(1) A paying bank that receives a cash item in the amount of $2,500 or more directly or indirectly from a Reserve Bank and determines not to pay it shall provide notice to the first bank to which the item was transferred for collection ("depositary bank") that the paying bank is returning the item unpaid.... (2) The paying bank shall provide the notice such that it is received ... by the depositary bank by midnight of the second banking day of the paying bank following the deadline for return of the item as specified in paragraph (a) of this section ... Notice may be provided through any means, including return of the cash item so long as the cash item is received by the depositary bank within the time limits specified in this subparagraph.

12 C.F.R. §210.12(c)(1) and (2). Instead, M & I merely returned the check to the Federal Reserve Bank of Chicago.

As the check was making its way back to First American, Martha Bonanni withdrew a total of $17,000.00 from her account. She withdrew the money on two separate occasions--$12,000.00 on January 9, 1987 and $5,000.00 on January 12, 198[7] at 11:59 a.m. First American did not receive notification of M & I's dishonor of the check until later in the day of January 12, 1987, at 1:45 p.m., when its correspondent, Provident National Bank, telephoned with the information. At that time, Mrs. Bonanni had only $1,800.00 left on deposit, thereby resulting in an overdraft of $17,000.00 when First American charged the check back against her account.

Subsequent to M & I's dishonor of the check, it was discovered that the payee's endorsement was forged. Although M & I dishonored the check because the account on which it had been drawn was closed, M & I nevertheless disclaimed any liability to First American for failure to notify because of the existence of the forgery. To date, First American has recovered only $500.00 of the overdraft, leaving a principal loss of $16,500.00.

First American commenced the present action in the district court to recover the balance of the overdraft, and moved for summary judgment on the basis of M & I's Regulation J violation. First American argued that had M & I given proper notification of dishonor, First American would have learned the check was being returned no later than midnight on January 8, 1987, and, therefore, could have prevented both of the withdrawals made by Mrs. Bonanni.

In defense, M & I cross moved for summary judgment arguing that First American was ultimately liable to M & I for breach of warranty of good title under the UCC and for breach of warranty that the check bore no forged endorsements under Regulation J. In keeping with prior common law, these warranties operate to place the loss suffered from a forged endorsement on the depositary bank as the party that took from the forger. Specifically, the UCC provides:

(a) *Warranties to Payor or Acceptor*--Each customer or collecting bank who obtains payment or acceptance of an item and each prior customer and collecting bank warrants to the payor bank or other payor who in good faith pays or accepts the item that: (1) He has a good title to the item or is authorized to obtain payment or acceptance on behalf of one who has good title.

13 Pa.C.S.A. §4207(a)(1). Similarly, Regulation J provides:

(a) *Sender's agreement.* By sending an item to a reserve bank, the sender: (2) warrants to each reserve bank handling the item (i) the sender has good title to the item or is authorized to obtain payment on behalf of one who has good title ...; but this subparagraph does not limit any warranty by a sender or other party arising under state law.

12 C.F.R. §210.5(a)(2).

The district court granted M & I's cross motion for summary judgment essentially holding that First American breached its presentment warranty. The court rejected First American's argument, in response to M & I's cross motion, that a breach of warranty can occur only when the payor bank *honors*, or pays, a check bearing a forged endorsement, reasoning that, by its terms, Regulation J's warranty is created upon a bank's "sending" as opposed to "paying" an item. Moreover, the court noted that in revising Regulation J in 1985 to incorporate the notice requirement, the Federal Reserve Board commented:

> Several commentators raised questions concerning how the liability provision of the notification requirement would overlap with the existing requirements in the U.C.C. The Board believes that it would be possible to have duplicative or overlapping liability if the payor institution fails to comply with the notification requirement and another depositary institution failed to comply with the U.C.C. requirements concerning the return of the physical check. *Similarly, the failure of the payor institution to satisfy the notification requirement should not defeat the claims that the institution otherwise would have against the institution of first deposit for breach of warranty.*

Amendment of Regulation J, 50 Fed.Reg. 5734 (February 12, 1985) (emphasis supplied).

Relying on that language, and on the judicial deference owed to the Board's interpretation of its own regulations, the court concluded that M & I's warranty claim should not be defeated by its notification violation. The court held that as the party closest in the collection chain to the person who forged the endorsement, First American should suffer the ultimate loss.

Our standard of review of the district court's grant of summary judgment, involving the application of law to undisputed facts, is plenary.

II.

It is undisputed that M & I violated the notification provisions of Regulation J, and as a result would ordinarily be required to assume First American's loss. Regulation J expressly provides:

> A paying bank that fails to exercise ordinary care in meeting the requirements of [timely notice] shall be liable to the depositary bank for losses incurred by the depositary bank, up to the amount of the item, reduced by the amount of the loss that the depositary bank would have incurred even if the paying bank had used ordinary care.

12 C.F.R. §210.12(c)(6). Indeed, the loss suffered by First American as a consequence of M & I's failure to notify it that the check had been dishonored is precisely the kind of loss the Federal Reserve Board sought to avoid when it promulgated the notification rule in 1985. As the Board explained at that time:

> The Board believes that timely notification of nonpayment will enable the institution of first deposit to take steps to protect itself from potential loss. Such measures may include extending a hold it may have placed on the account or placing a hold on other funds of the depositor. The Board believes that the proposal would provide significant public benefits by providing depositary institutions the opportunity to make funds available sooner to their customers. Accordingly, the Board has determined to adopt the notification proposal.

Amendment of Regulation J, 50 Fed.Reg. 5735 (February 12, 1985). In light of these considerations, we perceive no reason why the subsequently discovered forged endorsement should change in any way M & I's liability to First American for the balance of the overdraft.

The UCC makes clear that only a payor bank that *honors* a check later found containing a forged endorsement can recover for breach of warranty from the depositary bank. According to Section 4207(a)(1), collecting banks such as First American warrant good title only to "the payor bank or other payor *who in good faith pays or accepts* the item." Because M & I dishonored, and therefore did not "pay or accept," Mrs. Bonanni's check, it cannot claim that First American breached its warranty of good title under the UCC. Thus, although ordinarily a forged endorsement would shift any loss onto the depositary bank, in this case, the forgery is of no consequence as M & I dishonored the check and accordingly can not rely on the UCC's warranty provision.

We further find, in contrast to the district court, that a payor bank must also have paid a check in order to recover under Regulation J's warranty provisions. While no mention is made in §210.5(a)(2) of such a requirement and by its terms the section provides that by "*sending* an item" a bank warrants good title, we believe the difference in language is one of form and not of substance. In a context like this, the purpose of casting the rule of liability in terms of warranty is to make the usual rules of warranty law applicable, including the requirement that one seeking to recover must demonstrate a loss occasioned by reliance on the express or implied representation. As the drafters of the comparable UCC provision note in their Commentary:

> The obligations imposed by this section are stated in terms of warranty. Warranty terms, which are not limited to sale transactions, are used with the intention of bringing in all the usual rules of law applicable to warranties, and in particular the necessity of reliance in good faith and the availability of all remedies for breach of warranty, such as rescission of the transaction or an action for damages.
>
> ...

13 Pa.C.S.A. §3417 Comment 1.

In the situation before us, M & I suffered no loss in reliance on First American's implied representation that the endorsement was genuine. As a result, it has no meritorious warranty claim against First American and, accordingly, should not be permitted a set off against its liability to First American for the loss occasioned by its breach of duty under Regulation J to give notice of dishonor. Bailey, *Brady on Bank Checks* §26.20 (6th ed. 1987) ("where no loss results from payment on a forged endorsement, a payor bank has no right of recovery from a bank that collected on the forged endorsement.") The loss which M & I will thus be required to assume will be a loss incurred as a result of its failure to give prompt notice of dishonor, not one resulting from its reliance of the genuineness of the endorsement.

We further note that we find no indication in §210.5(a)(2)'s administrative history that it was intended to be more expansive than the UCC's warranty. More importantly, we can perceive no reason why the Federal Reserve Board would have wished to broaden the warranty in the manner suggested by M & I. Indeed, if we were to accept the reasoning of M & I and the district court, payor banks would be fully relieved of their obligation to notify depositary banks of a check's dishonor even when the reason for the dishonor is the detection of a forged signature. Such a result is at odds with the purpose of requiring prompt notification, specifically, to eliminate a depositary bank's avoidable loss occasioned by delay in notification.

M & I's reliance on the Reserve Board's commentary is similarly misplaced. The commentary, properly understood, states only that the additional burden placed on payor banks under the new notification rule does not alter liabilities under traditional warranty law. Under Section 210.12(c), notice of dishonor must ordinarily be provided to the depositary bank before midnight of the third banking day following receipt of a check by the payor bank. In a situation where the payor bank pays and only later discovers a forged endorsement, it will want to deny liability on the check but may be unable to do so by the required deadline. If the notification requirement were to be interpreted as barring recovery from the depositary bank in such circumstances, the rule placing the loss occasioned by a forged endorsement on the depositary bank would, in effect, be overruled. The quoted commentary makes it clear such a result was not intended--that the payor's rights under the UCC's warranty of good title in such circumstances are not affected by the failure to give timely notice of dishonor. However, the commentary need not, and should not in our judgment, be read to take the position that a payor bank who *does not pay* a check on presentment has a claim for breach of the UCC's warranty of good title even though it has incurred no loss.

We stress that the Board's opinion refers specifically to the "*UCC*" warranty. As we have explained, that warranty, by its express terms, arises only in favor of a payor bank that has paid or accepted a check. Accordingly, it is clear that the Board was not thinking of the situation before us when it opined that: "... the failure of the payor institution to satisfy the notification requirement should not defeat the claims the institution otherwise would have against the institution of first deposit for breach of warranty." Amendment of Regulation J, 50 Fed.Reg. 5734 (February 12, 1985).

III.

In sum, we hold that M & I violated its obligation under Regulation J to notify First American that it dishonored the check and is therefore liable for the balance of the overdraft. Accordingly, we will reverse the judgment of the district court and remand with instructions that judgment be entered in favor of First American.

practice

Case 1

D drew a check to P. P indorsed the check and deposited it in her account at Depositary Bank, DB, which credited P's account for the amount of the item. The law presumes that this credit is provisional. DB inexplicably held the check for a week before forwarding it to IB, an intermediary bank, for collection. IB promptly sent the check to the drawee or Payor Bank, PB, for payment. PB immediately dishonored the check because just the day before D had withdrawn all the funds from her account. PB returned the check to IB, and IB bounced the item back to DB. DB quickly notified P of the return of the check, and debited P's account for the amount of the item. This debit was pursuant to 4-214(a), which allows a collecting bank to revoke a provisional settlement given for an item even though the bank was negligent in handling the item. 4-214(d)(2). (Or, it was a setoff based on P's liability as indorser.) D is nowhere to be found.

a. P sued DB for negligence in handling the check. What result? See 4-202; 4-103(e); *Pan American World Airways v. Bankers Trust Co*, 99 A.D.2d 712, 472 N.Y.S.2d 315 (1984).

b. Is the result the same if the day after issuing the check D had ordered PB to stop payment on the item? See *Wertling v. Manufacturers Hanover Trust Co.*, 118 Misc.2d 722, 461 N.Y.S.2d 157 (N.Y.Civ.Ct.1983). "[T]he legal standard governing causation and damages under UCC §4-103 ***, while it permits reasoned deductions from probative facts, does not permit mere guesswork. Plaintiffs must show they would have had at least a *reasonable chance* to collect. It is not enough to show that by a fortuitous combination of unlikely events there was a dim hope of collection." *Marcoux v. Van Wyk*, 572 F.2d 651, 655 (8th Cir.1978) (emphasis in original); see also *Alioto v. United States*, 593 F.Supp. 1402 (N.D.Cal.1984); *Appliance Buyers Credit Corp. v. Prospect Nat'l Bank*, 505 F.Supp. 163 (C.D.Ill.1981), aff'd 708 F.2d 290 (7th Cir.1983); *White v. Hancock Bank*, 477 So.2d 265, 272 (Miss.1985) (collecting bank not liable for delay in presentment from February 15 to April 14 because "the check was just as worthless on February 15 as it was on April 14").

c. Same facts as in the beginning except that DB promptly forwarded the check to IB upon receiving the item. IB, however, held the check for a week. Is IB liable to P if the facts otherwise are the same? Is IB a collecting bank for purposes of 4-202(a)? If IB has a duty of ordinary care, is the duty owed to P? See 4-201(a); *Colonial Cadillac, Inc. v. Shawmut Merchants Bank*, 488 F.Supp. 283 (D.Mass.1980) (dictum).

d. Is DB vicariously liable to P for IB's negligence on the theory that IB was DB's agent? See 4-202(c). Could DB be liable for having selected IB as the intermediary bank? See 4-202 comment 4; but cf. *Hoke v. Pioneer State Bank*, 167 N.J.Super. 410, 400 A.2d 1217 (1979) (to recover from a collecting bank on the basis of negligence in choosing method of transmitting items for payment there must be a causal connection between the choice of method and the loss and no such connection was shown where person to whom items were forwarded for presentment filed bankruptcy before remitting proceeds of items to collecting bank).

e. Suppose that IB is the Federal Reserve Bank of Minneapolis. Can P recover from IB for IB's own negligence?

Case 2

Buyer drew a check to Seller in payment of goods bought and sold. Seller deposited the check in her account at First Bank, which credited Seller's account with the amount of the item. First Bank presented the item to the payor, Second Bank, for payment. Second Bank immediately settled for the item. Thereafter, however, the check was dishonored and returned in due course to First Bank. Buyer had issued a stop order covering the item because of a dispute with Seller over the quality of the goods purchased by Buyer. A week later, having taken no action of any kind against anyone, First Bank retains you to pursue the full range of First Bank's remedial options against its customer, the Buyer and Second Bank.

a. On these facts what are First Bank's options?

b. If First Bank has recourse against Seller, does Seller have a counterclaim against First Bank for the latter's delay in giving notice of the check's dishonor? See 4-214(a) & (d)(2); 4-202(a)(2) & (b); 4-103(e); see also *Appliance Buyers Credit Corp. v. Prospect Nat'l Bank*, 708 F.2d 290 (7th Cir.1983); *Northpark Nat'l Bank v. Banker's Trust Co*, 572 F.Supp. 524 (S.D.N.Y.1983); *Salem Nat'l Bank v. Chapman*, 64 Ill.App.3d 625, 21 Ill.Dec. 414, 381 N.E.2d 741 (1978). Regarding liability, compare *United Kentucky Bank, Inc. v. Eagle Machine Co., Inc*, 644 S.W.2d 649 (Ky.App.1983) (collecting bank failed for 48 days after learning of dishonor to so notify its depositor, the payee). On the question of proof of damages under the standard of 4-103(e), see *Royal Trust Bank v. All Florida Fleets, Inc*, 431 So.2d 1043, 1045-46 (Fla.App.1983) (listing array of material facts relevant to damages such as (1) evidence as to what efforts were actually made by the customer to recover from those liable on the check after the customer learned of dishonor; (2) whether the customer's actual collection efforts were all that were required as reasonable and timely efforts to collect on the dishonored check under the circumstances; (3) proof demonstrating how the failure of the bank seasonably to notify the customer of the dishonor proximately caused the customer to be unable to recover the full amount of the check from the drawer; and (4) how much of the deficiency in recovery was attributable to the bank's negligent delay in notifying the customer and how much to other possible factors). For a unique view on the relationship among 4-103(e), 4-202, and 4-214(a) and the effect of this relationship on the issue of damages in a case in which a depositary/collecting bank is negligent in giving its customer notice of dishonor, see *Appliance Buyers Credit Corp. v. Prospect Nat'l Bank*, 708 F.2d 290, 297 (7th Cir.1983) (Cudahy, J., dissenting) (argues that court should presume that bank's default caused injury equal to the face amount of the check, which presumption could be rebutted by the bank proving that the check would have been uncollectable even if timely notice had been given).

c. Suppose that Buyer and Seller both bank at First Bank. Seller deposits the check there and gets credit for the item, but very shortly thereafter Buyer directs First Bank to stop payment. What are First Bank's remedial options?

Case 3

Buyer drew a check to Seller in payment of goods bought and sold. Seller deposited the check in her account at First Bank, which credited Seller's account with the amount of the item. First Bank presented the item to the payor, Second Bank, for payment. Second Bank immediately settled for the item but bounced it three banking days later. Buyer had belatedly issued a stop order because of a dispute with Seller over the quality of the goods purchased by Buyer. A week later, having taken no action of any kind against anyone, First Bank retains you to pursue the full range of First Bank's remedial options against Seller, the Buyer and Second Bank.

a.   **What are First Bank's options?**

There is a very good argument that First Bank cannot charge back the item against Seller's account. Because Second Bank did not return the item to First Bank before Second Bank's midnight deadline, Second Bank failed to revoke the provisional settlement it made with First Bank in the time and mann er permitted by statute. See 4-301(a). Therefore, Second Bank finally paid the item, 4-215(a)(3), and the provisional settlement between Second Bank and First Bank became a final settlement. 4-213(c). Because the settlement between these banks became final, First Bank lost the rights to charge back the item against Buyer's account and to obtain refund. 4-214(a) (third sentence); see also 4-215(d); *Boggs v. Citizens Bank & Trust Co*, 32 Md.App. 500, 363 A.2d 247 (1976); but see generally *Yoder v. Cromwell State Bank*, 478 N.E.2d 131 (Ind.App.1985) (except when a check is paid in cash, a payor bank's accountability does not amount to a final settlement which would preclude a depositary bank from charging back the amount of the item); accord *Mercantile Bank & Trust Co. v. Hunter*, 31 Colo.App. 200, 501 P.2d 486 (1972).

There is some justice in the world, however. Second Bank's final payment under 4-215(a) may have caused First Bank to lose the 4-214(a) right of charge back against Seller's account. Yet, the same final payment gives First Bank a claim for the amount of the item against Second Bank.

b.   **Does Second Bank's final payment of the check affect First Bank's chances of recovering on the instrument from the Buyer (as drawer) or Seller (as indorser)? Consider 3-602(a). Is payment made for purposes of 3-602 when an item is finally paid under any of the subparts of 4-215(a); consider also 3-414 & 3-415, which condition the liability of drawers and indorsers on dishonor. Is dishonor (as defined in 3-502(b)(1)) possible in a case in which an item has been finally paid under 4-215?**

c.   **Suppose Second Bank orally notified First Bank of the check's dishonor within 24 hours after Second Bank received the item, but Second Bank did not actually return the check itself until three banking days after receiving it. Does this new fact change any of your answers? See 4-301(a). Banks can agree, however, to vary the requirements of this provision with respect to the procedures whereby a payor bank revokes settlements for items. 4-103. For a collection of cases dealing with the proper revocation procedure when there is an agreement or other law varying 4-301(a), see Annot., 22 A.L.R.4th 11 (1983) (construction and effect of laws making payors accountable for failing to act promptly on items presented for payment).**

d.   **Despite Second Bank's late return of the check, First Bank immediately upon receipt of it debited Seller's account for the amount of the item and delivered the check to her. What are Seller's remedial options?**

    i.   Specifically, does Seller have a cause of action against First Bank? See generally 4-214(a) (last sentence) (negative implication); cf. 4-215(d).

    ii.   Section 4-302(a) explains that a payor is accountable upon a late return of an item. To whom? Is Second Bank directly accountable to Seller? Yes (see generally, e g., *Horney v. Covington County Bank*, 716 F.2d 335 (5th Cir.1983); *Reynolds-Wilson Lumber Co. v. Peoples Nat'l Bank*, 699 P.2d 146 (Okl.1985)), but the technical basis for liability may be final payment rather than 4-302 accountability. In any event, how are damages measured? In the case of a late return, 4-302(a) explains that accountability means liability for the amount of the item. Suppose that upon First Bank debiting Seller's account, Seller sues Second Bank on the basis of the payor's accountability for the late return. Suppose also that First Bank can show that Seller ultimately collected part of the price of the goods from Buyer. Should Seller's recovery against First Bank be reduced by this amount? See *State & Savings Bank v. Meeker*, 469 N.E.2d 55 (Ind.App.1984) (yes). Suppose that First Bank can further show that Seller was unable to recover the balance of the price from Buyer because as to some of the goods Buyer had a defense based on Seller's breach of warranty. Will this showing affect First Bank's accountability to Seller? Consider 4-407. Cf. *Starcraft Co. v. C.J. Heck Co.*, 748 F.2d 982 (5th Cir.1984). Would the answer to the last question change if Buyer had not ordered Second Bank to stop payment on the check but Buyer's account had insufficient funds to cover the item?

Case 4

Buyer drew a check to Seller in payment of goods bought and sold. Seller deposited the check in her account at First Bank, which credited Seller's account with the amount of the item. First Bank presented the item to the payor, Second Bank, for payment on banking day Monday. Second Bank immediately settled for the item. Second Bank decided to dishonor the check at 11:30 p.m. on Tuesday. It did so by sending the item to First Bank by U.S. mail. This method of return is almost never used by any bank in the area. First Bank did not receive the dishonored check until Friday.

a.   Can First Bank lawfully charge the item against Seller's account?

b.   What are Seller's options if First Bank charges the item against her account?

c.   Suppose that Second Bank sent the check to First Bank via direct courier who picked up the check at 2:00 a.m. on Wednesday.

Case 5

"SOS during 1984 had an ongoing arrangement to sell wholesale petroleum products to Conlo Services Corporation. Owing to the large volume of sales, a 'running account' was maintained between SOS and Conlo. To facilitate Conlo's payments, SOS opened a checking account with Norstar, where Conlo also maintained an account, and Conlo deposited its payments directly into SOS's account, apparently retaining the deposit slips. Norstar thus functioned both as payor bank (UCC 4-105[b]) in accepting presentment of Conlo's checks for payment, and as depositary bank (UCC 4-105[a]) in accepting deposits of Conlo checks into SOS's account, although it performed its separate functions without regard to the fact that it was doing both. This appeal centers on Norstar's role as payor bank in paying Conlo's check, but the unusual facts call upon us also to take note of its role as depositary bank in encoding the check.

"In connection with opening its account, SOS completed and adopted a 'Corporate Resolution' on a Norstar form, which among other things named the SOS officers authorized to make loans and withdrawals on behalf of the corporation. The resolution began with a declaration that SOS designated Norstar 'as a depository,' and in paragraph 9 it established notification and time requirements for bringing suit against the bank for claimed errors in the customer's statements of account. Unless written notification were given to the bank within 14 days and suit commenced within one year of delivery of a statement, according to paragraph 9 of the 'Corporate Resolution' the statement as rendered would be considered correct for all purposes and Norstar would not be liable to SOS for any errors in that record.

"On July 9, 1984, Conlo deposited into SOS's account its check drawn on its account at Norstar, payable to SOS, in the amount of $255,000. The amount was correctly indicated on the deposit slip prepared by Conlo as well as on the check itself, both in numbers and in script. Norstar then encoded the check mechanically--meaning the bank wrote the amount on the check in computer-readable magnetic ink, which permitted automated processing.[*] Instead of $255,000, however, Norstar mistakenly encoded the amount of the check as $25,000, which amount was then credited to SOS and debited to Conlo. The $25,000 deposit appeared on SOS's July 31, 1984 statement from Norstar.

"Months later SOS discovered the error, when a dispute arose with Conlo as to how much of their 'running account' balance had been paid, whereupon SOS asked Norstar for a copy of the deposit slip and check for the July 9 transaction. On October 31, 1985, SOS brought the error to Norstar's attention and demanded the $230,000 difference. By that time, Conlo's

---

[*]   "Described as the most widespread technological advance in bank collections since the UCC was drafted (see Clark, The Law of Bank Deposits, Collections and Credit Cards, § 10.5, at 10-8 [Rev. ed.] 1981), the encoding of checks with magnetic ink has become an integral part of the automation of modern banking. In this process, a bank, using magnetic ink, will encode the amount of the check on the deposited check itself. When that is done, the amount of the check, the identity of the payor bank, and the identity of the drawer-depositor can be "read" electronically. As a consequence of magnetic encoding, checks do not generally require manual attention for most of the check collection process (see, Bailey, Brady on Bank Checks, § 19.2, at 19-3 [6th ed. 1987]; Clark, The Law of Bank Deposits, Collections and Credit Cards, supra; 1 White and Summers, Uniform Commercial Code, § 17.3, at 846-847 [3d ed.] 1988)." *SOS Oil Corp. v. Norstar Bank*, 152 A.D.2d 223, 548 N.Y.S.2d 308 548 N.Y.S.2d 308 (1989), further appeal, 76 N.Y.2d 561, 563 N.E.2d 258, 561 N.Y.S.2d 887 (1990).

account at Norstar had been closed for more than a year and Conlo had gone out of business.

"Norstar refused to pay, resulting in the present complaint on alternative theories of Norstar's UCC 4-302 liability as payor bank, breach of contract as depositary bank, and negligence in underencoding the check. Norstar denied liability and asserted both the notification requirements of the 'Corporate Resolution' and defenses of estoppel, account stated, contributory negligence and illegality of the underlying SOS-Conlo transaction. The trial court granted plaintiff's cross motion for summary judgment on its UCC 4-302 cause of action, concluding that neither the bank's contractual defense nor its remaining defenses were valid against that statutory claim. The Appellate Division affirmed ***." *SOS Oil Corp. v. Norstar Bank*, 76 N.Y.2d 561, 565-66 563 N.E.2d 258, 259-60, 561 N.Y.S.2d 887 (1990).

Should the New York Court of Appeals have affirmed or reversed?

Case 6

"Parkfair Pisa, Inc. ('Parkfair') maintained a checking account at First Westside Bank of Omaha ('Westside'). From November 28 through December 3, 1986, Parkfair drew five checks totalling $46,739.00 on Westside, the 'paying bank.' The checks were payable to Pisa Pizza ('Pisa') and were deposited in Pisa's checking account at the 'depository bank,' Northwest Bank and Trust Company ('Northwest'), an Iowa banking corporation located in Davenport, Iowa. Northwest sent the checks through the Federal Reserve System for collection. When the Federal Reserve Bank of Kansas City, Omaha branch, presented the checks to Westside, Westside refused to honor the Parkfair checks because they were drawn on uncollected funds. Westside, however, failed to give Northwest notice of its refusal to pay the checks as required under Federal Reserve Board Regulation J. After the Parkfair checks totalling $46,739.00 were returned by Westside, the Pisa account was overdrawn in the amount of $43,128.43. Northwest asserts that it would have dishonored $44,421.00 in checks drawn on Pisa's account and presented for payment by Northwest Bank of Kearney, Nebraska (the 'Kearney Bank') on December 5, 1986, if it had received timely notice of dishonor from Westside.

"On December 4, 1986, when the balance in the Pisa account at Northwest was $88,068.58 of which $86,555.00 represented uncollected funds, the Kearney Bank notified Northwest that an $11,133.00 check drawn on the Kearney Bank by MIMCO, a Kearney Bank customer, and deposited in the Pisa account was being returned. Northwest then placed a hold on the Pisa account in that amount. On December 5, 1986, however, Northwest paid by cashier's check five different checks totalling $44,421.00, which had been drawn on the Pisa account, to the Kearney Bank after representatives of the Kearney Bank presented the checks for payment in person.

"Northwest previously had returned the checks unpaid to the Kearney Bank because they were not endorsed properly. The Kearney Bank later flew representatives to Davenport to obtain, by cashier's check, the $44,421.00 from Northwest.

"Northwest paid the five checks to the Kearney Bank the day after the Regulation J notification deadline passed for Parkfair check number 1685 in the amount of $10,286.00. Regulation J did not require Westside to notify Northwest of its refusal to pay the other four Parkfair checks until after Northwest paid the five checks presented by the Kearney Bank. The Regulation J deadline for check number 1688 was December 8, 1986; the Regulation J deadline for check numbers 1690 and 1691 was December 9, 1986; and the Regulation J deadline for check number 1695 was December 10, 1986.

"Between December 9 and December 15, 1986, the Kearney Bank returned unpaid to Northwest five additional checks drawn on the MIMCO account totalling $39,816.00, which had been deposited in the Pisa account at Northwest prior to December 5, 1986. Northwest received timely notice from the Kearney Bank of the return of four of these checks after December 5, 1986. Westside and the Kearney Bank's failure to collect funds from Parkfair and MIMCO, respectively, combined with Northwest's payment of the cashier's check for $44,421.00, caused the Pisa account to be overdrawn by $43,128.43.

"Northwest brought an action against Westside to recover damages allegedly incurred due to Westside's failure to comply with the notice requirements of Regulation J. The district court found that Westside failed to exercise ordinary care by not notifying Northwest of its refusal to honor the five Parkfair checks within the time specified in Regulation J. The court held, however, that Northwest still would have lost $32,842.43 even if Westside had followed Regulation J. The court reasoned that as of the time Northwest paid the checks presented by the Kearney Bank, Westside had violated Regulation J only with regard to Parkfair check number 1685 in the amount of $10,286.00. Consequently, the court awarded Northwest $10,286.00 in damages.

"Westside concedes that it failed to exercise ordinary care in meeting the notification requirements of Regulation J.

"Northwest now appeals the district court's judgment limiting its recovery of damages against Westside to $10,286.00. Westside cross appeals on the ground that the district court should not have awarded Northwest any damages under its findings of fact." *Northwest Bank & Tr. Co. v. First Westside Bank*, 941 F.2d 722, 723-24 (8th Cir. 1991).

How should the Eighth Circuit have disposed of the appeal?

Case 7

Chicago Title Insurance Company (the Company) acted as escrow agent in numerous transactions initiated by a mortgage broker, Robert Dean Financial (RDF), and its principal client, George I. Benny. The Bank handled certain checks connected with these transactions, as a result of accounts RDF and Benny held at the Bank. Unfortunately, RDF and Benny were engaged in a massive check fraud operation. The Company brought this lawsuit alleging, inter alia, that the Bank had caused these losses to improperly fall upon the

Company. The Company contended the Bank belatedly returned as dishonored 28 bad checks payable to the Company, *after* the "midnight deadline" by which time the Bank must take such action or be held "accountable" under the Uniform Commercial Code. (Cal.U.Com.Code, §4302.) The Bank had its main Northern California office in San Francisco, and had a San Mateo County branch which returned the 28 checks in issue, totalling about $17 million. The checks were first deposited by the Company at the Bank of San Francisco. That bank then forwarded them via Crocker Bank to the San Francisco office of the Bank for presentment. The next day, they were sent by the Bank from its San Francisco office to its San Mateo branch. That branch (in which the makers of the 28 checks maintained the accounts on which they were drawn) decided to return the checks as dishonored. The checks *left* the Bank's San Mateo branch by courier for the Bank's in-house data processing and computer center in San Francisco before the "midnight deadline," but did not *arrive* at their ultimate destination -- 14 checks going to the San Francisco clearing house and another 14 going directly to Crocker Bank in San Francisco -- until the next day. The Bank claimed this return of the checks from the San Mateo branch was timely, since the checks left that *branch* for its in-house San Francisco processing and computer center before the midnight deadline; the Company contended, and the trial court ruled, that the checks were returned untimely since they did not actually arrive at the central clearing house in San Francisco or at Crocker Bank before the midnight deadline. The parties agree that the proper resolution of this issue of timeliness turns upon the interpretation of language contained in the formerly applicable version of certain regulations, issued by the California Bankers Clearing House Association (CBCHA) in order to implement section 4302. The most pertinent language of CBCHA regulation 7.04.b.2.(c) provides that checks, "drawn payable at a member bank office or branch located outside of the City and County of San Francisco [such as the Bank's San Mateo branch], shall be mailed or dispatched for return by the payor office or branch not later than midnight of the next business day ***." The trial court concluded that the Bank had indeed returned the checks late and was, therefore, "acccoutable" for the loss. The Bank appealed from a judgment of $25 million in favor of the Company. Part of the Bank's argument was that the midnight deadline had been met by getting the checks out of the branch proper before the deadline expired. *Chicago Title Ins. Co. v. California Candian Bank,* 1 Cal.App.4th 798, 2 Cal.Rptr.2d 422 (1992).

Who should prevail on the appeal?

Case 8

Appellant Los Angeles National Bank filed an action against respondent Bank of Canton of California seeking $2,257,965 in compensatory damages, plus punitive damages, for respondent's alleged failure either to pay the face amount of, or notify appellant it would not honor, 28 checks prior to the "midnight deadline" established by the Commercial Code, and for conversion arising from respondent's alleged wrongful failure to pay appellant the face amount of the checks. It is undisputed that appellant and respondent both use the Los Angeles branch of the Federal Reserve Bank of San Francisco as an intermediary "clearinghouse" to settle accounts for negotiable items which pass between appellant and respondent. In addition, respondent had entered into an agreement with the Federal Reserve Bank requiring the latter to send checks and other items to Decimus Corporation, an entity located outside the premises of respondent and employed by the latter to sort, collate, and otherwise process checks and various items for respondent. In a typical transaction, the U.S. Courier Corporation, a messenger service, would pick up items from the Federal Reserve Bank and deliver them to Decimus Corporation, where they would be processed before delivery to respondent. It was the responsibility of respondent to determine whether to return an item for insufficient funds.

In August or September of 1985, an entity known as Golden Fields Leasing Company, Inc., established a checking account with respondent, purportedly for use in a business consisting of selling and leasing Mercedes Benz automobiles. During the period from January 22 to January 25, 1986, Tony Lam and Peter Wong, principals in the business, executed 28 checks drawn on Golden Fields Leasing Company, Inc.'s account with respondent. These individuals deposited the checks, in three separate groups, in an account held by Golden Fields Leasing Company, Inc., in one of appellant's branch offices in Monterey Park, located three blocks from one of respondent's branch offices.

It was alleged in appellant's complaint that on January 22, 1986, a Wednesday, appellant processed three checks totalling $900,000, drawn by Golden Fields Leasing Company, Inc., on its account with respondent. Appellant sent the three checks for collection to the Federal Reserve Bank, which provisionally "settled" and delivered the checks to respondent before 2:00 p.m. on Friday, January 24th. Respondent, on the basis there were insufficient funds in the account of Golden Fields Leasing Company, Inc., returned the checks to appellant on Tuesday, January 28th, after expiration of the statutory "midnight deadline" for returning the items, which must be met in order to revoke the provisional settlement made by the Federal Reserve Bank. Appellant alleged that, after it subsequently returned each of the checks to respondent marked "Late Return Item Claim, Response," respondent again returned the checks, marking them "Paying Bank's Response To Late Return Item Claim," thus wrongfully denying that the checks were returned late and that appellant was due the face amount of the checks. In a separate cause of action, appellant alleged that respondent wrongfully had converted to its own use the face amount of these checks.

Appellant made similar allegations regarding a second group of 17 checks totalling $1,091,520 processed by appellant on Friday, January 24, 1986, which the Federal Reserve Bank provisionally settled and delivered to respondent before 2 p.m. on Monday, January 27th. It was alleged respondent returned these checks for insufficient funds on or after Wednesday, January 29th, after expiration of the midnight deadline. Appellant alleged a separate cause of action for conversion of the total face amount of this group of checks.

Appellant made similar allegations regarding a third group of eight checks totalling $266,445, which it had processed on Monday, January 27, 1986, and which the Federal Reserve Bank provisionally settled and delivered to respondent before 2 p.m. on Tuesday, January 28th. It was alleged respondent returned these checks for insufficient funds on or after Thursday, January 30th, after expiration of the midnight deadline. Appellant alleged a separate cause of action for conversion of the total face amount of this group of checks.

Appellant moved for summary judgment on the ground respondent was accountable for the face amount of the checks because it had failed to return the checks before the midnight deadline in accordance with the applicable provisions of the Commercial Code. Respondent in turn moved for summary judgment on the basis that appellant's loss was caused solely by the negligence of its employees in cashing the checks or giving credit to the principals of Golden Fields Leasing Company, Inc., without verifying that there were funds on deposit with respondent sufficient to pay the face amount of the checks.

In support of its motion for summary judgment, respondent submitted the following evidence. On January 22 and 23, 1986, the principals of Golden Fields Leasing Company, Inc., deposited with appellant three checks totalling $900,000. After appellant had transferred them to the Federal Reserve Bank, at 6 p.m. on Friday, January 24th, U.S. Courier Corporation picked up the first group of three checks from the Federal Reserve Bank and delivered them to Decimus Corporation. After processing by Decimus Corporation, respondent received this group of checks on Tuesday, January 28th, and returned them to the Federal Reserve Bank that day. Between 8:57 and 9:05 a.m. that day, respondent informed the Federal Reserve Bank by telephone that it would not honor the checks. The Federal Reserve Bank wired notice to that effect to appellant later that day.

On Friday, January 24th, the principals of Golden Fields Leasing Company, Inc., deposited with appellant 17 checks totalling $1,091,520. At 6 p.m. on Monday, January 27th, U.S. Courier Corporation picked up the second group of 17 checks from the Federal Reserve Bank and delivered them to Decimus Corporation. On Wednesday, January 29th, respondent received these checks and returned them to the Federal Reserve Bank that day. Between 3:28 and 3:38 p.m. that day, respondent informed the Federal Reserve Bank by telephone that it would not honor the checks. The Federal Reserve Bank wired notice to that effect to appellant on January 30th.

On Saturday, January 25th, the principals of Golden Fields Leasing Company, Inc., deposited with appellant eight checks totalling $266,445. At 6 p.m. on Tuesday, January 28th, U.S. Courier Corporation picked up the third group of 8 checks from the Federal Reserve Bank and delivered them to Decimus Corporation. On Thursday, January 30th, respondent received these checks, returning them to the Federal Reserve Bank that same day. Later that day, respondent informed the Federal Reserve Bank by telephone that it would not honor the checks, and the Federal Reserve Bank wired notice to that effect to appellant.

Respondent's evidence established that U.S. Courier Corporation typically picked up items from the Federal Reserve Bank and delivered them to Decimus Corporation on the same evening. These items would be processed during the following day, and on the third day Decimus Corporation would send them by courier to respondent.

Respondent furnished the following additional evidence. Ms. Pou San Au was an operations officer who worked for appellant in its branch office in Monterey Park. On Thursday, January 23, 1986, after Lam and Wong had deposited three checks totalling $900,000, Ms. Pou San Au gave Lam and Wong $400,000 in cash, in violation of the limitations placed on her authority to give immediate credit. The two men carried the cash out of the bank in brown paper bags. On the same day, other employees of appellant wire-transferred $488,000 in credit against the remaining uncashed checks to National Westminster Bank in New York. On Friday, January 24th, Lam and Wong deposited 17 checks payable to appellant, exchanging 15 of these for cashier's checks payable to the Bank of America. They also received $400,000 in cash from Ms. Pou San Au, which the two men carried from the bank in brown paper bags. On Saturday, January 25th, Lam and Wong deposited eight checks payable to appellant, immediately exchanging them for cashier's checks payable to the Bank of America.

On Monday, January 27th, Ms. Pou San Au walked the three blocks from the bank where she worked to the branch office of respondent, where she inquired of respondent's employees to verify that adequate funds were available in the checking account of Golden Fields Leasing Company, Inc., to cover the checks she had cashed. Ms. Pou San Au was advised by respondent's employees that the account of Golden Fields Leasing Company, Inc., lacked adequate funds, and that respondent would return, without honoring, any checks written on that account, with the designation "uncollected funds."

Ms. Pou San Au, immediately returning to appellant's branch office, notified the branch manager, Kevin Chan, and appellant's president of the loss and was thereupon suspended. (Subsequently, she was terminated for cause because of having granted immediate credit to Lam and Wong without first verifying whether the account of Golden Fields Leasing Company, Inc., had adequate funds to cover the amount of the checks which its principals had presented.) Mr. Chan went to the offices of Golden Fields Leasing Company, Inc., and found them deserted and wiped clean of fingerprints. On that date, appellant notified the Federal Bureau of Investigation of appellant's loss.

In opposition to respondent's motion for summary judgment, and incorporating evidence introduced in support of its own motion for summary judgment, appellant established that the first group of checks was made available for pick-up and was received by Decimus Corporation on January 24, 1986, but that respondent did not return the checks, with written notice they were dishonored, until January 28th. The second group of checks was made available for pickup and was received by Decimus Corporation on January 27th, but respondent did not return the checks until January 29th. The third group of checks was made available for pickup and was received by Decimus Corporation on January 28th, but respondent did not return the checks until January 30th. As to each group of checks, appellant provided evidence, in the form of expert and other testimony, that the Federal Reserve Bank made the checks available for pickup by Decimus Corporation before 2 p.m. on the dates in question, thereby effectuating presentation and delivery at that time.

Appellant also provided detailed information concerning its extensive prior dealings with Lam and Wong over the four to five-month period preceding the incidents involved in the present case, demonstrating that Ms. Pou San Au had handled numerous other items for Lam without incident. A number of the checks deposited during the three-day period were accepted in payment for "automobile drafts" and documents of title related to Golden Fields Leasing Company, Inc.'s business, rather than for cash. Ms. Pou San Au did not violate her credit authorization in cashing or allowing credit for at least some of the checks. When Ms. Pou San Au contacted respondent on January 27, 1986, it did not inform her that any further checks it received would be returned unpaid. The FBI was notified only on January 28, 1986, that there was a possible loss.

Additionally, appellant submitted evidence that on January 15, 1986, respondent had become suspicious of the activities of Golden Fields Leasing Company, Inc., and as of January 17th, began to scrutinize its account, instructing its tellers to hold all checks on this account. On January 23rd and 24th, respondent's employees contacted appellant's employees to verify cashier's checks drawn on Golden Fields Leasing Company, Inc.'s account with appellant. Nonetheless, respondent failed to notify appellant, any other bank, or any regulatory agencies of its suspicions.

The superior court denied appellant's motion for summary judgment, granted respondent's motion for summary judgment, and entered judgment in favor of respondent. Appellant filed a notice of appeal. Respondent's reasons for affirmance included these two arguments: (1) it had given timely oral notice of dishonor regardless of when the midnight deadline began to run and (2) it returned the items prior to the applicable midnight deadlines if the time is calculated from when it received the items from Decimus Corporation. *Los Angeles Nat'l Bank v. Bank of Canton*, 229 Cal. App.3d 1267, 280 Cal. Rptr. 831 (1991).

What should be the outcome of the appeal?

§ 2. Checking Accounts

The fundamental relationship in the check collection process is between the drawee-payor bank and the drawer of the check who, generally and technically, is a *customer* of the payor bank because she has an account there. See 4-104(a)(5). The account upon which the drawer writes a check is the source of funds to which the payor bank looks for reimbursement upon paying the check. Actually, the account is a balance sheet reflecting the amount of money the bank owes the customer (or vice versa if the account is overdrawn). Money deposited in an account is not really held *in species* by the bank for the customer's benefit. The money becomes the bank's funds, but the customer becomes a general creditor of the bank for the total of her deposits. Checks that can rightfully be charged against the account are debits that reduce the bank's indebtedness to the customer.

The debtor-creditor relationship that a checking account creates is basically founded upon a contract between the payor bank and the customer. The contract is typically expressed in a written deposit agreement which often takes the simple form of a signature card with an agreement in tiny print on the back. In exchange for having the use of the customer's money deposited in a checking account and, perhaps, for a further fee, the bank agrees to pay checks drawn on the account over the signature of the person or persons named in the deposit agreement.

DEPOSIT ACCOUNT SIGNATURE CARD

TYPE OF ACCOUNT (Personal)

☐ Individual ☐ Joint—Survivorship ☐ Joint—No Survivorship

☐ In Trust For ☐ Uniform Gift to Minor ☐ Other _____

TYPE OF ACCOUNT (Business)

☐ Sole Proprietorship ☐ Corporation—Profit ☐ Corporation—Not for Profit

☐ Partnership ☐ Unincorporated Ass'n. ☐ Other _____

TYPE OF SERVICE

☐ Checking ☐ N.O.W. ☐ Money Market Account

☐ Savings ☐ Super N.O.W. ☐ Other _____

DEPOSITS   **FEES**

Initial Minimum Deposit $ _____   Maintenance or Account Fee $ _____

Additional Deposits (Minimum) _____   Per Withdrawal Item   _____

INTEREST   Per Deposited Item   _____

Interest Calculation: Computed _____   Overdrafts—Per Item   _____

Compounded _____   Stop Payment—Per Item   _____

Change in Interest Rate   _____   Returned Item—Per Item   _____

Minimum Average Daily Balance   _____

DORMANT ACCOUNT FEE

A fee will be charged if there is no activity in the account for _____ consecutive days, and will be charged for each _____ day period that no activity occurs on the account.

WITHDRAWALS

_____ days prior written notice may be required to effectuate any withdrawals.

No more than _____ preauthorized transfers will be allowed per month.

No more than _____ checks may be drawn on the account.

ADDITIONAL FEES, CHARGES, OR SPECIAL INSTRUCTIONS

NAME NO. 1	ACCOUNT NUMBER
	DATE
NAME NO. 2 (Joint Account)	
	BUSINESS PHONE
MAILING ADDRESS	HOME PHONE
CITY, STATE, ZIP CODE	SOC. SEC. NO. or FED. TAX ID NO.

By signing this document, I (we) have opened the type of account designated above and have received a copy of that account's agreement and terms and agree to be bound by them. If this account is designated as a joint account, I acknowledge that I have received and read the terms related to joint accounts. Under penalty of perjury, I (we) certify (1) that the number shown on this card is my (our) correct taxpayer identification number and (2) that I (we) are not subject to backup withholding, either because I (we) have not been notified of backup withholding as a result of a failure to report all interest or dividends, or the Internal Revenue Service has notified me (us) that I (we) are no longer subject to backup withholding. (Instruction to signer: If you have been notified by the IRS that you are subject to backup withholding due to notified payee underreporting and you have not been notified that the backup withholding is terminated you should strike out the language in clause 2 above.)

CHECKS, DRAFTS, AND WITHDRAWALS TO BE SIGNED BY

☐ Any _____ of the signers.

☐ Signed by Number _____ and Countersigned by Number _____.

AUTHORIZED SIGNATURES

1 _____

2 _____

3 _____

4 _____

NAMES AND / OR TITLES

Form 1642 Rev. 03/85
© Copyright 1985

DEPOSIT ACCOUNT AGREEMENTS

General Agreement. As used herein, the terms ''I'', ''me'', ''my'', ''us'' and ''our'' refer to the depositor (whether joint or individual) and the terms ''you'' and ''your'' refer to the institution. The following agreement shall govern my account with you as reflected on the deposit account signature card, under ''type of service''. My agreement with you also includes signature cards; transfer authorization; and any other documents or notices executed and/or issued to establish and/or maintain my account (sometimes collectively called ''Agreement''). In addition, my agreement with you includes all applicable state and federal laws and regulations including Clearing House rules and the Uniform Commercial Code.

General Rules. The following rules apply to all types of accounts.

1. **Deposits.** Even though you may credit my account immediately upon my making a deposit, I understand except for cash deposits, you receive any other item as a collecting bank and you may handle the collection of any such item in accordance with your usual practices. I understand that if any item is returned, it should be debited back to my account and you may adjust the interest earned on my account, if any, accordingly. You may also refuse to honor any request I make, whether or not preauthorized, to withdraw funds from my account until you have received final settlement for the item deposited. I may make deposits to the account as often, and in such amounts as I wish, unless otherwise specified in the deposit account signature card. All deposits must be in U.S. dollars. All deposits to my account which are received by you after 3:00 p.m. on business days or on Saturdays, Sundays or Holidays, may be treated by you as if received at the opening of the next business/banking day. I understand that any deposit I make may be subject to a service charge.

2. **Withdrawals.** I understand that notwithstanding my right to withdraw from my account, you have the right to require prior written notice from me of my intent to withdraw, according to the minimum time for such notice set forth in the Agreement. I understand that any withdrawal I make may be subject to a service charge. I agree not to attempt to withdraw more than the amount available to me in the account.

3. **Set offs.** If I owe you any money, either directly or indirectly, you may use the funds in my account as payment upon such debt. If our account is a joint account, it is agreed that you are held harmless and indemnified by us in the event the account is set off for the debt of only one joint owner. Each joint owner hereby acknowledges your right to so offset for the debt of any one of the joint owners.

4. **Expenses.** I agree that, if you incur any expense due to an attachment, garnishment or levy upon my account, including, but not limited to, court costs and attorney's fees, I will reimburse you for such expense or you may charge any portion of such expense to my account.

5. **Dormant Accounts.** I understand that if my account is dormant for the period of time specified in the Agreement, I will be charged the fee specified and that you may stop paying interest on my account. I further agree that you are relieved of all further responsibility if my account balance is escheated.

6. **Joint Accounts, Trust Accounts and Custodial Accounts.** I acknowledge that if my account is set up as a joint account, trust account or custodial account, I have instructed you as to the proper title of the account and that you assume no legal responsibility to inform me as to how the creation of such account affects my legal interests. If I have any questions as to the legal effect of such types of accounts, I will consult my own attorney and I bear the sole responsibility as to the legal effect of the creation of the account or how it is maintained with you. The law governing the ownership rights of such accounts shall be the law of the state where your main office is located.

7. **Joint Account. If the account is designated as a joint account, deposits and any additions thereto shall be the property of any person named on the account. You may release the entire amount or any portion in this account to any person named on this account. You may honor checks, withdrawals, orders or requests from any person named on this account. You may, upon receipt of a court order or under other valid legal process remit funds held in the account to satisfy a judgement or other valid debt incurred by any person named on this account. In the event of death of any person named on this account you may continue to honor checks, withdrawals, orders or requests by any surviving person named on this account. In the event of death of any person named on this account you may treat the account as the sole property of any surviving person(s) named on this account. You may freeze the account if you receive written notice from any person named on the account instructing you not to pay or deliver any joint deposits or additions thereto or accrual of interest thereon. You will have no liability if you continue to honor checks, orders, withdrawals or requests prior to receiving written notification to freeze the account. The account would continue to be frozen until you receive written notification signed by all parties named on the account or a court orders you as to the disposition of the account.**

In the event this account is designated as a joint account with no survivorship (and state law where the account is opened allows such an account), then upon receipt of notice of the death of any person named on the account, you may freeze the account until you have satisfied yourself that all legal documents necessary to make payment have been delivered to you or a court orders you as to the dispostion of the account.

8. **Trust Account.** I understand that if I create the account as a trust that you may absolutely rely upon my representation to you, as I may change from time to time, as to who is the beneficiary of the trust. I warrant that all deposits and withdrawals upon the account will be made for the benefit of the beneficiary. I agree to comply with all applicable laws as to my actions as trustee for the account.

9. **Custodial Account.** If I have set the account up as a custodial account, I agree that the account shall be subject to the Uniform Gift to Minors Act, or similar law, as adopted in the state where your main office is located.

10. **Fees, Service Charges and Balance Requirements.** I agree to pay you, or have you deduct from my account, such fees and service charges as you may, from time to time, impose as set forth in the Agreement. I agree to comply with any minimum balance/deposit requirements you may from time to time impose.

11. **Amendment and Alterations.** I agree that you may change the terms of this agreement at any time by conspicuously posting a notice of such change at your main office or by mailing the notice to my address as shown on your records in either of which events, the changes will be binding upon me. Your ability to change the terms of the Agreement includes the right to increase or decrease any fees, minimum balance/deposit requirements or any other term or condition to which my account is or may be subject to.

12. **Closing Account.** I may withdraw all collected funds in the account at any time. You may close the account at any time by sending me a check for the collected balance in your possession and giving me a notice that you have done so.

13. **Assignment.** I understand that I cannot transfer or assign any interest I have in my account, except by withdrawal means, without your written consent.

14. **Effective Applicable Laws and Regulations.** I understand that if any of the provisions of this agreement are found to be in violation of, or restricted by, any applicable federal, state or local law, regulation, or ordinance, this agreement shall be so construed as to conform with such law, and that the remainder of this agreement shall not be affected by such laws, and shall remain in full force and effect.

15. **If my account is an interest bearing account**, my account deposits will earn interest paid on the collected balance of my account at such rate and time as established in the Agreement.

CHECKING, NOW, AND SUPER NOW ACCOUNTS

Specific Rules. In addition to the General Rules, my checking account, negotiable order of withdrawal (NOW) account, and Super NOW, will be subject to the following specific rules.

1. **Checks.** All negotiable paper presented for payment must be in a format that is processable or photographable using equipment which you presently have on hand for such work. You may refuse to accept any negotiable paper that is nonconforming.

2. **Non-Sufficient Funds.** If my account lacks a sufficient collected funds balance to cover the payment of any check presented for payment, you may return such check for non-sufficient funds. In such a case, you may charge me a fee for such returned item as then applicable to my account.

3. **Stop Payments.** I may request you not to pay a check which I have written. If I do so, I must advise you of my account number, the date, number and amount of the check, and the name of the payee. I must confirm such request in writing within 14 days. Stop payments will be effective for 6 months unless otherwise agreed. I will be charged a fee for any stop payment request as might then be applicable to my account. Each continuation of a stop payment request will be treated as a new request for the purpose of fee assessment. I agree to hold you harmless and indemnify you for any and all expenses and liability which you might incur if you pay an item upon which I have requested a stop payment provided that you have exercised ordinary care. I also agree that if you return any other item drawn by me due to non-sufficient funds which situation is caused because you have paid an item upon which I had requested a stop payment, you will not be liable for such action. I understand that you may accept the stop payment request from any of the joint owners of the account regardless of who signed the check.

4. **Statements.** I understand that you will provide me with a periodic statement showing account activity. I agree to promptly examine my statement and all cancelled checks (if returned) and to notify you of any discrepancies, including, but not limited to, forgeries or improper charges within fourteen (14) days after you mail the statement to me. If I fail to notify you of any such discrepancies, any claim I have against you will be waived. If the statement is returned to you because I have failed to claim it or if I have failed to provide you with a proper mailing address, you may discontinue sending me statements until I specifically make written request that you commence sending statements to me again, furnishing you with a proper address. I understand that you do not have to return my cancelled checks but that you will provide me copies upon written request and I may be charged for said photocopy service.

5. **Withdrawals.** I agree not to postdate any check drawn on the account. I hold you harmless for paying any stale, postdated or overdraft check and agree to reimburse you for any loss you might suffer because of such payment made in good faith.

6. **Check Safekeeping.** If offered by you, I may utilize your check safekeeping or similar service in which case my cancelled checks will not be returned with my statements and the original cancelled checks will be destroyed by you after a reasonable period of time. I may request a copy of any check. However, if I do, I may be charged a service fee for such service. If you cannot provide me with a copy of any check or satisfy me through other means, I agree that in any event you will not be liable for more than the face amount of the check or my actual damages, whichever is less. I agree that any time I request a copy of a check I may be required to prove the existence of such check by corroboration with your statement related to my account.

MONEY MARKET ACCOUNTS

In addition to the General Rules and Specific Rules, my money market account will be subject to the following additional rules:

1. **Withdrawals.** I understand, notwithstanding my right to withdraw from my account, you have the right to require prior written notice from me of my intent to withdraw according to the minimum time for such notice set forth in the Agreement. I understand that you will not allow more preauthorized transfers than the maximum number set forth in the Agreement. I further understand that I may not draw more checks on my account per month than the maximum number set forth in the Agreement. I agree that the date used to determine the maximum number of checks to be drawn per month limitation shall be the date of payment of the check. As used herein, the term month means the monthly statement period.

SAVINGS ACCOUNTS

In addition to the General Rules, my Savings Account will be subject to the following Specific Rules:

1. **Statement or Passbook Account.** I may choose between a statement or passbook account. If I choose a statement account I will receive a periodic statement showing activity in my account and interest paid, if any, since the prior statement. Statements will be mailed to me at the mailing address shown on your records. If I choose a passbook account and my passbook is lost or stolen, I will immediately provide you with written notice. Passbook account withdrawals requested without presentation of the passbook may at your option be refused or I may be required to provide whatever proof you require to effectuate a no book withdrawal.

2. **Transfers and Assignments.** In accordance with the provisions of Regulation D (12 CFR 204), my account is not transferrable except as provided therein or as revised or amended from time to time by the Federal Reserve Board. In no event, may I transfer or assign this account without your written consent. By law you must prohibit me from making more than three withdrawals a month from my account for purposes of transferring funds to another account or for making payments to a third party by means of a pre-authorized or telephone agreement, order or instruction, except that withdrawals from my account will be permitted for the purposes of repaying loans and associated expenses to you.

Certain aspects of the relationship are also governed by U.C.C. Article 4. Most importantly, Article 4 explains that, "[a] bank may charge against the account of a customer an item that is properly payable from the account even though the charge creates an overdraft. An item is properly payable if it is authorized by the customer and is in accordance with any agreement between the customer and bank." 4-401(a). On its face, this provision appears only to create a right in the bank's favor. As applied, however, 4-401(a) imposes a duty on a payor bank: *The bank must pay properly payable items.* Failing to do so makes the payor bank liable to its customers for *wrongful dishonor,* 4-402, which includes any unauthorized or unjustified refusal to pay a check.

The negative implication of 4-401(a) imposes another duty on a payor bank: *The bank cannot charge its customer's account for an item that is not properly payable, and the bank should therefore dishonor the item.* A variety of circumstances render an item not properly payable. A good example is a check that the drawer has ordered the bank not to pay by issuing a stop-payment order. See 4-403. Another good example is a check that bears a forged or otherwise ineffective signature of the drawer or an indorser. If a bank pays a check that is not properly payable, the item cannot rightfully be charged against the customer's account. If the account is nevertheless charged for the item, the bank thereby breaches 4-401(a) and on this basis the customer can ordinarily sue to force the bank to recredit her account.

These twin duties that a payor bank owes its checking account customer, i.e., to pay properly payable items and to dishonor items that are not properly payable, account for most of the instances in which a bank is liable to such a customer. Yet, a payor bank's liability for breaching either of these duties is not absolute. Article 4 and supplemental law establish a host of defenses and conditions to the bank's liability, some of which take the form of duties that are imposed on the customer.

story

Wrongful dishonor

1. The Meaning of "Wrongful Dishonor"

"A payor bank is liable to its customer for damages proximately caused by the wrongful dishonor of an item." 4-402(b). Simply put, *wrongful dishonor* is dishonoring a check that is properly payable and thus should have been paid. 4-402(a). (For the meaning of dishonor, see 3-502(b).) "An item is properly payable if it is authorized by the customer and is in accordance with any agreement between the customer and bank." 4-401(a). Put more fully, wrongful dishonor is any dishonor of a check by the drawee/payor bank that is not permitted or justified by law or the terms of the deposit contract between the payor bank and its customer. Thus, there is no wrongful dishonor where the drawer has no credit extended by the drawee, or where the draft lacks a necessary indorsement or is not properly presented. In contrast, a bank wrongfully dishonors by refusing to pay a check that is properly presented and properly drawn on an account having sufficient funds to cover the item.

The express terms of 4-402 describe the customer's recovery for wrongful dishonor as damages "proximately caused." 4-402(b). This includes consequential damages of all sorts, including damages for an arrest or prosecution of the customer (as when the customer is charged with writing bad or hot checks), for loss of credit, and for other mental suffering. Though punitive damages are not authorized by the statute, there is caselaw permitting recovery of such damages in appropriate circumstances, as when the payor bank acted intentionally or with malice. See also 4-402 comment 1 ("Whether a bank is liable for noncompensatory damages, such as punitive damages, must be decided by Section 1-103 and Section 1-106 ('by other rule of law').")

A statutory action for wrongful dishonor did not exist under pre-Code law. The wrong was addressed through a common-law action for breach of contract or an action in tort, such as defamation. In a defamation case, the customer could recover substantial damages without proving that damage actually occurred if she was a merchant, trader or fiduciary. Damages were presumed because defaming a person in her business, trade or profession was a defamation "per se." Presuming damages in such a case was known as the *Trader Rule*. Section 4-402 does not "retain" this Rule. 4-402 comment 1. By the terms of the statute, liability is limited to actual damages proved. 4-402(b). It could be argued that the common-law Trader Rule supplements 4-402; but it is likely that by not retaining the rule, 4-402 also displaces it.

The person who can complain of wrongful dishonor is the payor bank's "customer." 4-402(b). Defined most restrictively, this means the person who has the account on which the dishonored item was drawn. See 4-104(a)(5). Following the restrictive definition of customer, most courts have held that an individual who signed a check on behalf of a partnership or corporation cannot herself recover for wrongful dishonor of the item even though the individual maintains a separate personal account with the payor bank. A few courts have concluded, however, that upon the wrongful dishonor of a check of a business entity such as a partnership or a corporation, an individual member or officer of the entity is a customer for purposes of 4-402, and is entitled to recover damages thereunder in her own right, where -- in fact and as perceived by the payor bank -- the business entity had no viability as a separate and distinct legal creature; its affairs and the individual's were closely intertwined; and the individual was treated, for practical purposes, as the real customer. It is also possible that supplemental common law gives the individual a separate cause of action if the dishonor of the other entity's check actually impugns her own reputation. The statute does not displace such a common-law action. 4-402 comment 5.

A payee or other holder of a check that is wrongfully dishonored cannot recover from the payor bank under 4-402. See 4-402 comment 5. (The statute "confers no cause of action on the holder of a dishonored item.") Yet, if the payor bank finally pays a check or becomes accountable for it under other rules of Article 4, the bank is liable to the holder. It is not clear whether the holder could recover from the bank upon the dishonor of a check that, while not finally paid, was entitled to priority under 4-303. In this case the basis of recovery would have to be 4-303(a) itself. This provision contains no language expressly imposing accountability. On the other hand, the payor bank is culpable, in general terms, when it dishonors an item that is entitled to priority under 4-303(a), inasmuch as the bank thereby interferes with and frustrates the superior rights of the owner of the item.

2. The Connection To *Funds Availability*

The most common reason for dishonoring a check is insufficient funds in the drawer's account. Dishonor for this reason is wrongful, however, if the payor bank errs in deciding that the account is insufficient to cover the check. Whether or not an account is sufficient depends partly on how soon the bank must account for funds that the customer deposits in the account. This timing issue concerns the law of *funds availability*, which determines when the customer has the right to withdraw or apply credit to her account that results from deposits of cash, checks or other items. If a check is dishonored because funds are not counted that should have been available to the customer, the dishonor is wrongful under any applicable federal law that is violated and is also wrongful under state law 4-402.

Article 4

Article 4 says very little about funds availability and, in any event, is subject to preemptive federal law.

- Cash
  "[A] deposit of money becomes available for withdrawal as of right at the opening of the bank's next banking day after receipt of the deposit." 4-215(f).

- "On Us" Items
  When the customer deposits a check in a bank that is also the payor bank and the check is finally paid, credit given for the item in the customer's account becomes available for withdrawal as of right "at the opening of the bank's second banking day following receipt of the item." 4-215(e)(2). "[I]f A and B are both customers of a depositary-payor bank and A deposits B's check on Monday, time must be allowed to permit the check under the deferred posting rules of Section 4-301 to reach the bookkeeper for B's account at some time on Tuesday, and, if there are insufficient funds in

B's account, to reverse or charge back the provisional credit in A's account. Consequently this provisional credit in A's account does not become available for withdrawal as of right until the opening of business on Wednesday. If it is determined on Tuesday that there are insufficient funds in B's account to pay the check, the credit to A's account can be reversed on Tuesday. On the other hand if the item is in fact paid on Tuesday, the rule of subsection (e)(2) is desirable to avoid uncertainty and possible disputes between the bank and its customer as to exactly what hour within the day the credit is available." 4-215 comment 12.

- Other Checks

  When the customer deposits and gets credit for a check that is drawn on another bank, the credit becomes available for withdrawal as of right if and when

  > the settlement [to the depositary bank] becomes final and [also] the bank has had a reasonable time to receive return of the item and the item has not been received within that time.

  4-215(e)(1). In this context "reasonable" depends "on the distance the item has to travel and the number of banks through which it must pass (bearing in mind not only travel time by regular lines of transmission but also the successive midnight deadlines of the several banks) and other pertinent facts." 4-215 comment 11.

Federal Law – Expedited Funds Availability Act and Regulation CC

The federal Expedited Funds Availability Act, 12 U.S.C.A. 4001 - 4010, specifies the maximum length of time that a depositary bank can delay before making a customer's deposits "available for withdrawal." The Act does not require any delay and would approve immediate availability of all deposits. It sets an outside limit -- an *availability schedule* -- that shortens any longer state law and that varies the time of availability with the nature of the deposit. This law is greatly amplified -- in huge detail -- by Subpart B of Regulation CC. 12 CFR 229.10 - 229.21.

At such time as the law requires making funds "available for withdrawal," the bank must make them "available for *all* uses generally permitted to the customer for actually and finally collected funds under the bank's account agreement or policies, such as for *payment of checks drawn on the account,* certification of checks drawn on the account, electronic payments, withdrawals by cash, and transfers between accounts." 12 CFR 229.2(d) (emphasis added).

The mandated availability of funds is determined by a complicated schedule that turns on the nature of the deposit. Deposits that carry a low risk of fraud must be made available sooner than ordinary checks; and availability varies for ordinary checks depending on whether they are local or nonlocal. The schedule assumes that the time a depositary bank can hold credit for ordinary checks should roughly correspond to the time ordinarily required to collect the items. The time is longer for nonlocal checks because collection takes longer, and thus the time for availability of nonlocal checks is longer. Availability that is earlier than the time usually needed for collection increases the risk of fraud because of the greater chance that the funds will become available and will be withdrawn before notice of dishonor.

The statute and its regulations create six "safe guard" exceptions that allow depositary banks to extend the availability times in certain narrow situations involving high risks of fraud. The exceptions concern new accounts, large deposits, redeposited checks, repeated overdrafts, situations that create reasonable cause to doubt the collectibility of items, and certain emergency conditions. Also, "[a] depositary bank may provide availability to its nonconsumer accounts based on a sample of checks that represents the average composition of the customer's deposits, if the terms for availability based on the sample are equivalent to or more prompt than the [usually required] availability requirements * * *." 12 CFR 229.19(d).

Nothing prevents banks from making funds available sooner than the law requires. In truth, most banks generally make a customer's deposit available on the very day it is made or no later than the next day. They reserve the right, however, to deviate from this policy on a case-by-case basis. Whenever they do, the federal availability schedule fully applies, and they cannot deviate from it unless an appropriate exception to the federal schedule applies.

The Act and Regulation CC themselves provide for damages for violating the funds availability rules of federal law. A bank that fails to comply with any of these rules is liable to the injured person for:

+ Any actual damages sustained by that person as a result of the failure;
+ Such additional amount as the court may allow, except that in the case of an individual action this liability shall not be less than $100 nor greater than $1000; and
+ In the case of a successful action to enforce the foregoing liability, the costs of the action, together with a reasonable attorney's fee as determined by the court.

12 CFR 229.21(a)(1-3). Any action under this section may be brought either in federal or state court within one year after the date of the occurrence of the violation involved. Id. 229.21(d).

This federal liability is not the exclusive consequence for violating the funds availability rules. The Expedited Funds Availability Act preempts state law only narrowly, as where the state law allows longer holds than the federal law or contradicts the federal disclosure requirements. See 12 CFR 229.20. It does not preempt alternative, more generous recovery under state law when the wrongful refusal to make funds available results in wrongful dishonor of the customer's check.

3. The Problem Of Priority Between Checks

The sufficiency of an account with respect to a particular item can depend on when the item is considered in relation to other checks drawn against the account. This will be true, for example, in a case where several checks are presented at roughly the same time, and there are sufficient funds to cover one or more of the items but not all of them. Whether the item or items that are not paid were dishonored rightfully or wrongfully will depend on whether the bank dealt with the checks in the proper order. The proper order, however, is "any order." 4-303(b). "This is justified because of the impossibility of stating a rule that would be fair in all cases, having in mind the almost infinite number of combinations of large and small checks in relation to the available balance on hand in the drawer's account; the possible methods of receipt; and other variables. Further, where the drawer has drawn all the checks, the drawer should have funds available to meet all of them and has no basis for urging one should be paid before another ***." 4-303 comment 7.

4. Priority In Relation To Other Events

There are a variety of legal events that can eliminate or freeze a drawer's account. For example, an account is effectively frozen upon being garnished by a creditor of the account holder. Also, an account can be reduced or entirely wiped out by the payor bank itself exercising its equitable, self-help right of setoff to satisfy a matured debt the account holder owes the bank. Any such event can thereby compete with a check drawn on the affected account in the sense that if the event is recognized before the check is considered for payment, there may not be sufficient available funds to pay the check. Whether the resulting dishonor is rightful or wrongful in such a case depends on whether the legal event or the check was entitled to priority.

To solve this and similar conflicts, 4-303(a) determines priority between certain events that affect an account and checks drawn against the account. The provision rather awkwardly provides:

> Any knowledge, notice or stop-payment order received by, legal process served upon, or setoff exercised by a payor bank comes too late to terminate, suspend or modify the bank's right or duty to pay an item or to charge its customer's account for the item if the knowledge, notice, stop-payment order, or legal process is received or served and a reasonable time for the bank to act thereon expires or the setoff is exercised after the earliest of the following:
> (1) the bank accepts or certifies the item;
> (2) the banks pays the item in cash;

(3) the bank settles for the item without having a right to revoke the settlement under statute, clearing-house rule or agreement;

(4) the bank becomes accountable for the amount of the item under Section 4-302 dealing with the payor bank's responsibility for late return of items; or

(5) with respect to checks, a cutoff hour no earlier than one hour after the opening of the next banking day after the banking day on which the bank received the check and no later than the close of that next banking day or, if no cutoff hour is fixed, the close of the next banking day after the banking day on which the bank received the check.

4-303(a). In essence, the rule is that if any one of the circumstances listed in subsections (1) through (5) occurs before notice of the legal event is received or served and a reasonable time for the bank to act thereon expires or, in the case of setoff, before the setoff is exercised, the check has priority over the event. Dishonoring the check due to or after to the event would thus be wrongful as against the account customer. Violating 4-303 would not be wrongful, in itself, against the payee or other holder.

When the competing legal event is anything other than setoff by the payor bank, "the effective time for determining whether they [i.e., the legal events] were received too late * * * is receipt [of the knowledge, notice, stop-order or legal process] *plus* a reasonable time for the bank to act on any of these communications." 4-303 comment 6 (emphasis added). In the case of a setoff exercised by the payor bank, the effective time is not similarly extended because the setoff is itself action by the bank.

Be careful! It is easy to confuse 4-303(a) with 4-215(a) which describes the circumstances constituting final payment of an item. Certain of the tests determining the priority status of the item for purposes of 4-303(a) are the same as for final payment under Section 4-215(a), *but other tests apply in the context of 4-303(a)*. The tests for priority that are not tests for final payment are:

- acceptance or certification of the item; and,
- passing of the bank-fixed cut-off hour on the day after the check is received.

This means that an item can attain priority for purposes of 4-303(a) even before the item has been finally paid within the meaning of 4-215(a).

Overdraft liability

An *overdraft* is a check drawn on an account that contains insufficient funds to cover the item. Ordinarily, of course, the payor bank can and will dishonor an overdraft. The bank usually is not obligated to pay a check that is not fully backed by collected funds (e.g., cash and finally paid checks) in the drawer's account. An exception is the unusual case in which the bank has agreed to pay overdrafts in the deposit agreement or otherwise. The bank's right to dishonor an overdraft does not, however, create a duty to do so. A bank can pay an overdraft and charge the amount to the customer's account even in the absence of an agreement with the customer authorizing the payment of overdrafts. See 4-401(a) (as against its customer a payor bank may charge her account with an overdraft). In other words, paying an overdraft is *not* an instance of wrongful payment. The customer is personally liable to the bank for the amount of the negative balance created by an overdraft because the overdraft "itself authorizes the payment for the drawer's account and carries an implied promise to reimburse the drawee." 4-401 comment 1 (1989 Official Text & Comments).

1. Overdraft Liability Of Joint Account Holders

In the past the courts disagreed whether or not a joint owner of an account is liable for an overdraft that she did not sign or otherwise authorize and from which she received no benefit. Former law seemed to authorize such an overdraft "as against its customer." It defined "customer" broadly to include any person having an account with the bank, and "account" was broad enough to include a joint account. "There is [thus] some judicial authority for the proposition that *A* can be held personally liable for an overdraft in a joint account where the overdraft is created by *B*. Given the broad definition of 'customer' in Article 4, this decision seems correct." B. Clark, THE LAW OF BANK DEPOSITS, COLLECTIONS AND CREDIT CARDS ¶ 2.08[4] (1990).

On the other hand, the basis for imposing overdraft liability is the implied promise to reimburse the drawee which the instrument itself carries. Presumably, this implied promise is made only by the person who actually drew the instrument, not by other owners of the account against which the instrument is drawn. So there is contrary judicial authority holding that a joint account holder is not liable for overdrafts simply because she is joint owner of the account. She must have signed the check, authorized its issuance, benefited from its payment, or have agreed in the deposit contract or otherwise to be responsible for overdrafts created by another owner of the account.

Article 4 settled this disagreement in 1990. It "adopts the view of case authority holding that if there is more than one customer who can draw on an account, the nonsigning customer is not liable for an overdraft unless that person benefits from the proceeds of the item" 4-401 comment 2. The rule is: "A customer is not liable for the amount of an overdraft if the customer neither signed the item nor benefited from the proceeds of the item." 4-401(b). Expect the courts to define "benefit" fairly generously for this purpose.

2. Contrary Agreements Regarding Overdrafts

Bank Agreeing To Pay Overdrafts

A bank is obligated to pay an overdraft if it has made an enforceable agreement to do so. An overdraft that is within the terms of such an agreement is, in effect, properly payable, and the bank commits wrongful dishonor by not paying the item.

Customers often argue that an agreement to pay overdrafts resulted from the bank's habit and practice of gratuitously paying the customer's overdrafts in the past. It is true that as a matter of contract law, such a contract need not be expressed and can be inferred from circumstances such as a pattern of conduct between the parties. On the other hand, the pattern itself must be so well established as to imply a promise by the bank to pay future overdrafts; and there must be consideration, reliance, or some other legal basis for enforcing this promise. The deposit contract that the customer signed might very well argue against both promise and enforceability. In *Thiele v. Security State Bank*, 396 N.W.2d 295 (N.D. 1986), the deposit contract provided that "'[w]e [the bank] do not in any way oblige ourselves to pay any item which would overdraw this account regardless of the frequency with which we may do so hereafter as a matter of practice.'" Id. at 298. The court decided that this "language explains any course of dealing which may have occurred before the execution of the account agreement and negates any informal modification of express terms subsequent to the written agreement." Id. at 301. Moreover, an agreement to pay overdrafts is really a promise to loan money, and many states recently have enacted statutes of frauds that condition the enforcement of such a promise (often called a "credit agreement") on a writing signed by the bank.

Joint Account Customer Assuming Liability For Another Customer's Overdrafts

A customer on an account who neither signed an overdraft nor benefited from it is nevertheless liable for the overdraft, despite 4-401(b), if she agreed (before or after) to pay overdrafts drawn by another customer on the account, ratified the overdraft, or is estopped to deny liability for it.

Stopping payment (and closing an account)

Stopping payment refers to the drawer of a check or other authorized person ordering the payor bank, usually after the check has already been issued, to dishonor the item upon presentment for payment even though the item is otherwise properly payable. The intent of an order to close an account is the same with respect to outstanding items.

1. The Right To Stop Payment

"A customer or any person authorized to draw on the account if there is more than one person may stop payment of any item drawn on the customer's account or close the account by an order to the bank describing the item or account with reasonably certainty * * *." 4-403(a). "[S]topping payment or closing an account is a service which depositors expect and are entitled to receive from banks notwithstanding its difficulty, inconvenience and expense." 4-403 comment 1. The right is absolute, and is fettered only by certain procedural requirements that must be satisfied for the stop-order to be valid and effective. In other words, a customer can order payment stopped on any check she has written for whatever reason, or for no reason, without having to explain her motives to the payor bank.

The right to stop payment belongs to any customer on the account against which the item is drawn. This means:

- "[I]f there is more than one person authorized to draw on a customer's account any one of them can stop payment of any check drawn on the account or can order the account closed," 4-403 comment 5, even if the person did not sign the check on which she orders payment stopped.
- "[I]f there is a customer, such as a corporation, that requires its checks to bear the signatures of more than one person, any of these persons may stop payment on a check." Id.

Also, upon a customer's death, payment of her checks can be stopped by any person claiming an interest in the account, including a surviving relative or a creditor of the customer. See 4-405 comment 3. Otherwise, "a payee or indorsee has no right to stop payment." 4-403 comment 2.

The right to stop payment ordinarily is exercised against checks, but the right is not limited to checks and applies to any "item" drawn against a customer's account. Therefore, the right "extends to any item payable by any bank. If the maker of a note payable at a bank is in a position analogous to that of a drawer (Section 4-106) the maker may stop payment of the note. By analogy the rule extends to drawees other than banks." 4-403 comment 3.

2. Payor Bank's Liability For Payment Over A Valid Stop-Payment Order

A valid stop order renders the affected check not properly payable. Therefore, a "payment in violation of an *effective* direction to stop payment is an improper payment, even though it is made by mistake or inadvertence." 4-403 comment 7 (emphasis added). Banks would like to disclaim this liability and often will try to do so in the deposit agreement or otherwise, but any such agreement "is invalid * * * if in paying the item over the stop-payment order the bank has failed to exercise ordinary care." 4-403 comment 7; see also 1-102(3) & 4-103(a). Moreover, an agreement disclaiming or limiting a bank's liability "which is imposed upon a customer as part of a standard form contract would have to be evaluated in the light of the general obligation of good faith." 4-403 comment 7; see also 1-203 & 4-104(c).

Because a check covered by a valid stop order is not properly payable, it can be argued that a charge to the drawer's account is improper and must be reversed. By this argument the measure of the payor bank's liability is the amount of the item. It may be, however, that the bank's wrongful payment over the stop order actually caused the drawer no loss, as where the drawer has no reason for refusing to pay the payee or other holder. In such a case, holding the bank strictly liable for the amount of the item would give the drawer a windfall. So a payor bank is liable for paying over a stop order only if the drawer suffered actual loss. The question is whether the drawer's recovery should be conditioned on her proving the loss, or the absence of loss should be a defense proved by the payor bank.

The statute itself expressly provides: "The burden of establishing the fact and amount of loss resulting from the payment of an item contrary to a[n] [effective] stop-payment order or order to close an account is on the customer." 4-403(c).

Arguably, however, this provision is contradicted by 4-407, which gives subrogation rights of various parties to a payor bank that has paid over a stop order. The purpose is to prevent unjust enrichment. These rights include the rights of the payee (or any other holder of the check) against the drawer, either on the instrument or the underlying transaction. 4-407(2). The purpose of this specific subsection is to prevent unjust enrichment of the drawer by allowing the payor bank to recover from the drawer whatever is legitimately owed the payee or other person to whom the drawer would be liable in connection with the instrument. Naturally, when relying on 4-407, the payor bank would have the complete burden of proving the rights to which it is subrogated. It would seem, therefore, that the drafters intended that concerns about a windfall to the drawer should be addressed through 4-407, which puts the burden squarely on the payor bank to prove, in effect, the absence of loss from its failure to honor the drawer's stop order.

Several courts have resolved this apparent conflict between 4-403 and 4-407 by dividing the burden of proof. Under their compromise approach, the payor bank must plead the absence of loss as a defense and bear the burden of going forward with some evidence to substantiate the defense. Thereafter, the drawer bears the burden of persuading the trier of fact as to the fact and amount of loss.

Damages can be compounded by wrongful dishonor. An item covered by an effective stop-order must be ignored in determining the sufficiency of an account to cover other items. An account balance will be artificially and inaccurately low if the bank violates a stop-order, pays the check, and debits the account. If the bank then bounces checks due to this inaccurate insufficiency in the account, the bank is guilty of wrongful dishonor with respect to these items. The statute is explicit that the customer's loss for violating a stop payment order "may include damages for [wrongful] dishonor of subsequent items under Section 4-402." 4-403(c).

A bank has three main answers to liability for having paid over a valid stop order. The first is subrogation. As just mentioned, 4-407 gives to a payor bank, that has paid over a stop order, subrogation rights of various parties. The payor bank is subrogated to the rights

- of any holder in due course on the item against the drawer or maker;
- of the payee or any other holder of the item against the drawer or maker either on the item or under the transaction out of which the item arose; and
- of the drawer or maker against the payee or any other holder of the item with respect to the transaction out of which the item arose.

4-407(1-3). The purpose is to prevent unjust enrichment. This purpose is achieved because, by exercising the subrogation rights appropriate for the case, the payor bank can shift responsibility for the instrument or the underlying transaction to the party who properly should bear it.

Also, apart from and beyond subrogation, the payor bank retains common-law defenses against its customer who complains about the bank paying over an effective stop order. For example, the defense of ratification is available to the bank, e.g., "that by conduct in recognizing the payment the customer has ratified the bank's action in paying over a stop-payment order." 4-403 comment 7.

Finally, people whom the bank pays are potentially accountable to the bank for restitution -- unjust enrichment resulting from payment by mistake. Id. This accountability is subject, however, to the beneficiary's bona fide-purchaser defense of 3-418, which usually is a good and complete defense to restitution.

3. Requisites Of An Effective Stop-Payment Order

Payment in violation of a stop order is improper only if the stop order was effective with respect to the item. To be effective a stop order must be "received at a *time* and in a *manner* that affords the bank a reasonable opportunity to act on it before any action by the bank with respect to the item described in Section 4-303." 4-403(a) (emphasis added).

STOP PAYMENT ORDER

DATE RECEIVED		TIME RECEIVED	AM PM
TO:		FROM:	
	["Institution"]		["You, Your or Customer"]
ACCOUNT NUMBER	CHECK NUMBER	CHECK AMOUNT	DATE OF CHECK
PAYABLE TO		REASON FOR STOPPING PAYMENT	

☐ Oral stop payment orders are binding on Institution for fourteen (14) days only, unless confirmed by You in writing within that period. Written stop payment orders are effective for six months unless renewed by You in writing.

ORDER ENTERED BY:	DATE ENTERED	TIME ENTERED	AM PM	FEE $

X _____

CUSTOMER SIGNATURE   DATE

ORAL REQUEST
TAKEN BY

This Stop Payment Order is hereby released, withdrawn and cancelled.

X _____

CUSTOMER SIGNATURE   DATE

Front side

You have authorized, directed and requested Institution to stop payment on the check described on the reverse side. You agree to indemnify and hold the Institution harmless from any and all claims, liabilities, costs and expenses, including but not limited to court costs and reasonable attorney fees, resulting from or growing out of the Institution's refusal to pay the check described on the reverse side. Institution shall have no liability to You for the payment of the identified check contrary to this stop payment order if the indicated check number, dollar amount or account number are not accurate. You understand that if the stop payment order comes too late for the Institution to have a reasonable time to act on it prior to accepting, certifying, paying, settling for, posting or becoming accountable for the check described on the reverse side, that this stop payment order shall be of no effect. You agree that the Institution may charge you the fee indicated for processing this stop payment order as well as a similar fee for each renewal You make, such fee to be deducted from Your account. This stop payment order shall be governed by the provisions of the Uniform Commercial Code in effect in the state in which Institution is located. This stop payment order shall be valid for a period of six months from the date it is made if signed by You unless Institution has received a written revocation or renewal prior to expiration of such period. You agree not to make any claim whatsoever against the Institution if the identified check is processed by Institution through Your account by mistake. Phrases preceeded by a ☐ are only applicable if ☐ is marked.

Back side

Manner

A stop order can be oral or written, but a written order is effective for a longer time. A written order is effective for six months. An oral stop order lasts only 14 calendar days unless confirmed in writing within the 14-day period. 4-403(b). "If there is written confirmation within the 14-day period, the six-month period dates from the giving of the oral order." 4-403 comment 6.

- A stop-payment order may be renewed any number of times by written notice given during a six-month period while a stop order is in effect.
- A new stop-payment order may be given after a six-month period expires, but such a notice takes effect from the date given.
- "When a stop-payment order expires it is as though the order had never been given, and the payor bank may pay the item in good faith * * * even though a stop-payment order had once been given.

Id.

A stop order is effective only if it contains sufficient information to allow the bank to act. The order must describe the item with "reasonable certainty." 4-403(a). This "reasonableness standard * * * does not rise to the level of [complete or absolute] certainty," and it tolerates "certain discrepancies in the description of an otherwise adequate order" so that a stop order may be effective even though there are mistakes in the customer's description of the item. *Best v. Dreyfus Liquid Assets, Inc.*, 215 N.J.Super. 76, 81, 521 A.2d 352, 355 (1987). The reasonableness of an inaccurate description is ordinarily, of course, a factual question.

In the *Best* case, the customer erroneously stated the date of the check and the check number. The court nevertheless held that the customer's stop order was not unreasonable as a matter of law. Similarly, in the case *Kunkel v. First Nat'l Bank of Devils Lake*, 393 N.W.2d 265 (N.D. 1986), the court determined that a stop order was not necessarily unreasonable simply because the customer listed the amount of the check as $7400 when, in fact, the amount was $7,048.27. In contrast, the stop order was unreasonable in *Marine Midland Bank v. Berry*, 123 A.D.2d 254, 506 N.Y.S.2d 60 (1986), because the order misstated the check number, incorrectly named the payee, and misstated the amount of the check.

Time Of Receipt

To be effective, a stop order must be received a reasonable time before any of these circumstances has occurred:

- the bank accepts or certifies the item;
- the bank pays the item in cash;
- the bank settles for the item without having a right to revoke the settlement under statute, clearing-house rule or agreement;
- the bank becomes accountable for the amount of the item under Section 4-302 dealing with the payor bank's responsibility for late return of items; or
- with respect to checks, a cutoff hour no earlier than one hour after the opening of the next banking day after the banking day on which the bank received the check and no later than the close of that next banking day or, if

no cutoff hour is fixed, the close of the next banking day after the banking day on which the bank received the check.

4-303(a)(1-5). This section, which is discussed earlier in this chapter, determines priority between the right of a customer to stop payment and the right and duty of the payor bank to promptly process checks presented for payment. If any one of the circumstances in 4-303(a) has occurred with respect to a check before the bank has had a reasonable chance to act on a stop order covering the item, the stop order comes too late, which means that the order is ineffective and paying the item is not wrongful.

4. Stopping Payment Against A Holder In Due Course

Technically speaking, payment can be stopped against a holder in due course. On the other hand, "the drawer remains liable on the instrument * * * and the drawee, if it pays, becomes subrogated to the rights of the holder in due course against the drawer." 4-403 comment 7. The practical result is that the drawer cannot complain against the bank for violating the drawer's stop order if the drawer had no defense that was good against the holder in due course. At a minimum, the bank's recovery as subrogee is offset against its liability for wrongful dishonor.

5. Cashier's Checks

In a very large number of recent cases the courts have considered if payment can be stopped on a cashier's check, which is a draft drawn by a bank on itself. 3-104(g). This broad concern involves two entirely separate issues. The easier issue is whether the bank that issues the cashier's check becomes liable to the person who procured it, i.e., the remitter, by refusing to dishonor the instrument upon the remitter's request. The second and harder issue is whether an issuing bank that refuses payment of its cashier's check, either on its own or at the request of the remitter, can escape liability to the payee or other holder of the instrument.

Remitter's Right To Stop Payment

Suppose that B buys goods from S who demands payment in the form of a cashier's check. B purchases a cashier's check from Bank and delivers the instrument to S. B quickly learns that the goods are defective and asks Bank not to pay the cashier's check and to return to B the money she paid Bank for the check. Must Bank honor B's request?

The answer is no, unless Bank and B have an enforceable agreement giving B the right to stop payment of the check. B does not have the right apart from such an agreement. 4-403 does not apply for two reasons. First, 4-403 is limited to checks drawn on the customer's account. A cashier's check is drawn by the issuing bank against the bank's own account. Second, a stop order comes too late, i.e., is ineffective, if received after the item it covers has been accepted. See 4-303(a)(1). A draft drawn by the drawer on itself is accepted upon issuance. Therefore, there can never be a timely stop order of a cashier's check.

Issuer's Liability When Payment Denied

A bank that issues a cashier's check may wish to dishonor the item either as a courtesy to the remitter who requests that payment be stopped, or for the bank's own reasons. The problem in doing so is that the bank, as issuer of the check, is liable on the instrument to the payee or a subsequent holder. 3-412. In a conflict between the bank and a holder of the cashier's check, is the bank always and inevitably liable, or can the bank raise defenses to its liability on the instrument? The courts have disagreed on this issue.

The preferable view is that an issuing bank can raise defenses to the payment of a cashier's check according to the usual rules governing an obligor's liability on a negotiable instrument. Unless the holder is a holder in due course, the bank can raise the full range of its defenses permitted under 3-305 and 3-306, including the defenses of want or failure of consideration and all other defenses of the bank which would be available in an action on a simple contract. If the holder enjoys "due course" status, the bank can raise only its real defenses. Yet, even if the holder lacks due-course status, the bank can assert only its own defenses. It cannot raise defenses that are personal to the remitter, such as breach of contract between the remitter and the payee of the cashier's check. Such matters are properly left for decision in an action between those parties.

When a bank refuses payment of a cashier's, certified, or teller's check on which it is liable and for which it has no good defense, the damages against the bank naturally include the amount of the item; but the damages are not limited to this amount. The damages also can include "compensation for expenses and loss of interest resulting from the nonpayment and may [include] * * * consequential damages if the obligated bank refuses to pay after receiving notice of particular circumstances giving rise to the damages." 3-411(b). Expenses and consequential damages are not recoverable, however, even though the bank is liable on the instrument, if payment was refused because:

- the bank suspends payments;
- the obligated bank asserts a claim or defense of the bank that it has reasonable grounds to believe is available against the person entitled to enforce the instrument;

- the obligated bank has a reasonable doubt whether the person demanding payment is the person entitled to enforce the instrument; or
- payment is prohibited by law.

3-411(c).

Rights of a Claimant Who Lost a Cashier's Check

Because of the large damages that can flow from the wrongful dishonor of a cashier's check, the issuing bank naturally will be reluctant to honor the rights of a person who claims to have lost a cashier's check. To honor these rights requires the bank to risk (minimally) the truth of the person's claim, which can unduly burden honest people in some cases. By way of section 3-312, Article 3 attempts to accommodate the interests of the bank and original claimant in such a case.

In the typical situation, a person claims the right to receive the proceeds of a check that she has lost. The risk to the bank which honors the claim is that the check will end up in the hands of a holder in due course who can force the bank to pay the check. The bank will have paid twice. Perhaps the bank can recoup from the original claimant but the bank risks this person's solvency. The bank can protect itself by requiring the original claimant to provide security for any payment to her, but this procedure imposes a large burden on the claimant.

Essentially, 3-312 allows the claimant to make a claim for payment by providing the bank with a declaration of loss. The claim is enforceable at the later of the time the claim is made or the 90th day following the date or certification of the check. If the claim becomes enforceable before the check is presented for payment, the bank is obliged to pay the claim and is discharged of all liability with respect to the check. The claim is legally ineffective prior to the time the claim becomes enforceable, and the bank must pay the check if the check is presented prior to the time of the claim's enforceability. The reasoning seems to be that if 90 days pass without presentment of the check, the claim of loss is probably legitimate and the possibility is small that someone will appear as a holder in due course of the instrument. In the unlikely event that such a person appears after the bank has honored an enforceable claim, the claimant is accountable for the check.

Example

Obligated Bank (OB) issued a cashier's check to its customer, Payee (P). P indorsed and mailed the check to P's bank for deposit to P's account. P's bank never received it. P asserted a claim pursuant to 3-312(b). X found the check, indorsed and deposited it in her account in Depositary Bank (DB). DB presented the check for payment before the end of the 90-day period after its date. OB paid the check. Because of the unrestricted blank indorsement by P, X became a holder of the check and so did DB. Since the check was paid before P's claim became enforceable and payment was made to a person entitled to enforce the check, OB is discharged of all liability with respect to the check. Subsection (b)(2). Thus, P is not entitled to payment from OB. Subsection (b)(4) doesn't apply. 3-312 comment 4 (Case #4).

Untimely checks

1. Stale Checks

A *stale check* is an uncertified check of a customer which is presented more than six months after the check's date. There are two rules with respect to stale checks. First, the payor bank is not obligated to pay them. 4-404. Thus, dishonor of a stale check is not wrongful dishonor. Second, although not bound to pay a stale check, the payor bank has the right to do so *in good faith*. Id. Thus, paying a stale check in good faith is not wrongful payment and the item rightfully can be charged to the customer's account. A bank pays a stale check in good faith if, for example, the bank knows that the drawer wants payment made. "Certified checks are excluded [from these rules on stale checks] * * * because they are the primary obligation of the certifying bank * * * [which] runs directly to the holder of the check." 4-404 comment.

2. Postdated Checks

A postdated check is a check issued before the stated date of the instrument. It could be argued that premature payment of a postdated check is wrongful because the drawer ordered payment at a later date. Payor banks, however, cannot easily discover postdates. Finding them would be very costly in time and money. Therefore, in order to enforce a postdate against a payor bank, the customer "must notify the payor bank of its postdating in time to allow the bank to act on the customer's notice before the bank has to commit itself to pay the check." 4-401 comment 3. Here is the rule:

> A bank may charge against the account of a customer a check that is otherwise properly payable from the account, even though payment was made before the date of the check, unless the customer has given notice to the bank of the postdating describing the check with reasonable certainty. 4-401(c).

In effect, a notice of postdating is akin to a stop order that orders the bank to delay payment rather than to stop payment. Therefore, some of the procedural rules are the same:

- The period of effectiveness of a notice of postdating is the same as that for a stop order. See 4-401(c) & 4-403(b) (14 days oral and six months written).

- Like a stop order, a notice of postdating must be received at such time and in such manner as to afford the bank a reasonable opportunity to act on it before the bank takes any action with respect to the check described in Section 4-303, that is, before

  ✓ the bank accepts or certifies the item;
  ✓ the banks pays the item in cash;
  ✓ the bank settles for the item without having a right to revoke the settlement under statute, clearing-house rule or agreement;
  ✓ the bank becomes accountable for the amount of the item under Section 4-302 dealing with the payor bank's responsibility for late return of items; or
  ✓ with respect to checks, a cutoff hour no earlier than one hour after the opening of the next banking day after the banking day on which the bank received the check and no later than the close of that next banking day or, if no cutoff hour is fixed, the close of the next banking day after the banking day on which the bank received the check.

4-303(a)(1-5) & 4-401(c).

If a bank violates an effective notice of postdating by charging the check against the customer's account before the date stated in the notice, the bank is liable for damages for any resulting loss, including loss resulting from dishonor of subsequent items. 4-401(c).

As in the case where a stop order is violated, a payor bank that wrongfully pays a stale or postdated check should not be liable if the drawer suffered no actual loss as a result of the wrongful payment. Moreover, 4-407 subrogates the bank to the rights of various parties to the instrument.

Effect of a customer's incompetence or death

A check drawn by a customer who was then incompetent, or who later dies or becomes incompetent, is properly payable so long as the bank is unaware of the death or an adjudication of incompetency. The check becomes not properly payable, however, a reasonable time after the bank knows of the death or adjudication. That is, when a customer has been adjudged incompetent, or has died, the payor bank loses the authority to pay the customer's checks as of the time "the bank knows of the fact of death or of an adjudication of incompetence *and* has reasonable opportunity to act on it." 4-405(a) (emphasis added). There is an exception in the case of a customer's death: "Even with knowledge, a bank may for 10 days after the date of death pay or certify checks drawn on or before that date unless ordered to stop payment by a person claiming an interest in the account." 4-405(b).

Arguably, paying the checks of an incompetent or dead customer without authority, i.e., in violation of 4-405, is -- by analogy or otherwise -- a case in which the payor bank has paid an item "under circumstances giving a basis for objection by the drawer or maker." 4-407. In this event, as when there is wrongful payment over a stop order or payment of an untimely check, the payor bank is subrogated to the rights of various parties under 4-407 for the purpose of preventing unjust enrichment of the customer's estate.

Regulation CC Availability of Funds and Collection of Checks

12 CFR 229, App. E
Commentary

Section 229.10 -- Next-Day Availability

(a) *Cash Deposits*

This paragraph implements the Act's requirement for next- day availability for cash deposits to accounts at a depositary bank "staffed by individuals employed by such institution." This paragraph, as well as other provisions of this subpart governing the availability of funds, provides that funds must be made available for withdrawal not later than a specified number of "business days" following the "banking day" on which the funds are deposited. Thus, a deposit is only considered made on a banking day, i.e., a day that the bank is open to the public for carrying on substantially all of its banking functions. For example, if a deposit is made at an ATM on a Saturday, Sunday, or other day on which the bank is closed to the public, the deposit is considered received on that bank's next banking day.

Nevertheless, "business days" are used to determine the number of days following the banking day of deposit that funds must be available for withdrawal. For example, if a deposit of a local check were made on a Monday under the temporary schedule, which requires that funds be available for withdrawal on the third business day after deposit, funds must be made available on Thursday regardless of whether the bank was closed on Wednesday for other than a standard legal holiday as specified in the definition of "business day."

Under this paragraph, cash deposited in an account at a staffed teller station on a Monday must become available for withdrawal by the start of business on Tuesday. It must become available for withdrawal by the start of business on Wednesday if it is deposited by mail, at a proprietary ATM (or at a nonproprietary ATM under the permanent schedule), or by other means other than at a staffed teller station.

(b) *Electronic Payments*

The Act provides next-day availability for funds received for deposit by wire transfer. The regulation uses the term "electronic payment," rather than "wire transfer," to include both wire transfers and ACH credit transfers under the next-day availability requirement. (See discussion of definitions of "automated clearinghouse," "electronic payment," and "wire transfer" in §229.2.)

The Act requires that funds received by wire transfer be available for withdrawal not later than the business day following the day a wire transfer is received. This paragraph clarifies what constitutes receipt of an electronic payment. For the purposes of this paragraph, a bank receives an electronic payment when the bank receives both payment in finally collected funds and the payment instructions indicating the customer accounts to be credited and the amount to be credited to each account. For example, in the case of Fedwire, the bank receives finally collected funds at the time the payment is made. (See 12 CFR 210.36.) Finally collected funds generally are received for an ACH credit transfer when they are posted to the receiving bank's account on the settlement day. In certain cases, the bank receiving ACH credit payments will not receive the specific payment instructions indicating which accounts to credit until after settlement day. In these cases, the payments are not considered received until the information on the account and amount to be credited is received.

This paragraph also establishes the extent to which an electronic payment is considered made. Thus, if a participant on a private network fails to settle and the receiving bank receives finally settled funds representing only a partial amount of the payment, it must make only the amount that it actually received available for withdrawal.

The availability requirements of this regulation do not preempt or invalidate other rules, regulations, or agreements which require funds to be made available on a more prompt basis. For example, the next-day availability requirement for ACH credits in this section does not preempt ACH association rules and Treasury regulations (31 CFR Part 210), which provide that the proceeds of these credit payments be available to the recipient for withdrawal on the day the bank receives the funds.

(c) *Certain Check Deposits*

The Act generally requires that funds be made available on the business day following the banking day of deposit for Treasury checks; state and local government checks; cashier's, certified, and teller's checks; and "on us" checks, under specified conditions. (Treasury checks are checks drawn on the Treasury of the United States and have a routing number beginning with the digits "0000.") This section also requires next-day availability for additional types of checks not addressed in the Act. Checks drawn on a Federal Reserve Bank or a Federal Home Loan Bank and U.S. Postal Service money orders must also be made available on the next business day following deposit under specified conditions. For the purposes of this section, all checks drawn on a Federal Reserve Bank or a Federal Home Loan Bank that contain in the MICR line a routing number that is listed in Appendix A are subject to the next-day availability requirement if they are deposited in an account held by a payee of the check and in person to an employee of the depositary bank, regardless of the purposes for which the checks were issued. For all new accounts, even if the new account exception is not invoked, traveler's checks must be included in the $5,000 aggregation of checks deposited on any one banking day that are subject to the next-day availability requirement. (See §229.13 (a).)

Deposit in Account of Payee

One statutory condition to receipt of next-day availability of Treasury checks; state and local government checks; and cashier's, certified, and teller's checks is that the check must be "endorsed only by the person to whom it was issued." The Act could be interpreted to include a check that has been indorsed in blank and deposited into an account of a third party that is not named as payee. The Board believes that such a check presents greater risks than a check deposited by the payee and that Congress did not intend to require next-day availability to such checks. The regulation, therefore, provides that funds must be available on the business day following deposit only if the check is deposited in an account held by a payee of the check. For the purposes of this section, payee does not include transferees other than named payees. The regulation also applies this condition to Postal Service money orders, and checks drawn on Federal Reserve Banks and Federal Home Loan Banks.

Deposits Made to an Employee of the Depositary Bank

In most cases, next-day availability of the proceeds of checks subject to this section is conditioned on the deposit of these checks in person to an employee of the depositary bank. If the deposit is not made to an employee of the depositary bank on the premises of such bank, the proceeds of the deposit must be made available for withdrawal by the start of business on the second business day after deposit, under paragraph (c)(2) of this section. For example, second-day availability rather than next-day availability would be allowed for deposits of checks subject to this section made at a proprietary ATM (and at a nonproprietary ATM under the permanent schedule), night depository, through the mail or a lock box, or at a teller station staffed by a person that is not an employee of the depositary bank. Second-day availability may also be allowed for deposits picked up by an employee of the depositary bank at the customer's premises; such deposits would be considered made upon receipt at the branch or other location of the depositary bank.

The Act and regulation do not condition the receipt of next-day availability to deposits at staffed teller stations in the case of Treasury checks. Therefore, Treasury checks deposited at a proprietary ATM must be accorded next-day availability, if the check is deposited to an account of a payee of the check.

"On Us" Checks

The Act and regulation require next-day availability for on us checks, i.e., checks deposited in a branch of the depositary bank and drawn on the same or another branch of the same bank, if both branches are located in the same state or check processing region. Thus, checks deposited in one branch of a bank and drawn on another branch of the same bank must receive next-day availability even if the branch on which the checks are drawn is located in another check processing region but in the same state as the branch in which the check is deposited. For the purposes of this requirement, deposits at facilities that are not located on the premises of a brick-and-mortar branch of the bank, such as off-premise ATMs and remote depositories, are not considered deposits made at branches of the depositary bank.

First $100

The Act and regulation also require that up to $100 of the aggregate deposit by check or checks not subject to next-day availability on any one banking day be made available on the next business day. For example, if $70 were deposited in an account by check(s) on a

Monday, the entire $70 must be available for withdrawal at the start of business on Tuesday. If $200 were deposited by check(s) on a Monday, this section requires that $100 of the funds be available for withdrawal at the start of business on Tuesday. The portion of the customer's deposit to which the $100 must be applied is at the discretion of the depositary bank, as long as it is not applied to any checks subject to next day availability. The $100 next-day availability rule does not apply to deposits at nonproprietary ATMs.

The $100 that must be made available under this rule is in addition to the amount that must be made available for withdrawal on the business day after deposit under other provisions of this section. For example, if a customer deposits a $1,000 Treasury check, and a $1,000 local check in its account on Monday, $1,100 must be made available for withdrawal on Tuesday--the proceeds of the $1,000 Treasury check, as well as the first $100 of the local check.

A depositary bank may aggregate all local and nonlocal check deposits made by the customer on a given banking day for the purposes of the $100 next-day availability rule. Thus, if a customer has two accounts at the depositary bank, and on a particular banking day makes deposits to each account, $100 of the total deposited to the two accounts must be made available on the business day after deposit. Banks may aggregate deposits to individual and joint accounts for the purposes of this provision.

If the customer deposits a $500 local check, and gets $100 cash back at the time of deposit, the bank need not make an additional $100 available for withdrawal on the following day. Similarly, if the customer depositing the local check has a negative book balance, or negative available balance in its account at the time of deposit, the $100 that must be available on the next business day may be made available by applying the $100 to the negative balance, rather than making the $100 available for withdrawal by cash or check on the following day.

Special Deposit Slips

Under the Act, a depositary bank may require the use of a special deposit slip as a condition to providing next-day availability for certain types of checks. This condition was included in the Act because a number of banks determine the availability of their customers' check deposits in an automated manner by reading the MICR-encoded routing number on the deposited checks. Using these procedures, a bank can determine whether a check is a local or nonlocal check; a check drawn on the Treasury, a Federal Reserve Bank, a Federal Home Loan Bank, or a branch of the depositary bank; or a U.S. Postal Service money order. Appendix A includes the routing numbers of certain categories of checks that are subject to next-day availability. The bank cannot require a special deposit slip for these checks.

A bank cannot distinguish whether the check is a state or local government check or a cashier's, certified, or teller's check by reading the MICR-encoded routing number, because these checks bear the same routing number as other checks drawn on the same bank that are not accorded next-day availability. Therefore, a bank may require a special deposit slip for these checks.

The regulation specifies that if a bank decides to require the use of a special deposit slip (or a special deposit envelope in the case of a deposit at an ATM or other unstaffed facility) as a condition to granting next-day availability under paragraphs (c)(1)(iv) or (c)(1)(v) of this section or second day availability under paragraph (c)(2) of this section, and if the deposit slip that must be used is different from the bank's regular deposit slips, the bank must either provide the special slips to its customers or inform its customers how such slips may be obtained and make the slips reasonably available to the customers.

A bank may meet this requirement by providing customers with an order form for the special deposit slips and allowing sufficient time for the customer to order and receive the slips before this condition is imposed. If a bank provides deposit slips in its branches for use by its customers, it must also provide the special deposit slips in the branches. If special deposit envelopes are required for deposits at an ATM, the bank must provide such envelopes at the ATM.

Generally, a teller is not required to advise depositors of the availability of special deposit slips merely because checks requiring special deposit slips for next-day availability are deposited without such slips. If a bank only provides the special deposit slips upon the request of a depositor, however, the teller must advise the depositor of the availability of the special deposit slips, or the bank must post a notice advising customers that the slips are available upon request. If a bank prepares a deposit for a depositor, it must use a special deposit slip where appropriate. A bank may require the customer to segregate the checks subject to next-day availability for which special deposit slips could be required, and to indicate on a regular deposit slip that such checks are being deposited, if the bank so instructs its customers in its initial disclosure.

Section 229.12 -- Permanent Availability Schedule

(a) *Effective Date*

The permanent schedule supersedes the temporary schedule on September 1, 1990.

(b) *Local Checks and Certain Other Checks*

Under the permanent schedule, local checks must be made available for withdrawal not later than the second business day following the banking day on which the checks were deposited.

In addition, the proceeds of Treasury checks and U.S. Postal Service money orders not subject to next-day (or second-day) availability under §229.10(c); checks drawn on Federal Reserve Banks and Federal Home Loan Banks; checks drawn by a state or unit of general local government; and cashier's, certified, and teller's checks not subject to next-day (or second-day) availability under §229.10(c) and payable in the same check processing region as the depository bank, must be made available for withdrawal by the second business day following deposit.

Exceptions are made for withdrawals by cash or similar means and for deposits in banks located outside the 48 contiguous states. Thus, the proceeds of a local check deposited on a Monday generally must be made available for withdrawal on Wednesday.

(c) *Nonlocal Checks*

Under the permanent schedule, the time period for availability of nonlocal checks is also reduced. Nonlocal checks must be made available for withdrawal not later than the fifth business day following deposit, i.e., proceeds of a nonlocal check deposited on a Monday must be made available for withdrawal on the following Monday. In addition, a check described in §229.10(c) that does not meet the conditions for next-day availability (or second-day availability) is treated as a nonlocal check, if the check is drawn on or payable through or at a nonlocal paying bank. Adjustments are made to the schedule for withdrawals by cash or similar means and deposits in banks located outside the 48 contiguous states.

As described in the discussion of §229.11(c), the Board is required to shorten the schedules for any category of check where most of those checks can be returned to the depositary bank in a shorter period of time than provided in the schedule. Appendix B-2 sets forth the reductions to the schedule for certain nonlocal checks under the permanent schedule.

(d) *Time Period Adjustment for Withdrawal by Cash or Similar Means*

Unlike the temporary schedule, the Act applies the special cash withdrawal rule to all local and nonlocal checks under the permanent schedule. The regulation implementing this rule is described in the discussion of the temporary schedule at §229.11(b). Under the permanent schedule, if the proceeds of local and nonlocal checks become available for withdrawal on the same business day, the $400 withdrawal limitation applies to the aggregate amount of the funds that became available for withdrawal on that day.

* * *

Section 229.13 -- Exceptions

While certain safeguard exceptions (such as those for new accounts and checks the bank has reasonable cause to believe are uncollectible) are established in the Act, the Congress gave the Board the discretion to determine whether certain other exceptions should be included in its regulations. Specifically, the Act gives the Board the authority to establish exceptions to the schedules for large or redeposited checks and for accounts that have been repeatedly overdrawn. These exceptions apply to local and nonlocal checks as well as to checks that must otherwise be accorded next-day (or second-day) availability under §229.10(c).

Many checks will not be returned to the depositary bank by the time funds must be made available for withdrawal under the next-day (or second-day), local, and nonlocal schedules. In order to reduce risk to depositary banks, the Board has exercised its statutory authority to adopt these exceptions to the schedules in the regulation to allow the depositary bank to extend the time within which it is required to make funds available.

The Act also gives the Board the authority to suspend the schedules for any classification of checks, if the schedules result in an unacceptable level of fraud losses. The Board will adopt regulations or issue orders to implement this statutory authority if and when circumstances requiring its implementation arise.

(a) *New Accounts*

Definition of New Account

The Act provides an exception to the availability schedule for new accounts. An account is defined as a new account during the first 30 calendar days after the account is opened. An account is open when the first deposit is made to the account. An account is not considered a new account, however, if each customer on the account has a transaction account relationship with the depositary bank, including a dormant account, that is at least 30 calendar days old on September 1, 1988, or at any time thereafter (i.e., an established account), or has had an established account with the depositary bank or within the 30 calendar days prior to opening the account.

The following are examples of what constitutes, and does not constitute, a new account:

(1) If the customer has an established account with a bank and opens a second account with the bank, the second account is not subject to the new account exception.

(2) If a customer's account were closed and another account opened as a successor to the original account (due, for example, to the theft of checks or a debit card used to access the original account), the successor account is not subject to the new account exception, assuming

the previous account relationship is at least 30 days old. Similarly, if a customer closed an established account and opens a separate account within 30 days, the new account is not subject to the new account exception.

(3) If a customer has a savings deposit or other deposit that is not an account (as that term is defined in §229.2(a)) at the bank, and opens an account, the account may be subject to the new account exception.

(4) If a person that is authorized to sign on a corporate account (but has no other relationship with the bank) opens a personal account, the personal account is subject to the new account exception.

(5) If a customer has an established joint account at a bank, and subsequently opens an individual account with that bank, the individual account is not subject to the new account exception.

(6) If two customers that each have an established individual account with the bank open a joint account, the joint account is not subject to the new account exception. If one of the customers on the account has no current or recent established account relationship with the bank, however, the joint account is subject to the new account exception, even if the other individual on the account has an established account relationship with the bank.

Rules Applicable to New Accounts

During the new account exception period, the schedules for local and nonlocal checks do not apply, and, unlike the other exceptions provided in this section, the regulation provides no maximum time frames within which the proceeds of these deposits must be made available for withdrawal. Maximum times within which funds must be available for withdrawal during the new account period are provided, however, for certain other deposits. Deposits received by cash and electronic payments must be made available for withdrawal in accordance with §229.10.

Special rules also apply to deposits of Treasury checks; U.S. Postal Service money orders; checks drawn on Federal Reserve Banks and Federal Home Loan Banks; state and local government checks; cashier's, certified, and teller's checks; and, for the purposes of the new account exception only, traveler's checks. The first $5,000 of funds deposited to a new account on any one banking day by these check deposits must be made available for withdrawal in accordance with §229.10(c). Thus, the first $5,000 of the proceeds of these check deposits must be made available on the next business day following deposit, if the deposit is made in person to an employee of the depositary bank and the other conditions of next-day availability are met. Funds must be made available on the second business day after deposit for deposits that are not made over-the-counter, in accordance with §229.10(c)(2). (Proceeds of Treasury check deposits must be made available on the next business day after deposit, even if the check is not deposited in person to an employee of the depositary bank.) Funds in excess of the first $5,000 deposited by these types of checks on a banking day must be available for withdrawal not later than the ninth business day following the banking day of deposit. The requirements of §229.10(c)(1)(vi) and (vii) that "on us" checks and the first $100 of a day's deposit be made available for withdrawal on the next business day do not apply during the new account period.

Representation by Customer

The depositary bank may rely on the representation of the customer that the customer has no established account relationship with the bank, and has not had any such account relationship within the past 30 days, to determine whether an account is subject to the new account exception.

(b) *Large Deposits*

Under the large deposit exception, a depositary bank may extend the hold placed on check deposits to the extent that the amount of the aggregate deposit on any banking day exceeds $5,000. This exception applies to local and nonlocal checks, as well as to checks that would otherwise be made available on the next (or second) business day after the day of deposit under §229.10(c). Although the first $5,000 of a day's deposit is subject to the availability otherwise provided for checks, the amount in excess of $5,000 may be held for an additional period of time as provided in §229.13(h). When the large deposit exception is applied to deposits composed of a mix of checks that would otherwise be subject to differing availability schedules, the depositary bank has the discretion to choose the portion of the deposit to which it applies the exception. Deposits by cash or electronic payment are not subject to this exception for large deposits.

The following example illustrates the operation of the large deposit exception. If a customer deposits $2,000 in cash and a $9,000 local check on a Monday, $2,100 (the proceeds of the cash deposit and $100 from the local check deposit) must be made available for withdrawal on Tuesday. An additional $4,900 of the proceeds of the local check must be available for withdrawal on Wednesday in accordance with the local schedule, and the remaining $4,000 may be held for an additional period of time under the large deposit exception.

Where a customer has multiple accounts with a depositary bank, the bank may apply the large deposit exception to the aggregate deposits to all of the customer's accounts, even if the customer is not the sole holder of the accounts and not all of the holders of the customer's accounts are the same. Thus, a depositary bank may aggregate the deposits made to two individual accounts in the same name, to an individual and a joint account with one common name, or to two joint accounts with at least one common name for the purpose of applying the large deposit exception. Aggregation of deposits to multiple accounts is permitted because the Board believes that the risk to the depositary bank associated with large deposits is similar regardless of how the deposits are allocated among the customer's accounts.

(c) *Redeposited Checks*

The Act gives the Board the authority to promulgate an exception to the schedule for checks that have been returned unpaid and redeposited. Section 229.13(c) provides such an exception for checks that have been returned unpaid and redeposited by the customer or the depositary bank. This exception applies to local and nonlocal checks, as well as to checks that would otherwise be made available on the next (or second) business day after the day of deposit under §229.10(c).

This exception addresses the increased risk to the depositary bank that checks that have been returned once will be uncollectible when they are presented to the paying bank a second time. The Board, however, does not believe that this increased risk is present for checks that have been returned due to a missing indorsement. Thus, the exception does not apply to checks returned unpaid due to missing indorsements and redeposited after the missing indorsement has been obtained, if the reason for return indicated on the check (see §229.30(d)) states that it was returned due to a missing indorsement. For the same reason, this exception does not apply to a check returned because it was postdated (future dated), if the reason for return indicated on the check states that it was returned because it was postdated, and if it is no longer postdated when redeposited.

To determine when funds must be made available for withdrawal, the banking day on which the check is redeposited is considered to be the day of deposit. A depositary bank that made $100 of a check available for withdrawal under §229.10(c)(1)(vii) can charge back the full amount of the check, including the $100, if the check is returned unpaid, and the $100 need not be made available again if the check is redeposited.

(d) *Repeated Overdrafts*

The Act gives the Board the authority to establish an exception for "deposit accounts which have been overdrawn repeatedly." This paragraph provides two tests to determine what constitutes repeated overdrafts. Under the first test, a customer's accounts are considered repeatedly overdrawn if, on six banking days within the preceding six months, the available balance in any account held by the customer is negative, or the balance would have become negative if checks or other charges to the account had been paid, rather than returned. This test can be met based on separate occurrences (e.g., checks that are returned for insufficient funds on six different days), or based on one occurrence (e.g., a negative balance that remains on the customer's account for six banking days). If the bank dishonors a check that otherwise would have created a negative balance, however, the incident is considered an overdraft only on that day.

The second test addresses substantial overdrafts. Such overdrafts increase the risk to the depositary bank of dealing with the repeated overdrafter. Under this test, a customer incurs repeated overdrafts if, on two banking days within the preceding six months, the available balance in any account held by the customer is negative in an amount of $5,000 or more, or would have become negative in an amount of $5,000 or more if checks or other charges to the account had been paid.

The exception relates not only to overdrafts caused by checks drawn on the account, but also overdrafts caused by other debit charges (e.g. ACH debits, point-of-sale transactions, returned checks, account fees, etc.). If the potential debit is in excess of available funds, the exception applies regardless of whether the items were paid or returned unpaid. An overdraft resulting from an error on the part of the depositary bank, or from the imposition of overdraft charges for which the customer is entitled to a refund under §§229.13(e) or 229.16(c), cannot be considered in determining whether the customer is a repeated overdrafter. The exception excludes accounts with overdraft lines of credit, unless the credit line has been exceeded or would have been exceeded if the checks or other charges to the account had been paid.

This exception applies to local and nonlocal checks, as well as to checks that otherwise would be made available on the next (or second) business day after the day of deposit under §229.10(c). When a bank places or extends a hold under this exception, it need not make the first $100 of a deposit available for withdrawal on the next business day, as otherwise would be required by §229.10(c)(1)(vii).

(e) *Reasonable Cause to Doubt Collectibility*

In the case of certain check deposits, if the bank has reasonable cause to believe the check is uncollectible, it may extend the time funds must be made available for withdrawal. This exception applies to local and nonlocal checks, as well as to checks that would otherwise be made available on the next (or second) business day after the day of deposit under §229.10(c). When a bank places or extends a hold under this exception, it need not make the first $100 of a deposit available for withdrawal on the next business day, as otherwise would be required by 229.10(c)(1)(vii).

The following are several examples of circumstances under which the reasonable cause exception may be invoked:

If a bank received a notice from the paying bank that a check was not paid and is being returned to the depositary bank, the depositary bank could place a hold on the check or extend a hold previously placed on that check, and notify the customer that the bank had received notice that the check is being returned. The exception could be invoked even if the notice were incomplete, if the bank had reasonable cause to believe that the notice applied to that particular check.

The depositary bank may have received information from the paying bank, prior to the presentment of the check, that gives the bank reasonable cause to believe that the check is uncollectible. For example, the paying bank may have indicated that payment has been stopped on the check, or that the drawer's account does not currently have sufficient funds to honor the check. Such information may provide sufficient basis to invoke this exception. In these cases, the depositary bank could invoke the exception and disclose as the reason the exception is being invoked the fact that information from the paying bank indicates that the check may not be paid.

The fact that a check is deposited more than six months after the date on the check (i.e. a stale check) is a reasonable indication that the check may be uncollectible, because under U.C.C. §4-404 a bank has no duty to its customer to pay a check that is more than six months old. Similarly, if a check being deposited is postdated (future dated), the bank may have a reasonable cause to believe the check is uncollectible, because the check is not properly payable under U.C.C. §4-401. The bank, in its notice, should specify that the check is stale date or postdated.

There are reasons that may cause a bank to believe that a check is uncollectible that are based on confidential information. For example, a bank could conclude that a check being deposited is uncollectible based on its reasonable belief that the depositor is engaging in kiting activity. Reasonable belief as to the insolvency or pending insolvency of the drawer of the check or the drawee bank and that the checks will not be paid may also justify invoking this exception. In these cases, the bank may indicate, as the reason it is invoking the exception, that the bank has confidential information that indicates that the check might not be paid.

The Board has included a reasonable cause exception notice as a model form in Appendix C (C-13A). The model notice includes a number of reasons for which this exception may be invoked. The Board does not intend to provide a comprehensive list of reasons for which this exception may be invoked; another reason that does not appear on the model notice may be used as the basis for extending a hold, if the reason satisfies the conditions for invoking this exception. A depositary bank may invoke the reasonable cause exception based on a combination of factors that give rise to a reasonable cause to doubt the collectibility of a check. In these cases, the bank should disclose the primary reasons for which the exception was invoked in accordance with paragraph (g) of this section.

The regulation provides that the determination that a check is uncollectible shall not be based on a class of checks or persons. For example, a depositary bank cannot invoke this exception simply because the check is drawn on a paying bank in a rural area and the depositary bank knows it will not have the opportunity to learn of nonpayment of that check before funds must be made available under the availability schedules. Similarly, a depositary bank cannot invoke the reasonable cause exception based on the race or national origin of the depositor.

If a depositary bank invokes this exception with respect to a particular check and does not provide a written notice to the depositor at the time of deposit, the depositary bank may not assess any overdraft fee (such as an NSF charge) or charge interest for use of overdraft credit, if the check is paid by the paying bank and these charges would not have occurred had the exception not been invoked. A bank may assess an overdraft fee under these circumstances, however, if it provides notice to the customer, in the notice of exception required by paragraph (g) of this section, that the fee may be subject to refund, and refunds the charges upon the request of the customer. The notice must state that the customer may be entitled to a refund of any overdraft fees that are assessed if the check being held is paid, and indicate where such requests for a refund of overdraft fees should be directed.

(f) *Emergency Conditions*

Certain emergency conditions may arise that delay the collection or return of checks, or delay the processing and updating of customer accounts. In the circumstances specified in this paragraph, the depositary bank may extend the holds that are placed on deposits of checks that are affected by such delays, if the bank exercises such diligence as the circumstances require. For example, if a bank learns that a check has been delayed in the process of collection due to severe weather conditions or other causes beyond its control, an emergency condition covered by this section may exist and the bank may place a hold on the check to reflect the delay. This exception applies to local and nonlocal checks, as well as checks that would otherwise be made available on the next (or second) business day after the day of deposit under §229.10(c). When a bank places or extends a hold under this exception, it need not make the first $100 of a deposit available for withdrawal on the next business day, as otherwise would be required by §229.10(c)(1)(vii). In cases where the emergency conditions exception does not apply, as in the case of deposits of cash or electronic payments under §229.10(a) and (b), the depositary bank may not be liable for a delay in making funds available for withdrawal if the delay is due to a bona fide error such as an unavoidable computer malfunction.

(g) *Notice of Exception*

If a depositary bank invokes any of the safeguard exceptions to the schedules listed above, other than the new account exception, and extends the hold on a deposit beyond the time periods permitted in §§229.10(c), and 229.12, it must provide a notice to its customer. Except in the cases described in paragraphs (g)(2) and (g)(3) of the regulation, notices must be given each time an exception hold is invoked and must state the customer's account number, the date of deposit, the reason the exception was invoked, and the time period within which funds will be available for withdrawal.

With respect to paragraph (g)(1), the requirement that the notice state the time period within which the funds shall be made available may be satisfied if the notice identifies the date the deposit is received and information sufficient to indicate when funds will be available and the amounts that will be available at those times. For example, for a deposit involving more than one check, the bank need not provide a notice that discloses when funds from each individual check in the deposit will be available for withdrawal; instead, the bank may provide a total dollar amount for each of the time periods when funds will be available, or provide the customer with an explanation of how to determine the amount of the deposit that will be held and when the funds will be available for deposit. Appendix C (C-13) contains a model form of this exception notice.

For deposits made in person to an employee of the depositary bank, the notice generally must be given to the person making the deposit, i.e. the "depositor", at the time of deposit. The depositor need not be the customer holding the account. For other deposits, such as deposits received at an ATM, lobby deposit box, night depository, or through the mail, notice must be mailed to the customer not later than the close of the business day following the banking day on which the deposit was made.

Notice to the customer also may be provided at a later time, if the facts upon which the determination to invoke the exception do not become known to the depositary bank until after notice would otherwise have to be given. In these cases, the bank must mail the notice to the customer as soon as practicable, but not later than the business day following the day the facts become known. A bank is deemed to have knowledge when the facts are brought to the attention of the person or persons in the bank responsible for making the determination, or when the facts would have been brought to their attention if the bank had exercised due diligence.

If the depositary bank extends the hold placed on a deposit due to an emergency condition, the notice requirement generally applies; however, the regulation provides that the bank need not provide a notice if the funds would be available for withdrawal before the notice must be sent. For example, if on the last day of a hold period the depositary bank experiences a computer failure and customer accounts cannot be updated in a timely fashion to reflect the funds as available balances, notices are not required if the funds are made available before the notices must be sent.

In those cases described in paragraphs (g)(2) and (g)(3), the depositary bank need not provide a notice every time an exception hold is applied to a deposit. When paragraph (g)(2) or (g)(3) requires disclosure of the time period within which deposits subject to the exception generally will be available for withdrawal, the requirement may be satisfied if the one-time notice states when on us, local, and nonlocal checks will be available for withdrawal if an exception is invoked.

Under paragraph (g)(2), if a nonconsumer account (see Commentary to 229.2(n)) is subject to the large deposit or redeposited check exception, the depositary bank may give its customer a single notice at or prior to the time notice must be provided under paragraph (g)(1). Notices provided under paragraph (g)(2) must contain the reason the exception may be invoked and the time period within which deposits subject to the exception will be available for withdrawal (see Model Notice C-13B). A depositary bank may provide a one-time notice to nonconsumer customer under paragraph (g)(2) only if each exception cited in the notice (the large deposit and/or the redeposited check exception) will be invoked for most check deposits to the customer's account to which the exception could apply. A one-time notice may state that the depositary bank will apply exception holds to certain subsets of deposits to which the large deposit or redeposited check exception may apply, and the notice should identify such subsets. For example, the depositary bank may apply the redeposited check exception only to checks that were redeposited automatically by the depositary bank in accordance with an agreement with the customer, rather than to all redeposited checks. In lieu of sending the one-time notice, a depositary bank may send individual hold notices for each deposit subject to the large deposit or redeposited check exception in accordance with §229.13(g)(1) (see Model Notice C-13).

In the case of a deposit of multiple checks, the depositary bank has the discretion to place an exception hold on any combination of checks in excess of $5,000. The notice should enable a customer to determine the availability of the deposit in the case of a deposit of multiple checks. For example, if a customer deposits a $5,000 local check and a $5,000 nonlocal check, under the large deposit exception, the depositary bank may make funds available in the amount of (1) $100 on the business day after deposit, $4,900 on the second business day after deposit (local check), and $5,000 on the eleventh business day after deposit (nonlocal check with 6-day exception hold), or (2) $100 on the first business day after deposit, $4,900 on the fifth business day after deposit (nonlocal check), and $5,000 on the seventh business day after deposit (local check with 5-day exception hold).The notice should reflect the bank's priorities in placing exception holds on next-day (or second-day), local, and nonlocal checks.

Under paragraph (g)(3), if an account is subject to the repeated overdraft exception, the depositary bank may provide one notice to its customer for each time period during which the exception will apply. Notices sent pursuant to paragraph (g)(3) must state the customer's account number, the fact the exception was invoked under the repeated overdraft exception, the time period within which deposits subject to the exception will be made available for withdrawal, and the time period during which the exception will apply (see Model Form C-13C). A depositary bank may provide a one-time notice to a customer under paragraph (g)(3) only if the repeated overdraft exception will be invoked for most check deposits to the customer's account.

A depositary bank must retain a record of each notice of a reasonable cause exception for a period of two years, or such longer time as provided in the record retention requirements of §229.21. When paragraph (g)(2) or (g)(3) requires disclosure of the time period within which deposits subject to the execption generally will be available for withdrawal, the requiremen may be satisfied if the one-time notice states when on us, local, and nonlocal checks will be available for withdrawal if an exception is invoked. In many cases, such as where the exception was invoked on the basis of a notice of nonpayment received, the record requirement may be met by retaining a copy of the notice sent to the customer. In other cases, such as where the exception was invoked on the basis of confidential information, a further description to the facts, such as insolvency of drawer, should be included in the record.

(h) *Availability of Deposits Subject to Exceptions*

If a depositary bank invokes any exception other than the new account exception, the bank may extend the time within which funds must be made available under the schedule by a reasonable period of time. This provision establishes that an extension of up to one business day for on us checks, five business days for local checks, and six business days for nonlocal checks is reasonable. Under certain circumstances, however, a longer extension of the schedules may be reasonable. In these cases, the burden is placed on the depositary bank to establish that a longer period is reasonable.

For example, assume a bank extended the hold on a local check deposit by five business days based on its reasonable cause to believe that the check is uncollectible. If, on the day before the extended hold is scheduled to expire, the bank receives a notification from the paying bank that the check is being returned unpaid, the bank may determine that a longer hold is warranted, if it decides not to charge back the customer's account based on the notification. If the bank decides to extend the hold, the bank must send a second notice, in accordance with paragraph (g) of this section, indicating the new date that the funds will be available for withdrawal.

With respect to Treasury checks, U.S. Postal Service money orders, checks drawn on Federal Reserve Banks or Federal Home Loan Banks, state and local government checks, and cashier's, certified, and teller's checks subject to the next-day (or second-day) availability requirement, the depositary bank may extend the time funds must be made available for withdrawal under the large deposit, redeposited check, repeated overdraft, or reasonable cause exception by a reasonable period beyond the delay that would have been permitted under the regulation had the checks not been subject to the next-day (or second-day) availability requirement. The additional hold is added to the local or nonlocal schedule that would apply based on the location of the paying bank.

One business day for on us checks, five business days for local checks, and six business days for nonlocal checks, in addition to the time period provided in the schedule, should provide adequate time for the depositary bank to learn of the nonpayment of virtually all checks that are returned. For example, if a customer deposits a $7,000 cashier's check drawn on a nonlocal bank, and the depositary bank applies the large deposit exception to that check, $5,000 must be available for withdrawal on the next business day after the day of deposit and the remaining $2,000 must be available for withdrawal on the eleventh business day following the day of deposit (six business days added to the five- day schedule for nonlocal checks), unless the depositary bank establishes that a longer hold is reasonable.

In the case of the application of the emergency conditions exception, the depositary bank may extend the hold placed on a check by not more than a reasonable period following the end of the emergency or the time funds must be available for withdrawal under §§229.10(c) or 229.12, whichever is later.

This provision does not apply to holds imposed under the new account exception. Under that exception, the maximum time period within which funds must be made available for withdrawal is specified for deposits that generally must be accorded next-day availability under §229.10. This subpart does not specify the maximum time period within which the proceeds of local and nonlocal checks must be made available for withdrawal during the new account period.

Regulation CC Availability of Funds and Collection of Checks

12 CFR 229, App. C
Model Forms

C-13A--Reasonable cause hold notice

NOTICE OF HOLD

Account number: (*number*)
Date of deposit: (*date*)
Amount of deposit: (*amount*)
We are delaying the availability of the funds you deposited by the following check:
(*description cf check, such as amount and drawer*)
These funds will be available on the (*number*) business day after the day of your deposit.
The reason for the delay is explained below:
--We received notice that the check is being returned unpaid.
--We have confidential information that indicates that the check may not be paid.
--The check is drawn on an account with repeated overdrafts.
--We are unable to verify the endorsement of a joint payee.
--Some information on the check is not consistent with other information on the check.
--There are erasures or other apparent alterations on the check.
--The routing number of the paying bank is not a current routing number.
--The check is postdated or has a stale date.
--Information from the paying bank indicates that the check may not be paid.

--We have been notified that the check has been lost or damaged in collection.

--Other:

[If you did not receive this notice at the time you made the deposit and the check you deposited is paid, we will refund to you any fees for overdrafts or returned checks that result solely from the additional delay that we are imposing. To obtain a refund of such fees, (*description of procedure for obtaining refund*).]

Raymer v. Bay State National Bank
Supreme Judicial Court of Massachusetts, 1981
384 Mass. 310, 424 N.E.2d 515

Braucher, Justice. The plaintiff Raymer, as assignee of Raymer Products Corp. (company), brought this action against the defendant bank for damages for the wrongful dishonor of twenty-six checks, under the Uniform Commercial Code (UCC), G.L. c. 106, §4-402, and for unfair and deceptive acts and practices under G.L. c. 93A, §11. A judge of the Superior Court, sitting without a jury, awarded the plaintiff $36,463.73, the face amount of the dishonored checks, plus attorneys' fees and costs. Both parties appealed, and we transferred the case to this court on our own motion. We reverse the judgment and order the entry of judgment for the plaintiff for nominal damages plus attorneys' fees and costs.

We summarize the judge's findings of fact. Raymer was the president and principal shareholder of the company. The company became a customer of the bank in 1972, maintained a commercial checking account with the bank, and became indebted to the bank on three separate loans: (1) a real estate mortgage loan guaranteed by the Small Business Administration (SBA), (2) a second SBA-guaranteed loan secured by machinery, and (3) a "revolving" loan secured by accounts receivable and inventory. The first two were being repaid by monthly payments of principal and interest, and the revolving loan was maintained at varying levels, with interest payable monthly. The company did not miss any payments due. In the winter of 1975-1976 the company notified the bank that it expected an operating loss due to raw material shortages created by the oil embargo and to the bankruptcy of one of its customers. About May 23, 1976, after submission of the company's quarterly report, Raymer met with the bank's loan officer; they reviewed steps to be taken to restore profitable operations, to which the loan officer agreed. In June, 1976, a second loan officer took over the company's accounts, and he wanted further security. The balance on the revolving loan was then $229,000, and it was secured by more than $245,000 in accounts and more than $250,000 in inventory. The second loan officer was told to expect a loss of $15,000 for May and June, but an interim report showed a loss of less than $5,000. For the fiscal year ending April 30, 1976, the company had a net operating loss of some $122,000 on net sales of $1.7 million; for the three months ending July 31, 1976, the loss was $96,350.

On July 15, 1976, the second loan officer went to the company's plant and explained to Raymer that a separate account would be established the following week for the deposit of accounts receivable; until then the company should make deposits and pay bills as it normally would. Twenty-six checks drawn by the company before July 16, 1976, totalling $36,463.73, were presented to the bank, thirteen on Friday, July 16, and thirteen on Monday, July 19. The company's account contained sufficient available funds, and the twenty-six checks were "posted" by the bank's usual procedure then in force before 6 A.M. of the banking day following the day of receipt. On Tuesday, July 20, 1976, representatives of the company and the bank met at the bank at 3 P.M. to go over the company's earnings projections. Unknown to the company representatives, while the meeting was going on the bank's loan officer was at the company's plant taking possession of all its property. Later that day the bank returned all twenty-six checks for "uncollected funds," crediting the company's account and setting off some $78,000 of the revolving loan.

The company filed a petition under c. 11 of the Bankruptcy Act on August 10, 1976, and completed the petition on September 24, 1976. The bank had begun a proceeding in the United States Bankruptcy Court to compel the turnover of accounts receivable, and the company filed an answer but no counterclaim. The present claims were not scheduled as assets in the bankruptcy proceeding. A plan of arrangement was filed in December, 1976, and confirmed January 28, 1977; final decree was entered in May, 1977. On February 4, 1977, the company assigned the present claims to Raymer, and this action was begun on July 19, 1977.

The judge ruled that the company's claims were assignable and were not barred by what took place in the bankruptcy court, that the bank's set-off came too late under G.L. c. 106, §§4-303, and 4-109, and that the plaintiff could recover the face amount of the checks under G.L. c. 106, §4-402, as damages proximately caused by wrongful dishonor. He further ruled that the set-off was an unfair act or practice in violation of G.L. c. 93A, §2, and awarded the plaintiff attorneys' fees under G.L. c. 93A, §11. On the bank's appeal, it contests each of these rulings. On the plaintiff's appeal, he attacks the following rulings: that the plaintiff failed to show additional damages having the requisite causal connection under §4-402, and that the plaintiff was not entitled to multiple damages under G.L. c. 93A, §11. Except for the award of damages in the face amount of the checks, we uphold the actions taken by the judge. The result is that judgment is to be entered for the plaintiff for nominal damages plus attorneys' fees and costs.

* * *

2. *Wrongful dishonor.* The bank asserted a right to set off the balance of its revolving loan against the company's deposit. If the set-off was proper, there were insufficient funds, and the dishonor of the checks was not wrongful, although the stated reason, "uncollected funds," was inappropriate. The judge ruled, however, that the set-off came too late, and we agree. Under UCC §4-303(1), a set-off exercised by a payor bank "comes too late" to terminate the bank's duty to pay an item if it is exercised after the bank has done any one of several things. As to checks received on Friday, July 16, the bank's midnight deadline was at the end of Monday, July 19, under UCC §4-104(h), and the bank then became "accountable for the amount of the item" under UCC §§4-213(1)(d) and 4-302. The set-off on July 20 came thereafter and was "too late" under §4-303(1)(e). Hence the subsequent dishonor of these checks was wrongful.

As to the checks received by the bank on July 19, however, the set-off on the afternoon of July 20 came before the bank's midnight deadline at the end of July 20. The judge ruled that the set-off came too late under §4-303(1)(d), because before 6 A.M. on July 20 the bank had "completed the process of posting" the items to the indicated account of the company as drawer and had "evidenced by examination of such indicated account and by action its decision to pay the item." Those rulings rested on the judge's finding, pursuant to §4-109, that the bank's "usual procedure" involved completion of posting before 6 A.M. on the day following receipt of the item. That finding rested on the testimony of the responsible officer of the bank, which in the judge's view led to an "inescapable conclusion that the decision to pay on the checks presented was made during the 6 P.M. to 6 A.M. period." Although the testimony was not as clear as it might have been, we are unable to say that the judge's finding was clearly erroneous. It follows that the set-off came too late as to all the checks in controversy and that they were wrongfully dishonored.

* * *

3. *Damages*. The judge awarded damages in the face amount of the dishonored checks. In some circumstances such an award may be appropriate under UCC §4-402. But in the present case the net result of the wrongful dishonor was that the company's bank account was used to pay different debts from those the company sought to pay. The bank's right to set off the amount of its revolving loan is not disputed except on the ground that the set-off came too late to affect the checks that were dishonored on July 20. In this situation an award of damages in the face amount of the checks does not reflect any actual loss suffered by the depositor.

The plaintiff also sought consequential damages, and the judge ruled that such damages were recoverable under UCC §4-402 if "proximately caused" by the wrongful dishonor. He noted the company's "substantial and continuing financial difficulties beginning well before July 19, 1976," and said that, arguably, its worse performance in July, 1976, was a result of the bank's actions, but that close scrutiny did not support this conclusion. He concluded that the plaintiff had not shown the requisite causal connection. This is a factual conclusion, and we are unable to say that it is clearly erroneous.

Under UCC §4-402 the special rule for traders laid down in Wiley v. Bunker Hill Nat'l Bank, 183 Mass. 495, 496-497, 67 N.E. 655 (1903), is said to be abolished, and in cases of mistaken dishonor liability is limited to "actual damages proved." UCC §4-402 and Comment 3. See Holland, An Analysis of the Legal Problems Resulting from Wrongful Dishonors, 42 Mo.L.Rev. 507, 517-526 (1977). The present case is not one of mistake, and we think it proper, in accordance with the Wiley case, to order the entry of judgment for nominal damages.

* * *

5. *Disposition*. The judgment is reversed and the case is remanded to the Superior Court. Judgment is to enter for the plaintiff for $1.00, plus $4,500 attorneys' fees and costs of the action. No argument is made with respect to counsel fees and costs on these appeals, and such questions are left to further proceedings in the Superior Court.

So ordered.

Thrash v. Georgia State Bank

Court of Appeals of Georgia, 1988
189 Ga.App. 21, 375 S.E.2d 112

McMurray, Presiding Judge. In this "wrongful dishonor" case, we are called upon to decide whether plaintiff was a bank "customer" within the meaning of OCGA §11-4-402. We hold that he was not and affirm the trial court's grant of summary judgment to the bank.

On March 14, 1983, Tabb Auto Salvage Company was duly incorporated under the laws of the State of Georgia. "Tabb" was an acronym formed by the initial letters of the last names of the corporation's shareholders: Glenn Lamar Thrash, Sr., C. King Askew, Robert M. Brinson and Robert L. Berry.

The corporation's board of directors consisted of Askew, Brinson and Berry. Thrash, a minority shareholder in the corporation, held the office of president.

The corporation did business in Rome, Georgia, under the registered trade name "Thrash Tire Outlet." On April 1, 1983, it opened a commercial checking account with the bank. The name "Tabb Auto Salvage d/b/a Thrash Tire Co." appeared on the corporation's checks. Thrash, Askew, Brinson and Berry were all authorized to sign the checks.

On September 24, 1984, the corporation borrowed $71,678.09 from the bank. The note was signed by Thrash, as president, and Askew, as secretary of the corporation. It was personally guaranteed by Thrash, Askew, Brinson and Berry.

On May 15, 1985, the bank froze the corporation's checking account. (Apparently, the bank feared that corporate assets collateralizing the note were being removed from the corporation's premises.) As a result, corporate checks written by Thrash were dishonored.

Thrash was arrested subsequently on bad check charges. In the meantime, on May 16, 1985, Thrash was ousted from his office as president of the corporation by the other shareholders.

Thrash brought suit against The Georgia State Bank of Rome and Marc Duncan d/b/a Interstate Battery Systems of Northwest Georgia ("Interstate"). He alleged that the bank wrongfully dishonored checks which he had written; that one such check was delivered to Interstate; and that the wrongful dishonor of that check led to plaintiff's arrest and incarceration. It was also alleged that the bank wrongfully dishonored a check which plaintiff had written and delivered to the Employment Security Agency and that, as a result, plaintiff faced additional criminal or civil penalties. Defendants answered the complaint and denied any liability to plaintiff. Thereafter, following discovery, the bank moved for summary judgment.

In support of its motion for summary judgment, the bank submitted the affidavits of E. William Roberts, its Senior Vice-President. He averred that he was the bank officer responsible for the corporation's account; that he considered the corporation "to be the Bank's creditor"; that plaintiff represented himself to be the president of the corporation; that the corporation defaulted on its note with the bank; that Messrs. Askew, Brinson and Berry paid the corporation's obligation to the bank; and that plaintiff did not pay the corporation's obligation to the bank.

In opposition to the bank's summary judgment motion, plaintiff submitted an affidavit in which he averred: "To my knowledge, no stock of the corporation was ever issued to any stockholder. Additionally, this corporation was undercapitalized ... I made all of the decisions regarding the operations of the corporation. Specifically, I loaned the corporation money on several occasions; I saw to the daily operations of the corporation; I made all of the major decisions of the corporation. Indeed, I was the corporation."

The trial court granted the bank's motion for summary judgment. This appeal followed.
Held:

In pertinent part, OCGA §11-4-402 (which is identical to UCC §4-402) provides: "A payor bank is liable to its customer for damages proximately caused by the wrongful dishonor of an item ..." Was plaintiff a "customer" of the bank as that term is used in this Code section?

" 'Customer' means any person having an account with a bank ..." OCGA §11-4-104(1)(e). Plaintiff did not have an account with the bank. It was the corporation, Tabb Auto Salvage Co. d/b/a Thrash Tire Outlet, which had the account. Plaintiff was merely an officer and shareholder of the corporation. Accordingly, plaintiff cannot maintain an action against the bank for "wrongful dishonor."

Relying upon *Kendall Yacht Corp. v. United Cal. Bank*, 123 Cal.Rptr. 848, 50 Cal.App.3d 949 (1975), plaintiff contends he should be considered the bank's customer even though the corporation was the nominal depositor. In that case, the Kendalls brought suit against United California Bank for the wrongful dishonor of checks. Since the Kendalls' corporation was the nominal depositor, the bank defended on the ground that the Kendalls were not customers. The appellate court disagreed. It recognized that, as a general proposition, owners or officers of a depositor corporation are not customers of a bank within the meaning of UCC §4-402. It held, however, under the circumstances of that case, that the Kendalls were customers. What circumstances led the *Kendall* court to that conclusion? The

Kendalls' corporation was undercapitalized and it never issued stock. The Kendalls were the prospective principal shareholders of the corporation. They personally guaranteed the corporation's debts and they alone controlled the corporation's financial affairs. Essentially, the Kendalls and their corporation were one and the same. Moreover, the bank and others dealing with the corporation knew that that was the situation.

The facts in the case sub judice do not fit within the *Kendall* framework. Plaintiff was not the principal shareholder of the corporation. He was one of four shareholders and he owned a minority of the shares. Plaintiff guaranteed the corporation's debt to the bank but he was not alone in doing so. All of the shareholders guaranteed the corporation's debt to the bank. Moreover, the other shareholders, not plaintiff, paid that debt. Finally, the bank did not consider plaintiff to be its depositor. It viewed the corporation as its depositor. Based on these facts, it cannot be said that plaintiff and the corporation were one and the same. If they were, plaintiff would not have been ousted from the office of corporation president by the other shareholders.

Plaintiff's affidavit does not create a factual question with respect to the "customer" controversy. " 'Ultimate or conclusory facts and conclusions of law, as well as statements made on belief or "on information and belief," cannot be utilized on a summary judgment motion. Similarly, the mere reargument of a party's case or the denial of an opponent's allegations will be disregarded.' Wright & Miller, Federal Practice and Procedure: Civil §2738, p. 695." *Cel-Ko Bldrs. & Dev. v. BX Corp.*, 136 Ga.App. 777, 781, 222 S.E.2d 94. Thus, plaintiff's statement concerning the issuance of stock, made to his "knowledge," does not rise to the level of fact. Likewise, plaintiff's conclusions concerning undercapitalization and alter ego must be disregarded.

The evidence adduced upon the bank's motion for summary judgment demonstrates that plaintiff was not a "customer" of the bank within the meaning of OCGA §11-4-402 as a matter of law. Accordingly, the trial court did not err in granting the bank's motion for summary judgment.

JUDGMENT AFFIRMED.

Twin City Bank v. Isaacs
Supreme Court of Arkansas, 1984
283 Ark. 127, 672 S.W.2d 651

Hays, Justice. Twin City Bank has appealed from a judgment entered on a jury verdict against it in favor of Kenneth and Vicki Isaacs for damages sustained from the bank's wrongful dishonor of the Isaacs' checks resulting in a hold order against their account for a period of approximately four years.

On Sunday, May 13, 1979, the Isaacs discovered that their checkbook was missing. They reported the loss to Twin City promptly on Monday, May 14, and later learned that two forged checks totalling $2,050 had been written on their account and honored by the bank on May 11 and 12. The sequence of events that followed is disputed, but the end result was a decision by the bank to freeze the Isaacs' checking account which had contained approximately $2,500 before the forgeries occurred. A few checks cleared Monday morning before a hold order was issued leaving the balance at approximately $2,000. Mr. Isaacs had been convicted of burglary and the initial hold on the account was attributable to the bank's concern that the Isaacs were somehow involved with the two forged checks. The individual responsible for the forgeries was charged and convicted soon after the forgeries occurred and on May 30, 1979 the police told the bank there was nothing to connect the Isaacs with the person arrested. Two weeks later the police notified the bank a second time they could not connect the Isaacs to the forgeries. The bank maintains it continued to keep the account frozen on the advice of its attorneys. However that may be, the Isaacs were denied their funds for some four years. The Isaacs filed suit in mid-June of 1979 for wrongful dishonor of their checks and wrongful withholding of their funds.

The jury awarded the Isaacs $18,500 in compensatory damages and $45,000 in punitive damages. The bank made a motion for a new trial pursuant to ARCP Rule 59, which was denied. From that denial the bank brings this appeal contending error on three grounds: 1) Misconduct of a juror at trial, 2) the trial court's refusal to give two requested instructions, and 3) jury error in assessing excessive damages contrary to the evidence and the law.

* * *

On the issue of damages, the bank maintains there was insufficient evidence to support the $18,500 award for mental anguish, for loss of credit and loss of the bargain on a house, that the award of punitive damages should not have been given at all as there was not only insufficient proof of actual damages but insufficient evidence of malice or intent to oppress on the part of the bank. The bank does not challenge the sufficiency of the evidence of its wrongful dishonor, but contends only that there was no evidence to support an award of damages. These arguments cannot be sustained.

The statute upon which this suit was based is Ark.Stat.Ann. §85-4-402.

> Bank's liability to customer for wrongful dishonor -- A payor bank is liable to its customer for damages proximately caused by the wrongful dishonor of an item. When the dishonor occurs through mistake liability is limited to actual damages proved. If so proximately caused and proved damages may include damages for an arrest or prosecution of the customer or other consequential damages. Whether any consequential damages are proximately caused by the wrongful dishonor is a question of fact to be determined in each case.

The jury was instructed that if they found the bank liable they were to fix the amount of money which would compensate the Isaacs "for any of the following elements of damage sustained which were proximately caused by the conduct of Twin City Bank: 1) Any amounts of money wrongfully held by the defendant and remaining unpaid 2) any mental anguish and embarrassment suffered by the plaintiffs 3) any financial losses sustained by the (Isaacs)."

Initially, there can be no serious question as to certain losses: the $2,000 wrongfully withheld by the bank for four years, and the value of two vehicles repossessed because the Isaacs did not have access to their funds, resulting in a loss of approximately $2,200. Additionally, after the account was frozen the bank continued to charge the account a service charge and overdraft fees on checks written before the forgeries but presented after the account was frozen. The bank does not refute these damages but argues there is no showing of any financial deprivation from loss of credit or loss of the bargain on a house the Isaacs wanted to buy, and insufficient proof of mental anguish. We find, however, that in addition to the losses previously mentioned, there was sufficient evidence to sustain damages for mental suffering, loss of credit, and sufficient demonstration of some loss attributable to the inability to pursue the purchase of a home.

Mental suffering under §4-402 of the Uniform Commercial Code is relatively new and has not been frequently addressed by other courts, but of those a majority has allowed recovery. In general, the type of mental anguish suffered under §4-402 does not need to rise to the higher standard of injury for intentional infliction of emotional distress. Wrongful dishonors tend to produce intangible injuries similar to those involved in defamation actions. See *State Bank of Siloam Springs v. Marshall*, 163 Ark. 566, 260 S.W. 431 (1924). Damages of this kind are more difficult to assess with exactness. In *Wasp Oil v. Arkansas Oil and Gas*, 280 Ark. 420, 658 S.W.2d 397 (1983) we noted the general rule that damages may not be allowed where they are speculative, resting only upon conjectural evidence, or the opinions of the parties or witnesses, but there are instances where damages cannot be proven with exactness. In *Wasp* we recognized a different rule applies when the cause and existence of damages have been established by the evidence, that recovery will not be denied merely because the damages cannot be determined with exactness. We went on to say the plaintiff in the case at bar was not trying to prove the latter sort of damage such as *mental anguish* as a result of defamation, but loss of income.

Decisions upholding recovery for mental suffering under the code have found injury resulting from circumstances comparable to this case. In *North Shore Bank v. Palmer*, supra, for example, a $275 forged check was paid from Palmer's account. After the bank knew or should have known the check was forged, it charged Palmer with the $275 check and later wrongfully dishonored other checks. Part of the actual damages awarded was attributed to mental suffering for the "embarrassment and humiliation Palmer suffered from having been turned down for credit for the first time in his life."

In *Morse v. Mutual Federal Savings and Loan*, supra, $2,200 was awarded for "false defamatory implications arising from temporary financial embarrassment." And in *Farmers & Merchants State Bank of Krum v. Ferguson*, supra, the plaintiff's account in the amount of $7,000 was frozen for approximately one month for reasons not stated. The plaintiff was awarded $25,000 for mental anguish, $3,000 for loss of credit based on a denial of a loan, $5,000 for loss of time spent making explanations to creditors, and $1,500 for loss of use of his money. The court justified the mental suffering award because the dishonor was found to be with malice -- the bank had failed to notify Ferguson that the account was frozen, some checks were honored while others were not, and the bank continued to withdraw loan payments due it during the entire time.

In this case, prior to the forgery incident the Isaacs' credit reputation with Twin City Bank was described by the bank as "impeccable" and the freezing of their funds had a traumatic effect on their lives. They obviously lost their credit standing with Twin City, and were unable to secure credit commercially at other institutions because of their status at Twin City. The Isaacs had to borrow from friends and family, and were left in a precarious position financially. They did not have use of their $2,000 for four years. The allegation relative to the loss of a house resulted from the dishonor of an earnest money check for a home they were planning to buy, ending prospects for the purchase at that time. Though there may have been insufficient proof of loss of the bargain on the house, as the bank argues, nevertheless this evidence was admissible as an element of mental suffering. The denial of credit contributed to some monetary loss as occurred in *Ferguson*, supra, in addition to its being a reasonable element of mental suffering as was found in *Palmer*, supra. There was also testimony that the financial strain contributed to marital difficulties leading at one point to the filing of a divorce suit. The suit was dropped but there was testimony that the difficulties caused by the bank's action caused substantial problems in the marriage. Finally, the Isaacs lost equities in two vehicles repossessed as a result of the withholding of their funds. One of these, a new van, was repossessed by Twin City in June, 1979, before a five day grace period for a current installment had expired.

We believe there was substantial evidence to support the verdict. The jury heard the evidence of the amount wrongfully withheld, the loss of two vehicles, credit loss through loan denials, loss of the use of their money for four years, the suffering occasioned by marital difficulties, the inability to acquire a home they wanted, and the general anxieties which accompanied the financial strain. We recognize that our holding today presents some conflict with pre-code law by allowing recovery without exactness of proof as to damages. In *State*

Bank cf Siloam Springs v. Marshall, supra, a suit based on the predecessor to §85-4-402, we stated that the plaintiff must show the facts and circumstances which occasioned the damage and the amount thereof. However, *Marshall* itself recognized the nature of the damages in this action, and §85-4-402, although similar to its predecessor, has additional language which impliedly recognizes mental suffering and other intangible injuries of the type noted in *Wasp,* supra, as recoverable under this statute. See White, Summers, supra, §17-4, p. 675. To the extent that exactness in proof is not required, the law as stated in *Marshall* is displaced by §85-4-402.

The bank's objection to the award of punitive damages is three-fold: a) The instruction on punitive damages was in accordance with AMI 2217, which is intended for use in negligence cases and not applicable here; b) there was no evidence that the bank acted intentionally or with malice, and c) the verdict of $45,000 was excessive. However, we address only the question of the excessiveness of the verdict, as the other points were not raised in the trial court by objection to the instruction.

In *Holmes v. Hollingsworth,* 234 Ark. 347, 352 S.W.2d 96 (1961), we noted the elements that may be considered in assessing the amount of punitive damages, recognizing that the deterrent effect has some correlation to the financial condition of the party against whom punitive damages are allowed. In view of the circumstances in their entirety presented by this case, we cannot say the amount awarded was grossly excessive or prompted by passion or prejudice.

The judgment is affirmed.

Spencer Companies, Inc. v. Chase Manhattan Bank
United States District Court, District of Massachusetts, 1987
81 B.R. 194

Caffrey, Senior District Judge. * * * Plaintiff, Spencer Companies, Inc. ("Spencer"), is a Massachusetts corporation involved primarily in the footwear business. The defendants are Chase Manhattan Bank, N.A., ("Chase Bank") a national banking association having its principal place of business in New York, and Chase National Corporate Services, Inc., ("Chase Services"), a New York corporation affiliated with Chase Bank which maintains a regional office in Boston, Massachusetts. In 1983, Chase Bank became the primary lender for Spencer. Pursuant to the credit relationship established, Spencer executed two promissory notes dated June 1, 1983 and January 22, 1985. Each note was expressly governed by New York law. Spencer also opened two checking accounts with Chase Bank, one of which was entitled "Expense Account" and was used for payment of Spencer's general operating expenses. The other account was used primarily for inventory and salary purposes and has been labeled the "General Account" by Spencer.

The lending arrangement between Spencer and Chase ran smoothly until the spring of 1986 when Chase informed Spencer that it wished to terminate their banking relationship. At that time, Spencer owed $3.2 million under the promissory notes. After receiving notice that Chase wished to withdraw as Spencer's primary lender, Spencer sought alternative financing with another lender. Throughout the summer of 1986, Spencer and Chase participated in discussions and negotiations with several lenders and a venture capital firm concerning the refinancing of Spencer's business. During this period, Chase took several actions to better protect itself in its position as Spencer's primary lender. In addition, at the end of October, 1986, Chase announced that it would no longer continue its previous policy of allowing Spencer to draw checks against uncollected funds. Chase informed Spencer that no deposits would be available until six days after deposit. As a result of this new policy, several checks issued by Spencer were dishonored.

On November 4, 1986, Chase set off the balance of Spencer's General Account against the $3.2 million debt owed Chase by Spencer. Either after the set off or immediately before, Chase sent a letter to Spencer's offices in Boston demanding payment of the promissory notes. Eight days later, Chase set off the funds held in Spencer's Expense Account against the amounts remaining to be paid under the notes. As a result of the loss of the funds in both the General and Expense Accounts, Spencer was forced to file for bankruptcy.

* * *

Count VII of Spencer's complaint alleges that Chase breached its duty of good faith and fair dealing in the following manner: by dishonoring Spencer's checks wrongfully and in contravention of a longstanding course of dealing with Spencer, by accepting deposits with intent to benefit itself, by setting off the Expense Account, by failing to give notice of the setoffs and an opportunity to pay, by misrepresenting its intentions with respect to continued financing and by refusing to cooperate with Spencer and its lenders in restructuring Spencer's finances.

There is implied in every contract governed by the Uniform Commercial Code an obligation of good faith and fair dealing. See M.G.L. c. 106, §1- 203; N.Y.Uniform Commercial Code §1-203 (McKinney 1964). This obligation is implicit in the contract for deposit and the loan agreements governing the rights of the parties here.

Spencer alleges that Chase had a longstanding policy of honoring checks drawn on Spencer's accounts without regard to whether deposits to the accounts had cleared or were deemed collected. Approximately a week before Chase set off the General Account, Chase started to dishonor checks drawn on that account and insisted that no payments would be authorized until six days after each deposit. Spencer claims that this rule was imposed whether or not the deposits were in fact cleared or collected. Spencer further alleges that Chase dishonored checks drawn prior to the time that Spencer was notified of Chase's abrupt change in policy. Spencer asserts that these checks had been issued in reliance on Chase's longstanding policy of allowing Spencer to write checks against uncollected funds. Spencer further asserts that Chase dishonored the checks in an effort to increase the funds available for its intended set off of Spencer's accounts.

These facts, if proven, state a claim for a violation of the implied obligation of good faith. Although it seems to be conceded that Chase had the right to refuse to honor checks drawn on uncollected funds, where the course of dealing indicates that Chase had never asserted the right against Spencer, a jury could find that good faith required Chase to give notice to Spencer before the rule took effect. Spencer was entitled to rely on Chase's policy until such time as it received notice that the policy was no longer effective. Chase did not have unfettered discretion to abruptly change policies in order to benefit itself at Spencer's expense.

The complaint also indicates that Chase's demand for payment may not have been made in good faith. Spencer asserts that the letter demanding payment was sent to Spencer's officers at a time when Chase knew that the officers would not be available to receive the letter. The letter was also delivered immediately prior to the deadline set for payment, if not thereafter, ensuring that Spencer would not have an opportunity to respond to the demand before Chase set off the General Account. While Spencer was not entitled to notice of the setoff, Chase was required to exercise good faith in performing its contractual obligation to make a demand. If it deliberately sent the demand letter in a manner calculated to disadvantage Spencer, then a claim for the violation of good faith obligation imposed by the U.C.C. has been stated.

* * *

In accordance with memorandum filed this date, it is ORDERED:

The defendants' motion for dismissal of Counts III, IV, VI, and VIII is granted.

The defendants' motion for dismissal of Counts II and VII is denied.

The defendants' motion for dismissal or summary judgment on Count IX is denied.

Dunnigan v. First Bank

Supreme Court of Connecticut, 1991
217 Conn. 205, 585 A.2d 659

Borden, Associate Justice. In this appeal, we are called upon to define the meaning and scope of General Statutes §42a-4-403(3) of the Uniform Commercial Code (Code) as applied to the facts of this case. The defendant bank appeals, after a court trial, from the judgment of the trial court in favor of the plaintiff, the trustee in bankruptcy of Cohn Precious Metals, Inc. (Cohn), a customer of the bank. We transferred the appeal to this court pursuant to Practice Book §4023, and we now reverse the trial court's judgment.

The plaintiff brought this action against the bank for wrongfully paying a check issued by Cohn over Cohn's valid stop payment order. The trial court determined that the plaintiff had established a loss within the meaning of §42a-4-403(3) as a result of the bank's payment of the check, and that the subrogation provisions of General Statutes §42a-4-407 did not defeat the rights of Cohn. The court accordingly rendered judgment for the amount of the check. This appeal followed.

The bank claims that judgment was improperly rendered for the plaintiff because (1) as a matter of law, Cohn did not suffer a loss within the meaning of §42a-4-403(3), and (2) the bank was subrogated to the rights of the payee of the check and of the collecting banks, pursuant to §42a-4-407. We agree with the bank's first claim and therefore need not reach its second claim. Furthermore, it is not necessary to define the relationship between §§42a-4-403(3) and 42a-4-407.

The parties stipulated to the following facts. On November 8, 1978, pursuant to purchase order 1142, Lamphere Coin, Inc. (Lamphere), a trader in coins and precious metals, delivered to Cohn certain silver dollars with a unit price of $1.71 and with a total value of $27,492.07. Cohn's bookkeeper incorrectly recorded the unit price of those coins, however, as $17.10, resulting in an erroneous total value of $47,098.93. On November 9, 1978, Cohn paid Lamphere $47,098.93 by wire transfer to Lamphere's bank account, resulting in an overpayment to Lamphere by Cohn of $19,606.86. On November 10, 1978, Lamphere delivered three and one-half bags of silver dollars to Cohn pursuant to Cohn's purchase order 1145. The value of the silver dollars was $21,175. On the same day, Cohn issued two checks drawn on its account at the bank to Lamphere, one in the amount of $12,175 and one in the amount of $9000, totaling $21,175.

Between November 10 and November 15, Cohn discovered its bookkeeper's error and, on November 14, 1978, directed the bank to stop payment on the two checks totaling $21,175 that had been issued on November 10, 1978. The bank stopped payment on the $9000 check, but on or about November 20, 1978, the bank inadvertently honored the $12,175 check over the valid stop payment order. Cohn retained the three and one-half bags of silver dollars, but never recovered its overpayment from Lamphere. As of November 20, 1978, the date of the improper payment of the check by the bank, and at all times thereafter Lamphere owed Cohn in excess of $13,000 as a result of these transactions.

The merits of this controversy revolve around the meaning of §42a-4- 403(3), which provides that "[t]he burden of establishing the fact and amount of loss resulting from the payment of an item contrary to a binding stop order is on the customer." The bank argues that where there is good consideration for a particular check, or where the check was given as payment on a binding contract, the bank that paid the check over a valid stop payment order is not liable to its customer, because there was no "loss resulting from [its] payment...." General Statutes §42a-4-403(3). Thus, in the bank's view a customer cannot establish a loss under this provision of the code by relying on the loss of credits due the customer from prior unrelated transactions between the customer and the payee of the check. The plaintiff argues, as the trial court concluded, that whether a customer has incurred a "loss" within the meaning of §42a-4-403(3) cannot be determined solely by focusing on the transaction underlying the particular check involved, but must be determined by focusing on the entire relationship between the customer and the payee of the check. The plaintiff contends that it is unreasonable to disregard the relative positions of the parties, especially where they have demonstrated a continuing course of business dealings, where there are likely to be such credits. Under such circumstances, the plaintiff claims that focusing on a single transaction is contrary to the intent of the Code. Thus, in the plaintiff's view, Cohn would have had a good "defense" to a claim by Lamphere on the check because of the overpayment, and by paying the check the bank caused Cohn a loss within the meaning of §42a-4-403(3).

The issue, therefore, is whether, on the facts of this case, the bank customer who sought to establish "the fact and amount of loss resulting from the payment of an item contrary to a binding stop payment order" pursuant to §42a-4-403(3) was entitled to do so by resorting to credits from prior transactions unrelated to that for which the check was issued, or whether the customer was limited to the facts of the particular transaction for which the check was issued. We conclude that the customer was limited to the facts of the particular transaction for which the check was issued, and that §42a-4-403(3) does not contemplate taking into account a loss by the customer of credits that arose from prior unrelated transactions.

We note first that, contrary to the plaintiff's suggestion, there is nothing in the stipulated facts to indicate that Cohn and Lamphere had a "continual course of business dealings." Those facts disclose only the two separate transactions occurring on November 8 and 9, 1978, and on November 10, 1978. Furthermore, this is not a case involving a revolving credit, open account or ongoing contractual relationship between the customer of the bank and the payee of the check. Thus, we need not decide whether those facts would yield a different conclusion.

Under §42a-4-403(1), a bank customer has the right to order his bank to stop payment on a check, so long as he does so in a timely and reasonable manner, and, under §42a-4-403(2), an oral stop payment order is binding on the bank for a limited period of time. The fact that the bank has paid the check over the customer's valid stop payment order does not mean, however, that the customer is automatically entitled to repayment of the amount of the check. Under §4-403(3), the customer must also establish "the fact and amount of loss resulting from" the bank's improper payment.

The case law makes clear that "[t]he loss ... must be more than the mere debiting of his account." *Grego v. South Carolina National Bank*, 283 S.C. 546, 549, 324 S.E.2d 94 (1984). *** Otherwise, §42a-4-403(3) would be superfluous. Furthermore, whether the customer has suffered such a loss is in the first instance a question of fact.

The cases and commentators also agree that where the check in question was supported by good consideration, or where the payee has enforceable rights against the maker based on the transaction underlying the check, the customer has suffered no loss within the meaning of §42a-4-403(3). As then Professor Peters explained, it "is implicit in §4-403(3) that if a check was issued for good consideration ... failure to observe a stop payment order does no more than to accelerate the drawer's inevitable liability, and is therefore a defense to the payor bank." E. Peters, [A Negotiable Instruments Primer (1974) p. 79].

Applying these principles to the facts of this case, we conclude that as a matter of law Cohn suffered no "loss" within the meaning of §42-4-403(3). The check was supported by good consideration because it was issued in payment for the silver coins that Lamphere delivered to Cohn. Furthermore, on the basis of that underlying transaction Lamphere had enforceable rights to payment by Cohn for those coins.

The plaintiff argues, however, that, although the particular check was supported by valid consideration and although there were no defenses available to it arising out of that particular transaction, the previous transaction between Cohn and Lamphere had supplied Cohn with a defense to payment of the check based on Cohn's overpayment to Lamphere. We disagree.

First, the language of §42-4-403(3) suggests a narrower reading than would be required by the plaintiff's position. Section 42a-4- 403(3) places on the bank's customer the "burden of establishing the *fact and amount of loss resulting from the payment* of an item contrary to a binding stop payment order...." (Emphasis added.) By contrast, §42a-4-402, which deals with a bank's liability to its customer for a wrongful *dishonor*, as opposed to a wrongful payment, provides as follows: "A payor bank is liable to its customer for *damages proximately caused by the wrongful dishonor* of an item. When the dishonor occurs through mistake liability is limited to actual damages proved. If so proximately caused and proved damages may include damages for an arrest or prosecution of the customer or other consequential damages. Whether any consequential damages are proximately caused by the wrongful dishonor is a question of fact to be determined in each case." (Emphasis added.) Thus, pursuant to §42a-4-402 the wrongfully dishonoring bank may be liable for all consequential damages proximately caused by its wrongful conduct, including damages resulting from arrest or prosecution of the customer, whereas there is a conspicuous absence from §42a-4-403(3) of language indicating such a broad scope of liability for wrongful payment.

This difference in the scope of the language used in §42a-4-403(3), as compared to that used in §42a-4-402, is consistent with the notion that §42a- 4-403(3) is intended to impose a limited, rather than broad, form of liability on banks. "The trade-off for requiring banks to accept stop orders under §4-403(1) was the limitation of their liability under §§4-403(3) and 4- 407." E. Peters, supra.

The case law and commentary support this more restrictive view of the scope of §42a-4-403(3). In determining whether a customer has established a "loss" under this section of the code, they focus on the check itself and on the transaction underlying it, and not on whether there were other prior, unrelated transactions between the maker and payee of the check. "In order to prove a loss under [§42a-4-403(3) of] the Code, a customer must prove he was not liable to the payee *on the check*. Although Cohn had an offset or counterclaim available to it with respect to Lamphere, it did not have a defense to payment of the check itself.

Finally, we find guidance in *Siegel v. New England Merchants National Bank*, [386 Mass. 672, 437 N.E.2d 218 (1982)]. In that case, the court held that §42a-4-403(3) must be read together with the subrogation provisions of §42a-4-407. Id., 386 Mass. at 678, 437 N.E.2d 218. Although we need not go that far because on the facts of this case §42a-4-403(3) can be read independently of §42a-4-407, we are persuaded by the holding of *Siegel* that in order to establish a §42a-4-403(3) "loss" the customer must show that he had defenses to payment of the check that were good against a holder or holder in due course under §§42a-3-305 and 42a-3-306, as the case may be, or that he had a good defense to liability on the underlying transaction. Id. at 679, 437 N.E.2d 218. None of these defenses arise from facts outside the confines of the particular check in question or the transaction underlying it.

In this case, the plaintiff seeks more than to establish a loss caused by the bank's failure to honor Cohn's stop payment order. That "loss" occurred in fact on November 9, 1978, when

Cohn overpaid for the coins it had received. Rather, the plaintiff seeks to recoup a loss resulting from a prior transaction separate from and independent of the stopped check. Thus, the plaintiff's position would permit the customer to establish a "loss" based on offsets or counterclaims against the payee based on prior unrelated transactions, no matter how remote from the check in question or from the transaction underlying it. We do not believe that the intent of §42a-4-403(3) ranges that far.

The dissent reads the commentary of Peters and of White & Summers too broadly. Although both refer to the situation, unlike the case at bar, where a customer seeks to establish a loss resulting from the dishonor of subsequent checks, neither commentator states with any confidence that the customer would prevail under §42a-4-403(3). Peters discusses the hypothetical without coming to any conclusion other than "[w]hatever the inferences that may appropriately be drawn ... it can hardly alter the conviction that §4-403(3) accomplishes its purpose of severely limiting a drawer's power to stop payment." E. Peters, supra, 80. White & Summers do venture that they would find the bank liable, but "confess uncertainty about this conclusion, for it leaves little substance to §4-403(3)." J. White & R. Summers, [Uniform Commercial Code (3d ed. 1988) § 18-6, p.912]. In any event, that is a case where the purported "loss" *follows* the wrongful payment and thus could arguably be said to be the result thereof, and not, as in this case, where it *precedes* that payment. Furthermore, the dissent's equation of §42a-4-403(3) to the law of causation in negligence ignores the difference in statutory language between §42a-4-402, where that concept is incorporated, and §42a-4-403(3), where such language is absent.

A factual finding must be reversed as clearly erroneous if it was based on an incorrect rule of law. The trial court's finding in this case that the plaintiff had established a loss within the meaning of §42a-4- 403(3) was so based.

The judgment is reversed, and the case is remanded with direction to render judgment for the defendant.

In this opinion Callahan and Hull, JJ., concurred.

Shea, Associate Justice, with whom Glass, Associate Justice, joins, dissenting.

In this case it is undisputed that the drawer, Cohn Precious Metals, Inc. (Cohn), complied fully with General Statutes §42a-4-403(1) in stopping payment on the checks it had delivered to Lamphere Coin, Inc. (Lamphere), on November 10, 1978, while unaware of the overpayment of $19,606.86 on November 9, 1978. It is also clear that, but for the negligence of the bank in paying the $12,175 check contrary to the stop payment order, Cohn could have offset its overpayment of the previous day against the value of the coins received from Lamphere on November 10, 1978. Thus, as the trial court concluded, the plaintiff trustee, on behalf of Cohn, sustained his "burden of establishing the fact and amount of loss resulting from payment of an item contrary to a binding stop payment order" by the defendant bank, as §42a-4-403(3) requires.

The majority opinion does not challenge, as unsupported by the evidence, the trial court's factual finding that Cohn suffered a loss resulting from the bank's negligent payment of the $12,175 check to Lamphere, but rejects this straightforward "but for" causation analysis in favor of a narrower view of the "resulting from payment" provision of §42a-4-403(3). The majority would restrict a bank's liability for paying a check contrary to a stop order to losses arising from the transaction in which the check was issued, such as a failure of consideration. I disagree, because there is nothing in the text of §42a-4-403(3) or its history to support such an unjustifiable curtailment of the right of the drawer recognized by §42a-4-403(3) to stop payment on a check for any reason, so long as the order is given to the bank in a timely and reasonable manner, as in this case. The right, of course, would be illusory without recourse against the negligent bank.

"The right to stop payment is an established right that was recognized prior to the Code. The right is absolute." J. Reitman et al., 6 Banking Law §133.02. "If the drawer has a good defense on a check against a payee or holder, then the drawer suffers a loss when the bank wrongfully pays the check over a stop payment order." Id. The plaintiff trustee had the burden of proving that Cohn's loss resulted from noncompliance with the stop payment order, just as any negligence victim must prove causation. Even if the standard of causation applicable to breaches of contract should govern, reasonable foreseeability of the damages at the time the drawer and bank enter into this relationship; it is evident that a bank must be deemed to foresee that its payment of a check over a valid stop payment order is likely to cause a loss to the drawer in the amount of the payment. There is nothing in §4-403(3) that warrants a narrower approach to the issue of causation than that applicable to breaches of contract. In order to prevail against a bank that has ignored a stop payment order, "[t]he customer must show that (i) the account was debited, (ii) some other loss was suffered, if applicable, and (iii) bank's noncompliance with the stop order was the 'but for' cause." W. Hillman, Basic UCC Skills 1989, Article 3 and Article 4, p. 319. As the trial court found, those criteria were satisfied by the plaintiff trustee in this case.

In adopting its constricted view of the "loss resulting from the payment of an item contrary to a binding stop payment order" provision of §42a-4-403(3), the majority cites a plethora of authorities, none of which address the issue of whether a bank is excused from liability for failing to obey a stop payment order simply because the drawer had no defense arising out of the transaction in which the check was issued but only a right of set-off from another transaction. Most of the cases cited involve the principle that, when a bank has paid a check on which payment has been stopped, it becomes subrogated to the rights of the payee on the check. The quotation relied upon from E. Peters, A Negotiable Instruments Primer (1974) p. 79, it "is implicit in §4-403(3) that if a check was issued for good consideration ... failure to observe a stop payment order does no more than to accelerate the drawer's inevitable liability," is also based on the right of the bank to assert the rights of the payee on the check as a defense to an action by the drawer. Such a defense would not have been effective in this case, however, because the drawer, Cohn, had no such "inevitable liability," given its right to set off the previous overpayment to Lamphere against the bank's claim as subrogee of Lamphere's rights on the check.

Two of the commentators relied upon by the majority refer to the situation in which a bank has wrongfully debited a customer's account after a stop payment order and this action has resulted in dishonoring for insufficient funds subsequent checks issued by the drawer with the consequence of impairing his credit. E. Peters, supra; 1 J. White & R. Summers, Uniform Commercial Code (3d Ed.1988) p. 912. Although they disagree as to how this problem should be resolved under §42a-4-403(3), they implicitly recognize that the bank's liability for failing to obey a stop payment order may well subject it to liability with respect to other transactions resulting in damages to a drawer that have been caused by the bank's oversight. The narrow concept of causation adopted by the majority cannot be reconciled with the views of these commentators.

The majority stresses the difference between the "resulting from" causation language of §42a-4-403(3) and the more elaborate provision of §42a-4-402 that expressly makes the bank liable for consequential damages for wrongfully dishonoring a check, including such damages as may result from the arrest or prosecution of the customer. Such a provision in §42a-4-402 is probably necessary if liability for such damages is to be imposed because of the contract law limitation of damages to those that are reasonably foreseeable at the time of the contract. 3 Restatement (Second), Contracts §351(1). Such a provision in §42a-4-403(3) is unnecessary to make a bank liable for the amount of a check it has paid after a stop payment order, however, because it is obvious that such a loss to the drawer from the bank's oversight is readily foreseeable.

As the majority acknowledges in a footnote, the official commentary in §42a-4-403 takes the position "that stopping payment is a service which depositors expect and are entitled to receive from banks notwithstanding its difficulty, inconvenience and expense" and that "[t]he inevitable occasional losses through failure to stop should be borne by the banks as a cost of the business of banking." The view of the majority that a drawer should be made to bear a loss that would have been avoided but for the bank's neglect, because it did not arise from the transaction in which the check was issued, places a substantial restriction on the right to stop payment that §42a-4-403(1) purports to give.

With respect to §42a-4-407 and the defendant's claim to be a holder in due course, there is nothing in the record to indicate that the collecting bank ever allowed the payee to draw on the check after it was deposited. Since there is no proof that the collecting bank gave value, the defendant's claim to be subrogated to the status of a holder in due course is without foundation.

Accordingly, I dissent.

First State Bank v. Dixon

Court of Appeals of Arkansas, 1987
21 Ark.App. 17, 728 S.W.2d 192

Corbin, Chief Judge. Appellant, First State Bank of Warren, Arkansas, appeals the jury's award of damages to appellee, George Dixon, d/b/a Dixon Lumber Company & Builders Supply, contending there was not substantial evidence to show that appellee gave appellant a stop-payment order in a sufficient manner as to afford appellant a reasonable opportunity to act. We affirm.

On April 15, 1980, appellee called appellant bank to stop payment on a check he had written earlier that day. He gave appellant's employee, Frances Hargis, the correct account number, check number, date, and payee of the check but misstated the amount of the check as $1,828.73. The correct amount of the check was $1,868.15. A few weeks later, appellee received his bank statement and discovered the bank cashed his check despite his stop-payment order. He notified appellant and requested that appellant credit his account for the amount of the check. Appellant refused, and appellee filed suit for recovery of the check amount.

The record reflects appellee testified that when he gave appellant's employee, Frances Hargis, his stop-payment order, he stated it was his only check written to the payee and that it was drawn for $1,800.00 plus dollars. He stated that he was not advised by anyone at the bank that it needed the exact amount of the check in order to stop payment on it. He testified Frances Hargis advised him not to worry about it, that payment on it was stopped. Frances Hargis testified for appellant that appellant's stop-payment requests were computerized, and appellant had to have the exact amount of a check in order to stop payment. She stated that when appellee called her to stop payment on the check, she told him she would need the exact amount. The information she put on the stop-payment order, she testified, was the figure appellee gave her.

Arkansas Statutes Annotated §85-4-403 (Add.1961) provides [for stopping payment] ***. The Committee Commentary to the above statute is pertinent and provides:

2. The position taken by this section is that stopping payment is a service which depositors expect and are entitled to receive from banks notwithstanding its difficulty, inconvenience and expense. The inevitable occasional losses through failure to stop should be borne by the banks as a cost of the business of banking.

Appellant contends that the necessity of the exact amount of a check for which a stop-payment order is requested is critical because the computerized system it utilizes is a key feature of identification in its stop-payment procedure. We believe this argument, if allowed to prevail, would be inconsistent with the intent of the General Assembly in enacting Arkansas Statutes Annotated §85-4- 403. The commentary previously quoted indicates that the legislature clearly contemplated the burden being placed on the bank in the event of loss in such instances as the case at bar.

The issue of whether or not appellee's stop-payment order was received in such manner as to afford appellant a reasonable opportunity to act upon it was submitted to the jury based upon instructions which included:

> If you find that the [appellee], George Dixon, has complied with [Arkansas Statutes Annotated §85-4-403], then the burden falls on Mr. Dixon to prove the actual amount of his loss; however, if you find that Mr. Dixon failed to give the [appellant] a stop payment order in sufficient time and manner as to afford the [appellant] reasonable opportunity to act, then you must find in favor of the [appellant], First State Bank.
>
> You are instructed the [appellant] admits that on April 15, 1980, the [appellee] told an employee of the [appellant] he desired to stop payment on his check number 1346 drawn on the [appellant] bank on April 15, 1980, in an amount in excess of $1800.00 payable to Lloyd's Chevrolet-Olds.
>
> You are the sole judges on the issue of whether the [appellant] bank failed to exercise ordinary care in the transaction with the [appellee]. If you find the [appellant] failed to exercise ordinary care, then your verdict should be for the [appellee] in the amount you find by a preponderance of the [sic] [appellee] has lost.

After hearing the conflicting testimony of the parties and the instructions of the court, the jury found for appellee. It is within the province of the jury to believe appellee's theory over appellant's version, and on appeal, we only consider whether there is any substantial evidence to support the jury's findings. We hold there was substantial evidence to support the jury's decision that appellee gave his stop-payment order to appellant in a sufficient manner so as to afford appellant a reasonable opportunity to act upon it.

Affirmed.

Louis Falcigno Enterprises, Inc. v. Massachusetts Bank & Trust Co.

Appeals Court of Massachusetts, 1982
14 Mass.App.Ct. 92, 436 N.E.2d 993

[This opinion appears earlier, at pages 202-04 supra. Read it again.]

practice

Case 1

According to D's records, the balance in her general checking account was $1,750. On Tuesday she wrote a check for the purchase price of a new television, $800. In fact, the account contained only $750. D had made a record keeping mistake. On Wednesday the payor bank determined not to pay the $800 check and dishonored it. D had no agreement with the bank obligating the bank to pay overdrafts.

a.   On these facts is the bank liable for wrongful dishonor? 4-401(a); 4-402(a).   *No*

b.   Suppose that for many years the bank had almost always paid D's overdrafts notwithstanding the lack of an express agreement to do so. Same result?   *Probably not*

c.   Suppose that on Wednesday shortly after the bank had determined not to pay the check, D deposited $1,000 cash. Same result? 4-402(c).   *No liability*

d.   Suppose the $1,000 cash was deposited shortly before the bank determined not to pay the check? (Careful! There may be an issue of funds availability.)

e.   Suppose that instead of depositing cash, D deposited a $1,000 payroll check on Monday.

  i.   Does it matter if the bank's policy is next-day availability with respect to all checks?

  ii.   Does it matter that D had recently bounced several checks against her account and the bank reasonably suspected that D was insolvent?

  iii.   Suppose that the bank was aware that the drawer of the check had recently filed Chapter 11 bankruptcy.

f.   Suppose D had made no record keeping mistake. The check was dishonored because, unbeknownst to D, the bank had offset the entire account in satisfaction of an overdue personal loan the bank had made to D. The setoff occurred at the close of business on the very same day the $800 check was presented for payment. Is the bank liable for wrongful dishonor? See 4-303.   *No*

Case 2

On January 8, when D's checking account balance was $1,000, two checks drawn by D were presented to the payor bank for payme nt. One of the checks was dated January 2 and was drawn for $800 payable to D's mortgage company. The other check was drawn on January 4 payable to a finance agency affiliated with the payor bank and represented a $300 payment on an installment car loan. The bank first debited D's account for the $300 car loan payment and then dishonored the check to the mortgage company.

No

a. Was this dishonor wrongful? See 4-303(b).

b. Suppose the $800 mortgage company check arrived and was posted to D's account on Tuesday. The car loan check arrived the next day. At 2:30 p.m. on Wednesday the bank reversed the $800 debit, paid the car loan check, and, before its midnight deadline, returned the mortgage company check to the presenting bank unpaid and stamped "INSUFFICIENT FUNDS." Did the bank act wrongfully? If so, in what sense and as to whom?

Case 3

A is the president and majority stockholder of Z Corp. A's spouse owns the balance of the corporation's stock. Acting for Z Corp., A drew a check on the corporate account to pay for goods purchased from S. The check was wrongfully dishonored by the payor. As a result of the dishonor, neither S nor any other of Z Corp.'s usual suppliers will deal with Z Corp. or A individually.

a. Does A have a cause of action against the payor for wrongful dishonor for damages allegedly suffered by her personally? See 4-402 comment 5; compare *Koger v. East First Nat'l Bank*, 443 So.2d 141 (Fla.App.1983) with *Karsh v. American City Bank*, 113 Cal.App.3d 419, 169 Cal.Rptr. 851 (1980). Would the result be different or more certain if A maintained a perso nal account with the payor bank and thus was herself a "customer" of the bank? See *Casco Bank & Trust Co. v. Bank of New York*, 584 F.Supp. 763 (D.Me.1984). Could Z Corp. assign to A its claim for wrongful dishonor? See *Raymer v. Bay State Nat'l Bank*, 384 Mass. 310, 424 N.E.2d 515 (1981).

b. Does S have a cause of action against the payor

   i. Under 4-402? See *First American Nat'l Bank v. Commerce Union Bank*, 692 S.W.2d 642 (Tenn.App.1985) (neither payee of check nor depositary bank has a cause of action for drawee's wrongful dishonor).

   ii. Under the common law? See 1-103; Michael D. Sabbath, *Drawee Bank's Liability for Wrongful Dishonor: A Proposed Checkholder Cause of Action*, 58 ST. JOHN'S L.REV. 318 (1984).

c. Is the payor bank in *Raymer* liable to the payees of the checks? See 4-215; 4-302.

Case 4

B bought goods from S and paid for them with a $2,000 check drawn on PB Bank. S indorsed the check and deposited the item in her bank, DB Bank, which presented the check for payment to PB Bank, the drawee-payor bank. PB Bank immediately settled with DB Bank for the item. Eventually, PB Bank finally paid the check, but final payment was a mistake because B's account was empty.

a. Can PB Bank recover the $2,000 settlement from DB Bank?

No

b. Can PB Bank recover the $2,000 from B by suing B on the instrument? On some other theory? See 4-401(a) ("even though the charge creates an overdraft"); *Pulaski State Bank v. Kalbe*, 122 Wis.2d 663, 364 N.W.2d 162 (App.1985).

Yes; no

c. Suppose that PB Bank seeks to recover from B not only the amount of the overdraft, but also a $15 fee imposed for processing a check drawn on an account without sufficient funds. The signature card that B signed when she opened her account with PB Bank provided for this fee. See *Perdue v. Crocker Nat'l Bank*, 38 Cal.3d 913, 216 Cal.Rptr. 345, 702 P.2d 503 (1985) (signature card is a contract authorizing NSF charges but it is an adhesion contract and customer states claim for relief in alleging that six-dollar fee for NSF checks that actually cost bank thirty cents to process is unreasonable, unconscionable and unenforceable).

d. B, for her own personal use, bought goods from S and paid for them with a $2,000 check drawn on an account that B maintained jointly with C at PB Bank. The account empowered either B or C, acting alone, to draw against it. C was unconnected with, and unaware of, the transaction between B and S. S indorsed the check and deposited the item in her bank, DB Bank, which presented the check to PB Bank for payment. PB Bank settled with DB Bank for the item. Eventually, PB Bank finally paid the check, but final payment was a mistake because the account of B and C was empty. Can PB Bank recover the $2,000 overdraft from C? See 4-401(b).

Case 5

B purchased goods from S and paid for them by check. S deposited the check in her account at DB, and DB forwarded the item to PB for payment. In the meantime, B discovered that the goods were not as warranted and decided to stop payment on the check.

a. Must a payor bank obey a stop payment order only when the drawer of the check has a good reason for giving the order? Must B even explain to PB her reason for stopping payment? See 4-403(a).

b. Is a drawer criminally liable for stopping payment of a check for property or services? (State law commonly makes it a crime to issue issues a check which, at the time of issuance, the issuer intends not to pay. In addition, restitution can be ordered.)

c.   Suppose that PB obeys B's stop order, dishonors the check upon presentment, and bounces the item back to DB before PB's midnight deadline. DB reversed the provisional credit it had given S for the item and returned it to S before DB's midnight deadline. Can S recover from

No   i.   DB?

No   ii.   PB?

Yes   iii.   B?

Case 6

B purchased goods from S and paid for them by check. S deposited the check in her account at DB. DB forwarded the item to PB for payment. In the meantime, B discovered that the goods were not as warranted and ordered PB to stop payment. PB disobeyed B's stop order and paid the check. In theory, PB is prima facie liable to B. The theory is that, upon issuance of the stop order, the item was not properly payable, and that by paying the item the bank thereby violated 4-401. What defenses can PB possibly raise? PB has both procedural and substantive arguments.

a.   As to procedure, PB can argue that the stop order was not effective or binding, and thus the check remained properly payable, because:

i.   The stop order was not received in a manner sufficient to afford the bank a reasonable opportunity to act on it. 4-403. Here the bank complains about the content of the stop order. The typical complaint of this kind is that the customer supplied inaccurate information about the item that was the target of the stop order. Banks implement stop orders through computers. Computers are literal. So a stop order is practically impotent that does not accurately describe the target check. An inaccurate order may nevertheless have legal potency. See, e.g., *Staff Service Associates, Inc. v. Midlantic Nat'l Bank*, 207 N.J.Super. 327, 504 A.2d 148, 42 UCC Rep.Serv. 968 (1985) (stop order binding and effective against bank even though customer incorrectly reported the amount of the check); *Hughes v. Marine Midland Bank*, 127 Misc.2d 209, 484 N.Y.S.2d 1000 (City Ct.1985) (same where customer gave an incorrect check number).

ii.   The stop order was not received in time to afford the bank a reasonable opportunity to act on it. A stop order comes too late, meaning that the order is not effective and binding against the bank, if any one of the events listed in 4-303(a) occurs before the expiration of a reasonable time after receipt of the stop order.

iii.   The stop order expired by lapse of time. See 4-403(b).

b.   PB's arguments as to substance primarily concern whether the customer suffered any loss because of the bank having paid a check despite a procedurally effective and binding stop order. Who has the burden of proof on the issue of loss suffered by B? Is loss an element of B's cause of action, or is lack of loss a defense for PB? See 4-403(c); 4-407; *Siegel v. New England Merchants Nat'l Bank*, 386 Mass. 672, 437 N.E.2d 218, 33 U.C.C.Rep.Serv. 1601 (1982); *Mitchell v. Republic Bank & Trust Co*, 35 N.C.App. 101, 239 S.E.2d 867 (1978).

c.   If sued by B for paying over the stop order, why might PB file a third-party action against S? See 4-407(3).

Case 7

B buys goods from S and pays with a check. Without any reason whatsoever, B orders the payor bank not to pay the item. As B had hoped would happen, the payor bank paid over the stop order, i.e., it paid the check despite the valid stop order. B sues the payor, alleging that the bank paid an item that was not properly payable.

What prevents B from collecting a windfall? See 4-403(c); 4-407.

Case 8

B agreed to purchase goods from S who demanded a cashier's check in payment of the price. B purchased a cashier's check from State Bank payable to S's order and delivered the check to S in exchange for the goods. Before the check was presented for payment, B discovered that the goods were not as warranted.

a.   B asked State Bank to dishonor the cashier's check and return to B the amount she paid for the check. Must State Bank comply with this request? 4-403(a) ("any item drawn on the customer's account").   *No*

b.   Suppose State Bank complies with B's request and dishonors the cashier's check. S then sues State Bank on the instrument. Who prevails?

c.   Is the analysis any different if the reason for dishonor was failure of the check which B gave State Bank in exchange for the cashier's check? See, e.g., *Hotel Riviera, Inc. v. First Nat'l Bank & Trust Co*, 768 F.2d 1201 (10th Cir.1985) (cashier's check must be honored notwithstanding dishonor of instrument given in exchange for the cashier's check); *Da Silva v. Sanders*, 600 F.Supp. 1008 (D.D.C.1984) (same); Lary Lawrence,*Making Cashier's Checks and Other Bank Checks Cost Effective: A Plea for Revision of Articles 3 and 4 of the Uniform Commercial Code*, 64 MINN.L.REV. 275, 292-304 (1980).

d. Is the analysis any different if B purchased and gave to S a personal money order issued by State Bank rather than a cashier's check? See 4-403(a); *Interfirst Bank v. Northpark Nat'l Bank*, 671 S.W.2d 100 (Tex.App.1984)

Case 9

B purchased goods from S and paid for them with a check issued on the date of the sale, January 2. S mislaid the check which was not discovered until October 4. S presented the check for payment on October 6. The payor dishonored the item.

No

a. Is the payor bank liable to B, its customer, for wrongful dishonor? See 4-404.

Yes

b. Is it possible that the payor bank could incur liability to its customer B by paying the check? See 4-404; *Charles Ragusa & Son v. Community State Bank*, 360 So.2d 231 (La.App.1978).

c. If the check is not paid because it is stale within the meaning of 4-404, does B remain liable to S on the instrument? *Harik v. Harik*, 861 F.2d 139 (6th Cir. 1988) (4-404 has no effect on the drawer's liability to payee); *Wildman Stores, Inc. v. Carlisle Distributing Co., Inc*, 15 Ark.App. 11, 688 S.W.2d 748 (1985) (a drawer is not discharged merely because the check is stale).

Case 10

On January 2, D drew a $2,000 check postdated February 1. The check was presented for payment by a collecting bank on January 4 and was paid by the payor bank. This payment reduced D's account balance to zero. On January 3, D drew a check for $1,000 which was presented on January 5 and dishonored for insufficient funds.

a. Is the bank guilty of wrongful dishonor or otherwise accountable to D? See 4-401(c).

b. Same result if the payor bank had been warned of the postdate on the $2,000 check before this check was presented for payment?

c. If the payor bank is sued by its customer D for prematurely paying the $2,000 check, why might it file a third-party action against the payee of the check? See 4-407. Can the bank use 4-407 to supply it a good defense or counterclaim against D's action?

Case 11

"John purchased a new Vulture automobile from Sam's Auto and issued his personal check in full payment. John's wife, Helen, was violently opposed to this purchase while John was happy with his Vulture. On the following day, Sam endorsed [sic] this check to Bill in payment for some worthless stock which was sold to him in violation of the state's blue sky laws; Sam was a dupe in this purchase. Bill endorsed [sic] this check to Harry on the next day. Harry took the check in good faith, for value, and without knowledge of any of the foregoing events. Harry endorsed [sic] the check to his son, Ben, as a gift. Ben misplaced the check and five months after its issuance presented the check for payment to the drawee bank. Five days before Ben presented the check for payment, John died and the drawee-payee [sic] bank was informed of his death on the day it occurred. By sheer coincidence, Helen (still angry about her husband's purchase of a Vulture), telephoned the bank to stop payment of the check one hour before Ben presented the check for payment. Unfortunately, the teller who paid the check was not informed of the stop-order before payment was made. Helen has sued the bank for its alleged improper payment." Arkansas Bar Examination Question No. 2 (July, 1978).

The Bar Examination directed students to "[i]dentify and discuss and state your opinion on each issue involved." See 4-405.

§ 3. Check Fraud

Check fraud mainly refers to wrongfully altering checks or adding signatures that are unauthorized or otherwise ineffective. The result is that someone -- who usually is relatively innocent -- loses money. Who bears the loss in case of check fraud as between the payor bank and the customer whose account is charged with the tainted item? The usual answer is that the loss falls on the payor bank, unless the bank can establish a defense provided by Article 3 or 4 or extra-Code law. The outcome between these two parties is not the end of the matter, however. There are the further issues: if and how, in check fraud cases, the loss should properly be shifted to a third person. Usually, collecting the loss from the wrongdoer, who in every case is ultimately responsible, is practically impossible because she is financially or otherwise unavailable. Thus the real target in shifting the loss question is almost always another relatively innocent party (who hopefully is also solvent).

Payor bank's liability to its checking-account customer

1. Basis Of Liability

In every instance of check fraud the fundamental basis of a payor bank's accountability to its customer, where the item has been charged to the customer's account, is the rule that only properly payable items can be charged against a customer's account. See 4-401(a). Checks that have been materially altered, or that carry an ineffective signature, are not properly payable.

Ineffective Drawer's Signature

The deposit contract between a payor bank and its customer determines who can draw against the customer's account by specifying whose signature is necessary on checks that are chargeable against the customer's account. Therefore, a check drawn against the account of an individual customer that is signed by someone other than the customer, and without authority from her, is not properly payable and is not chargeable to the customer's account, inasmuch as any "unauthorized signature [on an instrument] is ineffective" as the signature of the person whose name is signed. 3-403(a). Similarly, a check is not properly payable that is drawn on the account of a corporate customer by someone other than the person or persons authorized to draw against the account. Also, in the case where a deposit contract requires multiple signatures on checks drawn against the account, a check not signed by all of the required signatories is unauthorized, 3-403(b), and is not properly payable.

Example

a. T steals D's checkbook. Using D's name or her own name, T draws a check against D's account. The drawee-payor bank pays the check and charges it to D's account. D can force the bank to recredit her account for the amount of the item.

b. The deposit contract between D Corp. and Bank provides that Bank can and will pay checks drawn on the account by the president *or* the comptroller of D Corp. Without authority, an employee of D Corp. draws a check on the account using the president's name. The check is not properly payable and cannot rightfully be charged against the account of D Corp.

c. The deposit contract between D Corp. and Bank provides that Bank can and will pay checks drawn on the account by the president *and* comptroller of D Corp. Both officers must sign the checks. Bank pays a check drawn against the account of D Corp. that is signed only by the comptroller. The check is not properly payable and cannot rightfully be charged against the account of D Corp.

d. Same facts (both officers must sign), except that the comptroller, without authority, also signs the president's name. The check is not properly payable. The unauthorized signature of the president is not operative as the president's signature. So the check lacks a necessary signature.

Ineffective Indorsement

A check that bears a forged or otherwise unauthorized or ineffective indorsement cannot rightfully be charged against the drawer-customer's account because the check was not paid consistently with the drawer's (or subsequent holder's) order and was not properly presented to the payor bank. (Presentment is a demand for payment made by or on behalf of the person entitled to enforce the instrument, usually a holder. 3-501(a). A transferee of a check with an ineffective indorsement cannot be a holder.) In short, a check with any forged indorsement, or an indorsement that is otherwise ineffective, is not properly payable because it was not properly presented and paid. Because the check is not properly payable, it cannot rightfully be charged against the customer's account.

Example

a. B drew a check to S in payment for goods. An employee of S indorsed the check and cashed it at the payor bank. This employee had no responsibilities with respect to D's checks, acted without any authority from S to enforce for S, and used her own name. The bank then charged the amount of the check against B's account. B can force bank to recredit her account. The result is the same if the employee used S's name or indorsed in both her name and S's name.

b. B drew a check to H and W jointly. H indorsed the check and also forged W's indorsement. The payor bank paid the check and charged B's account for the amount of the item. W never got a dime of the payment. Payor bank must recredit B's account, at least to the extent of W's interest in the check. (Remember: "[i]f an instrument is payable to two or more persons not alternatively, it is payable [only] to all of them and may be negotiated, discharged, or enforced only by all of them." 3-110(d).)

But why does B care? Why would B complain against the payor bank for charging the item to her account. The loss to S is obvious. Where is the loss to *B*? In the first example payment was improper because it was not made to a holder. In the second example payment was improper because payment was not made to all of the joint payees. As a result, B was not discharged on the instrument, see 3-602(a) (discharge requires payment to holder); so she was not discharged on the underlying obligation. 3-310(b). B thus remains liable to the payee. If this liability to the payee is enforced, B effectively will "pay" twice, inasmuch as her account has already been debited for the amount of the check. There is the loss to B. (The fuller truth, however, is that S usually enjoys additional actions against other people and often shifts the loss to them instead of B. These other actions are considered in the next chapter.)

Alteration

A check is properly payable only on the terms ordered by the drawer. So an altered check, i.e., a check on which the terms have been wrongfully changed by the payee or someone else, is not properly payable. In the usual case of alteration, the wrongdoer raises the amount of the check. In this case, the check is not properly payable to the extent of the alteration. The payor bank can charge the customer's account according to the original tenor of the item (i.e., in the amount ordered by the customer), 4-401(d)(1), but the difference between the original and raised amounts of the check cannot be charged against the account.

Example

B drew a $50 check to S who cleverly and fraudulently raised the amount to $500, and cashed it, for $500, at payor bank. The bank then charged B's account for $500. B can force the bank to recredit her account for $450.

Wrongfully Completed Checks

For some purposes, a check that is completed other than as authorized is treated as an altered instrument. See 3-115 & 3-407. This is not true in deciding who, as between a payor bank and its customer, bears the loss from a wrongfully completed check. The rule is: A bank which in good faith makes payment to a holder may charge the indicated account of its customer according to the tenor of the check as actually completed, not just in the amount or as otherwise authorized by the customer. 4-401(d)(2). It makes no difference that the bank knows that the item was completed by someone other than the customer so long as the bank was unaware that the *completion* itself was improper. Id.

Example

a. B drew a check to S, leaving the amount blank. S was authorized to complete the check in an amount not exceeding $50. S filled in the amount of $500 and cashed the item at payor bank. The bank can charge B's account to the full extent of $500.

b.   B drew a $500 check, leaving blank the name of the payee. B then gave the check to T and directed T to use the check to purchase certain goods for B, filling in the name of the seller. T filled in her own name and cashed the check at payor bank. The bank can charge the check to B's account.

2. Payor Bank's Defenses

The U.C.C. and other law provide an array of defenses for a payor bank or another defendant in a check fraud case as against a customer or other person who complains of a loss.

Authority

When a customer demands the recrediting of her account for the amount of an item that carried an allegedly ineffective signature, or that has been altered, the payor bank's most basic defense is that the alteration or signature was authorized by a proper person. Authority denies the wrong that is the foundation of the complaint.

The rules on signatures by agents are very important in establishing the defense of authority with respect to signatures. In practice, problem signatures usually are not made by strangers. Problem signatures commonly are made by wrongdoers who were associated with the person whose signature was necessary. They could have been authorized to sign for her. Here are the rules:

- A person's signature on an instrument may be made by an agent or other representative.
- The signature is deemed to be the signature of the represented person, and she is fully bound on the instrument as if she personally had signed it, if the represented person would be bound if the signature were on a simple contract. 3-402(a).
- Whether or not the represented person is so bound is determined by extra-Code agency law. "If under the law of agency the represented person would be bound by the act of the representative [or purported representative] in signing either the name of the represented person or that of the representative, the signature is the authorized signature of the represented person." 3-402 comment 1
- By reference to this extra-Code law, the defense that a signature on an instrument was authorized can be based on express authority, may be implied in law or in fact, or may rest merely on apparent authority.
- Article 3 does not bar parol evidence to prove or deny the authority.
- Article 3 requires no particular form of appointment or form of signature to establish the authority.

* In particular, if the represented person would be bound on a simple contract under extra-Code law, she is bound on the instrument whether or not she is identified in the instrument.

Example

a. B has a checking account with Payor Bank. The deposit contract specifies that B is the sole signatory on checks payable against the account. C drew a check on B's account, using C's own name or B's name. Payor Bank paid the check and charged B's account for the amount of the item. C fled with the proceeds of the check. B sued Bank to force the recrediting of her account. Bank proves at trial that B had expressly or implicitly authorized C to draw checks against the account. Bank wins.

b. The deposit contract between D Corp. and Bank provides that Bank can and will pay checks drawn on the account by the president or comptroller of D Corp. The contract also authorizes the bank to pay checks drawn over the facsimile signature of either of these people, as through the use of a rubber stamp. Without authority, an employee of D Corp. draws a check on the account using a rubber stamp bearing the president's name. The courts are split on whether the check in such a case is properly payable. Some authority says that the check is properly payable and chargeable to the corporation's account due to the terms of the deposit agreement. Other authority argues that the deposit agreement protects the bank only when the facsimile signature is used with appropriate authority. Perhaps the case is better resolved in the bank's favor on the basis of estoppel or the like rather than authority.

c. B drew a check to H and W jointly. H indorsed the check by signing his name and also W's name. Payor Bank paid the check and charged B's account for the amount of the item. W never got a dime of the payment. W complained to B who satisfied the amount she owed W. B then sued Payor Bank who established at trial that W had approved H indorsing the check on her behalf. Bank is not accountable to B. (In fact, B was not accountable to W. Inasmuch as H acted rightfully in dealing with the check, B was discharged on the instrument and the underlying obligation to both H and W.)

d. B gave P a check in settlement of a tort action. The check was payable to P and her attorney in the action, L. Unbeknownst to P, L indorsed the check, which was paid, and used the proceeds for her own purposes. P got nothing. Believing she remained obligated on the settlement, B paid P and attempted to shift the loss to Payor Bank. Whether or not the bank is accountable -- i.e., whether or not the item was properly payable -- depends on whether or not L, as P's attorney in the action, was authorized to sign the settlement check for P. Also, if L had this authority, payment of the check to L discharged B's liability on the instrument and on the underlying settlement.

Ratification

A customer cannot recover against a payor bank on the basis that her signature or an indorsement was forged if the person whose name was signed ratifies the signature. "An unauthorized signature may be ratified for all purposes of this Article." 3-403(a). The effect is that "[t]he unauthorized signature becomes valid so far as its effect as a signature is concerned." 3-403 comment 3. Ratification is retroactive and may be found in conduct as well as in express statements.

Example

The deposit contract between D Corp. and Bank provides that Bank can and will pay checks drawn on the account by the president or comptroller of D Corp. Without authority, an employee of D Corp. draws a check on the account using the president's name. The check is used to purchase widgets. The Bank pays the check and debits the account of D Corp. Upon discovering the fraud, D Corp. fires the employee and confiscates the widgets for the use of D Corp. By retaining the benefits received in the transaction with knowledge of the unauthorized signature, D Corp. thereby ratifies the employee's signature. The signature is thus effective even though the employee was not an authorized agent of D. Corp. So the check is deemed to have been properly payable and D Corp. cannot complain that the check was charged to the corporate account.

Ratification relieves the actual signer of liablity because the represented person adopts it as her own. Nevertheless:

♦ The ratification does not relieve the signer of liability to the person represented.
♦ It does not in any way affect the signer's criminal liability.

3-403 comment 3.

Preclusion By Estoppel

Former law expressly provided that an unauthorized signature could operate as the signature of the represented person when, because of the peculiar circumstances, the person was "precluded from denying it." 3-404(1) (1989 Official Text). It recognized "the possibility of an estoppel against the person whose name is signed, as where he expressly or tacitly represents to an innocent purchaser that the signature is genuine." 3-404 comment 4 (1989 Official Text). Even in the absence of this express provision in the new law, preclusion by estoppel remains possible because of 1-103, which allows principles of common law and equity to supplement the Code.

3-406 (Negligence)

The defense of 3-406 covers preclusion because of certain negligence:

A person whose failure to exercise ordinary care *substantially contributes* to an alteration of an instrument or to the making of a forged signature on an instrument is precluded from asserting the alteration or the forgery against a person who, in good faith pays the instrument or takes it for value or for collection.

3-406(a) (emphasis added).

Not just any negligence effects preclusion under 3-406. The negligence must actually "contribute" to the forgery or alteration. That is, it must afford an opportunity of which advantage is in fact taken. Moreover, the contribution must be *substantial*. The test is less stringent than direct and proximate cause. It is an easier test requiring only that the negligence was a substantial contributing factor in bringing about the alteration or forgery. 3-406 comment 2. "The Code has thus abandoned the language of the older cases (negligence which 'directly and proximately affects the conduct of the bank in passing the forgery') and shortened the chain of causation which the defendant bank must establish. * * * In the instant case, the trial court could readily have concluded that plaintiff's business affairs were conducted in so negligent a fashion as to have 'substantially contributed' to the * * * forgeries, within the meaning of 3-406." *Thompson Maple Products, Inc. v. Citizens Nat. Bank*, 234 A.2d 32, 34-35 (Pa.Super. 1967).

Example

a. Using a No. 2 soft-lead pencil, D draws a $100 check to P's order. With no trouble at all, P erases the amount of the check and raises it to $1,000. The check is properly chargeable to D's account in the amount of $1,000.

b. The deposit contract covering the checking account of D Corp. authorized the payor bank to pay checks drawn over the actual signature of the president of D Corp., or over her facsimile signature imprinted with a rubber stamp whenever the stamp was used by her personally or by someone else authorized to sign for her. Because the company was negligent in looking after the rubber stamp, it was used by an unauthorized person to draw several checks on the corporate account. These checks were paid and charged to the account. D Corp. cannot complain against the payor bank. The company is precluded by 3-406 from asserting the employee's lack of authority.

c. During a two-year period a secretary in the law partnership of Olson & Olsen embezzled more than $100,000 from the firm. He drew checks on the firm's trust account, forging the name of the managing partner who was the only authorized signatory on the account. The secretary was not authorized to draw against the account and had no responsibilities with respect to the firm's checks. The firm was aware that someone was stealing from the account as soon as two months after the secretary's embezzlement began, but took no action to prevent further forgeries. The firm is precluded from complaining about forgeries that occurred after it learned of the problem and had a reasonable time to take preventive action.

d. Jane Smith filed an insurance claim with her carrier, Assured Equity. Upon approval of the claim, the insurer drew a check to Jane Smith but negligently mailed it to the wrong person whose name was the same as the insured. The check was paid, upon the unauthorized signature of the intended Jane Smith, and charged to Assured Equity's account. The payor bank is not accountable to the insurer which is precluded, on the basis of 3-406, from asserting the unintended Jane Smith's lack of authority.

The defense of 3-406 does not entirely fail if the payor bank or other person asserting the preclusion also acted unreasonably in dealing with the instrument. A concept of comparative negligence applies.

[I]f the person asserting the preclusion fails to exercise ordinary care in paying or taking the instrument and that failure substantially contributes to loss, the loss is allocated between the person precluded and the person asserting the preclusion according to the extent to which the failure of each to exercise ordinary care contributed to the loss.

3-406(b). "'Ordinary care' in the case of a person engaged in business means observance of reasonable commercial standards, prevailing in the area in which the person is located, with respect to the business in which the person is engaged." 3-103(a)(7). Significantly, "[i]n the case of a bank that takes an instrument for processing for collection or payment by automated means, reasonable commercial standards do not require the bank to examine the instrument if the failure to do so does not violate the bank's prescribed procedures and the bank's procedures do not vary unreasonably from general banking usage not disapproved by this Article or Article 4." Id.

Example

Janitor steals Employer's blank check form that was negligently left on a desk in Employer's office. Janitor draws a check to herself, signing the name of Employer's president who is the only person authorized to draw on the account. The check is paid and charged to Employer's account. Employer may be precluded from complaining about the forgery because of Employer's negligence. It happens, however, that the payor bank did not attempt to verify the authenticity of the drawer's signature. This failure may be comparative negligence that dilutes the preclusion defense. It can be comparative negligence if the bank's own procedures were violated or, if they were met, if general banking practice was violated by not requiring verification. Banks commonly verify signatures only on items that exceed a certain dollar amount. The likelihood that verification is required increases with the amount of the check.

4-406(c-d) (Breach of Duty to Discover and Report Check Fraud)

Typically, a bank sends its checking-account customer a statement of account that shows payment of items from the customer's account. In so doing the bank returns or makes available to the customer either the items themselves or information sufficient to allow the customer reasonably to identify the items. Article 4 does not directly require this accounting; but if the bank provides such a statement, Article 4 imposes a duty on the customer to examine the items or information with "reasonable promptness * * * to *determine* whether any payment was not authorized because of an alteration of an item or because a purported signature by or on behalf of the customer was not authorized. If, based on the statement or items provided, the customer should reasonably have discovered the unauthorized payment, the customer must promptly *notify* the bank of the relevant facts." 4-406(c) (emphasis added).

The duty on the customer is not imposed unless the bank either (1) returns or makes available the checks paid or (2) provides information sufficient to allow the customer to identify them. Which course the bank follows is a matter of bank-customer agreement; but if their agreement requires the bank only to provide identifying information, the duty on the customer requires adequate information -- "sufficient to allow the customer reasonably to identify the items paid." 4-406 comment 1. Images of the items will do but are not required. It is sufficient that the bank describes the checks by item numbers, amount, and dates of payment. Id. It is not necessary for the bank to identify the payee of each item and the item's date. The customer should be able to determine these two pieces of information from her own records based on the number of the check, its amount and date of payment supplied by the bank.

The effect of a customer's breach of the 4-406(c) duty is described by 4-406(d). If the bank proves that the customer failed to discover or report an unauthorized payment, the customer is precluded from asserting the alteration or the customer's unauthorized signature against the bank. 4-406(d)(1).

Whether or not the bank can prove a loss, the customer is precluded from asserting her unauthorized signature or an alteration by the same wrongdoer on any item paid in good faith by the bank "if the payment was made before the bank received notice from the customer of the unauthorized signature or alteration and after the customer had been afforded a reasonable period of time, not exceeding 30 days, in which to examine the item or statement of account and notify the bank." 4-406(d)(2). This language covers the case of a string of forgeries or alterations by the same wrongdoer. The bank need not establish that it suffered a loss because, in this kind of case, the law presumes loss.

The 4-406(d) preclusion is limited to alterations and forgeries and unauthorized signatures of the customer -- the person who has the account and whose name should have been signed as drawer. The preclusion of (d) therefore never applies to forged indorsements. Typically, the checking account customer has no way of verifying indorsements.

Under former law, the courts were divided on whether or not the duty and preclusion of 4-406 applies in the case where multiple signatures on a check are required by the deposit contract, but the bank pays checks missing one or more of the required signatures. The decisive question is whether or not, in such a case, there is an "unauthorized signature." Article 3 now clearly ends this dispute because the statute expressly provides that "[i]f the signature of more than one person is required to constitute the authorized signature of an organization, the signature of the organization is unauthorized if one of the required signatures is lacking." 3-403(b). This rule will apply even when two natural persons jointly hold an account in their individual capacities because "organization" is a broad term. It includes "a corporation, government or governmental subdivision or agency, business trust, estate, trust, partnership or association, *two or more persons having a joint or common interest,* or any other legal or commercial entity." 1-201(28) (emphasis added).

Even if the customer was negligent so that the preclusion of 4-406(d) applies against her, the bank nevertheless shares the loss if the customer proves that the bank failed to exercise ordinary care in paying the item and that the failure substantially contributed to the loss. 4-406(e). In this event loss is allocated between the customer and the bank according to the extent to which the customer's negligence in not finding or reporting the wrong and the bank's negligence in paying the item contributed to the loss.

If the customer proves that the bank did not pay the item in good faith, the bank completely forfeits the 4-406(d) preclusion defense despite negligence by the customer. 4-406(e).

4-406(f) (One-Year Outside Limit on Customer's Complaints)

Applying the 4-406(d) preclusion rule depends upon determinations as to ordinary care of the customer and the bank. In contrast, 4-406(f) places an *absolute* limit on the right of a customer to make a claim for payment of altered or unauthorized checks *without regard to care or lack of care of either the customer or the bank.* In any event, "a customer who does not within one year after the statement or items are made available to the customer * * * discover and report the customer's unauthorized signature on or any alteration on the item is precluded from asserting against the [payor] bank the unauthorized signature or alteration." 4-406(f). On the other hand, subsection (f) is like 4-406(d) in that neither preclusion defense applies to indorsements. "Section 4-406 imposes no duties on the drawer to look for unauthorized indorsements." 4-406 comment 5. Customers' complaints about ineffective indorsements are covered, however, by the general three-year statute of limitations that applies to any action to enforce any obligation, duty, or right arising under Article 4. See 4-111.

Special Rules for Unauthorized Indorsements in Certain Circumstances

Section 3-404 and 3-405 provide three different rules whereby indorsements of payees are deemed effective in law even though, in fact, they are unauthorized. These rules cover circumstances where, for overriding policy reasons, the loss is generally better left with the drawer-customer -- she cannot shift her loss to the payor bank -- because, in the covered cases, the customer is in the best position to protect against it. Generally, the rules operate in the same way. When an indorsement involves fraud that a rule covers, an indorsement by *any person* in the name of the identified payee is deemed effective as the payee's indorsement in favor of the person who pays or people who take the instrument for value or collection. Section 3-404 applies in certain cases involving impostors and nominal or fictitious payees, and section 3-405 involves fraudulent indorsements by employees on instruments for which their employment gives them some responsibility. Although the main purpose of the statutes is to insulate payor banks from customers' complaints of losses in certain instances of unauthorized indorsements, neither 3-404 nor 3-405 is limited to this purpose, this situation, or to checks. Each statute is generally applicable to any instrument and in any situation that meets its peculiar requirements.

a. When Payees are Impersonated – The Impostor Rule – 3-404(a)

In the *impostor case*, a drawer is induced to issue an instrument because a thief impersonates someone else whom the drawer intends and names as payee. The thief indorses in the name of the payee and induces a third person to take or pay the instrument. Finally, the thief departs with her loot, and the law must determine which of the two innocent and defrauded parties must bear the cost of the wrong. The drawer often complains against her bank for paying the item, arguing that the indorsement was ineffective because the check was payable to the person whom the drawer intended rather than to the thief. Therefore, the item was not properly payable and not chargeable against the customer's account.

The answer to this argument is the *impostor rule* of 3-404(a):

> If an impostor, by use of the mails or otherwise, induces the issuer of an
> instrument to issue the instrument to the impostor, or to a person acting in
> concert with the impostor, by impersonating the payee of the instrument or
> a person authorized to act for the payee, an indorsement of the instrument
> by any person in the name of the payee is effective as the indorsement of the
> payee in favor of a person who, in good faith, pays the instrument or takes it
> for value or for collection.

Regardless of how the imposture is carried out, when the impostor or her confederate or anyone else indorses the instrument, it is as if the real payee of an ordinary order instrument indorsed it. If the indorsement is in blank, the instrument immediately becomes payable to bearer so that the impostor or anyone else in possession of it becomes the holder and the proper person to negotiate it or to receive payment. If the instrument is indorsed specially, by anyone, and delivered to the special indorsee, the latter becomes the holder; and if she otherwise qualifies, she becomes a holder in due course who is entitled to enforce the instrument -- free from defenses -- against the defrauded maker or drawer. If a drawee pays the holder, whether she be the impostor or anyone else, the drawee is entitled to charge the drawer's account because a payment to the holder is in accordance with the drawer's order. The net result is that the ultimate loss is normally borne by the defrauded maker or drawer rather than by the transferee from the defrauder or by the drawee who pays the impostor or a transferee.

Example

a. Upon answering a knock at her door, D, a religious fundamentalist, found a man who said his name was Pastor Oral Roberts and asked for a contribution to his cause of returning God to the classroom. The man represented himself as THE Oral Roberts who is a famous evangelist and faith healer. D thus gave the man a check for $500 payable to the order of Oral Roberts. In fact, the man was a crook who used the proceeds of the check for his own purposes. Upon discovering that she had been swindled, D demanded that the drawee-payor bank recredit her account. D argued that the indorsement on the check was not the signature of the intended payee, the real Oral Roberts, and that consequently the check was not properly payable. D loses. The crook's signature was effective under 3-404(a).

b. Same facts, except that the impostor had obtained the check as a result of a solicitation letter sent through the mail to D. The result is the same.

In a variant case, the defrauder, instead of misrepresenting herself to be another, misrepresents herself to be the agent of another, and thereby induces a maker or drawer to issue the negotiable instrument made payable to her alleged principal. The impostor rule of former law did not apply in this case, and effective negotiation of the instrument was not possible unless the alleged principal, herself, indorsed the instrument. The impostor rule of 3-404(a) changes this result. It is wider and expressly applies when an impostor impersonates "the payee of the instrument *or a person authorized to act for the payee*." 3-404(a) (emphasis added). An indorsement in the payee's name by the supposed "agent" or anyone else is effective. The defrauded maker or drawer again bears the loss.

Example

Suppose that the man at D's door falsely represented that he was an assistant minister to the real Oral Roberts and was authorized to act for Pastor Roberts. D gave the man a check payable to Oral Roberts. D indorsed the check using the name of Oral Roberts and cashed it. The check was paid and charged to D's account. 3-404(a) does protects the drawee against D's demand that her account be recredited with the amount of the check.

b. *When Payees Are Imagined – Rule of the Nominal or Fictitious Payee – 3-404(b)*

The *nominal or fictitious payee* is an entirely different kind of fraud but is handled similarly by 3-404. Suppose that X gives Y general authority to issue checks drawn on B Bank to pay X's creditors and employees. Intending to cheat X, and enrich herself, Y draws a check for $3,000 on B Bank payable to the order of F, and signs X's name as drawer. F is neither a creditor nor an employee, and Y intends F to have no interest in the check. Y indorses the check in the name of F naming herself as special indorsee. Y promptly cashes the check at B Bank and retains the proceeds. B Bank charges X's account for the $3,000. When X learns of Y's duplicity, X demands that the bank recredit her account for $3,000. When B Bank refuses, X sues B Bank. Both X and B Bank agree that X was liable on the check and that B Bank had a right to charge X's account if, but only if, the check was properly payable, which requires that Y was a holder. X contends that Y was not a holder because the check was payable to the order of F, who was therefore the only appropriate party to indorse. Because the instrument was never indorsed by F, Y could not become holder. Logically, there is much to be said for X's position.

As a matter of policy, however, the Code favors B Bank. It does so by this rule:

If (i) a person whose intent determines to whom an instrument is payable * * * does not intend the person identified as payee to have any interest in the instrument, or (ii) the person identified as payee of an instrument is a fictitious person, the following rules apply until the instrument is negotiated by special indorsement:

(1) Any person in possession of the instrument is its holder.

(2) An indorsement by any person in the name of the payee stated in the instrument is effective as the indorsement of the payee in favor of a person who, in good faith, pays the instrument or takes it for value or for collection.

3-404(b). In terms of this rule, Y's intent determined to whom the check was payable because Y was the person who signed the check, even though Y was signing on behalf of X. 3-110(a). At the time of issuing the check, Y did not intend F to have any interest in the check. Therefore, because of 3-404(b)(1), Y was a holder before the special indorsement. Also, the indorsement of Y (or her confederate or anyone else), in the name of F, the named payee, had the same effect as if F, the named payee, had indorsed. Consequently, after the special indorsement to herself, Y was a holder because she was still in possession of an instrument that ran to her. When a person draws a negotiable draft or check she orders the drawee to pay the holder. Therefore, when the bank in good faith paid Y who was a holder, the bank was obeying X's order and so was entitled to charge X's account.

The result is the same even with these variations in the problem:

- ◆ F was an actual creditor of X . The key is that Y did not intend F to have an interest in the check.
- ◆ F was nonexistent, made-up, fictitious. Ditto.
- ◆ Checks of X must be signed by two persons, Y and Z. They both sign the check to F. As far as Z knows, the check is intended to pay a legitimate debt owed F. Y intends to keep the check for himself.

On the other hand, section 3-404(b) would not apply if F, the payee, were a real person and Y did not decide to steal the check until after issuing it. If the payee is fictitious, it is irrelevant when Y makes the decision to steal the instrument.

The rule of 3-404(b) also would not apply if Y had not actually signed the check as, or for, the maker or drawer of the instrument. Suppose that, instead of actually drawing the check, Y merely prepared it for X's signature and that X signed it thinking that F was a creditor. Or suppose that instead of preparing the check, Y merely prepared a list or report on which F's name falsely appeared as creditor. In these situations, 3-404(b) does not apply because Y is not the person whose intent determined to whom the check is payable. It was X. The person to whom an instrument is "payable is determined by the intent of the person, whether or not authorized, signing as, or in the name or behalf of, the issuer of the instrument." 3-110(a). In effect, when the payee is a real person, 3-404(b) only applies if the actual "drawer or maker does not intend the payee to have any interest in the instrument." 3-404 comment 2.

It is a different case, however, if the payee is fictitious. In this event, 3-404(b) applies regardless of the intent of the actual drawer or maker. It is also a different case, even if the payee is a real person, if X's signature is made by a check-writing machine or other automated means that Y uses to issue the check payable to F. In this event, the payee is determined by the intent of the person supplying the name of the payee. 3-110(b). On these facts, this person is Y. It would seem, therefore, that 3-404(b) applies. 3-404 comment 2 (Case # 4). Section 3-405 may also apply if Y is an employee.

————

Take note that 3-404 works only on indorsements. Unauthorized drawer's signatures are not deemed effective by either 3-404(a) or (b). If in any of these examples the signature of X, the drawer, is ineffective, X is not liable to anyone on the check (but Y may be liable). The check, therefore, is not properly payable with respect to X's account and cannot be charged against this account by the drawee-bank whether or not 3-404 applies. Suppose, for example, that Y has no authority to act for X in any regard. Y drew a check on X's account using X's name. To hide the fraud, Y drew it payable to F, a person with whom X regularly does business. Y did not intend F to have an interest in the instrument. The drawee paid it. The check, however, is not properly payable because X did not draw it. Section 3-404 does not solve this problem. The bank cannot charge X's account.

Subsections 3-404(a) and (b) are also alike in that the only bogus indorsement that either rule makes effective is an indorsement "in the name of the payee." Under former law, some cases required the indorsement to be in exactly the same name as the named payee. These cases are rejected. Under 3-404(a) or (b), an indorsement is effective if in a name "substantially similar" to the name of the payee. 3-404(c). Moreover, an indorsement that is wildly different, or no indorsement at all, is effective if the instrument is deposited in a depositary bank to an account in a name substantially similar to that of the payee. Id. This allowance is based on the rule that checks may be deposited for collection without indorsement. See 4-205(1).

Another similarity between 3-404(a) and (b) is that they both protect not only a person who pays an instrument in circumstances to which the rules apply. Both rules also protect a person who takes an instrument for value or for collection.

Example

a. Suppose that X gives Y general authority to issue checks drawn on B Bank to pay X's creditors and employees. Intending to cheat X, and enrich herself, Y draws a check for $3,000 on B Bank payable to the order of F, and signs X's name as drawer. F is neither a creditor nor an employee, and Y intends F to have no interest in the check. Y indorses the check in the name of F naming herself as special indorsee. Y promptly cashes the check at B Bank and retains the proceeds. B Bank charges X's account for the $3,000. When X learns of Y's duplicity, X demands that the bank recredit her account for $3,000. When B Bank refuses, X sues B Bank. B Bank wins.

b. Suppose that instead of Y herself presenting the check and getting payment from the drawee bank, she promptly indorsed in F's name and cashed or deposited the check at C Bank. This bank presented the item for payment but B Bank, the drawee, dishonored. C Bank is a holder because of 3-404(b). It can sue Y as indorser and, more important, X as drawer. Moreover, if C Bank is a holder in due course, it can take free of X's defenses and claims, including any defense based on Y's tackiness.

Subsections 3-404(a) and (b) equally take into account the negligence of the person who pays or takes the instrument for value or collection. They do so by this qualification to both rules:

> With respect to an instrument to which subsection (a) or (b) applies, if a person paying the instrument or taking it for value or for collection fails to exercise ordinary care in paying or taking the instrument and that failure substantially contributes to loss resulting from payment of the instrument, the person bearing the loss may recover from the person failing to exercise ordinary care to the extent the failure to exercise ordinary care contributed to the loss.

3-404(d). Such negligence can be even more potent. Suppose that in the example immediately above, C Bank was negligent in not detecting the wrongdoing when Y deposited or cashed the check there. In this event, even if C Bank was a holder in due course, X could discount its liability by the value of C Bank's negligence. Yet, becoming a holder in due course requires taking the instrument in good faith, which "means honesty in fact *and the observance of reasonable commercial standards of fair dealing.*" 3-103(a)(4) (emphasis added). Arguably, then, C Bank's negligence prevents it from being a holder in due course so that X would have a complete defense to liability. The result is probably the same either way.

On the other hand, establishing that C Bank was negligent is not a slam dunk. Look at this definition of *"ordinary care,"* which certainly applies to 3-404 and maybe also applies to the meaning of good faith:

> "Ordinary care" in the case of a person engaged in business means observance of reasonable commercial standards, prevailing in the area in which the person is located, with respect to the business in which the person is engaged. In the case of a bank that takes an instrument for processing[,] for collection or payment by automated means, *reasonable commercial standards do not require the bank to examine the instrument if* the failure to examine does not violate the bank's prescribed procedures and the bank's procedures do not vary unreasonably from general banking usage not disapproved by this Article or Article 4.

3-103(a)(7) (emphasis added). The outcome in C Bank's case may depend on whether it dealt with Y through an individual who normally would be required to examine the instrument and check identification, or by some other means less likely to trigger such a duty.

c.   *When Employees Steal Checks for Which They Are Responsible – 3-405*

Section 3-405 focuses on employee fraud. It was added in 1990 and is among the two or three most important innovations of the 1990 changes in Article 3. Formerly, employers often could shift and avoid losses caused by employee fraud if the fraud did not fit the relatively narrow rules of 3-404 covering impostors, nominal or fictitious payees and did not involve employer negligence that would trigger 3-406. The drafters of the 1990 Article 3 reconsidered how fairly to distribute losses caused by employee fraud. The balance they reached is different from former law, and less favorable to employers. It is expressed in the policy and language of 3-405 that employers should be originally responsible for a wider range of employee fraud when, and solely because, the fraud is committed by an employee who was entrusted with responsibilities with respect to instruments. The basic reason is that employee fraud is really an employment matter and is better dealt with as such.

Although 3-405 applies to any kind of instrument, the normal case for applying 3-405 will involve checks, and will usually be between the employer, as drawer or payee, and a collecting bank that cashed the checks or a drawee bank that paid them. The issue is always who bears the loss between the employer and the bank. The loser always has a right to recover over from the wrongdoer; but, almost always, the wrongdoer is financially unavailable.

Section 3-404, which is discussed earlier, overlaps with 3-405. Some cases fit both sections. As to these cases, 3-405 may eclipse 3-404 because the elements of the former may be easier to prove. The eclipse is not total, however, because 3-404 is not limited to employee fraud. On the other hand, the kinds of fraud that 3-404 covers are usually committed by employees, so that 3-404 will not work nearly as hard as its statutory predecessors or be as important in Article 3's scheme for distributing fraud losses. Section 3-405 will be worked to death because, although it is limited to employee fraud, it alone covers a wider range of fraudulent conduct than all of the former rules of check fraud combined, and also because most check fraud is committed by employees.

Section 3-405 is big but the core rule of 3-405 is small and easy to understand. It is the first sentence of subsection (b):

> [I]f an employer entrusted an employee with responsibility with respect to the instrument and the employee or a person acting in concert with the employee makes a fraudulent indorsement of the instrument, the indorsement is effective as the indorsement of the person to whom the instrument is payable if it is made in the name of that person.

3-405(b). In some respects this rule is similar to the rules of 3-404. For both 3-404 and 3-405(b):

- The same standard determines if the indorsement is in the same name as the payee, "substantially similar."
- The indorsement is effective only in favor of a person who, in good faith, pays an instrument or takes it for value or for collection.
- Finally, the effectiveness is discounted by such a person's negligence in paying or taking the instrument.

These matters, however, are details. In the main, 3-405 is very different and much broader than 3-404, covering cases of employee fraud that would fit 3-404 and more. Most significantly, 3-405 covers the simple case in which an employee with certain responsibility does nothing more than steal checks that are issued *by* her employer for accounts payable, or checks that are issued *to* her employer for accounts receivable.

Example

a. Suppose that X gives Y, an employee, the job of verifying, electronically recording, and sending checks that X draws to pay accounts she owes other people. Y plays no role in deciding to whom these checks are payable. In fact, she plays no other role whatsoever with respect to the checks. One day, Y stole several checks and forged the payees' indorsement. The instruments were paid. Ordinarily, because of the missing indorsements of the payees, the checks are not properly payable; and the drawee bank cannot charge them to X's account. Because of 3-405, however, the indorsements are effective since X entrusted Y with responsibilities with respect to the checks. Because the indorsements are effective, the checks are properly payable and thus chargeable to X's account. The loss stays with X. She cannot shift it to anyone other than Y, who is financially unavailable. Of course, the result is the same if Y's duties include deciding to whom the checks are payable, as by determining and reporting accounts payable.

b. Suppose that the stolen checks were received by X rather than issued by X. Instead of drawer, X was payee. Y could easily take the checks because her job also involved processing payments on accounts receivable. Y forged X's indorsement and the checks were cashed by D Bank, a depositary bank, and paid by the drawee. Ordinarily, X could shift the loss to either bank by way of a conversion action based on her forged indorsements. Because of 3-405, however, the indorsements by Y are effective. There is no basis for conversion against anyone. The loss once again stays with X.

Both of these examples are beyond 3-404. In the absence of 3-405, the employer very likely could shift the losses to the banks, which frequently happened under former law. The loss now stays with the employer.

The real keys to 3-405, which largely determine its reach, are four terms:

Employee. There is no special definition of "*employee*." Its ordinary meaning controls, except that the term includes an independent contractor and employee of an independent contractor. 3-405(a)(1). Officers, executives, and other white-collar workers are included equally with other employees.

Entrusted. This term likewise lacks any special meaning. It probably includes any conduct whereby the responsibility is expressly given or assigned to the employee by the employer, and also the employer's acquiescence in the employee keeping responsibilities that she otherwise assumed. Cf. 2-403(3).

Responsibility With Respect to Instruments. The most critical term is "*responsibility with respect to instruments*." It is a new term of art with a special (and very long) definition which generally means having authority to act as to instruments in a responsible capacity. 3-405(a)(3)(vi). It includes authority:

- to sign or indorse instruments on behalf of the employer;
- to process instruments received by the employer for bookkeeping purposes, for deposit to an account, or for other disposition;
- to prepare or process instruments for issue in the name of the employer;
- to supply information determining the names or addresses of payees of instruments to be issued in the name of the employer; and
- to control the disposition of instruments issued in the name of the employer.

3-405(a)(3)(i-v). The term "does not include authority that merely allows an employee to have access to instruments or blank or incomplete instrument forms that are being stored or transported or are part of incoming or outgoing mail, or similar access." 3-405(a)(3). This access does not empower the employee to act in a sufficiently *responsible capacity* with respect to instruments. Thus, a janitor or mail room clerk does not have "responsibility with respect to instruments" even though the job gives her constant access to checks going from and coming to the employer.

Suppose that a janitor steals a batch of checks from the desk of the accounts payable clerk. They are properly drawn by the employer and payable to various of the employer's suppliers. The janitor's unauthorized indorsements in the suppliers' names are not made effective under 3-405. It is inapplicable because the janitor is not an employee entrusted with responsibility with respect to instruments. Section 3-404 is also inapplicable. Likewise, neither section applies if the mail room clerk steals and indorses incoming checks payable to the employer.

Fraudulent Indorsement. The last term, "*fraudulent indorsement*," also limits the kinds of fraud that 3-405 covers. It means:

- in the case of an instrument payable to the employer, a forged indorsement purporting to be that of the employer, or
- in the case of an instrument with respect to which the employer is the issuer, a forged indorsement purporting to be that of the person identified as payee.

3-405(a)(2). An indorsement is not fraudulent that a person is authorized to make. Therefore, 3-405 will not apply when the wrongdoer causes the employer to issue the checks payable to the wrongdoer herself that she then indorses. It is also inapplicable when the employee steals checks that, as part of her job, she stamped with the employer's unrestrictive, blank indorsement. In both cases the indorsements are authorized, not forged. In both cases there is fraud, but not in the indorsements themselves.

It is more obvious, but very significant, that 3-405 is also inapplicable to any forged or unauthorized signature of the employer as drawer, maker, or acceptor.

Thus, whenever an employee without authority issues checks in the name of the employer, 3-405 does not make the signatures effective against the employer even if the employee was entrusted with responsibility with respect to instruments. The rule of 3-405 applies only to indorsements, not signatures in any other capacity. Because of the ineffective drawer's signature, the drawee bank cannot charge the checks to the employer's account unless some other rule prevents the employer from shifting the loss to the bank.

———

Like 3-404 and 3-406, 3-405 also accounts for comparative fault. "If the person paying the instrument or taking it for value or for collection fails to exercise ordinary care * * * and that failure substantially contributes to loss resulting from the fraud, the person bearing the loss may recover from the person failing to exercise ordinary care to the extent the failure to exercise ordinary care contributed to the loss." 3-405(b) (second sentence).

Example

A computer that controls Employer's check-writing machine was programmed to cause a very large check to be issued to a well-known national corporation, such as General Motors, Inc. (GM), to which Employer owed money. Employee fraudulently changed the address of GM in the computer data bank to Employee's post office box. Employee was an accounts payable clerk whose duties included entering information into the computer. The check was subsequently produced by the check-writing machine and mailed to the Employee's box. She got the check, indorsed it in the name of GM, and deposited the check to an account in Depositary Bank which Employee had opened in GM's name. The Bank had opened the account without requiring Employee to produce any resolution of the corporation's board or other evidence of authorization of Employee to act for GM. In due course, the check is presented for payment; Depositary Bank receives payment; and Employee is allowed to withdraw the credit by wire transfer to a foreign bank. Employer remains obligated to General Motors, and cannot recover from the drawee bank because the indorsement was effective and thus the item was properly payable. Employer can recover from Depositary Bank, however, to the extent the finder of fact concludes (as it should) that Depositary Bank was negligent and that its negligence contributed to Employer's loss.

Payor bank versus people upstream in the collection chain (primarily, presentment warranties)

A check that has been altered, or that carries an unauthorized signature of the drawer or an indorser, is not properly payable and cannot rightfully be charged to the account against which it was drawn. Thus, if the payor bank pays the check, the payment cannot be recouped from the account. So, as against its checking account customer, the bank must bear the check fraud loss. Usually, the only way the payor bank can shift the loss to someone else is by a claim for breach of warranty based on 4-208. It establishes implied warranties that benefit payor banks which pay or accept items:

> If an unaccepted draft is presented to the drawee for payment or acceptance and the drawee pays or accepts the draft, (i) the person obtaining payment or acceptance, at the time of presentment, and (ii) a previous transferor of the draft, at the time of transfer, warrant to the drawee that pays or accepts the draft in good faith that:
> (1) the warrantor is, or was, at the time the warrantor transferred the draft, a person entitled to enforce the draft or authorized to obtain payment or acceptance of the draft on behalf of a person entitled to enforce the draft;
> (2) the draft has not been altered; and
> (3) the warrantor has no knowledge that the signature of the purported drawer of the draft is unauthorized.

4-208(a). As is apparent, these presentment warranties do not cover every kind of check fraud. Thus, the payor bank cannot unload every kind of check fraud loss.

The warranties, though limited as they are, are made by the person who obtains payment and also by every previous transferor. The warranties arise automatically, that is, the warranties are implied by law and are not conditioned on the warrantor expressly making them or even being aware that warranties are made as part of the collection process. The warranties are triggered whenever a check is presented and paid, but the person obtaining payment is not the only warrantor. Also making the presentment warranties to the bank is every previous transferor of the check. This means that a payor bank is not limited, in a breach of warranty action on a check, to suing the person who presented the item and obtained payment. The payor bank can recover from any collecting bank or other person in the collection chain or from any prior transferor if a 4-208 warranty was breached at the time of this person's transfer. A previous transferor would not be responsible for breach of the warranty against alteration if the check was altered after she transferred it.

1. Major Defenses In Warranty Action

Payor Bank's Lack of Good Faith

No one is liable to a payor bank for breach of warranty with respect to a check the bank paid if, in paying the item, the payor bank acted without good faith. The presentment warranties of 4-208 are made only to a payor which *in good faith* pays or accepts the item. On the other hand, the drawee's negligence -- failure to exercise ordinary care in making payment -- is irrelevant. 4-208(b).

Laches

In asserting breach of warranty, a payor bank must notify the warrantor within 30 days after acquiring "reason to know of the breach and the identity of the warrantor." 4-208(e). Otherwise, "the warrantor is discharged to the extent of any loss caused by the delay in giving notice of the claim." Id.

Failure to Assert Defenses Against Customer

Articles 3 and 4 provide a payor bank with various defenses in check fraud cases. In certain situations, ineffective indorsements are deemed valid; and for various reasons a drawer is precluded from complaining about an unauthorized indorsement or alteration. See 3-404, 3-405, 3-406 & 4-406. A payor bank should not be allowed to ignore these defenses, accept the check fraud loss from its customer, and then pass the loss to someone upstream in the collection process by way of a warranty or other action. To allow such shifting of the loss would undermine the purposes and policies behind the Code defenses or upset the balancing of liabilities that the whole scheme of defenses is designed to achieve. For this reason, Article 4 encourages a payor bank to assert its defenses against a customer by giving warrantors this derivative protection:

> If a drawee asserts a claim for breach of warranty under subsection (a) [4-208(a)] based on an unauthorized indorsement of the draft or an alteration of the draft, the warrantor may defend by proving that the indorsement is effective under Section 3-404 or 3-405 or the drawer is precluded under Section 3-406 or 4-406 from asserting against the drawee the unauthorized indorsement or alteration.

4-208(c).

Example

a.   B drew a check to S who fraudulently raised the amount of the item. S cashed the item at DB Bank which presented the item for payment to the drawee, PB Bank. The check, as altered, was paid and charged to B's account. B did not discover the alteration until 14 months after receiving from PB the canceled item and a statement of account covering it. B demanded that PB recredit her account, arguing that the check was not properly payable beyond the original tenor of the item. Although B's claim against PB was barred by 4-406(f), PB recredited B's account for the amount of the alteration and, in the process, waived the 4-406 defense against B's claim. PB then sued DB Bank for breach of the 4-208(a) payment warranty against alteration. DB wins. Because PB waived its 4-406 defense to B's claim, 4-208 and 4-406 preclude PB from asserting any claim against DB based on the alteration.

b.   B drew a check to S and negligently mailed it to another person named S. This person cashed the check at DB Bank, after indorsing the item in her name. PB Bank, the drawee, paid the check and charged it to B's account. After satisfying her debt to S, B sued PB Bank for charging her account with an item that was not properly payable, and PB Bank filed a third party claim against DB Bank for breach of the 4-208(a)(1) presentment warranty. PB Bank decided to recredit B's account, ignoring the advice of DB Bank that B's claim was precluded by 3-406 (negligence substantially contributing to unauthorized signature). In the third-party action, DB Bank can defend against PB's warranty action by proving that B was precluded by 3-406 from asserting the unauthorized indorsement against PB. It is uncertain whether or not this defense is pro tanto. Suppose that B's negligence would have reduced her recovery against PB but would not have provided a complete defense. Is DB's derivative reliance on 3-406 similarly reduced?

Signature Not Unauthorized

When a payor bank's breach of warranty claim is based on an unauthorized signature, it is a good defense that the signature was actually authorized (expressly or impliedly) by the person whose name was signed, or was otherwise effective under agency law or other extra-Code law. This defense is asserted by the warrantor in its own right and directly against the payor bank, and is not premised on the payor bank having failed to raise the defense against the bank's customer. The defense, if proved, undermines completely the very foundation of the payor bank's claim.

Example

B drew a check to S on an account at PB Bank. Signing S's name, T indorsed the check and cashed it at DB Bank. PB Bank paid the check and charged it to B's account. When B complained that the check was not properly payable because it lacked S's indorsement, PB Bank recredited B's account and sued DB Bank for breach of the 4-208(a)(1) warranty. DB Bank wins if it can establish that T had authority to indorse the check on S's behalf, just as DB would win (because of 4-208(c)) if the case were covered by 3-404 or 3-405 so that any person's indorsement in S's name was deemed effective.

2. Recovery Over Using 4-207 Transfer Warranties

A person who is liable to a payor bank for breaching a 4-208 presentment warranty can often pass the loss to someone else further upstream in the collection process on the basis of the transfer warranties implied by 4-207, which provides:

> A customer or collecting bank that transfers an item and receives a settlement or other consideration warrants to the transferee and to any subsequent collecting bank that:
> (1) the warrantor is a person entitled to enforce the item;
> (2) all signatures on the item are authentic and authorized;
> (3) the item has not been altered;
> (4) the item is not subject to a defense or claim in recoupment (Section 3-305(a)) of any party that can be asserted against the warrantor; and
> (5) the warrantor has no knowledge of any insolvency proceeding commenced with respect to the maker or acceptor or, in the case of an unaccepted draft, the drawer.

4-207(a). In addition, each customer and collecting bank that transfers an item and receives a settlement or other consideration is obligated to pay the item if the item is dishonored. 4-207(b).

As you can see, the 4-207 transfer warranties cover the same kinds of fraud and more that are covered by the presentment warranties of 4-208. So, in any case where a presentment warranty is breached, there is a corresponding transfer warranty. The transfer warranties thus ordinarily insure that any check fraud loss unloaded by a payor bank can be passed upstream to the very beginning of the collection chain, thereby protecting every collecting bank through which the check passed. This is possible because the transfer warranties are made, in seriatim order, by *each* customer and collecting bank who transfers an item and receives a settlement or other consideration for it, and they run in favor of the customer's or collecting bank's "transferee and to *any subsequent collecting bank*." 4-207(a). A transferee not protected by 4-207 may find protection among the similar warranties of 3-416 which covers transfers of instruments outside of the check collection process.

Example

B drew a check on her account at PB Bank, and gave it to S in payment for goods. T stole the check from S and cashed it at DB Bank, after forging S's indorsement. DB Bank forwarded the item for collection through an intermediary bank, IB Bank. IB presented the check for payment to PB Bank which paid the item and charged it to B's account. Upon learning of the theft, S demanded the price of the goods sold to B. B paid S in cash, and then demanded that PB Bank recredit her account for the amount of the check because the check was not properly payable. PB Bank did so. Now PB Bank can sue, for breach of the presentment warranty of 4-208(a)(1), any of the following: IB Bank, DB Bank, or T. Suppose that PB Bank sues IB Bank. IB Bank, in turn, can sue DB Bank or T for breach of the corresponding transfer warranty. See 4-207(a)(1). If IB Bank sues DB Bank, the latter bank can rely on the same transfer warranty to recover from T.

Upon scanning the 4-207 transfer warranties, you will notice that the list includes a warranty that "all signatures on the item are authentic and authorized," 4-207(a)(2), which is not limited by a requirement that the warrantor know of the problem. You might conclude that this warranty would permit a payor bank to shift a loss resulting from a forged drawer's signature where prior parties were unaware of the forgery. You are wrong! Remember: The 4-207 transfer warranties do not run in favor of payors. The only warranties to payors are the payment warranties of 4-208, which are less inclusive than the transfer warranties.

3. Payor Bank's Restitution Action To Shift Losses Not Covered By Payment Warranties

You surely will notice that certain check fraud and other kinds of losses that a payor bank can suffer are not covered by the 4-208 payment warranties. Most noticeable are losses resulting from checks bearing unauthorized drawers' signatures when the lack of authority is unknown to prior parties, payments over valid stop orders, and losses resulting from overdrafts (a/k/a NSF checks) that cannot be collected from customers because the customers are insolvent or otherwise unable or unavailable to satisfy the overdrafts.

Payor banks sometimes argue mistake and rely on restitution law or some other common-law theory to recoup these losses from persons who obtained payment of such items or who otherwise received the proceeds of them. Section 3-418 sanctions the common-law restitution claim in 3-418(b) and, to some extent, codifies restitutionary liability in 3-418(a) which covers the two most common cases of mistaken payment: payment of forged checks and checks on which the drawer has stopped payment. If the case does not fit within (a), however, the bank is then free under (b) to resort to the common law which, rather than 3-418.

On the other hand, 3-418 creates a huge defense to both common law and statutory restitution:

> The remedies provided by subsection (a) or (b) may not be asserted against a person who took the instrument in good faith and for value or who in good faith changed position in reliance on the payment or acceptance.

3-418(c). It is a defense to any action by any payor to recover payment or escape acceptance made on any instrument without regard to the nature of the error the payor made as to the state of the drawer's account. So the defense is available whether the loss to the payor was caused by a forged drawer's signature; an overdraft; payment over a stop order; or any other circumstance giving reason for the payor bank's complaint. Behind 3-418(c) is the argument for finality of payment, and this argument applies whatever the payor's reason for avoiding payment or acceptance. Also behind 3-418(c) is the additional reason that the drawee is responsible for knowing the state of the account before acceptance or payment.

There are two limitations on the 3-418(c) defense. First, the defense is only available to a holder in due course (or other good faith purchaser) or a person who in good faith changed her position in reliance on the payment. As against anyone else, the equities favor allowing the payor to recover payments mistakenly made. (Practically speaking, however, in most cases any solvent party who benefited from payment will have taken the check in good faith and for value so that the defense is available to her.) Second, 3-418(c) is no defense for anyone to a payor's recovery for breach of a presentment warranty or to recovery of a bank settlement under 4-301. In these cases other concerns override the policies behind 3-418(c).

Together, the 4-208 presentment warranties and the 3-418(c) defense to restitution allocate check losses on the basis of whether the payor bank or someone else was in a better position to protect against the loss. In the case of a forged drawer's signature or an overdraft, for example, the payor bank occupies the superior position because the bank should know the balance of the customer's account, and (in theory) can check the authenticity of a drawer's signature on a check by comparing it to the customer's signature on the deposit contract on file with the bank. For this reason, a loss caused by the payor bank paying an overdraft or a check bearing a forged drawer's signature is not covered by a warranty (except when the forgery is known to the prior party), and shifting the loss by way of a common-law action is barred by 3-418(c).

On the other hand, detecting forged indorsements is practically impossible (even in theory) for a payor bank. The person best able to uncover such an unauthorized signature is the person who deals with the forger. So, a payor bank can shift a loss resulting from paying a check with a forged indorsement because this problem is covered by a payment warranty. Moreover, recovery on this basis, i.e., warranty, is not barred by 3-418(c). The transfer warranties of 4-207 allow passing the loss to the start of the check collection process. If the loss is not thereby placed on the person who dealt with the forger, the loss can ultimately reach this person by way of the transfer warranties of 3-416, which are similar to 4-207 but apply to transfers beyond the check collection chain.

Payee versus depositary-collecting bank

The most common kind of check fraud involves forged indorsements. In the typical case, a thief steals checks payable to someone else, forges the payee's indorsements, and deposits the checks at a bank where the thief maintains an account. The thief may have opened the account in the name of the payee, posing as a representative of the payee who is authorized to deal with the account; or the thief may have opened the account in some other name, even her own name. The stolen checks are eventually paid by the payor bank. The thief's account thus swells, and the drawers' accounts correspondingly shrink.

Obviously, the payee is the person who initially suffers loss from this fraudulent scheme. We know, however, that the payee can shift the loss to the drawers of the stolen checks. Because the checks carried forged indorsements, the checks were not paid to a holder. Therefore, the drawers of the checks were not discharged on the instruments or on their underlying obligations to the payee. The drawers thus remain liable to the payee.

Upon satisfying their obligations to the payee, the drawers thereby assume the check fraud loss, inasmuch as their checking accounts have already been reduced by the amounts of the stolen checks. The drawers have, in effect, paid twice. The drawers, however, can pass the loss to the payor banks. The stolen checks paid by the banks were not properly payable and could not rightfully be charged to the drawers' accounts. Therefore, their accounts must be recredited.

The check fraud loss passes to the payor banks when they recredit the drawers' accounts. Of course, the payor banks can shift the loss back up the collection chain by relying on the presentment warranty that the warrantor was entitled to enforce the checks. 4-208(a)(1). The collecting banks that obtained payment of the checks, and each prior customer and collecting bank, made this warranty to the payor banks. They effectively warranted that the checks carried all necessary indorsements, and that the indorsements were authorized. Sooner or later, the loss will come to rest on the first collecting bank, i.e., the depositary bank, which is the bank where the thief deposited or cashed the stolen checks. In theory, this bank can recoup from the thief who herself breached the 4-207(a)(1) transfer warranty of right to enforce. By this time, however, the thief is long gone, physically or financially.

So the loss rests ultimately with the depositary-collecting bank in line with the policy of putting the loss on the person in the best position to protect against it. Yet, implementing this policy involves a very long, circuitous route of claims and recoveries over: payee v. drawers; drawers v. payor banks; payor banks v. depositary bank or intermediary banks; intermediary banks v. depositary bank. It would be much more efficient if the payee sued the depositary bank directly. After all, in this case the payee is the real victim of the check fraud, and the depositary bank is the entity who, in the end, is ultimately responsible.

The payee's theory in a direct action against the collecting bank is conversion. The holder of a check is the owner of it and the only rightful recipient of its proceeds unless she, or someone acting by her authority, directs otherwise. Therefore, when a check is stolen from a payee, her indorsement forged and the proceeds of the instrument are misappropriated, the thief is guilty of converting the payee's property and is liable to the payee for common-law conversion; and so is every transferee involved in the misappropriation even though the transferee acted innocently and without knowledge of the payee's superior rights. As a result, the bank at which the thief cashes the stolen check, or deposits it, is liable for conversion to the payee. Article 3 recognizes and codifies this conversion liability by providing:

> An instrument is * * * converted if it is taken by transfer, other than a negotiation, from a person not entitled to enforce the instrument or a bank makes or obtains payment with respect to the instrument for a person not entitled to enforce the instrument or receive payment.

3-420(a). "This covers cases in which a depositary or payor bank takes an instrument bearing a forged indorsement." 3-420 comment 1. "[T]he measure of liability is presumed to be the amount payable on the instrument, but recovery may not exceed the amount of the plaintiff's interest in the instrument." 3-420(b).

Example

a. T steals a check from Payee, forges Payee's indorsement, and cashes the check at DB Bank. The check is presented for payment and charged to the drawer's account at PB Bank. Payee sues DB Bank. In the absence of a defense, DB Bank is liable for the amount of the check. In case an instrument that pays interest is converted, the damages are presumed to include the loss of interest.

b. Same facts except that the check is payable jointly to two payees who are a building contractor and a supplier of building materials. The check is delivered to the contractor who forges the supplier's indorsement. "The supplier should not, without qualification, be able to recover the entire amount of the check from the bank that converted the check. Depending upon the contract between the contractor and the supplier, the amount of the check may be due entirely to the contractor, in which case there should be no recovery; due entirely to the supplier, in which case recovery should be for the entire amount; or part may be due to one and the rest to the other, in which case recovery should be limited to the amount due to the supplier." 3-420 comment 2.

Under former law the depositary-collecting bank's principal defense was 3-419(3), which provided:

> [A] representative, *including a depositary or collecting bank*, who has in good faith and in accordance with the reasonable commercial

standards applicable to the business of such representative dealt with an instrument or its proceeds on behalf of one who was not the true owner is not liable in conversion or otherwise to the true owner beyond the amount of any proceeds remaining in his hands.

3-419(3) (1989 Official Text) (emphasis added). According to the usual interpretation of 3-419(3), a depositary-collecting bank acted as a *representative* when it took checks for deposit and collection from a thief who had stolen them and forged the payee's indorsement, even though the person represented was not the owner of the items. So, when the payee sued the bank for conversion, the section operated as a defense, except to the extent of proceeds remaining in the bank's hands. As usually interpreted, however, "remaining proceeds" meant funds attributable to the forged checks that remained available in the wrongdoer's account. The bank thus was not liable for amounts attributable to the checks that had been withdrawn from the account. Ordinarily, most of the funds had been withdrawn, and 3-419(3) thus operated as a complete, or almost complete, defense for the bank. There were contrary interpretations of 3-419(3) that very narrowly defined the term "representative," or the "remaining proceeds" language, so that 3-419(3) did not apply to any extent as a defense for the depositary-collecting bank. Most cases, however, rejected these interpretations, with the ultimate effect that the payee's direct action against the depositary-collecting bank was usually fruitless -- except where the wrongdoer had left tainted funds in her account, or where the peculiar circumstances of the particular case made the 3-419(3) defense unavailable by its own terms.

In 1990, 3-419(3) became 3-420(c) and more than the number was changed. The section was rewritten to provide:

> A representative, *other than a depositary bank*, who has in good faith dealt with an instrument or its proceeds on behalf of one who was not the person entitled to enforce the instrument is not liable in conversion to that person beyond the amount of any proceeds that it has not paid out.

3-419(c) (emphasis added). This change in substance denies to depositary banks the defense of having acted reasonably and in good faith in dealing with converted items. The reason for the change is clear and sound, inasmuch as former law allowed the payee to shift the loss directly or indirectly to the payor bank which could shift it ultimately to the depositary bank:

> The depositary bank is ultimately liable in the case of a forged indorsement check because of its warranty to the payor bank under Section 4-208(a)(1) and it is usually the most convenient defendant in cases involving multiple checks drawn on different banks. There is no basis for requiring the owner of the check to bring multiple actions against the various payor banks and to require those banks to assert warranty rights against the depositary bank.

3-420 comment 3.

Other direct actions

1. Payee Versus Payor Bank

In the typical check fraud case involving a payee's unauthorized indorsement, there is no doubt that the payee can recover directly from the payor bank for conversion if the check is paid. Paying a check over a forged indorsement amounts to conversion. 3-420(a). Because the payee is the owner of the check and is entitled to its proceeds, she is a proper party to complain of the wrong by the payor bank. Section 3-420 covers any case in which a check is paid over an unauthorized or missing indorsement.

The defense of 3-420(c), which bars or limits a conversion action against a "representative" who deals with converted checks in good faith, is not available to the payor bank. The payor bank is not a "representative" within the meaning of the section, which has no applicability here whatsoever.

When the payee and payor bank are located in different states, the payee may be unable to sue the bank locally for jurisdictional reasons. Even if the local long-arm statute supports jurisdiction, constitutional due process will not permit exercising that jurisdiction if the bank's only connection with the payee's state is that checks drawn against the bank have circulated there. In this event, the payor bank has not purposefully acted in the payee's state or deliberately directed its activities at residents of the state. Therefore, traditional notions of justice and fair play, which define jurisdictional due process, would be offended by forcing the bank to answer for the conversion there. The payee would be required to sue where the payor bank is located.

Example

B draws a check to S whose employee, T, takes the check, forges S's indorsement and deposits the item in her account at DB Bank. The check is paid by the drawee, PB Bank. T cleans out her account and leaves town. S could recover from DB Bank but decides not to pursue this local bank. S can nevertheless recover from PB Bank. If, however, PB Bank is located in a different state and has insufficient local connections for jurisdictional purposes, S cannot pursue her conversion action against the bank locally. In case PB can be sued locally and "suit is brought against both the payor bank and the depositary bank, the owner, of course, is entitled to but one recovery." 3-420 comment 3.

2. Drawer Versus Depositary-Collecting Bank

The traditional view is that in the typical unauthorized indorsement case, the drawer of the check cannot directly recover from the depositary-collecting bank for conversion, money had and received, or otherwise. Article 3 expressly adopts this view, at least with respect to conversion. It provides that "[a]n action for conversion of an instrument may not be brought by * * * the issuer or acceptor of the instrument." 3-420(a). The explanation is that the drawer of the check is not the holder or owner of the item, and has no right to the proceeds of it. Moreover, even though the check was paid and the drawer's account charged with the item, this charge was not authorized or effective against the drawer because the check was not properly payable, inasmuch as it carried an unauthorized indorsement. Therefore, any wrong committed by the depositary-collecting bank in dealing with the check violated no valuable property or other rights of the drawer. The drawer's recourse is to recover from the payor bank for paying an item that was not properly payable.

Under former law, a few cases allowed the drawer of an altered check or a check with a forged indorsement to sue -- on other theories -- a depositary bank that took the check. The best example is *Sun 'N Sand, Inc. v. United California Bank*, 21 Cal.3d 671, 148 Cal. Rptr. 329, 582 P.2d 920 (1978), in which the California Supreme Court recognized that a drawer of a check might possibly recover directly from the depositary-collecting bank in a check fraud case on the basis of breach of warranty or negligence.

Sun 'N Sand held that the presentment warranties of former law ran in favor of the drawer of a check, as well as the payor bank. The technical analysis is that the drawer of a check pays the item, or is a payor of it, within the meaning of those warranty provisions. Because the payment warranties are made by any collecting bank in the collection chain of a check, the drawer could hold the depositary-collecting bank accountable in a forged indorsement case because the warranty against forged indorsements would have been violated directly as to the drawer. This theory will no longer hold. The 1990 Articles 3 and 4 make clear that no presentment warranties are made to the drawer of a check upon presentment to the drawee-payor bank. 3-417 & 4-208. With respect to the breach of warranty theory, *Sun 'N Sand* is flatly rejected.

Sun 'N Sand also holds, though much more narrowly, that a depositary-collecting bank owes a limited duty of reasonable care to the drawer of a check, and that the drawer can recover from the bank on a negligence theory if the bank acts unreasonably in dealing with the item. By the terms of the court's opinion, however, the duty is narrowly circumscribed and is activated only when checks drawn payable to a bank are presented to the same bank by a third person who seeks to negotiate them for her own benefit. This aspect of *Sun 'N Sand* is not so clearly rejected by the 1990 changes in Articles 3 and 4 and probably stands. Moreover, the duty of care has already been widened by the California Court of Appeals, holding that a drawer stated a cause of action in negligence against a depositary-collecting bank where an employee of the drawer stole checks payable to various persons, forged the payees' indorsements, and deposited the checks in the employee's personal account. *E.F. Hutton & Co., Inc. v. City Nat'l Bank*, 149 Cal. App.3d 60, 196 Cal. Rptr. 614 (1983). In *Hutton*, the key fact triggering the bank's duty of care to the drawer was that the bank knew, or should have known, that the employee worked for the drawer.

law

Five Towns College v. Citibank, N.A.

New York Supreme Court, Appellate Division, 1985
108 A.D.2d 420, 489 N.Y.S.2d 338

Gibbons, Justice. The issues raised on this appeal concern the propriety of Special Term's refusal to grant plaintiff partial summary judgment in its action to recover damages arising out of defendant's alleged improper payment of a series of checks bearing forged drawers' signatures, and its further decision to allow the defendant to amend its answer in order to assert, in effect, plaintiff's contributory negligence as an affirmative defense (CPLR 1411, 1412). In our view, the order, as amended, should be modified by deleting the provision granting leave to amend the answer in order to assert the aforementioned affirmative defense, and, as so modified, should be affirmed insofar as appealed from.

On or about September 3, 1979, plaintiff Five Towns College filed a signature card with defendant Citibank, N.A., designating its business manager (Mr. Martin Crafton), its president (Dr. Stanley G. Cohen), and its coordinator (Ms. Lorraine Kleinman) as the authorized signatories on its checking account No. 15107257. Previously, in March of 1979, the college had allegedly hired one Hilda Weisel as its new full-charge bookkeeper, and following the latter's untimely death in March of 1981, it was belatedly discovered that Ms. Weisel had embezzled in excess of $162,000 from the college by writing a series of checks to her own order and signing the names of either the college president (Dr. Cohen) or its coordinator (Ms. Kleinman). Citibank was notified of these forgeries on or about May 11, 1981, and following the latter's refusal to reimburse the plaintiff, this action was commenced in the Supreme Court, Nassau County, in which the college sought to recover the full amount of the forged checks. Issue was joined by the service of an answer in which the defendant bank successively pleaded Uniform Commercial Code §§3-406 and 4-406 as affirmative defenses, and following the service of answers to plaintiff's first set of interrogatories, the college moved for summary judgment in the principal amount of $104,625, representing the face amount of the 30 checks bearing the forged signature of Lorraine Kleinman which had been paid by the defendant during the 12 months preceding the first date of notification to the bank of the forgeries.

In support of its application, plaintiff annexed the affidavits of its business manager (Mr. Crafton) and its coordinator (Ms. Kleinman) to establish the facts regarding Ms. Weisel's employment, the forgeries, and her lack of authority to sign Ms. Kleinman's name, and also annexed copies of the defendant's answers to its first set of interrogatories. In them, the defendant admitted that it had not taken any steps whatsoever to verify the drawer's signatures on any of the plaintiff's checks, but claimed, in mitigation, that "(s)ignature verification would not have detected the alleged forgeries complained of in this action". Moreover, while no verification of any of these items was apparently attempted, Citibank did maintain that it had in effect at the operative time, a viable verification policy pursuant to which "(c)hecks drawn on end-of-month and special instruction accounts (were) signature verified".

In opposition, the defendant submitted an affidavit by an assistant manager of the defendant, employed at its Regional Processing Center, in which it was alleged, inter alia, that defendant presently lacked any knowledge or information regarding the existence or nonexistence of Hilda Weisel; that it had not, as yet, had the opportunity to depose Ms. Kleinman regarding either the fact of the "forgeries" or the existence of Ms. Weisel; that the "midnight deadline" for the acceptance or rejection of demand items imposed by UCC 4-302 (see also, UCC 4-104(1)(h)) renders the verification of signatures on every check impossible; that the verification procedure employed by Citibank constitutes the required exercise of "ordinary care" in the payment of customers' checks (see, UCC 4-406); and that there are other safeguards employed by Citibank in order to prevent the payment of unauthorized checks, e.g., the employment of Magnetic Ink Character Readers to make sure that every check which is actually paid is one of the preprinted checks which it sends to its depositors, thus insuring that if a check with a forged endorsement is paid "it would necessarily be (the) result of Citibank's customer having failed to exercise a sufficient degree of care to keep the magnetically encoded checks out of the hands of the forger or unauthorized signer". In addition, the defendant cross-moved for (1) partial summary judgment dismissing the complaint insofar as it pertained to the recovery of items paid more than one year prior to the date of its notification; and (2) for leave to amend its answer in order to assert a claim of contributory negligence against the plaintiff.

The plaintiff opposed the cross motion for leave to amend the answer, but on June 3, 1983, Special Term (Levitt, J.), granted the cross motion and denied the plaintiff's motion ***.

This appeal followed.

On appeal, it is the plaintiff's contention that Special Term erred in denying its motion for partial summary judgment on the 30 forged checks totaling $104,625 which the defendant had paid during the 12 months preceding its first notification of the forgeries (cf. UCC 4-406(4)), since the admitted failure to attempt to verify any of the signatures of any of the plaintiff's checks constituted a "lack of ordinary care on the part of the (defendant) bank in paying the (contested) item(s)" as a matter of law (see, UCC 4-406(3)). In addition, plaintiff maintains that the concepts of contributory negligence and comparative fault (CPLR arts. 14, 14-A) are wholly inapplicable to an action, as here, predicated on contract and arising under the Uniform Commercial Code.

In our view, the existence of triable issues of fact, including, e.g., the existence of the alleged forger, her lack of authority to sign the disputed checks, and presence or absence of ordinary care on the part of the defendant bank in paying the contested items, precluded the entry of partial summary judgment in plaintiff's favor. However, we agree with the plaintiff that the principles of comparative fault should not be extended to alter the careful adjustment of the respective rights and obligations of a bank and its customers regarding the payment of checks bearing unauthorized or forged signatures set forth in the UCC. Accordingly, that aspect of the defendant's cross motion which sought leave to amend its answer in order to assert a claim for an apportionment of responsibility was not properly granted, and should have been denied in toto.

Assuming, arguendo, that plaintiff is correct in contending that the admitted failure of the bank to attempt any signature verification on any of the checks written against its account No. 15107257 constituted a per se failure to exercise ordinary care in the payment of such items (see, UCC 4-406(3); see also, UCC 3-406, 4-401(1)), it is, nevertheless, plain that the plaintiff would not be entitled to partial summary judgment at this stage of the proceedings, as discovery has not, as yet, been completed, and the defendant is presently without sufficient knowledge to challenge either the existence of the alleged forger, the facts of her employment, or her lack of authority to sign the name of the plaintiff's authorized signatory, Ms. Kleinman. In fact, while the UCC provides, inter alia, that an unauthorized signature (including a forgery) is (with exceptions not here relevant) "wholly inoperative as that of the person whose name is signed" (UCC 3-404(1)), it also provides that an "unauthorized" signature is one which is made without the "actual, implied or apparent authority" of the person in whose name it is executed (UCC 1-201(43)), the knowledge of which factors are presently beyond the defendant's reach. It is well established that summary judgment will not be granted without an opportunity to complete discovery where, as here, the facts necessary to oppose the motion lie peculiarly within the knowledge of the moving party. [Citations omitted.]

Quite apart from the foregoing, however, there is another, more central reason why summary judgment may not be granted in this case, as the defendant has affirmatively pleaded as a defense UCC 3-406 and 4-406, which provide, inter alia, that "(a)ny person who by his (own) negligence substantially contributes *** to the making of an unauthorized signature is *precluded* from asserting the *** lack of authority *** against a drawee *** who pays the instrument in good faith and in accordance with the reasonable commercial standards of the drawee's *** business" (UCC 3-406, emphasis supplied), and that a customer's failure to exercise reasonable care and promptness in examining his bank statement and canceled checks for unauthorized signatures and in reporting the same to the drawee bank is precluded from asserting against said bank "an(y) unauthorized signature *** by the *same* wrongdoer on any other item paid in good faith by the bank *after* the first item and statement was available to the customer for a reasonable period not exceeding fourteen calendar days and before the bank receives notification from the customer of any such unauthorized signature" (UCC 4-406(2)(b), emphasis supplied). Here, it is not contended by either party that any of the 30 items in issue were actually paid by the defendant bank within 14 days after the return to the plaintiff of the earliest items bearing the allegedly forged drawer's signatures (i.e., those items as to which recovery is barred by the one-year period of limitation set forth in UCC 4-406(4)), and it is therefore apparent that but for the plaintiff's reliance on the statutory limitation imposed by UCC 4-406(3), precluding a bank from asserting its customer's lack of notice regarding unauthorized signatures in any case where the latter can establish a "lack of ordinary care on the part of the bank in paying the (contested) item(s)", that the bank would be entitled to summary judgment dismissing the complaint.

Moreover, given the extreme length of time which expired in this case before any of the alleged forgeries were reported to the defendant, it can certainly be argued that, at least as to some of these items, the prolonged lack of detection on the part of the plaintiff constituted "negligence (on its part which) substantially contribute(d) *** to the making of an unauthorized signature", thereby precluding the plaintiff from asserting the suspected forgeries against the defendant bank (see, UCC 3-406; [citations omitted]), but it is argued, inter alia, that the foregoing is not the case here due to the defendant's admitted failure to verify the signatures on any of the items cleared through plaintiff's checking account during the period from November 1979 through March 1981. Such conduct, according to plaintiff, precludes the defendant from establishing that it acted "in accordance with the reasonable commercial standards of (its) *** business" in paying the contested items, as required by UCC 3-406, as well as preventing the defendant from attempting to avoid liability by asserting as an affirmative defense plaintiff's apparent failure to detect the alleged forgeries (see, UCC 4-406(2)). In so arguing, plaintiff relies, inter alia, on UCC 4-406(3) which pertinently provides that "(t)he preclusion (set forth in) subsection (2) (regarding the customer's failure to detect unauthorized signatures) does not apply if the customer establishes (a) lack of ordinary care on the part of the (drawee) bank in paying the (contested) item(s)" (emphasis supplied). According to the plaintiff, defendant's lack of ordinary care has been conclusively established herein.

Notwithstanding the undoubted facial appeal of plaintiff's position, we conclude that the alleged lack of care on the part of the defendant bank presents a triable issue of fact, since it is impossible to determine on the present state of the record whether the admitted verification policy of the defendant bank (i.e., the signature verification of checks drawn on end-of-month and special instruction accounts) is commercially reasonable (UCC 3-406) given the existence of the "midnight deadline" for the payment of demand items (UCC 4-302(a)), and the realities of modern electronic banking in the New York Metropolitan area. Ironically, the same problem also prevents the entry of partial summary judgment based on the statutory preclusion set forth in UCC 4-406(3), for while the statute speaks in terms of a "lack of ordinary care" on the part of the drawee bank, UCC 4-103(3) provides, inter alia, that "action or nonaction consistent with clearing house rules *** or with a *general banking usage not disapproved by this Article*, prima facie constitutes the exercise of ordinary care" (emphasis supplied). Thus, the operative standard in either instance is much the same, and cannot be determined on the present record.

Notably, no case has been cited to this court in which partial summary judgment has been granted *against* a bank on the theory that it had failed to exercise the requisite degree of care in honoring customers' checks bearing unauthorized drawers' signatures. Moreover, in the one such case disclosed by our independent research, it appears that the plaintiff's moving papers contained uncontroverted documentary evidence that the defendant's conduct in cashing a check made payable to the plaintiff corporation in violation of a resolution on file with the bank, fell well below any acceptable standard of professional care. No comparable showing has been made in the case at bar. Apparently, with these lone exceptions, the extent of care exercised by a drawee bank under the UCC in honoring a forged check has routinely been held to present a triable issue of fact for the jury to determine.

Turning to a consideration of the second issue presented, it is our belief that leave to amend defendant's answer in order to assert the plaintiff's contributory negligence as an affirmative defense (CPLR 1411, 1412*) was not properly granted, for notwithstanding the fact that a claim for an apportionment of liability is no longer restricted solely to causes of action predicated on negligence, and has been extended, e.g., to include causes of action sounding in breach of warranty and strict products liability, the seminal issue, as we see it, is not whether, in the broadest sense, the breach of a duty arising out of contract is amenable to the interposition of such an affirmative defense, but, rather, whether the concept of comparative fault is a permissible vehicle to vary the respective rights and obligations under the UCC of the parties to a negotiable instrument. In our view, this question should be answered in the negative, as the balancing of rights under the UCC represents the ultimate distillation of a painstaking process of evolution, pursuant to which the risk of loss in commercial matters has been attempted to be adjusted in a fair and equitable manner.

Thus, it is specifically provided by statute that a drawee bank cannot, as a general rule, charge its customer for items paid upon a forged drawer's signature, but that where the drawer has, by his own negligence "substantially contribute(d) *** to the making of an unauthorized signature, (he) is precluded from asserting the *** lack of authority against *** a drawee or other payer who pays the instrument in good faith and in accordance with reasonable

---

* These laws provide:

> In any action to recover damages for personal injury, injury to property, or wrongful death, the culpable conduct attributable to the claimant or to the decedent, including contributory negligence or assumption of risk, shall not bar recovery, but the amount of damages otherwise recoverable shall be diminished in the proportion which the culpable conduct attributable to the claimant or decedent bears to the culpable conduct which caused the damages.

N.Y.Civ.Prac.Law § 1411 (McKinney 1976).

> Culpable conduct claimed in diminution of damages, in accordance with section fourteen hundred eleven, shall be an affirmative defense to be pleaded and proved by the party asserting the defense.

Id. § 1412.

commercial standards" (UCC 3-406). However, if the drawee has also acted unreasonably, the preclusion is withdrawn and the bank will remain liable to its depositor. Moreover, where, as in the case at bar, an unauthorized signature is in issue, the customer may still be precluded from recovering against his bank on those items whose payment could have been prevented had he acted reasonably in examining his bank statement and canceled checks (UCC 4-406(2)). Again, the preclusion is withdrawn if the bank has failed to employ "ordinary care *** in paying the (contested) item(s)" (UCC 4-406(3)), but, notwithstanding the foregoing, recovery is barred as to those items with respect to which the bank's customer "does not within one year from the time the statement and (the) items are made available to (him) *** discover and report his (own) unauthorized signature" (UCC 4-406(4)).

In our view, the foregoing balancing of the respective rights and duties was intended to be exclusive, and any alteration in the underlying pattern of liability should not be based upon the vague (in this application) language of CPLR 1411 and 1412.

* * *

Accordingly, the order appealed from, as amended, should be modified by deleting the provision granting leave to amend the defendant's answer and, as so modified, should be affirmed insofar as appealed from.

Payroll Check Cashing v. New Palestine Bank
Court of Appeals of Indiana, 1980
401 N.E.2d 752

[The court's opinion in this case is reprinted in Chapter 4, supra, at pages 219-21.]

United Carolina Bank v. First Union National Bank
Court of Appeals of North Carolina, 1993
109 N.C.App. 201, 426 S.E.2d 462

Greene, Judge. Plaintiff appeals from an 11 June 1991 judgment of the trial court, sitting without a jury, granting defendant's motion to dismiss made at the close of plaintiff's evidence pursuant to N.C.G.S. §1A-1, Rule 41(b), on the ground that plaintiff established no right to relief.

The evidence before the trial court established that on 29 March 1989, Mary S. Wood (Wood) drew a check on defendant First Union National Bank (First Union) in the amount of $23,000.00 payable to the order of Eagle Construction Company. Jack S. Allen and Sylvia P. Allen were partners of Eagle Construction Company. On 3 April 1989, Jack Allen deposited the check with plaintiff United Carolina Bank (UCB) to the account of Sylvia P. Allen, No. 43-541-009-1. The check was not indorsed by payee Eagle Construction Company or by Sylvia or Jack Allen. At the time the check was deposited, Eagle Construction Company did not have an account at UCB. UCB gave immediate credit for the check to the Sylvia Allen account, and by 4 April 1989, Sylvia Allen had withdrawn the entire $23,000.00 from the account.

UCB sent the check through the Federal Reserve System, and on 4 April 1989, it was presented to payor First Union. Upon presentment to First Union, the check still contained no payee indorsement. UCB, however, had stamped on the back of the check, "United Carolina

Bank, Monroe, N.C., pay any bank, P.E.G." ("P.E.G." meaning "prior endorsements guaranteed"). First Union posted the check to Wood's account and credited UCB's settlement account in the amount of $23,000.00. First Union sent the check to Wood with her monthly bank statement on 10 May 1989, whereupon she discovered the missing indorsement, returned the check to First Union, and asked First Union to credit her account in the amount of $23,000.00.

On 10 May 1989, First Union credited Wood's account in the amount of $23,000.00. First Union returned the check to UCB for lack of indorsement and debited UCB's settlement account in the amount of $23,000.00. On 12 May 1989, Wood issued to First Union a stop-payment order on the check. Upon receiving the check from First Union on 11 May 1989, UCB called Jack Allen to tell him that he needed to indorse the check. Jack Allen authorized UCB to indorse the check for him and to redeposit it. A UCB employee wrote on the back of the check "Eagle Construction Co., Deposit only to payee account 43- 5410091 Sylvia P. Allen," and UCB sent the check back to First Union for payment. Upon receiving the check on 16 May 1989, First Union honored Wood's stop-payment order and refused payment to UCB.

After First Union refused payment on the check, UCB brought the present action alleging that First Union "wrongfully had the check charged back against [UCB] after making final payment, and [First Union] is accountable to [UCB] under the provisions of N.C.G.S. Chapter 25." In its answer, First Union denied liability to UCB based in relevant part on UCB's alleged breach of presentment warranty of good title under N.C.G.S. §25-4-207 and asserted in the alternative a counterclaim against UCB on the same basis. The matter was heard in Brunswick County Superior Court by Judge Gregory Weeks sitting without a jury on 10 June 1991, and at the close of UCB's evidence, First Union made a Rule 41(b) motion to dismiss plaintiff's complaint.

Judge Weeks after making findings of fact concluded in relevant part that UCB breached its warranties and guarantee of prior indorsement "by the lack of indorsement by the payee and the lack of good title in UCB," and that therefore "payment by First Union did not become final and First Union properly honored the stop payment order." The court also concluded that, if payment had become final, First Union nonetheless would be entitled to recover from UCB the amount of the check for breach of presentment warranties and guarantee of prior indorsement by UCB and could do so by returning the check to UCB and charging the check back to UCB. Finally, Judge Weeks concluded that UCB was without authority to supply the indorsement of Eagle Construction Company.

––––––––

The dispositive issues are, under Chapter 25 of the North Carolina General Statutes, (I) whether UCB breached the presentment warranty of good title by obtaining payment from First Union on a check containing no payee indorsement; if so, (II) whether UCB cured its breach of warranty by supplying the indorsement of Eagle Construction Company before re-presenting the check for payment; and, if not, (III) whether UCB's breach of warranty entitled First Union to charge back to UCB the amount of the check.

I

UCB argues that the trial court erroneously concluded that UCB breached the presentment warranty of good title by obtaining payment of the Wood check from First Union when the check did not contain the indorsement of the payee. Specifically, UCB argues that "the true test of whether one has good title to an instrument lies in how he came into possession of it, and not in the presence or absence of indorsements." We disagree.

Pursuant to N.C.G.S. §25-4-207, each "collecting bank who obtains payment" of a check from a payor bank "warrants to the payor bank ... that ... he has good title" to the check. N.C.G.S. §25-4-207(1)(a) (1986). This is known as a presentment warranty of good title whereby the collecting bank warrants that the check contains neither forged indorsements, *North Carolina Nat'l Bank v. Hammond*, 298 N.C. 703, 708, 260 S.E.2d 617, 621 (1979), nor missing indorsements. See *Witten Prods., Inc. v. Republic Bank & Trust Co.*, 102 N.C.App. 88, 90, 401 S.E.2d 388, 390 (1991) (indorsement of the payee is required in order to pass good title); *Chilson v. Capital Bank*, 237 Kan. 442, 701 P.2d 903, 906 (1985) (collecting bank breached Article Four presentment warranty of good title by receiving final payment on check with missing payee's indorsement); accord *Stapleton v. First Sec. Bank*, 207 Mont. 248, 675 P.2d 83 (1983). Indeed, it is well established that this presentment warranty of good title, guaranteeing prior indorsements, applies "regardless of the type of indorsement or whether there was an indorsement." N.C.G.S. §25-4-207 N.C. comment (emphasis added).

In this case, it is undisputed that the indorsement of the payee was missing when First Union initially received the check for payment. Therefore, if final payment was obtained by UCB, the collecting bank, from First Union, the payor bank, UCB breached the presentment warranty of good title. See James J. White & Robert S. Summers, *Uniform Commercial Code* §17-2, at 722 (3d ed. 1988) (presentment warranty arises only when the collecting bank receives from the payor bank final payment for the check). Final payment of a check by a payor bank occurs when the payor bank has done any of the following, whichever happens first: (a) paid the item in cash; or (b) settled for the item without reserving a right to revoke the settlement and without having such right under statute, clearing house rule or agreement; or (c) completed the process of posting the item to the indicated account of the drawer, maker or other person to be charged therewith; or (d) made a provisional settlement for the item and failed to revoke the settlement in the time and manner permitted by statute, clearing house rule or agreement. Upon a final payment under subparagraphs (b), (c) or (d) the payor bank shall be accountable for the amount of the item. N.C.G.S. §25-4-213(1) (1986).

It is undisputed that First Union made final payment on the check. The evidence before the trial court established that First Union completed the process of posting the item to Wood's account and that First Union made a provisional settlement for the item and failed to revoke the settlement in the time and manner permitted by statute, that is, before its midnight deadline. N.C.G.S. §25-4-301(1) (1986); N.C.G.S. §25-4-104(1)(h) (1986). Thus, because UCB presented the check to First Union without the required indorsement and because First Union paid the check under Section 25-4-213(1), Judge Weeks properly concluded that UCB, as a collecting bank, breached its presentment warranty of good title. We note, however, that the stamp which UCB placed on the back of the check, "P.E.G.," does not affect UCB's liability for breach of warranty. A specific guarantee of prior indorsements is not necessary under the UCC because, as previously discussed, the effect obtained by such words now arises automatically under the Code as a part of the bank collection process. N.C.G.S. §25-4-207(3) & official comment 2; Henry J. Bailey & Richard B. Hagedorn, *Brady on Bank Checks* §12.10 (6th ed. 1987 & Supp.1992). In fact, the use of P.E.G. stamps by banks is discouraged as it "make[s] it more difficult to read the bank indorsements and identify the depositary bank in the event that the check is returned unpaid." Id.

II

UCB argues that any breach of the presentment warranty of good title was cured when UCB supplied the missing indorsement after the check was returned by First Union. We acknowledge that a depositary bank such as UCB which has taken a check for collection may supply the indorsement of its "customer." N.C.G.S. §25-4-205(1) (1986). In this case, however, assuming *arguendo* that UCB could have cured the breach of warranty by supplying the proper indorsement, UCB did not do so. Eagle Construction Company, the payee of the check, did not have an account at UCB and therefore was not a "customer" within the meaning of Section 25-4-205(1). See N.C.G.S. §25-4- 104(1)(e) (1986) ("customer" is any person having an account with the bank). Accordingly, we again agree with Judge Weeks that the indorsement provided by UCB was without effect and could not cure the breach of warranty.

III

UCB finally argues that even if it breached the presentment warranty of good title, First Union became accountable for the check upon final payment and could not charge the check back to UCB. In support of its argument, UCB directs our attention to Section 25-4-213(1) which provides that, except for certain exceptions not here applicable, "upon final payment, the payor bank shall be accountable" for the amount of the check. First Union argues, based on N.C.G.S. §25-3-418, that because UCB breached the presentment warranty of good title, payment of the check was not final and that, after discovering the missing indorsement, First Union had the legal right to return the check and to charge the amount of the check back to UCB.

North Carolina Gen.Stat. §25-3-418 in relevant part provides that *except for liability for breach of warranty on presentment* under the preceding section [GS 25-3-417], [and under GS 25-4-207] payment ... of any instrument is final in favor of a holder in due course, or a person who has in good faith changed his position in reliance on the payment. N.C.G.S. §25-3-418 & N.C. comment (1986) (emphasis added). This statute, on its face, seems to suggest that First Union is correct in its argument, that is, that a breach of warranty by the collecting bank prevents payment of a check by a payor bank from becoming final. Because, however, the warranties under Section 25-4-207(1) arise *only* when there has already been final payment of the check, it defies logic to assert that when a breach of presentment warranty exists, payment of the check is not final. In addition, although under Section 25-4-207(4) a payor bank may "make a claim" within a reasonable time for breach of warranty, there is no explicit or implied provision in the Code authorizing a payor bank to unilaterally charge back to the collecting bank on breach of warranty grounds the amount of a check after the payor bank has "finally paid" the check under Section 25-4-213(1). Finally, other jurisdictions addressing the question before us have concluded, and we agree, that UCC Section 3-418 operates as an exception to the final payment rule in Section 4-213(1) only to the extent that it permits the payor bank which has made final payment to seek a recovery against the collecting bank for breach of presentment warranties. See, e.g., *First Nat'l Bank of Arizona v. Continental Bank*, 138 Ariz. 194, 197, 673 P.2d 938, 941 (Ct.App. 1983). Damages in such an action include the consideration received by the collecting bank and finance charges and expenses related to the check, if any. N.C.G.S. §25-4-207(3).

In sum, First Union's right to recover for breach of presentment warranties does not undo or negate the final payment made by First Union to UCB under Section 4-213(1). To read Section 25-3-418 as doing so "would be to introduce a great amount of uncertainty to the finality of payment rule in any case where the [i]ndorsements are questioned." *First Nat'l*, 138 Ariz. at 197, 673 P.2d at 941. Accordingly, the trial court was incorrect in determining that First Union had the right to unilaterally charge the check back to UCB. The trial court, however, was correct in its alternative ruling that First Union was entitled to judgment on its counterclaim for breach of the presentment warranty of good title. In other words, although UCB is entitled to recover on its claim that First Union unlawfully charged back the check to UCB's account, First Union is entitled to recover on its claim against UCB for breach of warranty. The trial court determined that these were offsetting claims. Although both parties in their pleadings sought recovery of interest on the $23,000.00, neither UCB nor First Union argues before this Court that the trial court failed to properly account for any interest due. Thus, we deem the interest claim abandoned by the parties. N.C.R.App.P. 28(a) (1992). Therefore, we agree that the parties' claims are offsetting and, accordingly, the order of the trial court is

Affirmed.

Cooper v. Union Bank
Supreme Court of California, 1973
9 Cal.3d 371, 107 Cal. Rptr. 1, 507 P.2d 609

Mosk, Justice. We here consider the rights of the true owner of a negotiable instrument which has been collected and paid on a forged indorsement. The question has not previously arisen in this state under the Uniform Commercial Code, and has seldom been addressed in other jurisdictions.

The record recounts a typical tale of forgery. Plaintiff Joseph Stell, an attorney, employed one Bernice Ruff as a secretary and bookkeeper. During a period of approximately a year and one-half Ruff purloined some 29 checks intended for Stell and forged the necessary indorsements thereon. She cashed some of these checks at defendants Union Bank and Crocker Citizens National Bank and deposited the remainder (except one that was cashed elsewhere) to her personal account at the latter bank. The entire amount of such deposits was subsequently withdrawn by Ruff prior to discovery of the forgeries. Certain of the checks were forwarded to and paid by defendants Crocker Citizens National Bank, Security First National Bank, and First Western Bank and Trust Company; the remainder were drawn on payors who are not parties to this action.

Stell and his partners bring this action in conversion against both the collecting and the payor banks to recover the amounts of the instruments handled by them on the forged indorsements. The critical California Commercial Code provision is section 3419 which establishes that "(1) An instrument is converted when *** (c) It is paid on a forged indorsement." Notwithstanding this language, the superior court denied recovery on the basis of section 3419, subdivision 3, which provides:

"(3) Subject to the provisions of this code concerning restrictive indorsements a representative, including a depositary or collecting bank, who has in good faith and in accordance with reasonable commercial standards applicable to the business of such representative dealt with an instrument or its proceeds on behalf of one who was not the true owner is not liable in conversion or otherwise to the true owner beyond the amount of any proceeds remaining in his hands."

The court concluded that all defendants in the case, including payor as well as collecting banks, qualified as representatives, had acted in good faith and in accordance with reasonable commercial standards, and had no proceeds remaining in their hands. Thus defendants were held immune from liability. The court also found that plaintiffs had been negligent in failing to discover Ruff's defalcations by April 1, 1966, approximately six months following their commencement, and that such negligence substantially contributed to the making of the subsequent forged indorsements. On this additional basis it held plaintiffs were "precluded from asserting such forgeries or lack of authorized signatures against any of the respective Defendants herein on checks presented after April 1, 1966."

We hold that the trial court relied on an erroneous interpretation of section 3419 and that therefore the judgment must be reversed in part. Inasmuch as collecting banks and payor banks raise distinctive issues under section 3419, the application of this section to the two categories of banks will be discussed separately.

Collecting Banks

It is clear, excluding for the moment the issue of plaintiff's negligence, that defendant collecting banks are liable for conversion unless they can establish a defense under section 3419, subdivision (3). A careful study of this provision, however, reveals no possible defense in this case after it becomes evident that the court below erroneously held defendant collecting banks had parted with the proceeds of the fraudulently indorsed instruments. The code, unfortunately, fails to define the word "proceeds" in the context of bank collection. Therefore, to fully comprehend the code section we must examine the concept of proceeds as it was understood prior to enactment of the code and to general theory of bank collection found elsewhere in the code and in other parts of the law.

Whether defendant depositary banks have any proceeds of the fraudulently indorsed checks remaining in their hands is resolved through a bifurcated inquiry: first, did they receive any proceeds and second, have they parted with any proceeds they may have received? Each of these queries is more complex than superficially appears. A collecting bank obviously does not receive any proceeds of an instrument unless such proceeds are forwarded to it from a payor bank. Under the dominant theory of bank collection that preexisted the code and which the code has left unchanged, however, the amounts a payor bank remits on a forged indorsement are not considered the proceeds of the instrument. The explanation for this result lies in the relationship between a payor bank and its customer, the depositor-drawer. The relationship is one of debtor and creditor: the bank is indebted to the customer and promises to debit his account only at his direction. If the bank pays, on an instrument drawn by its customer, any person other than the designated payee or a person to whom the instrument is negotiated, the bank's indebtedness to the customer is not diminished. If the bank does debit the customer's account, the customer can compel the bank to recredit the sum. Inasmuch as the full amount of the instrument remains in the account of the drawer when the bank pays on a forged indorsement, the bank manifestly does not part with the proceeds of the instrument but merely remits other funds from its own account.

General bank collection theory also instructs us that the true owner, in bringing an action against a collecting bank for conversion of a check collected on a forged indorsement, is deemed to have ratified the collection of the proceeds from the payor bank. This ratification transmutes the remittance of funds by the payor bank into an authorized act for which it may debit its customer's account. In the case at bar, it appears that plaintiffs' action against defendant collecting banks constitutes such a ratification, and these banks, therefore, must be considered to have received the proceeds of the instruments.

Ratification of collection, however, does not constitute a ratification of the collecting bank's delivery of the proceeds to the wrong person. The dominant precode law established, on the contrary, that the proceeds were held, after collection by the collecting bank, for the benefit of the true owner. Again resorting to general banking theory, we find that the amounts a collecting bank remits to a person who transfers to the bank a check bearing a forged indorsement do not constitute the proceeds of the instrument. This result is quite clear in the case of an instrument cashed over the counter. At the time the bank takes such an instrument it has obviously not made any prior collection and, thus, has nothing that could be considered proceeds. The money paid over the counter is, consequently, the bank's own money. Upon collection of the instrument, the proceeds become merged with the bank's general funds and are therefore retained by the bank.

A bank that accepts an instrument for deposit likewise ultimately retains the proceeds of that instrument. Such a bank is initially considered to be an agent of the person who delivers the instrument to it for collection. When, however, the bank receives a final settlement for an item it has forwarded for collection, the agency status typically ends, and the bank becomes a mere debtor of its customer. As a mere debtor, it becomes entitled to use the proceeds as its own.

The foregoing view was expressed by Justice Cardozo for the United States Supreme Court in the following terms:

> "Whether a fiduciary relation continues even afterwards (when the collecting bank has completed the business of collection) upon the theory that the proceeds of the collection until remitted to the forwarder are subject to a trust, depends upon the circumstances. In the absence of tokens of a contrary intention, the better doctrine is, where the common law prevails, that the agency of the collecting bank is brought to an end by the collection of the paper, the bank, from then on being in the position of a debtor, with the liberty, like debtors generally, to use the proceeds as its own." (Jennings v. United States Fidelity & Guaranty Co. (1935), 294 U.S. 216, 219, 55 S.Ct. 394, 395, 79 L.Ed. 869.)

It is significant that the Commercial Code does not make a collecting bank accountable to its customer for the *proceeds* of an instrument but only for "the *amount* of the item." (§ 4213, subd. (3); italics added.) Justice Cardozo's conception of the post-collection status of collecting banks is clearly preserved: "(I)f a collecting bank receives a settlement for an item which is or becomes final the bank is accountable to its customer for the amount of the item. One means of accounting is to remit to its customer the amount it has received on the item. If previously it gave to its customer a provisional credit for the item in an account its receipt of final settlement for the item 'firms up' this provisional credit and makes it final. When this credit given by it so becomes final, in the usual case *its agency status terminates and it becomes a debtor to its customer for the amount of the item*." (§ 4213, U.Com.Code, com. 9; italics added.)

As suggested by Justice Cardozo, the parties can by mutual agreement extend the agency relationship until the amount of an instrument is received by the customer. Under such an agreement the proceeds would be maintained as a separate fund until paid over to the customer. The ordinary banking transaction, however, contains no such agreement, and it is apparent that there was none in the present case. Defendant collecting banks, on the contrary, became debtors, and the proceeds of the instruments were completely merged with the banks' own funds. The effect of this commingling is that the banks retain the proceeds of the instruments even though amounts set forth in the instruments, in the banks' own money, were remitted to Ruff. This conclusion is derived by reference to the law of constructive trusts. The cases in that area establish that money received by a bank and mingled with the bank's funds is traceable by a proper claimant into those funds. This result is unaffected by withdrawals so long as the amount of the cash on hand is not diminished below the amount of the claimant's money that has been mingled with the fund. Since it is obvious that no such severe diminution of funds occurred in the present case, defendant collecting banks must be deemed to retain the proceeds of the instruments transferred by Ruff, regardless of whether those instruments were cashed or accepted for deposit.*

---

* *Ervin v. Dauphin Deposit Trust Co.* (1965), 38 Pa.Dist. & Co.R.2d 473 (3 U.C.C.Rep. 311, 319), arrives at this same conclusion. The court states: "When (the collecting bank)

Our conclusion that defendant collecting banks did not part with the proceeds of the instruments in making the various payments to Ruff is reinforced by several additional factors. To begin with, had the draftsmen of the Commercial Code intended to absolve collecting banks from liability by virtue of such payments, it seems probable they would have employed language more explicit than that of retaining or parting with proceeds. Instead, the words "for value" could have been employed. The collecting banks in this case are in a situation comparable to that of a holder in due course under the Commercial Code or a bona fide purchaser under the law of constructive trusts inasmuch as they took property and in return gave consideration to the transferor. With respect to a holder in due course or a bona fide purchaser, however, this consideration is termed "value." (§ 3302) The fact that different terminology is contained in section 3419, subdivision (3), suggests that the ambiguous language of this provision was not intended to refer to the giving of such consideration. If the draftsmen and the Legislature had intended to protect collecting banks that had merely given value for an instrument, it may be assumed they would have clearly said so.

Secondly, an examination of the law existing prior to the enactment of the Uniform Commercial Code reveals a nearly unanimous agreement among the jurisdictions that the true owner of an instrument collected on a forged indorsement could recover in a direct suit against a collecting bank even though the bank had acted in good faith and with the highest degree of care and even though it had remitted the amount of the instrument to a prior party. Since the rule had apparently operated satisfactorily, there is no reason to believe the code draftsmen or the Legislature would have wished to modify it to make direct suits extremely difficult. As discussed below, the payor bank is in effect strictly liable to the true owner if it pays an instrument on a forged indorsement. The collecting banks that handled the instrument for collection are, in turn, strictly liable to the payor bank for breach of warranty of good title. (§ 4207).[*] Because liability ultimately rests with the first collecting bank, it is unlikely that

---

purchased or cashed the forged checks drawn on other banks it did so with its own money and then, in putting them through for collection it obtained from the drawee banks money which belongs to the plaintiff." Commentators have suggested that the *Ervin* case may stand for the rule that the collecting bank parts with the proceeds if it accepts an instrument for deposit in an account and later pays out the money in the account but does not part with the proceeds if it cashes the instrument. There appears to be no practical rationale for this arbitrary solution, and the *Ervin* decision clearly appears to negate it: "As far as the problem in the instant case is concerned we can find no distinction between the *cashing* of a forged check and the *accepting* of such check for deposit." (3 U.C.C.Ret. at p. 315.)

---

[*] The remedies of direct action by the true owner and of circuitous action through the payor bank are not strictly coincident inasmuch as the payor's warranty action may be barred by his failure to act in a timely fashion. Section 4207, subdivision (4), provides: "Unless a claim for breach of warranty under this section is made within a reasonable time after the person claiming learns of the breach, the person liable is discharged to the extent of any loss caused by the delay in making claim." This proviso is of small significance with respect to forged indorsements since the forgery is rarely, if ever, discovered soon enough to prevent loss. The fact that the direct action and the circuitous action might result in different allocation of liability in one improbable situation appears insufficient to justify the diseconomy and injustice created by circuitous action. Moreover, assuming the payor bank failed to make a timely claim to the collecting bank, which failure proximately resulted in the collecting bank's payment of the amount of an instrument on a forged indorsement, and that the true owner recovered from the collecting bank in a direct action, it would appear that the collecting bank should be able to recover its loss from the payor bank, if not under the code, in an action for

such a bank was intended to have a ready defense in a direct suit by the true owner. Requiring cumbersome and uneconomical circuity of action to achieve an identical result would obviously run contra the code's explicit underlying purposes "to simplify, clarify and modernize the law governing commercial transactions." (§ 1102, subd. (2)(a).)

Such a modification would also create a significant potential for injustice. In cases involving forged indorsements collecting banks are generally the most feasible defendants. A forger typically transfers instruments bearing forged indorsements to only one or two banks for collection. Often the banks are located near the true owner. Thus it would be practical for him to bring a suit against such banks. The payors, by contrast, may be situated in many and distant states or in foreign countries, and the drawers may be equally geographically diverse. Even though the collecting banks would be ultimately liable after initial suits were brought in all the various fora, the expense and difficulty of bringing such suits would have the actual effect of freeing the collecting banks from any responsibility. The true owner would be required to shoulder the loss that should have been that of the banks; thus the banks would receive a windfall. That section 3419, subdivision (3), was intended to produce this unjust result is highly doubtful.

Had such substantial and controversial deviation from prior law been intended, moreover, it could be expected that the official commentary to section 3419 would have so stated and would have included extensive explanation of the reasons for the change. Neither the California nor the uniform comment to this section, however, contains any such discussion. The comments, on the contrary, are brief and state that section 3419, subdivision (3), is merely a codification of prior decisions (U.Com.Code com. 5) and is entirely consistent with prior California law (Cal. com. 5).

The prior decisions to which the Uniform Commercial Code comment makes reference are presumably a line of cases primarily involving defendants that had acted as investment brokers and had marketed negotiable securities, remitting the consideration received to their customers. The relationships between the representatives and their customers in those cases appear to have been true agency relationships that did not merge into debtor-creditor relationships upon collection of the proceeds. Unlike the ordinary bank collection transaction, in which the collecting bank and its customer have tacitly agreed a debtor-creditor relationship will emerge upon collection, the ordinary agency transaction gives rise to no such debt when the agent receives funds intended for the principal. Such funds, instead of being mingled, must be kept separate from the agent's own funds and identified as the property of the principal. Thus, when the true agent remits the amount of an instrument to his customer, the agent actually does part with the proceeds. It is to this kind of situation, rather than to the typical bank collection transaction, that section 3419, subdivision (3), appears to be addressed.

Defendant collecting banks are, therefore, liable to plaintiffs for the amounts of those instruments received by them as of April 1, 1966. Plaintiffs' negligence, however, bars them from recovering for conversion of instruments received after that date. Plaintiffs do not dispute the trial court's finding that their negligence substantially contributed to the conversion of these instruments, and it appears, viewing the evidence in the light most favorable to the judgment, substantial evidence existed to justify such a finding. Stell had been retained by Ruff in 1963 because of her insolvency and because of litigation instituted against her by several creditors. She had informed Stell at that time that her financial difficulties were primarily due to considerable gambling losses she had sustained. A short time thereafter he hired her as a secretary and bookkeeper. He exercised practically no supervision over her, never reviewed the books, and never checked the bank reconciliation of

---

common law negligence or in a suit in equity to prevent unjust impoverishment.

deposits on the accounts she handled. Only during an annual examination made for tax return purposes by one of Stell's partners were Ruff's records reviewed, and even then, despite the suspicious absence of an entry, her accounts were accepted without checking for accuracy or veracity.

Section 3404 provides: "Any unauthorized signature is wholly inoperative as that of the person whose name is signed unless he ratifies it *or is precluded from denying it.* ***."* (Italics added.) The Uniform Commercial Code comment to this section adds the following explanation: "The words 'or is precluded from denying it' are retained in subsection (1) to recognize the possibility of an estoppel against the person whose name is signed, as where he expressly or tacitly represents to an innocent purchaser that the signature is genuine; *and to recognize the negligence which precludes a denial of the signature."* (§ 3404, U.Com.Code com. 4; italics added.) The preclusion language of section 3404 is essentially the same as that of section 23 of the Negotiable Instruments Law (former §3104 of the Civ.Code). This language had been interpreted to provide for equitable estoppel in order to avoid an unconscionable result. We conclude that the doctrine must be invoked in the present case. Plaintiffs' negligent failure to discover Ruff's patent defalcations was directly responsible for defendant depositary banks' detrimental change of position in paying Ruff the amount of the instruments. Defendants acted entirely in good faith, and, though their conduct with respect to certain of the instruments may have fallen somewhat below reasonable commercial standards, it was not sufficiently egregious to shift the balance of the scales in plaintiffs' favor.

For the purpose of this case, therefore, plaintiffs are precluded from denying the forged signatures are operative indorsements. ***

Payor Banks

All but three of the instruments paid by defendant payor banks had been transferred for collection by collecting banks that are also parties to this suit. As indicated above, plaintiffs ratified the collection of these instruments by bringing this action against the collecting banks. This ratification retroactively validates the payor banks' remission of proceeds and provides a defense to an action for conversion. With respect to these instruments, therefore, no liability exists as to any payor bank. Two of the instruments on which this action is based, however, were presented by Ruff directly to the payor, Crocker Bank. The one remaining instrument was collected through banks that are not parties to this action and was also paid by Crocker. With respect to these three instruments no ratification occurred, and we must therefore consider whether Crocker is liable for their conversion.

* * *

Inasmuch as the three instruments that concern us were all transferred by Ruff after April 1, 1966, plaintiffs' negligence stands as a bar to recovery. Section 3406 states that "Any person who by his negligence substantially contributes to a material alteration of the instrument or to the making of an unauthorized signature is precluded from asserting the alteration or lack of authority against a holder in due course or against a drawee or other payor who pays the instrument in good faith and in accordance with the reasonable commercial standards of the drawee's or payor's business."

The record contains substantial evidence to support the trial court's finding that Crocker acted in good faith and in accordance with reasonable commercial standards in handling the three instruments. Ruff held an account with Crocker, and at the time the account was opened, she had been introduced to the bank by one of its established customers. Nothing on the face of the instruments would have led the bank to suspect they were irregular in any way. A single branch of a large bank, as the testimony indicated, may handle several thousand instruments bearing third party indorsements in a single day. Considering this burden, it would be commercially unreasonable to expect payor banks to undertake foolproof efforts to verify ostensibly valid indorsements. Crocker's diligence with respect to the check received through bank collection channels is, of course, particularly evident, inasmuch as Crocker apparently received the instrument with all prior indorsements guaranteed by the collecting banks. Having acted in good faith and in accordance with reasonable commercial standards, Crocker is therefore entitled to invoke the defense of section 3406.

Conclusion

We conclude that defendant collecting banks are liable for the amount of any instrument received by them prior to April 1, 1966. The record reveals that only 7 of the 29 misappropriated checks were received by that date, and each of them was taken for collection by defendant Union Bank. The total amount of these seven checks is $2,791.11. The judgment is therefore reversed with directions to enter judgment against Union for $2,791.11 plus the appropriate interest due on the amounts of each of the seven checks. With respect to the other defendants the judgment is affirmed. The parties shall bear their own costs on appeal.

Stone & Webster Engineering Corp. v. First Nat'l Bank & Trust
Supreme Court of Massachusetts, 1962
345 Mass. 1, 184 N.E.2d 358

Wilkins, Chief Justice. In this action of contract or tort in four counts for the same cause of action a demurrer to the declaration was sustained, and the plaintiff, described in the writ as having a usual place of business in Boston, appealed. The questions argued concern the rights of the drawer against a collecting bank which "cashed" checks for an individual who had forged the payee's indorsement on the checks, which were never delivered to the payee.

In the first count, which is in contract, the plaintiff alleges that between January 1, 1960, and May 15, 1960, it was indebted at various times to Westinghouse Electric Corporation (Westinghouse) for goods and services furnished to it by Westinghouse; that in order to pay the indebtedness the plaintiff drew three checks within that period on its checking account in The First National Bank of Boston (First National) payable to Westinghouse in the total amount of $64,755.44; that before delivery of the checks to Westinghouse an employee of the plaintiff in possession of the checks forged the indorsement of Westinghouse and presented the checks to the defendant; that the defendant "cashed" the checks and delivered the proceeds to the plaintiff's employee who devoted the proceeds to his own use; that the defendant forwarded the checks to First National and received from First National the full amounts thereof; and that First National charged the account of the plaintiff with the full amounts of the checks and has refused to recredit the plaintiff's checking account; wherefore the defendant owes the plaintiff $64,755.44 with interest.

Count 2, also in contract, is on an account annexed for money owed, namely $64,755.44, the proceeds of checks of the plaintiff "cashed" by the defendant on forged indorsements between January 1, 1960, and May 15, 1960.

Counts 3 and 4 in tort are respectively for conversion of the checks and for negligence in "cashing" the checks with forged indorsements.

* * *

1. Count 1, the plaintiff contends, is for money had and received. We shall so regard it. "An action for money had and received lies to recover money which should not in justice be retained by the defendant, and which in equity and good conscience should be paid to the plaintiff."

The defendant has no money in its hands which belongs to the plaintiff. The latter had no right in the proceeds of its own check payable to Westinghouse. Not being a holder or an agent for a holder, it could not have presented the check to the drawee for payment. Uniform Commercial Code, enacted by St.1957, c. 765, §1, G.L. c. 106, §§3-504(1), 1-201(20). See Am.Law Inst. Uniform Commercial Code, 1958 Official Text with comments, §3-419, comment 2: "A negotiable instrument is the property of the holder." See also Restatement 2d: Torts, Tent. draft no. 3, 1958, §241A. The plaintiff contends that "First National paid or credited the proceeds of the checks to the defendant and charged the account of the plaintiff, and consequently, the plaintiff was deprived of a credit, and the defendant received funds or a credit which in equity and good conscience belonged to the plaintiff."

In our opinion this argument is a non sequitur. The plaintiff as a depositor in First National was merely in a contractual relationship of creditor and debtor. The amounts the defendant received from First National to cover the checks "cashed" were the bank's funds and not the plaintiff's. The Uniform Commercial Code does not purport to change the relationship. See G.L. c. 106, §§1-103, 4-401 to 4-407. Section 3-409(1) provides: "A check or other draft does not of itself operate as an assignment of any funds in the hands of the drawee available for its payment, and the drawee is not liable on the instrument until he accepts it." This is the same as our prior law, which the Code repealed. See, formerly, G.L. c. 107, §§150, 212. Whether the plaintiff was rightfully deprived of a credit is a matter between it and the drawee, First National.

If we treat the first count as seeking to base a cause of action for money had and received upon a waiver of the tort of conversion -- a matter which it is not clear is argued -- the result will be the same. In this aspect the question presented is whether a drawer has a right of action for conversion against a collecting bank which handles its checks in the bank collection process. Unless there be such a right, there is no tort which can be waived.

The plaintiff relies upon the Uniform Commercial Code, G.L. c. 106, §3-419, which provides, "(1) An instrument is converted when *** (c) it is paid on a forged indorsement." This, however, could not apply to the defendant, which is not a "payor bank," defined in the Code, §4-105(b), as "a bank by which an item is payable as drawn or accepted." See Am.Law Inst. Uniform Commercial Code, 1958 Official Text with comments, §4-105, comments 1-3; G.L. c. 106, §§4-401, 4-213, 3-102(b).

A conversion provision of the Uniform Commercial Code which might have some bearing on this case is §3-419(3). This section implicitly recognizes that, subject to defences, including the one stated in it, a collecting bank, defined in the Code, §4-105(d), may be liable in conversion. In the case at bar the forged indorsements were "wholly inoperative" as the signatures of the payee, Code §§3-404(1), 1-201(43), and equally so both as to the restrictive indorsements for deposits, see §3-205(c), and as to the indorsement in blank, see §3-204(2). When the forger transferred the checks to the collecting bank, no negotiation under §3-202(1) occurred, because there was lacking the necessary indorsement of the payee. For the same reason, the collecting bank could not become a "holder" as defined in §1-201(20), and so could not become a holder in due course under §3-302(1). Accordingly, we assume that the collecting bank may be liable in conversion to a proper party, subject to defences, including that in §3-419(3). But there is no explicit provision in the Code purporting to determine to whom the collecting bank may be liable, and consequently, the drawer's right to enforce such a liability must be found elsewhere. Therefore, we conclude that the case must be decided on our own law, which, on the issue we are discussing, has been left untouched by the Uniform Commercial Code in any specific section.

* * *

The authorities are hopelessly divided. We think that the preferable view is that there is no right of action.

* * *

We state what appears to us to be the proper analysis. Had the checks been delivered to the payee Westinghouse, the defendant might have been liable for conversion to the payee. The checks, if delivered, in the hands of the payee would have been valuable property which could have been transferred for value or presented for payment; and, had a check been dishonored, the payee would have had a right of recourse against the drawer on the instrument under §3-413(2). Here the plaintiff drawer of the checks, which were never delivered to the payee, had no valuable rights in them. Since, as we have seen, it did not have the right of a payee or subsequent holder to present them to the drawee for payment, the value of its rights was limited to the physical paper on which they were written, and was not measured by their payable amounts.

The enactment of the Uniform Commercial Code opens the road for the adoption of what seems the preferable view. An action by the drawer against the collecting bank might have some theoretical appeal as avoiding circuity of action. It would have been in the interest of speedy and complete justice had the case been tried with the action by the drawer against the drawee and with an action by the drawee against the collecting bank. So one might ask: If the drawee is liable to the drawer and the collecting bank is liable to the drawee, why not let the drawer sue the collecting bank direct? We believe that the answer lies in the applicable defences set up in the Code.[*]

The drawer can insist that the drawee recredit his account with the amount of any unauthorized payment. Such was our common law. This, is in effect, retained by the Code §§4-401(1), 4-406(4). But the drawee has defences based upon the drawer's substantial negligence, if "contributing," or upon his duty to discover and report unauthorized signatures and alterations. §§3-406, 4-406. As to unauthorized indorsements, see §4-406(4). Then, if the drawee has a valid defence which it waives or fails upon request to assert, the drawee may not assert against the collecting bank or other prior party presenting or transferring the check a claim which is based on the forged indorsement. §4-406(5). See Am.Law Inst. Uniform Commercial Code, Official Text with comments, §4-406, comment 6, which shows that there was no intent to change the prior law as to negligence of a customer. If the drawee recredits the drawer's account and is not precluded by §4-406(5), it may claim against the presenting bank on the relevant warranties in §§3-417 and 4-207, and each transferee has rights against his transferor under those sections.

If the drawer's rights are limited to requiring the drawee to recredit his account, the drawee will have the defences noted above and perhaps others; and the collecting bank or banks will have the defences in §4-207(4) and §4-406(5), and perhaps others. If the drawer is allowed in the present case to sue the collecting bank, the assertion of the defences, for all practical purposes, would be difficult. The possibilities of such a result would tend to compel resort to litigation in every case involving a forgery of commercial paper. It is a result to be avoided.

The demurrer to count 1 [and also to all other counts] was rightly sustained.

* * *

4. Count 4 alleges that "on divers dates between January 1, 1960, and May 15, 1960, the defendant by reason of its negligence in cashing checks with forged indorsements thereon

---

[*] Cases where a payee has acquired rights in an instrument may stand on a different footing.

4. Count 4 alleges that "on divers dates between January 1, 1960, and May 15, 1960, the defendant by reason of its negligence in cashing checks with forged indorsements thereon damaged the plaintiff the full amount of said checks, to wit $64,755.44. Wherefore, the plaintiff prays judgment against the defendant in the sum of $64,755.44, with interest." From the checks, we observe that, wholly apart from any duty on the part of the defendant toward the plaintiff, there is no allegation of legal damage. When the defendant "cashed" checks with its own funds, no legal harm befell the plaintiff. From what we have said in respect of counts 1 and 3, there would be difficulty in making such an allegation. The harm which befell the plaintiff was the charging of its account by the drawee bank. As has been noted above, the drawer has a cause of action, possibly subject to defences, against that bank. It does not appear that this right is impaired.

There was no error in sustaining the demurrer to count 4.

Order sustaining demurrer affirmed.

UNDERPINNING & FOUNDATION CONSTRUCTORS, INC. v. CHASE MANHATTAN BANK, 46 N.Y.2d 459, 386 N.E.2d 1319, 1321, 414 N.Y.S.2d 298 (1979). [The plaintiff, Underpinning, employed Walker in its accounting department. Sadly, Walker was dishonest. He prepared false invoices, prepared checks in payment of them, and obtained the necessary signatures from plaintiff's officers. Walker then forged the indorsements of the payees, adding to these indorsements the restriction "for deposit only." The checks were then either cashed or deposited in savings accounts opened at various banks by Walker or his associates, in names other than the names of the named payee-indorsers. Each of the depositary-collecting banks followed the instructions of the wrongdoer, wholly disregarding the restrictive indorsements. The checks were paid by the drawee bank. Plaintiff sued the depositary-collecting banks for disregarding the restrictive indorsements. Relying on New York authority similar to *Stone & Webester Engineering Corp. v. First Nat'l Bank & Trust*, the defendants moved to dismiss. The trial court denied the motion, and this decision was upheld by the intermediate appellate court. The Court of Appeals affirmed in an opinion by Judge Gabrielli, who wrote in part:]

[T]he reason why a drawer is normally held to have no cause of action against a depositary bank which wrongfully paid over a forged indorsement, is that the depositary bank is not deemed to have dealt with any valuable property of the drawer *** [because] the check will not authorize the drawee bank to pay it from the drawer's account. Absent such authority, the drawee may not charge the drawer's account and any payment made on the check is deemed to have been made solely from the property of the drawee, not the drawer. *** Moreover, since the check cannot be paid over a forged indorsement, the drawer is viewed as having no valuable interest in whatever right the check might otherwise be seen as transferring to the payee and to subsequent holders, for the simple reason that there exists no such right.

Whatever the intrinsic validity of these arguments in the typical forged indorsement case in which the forged indorsement is "wholly inoperative" (Uniform Commercial Code, §3-404), the applicable considerations change when the indorsement, although forged, is yet effective. In such cases, the check is both a valuable instrument and a valid instruction to the drawee to honor the check and debit the drawer's account accordingly. Since the result of valid payment on the check is the cancellation of a debt otherwise owed the drawer and the payment of funds otherwise claimable by the drawer, the drawer obviously does have an interest in the funds paid on the check. Where the indorsement is ineffective, the drawee is deemed to be paying out its own money because it cannot charge the drawer's account without authorization. Where, however, the indorsement is deemed effective, then the drawee is in fact paying out funds in which the drawer does have an interest and which may serve as the basis for an action against a depositary bank which has wrongfully obtained that money. Naturally, in such a case, since the indorsement is effective, no action would lie against the depositary bank for payment over the forged indorsement. Moreover, if the check was tainted in some other way which would put the drawee on notice, and which would make its payment unauthorized and subject it to suit, then the above rationale would not apply, since the payment would once again be from the drawee's funds rather than the drawer's account, and thus no action would lie against the depositary bank in favor of the drawer. Hence, it is only in those comparatively rare instances in which the depositary bank has acted wrongfully and yet the drawee has acted properly that the drawer will be able to proceed directly against the depositary bank.

Applying these principles to this case, we conclude that plaintiff has stated a cause of action against defendant Bank of New York sufficient to withstand a motion to dismiss for failure to state a cause of action [because the complaint indicates that the indorsements in this case were effective under U.C.C. §3-405(1)(c), and] hence the traditional reasons for refusing to allow a drawer to sue a depositary bank directly in a forged indorsement case are inapplicable, as the money paid to the depositary bank by the drawee was property in which the drawer had a very real interest.

* * *

In summary, we hold today that a drawer may directly sue a depositary bank which has honored a check in violation of a forged restrictive indorsement in situations in which the forgery is effective. This result is not only theoretically viable, but is in accord with principles of equity and sound public policy. It is basic to the law of commercial paper that as between innocent parties any loss should ultimately be placed on the party which could most easily have prevented that loss. Hence, in most forged indorsement cases, the party who first took the check from the forger will ultimately be liable, assuming of course that there is no solvent forger available. This is so because it is the party who takes from the forger who is in the best position to verify the indorsement. This is not always true, however, and if the forgery is the result of some other interested party's negligence, the burden may ultimately be placed on that party (see Uniform Commercial Code §3-406). In certain instances in which it is clear that the loss could have been most readily prevented by the drawer, the code may place the loss upon the drawer as a matter of law (Uniform Commercial Code, §3-405). One such situation might be that alleged to be present in this case, in which the indorsement of a named payee has been forged by "an agent or employee of the maker or drawer (who) has supplied him with the name of the payee intending the latter to have no such interest" (Uniform Commercial Code, §3-405, subd. (1) par. (c)). In such cases, the indorsement is deemed to be effective and the drawer is thus precluded from recovering solely on the basis of the forgery from banks which honor the check. The reason for this rule is that it is believed that as a practical matter the drawer is in a better position to prevent the fraud by utilizing proper accounting methods, than is even the first party to take from the forger. Although this presumption is not free from criticism, and may in some instances be less than sound, the language of the code makes it applicable.

Had the forger in this case not forged a check with a restrictive indorsement, it would appear that the loss might properly be placed upon the drawer alone. A restrictive indorsement, however, imposes a new and separate duty upon a transferee to pay the check only in accord with the restriction. In this case, the restrictive indorsements required that the checks be deposited only in the accounts of the respective restrictive indorsers, the named payees. This was not done and the failure to do so serves as a basis for liability independent of any liability which might be created by payment over a forged indorsement alone.

It has been suggested that it is illogical to reach a different result dependent only on whether the forger adds a restriction to the indorsement or not. Although superficially attractive, this argument could as readily serve as a challenge to the soundness of the code provisions imposing a liability upon the drawer where the forger has chosen to act in one way rather than another (see Uniform Commercial Code, §3-405). The obvious flaw in the argument made is that it ignores the prime function of all these rules and distinctions: to impose liability on the party which could most readily have prevented the fraud. Where the only defect is the forgery itself and the forgery could and should have been prevented by the drawer, liability is imposed on the drawer. Where, however, as here, the indorsement is not only forged, but is also restrictive, and the check is presented in what appears on its face to be an obvious violation of that restriction, then the situation is different, and the balance of obligations and potential liabilities shifts. That an indorsement is forged does not serve to justify a failure to apply normal commercial standards with respect to any restrictions imposed by the indorsement. The presence of a restriction imposes upon the depositary bank an obligation not to accept that item other than in accord with the restriction. By disregarding the restriction, it not only subjects itself to liability for any losses resulting from its actions, but it also passes up what may well be the best opportunity to prevent the fraud. The presentation of a check in violation of a restrictive indorsement for deposit in the account of someone other than the restrictive indorser is an obvious warning sign, and the depositary bank is required to investigate the situation rather than blindly accept the check. Based on such a failure to follow the mandates of due care and commercially reasonable behavior, it is appropriate to shift ultimate liability from the drawer to the depositary bank.

Accordingly, the order appealed from should be affirmed, with costs, and the question certified should be answered in the affirmative.

practice

Case 1

T steals D's checkbook. Using D's name, T draws a check payable to S in exchange for goods T purchased from S. S presents the check to D's bank for payment. The check is dishonored because the bank has been notified of the theft of D's checkbook.

a.   S sues D on the instrument. What result? 3-414(b); 3-401(a); 3-403(a).

b.   Suppose that D's bank does not learn of the theft before S presents the check for payment. The bank pays the item in good faith and debits D's account accordingly. Can D force the bank to recredit her account? See 4-401(a). (Ask yourself if the check is properly payable from D's account if D's signature as drawer is forged. See, e.g., *Indiana Nat'l Corp. v. Faco, Inc.,* 400 N.E.2d 202 (Ind.Ct.App.1980) ("[i]t is a general rule that a bank is presumed to know the signatures of its depositors and pays forged checks at its peril")).

Yes

c. Checks drawn on the checking account of D Corp. required the signatures of
    both the president and treasurer. If the drawee pays items drawn over the
    signature of only one of these people, can the company rightfully demand
    the recrediting of its account? See, e.g., *German Educ. Television Network,
    Ltd. v. Bankers Trust Co.*, 109 A.D.2d 684, 487 N.Y.S.2d 26, (1985) (summary
    judgment against payor bank was appropriate on the authority of 4-401
    because bank paid check with only one signatory and two signatories where
    required). For a vast collection of cases with holdings similar to *German
    Educational*, see James L. Rigelhaupt, Annotation, *Banks Liability for Payment
    or Withdrawal on Less Than Required Number of Signatures* 7 A.L.R. 4th 655
    (1981).

                                                                              Yes

Case 2

"On May 7, 1975, Mrs. Ray, an eighty-year-old lady, was awakened from a nap
by a man who was shaking the screen to her front door. He gave his name as
Robert Freeman, said he worked for the utility company, and that he needed to
check the electrical system of the home because the power was off along the
block. Mrs. Ray testified that when she unlatched the screen to look down the
street for a utility vehicle, Freeman pushed his way inside the house. He went
around the house placing a device in the electrical outlets and then went
outside to check in the garage. While he was outside, she later discovered, he
cut the telephone wire to her house. Upon returning, he told Mrs. Ray that he
was not through, but that he was awaiting the arrival of someone else from
the utility company. He said that he was going to get a hamburger and would
return after lunch, but that she should give him $1.50 for the service charge.
Mrs. Ray testified that she could not see what he had done to earn $1.50 but
was willing to give him the money to get him out of the house. She reached
for her purse, but Freeman picked up her checkbook that was lying on the
table telling her that his company required payment by check. He proceeded
to fill it in, then shoved it over to her to be signed. She noted to herself that
the check was for $1.50 and was in ink so that it couldn't be changed. She
signed the check and Freeman left.

"After waiting a considerable period of time, Mrs. Ray concluded that Freeman
was not going to return. She decided to phone the bank to stop payment on
the check because he had not earned the money. She then discovered the
phone was dead. Mrs. Ray walked down the street to use a neighbor's phone
but could find nobody at home. After two hours later, when she finally talked
to a lady at the bank, she learned that Freeman had cashed the check and that
it was for $1,851.50 instead of $1.50.

"When Freeman filled out the check at Mrs. Ray's home, he wrote the figures
'1.50' far to the right of the dollar mark, leaving space in which he later added
the figures '185.' That made the amount appear as $1,851.50. There is some
evidence that he also left space on the next line where he wrote the words
'one and 50/100.' He later placed in front of those words, 'Eighteen Hundred &
Fifty.'" *Ray v. Farmers' State Bank*, 576 S.W.2d 607, 607-08 (Tex.1979).

a. In this case, the trial court found as facts that, in paying the check as altered in the amount of $1,851.50, the payor bank acted in good faith and in accordance with reasonable commercial standards of the bank's business, and that the bank paid the check in due course of its banking business. Nevertheless, the trial court concluded, and the Texas Supreme Court agreed, that the bank could only charge Mrs. Ray's account according to the original tenor of the item, $1.50. What law supports this conclusion? See 4-401(d)(1).

b. Suppose that Mrs. Ray had signed a blank check which she instructed Freeman to complete in the amount of $1.50. Freeman later disobeyed her instructions and completed the check in the amount of $1,851.50. To what extent can the bank charge Mrs. Ray's account? See 4-401(d)(2); *Russello v. Highland Nat'l Bank,* 56 A.D.2d 772, 392 N.Y.S.2d 439 (1977) (4-401 fully protected drawee which paid checks drawn by its customer in blank that a relative of the customer had wrongfully completed); compare *Kings Premium Service Corp. v. Manufacturers Hanover Trust,* 115 A.D.2d 707, 496 N.Y.S.2d 524 (1985) (drawee liable to drawer for paying check that drawer had signed in blank where check was made payable to individual person despite legend on check specifying "only payable to automobile insurance plan or an insurance company").

$1,851.50

Case 3

D drew a check to P for the price of goods. An employee of P, acting without authority and using P's name, indorsed the check and cashed it at First Bank. The employee then fled with the proceeds. First Bank presented the check for payment. The payor bank paid the item and debited D's account accordingly.

a. Can P successfully sue D on the check or on the underlying sales transaction?

Yes

b. Can D force the payor bank to recredit her account in the amount of the stolen check which the bank paid and charged to her account?

c. Suppose the employee did not forge P's indorsement on the check. She cashed the check without indorsing it in any fashion.

Yes

i. Can D force the payor bank to recredit her account? See, e.g., *Tonelli v. Chase Manhattan Bank,* 41 N.Y.2d 667, 394 N.Y.S.2d 858, 363 N.E.2d 564 (1977) (a check presented without the payee's indorsement is not properly payable and the drawer's account cannot be charged for the amount of the item).

ii. Could you successfully argue for a different result in this part of the problem on the basis of 4-205?

d. Suppose the employee did not steal the check. P delivered the check to the employee and instructed her to cash the item. So the employee dutifully cashed the unindorsed item at First Bank, and then she absconded with the proceeds. The payor bank paid the check when First Bank presented it. D demands that the payor bank recredit her account. Is the payor obligated to comply with this demand?

e. Suppose the employee stole the check; cashed the unindorsed item; and, upon second thought, gave the proceeds to P. D, who is dissatisfied with her deal with P, demands that the payor bank recredit her account. D argues that, in paying the check without an indorsement by P, the bank paid an item that was not properly payable. Must the payor bank comply with D's demand?

Case 4

D drew a check payable to A and B. A indorsed the check by signing her name and also B's name. A lacked authority to act for B in this or any other regard. A then cashed the check at First Bank and absconded with all of the proceeds. B got nothing. Upon presentment of the check by First Bank, the payor bank paid the item and charged D's account accordingly.

a. Must the payor bank recredit D's account to some extent if so demanded by D? *Dykstra v. National Bank*, 328 N.W.2d 862 (S.D.1983) (drawer can recover from drawee that paid check over a "forged" indorsement of one of two payees of the instrument even though forged signature was that of a fictitious person).   *Yes*

b. Is the answer the same if A indorsed the check by signing only her name? *Travelers Ins. Co. v. Connecticut Bank & Trust Co*, 40 Conn.Supp. 70, 481 A.2d 111 (1984) (summary judgment against payor bank affirmed where bank paid check despite missing indorsement of one of two joint payees); *Cincinnati Ins. Co. v. First Nat'l Bank*, 63 Ohio St.2d 220, 407 N.E.2d 519 (1980) (checks payable to two payees jointly and not indorsed by both of them were not properly payable); *Murray Walter, Inc. v. Marine Midland Bank*, 103 A.D.2d 466, 480 N.Y.S.2d 631 (1984) (same); *Middle States Leasing Corp. v. Manufacturers Hanover Trust Co*, 62 A.D.2d 273, 404 N.Y.S.2d 846 (1978) (same).   *Yes*

c. Would the answers change if A and B were business partners with respect to the transaction involving the sale of the goods?

Case 5

D Corp. and Bank agreed that Bank should pay items drawn over the facsimile signature of D's treasurer. A thief stole check forms belonging to D and, using the device for imprinting the treasurer's facsimile signature on instruments, drew several items payable to herself. The thief then cashed the items at Bank.

a. Can D Corp. force the payor bank to recredit the company's account? See 3-110(a); *Perini Corp. v. First Nat'l Bank*, 553 F.2d 398 (5th Cir.1977);

Wilmington Trust Co. v. Phoenix Steel Corp, 273 A.2d 266 (Del.1971); compare *Cumis Ins. Soc'y, Inc. v. Girard Bank,* 522 F.Supp. 414 (E.D.Pa.1981).

b. Would the result be different or more certain if the thief had drawn the checks payable to a third person and indorsed them using that person's name? These circumstances describe a double forgery, i.e., the signatures of both the drawer and indorser are forged or otherwise defective. The courts treat a double-forgery case as if only the drawer's signature was forged. Thus, if the drawer's signature is deemed effective, or for other reasons cannot be complained of, the forged indorsement provides no basis for relief. See *National Credit Union Admin. v. Michigan Nat'l Bank,* 771 F.2d 154 (6th Cir.1985); *Perini Corp. v. First Nat'l Bank,* 553 F.2d 398 (5th Cir.1977).

⊓⊓⊓⊓⊓

Case 6

The bookkeeper in D's business office regularly stole blank check forms from the back of D's checkbook and issued instruments to himself over the forged signature of D. He cashed these items at a small suburban bank near his house, and this bank forwarded them to the drawee for payment. D's bank, the drawee, paid every one of them. This pattern of theft continued for two years without detection, largely because the bookkeeper's work was unsupervised, and he was the person responsible for reconciling the business books with statements of account sent by the drawee-payor bank. The scheme was finally uncovered during a surprise audit of D's books by the IRS. The bookkeeper embezzled $100,000, which is the amount that D argues the payor must recredit to her account.

a. Does the bank have a good defense under 3-406?

Probably   b. Does 4-406 provide defenses for the bank?

Probably   c. Is the bank's reliance on 3-406 or 4-406 affected by its failure to verify the drawer's signature on the checks? See 3-103(a)(7).

Maybe not

Case 7

D drew and mailed a check to P in payment for the price of goods. The bookkeeper in P's office stole the check, forged P's indorsement, and cashed the item which was paid by the drawee. Several months later D and P discovered the theft and forgery. D demanded that the drawee recredit its account for the amount of the item.

Does 4-406 provide the drawee bank any protection?

No

Case 8

D drew a check to Joan Smith whose address was 1134 South Hampton Drive. By mistake, D mailed the check to 1134 North Hampton Ave., which was listed in the telephone directory as the address of J. Smith. This person, whose first name is also Joan, received the check, indorsed it, and got the drawee to pay it. The Joan Smith whom D had intended to pay notified D that she had not received the expected check. D then discovered what had happened and demanded that the drawee recredit its account.

What is the bank's defense? See 3-406(a) & comment 3 *(Case #2).*

Case 9

Upon answering a knock at his door, D, a religious fundamentalist, found a man who said his name was Pastor Oral Roberts and asked for a contribution for his cause of returning God to the classroom. D mistakenly believed this man to be THE Oral Roberts who is a famous evangelist and faith healer. D thus gave the man a check for $500 payable to the order of Oral Roberts. The check was paid by the drawee. When D discovered his mistake, he demanded that the drawee recredit his account, arguing that the indorsement on the check was not the signature of the intended payee, the real Oral Roberts. Consequently, D concluded, the check was not properly payable.

a. **What result on these facts? See 3-404(a).**

b. **Would the result be different if the impostor had gotten the check as a result of a solicitation letter sent through the mail to D?** *No*

c. **Suppose that the man at D's door falsely represented that he was an assistant minister to the real Oral Roberts. D gave him a check payable to Oral Roberts. D indorsed the check using the name of Oral Roberts and cashed it. The check was paid by the drawee. Does 3-404(a) protect the drawee against D's demand that his account be recredited?** *No*

d. **Suppose that D drew the check payable not to Oral Roberts, but to the false agent. Is the wrongdoer's indorsement in his own name effective under 3-404(a)?** *Yes*

Case 10

T was the treasurer of D Corp. which had authorized T to draw checks on the company's behalf. T drew a check on the account of D Corp. payable to Zerox Co., which was a name pulled from T's imagination. T then indorsed the check, "Zerox Co., Inc., by John Smith," and deposited it in an account he had opened under his name d/b/a Zerox Company. The check was forwarded to the drawee which paid the item. T cleaned out the Zerox account and fled with the proceeds. D Corp. demands that the drawee recredit its account.

a. **In defense, the drawee relies on 3-404(b). What result?**

Probably   **b.**   Is 3-405 applicable, additionally or alternatively?

Same result   **c.**   Would the result be different if Zerox Company was a real entity from which D Corp. regularly purchased goods?

No   **d.**   Would the result be different if T drew the checks payable to herself?

Probably   **e.**   Would the result be different if D Corp. had not authorized T to issue checks on its behalf?

Case 11

Suppose that T was the invoice clerk of D Corp. with no authority to issue checks for the company. T's job was to keep track of D Corp.'s accounts payable and to prepare lists of verified, mature debts of D Corp. which would be paid by checks issued through the office of the company secretary. T prepared a false invoice purportedly received from a fictitious entity, Zerox Co. T then submitted this invoice, along with legitimate debts, to the secretary's office for payment by D. Corp. A check payable to Zerox Co. was issued and signed by the company secretary who was authorized to issue instruments on behalf of D Corp. T then took the check and cashed it at the bank where she had opened the account in the name of Zerox Corp. The check was paid by the drawee. D Corp. discovered what had happened only after T had quit and fled with the proceeds of the Zerox account.

a.   D Corp. demands that the drawee recredit its account. The drawee relies defensively on 3-405(b). What result?

No   **b.**   Would 3-404(b) apply, alternatively or additionally?

c.   Would the result be different if Zerox Co. was a real entity from which D Corp. regularly purchased goods?

d.   Would the analysis or result be different if Zerox Co. had submitted an invoice for goods sold to D Corp. and the check which T took was in payment of that account?

e.   Consider whether the results would be affected by evidence that, in paying the checks drawn against D Corp.'s account, the drawee failed to follow procedures dictated by reasonably prudent banking practice.

ᴑᴑᴑᴑᴑᴑ

Case 12

D's signature as drawer was forged by her secretary on a large check payable to the secretary's order. The item was cashed at CB Bank and was paid by the payor bank, PB Bank. The secretary is currently enjoying a vacation at some unknown spa. Two months later, D discovers the theft and demands that the payor recredit her account. PB Bank agrees and then sues CB which innocently cashed the item for the secretary.

a.   Is CB liable on the instrument itself?   *No*

b.   Can PB Bank recoup under 4-301?   *No*

c.   Did CB breach a warranty of presentment?   *No*

d.   Can PNB Bank recover from First Bank on a restitution theory? See 3-418;   *Probably not*
     Price v. Neal, [K.B. 1762] 3 Burr. 1354, 97 Eng.Rep. 871, which is reprinted in
     Chapter 2 supra.

Case 13

D bought goods from P and paid by check. An employee of P stole the check and forged P's indorsement. The employee then cashed the check at CB Bank which forwarded it for payment to the drawee, PB Bank. The item was paid. D issued P a second check for the price of the goods. (Why would D issue a second check?) PB recredited D's account for the amount of the first item. (Why?) PB then asks you if it can recoup its loss on the first check from CB. Consider these theories:

a.   Can PB sue CB on the instrument itself?

     i.   Did CB sign the instrument? In what capacity?

     ii.   Is an indorser's liability conditioned? Was the instrument dishonored?

b.   Can PB recover credit given CB for the item under 4-301. (When does the right to revoke a provisional credit expire? Was the instrument finally paid?)

c.   Can PB sue CB for breach of warranty under 4-208(a)? See, e.g., *KOUS-TV, Inc. v. Spot Time, Ltd.*, 599 F.Supp. 90 (S.D.N.Y.1984) (to the extent that drawee is liable to its customer for paying checks with forged indorsements, drawee can recover from depository bank for breach of the warranty of good title); *First Nat'l Bank v. Plymouth-Home Nat'l Bank*, 553 F.Supp. 448 (D.Mass.1982) (if a check contains a forged indorsement, the depositary bank does not have good title to the instrument and presentment warranty is breached).

     i.   If PB sues CB on a breach of warranty theory, why cannot CB successfully defend on the basis that PB finally paid the item under 4-215? (Ask if 3-418 protects CB from the warranty action.)

     ii.   Would PB's lack of good faith in paying the instrument provide a defense for CB?

     iii. Are there other defenses that CB possibly can raise?

iv. Can CB raise as a defense against PB any sort of culpability or accountability or responsibility of the drawer or payee of the instrument? See 4-208(c).

Case 14

D bought goods from P and paid by check. An employee of P stole the check and forged P's indorsement. The employee then cashed the check at CB Bank which forwarded it for payment to the drawee, PB Bank. The item was paid.

a. Instead of getting D to pay again, P can recover from the depositary bank, CB.

i. How so?

ii. P alternatively can recover from the drawee, PB Bank. How so?

iii. Can CB and PB raise as a defense any sort of culpability of the drawer or payee of the instrument?

b. Suppose that P authorized the employee to indorse the checks for deposit into P's account. See *Oswald Machine & Equip., Inc. v. Yip* 10 Cal.App.4th 1238, 13 Cal. Rptr.2d 193 (1992) (authority to make particular restrictive indorsements does not necessarily include authority to indorse in fictitious names for deposit to sham accounts); *Atena Casualty and Surety Co. v. Hepler State Bank*, 6 Kan.App.2d 543, 630 P.2d 721 (1981) (giving indorser authority to collect checks made payable to company exclusively pursuant to company policy and furnishing indorser rubber stamp to mark in payee's name on check fell short of demonstrating "implied intent" that indorser should have authority to indorse and cash company checks).

c.. Suppose the check was payable to the order of P and Q. P herself indorsed and forged Q's indorsement. To what extent can Q recover from CB Bank? See *Clark v. Griffin*, 481 N.E.2d 170 (Ind.App.1985) (joint payee whose indorsement was forged is entitled to recover from drawee only to the extent of the loss actually suffered, relying on common-law principles); *Quintana v. Allstate Ins. Co*, 378 N.W.2d 40 (Minn.App.1985) (same by implication).

Case 15

D bought goods from P and paid by check. An employee of P stole the check and forged P's indorsement. The employee then cashed the check at CB Bank which forwarded it for payment to the drawee, PB Bank. The item was paid. D issued P a second check for the price of the goods. P got payment.

a. Instead of recovering from PB Bank, can D recover from CB Bank?

b. Suppose that T, who was a dishonest employee of D, took the check before D had a chance to send it to P. T forged P's indorsement and cashed the check at CB Bank. PB Bank paid the item and charged it against D's account.

    i.   From whom can D recover?

    ii.   Can P recover from either bank?

c. Suppose that T took the check from D but did not forge P's indorsement. Instead, T used the check (which was payable to P's order) to pay for property she bought for herself from P. Is P accountable to D? See *Carrefour U.S.A. Properties Inc. v. 110 Sand Co.*, 918 F.2d 345 (2d Cir. 1990); *Eldon's Super Fresh Stores, Inc. v. Merrill Lynch, Pierce, Fenner & Smith, Inc.*, 296 Minn. 130, 207 N.W.2d 282 (1973), reprinted in Chapter 5 supra. These cases imply that the payee is immune to liability if the payee takes the instrument as a holder in due course. Compare cases in which checks payable to banks were misapplied to the credit of a third person and in which the courts suggested that the banks, depending on their notice, can be liable for not taking steps to see that checks were properly applied, such as *Terre Haute Indus., Inc. v. Pawlik*, 765 F. Supp. 925 (N.D. Ill. 1991); *Master Chemical Corp. v. Inkrott*, 563 N.E.2d 26 (Ohio 1990). The issue is the nature of the liability for which immunity is necessary. What is the theory of liability against the payee in the first instance?

d. Suppose that T forged a check on D's account, made it payable to her own order, and cashed the check at CB Bank. Can D recover from CB? See *G.F.D. Enter., Inc. v. Nye*, 37 Ohio.St.3d 205, 525 N.E.2d 10 (1988) (bank protected because of final payment rule,.that is, its status as holder in due course bars restitution action).

e. Suppose that T was authorized to draw checks on D's account. T drew a check on the account to her own order and cashed it at CB Bank. Is CB accountable? See *Penalosa Coop. Exch. v. A.S. Polonyi Co.*, 754 F. Supp. 722 (W.D. Mo. 1991) (issue is transferee's status as holder in due course); *Johnstown Mfg., Inc. v. Haynes*, 557 N.E.2d 1221 (Ohio Ct. App. 1988) (bank was protected as holder in due course).

Chapter 7. Special Uses Of Ordinary Drafts With Other Commercial Paper

§ 1. Payment Against Documents

A seller who takes the buyer's check in exchange for property or services is not certain to get payment from the drawee-bank. The check can be dishonored for a variety of reasons (insufficient funds, stop order, etc.) that leave the seller-payee with nothing more than a cause of action against the buyer-drawer. The result is that, although the seller intended a cash deal, she ends up having sold on credit. To make matters worse, this unintended credit is most often unsecured.

A seller of goods can insure that she is actually paid by not delivering the property until she gets cash, or its equivalent, in hand. Of course, the typical buyer will not wish to pay for the goods in advance of delivery. The answer is a simultaneous exchange of goods for cash. When the seller and buyer are located far apart, this kind of exchange is made possible through a payment scheme known as "payment against documents," which is powered by a combination of principles codified in U.C.C. Articles 3, 4 and 7.

The following description of payment against documents is designed to walk you through the three basic steps in the scheme and provide a general overview of how the scheme works. As you stroll along, pay close attention to the interrelationship of the principles of documents of title and negotiable instruments law, and observe how the two bodies of law combine to make the scheme work. Your main job is to consider the extent to which the different risks of the buyer and the seller are minimized so as to make the scheme attractive and useful to both of them.

story

Step one: creating the documentary draft

Upon shipping the goods to the buyer, the seller has the carrier issue a negotiable bill of lading to the seller's order. The bill of lading is a document of title that, when state law applies, is governed by U.C.C. Article 7.[*] The bill will probably direct the carrier to notify the buyer when the goods arrive in the buyer's vicinity. Yet, because the bill is a negotiable document, the carrier cannot properly deliver the goods to anyone except a holder of the document. 7-403(1) & (4). So, even though the seller has asked the carrier to notify the buyer of the arrival of the goods, the carrier cannot surrender the goods to the buyer unless the buyer holds the bill of lading.

At the time of shipment, the holder of the bill is the seller. 1-201(20) (defining "holder"). It was issued to her order, and she is in possession of it. So, even though the seller has shipped the goods, she remains in control of them because she holds the negotiable document covering the goods and thereby holds the key to getting possession of them from the carrier. Moreover, by shipping the goods under a negotiable document to her own order, the seller effectively retains, by law, a security interest in the goods. 2-505(1)(a). This interest is important to the seller because, if the contract is a shipment contract, title to the goods will pass to the buyer when they are shipped despite the seller having procured a negotiable document covering the goods. See 2-401(2)(a).

The seller will attach the bill of lading to an Article 3 draft, in the amount of the price of the goods, drawn against the buyer. The seller is both the drawer and payee of the draft, which is payable at sight or on demand. The draft with the accompanying bill of lading is referred to as a *documentary draft*. 4-104(a)(6). The seller will not send the documentary draft directly to the buyer. Rather, she will ask her bank to send the draft through banking channels for the purpose of collecting it from the buyer.

---

[*] Federal law often preempts the U.C.C. The Pomerene Bills of Lading Act governs "[b]ills of lading issued by any common carrier for the transportation of goods in any Territory of the United States, or the District of Columbia, or from a place in a State to a place in a foreign country, or from a place in one State to a place in another State, or from a place in one State to a place in the same State through another State or foreign country." 49 U.S.C.A. app. 81 (§§ 81 to 124). The Carriage of Goods by Sea Act applies to "[e]very bill of lading or similar document of title which is evidence of a contract for the carriage of goods by sea to or from ports of the United States, in foreign trade." 46 U.S.C.A. app. 1300 (§§ 1300-1315). These federal laws are mostly consistent with Article 7.

Step two: sending the documentary draft for collection

The collection activities of banks, and the scope of UCC Article 4, are not limited to checks. Banks collect, and Article 4 regulates, other kinds of items. "'*Item*' means an instrument or a promise or order to pay money handled by a bank for collection or payment." 4-104(a)(9) (emphasis added). A documentary draft is an item, and a seller who seeks payment against documents can have her bank collect the documentary draft she has drawn against the buyer. Part 5 of Article 4 deals with the collection of documentary drafts.

The seller will indorse both the draft and document that comprise her documentary draft and transfer them to her bank. The bank treats the draft, however, very different than a check. A check is treated as cash, and the depositor's account is credited with the amount of the item immediately upon deposit because the bank assumes that the item will be paid. Banks thus commonly refer to checks as *cash items*. There is no assumption that a documentary draft will be paid. So, when the bank takes a documentary draft from the seller for collection, the seller's account is not credited with the item. Thus, instead of referring to the draft as a cash item, the bank labels it a *collection item*, which means that credit will be given to the seller's account only if and when the draft is actually collected, that is, when the buyer makes payment and the payment is remitted to the depositary bank.

Upon taking a documentary draft for collection, the seller's bank, which in Article 4 terms is the depositary-collecting bank, "shall present or send the draft and accompanying documents for presentment." 4-501. The bank, however, does not send the documentary draft to the buyer. Rather, it is sent, through banking channels, to a bank where the buyer is located for the purpose of having the latter bank present the item to the buyer for payment. In this regard Article 4 requires the seller's bank, which is a collecting bank, to "exercise ordinary care in * * * sending [the item] for presentment," 4-202(a)(1), which requires the bank to "send [the item] by a reasonably prompt method," 4-204(a), and to send the item before the bank's midnight deadline. 4-202(b).

The documentary draft will end up in the hands of a bank where the buyer is located. This bank is known as the *presenting bank*, see 4-105(6). It is not a payor bank because the presenting bank is not the drawee of the draft. The buyer is the drawee. The presenting bank is acting solely as the agent, or sub-agent, of the owner of the item, i.e., the seller, for the purpose of collecting the item from the buyer. So, like the seller's bank, the presenting bank is a collecting bank whose duties are very different from a payor bank.

Step three: presenting the documentary draft for payment

The presenting bank is obligated to present the documentary draft to the buyer-drawee for payment. The bank can, and probably will, make presentment by sending the buyer, who is the drawee, a written notice that the bank holds the item for payment. See 4-212(a). In this event, the draft is deemed presented when the buyer-drawee receives the notice. 3-501(b)(1). To avoid dishonor of the draft, the buyer must make payment on the day of presentment, 3-502(b)(2), "except that payment * * * may be delayed without dishonor until no later than the close of the third business day of the drawee following the day on which payment * * * is required." 3-502(c). Upon receiving payment of the draft, the presenting bank is obligated to deliver the documents to the drawee. 4-503(1).

Here is the exact point at which the simultaneous exchange of goods for cash takes place. The buyer tenders actual payment, which typically is cash or a cash equivalent. This payment is sent back down the collection chain to the seller's bank which will credit it to the seller's account. In return, the buyer gets the bill of lading covering the goods. Remember that the bill was indorsed in blank by the seller to whose order the bill was issued. Thus, the buyer, by taking possession of the bill, becomes the holder of the document, and thus the holder of the key to the goods, because the carrier-bailee's obligation to deliver the goods now runs to the buyer qua holder of the negotiable bill of lading. 7-403(1) & (4).

Variations

1. Shipping Under a Non-Negotiable Document

So far, the discussion of payment against documents has assumed that the goods are covered by a negotiable document. Payment against documents can be structured, however, so that the goods are shipped under a non-negotiable bill of lading. In this event, the seller retains control of the goods by consigning them to herself or her agent so that the carrier is obligated to deliver the goods according to the seller's instructions. 7-403(1) & (4). The seller or her agent will instruct the carrier to surrender the goods to the buyer upon the buyer's payment of the draft.

This variation is less acceptable to the buyer for two basic reasons: First, paying the draft does not give the buyer exclusive control of the goods, as is true when she pays and gets a negotiable document covering them. Even after a buyer pays a draft against a non-negotiable document, the carrier can rightfully deliver the goods to whomever the seller instructs (at least if the carrier has not received notice of the buyer's claim). This is true even if the buyer receives, upon paying the draft, a delivery order in her favor. Second, a buyer who pays against a non-negotiable document cannot have the rights of a holder who takes through due negotiation. These rights are possible only when a negotiable document is negotiated. Thus, the buyer would have no protection against pre-existing claims to the document or the goods themselves.

2. Discounting Documentary Drafts

Typically, when a depositary bank takes a documentary draft for collection, the amount of the draft is not credited against the seller-customer's account until the draft is actually paid by the buyer-drawee and payment is remitted through banking channels to the depositary bank. The seller, however, may convince her bank to purchase the draft from her rather than simply take it for collection. This arrangement is referred to as *discounting the draft*.

Obviously, by discounting a documentary draft, the depositary bank assumes the risk of the buyer's dishonor. This risk is well insured, however. In effect, the goods become collateral for the bank's advance, inasmuch as the bank acquires a security interest in the document, 4-210(a); and the bank enjoys the control and rights of a holder of the document who acquired it through due negotiation. Also, upon the buyer's dishonor and notice to the seller-drawer, the latter party becomes liable on the draft to the bank. Arguably, though not certainly, the bank has the 4-214(a) right to charge back the amount of the item to the seller's account. 4-201(a) (last sentence). In any event, because the seller will be liable to the bank as drawer of the draft should the buyer dishonor it, the bank can debit the seller's account through its common-law right of setoff, whether or not the 4-214(a) right of charge back is available to the bank.

law

Hamby Co. v. Seminole State Bank
Court of Appeals of Texas, 1982
649 S.W.2d 81

Stephen F. Preslaw, Chief Justice. This case involves a bank's responsibility for the late return of a documentary draft. The First National Bank of Plainview, as agent for The Hamby Company, presented two drafts to the Seminole State Bank, the Appellee, who returned them unpaid two days after maturity. Appellant brought suit against Appellee for the face amount of the items under Section 4.302 of the Texas Business and Commerce Code. The trial court denied Appellant's motion for summary judgment and granted summary judgment for Appellee. We reverse and remand for trial on the merits.

The summary judgment proof is that Campbell Equipment Company purchased and received merchandise from The Hamby Company in June of 1979 in exchange for a "trade acceptance." On January 10, 1980, when this acceptance was due, the two acceptances involved in this suit were substituted for it in lieu of payment. These acceptances were drawn to the order of The Hamby Company for a total of $44,396.77, were payable at Seminole State Bank and matured on April 10, 1980.

The Hamby Company delivered the two acceptances to First National Bank of Plainview for collection. First National presented the acceptances along with corresponding invoices and a collection letter to Appellee, Seminole State Bank, on April 4. The letter accompanying the drafts stated that they were enclosed for collection and instructed Appellee not to hold the items after the date of maturity unless otherwise instructed and not to remit credit until actually paid. The summary judgment evidence is that Campbell had been doing business with Seminole State Bank for about two years and maintained a checking account which was not adequate to cover the drafts. In the past, Appellee would notify Campbell when an acceptance came in and Campbell would write a check to cover its amount. Upon the receipt of these two acceptances, Appellee notified Campbell. Campbell responded that he would be in to take care of it. Campbell was called daily and on Thursday, April 10, he was still making that response. On Monday, April 14, Appellant called Appellee to inquire why the drafts had not been paid. Appellee again contacted Campbell who said that he did not have the funds to pay and Appellee mailed the items back to the Appellant. Appellant then brought this suit under Section 4.302 of the Texas Business and Commerce Code, hereinafter referred to as the "Code." Section 4.302 provides: "In the absence of a valid defense, such as breach of a presentment warranty (Subsection (a) of Section 4.207), settlement effected or the like, if an item is presented on and received by a payor bank the bank is accountable for the amount of (1) A demand item other than a documentary draft whether properly payable or not if the bank, in any case where it is not also the depositary bank, retains the item beyond midnight of the banking day of receipt without settling for it or, regardless of whether it is also the depositary bank, does not pay or return the item or send notice of dishonor until after its midnight deadline; or (2) any other properly payable item unless within the time allowed for acceptance or payment of that item the bank either accepts or pays the item or returns it and the accompanying documents."

The parties agree that the items in question constitute "documentary drafts." Therefore, the provisions in paragraph (1) above do not apply. This, then, is not a midnight deadline case as was the case of *Continental National Bank v. Sanders,* 581 S.W.2d 293 (Tex.Civ.App.--El Paso 1979), and *Pecos County State Bank v. El Paso Livestock Auction Co., Inc.,* 586 S.W.2d 183 (Tex.Civ.App.--El Paso 1979, n.r.e.). Those two cases, although inapplicable here, cite the rule that there is strict liability on the part of the bank that does not timely act upon a demand item when presented to the payor bank. *Rock Island Auction Sales, Inc. v. Empire Packing Company, Inc.,* 32 Ill.2d 269, 204 N.E.2d 721 (1965).

In *Marfa National Bank v. Powell,* 512 S.W.2d 356 (Tex.Civ.App.--El Paso 1974, writ ref'd n.r.e.), this Court passed on a documentary draft case and applied Section 5.112 of the Code, which provides that a bank in which a documentary draft is presented under a letter of credit may defer acting until the close of the third banking day following receipt of the document. The case before us is not a letter of credit so we look elsewhere to determine the time element in which the draft must be paid or returned.

In the case of New Ulm State Bank v. Brown, 558 S.W.2d 20 (Tex.Civ.App.-- Houston [1st Dist.] 1977), it was held that in deciding whether or not a payor bank has made proper payment of an item, it is appropriate to look not only to the facts of the particular case but also to all appropriate sections of Article 3 and 4 of the Code, citing the official comment to Article 4.203. In its search for applicable time limits in which a bank must pay or return a documentary draft, the court turned to Section 4.501, sub-chapter E, entitled "Collection of Documentary Drafts." That section provides that a bank taking a documentary draft for collection must present or send the draft and accompanying documents for presentment, and, upon learning that the draft has not been paid or accepted in due course, the bank must seasonably notify its customer of such fact. It was then pointed out that an action is taken seasonably when it is taken "within a reasonable period of time." The court then applied Section 4.202(b) of the Code which provides that a collecting bank taking proper action before its midnight deadline following receipt of an item acts seasonably; and that "taking proper action within a reasonably longer period of time may be seasonable but the bank has the burden of so establishing." In the case before us, we have concluded that a fact question exists as to whether the bank acted seasonably or within a reasonable time.

The summary judgment is reversed and the cause is remanded for trial.

Memphis Aero Corp. v. First American National Bank

Supreme Court of Tennessee, 1983
647 S.W.2d 219

Harbison, Justice. This case arises under the Uniform Commercial Code. It involves a claim against a commercial bank for late return of a documentary draft which it had received by mail. The Chancellor and the Court of Appeals held that the bank was liable for the amount of the draft. We reverse and dismiss.

There were some disputed factual issues at the trial. However, the following material facts either were undisputed or have been resolved by the courts below.

Appellant, First American National Bank in Nashville (American), received from Trust Company of Georgia on November 14, 1974 the following instrument which is the subject of this suit.

The documents referred to as "Enclosures" accompanied the draft. Stamped on the back of the instrument was the following:

Also accompanying the document was the following "collection letter" or "advice":

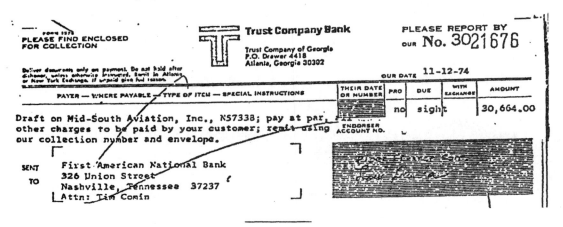

Mr. Tim Comin, an officer of American, received the draft and the other documents. He immediately notified an official of Mid-South Aviation with whom he had dealt on numerous occasions for more than a year. This official had previously advised Mr. Comin that he had authorized the draft. When the instrument arrived, however, Mid-South Aviation did not have sufficient funds to pay it. Although repeated promises were made to Mr. Comin that funds would be made available, this was never done.

The underlying commercial transaction involved the purchase of a Piper aircraft by Mid-South, a local retailer, from a regional Piper dealer, Memphis Aero Corporation. The latter had acquired it from the manufacturer, whose subsidiary, Piper Finance Corporation, retained a security interest. When the local dealer, Mid-South, sold the plane it advised Memphis Aero to draw a draft on First American. Memphis Aero actually had this done by Piper Finance. It and Piper supplied the necessary accompanying title documents to be delivered by American to Mid-South upon payment of the draft. Piper sent the draft and other papers through its own bank, Trust Company of Georgia. The record does not show whether or not that bank gave provisional credit therefor to Piper.

Mid-South, a relatively new but high-volume Piper retail dealer in Nashville, was a customer of First American. It maintained a checking account at that bank through which it passed large sums in connection with the purchase and sale of aircraft. The account was not under the control of any officer or official of American, was never frozen for any purpose, nor did American have authority to pay documentary drafts therefrom without approval from the depositor. American had made commercial loans to Mid-South from time to time, some collateralized and some not. It never at any time attempted to set off the customer's checking account against those loans. Only officials of Mid-South had authority to draw checks against the account. American had made no previous agreements with Mid-South or with Piper and Memphis Aero to finance the purchase of the aircraft in question by Mid-South or to carry overdrafts of the latter. It had on some prior occasions made loans to enable Mid-South to purchase planes, but the latter dealt with numerous other banks and also obtained financing from Memphis Aero.

Mr. Comin, the bank officer who handled the documentary draft upon its receipt, had little experience with such instruments. However he immediately notified Mid-South of its arrival and was advised that the latter would acquire sufficient funds to cover the draft but that such funds were not available on the day of presentment. Although he was in communication with both Piper and Memphis Aero by telephone no later than November 26 and advised them of the situation, Mr. Comin did not notify their agent Trust Company of Georgia of the dishonor of the draft, nor did he return it and the title documents until about December 20.

There were several questions presented in the courts below, but as the case comes here the only issue is whether appellant, a "payor bank" under the Code, is strictly liable for the amount of the draft under T.C.A. §47-4-302(b) or whether its liability is limited to damages proximately caused by its negligence under the general provisions of T.C.A. §47-4-103(5). If the latter measure is applied, no recovery is warranted because the bank customer, which owed the debt out of which the transaction arose, never had sufficient assets to pay the draft, and the item was essentially worthless at all relevant times. The Court of Appeals correctly held that "there is no evidence that, if First American had given timely notice of dishonor and made timely return of the draft and documents, Memphis Aero could have collected the amount due from Mid-South. That is, there is no evidence that Memphis Aero lost any amount as a proximate result of the action or inaction of First American."

On the other hand, the strict liability imposed under T.C.A. §47-4-302(b) is applicable only if the documentary draft was a "properly payable" item as contemplated in the Code, including the requirement stated in T.C.A. §47-4-104(i) of "availability of funds for payment at the time of decision to pay or dishonor."

Both the trial court and the Court of Appeals held that appellant, as a payor bank, was strictly liable under T.C.A. §47-4-302(b), but the Court of Appeals did not address the issue of whether the draft was "properly payable." The Chancellor resolved this issue by holding that the payor bank was also a "joint drawee" of the documentary draft with its customer. The bank was, in fact, solvent and, therefore, had sufficient funds *cf its own* to pay the draft. This was deemed to render it strictly liable under T.C.A. §47-4-302(b) as a *payor bank* --although, as we understand it, liability under that section is not liability *on the document itself* but is liability for the mishandling (delay in giving notice or return) of the item. Making no distinction between liability of a drawee *on the instrument* and liability for mishandling by a "*payor bank*," the Chancellor, following the insistence of appellee, virtually eliminated from the Code the requirement that before a payor bank can be held strictly liable for mishandling, a documentary draft must be "properly payable."

Appellee insists that the Code provision that "properly payable includes the availability of funds for payment at the time of decision to pay or dishonor" (T.C.A. §47-4-104(i)) means sufficient funds of the *payor bank* as well as sufficient funds of the *debtor* in the commercial transaction. Very little authority exists for this proposition. Some of the cases most relied upon by appellee and by the courts below arose and were decided under the equivalent of T.C.A. §47-4-302(a)--strict liability for not handling demand items by the banking "midnight deadline." Liability is imposed under that provision of the Code, however, for mishandling items "*other than a documentary draft*" and "*whether properly payable or not*." There is a distinct difference between liability under subsection (a) and that under (b) of this Code section.

In other cases cited by appellee where liability has been imposed upon a payor bank under subsection (b), there was no question that the debtor had on deposit with or made available to the payor bank sufficient funds to pay the draft. In still others, the issue was never discussed. One federal case, cited by appellee as a "leading case," merely stated that a payor bank is liable under subsection (b) if it does not pay or return an "item" within a reasonable time and made no reference to the "properly payable" requirement of that statute. This decision was followed by another from the same circuit, holding that the payor bank was obligated to pay late-returned drafts even though there were insufficient funds made available by the debtor and even though the payment would have created an overdraft.

In the present case the debtor at no time had or made available to the payor bank, appellant here, sufficient funds for payment of the draft, which was timely presented. In our opinion the draft was not a "properly payable" item under T.C.A. §47-4-302(b) so as to render the payor bank strictly liable for its late return. Liability, therefore, is governed by T.C.A. §47-4-103(5), and the action fails for insufficient proof for damages.

The Court of Appeals at several points drew an analogy between the liability of the drawee of a check and that of a payor bank respecting a documentary draft. There is a significant difference. Checks are usually referred to as "cash" or "demand" items, and the drawee must handle these under its midnight deadline, "whether properly payable or not." T.C.A. §47-4-302(a). Sight drafts, unaccompanied by title documents, may also fall within that provision. *Farmers Cooperative Livestock Market v. Second National Bank*, 427 S.W.2d 247 (Ky.1968). Both the Chancellor and the Court of Appeals correctly held in the present case, however, despite the contention of appellee to the contrary, that the instrument involved here was a "documentary draft" as defined in the U.C.C. It was described by some witnesses as an "envelope draft." As shown on its face, it was accompanied by a bill of sale to an airplane, a release of lien on the same, and an application for registration of title in the name of the vendee (the debtor in the transaction). The accompanying "advice" or "collection letter" from the transmitting bank called it a "Draft on Mid-South Aviation, Inc., N573 38" [the serial number of the plane], and instructed the appellant to "*Deliver documents only on payment.*" Clearly it was contemplated that the title papers were to be "delivered against honor of the draft," T.C.A. §47-4-104(f), and the draft was a "documentary draft," not a check or a simple sight draft which had to be processed under T.C.A. §47-4-302(a) "whether properly payable or not."

Further, there is no contention in this case that appellant had agreed that it would pay the draft out of its own funds, that it would lend funds to the purchaser of the airplane or "floor plan" the craft, or that it had obligated itself to the sellers (the drawer and payee) so as to render it liable *on the instrument* for not immediately accepting or paying the draft. It was instructed to present the draft to the purchaser of the plane and to deliver the title papers to the latter only upon payment. It did timely present the draft. It did not timely return the documents to the transferor bank or notify the latter that the purchaser had insufficient funds to meet its obligation. Therein it was negligent. Had this negligence caused loss to the creditor, liability would follow, but there is no evidence that this occurred. Eight business days elapsed between receipt of the draft by appellant and telephone communication between it and the creditor that the draft had been dishonored upon presentment. There is conflicting evidence as to whether this was or was not a reasonable time, but we accept the findings of the courts below that the appellant was negligent in this respect and in not notifying the transmitting bank, agent of the creditors. In that regard, however, we note that the creditors (Memphis Aero and its financing company Piper Finance) by-passed their own agent, Trust Company of Georgia, the transmitting bank, and dealt directly with appellant, the payor bank. While appellant held the draft for a total of thirty-six days, the fact that it was holding the dishonored draft was known to the creditors upon the eighth business day (the twelfth calendar day), at the latest. They thereafter tried to deal directly with the debtor, Mid-South Aviation, to repossess the aircraft and to arrange new financing for the debtor. Only after these efforts failed did they demand that appellant return the draft. It did so immediately.

It will be recalled that under T.C.A. §47-4-302(b) a payor bank becomes liable for a properly payable item "unless within the time allowed for acceptance or payment" of that item the bank either accepts, pays or returns it.

No specific time is provided under this section of the U.C.C. for the acceptance or payment of a documentary draft. Under special provisions of the Code dealing with the collection of documentary drafts, a collecting bank must "seasonably" notify "its customer" of dishonor. T.C.A. §47-4-501. Unless otherwise instructed, a bank presenting a documentary draft must deliver the documents "to the drawee" on acceptance of the draft if payable more than three days after presentment or, otherwise, only on payment. T.C.A. §47-4-503(a). Upon dishonor the presenting bank "... must use diligence and good faith to ascertain the reason for dishonor, must notify its transferor of the dishonor and of the results of its effort to ascertain the reasons therefor and must request instructions." T.C.A. §47-4- 503(b).

A non-payor bank, that is one which is merely a collecting or presenting bank, is liable for damages proximately caused by its negligence in failing to carry out these duties. T.C.A. §§47-4-103(5), -105(d), -105(e). A "payor bank" becomes liable for the amount of the instrument if it fails to carry out its duties and if it is a "properly payable item." T.C.A. §47-4-302(b).

It is clear that the "midnight deadline" applicable to the handling of checks and other demand items is not applicable to the handling of documentary drafts. Banking institutions are permitted a reasonable or "seasonable" time within which to present, remit or return. *Wiley, Tate & Irby v. Peoples Bank and Trust Co.*, 438 F.2d 513 (5th Cir.1971).

As noted by the Supreme Court of Virginia, and as abundantly illustrated by the testimony in the present record, "The custom followed by banks in handling documentary drafts is not uniform. And the time permitted for their payment or return varies. What is seasonable time, and what is due diligence and good faith, must necessarily depend upon the facts and circumstances of each case. The cashier of Citizens and Marine testified that while the policy of his bank was ten days without specific instructions, under certain circumstances, depending on the customer, an unpaid draft would be retained for a month before being returned." *Suttle Motor Corp. v. Citizens Bank of Poquoson*, 216 Va. 568, 221 S.E.2d 784, 786 (Va.1976).

A number of expert witnesses testified in the present case, representing banking institutions from different parts of this state. Others having knowledge of the subject testified to practices of banking institutions in New York, Atlanta and other parts of the United States. The time for holding a documentary draft, according to these witnesses, varies from two days to as much as ten days or longer. Witnesses from American testified that they customarily hold such drafts for about ten days.

We have already stated that we concur in the findings of the courts below that the holding period in the present case was unreasonable under all of the circumstances, although, in view of the direct communication between the creditors and the payor bank, it was not nearly so long or nearly so unreasonable as indicated by the courts below.

If, during the period while American was holding the draft, it had become "properly payable" and the bank had failed to pay or return, an entirely different case would be presented. That was the situation in *Suttle Motor Corp.*, supra. There, while the bank was holding the drafts, funds came into its hands which should have been applied directly to the payment of those specific drafts. The title documents attached to the drafts should have been detached, delivered to customers who had made loans from the bank to purchase their automobiles, and the drafts paid out of the proceeds. Instead the bank applied those proceeds to other debts owed to it by the drawer of the drafts. It served its own interests, proximately and directly damaging the payee of the drafts who had caused them to be sent to the bank for collection. In one instance a bank customer named Harrell borrowed funds from the bank to finance the purchase of a car, and those loan proceeds were credited directly to the drawer of a draft which the bank was holding. The title papers attached to the draft were not delivered to the borrower, and the Supreme Court of Virginia said: "Clearly the proceeds from the loan to Harrell should have been applied in payment of the Suttle draft, thereby enabling Harrell to obtain good title to her automobile." 221 S.E.2d at 787.

The Court further said: "We do not have here a mere delay in the return of a draft. There was delay and inaction at a critical time when Poquoson was making a tremendous effort in its own behalf to reduce the losses which it obviously faced on the Batts and Hockaday account." 221 S.E.2d at 788.

These facts differ drastically from those presented in the present case. While the debtor, Mid-South Aviation, was indebted to American, the latter did not at any time divert funds or assets of Mid-South to the payment of its own claims when these should have been used to pay the draft which the bank was holding. This, indeed, is a case involving nothing more than "a mere delay in the return of a draft," and there is no evidence of any dereliction of duty or neglect other than failure of the bank official to give notice to the transferor bank or to give more prompt notice than he did to the creditors who undertook to deal directly with him.

No question was made in the *Suttle Motor Corp.* case, supra, but that liability was fixed under §4-302(b) of the Uniform Commercial Code. The drafts in that case clearly were or became "properly payable" while the bank was holding them, because sufficient funds of the debtor did come into the possession of the bank to pay the drafts--a situation entirely different from that involved here.

We concur in the conclusions of the courts below that American was a "payor bank" and that it was negligent, but since we do not find that the item was "properly payable," in our opinion liability should not have been imposed under T.C.A. §47-4-302(b).

The judgments of the courts below are reversed and the suit is dismissed at the cost of appellee. The cause will be remanded to the trial court for collection of all costs accrued there.

Continental Time Corp. v. Merchants Bank of New York

Supreme Court, Special Term, New York County, 1983
117 Misc.2d 907, 459 N.Y.S.2d 396

Arthur E. Blyn, Justice.

Motion by plaintiff for summary judgment.

The following undisputed facts appear from the papers submitted. On January 10, 1980 one Georges Bloch ("Bloch") requested his Swiss bank, Credit Suisse ("Credit"), to issue an irrevocable letter of credit in favor of plaintiff Continental Time Corp. ("Continental") in the principal sum of $236,961.90 in order to facilitate payment for a shipment of watches sold by Continental to Bloch. Said letter of credit was issued and, as amended, was valid until February 11, 1980 and payable upon presentation of certain documents. Defendant The Merchants Bank of New York ("Merchants") acted as the collecting bank on behalf of Continental in the presentation and negotiation of the documents called for by the letter of credit.

On January 23, 1980 Continental delivered to Merchants the various documents for presentation to Credit including a sight draft for the full amount. Merchants forwarded the documents on that date to Credit for payment.

By telex dated January 29, 1980 Credit advised Merchants it was refusing the documents because of an alleged discrepancy in one of them (airway bill) which telex further provided, "documents at your disposal"--"please authorize us to present documents on collection basis". By telex of the same date Merchants authorized Credit to present the documents on a collection basis. Bloch refused to pay alleging a set-off against Continental.

In this action Continental seeks to recover the principal amount of the letter of credit alleging in its complaint two causes of action. The first sounds in negligence and the second claims breach of contractual duties under the Uniform Commercial Code (§§4-202, 4-501, 4-503, 5-111). Continental contends Merchants failed to (a) detect those material discrepancies claimed to exist by Credit in the documents delivered under the irrevocable letter of credit in the course of Merchants' review of the documents prior to delivery and presentment; (b) timely notify Continental of Credit's refusal to pay under the irrevocable letter of credit as well as the reasons therefor; (c) request instructions of Continental as to what to do following Credit's refusal to pay; (d) request the documents back for correction prior to the expiration date of the irrevocable letter of credit; and (e) receive authority from Continental to place the irrevocable letter of credit on a "collection basis". Simply stated Merchants takes the position it took all necessary and proper actions in presenting the documents for payment.

At the outset, since there appears to be some confusion in the parties' minds, it is necessary to identify the precise nature of the transaction at issue and the applicable legal standards. Article 4 of the Uniform Commercial Code ("UCC") is entitled "Bank Deposits And Collections". Part 2 of that Article deals with the obligations in general of collecting banks and Part 5 more specifically with the collection of documentary drafts. (defined in UCC §4-104(f) as "any ... draft with accompanying documents ... to be delivered against honor of the draft".) Article 5 of the UCC deals with letters of credit. The Court of Appeals in *United Bank Ltd. v. Cambridge Sporting Goods Corp.*, 41 N.Y.2d 254, 258, 259, 392 N.Y.S.2d 265, 360 N.E.2d 943 addressed the question of the law applicable to letters of credit and the relationship between them and documentary drafts as follows: "Article 5 of the Uniform Commercial Code, dealing with letters of credit, and the Uniform Customs and Practice for Documentary Credits promulgated by the International Chamber of Commerce set forth the duties and obligations of the issuer of a letter of credit. A letter of credit is a commitment on the part of the issuing bank that it will pay a draft presented to it under the terms of the credit, and if it is a documentary draft, upon presentation of the required documents of title (see Uniform Commercial Code, §5-103)". In the footnote (2) the court, citing UCC §5-102(4), pointed out that the Uniform Customs and Practice ("UCP") controls, in lieu of Article 5, when by its terms the letter of credit is made subject to the UCP. That is the case at bar. It is thus apparent that while it may be said that Merchants handled a single transaction for Continental, that transaction was duplex in nature, the documentary draft aspect being governed by the UCC (Art. 4) and the letter of credit aspect being governed by the UCP rather than the UCC (Art. 5).

With that analytical preamble the court turns to the various grounds advanced by Continental for recovery as a matter of law.

Continental's first contention focuses on the letter of credit and the supporting airway bill. The letter of credit contains specific requirements regarding the language of the airway bill. The document presented to Credit was not filled in in the portion entitled "Airport of Departure" and "Airport of Destination". (this was the basis for the rejection by Credit.) The letter of credit is silent in that regard. The parties' reliance on sections of Article 5 of the UCC on this issue is misplaced. The UCP, however, provides that banks assume no responsibility or liability for the form and sufficiency of documents (Art. 9). Further, Article 7 of the UCP provides "Banks must examine all documents with reasonable care to ascertain that they appear on their face to be in accordance with [the letter of credit]". On the basis of the foregoing it may not be said as a matter of law that Merchants breached any duty in its review of the airway bill prior to presentation of the documents to Credit.

The next contention, although couched in terms of notice of refusal to pay under the letter of credit, in fact deals with Merchants' obligation to notify Continental of dishonor of the documentary draft. UCC §4-501, relied upon by Continental, imposes an obligation upon Merchants to do so "seasonably". Continental maintains no such notice was given. Merchants, pointing principally to the deposition of Continental's president in this action, argues otherwise. This court need not determine whether a bona fide issue of fact exists on the issue of notice of dishonor as such issue is a red herring in view of the additional obligations imposed upon Merchants which, as hereinafter set forth, this court finds it did not meet.

Beyond notice of dishonor of the documentary draft Merchants was obligated under UCC §4-503, subd. b, to "... use diligence and good faith to ascertain the reason for dishonor, must notify its transferor [Continental] of the dishonor and of the results of its effort to ascertain the reasons therefor *and must request instructions.*" (Emphasis added.) Continental contends Merchants failed to request instructions of it. The opposing affidavit of a Merchants' officer, who fails to indicate any source of his knowledge, opines: "Upon rejection by CREDIT SUISSE of the documents, MERCHANTS, as is its custom, telephoned its customer of the discrepancies and awaited their instructions. After conferring with its customer, [as is its custom and practice] MERCHANTS authorized CREDIT SUISSE to re-present the documents on a collection basis as requested by CREDIT SUISSE in order to have the documents paid". (Matter in brackets handwritten.) Such a conclusory statement of a custom of the bank totally devoid of evidentiary facts by an affiant with no personal knowledge is hardly laying bare one's proof to demonstrate the existence of a triable issue.

Rather than request instructions, the record is clear that Merchants unilaterally and without authorization from Continental placed the irrevocable letter of credit on a collection basis. Testimony by experts from both Merchants as well as Credit in a related federal action unequivocally establish that the steps taken by Merchants were contrary to banking custom and practice in failing to afford Continental an opportunity to cure the claimed deficiency in the airway bill and resubmit the letter of credit for payment, which it had a right to do, as well as destroying the irrevocability of the letter of credit. (releasing Credit's obligation to pay.) Moreover, such conduct is violative of Article 3(c) of the UCP which provides that an irrevocable letter of credit cannot be cancelled without the agreement of all the parties thereto, as well as contrary to Decisions (1975-1979) of the International Chamber of Commerce Banking Commission under the UCP (References 13 and 14).

For the foregoing reasons the motion is granted and the Clerk is directed to enter judgment accordingly.

practice

Case 1

The buyer who pays against documents actually gets, at the time of payment, a piece of paper which, in itself, is worthless. The credibility of the document, and the value in it, are based on rights which accompany the transfer of the document to her and provide some protection, i.e., some insurance, that the buyer will get the goods she bargained for or, at least, compensation if she does not get the goods themselves.

What insurance of this kind does the U.C.C. provide the buyer, and who is the insurer in each instance? See 7-403 (exclusive access to the goods); 7-504(1) & 7-502 (title to the goods); 7-301(1), 7-507, 2-313, 2-314 & 2-315 (warranties); 2-711 & 2-714 (contract remedies).

Case 2

"The plaintiff and his wife stopped in Mobile, Alabama, while en route to Florida. Personal property was stored with the defendant, who was in the business of storing personal property. The storage occurred in March 1981. The plaintiff received a warehouse receipt from the defendant. The plaintiff signed the warehouse receipt as bailor of the goods. The plaintiff was listed on the warehouse receipt as the owner of the goods. The plaintiff paid the storage fee. In April of 1981, the plaintiff and his wife separated. Thereafter, plaintiff's wife went to the defendant and requested the goods and the defendant gave the goods to the wife. The plaintiff then contacted the defendant and requested the goods. The defendant was, in view of the above, unable to deliver the goods and the plaintiff filed the instant lawsuit." *Teague Bros. Transfer & Storage Co., Inc. v. Kinloch* 441 So.2d 968 (Ala. Ct. Civ. App. 1983).

Who should win in plaintiff's action against defendant for failure to deliver the goods?

Case 3

a. **Seller ships goods to Buyer, who has agreed to pay against documents. Upon presentment of the draft to Buyer, she pays it and the presenting bank gives her a negotiable document that describes the kind and quantity of goods she contracted to buy from seller. Buyer then contacted the carrier about taking delivery of the goods. The carrier explained that the seller had telephoned and given instructions to deliver the goods to an innocent buyer --BFP -- to whom Seller had sold the goods. Is the carrier or BFP accountable to Buyer?**

b. **Same facts except that Seller had not double-dealt. In other words there was no resale to BFP. The carrier had the goods and gladly surrendered them to Buyer. Yet, there was a small problem: The bill of lading described the shipment as ten cartons of widgets, which is the amount buyer had ordered from seller. The carrier, however, delivered to buyer only nine cartons. Further investigation revealed that seller only shipped nine cartons. Who among the seller, the presenting bank and the carrier is liable to Buyer?**

Case 4

The seller in a documentary transaction has released her own actual possession of the goods without getting payment for them. What protects her against loss if any of the following breakdowns in the scheme occur?

a. **The buyer dishonors the documentary draft. See 4-503; 4-504; 4-501; 2-703.**

b. **The carrier misdelivers the goods, as by delivering them to the buyer before the buyer has honored the documentary draft and properly acquired the bill of lading. See 7-403.**

c. **The presenting bank delivers the bill of lading to the buyer without getting payment of the draft. See 4-503; 4-202 & 4-103(e).**

Case 5

"Don Lloyd owns Lloyd's and Don L. Motors in Miami, Florida. The largest portion of his business includes buying used vehicles from car dealers and selling them to other car dealers. Lloyd's used envelope drafts to purchase these cars for resale and accepted them as payment when the cars were resold to other dealers. Envelope drafts are envelopes with a draft printed on the outside of the envelope. The envelopes have the buyer's bank's name and address and vehicle identification information on them, and are given to the seller of the automobile when the buyer takes possession. The seller then places the title to the vehicle in the envelope and deposits the draft in his bank for forwarding to the buyer's bank. The seller may be given immediate credit upon deposit of the draft. When the buyer's bank receives the envelope draft, it contacts its customer and notifies him that the draft has arrived and should be picked up. The buyer must pay for the draft before the title is released, either by giving the bank funds or by authorizing the bank to debit his account.

"Leon Campbell owns Campbell's Cleanup ("Campbell's") in Darlington, South Carolina. Campbell's buys used cars from dealers like Lloyd's and cleans and refurbishes them for resale at Clanton's Auto Auction ("Clanton's") in Darlington. Campbell's had an ongoing relationship with Lloyd's since 1986, dealing for the most part with Mike Drotch. Typically, Drotch would call Campbell's by phone and offer to sell a car. Once the price was agreed upon, Drotch would fill out an envelope draft previously signed by Campbell's. Delivery to Campbell's in Darlington occurred when 8 cars were sold. Once the cars were shipped to Campbell's, the titles would be placed in the envelope drafts and the drafts would be deposited in Lloyd's account in the Jefferson National Bank ("JNB") in Florida. Lloyd's received immediate credit for these drafts. JNB would then mail the drafts to [South Carolina National Bank] SCN with a collection advice or ticket instructing SCN to pay or return the drafts within 72 hours. Lloyd's gave SCN written instructions to hold the drafts up to seven days.

"When Campbell's first started buying cars from Lloyd's in 1986, Clanton's provided financial backing for Campbell's by advancing the funds to pick up drafts as soon as they arrived at SCN. Campbell's would repay Clanton's following the sale of an automobile. When Clanton's ceased the financial backing, Campbell's informed Drotch, who stated, 'Don't worry, we will back you.' Campbell's interpreted this statement as permitting time to sell the vehicle before picking up the drafts from SCN.

"Veronica Barcus was the supervisor over the drafts at SCN. After the customer was informed that the drafts had arrived, they would be given to Ms. Barcus to hold until they were picked up or returned to the sending bank. When the customer paid for and picked up the draft, SCN would issue and mail its cashier's check to the sending bank. Campbell's picked up and paid for all the drafts except the 24 involved in this lawsuit. When it picked up a draft, it would give Ms. Barcus a check drawn on the account of Clanton's. Clanton's was an SCN customer which maintained a substantial balance in its account and thus immediate credit was given to its checks. The check from Clanton's would be in an amount just over the amount of the draft, the difference being the profit Campbell's made on the transaction. Simultaneously with the deposit of Clanton's checks to Campbell's account, Campbell's would issue a check payable to SCN to pay for the drafts. SCN debited this check against Campbell's account and issued a cashier's check payable to SCN which in turn was used to purchase SCN's own cashier's check payable to JNB.

"If Campbell's could not sell a car at a price which would cover its expenses, it would keep the car and try to sell it the following week. Ms. Barcus explained that drafts were held more than seven days because Campbell's told her it had not sold the cars and that it would contact Drotch at Lloyd's to get permission to hold the drafts. She testified that she received calls from Lloyd's telling her to hold the drafts.

"JNB put tracers on the drafts. When the tracers were received by SCN, SCN returned the remaining drafts to JNB. The first set of five or ten tracers arrived in April 1987 and the second set of 13 came in May 1987. Lloyd's continued to sell and ship cars to Campbell's throughout the summer of 1987. Upon demand from JNB, each of these drafts was returned to it unopened with the title to the automobile inside. All of the automobiles represented by the drafts were retrieved by Lloyd's and sold either in Florida or Darlington. The 24 drafts which are the subject of this action total $184,750. Lloyd's received a total of $169,650 from the sale of the cars or $15,100 less than the face amount of the drafts.

"On March 2, 1988, Lloyd's filed this action against South Carolina National Bank (SCN) to recover the face amount of documentary drafts (automobile envelope drafts) held beyond the period allowed for payment or return under South Carolina Code of Laws §§36-3-419 and 36-4-302 and on a theory of negligence. On October 6, 1989, a jury returned a verdict in favor of Lloyd's in the amount of $15,100, the face amount of 24 drafts, in actual damages and awarded Lloyd's $34,900 in consequential damages. Lloyd's motion for judgment notwithstanding the verdict for $219,600, which represented the face amounts of all the drafts, plus consequential damages, and costs and attorney's fees and SCN's motion to reduce the verdict were denied." *Lloyd's Excellent Automobiles, Inc. v. South Carolina Nat'l Bank*, 931 F.2d 887 (4th Cir. 1991) (Table) (unpublished disposition) (text in WestLaw).

How would you decide the appeal?

Case 6

Seller ships goods to Buyer, who has agreed *to pay* against documents. Upon presentment of the *demand draft* to Buyer, she accepts it instead of paying the instrument. The presenting bank then surrenders to Buyer the negotiable document, in bearer form, which had accompanied the draft. The bank returns the accepted draft through banking channels to Seller. Buyer gets possession of the goods from the carrier.

a. **Is the carrier liable to Seller?**

b. **Is the presenting bank liable to Seller?**

§ 2. Credit Against Documents: Trade Acceptances

Payment against documents requires the buyer to pay the documentary draft upon presentment to her. The seller may agree, however, that the buyer can acquire the documents accompanying the draft by accepting the instrument upon presentment instead of paying it. "'Acceptance' means the drawee's signed agreement to pay a draft as presented," and is accomplished by the drawee signing the draft. 3-409(a). The buyer qua acceptor "is obliged to pay the draft *** according to its terms at the time it was accepted." 3-413(a). A draft accepted by a buyer in a sale of goods arrangement as described here is called a *trade acceptance*. The arrangement as whole a could be labelled, quite accurately, credit against documents because the effect is an extension of credit to the buyer for a period of time specified by the terms of the draft. For example, if the draft provides for payment "60 days after sight," the drawee turned acceptor must pay the draft, to the payee or her transferee, 60 days after accepting it.

The procedure for getting the buyer's acceptance is basically the same as that involved in getting payment from the buyer when she is to pay against documents. There are only two basic differences, both of which are obvious. First, in credit against documents, the seller draws a time draft, rather than a demand draft, ordering the buyer to pay the instrument a specified period after acceptance. Second, although the documentary draft is routed to the buyer through banking channels (just as in the case of a draft requiring payment), the presenting bank presents the draft for acceptance rather than for payment. See 4-503(1).

The obvious question is why the seller would insist on a trade acceptance instead of simply sending the goods to the buyer on unsecured credit and relying on the buyer's Article 2 obligation to pay the price. In either case the seller depends on the buyer's promise to pay. The difference is that a trade acceptance captures the buyer's promise to pay in a negotiable form, which is easier to enforce (even for the seller-payee) than a mere contractual promise, see 3-308, and for which there may be a wider market should the seller-payee decide to discount her rights against the buyer.

In the event the seller discounts the draft, the purchaser will acquire the buyer's obligation thereon as acceptor, 3-413(a), and also the obligations of the seller as drawer turned indorser. 3-414(d). Moreover, the typical purchaser would satisfy the requirements for holder-in-due-course status, see 3-302(a), so that she would acquire the draft free from claims and defenses. 3-305. Thus, the purchaser of the draft could enforce it against the buyer-acceptor notwithstanding that the seller breached the underlying sales contract between her and the buyer.

From the buyer's perspective, credit against documents is preferable to signing a note at the time the sales contract is made because, in accepting a documentary draft, her engagement on an instrument is concurrent with acquiring control of the goods. In signing an instrument beforehand, as when the contract is made, the buyer risks having to pay a holder in due course for goods she never received.

§ 3. Bankers' Acceptances

Another means for financing the buyer's purchase of goods is the *bankers' accep-tance*. By this means the buyer usually can get funds more easily and more cheaply because the buyer's draft is accepted by a bank and thereby is backed by the credit of the acceptor-bank as well as the buyer's own credit. Here is the very best explanation of bankers' acceptances given by a top expert, Reade H. Ryan, Jr.

Take a very simple example--that of a bank customer which is an importer or buyer of oil. The importer wants to finance its importation of oil for 120 days, the time it takes the importer to import, re-sell and get paid for the oil purchased from the exporter. To extend the acceptance financing, the bank first has the importer execute an appropriate acceptance credit agreement under which the importer agrees that, in consideration for the bank's accepting one or more drafts drawn by the importer on the bank, the importer will pay the bank the amount of each draft the bank may accept and will pay that amount on or before the last business day before its maturity (or at maturity in same day funds), together with an appropriate acceptance commission for the bank's taking the credit risk of its customer. Technically, the acceptor bank does not need the acceptance credit agreement in order to have the drawer's reimbursement obligation. Such obligation is imposed by law. See UCC, § 4-401. The draft sometimes makes this obligation clear by expressly authorizing the drawee to 'charge' the draft 'to account of' the drawer. However, the acceptance credit agreement is important to make clear the terms of payment, of the acceptance commission and other amounts payable by the customer, and of the other agreements, representations, and provisions which protect the credit position of the bank.

Having executed the acceptance credit agreement, the importer will draw a 120-day time draft on the bank payable to the order of the importer (though the draft could be payable to the order of the bank or to the order of bearer). Then the bank accepts that draft by stamping 'Accepted', and dating and signing, across the face of the draft. Once accepted, the draft, now a negotiable instrument known as a banker's acceptance, may be transferred by the importer by its endorsement and delivery. The importer will get the money to pay for the imported oil either by selling or having the acceptor bank (as the importer's agent) sell, at a discount, the banker's acceptance in the acceptance market or, typically, by having the acceptance discounted by the acceptor bank, which may then or later rediscount the acceptance in the acceptance market.

The market for bankers' acceptances is an over-the-counter market made by about 30 dealers and a dozen brokers, with investors ranging from foreign central banks and foreign governments to domestic and foreign private investors of all kinds. Dealers quote bid and asked prices for round lots of $5 million. If the transaction to be financed is large, several drafts of $5 million each will be drawn. For smaller transactions, a number of drafts of similar maturities drawn on the same bank will be packaged to trade as a round lot. Typical maturities are one, three and six months, with the average reportedly around three months.

The acceptor bank which discounts its acceptance may hold the acceptance until maturity, but commonly the bank will, on the same day it discounts the acceptance, rediscount the acceptance in the market to put itself back in funds. The rediscount rate will normally be lower than the discount rate. In theory that is because the rediscounted paper carries with it the obligation of at least two parties, the acceptor and the drawer, and possibly a third, an endorser; in practice, the discounting bank sets its discount rate by applying a margin over the rediscount rate. Thus, in ordinary course, a bank will make a small profit on rediscount at the same time that it converts its paper into cash.

Ultimately the accepted draft will mature--in our example, after 120 days -- but by then (hopefully) the importer will have sold its oil acquired with the proceeds of the acceptance and will, pursuant to the acceptance credit agreement, have paid the acceptor bank an amount equal to the face amount of the accepted draft.

Upon its payment of its acceptance, the acceptor bank can look back on a transaction in which the bank never had to use its own funds, only its credit, and received an acceptance commission and made profit on the discount and rediscount of the acceptance. (Of course, if the acceptor bank holds its acceptance for a day or more without rediscounting the acceptance, the bank will use its own funds.) The bank's customer, the importer, can look back on a transaction in which it financed the importation of oil using the bank's credit and paid an acceptance commission and the discount.

An exporter can also use acceptance financing. Assume the customer is an oil exporter which has a sales contract with a foreign buyer for its oil and expects to export, sell and get paid for its oil in 120 days. At the outset the bank will require the customer to execute an acceptance credit agreement under which the customer agrees to furnish the bank the funds with which to pay the acceptance at maturity. Having executed this agreement, the exporter will draw a 120-day draft on the bank, will have the draft accepted by the bank, and will realize the proceeds of the oil sale by having the accepted draft discounted. Upon maturity of the acceptance, the exporter repays the bank out of the oil proceeds from the foreign buyer.

* * *

A banker's acceptance is often connected to a letter of credit issued by the accepting bank to finance the sale of goods. For example, the importer-buyer could instruct its bank to issue to the exporter-seller a commercial documentary letter of credit under which the bank issuer is not to pay cash against a sight draft, but rather to accept time drafts drawn by the exporter- seller on the bank against stipulated documents and in accordance with specified terms. When the exporter presents the stipulated documents, together with its time drafts drawn on the issuing bank, the bank would accept the drafts, and the exporter would receive its cash payment from the sale of the bankers' acceptances.

Letters of credit and bankers' acceptances may be used separately or in conjunction.

Reade H. Ryan, *Bankers' Acceptances,* in PLI COMMERCIAL LAW AND PRACTICE COURSE HANDBOOK ON LETTERS OF CREDIT AND BANKERS' ACCEPTANCES (1988); see also *United*

States v. Dougherty, 763 F.2d 970, 972 (8th Cir. 1985) (discussing exporter's use of bankers' acceptances to finance foreign sales).

Bankers' acceptances ordinarily are used only to finance international sales of goods. The reason is that certain advantages attach to acceptances that are "eligible" for discount or purchase by the Federal Reserve. Federal law limits eligible acceptances to those

> having not more than six months' sight to run, exclusive of days of grace-- (i) *which grow out of transactions involving the importation or exportation of goods*; (ii) which grow out of transactions involving the domestic shipment of goods; or (iii) which are secured at the time of acceptance by a warehouse receipt or other such document conveying or securing title covering readily marketable staples.

12 U.S.C.A. §372(a) (emphasis added). Import or export transactions mean sales between the United States and another country or between foreign countries. Domestic acceptances are eligible to finance shipment alone and not to provide working capital, i.e., finance purchases of goods.

Ineligible acceptances are not necessarily illegal and banks sometimes create them, but they do not qualify for Federal Reserve discount. In truth, the Federal Reserve no longer rediscounts acceptances to any significant extent, but the eligibility of acceptances for discount remains important to banks for reasons of reserve requirements and lending limits. See generally W. Todd, *A Regulator's View of Bankers' Acceptances* in PLI COMMERCIAL LAW AND PRACTICE COURSE HANDBOOK ON LETTERS OF CREDIT AND BANKERS' ACCEPTANCES (1988).

§ 4. Letters of Credit

A vehicle for financing sales of goods that lacks the imperfections of bankers' acceptances is the *letter of credit*. A letter of credit is, in general terms, a bank's present, absolute commitment to pay or accept drafts -- usually documentary drafts -- presented to it in the future; but, until the future arrives and the letter of credit is actually drawn upon, it is only a contingent liability of the bank. The letter of credit is so important and distinctive that the whole of U.C.C. Article 5 is devoted exclusively to it. This statute mostly sets out principles that are wide and loose. They allow a letter of credit to be a versatile device that can be tailored to the parties' specific needs, and that can used for a variety of purposes other than sales financing, including providing insurance for the nonperformance of contracts involving services, loans, and sales of every kind of property. The principal use, however, is in financing sales of goods.

story

Overview

Suppose that seller and buyer are negotiating a contract for the sale of goods. Seller is unwilling or unable to commit herself without payment in advance. Buyer does not wish to pay for the goods until she gets them. This impasse can be broken by the buyer having her bank issue the seller an Article 5 *letter of credit,* which is "an engagement by a bank or other person made at the request of a customer *** that the issuer will honor drafts or other demands for payment upon compliance with the conditions specified in the credit." 5-103(1)(a).

This engagement, which is an enforceable promise, runs directly to the person named as beneficiary in the letter of credit, which would be the seller in the hypothetical case described here. The engagement is an independent obligation of the issuer to the beneficiary. The obligation is separate from the sales contract between the buyer and seller and separate from the bank's relationship with its customer who requested the credit. The seller thereby acquires, up front, a bank's promise to pay her upon the seller satisfying conditions described in the letter of credit. These conditions are decided by the buyer and seller, although nothing requires the buyer's bank to issue a credit on conditions that are objectionable to it. Typically, the principal condition is the presentation of documents of title covering goods the customer has ordered from the seller. Satisfaction of the conditions of the credit trigger the issuer's obligation to pay without the seller first looking to the buyer for payment. In this sense, the issuer's obligation to the seller is primary rather than secondary, which distinguishes a letter of credit from a guaranty.

Under the letter of credit arrangement the seller does not get payment in advance, but she gets the next best thing: A virtually undeniable promise by a person likely to remain solvent that the seller will be paid once control of the goods passes to the buyer by the transfer of appropriate documents.

The buyer is required to reimburse the issuer for paying the letter of credit. In effect, therefore, the buyer is paying for the goods when the bank honors the seller's demand for payment under the letter of credit. Thus, the buyer must pay for the goods before actually getting them. The buyer, however, gets the next best thing. She gets control of the goods upon payment because the bank will not pay the seller unless the seller transfers documents covering the goods.

If the goods are nonconforming, the buyer can sue the seller for breach of contract. Herein, however, is the ultimate effect of using a letter of credit. Ordinarily, a buyer is not required to pay for goods until after she has inspected them following delivery. The seller thus bears the risk of the buyer's dissatisfaction and the burden of having to sue to recover the price or other damages if the buyer breaches by rejecting conforming goods. When a letter of credit is used, the seller is paid regardless of the buyer's dissatisfaction with the goods. The buyer must sue to recoup her damages if the seller has breached the contract, as by shipping nonconforming goods. In effect, therefore, using a letter of credit shifts, from the buyer to the seller, the advantage of holding the price of the goods pending the resolution of contractual disputes between the parties. Significantly, the risk of insolvency also shifts. The buyer, rather than the seller, gambles that the other party will have available assets from which to satisfy her damages in the event she is the victim of a breach of contract.

The foregoing overview illustrates the traditional use of a letter of credit -- facilitating sales of goods (especially in international transactions) by insuring payment of the price to the seller-beneficiary upon her performance in accord with the terms of the letter of credit. A letter of credit so used is referred to as a *commercial credit*. A *standby credit* is a different use of Article 5. A *standby credit* is a letter of credit that insures payment to the beneficiary not for her performance in a sale or other transaction with the customer, but for the customer's default in the transaction.

The principal source of law for the discussion here is UCC Article 5.[*] In practice, an equally important source of law is the Uniform Customs and Practice for Commercial Documentary Credits (UCP), promulgated by the International Chamber of Commerce. The UCP often governs rights and duties under letters of credit, and the interpretation of their terms, either because the credit itself declares that it is issued subject to the UCP, or because the courts rely on the UCP as evidence of trade usage and common understanding with respect to letters of credit. In most important respects, Article 5 and the UCP are entirely consistent.

Commercial credits

1. The Main Players

In the commercial letter of credit, the *issuer,* 5-103(1)(c), usually a commercial bank, issues the *credit* (shorthand for *letter of credit)* in favor of the seller of goods. The bank acts in response to a request or application of the buyer, who is known as the *customer.* 5-103(1)(g). The seller is known as the *beneficiary* of the credit. 5-103(1)(d). The *credit* is a writing in which the issuer engages that it will pay or accept drafts or other demands for payment that comply with the terms of the credit. See 5-102(1), 5-103(1)(a) & 5-104. Typically, the terms require the seller to present documents, which usually consist of the seller's invoice; a shipping document (e.g., bill of lading, airway bill); an insurance certificate; various additional certificates (e.g., of inspection or origin); and consular documents, if necessary. The terms of credit also typically require presenting the documents together with a draft, or other form of a demand, ordering the issuer to pay or accept.

The nature of the draft gives rise to an important distinction in credit law: The distinction between *payment credits* and *time, usance,* or *acceptance credits.* With a payment credit, the beneficiary presents a sight or demand draft calling for payment,

---

[*]   As this book is written, Article 5 is being revised by the National Conference of Commissioners on Uniform State Laws (NCCUSL) and the American Law Institute (ALI). A new official text is expected in 1993 or 1994, but fundamental changes are unlikely.

and the issuer honors the credit by paying the draft. With a time, usance, or acceptance credit, the beneficiary draws a draft payable at a specified future date after presentation, and the issuer honors the draft by accepting it, thereby creating a *bankers' acceptance.* (Bankers' acceptances are discussed earlier in this chapter in §3 supra.) In either case, the seller-beneficiary gets her money sooner or later, but the delay in payment under an acceptance credit is a cost to the seller which she may shift to the buyer in negotiating the price of the goods. This cost is incurred whether the seller holds the accepted draft until maturity or sooner discounts the draft to a third party.

The terms of a letter of credit, including the required documents and whether drafts are presented for payment or acceptance, are really decided by the seller and buyer. They decide how little, or how much, is required of the seller in order to get payment or acceptance of drafts drawn under a credit. The buyer then asks her bank, through an *application agreement,* to issue a letter of credit containing the terms agreed to by the seller. In this role the buyer is known, technically, as the *customer.* 5-103(1)(g). In practice the buyer is also referred to as the *applicant,* because of the application agreement she makes with the issuer-bank, or the *account party,* because it is on the buyer's account that the issuer-bank issues the credit.

If the buyer's bank is unwilling to establish a credit on the terms agreed to by the buyer and seller, they must find another bank willing to accept their terms or change the terms to suit the bank.

2. The Relationship Between Issuer and Beneficiary: Duty to Honor

A letter of credit is *established* as regards the beneficiary, meaning that the issuer becomes liable thereon to the beneficiary, when the beneficiary receives the credit itself from the issuer, or when she receives written advice, i.e., notice, from another bank acting for the issuer that the credit has been issued. 5-106(1)(b). A credit that has been established cannot be modified or revoked unilaterally by the issuer unless the credit is a *revocable credit.* See 5-106(3). Practically speaking, however, a revocable credit is not really a letter of credit because it has no legal significance. See 5-106 comment 2. So nothing more is said here about revocable credits. The entire discussion before and after this paragraph refers to *irrevocable credits,* which cannot be modified or revoked as regards the customer or the beneficiary without her consent. See 5-106(2).

Once a credit is established, the issuer owes a statutory *duty to honor* directly to the beneficiary. This duty is stated in 5-114(1), which is the heart and soul of Article 5 and the statute's most important provision: "An issuer must honor a draft or demand for payment which complies with the terms of the relevant credit *regardless* of whether the goods or documents conform to the underlying contract for sale or other contract between the customer and the beneficiary."

The clause in 5-114(1) that begins with the word "regardless" is terribly important because it states the *independence principle,* which is that:

The letter of credit is *** independent of the underlying contract between the customer [buyer] and the beneficiary [seller]. *** [T]he issuer is under a duty to honor the drafts or demands for payment which in fact comply with the terms of the credit without reference to their compliance with the terms of the underlying contract. * * * The duty of the issuer to honor where there is factual compliance with the terms of the credit is also independent of any instructions from its customer once the credit has been issued and received by the beneficiary.

5-114 comment 1.

An issuer that violates the duty to honor is guilty of *wrongful dishonor* and is liable to the beneficiary for "the face amount of the draft or demand * * * less any amount realized by resale or other use or disposition of the subject matter of the transaction [i.e., the goods]." 5-115(1). Moreover, "the customer is entitled to compensation for the issuer's failure to perform the customer/issuer contract [i.e., the application agreement], and thus to recover as if for nondelivery under a contract for the sale of goods." H. Harfield, LETTERS OF CREDIT 62 (1979).

3. The Relationship Between Issuer and Customer: The Right of Reimbursement

Upon duly honoring a draft or demand for payment under a credit, the issuer acquires a *right of reimbursement* against the customer. 5-114(3). This right entitles the issuer to recoup "any payment made under the credit and to be put in effectively available funds not later than the day before maturity of any acceptance made under the credit." Id. Usually, the issuer's right of reimbursement is also confirmed in the application agreement or another writing that is part of the contract between it and the customer. Their contract will also provide for a commission to be paid to the issuer for issuing the credit, and the means for securing the right of reimbursement and the commission. Significantly, the right of reimbursement depends on the issuer having "duly honored" a demand under a credit. The issuer cannot recoup payment from its customer in the event of *improper payment* or *wrongful* or *improper honor*, meaning payment or acceptance against documents that did not factually comply with the terms of the credit. In this event, the issuer is left with pursuing the beneficiary, who may be liable for restitution or for breach of warranty. See, e.g., 5-111(1) (warranty that the necessary conditions of the credit have been complied with); 7-507 (warranties upon transfer of documents, including genuineness of documents and lack of knowledge of facts which would impair validity or worth of documents). The issuer also is secured by the documents and the goods they represent either through a common-law bankers' lien or otherwise, such as by the issuer's rights to the documents and the goods by virtue of its status as a holder through due negotiation. 7-502(1).

4.   Dishonor: Rightful or Wrongful

Overview

An issuer must honor a draft or demand for payment that complies with the terms of the relevant credit. 5-114(1). Compliance means that the draft or demand, and the documents presented with it, appear on their face to satisfy the terms of the credit. Thus, as a general rule, an issuer is guilty of wrongful dishonor, and is accordingly liable to the beneficiary, by refusing to pay a demand that facially complies with the credit. On the other hand, mainly to safeguard the issuer's right of reimbursement and also to limit the issuer's obligation to the terms it agreed to, the courts generally follow the rule that a beneficiary is not entitled to acceptance or payment unless the documents she presents *comply literally, precisely and strictly* with the terms of the credit. A dishonor in the face of less than strict compliance with the terms of the credit is not wrongful. Only in a few cases have the courts embraced a less stringent test of "reasonable" or "substantial" compliance.

Moreover, there are a few exceptions, themselves qualified, which justify an issuer dishonoring a letter of credit despite facial compliance with the credit's terms. Dishonor is rightful, despite facial compliance, when:

- a required document does not in fact conform to the warranties made on negotiation or transfer of a document of title (7-507) or a certificated security (8-306);
- a required document is forged or fraudulent; or,
- there is fraud in the transaction.

5-114(2).

Remember! For purposes of the immediate discussion, the assumption is that the demand for payment and accompanying documents appear on their face to comply with the terms of the credit. The reasons for dishonor under 5-114(2) involve latent or hidden problems that the issuer is not obligated to search for when a demand is made. See 5-109. How then will the issuer know of these problems so that, on the basis of them, it can dishonor? The informant is usually the customer who asks the issuer to dishonor a credit because, the customer alleges, there is a hidden defect or problem that justifies dishonor under 5-114(2).

All's well if the customer is right. If the customer is wrong, however, the issuer will have wrongfully dishonored and thus will be liable to the beneficiary. The credibility and overall utility of credits would be seriously undermined if the issuer were allowed to dishonor solely on the basis of the customer's allegations, or if the issuer were required, or even allowed, to suspend a credit while it investigated the customer's allegations "since these matters frequently involve situations in which the determination of the fact of the non-conformance may be difficult or time-consuming." 5-114 comment 2.

Article 5 resolves this problem, in the first instance, against the customer by providing: "[In all] cases as against its customer, an issuer acting in good faith may honor the draft or demand for payment despite notification from the customer of fraud, forgery or other defect not apparent on the face of the documents." 5-114(2)(b). This means that when an issuer honors a credit despite the customer's warning of a hidden defect, the issuer nevertheless has a right of reimbursement against the customer even though, in fact, the customer was right. The only requirement is that the issuer must have acted in good faith, which is judged by a subjective standard. See 1-201(19).

The customer is not completely without recourse in this situation. If the issuer decides to ignore the customer's warning and honor the credit, "a court of appropriate jurisdiction may enjoin such honor." 5-114(2)(b). To win an injunction, however, the customer must establish a hidden defect that justifies dishonor under Article 5 and must also satisfy the usual prerequisites for an injunction under the local, extra-Code law of remedies.

Notwithstanding the foregoing, a hidden defect never justifies an issuer's dishonor, and never supports an injunction against honor, when the person demanding honor is "a negotiating bank or other holder of the draft or demand which has taken the draft or demand under the credit and under circumstances which would make it a holder in due course (Section 3-302) and in an appropriate case would make it a person to whom a document of title has been duly negotiated (Section 7-502) or a bona fide purchaser of a certificated security (Section 8-302)." 5-114(2)(a). The person will have purchased drafts that the beneficiary has drawn under the credit, as is explained below in a discussion of the alienability of credits. In essence, the person is a good faith purchaser for value who has innocently relied on the issuer's engagement to honor the credit. Thus, the issuer must honor the credit despite hidden defects, and the customer must then reimburse the issuer. In effect, therefore, "[t]he risk of the original bad-faith action of the beneficiary is thus thrown upon the customer who selected him rather than upon innocent third parties or the issuer. So, too, is the risk of fraud in the transaction placed upon the customer." 5-114 comment 2.

Fraud in the Transaction

The reason for dishonor that the courts most often debate is "fraud in the transaction" within the meaning of 5-114(2). Indeed, the most troubling issue under the whole of Article 5 is the meaning of "fraud in the transaction," which justifies dishonoring a credit even though the documents appear on their face to comply with the terms of a credit. The source of the phrase is well-known. It codifies the holding of *Sztejn v. J. Henry Schroder Banking Corp.*, 177 Misc. 719, 31 N.Y.S.2d 631 (Sup. Ct. 1941).

In the *Sztejn* case, Schroder had issued, for the account of Sztejn, an irrevocable credit in favor of Transea Trading. The credit required the beneficiary to present, among other things, a bill of lading covering a quantity of bristles. The issue in the case was whether the issuer was required to honor the credit if the beneficiary presented a document in perfect order, that is, a genuine bill of lading describing the goods as bristles, when, in fact, the seller-beneficiary had shipped cow hairs and other worthless materials. The court decided that, on these facts, payment of the credit should be enjoined.

Neither the *Sztejn* case nor the phrase "fraud in the transaction" justifies dishonor simply because of a breach of warranty or other breach of contract in the underlying transaction between the customer and the beneficiary. What is required is *intentional, active fraud on the part of the seller.* Moreover, the fraud must be serious, that is, *of such an egregious nature as to vitiate the entire transaction.*

Look at it this way: The very purpose of the letter of credit is to insure that the money is in the seller's hands during any period of dispute between the buyer and seller as to performance of their underlying contract. The risk of recovering for nonperformance is therefore on the buyer. She agrees to assume this risk by agreeing to the letter of credit arrangement. So, breach of contract is not "fraud in the transaction" justifying dishonor of a credit. The buyer does not accept the risk of recovering the price in circumstances where the seller hoodwinked her. Putting the money in the seller's care in such a case is thus beyond the purpose of the letter of credit, and therefore dishonoring the credit in such a case does not undermine its legitimate commercial utility.

Standby credits

The main players, and the basic rights and duties of the issuer, are the same in both commercial and standby letters of credit. Yet, a standby credit differs fundamentally from a commercial credit. While the traditional commercial credit directs a bank to pay the beneficiary upon the shipment of goods or other performance by her in favor of the customer, the standby credit "directs the bank to pay the beneficiary not for his own performance but upon the customer's default, thereby serving as a guarantee device." Note, *Fraud in the Transaction: Enjoining Letters of Credit During the Iranian Revolution,* 93 HARV. L. REV. 992, 993 (1980). For this reason, standby credits are often referred to as *guaranty letters of credit.* A standby credit differs from a common-law guaranty, however, in "that the former is a direct obligation to pay upon 'specified documents showing default' while the latter is a secondary obligation requiring proof of the fact of default." *American Nat'l Bank & Trust Co. v. Hamilton Indus. Int'l, Inc.,* 583 F.Supp. 164, 169 (N.D. Ill. 1984), *rev'd on other grounds,* 767 F.2d 380 (7th Cir. 1985).

For example, O hires C to construct a building. Pursuant to their agreement, C, the customer, gets her bank, the issuer, to establish a letter of credit in favor of O, the beneficiary. The credit provides that the issuer will honor drafts presented by O together with O's certified statement that C has breached the terms of the construction contract.

Often, however, the beneficiary of a standby credit is a bank or other financer that gives credit to a third party. For example, C borrows money from State Bank to begin construction of a building for O. As collateral for the loan, C assigns to State Bank her right to payment from O. State Bank worries that O might be unwilling or unable to pay sums owed C under the construction contract. So C convinces O to get National Bank to issue a letter of credit in favor of State Bank. The credit provides that National Bank will pay drafts drawn against it by State Bank and accompanied by certificates to the effect that C has performed and is entitled to payment from O.

Here is a more elaborate example by Professor John Dolan, who is a top expert on letters of credit:

> Defense Contractor (Contractor) negotiates the sale of high technology optical equipment with Foreign Government (Buyer). * * * Contractor insists on a twenty percent downpayment, progress payments of an additional sixty percent during the course of performance, and the balance upon installation and satisfactory operation of the equipment. Buyer balks at these terms. It is concerned that Contractor may not perform at all or may perform unsatisfactorily. In these events Contractor will have Buyer's money, and Buyer will have a cause of action that it will have to pursue in a distant jurisdiction, Buyer being situated in one country, Contractor in another. Buyer is also concerned that its cause of action may become worthless in the face of Contractor's insolvency. * * *

> [T]he parties agree that a strong financial institution, usually a foreign bank or the foreign subsidiary of a United States bank, will issue two guaranties in favor of Buyer, one to cover return of the downpayment, the other to cover return of progress payments. Under those guaranties * * * the guaranty issuer will pay Buyer promptly and without inquiry upon Buyer's demand, provided that the demand is made in the time and manner specified in the guaranty. [These guaranties are not letters of credit. Rather, they are more like bonds or other suretyship contracts governed by the common law.]

> The guaranty issuer insists that it have security for its guaranty, so the parties agree further that Contractor will cause a financially strong party (usually a commercial bank) to issue two standby credits in favor of the guaranty issuer. The first credit engages to pay the guaranty issuer a sum equal to the downpayment upon the guaranty issuer's order. The second engages to pay a sum equal to or less than the progress payments, as the guaranty issuer orders. If Buyer draws on a guaranty, the guaranty issuer will draw on the corresponding standby.

> Contractor is concerned that there may be a draw on the credits when Contractor is not in default and asks that the credits contain conditions that protect against unauthorized drafts. Buyer refuses. It argues that any attempt to condition payment of the credit on the question of performance may force Buyer to litigate performance questions before payment and may force Buyer to litigate them in Contractor's forum. It is against these risks that Buyer is attempting to guard, and Buyer insists that the credits contain only paper conditions and that they are to be simple. The bank issues, then, two credits under which it engages to pay * * * drafts provided that they: (1) are presented prior to the respective credit's expiry; (2) bear a legend identifying the credit; and (3) are accompanied by a certificate reciting, in the downpayment credit, that the guaranty issuer paid on the downpayment guaranty, and in the performance credit, that the guaranty issuer paid on the progress-payments guaranty. Ultimately, Contractor will bear the cost of draws under the guaranties, for when Buyer draws on a guaranty, the guaranty issuer will draw

on the standby; and in the event of draw under the standby, the bank issuer [of the letters of credit] will seek reimbursement from Contractor.

John F. Dolan, *Standby Letters of Credit and Fraud (Is the Standby Only Another Invention of the Goldsmiths in Lombard Street?)*, 7 CARDOZO L. REV. 1, 2-5 (1985).

Back-to-back credits

Back-to-back credits describes a financing and security arrangement in which a bank issues a letter of credit on the strength of an assignment of the right to proceeds of a separate credit. Barkley Clark, another top expert, gives this example:

Distributor is the beneficiary of a letter of credit issued by Retailer's bank. Under the terms of the letter, Distributor is to ship widgets to Retailer under documentary drafts. The letter requires that the drafts be accompanied by proper bills of lading, invoices, and insurance certificates. If the documents are in order, the issuing bank is obligated to pay drafts to Distributor * * *. In order to help finance Distributor's operation, Distributor's bank extends to Distributor a line of credit secured by an assignment of Distributor's rights to proceeds of drafts drawn under the letter [issued by Retailer's bank]. * * * Distributor's bank could use the security interest in proceeds under the *** letter as collateral to support either a direct line of credit to Distributor or the issuance of a *second* letter with Distributor as customer and Distributor's supplier as beneficiary. In this way, Distributor's bank could finance the purchase of inventory one link up the chain of distribution. Under such an arrangement, Distributor's bank would be required to honor drafts drawn by Supplier that conform to the second letter, but in turn could be assured of the proceeds from drafts drawn by Distributor upon Retailer that conform to the first letter.

Barkley Clark, THE LAW OF BANK DEPOSITS, COLLECTIONS AND CREDIT CARDS ¶¶ 10.12[2] & [3] (3d ed. 1991).

law

Courtaulds North America, Inc. v.
North Carolina National Bank
United States Court of Appeals, Fourth Circuit, 1975
528 F.2d 802

Bryan, Senior Circuit Judge. A letter of credit with the date of March 21, 1973 was issued by the North Carolina National Bank at the request of and for the account of its customer, Adastra Knitting Mills, Inc. It made available upon the drafts of Courtaulds North America, Inc. "up to"

$135,000.00 (later increased by $135,000.00) at "60 days date" to cover Adastra's purchases of acrylic yarn from Courtaulds. The life of the credit was extended in June to allow the drafts to be "drawn and negotiated on or before August 15, 1973."

Bank refused to honor a draft for $67,346.77 dated August 13, 1973 for yarn sold and delivered to Adastra. Courtaulds brought this action to recover this sum from Bank.

The defendant denied liability chiefly on the assertion that the draft did not agree with the letter's conditions, viz., that the draft be accompanied by a "Commercial invoice in triplicate stating [*inter alia*] that it covers *** 100 acrylic yarn"; instead, the accompanying invoices stated that the goods were "Imported Acrylic Yarn."

Upon cross motions for summary judgment on affidavits and a stipulation of facts, the District Court held defendant Bank liable to Courtaulds for the amount of the draft, interest and costs. It concluded that the draft complied with the letter of credit when each invoice is read together with the packing lists stapled to it, for the lists stated on their faces: "Cartons marked: -- 100 Acrylic." After considering the insistent rigidity of the law and usage of bank credits and acceptances, we must differ with the District Judge and uphold Bank's position.

The letter of credit prescribed the terms of the drafts as follows:

"Drafts to be dated same as Bills of Lading. Draft(s) to be accompanied by:

1. Commercial invoice in triplicate stating that it covers 100,000 lbs. 100% Acrylic Yarn, Packaged Dyed at $1.35 per lb., FOB Buyers Plant, Greensboro, North Carolina Land Duty Paid.
2. Certificate stating goods will be delivered to buyers plant land duty paid.
3. Inland Bill of Lading consigned to Adastra Knitting Mills, Inc. evidencing shipment from East Coast Port to Adastra Knitting Mills, Inc., Greensboro, North Carolina."

The shipment (the last) with which this case is concerned was made on or about August 8, 1973. On direction of Courtaulds bills of lading of that date were prepared for the consignment to Adastra from a bonded warehouse by motor carrier. The yarn was packaged in cartons and a packing list referring to its bill of lading accompanied each carton. After the yarn was delivered to the carrier, each bill of lading with the packing list was sent to Courtaulds. There invoices for the sales were made out, and the invoices and packing lists stapled together. At the same time, Courtaulds wrote up the certificate, credit memorandum and draft called for in the letter of credit. The draft was dated August 13, 1973 and drawn on Bank by Courtaulds payable to itself.

All of these documents -- the draft, the invoices and the packing lists -- were sent by Courtaulds to its correspondent in Mobile for presentation to Bank and collection of the draft which for the purpose had been endorsed to the correspondent.

This was the procedure pursued on each of the prior drafts and always the draft had been honored by Bank save in the present instance. Here the draft, endorsed to Bank, and the other papers were sent to Bank on August 14. Bank received them on Thursday, August 16. Upon processing, Bank found these discrepancies between the drafts with accompanying documents and the letter of credit: (1) that the invoice did not state "100% Acrylic Yarn" but described it as "Imported Acrylic Yarn," and (2) "Draft not drawn as per terms of [letter of credit], Date [August 13] not same as Bill of Lading [August 8] and not drawn 60 days after date" [but 60 days from Bill of Lading date 8/8/73]. Finding of Fact 24. Since decision of this controversy is put on the first discrepancy we do not discuss the others.

On Monday, August 20, Bank called Adastra and asked if it would waive the discrepancies and thus allow Bank to honor the draft. In response, the president of Adastra informed Bank that it could not waive any discrepancies because a trustee in bankruptcy had been appointed for Adastra and Adastra could not do so alone. Upon word of these circumstances, Courtaulds on August 27 sent amended invoices to Bank which were received by Bank on August 27. They referred to the consignment as "100% Acrylic Yarn", and thus would have conformed to the letter of credit had it not expired. On August 29 Bank wired Courtaulds that the draft remained unaccepted because of the expiration of the letter of credit on August 15. Consequently the draft with all the original documents was returned by Bank.

During the life of the letter of credit some drafts had not been of even dates with the bills of lading, and among the large number of invoices transmitted during this period, several did not describe the goods as "100% Acrylic Yarn." As to all of these deficiencies Bank called Adastra for and received approval before paying the drafts. Every draft save the one in suit was accepted.

Conclusion of Law

The factual outline related is not in dispute, and the issue becomes one of law. It is well phrased by the District Judge in his "Discussion" in this way:

"The only issue presented by the facts of this case is whether the documents tendered by the beneficiary to the issuer were in conformity with the terms of the letter of credit."

The letter of credit provided:

"Except as otherwise expressly stated herein, this credit is subject to the 'Uniform Customs and Practice for Documentary Credits (1962 revision), the International Chamber of Commerce, Brochure No. 222'." Finding of Fact 6.

Of particular pertinence, with accents added, are these injunctions of the Uniform Customs:

"*Article 7.* -- Banks must examine all documents with reasonable care to ascertain that they *appear on their face* to be in accordance with the terms and conditions of the credit.
"*Article 8.* -- In documentary credit operations all parties concerned deal in documents and not in goods.
***
"If, upon receipt of the documents, the issuing bank considers that they *appear on their face* not to be in accordance with the terms and conditions of the credit, that bank must determine, on the basis of the documents alone, whether to claim that payment, acceptance or negotiation was not effected in accordance with the terms and conditions of the credit.
***
"*Article 9.* -- Banks *** do [not] assume any liability or responsibility *for the description*, *** quality, *** of the goods represented thereby ***.
***
"The description of the goods in the commercial *invoice* must correspond with the description in the credit. *In the remaining documents the goods may be described in general terms.*"

Also to be looked to are the North Carolina statutes, because in a diversity action, the Federal courts apply the same law as would the courts of the State of adjudication. Here applicable would be the Uniform Commercial Code -- Letters of Credit, [Article 5]. Especially to be noticed are these sections:

"§5-109. Issuer's obligation to its customer.

(1) An issuer's obligation to its customer includes good faith and observance of any general banking usage but unless otherwise agreed does not include liability or responsibility

(a) for performance of the underlying contract for sale or other transaction between the customer and the beneficiary; or

***

(c) based on knowledge or lack of knowledge of any usage of any particular trade.

(2) An issuer must examine documents with care so as to ascertain that on their face they appear to comply with the terms of the credit but unless otherwise agreed assumes no liability or responsibility for the genuineness, falsification or effect of any document which appears on such examination to be regular on its face."

In utilizing the rules of construction embodied in the letter of credit -- the Uniform Customs and State statute -- one must constantly recall that the drawee bank is not to be embroiled in disputes between the buyer and the seller, the beneficiary of the credit. The drawee is involved only with documents, not with merchandise. Its involvement is altogether separate and apart from the transaction between the buyer and seller; its duties and liability are governed exclusively by the terms of the letter, not the terms of the parties' contract with each other. Moreover, as the predominant authorities unequivocally declare, the beneficiary must meet the terms of the credit -- and precisely -- if it is to exact performance of the issuer. Failing such compliance there can be no recovery from the drawee. That is the specific failure of Courtaulds here.

Free of ineptness in wording the letter of credit dictated that each invoice express on its face that it covered 100% acrylic yarn. Nothing less is shown to be tolerated in the trade. No substitution and no equivalent, through interpretation or logic, will serve. Harfield, *Bank Credits and Acceptances* (5th Ed.1974), at p. 73, commends and quotes aptly from an English case: "There is no room for documents which are almost the same, or which will do just as well." Although no pertinent North Carolina decision has been laid before us, in many cases elsewhere, especially in New York, we find the tenet of Harfield to be unshaken.

At trial Courtaulds prevailed on the contention that the invoices in actuality met the specifications of the letter of credit in that the packing lists attached to the invoices disclosed on their faces that the packages contained "cartons marked: -- 100% acrylic". On this premise it was urged that the lists were a part of the invoice since they were appended to it, and the invoices should be read as one with the lists, allowing the lists to detail the invoices. But this argument cannot be accepted. In this connection it is well to revert to the distinction made in *Uniform Customs*, supra, between the "invoice" and the "remaining documents", emphasizing that in the latter the description may be in general terms while in the invoice the goods must be described in conformity with the credit letter.

The District Judge's pat statement adeptly puts an end to this contention of Courtaulds:

"In dealing with letters of credit, it is a custom and practice of the banking trade for a bank to only treat a document as an invoice which clearly is marked on its face as 'invoice.'" Finding of Fact 46.

This is not a pharisaical or doctrinaire persistence in the principle, but is altogether realistic in the environs of this case; it is plainly the fair and equitable measure. (The defect in description was not superficial but occurred in the statement of the *quality* of the yarn, not a frivolous concern.) The obligation of the drawee bank was graven in the credit. Indeed, there could be no departure from its words. Bank was not expected to scrutinize the collateral papers, such as the packing lists. Nor was it permitted to read into the instrument the contemplation or intention of the seller and buyer. Adherence to this rule was not only legally commanded, but it was factually ordered also, as will immediately appear.

Had Bank deviated from the stipulation of the letter and honored the draft, then at once it might have been confronted with the not improbable risk of the bankruptcy trustee's charge of liability for unwarrantably paying the draft money to the seller, Courtaulds, and refusal to reimburse Bank for the outlay. Contrarily, it might face a Courtaulds claim that since it had depended upon Bank's assurance of credit in shipping yarn to Adastra, Bank was responsible for the loss. In this situation Bank cannot be condemned for sticking to the letter of the letter.

Nor is this conclusion affected by the amended or substituted invoices which Courtaulds sent to Bank after the refusal of the draft. No precedent is cited to justify retroactive amendment of the invoices or extension of the credit beyond the August 15 expiry of the letter.

Finally, the trial court found that although in its prior practices Bank had pursued a strict-constructionist attitude, it had nevertheless on occasion honored drafts not within the verbatim terms of the credit letter. But it also found that in each of these instances Bank had first procured the authorization of Adastra to overlook the deficiencies. This truth is verified by the District Court in its Findings of Fact:

"42. It is a standard practice and procedure of the banking industry and trade for a bank to attempt to obtain a waiver of discrepancies from its customer in a letter of credit transaction. This custom and practice was followed by NCNB in connection with the draft and documents received from Courtaulds.

"43. Following this practice, NCNB had checked all previous discrepancies it discovered in Courtaulds' documents with its customer Adastra to see if Adastra would waive those discrepancies noted by NCNB. Except for the transaction in question, Adastra waived all discrepancies noted by NCNB.

"44. It is not normal or customary for NCNB, nor is it the custom and practice in the banking trade, for a bank to notify a beneficiary or the presenter of the documents that there were any deficiencies in the draft or documents if they are waived by the customer."

This endeavor had been fruitless on the last draft because of the inability of Adastra to give its consent. Obviously, the previous acceptances of truant invoices cannot be construed as a waiver in the present incident.

For these reasons, we must vacate the decision of the trial court, despite the evident close reasoning and research of the District Judge.

Sztejn v. J. Henry Schroder Banking Corp.
Supreme Court, Special Term, New York County, 1941
177 Misc. 719, 31 N.Y.S.2d 631

Shientag, Justice. This is a motion by the defendant, the Chartered Bank of India, Australia and China, (hereafter referred to as the Chartered Bank), made pursuant to Rule 106(5) of the Rules of Civil Practice to dismiss the supplemental complaint on the ground that it fails to state facts sufficient to constitute a cause of action against the moving defendant. The plaintiff brings this action to restrain the payment or presentment for payment of drafts under a letter of credit issued to secure the purchase price of certain merchandise, bought by the plaintiff and his coadventurer, one Schwarz, who is a party defendant in this action. The plaintiff also seeks a judgment declaring the letter of credit and drafts thereunder null and void. The complaint alleges that the documents accompanying the drafts are fraudulent in that they do not represent actual merchandise but instead cover boxes fraudulently filled with worthless material by the seller of the goods. The moving defendant urges that the complaint fails to state a cause of action against it because the Chartered Bank is only concerned with the documents and on their face these conform to the requirements of the letter of credit.

On January 7, 1941, the plaintiff and his coadventurer contracted to purchase a quantity of bristles from the defendant Transea Traders, Ltd. (hereafter referred to as Transea) a corporation having its place of business in Lucknow, India. In order to pay for the bristles, the plaintiff and Schwarz contracted with the defendant J. Henry Schroder Banking Corporation (hereafter referred to as Schroder), a domestic corporation, for the issuance of an irrevocable letter of credit to Transea which provided that drafts by the latter for a specified portion of the purchase price of the bristles would be paid by Schroder upon shipment of the described merchandise and presentation of an invoice and a bill of lading covering the shipment, made out to the order of Schroder.

The letter of credit was delivered to Transea by Schroder's correspondent bank in India, Transea placed fifty cases of material on board a steamship, procured a bill of lading from the steamship company and obtained the customary invoices. These documents describe the bristles called for by the letter of credit. However, the complaint alleges that in fact Transea filled the fifty crates with cowhair, other worthless material and rubbish with intent to simulate genuine merchandise and defraud the plaintiff and Schwarz. The complaint then alleges that Transea drew a draft under the letter of credit to the order of the Chartered Bank and delivered the draft and the fraudulent documents to the 'Chartered Bank at Cawnpore, India, for collection for the account of said defendant Transea'. The Chartered Bank has presented the draft along with the documents to Schroder for payment. The plaintiff prays for a judgment declaring the letter of credit and draft thereunder void and for injunctive relief to prevent the payment of the draft.

For the purposes of this motion, the allegations of the complaint must be deemed established and 'every intendment and fair inference is in favor of the pleading.' Therefore, it must be assumed that Transea was engaged in a scheme to defraud the plaintiff and Schwarz, that the merchandise shipped by Transea is worthless rubbish and that the Chartered Bank is not an innocent holder of the draft for value but is merely attempting to procure payment of the draft for Transea's account.

It is well established that a letter of credit is independent of the primary contract of sale between the buyer and the seller. The issuing bank agrees to pay upon presentation of documents, not goods. This rule is necessary to preserve the efficiency of the letter of credit as an instrument for the financing of trade. One of the chief purposes of the letter of credit is to furnish the seller with a ready means of obtaining prompt payment for his merchandise. It would be a most unfortunate interference with business transactions if a bank before honoring drafts drawn upon it was obliged or even allowed to go behind the documents, at the request of the buyer and enter into controversies between the buyer and the seller regarding the quality of the merchandise shipped. If the buyer and the seller intended the bank to do this they could have so provided in the letter of credit itself, and in the absence of such a provision, the court will not demand or even permit the bank to delay paying drafts which are proper in form. Of course, the application of this doctrine presupposes that the documents accompanying the draft are genuine and conform in terms to the requirements of the letter of credit.

However, I believe that a different situation is presented in the instant action. This is not a controversy between the buyer and seller concerning a mere breach of warranty regarding the quality of the merchandise; on the present motion, it must be assumed that the seller has intentionally failed to ship any goods ordered by the buyer. In such a situation, where the seller's fraud has been called to the bank's attention before the drafts and documents have been presented for payment, the principle of the independence of the bank's obligation under the letter of credit should not be extended to protect the unscrupulous seller. It is true that even though the documents are forged or fraudulent, if the issuing bank has already paid the draft before receiving notice of the seller's fraud, it will be protected if it exercised reasonable diligence before making such payment. However, in the instant action Schroder has received notice of Transea's active fraud before it accepted or paid the draft. The Chartered Bank, which under the allegations of the complaint stands in no better position than Transea, should not be heard to complain because Schroder is not forced to pay the draft accompanied by documents covering a transaction which it has reason to believe is fraudulent.

Although our courts have used broad language to the effect that a letter of credit is independent of the primary contract between the buyer and seller, that language was used in cases concerning alleged breaches of warranty; no case has been brought to my attention on this point involving an intentional fraud on the part of the seller which was brought to the bank's notice with the request that it withhold payment of the draft on this account. The distinction between a breach of warranty and active fraud on the part of the seller is supported by authority and reason. As one court has stated: 'Obviously, when the issuer of a letter of credit knows that a document, although correct in form, is, in point of fact, false or illegal, he cannot be called upon to recognize such a document as complying with the terms of a letter of credit.'

No hardship will be caused by permitting the bank to refuse payment where fraud is claimed, where the merchandise is not merely inferior in quality but consists of worthless rubbish, where the draft and the accompanying documents are in the hands of one who stands in the same position as the fraudulent seller, where the bank has been given notice of the fraud before being presented with the drafts and documents for payment, and where the bank itself does not wish to pay pending an adjudication of the rights and obligations of the other parties. While the primary factor in the issuance of the letter of credit is the credit standing of the buyer, the security afforded by the merchandise is also taken into account. In fact, the letter of credit requires a bill of lading made out to the order of the bank and not the buyer. Although the bank is not interested in the exact detailed performance of the sales contract, it is vitally interested in assuring itself that there are some goods represented by the documents.

On this motion only the complaint is before me and I am bound by its allegation that the Chartered Bank is not a holder in due course but is a mere agent for collection for the account of the seller charged with fraud. Therefore, the Chartered Bank's motion to dismiss the complaint must be denied. If it had appeared from the face of the complaint that the bank presenting the draft for payment was a holder in due course, its claim against the bank issuing the letter of credit would not be defeated even though the primary transaction was tainted with fraud. This I believe to be the better rule despite some authority to the contrary.

The plaintiff's further claim that the terms of the documents presented with the draft are at substantial variance with the requirements of the letter of credit does not seem to be supported by the documents themselves.

Accordingly, the defendant's motion to dismiss the supplemental complaint is denied.

First Commercial Bank v. Gotham Originals, Inc.

Court of Appeals of New York, 1985
64 N.Y.2d 287, 475 N.E.2d 1255, 486 N.Y.S.2d 715

Simons, Judge. This is a special proceeding instituted pursuant to CPLR 6221 to determine adverse claims to attached property. The disputed property consists of funds and assets held by respondent Bank Leumi Trust Company of New York. Petitioner, First Commercial Bank, claims the proceeds because Bank Leumi accepted drafts it presented in the amount of $70,978.50 which had been drawn in connection with a letter of credit. Respondent Gotham Originals, Inc., the customer of Bank Leumi which obtained the letter of credit, claims that Bank Leumi may not transfer the proceeds because the court enjoined it from doing so before it honored the drafts. Petitioner bases its claim to the funds on the provisions of Uniform Commercial Code §4-303(1)(a) which provides that legal process comes too late to suspend the bank's duty to pay an item if it comes, as this order did, after the bank has accepted it. Gotham contends, however, that the restraining order was timely under section 5-114(2)(b) of the Code because the order was served upon the Bank before it honored the drafts. The Code defines honor as "to pay or to accept and pay" (Uniform Commercial Code §1-201[21]). Thus, the order was untimely under section 4-303 because Bank Leumi had accepted the drafts before enjoined but timely under section 5-114 because it had not yet honored them. The Appellate Division held that under these circumstances section 4-303 prevails. We agree and therefore affirm its order.

I

In June 1981 respondent Gotham Originals, Inc. agreed to purchase approximately 24,000 pairs of ladies leather and snakeskin shoes from Teng Shih Industries Company, Ltd., and other Taiwanese shoe manufacturers. To finance the purchase, it obtained an irrevocable letter of credit from Bank Leumi designating Teng Shih Industries as beneficiary and petitioner First Commercial Bank, a banking corporation organized under the laws of the Republic of China and having its principal place of business in Taipei, as advising bank. The total amount of the letter of credit, as amended, was $172,026. It was transferrable and contained an expiration date of September 5, 1981. On September 10, 1981, R. Bore International, Inc., a transferee beneficiary of Teng Shih Industries, negotiated to petitioner two drafts in the amount of $70,978.50, payable on sight 60 days from date, together with the other documents required by the letter of credit. Petitioner paid for the drafts in Taiwanese currency and credited the amounts to R. Bore's checking account although it did so "under reserve" because the letter of credit had expired on September 5, 1981. On September 21st, Bank Leumi received from petitioner the two drafts, the required documentation and transmittal letters and a request for payment of the drafts on Gotham's letter of credit. Petitioner disclosed the discrepancy in the expiration date, noted that it had negotiated the drafts "under reserve" and requested advice as to when it could lift the reserve and make final payment to R. Bore. Bank Leumi subsequently obtained a waiver of the discrepancy in the expiration date from Gotham and on September 24th it notified petitioner by letter that the drafts had been accepted and that payment would be made on November 23, 1981.

After Bank Leumi had accepted the drafts, but before it had paid them, Gotham instituted an action against Teng Shih, R. Bore and the other shoe manufacturers-sellers in Supreme Court, New York County, claiming they had sold it worthless merchandise and charging them with fraud and breach of contract. It simultaneously obtained a temporary restraining order enjoining Bank Leumi from transferring the letter of credit or any moneys or assets of the sellers and sought orders attaching the proceeds of the drafts. After the restraining order was served on Bank Leumi and the attachment was perfected, Bank Leumi refused to pay petitioner.

Petitioner first attempted to recover the funds by a plenary action against Bank Leumi and the bank, in turn, impleaded Gotham. Petitioner then moved for summary judgment and when its motion was denied it commenced this proceeding. In it petitioner seeks to vacate and discharge the restraining order and the orders of attachment, to void the Sheriff's levy and to obtain a determination that section 4-303 of the Code controls this transaction and requires Bank Leumi to pay the accepted drafts. Before answering, Gotham moved to dismiss the petition contending that it failed to state a cause of action and that granting the relief sought would violate a prior order of the same court (i.e., the order denying petitioner summary judgment in the plenary action). It requested leave to answer if its motion was denied. Bank Leumi appeared and answered the petition.

On November 15, 1983 Special Term granted Gotham's motion and dismissed the petition holding that (1) petitioner's plenary action involved the same parties and issues and was still pending, (2) no judgment had been obtained in it, which it viewed as a necessary predicate to a

CPLR 6221 petition, and, (3) petitioner failed to name as necessary parties the defendants in the Gotham action and the Sheriff of New York City.

The Appellate Division, First Department, unanimously reversed and granted the petition (101 A.D.2d 790, 476 N.Y.S.2d 835). It held that there were no procedural bars to reaching the merits and, on the merits, it held that the attachment order was untimely under Uniform Commercial Code §4-303 and was therefore ineffective to terminate or suspend Bank Leumi's duty to pay the accepted drafts.

II

The purpose of a letter of credit is to substitute for, and therefore support, an engagement to pay money. Letters of credit are used in various ways in modern business practice, but when used in the traditional manner to finance a sale of goods, the credit subsumes a separate agreement by a buyer to pay money to a seller (for illustrations of other uses see J. White & R. Summers, Handbook on Uniform Commercial Code §18-1, at 708-09 [2d ed.]). By issuing a letter of credit, the issuer undertakes an obligation to pay the beneficiary, or his transferee if the letter is negotiable, from the account of its customer. Thus, a commercial letter of credit transaction involves three separate contractual relationships and undertakings: first, the underlying contract for the purchase and sale of goods between the customer (the buyer, Gotham in this case) and the beneficiary (the seller Shih): second, the agreement between the issuer (Bank Leumi), customarily a bank but frequently some other institution or person, and its customer (Gotham) in which the issuer typically agrees to issue the letter of credit in return for its customer's promise to reimburse it for any payments made under the credit plus a commission; and third, the letter of credit itself which is an engagement by the bank or other issuer that it will honor drafts or other demands for payment presented by the beneficiary or a transferee beneficiary upon compliance with the terms and conditions specified in the credit.

The fundamental principle governing these transactions is the doctrine of independent contracts. It provides that the issuing bank's obligation to honor drafts drawn on a letter of credit by the beneficiary is separate and independent from any obligation of its customer to the beneficiary under the sale of goods contract and separate as well from any obligation of the issuer to its customer under their agreement. Stated another way, this principle stands for "the fundamental proposition * * * that all parties [to a letter of credit transaction] deal in documents rather than with the facts the documents purport to reflect." Thus, the issuer's obligation to pay is fixed upon presentation of the drafts and the documents specified in the letter of credit. It is not required to resolve disputes or questions of fact concerning the underlying transaction.

A limited exception to this rule of independence is provided in section 5-114 of the Code (see also, *Sztejn v. Schroder Banking Corp.*, 177 Misc. 719, 31 N.Y.S.2d 631). Under the general rule the issuer must honor the draft when the documents presented comply with the terms of the letter of credit (Uniform Commercial Code §5-114[1]). But when a required document does not conform to the necessary warranties or is forged or fraudulent or there is fraud in the transaction, an issuer acting in good faith may, but is not required to, refuse to honor a draft under a letter of credit when the documents presented appear on their face to comply with the terms of the letter of credit. Further than that, a customer may also enjoin an issuer from honoring such a draft if the issuer fails to do so on its own. . Notwithstanding this exception, if the person presenting a draft drawn on a letter of credit is a holder in due course (see, Uniform Commercial Code §3-302), the issuer must pay the draft, whether it has notice of forgery or fraud or not (Uniform Commercial Code §5-114[2][a]).

Thus, if petitioner had taken the drafts under circumstances which made it a holder in due course, it would have acquired greater rights than the beneficiary and Bank Leumi would be obligated to honor the drafts despite Gotham's allegations of fraud in the transaction. Petitioner has neither pleaded nor proved its status as a holder in due course, however. Indeed it asserts that its status as such is irrelevant and maintains that it is entitled to recover on the facts presented in any event.

Petitioner was initially designated as an advising bank and stood in a neutral position; its only obligation was to convey accurate information of the issuance, amendment and terms and conditions of the credit to its beneficiaries (see, Uniform Commercial Code §5-103[1][e]; H. Harfield, Letters of Credit 10-111; PLI, Letters of Credit and Bankers' Acceptances 43). By purchasing the signed drafts drawn under the letter of credit by the transferee-beneficiary, R. Bore, it became a negotiating bank and because of Bank Leumi's express engagement in the letter of credit to honor drafts presented by a negotiating bank, petitioner acquired rights against Bank Leumi, as issuer, "to the same extent as if it were named as beneficiary of the credit" (H. Harfield, Letters of Credit 14; see, PLI, Letters of Credit and Bankers' Acceptances 45-46).

Thus, although the parties agree subdivision (2)(b) is the provision of section 5-114 pertinent to this appeal because petitioner does not claim to be a holder in due course, they disagree on its significance. Gotham contends that the court was authorized to enjoin payment of the drafts pursuant to it because there was fraud in the transaction. Petitioner asserts that section 4-303 prevails in the case of conflict and that because the drafts were accepted before the restraining order was issued or served on Bank Leumi, its rights became fixed and are paramount to Gotham's, notwithstanding its status and the statutory authorization to enjoin payment found in section 5-114.

III

Section 4-102 of the Code specifically provides that if the provisions of article 4 conflict with those of article 3 then article 4 shall govern and that if they conflict with the provisions of article 8 then the provisions of article 8 shall govern. It contains no similar provision with respect to a conflict with the provisions of article 5 nor does any section in article 5 deal with the conflict. The controlling language must be found in section 4-303(1). It states that any legal process served upon a payor bank, "*whether or not effective under other rules of law*" to terminate or suspend the bank's duty to pay the item comes too late to terminate or suspend that duty if the bank has previously accepted the item (Uniform Commercial Code §4-303[1][a]). Section 5-114 contains no similar provision. Indeed, the Legislature made clear that article 5 and the UCP do not control every aspect of a transaction that involves a letter of credit when it provided that article 5 was intended to deal "with some but not all of the rules and concepts of letters of credit" (Uniform Commercial Code §5-102[3]). Accordingly, section 4-303, by its terms, supersedes section 5-114 and when Bank Leumi accepted the drafts on September 24, 1981, it became directly, primarily and unconditionally obligated to the holder to pay them at maturity (Uniform Commercial Code §3-413[1]; for the definition of "acceptance" see Uniform Commercial Code §3-410[1]). Because the restraining order was served on it on October 30, 1981, 36 days after the act of acceptance, it came "too late" to prevent payment to petitioner.

This view is reinforced by authorities holding that article 4 continues to apply in letter of credit transactions to the rights and liabilities on documentary drafts. So, also, in *Key Intl. Mfg. v. Stillman*, 103 A.D.2d 475, 480 N.Y.S.2d 528, the Appellate Division, Second Department, noted that it was improper for the lower court to restrain the issuing bank from paying cashier's checks it had previously issued to the beneficiary following presentment of a draft and necessary documents under a letter of credit. A cashier's check is accepted upon its issuance and therefore the court, citing section 4-303(1)(a) of the Code, stated that the restraining order was not timely. Similarly, in *Voest-Alpine Intl. Corp. v. Chase Manhattan Bank*, 2nd Cir., 707 F.2d 680, the Second Circuit, applying New York law, reversed and remanded an award of summary judgment for a confirming bank in an action by the beneficiary of a letter of credit, because there was an issue of fact whether the bank had accepted the beneficiary's drafts prior to its refusal to pay them (707 F.2d at pp.

685-686). Implicit in the court's decision is the determination that if the bank had accepted the drafts, it would be precluded from subsequently refusing payment.

Important policy considerations suggest the result also. Letters of credit provide a quick, economic and predictable means of financing transactions for parties not willing to deal on open accounts by permitting the seller to rely not only on the credit of the buyer but also on that of the issuing bank. By its terms, the credit often reflects a conscious negotiation of risk allocation between customer and beneficiary and its utility rests heavily on strict adherence to the agreed terms and the doctrine of independent contract. It is this predictability of credit arrangements which permits not only the financing of sale of goods transactions between widely separated parties in different jurisdictions but also has permitted the development of a market in trade or bankers' acceptances of time drafts. Once a draft payable in the future is accepted by a bank, it becomes known as a bankers' acceptance, and such acceptances can be, and regularly are, sold in conjunction with letter of credit transactions to obtain financing prior to the date of maturity in a market sanctioned by the Federal Reserve Board (see, 12 U.S.C. §372). If the courts intervene to enjoin issuing banks from paying drafts they have previously accepted they seriously undermine this market and limit the use of acceptances as a financing tool.

IV

Our decision in *United Bank v. Cambridge Sporting Goods Corp.*, 41 N.Y.2d 254, 392 N.Y.S.2d 265, 360 N.E.2d 943, does not compel a contrary conclusion. In *United Bank*, the presenters claimed to be holders in due course and asserted their right to payment under section 5-114(2)(a). They did not rely on section 4-303 as a basis for relief and we expressly noted that the petitioning banks did not "dispute the validity of the prior injunction" and that we did not reach "the question of the availability and the propriety of this relief" (41 N.Y.2d, at 260, 392 N.Y.S.2d 265, 360 N.E.2d 943).

Accordingly, the order of the Appellate Division should be affirmed, with costs.

Order affirmed, with costs.

Rose Developments, Inc. v. Pearson Properties, Inc.
Court of Appeals of Arkansas, 1992
38 Ark.App. 215, 832 S.W.2d 286

Mayfield, Judge. Rose Developments appeals from the order of the circuit court which permanently enjoined the drawing on, or honor of, a letter of credit, pursuant to Ark.Code Ann. §4-5-114(2)(b) (Repl.1991), on the finding that appellant had committed fraud.

On December 6, 1988, appellee Pearson contracted with the appellant Rose to provide material and labor in connection with the construction of building "K" in a condominium project known as Solomons Landing Project. The amount of the contract was $458,200.00. In lieu of a performance bond, Pearson delivered an irrevocable letter of credit in the amount of $25,000.00 to secure its performance under the contract. The letter of credit authorized Rose to draw up to $25,000.00 available by "your drafts at sight" accompanied by an authorized statement that Pearson (d/b/a Homes, Inc.) had failed to perform its obligations as required under the terms and conditions of its construction contract and the original of the letter of credit. Under the terms of the letter of credit, drafts had to be drawn and negotiated no later than July 15, 1989. Subsequently, buildings "E" and "L" were made addendum to the original contract. The only change was an increase in the price.

On July 5, 1989, S. Brooks Grady, Sr., Vice-President of Rose, stated in a letter to First National Bank (Bank) that "Homes, Inc. has been working on our job at Solomons Landing in Maryland since November 1988. We have been very satisfied with their work, and they are presently working on our third building." On July 15, 1989, the letter of credit was extended until January 12, 1990, for the purpose of working on buildings "E" and "L".

On December 4, 1989, the Bank was notified that Homes, Inc., had failed to perform its obligations as required under the terms and conditions of its construction contract and immediate payment of $25,000.00 was requested under the letter of credit.

On December 12, 1989, Pearson filed a petition for a temporary restraining order against Rose and the Bank alleging among other things that the draft was fraudulently presented upon misrepresentations by Rose, and alternatively that "Ark.Code Ann.Section 4-5-114 specifically grants the Court authority to enjoin the honor of a draft or demand based on 'fraud, forgery, or other defect not apparent on the face of the documents.' "

On December 13, 1989, the court granted the petition. Subsequently, the Bank filed an answer admitting its obligation to honor the draft drawn against the letter of credit unless enjoined by the court and tendered a cashier's check for $25,000.00 to the clerk of the court for safekeeping until further orders.

After a hearing, held May 31, 1990, the trial court found Rose had committed fraud which should prevent it from drawing on the letter of credit and permanently enjoined the Bank from honoring the draft and Rose from drawing on the letter of credit.

A letter of credit is a three-party arrangement involving two contracts and the letter of credit: 1) the underlying contract between the customer and the beneficiary, in this case between Pearson and Rose; 2) the reimbursement agreement between the issuer and the customer, in this case between First National Bank and Pearson; and 3) the letter of credit between the issuer and the beneficiary, in this case between First National Bank and Rose. The significant part of this arrangement is the "independence principle" which states that the bank's obligation to the beneficiary is independent of the beneficiary's performance on the underlying contract. 2 J. White & R. Summers, *Uniform Commercial Code* §19-2 (3d ed.1988). "Put another way, the issuer must pay on a proper demand from the beneficiary even though the beneficiary may have breached the underlying contract with the customer." Id. at 8. "It is not a contract of guarantee ... even though the letter fulfills the function of a guarantee." Id. at 9.

The letter of credit involved in this case is a standby letter of credit which has been characterized as a "back-up" against customer default on obligations of all kinds. Id. §19-1, at 4. Such letters function somewhat like guarantees because it is the customer's default on the underlying obligation that prompts the beneficiary's draw on the letter. Id. at 4. The risk to the issuer is somewhat greater than in a commercial letter of credit in that the commercial letter gives the issuer security in goods whereas the standby letter gives no ready security, and the banker behaves as a surety. Id. at 6. The standby letter of credit is somewhat akin to a performance bond in that:

In place of a performance bond from a true surety, builder (customer) gets his bank (issuer) to write owner (beneficiary) a standby letter of credit. In this letter, issuer engages to pay beneficiary-owner against presentment of two documents: 1) a written demand (typically a sight draft) which calls for payment of the letter's stipulated amount, plus 2) a written statement certifying that customer-builder has failed to perform the agreed construction work.

Id. at 4. One difference between the standby letter of credit and the surety contract is that the standby credit beneficiary has different expectations.

In the surety contract situation, there is no duty to indemnify the beneficiary until the beneficiary establishes the fact of the obligor's nonperformance. The beneficiary may have to establish that fact in litigation. During the litigation, the surety holds the money and the beneficiary bears most of the cost of delay in performance. In the standby credit case, however, the beneficiary avoids that litigation burden and receives his money promptly upon presentation of the required documents. It may be that the account party has in fact performed and that the beneficiary's presentation of those documents is not rightful. In that case, the account party may sue the beneficiary in tort, in contract, or in breach of warranty; but during the litigation to determine whether the account party has in fact breached his obligation to perform, the beneficiary, not the account party, holds the money.

J. Dolan, *The Law of Letters of Credit*, at 1-18, 1-19 (2d ed.1991).

Letters of credit are governed by the "Uniform Commercial Code--Letters of Credit," Ark.Code Ann. §4-5-101 through 117 (Repl.1991). Section 4-5-114(1) provides that an issuer must honor a draft which complies with the terms of the relevant credit regardless of whether the goods or documents conform to the underlying contract between the customer and the beneficiary. However, the issuer does not have an absolute duty to honor a draft authorized by the letter of credit. An exception is provided by §4-5-114(2) which provides that an issuer need not honor the draft if "a required document does not in fact conform to the warranties made on negotiation or transfer of a document of title (§4-8-306) or of a certificated security (§4-8-306) or is forged or fraudulent or there is fraud in the transaction." Section 4-5-114(2)(b) provides that in all other cases as against its customer an issuer may honor the draft despite notification from the customer of fraud, forgery, or other defect not apparent on the face of the documents but a court of appropriate jurisdiction may enjoin such honor.

On appeal, it is argued that the trial court erred in finding the appellant committed fraud which would prevent it from drawing on the letter of credit. Appellant admits that courts have allowed injunctions for "fraud in the transaction" but argues an injunction is proper only if there is no bona fide claim to payment, and the wrongdoing of the beneficiary has so vitiated the entire transaction that the legitimate purposes of the independence principle would no longer be served. See *Intraworld Industries, Inc. v. Girard Trust Bank*, 461 Pa. 343, 336 A.2d 316 (1975); *Sztejn v. Henry Schroder Banking Corp.*, 177 Misc. 719, 31 N.Y.S.2d 631 (1941). Appellant contends that Pearson has established only that there may be a dispute as to some of the "back charges". (Back charges have to do with material and labor that needs or needed to be performed, that Pearson was supposed to be responsible for, but appellant had to take over.)

Appellees agree the only issue on appeal is whether appellant committed fraud which would justify the issuance of the injunction and argue the injunction was proper. Appellee Pearson contends that in December 1989 or January 1990 it received a number of back charges dating as far back as December 1988; that it had never previously received these charges; that appellant, while in possession of documents it claimed were back charges, wrote a letter to obtain an extension of the letter of credit stating it was "very satisfied with the work of Homes, Inc."; and that appellant knowingly misrepresented the facts in order to obtain an extension of the letter of credit.

In support of its argument, appellee Pearson cites *W.O.A. Inc. v. City National Bank of Fort Smith, Ark.*, 640 F.Supp. 1157 (W.D.Ark.1986), and *Shaffer v. Brooklyn Park Garden Apartments*, 311 Minn. 452, 250 N.W.2d 172 (1977). Those cases, however, involved false certification accompanying drafts for payment and have no application here. In *City National Bank* the appellant intentionally misrepresented the state of affairs when, though it had been paid, it presented drafts for payment under a letter of credit. That case relied on *Roman Ceramics Corp. v. Peoples National Bank*, 714 F.2d 1207 (3d Cir.1983), which held that a beneficiary who tenders a draft knowing that its certification of nonpayment by the buyers is false, is guilty of fraud in the transaction. Similarly, *Shaffer* involved a situation where letters of credit guaranteed payment of certain promissory notes. The issuer received documents which appeared to comply with the presentation requirements under the letters of credit; however, the certifications which stated the customers had defaulted on their loans were false.

In the instant case, the certification stated that "Homes, Inc., has failed to perform its obligations as required under the terms and conditions of their construction contract." At trial, Robert Pearson III, Vice-President of Homes, Inc., testified they did not allege that there were forgeries "or anything like that" involved in the demand for payment on the letter of credit. Pearson admitted the letter of credit was to protect appellant in the event Pearson did not pay for labor, materials and other supplies that might be incorporated into the structure; that there were outstanding materialmen's and laborers' liens against the project; and that some of those liens were for materials, labor, and supplies that were the responsibility of Pearson. Pearson testified his allegation of fraud was based on the contention that he had been billed for work outside his contract and that Rose had called upon the letter of credit based upon certain back charges. Pearson said the majority of the back charges were unacceptable, but acknowledged that 10% of the charges were legitimate.

Appellee Bank admits this case does not involve forgery or "other defect not apparent on the face of the documents". John Thornton, Executive Vice-President of the Bank, testified he would not have extended the original letter of credit without Rose's statement that the jobs were being done in a satisfactory manner. Appellee Bank argues that none of the back charges, that predated the extension of the letter of credit, were mentioned in appellant's letter which induced the Bank to extend the letter of credit. And the Bank contends that Rose's fraud can be categorized as both egregious and intentional and that the injunction was a proper statutory remedy.

The narrow question to be decided by this court is whether the evidence will support a finding that there was "fraud in the transaction." Our research has revealed no Arkansas cases containing a definition of "fraud in the transaction" as used in the section of the Uniform Commercial Code that is involved in this case. Some courts have held that fraud in the transaction must be of such an egregious nature as to vitiate the entire underlying transaction so that the legitimate purposes of the independence of the bank's obligation would no longer be served. See *Roman Ceramics Corp. v. Peoples National Bank*, 517 F.Supp. 526 (M.D.Pa.1981), aff'd, 714 F.2d 1207 (3d Cir.1983); *Intraworld*, supra; *Sztejn*, supra. Other cases and writers have suggested intentional fraud should be sufficient to obtain injunctive relief in letter of credit cases. See *NMC Enterprises, Inc. v. Columbia Broadcasting System, Inc.*, 14 U.C.C.Rep.Serv. 1427 (N.Y.Sup.Ct.1974); 6 W. Hawkland, *Uniform Commercial Code Series*, §5-114:09 (1984); Edward L. Symons, Jr., *Letters of Credit: Fraud, Good Faith and the Basis for Injunctive Relief*, 54 Tul.L.Rev. 338 (1980). Professor Symons concludes "a proper definition of fraud will necessarily encompass and be limited by the requirement of scienter: that there be an affirmative, knowing misrepresentation of fact or that the beneficiary state a fact not having any idea about its truth or falsity, and in reckless disregard of the truth." Symons, supra at 379. It has also been suggested that the lesson to be learned from this section of the Uniform Commercial Code (Ark.Code Ann. §4-5-114(2) (Repl.1990)), is that a court should seldom enjoin payment under a letter of credit on the theory that there is fraud in the documents or fraud in the underlying transaction. See 2 J. White & R. Summers, *Uniform Commercial Code* §19-7 (Supp.1991).

From our consideration of the law and the evidence in this case, we think the trial court erred in enjoining payment under the letter of credit. In the first place, we do not believe appellant's general statement "we have been very satisfied with their work" is sufficient for a finding of fraud. At the time this statement was made, appellant had extended Pearson's contract for building "K" to include buildings "E" and "L", and it seems obvious that appellant's statement was truthful or appellant would not have extended the contract. Also, the testimony shows that the total amount of the contract for building "K" was $458,200.00 and that the back charges which pre-date the statement complained of totalled only approximately $1,944.81. We do not believe the existence of back charges in that small amount supports a finding that appellant committed fraud when it said "we have been very satisfied with their work."

As to the argument that appellant's fraud consisted of billing for work that was outside its contract and other disputed back charges, Robert Pearson III testified his allegation of fraud was that the letter of credit was being called upon because appellant said that based upon "these back charges" they were still owed money, but Pearson testified that as far as "these back charges" are concerned "the majority of them are unacceptable." Pearson testified appellant was claiming a total of $50,000.00 to $60,000.00 in back charges on a project which totaled over $1.2 million. This is simply a contract dispute relating to back charges which may have to be resolved in litigation. However, as explained in Dolan, supra, in the standby letter of credit case "the beneficiary avoids that litigation burden and receives his money promptly" and during the litigation "the beneficiary, not the account party, holds the money."

When we apply the law to the evidence in this case, we think it was clearly erroneous to find that appellant committed fraud that should prevent it from drawing on the letter of credit; therefore, it was error to grant permanent injunctive relief to appellee Pearson and prevent the Bank from honoring the draft drawn on the letter of credit.

Reversed and remanded for any necessary proceedings consistent with this opinion.

Bank of Newport v. First National Bank & Trust Co.
United States Court of Appeals, Eighth Circuit, 1982
687 F.2d 1257

Gibson, Senior Circuit Judge. Bank of Newport appeals from the dismissal by the district court after a bench trial of Bank of Newport's diversity action against First National Bank and Trust Company of Bismarck (First National) for alleged wrongful dishonor of a draft drawn under a letter of credit issued by First National. We affirm the district court.

I

The events leading to this action began when First National at the request of Drs. Robert Honkola, Ralph Honkola, and Richard Fettig (the doctors) issued an irrevocable letter of credit, dated June 30, 1976, in the amount of $125,775.00 to Fiscal Concepts, Inc., a California corporation (Fiscal). The doctors sought issuance of the letter of credit pursuant to an investment program under which they were to provide Fiscal with $60,000.00 in cash and a letter of credit in the amount of $125,775.00 in exchange for the ownership interest in distributorships of coin-operated blood pressure machines. Specifically, the doctors were to receive forty-five blood pressure machines for sale or lease in Minnesota, North Dakota, South Dakota, and Wisconsin.

Fiscal and the doctors agreed that the First National letter of credit was to guarantee the manufacture and delivery of the blood pressure machines and, therefore, should serve as collateral for a second letter of credit issued at Fiscal's request for the benefit of Filac Corporation (Filac), the manufacturer of the machines. However, Fiscal made a commitment to the doctors that the First National letter of credit would never be drawn upon. The First National letter of credit,* issued

---

* The letter of credit provides as follows:
      "Gentlemen:
          "Our Irrevocable Letter of Credit No. 30 Amount -- $125,775.00 -- U.S.
    Funds for account of Drs. Honkola, Fettig, and Honkola
          "For guaranty that Drs. Honkola, Fettig, and Honkola will sell 25 BPM-1200
    Systems in Minnesota, North Dakota, and South Dakota, and 20 like machines in

June 30, 1976, provides that the letter was issued " *** [f]or guaranty that Drs. Honkola, Fettig, and Honkola will sell 25 BPM-1200 systems in Minnesota, North Dakota, and South Dakota, and 20 like machines in Wisconsin ***." The letter further provides that drafts drawn under the credit must be endorsed and state the reason for the draw.

On June 14, 1976, Fiscal entered into a general loan and blanket collateral agreement with the Bank of Newport, giving the bank a security interest in Fiscal property. At this time, Fiscal also assigned the proceeds of the First National letter of credit to the bank. The doctors were not told of the assignment until the summer of 1977 and of the security agreement until after this action was commenced.

In December of 1976, Bank of Newport issued, at Fiscal's request, a letter of credit in the amount of $125,760.00 to Filac to guarantee the shipment of ninety-six blood pressure machines to Fiscal. The First National letter of credit was designated as collateral for this letter of credit. In March 1977, Fiscal executed a promissory note in favor of the Bank of Newport in the amount of $125,750.00. This note was secured by the proceeds of the First National letter of credit pursuant to the general loan and collateral agreement of June 14, 1976. Bank of Newport made periodic disbursements under this note to cover draws made by Filac on the Bank of Newport letter of credit.

First National first became aware that the letter of credit had been assigned to Bank of Newport as collateral for Bank of Newport loans to Fiscal in July 1977. Consequently, First National's attorney Jerome Zamos wrote Bank of Newport a letter, stating that the First National letter of credit was not to be used as security for any loans by Bank of Newport to Fiscal, that such use would violate the terms of the letter of credit, and that First National would not honor calls upon its letter of credit. In this letter, Zamos referred to the Fiscal's earlier written commitment to the doctors that the First National letter of credit would never be drawn upon and would only be used "to guarantee manufacturing [of the blood pressure machines] in the first instance."

Despite receiving this notice from First National, on September 13, 1977, Bank of Newport prepared a sight draft, executed by Fiscal's president, authorizing First National to pay Bank of Newport $125,775.00 under the letter of credit. The front side of the draft provided that it was "[d]rawn under the First National Bank and Trust Company of Bismarck Letter of Credit # 30 dated 6/30/76 and subsequent amendments thereof." On November 30, 1977, Bank of Newport endorsed the reverse side of the draft, stating that it was "[d]rawn for Letter of Credit face value for application to beneficiary's obligation incurred for the purchase of merchandise in accordance with the letter of credit purpose." When Bank of Newport made this endorsement, it had no knowledge that any blood pressure machines had been purchased by Fiscal for eventual delivery to the doctors and made no effort to determine whether such purchases had been made. Further, at this time, the Bank of Newport retained possession of some 200 blood pressure machines warehoused pursuant to its blanket security agreement with Fiscal and knew that the doctors had not received their forty-five blood pressure machines as required by the agreement between Fiscal and the doctors, the agreement which was the underlying purpose for the letter of credit.

Bank of Newport subsequently presented the draft to First National along with Fiscal's assignment statement and the letter of credit. First National refused to honor the draft because: (1)

Wisconsin.
"The drafts drawn under this Credit are to be endorsed thereon and must bear the clause, drawn under the First National Bank and Trust Company of Bismarck Letter of Credit No. 30 dated June 30, 1976. [sic]
"The drafts drawn under this Credit should state the reason for the draft.
"We hereby agree with drawers, endorsers, and bona fide holders of drafts drawn under and in compliance with the terms of this credit that the same shall be duly honored upon presentation at the First National Bank and Trust Company of Bismarck, Bismarck, North Dakota if drawn and negotiated on or *before December 30, 1977.*"

the condition of the letter of credit had not been met -- i.e., the blood pressure machines had not been delivered to the doctors; and (2) Bank of Newport had received notice that the letter of credit was being improperly used to repay loans from Bank of Newport to Fiscal rather than to guarantee delivery of the machines to the doctors.

The District Court dismissed both of Bank of Newport's claims, holding that First National's dishonor was justified on two independent grounds: First, Bank of Newport failed to provide documentation evidencing delivery of the machines to the doctors as was required under the court's interpretation of the letter of credit. Second, prior to drawing the draft, Bank of Newport had actual knowledge of nondelivery of the machines to the doctors, had possession and control of 200 such machines warehoused pursuant to its security agreement with Fiscal, and had notice that the letter of credit was being improperly used by Fiscal as security for loans from Bank of Newport to Fiscal.[*] As to the second grounds for dishonor, the court concluded that Bank of Newport was "attempting to manipulate the requirements of [the] letter of credit *** to recover its loan to Fiscal without giving up any of the machines it held as collateral."

Bank of Newport now appeals from the district court's dismissal of its claim for wrongful dishonor; it does not appeal the district court's dismissal of its claim for declaratory relief as to its status as a holder in due course.

II

(A)

This appeal focuses on the question of whether Bank of Newport's draft on the First National letter of credit was tainted by "fraud in the transaction," giving First National the right to dishonor that draft under Uniform Commercial Code §5-114(2). Bank of Newport makes two arguments in support of its position that there was no "fraud in the transaction." First, Bank of Newport argues that it complied fully and truthfully with the terms of the letter of credit by providing the following statement of reason for the draw:

> "Drawn for letter of credit face value for application to beneficiaries' obligation incurred for purchase of merchandise in accordance with the letter of credit purpose."

Bank of Newport urges that the veracity of this statement was not impaired by the fact that the purpose for which the draft was drawn -- to repay loans Bank of Newport made to Fiscal -- was wholly inconsistent with the purpose for which the letter of credit was issued -- to assure delivery of blood pressure machines to the doctors. Bank of Newport further argues that its actual knowledge of nondelivery of the blood pressure machines, its retained possession and control of such machines, and its knowledge of the improper use of the letter of credit did not impair its right to receive payment on the draft presented to First National. Both of these arguments are hinged upon the long-standing principle that a letter of credit is completely divorced from the underlying transaction between the issuing bank's customer (the doctors) and the beneficiary under the letter of credit (Fiscal).

We do not accept Bank of Newport's arguments and conclude that where, as here, no innocent third parties are involved and where the draft itself and the underlying transaction are tainted with fraud or actual knowledge that the underlying transaction is being wholly thwarted by the

---

* The court further found that:

"[P]laintiff had knowledge that delivery of the machines may have been required under the [First National] letter of credit and a number of other letters of credit for the benefit of Fiscal issued for other investors not party to this action. In situations when plaintiff found such letters of credit to be ambiguous in regard to conditions precedent, plaintiff informed Fiscal of the fact and requested Fiscal to seek revision of the letters of credit to provide simply that funds be used 'for general corporate purposes.'"

beneficiary or its assignee, the draft need not be honored. Under the circumstances here presented, the salutory commercial doctrine of the independence of the letter of credit from the underlying transaction has no application. Bank of Newport, as assignee, stands in the shoes of Fiscal, and obviously Fiscal had no right to draw on the letter of credit without making provision for the delivery of the machines. Bank of Newport, as assignee, only had the right to receive payment on drafts properly drawn by the beneficiary, Fiscal.

(B)

A letter of credit is a commitment on the part of the issuing bank that it will pay a draft or demand for payment presented to it under the terms of the credit. Typically, three separate and distinct contracts are involved:

> (1) The contract of the bank (First National) with its customer (the doctors) by which the bank agrees to issue the letter of credit to the beneficiary (Fiscal).
> (2) The underlying contract between the customer and the beneficiary which results in the letter of credit issuance.
> (3) The letter of credit itself, which is a contract between the issuing bank and the beneficiary by which the bank agrees to pay the drafts drawn under the letter of credit and presented to it by the beneficiary if they are accompanied by the requisite documents.

Long-standing case law, codified in the Uniform Commercial Code, establishes that the letter of credit is separate and distinct from the underlying contractual transaction between the issuing bank's customer and the beneficiary. Accordingly, the issuing bank's duty to honor drafts presented for payment is dependent only on the terms and conditions of the letter of credit and not the underlying contract between the bank's customer and the beneficiary. The rule of the independence of the letter of credit from the underlying transaction is based on two policy considerations. First, the issuing bank can assume no liability for the performance of the underlying contract because it has no control over making the underlying contract or over selection of the beneficiary. Second, the letter of credit would lose its commercial vitality if, before honoring drafts, the issuing bank were obliged to look beyond the terms of the letter of credit to the underlying contractual controversy between its customer and the beneficiary.

In the instant case, First National's duty to honor Bank of Newport's draft is governed by §5-114(1) of the Uniform Commercial Code, which provides that:

> "An issuer must honor a draft or demand for payment which complies with the terms of the relevant credit regardless of whether the goods or documents conform to the underlying contract for sale or other contract between the customer and the beneficiary."

However, §5-114(2) of the Uniform Commercial Code permits an issuer to dishonor where "fraud in the transaction" has been shown and the holder has not taken the draft in circumstances that would make it a holder in due course. Here, because Bank of Newport does not (and cannot in this factual context) claim holder in due course status, we only address whether or not the defense of "fraud in the transaction" has been shown.

The "fraud in the transaction" defense is a statutory codification of the landmark case of *Sztejn v. J. Henry Schroder Banking Corp.*, 177 Misc. 719, 31 N.Y.S.2d 631 (N.Y.Sup.Ct.1941). In *Sztejn*, a letter of credit was issued to a seller to insure payment for a quantity of bristles. The letter of credit provided that drafts would be paid upon presentation of invoices and a bill of lading showing that shipment of the bristles had been made. The buyer who had procured the letter of credit sued to enjoin payment of the drafts drawn under the letter of credit. The buyer's complaint alleged that while the documents complied on their face with the terms of the letter of credit, the seller shipped worthless cowhairs instead of bristles. Thus, the buyer claimed the seller had engaged in "active fraud" in presenting the documents. The seller's correspondent bank who presented the draft moved to dismiss the buyer's injunction claiming that in a letter of credit transaction, the issuing bank was required to honor drafts where the accompanying documents on their face conformed to the requirements of the letter of credit, notwithstanding fraud in the underlying transaction.

The *Sztejn* court denied the correspondent bank's motion. The court stated that although a letter of credit is independent of the primary contract of sale between the buyer and the seller, and a bank is not required to go behind documents presented for payment before honoring drafts, "[t]he application of this doctrine presupposes that the documents accompanying the drafts are genuine."

The court went on to conclude that where no innocent parties are involved and where the documents and underlying transaction are tainted with intentional fraud, the draft need not be honored, even though the documents conform on their face. The court remarked that "the principle of the independence of the bank's obligation under the letter of credit should not be extended to protect the unscrupulous [beneficiary]." The court accordingly held that a bank presenting a draft on the beneficiary's behalf rather than as a holder in due course stood in no better position than the beneficiary charged with fraud. In the instant case no goods had been shipped at all.

Courts applying *Sztejn's* "fraud in the transaction" defense, as codified in UCC §5-114(2), have given varying interpretations to the term "fraud in the transaction." Some courts interpret the "fraud in the transaction" defense to permit an issuer to dishonor where fraud in the *underlying transaction* has been shown *and no innocent parties are involved.*

Other courts have interpreted the "fraud in the transaction" defense to apply only where fraud has been found in respect to the documents presented to the issuer and not as to the underlying transaction.

Bank of Newport urges that the "fraud in the transaction" defense is available only where the required documents presented along with the draft for payment are intentionally misleading or false, and, fraud in the underlying transaction cannot give rise to a defense to payment. Thus, Bank of Newport suggests that the only issue raised in this case is whether the required document, the draft setting forth the reason for the draw, was itself false; and contends that the statement was true, even though the purpose for the draw -- to repay Bank of Newport loans to Fiscal -- may have been inconsistent with the purpose underlying the letter of credit issuance -- delivery of the machines to the doctors.

(C)

Even accepting Bank of Newport's framing of the issue, we cannot agree that the statement of reason for the draw was itself truthful and that the purpose underlying the letter of credit was of no importance. The statement for the draw may have been artfully worded, but it was in total variance from the purpose of the transaction and not at all in keeping with the obligations of the beneficiary to manufacture and deliver the machines. We analyze this issue in three steps.

First, the purpose underlying the letter of credit is important in determining the truthfulness of the statement of reason because in that statement Bank of Newport explicitly warrants that its draft is "drawn *** in accordance with the letter of credit purpose." Clearly, the ultimate purpose behind the letter of credit issuance here was to assure delivery of the machines to the doctors. Bank of Newport's suggestion that the district court found that the letter of credit was intended merely to serve as collateral to secure manufacture of the machines is based on an incomplete reading of the district court's decision. Furthermore, the district court expressly found that Fiscal and the doctors agreed that the letter of credit was issued "to guarantee the manufacture and delivery of the BPM machines." That court also concluded that "it would be incongruous for the doctors to guarantee to sell machines without being able to acquire the machines to complete their sale."

Second, Bank of Newport knew or at least had reason to know that the purpose behind the letter of credit issuance was delivery of the machines to the doctors. The letter of credit itself indicates that its purpose was to "guaranty that the doctors will sell [blood pressure machines]." Even though the language may have been insufficient to impose a documentary evidence of delivery requirement, it clearly put Bank of Newport on notice that the *purpose* underlying the letter of credit issuance was to assure delivery of the machines. Furthermore, as the district court found, "Bank of Newport was intrinsically involved in the financing and supervising of Fiscal Concepts, Inc. *** and was aware that a number of letters of credit *** may have required delivery of machines as a condition precedent." In view of Bank of Newport's close supervision over Fiscal's financing, it is reasonable to assume that Bank of Newport was aware of the purpose behind a sizable letter of credit made in Fiscal's favor, particularly where Bank of Newport was an assignee of proceeds under that credit. Finally, the letter sent by First National's attorney, Jerome Zamos prior to presentation of the draft put Bank of Newport on notice of the purpose behind the letter of credit. In that letter Zamos indicated that the letter of credit was not to be used to secure loans by Bank of Newport to Fiscal. The Zamos letter also referred to the letter of agreement between Fiscal and the doctors in which Fiscal promised never to draw against the letter of credit.

Third, as the district court found and Bank of Newport concedes, Bank of Newport had knowledge of nondelivery of the machines when it submitted its draft including the statement of reason for the draw. Furthermore, Bank of Newport made no effort to determine whether any machines were *ever* going to be delivered to the doctors.

Therefore, synthesizing steps one through three, the following conclusion emerges: when Bank of Newport submitted its statement of reason that the draft was drawn "in accordance with the letter of credit purpose," it knew that the purpose for which the draft was drawn -- repayment of loans Bank of Newport made to Fiscal -- could not possibly be "in accordance with" the purpose for which the letter of credit was issued -- delivery of the machines to the doctors. Hence, the statement was itself intentionally inaccurate. However, the real fraudulent effect of this statement is amplified when it is considered in conjunction with Bank of Newport's participation in frustrating the letter of credit purpose by retaining possession and control over the machines rather than shipping them to the doctors. Thus, while expressly warranting on its draft that the draft was made in accordance with the letter of credit purpose, Bank of Newport knew that such purpose would be frustrated by its own refusal to ship the machines.* We therefore conclude that Bank of Newport's draft was tainted by "fraud in the transaction"** and affirm the district court, with costs assessed against appellant.

Affirmed.

---

* This case is therefore distinguishable from cases Bank of Newport relies upon which hold that the purposes for the draw on a letter of credit need not be consistent with the purpose of the underlying transaction. Indeed, this case falls squarely within the exception enunciated in *Sztejn* that "the principle of the independence of the bank's obligation under a letter of credit should not be extended to protect the unscrupulous [beneficiary]." *Sztejn*, 31 N.Y.S.2d at 634. Bank of Newport, as an assignee, had a direct interest in payment under a letter of credit, the purpose of which the Bank knew was being frustrated by its own actions. Bank of Newport stands in no better position than Fiscal, which clearly had no right to draw the draft under these circumstances.

** While not expressly characterizing the Bank of Newport's actions as constituting "fraud in the transaction," the district court did conclude:

> "It is clear that [Bank of Newport] had control of the machines and was attempting to manipulate the requirements of [the] letter of credit in regard to the machines. [Bank of Newport's] intent was obviously to recover its loan to Fiscal without giving up any of the machines it held as collateral."

practice

Case 1

a. The appellant issued an irrevocable letter of credit to Hobbs Construction and Development Company for the benefit of the appellee, who was to tow a ship from Puerto Rico to Boston for Hobbs. The letter of credit specified two conditions of honor: the original letter and a document certifying the failure of Hobbs to make satisfactory payment. The letter of credit required that the certification be made in specific terms, as follows:

> "The Undersigned, being President or Treasurer of Cashman Brothers Marine Contracting Co., Inc., *hereby certifies* that Hobbs Construction and Development, Inc., has failed to make satisfactory arrangements for the payment of the towage of the dump scow ZB-1004 (O.N. 505974) from Puerto Rico to a port designated by us pursuant to paragraph 5 of the Charter Party between Weymouth Equipment Corporation and Hobbs Construction and Development, Inc., dated November 21, 1984 as amended." (Emphasis added.)

Appellee presented the letter for payment on the day before the letter was set to expire. The requisite certifying document failed to precisely follow the language set out in the original letter, for it contained the additional words: "I have determined." The language of the affidavit submitted is as follows:

> The Undersigned, being President or Treasurer of Cashman Brothers Marine Contracting Co., Inc., *hereby certifies that I have determined that* Hobbs Construction and Development, Inc., has failed to make satisfactory arrangements for the payment of towage of the dump scow ZB-1004 (O.N. 505974) from Puerto Rico to a port designated by us pursuant to paragraph 5 of the Charter Party between Weymouth Equipment Corporation and Hobbs Construction and Development, Inc., dated November 21, 1984, as amended. (Emphasis added.)

The appellant bank, upon receiving the original letter and the nonconforming document, deferred honor pursuant to section 675.112, Florida Statutes (1987). Upon being told that the bank was deferring honor, the appellee's counsel made a demand and then left the bank with the original letter in hand. Three days later, appellant notified the appellee through appellee's counsel that it was refusing to honor the letter because presentment was not made during the term of the letter, the affidavit tendered was nonconforming, and the term of the letter had expired. The appellee subsequently filed suit for wrongful dishonor seeking in damages the face value of the letter of credit. The trial court granted summary judgment in favor of the appellee, finding that the deviation of language did not affect the meaning of the affidavit and that the other reasons given for dishonor were simply without merit. *American Nat'l Bank v. Cashman Bros. Marine Contracting,* 550 So.2d 98 (Fla. App. 1989).

b. "Paris issued an irrevocable documentary letter of credit on June 12, 1986, for $250,000.00, naming First Bank as beneficiary. The terms of the credit required that funds would be available until January 18, 1987, upon tender of a draft with certain requirements and accompanying documents. The required documents were the original letter of credit and an affidavit specifying that a default had occurred. On January 15, 1987, First Bank presented a draft for $250,000.00, the original letter of credit, and a document entitled "AFFIDAVIT" stating there had been a default. Paris gave First Bank notice of dishonor on January 20, 1987, stating that the draft and documents did not comply with the terms of the credit.
* * *

"The letter of credit drawn by Paris on its stationery provides in pertinent part:

IRREVOCABLE LETTER OF CREDIT
NO. 1033--2nd Revision & Amendment

DATE: June 12, 1986
FOR THE ACCOUNT OF: Casa Loma Estates Joint Venture
TO BENEFICIARY: First Bank of Rowlett
AMOUNT: $250,000.00
EXPIRATION DATE: January 18, 1987

GENTLEMEN: We hereby establish, at the request and for the account of Casa Loma Estates Joint Venture our Irrevocable Letter of Credit No. 1033 in your favor. Funds under this Letter of Credit are available to you against one draft at SIGHT on us, accompanied by the original of this Letter of Credit. This draft must be marked, 'Drawn under Paris Savings and Loan Association Letter of Credit No. 1033'. This draft must be accompanied by the following documents: 1. An affidavit by an official of the Beneficiary stating that a default has occurred pursuant to the terms of that certain Promissory Note dated June 18, 1986, payable to First Bank of Rowlett in the original principal sum of One Million Seven Hundred Thirty Three Thousand Nine Hundred Ninety Two and 76/100 Dollars ($1,733,992.76) and all renewals and modifications thereof if any.

"On January 15, 1987, First Bank presented a draft for $250,000.00 to Paris with the notation on the draft: "Drawn under Paris Savings and Loan Association Letter of Credit No. 1033, *dated June 12, 1986, i/a/o $250,000.00* Accompanying the draft, First Bank sent a document printed on First Bank's stationery entitled 'AFFIDAVIT', addressed to Paris which states the following:

This letter shall serve as written notice that Casa Loma Estates Joint Venture is in default pursuant to the terms of that certain Promissory Note dated June 18, 1986, payable to First Bank of Rowlett in the original principal sum of One Million Seven Hundred Thirty Three Thousand Nine Hundred Ninety Two and 76/100 Dollars ($1,733,992.76) and all renewals and modifications. *It is expressly understood there have been no renewals or modifications to the indebtedness described above.* First Bank of Rowlett hereby respectfully requests the sum of Two Hundred Fifty Thousand and no/100 Dollars ($250,000.00) due it under the terms of Paris Savings &

Loan Association original Letter of Credit No. 1033 (2nd Revision & Amendment). (Emphasis added.)

"The document is signed by a First Bank senior vice- president and includes a jurat." *First Bank v. Paris Sav. and Loan Ass'n,* 756 S.W.2d 329 (Tex. App. 1988).

First Bank of Rowlett (First Bank) sued Paris Savings and Loan Association (Paris) for wrongful dishonor and breach of contract after Paris refused to honor First Bank's draft. Paris and First Bank both moved for summary judgment and the trial court granted the Paris motion for summary judgment from which First Bank appeals. How should the appeals court decide the case?

Case 2

a. "Sometime prior to August 26, 1986, Union, a Nashville based company, agreed to purchase 1500 metric tons of calcium chloride, a chemical used in snow removal, from N.I.B., a Swedish exporter. In order to guarantee payment, Union had First American issue N.I.B. an irrevocable letter of credit in the amount of $345,000. The letter of credit required the presentment of a draft payable 150 days after sight along with certain other documents.

"On December 1, 1986, First American received from Skanska Banken (Skanska) a $345,000 time draft, drawn and endorsed in blank by N.I.B., together with other documents, all of which complied with the letter of credit. First American accepted the draft on December 1, 1986 by affixing its signature thereto, and on the next day, December 2, sent notice of its acceptance by Telex to Skanska. The acceptance had a maturity date of April 30, 1987.

"Upon receiving notice of the acceptance, Skanska made two loans to N.I.B. totaling $345,000, taking as security N.I.B.'s claim under the letter of credit.

"In February, 1987, Union notified First American that the shipment of chemicals it purchased from N.I.B. was defective. Because First American indicated it would pay its acceptance when it matured, Union commenced this action." *Union Export Co. v. N.I.B. Intermarket,* 786 S.W.2d 628, 629 (1990)

i.   Suppose First American had been informed of the defective goods before the draft was presented. Could First American have freely refused to pay or accept?

ii. Suppose Union sought an injunction before First Ameircan had paid or accepted the draft. Would an injunction have been appropriate on these facts?

iii. Suppose the seller had committed fraud. The chemical that it shipped was worthless chalk. Would an injunction to prevent payment or acceptance be appropriate?

iv. Take the facts as they are reported. First American has already accepted the draft, and did so innocently. If the seller has committed fraud, is an injunction proper to prevent First American from paying its acceptance?

b. "June 1990, MMI and All Service entered into a written agreement, whereby MMI agreed to sell 15,000 metric tons of 'black beans' for $8,250,000. The price included the cost of freight from Tianjin, China to Rio de Janeiro, Brazil. To pay for the shipment, All Service arranged for an irrevocable letter of credit from Banco in favor of MMI, payable 90 days after shipment of the black beans and upon presentation of certain designated documents. The import license, referred to in the relevant papers, describes the items to be shipped as 'Phaseolus vulgaris,' the scientific name for a type of black bean that is a staple food in Brazil.

"The beans were inspected and loaded for delivery in late July. All Service permitted the transaction to go forward without a preshipment inspection by its technical expert, as provided in the contract, because the Chinese government prevented the expert from entering the country.

"Prior to the cargo's arrival in Brazil, MMI forwarded the necessary papers to First Chicago, the advising bank to MMI, together with a draft dated July 29, 1990 in the amount of $8,250,000. The documents appeared on their face to comply with the conditions set forth in the letter of credit. In August, at the request of First Chicago, Banco accepted the draft and retained physical possession of it.

"The saga of the beans continued. After the shipment arrived in port, an independent inspection agency determined the beans were soybeans, rather than black beans, and presented 'a general mouldy or fermented aspect, improper for human consumption.' On the basis of this report, All Service decided that a fraud in the transaction had occurred. Accordingly, it sought to prevent payment pursuant to the letter of credit by seeking an injunction in a Brazilian court. On October 19, that court issued the requested injunction. One day later, MMI's agent recovered physical possession of the draft.
* * *

"October 21, All Service commenced this action in the New York Supreme Court where a temporary restraining order prohibiting payment of the draft was entered. Banco subsequently removed the proceedings to federal court * * * based on the presence of a federal question involving an issue of international banking. MMI was permitted to intervene.

"Judge Haight found that under applicable New York law, once Banco accepted the draft drawn upon the letter of credit, the defense based on fraud in the underlying transaction was not available. Accordingly, without holding an evidentiary hearing, he denied All Service's motion for a preliminary injunction, vacated the temporary restraining order, and entered a fifteen day stay to enable the parties to accelerate their appeal." *All Service Exportacao, Importacao Comercio, S.A. v. Banco Bamerindus Do Brazil*, 921 F.2d 32 (2d Cir. 1990).

Should the appeals court affirm, reverse, or remand?

c.   "Plaintiff Andina Coffee, Inc., a New York corporation, was engaged in the importation of coffee from defendant Gonchecol, Ltda., at one time a major Colombian exporter of coffee. To pay for its purchases, Andina delivered to Gonchecol letters of credit which it obtained from a number of commercial banks in New York, including defendants National Westminster Bank USA (NatWest) and Cooperatieve Centrale Raiffeisenboerenleenbank B.A. (Rabobank). As the beneficiary of the letters of credit, Gonchecol apparently used all or some of the funds to borrow money from defendant Banco Credito y Commercio de Colombia (BCCC) and other Colombian banks in order to finance its business operations. In June of 1986, BCCC advanced $2,100,000 to Gonchecol in exchange for which it was to be reimbursed through a $2,100,000 check drawn on a Panamanian Bank. However, Gonchecol's check bounced, and BCCC was left with an unpaid $2,100,000 loan. According to NatWest and Rabobank, this event could only have served to confirm what BCCC had already learned from its own sources; that is, that Gonchecol had already lost millions of dollars and was experiencing severe financial difficulties. As was the situation with most of the moneys made available by BCCC to Gonchecol, the source of repayment would have to be proceeds from the letters of credit provided to Gonchecol from the issuing banks.

"Beginning in May of 1986, coffee financed under the various letters of credit, which were to be paid on the presentation of interior truck bills of lading, failed to materialize. Consequently, representatives of the New York banks were dispatched to Colombia in August of 1986 when it was discovered that Gonchecol had caused fraudulent truck bills of lading to be furnished for large quantities of coffee which were, in fact, never shipped, thereby resulting in substantial financial losses to New York banks. The four letters of credit involved here are the last outstanding instruments which were not drawn against prior to the disclosure of the exporter's dishonest practices. In that regard, NatWest and Rabobank had each supplied two of the letters of credit, one for $2,104,000 and the other three in the amount of $1,000,000, pursuant to which they agreed to make payment upon the presentation within a specified period of time of drafts and certain documents, among which were to be the 'original railroad and/or truck bill of lading'. The bill of lading was supposed to show that the coffee was actually in existence, that it had left the control of the growers and that it was in the hands of the shipper and en route from the interior of Colombia to a seaport.

"On July 9, 1986, fifteen days after BCCC had already advanced $2,100,000 to Gonchecol against the latter's bad check, it received from NatWest a letter of credit in the amount of $2,104,000. The following day, almost six weeks before the earliest possible date for presentment under that instrument, BCCC accepted from Gonchecol its draft and accompanying documents. These documents included truck bills of lading which were dated August 22, 1986, almost six weeks after the date submitted to BCCC, and purported to show that 8,000 bags of coffee had been delivered to a trucking company for transport to a Colombian port. BCCC sent the draft and documents to NatWest with a cover letter dated July 15, 1986. By telex dated July 22, 1986, NatWest advised BCCC that it would not pay under the letter of credit because of four enumerated discrepancies in the documents, including the fact that the draft and documents were presented prior to the earliest date mentioned in the letter of credit and that the truck bills of lading were post-dated.

"BCCC thereupon requested that the bills of lading and other documents be returned to it by mail. It then reviewed the documents received under the other three letters of credit and per ceived that the bills of lading in those instances were similarly post-dated. Consequently, it sent all of the bills of lading back to Gonchecol so that the exporter could revise the dates to comply with the letters of credit. Indeed, some of the changes were made twice in an attempt to bring the documents into conformity with both the form and date mandates of the letters of credit. Thus, it appears that the documents were designed more to effect payment under the letters of credit than to reflect accurately the business transactions that they were intended to evince. In any event, by the time that the documents had been altered and re-altered, the full extent of Gonchecol's fraud had been detected, and payment was rejected by NatWest and Rabobank on the ground that, in part, the bills of lading were post-dated and fraudulent.

"The instant appeal concerns respective motions and cross-motions for summary judgment with respect to the letters of credit. The Supreme Court, in granting BCCC's cross-motion for summary judgment and denying the motions of NatWest and Rabobank for the same relief, was persuaded that BCCC took the drafts for value, in good faith and without any knowledge of any fraud defenses and was, therefore, a holder in due course entitled to payment under the letters of credit." *Andina Coffee, Inc. v.Nat' l WestminsterBank USA,* 160 A.D.2d 104, 560 N.Y.S.2d 1 (1990).

What is the proper resolution on appeal?

Case 4

a.   "Invoil LA-TX Drilling Fund 1981, Ltd. (Invoil), was a limited partnership to be formed in Oklahoma for drilling development oil and gas wells. * * * Invoil Inc., an Oklahoma corporation, was the general partner of Invoil, the proposed limited partnership.

"To finance operations, Invoil negotiated a 'Loan Agreement' with Guaranty of Oklahoma City. As collateral for its loan to Invoil, Guaranty agreed to accept certain letters of credit from Invoil's limited partners. The Invoil-Guaranty loan agreement contained the following provisions:

> *Draw on Letter of Credit*.... If any other event of Default occurs, [Guaranty] will have the right to draw down the entire outstanding balance of each of the Letters of Credit. The amount received from such draw down will be credited by [Guaranty] to the Note together with interest thereon and costs of collection thereof, including a reasonable attorney's fee, with any excess, after the payment thereof, to be paid by [Guaranty] to the respective Limited Partner or refunded to the Issuing Bank for the respective Limited Partner's account.... .... *Disclaimer*.... (a) [Guaranty] has made no evaluation of [Invoil] and will not be deemed to have made any representation as to the proposed activities of [Invoil] or the financial strength or integrity of the [Invoil Inc.]; (b) [Guaranty] has no responsibility or liability for the issuance, offer or sale of the interests in [Invoil]; and (c) nothing herein contained or

contained in any Loan Document or the Private Placement Memorandum is intended by the parties hereto to impose such liability or responsibility on [Guaranty]. [Guaranty] has made no representation, warranty or statement regarding the advisability of the Limited Partners' purchasing the Limited Partnership interest. [Guaranty] did not participate in the preparation of the Private Placement Memorandum and is not responsible for any statements contained therein or the accuracy or completeness thereof. [Guaranty] will not in any way be responsible or liable to [Invoil], [Invoil Inc.] or any other party for determination of the amount, type, source or what constitutes revenue or income from [Invoil]. [Guaranty] may rely on the representations made by [Invoil Inc.] in the Private Placement Memorandum for [Invoil] as if such representations were made directly to [Guaranty] by [Invoil Inc.]. This Disclaimer and this paragraph must be set forth in the Private Placement Memorandum.

"Invoil issued a 'Private Placement Memorandum' summarizing the 'program,' that is, subscription in the limited partnership ***.
* * *
"A Prudential-Bache representative gave Invoil's private placement memorandum to James Schumacher, Brown's attorney. After Schumacher's examination of the private placement memorandum, Brown signed the Invoil limited partnership agreement and purchased two units of Invoil under the 'Subscription Payment Option.' Pursuant to such option Brown paid $30,000 in cash and directed U.S.N.B. to issue two irrevocable letters of credit, Nos. 02414 and 02415. Each letter of credit had a face amount of $70,000, expired on July 31, 1983, and authorized Guaranty to sight draw $70,000, when an officer of Guaranty signed a statement 'certifying that the amount drawn is due [Guaranty] in connection with the loan to [Invoil].' Interests in Invoil were not registered.

"Invoil and Guaranty signed the loan agreement on August 4, 1981. Invoil borrowed $1,860,000 from Guaranty, which, according to Invoil's promissory note, was payable on July 1, 1983. As the result of an inquiry by the Federal Deposit Insurance Corporation, Invoil's general partner, on March 30, 1983, wrote to the FDIC and indicated that unless Guaranty restructured its loan to Invoil bankruptcy was 'the only alternative.' Guaranty deemed itself 'insecure' and, as provided in its loan agreement with Invoil, declared a default regarding the Invoil loan.

"On April 13, 1983, Guaranty sent U.S.N.B. two letters stating that Brown's letters of credit were due and enclosed a sight draft in the amount of $70,000 with each letter. In its letter to U.S.N.B. regarding letter of credit No. 02414, Guaranty stated: 'We certify the amount drawn is due Guaranty ... in connection with the loan to Invoil....' Regarding letter of credit No. 02415, Guaranty's letter in part read: 'The amount drawn is due Guaranty ... in connection with the loan [to] Invoil....' Each of Guaranty's letters to U.S.N.B. was signed by the senior executive vice president of Guaranty. Among other documents sent to U.S.N.B. by Guaranty was an 'Assumption of Personal Liability' signed by Brown, limiting Brown's share of Invoil's indebtedness to $60,000.

"On April 21, Brown filed an action in the district court for Douglas County, seeking to enjoin U.S.N.B. from honoring the letters of credit, and obtained a temporary restraining order enjoining U.S.N.B. from honoring Guaranty's draw authorized by the letters of credit.

"In an amended petition, Brown alleged * * * misrepresentations in the private placement memorandum of Invoil and a deliberate nondisclosure that Guaranty might call the 'full face value of the letter of credits even though the loan secured thereby is substantially less than the face value of the letter of credits to in essence use one investor's credit to pay off another investor's loan or the cost of collecting another investor's loan.' Such fraud, Brown alleged, was perpetrated with the 'actual knowledge and consent' of Guaranty. In a supplemental petition Brown alleged Guaranty's documentation accompanying its sight draft No. 02415 did not include 'certification' of the amount due Guaranty on the Invoil loan. Having filed companion actions in federal courts for rescission of the sale involving Invoil's unregistered securities, Brown requested an injunction prohibiting U.S.N.B. from paying Guaranty's sight draft or that U.S.N.B. 'be allowed to honor said letters of credit only to the extent of [Brown's] respective $60,000 participation interest' in Invoil.

"U.S.N.B. filed an answer in the form of a general denial. Guaranty filed a petition of intervention, requesting dismissal of Brown's petition." *Brown v. United States Nat'l Bank*, 220 Neb. 684, 371 N.W.2d 692 (Neb. 1985).

What should the outcome be?

b. "Woodmoor planned to develop a mountain recreation community in Routt County, Colorado (the County), to be known as Stagecoach. Early in 1973, Woodmoor obtained plat approval from the Routt County Board of County Commissioners (the Commissioners) for several Stagecoach subdivisions. Pursuant to section 30-28-137, C.R.S.1973 (1977 Repl. Vol. 12), and county subdivision regulations, approval of three of these subdivision plats was conditioned upon Woodmoor's agreement to provide a bond or other undertaking to ensure the completion of roads in accordance with the subdivision design specifications. Accordingly, subdivision improvements agreements were executed between Woodmoor and the County.

"At Woodmoor's request, the Bank issued three letters of credit to secure Woodmoor's obligations under the agreements. The first two letters of credit, No. 1156 and No. 1157, were issued January 23, 1973 in the respective amounts of $158,773 and $77,330 bearing expiry dates of December 31, 1975. The third letter of credit No. 1168 was issued March 7, 1973 in the amount of $113,732 bearing an expiry date of December 31, 1976. The face amounts of the letters of credit were identical to the estimated costs of the road and related improvements in the respective subdivision improvements agreements. The County was authorized by each letter of credit to draw directly on the Bank, for the account of Woodmoor, up to the face amount of each letter of credit. Each letter of credit required the County, in order to draw on the letters of credit, to submit fifteen-day sight drafts accompanied by: 'A duly-signed statement by the Routt County Board of Commissioners that improvements have not been made in compliance with a Subdivision Improvements Agreement between Routt County and the Woodmoor Corporation dated (either January 9, 1973 or March 7, 1973) and covering the (respective subdivisions) at Stagecoach and that payment is therefore demanded hereunder.'

"Woodmoor never commenced construction of the roads and related improvements. On December 31, 1975, the expiry date of letters of credit No. 1156 and No. 1157, the County presented two demand drafts to the Bank for the face amounts of $158,773 and $77,330. The demand drafts were accompanied by a resolution of the Commissioners stating that Woodmoor had failed to comply with the terms of the subdivision improvements agreements and demanded payment of the face amounts of the letters of credit. On January 5, 1976, within three banking days of the demand, the Bank dishonored the drafts. The Bank did not specifically object to the County's presentation of demand drafts rather than fifteen-day sight drafts as required by the letters of credit.

"On December 22, 1976, the County presented the Bank with a demand draft on letter of credit No. 1168 which was accompanied by the required resolution of the Commissioners. The Bank dishonored this draft because of the County's nonconforming demand, viz., that a demand draft was submitted rather than a fifteen-day sight draft. On December 29, 1976, the County presented a fifteen- day sight draft to the Bank. This draft was not accompanied by the resolution of the Commissioners. On December 31, 1976, the Bank dishonored this draft.

"The County sued to recover the face amounts of the three letters of credit plus interest from the dates of the demands. The Bank answered the County's complaints alleging several affirmative defenses. The fundamental premise of the Bank's defenses was the assertion that the County would receive a windfall since it had not expended or committed to spend any funds to complete the road improvements specified in the subdivision improvements agreements." *Colorado Nat'l Bank v. Bd. of County Comm'rs*, 634 P.2d 32 (Colo. 1981).

Who should prevail, the County or the Bank?

Chapter 8. Credit Cards (Primarily, General Bank Cards)

In the past twenty-five years, credit cards, and credit card debt, have become as American as apple pie. The average creditworthy American over the age of eighteen has approximately one dozen credit cards and over one billion credit cards are currently in use in the United States. In 1992, consumers charged over $300 billion on their credit cards (a fivefold increase from 1980) and the average consumer had an outstanding balance of approximately $7,000, while paying over $450 during the year in credit card interest. The significance of credit cards and credit card debt to American commerce simply cannot be overstated. To a great extent, credit cards have come to embody commerce, at least on the consumer level, in late twentieth-century America.

Currently, there exist three primary types of credit cards: the "bank credit card," dominated principally by Visa and MasterCard; "travel and entertainment charge cards," such as American Express or Diner's Club; and "two-party credit cards," such as department store or oil company cards. These three types of cards account for over fifteen cents of every consumer-dollar transaction made in the United States today. Bank and two-party cards are distinct from travel and entertainment cards principally because they provide for a revolving credit option. That is, the cards do not have to be paid off in full at the end of the grace period during which charges were incurred. As a rule, moreover, the credit limits and the fees charged for the use of these cards (if any) tend to be lower than those on travel and entertainment cards. Additionally, because the issuers of these cards charge interest to card-users for payments made past the customary grace period (usually twenty-five to thirty days from the time the charge is made), and hence earn substantial revenue from these charges, the issuers tend to charge merchants (in the case of bank credit cards) less for their services than those charged by issuers of travel and entertainment cards.

A new card to watch, growing in use by almost fifty percent each year, is the debit card, which allows consumers to effect point-of-sale transfers from their deposit accounts directly to merchant deposit accounts. Presently, debit card use accounts for one-half cent of every consumer-dollar transaction. Debit cards are distinct from credit cards in that consumers can only spend the amount of money that they have available in their deposit account at the time in question. No credit is extended to them by the relevant financial institution. These cards offer the obvious advantage of removing temptation from the consumer.

The use of a credit card to purchase a good or service raises numerous issues of interest to us. Most fundamentally, what is a credit card transaction and how does it work? Second, how is the issuance and use of credit cards regulated and who is responsible for such regulation? Third, what is the nature of the relationships and liability created by the issuance and use of credit cards?

story

General bank credit cards: the players and the system

Suppose that Mike Monahan, who lives in Minneapolis, Minnesota, plays golf with his former law school professor and good friend three times each week. On virtually every occasion, however, Mike fails to outscore his friend. Deciding that his friend's clubs, and not his innate ability, are responsible for his winning scores, Mike decides to buy a new set of golf clubs for himself from Nickles SuperSports, owned by Elton Nickles. The price is $500. Mike does not have this amount in cash so he offers Nickles a check drawn on Norwest Bank Minnesota. Nickles, however, is unwilling to take the check unless Mike is willing to wait three days for the check to clear. Because Mike cannot wait this long to beat his friend, he asks Nickles if he would accept his VISA card issued by Norwest. Nickles readily agrees, even though he, as a merchant, will incur a charge for his customer's use of the credit card.

Norwest is a member of VISA U.S.A., Inc., the organization that sponsors and promotes the VISA card system. As a member, Norwest regularly pays membership fees and agrees to an elaborate set of by-laws which include very detailed operating regulations. These by-laws and regulations are too voluminous to publish here. Moreover, VISA U.S.A. considers the information confidential. In any event, Norwest's principal obligation under the by-laws of the system is to develop contractual relationships with cardholders and merchants for the issuance and honoring of VISA's credit card. In fulfilling the first part of this obligation, Norwest issues credit cards to creditworthy customers pursuant to a written cardholder agreement that, essentially, obligates the cardholder to pay the bank for all charges (purchases and advances) to his or her credit card.

Mike entered into such an agreement with Norwest when it issued him his VISA credit card. He thereby promised to pay Norwest, known as the "issuing bank," for charges to his credit card account.

Bank members of VISA U.S.A. also solicit merchants such as Nickles SuperSports to enroll in the card system. Merchant members agree to honor the cards of the system or systems in which they enroll. In exchange the merchants get the soliciting bank's commitment to give them credit for purchases of property and services that a customer makes using a system card. In effect, the merchant bank finances the merchant's accounts receivable by discounting the merchant's sales slips, after which the issuing bank collects payments from the cardholders on a deferred, revolving credit basis. The merchant bank may be the same as the issuing bank or another member of the bank card system. First Bank National Association, known as the "acquiring bank" here, enrolled Nickles in the VISA U.S.A. system. The agreement Nickles signed as a merchant member of the bank card system is completely comprehensive, covering everything from the procedures Nickles must use for hadling credit card transacyions to the details of presentation, payment and repayment of sales slips.

The sale aspects of the transaction between Mike and Nickles SuperSports are governed by Article 2 of the U.C.C. This law obligates Mike to accept the golf clubs, and to pay the price according to the contract of sale between him and Nickles. U.C.C. 2-507(1); 2-709(1). If Mike would have leased the golf clubs from Nickles, then Article 2A of the U.C.C. would have governed the transaction; if Mike would have purchased golf lessons from Nickles, then the common law of contracts would have applied because Article 2 only "applies to transactions in goods," not to the sales of services. U.C.C. 2-102.

When Mike decides to pay for the golf clubs at Nickles SuperSports using his VISA card, he signs a credit card sales slip prepared by Nickles. Nickles uses an imprinting machine or similar device to reproduce the information embossed on Mike's VISA card to the sales slip, including a 16 digit number. The first ten digits identify the issuing bank, Norwest. The other six digits identify Mike's credit card account at Norwest. The machine also reproduces Nickles' name and address and the merchant number assigned to him by First Bank on the sales slip. These numbers are important in processing the slip through the interchange network, discussed later. In sum, they help in getting Nickles' account credited with the amount of the sales slip; sending the slip to Norwest for payment; sending the payment to First Bank; and charging Mike's credit card account.

A credit card sales slip is commonly referred to by member banks and merchants as a draft. Actually, however, the slip is not a draft or other negotiable instrument within the scope of U.C.C. Article 3. The writing does not fulfill the requisites of negotiability spelled out in U.C.C. section 3-104(a). Rather, the slip evidences the sale transaction and authorizes Norwest to charge the amount of the slip to Mike's credit card account.

In order to complete the transaction with Mike, Nickles will (directly or through First Bank) contact Norwest or its agent, by phone or electronically, for authorization to allow Mike to charge the price of the golf clubs to his VISA card. (Each bank card Association maintains an authorization system to which member banks can subscribe.) Whether or not this authorization is forthcoming depends on the available credit that Norwest has agreed to extend Mike with respect to his VISA card. If authorization is given, Nickles will receive an authorization code for the transaction which will be recorded on the sales slip.

How might one characterize this transaction involving Norwest, Mike, Nickles and First Bank under the U.C.C.? The slip is not a draft or other instrument within the scope of Article 3. Clearly then, Norwest's authorization for Mike to charge the price of the golf clubs to his VISA card does not amount to acceptance of the sales slip within the meaning of U.C.C. 3-409(a). Second, the authorization does not amount to Norwest issuing a letter of credit to Nickles under the provisions of the U.C.C. Article 5. Neither the credit card issued by Norwest to Mike, nor the authorization given by Norwest, nor the merchant agreement is an engagement of a kind within the scope of Article 5. While the letter of credit "is essentially a contract between the issuer and the [merchant]," U.C.C. 5-114, comment 1, the credit card itself represents the issuer-cardholder agreement. Likewise, while the letter of credit is purchaser-specific, the acquirer-merchant agreement covers *all* purchasers who are credit card holders. Finally, the credit card does not seem to constitute a factoring of Nickles' accounts receivable; if it were a sale of accounts receivable, under Article 9 of the U.C.C. First Bank, the merchant bank, would have to file a separate financing statement for every one of its merchants.

Rather, the credibility behind Mike's authorized use of his VISA card comes from the merchant agreement between Nickles and First Bank, and also from the agreement among VISA U.S.A., First Bank and Norwest as parties to the VISA by-laws. Through the merchant agreement First Bank promised, upon certain conditions, to "make payment to the Merchant for sales slips physically presented by the Merchant to the Bank." By agreeing to the VISA by-laws Norwest agreed to purchase or otherwise pay sales slips signed or otherwise authorized by persons holding credit cards issued by Norwest. Moreover, VISA U.S.A. promises member banks that it will indemnify and reimburse them for loss or expense they suffer by reason of any member's failure properly to honor any sales slip processed in accordance with VISA by-laws and regulations.

So Nickles will gladly accept the authorized use of Mike's VISA card in payment for the golf clubs because Nickles has the commitment of First Bank to give him credit, less a discount, for the sales slip that Mike signs. First Bank makes this commitment because Norwest is bound by contract to buy the sales slip; and, if Norwest breaches this contractual obligation, VISA U.S.A. will indemnify First Bank. Norwest will not likely breach, however, because it expects to collect the sales slip, plus interest, from Mike. Moreover, if Norwest breached by failing to pay First Bank, it could be expelled from the VISA system--a terrible outcome from Norwest's perspective because it very much desires to continue as a member in good standing of the VISA system. Norwest earns interest from Mike and other customers who use credit cards issued to them by Norwest. In addition, Norwest earns a fee every time one of its cardholders uses her credit card in a transaction with a merchant who deposits the sales slip with another bank. This fee, which VISA calls an *interchange reimbursement fee*, is paid to Norwest by the bank which acquires the sales slip from a merchant who honored the credit card of a Norwest cardholder, in this example First Bank.

The inter-bank collection of sales slips is accomplished not through the Federal Reserve or other systems for collecting checks, but through entirely different and independent, completely private interchange networks maintained separately by VISA U.S.A. and MasterCard International. These bank card collection networks are not governed by U.C.C. Article 4 or federal law. *But see First United Bank v. Philmont Corp.*, 533 So.2d 449, 453-54 (Miss. 1988) (holding that credit card slips are "items" within the meaning of U.C.C. 9-104(1)(g); therefore the credit card network relationship is governed by U.C.C. Article 4); *see also Broadway National Bank v. Barton-Russell Corp.*, 585 N.Y.S.2d 933, 938-39 (N.Y. Sup. Ct. 1992) (adopting the court's reasoning in *Philmont*). Rather, they are governed exclusively by contract, primarily by the by-laws and operating regulations of the bank card Associations. Although VISA and MasterCard operate separately in collecting sales slips, the essentials of the two systems' interchange networks are very similar, and both networks are much more efficient than the processes used to collect checks under Article 4 and through the Federal Reserve System. The following discussion, however, is mainly based on the VISA network.

At the end of the day, Nickles will include Mike's sales slip among the cash, checks, and other credit card sales slips included in the deposit he makes at First Bank, which is known as the "acquiring bank" with respect to slips deposited with it. Nickles actually separates all the day's credit card sales slips from the other cash items and bundles them together with a "batch header" which shows the total of the slips. This header also includes Nickles' name, his merchant number, and a number that identifies First Bank. Alternatively, Nickles will electronically send and receive authorization and credit from the bank during the course of each transaction.

First Bank (perhaps with the help of a processing agent) will credit Nickles' SuperSports account for the amount of Mike's sales slip, less a discount. The credit may be available for withdrawal immediately, or it may harden, i.e., firm up, after only two or three banking days. This detail depends on the merchant agreement between Nickles and First Bank.

First Bank will then separate the VISA and MasterCard sales slips from the daily deposits of all its merchant customers. Following this separation, the slips are bundled and sent by courier to the appropriate bankcard association for processing. When bank credit cards first appeared, many regional banks formed non-profit associations to share the expenses associated with processing credit card accounts. Gradually over the past twenty years, for-profit vendors of processing services have bought up virtually all of the major non-profit associations. These entities exist in every region of the country, although the credit card operations of some banks are so large that each of them functions independently in the national interchange processes maintained by the bank card systems.

On a daily basis the applicable association electronically records the credit card sales slips received from member banks. Intra-association settlements are then determined and effected through accounts association member banks maintain for this purpose at a designated bank. Sales slips drawn on banks that are not association members are presented electronically to each card system's national switch which is maintained and operated by the system, pursuant to its by-laws and operating regulations, as part of the system's national interchange process. The MasterCard switch is in St. Louis, Missouri. VISA's national switch is in San Mateo, California. VISA also maintains a regional switch for eastern banks in McLean, Virginia.

The national switch is the central bookkeeper or clearing house for the entire system. It determines daily net settlements among member banks, addressing the banks directly or through regional processing centers. The system maintains a settlement account, and each member bank, or a representative of the bank, maintains its own clearing account for inter-bank settlement. If a bank's net settlement position is a credit, the switch will transfer funds from the system's settlement account to the bank's clearing account. If the bank's net settlement position is a debit, the switch will request the bank to transfer funds to the system settlement account. Transfers of funds are usually accomplished electronically by wire, and funds transferred are same day (collected) funds in United States dollars. The switch also determines, collects, and distributes interchange reimbursement fees as part of effecting net settlements.

Remember that the bank credit card interchange system is largely truncated: the sales slips, if applicable, are impounded by the acquiring bank, or its agent (e.g., the applicable association), and the remaining operations are handled electronically. So Norwest will not in the ordinary course receive the paper sales slip Mike signed when he bought the golf clubs from Nickles SuperSports. Rather, Norwest will learn of the transaction when the information about the purchase of the golf clubs is relayed electronically to Norwest by the VISA switch, which received the information in the same fashion from the applicable association. (Norwest's credit card operation is so large that it deals directly with the switch rather than through an agent.) Norwest will then charge the amount of the sales slip to Mike' credit card account. Mike is bound to pay this charge, plus interest and other fees, by the terms of the cardholder agreement between him and Norwest.

The cardholder agreement does not give Mike a right to "stop payment" of a sales slip. There is nothing in the agreement comparable to U.C.C. section 4-403. Moreover, the bank card system's operating regulations do not allow an issuing bank to dishonor a sales slip upon presentment. The consequence, however, is not that the issuing bank, or ultimately the cardholder, bears all the risks of fraud and other losses such as those common to the check collection system.

An issuing bank that pays a sales slip can return it to the acquiring bank for a wide variety of reasons and receive a corresponding credit. This right of return is granted by the operating regulations of the bank card system. The regulations refer to the right as a "charge back" which is conditioned on the issuing bank satisfying certain procedural conditions. The principal condition is timely action to effect the charge back. The period for acting is variable, depending on the reason for the action, but is always much longer than the midnight deadline associated with the check collection system. The time for making charge backs of credit card sales slips ranges from thirty to one hundred and eighty calendar days from the time the acquiring bank entered the sales slip in the system's interchange network. Whether the acquiring bank can pass along a charge back to the merchant depends on the terms of the agreement the merchant signed when she enrolled in the bank card system.

Charge backs are transmitted through the interchange system as a debit against the acquiring bank and a credit in favor of the card issuer. Upon receiving a charge back, the acquiring bank can either accept responsibility, whereupon it will most likely pass the loss to the merchant if the reason for the charge back is among the risks the merchant agreed to accept in the merchant agreement. Alternatively, the acquiring bank can re-present the sales slip to the issuing bank through the interchange system. The issuing bank can respond to the re-presentation by charging back the item a second time. Most charge backs and re-presentations must be accompanied by "adjustment advices" (means of formal notice) and other documentation that explain or support the reason for the action.

Sales slips cannot be presented more than twice. So, if the acquiring bank is still unwilling to accept a charge back following re-presentation, its remedy under the system's operating regulations is to appeal for private resolution of the dispute through an arbitration mechanism maintained by the bank card system. The loser pays the costs of arbitration.

In deciding the legitimate reasons for charging back sales slips, and the ease with which the charge backs can be accomplished, each bank card system effectively determines the distribution of various kinds of risks and losses between the issuing and acquiring banks in a card transaction. Whether the banks in any event can pass on these risks and losses to the cardholder or merchant depends, to a large extent, on the agreements these people make with the banks upon enrolling in the credit card systems, and also depends, to a lesser extent, on state and federal law.

Unauthorized use of credit cards poses the greatest risk of significant loss in every bank card system. The problem is akin to forged drawers' signatures in the check collection process. U.C.C. Article 4 generally places this risk on the payor bank inasmuch as a collecting bank does not warrant the genuineness of such signatures, and the payor bank cannot usually charge to its customer's account a check that lacks the customer's signature or the signature of someone authorized to sign for the customer. Similarly, in the credit card system, an issuing bank cannot charge its cardholder's account in full for sales slips produced through unauthorized use of a credit card. On the other hand, an issuing bank, though it lacks the right to dishonor upon presentation, may, in some circumstances, enjoy the right to charge back, within one hundred and twenty days, a sales slip generated through the unauthorized use of a credit card. Thus, to a greater extent in the bank card system than in the check collection process, the issuing bank bears less of the risk of loss associated with unauthorized access to customers' accounts. The lessened load may ultimately be shifted, however, to the merchants. The merchant agreement illustrated above provides that the merchant must repay the bank for "[a]ny sales slips as to which the card account holder disputes the transaction in any manner, regardless of whether the dispute is valid or not."

An important risk assumed by a paying bank in the check collection system is the sufficiency of the drawer's account. The comparable risk in the bank card system, likewise borne by the issuing bank, is the risk of paying sales slips when the cardholder's credit limit has been exceeded. There is no general right of charge back covering slips drawn against a credit-exhausted bank card account. Yet, this risk is greatly reduced in the bank card system by various safeguards built into the merchant agreement, principally the requirement that the merchant have the issuing bank authorize the use of a credit card to purchase property or services when the amount exceeds a threshold amount of $50 or $100. In fact, many merchants request authorization for *all* transactions. Merchants are careful to satisfy this requirement because, if a necessary authorization is not obtained, a sales slip can be charged back to the acquiring bank which can pass the loss to the merchant. If, however, an issuing bank mistakenly gives its authorization, this mistake is no reason for a charge back. The problem stays with the issuing bank. In any event, just as a customer is liable to her bank for paying an overdraft on the customer's checking account, a cardholder is liable to the issuing bank for an "overcredit" charge to her credit card account because, in the cardholder agreement, the cardholder assumed "complete responsibility for any credit extended by the Bank on the basis of this card."

Issuing banks in a card system are exposed to a significant risk that is unknown in the check collection process: the risk that, after making payment of a sales slip, the cardholder will shift to the issuing bank losses the customer suffered because of the merchant's breach or other culpability with respect to the underlying sales contract between merchant and cardholder. Federal law provides that, subject to certain substantive and procedural conditions, a cardholder's claims and defenses against a merchant can be asserted against the issuer. So, in certain cases, a cardholder can legitimately avoid having to pay a charge to her credit card account to the extent she has a claim or defense against the merchant who sold her the property or services that gave rise to the charge. A drawer of a check cannot protest the debiting of her checking account on a similar basis.

This loss, however, does not remain long with the issuing bank. When a cardholder invokes this federal right to assert against the bank claims or defenses she has against a merchant, the bank, pursuant to the bank card system's operation regulations, can charge back the affected sales slip to the acquiring bank, so long as the issuing bank acts within sixty calendar days of the time the customer asserts the claim or defense against it. The loss ultimately finds its way to the place where it properly belongs, that is, with the merchant. The merchant, upon enrolling in the bank card program, agrees to repay the acquiring bank for "[a]ny sales slips as to which the bank card holder disputes the transaction in any manner, regardless of whether the dispute is valid or not." The merchant also agrees, more specifically, to repay the acquiring bank for "[a]ny sales slips for which the goods have not been delivered or the services have not been performed as agreed."

Apparently, the bank card interchange system works extremely well in adjusting risks and losses between banks. There are few reported cases of inter-bank disputes concerning the collection or charge back of sales slips. One reason is the arbitration system established and maintained by the system; another reason is the banks' fear that causing trouble will lead to expulsion from the system; also, as suggested by the foregoing discussion, most risks and losses suffered by either an acquiring or issuing bank can usually be shifted to that bank's customer, either the merchant or the cardholder.

Regulating the issuance and use of credit cards

Both national and state banks have the power to issue credit cards. Since 1976, the law has allowed a single bank to issue both VISA and MasterCard. When credit cards were initially issued in the 1960s, unsolicited mailings to potential cardholders created troublesome questions of offer and acceptance. The mailing itself seemed to constitute an offer to the recipient which was accepted by the recipient's use of the card. This use of the card triggered all the terms and conditions of the cardholder agreement itself. However, if the recipient did not use the card, then there was arguably no contract formed. This meant, for example, that fraudulent use of the card by a thief might not subject the intended holder to a provision in the card that placed fraudulent losses on the holder until the issuer was notified.

To clarify issues such as this and many others, Congress enacted the Truth-in-Lending Act (TILA) in 1970, 15 U.S.C. §§1601-67e. As structured, TILA applies principally to open end credit plans. An open end plan under TILA is defined as "a plan under which the creditor reasonably contemplates repeated transactions, which prescribes the terms of such transactions, and which provides for a finance charge which may be computed from time to time on the outstanding unpaid balance." 15 U.S.C. §1602(i) (1988). A credit card is a quintessential open end credit plan for TILA purposes.

TILA not only expressly prohibits the issuance of unsolicited credit cards but more importantly, in connection with Federal Reserve Board Regulation Z, 12 C.F.R. §226 (1993), provides initial and periodic disclosure requirements for card issuers. Under TILA, before a consumer uses a credit card account, the issuer must disclose certain information, such as when a finance charge will be imposed, how the balance subject to the finance charge will be computed, and how the finance charge will be computed. 15 U.S.C. §1637(a) (1988). Additionally, the issuer must send the cardholder a billing statement for each billing cycle at the end of which there is an outstanding balance or during which a finance charge is imposed, disclosing such information as the beginning balance, all transactions that occurred during the billing cycle, the ending balance, the amount of finance charges imposed, how the finance charge was computed, and the amount and due date of any required minimum payment. 15 U.S.C. §1637(b) (1988). The Fair Credit and Charge Card Disclosure Act, Pub. L. 100-583, sec. 2(a), §1637, 102 Stat. 2960, 2960-66 (1988), signed into law by former President Reagan on November 3, 1988, includes additional disclosure requirements mandating more detailed disclosures by issuers at an earlier point in their relationship with the consumer.

Importantly, the TILA disclosure provisions only apply to "consumer" credit transactions. 15 U.S.C. §§1602(h), 1637 (1988) . A credit card issued and used by an individual for business purposes does not subject the issuer to TILA disclosure obligations. See Baskin v. G. Fox & Co., 550 F.Supp. 64, 65-66 (D. Conn. 1982); cf. American Express Co. v. Koerner, 452 U.S. 233 (1981) (corporate credit cardholder not entitled to correction of billing errors pursuant to 15 U.S.C. §1666(a) because Congress restricted operation of that provision of TILA to extensions of consumer credit).

Moreover, with respect to the important question of what interest rates can be charged to consumers in connection with a credit card account, state law provides for most of the regulation of maximum rates. As with other transactions, the primary problem that arises in these instances is one of transaction characterization: the use of a bank credit card or other tripartite credit card may be governed by the time-price doctrine or subject to special legislation, depending on the particular state involved.

The applicable law may also differ depending on the type of card and the particular transaction involved, such as where a bank card is used both to purchase goods and to secure cash advances. *See, e.g., Attorney General of Maryland v. Equitable Trust Co.,* 450 A.2d 1273, 1289-90 (Md.1982) and Comptroller of the Currency, Staff Interpretation Letter No. 178, Consumer Cred. Guide (CCH) ¶ 97,239 (Jan. 21, 1981).

With respect to rate regulation, for a long time, issuers of bank credit cards had an advantage over issuers of other credit cards. Section 85 of the National Banking Act, as interpreted by the Supreme Court in *Marquette National Bank of Minneapolis v. First of Omaha Service Corp.*, 439 U.S. 299 (1978), allowed a national bank to "export" higher rates from the state where the bank was located to customers in other states with lower limits. 12 U.S.C. §1831d(a). This benefit created an incentive for institutions to shop among the states for desirable locations and to relocate their credit card operations where the state's rates were most favorable. For example, Citibank moved its operations to South Dakota. Title V of the Depository Institutions Deregulation and Monetary Control Act of 1980 extended this benefit to *all federally insured institutions*, see 12 U.S.C. §1831d(a) (1988 & Supp. 1990). *See also Greenwood Trust Co v. Commonwealth of Massachusetts*, 971 F.2d 818 (1st Cir. 1992) *cert. denied*, 113 S.Ct. 974 (1993) (holding that 12 U.S.C. §1831d(a) preempted a Massachusetts law that, as applied, prohibited a federally-insured state bank, chartered out of state, from charging its Massachusetts cardholders a late fee on delinquent accounts). Other credit card issuers, such as Diner's Club, Carte Blanche, Penney's, and Sears, however, are not so favored.

Relationships created by issuance and use of credit cards

As noted above, the typical bank credit card transaction involves four separate agreements:

- The cardholder agreement between the cardholder and the issuer (issuing) bank;
- The merchant agreement between the merchant and the merchant (acquiring) bank;
- The sales agreement between the merchant and the cardholder (the sales slip); and
- The interchange agreement between the requisite banks, governing settlement times, minimum standards and charge-backs.

Of these agreements, those between merchants and merchant (acquiring) banks, and cardholders and issuing banks, are virtually the only sources of public squabbles arising from the bank card system. Aspects of these two sets of relationships are explored more fully in the remaining materials in this chapter. The focus throughout, however, is on the issuer/cardholder relationship because it is the only component of the bank card system, or any other credit card system, that is specially regulated by law and also because the cardholder is arguably the participant in the system who is most in need of special protection.

1.   Cardholder-Issuer Agreement

The typical cardholder-issuer agreement entered into by Mike above will include the following provisions:

+ A promise by the cardholder to repay the issuer the amounts financed, together with finance charges at the rates disclosed in the agreement;
+ A provision imposing limited liability on the cardholder for unauthorized use, loss or theft of the card;
+ A provision whereby the issuer retains the right to deny the cardholder use of the card and to demand surrender of the card;
+ A provision providing that the issuer will provide monthly billing statements to the cardholder, summarizing the transactions entered into by the cardholder;
+ Disclosures required by federal law; and
+ A provision providing that the agreement is subject to the laws of the state where the issuing bank is domiciled, allowing the issuer to export higher rates to consumers who live in states where ceilings may be lower.

Controversy has often revolved around the interpretation, meaning and effect of many of these provisions. One common area of controversy involves the allocation of fraud losses. Suppose, for example, that a thief steals and uses Mike's credit card to make several purchases in Minneapolis.   Is Mike liable for these purchases? If so, what is the extent of his liability? What if the card is not stolen from Mike, but used by a friend in excess of the amount that Mike authorized for the friend's use? To what degree is Mike liable in that instance?

The federal Consumer Credit Protection Act, 15 U.S.C. §1643, handles just such problems. Under the law, a cardholder is liable for unauthorized use of his credit card only if: 1) the credit card has been accepted by the cardholder for his use; 2) the liability does not exceed $50; 3) the issuer gives adequate notice of the potential liability; 4) the issuer provides the cardholder with a description of a means by which the issuer may be notified of loss or theft of the card; 5) the unauthorized use occurs before the cardholder has notified the issuer of the loss or theft; and 6) the issuer has provided a means to identify (i.e., signature or photograph) the person, the cardholder, who is authorized to use the card. 16 U.S.C. §1643(a)(1) (1988). Thus, unlike when cash is stolen, the cardholder's liability is limited to $50 for unauthorized use if the card was an "accepted" credit card, the issuer gave the cardholder "adequate notice" of the potential liability and the "means by which the card issuer may be notified of loss or theft" and the unauthorized use occurred before the issuer has been notified that an unauthorized use has or might occur. Moreover, to further protect consumers such as Mike, the Act expressly defers to any state statute that is even more consumer-protective. 15 U.S.C. §1643(c) (1988).

Importantly, however, section 1643 is not applicable where the cardholder voluntarily and knowingly allows another to use his card and that person goes on a spending spree of her own. Unauthorized use occurs only where there is no actual, implied or apparent authority for such use by the cardholder. In the case of unauthorized use, the unauthorized user of the credit card is then accountable to the card issuer under the law of unjust enrichment for charges incurred through the wrongful use of the card. *See Fifth Third Bank v. Gilbert*, 478 N.E.2d 1324 (Ohio Mun.Ct.1984); Restatement of Restitution §§28 (mistake due to fraud or misrepresentation); 39 (transfer of land, chattels, or choses in action); 40 (restitution for services); 128 (conversion and other tortious dealings with chattels) 134 (services tortiously obtained) (1937). The unauthorized user also is accountable to society under federal and state criminal laws. *See, e.g.*, 15 U.S.C. §1644 (1988) (criminal penalties for fraudulent use of credit cards); *United States v. Kay*, 545 F.2d 491 (5th Cir.), *cert. denied* 434 U.S. 833 (1977) (affirming conviction for violation of §1644); Annot., 72 A.L.R.Fed. 875 (1985) (meaning of fraudulent use for purposes of §1644). If the cardholder's authority for the use of card exists, of course, the cardholder will be responsible for any purchases made through the use of her card.

Because section 1643 was enacted as an amendment to the Truth in Lending Act, which expressly excludes from its scope "[c]redit transactions involving extensions of credit primarily for business, commercial, or agricultural purposes *** or to organizations," 15 U.S.C. §1603(1), card issuers have argued in the past that the section 's limitation on liability for unauthorized use did not apply when the cardholder was a corporation, or when a credit card was used by an individual for business purposes. Yet, in 1974 Congress amended TILA expressly to provide that the exemption of section 1603(1) does not apply to the provisions relating to the issuance of credit cards and their unauthorized or fraudulent use. 15 U.S.C. §1645 (1988). As a result of this, courts have applied section 1643 across-the-board to all cardholders who are the victims of unauthorized use regardless of the purposes for which a card is used. *See generally Credit Card Service Corp. v. Federal Trade Commission*, 495 F.2d 1004 (D.C.Cir.1974); *American Airlines, Inc. v. Remis Industries, Inc.*, 494 F.2d 196 (2d Cir.1974); 12 C.F.R. §§226.2(a)(8), 226.12(b) (1993) (defining a cardholder as "any person to whom a credit card is issued for any purpose, including business, commercial or agricultural use" for the purpose of limiting the liability of a cardholder for unauthorized use).

From a procedural standpoint, also recall from our earlier discussion in Chapter 3 that the rule under Article 3 is that no person is liable on an instrument unless she herself signed the writing, or it was signed for her by someone with authority to do so. U.C.C. 3-401(a); 3-404(a). Yet, forgery or lack of authority is an affirmative defense that a defendant must specifically assert in a suit on an instrument. Moreover, even when the defense is properly asserted, the defendant's signature is presumed genuine or authorized. She thus has the burden of producing evidence to the contrary. Only then must the plaintiff-holder worry about proving authenticity or authority. U.C.C. 3-307(a) & comment 1. Consequently, if the defendant claims that the signature on the instrument is forged or otherwise was made without authority but offers no proof to support the claim, the plaintiff can recover without putting on a scintilla of evidence to rebut the defense. While Article 3 does not apply when a card issuer sues to enforce liability for the use of a credit card, section 1643(b) expressly provides that in such a case "the burden of proof is upon the issuer to show that the use was authorized or, if the use was unauthorized, then the burden of proof is upon the card issuer to show that the conditions of liability for the unauthorized use of a credit card, as set forth in subsection (a) of this section, have been met." 15 U.S.C. §1643(b) (1988).

In addition to the important protection offered cardholders by section 1643, card-holders are further protected by the provisions of the Fair Credit Billing Act. 15 U.S.C. §1666 (1988). The Fair Credit Billing Act seeks to prescribe an orderly procedure for identifying and resolving disputes between a cardholder and a card issuer as to the amount due at any given time. Under the Act, if the cardholder believes that the statement contains a billing error (as defined in 15 U.S.C. §1666(b)), she then may send the creditor a written notice setting forth that belief, indicating the amount of the error and the reasons supporting her belief that it is an error. If the creditor receives this notice within sixty days of transmitting the statement of account, section 1666(a) then imposes two separate obligations upon the creditor. First, within thirty days, it must send a written acknowledgment that it has received the notice. Second, within ninety days or two complete billing cycles, whichever is shorter, the creditor must investigate the matter and either make appropriate corrections in the cardholder's account or send a written explanation of its belief that the original statement sent to the cardholder was correct. The creditor must send its explanation before making any attempt to collect the disputed amount. A creditor that fails to comply with section 1666(a) forfeits its right to collect the first $50 of the disputed amount including finance charges. 15 U.S.C. §1666(e) (1988). In addition, section 1666(d) provides that, pursuant to regulations of the Federal Reserve Board, a creditor operating an "open end consumer credit plan" may not restrict or close an account due to a cardholder's failure to pay a disputed amount until the creditor has sent the written explanation required by section 1666(a).

Other obligations also attach. First, if "appropriate corrections" are made, the card issuer also must credit any finance charge on accounts erroneously billed. 15 U.S.C. §1666(a)(B)(i) (1988). Second, the card issuer must notify the cardholder on subsequent statements of account that she need not pay the amount in dispute until the card issuer has complied with section 1666. 15 U.S.C. §1666(c)(2) (1988). Third, the card issuer may not report, or threaten to report, adversely on the cardholder's credit before the card issuer has discharged its obligations under section 1666, 15 U.S.C. §1666a(a), and, if the cardholder continues to dispute the bill in timely fashion, the card issuer may report the delinquency only if it also reports that the amount is in dispute and tells the cardholder to whom it has released this information. 15 U.S.C. §1666a(b) (1988). The card issuer is further obliged to report any eventual resolution of the delinquency to the same third parties with whom it earlier had communicated. 15 U.S.C. §1666a(c) (1988). Finally, a card issuer that fails to comply with any requirements of the Act is liable to the cardholder for actual damages, twice the amount of any finance charge, and costs of the action and attorney's fees. 15 U.S.C. §1640(a) (1988).

One final important area of controversy involves the issue of whether cardholders should be allowed to raise merchandise defenses against the issuer if the goods or services purchased with her card prove to be unsatisfactory or the cardholder encounters some other problem in connection with the transaction. While cardholder agreements generally provide that a cardholder is obligated to pay the bank regardless of any dispute which may exist respecting the merchandise, a significant exception to this rule arises under a provision in the Truth in Lending Act which allows claimants whose transactions exceed $50 and who have made a good faith attempt to obtain satisfactory resolution of the problem, to assert claims and defenses arising out of the credit card transaction, if the place of the initial transaction is in the same state or within 100 miles of the cardholder. 15 U.S.C. §1666i (1988).

2.   Merchant and Merchant-Bank Agreement

A separate written agreement also governs the relationship between the merchant and merchant bank. The typical merchant agreement signed by Nickles Super-Sports and First Bank will contain the following provisions:

- ◆ A provision providing that the merchant is under a duty to sell goods or services in the ordinary course of business to any cardholder upon the cardholder's tender of the credit card, within certain limits;
- ◆ A provision whereby the merchant agrees to evidence each sale by a sales slip signed by the cardholder and to transfer all sales slips to the merchant bank at a stated discount rate, such as 3 percent;
- ◆ A provision providing that the merchant will maintain a regular depository account with the merchant bank, to which all charges and credits derived from bank card transactions must be made;
- ◆ A provision whereby the merchant warrants as to each sales slip, that the slip was actually signed by the person presenting the card; that it represents a bona fide sale as itemized in the sales slips; that the slip represents an unconditional obligation of the cardholder; that the merchandise was actually delivered to the party who signed the sales slip; and that the merchant has no knowledge of any fact that would impair the validity of the slip; and
- ◆ A provision providing that every sales slip must contain a brief description of the merchandise or services involved and must be signed or initialed by the appropriate salesperson.

The merchant agreement is a mutually beneficial one for both parties. In essence, the merchant bank agrees for a certain fee to process credit card transactions between an individual merchant and the network of other financial institutions which both issue credit cards to their customers and represent other merchants who accept credit cards in payment for their goods and services. The merchant profits from the agreement by increased sales volume due to her acceptance of a form of payment from her customer other than cash. The merchant also receives immediate credit to her account for credit card sales, even before they are sent through the interbank processing system. The merchant bank, in turn, receives fees for this service. Inasmuch, of course, as the credit card holder has the right under Federal law to refuse payment to the issuing bank pursuant to section 1661, the merchant bank, which is one step removed from the actual transaction giving rise to the credit card debit or credit, obtains from the merchant an agreement to the effect that all charge backs, or disputed amounts, for which the depository bank is not paid, may be deducted from the merchant's account. By this means, the risk that a credit card customer may dispute the transaction and refuse to pay is borne by the party who actually accepted payment by credit card. Indeed, the risk is not unlike that taken by a merchant who accepts a check which is later dishonored. While for the most part charge backs occur without difficulty, on occasion problems do develop. The typical problems which may arise are detailed below.

law

Cardholder Liability for Unauthorized Use

Liability of Holder of Credit Card
15 U.S.C.A. §1643

(a) Limits on liability

(1) A cardholder shall be liable for the unauthorized use of a credit card only if--

(A) the card is an accepted credit card;

(B) the liability is not in excess of $50;

(C) the card issuer gives adequate notice to the cardholder of the potential liability;

(D) the card issuer has provided the cardholder with a description of a means by which the card issuer may be notified of loss or theft of the card, which description may be provided on the face or reverse side of the statement required by section 1637(b) of this title or on a separate notice accompanying such statement;

(E) the unauthorized use occurs before the card issuer has been notified that an unauthorized use of the credit card has occurred or may occur as the result of loss, theft, or otherwise; and

(F) the card issuer has provided a method whereby the user of such card can be identified as the person authorized to use it.

(2) For purposes of this section, a card issuer has been notified when such steps as may be reasonably required in the ordinary course of business to provide the card issuer with the pertinent information have been taken, whether or not any particular officer, employee, or agent of the card issuer does in fact receive such information.

(b) Burden of proof

In any action by a card issuer to enforce liability for the use of a credit card, the burden of proof is upon the card issuer to show that the use was authorized or, if the use was unauthorized, then the burden of proof is upon the card issuer to show that the conditions of liability for the unauthorized use of a credit card, as set forth in subsection (a) of this section, have been met.

Society National Bank v. Kienzle
Ohio State Court of Appeals, 1983
463 N.E.2d 1261

Stillman, Judge. Defendant credit cardholder appeals from a municipal court judgment in favor of plaintiff credit card issuer for alleged authorized transactions involving defendant's credit card.

Defendant testified at trial that he was issued a single MasterCard charge card from plaintiff. He stated that after incurring a large charge bill, he decided to cease using the card until he reduced his indebtedness. Defendant asserted that he did not use the card for approximately eight months, and that he telephoned plaintiff to notify it of his credit card's apparent theft after he discovered a cash advance on his monthly statement which he did not make.

The testimony of plaintiff's employee acknowledged defendant's telephone notification of his stolen credit card. This witness testified regarding the procedures implemented to protect against further unauthorized use of the stolen card. She stated that even though the card was listed as stolen in the bank bulletins, charges were incurred without being charged back to the respective merchant's account. The witness further stated that defendant's account had a balance due and owing of $2,431.18. Bank records indicated that defendant owed $354.54 prior to his discovery of the unauthorized cash advance.

Defendant's further testimony implicated his estranged wife as the alleged thief of his card. Plaintiff contended at trial that her use of the card was authorized. Testimony by defendant and plaintiff's employee established defendant's credit limit to be $1,000, yet evidence exhibited that $4,057.76 was charged to defendant's account.

Defendant *** asserts that at most, he was liable only to the extent mandated by the Federal Truth in Lending Act, §1601 *et seq.*, Title 15, U.S. Code. We agree.

[According to] §1643, Title 15, U.S. Code,[*] *** a cardholder is liable for a limited amount if certain conditions are met and if the use of the credit card was unauthorized. Pursuant to §§1643(b), (c) and (d), Title 15, U.S. Code, " *** the burden of proof is upon the card issuer to show that the use was authorized or, if the use was unauthorized, then the burden of proof is upon the card issuer to show that the conditions of liability for the unauthorized use of a credit card, as set forth in subsection (a) of this section, have been met." §1643(b), Title 15, U.S. Code; *First National City Bank v. Mullarkey* (1976), 87 Misc.2d 1, 2, 385 N.Y.S.2d 473. Accordingly, the initial determination is whether the use of a credit card is unauthorized. *Transamerica Ins. Co. v. Standard Oil Co.* (N.D.1982), 325 N.W.2d 210, 213. " *** The test for determining unauthorized use is agency, and State agency law must be used to resolve this issue." *Transamerica Ins. Co. v. Standard Oil Co., supra*, at 214.

---

[*]   As noted in Part I of this opinion, state courts must apply federal law. When the federal government in the exercise of its delegated powers has enacted a complete scheme of regulation, states cannot, inconsistently with the purpose of Congress, conflict or interfere with, curtail or complement the federal law, or enforce additional or auxiliary regulations. However, our legislature has not attempted to regulate anything in this area. Therefore, there is no preemption problem.

In Ohio, a husband is not answerable for the acts of his wife unless the wife acts as his agent or he subsequently ratifies her acts. 28 Ohio Jurisprudence 2d 227, Husband and Wife, §100. In this case, there was no evidence introduced that defendant's wife acted as his agent, or that he ratified her conduct. Indeed, the transcript reveals that defendant notified plaintiff immediately after his discovery of someone else using his credit card. The transcript is devoid of any other evidence of agency or ratification. Thus, plaintiff failed in its burden of proof.

Further, if plaintiff fails to prove that the card use was authorized, defendant must elicit facts which prove the factors delineated in §1643(a), Title 15, U.S. Code. Based upon the testimony and evidence adduced at trial, we conclude that defendant has met the burden of proof in regard to §1643(a), Title 15, U.S. Code, and we must reduce the judgment rendered to the maximum delineated in that subsection--*i.e.*, fifty dollars.

Judgment modified, and affirmed as modified.

Walker Bank & Trust Co. v. Jones
Supreme Cour t of Utah, 1983
672 P.2d 73

HALL, CHIEF JUSTICE. At issue in these consolidated cases is the liability of defendants to plaintiff Walker Bank for expenses allegedly incurred by defendants' separated spouses upon credit card accounts established by the plaintiff bank in the names of the defendants. Defendants appeal from adverse summary judgment orders on the grounds that their rights under the Federal Truth in Lending Act were violated.

A. DEFENDANT BETTY JONES

In 1977, Defendant Jones established VISA and Master Charge accounts with plaintiff Walker Bank (hereinafter "Bank"). Upon her request, credit cards were issued on those accounts to herself and her husband in each of their names.

On or about November 11, 1977, defendant Jones informed the Bank, by two separate letters, that she would no longer honor charges made by her husband on the two accounts, whereupon the Bank immediately revoked both accounts and requested the return of the credit cards.[*] Despite numerous notices of revocation and requests for surrender of the cards, both defendant Jones and her husband retained their cards and continued to make charges against the accounts.

It was not until March 9, 1978, that defendant Jones finally relinquished her credit cards to the Bank, and then only after a persuasive visit to her place of employment by a Bank employee. At the time she surrendered her cards, the balance owing on the combined accounts (VISA and Master Charge) was $2,685.70. Her refusal to pay this balance prompted the Bank's institution of this suit to recover the same.

B. DEFENDANT GLORIA HARLAN

In July, 1979, defendant Harlan, who was prior to that time a VISA cardholder at plaintiff Bank, requested that her husband, John Harlan, be added to the account as an authorized user. The Bank honored this request and issued a card to Mr. Harlan. Shortly thereafter, at some point between July and the end of 1979, the Harlans separated and defendant (Mrs.) Harlan informed the Bank by letter that she either wanted the account closed or wanted the Bank to deny further extensions of credit to her husband.

---

[*] By the terms of the credit card account agreement, an account can be closed by returning to the Bank all outstanding credit cards.

Notwithstanding the explicit requirement in the account agreement that all outstanding credit cards be returned to the Bank in order to close the account, defendant Harlan did not tender either her card or her husband's at the time she made the aforementioned request. As to her card, she informed the Bank that she could not return it because it had been destroyed in the Bank's automated teller. Notwithstanding, however, she returned the card to the Bank some three months later (March, 1980).

In the interim period, i.e., after defendant's correspondence with the Bank regarding the exclusion of her husband from her account and prior to the relinquishment of her card, several charges were made (purportedly by Mr. Harlan) on the account for which the Bank now seeks recovery. The Bank has sued only Mrs. Harlan, as owner of the account.

Defendants' sole contention on appeal is that the Federal Truth in Lending Act (hereinafter "TILA") limits their liability, for the unauthorized use of the credit cards by their husbands, to a maximum of $50. The specific section of the Act upon which this contention rests is 15 U.S.C. §1643. ***

The Bank's rejoinder is that section 1643 does not apply, inasmuch as defendants' husbands' use of the credit cards was at no time "unauthorized use" within the meaning of the statute. Whether such use was "unauthorized," as that term is contemplated by the statute, is the pivotal question in this case.

The term "unauthorized use" is defined in 15 U.S.C. §1602(o) (1974) as:

> [U]se of a credit card by a person other than the cardholder who does not have actual, implied, or apparent authority for such use and from which the cardholder receives no benefit.

A "cardholder" is described in 15 U.S.C. §1602(m) as:

> [A]ny person to whom a credit card is issued or any person who has agreed with the card-issuer to pay obligations arising from the issuance of a credit card to another person.

Defendants contend that they alone occupied the status of "cardholder," by reason of their request to the bank that credit cards be issued to their husbands and their assumption of liability therefor. Accordingly, they maintain that their husbands were no more than authorized users of defendants' accounts.

Defendants' further aver that the effect of their notification to the Bank stating that they would no longer be responsible for charges made against their accounts by their husbands was to render any subsequent use (by their husbands) of the cards unauthorized. This notification, defendants maintain, was all that was necessary to revoke the authority they had once created in their husbands and thereby invoke the section 1643 limitations on cardholder liability.

The Bank's position is that unauthorized use within the meaning of section 1643 is precisely what the statutory definition (§1602(o) *supra*) says it is, to wit: "[U]se *** by a person *** who does not have actual, implied, or apparent authority ***," and that notification to the card issuer has no bearing whatsoever on whether the use is unauthorized, so as to entitle a cardholder to the statutory limitation of liability. We agree with this position.

Where section 1643 governs, the liability of the cardholder for unauthorized charges is limited to $50 regardless of any notification to the card issuer. Notification, if given prior to the unauthorized charges, serves only to eliminate the $50 liability and not, as defendants argue, to render a use unauthorized. Unless and until the unauthorized nature of the use has been established, the notification provision, as well as the statute itself, is irrelevant and ineffectual.

The language of the statute defining unauthorized use (§1602(o) *supra*) is clear and unambiguous. It excludes from the category of unauthorized users, any person who has "actual, implied, or apparent authority."

The Bank maintains that defendants' husbands clearly had "apparent" authority to use the cards, inasmuch as their signatures were the same as the signatures on the cards, and their names, the same as those imprinted upon the cards. Accordingly, it contends that no unauthorized use was made of the cards, and that defendants therefore cannot invoke the limitations on liability provided by the TILA.

Again, we find the Bank's position to be meritorious. Apparent authority exists:

> [W]here a person has created such an appearance of things that it causes a third party reasonably and prudently to believe that a second party has the power to act on behalf of the first person ***.

As previously pointed out, at defendants' request their husbands were issued cards bearing the husbands' own names and signatures. These cards were, therefore, a representation to the merchants (third parties) to whom they were presented that defendants' husbands (second parties--cardbearers) were authorized to make charges upon the defendants' (first parties--cardholders) accounts. This apparent authority conferred upon defendants' husbands by reason of the credit cards thus precluded the application of the TILA.

In view of our determination that the TILA has no application to the present case, we hold that liability for defendants' husbands' use of the cards is governed by their contracts with the Bank. The contractual agreements between defendants and the Bank provided clearly and unequivocally that *all* cards issued upon the accounts be returned to the Bank in order to terminate defendants' liability. Accordingly, defendants' refusal to relinquish either their cards or their husbands', at the time they notified the Bank that they no longer accepted liability for their husbands' charges, justified the Bank's disregard of that notification and refusal to terminate defendants' liability at that time.

The dissent expresses concern that the decision of the Court imposes an unreasonable burden on the cardholder. We disagree because in our opinion justice is better served by placing the responsibility for the credit escapades of an errant spouse (or son, daughter, mother, father, etc.) on the cardholder rather than the Bank. The cardholder is not left powerless to protect against misuse of the card. He or she need only surrender the cards and close the account, just as the defendants in the instant case were requested by the Bank to do.

Affirmed. No costs awarded.

Durham, Justice (dissenting):

[T]he pivotal issue in this case is whether the defendants' notification to the Bank was sufficient to revoke the defendants' husbands' "actual, implied, or apparent authority" to use the credit cards, thereby rendering the husbands' use unauthorized. The majority opinion responds in the negative by contending that the defendants' husbands were clothed with apparent authority because they carried credit cards imprinted with the husbands' names and bearing the husbands' signatures. The majority opinion holds that, despite notification to the Bank by the defendants that all authority has been expressly revoked, this apparent authority continues to exist until the defendants obtain the cards from their estranged husbands and return them to the Bank. I disagree with that holding for three reasons.

First, the result of the majority opinion runs counter to the purpose of section 1643 of the TILA, which has been described as follows:

> The federal credit card statute reflects a policy decision that it is preferable for the issuer to bear fraud losses arising from credit card use.

*** [I]ssuers are in a better position to control the occurrence of these losses. They not only select the merchants who may accept the card and the holders who may use it, but also design the security systems for card distribution, user identification, and loss notification. Hence, *the statutory choice of issuer liability assures that the problem of credit card loss is the responsibility of the party most likely to take efficient steps in its resolution.*

Weistart, *Consumer Protection in the Credit Card Industry: Federal Legislative Controls*, 70 Mich.L.Rev. 1475, 1509-10 (1972) (citations omitted) (emphasis added). *Cf. First National Bank of Mobile v. Roddenberry*, 701 F.2d 927 (11th Cir.1983) (stating that, by issuing a credit card, a bank assumes the risk of nonpayment and that only the bank can decide when and if credit will be revoked). Under the present circumstances, I acknowledge that the burden or risk of liability should initially fall on the cardholder because use of the credit card by a spouse is, and remains, authorized until notice is given to the card issuer that the authority to use the credit card is revoked. However, once the cardholder notifies the card issuer of the revocation of that authority, it is clear that the card issuer is in the best position to protect itself, the cardholder and third parties. The card issuer can protect both itself and the cardholder by refusing to pay any charges on the account, and it can protect third parties by listing the credit card in the regional warning bulletins. *See* Weistart, *supra*; *Standard Oil Co. v. State Neon Co.*, 120 Ga.App. 660, 171 S.E.2d 777 (1969). The issuer need only terminate the existing account, transfer all existing charges to a new number, and issue a new card to the cardholder.

* * *

Second, the language of section 1643 and the law of agency require that the defendants be relieved of liability. As the majority opinion recognizes, state law determines the question of whether the defendants' husbands are clothed with "apparent authority." *See, e.g.*, FRB Letter of July 23, 1974, No. 822, by J. Kluckman, Chief, Truth-in-Lending Section (excerpted in Consumer Credit Guide (CCH) §31,144 (October 8, 1974)). Under Utah law, a husband or wife may terminate an agency created in the spouse in the same manner as any other agency. *See* U.C.A., 1953, §30-2-8. The majority opinion holds that the defendants' husbands' use was authorized because the husbands had "apparent authority." This is apparently a reference to the relationship between the husband and third-party merchants who rely on the husband's possession of a credit card with his name and matching signature on it. It cannot refer to the existence of apparent authority vis-à-vis the Bank, because the Bank has been *expressly notified* of the revocation of all authority. I fail to see why the existence of "apparent authority" as to third-party merchants should govern the liability of a cardholder whose spouse "steals" a card in the context of marital difficulties, any more than it would govern in the case of a cardholder whose card is stolen before delivery and bears a "matching signature" forged thereon by a thief.

It is well recognized that apparent authority exists only to the extent that the *principal* represents to a third person that another is one's agent. *See, e.g.*, Restatement (Second) of Agency §8 & comments (1958). In the present case, with respect to the Bank, the husbands' authority, actual, implied and apparent, was specifically terminated by the defendants (the principals) when the Bank was notified that the husbands' authority to use the defendants' credit cards was revoked. *See, e.g., id.* §§124A, 125 & 130. Thus, after notification, the husbands' use was unauthorized and both section 1643 and the provisions of the cardholder agreements relieved the defendants of all liability for charges incurred by their husbands subsequent to that notification. *See, e.g., In re Shell Oil Co.*, 95 F.T.C. 357 (1980); *Socony Mobile Oil Co. v. Greif, supra. Accord Neiman-Marcus Co. v. Viser*, La., 140 So.2d 762 (1962).

* * *

The majority opinion sanctions the Bank's refusal to terminate the defendants' liability based on the majority opinion's interpretation that the cardholder agreements require "clearly and unequivocally that *all* cards issued upon the accounts be returned to the Bank in order to terminate defendants' liability." To the contrary, the cardholder agreements do not mandate the return of the credit cards as a condition precedent to termination of *liability*. The cardholder agreements provide that "Cardholder may terminate this *Agreement* at any time by returning the cards issued under this Agreement to the Bank." (Emphasis added.) This provision deals with termination of the "account," not termination of liability for unauthorized use. In fact, like section 1643, the relevant portions of the cardholder agreements, quoted above, provide specifically that the cardholder is not liable for charges incurred *after* notice of the possible unauthorized use is given to the Bank. Contrary to the majority opinion's suggestion, there are no provisions in the cardholder agreements that require the return of the credit cards to the Bank as a prerequisite to relieving the defendants of "liability" for the unauthorized use of their credit cards.

Finally, the majority opinion ignores the impracticality of imposing the burden on a cardholder of obtaining a credit card from an estranged spouse in order to return it to the Bank. It is unrealistic to think that estranged spouses will be cooperative. Moreover, it is extremely unwise to arm one spouse with a weapon which permits virtually unlimited spending at the expense of the other. As is illustrated by the facts of these cases, where the whereabouts of the unauthorized spouse are unknown, the cardholder may be powerless to acquire possession of his or her card and return it to the Bank, which, according to the majority opinion, is the only way to limit liability. One result of the majority opinion will surely be to encourage the "theft" by divorcing spouses of credit cards they were authorized to use during the marriage and the liberal use of those cards at the other spouse's expense.

In conclusion, *** I believe that section 1643 of the TILA and the provisions of the cardholder agreements relieve the defendants from liability for the unauthorized charges incurred by their husbands subsequent to the notification given to the Bank.

Martin v. American Express, Inc.
Alabama Civil Appellate Court, 1978
361 So.2d 597

Bradley, Judge. This appeal is the result of an order by the Circuit Court of Montgomery County granting appellee's (American Express, Inc.) motion for summary judgment.

In the summer of 1972 appellant (Robert A. Martin) applied for and was issued an American Express credit card. Approximately three years later, in April of 1975, Martin gave his credit card to a business associate named E.L. McBride. The reason for this action by Martin was apparently to enable McBride to use the card for the purpose of a joint business venture into which the two men had entered. Martin claimed that he orally authorized McBride to charge up to $500 on the credit card. However, in June of 1975 Martin received a statement from American Express which indicated that the amount owed on his credit card account was approximately $5,300. Martin denied that he had signed the credit card invoices which demonstrate that an amount has been charged to the cardholder's account. Upon learning of Martin's refusal to pay the charges incurred through the use of his credit card, American Express filed suit against Martin to obtain the money which it claimed Martin owed.

As the suit proceeded, American Express deposed Martin. In his deposition Martin admitted that he had given his credit card to McBride for use in a joint venture. Martin further stated that he did not know McBride very well, but that he (Martin) was not concerned about that fact because he told McBride not to charge more than $500 to his (Martin's) credit card account. Martin was also relying on a letter which he had sent to American Express prior to giving his card to McBride. Martin testified that in this letter he asked American Express not to allow the total charges on his account to exceed $1,000. Moreover, in his deposition Martin indicated that McBride subsequently returned the credit card to him (Martin) and shortly thereafter disappeared.

On the basis of this deposition American Express moved for a summary judgment pursuant to Rule 56, ARCP. The trial court granted this motion and Martin filed an appeal to this court.

We believe that the trial court properly entered an order granting a summary judgment in favor of American Express and therefore affirm the trial court's action.

Despite the various arguments presented by the attorneys in this case, we perceive only one issue before us on this appeal. That issue is whether the use of a credit card by a person who has received the card and permission to utilize it from the cardholder constitutes "unauthorized use" under the Truth in Lending Act, 15 U.S.C.A. §1602(o) and §1643(a). We hold that in instances where a cardholder, who is under no compulsion by fraud, duress or otherwise, voluntarily permits the use of his (or her) credit card by another person, the cardholder has authorized the use of that card and is thereby responsible for any charges as a result of that use.

Section 1643(a), which is of principal concern in this case, limits a cardholder's liability to $50 for the "unauthorized use of a credit card." However, the statutory limitation on liability comes into play only where there is an "unauthorized use" of a credit card. *Credit Card Service Corp. v. Federal Trade Comm'n*, 161 U.S.App.D.C. 424, 495 F.2d 1004 (1974). And section 1602(o) defines "unauthorized use" as the "use of a credit card by a person other than the cardholder [a] who does not have actual, implied, or apparent authority for such use, and [b] from which the cardholder receives no benefit."

American Express argues that the actions of Martin in giving McBride the credit card clearly demonstrated that Martin was not entitled to rely on the $50 limitation for unauthorized use of a credit card. Conversely, Martin relies on the familiar principle of agency law that a principal has the right to presume that his agent will act only within the sphere of his authority, and that in the absence of circumstances sufficient to place him on notice, a principal will not be held liable for his failure to ascertain that his agent is acting beyond the scope of his authority. *University Chevrolet Company v. Bank of Moundville*, 25 Ala.App. 506, 150 So. 557, *cert. denied* 227 Ala. 516, 150 So. 560 (1933). Thus, Martin submits that he cannot be held liable for the acts of his agent in that the latter was authorized to charge only $500 to Martin's American Express account, yet exceeded his authority by charging in excess of that amount.

We fail to see the applicability of common law principles regarding agents and the scope of their authority to the statutory provisions in question. The Truth in Lending Act is to be liberally construed in favor of the consumer. *Irvin v. Public Finance Company of Alabama*, Ala.Civ.App., 340 So.2d 811 (1976). And its terms are to be strictly enforced. *Irvin v. Public Finance Company of Alabama, supra.* However, it is a well-settled rule of statutory construction that the plain language of a statute offers the primary guidance to its meaning. *American Airlines, Inc. v. Remis Industries, Inc.*, 494 F.2d 196 (2d Cir.1974). Accordingly, where the language found in the statute is clear and unambiguous and the words used therein plainly and distinctly demonstrate the intent of the framers of the statute, there is no occasion to resort to any other means of interpretation or to interject common law principles into the statutory provisions in question. *See American Airlines, Inc. v. Remis Industries, Inc., supra.*

We believe Congress clearly indicated that "unauthorized use" of a card would occur only where there was no "actual, implied or apparent authority" for such use by the cardholder. In the present case Martin maintains that the actual, implied or apparent authority given by him to McBride was limited to the $500 amount which Martin told McBride not to exceed. Thus, Martin says he gave no authority for McBride to charge the large sum which eventually resulted in this suit. Furthermore, Martin asserts that prior to giving the card to McBride, he (Martin) wrote American Express and requested that its employees not allow the amounts charged to his credit card account to exceed $1,000. And since no such action was taken, Martin argues that any sum charged in excess of $1,000 constituted an "unauthorized" charge on his credit card.

We cannot accept either of the above contentions. McBride was actually authorized by Martin to use the latter's card. Martin admitted this fact. And the authority to use it, if not actual, remained apparent even after McBride ignored Martin's directions by charging over $500 to Martin's credit card account. Consequently, Martin was not entitled to rely on the provisions contained in section 1643(a) and he must be held responsible for any purchases made through the use of his card.

Nor are we aware of any requirement, either by statute, contract or trade usage, which would compel a credit card issuer to undertake a policy whereby the issuer would see to it that charges on a cardholder's account do not exceed a specified amount. Such a policy would place a difficult and potentially disastrous burden on the issuer. We know of no authority which requires a card issuer to perform services of this nature and Martin has provided us with none. Rule 28(a)(5), ARAP.

The express intent of Congress in enacting the Truth in Lending Act was to protect the consumer or cardholder against charges for the unauthorized use of his or her credit card and to limit his or her liability for such unauthorized use to a maximum of $50 providing, however, that the conditions set forth in the statute are complied with. *First National City Bank v. Mullarkey*, 87 Misc.2d 1, 385 N.Y.S.2d 473 (1976). We believe that section 1643(a) clearly indicates that such protection is warranted where the card is obtained from the cardholder as a result of loss, theft or wrongdoing.* However, we are not persuaded that section 1643(a) is applicable where a cardholder voluntarily and knowingly allows another to use his card and that person subsequently misuses the card.

Were we to adopt any other view, we would provide the unscrupulous and dishonest cardholder with the means to defraud the card issuer by allowing his or her friends to use the card, run up hundreds of dollars in charges and then limit his or her liability to $50 by notifying the card issuer. We do not believe such a result was either intended or sanctioned by Congress when it enacted section 1643(a).

Based on the pleadings and deposition before it, the trial court concluded that there was no genuine issue as to any material fact and that the moving party (American Express) was entitled to a judgment as a matter of law. The court did not err in reaching such a conclusion. Accordingly, the judgment of the trial court granting American Express's motion for summary judgment is affirmed.

AFFIRMED.

Towers World Airways Inc. v. PHH Aviation Systems Inc.

United States Court of Appeals, Second Circuit, 1991
933 F.2d 174

Newman, Circuit Judge.   The Truth-in-Lending Act, 15 U.S.C .s 1643(a) (1988), places a limit of $50 on the liability of a credit cardholder for charges incurred by an "unauthorized" user. This appeal concerns the applicability of this provision to a card bearer who was given permission by the cardholder to make a limited range of purchases but who subsequently made substantial

---

*   This construction is supported by two of the conditions for limitation of liability in unauthorized use situations under section 1643(a). Those conditions are: (1) that the card issuer has provided the cardholder with a self-addressed, pre-stamped notification to be mailed by the cardholder in the event of *loss* or *theft* of the credit card; and (2) that the unauthorized use occurs before the cardholder has notified the card issuer that an unauthorized use of the credit card has occurred or may occur as the result of *loss, theft* or otherwise.

additional charges on the card. The appeal is brought by Towers World Airways, Inc. ("Towers"), a credit cardholder, and two related corporations from the June 19, 1990, judgment of the District Court for the Southern District of New York (Kevin Thomas Duffy, Judge) denying their request for a declaratory judgment to absolve them of liability for the sums charged and granting judgment for the card issuer, PHH Aviation Systems ("PHH"), on its counterclaim for the amounts charged. We conclude that the person incurring the charges was not an "unauthorized" user within the meaning of section 1643(a) and therefore affirm.

BACKGROUND

In February 1988, PHH issued a credit card to Towers to purchase fuel and other aircraft-related goods and services for a corporate jet leased by Towers from PHH. World Jet Corporation, a subsidiary of United Air Fleet, was responsible for maintaining the aircraft. An officer of Towers designated Fred Jay Schley, an employee of World Jet, as the chief pilot of the leased jet and gave him permission to make purchases with the PHH credit card at least in connection with non-charter flights, which were used exclusively by Towers' executives. Notwithstanding United Air Fleet's agreement to pay the cost of fuel on chartered flights, which provided service for other clients, Schley used the credit card to charge $89,025.87 to Towers in connection with such flights, prior to the cancellation of the card in August 1988.

Towers filed a complaint in state court seeking a declaratory judgment (i) absolving it of liability for any charges incurred in connection with fuel purchases for chartered flights, (ii) holding PHH responsible for knowingly permitting these purchases and consequently for breaching the credit agreement issued in connection with the PHH credit card, and (iii) requiring an accounting and disgorgement of all improperly charged amounts. After removing to federal court, PHH moved for summary judgment on its counterclaims seeking recovery for the $89,025.97 in unpaid charges.

The District Court granted PHH's motion, denied Towers' prayer for declaratory relief, and entered judgment for the full amount in dispute. Judge Duffy held Towers liable under the terms of the credit agreement between Towers and PHH, which provided that "[the] Aircraft Operator shall be responsible for all purchases made with a Card from the date of its issuance until the Aircraft Operator reports that a card is lost, stolen, misplaced or canceled by calling PHH." Judge Duffy further held that the Truth-in-Lending Act, which limits a cardholder's liability for "unauthorized" uses, was inapplicable to charges incurred by one to whom the cardholder has "voluntarily and knowingly allow[ed]" access for another, limited purpose.

On appeal, Towers concedes liability under its credit agreement with PHH but contends that summary judgment was improperly granted on the question of whether the Truth-in-Lending Act limits its liability to $50. The issues on appeal are whether Schley's use of the card to incur the $89,025.97 in connection with chartered flights was "unauthorized" within the meaning of the Truth-in-Lending Act and whether that question was properly decided on summary judgment.

DISCUSSION
***

B. Was Apparent Authority Limited by Notice to the Card Issuer?

Towers contends that, despite its own failure to have the card canceled, once PHH, as the card issuer, learned, either through Towers or a third party, that Schley lacked authority to make certain charges, any such transaction that Schley entered into becomes an unauthorized use even if fuel sellers reasonably perceived that Schley had apparent authority to charge fuel purchases. Whether notifying the card issuer that some uses (or users) of a card are unauthorized makes them so has divided those courts that have considered the issue. *Compare Cities Service Co.*, 452 So.2d at 320-22 (authority terminated), *and Standard Oil Co.*, 489 N.E.2d at 844 (same), *with Martin*, 361 So.2d at 600-01 (notice to card issuer ineffective), *and Walker Bank*, 672 P.2d at 75 (same).

With respect to this claim as well, the agency principles incorporated in section 1602(o) remain Congress's chosen vehicle for establishing a card bearer's authority, and whether a cardholder can limit a card bearer's authority by notifying the card issuer must be resolved by looking first to these principles and then to other indicia of Congressional intent that might qualify the application of agency principles to credit card transactions. Under well-established principles of agency law, codified in Restatement (Second) of Agency §166 (1958), notice to a third party of limitations on an agent's authority qualifies the agent's apparent authority to act on the principal's behalf. *See Warner v. Central Trust Co.*, 798 F.2d 167, 171 (6th Cir.1986); *Cox v. Pabst Brewing Co.*, 128 F.2d 468, 472 (10th Cir.1942); H. Reuschlein & W. Gregory, Agency and Partnership 164 (1979). However, in making a purchase with a third-party credit card, where the card issuer and the selling merchant are distinct entities, a card bearer not only reaches an agreement with one third party, the merchant, but also indirectly deals with a different third party, the card issuer. Use of a third-party credit card by its bearer is made possible by arrangements, previously entered into by both the merchant and the card issuer, that simultaneously obligate the cardholder and the issuer to the merchant and the cardholder to the card issuer each time the card is used to charge purchases. ***

The rule of agency law contained in section 166 of the Restatement would permit the principal to qualify the authority of an agent to make purchases from a merchant by giving the merchant notice of the limitation. The limitation would surely be effective in an ordinary three-party arrangement in which an agent charges purchases on a principal's running account with a merchant. It is more doubtful whether a principal can similarly avoid liability by notifying the merchant of limitations on an agent's authority when an agent makes purchases using a credit card. Both cardholders and merchants normally regard anyone voluntarily entrusted with a credit card as having the right to make any purchases within the card's contractually specified limits. But to whatever extent a cardholder can limit the authority of a card user by giving notice to a merchant, we do not believe he can accomplish a similar limitation by giving notice to a card issuer. In four-party arrangements of this sort, it is totally unrealistic to burden the card issuer with the obligation to convey to numerous merchants whatever limitations the cardholder has placed on the card user's authority.*

Finally, there is no substance to the argument that our construction of the 1970 Amendments inadequately protects cardholders against liability for charges made without their consent. Admittedly, third-party credit cards ordinarily permit the bearer to charge purchases made from a vast number of merchants, and cardholders, who typically do not know which merchants have contracted to accept the card, cannot contact each merchant to selectively revoke a card bearer's authority. However, a cardholder need not do so to prevent unauthorized use by one entrusted with the card. In many cases, the cardholder can avoid unwanted charges simply by repossessing the card. Where a card issuer permits a cardholder to cancel the card, and thereby any contractual obligation to pay, a cardholder can limit his liability even if unable to regain possession by canceling his card. Even where the card issuer also requires return of the card prior to cancellation of the agreement, a cardholder who has tried and failed to recover a card from an "estranged spouse, a dishonest employee, or a disappeared 'friend,' " R.J. Rohner, F.H. Miller, J.H. Mancuso, The Law of Truth-in-Lending P 10.03[2][a], at S10-9 (Supp.1989), likely can prevail on the claim that the card user has stolen the card and that any subsequent charges are for that reason unauthorized. Finally, we note that by foreclosing card issuers from recovering unauthorized

---

* As framed by the Restatement, the notice rule is subject to certain restrictions, such as the requirement that the principal's communication of the limits on the agent's authority must be clear. But the existence of these restrictions does not necessarily mean that the notice rule itself is applicable in all contexts where those restrictions are satisfied. See Restatement of Agency (Second) at section 166, comment e.

charges from cardholders, section 1643(a)(1) undoubtedly encourages card issuers to facilitate the cancellation of cards once a possible unauthorized use has been reported.

Because the disputed charges were not unauthorized within the meaning of 15 U.S.C. §§1602(o) and 1643(a)(1), PHH was entitled to recover their full value from Towers under their credit agreement.

The judgment of the District Court is affirmed.

Transamerica Insurance Co. v. Standard Oil Co.
Supreme Court of North Dakota, 1982
325 N.W.2d 210

Vande Walle, Justice. Robert Smith, former office manager of Minot Builders Supply Association (hereinafter "MBS"), fraudulently used a credit card issued to MBS by Standard Oil Company of Indiana, doing business as Amoco Oil Company (hereinafter "Amoco"), for his personal gain. Because Transamerica Insurance Company (hereinafter "Transamerica") insured MBS for wrongful acts by MBS employees, Transamerica paid MBS for the loss caused by Smith's fraud. As a result Transamerica became subrogated to MBS's claims. Transamerica brought an action against Amoco alleging that it was not liable for Smith's fraudulent charges under Federal and State credit-card laws. The district court of Ward County agreed and awarded Transamerica $26,376.53 plus costs. We reverse and remand for a reconsideration of the amount of damages consistent with this opinion.

In March 1967 MBS first obtained an Amoco credit card for use in its business. As office manager Smith's duties included requesting credit cards for MBS employees and paying bills. The cards were renewed periodically, and the charges were paid by MBS.

On May 16, 1975, Smith made a written request to Amoco for a Torch Club credit card. A Torch Club credit card is comparable to a Diner's Club card because it may be used for purchases of consumer goods and services other than those furnished at gasoline service stations. The Torch Club application was signed by Smith as office manager. It also contained the signature of Mr. Switzer as general manager and secretary-treasurer of MBS; however, the trial court determined that Mr. Switzer's signature was forged by Smith.

After receiving the application Amoco did not contact the credit references listed in the application letter or any officer of MBS. Amoco issued the Torch Club card after reviewing MBS's record of payment on its Amoco gasoline credit cards.

During the period from May 1975 until July 1978 Smith wrongfully and fraudulently used the Torch Club card to obtain goods and services in the amount of $26,376.53. MBS paid for these purchases with checks signed by Smith and an authorized officer. There is some indication that Smith forged a portion of the necessary second signatures and that he altered the records to cover his wrongful acts. During this time MBS employed accountant firms to perform annual audits, but they did not discover the fraud.

After Smith's dishonesty was revealed, he was fired. MBS's fidelity-bond carrier, Transamerica, paid MBS its claim in full for the loss caused by Smith's fraudulent acts. Transamerica brought an action against Amoco as a subrogee under MBS's claim, alleging that it was not liable for the charges under Federal and State credit-card law. The trial court ruled in favor of Transamerica, and Amoco appealed.

The version of 15 U.S.C. §1643(a) (1977) in effect during the time of the transaction in issue is as follows:

A cardholder shall be liable for the unauthorized use of a credit card only if the card is an accepted credit card, the liability is not in excess of $50, the card issuer gives adequate notice to the cardholder of the potential liability, the card issuer has provided the cardholder with a self-addressed, prestamped notification to be mailed by the cardholder in the event of the loss or theft of the credit card, and the unauthorized use occurs before the cardholder has notified the card issuer that an unauthorized use of the credit card has occurred or may occur as the result of loss, theft, or otherwise. ***

The North Dakota Legislature also has enacted a credit-card statute, §51-14.1-02, N.D.C.C., which provides, in part:

A provision imposing liability on a cardholder for the unauthorized use of a credit card shall be effective only if the card is an accepted credit card, the liability imposed is not in excess of one hundred dollars, the card issuer gives adequate notice to the cardholder of the potential liability, and the unauthorized use occurs before the cardholder has notified the card issuer of the loss or theft of the card or of any unauthorized use.

*** [T]he Federal statute supersedes the State statute to the extent the provisions regarding the amount of maximum cardholder liability for an unauthorized use actually conflict. *See, generally*, 16 Am.Jur.2d, *Constitutional Law*, §291 (1979).

In 15 U.S.C. §1643(a) and §51-14.1-02, N.D.C.C., a cardholder is liable for a limited amount if certain conditions are met and if the use of the credit card was unauthorized. Accordingly, the initial determination is whether or not the use of the credit card in the case at hand was unauthorized. The Federal and State definitions of "unauthorized use" are identical: "a use of a credit card by a person other than the cardholder who does not have actual, implied, or apparent authority for such use and from which the cardholder receives no benefit." 15 U.S.C. §1602(o) (1977); Sec. 15-14.1-01(7), N.D.C.C. The test for determining unauthorized use is agency, and State agency law must be used to resolve this issue.

Smith did not have actual or implied actual authority to request an Amoco Torch Club credit card. The trial court correctly determined that the doctrine of ostensible authority controls in this case. The party who alleges the existence of agency based upon ostensible authority--here, Amoco--has the burden of proving agency by clear and convincing evidence. *Farmers Union Oil Co. of Dickinson v. Wood*, 301 N.W.2d 129, 133 (N.D.1980).

"Ostensible authority" is also called "apparent authority" and it "is such as the principal [MBS] intentionally or by want of ordinary care causes or allows a third person [Amoco] to believe the agent [Smith] to possess." Sec. 3-02-02, N.D.C.C. MBS is bound by Smith's acts under ostensible authority only to third persons who have incurred a liability in good faith and without ordinary negligence. See Sec. 3-03-03, N.D.C.C. The trial court determined that Amoco acted negligently by issuing MBS a Torch Club credit card without independently verifying Smith's authority. Because of this negligence the trial court determined that Amoco could not rely upon Smith's ostensible authority to establish the existence of agency.

The trial court's finding of fact that Amoco was negligent in issuing Smith the Torch Club card was not clearly erroneous. Credit-card issuers should make the necessary investigation prior to issuing a credit card. *First National City Bank v. Mullarkey*, 87 Misc.2d 1, 385 N.Y.S.2d 473 (1976). Amoco did not use the requisite reasonable diligence to ascertain whether or not Smith was acting within the scope of his authority. Therefore, Amoco is unable to rely upon the doctrine of ostensible authority when claiming Smith was authorized to request and use the Torch Club card. In *Hagel v. Buckingham Wood Products*, 261 N.W.2d 869, 875 (N.D.1977), this court quoted 3 Am.Jur.2d, *Agency*, §78, as follows: "[A] third person dealing with a known agent must bear the burden of determining for himself, by the exercise of reasonable diligence and prudence, the existence or nonexistence of the agent's authority to act in the premises." Smith's request for a Torch Club credit card was "unauthorized" under the Federal and State credit-card legislation.

A second requirement for imposing limited cardholder liability under Federal and State law is that the card must be an accepted credit card. An "accepted credit card" is any credit card which the cardholder has requested, signed, used, or authorized another to use for the purpose of obtaining money, property, labor, or services on credit. 15 U.S.C. §1602(l) (1977); Sec. 51-14.1-01(1), N.D.C.C. In the case at hand, MBS did not sign, use, or authorize Smith to use the credit card. The trial judge's finding that the Torch Club card was not an accepted credit card belonging to MBS was not clearly erroneous.

Both the Federal and the State statutes provide that when all the statutory requirements for limited liability are not met, the cardholder incurs no liability based upon the unauthorized use of any credit card. 15 U.S.C. §1643(d) (1977); Sec. 51-14.1-02, N.D.C.C. Because the Torch Club card issued to Smith was not an accepted card, MBS and its subrogee, Transamerica, are not liable for the initial fraudulent charges made by Smith.

However, the trial court erred in not looking beyond Amoco's negligence in issuing Smith the card. After receiving the first statement from Amoco containing the fraudulent charges, MBS was negligent in not finding and reporting the fraud. If the person to whom a credit card is issued is careless, he may be held liable. 50 Am.Jur.2d, *Letters of Credit*, §39 (1970). For example, in *Martin v. American Express, Inc.*, 361 So.2d 597 (Ala.Civ.App.1978), a cardholder voluntarily permitted another who was involved in a business venture with him to use his credit card. The court held that the limit on liability in 15 U.S.C. §1643(a) was inapplicable to these facts for policy reasons. Otherwise, an unscrupulous cardholder could allow another to charge hundreds of dollars in goods and services and then attempt to limit his liability to 50 dollars.

The Federal Truth in Lending Act does not answer the question of whether or not cardholder negligence removes the statutory liability limit. See Weistart, *Consumer Protection in the Credit Card Industry: Federal Legislative Controls*, 70 Mich.L.Rev. 1476, 1526 (1972). We believe that MBS's negligence in not examining its monthly statements from Amoco removes this case from the statutory limit on cardholder liability.

A bank customer has a duty to examine his bank statement promptly, using reasonable care to discover unauthorized signatures or alterations. Sec. 41-04-33(1), N.D.C.C. If the bank uses reasonable care in making the statement and if the bank customer fails to examine his statement, the customer is precluded from asserting his unauthorized signature against the bank after a certain time. Sec. 41-04-33(2), (4), N.D.C.C.*** This commercial-paper situation parallels the facts at hand. Amoco was not negligent in billing MBS. If someone at MBS other than Smith had examined its statements from Amoco, he would have discovered Smith's fraud. It was the responsibility of MBS to institute internal procedures for the examination of the statements from Amoco which would have disclosed Smith's defalcation. It was solely within MBS's power to do so. The failure of MBS to institute such procedures is the cause of that portion of the defalcation which occurred following the billing from Amoco which contained the first evidence of Smith's fraud

Because of MBS's negligence, we will reexamine whether or not Smith acquired ostensible authority in his use of the Torch Club card after MBS became negligent. In *Farmers Union Oil Co. of Dickinson v. Wood, supra*, this court set forth the test to determine whether or not an ostensible authority existed. The authority must be based upon a principal's conduct which, reasonably interpreted, causes a third person to believe the agent has authority to act for the principal.

In *Hagel v. Buckingham Wood Products, Inc., supra*, 261 N.W.2d at 875, this court quoted with approval *McGee v. Breezy Point Estates*, 283 Minn. 10, 22, 166 N.W.2d 81, 89 (1969) as follows:

[T]he scope of apparent [ostensible] authority is determined not only by what the principal knows and acquiesces in, but also by what the principal should, in the exercise of ordinary care and prudence, know his agent is doing.

Thus, if a principal acts or conducts his business either intentionally or through negligence, or fails to disapprove of the agent's acts or course of action so as to lead the public to believe that his agent possesses authority to act or contract in the name of the principal, the principal is bound by the acts of the agent within the scope of his apparent authority as to persons who have reasonable grounds to believe that the agent has such authority and in good faith deal with him. 3 Am.Jur.(2d) Agency, §74.

Amoco was negligent in issuing Smith the Torch Club card and therefore Amoco initially could not rely on the doctrine of ostensible authority. However, during Smith's fraudulent use of the card, Amoco was not negligent. Rather, MBS was negligent in not requiring that someone other than Smith examine its monthly statements. Smith embezzled money from MBS for three years through his fraudulent use of the Torch Club credit card. During this lengthy period of embezzlement, MBS always paid its monthly bill to Amoco. MBS contends that it is not proper for the court to consider the fact that MBS paid all the Amoco credit card charges. That contention is without merit. As a result of MBS's acts of paying for the charges and its failure to examine its statements so that it could notify Amoco of the fraud, MBS allowed Amoco to reasonably believe that Smith was authorized to use the credit card.

MBS claims that it relied upon its accountants to find fraud during annual audits. MBS made the decision to hire and rely upon accountants. This decision does not protect MBS from the inability of these accountants to discover the fraud.

We conclude that Amoco is liable for Smith's fraudulent purchases from the time the credit card was issued until MBS received the first statement from Amoco containing Smith's fraudulent charges plus a reasonable time to examine that statement. After that time, MBS's subrogee, Transamerica, is liable for the remaining fraudulent charges. We reverse the judgment and remand this case for a determination of when MBS should have examined its statements and discovered Smith's fraud, and, consistent with this opinion, for a new calculation of the damages.

Wrongful Dishonor

Gray v. American Express Co.
United States Court of Appeals, District of Columbia Circuit, 1984
743 F.2d 10

Mikva, Circuit Judge. We are called upon to determine what rights, if any, appellant Oscar Gray has against American Express arising from the circumstances under which it canceled his American Express credit card. The District Court granted summary judgment to American Express; we vacate that judgment and remand for further proceedings.

I. BACKGROUND
Gray had been a cardholder since 1964. In 1981, following some complicated billings arising out of deferred travel charges incurred by Gray, disputes arose about the amount due American Express. After considerable correspondence, the pertinence and timeliness of which we will detail below, American Express decided to cancel Gray's card. No notification of this cancellation was

communicated to Gray until the night of April 8, 1982, when he offered his American Express card to pay for a wedding anniversary dinner he and his wife already had consumed in a Washington restaurant. The restaurant informed Gray that American Express had refused to accept the charges for the meal and had instructed the restaurant to confiscate and destroy his card. Gray spoke to the American Express employee on the telephone at the restaurant who informed him, "Your account is canceled as of now."

The cancellation prompted Gray to file a lengthy complaint in District Court, stating claims under both diversity and federal question jurisdiction. *See* 28 U.S.C. §§1331, 1332; *see also* 15 U.S.C. §1640. He alleged that the actions of American Express violated the contract between them, known as the "Cardmember Agreement," as well as the Fair Credit Billing Act (the "Act"), 15 U.S.C. §§1666-1666j, Pub.L. 93-495, Tit. III, 88 Stat. 1511 (1974).*** The District Court granted summary judgment for American Express and dismissed the complaint.

The surge in the use of credit cards, the "plastic money" of our society, has been so quick that the law has had difficulty keeping pace. It was not until 1974 that Congress passed the Act, first making a serious effort to regulate the relationship between a credit cardholder and the issuing company. We hold that the District Court was too swift to conclude that the Act offers no protection to Gray and further hold that longstanding principles of contract law afford Gray substantial rights. We thus vacate the District Court's judgment and remand.

II. DISCUSSION
A. THE STATUTORY CLAIM

1. *The Billing Error*

The billing dispute in issue arose after Gray used his credit card to purchase airline tickets costing $9312. American Express agreed that Gray could pay for the tickets in 12 equal installments over 12 months. In January and February of 1981, Gray made substantial prepayments of $3500 and $1156 respectively. He so advised American Express by letter of February 8, 1981. There is no dispute about these payments, nor about Gray's handling of them. At this point the numbers become confusing because American Express, apparently in error, converted the deferred payment plan to a current charge on the March bill. American Express thereafter began to show Gray as delinquent, due at least in part to the dispute as to how and why the deferred billing had been converted to a current charge.

The District Court held that Gray failed to trigger the protection of the Act because he neglected to notify American Express in writing within 60 days after he first received an erroneous billing. Gray insists that his first letter to American Express on April 22, 1981, well within the 60 day period set forth in the statute, identified the dispute as it first appeared in the March, 1981 billing. According to Gray's complaint, the dispute continued to simmer for over a year because American Express never fulfilled its investigative and other obligations under the Act.

The District Court made no mention of the April 22, 1981 letter, deeming instead a September, 1981 letter as the first notification from Gray as to the existence of a dispute. We conclude that the District Court erred in overlooking the April letter.

Gray's April 22, 1981 letter complained specifically about the March bill and the miscrediting of the prepayments. Whatever the import and impact of other correspondence and actions of the parties, we hold that, through this earlier letter, Gray triggered the procedural protections of the Act. The letter enabled the card issuer to identify the name and account number, indicated that the cardholder believed that an error existed in a particular amount and set forth the cardholder's reasons why he believed an error had been made. 15 U.S.C. §1666(a); *see Lincoln First Bank, N.A. v. Carlson*, 103 Misc.2d 467, 426 N.Y.S.2d 433 (1980) (returned credit slip, with nothing more, could suffice as notice under the Act). The later correspondence and activities may be treated as evidentiary in nature--sufficient perhaps to show that American Express fulfilled all of its obligations under the Act, but not pertinent to the question of whether the Act was triggered in the first place. *See Byers v. Burleson*, 713 F.2d 856, 859 (D.C.Cir.1983) (appellate court reviewing summary judgment determines whether there is genuine issue of material fact and, if not, whether the law was correctly applied).

* * *

3. *The Act and the Cardmember Agreement*

* * * On appeal, American Express also urges that, even if the Act is otherwise pertinent, Gray was bound by the terms of the Cardmember Agreement which empowered American Express to cancel the credit card without notice and without cause. The contract between Gray and American Express provides:

> [W]e can revoke your right to use [the card] at any time. We can do this with or without cause and without giving you notice.

American Express concludes from this language that the cancellation was not of the kind prohibited by the Act, even though the Act regulates other aspects of the relationship between the cardholder and the card issuer.

Section 1666(d) of the Act states that, during the pendency of a disputed billing, the card issuer, until it fulfills its other obligations under section 1,666(a)(B)(ii), shall not cause the cardholder's account to be restricted or closed because of the failure of the obligor to pay the amount in dispute. *See also* 12 C.F.R. §226.14(d). American Express seems to argue that, despite that provision, it can exercise its right to cancellation for cause unrelated to the disputed amount, or for *no* cause, thus bringing itself out from under the statute. At the very least, the argument is audacious. American Express would restrict the efficacy of the statute to those situations where the parties had not agreed to a "without cause, without notice" cancellation clause, or to those cases where the cardholder can prove that the sole reason for cancellation was the amount in dispute. We doubt that Congress painted with such a faint brush.

The effect of American Express's argument is to allow the equivalent of a "waiver" of coverage of the Act simply by allowing the parties to contract it away. Congress usually is not so tepid in its approach to consumer problems. *See* 118 Cong.Rec. 14,835 (1972) (remarks by Sen. Proxmire, principal proponent of the Act, concerning a technical amendment to a predecessor bill later carried over into the Act; its purpose was to prevent "possible evasion" by precluding the creditor from including a predispute waiver provision in the card agreement); 119 Cong.Rec. 25,400 (1973) (remarks by Sen. Proxmire on S. 2101, another predecessor: "The legislation seeks to establish a system for *insuring* that billing disputes or inquiries are resolved in a fair and timely manner.") (emphasis added); *see also Mourning v. Family Publications Service, Inc.*, 411 U.S. 356, 375-77, 93 S.Ct. 1652, 1663-64, 36 L.Ed.2d 318 (1973) (Truth-in-Lending Act should not be narrowly construed); *Koerner v. American Express Co.*, 444 F.Supp. 334, 341 (E.D.La.1977) (*Koerner* trial court's recitation of Act's legislative history reflecting congressional concern about card issuers' "highhanded tactics" in handling of consumer billing disputes).

Moreover, the consumer-oriented statutes that Congress has enacted in recent years belie the unrestrained reading that American Express gives to the Act in light of its contract. Waiver of statutory rights, particularly by a contract of adhesion, is hardly consistent with the legislature's purpose. The rationale of consumer protection legislation is to even out the inequalities that consumers normally bring to the bargain. To allow such protection to be waived by boiler plate language of the contract puts the legislative process to a foolish and unproductive task. A court ought not impute such nonsense to a Congress intent on correcting abuses in the market place.

Finally, American Express also contends that, even if the Act is not waived totally, its cancellation was proper because it was for reasons other than those prohibited by the statute. A showing of whatever limited grounds for cancellation remain available under section 1666(d) while a dispute is pending calls for substantial evidentiary proceedings, however. If American Express seeks to avail itself of these grounds, a more substantial factual predicate than that established through summary judgment is necessary. *See Harlow v. Fitzgerald*, 457 U.S. 800, 816, 102 S.Ct. 2727, 2737, 73 L.Ed.2d 396 (1982).

Thus we hold that the Act's notice provision was met by Gray's April 22, 1981 letter and remand the case to the District Court for trial of Gray's statutory cause of action. American Express will be obliged to justify its conduct in this case as fully satisfying its obligations under the Act.

B. THE CONTRACT CLAIM

Gray stated a second cause of action in diversity, a contract claim, in which he alleged that American Express violated the Cardmember Agreement by wrongfully canceling it. Notably, in *American Express Co. v. Koerner*, 452 U.S. 233, 101 S.Ct. 2281 (1981), the Supreme Court on very similar facts observed that a cardholder could state, in addition to, and separate from, his federal claim under the Act, a claim under state law for cancellation arising out of a credit card billing dispute. 452 U.S. at 239-40 & n. 6, 101 S.Ct. at 2285, & n. 6. *See also Hill v. American Express Co.*, 257 S.C. 86, 184 S.E.2d 115 (1971). Although a state law claim was raised, and addressed, in this case, neither the parties nor the District Court considered the preliminary question of choice of law. The parties failed again to address it on appeal. As a court sitting in diversity, we are obliged, however, to examine that issue.

1. *Choice of Law*

* * *

The American Express contract contains a specific provision which states that the agreement will be governed by the law of New York. The District of Columbia courts apparently have not had occasion to consider the efficacy of such a contractual choice of law provision. *Flintkote, supra*, 593 F.2d at 1279 n. 16. When District of Columbia law is silent, it has been the practice of the federal courts in this Circuit to turn to the law of Maryland for historical and geographical reasons. *Conesco Industries, Ltd. v. Conforti & Eisele, Inc.*, 627 F.2d 312, 315-16 (D.C.Cir.1980). Like most other jurisdictions, Maryland recognizes the ability of parties to agree upon the law which will govern their contract, provided, of course, that the choice bears some substantial relation to the parties or their transaction. *Kronovet v. Lipchin*, 288 Md. 30, 415 A.2d 1096, 1103-06 (1980); *see* Restatement (Second) of Conflict of Laws §187 (1971). Because American Express is a New York corporation, we find sufficient basis for deferring to the parties' choice of law. We therefore look to the law of New York to interpret this contract.

2. *Notice*

We are asked to interpret the "without notice" provision in the Cardmember Agreement. Gray challenges the card issuer's extreme and, in our view, unreasonable interpretation of this language. The District Court concluded that the notice provision was enforceable. We disagree.

It is certainly true that, from the common law immemorial, parties have been free to include whatever conditions and limitations that they may desire in a contract. *See* Restatement (Second) of Contracts, Introductory Note, ch. 8, at p. 2 (1981); *see also id.* §72 comment b (contract provides opportunity for freedom of action and exercise of judgment). Absent a statutory prohibition or some public policy impediment, *id.* §178, the very essence of freedom of contract is the right of the parties to strike good bargains and bad bargains. *See id.* §79 comment c (exchange of unequal values); *see also Dorman v. Cohen*, 66 A.D.2d 411, 413 N.Y.S.2d 377 (1st Dept.1979) ("mutuality of obligation" does not mean equality). However traditional "cancellation for cause" and "with notice" provisions are to a contract, parties sometimes agree to give them up. *See, e.g.,*

A.S. Rampell, Inc. v. Hyster Co., 3 N.Y.2d 369, 165 N.Y.S.2d 475, 144 N.E.2d 371 (1957) (merchant-to-merchant context). Appellant thus would not be the first nor the last cardholder to have surrendered substantial rights. Nor does the fact that Gray paid $35.00 per year for his cardholding privileges automatically entitle him to receive notice or to insist on some showing of cause before his card is canceled. Indeed, American Express generously provides for a pro-rata refund of the annual charge in the event of cancellation.

The problem, then, is not, as Gray would suggest, the unconscionable nature per se of this clause. Nor is it that this clause contradicts in any actionable way the advertising and puffing that he claims American Express used to entice him into the relationship. (*e.g.*, "When you're out of cash, you're not out of luck."; " *** flexibility to travel and entertain when and where you want, virtually without interruption.") The problem stems from the card issuer's attempt to interpret the "without notice" provision so as to give the creditor's internal cancellation decision effect as against irreversible transactions that already have been completed.

Commonly understood, the function of notice is to provide forewarning of an event. Similarly, in the context of contractual relations, notice allows the party notified to contemplate, and to prepare for, an action that will occur. *See* 1 M. Merrill on Notice §§1, 526 (1952). By contrast, and reasonably interpreted, a contract that is cancelable without notice implies that it can be terminated without forewarning. Such a contract provision ordinarily does not suggest, however, that the cancellation is effective retrospectively to events that transpired prior to notification of the decision to cancel. *Cf. Fifty States Management Corp. v. Public Service Mut. Ins. Co.*, 67 Misc.2d 778, 324 N.Y.S.2d 345 (1971) (after loss occurs, rights of parties become fixed; cancellation may not be effected retroactively) (citing *Duncan v. N.Y. Mut. Ins. Co.*, 138 N.Y. 88, 33 N.E. 730 (1893)); *Marjean, Inc. v. Ammann*, 6 A.D.2d 878, 177 N.Y.S.2d 882 (2d Dept.1958) ("[N]otice given pursuant to the 'escape clause' in the contract did not terminate liability as to obligations already accrued, but only as to liabilities thereafter accruing."). Indeed, counsel for American Express made this point for us indirectly at oral argument. When he was asked whether, based on his client's interpretation of the "without notice" clause, American Express was empowered to cancel the agreement "retroactively," he answered "yes," but was quick to add that his client would never take such action against a cardholder. We see little, if any, principled distinction, however, between admittedly "retroactive" cancellation and cancellation effective against irreversible obligations incurred after cancellation but before the cardholder learns his card has been canceled.

***

There can be no dispute that American Express drew the language for a broad application. But if American Express were correct in its interpretation, it even could refuse to honor past charges long since incurred--an outcome that must be rejected even in application of *strictum jus*. The right to cancel "without giving you notice" means that the decision to cancel can be entirely unilateral and instantaneous. It cannot, however, be an internalized decision which is never communicated to the cardholder. Such a reading defies any reasonable expectation that the parties could have had about their contractual relationship. *** Thus, we think that the "without notice" provision is given full weight by allowing the cancellation to be unilateral and to be given contemporaneous effect upon communication. To say that "without notice" also means that it never need be communicated to the cardholder extends the clause, and the waiver it contains, "to circumstances not covered." 2 M. Merrill, *supra*, §899 at p. 427 (waiver of notice construed narrowly).

Indeed, the interpretation of the language urged by American Express would subsume the entire contract and make the underlying contractual relationship illusory. *See Niagara Mohawk Power Corp. v. Graver Tank & Mfg. Co.*, 470 F.Supp. 1308, 1316 (N.D.N.Y.1979) (applying New York law; presence of notice requirement in otherwise broad termination provision prevents promise from being illusory); Restatement (Second) of Contracts §77 comment a (illusory promises); 1A Corbin on Contracts §163 at p. 76 (1963) ("If a promisor reserves the power to cancel at any time without notice, his promise seems to be unenforceable, ***."); 1 Williston, *supra*, §105 at p. 418 ("An agreement wherein one party reserves the right to cancel at his pleasure cannot create a contract.") (footnote omitted). We therefore hold that, even as a contract of adhesion, the language quoted above has limitations. The card can be revoked without cause and without any waiting period, but it cannot be revoked for transactions that already have occurred.

American Express suggests that if the clauses are not upheld in the manner it urges, there will be a great risk thrown on the credit card business. We think they protest too much. Within the limits of state and federal statutes, credit cards can still be canceled without cause and without notice. But the cancellation can affect only transactions which have not occurred before the cancellation is communicated to the cardholder. In practical terms American Express will have to make an effort to communicate its cancellation decision to the cardholder. The effort may be as informal as a phone call or a telegram. We leave to future cases the question of what constitutes a good faith effort to communicate the cancellation decision to the cardholder.

Nor need we decide what fact situations would allow the communication of the cancellation to take place through the merchant involved in the transaction. If a cardholder seeks to use his American Express card to buy a car, for example, we think that a communication, through the car dealer, that the card has been canceled prior to title passing to the cardholder may effect notice in reasonable fashion. But where the meal has been consumed, or the hotel room has been slept in, or the service rendered, the communication through the merchant comes too late to void the credit for that transaction.

* * *

We therefore hold that the cancellation without notice provision, as interpreted by American Express, is unenforceable. We remand the case to the District Court to resolve Gray's claims under the contract.

III. CONCLUSION

The District Court's order of summary judgment and dismissal is hereby vacated. The case is remanded for further proceedings consistent with this opinion.

So Ordered.

Asserting Claims and Defenses Against the Issuer

Assertion By Cardholder Against Card Issuer Of Claims And Defenses Arising Out Of Credit Card Transaction
15 U.S.C.A. §1666i

(a) Subject to the limitation contained in subsection (b) of this section, a card issuer who has issued a credit card to a cardholder pursuant to an open end consumer credit plan shall be subject to all claims (other than tort claims) and defenses arising out of any transaction in which the credit card is used as a method of payment or extension of credit if (1) the obligor has made a good faith attempt to obtain satisfactory resolution of a disagreement or problem relative to the transaction from the person honoring the credit card; (2) the amount of the initial transaction exceeds $50; and (3) the place where the initial transaction occurred was in the same State as the mailing address previously provided by the cardholder or was within 100 miles from such address, except that the limitations set forth in clauses (2) and (3) with respect to an obligor's right to assert claims and defenses against a card issuer shall not be applicable to any transaction in which the person honoring the credit card (A) is the same person as the card issuer, (B) is controlled by the card issuer, (C) is under direct or indirect common control with the card issuer, (D) is a franchised dealer in the card issuer's products or services, or (E) has obtained the order for such transaction through a mail solicitation made by or participated in by the card issuer in which the cardholder is solicited to enter into such transaction by using the credit card issued by the card issuer.

(b) The amount of claims or defenses asserted by the cardholder may not exceed the amount of credit outstanding with respect to such transaction at the time the cardholder first notifies the card issuer or the person honoring the credit card of such claim or defense. For the purpose of determining the amount of credit outstanding in the preceding sentence, payments and credits to the cardholder's account are deemed to have been applied, in the order indicated, to the payment of: (1) late charges in the order of their entry to the account; (2) finance charges in order of their entry to the account; and (3) debits to the account other than those set forth above, in the order in which each debit entry to the account was made.

Izraelewitz v. Manufacturers Hanover Trust
New York City Civil Court, 1983
465 N.Y.S.2d 486

Ira B. Harkavy, Judge. As the texture of the American economy evolves from paper to plastic, the disgruntled customer is spewing its wrath upon the purveyor of the plastic rather than upon the merchant.

Plaintiff George Izraelewitz commenced this action to compel the Defendant bank Manufacturers Hanover Trust Company to credit his Mastercharge account in the amount of $290.00 plus finance charges. The disputed charge, posted to Plaintiff's account on July 16, 1981, is for electronic diagrams purchased by Plaintiff via telephone from Don Britton Enterprises, a Hawaii-based mail order business.

On September 9, 1981 Plaintiff advised Defendant bank, Manufacturers Hanover Trust Company (Trust Company), that the diagrams had been unsuitable for his needs and provided Defendant with a UPS receipt indicating that the purchased merchandise had been returned to Don Britton. Defendant's Customer Service Department credited Plaintiff's account and waived finance charges on the item. Trust Company subsequently proceeded to charge back the item to the merchant. The merchant refused the charge back through The 1st Hawaii Bank, and advised Defendant bank of their strict "No Refund" policy. Don Britton also indicated that Plaintiff, during the course of conversation, had admitted that he was aware of this policy. On April 1, 1982 Defendant advised Plaintiff that his account would be redebited for the full amount. At two later dates, Plaintiff advised Trust Company of said dispute, denied knowledge of the "No Refund" policy and stated that the goods had been returned. The Trust Company once again credited Plaintiff's account and attempted to collect from Don Britton. The charge back was again refused and Plaintiff's account was subsequently redebited.

Bank credit agreements generally provide that a cardholder is obligated to pay the bank regardless of any dispute which may exist respecting the merchandise. An exception to this rule arises under a provision in the Truth in Lending Law which allows claimants whose transactions exceed $50.00 and who have made a good faith attempt to obtain satisfactory resolution of the problem, to assert claims and defenses arising out of the credit card transaction, if the place of the initial transaction is in the same state or within 100 miles of the cardholder. Consumer Credit Protection Act, 15 U.S.C.A. §1666i.

It would appear that Plaintiff is precluded from asserting any claims or defenses since Britton's location exceeds the geographical limitation. This assumption is deceiving. Under Truth in Lending the question of where the transaction occurred (e.g. as in mail order cases) is to be determined under state or other applicable law. Truth in Lending, 12 CFR, §226.12(c).

Furthermore, any state law permitting customers to assert claims and defenses against the card issuer would not be preempted, regardless of whether the place of the transaction was at issue. In effect, these federal laws are viewed as bare minimal standards.

In *Lincoln First Bank, N.A. v. Carlson*, 103 Misc.2d 467, 426 N.Y.S.2d 433 (1980), the court found that:

> (T)he statement that a card issuer is subject to all defenses if a transaction occurred less than 100 miles from the cardholder's address, does not automatically presume a cardholder to give up all his defenses should the transaction take place at a distance of greater than 100 miles from the mailing address. *Id.* at 436.

The facts at bar do not warrant a similar finding. Whereas in *Lincoln, supra*, the cardholder's defense arose due to an alleged failure of the card issuer itself to comply with statutory rules, the Defendant herein is blameless. The geographical limitation serves to protect banks from consumers who may expose them to unlimited liability through dealings with merchants in faraway states where it is difficult to monitor a merchant's behavior. These circumstances do not lend the persuasion needed to cast-off this benefit.

Considering, arguendo, that under the Truth in Lending Act, Plaintiff was able to assert claims and defenses from the original transaction, any claims or defenses he chose to assert would only be as good as and no better than his claim against the merchant. Accordingly, Plaintiff's claim against the merchant must be scrutinized to ascertain whether it is of good faith and substantial merit. A consumer cannot assert every miniscule dispute he may have with a merchant as an excuse not to pay an issuer who has already paid the merchant.

The crux of Plaintiff's claim, apparently, is that he returned the diagrams purportedly unaware of merchant's "No Refund" policy. The merchant contends that Plaintiff admitted that he knew of the policy and nonetheless used deceptive means to return the plans; in that they were sent without a name so they would be accepted; were not delivered to an employee of the company; were not in the original box; and showed evidence of having been xeroxed.

"No Refund" policies, per se, are not unconscionable or offensive to public policy in any manner. Truth in Lending Law "(n)either requires refunds for returns nor does it prohibit refunds in kind." Truth in Lending Regulations, 12 CFR, §226.12(e). Bank-merchant agreements, however, usually do contain a requirement that the merchant establish a fair policy for exchange and return of merchandise.

To establish the fairness in Don Britton's policy, the strength of the reasons behind the policy and the measures taken to inform the consumer of it must necessarily be considered. Don Britton's rationale for its policy is compelling. It contends that printing is a very small part of its business, which is selling original designs, and "once a customer has seen the designs he possesses what we have to sell." Britton's policy is clearly written in its catalog directly on the page which explains how to order merchandise. To compensate for not having a refund policy, which would be impractical considering the nature of the product, Britton offers well-advertised backup plans with free engineering assistance and an exchange procedure, as well, if original plans are beyond the customer's capabilities. The Plaintiff could have availed himself of any of these alternatives which are all presumably still open to him.

On the instant facts, as between Plaintiff and the Defendant bank, Plaintiff remains liable for the disputed debt, as he has not shown adequate cause to hold otherwise.

Judgment for Defendant dismissing the complaint.

Lincoln First Bank v. Carlson

Supreme Court of New York, 1980

426 N.Y.S.2d 433

Joseph P. Kuszynski, Justice. Plaintiff Lincoln First Bank moves pursuant to CPLR 3212 for summary judgment against the defendant Herbert Carlson. The third-party defendant Marine Midland Bank moves pursuant to CPLR 3211(a)(7) to dismiss the third-party complaint against it upon the grounds it does not state a cause of action.

It appears that on June 6, 1978, defendant purchased a ring by telephone from Constantine Gems of Cleveland, Ohio and charged the amount of the purchase, in the sum of $379.00 to his Visa Charge Card account with plaintiff Lincoln.

According to his answer, defendant returned the ring to the merchant in Cleveland, Ohio on June 16, 1978 and received a credit slip from the store on June 21, 1978. The credit slip, however, showed defendant's identification number to be his Master Charge Card account with the third-party defendant Marine, rather than his Visa account with plaintiff, Lincoln.

Defendant states in his answering affidavit that the first statement he received from Visa after obtaining the credit slip was on about July 26, 1978, and it showed no credit for the ring. He presumed, he states, that it was because the attendant paperwork had not been processed. Mr. Carlson claims that afterward he moved and heard nothing from Visa until his wife was contacted by phone by plaintiff on September 16, 1978. A letter to plaintiff from the Carlsons postmarked September 17, 1978 contained the purchase and credit slips.

The next apparent contact between the parties was on December 11, 1978, when a letter from plaintiff advised defendant that his "time limit *** has expired", referring to the "Federal Truth in Lending Act", which is 15 United States Code (U.S.C.) §1666. The letter also suggested he contact Constantine Gems "regarding the non-receipt of credit". According to the answering papers, Mr. Carlson did attempt to contact Constantine Gems, only to find that the company had since gone bankrupt. Further attempts by defendant to secure an amended credit from Constantine Gems failed.

Thereafter in October, 1979 plaintiff Lincoln commenced an action against the defendant Carlson under the terms of the charge card agreement. Defendant served an answer asserting as an affirmative defense the merchant's failure to issue a credit slip to his Visa account for a returned purchase.

Defendant then commenced a third-party action against Marine Midland Bank for indemnification asserting that because the Cleveland merchant had placed his Master Charge account number on a credit slip that Marine should indemnify.

Plaintiff Lincoln First Bank's motion for summary judgment is grounded in the main on two sections of the Federal Truth in Lending Act dealing with credit billing, viz., 15 U.S.C. §1666 and 15 U.S.C. §1666i.

Plaintiff maintains that section 1666(a) placed an obligation upon defendant to notify plaintiff of the billing problem in writing within 60 days of defendant's receipt of the account statement reflecting the billing error. Counsel for the Bank contends that the only notice plaintiff received was on September 16, 1978 when one of its employees contacted Mrs. Carlson by telephone. The fact that plaintiff received copies of the purchase and credit slips from defendants in a letter postmarked September 17, 1978 is, however, not disputed.

This Court finds that sufficient and timely notice of the situation might be found to have been received by the plaintiff. Viewed in a light most favorable to the defendant, Mr. Carlson's first statement from plaintiff which reflected the billing error was received on July 26, 1978, less than 60 days prior to the September 16th telephone conversation and the September 17th letter. Depending on facts adduced at trial, a trier of fact could well find that the plaintiff waived its requirement of full written notice in only requesting copies of the purchase and credit slips, or that in fact the slips were sufficient written notice.

Moreover, timely notice by defendant, under section 1666(a) required the Bank to take steps, within certain specific time limits, to rectify the billing error. *Neal v. United States*, 402 F.Supp. 678 (D.C.N.J., 1975). If plaintiff is found not to have met such requirements, it forfeits its right to collect $50.00 of any amount owing it by the defendant. 15 U.S.C. §1666(e).

Plaintiff's second ground is based on 15 U.S.C. §1666i which reads in pertinent part, " *** a card issuer who has issued a credit card to a cardholder pursuant to an open end consumer credit plan shall be subject to all claims (other than tort claims) and defenses arising out of any transaction in which the credit card is used as a method of payment or extension of credit if *** (3) the place where the initial transaction occurred was in the same State as the mailing address previously provided by the cardholder or was within 100 miles from such address *** ." The Bank maintains that since Cleveland is out of New York State and more than 100 miles from Jamestown, New York, the defendant is precluded from asserting any defense in the present action.

A review of federal cases indicates that no interpretation of section 1666i has been made to date. To this Court's mind, the statement that a card issuer is subject to all defenses if a transaction occurred less than 100 miles from the cardholder's address, does not automatically presume a cardholder to give up all his defenses should the transaction take place at a distance of greater than 100 miles from the mailing address.

While the line between which defenses may or may not be asserted by a credit cardholder living more than 100 miles from the place of the purchase has not yet been clearly drawn, it would seem that the cardholder can clearly assert a defense which arose due to an alleged failure of the card issuer itself to comply with the statutory requirements of 15 U.S.C. §1666 to correct an obvious billing error.

While it may be found that plaintiff was in fact not culpable in failing to correct the error in light of the date it received defendant's notification and the time limits for response contained in 15 U.S.C. §1666, this is a factual question for a trier of fact to determine.

As for the companion motion made by the third-party defendant, Marine, to dismiss the third-party complaint against it upon the ground it does not state a cause of action, it is granted. There is claim on the part of the defendant Carlson that Marine had received the credit from the merchant on defendant's Master Charge account and denied him its use.

It is set forth on behalf of Marine that in June, 1979 about one year after defendant had received the improperly issued credit slip and after the bankruptcy of Constantine Gems, he did contact Marine "about a possible credit to this Master Charge". Marine did not credit defendant's account because defendant's Master Charge account was never charged for the purchase for which he sought a credit, no check was received by Marine from the merchant for the purchase for which a credit was sought, the 120 day period in which to charge back to a merchant the amount of a credit slip issued by the merchant but not processed against the cardholder's account had expired, and Marine's voluntary attempt on behalf of defendant to collect the amount of the returned Visa purchase from the merchant had been unsuccessful.

Defendant does not state a cause of action in his third-party action. There is no claim that Marine received any benefit from the credit slip issued by the merchant nor is there any claim of negligence or intentional tortious conduct on the part of Marine. Even if there was one, the facts alleged could not support such a claim. Marine was not under any duty to credit a Master Charge cardholder's account for the amount of returned goods purchased on a Visa charge account with another bank as Master Charge account slips are not negotiable instruments. *See* UCC §3-104. Furthermore, defendant does not allege a breach of any contractual obligation by Marine. *See Lupinski v. Village of Ilion*, 59 A.D.2d 1050, 399 N.Y.S.2d 956; *Cohn v. Lionel Corp.*, 21 N.Y.2d 559, 289 N.Y.S.2d 404, 236 N.E.2d 634.

Plaintiff's motion for summary judgment is denied. Defendant's third-party action against Marine Midland Bank is dismissed.

Banks' Right of Charge Back in Bank Card System

Schorr v. Bank Of New York

New York Appellate Division Court, 1983
458 N.Y.S.2d 244

Niehoff, Justice. This case, which is here by leave of this court, originated in the City Court of the City of White Plains. In his opinion, the City Court Judge wrote that the case, which concerns itself with the sum of $761.25, "involves a question of law which goes to the heart of the credit card operation and appears to be one of first impression in this State." It was because of the importance of the question presented that this court determined to grant leave.

There is no dispute as to the facts. The plaintiff, who owns and operates a transmission repair shop, performed certain work on a customer's car. The customer paid for the work by use of his credit card and the car was released to him by the repair shop.

On February 8, 1980 the plaintiff deposited the credit card sales slip, signed by the customer in the amount of $761.25, into a checking account which he maintained with the defendant, The Bank of New York. Thereafter, on March 29, 1980, the customer executed a form entitled "CARDHOLDER DISPUTE" provided by Marine Midland Bank, at which he maintained his Master Charge account. On that form the customer stated that he had paid the plaintiff for certain automotive repair work using his Master Charge card, that the car was never repaired, that he was disputing the entire charge, and that such charge came to $765. Eventually, through banking procedures, the customer's action came to the defendant bank's attention. As a consequence, on April 15, 1980, the defendant debited plaintiff's account in the sum of $761.25. The bank's action was taken pursuant to a written agreement which it had with the plaintiff entitled "CHARGE PLAN MERCHANT AGREEMENT". Insofar as pertinent, paragraph 10 of the agreement reads as follows:

> On demand Merchant [plaintiff] will pay to BNY [defendant Bank of New York] the amount paid or credited for, and will indemnify BNY against all liability, loss claims and demands whatsoever arising in connection with "unqualified Sales Slips," i.e., Sales Slips and the transactions evidenced thereby *** in connection with which *** there is any dispute or defense (whether or not valid) between Merchant and Cardholder *** BNY may charge any Unqualified Sales Slip to the Merchant and offset the amount of any Unqualified Sales Slip against the net proceeds due to Merchant from other Sales Slips deposited with BNY and BNY is authorized to debit Merchant's account for the amount thereof.

Insofar as pertinent paragraph 13 of the agreement states:

> Merchant waives notice of default or non-payment, protest or notice of protest, demand for payment and any other demand or notice in connection with any Credit Sale, Sales Slips, Credit Memo or this Agreement.

In the present action by the plaintiff repair shop owner to recover the $761.25 debited against his account, it is not disputed that the aforesaid agreement with the bank permitted it to make the charge back. However the plaintiff's argument before the City Court was that the agreement was invalid and unenforceable and he continues to press that contention on this appeal.

By a decision dated November 14, 1980, 107 Misc.2d 132, 433 N.Y.S.2d 546, the City Court granted the plaintiff's motion for summary judgment stating, in part:

> The issue *** narrows down to the validity of the agreement between plaintiff and defendant. There is no doubt that the agreement itself permitted the defendant to make the deduction which it did. The agreement before the Court contained no time limit at all within which the bank will honor a cardholder dispute claim, even from a cardholder whose card was issued by another bank. This is not merely a case of a depositor waiving certain notices and demands but results in the depositor having no security or finality in his account for an infinite period of time.
>
> The Court, therefore, holds that the agreement is unreasonable and unenforceable and grants the plaintiff's motion for summary judgment.

On July 9, 1981, 112 Misc.2d 684, 449 N.Y.S.2d 824, the Appellate Term for the 9th and 10th Judicial Districts unanimously reversed the order and judgment (one paper) entered upon the foregoing decision, stating in relevant part:

> The charge card agreement between plaintiff merchant and defendant bank provided that in the event of a dispute between the merchant and a customer who paid by credit card, the bank could debit the merchant's account for the amount involved. Given federal regulations permitting a card holder to withhold payment to the card issuing bank for the amount in controversy to the extent of the credit extended (see 12 CFR 226.13) this part of the agreement cannot be deemed unconscionable. Nor does the lack of a time limit for taking such action nullify the agreement, since a reasonable time will be implied (see *City of New York, v. New York Central RR Co.*, 275 N.Y. 287 [9 N.E.2d 931]). The defendant debited plaintiff's account less than three weeks after the date of the form in which the customer notified the issuing bank of the existence of the controversy. This time period should not be deemed unreasonable. Since no issue of fact exists and since, even on appeal, summary judgment may be awarded the nonmoving party, judgment should be entered in favor of defendant (see *Wiseman v. Knaus*, 24 A.D.2d 869 [264 N.Y.S.2d 331]; Siegel, Practice Commentaries, McKinney's Cons. Laws of N.Y., Book 7B, CPLR 3212:23, p. 443).

We affirm the order of the Appellate Term.

In arguing for a reversal of the order of the Appellate Term, the plaintiff contends that the mere notification by Marine Midland Bank, that one of its credit card customers had disputed a charge transaction, furnished no basis for the unilateral action on the part of the defendant depository bank to charge back the deposit credited to his checking account almost two months earlier, and that an effective investigation of the matter should have been made by the defendant depository bank before taking that action.

The difficulty with such argument is that it is obvious that the agreement between the plaintiff, as depositor, and defendant, as the depository bank, was designed to absolve the latter from any responsibility for investigating or determining the validity of a customer's complaint. Since both the card issuing bank and the depository bank are merely acting as financial intermediaries between the primary parties to the transaction, the cardholder and the merchant, the banks involved have no way of knowing the legal rights as between the parties. Therefore, it is not at all surprising that the depository bank should procure an agreement from the merchant allowing that bank to step away from the situation and permit the real parties to the controversy, the merchant and the customer, to battle it out themselves. In short, it is the defendant bank's position that this is not its war and that it should not be faulted for refusing to fight in it.

***

It is true, as plaintiff asserts, that in debiting his account for the sum of $761.25, the defendant acted "unilaterally". But, the bilateral written agreement of the parties authorized that very action by the defendant and we are unable to perceive anything wrongful in the conduct of the defendant, which simply exercised the rights given to it under the agreement.

Plaintiff also complains of the fact that he accepted the customer's credit card charge in full payment for his services, relying upon the expectation of payment from the defendant, that he thereby surrendered his "possessory lien", which by law was his guaranty of payment, and that at this late date he cannot regain that security. That may well be, but that is a risk the merchant assumes when he determines to engage in credit card transactions.

Manifestly, the plaintiff's remedy in this dispute is an action against the customer whose credit card payment he accepted, and not against the defendant bank which merely processed the credit card sales slip. The fact that some credit charges are not collected because of a dispute between the customer and the merchant, and are eventually charged back to the merchant's account by the bank, is a normal contingency of many commercial sales transactions in which methods of payment other than cash are accepted. Certainly, neither the card issuing bank nor the depository bank should suffer any loss as the result of a dispute between the merchant and the customer.

Accordingly, we hold that so much of the agreement as authorizes the charge back cannot be characterized as unconscionable.

Although it is true that the agreement places no time limitation on the defendant bank's right to debit the plaintiff merchant's account, it does not follow that the agreement is thereby rendered invalid. The absence of a time limitation is due to the fact that the Federal statutes and regulations contain no time limitation within which the customer is required to dispute the charge and the bank has no way of knowing when the customer will exercise his or her right to claim that the merchant's goods or services were defective. However, it is reasonable to presume that the consumer will assert his right to withhold payment to the card issuing bank when he receives his bill containing the charge in question. This, of course, will, in turn, depend on when the merchant deposits the charge slip. That step is likely to be taken quite promptly after the credit card transaction occurs. Thus, it would seem that the dispute, the raising of the defense of defective goods or services, and the ultimate charging back to the merchant can be expected to occur within reasonable time limits.

In the case at bar, the bank debited the plaintiff's account less than three weeks after the date that the customer signed the form notifying the issuing bank of the existence of a controversy. As the Appellate Term said, "[t]his time period should not be deemed unreasonable."

For the reasons stated above, we hold that the provision of paragraph 10 of the agreement authorizing the defendant to debit plaintiff's account in the circumstances at bar is valid and that summary judgment was properly granted in favor of the defendant bank. Accordingly, the order of the Appellate Term should be affirmed.

Upon appeal by permission, order of the Appellate Term of the Supreme Court, 9th and 10th Judicial Districts, dated July 9, 1981, affirmed, with $50 costs and disbursements.

In Re Standard Financial Management Corp.

Bankruptcy Court of Massachusetts, 1988
94 B.R. 231

Harold Lavien, Bankruptcy Judge. The debtor, Standard Financial Management Company, d/b/a New England Rare Coin Galleries (NERCG) sold rare coins through its store as well as over the telephone. Payments for the rare coins were made by cash, check, credit cards or wire transfers. On February 13, 1987, the Federal District Court of Massachusetts, at a hearing on the complaint of the Federal Trade Commission, appointed Joseph Ryan special counsel to take possession of NERCG's assets and authorized him to file a Chapter 11, which he did on the same day and at the same time, substantially, closed down the business operation.

The Bank of New England (BNE) processed the credit card, VISA and Master Charge, transactions of NERCG pursuant to two contracts, one pertaining to VISA and one pertaining to Master Charge. The contracts were signed by representatives of NERCG and BNE on June 27, 1983 and renewed on March 21, 1985.

The BNE provided other financial services to NERCG, including a revolving loan, lease equipment financing, depository and checking. At the commencement of the case, February 13, 1986, the NERCG maintained a balance of $179,948.47 including $109,894.32 in a segregated payroll account. BNE turned over the funds to NERCG on February 26, 1987 pursuant to a written stipulation that provided BNE did not prejudice it's right to later assert any lien, pledge, right or interest against the $179,948.47.

In 1985, customers charged back 24 times, for a total of $22,546.24. In 1986, customers charged back 25 times, for a total of $35,095.00. In the first quarter of 1987, during which, on February 13th, NERCG closed and the Chapter 11 was filed, customers charged back 9 times, for a total of $7,390.00. Over the next two quarters of 1987 post-filing in the Chapter 11, customers sought to charge back 62 times, for a total of $114,743.00. The total post-petition charge backs over the first three quarters of 1987 was $115,168.00 representing 63 transactions. BNE seeks to recover $115,168.00 in post-petition chargebacks and an additional $5,100.06 in bank service fees from the $179,948.47 that NERCG had on deposit with BNE on the date the case was commenced.

While the evidence was skimpy, BNE has introduced unrebutted evidence that NERCG solicited the credit card sales through telemarketing over the telephone, that were later charged back. In the absence of contrary evidence, the Court so finds.

The Court has held two hearings, reviewed eight memoranda of close to 200 pages, plus copious attachments, not counting a further unconsidered memorandum submitted by special counsel beyond the briefing schedule. It would appear that each side is literally trying to convince the Court by the sheer weight of their arguments.

BNE's claims rest on the provisions of the VISA and Master Charge standard form agreements which, in turn, refer to the terms and conditions set forth in other documents including the respective Operating Rules. The bank's position is that the express terms of the contracts gives it a secured position[*] in the funds of the debtor if, in fact, they are really funds of the debtor and

---

[*] Visa Merchant Agreement, P 3.4: 1. Security Interest: Merchant hereby grants to Bank a security interest in any deposits or other sums at any time credited by or due from Bank to Merchant security for any and all obligations of Merchant to Bank arising out of the terms of this Agreement or otherwise, whether direct or indirect, absolute or contingent, due or to become due, now existing or hereafter arising or acquired. Master Charge Merchant Agreement P III(e): (e) Merchant hereby grants to Bank a security interest in any deposits, balance of deposits or other sums at any time credited by or due from Bank to Merchant as security for any and all obligations of Merchant to Bank arising out of the terms of this Agreement, whether direct or indirect, absolute or contingent, due or to become due, now existing or hereafter arising or acquired.

not merely provisional credits subject to being canceled until the expiration of the charge back period.*

***

BNE relies on provisions in the VISA Operating Rules and Master Charge Rules and Regulations while Special Counsel relies on the Truth in Lending Laws, to delineate when a customer may chargeback, 15 U.S.C. §1601 *et seq. In re Twenty-Four Hour Nautilus Swim and Fitness Center, Inc.*, 81 B.R. 71 (D.Colo.1987). The former allows the customer to cancel a charge in 120 to 180 days, while the latter requires a written report and has stricter provisions including 100 mile and 60-day limitation. BNE contends that the TILA does not apply since it is limited to the relationship between the card user and its issuing bank and not the merchant. Further, it is argued, the debtor in the contracts agreed to be bound by the Operating Rules. Finally, BNE states that Congress did not provide a maximum protection for the consumer but, rather, a minimum which the Operating Rules improve.

Special Counsel argues that the VISA Operating Rules and Master Charge Rules and Regulations cannot apply to NERCG because NERCG did not and could not, after trying, have known that it was obligated to provide these additional protections.

The *Twenty-Four Hour Nautilus Swim and Fitness Center, Inc.* decision is not applicable because of the unique circumstances of this case. The Master Charge agreement provides that credit card holders can charge back from a card accepting merchant pursuant to the "Operating Guide" given to merchants who use Master Charge or VISA. The VISA card agreement does state that chargebacks are governed by VISA Operating Regulations; however, BNE only gives the merchants the Operating Guide for guidance. Section 11 of the "Operating Guide", which governs chargebacks, only discusses chargebacks that result from the merchant's failure to properly submit credit slips. Significantly, no mention is made that consumers are entitled to chargeback, or the time or under which conditions this can be done or, for that matter, if anything other than the merchant's normal business practices governed. The end of Section 11 does tell the merchant to refer to Master Charge Rules and Regulations and VISA Operating Rules, available upon request, for further information on chargebacks. This is not enough to put the merchant on notice that chargebacks may be allowed for reasons other than technical flaws in the credit slip or the merchant's normal business practices.

NERCG did attempt to obtain further information on the basis of credit card transactions. Mr. Richard Fried, chief financial officer of NERCG, sometime in 1985 or early 1986, wanted to program NERCG computers to transact credit card sales and to keep track of daily balances. He wanted information respecting the NERCG--BNE credit card relationship. After failing to find the

---

* VISA Merchant Agreement P 3.3: 1. Chargebacks: VISA's Operating Regulations govern presentment of sales drafts by Bank and chargebacks of sales drafts by card-issuing banks to Bank, and Bank shall have the right to collect from Merchant or to charge back directly to Merchant or Merchant's account with Bank the full amount of any sales draft which is in violation of this Agreement, which Bank is unable to present pursuant to the Operating Regulations or which is rejected or charged back to Bank by NEBA or by a card-issuing bank pursuant to the Operating Regulations or any Instructions. Master Charge Merchant Agreement P III(b): (b) If Merchant is a Multiple Location Merchant, it shall present each sales slip and credit slip to Bank within the time period (not to exceed 30 calendar days) prescribed by NEBA for Merchant's class of Multiple Location Merchant. If Merchant is not a Multiple Location Merchant, it shall present each sales slip and credit slip to Bank within three (3) Bank business days following the Effective Date of the slip. Bank shall pay Merchant for sales slips not later than the next Bank business day following the day of deposit. Payment may be effected by cash, Bank check or credit to Merchant's account with Bank. All figures submitted by Merchant to Bank are subject to final checking and audit by Bank and Bank may debit or credit deficiencies or overages to Merchant's account with Bank. Bank may also debit Merchant's account for all amounts due Bank by reason of any charge-back, breach of warranty or other obligation of Merchant to Bank hereunder.

relevant documentation within NERCG, Mr. Fried spoke to various people in BNE and was told that no material was available. Finally, he convinced one bank employee, on the condition he return the materials directly to her, to send him some dog eared papers. There is no evidence of exactly what those papers contained and Mr. Fried testified that they were of minimal assistance. In fact, when produced as evidence, the thick volume of the VISA Operating Rules had a caption in it's front cover that states:

> NOTICE: The information furnished herein by Visa is CONFIDENTIAL and is distributed to Visa Members for their exclusive use in operating their Visa sponsored programs, and shall not be duplicated, published or disclosed in whole or in part without the prior written permission of Visa. Only banks and related entities can be members of VISA.*** Alfred M. Tringali, an assistant vice president of BNE who supervised the provision of credit card services to NERCG, stated that the BNE does not let merchants look at the VISA Operating Rules because it contains confidential information that could be used to forge credit cards. BNE seeks to obligate merchants to regulations that it gives no notice of, does not supply upon request, and pursues a specific policy to keep the regulations confidential. In fact, the direct testimony of Mr. Tringali was that the information the merchant needed to understand the basis of chargebacks was summarized in the guide which, as previously indicated, had no information on customer chargebacks. No one testified on behalf of the bank that the charge back processes were explained orally to debtor.

To find a contract provision invalid because it is unconscionable "... involves determining whether there was an 'absence of meaningful choice on the part of one of the parties together with contract terms which are unreasonably favorable to the other party." *Zapatha v. Dairy Mart, Inc.*, 381 Mass. 284, 293, fn. 13, 408 N.E.2d 1370 (1980), *citing Williams v. Walker Thomas Furniture Co.*, 350 F.2d 445, 449 (D.C.Cir 1965). BNE's failure to give any notice of the chargeback policy deprived NERCG of any choice and the expansion of BNE security interests undeniably favors BNE and created hidden and potentially serious liability to the debtor, especially when reference is simply included in this pre-printed standard form multi-paragraph contract. There was nothing in the previous minimal chargebacks of the debtor to alert it to the undisclosed charge back provision; there was no meeting of the minds on those terms which can control the relationship of the parties. Incidentally, there was no evidence offered by the bank that these charge back terms were even brought to the attention of credit card holders.

BNE, nonetheless, claims the debtor should be held liable because NERCG breached its duty of good faith. *Rand-Whitney Packaging Corp. v. Robertson Group*, 651 F.Supp. 520 (D.Mass.1986). BNE makes the allegation, with exhibits not admitted in the trial, that NERCG fraudulently used credit cards, which is a criminal offense. 15 U.S.C. §1644. In addition, BNE states that NERCG submitted its credit slips later than the seven days provided under TILA. 15 U.S.C. §1666e; 12 C.F.R. §226.12(e). On the basis of these assertions, BNE would have the Court find NERCG has unclean hands and cannot contest the BNE right to collect. There is no need for the Court to abrogate all of the debtor's rights for BNE to be made whole. BNE can recover the amounts that NERCG fraudulently charged pursuant to its security interest as a valid chargeback and may even have a criminal remedy under 15 U.S.C. §1644. The failure of NERCG to timely deposit the return slips has no real importance. BNE suffered no harm because of the delay. The slips were submitted in early February. The first post petition chargeback did not occur until March. BNE had full notice of returns when consumers charged back post petition. Furthermore, the Court has determined that the bank is entitled to charge back regardless of the issuance of credit memos, so that no harm is suffered by the bank.

Since there was no consensual agreement between the card holder, the banks, and the merchant in this case, the right of the merchant's bank to chargeback against the merchant for some claim initiated by the card holder must be based on some other controlling law other than the unrevealed VISA and Master Charge Regulations. In this case, Congress has addressed the problem in the TILA.

While it is not explicit that the TILA applies to the merchant who is not the traditional consumer, the application between the card holder and the issuing bank of necessity sets of a train of events.[*] If the card holder has a right to charge back against the issuing bank, then that bank has a right against the merchant's bank who has a right against the merchant. It follows that conversely if the card holder has no right for a chargeback against the issuing bank, there is nothing to charge back against the merchant's bank or the merchant..

TILA grants eligible credit card holders the right to chargeback purchases if the holder (1) objects in writing to the charge, 15 U.S.C. §1666; (2) the holder objects within 60 days of receiving the statement listing the charge, 15 U.S.C. §1666i; (3) initial transaction took place within 100 miles or the same state as the customer, 15 U.S.C. §1666i, or (4) the use of the credit card was unauthorized, 15 U.S.C. §1643. The credit card customer cannot recover amounts already paid, 15 U.S.C. §1666i(b). The credit card holder who complies with the requirements of TILA can chargeback a purchase if the credit card holder can present a bona fide defense to payment. *** 15 U.S.C. §1666i; *Izraelewitz v. Manufacturers Hanover Trust Co.*, 120 Misc.2d 125, 465 N.Y.S.2d 486 (1983).

The claimed chargebacks fall into several categories which provide a convenient format for analysis. First, the merchant is not liable for a chargeback unless the card holder files a written objection, 15 U.S.C. §1666(a); *Himelfarb v. American Express Company*, 301 Md. 698, 484 A.2d 1013 (1984); *Contra Lincoln First Bank v. Carlson*, 103 Misc.2d 467, 426 N.Y.S.2d 433 (1980). Companies in bankruptcy especially need written objections to be able to review the basis of chargebacks. Chargebacks which are questionable may be borne by companies outside of bankruptcy as a cost of business, but they cannot automatically be allowed in bankruptcy because they deplete the estate from which honest creditors will receive a pro rata share and frustrate the equitable distribution of assets to all creditors which is the essence of the bankruptcy process. Credit card holders failed to give written notice of $19,615 of the chargebacks.

Second, the customer cannot recover if he lives more than 100 miles or a different state from the address that the initial transaction took place. 15 U.S.C. §1666i(b)(3). "The question of where a transaction occurs (as in case of mail or telephone orders, for example) is to be determined by state or other applicable law." *Izraelewitz v. Manufacturers Hanover Trust Company*, 120 Misc.2d 125, 465 N.Y.S.2d 486 (1983), citing, Federal Reserve Board Official Staff Commentary on 12 C.F.R. §226.12(c)(3)(iii), 12 C.F.R. §266 Supplement I (1988).***

Special Counsel argues that the NERCG mailing an acknowledgement to credit card customers is the last material act of the contract and so the transaction should be considered taking place in Boston and cites, in support, *Roto-Lith Ltd. v. F.O. Bartlett & Co.*, 297 F.2d 497 (1st Cir.1962). This case is not applicable since it involves the question of which form should prevail when the buyer and seller have exchanged many forms.

BNE argues that the transaction should be considered to take place in the customer's house. In answer to BNE's counsel, the representatives of the debtor said that orders for coins were solicited by telemarketing which, of course, means the debtor's sales personnel offered to sell coins to customers contacted by telephone who accepted the offer by providing their charge card information. Special Counsel offered no evidence that the orders subject to chargebacks were

---

[*]   TILA, itself, does reach and directly regulate at least part of the relationship between the merchant and the merchant's bank. The merchant is required to submit credit statements for forgiveness of credit card debt within seven days of the credit being allowed. 15 U.S.C. section 1666(e); 12 C.F.R. section 226.12(e)

obtained in any different manner. While there is no Massachusetts case on point, the overwhelming majority of cases considering this issue have found that when a contact is made on the telephone, the transaction takes place where the person utters his acceptance.***

Courts in New York have twice considered the question of under what conditions the geographic limitations apply. In its first decision, the state court found that if the card issuer violated TILA, then the credit card holder can assert that violation of TILA to refuse to pay even if the card holder lives more than 100 miles or lives in another state from the initial transaction. *Lincoln First Bank v. Carlson*, 103 Misc.2d 467, 426 N.Y.S.2d 433 (1980).

In its second decision, the Court found that geographic limitations precluded a credit card customer in New York disputing a telephone order he made to a merchant in Hawaii, *Izraelewitz v. Manufacturers Hanover Trust Company*, 120 Misc.2d 125, 465 N.Y.S.2d 486 (1983). The case is not applicable for two reasons. The court did not consider the legal significance of a telephone order. More importantly, in *Izraelewitz*, the merchant uttered his acceptance of the offer in Hawaii while the credit card customer, in this case, uttered his acceptance of the offer in the comfort of his own home.

Social policy favors finding that the transaction took place in the customer's home. TILA, it is true, intended to limit the liability of merchants to far away customers who might fraudulently chargeback a purchase, secure in the knowledge that the company will not sue because the sum is usually too minor. In this case, however, the seller came into the customer's house by calling the customer. The seller, by soliciting the sale in distant regions, implicitly states that doing business in those areas is not too minor for the seller to take whatever action it needs to protect its rights. Conversely, the customer who is solicited at home has a reasonable expectation that future contacts can likewise be adjusted at or near his home. The Court finds the transaction took place at the customer's home and, therefore, does not find under the facts of this case that the 100 mile limitation applies.

Third, TILA limits the amount of the possible chargeback to the amount of the bill not yet paid. 15 U.S.C. §166i(b). This provision makes TILA compatible with equity and the bankruptcy process. On one hand, the estate retains any assets, such as payment, it has as of the date the case was commenced. On the other hand, the customer is not made to pay the remainder of the outstanding amount, post-petition, on the contract unless the seller fully performs. As for the failed performance, the buyer has a claim. This result is both equitable and comports with bankruptcy's goal of treating all creditors of the same class equally. A customer who paid for a coin, pre-filing, and then had a dispute with the merchant, post-filing, would not be able to recover 100 cents on the dollar but would simply have an unsecured claim against the bankruptcy estate. This is different from the unpaid credit card bill because of the still conditional nature of the credit, both between the card holder, the issuing bank, and the merchant and its bank. At any rate, this distinction was considered important by Congress and is made explicit in the TILA, 15 U.S.C. §1666i(b). Thus, the $4,100 of these chargebacks of already paid charges are not allowed. They are in addition to and not included within the excluded chargebacks over 60 days.

Fourth, the credit card consumer is limited to 60 days from after he receives a bill to charge back a purchase, 15 U.S.C. §1666i; *Pinner v. Schmidt*, 805 F.2d 1258, 1264 (8th Cir.1986); *Gray v. American Express Company*, 743 F.2d 10, 14 (D.C.Cir.1984). It is agreed that chargebacks for $52,240 were more than 60 days after the receipt of their bills and, therefore, are improper chargebacks.***

Fifth, chargebacks for unauthorized use of credit cards are clearly appropriate.

Sixth, Special Counsel makes a contention that the bank cannot charge back where the debtor had previously issued a credit to the customer. That sounds appealing on the surface but does not fly. The issuing bank would have to credit the card holder and then seek reimbursement from the merchant bank who, in turn, would charge back the merchant. That right is no more effected by bankruptcy than any other TILA claim made post-filing by the card holder against the issuing bank when the merchant's bank has both a security interest in undisbursed credits and a charge back right. The bank may need to secure relief from automatic stay to exercise its right but its ultimate right is not diminished.

BNE claims it can charge back for coins returned both pre and post-petition. Nothing in TILA or in the agreement between the bank and merchant authorizes a credit card holder to unilaterally return merchandise and obtain a chargeback. That transaction is controlled by the merchant's own policy. The buyer where, here, the merchant does not recognize a right of return, simply has an unsecured claim. *Izraelewitz v. Manufacturers Hanover Trust Company*, 120 Misc.2d 125, 465 N.Y.S.2d 486 (1983). A chargeback for returns of $4,975.00, the amount not subsumed, is not appropriate.

Thus, BNE charged back $63,315 which represents the net total of chargebacks from people who either charged back after paying the bill, or those who claimed a chargeback after 60 days of the receipt of the bill, or those who unilaterally sought to return coins. The appropriate chargeback would be $115,168 less $63,315 or $51,853 plus bank fees of $5,070.06, a total of $56,923.06.

practice

Case 1

Jon Krahulik traveled the world as a successful attorney. On a visit to Thailand, Jon's VISA card was stolen from him by a thief. A few hours later the thief used Jon's card to purchase a $4,000 Rolex watch.

a. Is Jon liable for the purchase? If so, to what extent?

b. Would it matter if the VISA card Jon used was his law firm's credit card? That is, the card had been issued by Jon's law firm and was only to be used for law firm business.

c. Suppose that instead of a thief stealing Jon's credit card, he had delivered the card to one Liz Cumming for her use in Thailand. In doing so, Jon instructed Liz to purchase some rare jade for his trip back to the United States. As he expressly noted, he did not want Liz to spend more than $4,000 on the purchase of a necklace and earrings. Liz, however, proceeded to her Uncle's shop and promptly charged $46,000 on the credit card for jade valued at a little over $1,000. What is the extent of Jon's liability? What if Jon had notified the issuing bank that Liz could only charge up to $4,000 on the card?

Case 2

"In June 1983, defendant was in St. Thomas Hospital, Akron, Ohio. While she was hospitalized, Anita Zavodny, a friend of the defendant, telephoned her and explained that she needed to get to Cleveland and asked defendant if she could use defendant's Sohio credit card (the "card") to purchase one tank of gas for the trip. Defendant thought that it would be impossible for Zavodny to use the card without defendant being present to sign, but that a gas station in Mogadore where defendant was known would honor the card because the attendants knew both defendant and Zavodny. Defendant gave Zavodny the card and permission to use it to buy one tank of gasoline for the trip. No arrangements were made for the return of the card. Zavodny sent a third party, a woman unknown to defendant, to pick up the card. Defendant turned over the card without further discussion on June 28, 1983.

"Zavodny used the card for many purchases in addition to the gasoline. Other unknown parties also charged items on the card subsequent to June 28, 1983. Defendant notified plaintiff that her card was being misused on August 12, 1983.

"Plaintiff seeks to recover all charges made by use of the card occurring between June 28, 1983, and August 12, 1983," contending that the use of the card between June 28, 1983 and August 12, 1983 was authorized rather than unauthorized use. *Standard Oil Co. v. Steele,* 489 N.E.2d 842 (Ohio Mun. Ct. 1985).

Will plaintiff prevail here?

Case 3

"Plaintiff furnished his VISA card and personal identification number to Riley, his brother's girlfriend, two or three times in February and March, 1983. Plaintiff did so to enable Riley to obtain cash from defendant's automatic teller in order to make purchases on plaintiff's behalf. Each time, Riley did what plaintiff requested her to do and then returned the card to him, along with the teller receipt and the change that plaintiff had coming. In April, Riley moved into the house that plaintiff shared with his brother. On three occasions thereafter, she stole plaintiff's card from his wallet, used it to obtain money for her own use from defendant's machines and then put the card back into plaintiff's wallet.

"The money that Riley obtained through use of the card after she moved into plaintiff's house is the subject of this action. Defendant acknowledges that that use of the card was "without [plaintiff's] knowledge or approval." Defendant has procedures whereby a person who has reason to believe that someone is using his card without authorization can telephone and "block" the transaction or obtain a new identification number for activating the automatic teller. Plaintiff did not avail himself of those procedures. He was not aware of Riley's defalcation until defendant notified him that his account was overdrawn." *Vaughn v. United States National Bank,* 718 P.2d 769 (Ore. Ct. App..1986).

Who is likely to prevail in this instance?

Case 4

"Plaintiff [Blaisdell Lumber Company, Inc.] brought this action in April 1989 to recover payment for purchases made at its hardware store with defendant Karen Horton's American Express (AMEX) credit card in June and July 1987. Defendant alleged that her former male friend, Daniel Calvin, made the purchases without her permission or authority. She said that he was never permitted to use her AMEX card but stole it from her.

"Bruce Blaisdell, vice-president of Blaisdell Lumber Company of Red Bank, testified that seven transactions, resulting in AMEX credit card charges totalling $925.25, were made at his store from June 18 to July 18, 1987. He handled the first transaction personally on June 18. He was the only witness for plaintiff. He said that during the June 18 transaction Calvin signed only his name on the two charge slips for that date after "a woman" handed the credit card to Calvin. Only Karen Horton's name and signature appeared on the credit card itself. Blaisdell did not ask the woman either to sign the charge slips or to identify herself. At trial Blaisdell could not identify defendant Horton as the woman with Calvin on the day of the first purchase. The other six purchases were made by Calvin from other clerks in the hardware store on separate dates continuing through July 18, 1987. There was no proof offered at trial concerning the circumstances surrounding those purchases other than the credit card slips also signed by Calvin only in his own name.

"Blaisdell said that in August 1987 American Express refused to reimburse Blaisdell Lumber because Horton had "denied the signature" in early August by notifying AMEX that it was not her signature on the card slips. Blaisdell then telephoned Horton. He claimed that she said that the signature was not valid, that she had never reported her card stolen, and that "the bill" was Daniel Calvin's. Blaisdell testified that Horton also said that Calvin was out but that he would return soon and call him, suggesting to Blaisdell that the two were still living together. At the close of plaintiff's case, the defendant's motion to dismiss for failure to prove agency was denied.

"Karen Horton then testified. She said that she had first met Daniel Calvin around Christmas 1986. He had moved into her apartment in Long Branch in January 1987. She testified that their "romance" abruptly ended in early March 1987 when Calvin stole her car, changed the bill of sale to his name, and drove off to Mississippi. At that time, on March 4, 1987, Horton signed a complaint in the Long Branch Municipal Court alleging that Calvin had stolen her car, a gasoline credit card, a brief case, and had obtained $4,000 from her by misrepresentation.

"Calvin soon returned to Horton's New Jersey apartment and continued living there, although not on the same friendly and "romantic" terms as before. On August 11, 1987 Calvin pled guilty in the Long Branch Municipal Court to the offenses involving the March thefts. He was fined, received a suspended sentence and was ordered to make restitution.

"Horton testified that in August 1987 she was at a gas station and realized that she could not pay for her gas as she was unable to find her AMEX card in her wallet. The attendant who knew Horton then told her that he had seen Calvin with the credit card that morning. Horton said that she immediately called AMEX and reported her card missing. She did not know for how long it had been gone. She said that a Ms. Douglas of AMEX's fraud control department told her and confirmed in writing that the balance due was $5,496 of which only $218 was Horton's legitimate charges. See Evid.R. 2(2). An AMEX memo to Horton, dated August 13, 1987, placed in evidence, corroborates Horton's testimony regarding her conversation with Douglas. Horton said that she then signed a criminal complaint against Calvin based on the AMEX fraud.

"Horton said she previously had hidden her credit cards in a metal box in her bedroom. After Calvin stole her car and her gas credit card in March, she began carrying her credit cards on her person in her wallet. She denied ever dealing with or going to Blaisdell Lumber. She denied any benefit from or receipt of the hardware items purchased from plaintiff. All of the Blaisdell charges (eight slips in all) were signed by Calvin in his name only.

"Judgment was entered for plaintiff." *Blaisdell Lumber Company, Inc. v. Horton*, 575 A.2d 1386 (Sup. Ct. N.J. 1990).

How is the case likely to be disposed of on appeal?

Case 5

Tom Osteraas was a star law student and class favorite. Upon graduation, he began work at the law firm of Kramer and Kramer, a famous firm headed by Denise Kramer. On a business trip to Washington D.C. Tom decided to take one of the firm's most prestigious clients to dinner. Following dinner, Tom presented his MasterCard for payment. MasterCard, however, refused to honor the card because of an outstanding billing dispute it had with Tom. Tom had discussed the dispute over the phone with MasterCard but had received nothing in writing from them regarding the matter.

Is MasterCard liable under any statute for its behavior? What is the potential extent of its liability?

Case 6

Tracy Palmer bought an expensive stereo at a store near her house using her VISA credit card. When she arrived at home with the stereo and plugged it in, it failed to operate properly. The store refuses to refund Tracy's money because they maintain she broke the stereo while assembling it.

a. **Can Tracy refuse to pay the issuer of her credit card?**

b. **What if Tracy had purchased the stereo while on a vacation in another state?**

c. **What if Tracy had purchased a set of headphones for $25 from her neighborhood store instead of an expensive stereo system?**

Case 7

"The plaintiff received a postcard from Holiday Magic Travel Club, Inc. (herein "Holiday") of Miami, Florida, stating that he had been selected to receive a pre-paid luxury cruise plus hotel accommodations. The plaintiff called "Holiday" on December 19, 1986 and received details of the vacation offer and "Holiday's" money back guarantee, as well as assurances of the company's good standing, including bank references.

"The plaintiff obtained membership in "Holiday's" discount travel club via telephone by giving the number of his European American Bank (herein "EAB") mastercard to a representative of 'Holiday'" He paid $249.00 by credit card. 'Holiday' thereafter sent membership materials to the plaintiff, who decided that he did not want to obtain membership in the club. The plaintiff requested a refund from "Holiday," but received no reply. Apparently, plaintiff was lured into a scam, and recovery of the $249.00 from "Holiday" appears to be impossible since "Holiday" cannot be located.

"Plaintiff had purchased the membership over the telephone on December 19, 1986. The defendant claims that plaintiff received a statement reflecting his purchase on January 3, 1987. The plaintiff contends that the credit statements received on January 3, 1987 and April 3, 1987, did not contain the $249.00 purchase. Plaintiff concedes that he did not notify the defendant of the requested billing correction until April 25, 1987. The Court notes that neither the plaintiff nor defendant submitted into evidence a copy of the EAB credit statements sent to plaintiff on January 3, 1987 and on April 3, 1987." *Plutchok v. European American Bank*, 540 N.Y.S.2d 135 (N.Y. Dist. Ct. 1989).

Who is likely to prevail in this instance?

Chapter 9. Commercial And Consumer Electronic Funds Transfers

The swift and certain transfer of payments is vital to the wheels of commerce in a modern society. Historically, checks have been the device used to effectuate payment. The speed of check collection, however, has reached its limits because of the check's physical characteristics. Accordingly, checks have been supplanted by a new payment device: the electronic funds transfer. An electronic funds transfer, most basically, is any transfer of money not made in cash or other legal tender or by written instrument. Today, the greatest dollar volume of commercial obligations is satisfied through the use of this electronic means of payment.

While Article 4 of the U.C.C. governs the collection of checks and other "items," 4-104(1)(g), two other principal statutes govern electronic funds transfers. The Electronic Funds Transfer Act of 1978 (EFTA), 15 U.S.C. §§1693-1693r (1988 & Supp. III 1991), governs point of sales transactions such as credit and debit card purchases and consumer funds transfers. Article 4A of the U.C.C., in turn, covers wholesale wire transfers. This chapter explores the scope and coverage of each of these provisions, their operation and the manner in which relevant loss allocation issues are handled.

§ 1. Wholesale Funds Transfers

story

A wholesale funds transfer is characterized as a transfer of funds electronically between two banks or a business and financial institution. In a simple case, a bank will make the transfer on behalf of a customer, usually a business, to the account of another business at the same or another bank. Suppose, for example, that Addie Adams wishes to purchase $5,000,000 in veterinarian equipment from Pooch Pound Inc. To pay for her purchase, Addie (the Originating Sender, see

4A-103(a)(5)) wishes to transfer funds from her account at First Federal Bank (the Receiving Bank, see 4A-103(a)(4)) to the account Pooch Pound (the Beneficiary, see 4A-103(a)(2)) has at its bank, CitiCenter Bank (the Beneficiary Bank, see 4A-103(a)(3)). To accomplish this transfer, Originating Sender would issue a payment order (defined in 4A-103(a)(1) as "an instruction of a sender to a receiving bank, transmitted orally, electronically, or in writing, to pay, or to cause another bank to pay, a fixed or determinable amount of money to a beneficiary") to Receiving Bank to transfer $5,000,000 to Beneficiary. Receiving Bank would then debit Originating Sender's account and accept the payment order by transmitting by Fedwire a new payment order (the actual funds are not transferred) to Beneficiary Bank to credit Beneficiary's account in the amount of $5,000,000. On the same day, Beneficiary Bank would accept the payment order and credit the Beneficiary's account. The obligations of the banks would then be settled by appropriate debits and credits in their Federal Reserve accounts.

While checks and credit cards are the most common form of payment as measured by the number of transactions per day, wholesale wire transfers far exceed all other payment systems as measured by dollar volume on a daily basis. Each wholesale wire transfer usually exceeds six figures and payments over the two principal wire transfer services--Fedwire and Clearing House Interbank Payment System (CHIPS)--exceed over $1 trillion per day.

Fedwire and CHIPS are both wire transfer networks through which a payment order from one bank may be transmitted to another bank to which the order is addressed. Fedwire is operated by the Federal Reserve System and is an automated network composed of thirteen switches: one switch is located in each of the twelve Federal Reserve Banks and one switch is located in the Board of Governors Office in Washington D.C. Transfers made by Fedwire are governed by Federal Reserve Regulation J. 12 C.F.R. §210 (1993). In a typical Fedwire transfer, Bank A (with an account at the Chicago Federal Reserve Bank) wants to pay Bank B (with an account at the New York Federal Reserve Bank). Bank A will send a payment order to Chicago Federal Reserve Bank which will then debit Bank A's account and credit the account of the New York Federal Reserve Bank. The Chicago Federal Reserve Bank will then issue an instruction to the New York Federal Reserve Bank to credit the account of Bank B and debit the account of the Chicago Federal Reserve Bank. The New York Federal Reserve Bank will then advise Bank B of the credit. If Addie is the originator and Pooch Pound is the beneficiary, then Fedwire will not only transfer the requested amount from Bank A to Bank B but will also simultaneously instruct Bank B to pay the requisite amount to Pooch Pound's account.

In contrast to Fedwire, CHIPS is privately owned by twelve New York banks that constitute the New York Clearing House. Transfers over CHIPS are governed by the CHIPS rules.

Although CHIPS processes some domestic funds transfers, its main purpose is to process international transfers between its members that act as intermediaries for foreign banking organizations [that] have a corresponding relationship. Unlike Fedwire, a transfer through CHIPS is not a present transfer of funds. In a CHIPS transaction, the sending bank will send its payment message to the receiving bank sometime during the banking day. The receiving bank will usually accept the order immediately, *** but payment by the sending bank is not then made until the end of the banking day, when settlement is effected through the Federal Reserve System. As a result, the receipt of the payment message does not guarantee that the receiving bank will receive actual funds. *** Because large dollar amounts are involved, if the sending bank suspends payments before settling its liabilities at the end of the day, the financial stability of receiving banks may be jeopardized. [To protect against such situations, in 1990 CHIPS adopted a loss sharing plan pursuant to] which CHIPS participants must provide funds necessary to complete settlements for participants unable to meet their obligations.

[Transfers can also be made] through an automated clearinghouse (ACH) transaction. [In an ACH transaction,] an originator instructs her bank to pay a beneficiary at a specific bank. The originator's instruction is [then] carried to the originator's bank together with instructions to pay any other beneficiaries at other banks. All of these instructions are contained either on a magnetic tape or in an electronic device. An ACH then accomplishes these transfers by processing and repackaging the originator's instructions to a particular beneficiary's bank together with instructions from other originators to the same bank so that they can be transmitted together to that bank. ACHs are operated by the Federal Reserve banks and by other associations of banks.

Thomas Crandall, Michael Herbert & Lary Lawrence, 3 UNIFORM COMMERCIAL CODE §20.2 at 20:12 - 20:13 (1993) (footnotes omitted).

While Article 4A of the U.C.C. governs funds transfers of the type engaged in by Addie and the Pooch Pound, it specifically does not apply to a funds transfer *any part of which* is governed by EFTA. 4A-108. The emphasized language of 4A-108 is crucial. A corporate dividend payment, for example, may begin with a payment order (usually in the form of a magnetic tape) from a corporation to its bank. The tape will sometimes be processed by an ACH, which could result in transactions by one or more other banks. Ultimately, the account of the beneficiary, who could be a natural person, is credited. If the beneficiary is a natural person who has "established [the account] primarily for personal, family or household purposes," 15 U.S.C. §1693a(2), then the ACH transfer will not be governed by Article 4A. Rather, EFTA would apply in this instance. The reason is that a "part" of the overall transaction--the beneficiary's payment by the beneficiary bank--is governed by EFTA. Of course, if another dividend payment on the same magnetic tape is for a corporate shareholder, then that transfer will be governed by Article 4A because no consumer account is affected.

Rights and obligations under Article 4A arise as a result of "acceptance" of a payment order by the bank to which the order is addressed. 4A-209. In the case of a payment order sent to a receiving bank *other than* the beneficiary's bank, acceptance occurs when the receiving bank "executes" the payment order of the sender by sending a payment order to some other bank intended to carry out the payment order received by the receiving bank. 4A-209(a); 4A-301(a). In the case of a payment order sent to the *beneficiary's bank*, acceptance usually occurs when the bank receives payment of the sender's payment order or when the bank pays the beneficiary or notifies the beneficiary of receipt of the payment order. 4A-209(b)(1) and (2). When a payment order is accepted, the sender of the order must pay the amount of the order to the receiving bank. 4A-402(b) and (c). If the beneficiary's bank accepts a payment order, that bank must pay the amount of the order to the beneficiary. 4A-404(a). Acceptance by the beneficiary bank also means that the funds transfer has been completed; when acceptance occurs, payment by the originator of the funds transfer to the beneficiary occurs. 4A-406(a). Thus, under Article 4A, if a funds transfer is made to pay an obligation, the obligation is paid by the originator at the time the beneficiary bank incurs an obligation to pay the beneficiary and in the amount of the payment order accepted by the bank. 4A-406(b). See generally Ballen & Diana, Duties of the Beneficiary Bank, 45 Bus. Law. 1467 (1990). Importantly, Article 4A imposes a duty on a beneficiary bank promptly to pay the beneficiary; breach of this duty may subject the beneficiary's bank to liability for consequential damages in the appropriate circumstances. 4A-404(a).

If, by contrast, a bank other than the beneficiary's bank accepts a payment order, the obligations and liabilities are owed to the originator of the funds transfer. 4A-209 comment 1; 4A-302(a)(1). The primary obligation of the receiving bank is to issue a payment order to the beneficiary's bank on the execution date that complies with the sender's order. 4A-302(a)(1). The "execution date" of a payment order is the day on which the receiving bank properly may issue a payment order executing the sender's order and refers to the time that the payment order should be executed rather than the day that it is actually executed. 4A-301(b). The sender by its instruction may set an execution date, but the date cannot be earlier than the day the order is received by the receiving bank. Id. If no payment date or execution date is set, the order usually is intended to be executed immediately. 4A-301 Comment 2. In this instance, the execution date is the date the order is received. Id. Significantly, absent an express written agreement to the contrary, consequential damages are not available to the originator if the receiving bank delays execution of an order, 4A-305(a), fails to complete an order it has accepted, 4A-305(b), or fails to execute a payment order it was obligated to execute under an express agreement with the originator or sender. 4A-305(d). Of course, if a receiving bank fails to fulfill its obligations concerning acceptance, it may be liable for damages as provided in the agreement or in 4A-305.

The payment order is Article 4A's equivalent of a check. See 4A-103(a)(1). In a large percentage of cases, the payment order of the originator of the funds transfer is transmitted electronically to the originator's bank. An important issue addressed in 4A-202 and 4A-203 is how the risk of loss from unauthorized payment orders is to be allocated. Suppose, for example, that a thief, Farmer D. Linares, manages to obtain Addie's payment order code and issues an unauthorized payment order, see 4A-202(a), to Receiving Bank and the funds are ultimately transferred from Addie's account at Receiving Bank to Farmer's account in Beneficiary Bank. To what extent is Addie liable?

First, the analysis depends upon whether Sender and Receiving Bank have agreed in advance that the authenticity of a payment order issued in Sender's name is to be verified by a commercially reasonable "security procedure." See 4A-201, which defines "security procedure," and 4A-202(c) which provides a test for commercial reasonableness. If such a security procedure is agreed, the unauthorized payment order is "effective" if the "bank proves that it accepted the payment order in good faith and in compliance with the security procedure and any written agreement or instruction of the customer restricting acceptance of payment order issued in the name of the customer." 4A-202(b).

Second, if the payment order is unauthorized but "effective" under 4A-202(b), it still may be "unenforceable" against the purported Sender if the conditions of 4A-203(a) are satisfied. Read those conditions carefully. Note that 4A-203(a)(2) tracks the concept of a "responsible" employee employed in 3-405. Receiving Bank cannot enforce the unauthorized but effective payment order unless an "entrusted" person caused the order or access to key transmission facilities were obtained from a "source controlled" by the customer. Thus, the person who denies enforcement to the payment order must be an outsider or a brilliant computer "hacker" who is able to pierce the security procedure.

Third, if the unauthorized payment order is neither "effective" under 4A-202 nor "enforceable" under 4A-203, the "bank shall refund any payment of the payment order received from the customer to the extent the bank is not entitled to enforce payment and shall pay interest on the refundable amount calculated from the date the bank received payment to the date of the refund." 4A-204(a). This rule applies where the parties have not agreed in advance to a commercially reasonable security procedure. In short, in the absence of the agreed security procedure, the loss from an unauthorized payment order is treated like a forged check under Article 4--it is left to be borne by the Receiving Bank.

law

Banque Worms v. Bankamerica International
Court of Appeals of New York, 1991
77 N.Y.2d 362, 570 N.E.2d 189, 568 N.Y.S.2d 541

Alexander, Judge. On April 10, 1989, Security Pacific International Bank (Security Pacific), a Federally chartered banking corporation with offices in New York City, mistakenly wired $1,974,267.97 on behalf of Spedley Securities (Spedley), an Australian corporation, into the account of Banque Worms, a French Bank, maintained with BankAmerica International (BankAmerica), another Federally chartered bank with New York offices. Initially intending to make payment on its debt to Banque Worms under a revolving credit agreement, Spedley instructed Security Pacific, which routinely effected wire transfers for Spedley, to electronically transfer funds from Security Pacific to Banque Worms' account at BankAmerica.

A few hours after directing this wire transfer, Spedley, by a second telex, directed Security Pacific to stop payment to Banque Worms and to make payment instead to National Westminster Bank USA (Natwest USA) for the same amount. At the time Security Pacific received the telexes, Spedley had a credit balance of only $84,500 in its account at Security Pacific, but later that morning, Security Pacific received additional funds sufficient to cover the transaction and then began to execute the transaction. However, in mistaken disregard of Spedley's second telex canceling the wire transfer to Banque Worms, Security Pacific transferred the funds into Banque Worms' account at BankAmerica. The funds were credited to the account after Banque Worms was notified through the Clearing House Interbank Payment System (CHIPS) that the funds had been received. That afternoon, Security Pacific executed Spedley's second payment order and transferred $1,974,267.97 to Natwest USA. Spedley's account at Security Pacific was debited twice to record both wire transfers thus producing an overdraft.

Meanwhile, at Security Pacific's request made prior to the transfer to Natwest USA, BankAmerica agreed to return the funds mistakenly transferred, provided Security Pacific furnished a United States Council on International Banking, Inc. (CIB) indemnity. The indemnity was furnished and the funds returned to Security Pacific on the following day. Banque Worms, however, refused BankAmerica's request that it consent to its account being debited to reflect the return of the funds. Consequently BankAmerica called upon Security Pacific to perform pursuant to the CIB indemnity and return the funds. Security Pacific's attempt to obtain funds from Spedley to cover this indemnity was unavailing because by that time, Spedley had entered into involuntary liquidation.

Banque Worms brought suit against BankAmerica in the United States District Court for the Southern District of New York seeking to compel BankAmerica to recredit $1,974,267.97 to Banque Worms' account. BankAmerica instituted a third-party action against Security Pacific for return of the funds, and Security Pacific counterclaimed against Banque Worms seeking a declaration that neither Banque Worms nor BankAmerica were entitled to the $1,974,267.97. Eventually, for reasons not here pertinent, Security Pacific returned the funds to BankAmerica, BankAmerica recredited Banque Worms' account and was voluntarily dismissed from the case leaving only Banque Worms and Security Pacific as the sole contestants seeking entitlement to the $1,974,267.97.

On their respective motion and cross motion for summary judgment, the District Court, applying the "discharge for value" rule, granted judgment for Banque Worms. Security Pacific appealed to the United States Court of Appeals for the Second Circuit, arguing that New York neither recognized nor applied the "discharge for value" rule in situations such as this; that the controlling rule under New York law was the "mistake of fact" rule pursuant to which, in order to be entitled to retain the mistakenly transferred funds, Banque Worms was required to demonstrate detrimental reliance. The case is before us upon a certified question from the Second Circuit (see, section 500.17 of the Court of Appeals Rules of Practice [22 NYCRR]) inquiring "[w]hether in this case, where a concededly mistaken wire transfer by [Security Pacific] was made to [Banque Worms], a creditor of Spedley, New York would apply the 'Discharge for Value' rule as set forth at section 14 of the Restatement of Restitution or, in the alternative, whether in this case New York would apply the rule that holds that money paid under a mistake may be recovered, unless the payment has caused such a change in the position of the receiving party that it would be unjust to require the party to refund."

For the reasons that follow, we conclude that, under the circumstances of this case, the "discharge for value" rule should be applied, thus entitling Banque Worms to retain the funds mistakenly transferred without the necessity of demonstrating detrimental reliance.

I

A

In the area of restitution, New York has long recognized the rule that "if A pays money to B upon the erroneous assumption of the former that he is indebted to the latter, an action may be maintained for its recovery. The reason for the rule is obvious. Since A was mistaken in the assumption that he was indebted to B, the latter is not entitled to retain the money acquired by the mistake of the former, even though the mistake is the result of negligence." (Ball v. Shepard, 202 N.Y. 247, 253, 95 N.E. 719.) This rule has been applied where the cause of action has been denominated as one for money had and received (Parsa v. State of New York, 64 N.Y.2d 143, 148, 485 N.Y.S.2d 27, 474 N.E.2d 235), for unjust enrichment or restitution (Paramount Film Distrib. Corp. v. State of New York, 30 N.Y.2d 415, 421, 334 N.Y.S.2d 388, 285 N.E.2d 695), or upon a theory of quasi contract (Miller v. Schloss, 218 N.Y. 400, 113 N.E. 337). Where, however, the receiving party has changed its position to its detriment in reliance upon the mistake so that requiring that it refund the money paid would be "unfair," recovery has been denied (Paramount Film Distrib. Corp. v. State of New York, supra, 30 N.Y.2d at 422, 334 N.Y.S.2d 388, 285 N.E.2d 695; Ball v. Shepard, supra, 202 N.Y. at 254, 95 N.E. 719).

This rule has evolved into the "mistake of fact" doctrine, in which detrimental reliance is a requisite factor, and which provides that "money paid under a mistake of fact may be recovered back, however negligent the party paying may have been in making the mistake, unless the payment has caused such a change in the position of the other party that it would be unjust to require him to refund." (National Bank v. National Mechanics' Banking Assn., 55 N.Y. 211, 213; see also, Hathaway v. County of Delaware, 185 N.Y. 368, 78 N.E. 153; Mayer v. Mayor of City of N.Y., 63 N.Y. 455, 457 ["general rule that money paid under a mistake of material fact may be recovered back * * * is subject to the qualification that the payment cannot be recalled when the position of the party receiving it has been changed in consequence of the payment, and it would be inequitable to allow a recovery."].)

The Restatement of Restitution, on the other hand, has established the "discharge for value" rule which provides that "[a] creditor of another or one having a lien on another's property who has received from a third person any benefit in discharge of the debt or lien, is under no duty to make restitution therefor, although the discharge was given by mistake of the transferor as to his interests or duties, if the transferee made no misrepresentation and did not have notice of the transferor's mistake" (Restatement of Restitution §14 [1]).

The question as to which of these divergent rules New York will apply to electronic fund transfers divides the parties and prompts the certified question from the Second Circuit. Security Pacific argues that New York has rejected the "discharge for value" rule and has required that detrimental reliance under the "mistake of fact" rule be demonstrated in all cases other than where the mistake was induced by fraud. Banque Worms, on the other hand, invokes the "discharge for value" rule, arguing that because it is a creditor of Spedley and had no knowledge that the wire transfer was erroneous, it is entitled to keep the funds. It points out, as indicated by the official comment to section 14(1) of the Restatement of Restitution, that the "discharge for value" rule is simply a "specific application of the underlying principle of bona fide purchase" set forth in section 13 of the Restatement (Restatement of Restitution §14, comment a).

Banque Worms cites to various decisions of New York courts in support of its contention that New York has adopted and applied the "discharge for value" rule (see, e.g., Ball v. Shepard, 202 N.Y. 247, 95 N.E. 719, supra; Consolidated Natl. Bank v. First Natl. Bank, 199 N.Y. 516, 92 N.E. 1081, affg. 129 App.Div. 538, 114 N.Y.S. 308; Oddie v. National City Bank, 45 N.Y. 735). Indeed, both parties rely to a significant degree upon Ball v. Shepard in support of their respective positions. Security Pacific relies upon the Court's observation in the first of two classes of cases discussed, that "the mistake of fact is usually one which arises inter partes, and in order to justify recovery in any such case it must appear that the defendant was not, in the first instance, entitled to receive the money; and that his circumstances have not been so changed through its receipt as to render it unjust to compel him to refund." (202 N.Y. at 256, 95 N.E. 719 [emphasis added].) Banque Worms, on the other hand, refers to the same discussion but relies upon the Court's description of the second class where "the mistake of the payor is usually superinduced by the fraud of a third person and the payee is not only ignorant of the fraud or mistake, but receives the money in good faith in the regular course of business and for valuable consideration." (Id. [emphasis added].)

Indeed one may find, as does Banque Worms, language in a myriad of cases that arguably lends support to the proposition that New York, long ago, embraced the "discharge for value" rule (see, e.g., Carlisle v. Norris, 215 N.Y. 400, 415, 109 N.E. 564 ["If defendants received the proceeds in good faith and without any notice of any wrong and credited them on an indebtedness due them, plaintiff is not entitled to recover them back."]; White v. Continental Natl. Bank, 64 N.Y. 316 [right of a party paying money to another to recover it from one who is not entitled to receive it, is well established]; Smith & McCrorken v. Chatham Phenix Natl. Bank & Trust Co., 239 App.Div. 318, 320, 267 N.Y.S. 153 ["where a bank honors and pays a check under a mistake of fact, it may sue for recovery of the money, at least, against one receiving payment thereon, who is not a bona fide holder for value."]; see also, New York Tit. & Mtge. Co. v. Title Guar. & Trust Co., 206 App.Div. 490, 201 N.Y.S. 529, affd. 237 N.Y. 626, 143 N.E. 769; State Farm Mut. Auto. Ins. Co. v. Stokos, 65 Misc.2d 316, 317 N.Y.S.2d 706; see generally, 44 NY Jur. Payment, §107).

On the other hand, cases can also be cited where the language employed supports the contrary view--that New York not only eschews the "discharge for value" rule, as Security Pacific argues, but also embraces exclusively the detrimental reliance rule-mistake of fact doctrine (see, e.g., Hathaway v. County of Delaware, 185 N.Y. 368, 78 N.E. 153, supra; Mayer v. Mayor of City of N.Y., 63 N.Y. 455, supra; National Bank v. National Mechanics' Banking Assn., 55 N.Y. 211, supra; Citibank v. Warner, 113 Misc.2d 748, 449 N.Y.S.2d 822). These cases for the most part, however, present issues involving more traditional aspects of mistake and restitution, and do not satisfactorily address the unique problems presented by electronic funds transfer technology.

While courts have attempted in wire transfer cases to employ, by analogy, the rules of the more traditional areas of law, such as contract law, the law of negotiable instruments and the special relations between banks, these areas are governed by principles codified in articles 3 and 4 of the Uniform Commercial Code. Various commentators found these efforts ineffective and inadequate to deal with the problems presented (see, Official Comment to UCC 4A-102; Revisions of UCC Article 4A Postponed Due to Federal Preemption, ABA is Told, 51 Banking Rep. 282 [BNA] [Aug. 15, 1988]). As pointed out by the Official Comment to article 4A, "attempts to define rights and obligations in funds transfers by general principles or by analogy to rights and obligations in negotiable instruments law or the law of check collection have not been satisfactory" (Official Comment to UCC 4A-102, 2A ULA [Master ed.], 1990 Supp.Pamph.; see also, Revisions of UCC Article 4A Postponed Due to Federal Preemption, ABA is Told, 51 Banking Rep. 282 [BNA] [Aug. 15, 1988]). Consequently, it was concluded, as the Prefatory Note to the new article 4A of the UCC approved by the National Conference of Commissioners on Uniform State Law and the American Law Institute observes, that a new article was needed because "[t]here is no comprehensive body of law that defines the rights and obligations that arise from wire transfers." (2A ULA [Master ed.], at 143, 1990 Supp.Pamph.)

B

Electronic funds transfers have become the preferred method utilized by businesses and financial institutions to effect payments and transfers of a substantial volume of funds. These transfers, commonly referred to as wholesale wire transfers, * * * differ from other payment methods in a number of significant respects, a fact which accounts in large measure for their popularity. Funds are moved faster and more efficiently than by traditional payment instruments, such as checks. The transfers are completed at a relatively low cost, which does not vary widely depending on the amount of the transfer, because the price charged reflects primarily the cost of the mechanical aspects of the funds transfer (Prefatory Note to UCC art. 4A). Most transfers are completed within one day and can cost as little as $10 to carry out a multimillion dollar transaction (see generally, Farley, Article 4A: Funds Transfers, NYS 7720-A, NYA 10431-A; Prefatory Note to UCC art. 4A). The popularity of wholesale wire transfers is evidenced by the fact that nearly $1 trillion in transactions occur each day, averaging $5 million per transfer and on peak days, this figure often approaches $2 trillion (see generally, Ring, Wholesale Funds Transfers: New Article 4A to the UCC, NYA 10431-A, NYS 7720-A).

Wholesale wire transfers are generally made over the two principal wire payment systems: the Federal Reserve Wire Transfer Network (Fedwire) and the CHIPS. * * * The CHIPS network handles 95% of the international transfers made in dollars, transferring an average of $750 billion per day (see generally, Note, Liability for Lost or Stolen Funds in Cases of Name and Number Discrepancies in Wire Transfers: Analysis of the Approaches Taken in the United States and Internationally, 22 Cornell Intl.L.J. 91 [1990]). These funds are transferred through participating banks located in New York because all of the banks belonging to the CHIPS network must maintain a regulated presence in New York. As a result, this State is considered the national and international center for wholesale wire transfers.

The low cost of electronic funds transfers is an important factor in the system's popularity and this is so even though banks executing wire transfers often risk significant liability as a result of losses occasioned by mistakes and errors, the most common of which involve the payment of funds to the wrong beneficiary or in an incorrect amount (see, American Law Institute Approves UCC Article Governing Wire Transfers, 52 Banking Rep. 1150 [BNA] [June 5, 1989]). Thus, a major policy issue facing the drafters of UCC article 4A was determining how the risk of loss might best be allocated, while preserving a unique price structure. In order to prevent or minimize losses, the industry had adopted and employed various security procedures designed to prevent losses * * * such as the use of codes, identifying words or numbers, call-back procedures and limits on payment amounts or beneficiaries that may be paid.

As indicated above, it was the consensus among various commentators that existing rules of law did not adequately address the problems presented by these wholesale electronic funds transfers. Thus, the National Conference of Commissioners on Uniform State Laws (NCCUSL) and the American Law Institute (ALI) undertook to develop a body of unique principles of law that would address every aspect of the electronic funds transfer process and define the rights and liabilities of all parties involved in such transfers (Prefatory Note to UCC art. 4A, op. cit.). After extensive investigation and debate and through a number of drafts, in 1989, both the NCCUSL and the ALI approved a new article 4A of the Uniform Commercial Code (see generally, Ballen, Baxter, Davenport, Rougeau, and Veltri, Commercial Paper, Bank Deposits and Collections, and Other Payment Systems, 45 Bus.Law 2341 [Aug. 1990]). In 1990, the New York State Legislature adopted the new article 4A and incorporated it into the New York Uniform Commercial Code (N.Y. UCC art. 4-A). * * * Although the new statute, which became effective January 1, 1991, may not be applied retroactively to resolve the issues presented by this litigation, the statute's legislative history and the history of article 4A of the Uniform Commercial Code from which it is derived and the policy considerations addressed by this legislation, can appropriately inform our decision and serve as persuasive authority in aid of the resolution of the issue presented in this case (see, Matter of Pell v. Coveney, 37 N.Y.2d 494, 373 N.Y.S.2d 860, 336 N.E.2d 421; Matter of Albano v. Kirby, 36 N.Y.2d 526, 369 N.Y.S.2d 655, 330 N.E.2d 615; MVAIC v. Eisenberg, 18 N.Y.2d 1, 271 N.Y.S.2d 641, 218 N.E.2d 524; see also, Shawmut Worcester County Bank v. First Am. Bank & Trust, 731 F.Supp. 57 [D Mass 1990]).

II

Both the NCCUSL and ALI drafters of article 4A and the New York Legislature sought to achieve a number of important policy goals through enactment of this article. National uniformity in the treatment of electronic funds transfers is an important goal, as are speed, efficiency, certainty (i.e., to enable participants in fund transfers to have better understanding of their rights and liabilities), and finality. Establishing finality in electronic fund wire transactions was considered a singularly important policy goal (American Law Institute Approves UCC Article Governing Wire Transfers, 52 Banking Rep. 1150 [BNA] [June 5, 1989]). Payments made by electronic funds transfers in compliance with the provisions of article 4A are to be the equivalent of cash payments, irrevocable except to the extent provided for in article 4A (see, Assn of Bar of City of NY, Committee on Banking Law, Report on proposed New York UCC art. 4-A; see also, Delbrueck & Co. v. Manufacturers Hanover Trust Co., 609 F.2d 1047, 1049-1051 [2d Cir.] [once an electronic fund transfer is completed and the funds released, the transaction is final and irrevocable under the CHIPS system]).

This concern for finality in business transactions has long been a significant policy consideration in this State. In a different but pertinent context, we observed in Hatch v. Fourth Natl. Bank, 147 N.Y. 184, 192, 41 N.E. 403 that "to permit in every case of the payment of a debt an inquiry as to the source from which the debtor derived the money, and a recovery if shown to have been dishonestly acquired, would disorganize all business operations and entail an amount of risk and uncertainty which no enterprise could bear".

A consequence of this concern has been the adoption of a rule which precludes recovery from a third person, who as the result of the mistake of one or both of the parties to an original transaction receives payment by one of them in good faith in the ordinary course of business and for a valuable consideration (see, Ball v. Shepard, 202 N.Y. 247, 95 N.E. 719, supra). This rule is grounded in "considerations of public policy and convenience for the protection and encouragement of trade and commerce by guarding the security and certainty of business transactions, since to hold otherwise would obviously introduce confusion and danger into all commercial dealings" (44 N.Y.Jur., Payment, §107; see also, Southwick v. First Natl. Bank, 84 N.Y. 420). We have previously held that from these considerations, "[t]he law wisely * * * adjudges that the possession of money vests the title in the holder as to third persons dealing with him and receiving it in due course of business and in good faith upon a valid consideration." (Stephens v. Board of Educ., 79 N.Y. 183, 187-188.)

The "discharge for value" rule is consistent with and furthers the policy goal of finality in business transactions and may appropriately be applied in respect to electronic funds transfers. When a beneficiary receives money to which it is entitled and has no knowledge that the money was erroneously wired, the beneficiary should not have to wonder whether it may retain the funds; rather, such a beneficiary should be able to consider the transfer of funds as a final and complete transaction, not subject to revocation.

We believe such an application accords with the legislative intent and furthers the policy considerations underlying article 4-A of the New York Uniform Commercial Code. Although no provision of article 4-A calls, in express terms, for the application of the "discharge for value" rule, the statutory scheme and the language of various pertinent sections, as amplified by the Official Comments to the UCC, support our conclusion that the "discharge for value" rule should be applied in the circumstances here presented.

Subject to certain exceptions not here relevant, N.Y. UCC 4-A-209(2) provides that a beneficiary's bank accepts a payment order when the bank pays the beneficiary by crediting the beneficiary's account and notifying the beneficiary of the right to withdraw the credit (see, UCC 4-A-209[2][a]; 4-A-405[1][i]). When a payment order has been accepted by the beneficiary's bank, cancellation or amendment of that payment order is not effective unless, for example, the order was issued because of a mistake of the sender resulting in a duplicate payment order or an order that directs payment to a beneficiary not entitled to receive the funds (see, UCC 4-A-211[3][b][i], [ii]). Where a duplicate payment order is erroneously executed or the payment order is issued to a beneficiary different from the beneficiary intended by the sender, the receiving bank in either case is entitled to recover the erroneously paid amount from the beneficiary "to the extent allowed by the law governing mistake and restitution" (see, UCC 4-A-303[1], [3]).

More specifically, UCC 4-A-303(3) instructs that "[i]f a receiving bank executes the payment order of the sender by issuing a payment order to a beneficiary different from the beneficiary of the sender's order and the funds transfer is completed on the basis of that error, the sender * * * [is] not obliged to pay the payment order[ ]. The issuer of the erroneous order is entitled to recover from the beneficiary * * * to the extent allowed by the law governing mistake and restitution." The Official Comment to UCC 4A-303 from which the identical New York statute is derived, explains that although section 4A-402(c) obligates the sender to pay the transfer order to the beneficiary's bank if that bank has accepted the payment order, section 4A-303 takes precedence and "states the liability of the sender and the rights of the receiving bank in various cases of erroneous execution" (see, Official Comment to UCC 4A-303, comment 1, 2A ULA [Master ed.], 1990 Supp.Pamph.).

Thus, as in the example discussed in comment 2, where the originator's bank mistakenly directs payment of $2,000,000 to the beneficiary's bank but payment of only $1,000,000 was directed by the originator, the originator's bank is obligated to pay the $2,000,000 if the beneficiary's bank has accepted the payment, although the originator need only pay its bank the $1,000,000 ordered. The originator's bank ordinarily would be entitled to recover the excess payment from the beneficiary. The comment points out, however, that "if Originator owed $2,000,000 to Beneficiary and Beneficiary received the extra $1,000,000 in good faith in discharge of the debt, Beneficiary may be allowed to keep it. In this case Originator's Bank has paid an obligation of Originator and under the law of restitution * * * Originator's Bank would be subrogated to Beneficiary's rights against Originator on the obligation paid by Originator's Bank" (see, Official Comment to UCC 4A-303, comment 2, 2A ULA [Master ed.], 1990 Supp.Pamph.).

A further example discussed in comment 3 of the Official Comment is of a duplicate payment order erroneously made, which transfers a second $1,000,000 payment to beneficiary's bank and beneficiary's bank accepts the payment. Although the originator's bank is only entitled to receive $1,000,000 from the originator, it must pay $2,000,000 to beneficiary's bank and would be relegated to a remedy the same as "that of a receiving bank that executes by issuing an order in an amount greater than the sender's order. It may recover the overpayment from Beneficiary to the extent allowed by the law governing mistake and restitution and in a proper case * * * may have subrogation rights if it is not entitled to recover from Beneficiary" (Official Comment to UCC 4A- 303, comment 3, 2A ULA [Master ed.], 1990 Supp.Pamph.).

Although it seems clear from these provisions of article 4A and the Official Comments that the drafters of UCC article 4A contemplated that the "discharge for value" rule could appropriately be applied in respect to electronic fund transfers, Security Pacific argues that to do so would undermine the low cost structure of wholesale electronic fund transfers and impose extraordinary risks upon banks implementing these enormously large transactions. This argument is unpersuasive. Article 4A contemplates, in the first instance, that a mistake such as occurred here can be effectively held to a minimum through the utilization of "commercially reasonable" security procedures in effecting wire transfers. These security procedures are for the purpose of verifying the authenticity of the order or detecting error in the transmission or content of the payment order or other communication (see, e.g., N.Y. UCC 4-A-201).

For example, under N.Y. UCC 4-A-202(2), if a bank accepts a payment order that purports to be that of its customer after verifying its authenticity through an agreed upon security procedure, the customer is bound to pay the order even if the payment order was not authorized. The customer will be liable, however, only if the court finds that the security procedure was a "commercially reasonable" method of providing security against unauthorized payment orders (id.). If the bank accepts an unauthorized payment order without verifying it in compliance with a security procedure, the loss will fall on the bank. * * *

Other mechanisms for preventing loss are also provided for in the statute. A bank may avoid a loss resulting from the insolvency of a sending bank by accepting the payment order on the condition that it first receives payment from the sending bank (see, N.Y. UCC 4-A-209[2][a][ii]; [c]; 4-A-403 [1][a], [b]; see also, American Law Institute Approves UCC Article Governing Wire Transfers, 52 Banking Rep 1150 [BNA] [June 5, 1989]; Prefatory Note to UCC art. 4A [a receiving bank can always avoid this risk by accepting a payment order after the bank has received payment]). Risk of loss can also be minimized by the institution keeping track of all transactions with a particular bank so that over-all debits and credits can be netted.

Application of the "discharge for value" rule to the circumstances presented here is particularly appropriate. The undisputed facts demonstrate that Security Pacific executed Spedley's initial order directing payment to Banque Worms notwithstanding having already received a cancellation of that order. The District Court also found that the second transfer to Natwest USA was executed despite the fact that Spedley's account did not have sufficient funds to cover this second transfer. Moreover, it appears that, as a creditor of Spedley, Banque Worms was a beneficiary entitled to the funds who made no "misrepresentation and did not have notice of the transferor's mistake."

Accordingly, we conclude, in answer to the certified question, that the "discharge for value" rule as set forth at section 14 of the Restatement of Restitution, should be applied in the circumstances in this case.

Bank Of America National Trust And Savings Association v. Sanati

California State Court of Appeals, Second District, 1992
11 Cal.App.4th 1079, 14 Cal.Rptr.2d 615

Johnson, Associate Justice. * * * In 1963 Hassan and Fatane Sanati were married in Tehran, Iran. They lived in Iran until Mrs. Fatane Sanati moved with their two children to Los Angeles in 1983. Between 1983 and 1987 Mr. Sanati spent nearly half his time living in Los Angeles. In 1987 Mr. Sanati permanently left the United States.

When Mr. Sanati left, he arranged for payments to be made to Mrs. Sanati in Los Angeles. He instructed Bank of America in London to send interest, as it accrued monthly from an account held in his name only, to an account he held jointly at Bank of America with Mrs. Sanati in Tarzana, California. The amount of each interest payment was between $2,000 and $3,000.

On April 30, 1990, Bank of America in London erroneously sent the principal of Mr. Sanati's bank account as well as the accrued interest to the joint Sanati account in Tarzana, California. The amount of the erroneous fund transfer was $203,750. The next day Mrs. Sanati authorized her children to withdraw $200,000 from this account. These funds were then deposited into various bank accounts under Mrs. Sanati's and her children's names.

Bank of America (bank) immediately realized its error and requested reimbursement for the erroneous payment. Mrs. Sanati and her children, Babak and Haleh Sanati (collectively Sanatis or defendants) refused the bank's requests.

In July 1990, the bank filed a complaint against the Sanatis seeking restitution for the amount of the erroneous payment. Eventually Mr. Sanati's bank account in London was re-credited the amount of the principal transferred without his authority and he was dismissed as a defendant in the action. The remaining parties stipulated the funds from the erroneous transfer would be placed in a blocked account at Bank of America pending resolution of the litigation.
* * *

The bank then moved for summary judgment. The trial court denied the bank's motion in order to allow the defendants to depose Mr. Sanati to determine whether he had altered his payment instructions to Bank of America London in this instance. The trial court allowed an additional 90 days continuance for this purpose. When 90 days elapsed and Mr. Sanati had not been deposed, the bank again moved for summary judgment, claiming it was entitled to judgment as a matter of law because the Sanatis had no defense to the bank's claim for restitution.

The trial court granted the bank's motion and this appeal followed.

I. REVIEW OF THE COMMON LAW GOVERNING ERRONEOUS FUND TRANSFERS.

At the time of the fund transfer in this case the law controlling the risks and liabilities of banks, beneficiaries and originators was general common law and equitable principles. Courts often borrowed concepts from Articles 3 and 4 of the Uniform Commercial Code governing commercial paper and negotiable instruments as well. This sometimes resulted in inconsistent decisions and was generally determined to be an unsatisfactory method of allocating risks and responsibilities in these widely used transactions generally involving large sums of money. Ultimately the American Law Institute developed article 4A of the Uniform Commercial Code to specifically deal with fund transfers. * * *   In 1990 the California

Legislature adopted article 4A of the Uniform Commercial Code as division 11 of the California Uniform Commercial Code.

However, as stated, under the law in effect at the time of the fund transfer in this case, the general common law and equitable principles controlled. Under the law as it then existed, the bank was entitled to restitution from the beneficiaries for the amount of the unauthorized transfer despite its negligence under general legal principles of mistake and unjust enrichment. (Rest., Restitution, §59, com. a, p. 232; American Oil Service, Inc. v. Hope Oil Co. (1965) 233 Cal.App.2d 822, 830, 44 Cal.Rptr. 60; Frontier Refining Co. v. Home Bank (1969) 272 Cal.App.2d 630, 634, 77 Cal.Rptr. 641; Aebli v. Board of Education (1944) 62 Cal.App.2d 706, 724- 725, 145 P.2d 601; see also Annot., Recovery by Bank of Money Paid Out to Customer by Mistake (1981) 10 A.L.R.4th 524 §§6-7 and cases collected.)

This rule, however, was subject to certain defenses. The most widely acknowledged defense to a claim for restitution for an erroneous transfer of funds was detrimental reliance by an innocent beneficiary. (Rest., Restitution §142, com. c; 1 Witkin Summary of Cal.Law (9th ed. 1987) Contracts, §94, pp. 124-125; Doyle v. Matheron (1957) 148 Cal.App.2d 521, 522, 306 P.2d 913.)

A less widely acknowledged defense to a claim for restitution was the "discharge for value" rule. (Rest., Restitution, §14.) This defense arises where there is a preexisting liquidated debt or lien owed to the beneficiary by the originator of the payment. If the originator or some third party erroneously gives the beneficiary funds at the originator's request, and the beneficiary in good faith believes the funds have been submitted in full or partial payment of that preexisting debt or lien and is unaware of the originator's or third party's mistake, the originator or third party will not be entitled to seek repayment from the beneficiary of the erroneously submitted funds. (1 Witkin (9th ed. 1987) Contracts, §§94, 100, 102, pp. 124, 129-130.)

The bank contends California courts have not adopted this rule and therefore it should not be applied in this case. A review of the cases, however, indicates to the contrary. For example, the decision in California Pacific Title & Trust Co. v. Bank of America NT & SA (1936) 12 Cal.App.2d 437, 55 P.2d 533 was specifically referred to in the reporter's notes to the Restatement of Restitution section 14 on the "discharge for value" rule as the basis for illustration six of comment (b). (See Rest., Restitution §14, reporter's notes, p. 11.) * * *

Other California cases have invoked the principle without specifically mentioning the "discharge for value" rule. The decision in Montgomery v. Meyerstein (1921) 186 Cal. 459, 199 P. 800 is one such example. In that decision the court held a plaintiff who sought to rescind a land sale contract due to fraud was not entitled to seek restitution from preexisting lienholders whose liens had been satisfied out of the sales proceeds and who were unaware of the fraud. (See also Hilliard v. Bank of America NT & SA (1951) 102 Cal.App.2d 730, 228 P.2d 327.)

Thus, under existing law the bank was entitled to seek restitution for the overpayment to defendants despite its negligence, unless defendants had detrimentally relied on the additional payment without notice of the mistake or unless the defendants had applied in good faith the additional erroneous payment to a preexisting debt or lien owed to them from Mr. Sanati.

II. THE BANK WAS ENTITLED TO JUDGMENT EVEN IF THE STATUTORY PROVISIONS GOVERNING ERRONEOUS FUND TRANSFERS CONTROLLED.

On appeal defendants vigorously argue the trial court erred in applying to a fund transfer case the general common law pertaining to commercial paper and negotiable instruments. They argue the court should have applied Division 11 of the California Uniform Commercial Code which governs the consequences of an erroneous execution of a payment order.

Defendants also suggest that had the court applied the new law, summary judgment would have been inappropriate because there would have been a triable issue of material fact whether defendants believed in good faith the additional erroneous payment was sent in satisfaction or discharge of a preexisting debt or lien from Mr. Sanati.

Defendants' argument fails for two reasons. First, the trial court did not err in failing to apply the new fund transfer provisions of Division 11 of the California Uniform Commercial Code. The Legislature expressly stated that division only applied to fund transfers in which the originator's payment order was transmitted on or after January 1, 1991. (Stats.1990, c. 125, §3.) The payment order in the present case was transmitted in April of 1990. Thus, by its terms the new fund transfer provisions of the California Uniform Commercial Code did not apply to the transfer in this case.

Secondly, even if the new fund transfer provisions were applied to this case, we conclude defendants have failed to create a triable issue of material fact whether Mr. Sanati owed them a preexisting debt or lien even assuming their good faith.

Section 11303 of the California Uniform Commercial Code discusses the effect of an erroneous transfer. That section merely restates existing law governing such errors and provides in pertinent part:

> (a) A receiving bank that (i) executes the payment order of the sender by issuing a payment order in an amount greater than the amount of the sender's order, ... is entitled to payment of the amount of the sender's order.... The bank is entitled to recover from the beneficiary of the erroneous order the excess payment received to the extent allowed by the law governing mistake and restitution.

The comment to the Uniform Commercial Code which was incorporated into the comments in the California Uniform Commercial Code provides examples illustrating how this section should operate. The effect of the comment explicating this section is to expressly adopt the "discharge for value" rule found in section 14 of the Restatement of Restitution.

The relevant comment provides:

> Subsections (a) and (b) deal with cases in which the receiving bank executes by issuing a payment order in the wrong amount. If Originator ordered Originator's Bank to pay $1,000,000 to the account of Beneficiary in Beneficiary's Bank, but Originator's Bank erroneously instructed Beneficiary's Bank to pay $2,000,000 to Beneficiary's account, subsection (a) applies. If Beneficiary's Bank accepts the order of Originator's Bank, Beneficiary's Bank is entitled to receive $2,000,000 from Originator's Bank, but Originator's Bank is entitled to receive only $1,000,000 from Originator. Originator's Bank is entitled to recover the overpayment from Beneficiary to the extent allowed by the law governing mistake and restitution. Originator's Bank would normally have a right to recover the overpayment from Beneficiary, but in unusual cases the law of restitution might allow Beneficiary to keep all or part of the overpayment. For example, if Originator owed $2,000,000 to Beneficiary and Beneficiary received the extra $1,000,000 in good faith in discharge of the debt, Beneficiary may be allowed to keep it. In this case Originator's Bank has paid an obligation of Originator and under the law of restitution, which applies through section 1-103, Originator's Bank would be subrogated to Beneficiary's rights against Originator on the obligation paid by Originator's Bank. * * *

Thus, under this section defendants would be entitled to retain the erroneously sent funds if in good faith they believed the funds were sent to them in satisfaction of or in discharge of a valid preexisting debt or lien.

Toward this end, Fatane Sanati asserted she had a quasi community property interest in Mr. Sanati's London bank account as well as in all other property accumulated during their marriage. In an affidavit offered in opposition to the bank's motion for summary judgment Mrs. Sanati declared:

> "3. I was married to Hassan Sanati, ('husband') ... on September 7, 1963 in Tehran, Iran where we resided until I came to Los Angeles with our two children.
>
> "4. My husband and I lived with our children, also defendants in this action, in Los Angeles since 1983. My husband was travelling in and out of the United States and until November of 1987, he had collectively spent 22 months in California during that period.
>
> "5. During our marriage we accumulated a substantial amount of money and real property, most of which was located in Iran and England.
>
> "6. My husband has always kept all of the bank accounts and most of the real property, wherever situated, in his own name.
>
> "7. Since he left in November, 1987, my children and I have been receiving interest monthly from our bank account in London, England to our account ... at Bank of America, Tarzana branch. The account in London was opened by my husband with funds derived from our bank accounts and real property in Iran.
>
> "8. I had asked my husband on numerous occasions to transfer the London account to me in Los Angeles. Although he had agreed to do so on several occasions he had never done it.
>
> "9. My children and I have been virtual prisoners here and completely at my husband's mercy with regard to financial matters. For the last twenty five years, my husband has always exercised complete control over all of our marital community assets worldwide.
>
> "... "11. In May, 1990, the Bank of America in London transferred the monthly interest and the entire principal of the account to my and my husband's account in Bank of America in Tarzana.
>
> "12. I used some of these funds for the family and I removed the remainder to accounts under my control.
>
> "... "17. Since the London account was transferred to our joint account in California, I have spoken to my husband via telephone. On several occasions, he agreed to keep the transferred money in our joint account under both our names. However, to this date, he has not done so.
>
> "... "19. I have filed a petition for Dissolution of Marriage at the Los Angeles Superior Court on July 2, 1990.... The Summons and Complaint were personally served upon my husband, in Tehran, Iran, by Rosy Shahbodaghi, on September 24, 1990. I have instructed my counsel to enter his default therein...."

Thus, Mrs. Sanati's declaration raises a reasonable inference of a potential quasi community property interest in the funds in the London bank account held in Mr. Sanati's name alone. However, this evidence does not raise a reasonable inference of a preexisting debt or lien at the time of the transfer of the type recognized in those decisions applying the "discharge for value" rule.

For example, in Banque Worms v. Bank America International (S.D.N.Y.1989) 726 F.Supp. 940, aff'd. (2d Cir.1991) 928 F.2d 538, the case upon which defendants primarily rely, the debt was a bank loan. In that case the originator had an outstanding loan for $2,000,000 from Banque Worms. On the day before the erroneous transfer, Banque Worms notified the originator it was calling the loan. The next day Banque Worms received a wire transfer for $2,000,000 from Security Pacific International Bank (SPIB), the originator's bank, and applied it to the originator's outstanding loan balance. Shortly thereafter Banque Worms received a second wire transfer from the originator's bank for $1,974,267.97 which was the amount the originator actually requested to be sent. Because it only had instructions for the latter payment, SPIB could not debit the originator's bank account for the first erroneous payment. Because Banque Worms received the payment in the good faith belief it was in response to their demand for repayment of the loan, the court held SPIB had to suffer the loss for the mistaken payment under the "discharge for value" rule.

Examples in the Restatement of Restitution describing the "discharge for value" rule describe debts that are liquidated, concrete and preexisting, not merely probable and undetermined. (E.g., Rest., Restitution, §14, com. b, illus. 1 [no restitution for proceeds erroneously used to pay existing mortgage on real estate]; illus. 2 [no restitution from city for property taxes paid on property not actually owned]; illus. 3 [no restitution where bank erroneously cashes customer's check given to payee in payment for services rendered]; illus. 4 [no restitution from judgment creditor for execution of judgment of wrong person's property].) No decision we are aware of has applied the discharge for value rule where the debt or lien in question was anything less than an objectively verifiable, preexisting, liquidated obligation. (See Rest., Restitution, (append.) §14 and cases collected.) Indeed, allowing the rule to apply to debts or obligations any less substantial would risk destroying the certainty of the rule and allow the exception to control its application.

Consequently, it does not appear the "discharge for value" rule can be properly invoked in a case such as this where the alleged preexisting debt or lien is at best a probable yet undetermined interest in a portion of the funds in Mr. Sanati's bank account in London.[*]

The defendants do not contend they changed their position to their detriment in reliance on the erroneously transmitted funds. Nor do the defendants' opposition papers raise any other potential defense to the bank's action for restitution. Thus, in the absence of any viable defense, the bank was entitled to restitution from the beneficiaries for the erroneously transmitted funds. We therefore conclude the trial court did not err in finding the bank was entitled to judgment as a matter of law.

The judgment is affirmed. Each side to bear its costs of appeal.

Shawmut Worcester County Bank
v. First American Bank & Trust
United States District Court, District of Massachusetts, 1990
731 F.Supp. 57

Young, District Judge. This action arises out of an error made by the plaintiff, the Shawmut Worcester County Bank ("Shawmut" or "transferor"). As is often the case with bank errors concerning money, restoring the status quo ante is somewhat more complicated

---

[*] This case would raise entirely different issues if, for example, there was a preexisting judgment dividing the parties' marital assets decreeing a sum certain of $200,000 or more in cash to be transferred to Mrs. Sanati as part of the settlement and that this amount was due and owing to her at the time of the erroneous wire transfer. But those are not the facts of this case. In fact, Mrs. Sanati did not file for dissolution of marriage until several months after the erroneous fund transfer.

than the slip that created the problem. In the instant case, Shawmut mistakenly transferred $10,000 from the account of American Optical Corporation, not a party to this action, to First American Bank & Trust in West Palm Beach, Florida ("First American" or "transferee"), purportedly for the benefit of one Fernando Degan ("Degan" or "beneficiary"), also not a party to this action, by means of an Electronic Funds Transfer System known as "Fedwire." Although Degan was the sole named beneficiary of the transfer, the payment order issued from Shawmut to First American also indicated that First American should credit account number 100 205 001 633, an account, it turns out, which is jointly held by Degan and one Joseph Merle. Shawmut discovered its error one hundred six (106) days after the mistaken transfer, credited the account of its customer American Optical the sum of $10,000.65, and asked First American to "reverse" a "previous day's" transfer, i.e., credit Shawmut the amount mistakenly transferred. First American asked Merle, its customer, if he would authorize the "reversal." Merle refused. Accordingly, American told Shawmut it would not reverse the transfer. Merle has already been adjudicated liable to Shawmut for $10,000. Apparently unsatisfied, Shawmut also seeks judgment against First American and its employee Michael Woods ("Woods").

Shawmut asserts claims of conversion against First American (Count I) and Woods (Count III) in handling the transfer. Shawmut also claims that First American is liable to it for breaching a principal-agent relationship (Count V) and for negligence (Count VI). Finally, Shawmut seeks recovery under rights purportedly derived from a federal statute, the Electronic Funds Transfers Act, 15 U.S.C. §1693 (1982) et seq., (Counts VII, VIII, X, and XI), as well as two Massachusetts statutes: Mass.Gen.Laws ch. 93A (the Massachusetts "consumer protection statute") (Count II) and Mass.Gen.Laws ch. 106 (the Massachusetts Uniform Commercial Code) (Counts XIII and XIV). First American and Woods have moved either to dismiss or for summary judgment with respect to all claims.

* * *

Shawmut's claim based on rights allegedly secured by the Electronic Funds Transfer Act, 15 U.S.C. §1693 (1982) ("Transfer Act") is also without merit. Although the statute does indicate that a subsidiary purpose of the Transfer Act is to "provide a basic framework establishing the rights, liabilities and responsibilities of participants in [electronic funds transfer] systems," the Transfer Act was primarily created for the especial benefit of consumers. 15 U.S.C. §1693(b). The Transfer Act evidently is aimed at providing a framework of law regulating the rights of consumers as against financial institutions in electronic funds transfers. The Transfer Act contains civil remedies only for consumers, with "consumers" being statutorily defined as "natural persons." 15 U.S.C. §1693a(5).

This dispute is between two financial institutions and there is no evidence before the Court, even after ample discovery, that First American "directly or indirectly holds an account belonging to a consumer" that conceivably might create the kind of financial institution and consumer relationship between First American and Shawmut that the Act regulates. See 15 U.S.C. §1693a (8). In the absence of such evidence, it is evident that this sort of funds transfer--a garden-variety wire transfer between financial institutions-- is specifically excepted from Transfer Act coverage by the provisions of section 1693a(6)(B). See Bradford Trust Co. v. Texas-American Bank-Houston, 790 F.2d 407 (5th Cir.1986) (Transfer Act does not apply to a wire of funds from an account held by a Boston bank to a Houston bank for the benefit of a Houston bank customer). Therefore, summary judgment must now be entered for Woods and First American on counts VII, VIII, X, and XII which allege a cause of action under the Transfer Act.

The counts that rest on the application of Massachusetts statutory law to this interbank dispute must also be dismissed. The provisions of the Massachusetts Consumer Protection Act, as amended, Mass.Gen.Laws ch. 93A, §11 (1989), preclude application of that

Massachusetts statute to this dispute, since the transaction constituting the alleged unfair or deceptive act or practice--First American's refusal to act on Shawmut's belated "reversal" request--occurred in Florida. * * * Since the conduct complained of did not occur "primarily and substantially within the Commonwealth [of Massachusetts]," this action cannot be maintained under Mass.Gen.Laws ch. 93A. The Massachusetts version of the Uniform Commercial Code has no application in the premises since Mass.Gen.Laws ch. 106, §4-102(2) specifically states that "[t]he liability of a bank for action or non-action with respect to any item handled by it for purposes of presentment, payment or collection is governed by the law of the place where the bank is located." First American, the bank whose liability for action or non-action is at issue here, is located in Florida. Therefore, if electronic funds transfers are governed by the Uniform Commercial Code, the law of Florida and the Florida Commercial Code, Fla.Stat. chapters 671-673 (1966), applies. The Circuits that have considered the matter have uniformly concluded that the Uniform Commercial Code does not apply to Electronic Funds Transfers, except perhaps by analogy. See Delbrueck & Co. v. Manufacturers Hanover Trust Co., 609 F.2d 1047 (2d Cir.1979), Evra Corp. v. Swiss Bank Corp., 673 F.2d 951 (7th Cir.1982), Bradford Trust, 790 F.2d at 409. An electronic funds transfer is not within Article 3 of the Uniform Commercial Code because it is not a signed negotiable instrument. See Fla.Stat. secs. 673.3-102(1)(e); 673.3-104; 673.3-401; Mass.Gen.Laws ch. 106, secs. 3-102(1)(e); 3-104; 3-401. Although the language of Article 4 could be stretched to include electronic funds transfers, they were surely not within the contemplation of the draftsmen. Evra Corp. v. Swiss Bank Corp., 673 F.2d 951, 955 (7th Cir.1982); see also Delbrueck & Co. v. Manufacturers Hanover Trust Co., 609 F.2d 1047 (2d Cir.1979) (Article 4 inapplicable to interbank wire transfer dispute, although Commercial Code finality concepts support irrevocability of electronic funds transfers).

What remains is the negligence claim (Count VI). The state of the common law in regard to electronic funds transfers generally and the liabilities concomitant to erroneous payment orders in particular is not yet well developed. There is no comprehensive body of law to define the rights and obligations that arise from wire transfers. More particularly, Florida decisions offer no specific guidance on the negligence issue in these circumstances.

Were it Massachusetts common law that supplied the rule of decision here, this Court could turn confidently to the American Law Institute Restatements as they so frequently guide the growth of the common law in this Commonwealth. See Recent Developments in Federal and Massachusetts Law (MCLE, Inc., 1989), §X; Recent Developments in Massachusetts Law (MCLE, Inc.1985), §III; Recent Developments in Massachusetts Law (MCLE, Inc.1984), §III. Florida common law decisions do not, however, so frequently advert to the Restatements. This Court is not nearly so sure, therefore, that the Florida Supreme Court will follow the Restatements as adopted. Nevertheless, given the dearth of decided cases, this Court will be guided * * * by the American Law Institute, Proposed Article 4A, Uniform Commercial Code, Proposed Final Draft (April 20, 1989) ("ALI Article 4A"). * * *

Shawmut argued first that First American was negligent in facilitating payment to an account number not peculiarly identified to the name of the transfer beneficiary. This is precisely the argument the Court has already considered--and rejected as matter of law--in evaluating whether First American violated any duty imposed on it as a possible agent of Shawmut. Supra at 61. The same result follows in the negligence context under the American Law Institute proposal. ALI Article 4A-209(3)(b) provides that duplicate transfers * * * may be subject to cancellation if the sender discovers a mistake has been made. * * * Section 4A-209(3) also cross references Fedwire rules, and reads, in pertinent part, as follows:

(3) Cancellation or amendment of a payment order accepted by the receiving bank is effective only if the bank agrees or a funds transfer system rule allows cancellation or amendment without agreement of the bank....

Fedwire rules do not permit a cancellation, "revocation," or "reversal" of a previous day's funds transfer without permission of the receiving bank. The transferee or receiving bank is under no obligation under Regulation J to comply with a request, even if the transferor provides indemnity. 12 C.F.R. §210. Both the ALI Article 4A and the Fedwire rules recognize that even with indemnity, the beneficiary's bank may be reluctant to alienate its customer, the beneficiary, by denying the customer the funds. See ALI Article 4A-209, Comment 5. * * * The language of section 4A-209 is permissive, not mandatory, where, as here, the funds transfer system rules do not permit cancellation without the permission of a receiving bank. Even if a receiving bank is the sender's "agent" on the day of the transfer, the regulatory framework that undergirds the parties' relationship cannot support the conclusion that the receiving bank is an agent for the sender charged with a duty broader than simply to credit promptly the beneficiary's account. The policies underlying this arrangement are even more compelling where a sending bank requests cancellation of a payment order three and one half months after the receiving bank has credited its customer's account. This Court rules that, as matter of law, a receiving bank is not negligent where it credits a payment order to the joint account as set out in the order.

Shawmut next argues that First American should have acted to prevent the reasonably foreseeable harm that proximately resulted from its negligent failure to notice that Shawmut's second payment order was a mistake and duplicative. The issue before the Court, thus, is whether First American was somehow put on notice that the transaction was so irregular that it should have investigated the circumstances prior to crediting the account a second time.

If Shawmut's own contributory negligence is put to one side for a moment, this last argument has some appeal. As a practical matter, the receiving bank probably is in a better position to recover the funds from the beneficiary, especially where the beneficiary is a customer of that bank. It thus makes sense that the risk of loss for duplicative payment orders such as the one involved in the instant case be shifted in some instances to a bank which blithely executes payment orders without exercising even ordinary care. The American Law Institute is considering this matter. See ALI Article 4A-205 permitting such a shift of the risk of loss where the sender can show that it complied with applicable security procedures and that the error would have been detected by the receiving bank had that bank complied with similar security procedures. * * * Here, however, there is no evidence before the Court that First American failed to comply with one of its own security procedures and no evidence that the lack of a reasonable security procedure may have caused the error to have gone undetected.

SO ORDERED.

Manufacturas International, Ltda v. Manufacturers Hanover Trust Co.

United States District Court, Eastern District of New York, 1992
792 F.Supp. 180

Weinstein, District Judge. * * * As part of a suspected drug money-laundering operation, large amounts of funds were being electronically transferred from Europe to South America via New York banks. The banks cooperated with government requests, subpoenas, and court orders by stopping transmission and turning the funds over to the court. The claimants to the funds--primarily Colombian business concerns--sue the banks in these Bank Cases for loss of the use of their funds and other claimed violations.

The banks move to dismiss. Their argument is elementary and correct: those who assist the government are not liable to those who claim ownership of what the government contends is already forfeited by the taint of drug trafficking. Faced with competing claims to the same funds, the banks followed instructions and took the sensible step of paying the moneys into court in a form of interpleader. Even if after adjudication it is determined that the funds are not tainted, no fault can be attributed to the banks.

I. FACTS

The electronic funds transfers at issue were seized based on complaints in United States v. All Funds on Deposit at Merrill Lynch, Pierce, Fenner & Smith, Inc., CV 90-2510 (All Funds). These funds are alleged by the government to be the proceeds of illegal narcotics transactions forfeited under 21 U.S.C. §881 et seq. (1988 & Supp. III 1991), and 18 U.S.C. §981 et seq. (1988 & Supp. III 1991). The instant parallel private actions against Manufacturers Hanover Trust, Banco Atlantico, and the Bank of New York are consolidated as the Bank Cases.

The first government document to mention these plaintiffs was the Third Amended All Funds Complaint filed July 18, 1990, with its accompanying Supplemental Warrant for Arrest of Articles in Rem issued pursuant to Rule C(3) of the Supplementary Rules for Certain Admiralty and Maritime Claims. An individual named Jose Santacruz-Londono and others working with him had allegedly "conducted extensive narcotics trafficking and money-laundering enterprises, involving millions of dollars and multi-kilograms of cocaine smuggled into the United States and distributed, in part, in the New York metropolitan area."

Santacruz-Londono is said to hold a high position in the Cali drug cartel of Colombia. In 1985, he was indicted in the Eastern District of New York for conspiring to distribute cocaine, distributing cocaine, and operating a continuing criminal enterprise. He is a fugitive.

The complaint alleged that in connection with Santacruz-Londono's narcotics trade, substantial sums of money have been deposited in, withdrawn from, and transferred to and from accounts located in the United States, including the defendant accounts, and other accounts located in Europe, Panama, and Colombia.

During the month of June 1990, three individuals believed to be connected with the Santacruz-Londono organization had been observed meeting and depositing large sums in accounts* * *.

On June 29, 1990, two of the alleged Londono compatriots were arrested on money-laundering charges. A flurry of wire transfer activity followed these arrests.

On July 12, 1990, the Eastern District of New York issued an International Letter Rogatory to the Federal Republic of Germany on information that Santacruz-Londono and others had imported and distributed cocaine in the United States and conspired to disguise the sources and ownership of the proceeds. The government claimed that the Santacruz-Londono organization was importing approximately 3,000 kilograms of cocaine a month into the United States.

A district judge of this court signed the Letter Rogatory and subsequent arrest warrants. The banks which are defendants in these Bank Cases were instructed in the Supplemental Warrants for Arrest of Articles in Rem accompanying the Third through Seventh Amended Complaints filed July 18 through August 3, 1990 to attach all funds on deposit in the name of various named individuals and entities and "all related entities and individuals." The United

States Attorney also requested by telephone that the banks inform him of all electronic funds transfers received for third-party beneficiaries, only some of whom were named.

From the third week of July through the month of August 1990, the banks faxed copies of each transaction to the United States Attorney, who then instructed the banks whether the beneficiaries were "related entities or individuals" and whether the transfers should be attached. The same or the next day the bank would get official notification to seize. Each of the successive Amended Complaints in All Funds named more beneficiaries as their identities became known.

There are now twenty-three claimants in All Funds, ten of whom are plaintiffs in these Bank Cases. None of the plaintiffs in the Bank Cases maintained accounts at the defendant banks. Rather, the plaintiffs were customers of Colombian banks that maintained correspondent banking relationships with the defendant banks. The defendant banks were intermediary banks between the European originating banks and the Colombian receiving banks.

To effect the wire transfers, the defendant banks were supposed to credit the Colombian banks' correspondent accounts. In turn, the Colombian banks were to advise the beneficiaries of the credits. Instead, the defendant banks complied with the requests of the United States Attorney and the instructions of the court and seized the funds on deposit and the wire transfers.

On July 24, 1990, a show cause order presented by the government why the funds should not be paid into court was not opposed by the claimants. The court on July 30, 1990 ordered the banks to pay all attached funds into court. The order also instructed that funds submitted to the court should be accompanied by identifying information such as the beneficiary and the ordering party. During August 1990, the banks complied, and the seized funds were transmitted to the Clerk of the Court of this district. The funds are being maintained in an interest-bearing account pending the outcome of the All Funds trial set to begin on March 9, 1992.

On March 26, 1991, the All Funds claimants moved for summary judgment and to dismiss the government's complaint on the ground that the government lacked probable cause to seize the funds, that wire transfers are not a res, and that the funds were seized without a warrant. On April 12, 1991, this court denied the motions to dismiss and for summary judgment. The case was remanded to a Magistrate Judge for a decision on whether there was probable cause to seize the funds as proceeds of narcotics trafficking and money-laundering. A supplemental hearing before the court was to be scheduled in the event that the Magistrate Judge found probable cause.

After a hearing, the Magistrate Judge found that the government had probable cause to seize the funds. On May 28 and 29 and June 6, 1991, a district judge also held a hearing on the probable cause issue. On June 13, 1991 this court issued an order finding that, based on the documentary evidence and the testimony of witnesses and experts, probable cause existed to believe that all the funds seized by the government and the subject of the verified claims are subject to forfeiture, except one Merrill Lynch account in the name of Jaime and Cecilia Vargas in the amount of $8,542.35. That small amount was released. The subject funds of the June 13 order were those on deposit in certain identified accounts and the wire transfers at issue in these Bank Cases.

The Bank Cases were then pending in the district court for the Southern District of New York. On October 30, 1991, that court transferred the consolidated Bank Cases to the Eastern District of New York on the grounds that the cases were legally and factually related to United States v. All Funds. See 28 U.S.C. §1404(a) (1988). In the Bank Cases, plaintiffs argue that the banks violated several federal statutes by seizing the funds: the Right to Financial Privacy Act, 12 U.S.C. §3401 et seq., the Omnibus Crime Control and Safe Streets

Act, 18 U.S.C. §2510 et seq. (as amended by the Electronic Communications Privacy Act of 1986), the Federal Reserve Act, 12 U.S.C. §464 et seq., and the Foreign Intelligence Surveillance Act, 50 U.S.C. §1801 et seq. In addition, plaintiffs have several state law claims based on the right to privacy, article 4A of the Uniform Commercial Code, conversion, breach of a third-party contract, and gross and ordinary negligence. None of these federal or state claims has merit.

* * *

III. MECHANICS OF ELECTRONIC FUNDS TRANSFERS

An electronic funds transfer begins with the sending bank. It normally receives a telex from the bank, individual, or corporate entity that is originating the transaction, instructing the sending bank to send funds. The sending bank tests and verifies the telex before transmitting the request, with all the identifying information, from its local computer operator to a central computer network. The central computer for the transfer system stores the information and causes a sending message to be automatically printed at the sending bank.

The sending bank, having determined that payment is appropriate, returns the sending message to its local computer operator to reinsert the message into the computer and press a release key. When the central computer receives this message, it causes the simultaneous printing of a debit ticket at the sending bank and a credit ticket at the receiving bank. The central computer creates a permanent record of the transaction and adjusts the accounts of the sending and receiving banks. These steps are almost instantaneous.

Once the receiving bank has received the credit ticket, the individual or corporate beneficiary of the transfer is notified and the funds are made available to the recipient--generally the same day. The funds transfer is considered completed at the moment the receiving bank receives the credit message, not when the beneficiary acquires the funds. See generally Richard M. Gottlieb, Payment, Settlement, and Finality, in UCC Article 4-A, A Practical Guide for Bankers and Bank Counsel (Am. Bankers Ass'n 1991) [hereinafter Bankers Guide].

The receiving bank may be acting as an intermediary bank for a third bank, such as an overseas correspondent bank. If so, another transaction is necessary between the intermediary bank and the correspondent bank. Once the intermediary bank receives the funds, it should credit the account of the correspondent bank. In the instant case the sending banks are in Europe, the intermediary banks are in New York, and the correspondent banks are in Colombia. The funds transfers were seized at the intermediary banks before the funds were credited to the Colombian correspondent banks.

As already indicated, acting on its own investigation, the United States Attorney notified the defendant intermediary banks by telephone that certain electronic funds transfers would be credited to those banks from sending banks. The intermediary banks examined all incoming wire transfers for their correspondent banks in Colombia, notifying the United States Attorney of all transfers designated for the identified beneficiaries. In addition, the banks notified the United States Attorney of other wire transfers to third-party beneficiaries, awaiting notification whether those funds were intended for "related individuals and entities" and should also be seized. Upon instruction from the United States Attorney, the intermediary banks seized the funds and turned them over to the Clerk of the Court for this district.

* * *

V. STATE LAW CLAIMS
* * *

B. U.C.C. ARTICLE 4A

Article 4A of the Uniform Commercial Code was enacted in the State of New York with an effective date of January 1, 1991. For the first time 4A put into place specific rules for the regulation of funds transfers. It cannot be relied upon in the instant case since the wire transfers were seized in July and August of 1990. The statute does not apply retroactively. See Banque Worms v. BankAmerica Int'l, 77 N.Y.2d 362, 371, 568 N.Y.S.2d 541, 547, 570 N.E.2d 189, 195 (Ct.App.1991).

In any event, section 4A-503 of the U.C.C., entitled "Injunction or Restraining Order With Respect to Funds Transfer," recognizes that banks have an obligation to respond to court orders. See Thomas J. Greco, Miscellaneous Provisions: Creditor Process, Injunction, Finality of Account Statement, and Choice of Law, in Bankers Guide, supra, at 56. The Official Comment states that "intermediary banks are protected," meaning that since the time in transit for funds transfers is brief, intermediary banks cannot be expected to comply with injunctions by creditors. Instead, creditor process should be directed at the originating and receiving banks. The Comment suggests that intermediary banks should not be exposed to liability under article 4A for declining to stop funds transfers where creditors are seeking the funds. In the instant case, the opposite situation is presented. Plaintiffs wish to hold the intermediary banks liable for agreeing to seize the funds. No such liability is justified. Article 4A was enacted to enable all parties to funds transfers to "predict risk with certainty, to insure against risk, to adjust operational and security procedures, and to price funds transfer services accordingly." Official Comment to U.C.C. §4A-102. The policies of article 4A are served by protecting the intermediary banks in forfeiture cases. The courts should hesitate to provide restrictions on their own powers to act swiftly. Cf. Sir Nicolas Browne-Wilkinson, Territorial Jurisdiction and the New Technologies, 25 Israel L.Rev. 145, 147 (1991) ("[T]he speed at which modern technology works is ... threatening the roots of justice itself."). Finally, even if the U.C.C. were applicable, under the Supremacy Clause a state could not in its regulation of commercial activity inhibit federal law enforcement agencies in applying federal drug laws.

* * *

VI. CONCLUSION

Plaintiffs have failed to state a claim under any state or federal theory. No liability can be found where the banks were in good faith following government orders respecting claimed government funds. There is not the slightest suggestion of bad faith by the banks. Summary judgment for the defendants is granted. The complaint is dismissed.

SO ORDERED.

practice

Case 1

Otto Inc. wishes to purchase $3,000,000 in dental supplies from Dentures 'R Us. To pay for the supplies, Otto wishes to transfer the money directly from its bank, Second Bank and Trust, to Dentures' bank, Intercity Express Bank

How are the relevant parties identified for Article 4A purposes?

Case 2

Greg Spitzer is an astute investor. He owns numerous securities and mutual funds and holds himself out to his friends as a financial planner. Among the stocks that Greg owns through his investment company, A-S Investors, Ltd., are 1,000 shares of IBM. IBM's bank pays dividends from its shares directly to the investment company's account.

a.   What legislation governs such a transaction?

b.   Does it matter if Greg holds the shares in his individual capacity?

c.   What if A-S Investors' bank receives the funds from IBM's bank but fails to promptly credit the investment company's account because of an ongoing dispute with Greg regarding an unrelated matter?

  i.   Is the beneficiary bank potentially liable here?

  ii.   What if their failure to properly credit the account means that A-S Investors cannot purchase shares of Microsoft on March 1, and the shares quickly climb in value $25/share by March 15, when A-S Investors is finally able to purchase them?

Case 3

Suppose that a thief, Randi Soggs, manages to obtain Joanna Smith's payment order code and issues an unauthorized payment order, see 4A-202(a), to Joanna's bank, resulting in funds being transferred from Joanna's account to Randi's account in her bank.

a.   To what extent is Joanna liable?

b.   Does your answer depend upon whether Sender and Receiving Bank have agreed in advance that the authenticity of a payment order issued in Sender's name is to be verified by a commercially reasonable "security procedure?" See 4A-201; 4A-202(c); 4A-202(b).

c.   What if the payment order is unauthorized but "effective" under 4A-202(b), may it still be "unenforceable" against the purported Sender? See 4A-203(a).

d.   What if the unauthorized payment order is neither "effective" under 4A-202 nor "enforceable" under 4A-203?

Case 4

On January 2, 1993, at the instruction of PlayDough Enterprises, FirstBanc wires $10,000,000 into the account of KneeJerk, Inc. at Albany Bank. A few hours after directing this wire transfer, PlayDough, by a second telex, directs FirstBanc to stop payment to KneeJerk and to make the same payment instead to Newsprint, Corp. That afternoon, FirstBanc executes PlayDough's second payment order and transfers $10,000,000 to Newsprint. PlayDough's account is debited twice to record both wire transfers thus producing an overdraft.

a.   If PlayDough indeed owed KneeJerk the transferred amount who is responsible for the amount transferred?

b.   Would it matter if KneeJerk was only owed $1,000,000 by PlayDough?

§ 2. Consumer Funds Transfers

story

While wholesale wire transfers have become a dominant method of transferring funds between businesses and financial institutions, the use of electronic funds transfers to make payments has also become an increasingly important substitute for the use of checks at the consumer level. In 1978 Congress enacted EFTA, establishing a comprehensive federal framework of consumer rights and liabilities in electronic funds transfer transactions. The purpose of EFTA is to define the legal relationships between the provider of electronic funds transfer services such as a commercial bank and the consumer whose funds will be transferred by electronic means. To implement the statute, the Federal Reserve Board promulgated Regulation E, 12 C.F.R. §205 (1993). Regulation E is amended from time to time to deal with issues arising under EFTA. The Federal Reserve also issues official commentary to Regulation E to address in detail specific problems faced by the institutions that are subject to EFTA. To date, there is very little litigation with respect to EFTA and the courts have played only a minor role in interpreting EFTA.

EFTA and Regulation E govern "electronic fund transfers" defined by Regulation E to mean "any transfer of funds, other than a transaction originated by check, draft, or similar paper instrument, that is initiated through an electronic terminal, telephone, or computer, or magnetic tape for the purpose of ordering, instructing, or authorizing a financial institution to debit or credit an account." 12 C.F.R. §205.2(g). In short then, EFTA and Regulation E take over where article 4A leaves off, governing consumer electronic transfers that are not executed through pieces of paper. Specifically, the five primary consumer electronic fund transfer transactions governed by the legal framework are:

* Automated Teller Machine (ATM) transactions such as cash withdrawals, deposits, transfers between accounts, and payments through an ATM;

- Debit cards and Point-of-Sale transactions involving transfers of funds from the customer's account to the merchant's account in payment for goods or services;
- Telephone bill-paying services where the customer directs payment by her bank or financial institution to designated creditors for recurring expenditures;
- Consumer wire service transfers such as that conducted by Western Union; and
- ACH transactions governing preauthorized payments from the customer's account to a third party, or direct deposit of wages, government benefits, dividends or other payments to the customer's account.

EFTA and Regulation E also exempt a number of familiar banking services from coverage, see 12 C.F.R. §205.3 (1993), including:

- Wire transfers through the Federal Reserve Communications System or similar network used primarily for transfers between financial institutions or between businesses, governed in large part by Article 4A and Regulation J, 12 C.F.R. §210 (1993);
- Purchases or sales of securities regulated by the Securities and Exchange Commission;
- Automatic transfers of funds between accounts of the same customer in the same institution, or between a customer account and an account of the financial institution such as automatic transfer from savings to checking account to cover overdrafts;
- Transfers initiated by telephone conversation between a consumer and an employee of the financial institution, so long as the transfer is not pursuant to a periodic, recurring payment;
- Check guaranty or authorization services that do not directly result in a debit or credit to the customer's account;
- Transfers in connection with trust accounts held by the financial institution; and
- Preauthorized transfers to financial institutions whose total assets are $25 million or less.

One important issue concerning EFTA is consumer liability for unauthorized transfers. Suppose, for example, that Gordon Brumwell is in possession of an ATM card that permits Gordon to withdraw cash from an ATM machine from an account with Issuing Bank and to purchase goods by authorizing Issuing Bank to transfer funds from that account to Merchant's account at the point of sale. If the card is stolen by a thief, then Gordon has no liability for unauthorized use unless (1) the card was accepted and (2) Issuing Bank has provided a means whereby the user of the card "can be identified as the person authorized to use it." 15 U.S.C. §1693g(a). That means is normally a Personal Identification Number (PIN). If, however, the use was unauthorized and these two conditions are satisfied, then Gordon is liable, but only for up to $50 or the amount of the transaction, whichever is less. Thus, the Issuing Bank must recredit Gordon's account for any loss in excess of $50.

Unlike the legislation dealing with credit cards, however, Gordon's loss may be greater in two circumstances. First, if Issuing Bank furnishes a periodic statement that contains the unauthorized transfer, Gordon cannot obtain reimbursement for losses that "the financial institution establishes would not have occurred but for the failure of the consumer to report within sixty days of transmittal of the statement" the unauthorized transfer. Id. Compare 4-406. This could be all or none of the reported unauthorized transfer. Second, if Gordon learns of the loss or theft of his card and fails to report the loss or theft "within two business days," he cannot obtain reimbursement for losses up to $500 "which the financial institution establishes would not have occurred *but for the failure of the consumer* to report" the loss or theft. Id. (emphasis added). Here, of course, the loss ceiling is $500, but it might be less if the "but for" test is not satisfied. It should be emphasized that any transfer initiated by someone to whom Gordon has furnished his card and PIN is not considered unauthorized until Gordon notifies the financial institution that the person no longer has permission to use the card. However, Gordon need not recover the card and, based on the "mailbox" rule, the financial institution need not receive the notification, which is effective when sent.

These loss limitations, like the credit card legislation, require extensive disclosure by Issuing Bank, 15 U.S.C. §1693c, and also provide a procedure for error resolution. 15 U.S.C. §1693f. As with truth in lending, EFTA and Regulation E, 12 C.F.R. §205.7 (1993), require various disclosures, particularly when a consumer initially contracts for an electronic funds transfer service. The mandated disclosures include:

- A summary of the consumer's potential liability for unauthorized transfers;
- Information regarding procedures for notifying the issuer if an unauthorized transfer has or may occur;
- The type of services provided by the issuer;
- Any service charges;
- A summary of consumer's right to receive documentation of transfers;
- A summary of the consumer's right to stop payment of a preauthorized transfer; and
- A summary of the issuer's liability for failure to honor a valid stop order.

EFTA and Regulation E, moreover, provide a set of detailed rules for resolving alleged account errors. See 12 C.F.R. §205.11 (1990). Possible errors include an unauthorized transfer, an incorrect transfer, or the consumer's receipt of an incorrect amount of money from an electronic terminal. Pursuant to the relevant EFTA provisions, if a consumer feels that an error has been made she must notify the financial institution orally or in writing within sixty days after the documentation has been transmitted to her. The institution must then correct the error within eleven business days of receiving the notice or, alternatively, give the consumer a provisional credit within ten business days of receiving notice and correct the error within forty-five days of receipt of the notice. If, however, the institution determines that no error has occurred, it must explain its conclusion to the consumer within three business days after completing the investigation. In this case, the burden is then on the consumer to make the next move.

law

Scope of the Law

Regulation E -- Electronic Fund Transfers
12 C.F.R. §205.3

Exemptions.

This Act and this regulation do not apply to the following:

(a) Check guarantee or authorization services. Any service that guarantees payment or authorizes acceptance of a check, draft, or similar paper instrument and that does not directly result in a debit or credit to a consumer's account.

(b) Wire transfers. Any wire transfer of funds for a consumer through the Federal Reserve Communications System or other similar network that is used primarily for transfers between financial institutions or between businesses.

(c) Certain securities or commodities transfers. Any transfer the primary purpose of which is the purchase or sale of securities or commodities regulated by the Securities and Exchange Commission or the Commodity Futures Trading Commission.

(d) Certain automatic transfers. Any transfer under an agreement between a consumer and a financial institution which provides that the institution will initiate individual transfers without a specific request from the consumer.

(1) Between a consumer's accounts within the financial institution, such as a transfer from a checking account to a savings account;

(2) Into a consumer's account by the financial institution, such as the crediting of interest to a savings account;

(3) From a consumer's account to an account of the financial institution, such as a loan payment; or

(4) From a consumer's account to an account of another consumer, within the financial institution, who is a member of the transferor's family.

(e) Certain telephone-initiated transfers. Any transfer of funds that (1) is initiated by a telephone conversation between a consumer and an officer or employee of a financial institution and (2) is not under a telephone bill-payment or other prearranged plan or agreement in which periodic or recurring transfers are contemplated.

(f) Trust accounts. Any trust account held by a financial institution under a bona fide trust agreement.

(g) Preauthorized transfers to small financial institutions. (1) Any preauthorized transfer to or from an account if the assets of the account- holding financial institution are $25 million or less on December 31. (2) If the account-holding financial institution's assets subsequently exceed $25 million, the institution's exemption for this class of transfers shall terminate one year from the end of the calendar year in which the assets exceed $25 million.

Kashanchi v. Texas Commerce Medical Bank, N.A.
United States Court of Appeals, Fifth Circuit, 1983
703 F.2d 936

Randall, Circuit Judge. The plaintiff, Morvarid Paydar Kashanchi, appeals from a final judgment of the district court dismissing her complaint for lack of subject matter jurisdiction. The issue on appeal is whether the term "electronic fund transfer" as used in the Electronic Fund Transfer Act ("EFTA" or "the Act"), 15 U.S.C. §1693 (Supp. V 1981), includes a transfer of funds from a consumer's account, initiated by a telephone conversation between someone other than the owner of the account and an employee of a financial institution, when that transfer is not made pursuant to a prearranged plan or agreement under which periodic transfers are contemplated. For the reasons set forth below, we affirm.

On or about February 9, 1981, the plaintiff and her sister, Firoyeh Paydar, were the sole owners of a savings account at Texas Commerce Medical Bank in Houston, Texas. On or about that date, $4900 was transferred from their account. The transfer was allegedly initiated by a telephone conversation between an employee of the bank and someone other than the plaintiff or her sister. Upon receipt of a March 31, 1981, bank statement showing the $4900 withdrawal, Firoyeh Paydar sent a letter to the bank, dated April 15, 1981, notifying the bank · that the withdrawal was unauthorized.

After the bank refused to recredit the account with the amount of the allegedly unauthorized withdrawal, the plaintiff filed this action on December 4, 1981, alleging violations by the bank of the EFTA. The district court granted the defendant's motion to dismiss on the ground that the plaintiff's cause of action was excluded from the coverage of the Act under 15 U.S.C. §1693a(6)(E). The plaintiff timely appealed.

This is apparently the first case in which we have been called upon to interpret any of the substantive provisions of the EFTA. We begin our inquiry with the language of the statute itself, recognizing that "absent a clearly expressed legislative intent to the contrary, the plain meaning of the language is ordinarily controlling." Johnson v. Department of Treasury, Internal Revenue Service, 700 F.2d 971 (5th Cir.1983); see also United States v. Martino, 681 F.2d 952, 954 (5th Cir.1982) (en banc).

The parties agree that the telephonic transfer that allegedly occurred in this case falls within the broad definition of "electronic fund transfers" in the Act: [T]he term "electronic fund transfer" means any transfer of funds, other than a transaction originated by check, draft, or similar paper instrument, which is initiated through an electronic terminal, telephonic instrument, or computer or magnetic tape so as to order, instruct, or authorize a financial institution to debit or credit an account. Such term includes, but is not limited to, point-of-sale transfers, automated teller machine transactions, direct deposits or withdrawals of funds, and transfers initiated by telephone. 15 U.S.C. §1693a(6). Some of what Congress has given, however, it has also taken away. Excluded from the definition of an electronic fund transfer is any transfer of funds which is initiated by a telephone conversation between a consumer and an officer or employee of a financial institution which is not pursuant to a prearranged plan and under which periodic or recurring transfers are not contemplated .... 15 U.S.C. §1693a(6)(E). The plaintiff concedes that the unauthorized transfer of her funds was not made "pursuant to any prearranged plan," and that it was made by an employee of the bank. The question in this case is whether the telephone conversation was between the employee and a "consumer." * * *

The Act defines a consumer as "a natural person." 15 U.S.C. §1693a(5). If we were to apply this definition to the language in the exclusion, we would have to conclude that the withdrawal of the plaintiff's funds was excluded from the coverage of the Act since a natural person, even if the person was neither the plaintiff nor her sister, made the withdrawal. The plaintiff argues, however, that we should read the term "consumer" more narrowly in this portion of the Act; she would have us interpret the provision to exclude only transfers made by the account holder.

The plaintiff maintains that the legislative history of the Act supports her narrow reading of the exclusion. She points out that the House version of the bill used the word "holder," meaning "the individual who is recognized as the owner of the account by the financial institution where the account is held," H.R. 13007, §903(i), 95th Cong., 2d Sess., 124 Cong.Rec. 25737 (1978), where the Senate version, eventually adopted by Congress as the EFTA, uses the word "consumer." The plaintiff would have us infer that the Senate intended the word "consumer" to be synonymous with "holder." There is no indication in the legislative history, however, that this is what the Senate intended. * * * The only criticism leveled at the definition of consumer concerned the exclusion of corporations, particularly nonprofit corporations, from that definition. See The Electronic Funds Transfer Consumer Protection Act, 1977: Hearings on S. 2065 Before the Subcomm. on Consumer Affairs of the Senate Comm. on Banking, Housing and Urban Affairs, 95th Cong., 1st Sess. 37 (1977) (Statement of Linda Hudak, Legislative Director, Consumer Federation of America).

Secondly, Congress demonstrated in other sections of the EFTA that when it wanted to limit a particular provision of the Act to an account holder, rather than to all natural persons, it was perfectly capable of adding language to do so. For example, the Act defines an "unauthorized electronic fund transfer" as "an electronic fund transfer from a consumer's account initiated by a person other than the consumer without actual authority to initiate such transfer ...." 15 U.S.C. §1693a(11). It is a well-established principle of statutory construction that "where Congress includes particular language in one section of a statute but omits it in another section of the same Act, it is generally presumed that Congress acts intentionally and purposely in the disparate inclusion or exclusion." United States v. Wong Kim Bo, 472 F.2d 720, 722 (5th Cir.1972). * * * In addition, reading "consumer" as the equivalent of "holder" would create redundancies in other portions of the Act. See, e.g., 15 U.S.C. §1693a(8). * * * "[W]ords in statutes should not be discarded as 'meaningless' and 'surplusage' when Congress specifically and expressly included them, particularly where the words are excluded in other sections of the same act." Wong Kim Bo, 472 F.2d at 722; see also Meltzer v. Board of Public Instruction, 548 F.2d 559, 578 n. 38 (5th Cir.1977), cert. denied, 439 U.S. 1089, 99 S.Ct. 872, 59 L.Ed.2d 56 (1979). In short, the language of the statute would seem to exclude the transfer in this case from the coverage of the Act.

Further, the legislative history of the EFTA is consistent with the plain meaning of the language in the statute and with the presumption arising from Congress's disparate inclusion and exclusion of words of limitation. The plaintiff emphasizes that Congress designed the Act to provide a comprehensive scheme of federal regulation for all electronic transfers of funds. See H.R.Rep. No. 1315, 95th Cong., 2d Sess. 2 (1978); see also E. Broadman, Electronic Fund Transfer Act: Is the Consumer Protected?, 13 U.S.F.L.Rev. 245 (1979). Congress undoubtedly intended the Act's coverage to be broad; the Act itself provides that its list of electronic fund transfers is not all- inclusive. 15 U.S.C. §1693a(6). Aware that computer technology was still in a rapid, evolutionary stage of development, Congress was careful to permit coverage of electronic services not yet in existence: "The definition of 'electronic fund transfer' is intended to give the Federal Reserve Board flexibility in determining whether new or developing electronic services should be covered by the act and, if so, to what extent." S.Rep. No. 915, 95th Cong., 2d Sess. 9 (1978), U.S.Code Cong. & Admin.News 1978, pp. 9273, 9411; see also National Commission on Electronic Fund Transfers, EFT in the United States, 4 (Final Rep.1977).

Congressional concern about electronic systems not specifically mentioned in the Act was focused, however, on future and as yet undeveloped systems, not on systems that Congress had simply failed to discuss. For example, the report on the House version of the Act explained the need for flexibility in dealing with future electronic systems: Many aspects of electronic fund transfer systems are undergoing evolutionary changes and, thus, projections about future events necessarily involve a degree of speculation. Consequently, the appropriate approach to those new financial service concepts is, in general, to permit further development in a free market environment and, to the extent possible, in a manner consistent with the nature and purpose of existing law and regulations governing financial services. H.R.Rep. No. 1315, supra, at 33. The absence of discussion about informal personal phone transfers would seem to indicate an intent not to cover these transfers, or at least an absence of congressional concern about them, in light of the extensive discussion throughout the hearings and reports of the other existing types of electronic transfers. It is highly unlikely that this silence was a result of congressional ignorance of the problem since these informal phone withdrawals presumably had been occurring since shortly after the time of Alexander Graham Bell.

The exclusion of these informal transactions was not in the House version of the EFTA, and presumably it was not in the original version of the Senate bill either, since the minority report criticized the bill's coverage of incidental telephone instructions: In an attempt to reach the automatic telephone payments (transfers through a touch-tone telephone and computer network routing instructions to the financial institution) the Committee has also covered incidental telephone instructions by (a) depositor to a teller to make a transfer from a savings account to cover an overdraft or pay a bill. S.Rep. No. 915, supra, at 24, U.S.Code Cong. & Admin.News 1978, p. 9425. Apparently, this criticism led to the inclusion in the final version of the EFTA of the exemption which is the subject of this suit. Focusing on the Federal Reserve Board's statement that phone transfers made as an "accommodation to the consumer" are not covered by the Act, 46 Fed.Reg. 46880 (1978), and the Senate minority report's discussion of telephone instructions made by a "depositor," the plaintiff would have us conclude that only transactions made as a favor to the actual account holder were excluded from the Act.

These transfers were more probably excluded, however, not because they are made as a favor to the account holder, but because of the personal element in these transfers. On the one hand, as the plaintiff points out, all phone transfers are particularly vulnerable to fraud because there is no written memorandum of the transactions; there is no signature to be authenticated. This lack of a written record was one of the factors that motivated Congress to pass the EFTA. See H.R.Rep. No. 1315, supra, at 2, 4. The other factor, however, was the dependency of electronic fund transfer systems on computers and the resulting absence of any human contact with the transferor. The House report explains: "Consequently, these impersonal transactions are much more vulnerable to fraud, embezzlement, and unauthorized use than the traditional payment methods." Id. at 2. Senator Proxmire opened the hearings on the Senate bill with the warning that "[c]omputer systems are far from infallible, and electronic fund transfers--so totally dependent on computers--will also be error prone." The Electronic Funds Transfer Consumer Protection Act, 1977: Hearings on S. 2065 Before the Subcomm. on Consumer Affairs of the Senate Comm. on Banking, Housing and Urban Affairs, 95th Cong., 1st Sess. 2 (1977); see also 124 Cong.Rec. 25731 (1978) (statement of Rep. Annunzio, bill sponsor). As one commentator explains, telephonic communications were included in the definition of electronic fund transfers in order to extend coverage over computerized pay-by-phone systems; informal non-recurring consumer-initiated transfers were excluded, however, because they are not prone to computer error or institutional abuse since they are handled on a personal basis: The final exemption from the purview of the EFT Act is an exclusion for nonrecurring transfers of funds that are initiated by an ordinary telephone conversation between a consumer and an officer or employee of the financial institution. In order to extend coverage over computerized "pay-by-phone" systems, the general definition of the term "electronic fund transfer" had to be broad enough to encompass transactions initiated through a telephone. Like automatic debiting of service charges and automatic crediting of interest, however, ordinary nonrecurring transfers informally initiated by a consumer's call to an officer or employee of his neighborhood bank or savings and loan association was not considered to pose a serious threat warranting the coverage and additional costs of the EFT Act. Such requests are handled on a personal basis, so the possibility of computer error or institutional abuse, believed to exist with respect to some other EFT systems, was deemed to be absent. Brandel & Oliff, The Electronic Fund Transfer Act: A Primer, 40 Ohio St.L.J. 531, 545 (1979). Telephonic transfers made between a natural person and an employee of the financial institution share this element of human contact, regardless of whether the transfer is made by the account holder or someone else.

Finally, we note that the EFTA was passed because "[e]xisting law and regulations in the consumer protection area are not applicable to some aspects of the new financial service concepts." H.R.Rep. No. 1315, supra, at 33. See also 15 U.S.C. §1693a. The plaintiff suggests in her reply brief that she would have no adequate legal remedy for the wrong she has suffered if she were denied relief under the EFTA. While she conceded at oral argument that she might have an action under state law for conversion or breach of contract (her deposit agreement with the bank), she maintained that a person suffering a loss resulting from the abuse of one of the other electronic fund transfer systems * * * would also have such an action under state law.

The plaintiff ignores the essential difference between electronic fund transfer systems and personal transfers by phone or by check. When the bank employee allegedly agreed to withdraw funds from the plaintiff's account, he or she presumably could have asked some questions to ascertain whether the caller was one of the account holders. The failure to attempt to make a positive identification of the caller might be considered negligence or a breach of the deposit agreement under state law. When someone makes an unauthorized use of an electronic fund transfer system, however, the financial institution often has no way of knowing that the transfer is unauthorized. * * * For example, in order to make a transfer at an automatic teller machine, a person need only possess the machine card and know the correct personal identification number. The computer cannot determine whether the person who has inserted the card and typed in the magic number is authorized to use the system. What might be a withdrawal negligently permitted by the financial institution in one situation might not be a negligent action in the other.

Our analysis of both the language of the EFTA and the legislative history of the Act leads us to conclude that Congress intended to exclude from the Act's coverage any transfer of funds initiated by a phone conversation between any natural person and an officer or employee of a financial institution, which was not made pursuant to a prearranged plan and under which periodic and recurring transfers were not contemplated. Accordingly, we hold that the withdrawal of funds from the plaintiff's account is not covered by the Act even though said withdrawal allegedly was not made by either the plaintiff or her sister. The district court's dismissal of the plaintiff's action for lack of subject matter jurisdiction is AFFIRMED.

Curde v. Tri-City Bank & Trust Company

Supreme Court of Tennessee, 1992
826 S.W.2d 911

Drowota, Justice. This case presents an issue of first impression, namely, whether the Electronic Fund Transfers Act, 15 U.S.C. §1693 et seq. (1988) (the "Act"), applies to the attempted deposit of a check via a bank automated teller machine. The trial court granted partial summary judgment to Plaintiffs-Appellants, Melanie and Tommy Curde, holding that the Act applied. The Court of Appeals granted Defendant-Appellee, Tri-City Bank & Trust Company, an interlocutory appeal pursuant to Rule 9, T.R.A.P., and reversed, holding that the Act did not apply. We granted Plaintiffs' application for permission to appeal, pursuant to Rule 11, T.R.A.P., and affirm on different grounds.

On May 24, 1987, Plaintiff Melanie Curde attempted to deposit a $200.00 check at Defendant-Bank's automatic teller machine (the "ATM"). The parties stipulated for purposes of the present summary judgment determination that Plaintiff cancelled the attempted deposit. Plaintiff received a receipt from the ATM indicating, in code, that the attempted deposit had been cancelled. While there is some dispute as to Plaintiff's particular actions in attempting to make the deposit, the check was discovered some seven months later behind the front cover of the ATM. The sole issue before us is whether the Act applies in these circumstances.

The purpose of the Electronic Fund Transfers Act is to "provide a basic framework establishing the rights, liabilities, and responsibilities of participants in electronic fund transfer systems." 15 U.S.C. §1693(b)(1988). Its primary objective "is the provision of individual consumer rights." Id.

The pivotal question presented here is whether a check deposit via an ATM is an "electronic fund transfer." Under the Act, an "electronic fund transfer" means any transfer of funds, other than a transaction originated by check, draft, or similar paper instrument, which is initiated through an electronic terminal, telephonic instrument, or computer or magnetic tape so as to order, instruct, or authorize a financial institution to debit or credit an account. Such term includes, but is not limited to, point-of-sale transfers, automated teller machine transactions, direct deposits or withdrawals of funds, and transfers initiated by telephone. Id. at §1693a(6) (1988). This definition specifically includes automatic teller machine transactions. Unmistakedly, there was an ATM transaction here, notwithstanding that the attempted deposit was ultimately cancelled. However, we must decide whether (1) the phrase "other than a transaction originated by check, draft, or similar paper instrument," or (2) the stipulated cancellation, removes this transaction from the scope of the Act.

I.

Plaintiffs assert that the phrase "other than a transaction originated by check, draft, or similar paper instrument" is intended only to exclude a bank's internal electronic processing of checks. The Bank urges an interpretation based on the "plain-meaning rule" and a resultant finding that all transactions involving checks are outside the purview of the Act.

When the interpretation of federal law depends upon a statute and the intention of Congress, we must first examine the statutory language. See Blum v. Stenson, 465 U.S. 886, 896, 104 S.Ct. 1541, 1548, 79 L.Ed.2d 891 (1984). If the statutory language is unclear, we then look to the legislative history. See id. Further, we note that the plain-meaning rule is "an axiom of experience [rather than] a rule of law, and does not preclude consideration of persuasive evidence if it exists." Boston Sand & Gravel Co. v. United States, 278 U.S. 41, 48, 49 S.Ct. 52, 54, 73 L.Ed. 170 (1928) (Holmes, J.), quoted with approval in Watt v. Alaska,

451 U.S. 259, 266, 101 S.Ct. 1673, 1678, 68 L.Ed.2d 80 (1981). Because we find the statutory language unclear as to whether the Act applies to check deposits via an ATM, we proceed to consider the related legislative history, Federal Reserve Board regulations, and caselaw.

The Senate Committee on Banking, Housing, and Urban Affairs, in its report recommending passage of the Act, stated that: "This bill applies to four common EFT services: automated teller machine transactions, such as cash withdrawals or deposits or transfers between accounts; pay-by-phone services, in which a consumer orders his financial institution to make payments to another; point-of-sale systems, where funds are transferred from a consumer's account to a merchant's through use of a computer terminal at the merchant's place of business; and automated clearing house transactions through which a consumer's account is automatically debited for a recurring payment, like insurance premiums, or is regularly credited with wages, pension benefits, and the like. Each of these EFT transactions is initiated and carried out primarily by electronic means." S.Rep. No. 95-915, 95th Cong., 2d Sess. 3, reprinted in 1978 U.S.Code Cong. & Admin.News 9403, 9405. The report goes on to state that the bill does not cover "check truncation systems in which paper checks or drafts are routed or processed electronically." Id. at 9406.

Two points are instructive. First, the bill was intended to cover cash deposits; second, the types of transactions covered were those "initiated and carried out primarily by electronic means." Note that a cash deposit is no more "carried out primarily by electronic means" than a check deposit. Both deposits are placed in envelopes and inserted into the ATM. Both envelopes must be physically removed from the ATM and have their contents checked by bank personnel. It would be a spurious distinction at best which justified a finding that while the cash deposit is "initiated and carried out primarily by electronic means," the check deposit is not.

The Act provides that "[t]he [Federal Reserve] Board shall prescribe regulations to carry out the purposes of this subchapter." 15 U.S.C. §1693b(a) (1988). Further, the Board's regulations "may provide for such adjustments and exceptions for any class of electronic fund transfers, as in the judgment of the Board are necessary or proper to effectuate the purposes of this subchapter." Id. at §1693b(c) (1988).

The regulations do not alter the Act's definition of "electronic fund transfer" except to exclude "payments made by check ... at an electronic terminal." 12 C.F.R. §205.2(g) (1991). However, the Official Staff Interpretations specifically state that a check deposit to an ATM is covered by the Act: "2-11 Q: Fund Transfer--Deposits of Currency, Checks. Does the term electronic fund transfer include deposits of currency and checks at an automated teller machine (ATM)? A: A deposit made at an ATM or other electronic terminal is an electronic fund transfer for purposes of the regulation if there is a specific agreement between the financial institution and the consumer for the provision of E.F.T. services to or from the particular account to which the deposit is made." Federal Reserve Official Staff Interpretation Q2-11, reprinted in 12 C.F.R. Pt. 205, Supp. II, at 130 (1991).

Although the Court of Appeals dismissed the above official staff interpretation as an erroneous opinion of a staff attorney contrary to the plain language of the statute, we are satisfied that the Federal Reserve Board could, in the exercise of its judgment under section 1693b(c), determine that check deposits should be covered in order to effectuate the purposes of the Act.

Additionally, during consideration of the Act in Congress, an amendment was added specifying that an institution would not be liable if it relied in good faith on official interpretations of the Federal Reserve regulations. See 124 Cong.Rec. 25743 (1978); 15 U.S.C. §1693m(d)(1) (1988) * * *. This good faith reliance exception was founded on the belief that "[a]n institution should have a clear reference source to enable it to know what it must do to comply with the Act." 124 Cong.Rec. 25743 (1978) (statement of Rep. Barnard). This safe harbor is a two-way watercourse; if institutions are entitled to rely upon the official interpretations, so should consumers be entitled. A financial institution should not be permitted to wait until a consumer brings suit, and then challenge the consumer's reliance on an Official Staff Interpretation clearly granting consumers protection under the Act.

There has been little prior judicial construction of the Act. Kashanchi v. Texas Commerce Medical Bank, N.A., 703 F.2d 936 (5th Cir.1983), dealt with whether the Act applied in a situation where an unauthorized withdrawal of funds was executed via telephone. Holding the Act inapplicable, the Court stated that "[t]he plaintiff ignore[d] the essential difference between electronic fund transfer systems and personal transfers by phone or by check." Kashanchi, 703 F.2d at 941 (emphasis added).

There was no personal contact between Ms. Curde and the Bank respecting her attempted deposit of the check. The absence of human contact between the parties was a major factor motivating Congress to pass the Act. See Kashanchi, 703 F.2d at 940; H.R.Rep. No. 95-1315, 95th Cong., 2d Sess. 2 (1978) (impersonal transactions are particularly vulnerable to fraud, embezzlement, and unauthorized use).

Another factor motivating passage of the Act was that consumers utilizing electronic transfers do not receive traditional written records of their transactions. See Kashanchi, 703 F.2d at 940; S.Rep. No. 95-915, 95th Cong., 2d Sess. 5, reprinted in 1978 U.S.Code Cong. & Admin.News 9403, 9407. Because of the "faceless" transaction with the ATM, a consumer does not, at the time of the deposit, receive the same receipt she would when dealing with a human teller. That a check deposit to an ATM is an impersonal transaction which does not supply the consumer with a traditional bank receipt weighs toward a finding that Congress intended these transactions to be within the scope of the Act.

In Bisbey v. D.C. National Bank, 793 F.2d 315 (D.C.Cir.1986), a consumer informed her bank that she believed an error had occurred with regard to a preauthorized transfer agreement. 793 F.2d at 316. The bank was held liable under the Act for its failure "to comply with provisions in the Act when addressing a lawful inquiry about possible mistaken fund transfers." Id. at 318 (emphasis in original) (bank failed to fulfill its duty under the Act to provide the consumer with written notice of the results of its investigation into the alleged error).

Ms. Curde asserts that the Act applies to her attempted deposit because, as in Bisbey, she made a "lawful inquiry regarding a possible mistaken fund transfer." The Bank replies that Bisbey is distinguishable because, there, (1) funds were actually transferred electronically and (2) there was a preauthorized transfer agreement. We find neither of the factors urged by the Bank must be present for the Act to apply. First, a completed transfer of funds is not a necessary prerequisite for a transaction to be an electronic fund transfer under the Act; if it were, a mistake by a financial institution that prevented actual transfer would remove the attempted transaction from the scope of the Act, thereby defeating the Act's purpose in "establishing the rights, liabilities, and responsibilities of participants in electronic fund transfer systems." See 15 U.S.C. §1693(b) (1988). Second, the Act's coverage is not limited to transactions surrounding preauthorized transfer agreements.

In Spain v. Union Trust, 674 F.Supp. 1496 (D.Conn.1987), plaintiff alleged that the Act applied when a bank made an unauthorized charge to her account. A "debit slip" had been prepared by a teller and sent to the bank's operation center for electronic processing. The court emphasized that the transactions were handled by bank employees, not electronic terminals. Id. at 1500 ("face-to-face personal banking transaction[s]" are not covered; stating that the presence of human contact removed the transaction from the Act's coverage). The Spain court held that the transaction was "more closely akin to an internal processing of a check ... than ... to an electronic terminal transfer," and thus not covered by the Act. Id.

In Wachter v. Denver National Bank, 751 F.Supp. 906 (D.Colo.1990), a customer brought suit against her bank for allegedly mishandling a wire transfer. The plaintiff gave cash to a bank employee who then initiated the wire transfer. Wachter, 751 F.Supp. at 907. The court found that the presence of personal contact with a bank employee between the consumer and the electronic transfer device removed the transaction from the scope of the Act. See id. at 908. There is no analogous personal contact here that would remove Ms. Curde's attempted deposit from coverage under the Act.

We find that under the rationale of both Spain and Wachter, there was no face-to-face personal contact which would remove Ms. Curde's attempted check deposit from the Act's coverage. Further, a completed transfer of funds is not necessary for coverage under the Act. See 15 U.S.C. §1693h(a) (1988) (imposing liability on financial institutions for failure to make certain electronic fund transfers). Therefore, we find that an attempted check deposit to a ATM is an "electronic fund transfer" covered by the Act. Here, Ms. Curde had a dispute with Tri-City Bank & Trust over whether a deposit had been made to her account. Imposing a duty on a bank to investigate and report disputed transactions at faceless automated teller machines is precisely the kind of consumer protection the Act is meant to afford.

II.

However, because for the purpose of this partial summary judgment motion, Ms. Curde admitted (via stipulation) that she cancelled the attempted deposit (transfer of funds), we hold that the Act does not apply. Once the consumer, by her own action, cancels a transaction, she has prevented the automatic teller transaction from becoming an electronic fund transfer under the Act. In order to come within the Act, the automatic teller transaction must "order, instruct, or authorize a financial institution to debit or credit an account." See 15 U.S.C. §1693a(6) (1988); Wachter, 751 F.Supp. at 908. Once the transaction was cancelled by Ms. Curde, the financial institution was no longer instructed to credit her account; it therefore was not an electronic fund transfer under the Act. * * *

For the foregoing reasons, on the facts presented to us, we find that the trial court erred in granting partial summary judgment for Plaintiff. The case is remanded to the trial court for proceedings consistent with this opinion. The costs will be divided equally by the parties to this appeal.

Unauthorized Transfers

Regulation E -- Electronic Fund Transfers
Supplement II to Part 205--Official Staff Interpretations
12 C.F.R. 205.6--Liability of Consumer for Unauthorized Transfers
(1-1-93 Edition)

6-1 Q: Unauthorized Transfers--access device not involved. If unauthorized transfers do not involve the use of an access device such as a debit card, may any liability be imposed on the consumer?

A: If the consumer fails to report an unauthorized electronic fund transfer within 60 days of transmittal of the periodic statement reflecting the transfer, the consumer could be subject to liability.[§205.6(a) and (b)]

6-2 Q: Failure to disclose business days. If a financial institution meets other conditions (including disclosure of liability) but fails to disclose its business days, can it hold the consumer liable for uanauthorized transfers involving a lost or stolen access device?

A: No, unless applicable state law or an agreement between the consumer and the financial institution sets a liability limit of $50 or less. [§205.6(a)(3)(iii)]

6-3 Q: Means of identification--multiple users. If more than one access device is issued to access a particular consumer account, must the financial institution provide a means to identify each separate user in order to impose liability for unauthorized transfers?

A: No. The financial institution may provide means to identify the separate users, but is not required to do so. [§205.6(a)(2)]

6-4 Q: Means of identification--use of PIN. Does the use of a personal identification number (PIN) or other alphabetical or numerical code satisfy the requirement of electronic or mechanical confirmation for identifying the consumer to whom an access device was issued?

A: Yes. [§205.6(a)(2)]

6-5 Q: Application of liability provisions--examples. What are some examples of when and how the following would apply: (1) The $500 liability limit provision, (2) both the $500 limit and the unlimited liability provisions, and (3) only the $50/unlimited liability provisions? [§205.6(b)(1), (2) and (3)]

Situation 1--$500 Limit Applies

Date and Event
June 1--C's card is stolen
June 2--$100 unauthorized transfer
June 3--C learns of theft
June 4--$25 unauthorized transfer
June 5--Close of 2 business days
June 7-8--$600 in unauthorized transfers that could have been prevented had notice been
        given by June 5
June 9--C notifies bank

Computation of C's liability:
Paragraph (b)(1) will apply to determine C's liability for any unauthorized transfers that occur before notice is given.

Amount of transfers before close of
    2 business days: $125 .... $ 50[1]
Amount of transfers, after close of 2
    business days and before notice
    to institution, that would not have
    occurred but for C's failure to
    notify within 2 business days: $600 ..... 450[2]
                                     ——
C's total liability   500

[1] Maximum liability for this period.
[2] Because maximum liability is $500.

Situation 2--Both $500 and unlimited liability provisions apply

Date and Event
June 1--C's card is stolen
June 3--C learns of theft
June 5--Close of 2 business days
June 7--$200 unauthorized transfer that could have been prevented had notice been given by June 5
June 10--Periodic statement is transmitted to C (for period from 5/10 to 6/9)
June 15--$200 unauthorized transfer that could have been prevented had notice been given by June 5
July 10--Periodic statement of C's account is transmitted to C (for period from 6/10 to 7/9)
August 4--$300 unauthorized transfer that could have been prevented had notice been given by June 5
August 9--Close of 60 days after transmittal of statement showing unauthorized transfer
August 10--Periodic statement of C's account is transmitted to C (for period 7/10 to 8/9)
August 15--$100 unauthorized transfer that could have been prevented had notice been given by August 9
August 20--C notifies bank

Computation of C's liability:
Paragraph (b)(1) will apply to determine C's liability for unauthorized transfers that appear on the periodic statement and unauthorized transfers that occur before the close of the 60-day period. (The transfers need not both appear on the periodic statement and occur before the close of the 60-day period.) The maximum liability under (b)(1) is $500.

Amount of transfers before close of
    2 business days: $0 .... $ 0

Amount of transfers, after close of 2
    business days and before close of
    60-day period, that would not have
    occurred but for C's failure to
    notify within 2 business days: $700 .....   500[1]

[1] Maximum liability.

Paragraph (b)(2)(ii) will apply to determine C's liability for transfers occurring after the close of the 60-day period. There is no dollar ceiling on liability under paragraph (b)(2)(ii).

Amount of transfers, after close of 60 days and
    before notice, that would not have occurred
    but for C's failure to notify within 60 days:
    $100.. $ 100

    C's total liability.................................   600

Situation 3--$50/unlimited liability provisions apply acts same as in Situation 2, except that C does not learn of the card theft, but questions the account balance and notifies bank on August 20 of possible unauthorized transfers.

Computation of C's liability
In this situation only paragraph (b)(2) applies.

Amount of transfers appearing on the periodic statement or occurring during the 60-day period: $700	$ 50[1]
Amount of transfers, after close of 60-day period and before notice, that would not have occurred but for C's failure to notify within 60 days: $100	100
C's total liability	150

[1] Maximum liability for this period.

Kruser v. Bank Of America
California Court of Appeals, Fifth District, 1991
230 Cal.App.3d 741, 281 Cal.Rptr. 463

Stome (Wm. A.), Associate Justice. In this appeal we interpret the language of a federal banking regulation establishing the respective liabilities of a bank and a consumer for unauthorized electronic transfers of funds from the consumer's account.

THE CASE

Appellants, Lawrence Kruser and Georgene Kruser, filed a complaint against Bank of America NT & SA (Bank) claiming damages for unauthorized electronic withdrawals from their account by someone using Mr. Kruser's "Versatel" card. The trial court entered summary judgment in favor of the Bank because it determined appellants had failed to comply with the notice and reporting requirements of the Electronic Fund Transfer Act (EFTA). (15 U.S.C. §§1693-1693r; 12 C.F.R. §205.6(b)(2).)

THE FACTS

The facts are undisputed. The Krusers maintained a joint checking account with the Bank, and the Bank issued each of them a "Versatel" card and separate personal identification numbers which would allow access to funds in their account from automatic teller machines. The Krusers also received with their cards a "Disclosure Booklet" which provided to the Krusers a summary of consumer liability, the Bank's business hours, and the address and telephone number by which they could notify the Bank in the event they believed an unauthorized transfer had been made.

The Krusers believed Mr. Kruser's card had been destroyed in September 1986. The December 1986 account statement mailed to the Krusers by the bank reflected a $20 unauthorized withdrawal of funds by someone using Mr. Kruser's card at an automatic teller machine. The Krusers reported this unauthorized transaction to the Bank when they discovered it in August or September 1987.

Mrs. Kruser underwent surgery in late December 1986 or early January 1987. She remained hospitalized for 11 days. She then spent a period of six or seven months recuperating at home. During this time she reviewed the statements she and Mr. Kruser received from the bank. In September 1987, the Krusers received bank statements for July and August 1987 which reflected 47 unauthorized withdrawals, totaling $9,020, made from an automatic teller machine, again by someone using Mr. Kruser's card. They notified the bank of these withdrawals within a few days of receiving the statements. The Bank refused to credit the Krusers' account with the amount of the unauthorized withdrawals.

DISCUSSION

* * *

The ultimate issue we address is whether, as a matter of law, the failure to report the unauthorized $20 withdrawal which appeared on the December 1986 statement barred appellants from recovery for the losses incurred in July and August 1987. Resolution of the issue requires the interpretation of section 909 of the EFTA (15 U.S.C. §1693g) and section 205.6 of Regulation E (12 C.F.R. §205.6), one of the regulations prescribed by the Board of Governors of the Federal Reserve System in order to carry out the purposes of the EFTA. (15 U.S.C. §1693a(3); 15 U.S.C. 1693b(a).)

* * *

The trial court concluded the Bank was entitled to judgment as a matter of law because the unauthorized withdrawals of July and August 1987 occurred more than 60 days after appellants received a statement which reflected an unauthorized transfer in December 1986. The court relied upon section 205.6(b)(2) of Regulation E.

Appellants contend the December withdrawal of $20 was so isolated in time and minimal in amount that it cannot be considered in connection with the July and August withdrawals. They assert the court's interpretation of section 205.6(b)(2) of Regulation E would have absurd results which would be inconsistent with the primary objective of the EFTA--to protect the consumer. (See 15 U.S.C. §1693.) They argue that if a consumer receives a bank statement which reflects an unauthorized minimal electronic transfer and fails to report the transaction to the bank within 60 days of transmission of the bank statement, unauthorized transfers many years later, perhaps totaling thousands of dollars, would remain the responsibility of the consumer.

The result appellants fear is avoided by the requirement that the bank establish the subsequent unauthorized transfers could have been prevented had the consumer notified the bank of the first unauthorized transfer. (12 C.F.R. §205.6(b)(2)(ii).) Here, although the unauthorized transfer of $20 occurred approximately seven months before the unauthorized transfers totaling $9,020, it is undisputed that all transfers were made by someone using Mr. Kruser's card which the Krusers believed had been destroyed prior to December 1986. According to the declaration of Yvonne Maloon, the Bank's Versatel risk manager, the Bank could have and would have canceled Mr. Kruser's card had it been timely notified of the December unauthorized transfer. In that event Mr. Kruser's card could not have been used to accomplish the unauthorized transactions in July and August. Although appellants characterize this assertion as speculation, they offer no evidence to the contrary.

In the alternative, appellants contend the facts establish that Mrs. Kruser, who was solely responsible for reconciling the bank statements, was severely ill and was also caring for a terminally ill relative when the December withdrawal occurred. Therefore they claim they were entitled to an extension of time within which to notify the bank. They argue these extenuating circumstances as recognized in both EFTA, 15 United States Code section 1693g(a)(2) and Regulation E, section 205.6(b)(4) present a question of fact about the reasonableness of the time in which they gave notice.

The evidence appellants rely upon indicates in late 1986 or early 1987 Mrs. Kruser underwent surgery and remained in the hospital for 11 days. She left her house infrequently during the first six or seven months of 1987 while she was recuperating. Mrs. Kruser admits, however, she received and reviewed bank statements during her recuperation. Therefore, we need not consider whether Mrs. Kruser's illness created circumstances which might have excused her failure to notice the unauthorized withdrawal pursuant to the applicable sections. She in fact did review the statements in question.

Appellants cite no evidence in support of their contention Mrs. Kruser was also caring for her ill relative during the relevant time period. We need not determine whether that fact might have excused her failure to notice the unauthorized withdrawal.

Moreover, nothing in the record reflects any extenuating circumstances which would have prevented Mr. Kruser from reviewing the bank statements. The understanding he had with Mrs. Kruser that she would review the bank statements did not excuse him from his obligation to notify the bank of any unauthorized electronic transfers.

In Sun 'n Sand, Inc. v. United California Bank (1978) 21 Cal.3d 671, 148 Cal.Rptr. 329, 582 P.2d 920, the Supreme Court held in the case of a dishonest employee who altered her employer's checks to her benefit: "We made clear in Basch v. Bank of America (1943) supra, 22 Cal.2d 316, 327-328 [139 P.2d 1], that an employer is charged with the knowledge that an honest agent would have gained in the course of a reasonably diligent examination; we explained that 'this rule reasonably imposes upon the depositor the further duty of properly supervising the conduct of his trusted employee....' Sun 'n Sand's failure to discover its mistake within three years of the issuance of the first three checks thus derived from its failure to discharge with reasonable care its duty to supervise its employees." (Id. 21 Cal.3d at p. 702, 148 Cal.Rptr. 329, 582, P.2d 920.)

Although the record is clear Mrs. Kruser did nothing dishonest which led to the failure to report the unauthorized transaction, we see no distinction between the employer's inability to avoid liability by claiming it delegated that duty and Mr. Kruser's inability to avoid liability by claiming he delegated to his wife his duty to discover unauthorized withdrawals on his Versatel card.

Finally, appellants contend evidence of mailing the December bank statement was insufficient to establish "transmittal" as that word is used in section 205.6(b)(2) of Regulation E. They contend actual knowledge is required and rely on the Federal Reserve Board's official staff interpretation of Regulation E relating to the loss or theft provision of section 205.6(b)(1). (See official staff interpretation, 12 C.F.R. part 205, supp. II (Jan. 1, 1987 ed.) p. 125.)

Section 205.6(b)(1) requires the consumer to notify the bank "within 2 business days after learning of the loss or theft of the access device...." (Emphasis added.) The question addressed by the staff comment is whether the consumer's receipt of a periodic statement that reflects unauthorized transfers is sufficient to establish knowledge of loss or theft of an access device. The comment provides: "Receipt of the periodic statement reflecting unauthorized transfers may be considered a factor in determining whether the consumer had knowledge of the loss or theft, but cannot be deemed to represent conclusive evidence that the consumer had such knowledge." (Official staff interpretation, 12 C.F.R. part 205, supp. II, (Jan. 1, 1987 ed.) §205.6(b), p. 125.)

Here we are not concerned with the loss or theft of an access device. Rather, our question is whether the bank has established the loss of $9,020 in July and August 1987 would not have occurred but for the failure of appellants to report timely the $20 unauthorized transfer which appeared on the December 1986 statement. (15 U.S.C. §1693g(a)(2).)

Appellants cite no authority which supports their claim the consumer must not only receive the statement provided by the bank, but must acquire actual knowledge of an unauthorized transfer from the statement. Such a construction of the law would reward consumers who choose to remain ignorant of the nature of transactions on their account by purposely failing to review periodic statements. Consumers must play an active and responsible role in protecting against losses which might result from unauthorized transfers. A banking institution cannot know of an unauthorized electronic transfer unless the consumer reports it.

The Bank has established that the losses incurred in July and August 1987 as a result of the unauthorized electronic transfers by someone using Mr. Kruser's Versatel card could have been prevented had appellants reported the unauthorized use of Mr. Kruser's card as reflected on the December 1986 statement. The Bank is entitled to judgment as a matter of law.

DISPOSITION

We affirm the judgment and award costs on appeal to respondent.

Disclosure

Bisbey v. D.C. National Bank
United States Court of Appeals, District of Columbia Circuit, 1986
793 F.2d 315

Harry T. Edwards, Circuit Judge. Sandra Bisbey challenges the refusal of the District Court to hold the District of Columbia National Bank ("the Bank") liable for a violation of the Electronic Fund Transfer Act of 1984 ("the Act"). * * * The District Court found that the Bank, in its resolution of Ms. Bisbey's inquiry about her account, erroneously failed to deliver or mail to her an explanation of its investigative findings. However, the trial court concluded that the Act did not contemplate a finding of civil liability for this type of procedural mistake.

We reverse the District Court. Although there is no evidence of bad faith in this case, it is nonetheless clear that Bank officials failed to comply with provisions of the Act. Therefore, the case must be remanded for a determination of civil liability and attorney's fees.

I. BACKGROUND
A. Facts

Ms. Bisbey opened a checking account with the defendant Bank in January 1981. Subsequently, she authorized the Bank to debit her checking account for fund transfer directives submitted monthly by the New York Life Insurance Company ("NYLIC") for payment for her insurance premiums.

In September 1981, Ms. Bisbey's account lacked sufficient funds to cover the NYLIC directive, and no transfer was made. Thus, the September request was resubmitted by NYLIC in October, along with the latter month's directive. Appellant's funds were insufficient to satisfy either submission, both of which were covered by the Bank. As a result, two overdraft notices were sent to Ms. Bisbey, each in the amount of her monthly insurance premium. The appellant, having forgotten her nonpayment in September, believed that the Bank had erroneously made two payments in October.

At this point, Ms. Bisbey informed a customer representative of the Bank that she believed that an error had occurred with regard to these preauthorized transfers. Upon request by the Bank, she confirmed her inquiry by letter. Approximately ten days later, an official of the Bank telephoned appellant and orally explained that there had been no improper duplication of her premium payments. Ms. Bisbey, however, still considered the matter unresolved, and she filed suit under the EFTA.

B. Procedural History

In her complaint, plaintiff alleged that the Bank unlawfully failed to properly inform her about the result of its investigation into the alleged duplication error in her checking account. * * * She sought compensatory, treble and liquidated damages; the Bank filed a counterclaim for costs and attorney's fees, alleging that the plaintiff had brought suit in bad faith.

In relevant part, the opinion of the District Court held that the Bank had failed to comply with its statutory obligation to provide written notice of its findings when it concluded that no electronic funds transfer error had occurred. However, the trial court determined that section 915 of the Act, * * * which provides for civil liability and attorney's fees for certain violations, was, by its own terms, not applicable to the mistake at issue. Finally, neither party was deemed to have acted in bad faith; thus, the District Court found that an award of attorney's fees was unwarranted.

II. ANALYSIS

Section 908(d) of the Act provides: If [a] financial institution determines after its investigation ... that an error did not occur, it shall deliver or mail to consumer an explanation of its findings within 3 business days after the conclusion of its investigation, and upon request of the consumer promptly deliver or mail to the consumer reproductions of all documents which the financial institution relied on to conclude that such error did not occur. The financial institution shall include notice of the right to request reproductions with the explanation of its findings. * * * This section imposed a duty upon the Bank to "deliver or mail" the results of its investigation to Ms. Bisbey and to advise her of her right to request reproductions of all documents which it relied upon to conclude that no error occurred. The oral notice given to appellant was insufficient with respect to the required "explanation," and it did not even purport to give "notice of the right to request reproductions" as required by the statute.

The Bank's foregoing failures to comply with the statute give rise to civil liability under section 915 of the Act. That section provides that "any person who fails to comply with any provision of [the Act] with respect to any consumer, except for an error resolved in accordance with section 908, is liable to such consumer" for actual damages or for a symbolic award. Thus, under the plain terms of the Act, civil liability attaches to all failures of compliance with respect to any provision of the Act, including section 908.

An examination of other provisions of the Act supports this analysis. We note, for example, that section 908(e) specifies certain egregious violations of section 908 which would result in an award of treble damages, such as a failure to provisionally recredit a consumer's account while simultaneously failing to perform a good faith investigation. The singling out of these particular violations and their focus on willful unlawfulness for an award of treble damages suggests that other failures to comply with the statute in the application of section 908 give rise to standard civil liability.

The Bank contends that the only "fail[ure]s to comply" to which civil liability should adhere are those which may be cured by the error resolution process of section 908. And, appellee maintains, it is unlikely that such procedural mistakes as occur in the course of an attempt to utilize the error resolution process would, in turn, be resolved by that same process.

This argument is patently flawed. There are "fail[ure]s of compliance" with the Act which cannot be or are unlikely to be resolved under section 908--such as a violation of section 908 itself--and which nonetheless give rise to civil liability. For example, section 910 sets forth the liability of financial institutions for damages caused by certain acts and omissions with regard to electronic fund transfers. These acts and omissions plainly constitute "fail [ure]s to comply" with the Act, yet they do not fall within the statutory definition of "error" for purposes of utilizing the error resolution procedures set forth in section 908. * * * But surely a financial institution cannot escape civil liability for a breach of section 910 merely because the breach cannot be resolved under section 908 pursuant to the "error" correction procedures. Civil liability attaches due to the "fail[ure] to comply" with the law.

Section 915 provides for an exception to civil liability for "an error resolved in accordance with section 908." Plainly, this exception has no play in this case. The Bank's failures to comply (i.e. the failure to "deliver or mail ... an explanation" and the failure to give "notice of the right to request reproductions") were never cured. Therefore, these failures cannot be viewed as "errors resolved in accordance with section 908" within the exception to civil liability enunciated in section 915. The District Court's ruling to the contrary is simply wrong as a matter of law.

If the Bank had made a mistake in transferring funds from appellant's account and then had redressed the error pursuant to section 908 (without otherwise failing to comply with section 908), then the exception to section 915 would have to come into play. In such a case, the Bank could not be charged with civil liability for the mistaken transfer of funds because the "error" would have been fully cured pursuant to section 908. In this case, however, there is no problem with mistaken fund transfers; rather, the problem here has arisen because the Bank failed to comply with provisions in the Act when addressing a lawful inquiry about possible mistaken fund transfers.

It may seem odd that the Bank is held liable for a transaction that benefited the plaintiff. Ms. Bisbey's account contained insufficient funds to cover either of the premium requests submitted by NYLIC. Though she had no overdraft agreement, the Bank did not charge an overdraft fee. Thus, the effect of the Bank's payments was to provide her, at no cost, with insurance coverage she would not have had otherwise. Upon Bisbey's inquiry, the Bank gave her a correct report but neglected to send it in writing, as the statute requires. Ms. Bisbey conceded below that she had suffered no damage and the District Court's surmise that she may have been benefited * * * seems correct. Despite this, the litigation has continued for nearly three years, and the statute compels a finding that the Bank is liable. Doubtless the discretion given the District Court to award only nominal damages and a "reasonable" attorney's fee * * * was designed to mitigate the results of strict liability in cases such as this, involving a technical and non-damaging violation.

III. CONCLUSION

The "fail[ure]s to comply" with the EFTA in the instant case are plain; moreover, they are failures to which civil liability attaches for they have not been resolved in accordance with section 908. We therefore remand this case to the District Court for a determination of civil liability and attorney's fees pursuant to section 915.

So ordered.

practice

Case 1

"This suit concerns a wire transfer of funds made by Denver National Bank ("the bank") for the plaintiff. On December 1, 1988, the plaintiff paid $153.42 in cash to the bank for a $143.42 wire transfer to California. Bank personnel initiated the transfer and the funds were received in California that same day. Plaintiff later requested confirmation from the bank that the funds had reached their intended destination. The bank provided the plaintiff a copy of the actual wire transfer, and then confirmed and orally notified her that the transfer had been received. The bank followed oral confirmation with a copy of a letter from the recipient California bank confirming that the transferred funds indeed had reached the person intended. Still dissatisfied, the plaintiff traveled to California and confirmed that the funds appropriately had been transferred.
* * *

"Plaintiff's allegations and claim for relief are based solely on alleged violations of the Electronic Fund Transfer Act ("the Act"), 15 U.S.C. §1693 et seq. Therefore, the question whether the Act applies here to provide the plaintiff grounds for relief controls my decision." *Wachter v. Denver National Bank*, 751 F.Supp. 906 (D. Col.1990).

Does the EFTA govern this transaction?

Case 2

"Plaintiff maintained a bank account with defendant, to which she had access through an electronic terminal. On May 17, 1985, a paycheck, made out to and endorsed by plaintiff, was presented to teller number 5255 (Sharon Young), together with a deposit slip. The deposit slip is a three-part form consisting of a top copy (white), a middle copy (pink), and a bottom copy (yellow). One hundred and thirty-five dollars of the check was deposited into plaintiff's account; $110.51 was disbursed in cash. This transaction occurred at 11:50 a.m. On that same day, at 11:51 a.m., a check payable to Michiko Fischer in the amount of $50 was also presented to Young and $50 was disbursed in cash. The back of that check contained the handwritten names of 'Michiko Fischer' and 'Inez Spain.' That check was not deposited into plaintiff's account.

"On June 24, 1985, defendant's agent, Shirley Veronneau, debited plaintiff's account for $50, representing the amount of the Fischer check, without plaintiff's knowledge. Prior to taking such action, Veronneau ascertained from the teller tape that plaintiff's paycheck had been deposited immediately prior to the cashing of the Fischer check. Veronneau also compared the signature on the Fischer check with plaintiff's signature card which was on file with the bank. Based on her conclusion that plaintiff had endorsed the Fischer check, Veronneau prepared a debit slip in the amount of $50. The debit slip, like the deposit slip, is a three-part form consisting of a top copy (white), middle copy (pink), and bottom copy (yellow). The yellow copy is sent to the person whose account is being charged when the debit is made; the white copy is sent to that person with his/her monthly statement; the pink copy is retained by the branch office. The debit slip is not put through a teller machine, but is sent instead to defendant's Operations Center. At the Operations Center, the debit slip is coded and sent to a sorting area. The debit slip is then recorded on a sorting machine which is connected electronically with the bank records. (No money goes into or out of an account except by computer). At the end of the evening, if the credits and debits recorded on the electronic sorting machine are in balance, the credit and debits are released and the accounts are thereby affected.

"Defendant admits that it did not inform plaintiff of the circumstances under which it would disclose information concerning a customer's account to a third party. It further admits that it did not disclose that it would give information about plaintiff's account to her employer. Finally, the bank also admits that, after plaintiff claimed that the transfer of $50 out of her account was in error, it did not send to plaintiff a written explanation of its finding." *Spain v. Union Trust*, 674 F.Supp. 1496 (D. Conn.1987).

Does the EFTA govern this transaction?

Case 3

Suppose that Mary Jones is in possession of an ATM card.

a. **If Mary's card is stolen by a thief, is she liable for its unauthorized use? What if the Issuing Bank has provided a means whereby the user of the card "can be identified as the person authorized to use it?"**

b. **What is the extent of Mary's liability in that instance?**

Suppose now that the Issuing Bank furnishes a periodic statement that contains the unauthorized transfer.

c. **Can Mary obtain reimbursement for losses that "the financial institution establishes would not have occurred but for the failure of the consumer to report within sixty days of transmittal of the statement" the unauthorized transfer? 15 U.S.C. §1693g(a); compare 4-406.**

d. **What if Mary learns of the loss or theft of her card and fails to report the loss or theft "within two business days?" 15 U.S.C. §1693g(a).**

e.   What if a transfer is initiated by someone to whom Mary has furnished her card and PIN?

   i.   Is transfer unauthorized in that scenario?

   ii.   What if Mary notifies the financial institution that the person no longer has permission to use the card?

Index Of Key Terms

References are to Pages

Annex of Supplemental Materials

1. Demand installment notes

The problem "arises from the formation and demise of nine limited partnerships organized to redevelop property in Atlantic City, New Jersey. Investors who purchased partnership interests sought tax benefits from their investments. To finance their purchases, the investors executed promissory notes payable to American Funding Limited. With the collapse of the redevelopment scheme, many of the investors ceased making payments on their notes which had been purchased from American Funding by various banks. The investors claim that they were defrauded in the promotion and sale of partnership interests, but the banks, seeking collection on the notes, assert that they are holders in due course and accordingly are immune from most of the defenses raised by the investors.

"On February 18, 1987 the Judicial Panel on Multidistrict Litigation transferred to this district many of the cases arising from this scheme. Jurisdiction in these cases is based on diversity. To date, their number exceeds 300 and is increasing. Most of the actions are suits initiated by banks against defaulting investors. Some were initiated by investors suing the promoters, their professional advisors (lawyers and accountants) and the banks.

"A threshold issue is whether the banks as purchasers of the investors' notes are holders in due course. Central to that issue is the determination of whether the notes are negotiable instruments. The investors, whether aligned as plaintiffs or defendants, have moved for "partial summary judgment" asserting that the notes are not negotiable.

* * *

"Under the Code, a holder in due course is one who takes an instrument for value, in good faith and without notice that it is overdue or has been dishonored or of any defense against or claim to it on the part of any person. Section 3-302. Throughout Article Three, "instrument" means negotiable instrument. Section 3-102(1)(e). To be negotiable, an instrument:

> must (a) be signed by the maker or drawer; and (b) contain an unconditional promise or order to pay a sum certain in money and no other promise, order, obligation or power given by the maker or drawer except as authorized by this

article; and (c) be payable on demand or at a definite time; and (d) be payable to order or bearer.

Section 3-104(1).
"The sole focus of the investors' challenge to the negotiability of these notes is Section 3-104(1)(c). The notes are relatively simple. See Appendix A. The relevant portions read as follows:

3. PAYMENTS
I will pay _____ monthly installments of Principal and interest, each in the amount of $_____, commencing on the _____ day of _____ 19_____ e
In the event I purchased Credit Life Insurance, the premium is included in the monthly installment.

e--estimated first payment date. ....

5. PAYMENT DUE DATE.
Lender will notify me in writing of the first payment due date, the amount of the first payment, the date of the first payment, the date of the final payment and the amount of the final payment. Interest shall not begin to be due to the Lender until the date of the notice to me, the first payment due date shall not be earlier than 30 days from the date of the notice to me.
I will begin making payments on the date set forth in the notice from the Lender to me, and continue to pay on the same day of each month until I have paid all the principal and interest and any other charges, described below, that I may owe under this Note.
If on the final payment due date as provided to me by the Lender in its notice, I still owe amounts under this Note, I will pay all those amounts, in full, on that date. I will make my monthly payments at the office of the Lender, 7 Lincoln Avenue, Greenwich, Connecticut 06830 or at a different place if required by the Note Holder.

In the blanks in paragraph 3 of each note are handwritten figures representing the number of monthly payments, the amount of each payment, and an estimated date on which the payments are to begin.
"The investors pose a narrow challenge to the notes' claimed negotiability, alleging that in contravention of Section 3-104(1)(c) they are neither payable on demand nor at a definite time." *In re Boardwalk Marketplace Securities Litigation*, 668 F. Supp. 115, 115-18 (D. Conn. 1987), *issue certified to state court*, 849 F.2d 89 (2d Cir. 1988).

In re Boardwalk Marketplace Securities Litigation
United States Court of Appeals, Second Circuit, 1988
849 F.2d 89

This case involves an appeal from an interlocutory ruling of the United States District Court for the District of Connecticut, Warren W. Eginton, J., reported at 668 F.Supp. 115 (D.Conn.1987), that certain promissory installment notes at issue in a complex, multidistrict litigation arising from the formation and demise of several tax shelter limited partnerships are not negotiable instruments under Connecticut law. The original lender on the notes was a Connecticut financial institution. Many of the notes have since found their way into the hands of the banks that are the appellants in this action. The tax shelter investors claim they have been defrauded and many of them have ceased making payments on the notes. Over 300 suits, most initiated by the banks against defaulting investors, have been consolidated in this litigation.

A threshold question in the litigation is whether the banks as purchasers of the investors' notes are holders in due course and thus immune from most of the defenses raised by the investors. Central to that issue is the narrow question of whether the notes are negotiable instruments. As the district court stated, "[t]he investors pose a narrow challenge to the notes' claimed negotiability, alleging that in contravention of [UCC] Section 3-104(1)(c) they are neither payable on demand nor at a definite time." 668 F.Supp. at 118. The district court determined that the notes were not negotiable instruments, holding that the notes were not due at a definite time and were not demand notes within the meaning of UCC §§3-104(1), 3-108, 3-109. In December 1987, the district court certified the negotiability question for immediate appeal pursuant to 28 U.S.C. §1292(b) on the ground that it was a controlling question of law and that a final resolution of the question would greatly advance the resolution of the entire litigation. The court stressed that there are more than 1,000 notes in the multidistrict litigation that are affected by the answer to this question. The court also stressed that it was a close question as to whether the notes were negotiable and that there is little case law on point. It stated that:

> there is substantial difference of opinion on whether the notes are negotiable, precisely because this is a case of first impression and so few reported decisions provide any analysis of the Code's negotiability requirements that can guide their application in new settings.

> The dearth of case law on this question is reflected in the conclusion of the Code's leading commentators that the condition that a note be payable on demand or at a definite time "seem[s] to have caused little difficulty recently and we devote no space to them." J. White and R. Summers, Handbook of the Law Under the Uniform Commercial Code 554 (2d ed. 1980). One can speculate that the Code's clear requirements for negotiability are easy to comply with and therefore do not produce a great amount of litigation. When notes are drafted which tread the line marking the outer limits of negotiability, however, the Code's language must be carefully parsed. At this point, differences of opinion become substantial.

In January 1988, this court granted leave to appeal.

We believe that the question whether the notes are negotiable instruments should be decided by the Connecticut Supreme Court. The notes provide that they are to be governed by Connecticut law and that the parties agree to submit to federal or state jurisdiction, and none of the parties dispute that Connecticut law governs.

There is little room for dispute that the notes do not fit squarely within the UCC definition of notes payable at a definite time, UCC §3-109, or demand notes, UCC §3-108. Although each note apparently contains a stated handwritten date on which installment payments are to commence, the notes also indicate that this date is an estimated date and that the actual date for commencement of payment will be provided to the investor in written notice from the lender. And, while the banks argue that the provision permitting the lender (and arguably the holder banks) to set the date for the first installment payment makes the notes demand notes, it is not entirely clear that the UCC envisions demand installment notes--that is, notes for which the first installment payment is due on demand and the remaining installments are due at stated intervals thereafter, as opposed to notes in which the entire principal amount is due on demand. There appear to be good arguments on both sides of the negotiability question.

The negotiability question presented here is apparently one of first impression for which there appears to be no controlling precedent in Connecticut, affects a significant number of notes in this litigation, is likely to recur and will have a potentially significant impact on commercial practices. Its resolution by the Connecticut Supreme Court at this time would aid in the administration of justice.

The foregoing is hereby certified to the Connecticut Supreme Court pursuant to Conn.Gen.Stat. §51-199a.

2. Nonrecourse notes

The case *United Nat'l Bank v. Airport Plaza Ltd. Partnership*, 537 So.2d 608 (Fla. Ct. App. 1988), perfectly illustrates the use of a nonrecourse note. In this case the Bank sued to foreclose a real estate mortgage after a default in payments. The defendant, Airport Plaza, "claimed that Milam Dairy Warehouse, the assignor of the note and mortgage to United National, had committed acts of fraud which Airport Plaza could assert against United National because the latter was not a holder in due course. Contending that the note lacks the negotiable character necessary to make United National a holder in due course as defined by section 673.302, Florida Statutes (1985), Airport Plaza relies principally on a clause in the note which provides:

> It is expressly understood and agreed by each original and successive owner or holder of this Note that nothing herein contained shall be construed as creating any personal liability on Borrower, or any Shareholders therein, to pay this Note or any interest that may accrue hereunder, all such liability, if any, being expressly waived.

Airport Plaza argues that this nonrecourse clause, which insulates the maker from personal liability on the note, destroys the negotiability of the note thereby depriving United National of its holder-in-due-course status." Id. at 609.

The court agreed. "In order to qualify as a negotiable instrument a promissory note must contain an unconditional covenant to pay a sum certain in money. §673.104(1)(b), Florida Statute (1985). Section 673.105(2)(b) provides further that a promise is conditional if the instrument "[s]tates that it is to be paid only out of a particular fund or source except as provided in this section." Because the note made by Airport Plaza specifically provides that the borrower shall have no personal liability, recourse for payment in the event of a default is limited to foreclosure against the secured property. The promissory note is thus rendered conditional. A conditional instrument is not negotiable. Since under this analysis the note is not negotiable, the bank is not a holder in due course and took the note subject to Airport Plaza's defense of fraud.." Id. at 609-10. As a result, the summary judgment against Airport Plaza in the foreclosure action was reversed.

Article 3 no longer provides that a promise or order is condition that limits payment to a particular source or fund. Rather, it is now the law that "[a] promise or order is not made conditional * * * because payment is limited to resort to a particular fund or source." 3-106(b). The explanation is:

> There is no cogent reason why the general credit of a legal entity must be pledged to have a negotiable instrument. Market forces determine the marketability of instruments of this kind. If potential buyers don't want promises or orders that are payable only from a particular source or fund, they won't take them, but Article 3 should apply.

3-106 comment 1.

This explanation argues too much. More to the point, we are not fully convinced that this change in the law completely insures the negotiability of nonrecourse notes. Clearly, if there is a promise, it is not conditional. We worry, however, that language disclaiming personal liability negates promise. If so, we are uncertain that 3-106(b) is broad enough to excuse the lack of promise.

3. Joint and several liability and liability between the parties

As a general rule, "two or more persons who have the same liability on an instrument as makers, drawers, acceptors, indorsers who indorse as joint payees, or anomalous indorsers are jointly and severally liable in the capacity in which they sign." 3-116(a). Therefore, for example, each co-maker of a note is liable for the whole to a person entitled to enforce the instrument.

Notice that this list of signers does not include indorsers, except when they are joint payees or anomalous indorsers. "Indorsers normally do not have joint and several liability. Rather, an earlier indorser has liability to a later indorser. 3-116 comment 2.

A different issue is the liability between themselves of parties who are jointly and severally liable on the instrument. *Inter se*, they share liability:

(a) Except as provided in Section 3-419(e) or by agreement of the affected parties, a party having joint and several liability who pays the instrument is entitled to receive from any party having the same joint and several liability contribution in accordance with applicable law.

(c) Discharge of one party having joint and several liability by a person entitled to enforce the instrument does not affect the right under subsection (b) of a party having the same joint and several liability to receive contribution from the party discharged..

3-116(b-c). With respect to the amount of contribution, the commonly "applicable law" provides that as a general rule:

> apportionment in contribution is that all co-obligors must contribute equally in discharging their common obligation. This has been called a presumption which may be rebutted by showing that one signed for the accommodation of the other or that one received all the proceeds of the loan, or by showing an inequality of benefits received, in which case each is liable to contribute in proportion to the amounts actually received.

Wilner v. Croyle, 214 Pa.Super. 91, 99, 252 A.2d 387, 391 (1969); see also *Siegler v. Ginther*, 680 S.W.2d 886 (Tex.App.1985) (the liability between principal co-makers is governed by the common law which makes the nonpaying co-maker impliedly liable for a pro rata contribution in assumpsit, i.e., the non-paying co-maker's share of the joint and several liability); *Dittberner v. Bell*, 558 S.W.2d 527, 534 (Tex.Civ.App.1977) (contribution may be prorated between co-obligors according to the benefits each received).

The rule of sharing among co-obligors does not apply a co-obligor who is a surety. A surety, whom Article 3 calls an accommodation party, is not liable for any amount to a co-obligor who is the principal debtor; and, if it is the surety who pays the instrument, she can recover the whole amount from the principal debtor. See 3-419(e).

Wilson v. Turner
Court of Appeals of North Carolina, 1976
29 N.C.App. 101, 223 S.E.2d 539

In his complaint plaintiff alleged that on 25 October 1967 he and defendant indorsed a note for $27,900. The note was executed by Landmark Inns of Charlotte, Inc. to the Bank of Commerce, and it was a renewal of an earlier note. Plaintiff also alleged that he and defendant had agreed that they would be jointly liable for $13,500, while plaintiff would be primarily liable for the balance. In April 1968 plaintiff paid the note and this action is to collect one- half the $13,500. Defendant admitted that he indorsed the note but denied that he was liable to plaintiff for any amount.

The case was tried without a jury and plaintiff's evidence was as follows:

On 27 November 1963 Landmark Inns of Charlotte, Inc. (Landmark) executed a note to the Bank of Charlotte for $22,500, and plaintiff and defendant signed the note on the back. This note was renewed and reduced as payments were made by Landmark. In December 1965 Landmark executed a renewal note for $12,500 and both parties again signed on the back.

In February 1964 Landmark executed a $3,000 note to the Bank of Commerce which plaintiff did not indorse. This note was periodically renewed and increased as additional loans were made. Plaintiff signed some of the renewal notes. On 25 October 1967 Landmark executed a renewal note to the Bank of Commerce for $27,900, and plaintiff and defendant signed it on the back. Plaintiff signed before defendant, and his signature appears above defendant's signature.

On 4 April 1966 plaintiff and defendant signed an "Indemnification Agreement" in which they "guaranteed" the payment of a $12,500 note from Landmark to the Bank of Charlotte, and a $16,000 note from Landmark to the Bank of Charlotte. This agreement stated that the parties had orally agreed that plaintiff should be primarily liable for these debts and the parties desired to reduce their agreement to writing, and it was agreed that plaintiff would indemnify defendant for any liability defendant might incur in connection with the two notes.

On 15 March 1967 the parties signed a "Stipulation and Agreement" which provided that they had "guaranteed" payment of a $12,500 note from Landmark to the Bank of Charlotte and a $29,500 note from Landmark to the Bank of Commerce. It further provided that plaintiff had agreed to be primarily liable for the $12,500 note and $16,000 of the $29,500 note, but that a dispute had arisen as to the remaining $13,500; and that each would thereafter be free to "guarantee" renewals of the $29,500 note without waiving any claims against the other.

Plaintiff personally paid the October 1967 note to the Bank of Commerce on 2 April 1968.

Defendant offered evidence to show that he signed the 25 October 1967 note after plaintiff signed it, and.that he never agreed to be jointly liable with plaintiff for any portion of Landmark's debt.

The court found that defendant had not agreed to be jointly liable and that plaintiff and defendant did not indorse the note as part of the same transaction. It concluded that the parties were liable in the order of their indorsement, and judgment was entered for defendant. Plaintiff appealed to this Court.

ARNOLD, JUDGE. Since the particular note for which contribution is sought was executed following the effective date of Chapter 25 of the N.C. General Statutes, the liabilities of the parties will be determined by the Uniform Commercial Code.

It is maintained by plaintiff that the judgment for defendant was in error for two reasons. First, he contends that there was an agreement by which the parties agreed to be jointly and severally liable. Under the provisions of G.S. 25-3-414(2) indorsers are liable to one another in the order in which they indorse unless they agree otherwise. The order of indorsement is presumed to be the order in which the signatures appear on the instrument.

The trial court found as a fact that there was no agreement, written or oral, by which defendant agreed to be jointly liable with plaintiff. This finding is supported by competent evidence and it is conclusive on appeal. Goggins v. City of Asheville, 278 N.C. 428, 180 S.E.2d 149 (1971); Laughter v. Lambert, 11 N.C.App. 133, 180 S.E.2d 450 (1971). Plaintiff's first argument is without merit.

In his second argument plaintiff contends that the court erred in finding that he and defendant did not indorse the note as part of the same transaction. Plaintiff reasons that if he and defendant signed the note "as a part of the same transaction" they would be jointly and severally liable. He relies on G.S. 25-3-118(e) which reads as follows:

> Unless the instrument otherwise specifies two or more persons who sign as maker, acceptor, or drawer or indorser and as a part of the same transaction are jointly and severally liable even though the instrument contains such words as "I promise to pay."

According to plaintiff the loan transaction was not completed until the note was executed by the corporate maker, and indorsed by both plaintiff and defendant. It was intended from the beginning that both parties indorse the note, and thus, plaintiff argues, there was only one transaction.

Assuming *arguendo* that it was intended that both parties indorse the note before the loan was closed it does not follow that plaintiff and defendant indorsed the instrument "as part of the same transaction" within the meaning of G.S. 25-3-118(e). This statute has not changed the rule in North Carolina that a prior indorser is not entitled to recover from a subsequent indorser in the absence of an agreement otherwise establishing liability. (See Lancaster v. Stanfield, 191 N.C. 340, 132 S.E. 21 (1926).

The Official Comment to G.S. 25-3-118(e) declares that the statute "applies to any two or more persons who sign in the same capacity, whether as makers, drawers, acceptors, or indorsers. It applies only where such parties sign as part of the same transaction; *successive indorsers are, of course, liable severally but not jointly.*" (Emphasis added)

Moreover, the North Carolina Comment to G.S. 25-3-118(e) provides that this section is not intended to affect the rules governing:

(1) Contribution between parties jointly and severally liable.

(2) The order of liability of parties signing in different capacities or at different times.
See North Carolina Comment to G.S. 25-3-414 (contract of indorser; order of liability).

From the North Carolina Comment to G.S. 25-3-414(2) it is clear that the Uniform Commercial Code did not change the North Carolina rule relating to the presumption of liability between prior and subsequent indorsers:

"This continues the rule of G.S. 25-74 (N.I.L. 68) that indorsers are presumed to be liable in the order in which their signatures appear on the instrument. However, parol evidence is admissible to show the true order of indorsement." Plaintiff's second argument is also without merit.

We hold that the conclusion by the trial court that plaintiff and defendant were indorsers and liable to each other in the order of their indorsement, according to G.S. 25-3-414, was correct. The judgment appealed from is

Affirmed.

4. Using extrinsic evidence to vary liability from the terms of an instrument

Robert Hillman, Julian McDonnell & Steve Nickles,
**Common Law And Equity Under The
Uniform Commercial Code**
¶12.02[1]-[3] (1985)

The negotiable instruments governed by Article 3 are, in the most fundamental sense, contracts. However, in contrast to the sales article, Article 3 makes no attempt to formulate comprehensively one of the most intricate of contract doctrines, the parol evidence rule. That rule -- or more accurately the matrix of rules -- specifies what evidence may and may not be considered as defining the contract. The writing, to the extent that it expresses the agreement of the parties ("is integrated"), is not as a matter of the substantive law of contracts to be contradicted by other evidence. This "integrated writing" is to be protected. The comparative silence of Article 3 with respect to this subject does not mean that the parol evidence rule is inapplicable to Article 3 paper. On the contrary, insofar as negotiable instruments are concerned, the parol evidence rule is one of the most significant common-law doctrines preserved by Section 1-103.

The drafters of Article 3, aware that the parol evidence rule stood in the background, provided a running commentary on the parol evidence implications of a number of Article 3 provisions. * * * [Yet] [e]ven in the light of the foregoing provisions and comments, Article 3 "does not attempt to state general rules as to when an instrument may be varied or affected by parol evidence." Article 3 has no counterpart to Section 2-202. There is, however, a substantial volume of parol evidence litigation dealing with negotiable instruments. This is typically litigation between the immediate parties to the instrument rather than with a third-party holder in due course. Since Article 3 lacks a general parol evidence provision, it is the common-law parol evidence doctrine of the particular jurisdiction that is most frequently brought to bear in these negotiable instruments cases. This doctrine is expressed in an array of general formulas that create the impression of a consensus. A list of the rubrics would include at least the following: Parol may be used to "explain" ambiguous terms in the instrument * * * to show want or failure of consideration, or fraud, or additional "collateral" agreements. The rule does not bar proof of agreement or waiver made subsequent to the execution of the writing. Conditions precedent to the effectiveness of the instrument may be shown provided they do not contradict the writing itself. Similarly, delivery for a special purpose may be established. However, alleged conditions subsequent that would divert or alter payment duties expressed in the instrument must be disregarded, although North Carolina openly adheres to a different view. Of course, elusive "contradiction" is always forbidden.

NORTHWESTERN STATE BANK v. GANGESTAD, 289 N.W.2d 449, 451-52 (Minn.1979). "Between 1975 and 1977, the defendant entered into 24 promissory notes with the plaintiff [bank], totaling approximately $275,000, to finance the purchase of cattle, seed and fertilizer and for other farm expenses. All of these notes were payable 'on demand,' and all bore interest at 9 per annum. * * * Towards the end of 1976, the bank began to feel insecure about the loans. It offered suggestions to the defendant for improving his farm operations and attempted to obtain refinancing for the defendant through the Farmers' Home Administration. In March 1977, when these efforts had failed, the bank made demand for payment of the notes. When payment was not made, it demanded surrender of the collateral and brought this action. *** Although they were all 'demand notes', the defendant claims plaintiff verbally agreed that the notes would not be paid until a certain time or would only be payable out of the proceeds of certain sales. However, the maker of a promissory note is barred from showing an agreement contrary to the terms of the note by the parol evidence rule. Thus the defendant cannot show that the demand notes were to be payable only at a certain time or after a certain event nor that the notes were only to be paid with certain funds."

ㅁㅁㅁㅁㅁ

Under pre-Code law, it was generally held that, as against parties not holders in due course, extraneous evidence is admissible to show that an instrument was delivered on a condition precedent which had not been satisfied. See, e.g. *Towle-Jamieson Inv. Co. v. Brannan,* 165 Minn. 82, 205 N.W. 699 (1925); *Rule v. Connealy,* 61 N.D. 57, 237 N.W. 197 (1931); *Dickson v. Protzman,* 123 Wash. 247, 212 P. 249 (1923). Indeed, the Negotiable Instruments Law explicitly provided:

> Every contract on a negotiable instrument is incomplete and revocable until delivery of the instrument for the purpose of giving effect thereto. As between the immediate parties, and as regards a remote party other than a holder in due course, *** the delivery may be shown to have been conditional, or for a special purpose only ***.

N.I.L. §16. There is no comparable provision in Article 3, but it is generally thought that the rule in principle, if not in letter, continues to apply today. Restatement (Second) of Contracts §217 (1981); *Participating Parts Associates, Inc. v. Pylant,* 460 So.2d 1299 (Ala.Civ.App.1984) (extrinsic evidence may be introduced as to an agreement between original parties to a note that liability was conditional and that delivery of the note was not effective until the happening of some agreed upon event); *Ketchian v. Concannon,* 435 So.2d 394 (Fla.Dist.Ct.App.1983) (court admitted evidence that effectiveness of note representing real estate broker's commission was conditioned on consummation of sale arranged by broker); cf. *Simpson v. Milne,* 677 P.2d 365 (Colo.App.1983) (extraneous evidence admissible against payee to show that parties did not intend for note to be legally enforceable debt); *Labar v. Cox,* 635 S.W.2d 801 (Tex.App.1982) (parol evidence admissible in suit between original parties to show that note was delivered for a special purpose which never occurred); but see *Evenson v. Hlebechuk,* 305 N.W.2d 13 (N.D.1981) (recognizes that evidence of conditions precedent to note generally are admissible but not when the condition conflicts with the terms of a note and is "so inconsistent"). The Restatement rejects reasoning such as that in *Evenson.*

RESTATEMENT (SECOND) OF CONTRACTS § 217
(1981)

Where the parties to a written agreement agree orally that performance of the agreement is subject to the occurrence of a stated condition, the agreement is not integrated with respect to the oral condition.

Comment:

b. Requirement of a condition inconsistent with a written term. The rule of this Section *** has sometimes been limited to requirements of conditions consistent with the written terms. But an oral agreement of a condition is never completely consistent with a signed agreement which is complete on its face; in such cases evidence of the oral requirement bears directly on the issues whether the writing was adopted as an integrated agreement and if so whether the agreement was completely integrated or partially integrated. Inconsistency is merely one factor in the preliminary determination of those issues. If the parties orally agreed that performance of the written agreement was subject to a condition, either the writing is not an integrated agreement or the agreement is only partially integrated until the condition occurs. Even a "merger" clause in the writing, explicitly negating oral terms, does not control the question whether there is an integrated agreement or the scope of the writing.

Herzog Contracting Corp. v. McGowen Corp.
United States Court of Appeals, Seventh Circuit, 1992
976 F.2d 1062

Posner, Circuit Judge. The district judge granted summary judgment in favor of Herzog Contracting Corporation in its diversity suit to enforce two promissory notes, aggregating $400,000, against the issuer, McGowen Corporation. The appeal raises a tangle of jurisdictional and substantive questions, the latter governed, the parties agree, by Indiana law.

* * *

In 1989 Herzog, the plaintiff, bought the assets of Tru-Flex Metal Hose Corporation from McGowen, the defendant, and formed a wholly owned subsidiary of Herzog (also called Tru-Flex) to hold them, to which Herzog assigned the asset purchase agreement. The agreement called for annual payments from Tru- Flex to McGowen of $500,000 for five years. The two promissory notes, both demand notes, were issued by McGowen to Tru-Flex later in 1989. The parties have radically different positions on the purpose of the notes. Herzog claims that it loaned McGowen $400,000 and the notes are McGowen's promises to repay the loan. McGowen acknowledges having received the $400,000 but denies that it was a loan, contending instead that it was partial prepayment of the next year's installment due under the asset purchase agreement and that the only purpose of the notes that it gave Tru-Flex was to enable it (that is, McGowen) to postpone the realization of taxable income to the following year by making the $400,000 payment look like a loan.

The parties soon fell to squabbling and Herzog refused to make further payments under the asset purchase agreement, precipitating a suit by McGowen against Herzog in an Indiana state court for breach of contract that remains pending. At about the same time that the state court suit was brought, Tru- Flex assigned McGowen's promissory notes to Herzog, which shortly afterward brought this suit to enforce them.

* * *

The question is whether, as the district judge held, solely on the basis that the notes are "clear and unambiguous," they are enforceable regardless of what the parties actually intended.

They would be if enforcement were being sought by a holder in due course, UCC §3-305, Ind.Code §26-1-3-305, but Herzog concedes that it is not that. It places its case on the parol evidence rule. The promissory notes are unambiguous--they promise Herzog a specified sum of money on demand--and their terms cannot be varied by extrinsic evidence. At first glance Herzog's argument seems a complete nonstarter. A holder of a promissory note who is not a holder in due course takes the note subject to "all defenses of any party which would be available in an action on a simple contract," UCC §3-306(b), Ind.Code §26-1-3-306(b), and one of those defenses, notwithstanding the parol evidence rule, is that the parties did not intend to create an enforceable contract. "It is well settled that whatever the formal documentary evidence, the parties to a legal transaction may always show that they understood a purported contract not to bind them; it may, for example, be a joke, or a disguise to deceive others." The deceived others may, of course, be able to object to the attempt to prove the contract a sham, but that is not a factor here. More to the point, a minority of jurisdictions "have refused to admit such evidence [i.e., that the purported contract was a joke, a disguise, in short a sham of some sort] where the purpose of the sham agreement was offensive to public policy."

However, we prefer the majority rule, * * * so will apply it here in default of any Indiana cases on the question. Apart from the fact that the minority rule rewards a party to the sham agreement and imposes a punishment that may be disproportionate to the promisor's misconduct, it invites a collateral inquiry into the character of the alleged "sham." Here the party accused of shamming by his fellow shammer was angling for a tax advantage. Did that make the transaction a "sham"? Despite the doctrine of tax law that substance prevails over form, many transactions that would strike a nonspecialist as contrived purely to avoid taxes are entirely lawful. Must we therefore, to resolve this case, decide whether McGowen's effort to postpone its tax liability for the sale of Tru-Flex was one of them? We trust not.

But we are not done. In the face of the principle that any defenses to a contract are available in a suit on a promissory note unless the plaintiff is a holder in due course, some courts enforce the parol evidence rule more broadly in such suits than in suits to enforce ordinary contracts. In Perez-Lizano v. Ayers, 215 Mont. 95, 695 P.2d 467, 469 (1985), for example, the court refused to allow the admission of parol evidence to show that the note was a sham. One of the cases in this line is an Indiana case, Highfield v. Lang, 182 Ind.App. 77, 394 N.E.2d 204, 206 (1979). But it is readily distinguishable from our case; and we have found two recent cases from other jurisdictions in which courts admitted parol evidence to show that a promissory note was not intended to be enforceable. American Underwriting Corp. v. Rhode Island Hospital Trust Co., 111 R.I. 415, 303 A.2d 121, 125 (1973); Simpson v. Milne, 677 P.2d 365, 368 (Colo.App.1983). The second was a case of a sham; the parol evidence was that the notes in suit "were executed as a fiction to satisfy plaintiff's wife, who was near death, and who strongly felt that [the defendant and his wife] still owed [the plaintiff and his wife] money from prior business transactions." Id.

Despite these last two cases and despite UCC §3-306(b), the parties have tacitly agreed that the applicability of the parol evidence rule to this case is governed not by general contract law but by a special doctrine that allows in parol evidence to show, against a plaintiff who is not a holder in due course, that the delivery of the negotiable instrument that he is suing to collect was "for a special purpose." UCC §3-306(c); Ind.Code §26-1-3-306(c). This approach is understandable though not inevitable. While section 3-306(b) subjects the promisee who is not a holder in due course to "all defenses" that the original promisor would have had, implicitly including the defense that the promise was not intended to create enforceable rights, section 3-306(c) deals with some of these defenses in greater detail. This could be taken to imply that the defense that no enforceable rights were intended to be created is to be analyzed in accordance with the "special purpose" doctrine that predates the Code, though a likelier inference is that the draftsmen wanted simply to make sure that no defense was overlooked.

However this may be, Herzog argues that the special-purpose doctrine is limited to allowing the promisor (McGowen here) to defend by showing that his obligation to make good on the note was subject to a condition precedent, which is not the case here. For it is McGowen's contention not that something had to happen before Herzog could demand payment, but that Herzog could never demand payment. Parol evidence is always admissible to prove a fraud, but McGowen does not contend that when Herzog agreed to the scheme for making the prepayment of the purchase installment look like a loan it intended to double- cross McGowen by demanding payment of the notes. If there was a fraud, it was against the Internal Revenue Service, though no one is arguing this. With fraud out of the picture and the scope of the parol evidence rule applicable to promissory notes conceded by McGowen to be governed by section 3-306(c) rather than 3-306(b), McGowen is left with the special-purpose doctrine and Herzog concludes that a sham case is outside that doctrine, which, as we have noted, he believes to be limited to conditions precedent.

There are cases, none from Indiana, on both sides of the question whether "delivery for a special purpose" is limited to conditions precedent, although the majority view is that it is not. Text and history can help us choose between these positions, though history more than text. Section 3- 306(c) expressly recognizes a defense of "nonperformance of any condition precedent," making the "special purpose" defense redundant on Herzog's construal of it. But redundancy is built into section 3-306(c), as we have seen, and maybe this is another example of it. So let us turn to history.

Until sometime after the middle of the nineteenth century, courts were highly reluctant to admit parol evidence, in suits on promissory notes, for any purpose other than to prove fraud or mistake. A little later, they were allowing such evidence in three additional types of case: delivery of the note together with a mortgage deed, with the note as additional security for payment of the mortgage; delivery of the note to escrow; and delivery contingent on the satisfaction of a condition precedent. Some courts also allowed the admission of parol evidence "to show that a contract signed and delivered was never intended to be the real contract between the parties." One case--oddly enough it is factually similar to ours--used the term "special purpose" to describe the defense in a "no obligation" or "sham" case. And when the English codified their law of negotiable instruments in 1882, they expressly allowed evidence (other than against a holder in due course) that delivery had been "conditional or for a special purpose only, and not for the purpose of transferring the property in the bill." The meaning brought out by the words that we have italicized seems unmistakable: the "special purpose" defense encompassed all cases in which the negotiable instrument had not been intended to create an enforceable obligation.

The American Negotiable Instruments Law--the first statute drafted by the National Conference of Commissioners on Uniform State Laws--copied the English provision word for word. Later, however, darkness descended, and we find some authorities distinguishing among condition cases, no-obligation cases, and special-purpose cases. This proliferation of unhelpful distinctions was abetted by the fact that the Uniform Commercial Code, in recodifying negotiable instruments law, dropped the explanatory phrase "and not for the purpose of transferring the property in the bill" from the formulation of the special purpose defense. But this was done without any intention of changing the meaning of the defense as it had appeared in the Negotiable Instruments Law. Certainly nothing in the history of the Uniform Commercial Code suggests a purpose of abolishing the "no obligation" defense and returning to the law as it existed before the Civil War. The tendency of our law for almost a century has been to relax strict rules, perhaps because of growing (though possibly misguided and even sentimental) confidence in the ability of judges and juries to resolve factual questions (such as, What was the purpose of McGowen's notes?), with reasonable accuracy and at reasonable cost, by sifting testimony. The legal realists who, led by Karl Llewellyn, drafted the Uniform Commercial Code were leaders in the movement to soften the contours of strict common law rules. See, e.g., UCC §§2-103(1)(b), 2-204, 2-205.

It hardly matters whether the no-obligation cases are subsumed under the special-purpose defense or set off by themselves or, as seems simplest and therefore--no other values being at stake so far as we can see--preferable, assimilated to the general contract doctrine that allows parol evidence to show that a contractual-looking document was not intended to be binding. The office of the parol evidence rule is to prevent parties to a written contract from seeking to vary its terms by reference to side agreements, or tentative agreements reached in preliminary negotiations. In the case of a condition precedent the promisor is not trying to vary the terms, but to deny the enforceability of the promise by pointing to some condition that has not been fulfilled. The distinction may seem fine-spun and even arbitrary, but it has been deemed consistent with the policy behind the parol evidence rule, or at least a tolerable qualification of it. Two points can be made on behalf of the distinction. The weaker, as it seems to us, is that without such an exception the rule would work dramatic forfeitures, by preventing a party from showing not merely that the terms were somewhat different from what they appeared to be but that he had never agreed to do or pay anything. The stronger point is that the parol evidence rule, properly understood, is not a rule imposed on contracting parties from without but merely an inference, drawn from the language of the document, that the parties intended it to be the complete statement of their agreement, extinguishing any agreements that might have emerged from the preliminary negotiations. The document is unlikely to reveal whether the parties intended it to be taken seriously, and if it does not, there is no basis for applying the rule.

At all events, to allow parol evidence to expose a sham case such as this is alleged to be would make no greater inroads into the parol evidence rule than the cases on conditions precedent do. McGowen is not trying to change the terms in the promissory notes, but to show that the notes were not in fact intended to create a legally enforceable obligation. They were, not to put too fine a point on it, intended to fool the Internal Revenue Service. Herzog, perhaps fearing that it will be found to have been a party to this little deception, does not argue that McGowen's unclean hands should forfeit its right to make a sham-transaction defense, if there is such a defense, and we think there should be because we can think of no principled distinction between it and the condition-precedent defense that Herzog concedes is valid.

The policy of the law is to facilitate negotiability by allowing assignees of negotiable instruments to take free of defenses not obvious on the face of the note. But that policy is expressed in the doctrine of holders in due course. Herzog made no effort to discount the notes to one who would have been such a holder and therefore could have enforced the notes against McGowen regardless of the oral agreement not to enforce them on which McGowen relies in this suit.

The judgment is reversed and the case remanded for further proceedings consistent with this opinion.

REVERSED AND REMANDED.

Questions and Hypotheticals

1.   What rule of parol evidence governed the *Gangestad* case?

2.   In deciding whether to admit the proffered evidence of the alleged verbal agreement, should the court in *Gangestad* have considered whether the agreement was made before or after the notes were signed? The parol evidence rule renders

inoperative *prior* agreements. Restatement (Second) of Contracts §213 (1981); *In Re Estate of Giguere*, 366 N.W.2d 345 (Minn.App.1985) (oral agreement to extend time of payment of note was valid and binding modification which offends neither the parol evidence rule nor the Statute of Frauds).

3. Suppose that the parties in the *Gangestad* case had agreed orally before signing the notes that the maker would not be liable on the instruments unless the price of beef reached a certain level which was never reached. Should evidence of this oral agreement be admitted?

4. Suppose that, prior to executing the note, the parties orally agreed to condition the maker's liability such that he would completely avoid liability if the price of beef failed to reach a certain level by the time the maker's cattle should, in due course, have been sold. Should a court admit evidence that this condition was not satisfied? Should evidence of a condition subsequent be treated differently from evidence of a condition precedent? E. Farnsworth, CONTRACTS §7.4 (1982) (extrinsic evidence is admissible to show an oral agreement that the written agreement is to take effect only if a stated condition occurs, but inadmissible to show that the duty of one party under agreement already in effect is conditional rather than absolute); Note, 34 NEB.L.REV. 141 (1954) (courts traditionally have admitted parol evidence to show delivery of a negotiable instrument on a condition precedent but not to show delivery on a condition subsequent). On the difficult distinction between conditions precedent and subsequent with respect to instruments and for suggested solutions to the problem, see Hutchinson, *Conditional Delivery of Negotiable Instruments in Colorado*, 13 U.COLO.L.REV. 248 (1941) (noting Beutel's call for abandoning the distinction and admitting evidence of all conditions).

5. M executed a note in payment for stock purchased from the payee, P. The note was unconditional on its face, but the parties had agreed orally that payment would be made from corporate dividends and that M would have no personal liability if the dividends were insufficient to pay the note. Is evidence of this agreement admissible if P sues to enforce the note after M dishonors because no dividends were earned? Is the condition on liability a condition precedent or a condition subsequent? The facts of this part of the problem are based on *Scafidi v. Johnson*, 420 So.2d 1113 (La.1982), in which the evidence was admitted as a condition precedent to the maker's obligation under the note.

6. Reconsider the *Gangestad* case. Make the argument that the court was wrong in excluding evidence of the oral agreement that the notes would be paid from the proceeds of certain sales of the cattle. Make the opposite argument. Which is the better argument? The parol evidence rule allows parties to a contract to rely on the terms of their written agreement and thus promotes certainty and predictability. The effect of applying the rule, however, may be to thwart actual intentions. Which is the weightier concern, insuring certainty in contractual relations generally or giving effect to the true understanding of the parties to a particular transaction? Is insuring certainty and predictability more or less important in transactions involving negotiable instruments than in transactions involving ordinary contracts? Is a negotiable instrument more or less likely to express the parties' whole agreement than a full-blown, detailed written contract? Should the parol evidence rule be applied more strictly or more leniently to negotiable instruments than it is

to ordinary written contracts? For a very good discussion of the clash between certainty and fairness in applying the parol evidence rule under Article 3, see Jordan, *Just Sign Here -- It's Only a Formality: Parol Evidence in the Law of Commercial Paper*, 13 GA.L.REV. 53 (1978).

7. In the *Gangestad* case, the defendant argued in the alternative that he was fraudulently induced to sign the notes through the misrepresentations of the bank regarding terms of liability. *Northwestern State Bank v. Gangestad*, 289 N.W.2d 449, 453-54 (1979). The court recognized that "[t]he defendant could avoid the parol evidence rule by proving fraudulent inducement," id. at 453, but upheld the trial court's directed verdict against the defendant on his fraud claim because there was "no evidence which could have supported a verdict of fraud as to the nature of the notes or as to the bank's intentions regarding future financing." Id. at 453-54. The parol evidence rule does not generally bar extrinsic evidence to show fraud, mistake or other invalidating cause as a ground for rescission or reformation of even a completely integrated contract. Restatement (Second) of Contracts §214 (1981). If a maker of an instrument is precluded by the parol evidence rule from proving a side agreement that frees her from liability on the instrument or changes her liability, will not this exception to the rule always give her a way around it so as to accomplish indirectly what she cannot achieve directly? Does this "invalidating cause" exception to the common-law parol evidence rule, or any other exception to the rule, apply in an Article 3 case when an applicable provision of the statute seems clearly to bar completely extrinsic evidence?

8. Suppose that the side agreement in the *Gangestad* case had been in writing.

   a. How should the court in the *Gangestad* case have ruled on the admissibility of the alleged side agreement, as between the immediate parties, if the agreement had been in a writing executed along with the notes? See 3-117? Are an instrument and a separate written agreement part of the "same transaction" if there is a two-year gap between them? See *Gensplit Finance Corp. v. Link Power & Machinery Corp*, 36 UCC Rep.Serv. 588 (S.D.N.Y.1983). As to reliance on evidence of an oral understanding to show that a separate written agreement modifies or affects the terms of an instrument, see *Federal Deposit Ins. Corp. v. Borne*, 599 F.Supp. 891 (E.D.N.Y.1984) (suggests cannot rely on extrinsic evidence to link instrument and another agreement); *Main Bank of Chicago v. Baker*, 86 Ill.2d 188, 427 N.E.2d 94 (1981). The court in the *Main Bank* case observed that Article 3 "applies the general rule to negotiable instruments that courts will look to the entire contract in writing and thus construe instruments executed as part of the same transaction, between the same parties, for the same purpose, as a single agreement." Id. at 200, 427 N.E.2d at 99. For exhaustive analysis, and considerable criticism, of this rule's applicability to negotiable instruments, see Bailey, *Negotiable Instruments and Contemporaneously Executed Written Contracts*(pts. 1 & 2), 13 TEX.L.REV. 278, 14 TEX.L.REV. 307 (1936).

   b. Does the existence of this written side agreement affect the negotiable form of the notes under 3-104? Do the terms of the separate agreement, which conditions the maker's liability by limiting payment, affect the negotiable form of the notes?

c. Suppose that the bank in the case had assigned the notes to a third person who sued the defendant to enforce the notes. The defendant proffers the written side agreement to establish that her liability was conditioned. The plaintiff argues that, even if the evidence is admitted and a condition is established in fact, she is a holder in due course and thus takes free of such a defense.

  i. If the plaintiff knew when she took the notes that there was a side agreement between the immediate parties to the notes, did this knowledge preclude plaintiff from being a holder in due course?

  ii. Suppose that the plaintiff also knew that the side agreement conditioned defendant's liability. Did this knowledge of itself preclude holder in due course status if plaintiff at the time she took the notes was unaware that the condition had not been satisfied? Was plaintiff in any event subject to the written side agreement? Does the condition in the agreement amount to a "defense"? If so, are the consequences to plaintiff the same as the consequences of not being a holder in due course?

5. Effect of a renewal note with respect to the maker's liability on the original instrument

The common-law rule is that, ordinarily, "the mere execution of a renewal note evidences the same debt by a new promise and does not constitute payment or discharge of the original note but operates only as an extension of time for payment." *State Bank of Young America v. Vidmar Iron Works, Inc.*, 292 N.W.2d 244, 248 (Minn.1980), quoting *Farmers Union Oil Co. v. Fladeland*, 287 Minn. 315, 319, 178 N.W.2d 254, 257 (1970); see also J. Brannan, Negotiable Instruments Law §119(4) at 1131-32 (F. Beutel 7th ed. 1948); W. Britton, HANDBOOK ON THE LAW OF BILLS AND NOTES §263 at 641-43 (2d ed. 1961); 3 J. Daniel, A TREATISE ON THE LAW OF NEGTOTIABLE INSTRUMENTS §1454 at 1469-1500 (T. Calvert 7th ed. 1933). In other words, taking one instrument in place of another does not in itself constitute payment and thus discharge of the original instrument under 3-602. Liability on the original note is simply suspended. 3-310(b); *Aluminum Co. of America v. Home Can Manuf. Corp.*, 134 Ill.App.3d 676, 89 Ill.Dec. 500, 480 N.E.2d 1243 (1985).

Yet, there is authority that accepting a renewal note will discharge the original instrument if this effect was intended by the parties. *Slaughter v. Philadelphia Nat'l Bank*, 290 F.Supp. 234 (E.D.Pa.1968), reversed on other grounds, 417 F.2d 21 (3d Cir.1969); *Cipra v. Seeger*, 215 Kan. 951, 529 P.2d 130 (1974); 3 J. Daniel, A TREATISE ON THE LAW OF NEGOTIABLE INSTRUMENTS §1458 (T. Calvert 7th ed. 1933). Such an intention might be inferred from the holder's surrender to the maker of the original instrument. Indeed, vintage authority teaches that "[w]here the old note is surrendered in exchange for the new note the presumption is that the old note is thereby discharged." W. Britton, HANDBOOK ON THE LAW OF BILLS AND NOTES §263 at 642 (2d ed. 1961); but see 3 J. Daniel, A TREATISE ON THE LAW OF NEGOTIABLE INSTRUMENTS §1455 (T. Calvert 7th ed. 1933); see also 3-604(a)(ii).

Upon the execution of a renewal note, liability on the original note will be discharged, albeit indirectly, if in executing the new note the parties effected a novation, substitute contract, or accord and satisfaction with respect to the obligation underlying the original note. In this event, the underlying obligation would be discharged; and, concomitantly, liability on the original note would be discharged. 3-601(a). This result depends, however, on satisfying the requirements of the common law or other applicable law governing novation, accord and satisfaction, or the like. See generally, e.g., *Ampex Corp. v. Appel Media, Inc.*, 374 F.Supp. 1114 (W.D.Pa.1974); *Wolfe v. Eaker*, 50 N.C.App. 144, 272 S.E.2d 781 (1980), cert. denied, 302 N.C. 222, 277 S.E.2d 69 (1981); *First Pennsylvania Bank v. Triester*, 251 Pa.Super. 372, 380 A.2d 826 (1977).

Hypothetical

A and B execute a note. Shortly before the note matures, B alone executes a renewal note. B dishonors the renewal note when it becomes due. The payee sues on the original note, and A defends by arguing that the taking of the renewal note freed her of liability.

a. Should this defense succeed? See *First Pennsylvania Bank v. Triester*, 251 Pa.Super. 372, 380 A.2d 826 (1977).

b. Collateral secured the original note, but nothing in the renewal note suggested that it, too, was secured by the property. Can the payee rely on the collateral if she seeks to enforce the renewal note against B? See U.C.C. 9-203(1); 9-204(1); see also *Matter of Cooley*, 624 F.2d 55 (6th Cir.1980); *Mid-Eastern Elec., Inc. v. First Nat'l Bank*, 455 F.2d 141 (4th Cir.1970); *In re Cantrill Constr. Co.*, 418 F.2d 705 (6th Cir.1969), cert. denied sub nom. , 397 U.S. 990 (1970). For discussion, see R. Hillman, J. McDonnell & S. Nickles, COMMON LAW AND EQUITY UNDER THE UNIFORM COMMERCIAL CODE ¶21.01[2] (1985).

c. Would the answers be different if the payee accepted the renewal note with the understanding that it effected a full and complete discharge of the original note?

6. Accord and satisfaction

Suppose that B buys goods on credit from S. Thereafter, a dispute arises over the amount that B had agreed to pay for the property. B sends S a check for less than the amount that S has demanded. The check bears the legend, "IN FULL

SETTLEMENT OF MY ACCOUNT." S indorses and cashes the check and later sues B for the balance of S's demand. What is the proper result? Should the result change if S had written "under protest" beneath her indorsement on the check? Here is the common law:

> An accord is a contract under which an obligee promises to accept a stated performance in satisfaction of the obligor's existing duty. Performance of the accord [satisfaction] discharges the original duty.

RESTATEMENT (SECOND) OF CONTRACTS §281(a) (1981).

> A recurring situation involves the creditor who indorses and cashes a check sent by the debtor and marked "payment in full." The debtor then argues that the creditor, by exercising dominion over the check, has made an accord under which he has promised to accept payment of the check in satisfaction of the debt. Assuming that the transaction is not subject to objections such as those based on the absence of consideration, on lack of good faith and fair dealing and on unconscionability, such a notation by the debtor, if prominent enough ***, may form the basis of an enforceable accord ***. The creditor cannot generally avoid the consequences of his exercise of dominion by a declaration that he does not assent to the condition attached by the debtor.

Id. §281 comment d.

Revised Article 3 specifically addresses this "recurring situation" that the Restatement describes -- accord and satisfaction by check. The section is 3-311 which is mostly a restatement of the common law "with some minor variations to reflect modern business conditions." 3-311 comment 3. It "is based on the belief that the common law rule produces a fair result and that informal dispute resolution by full satisfaction check should be encouraged." Id.

The general rule is that the full-payment check fully discharges the claim for which it is given if these requirements are met:

- the check was tendered in good faith to the claimant as full satisfaction of the claim,
- the instrument or an accompanying written communication contained a conspicuous statement warning that the instrument was tendered in full satisfaction,
- the amount of the claim was unliquidated or subject to a bona fide dispute, and
- the claimant obtained payment of the check.

3-311(a-b). The discharge results even if the claimant expresses orally or in writing, on the instrument or elsewhere, that she rejects the settlement or that she still demands the balance of her claim.

There are two small exceptions. First, if the claimant is an organization, no discharge results unless the check is sent to the organization's office that handles disputed debts, so long as the other person had prior warning to send full-payment checks there. 3-311(c)(1). Second, whether or not the claimant is an organization, a discharge can be undone by the claimant tendering repayment of the full-payment check within 90 days after the check was paid. 3-311(c)(2). This exception is designed for claimants who were unaware that the check was for full payment, not for claimants who have second thoughts about settling.

Both exceptions are subject to a limitation. Neither exception applies, and the discharge stands, if the claimant actually knew within a reasonable time before trying to collect the check that it was tendered in full satisfaction of the claim. 3-311(d).

Warning! There is no 3-311 discharge in the first instance unless the statute applies, which assumes that the instrument was negotiable so that Article 3 is applicable and that the four requirements for 3-311 discharge were met. When 3-311 is inapplicable for any reason, other law applies to determine if there was a valid accord and satisfaction. The other applicable law will almost certainly be common law, which is very unlikely to provide a discharge on facts that would fail the requirements of 3-311.

Hypothetical

B buys goods on credit from S. Thereafter, a dispute arises over the amount that B owes for the property. B sends S a check for less than the amount that S has demanded. The check bears the legend, "IN FULL SETTLEMENT OF MY ACCOUNT." S indorses and cashes the check and later sues B for the balance of S's demand.

a. On these facts who should win?

b. Does the result change if S had written "under protest" beneath her indorsement on the check?

c. Would it matter that S is a large corporation and B had sent the full payment check directly to the corporation's CEO. 3-311(c)(1) & (d).

d. What if 60 days after having cashed B's check, S tried to undo the situation by sending S's own check in the same amount to B, which check B returned. 3-311(c)(2).

e. Go back to the beginning. What result if the offer of accord had been written in a latter accompanying the check rather than on the check itself? Or if there had been no genuine dispute about the amount that B owed?

7. Liability on certain extraordinary instruments

a. Insurance Drafts

Canal Ins. Co. v. First Nat'l Bank

Court of Appeals of Arkansas, 1979
266 Ark. 1044, 596 S.W.2d 710

HOWARD, JUDGE. This is an appeal from a summary judgment rendered in behalf of First National Bank of Fort Smith against Canal Insurance Company for $2,412.99 * * *.

The facts are not in dispute. However, the pertinent facts for a resolution of the issues tendered are: Canal Insurance Company, on January 24, 1974, issued an insurance policy to Jim Marler insuring a utility refrigeration trailer. On April 5, 1974, International Harvester Credit Corporation, the lienholder, was added as a loss payee by an endorsement to the policy.

Following an accident involving the trailer on August 18, 1974, Marler filed a claim with Canal for the damages sustained. On April 22, 1975, Canal issued its draft, No. 414449, for $2,412.99. The following language was printed on the face of the draft: "Upon Acceptance Pay To The Order Of Jim Marler" and "Payable Through the South Carolina National Bank, Greenville, South Carolina." Marler deposited the draft on May 5, 1975, in a checking account of Nationwide Refrigerated Express, Inc., maintained at First National Bank of Fort Smith. First National permitted Marler to withdraw funds from the account, and moreover, the account was closed before First National received a reply to its tender of the draft to South Carolina National Bank for payment.

On May 16, 1975, the draft was presented for payment, but was not accepted because Canal had issued a stop payment order. * * *

* * *

First National filed its lawsuit against Canal on December 30, 1975, seeking judgment for $2,412.99. Canal informed International of the action on January 15, 1976, and requested International to intercede in the lawsuit and defend Canal's interest. International denied any obligation to respond to Canal's request contending that the hold harmless agreement did not provide for a defense "to any action as a result of the alleged wrongfully stop-payment of a draft issued in settlement of the subject claim."

On February 12, 1976, Canal filed its answer to First National's complaint and a third party complaint against International for judgment of its expenses incurred in defending the action and for whatever sum of money Canal may be required to pay First National.

Canal argues rather persistently that its initial draft, No. 414449, made payable to Jim Marler only was not a negotiable instrument inasmuch as the draft was conditional "Upon Acceptance" and "Payable Through the South Carolina National Bank, Greenville, South Carolina." Consequently, argues Canal, Canal had no affirmative obligation under the instrument until Canal had accepted the draft and, furthermore, until acceptance, Canal had every right to stop payment on the draft. Accordingly, reasons Canal, the trial court erred in rendering a judgment against it in behalf of First National.

In support of this position, Canal cites, among other things, Ark.Stat.Ann. §85-3-410(1) which provides essentially that "acceptance" is the drawee's signed engagement to honor the draft as presented; and there must be some manifestation of the drawee's acceptance on the draft.

Canal further contends that the language "Payable Through the South Carolina National Bank, Greenville, South Carolina" on the face of its initial draft simply designated South Carolina National Bank as a collecting bank without authority to pay the draft. Consequently, the bank is not a drawee and is not ordered or even permitted to pay the instrument out of any of the drawer's funds, if any, on hand. Canal relies on Ark.Stat.Ann. §85-3-120 to support its argument here. Ark.Stat.Ann. §85-3-120, (Add.1961), in material part, provides: An instrument which states that it is 'payable through' a bank or the like designates that bank as a collecting bank to make presentment but does not of itself authorize the bank to pay the instrument.

While Canal's argument is interesting and on first blush seems plausible, after close scrutiny of the circumstances existing in this case and consideration of the applicable law, we are not persuaded by Canal's argument and it is, therefore, rejected.

In First National Bank of Huttig v. Rhode Island Insurance Company, 184 Ark. 812, 43 S.W.2d 535 (1931), the Arkansas Supreme Court, in disposing of an identical issue under §7896, Negotiable Instrument Act of Crawford and Moses' Digest, made the following observation:

> . . . A bill of exchange drawn by the maker upon himself is in legal effect a promissory note, and cannot be countermanded. Where a bill of exchange is drawn by a corporation upon itself, the instrument may be treated as an accepted bill or as a promissory note at the election of the holder. In the present case, the instrument which is the basis of the suit was in form a bill of exchange. It was drawn by the corporation, Rhode Island Insurance Company, under the signature of its president upon itself. In other words, it was a bill of exchange drawn by the corporation through its proper officer upon itself, and was not therefore subject to countermand. It is claimed, however, that it was conditional because of the words 'upon acceptance' in it. . . . (T)hese words had no legal effect on the instrument. They were in the instrument when it was signed by the president of the corporation, and the very act of drawing the bill is deemed an acceptance of it, and the holder may treat it as an accepted bill of exchange or as a promissory note.
> * * *

We conclude that Canal remained liable on its initial draft made payable to Jim Marler only although a stop payment order was issued. As maker and drawee of the instrument, Canal could not countermand the draft. Moreover, where, as here, a bill of exchange is drawn by the maker upon itself, the mere execution of the bill is deemed an acceptance of it and the holder has an option to treat the draft as an accepted bill or as a promissory note.

It is plain that Canal's draft contained all the elements of negotiability and was not drawn without recourse. The record is deficient of any proof that First National had notice of any defense against the instrument. First National was, indeed, a holder in due course. Accordingly, the judgment of the trial court in behalf of First National is affirmed.

HAYS, JUDGE, dissenting. I respectfully dissent to the decision of the majority * * *. I would reverse as to First National Bank * * *.

I believe that the majority is overlooking a long-standing and recognized practice, particularly with the insurance industry, of issuing drafts bearing the words "upon acceptance" and "payable through" a specific bank and that such instruments are not treated as negotiable until actually accepted by the issuer. The reasons for this treatment of such drafts are practical to the problems of covering drafts in settlement of claims being issued at many separate branches across the country and providing efficiently, at the paying end, the necessary funds to cover the drafts being processed. I believe the Uniform Commercial Code framers recognized the custom and made allowance for it by the language of and comment to §85-3-120.

The record is silent, but I suspect this matter is before us only because appellee inadvertently treated the draft deposited by Marler as a cash item and immediately credited the account, rather than treating it conditionally. Its normal practice, I believe, would be to forward the draft for collection before crediting the account.

The effect of the majority opinion is to invalidate a practice I consider to be widespread and of near universal acceptance, with nothing to replace it all for no good reason. I recognize that there are decisions from other jurisdictions, which the majority cites, that reach a different conclusion; however, the opinions of Pennsylvania and New York are not binding upon us and, in this instance, are not even persuasive, where they contain nothing to commend them except that they exist. Nor am I willing to impose what I hold to be an extreme alteration of a custom and practice of commerce on the strength of an arcane decision handed down half a century ago, more than forty years before the adoption of the Uniform Commercial Code and decades before it was even conceived of. I refer to the case of First National Bank of Huttig v. Rhode Island Insurance Company, 184 Ark. 812, 43 S.W.2d 535, decided in 1931.

As I interpret the majority opinion, the determining factor is that where the drawer and drawee are the same person (as in the case before us) the words "upon acceptance" have no meaning and the issuer of such a draft is immediately liable upon the instrument to a holder in due course. Yet the opinion cites dicta from decisions, including an early decision of this state, which permit the same result by using different words, i. e., "without recourse." Thus a drawer and drawee can be identical and accomplish the same result if different words are used. I believe that in practice the words "upon acceptance" have been treated as having the same effect. If this is so, why insist on substituting two words more to our own liking, when those involved in this area of commercial dealing have come to recognize two different words as achieving the same result, and the practice is not objectionable under the U.C.C.?

* * *

I am authorized to state that Newbern, J., joins in this dissent.

b. Money Orders

Sequoyah State Bank v. Union Nat'l Bank
Supreme Court of Arkansas, 1981
274 Ark. 1, 621 S.W.2d 683

Adkisson, Chief Justice. The only issue in this case is whether Union Bank by its own initiative can stop payment on a personal money order it had issued in exchange for a hot check and, thereby, cause Sequoyah Bank, a holder in due course, to bear the loss. Under these circumstances the loss must be borne by Union Bank which issued the negotiable instrument to be circulated in commerce.

We do not decide the question of whether the purchaser may stop payment, but we do hold that after the sale of a personal money order, the issuing bank cannot stop payment on the instrument.

A personal money order is issued with unfilled blanks for the name of the payee, the date, and the signature of the purchaser. Only the amount is filled out at the time of issue, usually by checkwriter impression as was done in this case.

The Uniform Commercial Code apparently did not directly contemplate the use of money orders and made no specific provision for them. It was recognized in Mirabile that it is the custom and practice of the business community to accept personal money orders as a pledge of the issuing bank's credit. We may consider this custom and practice in construing the legal effect of such instruments. See Ark.Stat.Ann. §85-1-103 (Add.1961).

Appellee relies on the cases of Garden Check Cashing Service, Inc. v. First National City Bank, 25 A.D.2d 137, 267 N.Y.S.2d 698 (1966), aff'd. 18 N.Y.2d 941, 223 N.E.2d 566, 277

N.Y.S.2d 141 (1966) and Krom v. Chemical Bank New York Trust Co., 63 Misc.2d 1060, 313 N.Y.S.2d 810 (1970), rev'd. 38 A.D.2d 871, 329 N.Y.S.2d 91 (A.D.1972) which held that a purchaser of a personal money order may stop payment on it. However, the only cited case to specifically address the issue of whether the issuing bank, on its own initiative, may stop payment on a personal money order is Rose Check Cashing Service, Inc. v. Chemical Bank N. Y. Trust Co., 40 Misc.2d 995, 244 N.Y.S.2d 474, 477 (1963). In holding that the issuing bank could not stop payment and therefore must suffer the loss the court stated: All of these differences between the instrument at issue and an ordinary check would seem to indicate that the bank would honor the order to pay no matter who signed the face of the instrument, assuming of course an otherwise valid negotiation of the instrument. .... In the instrument in suit, the drawer purchases the instrument from the bank. The transaction is in the nature of a sale. No deposit is created. The funds to pay the instrument, immediately come within the bank's exclusive control and ownership.... The bank's contention that the instrument is a check is inconsistent with its own acts. The bank (drawee) stamped "Stop Payment" on the instrument in suit on its own order. Nowhere in the Negotiable Instruments Law is there any provision that a drawee (bank) may "Stop Payment" of a check unless ordered to do so by the drawer.

Appellee also denies liability on the instrument based upon Ark.Stat.Ann. §85-3-401(1) which states that "No person is liable on an instrument unless his signature appears thereon." Subdivision (2) of this same section provides that a signature may be "any word or mark used in lieu of a written signature." The authenticity of the instrument involved here is not in question. The issuance of the money order with the bank's printed name evidences the appellee's intent to be bound thereby.

Appellee also relies on Ark.Stat.Ann. §85-3-409 for the proposition that it is not liable on the personal money order since it did not accept it. In our opinion, however, the appellee accepted the instrument in advance by the act of its issuance.

The personal money order constituted an obligation of Union from the moment of its sale and issuance. The fact that Union was frustrated in retaining the funds because instead of cash it accepted a check drawn on insufficient funds is no reason to hold otherwise. We note by analogy that the Uniform Commercial Code on sales Ark.Stat.Ann. §85-2-403(1)(b) provides that a purchaser of goods, who takes delivery in exchange for a check which is later dishonored, transfers good title to the goods.

Union placed the personal money order in commerce for a consideration it accepted as adequate and was, thereafter, liable on it. Banks are not allowed to stop payment on their depositor's checks and certainly should not be allowed to stop payment on personal money orders.

Reversed.

Dudley, Justice, dissenting. This case involves a personal money order, not a bank money order, not a certificate of deposit and not a certified check. A personal money order is for the convenience of anyone who does not have an ordinary checking account and needs a safe, inexpensive and readily acceptable means of transferring funds. The bank simply sells to the individual a check-sized form which has the amount impressed into the face of the paper, an identification number and the name of the issuing bank. No authorized representative of the bank signs the instrument. When the purchaser of the instrument decides to pass it, he dates it, enters the name of the payee and signs the instrument.

Ark.Stat.Ann. §85-3-104(1)(a) (Add.1961) requires that a writing be signed by the drawer or maker in order to be negotiable. Any item which is an order to pay is considered a "draft" and any draft drawn on a bank and payable on demand is a "check." §85-3-104(2)(a), (b). Since the only signature on a personal money order is that of the purchaser, since the instrument takes the form of an order to pay, and since it is drawn on a bank and payable on demand, it is clearly within the classification of a check. The absence of the bank's signature as a "maker" and the absence of any express "undertaking" to pay by the bank, §85-3-102(1)(c) and §85-3-104(2)(d) preclude a finding that the instrument is a note. Aside from "draft," "check" and "note" the only other form of negotiable instrument recognized by the Uniform Commercial Code is a "certificate of deposit" and that requires an acknowledgment that the bank will repay it. §85-3-104(2)(c). Under these code provisions a personal money order must be classified as a check. There is no other code classification of negotiable commercial paper. §85-3-104. For the sake of clarity in the law of commercial paper this personal money order should be classified as a check.

However, the matter of classification is not nearly as important as the issue of liability. No authorized representative of appellee bank signed this check: Section 85-3-401 states: "No person is liable on an instrument unless his signature appears thereon." Section 85-3-409(1) states that a check or other draft is not an assignment of funds held by the drawee (appellee Union Bank) and the drawee is not liable until it accepts the check or draft. Appellee did not accept this instrument. It stopped payment. The language of these statutes, a part of the Uniform Commercial Code, is unmistakable.

The majority opinion holds: The personal money order constituted an obligation of Union from the moment of its sale and issuance. I respectfully submit that statement is supported by absolutely no authority and it creates an unnecessary legal quagmire. Assume that a purchaser of a personal money order has not filled in the name of the payee or has not signed the check and it is lost or stolen. The purchaser then wants to stop payment before it is negotiated to a third party. The majority has stated that it was an obligation of the bank from the moment of sale and issuance. Fairness and logic dictate that the purchaser should not be allowed to stop payment and leave the bank liable. Yet, §85-4-403(1) provides: Customer's right to stop payment Burden of proof of loss. A customer may by order to his bank stop payment of any item payable for his account but the order must be received at such time and in such manner as to afford the bank a reasonable opportunity to act on it prior to any action by the bank with respect to the item described in Section 4-303.

Comment 4 to this statute makes it abundantly clear that personal money orders are intended to be covered by this broad language.

One of the three explanations given for the holding is: The issuance of the money order with the bank's printed name evidences the appellee's intent to be bound thereby.

That notion will echo because the name of the drawee bank is printed on every ordinary check in circulation.

The other two explanations are that banks should not be allowed to stop payment and business custom. Both explanations are dead letters. Assume, for the sake of argument only, that banks should not be allowed to stop payment. That occurrence takes place after the sale and issuance of the instrument. The majority has held that liability attached upon issuance. Therefore this subsequent event logically cannot have any effect on liability. It very simply is not a reason for a decision that liability attached at the time of issuance. Business custom is not proven. There is not one single word in the transcript or abstract about business custom. Even if this defense had been proven it would be an estoppel defense, or a defense which accrues after the sale and, once again, it would not be a reason for a decision that liability attached at the time of issuance.

The master purpose of the Uniform Commercial Code is to clarify the law governing commercial transactions. The tragedy of this case is that both the purpose and the Code are emaciated for no reason.

I dissent.

c. Teller's Checks

Guaranty Federal Savings Bank v.
Horseshoe Operating Co.
Supreme Court of Texas, 1990
793 S.W.2d 652

Hightower, Justice. * * * These consolidated cases concern a savings and loan association's liability on its so-called "teller's check." A "teller's check" is a check drawn by a savings association on its account at another financial institution and made payable to the person designated by the customer purchasing the check. In each case, the customer delivered the teller's check to the designated payee, but later sought to stop payment. The savings association, as drawer of the check, timely requested its drawee institution to stop payment. The payee brought suit, not against the customer who remitted the check or against the drawee that refused payment, but against the savings association. In each case, the trial court granted summary judgment holding the savings association liable on the check. The courts of appeal, however, reached conflicting results.

In Guaranty Federal Savings & Loan Association v. The Horseshoe Operating Co., the Fifth Court of Appeals affirmed, holding that such checks are equivalent to cashier's checks or cash, and therefore not subject to countermand. As a result of this analysis, the court of appeals apparently deemed irrelevant all factual issues concerning the payee's possible status as a holder in due course and the savings association's possible defenses under the Texas Business and Commerce Code. In University Savings Association v. Intercontinental Consolidated Companies, the First Court of Appeals rejected the "cash equivalent" analogy, and concluded that the savings association, as a "customer" of a "bank," had a statutory right to stop payment on its check, and assert its own limited defenses to payment. Insofar as the savings association's customer intervened to assert its own claim to the instrument, its claims were also available as defenses to payment. Thus, the court of appeals held that there were relevant factual issues precluding summary judgment. * * *
* * *

The University Savings Case

Petrolife, Inc. (Petrolife) contracted to buy blending gasoline from Intercontinental Consolidated Companies, Inc. (ICC). Allegedly as part of an ongoing fraud, ICC promised to deliver the gasoline between November 7 and 10, 1986, if it received a check for $2,008,125, half the total purchase price. Petrolife purchased a check for that amount, payable to ICC, from University Savings Association (University Savings) by borrowing on the revolving line of credit Petrolife maintained at University Savings. University Savings drew the check on one of its accounts with the Federal Home Loan Bank of Little Rock (FHLB). Petrolife delivered the check to ICC, but ICC never delivered the gasoline.

On November 12, after investigating ICC's failure to deliver the gasoline and discovering its alleged fraud, Petrolife requested University Savings to stop payment. University Savings, the drawer of the check, contacted FHLB, the drawee, and requested that payment be stopped. FHLB honored the request to stop payment. Subsequently, University Savings credited Petrolife's line of credit for the amount of the check. ICC ultimately brought suit on the check, not against FHLB, but against University Savings. Petrolife filed a plea in intervention which the trial court struck.

The Guaranty Federal Case

Alan Parmet opened an account at Guaranty Federal Savings and Loan Association (Guaranty Federal). Later that day he used his new account to purchase a teller's check, referred to as an "official check" by Guaranty Federal, for $900,000. The payee on the check was designated as "Binnon & Co." Guaranty Federal drew the teller's check on its account at Citibank of New York. On the same day, Parmet cashed the check for gambling chips at "Binion's Horseshoe Casino" in Las Vegas. The next morning, Parmet was at Guaranty Federal when it opened, seeking to stop payment on the teller's check. Guaranty Federal immediately called Citibank to request that payment be stopped on Guaranty Federal's check. Thus, when the casino credit manager called the Citibank number listed on the teller's check, he was told that payment had been stopped. Undaunted, the casino attempted to negotiate the check. The check was endorsed "Binnon & Co. Jack B. Binion. Pay to the order of the Horseshoe Club Operating Co."; below that, it was further restrictively endorsed "Pay to the Order of Valley Bank of Nevada Main Office For Deposit Only The Horseshoe Club Operating Co. Hotel General Account 2100322." The Horseshoe Operating Company (Horseshoe) brought suit on the check, not against Parmet and his alleged co-conspirators, or against Citibank, but against Guaranty Federal. Guaranty Federal brought a third party claim against Parmet and his alleged co-conspirators. The trial court severed Horseshoe's action on the check against Guaranty Federal from Guaranty Federal's third party action.

* * *

Teller's checks have been described as "checks drawn by ... savings and loan associations on commercial banks with which they maintain checking accounts." A "teller's check" is an instrument used in the savings and loan industry and is analogous to a "bank draft" in the banking industry in which a "check" is drawn by a bank on an account maintained in another bank or financial institution. * * *

Although University Savings and Guaranty Federal stopped payment of the teller's checks, they remain liable on the checks and ICC and Horseshoe may pursue an action on the checks against them. See Tex.Bus. & Com.Code Ann. §§3.413, 3.802 (Vernon 1968). ICC and Horseshoe argue that University Savings and Guaranty Federal may not assert any defenses (including their customers' defenses) to payment of the teller's checks. We disagree. If ICC and Horseshoe are holders and not holders in due course, they take the checks subject to all valid claims and many defenses. Tex.Bus. & Com.Code Ann. §3.306 (Vernon 1968). These include the claims and defenses of third persons who are willing to defend and intervene on behalf of the savings associations to assert their claims and defenses to the teller's checks. Tex.Bus. & Com.Code Ann. §3.306(4) (Vernon 1968). If ICC and Horseshoe are holders in due course, they take the checks free from "all defenses of any party to the instrument with whom the holder has not dealt except" infancy, incapacity, duress, illegality of the transaction, fraud, discharge in insolvency, and any other discharge of which the holder has notice. Tex.Bus. & Com.Code Ann. §3.305 (Vernon 1968). We hold that University Savings and Guaranty Federal may assert the applicable defenses to payment of the teller's checks.

* * *

Mauzy, Justice, concurring and dissenting.

I concur with the majority's disposition of University Savings, but I respectfully dissent from the decision in Guaranty Federal. In my view, the record in Guaranty Federal shows plainly that the "official check" involved there was an executed sale of credit and was not subject to rescission and countermand under the facts presented. I agree with the court of appeals that it blinks reality for the courts not to treat ... an "official check" [sold for a two-dollar fee] of a savings and loan association in Texas as the equivalent of cash. Too much of the personal and commercial business of this State is transacted with such checks with the expectation that they do represent cash. Certainly Guaranty considered that this "official check" was the equivalent of a cashier's check and thus was delivered as the equivalent of cash. In this connection, the record contains various evidence indicating that Guaranty treated its "official check" as analogous to a cashier's check. * * * Plainly, both Parmet and Horseshoe had sufficient reason to rely on the savings and loan's check being the equivalent of cash. Accordingly, I dissent. I would affirm the Court of Appeals in Guaranty Federal.

d. Traveler's Checks

Citicorp v. Interbank Card Ass'n
United States District Court, S. D. New York, 1979
478 F.Supp. 756

A travelers check is a device for payment. Its "issuer" is the company that prints the check and offers it for sale, usually through a bank acting as selling agent. The check, which is customarily issued in various standard denominations of American or foreign currency, is much like a cashier's check in that the issuer is, in effect, drawer and drawee. Upon purchasing a travelers check, the purchaser must sign it in the presence of the selling agent. Then, upon negotiating the check, the purchaser must fill in the date and countersign it in the presence of the person who accepts it as payment. He may also designate that person as payee. The extent of the issuer's promise is to pay on demand the amount indicated by the denomination of the check, provided that the check is properly countersigned, and, in the event that the check is lost or stolen, after having been signed at purchase, but before being countersigned, to provide the purchaser with an immediate refund or replacement.

Although they have been in use since 1891, the legal status of travelers checks remains largely unresolved. They have been characterized as "contracts," "money," and various types of "negotiable instruments," including "cashier's checks" and "certificates of deposit." * * * Because they are issued in standard denominations, easily negotiated, and readily accepted worldwide, they are the virtual equivalent of money, but because of the issuer's promise to refund or replace lost or stolen checks, they are safer.

The issuer's gain from the sale of travelers checks derives from two sources. One is a "commission," as much as one percent of the face amount of the check, charged to the purchaser, a portion of which the selling agent retains. The other is the "float," which is the money paid for the checks which remains at the disposal of the issuer until the purchaser negotiates them. An established issuer doing a steady business can expect a steady "float," and thus will have a fairly constant amount of money available for investment. According to one estimate, American Express had a $1.9 billion float at the end of 1977.

The market in United States dollar travelers checks is highly concentrated. Estimates vary, and, of course, ultimate proof on this question must await trial, but many sources suggest that 90% To 95% Of the United States dollar travelers checks sold are issued by three companies: American Express, with approximately 55% To 60% Of sales; Citicorp, with approximately 20%; and BankAmerica Corp., with approximately 15%. Other issuers with small market shares are Thos. Cook & Son (Bankers) Ltd., Barclays Bank, and Republic Money Orders, Inc.

Xanthopoulos v. Thomas Cook, Inc.
United States District Court, S.D. New York, 1985
629 F.Supp. 164

SAND, District Judge. With a background of foreign intrigue and mystery more reminiscent of "The Maltese Falcon" than of a classic bills and notes dispute, plaintiff seeks to collect from defendant $150,000 and damages resulting from Cook's dishonoring 150 $1,000 travelers checks

which Cook claims were stolen and bear forged countersignatures. * * * [O]n August 12, 1982 a person holding a Saudi Arabian passport showing the transliterated name "Majid Barghouthi" bought 150 U.S. $1,000 Thomas Cook Travelers Checks from Bank Indosuez in London, England. * * * On August 13, 1982, Barghouthi reported that the checks had been lost or stolen at Heathrow Airport in London and made a claim for a refund. [He got replacement checks.] * * * The tale now shifts to plaintiff and to Athens, Greece. [In Greece the original 150 checks were sold to plaintiff, Nicolaos Xanthopoulos, an architect. He bought them for a client who had hired him for design services on a real estate project. This man identified himself as Majid Barghouthi, who for convenience we will refer to as "Barghouthi II." The checks were countersigned but not in plaintiff's presence and, it turns out, the countersignatures were forged. Cook dishonored the checks when plaintiff sought payment of them.]
       * * *

III. Defendant Cook is Not Liable to Plaintiff Xanthopoulos on the Travelers Checks

A. The Nature of a Travelers Check

It is necessary to begin with a brief description of travelers checks in general and Cook travelers checks in particular. A travelers check is an instrument for payment that combines the marketability of cash with the safety of a bank draft. Its issuer, here defendant Cook, prints the check, customarily in one of several standard denominations, and offers it for sale. The purchaser, here Barghouthi I, buys the instrument and signs it in the presence of the issuer. The nature of the agreement between the issuer and the purchaser is that the issuer will replace the check if it is lost or stolen, thus providing a safety net to the purchaser that is unavailable with cash. To use the check, the purchaser need only countersign it in the presence of the person to whom he is tendering it (hereinafter "the acceptor"). The acceptor, here Xanthopoulos, is required to have the countersigner countersign in the acceptor's presence so that the acceptor can compare the two signatures for similarity. This offers some protection against the thief who would find it difficult to artfully forge the purchaser's signature while under observation. The acceptor then redeems the check with the issuer, usually through the intermediary of the acceptor's own bank, and receives cash equalling the face value of the check.

B. The Uniform Commercial Code

Commercial paper is governed by Article 3 of the Uniform Commercial Code. It provides that if a given type of commercial paper is found to be a "negotiable instrument" and it is "negotiated" to a "holder" who qualifies as a "holder in due course" ("HIDC") then that "holder in due course" takes the instrument free from many of the defenses that the issuer could have raised against previous holders of the instrument, such as the defense here that the instrument was stolen.

We find that the travelers checks in issue are indeed negotiable instruments, but that Xanthopoulos never became their holder. Since he was not a holder, he could not have been a holder in due course. Therefore, he cannot collect on the travelers checks.

1. Cook's Travelers Checks are Negotiable Instruments

Official Comment 4 to UCC §3-104 makes clear that "[t]raveler's checks in the usual form ... are negotiable instruments under this Article when they have been completed by the identifying signature." Plaintiff has urged that the "identifying signature" noted in the comment refers to the countersignature made when the purchaser tenders the check to the acceptor. We reject his argument, finding instead, as defendant contends, that the check becomes negotiable at the time the purchaser first signs. The four required characteristics for an instrument to be considered negotiable under the Code, set forth at UCC 3-104(1), are met when the purchaser's initial signature is placed on the check. First, the instrument has been "signed by the maker or drawer." UCC 3-104(1)(a). The "maker" of a travelers check, like the maker of a bank check, is the bank upon which the check is drawn, here Cook. The purchaser has given Cook cash and Cook in turn has given him a note for that amount. The note is effectively "payable to [the] order" of the purchaser, satisfying the second requirement of negotiability. UCC 3- 104(1)(d). The note is "payable on demand," satisfying the third requirement, UCC 3-104(1)(c), and finally, it contains "an unconditional promise or order to pay a sum certain in money and no other promise, order, obligation or power given by the maker or drawer except as authorized by this Article." Effectively Cook has given a negotiable check to the purchaser, here Barghouthi I. In transferring the check to the acceptor, Xanthopoulos, Barghouthi II simply attempted to negotiate it. As one commentator has noted: "The [first] signature, in effect, put the check in 'order' form. The countersignature converts it to bearer paper because it makes it negotiable by delivery alone [pursuant to UCC §3-202(1)]."

For purposes of determining whether Xanthopoulos was a holder of the travelers checks, however, it matters not at which point the checks could have become negotiable instruments. By the time plaintiff took them, they were sufficiently completed so that were all the signatures valid, the checks would have been negotiable.

2. Xanthopoulos is Not a Holder

The holder of a negotiable instrument may "enforce payment in his own name." U.C.C. 3-301. The question that is really at the heart of this case is whether Xanthopoulos is such a "holder." We find that he is not.

A "holder" is defined in section 1-201(20) of the Code as "a person who is in possession of ... an instrument ... issued or indorsed to him or to his order or to bearer or in blank." When Cook first issued the traveler's checks in question to Barghouthi I, Barghouthi I thus became a holder. Had Barghouthi I--like countless travelers each day--properly countersigned, i.e., indorsed, his checks over to Xanthopoulos, Xanthopoulos would have then become the uncontested holder of properly negotiated travelers checks. But because the countersigner was not Barghouthi I but rather the imposter Barghouthi II, Cook is not liable on the instrument.

The crux of Cook's argument is that "a forged countersignature on a travelers check ... [is] the equivalent of a forged indorsement on a check [;] ... and the U.C.C. entitles an issuer to refuse payment on such checks." Defendant's Trial Memorandum at 8. Cook cites to several provisions in the Code that make it clear that as a general matter a forged signature is tantamount to no signature and, therefore, cannot be used to effectively negotiate a negotiable instrument. Cook then adds, correctly, that generally under the U.C.C. if there is a forgery, "the loss falls not upon the bank or issuer, but upon the first solvent party in the transfer stream after the one who forged the indorsement ... i.e., the person who cashed the instrument for the forger." Defendant's Trial Memorandum at 8. Thus, under Cook's analysis, with Barghouthi II gone with the money, Xanthopoulos should bear the loss.

Xanthopoulos attempts to escape Cook's generalizations by contending that despite the forgery he is a holder because Cook should be precluded from questioning the authenticity of the Barghouthi countersignature. In support of this contention, plaintiff puts forward several theories: first, that the terms of the "payment guarantee" provide that Cook will pay on latent forgeries. Second, that the custom of trade in the travelers check industry is to pay on latent forgeries. And finally, that Cook's own negligence contributed to the making of the forged countersignatures and thus Cook should be precluded from questioning their authenticity. Because, however, Xanthopoulos did not prove that he had Barghouthi II countersign the checks in his presence under circumstances that did not put him on notice of the forgery, none of plaintiff's theories can prevail.

a. The Payment Guarantee

One of the conditions of the payment guarantee is that the acceptor have the countersigner countersign in the acceptor's presence. This condition is obviously material and we find it was not met. Therefore the guarantee was not put into effect.

b. The Custom of Trade in the Travelers Check Industry

Plaintiff also contends that the "custom of trade" in the travelers check industry is "to honor travelers checks even with forged endorsements when presented by a holder in due course if countersigned in the presence of the holder." Plaintiff's Pre-Trial Brief at 26. While defendant recognizes that the Code provides that a "usage of trade" in an industry shall be used by the court in interpreting an agreement between parties, it disputes plaintiff's contention about what the usage is in the travelers check industry. The court, however, need not resolve this factual issue as plaintiff has failed to put forward any evidence that issuers of travelers checks pay on checks bearing forged countersignatures made outside of the presence of the acceptor or under circumstances that put the acceptor on notice of the forgery.

The Court is mindful of several cases that have said that travelers checks should be treated more like cash than should other negotiable instruments. None of these cases, however, involved a forged countersignature made outside of the acceptor's presence or under circumstance which put the acceptors on notice of the forgery. Nor has such a case been brought to the Court's attention. There is much to be said for the proposition that the public has come to accept travelers checks as a cash equivalent and so the checks have acquired "negotiable characteristics" not found in other instruments, see Ashford, supra. Nevertheless, when a travelers check has been countersigned out of the acceptor's presence, it creates a risk for which the issuer has not bargained. This is also true if the checks are countersigned in the acceptor's presence under circumstances putting the acceptor of the checks on notice of the forgery.

c. Defendant's Alleged Negligence

Plaintiff contends that pursuant to U.C.C. §3-406 Cook should be precluded from questioning the forged countersignatures because Cook's own negligence "substantially contribute[d] to" their making. In support of this proposition, plaintiff cites many measures that Cook could have taken to insure that innocent acceptors did not take checks that were reported lost or stolen. Cook's failure to take any of these measures, however, does not rise to the level of negligence. Acceptors who have had the checks properly countersigned in their presence are sufficiently protected by Cook's guarantee and possibly by the custom of the travelers check industry. The cases cited by plaintiff in support of his contention, Savemart v. Bowery Savings Bank, 117 Misc.2d 947, 461 N.Y.S.2d 144 (App.Term 1982) and Michaeli v. The Greater New York Savings Bank, 121 Misc.2d 840, 469 N.Y.S.2d 279 (Queens Co.Civ.Ct.1983) are easily distinguishable from the case at hand. Those cases involved teller's checks stolen in blank from defendant banks. They were signed by persons who forged the bank's authorized signatures before negotiating the checks to the plaintiffs. In Michaeli, the court held that the defendant bank was precluded from contesting the forged signature because the "bank's failure to take any precautions other than the self-protecting expedient of a stop payment order substantially contributed to the making of the ... unauthorized ... check." 469 N.Y.S.2d at 281. The Savemart court held similarly on the law, remanding the case to determine whether the bank had indeed been negligent.

Signed teller's checks, however, differ from the Cook travelers checks as Xanthopoulos took them. Signed tellers checks are the equivalent of cash. Travelers checks do not become cash equivalents until they are signed in the presence of the acceptor under circumstances that do not put the acceptor on notice of the forgery. Indeed, this difference between the two instruments is the reason travelers carry travelers checks rather than teller's checks. Had Cook's travelers checks been stolen in blank from Cook, signed by the thief and then countersigned in the presence of an acceptor, who was a holder in due course, only then would we have a situation analogous to Savemart and Michaeli.

IV. Defendant is Not Liable to Plaintiff in Tort for Negligence

The parties agree that absent a duty of care there can be no tort of negligence. Palsgraf v. Long Island Railroad Co., 248 N.Y. 339, 162 N.E. 99 (1928). Whatever the level of care that may be owed to an innocent acceptor in whose presence travelers checks are countersigned under non-suspicious circumstances, no duty of care was owed by Cook to plaintiff.

For the reasons stated above, judgment will enter for defendant dismissing the complaint.

SO ORDERED.

Ashford v. Thos. Cook & Sons (Bankers) Ltd.

Supreme Court of Hawaii, 1970
52 Haw. 113, 471 P.2d 530, 533-34

On June 24, 1964, defendant, Thos. Cook & Son (Bankers) Ltd., sold and delivered travelers checks totaling $25,000 to Mr. and Mrs. Kochton at their home in the suburb of Chicago, Illinois. Mr. Kochton was at home at the time of delivery and he signed his name to one-half of the checks on the lower left hand corner in the presence of an agent for Thomas Cook & Son (Bankers) Ltd., as required by its regulation. However, Mrs. Kochton was not at home and her unsigned travelers checks for the amount of $12,500 were left with Mr. Kochton. In spite of an instruction to have the checks signed as provided before her departure, Mrs. Kochton failed to do so and unsigned travelers checks amounting to $11,900 were stolen from her in Tahiti in July, 1964.

On May 3, 1966, Curtis H. Ashford, plaintiff, who was then living in Tahiti, inquired of the Indo-China Bank, the only bank at Papeete, Tahiti, whether he could exchange New Zealand pounds and Polynesian francs for United States dollars and was informed that he could not. He returned to his boat to have lunch. Shortly thereafter a young Tahitian male came on board his boat and stated that he had been informed that plaintiff desired to exchange Polynesian francs for United States dollars and suggested that plaintiff purchase travelers checks. Plaintiff inquired whether that was possible because when he was informed at the bank that he couldn't make the exchange of Polynesian francs for United States dollars he had assumed he couldn't buy travelers checks with francs. When plaintiff was assured that he could purchase travelers checks, assuming that the Tahitian was connected with the bank, he asked if he should go to the bank during the noon hour. The Tahitian told plaintiff that was not necessary and that he and a director from the bank would come to the boat to consummate the transaction.

Subsequently the Tahitian returned to plaintiff's boat with a European male, who introduced himself as a Cook's agent and flashed an identification card. Thereafter the transaction was consummated whereby plaintiff paid Polynesian francs and New Zealand pounds valued between $8,450 to $8,600 for United States travelers checks with face value of $8,300. The overcharge, according to the 'agent', was for fee, premium and difference in exchange rate.

Thereafter he remained in Tahiti for a short time before leaving for Hawaii. After coming to Hawaii, plaintiff kept the travelers checks until January 1967, when he deposited them with the Liberty Bank in Honolulu. When the checks were forwarded to New York for collection, they were not honored and Liberty Bank debited plaintiff's account.

Plaintiff brought this action against defendants Thos. Cook & Son (Bankers) Ltd., and Thos. Cook & Son, Inc. The case was tried by a jury and after the jury returned a verdict, the trial court entered judgment for plaintiff for the sum of $8,300 plus interest, costs, etc., or $9,609.06. Defendants appealed.

     * * *

It is common knowledge that any establishment issuing travelers checks intends its checks to be readily and freely passable from one person to another as money. This is not only intended, but it is widely advertised that travelers checks are readily accepted in commerce as money and that they are safer. The public is made to believe that travelers checks are a substitute for money, a medium of exchange, which are self-identifying and accepted everywhere, but, unlike currency, they can be carried without danger of loss or theft because of the protective device of signature and countersignature. We believe that if travelers checks are intended by the issuer and accepted by the public as a medium of exchange to take the place of money, they should be subjected to the same rules of law applicable to money under like circumstances. We therefore hold that travelers checks upon being printed become a medium of exchange or acquire negotiable characteristics and all the risk of theft is with the issuer. The issuer is thus liable to any bona fide holder of stolen travelers checks who has paid valuable consideration. * * * Affirmed.

8. Accommodation parties, indorsers, and their "suretyship defenses"

a. Role and Liability of Accommodation Party

An *accommodation party* is someone who signs an instrument for the purpose of being a *surety* for another party to the instrument. The common law refers to the other person as the *principal debtor*, and Article 3 refers to this person as the *accommodated party*. Officially, their roles are explained as follows:

> If an instrument is used for value given for the benefit of a party to the instrument ("*accommodated party*") and another party to the instrument ("*accommodation party*") signs the instrument for the purpose of incurring liability on the instrument without being a direct beneficiary of the value given for the instrument, the instrument is signed by the accommodation party "*for accommodation.*"

3-419(a)(emphasis added). Whether or not the accommodation party is paid for being a surety is unimportant to accommodation status. 3-419(b). The key is that someone else -- the accommodated party -- gets the *direct benefit* of the value *given for the instrument*. A party trying to prove accommodation status is aided by the presumption that anybody signing an instrument is an accommodation party "if the signature is an anomalous indorsement or is accompanied by words indicating that the signer is acting as surety or guarantor * * *." 3-419(c). The effect is to put the burden on the person who argues against accommodation whenever the issue arises.

"Accommodation party" is not the capacity of a party to an instrument. Capacity refers to a party's role as drawer, maker, acceptor, or indorser. Accommodation is beyond and independent of capacity. Capacity refers to the nature or terms of a party's liability on the instrument. Accommodation refers to purpose of incurring the liability. It is a label over a party's capacity that signals the reason or motivation for her having signed the instrument, which is to serve as surety.

An accommodation party can sign in any capacity that is appropriate for the kind of instrument involved, but the accommodation status does not change the contract of liability that the capacity dictates. Here is the rule:

> An accommodation party may sign the instrument as maker, drawer, acceptor, or indorser and * * * is obliged to pay the instrument in the capacity in which the accommodation party signs.

3-419(b). It makes no difference that the person enforcing the instrument was aware of the accommodation when she took the instrument. 3-419(c). Thus, if A signs a note to accommodate P, A would be an accommodation party if A and P signed as co-makers; P signed as maker and A as indorser; or A signed as maker and P as indorser. Similarly, A could accommodate P on a draft by signing as drawer, acceptor, or indorser. In each case, A's liability -- as maker, drawer, acceptor, or indorser -- is the standard liability of such a party and is unmodified by her role as an accommodation party. In the real world, accommodation is more common on notes, and the accommodation party will usually sign as co-maker or anomalous indorser.

With a single exception, the holder of an instrument is not required to exhaust remedies against the accommodated party before enforcing the instrument against the accommodation party. The exception applies only when the accommodation party embellishes her signature with "words indicating unambiguously that the party is guaranteeing collection rather than payment of the obligation of another party to the instrument * * *." 3-419(d). The words "collection guaranteed" are sufficient. When anybody adds these words to their signature on an instrument, the effect is:

> the signer is obliged to pay the amount due on the instrument to a person entitled to enforce the instrument only if (i) execution of judgment against the other party has been returned unsatisfied, (ii) the other party is insolvent or in an insolvency proceeding, (iii) the other party cannot be served with process, or (iv) it is otherwise apparent that payment cannot be obtained from the other party.

3-419(d).

So far, there are no advantages of accommodation. The advantages are elsewhere, in providing remedies and defenses rather than in defining liability. The advantages are in the special rights against the accommodated party if the accommodation party pays the instrument, and also in the special defenses that may reduce or eliminate, in the first instance, the accommodation party's obligation to pay the instrument.

b. Rights of Accommodation Party Against Principal Debtor

The common law gives a surety three major rights or remedies against the principal debtor. They are *exoneration, reimbursement,* and *subrogation. Exoneration* is a right to equitable relief compelling the principal debtor to pay the debt if she is able to do so. "Among the courses open to the court are to direct a payment by the principal to the creditor, to require that the sum be paid into court for the creditor, or that the principal give the surety adequate security for his ultimate reimbursement." Restatement of Security § 112 comment b (1941). It does not interfere with the creditor's rights against the surety but intends to force the principal debtor to pay the debt before the surety is required to pay it.

Reimbursement is the surety's direct, personal right to recoup duly made payment from the principal debtor. *Subrogation* is derivative. It gives the surety the creditor's rights against the principal debtor, including the creditor's right to payment and any collateral for the debt. It puts the surety, upon performance, in the creditor's former position.

Article 3 confirms that "[a]n accommodation party who pays the instrument is entitled to reimbursement from the accommodated party * * *." 3-419(e). It also allows the accommodation party to enforce the instrument itself against the accommodated party, regardless of the capacities in which the two of them signed the instrument. Id. Therefore, if A signed a note to accommodate P and they signed as co-makers, or A signed as maker and P as indorser, A can enforce the note against P. It makes no difference that, ordinarily, neither a co-maker nor an indorser is liable on the instrument to another maker. The accommodated party's liability in these circumstances is not based on capacity; rather, it is based on the principal debtor's accountability to a surety and, impliedly, on subrogation -- putting the accommodation party in the place of the holder whom she paid. This subrogation to the instrument is complete. "Since the accommodation party that pays the instrument is entitled to enforce the instrument against the accommodated party, the accommodation party also obtains rights to any security interest or other collateral that secures payment of the instrument." 3-419 comment 5.

If the accommodated party pays the instrument, she never can recoup from the accommodation party no matter how they are situated on the instrument. The accommodation party is immune even though she signed in a capacity that ordinarily would make her liable to the accommodated party, either on the instrument or for contribution under the common law. The accommodation cancels this liability which, as between the two of them, is form only and not substance. The rule is that "[a]n accommodated party who pays the instrument has no right of recourse against, and is not entitled to contribution from, an accommodation party." 3-419(e). The contract between the two of them, in substance, was that the accommodation party signed the instrument only to support the accommodated party, not to incur liability to her or to share liability for the instrument.

c. Derivative Defenses Available to Accommodation Party

Under the common law, a surety can assert most of the principal debtor's defenses against the creditor. Article 3 follows the common law in this regard by codifying this rule:

> In an action to enforce the obligation of an accommodation party to pay an instrument, the accommodation party may assert against the person entitled to

enforce the instrument any defense or claim in recoupment * * * that the accommodated party could assert against the person entitled to enforce the instrument, except the defenses of discharge in insolvency proceedings, infancy, and lack of legal capacity.

3-305(d). This means that the surety can assert the principal debtor's defenses of want or failure of consideration, impossibility, illegality, fraud, duress or the like.

There was doubt under the common law that the surety could assert counter-claims of the principal debtor against the creditor. Article 3 is clear on this issue. The surety can assert counterclaims but only as claims "in recoupment." They can be asserted defensively only and not to recover affirmatively from the creditor. 3-305(a). The surety cannot use for any purpose the principal debtor's unrelated setoffs.

The surety cannot assert the principal debtor's defenses of bankruptcy discharge and lack of legal capacity, including infancy. These are unavailable to the surety even though they are, or can be, real defenses that the principal debtor herself can assert even against a holder in due course. The explanation is that the very purpose of the accommodation was to shift the risk of these defenses from the creditor to the surety. See Peters, *Suretyship Under Article 3 of the Uniform Commercial Code*, 77 Yale L.J. 833, 862 (1968). Moreover, when the principal debtor enjoys one of these defenses and the surety is forced to pay the debt, the surety is not entitled to reimbursement from the principal debtor. Restatement of Security §108(3-4) (1941).

On the other hand, if the surety herself is discharged in bankruptcy, or if she lacked legal capacity in agreeing to the accommodation, she can assert the defense against the creditor. A surety does not waive her own defenses simply because she is a surety.

There is a very important limit, however, on an accommodation party asserting anybody's defenses, whether her own or the defenses of the accommodated party. She cannot assert personal defenses against a person who has the rights of a holder in due course which are not subject to the defense. Only real defenses are good against such a holder, except the bankruptcy or legal incapacity of the accommodated party.

d. Discharge Based on Status As Accommodation Party or Ordinary Indorser -- "Suretyship Defenses"

An accommodation party may have her own defenses to liability on the instru-ment that are Article 3 defenses or that arise under other law. The most common de-fense of other law probably is that the creditor or the principal debtor defrauded her into the accommodation. The creditor's right to enforce the instrument is subject not only to her own fraud, but also the fraud of the principal debtor toward the surety. The rights of any transferee of the instrument are likewise limited, except a holder in due course.

Accommodation parties often defend on the basis that they themselves received no consideration for the accommodation. It never works. First, as a matter of common law, any consideration running to the principal debtor as a result of the accommodation is also consideration to the surety. Second, as a matter of Article 3 law, lack of consideration to the accommodation party herself is no defense to her liability on the instrument. Here is the rule:

> The obligation of an accommodation party may be enforced notwithstanding any statute of frauds and whether or not the accommodation party receives consideration for the accommodation.

3-419(b).

The defenses of accommodation parties that are most commonly successful are the defenses of Article 3, principally discharge. An accommodation party is, first, a party to an instrument, and she can rely on any provision of Article 3 that gives her a defense in the capacity in which she signed the instrument. Because she is also a surety, an accommodation party is eligible for additional, special defenses -- special reasons for discharge that are intended to guard against increasing risks to sureties beyond what they agreed to undertake. These defenses are commonly referred to as the "*suretyship defenses*" and are collected in 3-605.

Significantly, the 3-605 suretyship defenses are also extended to *ordinary indorsers* -- anybody who indorses an instrument whether or not for accommodation. It also includes a drawer of a draft that is accepted by a nonbank because the law treats her, upon the acceptance, as an indorser. 3-414(d), 3-605(a). The reason 3-605 covers indorsers is that, functionally, every indorser to some extent is a surety, a guarantor of payment. 3-605 comment 1. This is not to say that every indorser is, by law, an accommodation party within the meaning of 3-419. An indorser is an accommodation party only if she meets the definitional test for such status. An indorser who fails this test is treated like a surety for purposes of 3-605 only, and not for purposes of 3-419.

Section 3-605 basically creates three special reasons for discharging a surety, which here means either an accommodation party or indorser. Simply put, the reasons are conduct by a person entitled to enforce the instrument that affects, in the following ways, the obligation of any other party to the instrument against whom the surety has a right of recourse:

- with or without consideration, agrees to extend the due date of the party's obligation;
- otherwise materially modifies the obligation; or
- impairs the value of an interest in collateral that secures the obligation.

3-605(c-e). In one way or another, the discharge is pro tanto, to the extent the conduct harms the surety. Except in the case of an indorser, the suretyship defenses of 3-605(c-e) further require that the holder knows of the accommodation, or has notice that the instrument was signed for accommodation, when she takes the action that is the basis for the defense. 3-605(h).

The truth is that the "suretyship defenses" of 3-605 rarely apply because they can be waived, 3-605(i), and usually are waived in the instrument or by

a separate writing. The whole truth is that sureties more often sign separate agreements of suretyship, commonly known as *side guaranties*, instead of or in addition to signing the instrument with the principal debtor. Especially in business and commercial transactions, these agreements waive the kinds of defenses that 3-605 covers, any derivative defenses that might arise, and every other defense possibly available to the surety against the creditor. The effect is that the surety agrees to pay "come hell or high water," and usually the courts fully enforce these agreements according to their terms. This explains why in the typical case, the "defense" that the surety asserts is some very durable, tort-like claim, usually arguing that the creditor is guilty of some level of fraud toward the surety.

ㅡㅡㅡㅡㅡ

Restatement of Security (1941)

§103. Principal's Duty to Surety: In General. Where suretyship exists, it is the duty of the principal [debtor] to the surety to satisfy the surety's obligation by performing his own duty to the creditor, in the absence of a defense between himself and the surety, or of a defense between himself and the creditor, which is also available to the surety.

§104. Reimbursement By Principal: In General.
(1) Where the surety makes a payment or otherwise performs on default by the principal, or where the surety's property is used to satisfy the principal's duty, it is the duty of the principal to reimburse the surety to the extent of his reasonable outlay if
(a) the surety's obligation has been incurred, or his property has been subjected to a charge, with the consent of the principal, or
(b) the principal has assumed an obligation which was once the primary obligation of the surety.
(2) Where a surety who has undertaken his obligation without the consent of the principal makes a payment or otherwise performs on account of the principal, it is the duty of the principal to reimburse the surety to the extent that the principal has been unjustly enriched.
* * *

§112. Exoneration. Where the surety is under an obligation to the creditor which has matured and which he has undertaken with the consent of the principal, and the surety, if he performed would be entitled to reimbursement from the principal, the surety has the right to exoneration.

Comment:
a. The principal owes the surety a duty to perform as soon as the performance is due. It is inequitable for the surety to be compelled to suffer the inconvenience and temporary loss which a payment by him will entail if the principal can satisfy the obligation. The surety is entitled to equitable relief without alleging any particular reason for fearing that he will not be reimbursed in the event of payment. The right to such equitable relief is called the right of exoneration.
b. It is beyond the scope of the Restatement of this subject to state in detail the procedure which will be followed in respect of exoneration. It is understood that the court must be able

to grant an effective decree and that the decree will properly protect the interests of principal and creditor as well as those of the surety. Among the courses open to the court are to direct a payment by the principal to the creditor, to require that the sum due be paid into the court for the creditor, or that the principal give the surety adequate security for his ultimate reimbursement.

c. An action in equity by the surety to compel exoneration by the principal does not prevent the creditor from suing the surety or principal on their obligations, unless the procedure followed by the surety brings in the creditor as a party to the action. In such a case a possible procedure is to permit the creditor to sue the principal at law for the purpose of establishing his rights.

* * *

§141. Subrogation. Where the duty of the principal to the creditor is fully satisfied, the surety to the extent that he has contributed to this satisfaction is subrogated

(a) to the rights of the creditor against the principal, and

(b) subject to the rule stated in Clause (d), to the interests which the creditor has in security for the principal's performance and in which the creditor has no continuing interest, and

(c) to the rights of the creditor against persons other than the principal whose negligence or willful conduct has made them liable to the creditor for the same default, and

(d) to the rights of the creditor against cosureties and to the creditor's interest in security held by them, but in such case the cosurety's personal liability is limited to the amount which will satisfy his duty to contribute his share of the principal's default.

Comment:

a. Subrogation. Subrogation is a term describing the equitable remedy by which, where the property of one person is used to discharge a duty of another or a lien upon the property of another, under such circumstances that the other will be unjustly enriched by the retention of the benefit thus conferred, the former is placed in the position of the obligee or lienholder. See Restatement of Restitution, §162. Subrogation is based on general principles of justice and does not spring from contract although it may be confirmed or qualified by contract. It is a mode which equity adopts to compel the discharge of a debt by the one who in good conscience ought to pay it. As applied to suretyship, subrogation denotes that the surety, upon performance, is placed in the position of the creditor both in respect of the creditor's right against the principal and of security held by the creditor. The surety also, subject to equitable limitations succeeds to the creditor's rights against others than the principal who may be liable for the principal's default. Where the surety performs so that he satisfies the duty of the principal to the creditor, or where a combination of performance by principal and surety satisfies the principal's duty, the principal's duty although discharged so far as the creditor is concerned, is kept alive against the principal or, subject to equitable limitations, against others, for the benefit of the surety. Equity, in effect, creates in the surety who has performed, rights similar to those of the creditor before the duty to him was discharged. This is sometimes called an assignment by operation of law. It does not depend upon an actual assignment, however, although where necessary to give the surety procedural or other advantages, the creditor can be required to make an assignment.

* * *

§144. Cosuretyship Defined. Cosuretyship is the relationship between two or more sureties who are bound to answer for the same duty of the principal, and who as between themselves should share the loss caused by the default of the principal.

* * *

§149. Contribution: General Rule. A surety who in the performance of his own obligation discharges more than his proportionate share of the principal's duty is entitled to contribution from a cosurety.

* * *

§154. Computation Of Contribution.

(1) A surety who has discharged more than his proportionate share of the principal's duty is entitled to contribution from a cosurety

(a) who has consented to the surety's becoming bound, in the proportionate amount of the net outlay properly expended,

(b) who has not consented to the surety's becoming bound in the proportionate amount by which the cosurety has benefited from the performance. * * *

Comment:

b. Consent of cosurety as affecting contribution. The surety seeking contribution from cosureties is entitled to an amount which will equalize the loss among those equally bound.

❑❑❑❑❑❑

Rahall v. Tweel

Supreme Court of Appeals of West Virginia, 1991
186 W.Va. 136, 411 S.E.2d 461

Miller, Chief Justice: N. Joe Rahall, the plaintiff below, appeals from a final order of the Circuit Court of Kanawha County, dated August 13, 1990, denying his motion to set aside a jury verdict. On appeal, the plaintiff contends that the trial court erroneously instructed the jury that a party who signs a promissory note, but receives no direct benefit by signing it, is an accommodation party, and, as such, is not liable to the principal on the note. We agree that the instruction was erroneous; accordingly, we reverse and remand the case for further proceedings consistent with this opinion.

I.

In 1984, the plaintiff and Nicholas Tweel, the defendant below, obtained two unsecured loans totaling $80,000 from the Charleston National Bank (the Bank). The loan was procured to keep a hotel in Huntington operational. Both parties testified that it was to their benefit that the hotel remain open.

Both notes were prepared by the Bank. The front of each note stated the value received, the date the note was signed, its due date, and the annual interest. There were two signature lines, where each party signed, and beneath each line was the printed phrase "Signature of Maker." The back of the notes contained covenants and conditions, language involving endorsers, and two lines for signatures. The phrase "Endorser's Signature" was printed under each of the lines on the back of the notes, both of which were blank.

When the notes became due, the plaintiff paid the Bank the total amount owed, and then filed suit against the defendant to collect one-half of this amount. At trial, the defendant claimed that because he had not directly received the proceeds from the two loans, he was merely an accommodation party. The trial court agreed and, over the plaintiff's objection, instructed the jury that an accommodation party is not liable to the principal, i.e., the person accommodated, unless he received a direct benefit.[*] By way of a special interrogatory, the jury found that Mr. Tweel received no direct benefit from signing the promissory notes; therefore, he was not liable to the plaintiff.

II.

Our inquiry is to determine Mr. Tweel's status on the two notes. Ordinarily, a party's status or capacity on commercial paper is determined solely from the face of the instrument. * * * On the face of the two notes in question, it is clear that the defendant signed as a co-maker. This was the capacity identified under his signature. Moreover, his signature appeared on the front of the note in the lower right hand corner, which, as the official comment to W.Va.Code, 46-3-402, states, is judicially noted as an intent to sign as a maker.

We explained the obligations of co-makers in Syllabus Points 2 and 3 of Estate of Bayliss v. Lee, 173 W.Va. 299, 315 S.E.2d 406 (1984): "2. 'Under our law, co-obligors on a note are jointly and severally liable. If one co-obligor is required to pay the entire obligation, he may seek contribution or reimbursement from his co-obligor for fifty per centum of the amount paid.' Syllabus Point 4, Newton v. Dailey, [167 W.Va. 347], 280 S.E.2d 91 (1981). "3. The rule of equal or pro tanto contribution is not absolute if it can be shown that the co-obligors have by agreement made a different allocation as to their liability inter se or one or more of the co-obligors have received a disproportionate benefit from the transaction, then disproportionate contribution may be allowed."

Having found Mr. Tweel to be a maker on the two notes, we must now decide whether he was only an accommodation maker. Under W.Va.Code, 46-3-415(5) (1963), an "accommodation party is not liable to the person accommodated." Thus, where the person accommodated, in this case Mr. Rahall, pays the entire amount owed on a promissory note, he cannot then recover from the defendant. Obviously, the defendant's contention that he was an accommodation party, if true, would relieve him of any obligation to reimburse the plaintiff.

In Syllabus Point 6 of Peoples Bank of Point Pleasant v. Pied Piper Retreat, Inc., 158 W.Va. 170, 209 S.E.2d 573 (1974), we defined an accommodation party: "An accommodation party is one who signs an instrument in any capacity for the purpose of lending his name to another party to the instrument."

The clearest example of this type of endorsement is where a creditor refuses to lend money to a debtor unless the debtor has someone co-sign the instrument as additional security on the debtor's obligation. The holding in Peoples Bank is derived from W.Va.Code, 46-3-415, which outlines the general rules regarding accommodation parties and their rights and obligations. Under W.Va.Code, 46-3-415(3), oral proof that a person is an accommodation party is not admissible against a holder in due course without notice of the accommodation. However, the accommodation status of a party may be established by oral proof against the party accommodated, holders not in due course, or any party with notice of the accommodation. Because the defendant was not a holder in due course, parol evidence was admissible to prove his accommodation status.

In determining whether a person signed a note merely to lend his name to another party on it, courts have considered several factors. These include the party's purpose in signing the note, the

---

* Defendant's Instruction No. 3 provided: "The Court further instructs the jury that the fact that a party signs an instrument, such as a promissory note, but does not receive any direct remuneration or consideration for signing establishes that party as an accommodation party under the West Virginia Uniform Commercial Code, and, an accommodation party is not liable to the principal, or person who receives the benefit arising under the instrument. "Accordingly, if you find that Nicholas J. Tweel signed the promissory notes involved herein, but did not receive any direct remuneration or consideration for signing those notes, then he is an accommodation party; as such, he is not liable to Nick Joe Rahall, the principal on those notes, and your verdict may be, 'We, the jury, agree and find for the defendant, Nicholas J. Tweel.' "

intent of the other parties, whether the party took part in the negotiations leading to the financing, the purpose of the loan, whether the accommodation party received any benefit from the transaction, and whether the party's signature was necessary to secure the loan. Finally, the party asserting that he is accommodation maker has the burden of proof.

Nor is it necessary that a party receive a direct benefit from a loan in order to be an accommodation party. If a party signs as a co-maker and his business interest benefits, this benefit may preclude him from alleging accommodation status. As the Utah Supreme Court explained in Utah Farm Production Credit Association v. Watts, 737 P.2d at 159, the receipt of benefits is only one factor: "[W]e believe a more accurate statement of the law is that whether or not a party to an instrument receives a benefit directly or indirectly, and if so to what extent, is one of several factors to be considered in determining the parties' intent."

In the present case, the trial court erred in giving Defendant's Instruction No. 3, which restricted the jury's consideration of an accommodation party solely to whether the defendant received any direct remuneration for signing the instrument. This error was compounded when the jury was asked in a Special Interrogatory whether the defendant "receive[d] any direct benefit by virtue of signing the promissory notes to the Charleston National Bank." Because Defendant's Instruction No. 3 and the accompanying special interrogatory focused exclusively on this one factor, the test for ascertaining whether the defendant was an accommodation party was too constricted. The jury was not instructed to consider the intention of the parties, the purpose of the loan, or whether the Bank would have given the plaintiff the loans without the defendant's signature.

Our traditional rule regarding the effect of an erroneous instruction is contained in Syllabus Point 5 of Yates v. Mancari, 153 W.Va. 350, 168 S.E.2d 746 (1969): " 'An erroneous instruction is presumed to be prejudicial and warrants a new trial unless it appears that the complaining party was not prejudiced by such instruction.' Point 2, syllabus, Hollen v. Linger, 151 W.Va. 255 [151 S.E.2d 330 (1966)]."

We cannot conclude that the plaintiff was not prejudiced by the erroneous instruction. Had the jury been properly instructed, it might have reached a different result. For example, the Bank officer at trial unequivocally stated that the plaintiff was known as a person of considerable wealth and that his loan would have been approved without the defendant's signature. Furthermore, both parties testified that the loan proceeds were used to keep the hotel operating, which was to everyone's benefit. The plaintiff had an ownership interest in the hotel. The defendant had an option under which he would acquire an ownership interest in the hotel if he could arrange the necessary financing. Moreover, the defendant acknowledged that if the hotel were sold, he would receive a commission if he secured the buyer.

III.

For the foregoing reasons, the judgment of the Circuit Court of Kanawha County is reversed, and this case is remanded for further proceedings consistent with this opinion.

Reversed and remanded.

Chemlease Worldwide, Inc. v. Brace, Inc., 338 N.W.2d 428 (Minn. 1983). [The secured party, Worldwide, disposed of certain equipment that was collateral and used the sureties, Charles and Clayton Brace, for the deficiency. Their defense was that Worldwide violated Part 5 of Article 9 by failing to given them reasonable notice of the disposition of the collateral. The trial court directed a verdict for Wprldwode. The Braces appealed.] "As the secured party, Chemlease had, on default, a right to take possession of the computer equipment. U.C.C. §9-503. Chemlease also had a right to dispose of the equipment, either by private or public sale, pursuant to section 9-504. Section 9-504(3) provides in part:

Unless collateral * * * is of a type customarily sold on a recognized market, reasonable notification of the time and place of any public sale or reasonable notification of the time after which any private sale or other intended disposition is to be made shall be sent by the secured party to the debtor, if he has not signed after default a statement renouncing or modifying his right to notification of sale.

This provision entitled Brace, Inc., as debtor to the lease agreement, to receive reasonable notice of sale. But are Charles and Clayton Brace, as guarantors on the lease, also entitled to receive such notice? While we have not heretofore considered the question, the New York courts and a majority of jurisdictions addressing the issue hold that a guarantor is a debtor within the meaning of section 9-504. In our view, this construction is consistent with the purpose of the reasonable notification requirement, that is, to enable the debtor to protect his interest in the secured property by paying the debt, finding a buyer, or bidding on the property. A guarantor faces potential liability when the sale price does not cover the deficiency. Additionally, a personal guaranty given by a primary participant in a family-owned corporation often means the guarantor is, in essence, the debtor. The view that a guarantor is a debtor under section 9-504 should be applied to Charles and Clayton Brace. Thus, we conclude they were entitled to receive notice of the proposed sale of the collateral.

"Chemlease argues that by the terms of the guaranty the guarantors waived their rights to the collateral and therefore to notice of sale. It appears to us, however, that the fact the guarantors had no rights to the collateral is irrelevant to their interest in insuring Chemlease made the best sale available. The interest Charles and Clayton Brace have in the best sale price is their interest in their potential liability on the guaranty. The waiver in the guaranty does not waive any right to notice they may have under the Uniform Commercial Code. Additionally, by virtue of section 9-501(3)(b), the provisions of section 9-504(3) may not be waived or varied by agreement. See Minn.Stat.Ann. §336.9-504(3) Code Comment (West 1966). * * * Reversed and remanded."

Continental Bank v. Everett

United States Court of Appeals, Seventh Circuit, 1992
964 F.2d 701

Easterbrook, Circuit Judge. Guilford Telecasters, Inc., which operates WGGT-TV in Greensboro, North Carolina, borrowed $4.2 million from Continental Bank in 1984. Continental obtained guarantees from the firm's stockholders, each of whom is jointly and severally liable up to a limit based on his proportional ownership of the stock. Robinson Everett and the estate of Kathrine Everett, his mother, own 65% of the stock between them. Each guaranteed roughly $1.6 million of Guilford's debt. J.H. Froelich, who owns a smaller bloc, guaranteed about $545,000 of the debt. Other investors assumed proportional obligations.

Guilford encountered cash flow problems and in 1986 filed a bankruptcy petition. Continental, which had a security interest in Guilford's receivables, consented to their use in operating the business, if Guilford remained current on the loan--which it did, until May 1987. Then the guarantors took over, in order to fulfill the condition on which Guilford had access to cash. During 1989 the guarantors and Continental reached a pass over two topics. First, Continental insisted that the guarantors pay according to the schedule negotiated before the bankruptcy, under which the payments increase with time to retire additional principal. The guarantors insisted that they had to pay only the amount due each month when the bankruptcy began. Second, Continental as creditor voted against the plan of reorganization proposed by the debtor and supported by the guarantors in their roles as its investors and managers. (Robinson

Everett, a professor of law who was at the time the Chief Judge of the United States Court of Military Appeals, was not a manager of the TV station but took an active role as an investor.) At the beginning of 1990 the guarantors stopped paying. Continental responded with this diversity action. All guarantors except Froelich and the two Everetts paid up. From now on, we refer to these three collectively as "the guarantors."

* * *

On to the merits. All of the guarantors' defenses (and mirror-image counterclaims) are variations on the theme that the Bank left the loan undersecured, exposing the guarantors to more risk than they anticipated. Continental's obligation to Guilford was contingent on Guilford's providing the Bank with security interests in, among other things, its broadcasting license and its leased broadcasting facilities. Continental funded the loan without obtaining a security interest in the license, having concluded that such an interest is legally impossible. And although Guilford took the steps necessary to grant a security interest in its leaseholds, the Bank failed to perfect that interest. The Bank obtained an interest in Guilford's receivables and other assets, but the guarantors say this is insufficient, that the Bank's taking the full security was essential for their protection. They add that the Bank defrauded them by not revealing what it knew and they did not: that because a broadcast license is not property, 47 U.S.C. §301, and may not be assigned or transferred without the FCC's permission, 47 U.S.C. §310(d), the license itself is not a store of value on which the Bank could levy.

Although the guarantors argue that the Bank defrauded them, that effective security was a condition precedent to the effectiveness of the loan and guarantees, and that the Bank impaired the value of the collateral, these amount to the same thing, and we treat the position as one argument. Professor Everett, arguing on behalf of all three guarantors, conceded that he had not found a case in Illinois (or any other jurisdiction) requiring a lender to reveal to a guarantor the value of the borrower's assets as collateral. No surprise. It amounts to saying that a potential debt investor in a firm (which a bank is) owes a duty of care, perhaps even a duty of loyalty, to the existing equity investors (which Guilford's guarantors are) or contingent debt investors (which all guarantors are, given the possibility of subrogation, see Levit v. Ingersoll Rand Financial Corp., 874 F.2d 1186, 1194-97 (7th Cir.1989)). That is unheard-of in either corporate or banking law. A bank making a commercial loan depends largely on the success of the business for repayment. The firm has the best information about its business and prospects and accordingly may be obliged to disclose some details to the bank and the guarantors. Even that duty is attenuated, for persons negotiating for a contract usually may keep valuable information to themselves. They may not lie, but they need not volunteer. The ability to capitalize on private information is an important goad to create that knowledge, which may be important in matching assets with their most productive use. Banks' self-interest leads them to nose out the value of collateral; if they do not, they are apt to suffer loss. Borrowers and guarantors have their own reasons to know the value of the assets. None acts as fiduciary of another.

The general principle that parties to arms' length negotiations need not open their files to each other is especially apt here, because the bit of information the guarantors wanted Continental to reveal--that it could not obtain a security interest in a broadcast license--is both public and irrelevant. It is public because it is a legal conclusion, having nothing to do with facts peculiar to WGGT-TV or information buried in Continental's vaults. One side in negotiations need not disclose the United States Code to the other; the statutes, regulations, and cases are available to all. Like other states, Illinois takes the position that failure to disclose the law cannot be the foundation for redress. If Guilford and the guarantors wanted to know whether a broadcast license may be used as collateral, they had only to ask their own lawyer. Not surprisingly, they had counsel to advise them about the intricacies of communications law. If as the guarantors now say the use of a license as collateral is a debatable issue, so that their lawyer's views were unreliable, it is all the more reason why Continental cannot be accused of "fraud" for failing to "reveal," as if it were a fact, its view of the law. But the whole subject is irrelevant. A broadcast license is not a tangible asset. It can't be melted down, sold as scrap, or packed up and sent to Alaska. Its value lies in access to a given frequency in a specific place, which yields time that may be sold by the minute to advertisers. The value of the license to Guilford lay in the income stream from those advertisers. Continental wanted, and got, a security interest in that income, which it could enjoy while Guilford remained the owner of the license and operator of WGGT-TV. What more would it have had with a security interest in the license? An ability to sell the license to someone able to extract greater revenues is not much different from the ability to replace Guilford's managers in the bankruptcy. This makes it hard to see how the Bank's failure to reveal 47 U.S.C. §301 to the guarantors did them injury.

In the end the parties' rights are fixed by their contracts, which contain three dispositive provisions. First, they say that the security is for the benefit of the lender, not of the borrower or guarantors. Second, they provide that the "Bank shall have no duty as to the collection or protection of the Collateral or any part thereof or any income thereon, or as to the preservation of any rights pertaining thereto, beyond the safe custody of any Collateral actually in the Bank's possession." Third, the guarantors "expressly waive[ ] ... all diligence in collection or protection of or realization upon ... any security for" the loan to Guilford, and permit the Bank to "release ... any property securing" the loan without notice to them. It could hardly be clearer that the lender is free to do what it wants with the collateral. Illinois enforces clauses of this kind, which are fatal to the guarantors' position. Guarantors may elect to rely on the lender's attention to its own interests as their best protection, preferring market incentives over legal remedies and receiving lower interest rates in exchange.

The guarantors rely on cases such as Langeveld v. L.R.Z.H. Corp., 74 N.J. 45, 376 A.2d 931 (1977), and First Citizens Bank & Trust Co. v. Sherman's Estate, 250 App.Div. 339, 294 N.Y.S. 131 (1937), in which the contracts were silent, and the courts concluded that in the absence of agreement the bank had to maximize its realization on the collateral to reduce the guarantors' risk. Judicial attempts to draft standby terms that will govern when the parties neglect to address the subject are just guesses about what the parties would prefer. When the contracting parties draw up their own provisions, courts enforce them. People write things down in order to assign duties and allocate risks--functions vital to economic life yet defeated if courts prefer hypothetical bargains over real ones or use the ambiguities present in all language to frustrate the achievement of certainty.

What about the requirement of good faith that is part of every contract? The guarantors say that they are entitled to a jury trial to determine whether the Bank acted throughout in good faith. Once again, the guarantors misunderstand how courts use such principles. The Uniform Commercial Code defines good faith as honesty in fact. UCC §1-201(19). Beyond that, and the obligation to be prudent in the exercise of discretion conferred by contract, good faith is another way to describe the effort to devise terms to fill contractual gaps. As a method to fill gaps, it has little to do with the formation of contracts * * * and nothing to do with the enforcement of terms actually negotiated. Because this duty is an estimate of "what parties would agree to if they dickered about the subject explicitly, parties may contract with greater specificity for other arrangements." Our guarantors negotiated with the Bank and agreed to language establishing precisely what duties Continental would have with respect to security: it must safeguard collateral in its possession but has no other obligations. Gap-filling methods such as good faith do not "block use of terms that actually appear in the contract". Kham & Nate's Shoes No. 2, Inc. v. First Bank of Whiting, 908 F.2d 1351, 1357 (7th Cir.1990). The guarantors released Continental from any obligation to use the collateral for their benefit. The guarantors may rue their decision but cannot escape it.

* * *

AFFIRMED AND REMANDED

Gant v. NCNB National Bank

Court of Appeals of North Carolina, 1989
94 N.C.App. 198, 379 S.E.2d 865

Eagles, Judge. [This case arose out of a contract of guaranty signed by plaintiff in favor of defendant, guaranteeing loans made by defendant to a company owned by plaintiff's husband. Plaintiff's complaint alleged a breach by defendant of its duty of good faith, fraud, negligence and wrongful withholding of stock certificates. Defendant moved to dismiss for failure to state a claim upon which relief can be granted. Defendant's motion was granted and plaintiff appeals.]

Plaintiff argues on appeal that the trial court erred in dismissing her complaint. After careful consideration of the record on appeal and the applicable law, we agree in part.

* * *

The crux of plaintiff's complaint is that defendant failed to fulfill its obligation to inform her of the financial condition of the company whose loans she guaranteed. Although there is no fiduciary relationship between creditor and guarantor, in some instances a creditor owes a duty to the guarantor to disclose information about the principal debtor. If the creditor knows, or has good grounds for believing that the surety [or guarantor] is being deceived or misled, or that he is induced to enter into the contract in ignorance of facts materially increasing the risks, of which he has knowledge, and he has an opportunity, before accepting his undertaking, to inform him of such facts, good and fair dealing demand that he should make such disclosure to him; and if he accepts the contract without doing so, the surety [or guarantor] may afterwards avoid it.

Plaintiff has alleged the defendant knew that she was unaware of the financial condition of the principal debtor and knew that she was relying on defendant's "good faith and financial expertise" in making the loans. Further, plaintiff alleged the defendant at all times knew or had sufficient information to know the principal debtor was insolvent. Plaintiff has alleged sufficient facts to state a claim against defendant, whether the cause of action is ultimately determined to be one for negligence or "breach of duty of good faith," as plaintiff has labeled her claims. Allegations of sufficient facts to state any legal claim are all that is generally required to withstand a Rule 12(b)(6) motion.

* * *

Plaintiff has also alleged a cause of action based on fraud. The essential elements of actionable fraud are well established. There must be a misrepresentation of material fact, made with knowledge of its falsity and with intent to deceive, which the other party reasonably relies on to his deception and detriment. Equally well-established is the requirement that the plaintiff allege all material facts and circumstances constituting the fraud with particularity in the complaint. Mere generalities and conclusory allegations of fraud will not suffice. The pleader must state with particularity the time, place and content of the false representation.

Here because plaintiff has failed to allege the circumstances constituting fraud with sufficient particularity, the trial court was correct in granting defendant's Rule 12(b)(6) motion on the fraud claim. The fatal deficiency in plaintiff's allegations is that the complaint contains no facts whatsoever setting forth the time, place or specific individuals who purportedly made the fraudulent misrepresentations to plaintiff. It is not sufficient to allege conclusorily that a corporation made fraudulent misrepresentations.

* * *

For the reasons stated, the trial court's order of dismissal is affirmed in part and reversed in part, and the case remanded for proceedings on the breach of duty of good faith claim and the negligence claim.

Affirmed in part, reversed in part and remanded.

Restatement of Security
(1941)

§ 124.   NON-DISCLOSURE BY CREDITOR.

(1) Where before the surety has undertaken his obligation the creditor knows facts unknown to the surety that materially increase the risk beyond that which the creditor has reason to believe the surety intends to assume, and the creditor also has reason to believe that these facts are unknown to the surety and has a reasonable opportunity to communicate them to the surety, failure of the creditor to notify the surety of such facts is a defense to the surety.

(2) Where, during the existence of the surety ship relation, the creditor discovers facts unknown to the surety which would give the surety the privilege of terminating his obligation to the creditor as to liability for subsequent defaults, and the creditor has reason to believe these facts are unknown to the surety and has a reasonable opportunity to communicate them to the surety without a violation of a confidential duty, the creditor has a duty to notify the surety, and breach of this duty is a defense to the surety except in respect of his liability for defaults which have occurred before such disclosure should have been made.

Comment:

a   Nondisclosure of material facts in the circumstances of the rule stated in this Section constitutes fraud on the surety. The rule is merely a special application in suretyship of the rule of Contracts that fraud creates a defense. See Restatement of Contracts, §§475 and 476.

b.   Although in applying the rule stated in this Section to particular situations there is often considerable difficulty in ascertaining the precise degree of knowledge of surety and creditor and even in deter mining the materiality of the facts alleged to be concealed, the rule itself is simple. It does not place any burden on the creditor to investigate for the surety's benefit. It does not require the creditor to take any unusual steps to assure himself that the surety is acquainted with facts which he may assume are known to both of them. Among facts that are material are the financial condition of the principal, secret agreements between the parties, or the relations of third parties to the principal. If the surety requests information, the creditor must disclose it. Where he realizes that the surety is acting or is about to act in reliance upon a mistaken belief about the principal in respect of a matter material to the surety's risk, he should afford the surety the benefit of his information if he has an opportunity to do so.

Every surety by the nature of his obligation undertakes risks which are the inevitable concomitants of the transactions involved. Circumstances of the transactions vary the risks which will be regarded as normal and contemplated by the surety. While no surety takes the risk of material concealment, what will be deemed material concealment in respect of one surety may not be regarded so in respect of another. A creditor may have a lesser burden of bringing facts to the notice of a compensated surety who is known to make careful investigations before taking any obligation than to a casual surety who relies more completely upon the appearances of a transaction. The rule stated in this Section applies an objective test of the materiality of the facts not disclosed rather than the intent of the creditor in failing to make the disclosure.

Illustrations:

1. P requests S to act as surety to C in connection with proposed purchases of merchandise. S asks C whether his earlier dealings with P have been satisfactory. C answers in the affirmative although he has had constant difficulties with P in respect of dilatory payments, unfair rejections, and the like. S, who knows little about P, accepts C's statement and becomes a surety. P subsequently defaults. C's nondisclosure and misrepresentations are a defense to S in any action against him by C.

2. P is the cashier of C to whom S is bound as surety for P's fidelity. Before S undertook his obligation, P had embezzled a sum of money from C, but C had excused this embezzlement. P subsequently embezzles other sums. S cannot be held on the fidelity bond.

Comment on Subsection (1):

c. The rule stated in Subsection (1) applies not only to cases where the surety has made an offer for a single obligation but also to offers to guarantee successive extensions of credit. The fact that the surety is already bound on one obligation does not excuse the creditor from disclosing material facts before the second obligation is incurred.

3. S is surety to C for P on a continuing guaranty which S may revoke at any time by notice to C. After C has made several extensions of credit to P he learns that P is insolvent. S does not know this and C is aware of S's ignorance. C, without disclosing the fact of C's insolvency, makes further advances to P. S's liability is limited to P's defaults in advances occurring before C could have notified S of P's insolvency.

d. *Disclosure breach of legal duty by creditor.* Where the creditor cannot without a breach of a confidential duty disclose facts about the principal which have a material bearing on the surety's risk, the creditor is not entitled to accept the obligation of the surety. The mere fact that the creditor should not disclose information should not enable him to take advantage of the information to the detriment of the surety.

Comment on Subsection (2):

e. Where the surety has offered to become bound on successive extensions of credit, each extension of credit creates a new obligation. This situation is covered by Subsection (1). Subsection (2) is meant to cover any situation where the surety has the power upon the happening of certain events to terminate his liability as to future defaults. Such a power may arise because of an express reservation, as is generally true in fidelity bonds, or may be implied from the type of surety contract. The creditor's nondisclosure must affect a fact which, if known to the surety, would entitle the surety to terminate his liability as to future defaults. Subsection (2) has its chief application in respect of fidelity bonds. The facts which the creditor must make a reasonable effort to disclose include dishonesty and other criminal conduct of an employee which affect the risk the surety has under taken. Mere inefficiency of the employee or irregularities of conduct within or without the scope of employment need not be disclosed unless they affect the surety's risk or have been made the subject of specific reservations. There is no general rule of suretyship that the creditor must keep the surety informed of natural facts affecting the surety's risk when they do not give the surety the power to terminate his liability. If the surety wishes the creditor to accept any such duty, he must make it a part of his contract with the creditor. Where the creditor has properly accepted the obligation of a surety but subsequently discovers material facts which he cannot disclose without a violation of a confidential relation, nondisclosure is not a defense to the surety.

Hypotheticals

1. A and B borrowed money from Bank to finance a joint business venture. They signed a note as co-makers. Is A an accommodation party?

2. A and B borrowed money from Bank to finance a business venture. They signed a note as co-makers. A applied all of the loan proceeds to the venture which is totally her enterprise. B joined in borrowing the money and in signing the note because A's credit alone would not support the loan.

a. Is B an accommodation party?

b. Is the answer different if B paid A for co-signing the note?

c. What is B's liability on the note if:

    i. just as the problem is structured, B signed as a co-maker?

    ii. A signed as maker and B indorsed irregularly?

    iii. B signed as maker and A indorsed irregularly?

    iv. B issued the note as maker payable to the order of A who indorsed the instrument to the Bank?

d. In deciding if B is an accommodation party, would it matter that A is a corporation in which B owns stock?

3. Suppose B agreed to serve as A's surety for a bank loan. A signed a note. B signed a separate contract of suretyship.

a. Is B an accommodation party?

b. Is B a surety?

c. Suppose that the deal was structured so that B issued a note to the Bank's order. A was not a party to the instrument, but A got the proceeds directly from Bank. Is B an accommodation party? Is B a surety? Pioneer Ins. Co. v. Gelt, 558 F.2d 1303 (8th Cir.1977) (applying Nebraska law).

d. Suppose the deal was structured so that Bank loaned the money to B, and A actually got the loan proceeds through B. Is B even a surety in this case?

4. A got a loan from Bank and issued a note to Bank's order. B also signed as accommodation maker. The note is collateralized by an Article 9 security interest in all of A's personal property. The note is not paid when due.

a. Must Bank pursue the collateral before expecting B to pay?

b. Must Bank sue A before going against B?

c. Must Bank even ask A to pay before looking to B?

d. Suppose B had signed as indorser rather than maker.

e. Suppose B signed as maker but added to her maker's signature the words "collection guarantee." See 3-419(d).

5. A got a loan from Bank and issued a note to Bank's order. B also signed as accommodation maker. The note is collateralized by an Article 9 security interest in all of A's personal property. The note is not paid when due. A files bankruptcy.

    a. Does the automatic stay of A's bankruptcy affect Bank's efforts to collect from B?

    b. B pays the note. What are her rights against A and A's bankruptcy estate?

    c. Suppose that C also has cosigned the note as another accommodation maker.

        i. Can Bank nevertheless expect B to pay the whole thing?

        ii. Can B expect anything from C?

6. Bank had filed an Article 9 financing statement to perfect its security interest in A's personal property, but the filing lapsed before A's bankruptcy. Consequently, the interest became unperfected and was avoided by the debtor in possession or trustee in A's bankruptcy case. In effect, the debt became unsecured.

    a. How does the lapse and resulting avoidance affect B's rights against the bankruptcy estate?

    b. How does the lapse affect Bank's rights against B?

    c. How would it matter if the note contained a clause providing that "Sureties to this instrument hereby waive their rights to collateral security"?

7. How would it matter if, before the bankruptcy, Bank and A had entered into a series of workout agreements that several times extended the time for A to pay the note and, in the end, completely discharged A's liability on the note?

8. It turns out that at the time B cosigned the note, A was already heavily indebted to Bank. The loan proceeds were never actually paid to A. They were applied to the preexisting debt that A owed Bank. B was completely unaware. She thought that the loan was to be used to buy new equipment for A's enterprise. She was also unaware that at the time she got involved, A was experiencing a negative cash flow and was already headed toward bankruptcy. Bank was fully knowledgeable of everything the whole time. Indeed, A's doubtful financial condition was the very reason that Bank had required A to find a surety to back A's debt to Bank. Bank never disclosed any of this information to B. Does the Bank's silence matter?

9. On the differences between being transferee and holder and the importance of due course

Milton Copeland, *A Statutory Primer: Revised Article 3 of the U.C.C. -- Negotiable Instruments*
1992 Ark. L. Notes 65

* * *

A. Transferees.

Article 3 states rights for many more parties than just holders in due course. In fact, the Article states the rights of transferees who do not even qualify as holders. However, the basic transfer rule for instruments has not always been understood or stated clearly. For example, in 1972 the Arkansas Supreme Court, in *McIlroy Bank v. First National Bank*, said that "the UCC does not permit assignments of negotiable instruments" but does permit instruments to be "transferred or negotiated." [252 Ark. 558, 560, 480 S.W.2d 127, 128 (1972)] But--isn't an assignment a transfer? In fact, isn't a negotiation a special type of transfer (rather than an alternative to a transfer as suggested by the "or" in the McIlroy Bank quotation)?

For the moment, forget McIlroy Bank (and other cases decided under former Article 3) and think about language in revised Article 3. "Negotiation" is defined as "a transfer of possession ... to a person who thereby becomes its holder." [3-201(a)] So, a negotiation is a special type of transfer; and the transferee of this type of transfer is called a "holder." Revised Article 3 also refers to "transfer of an instrument," and then adds, "whether or not the transfer is a negotiation"; [3-203(b)] thus, there is a type of transfer that is not a negotiation. There is even some merit in calling such a transfer an "assignment" and such a transferee an "assignee" (in contrast to a "negotiation" and the resulting "holder"), and the use of such terminology is consistent with revised Article 3. [3-203]

But is talk of an "assignment" of an instrument consistent with McIlroy Bank? Yes, if we read that opinion--particularly in light of other supreme court opinions--to hold merely that the particular type of assignment at issue in that case is not permitted by the UCC. The contention of First National Bank was that it had an equitable assignment of the promissory note in question even though it had given up possession of the note. The idea of being an assignee without "control of the note" was apparently what the court found unacceptable; the corollary of this is that the "transfer" permitted by the court requires a transfer of possession of the instrument. This is clearly the approach of revised Article 3, which states that an instrument is transferred "when it is delivered ... for the purpose of giving to the person receiving delivery the right to enforce the instrument." [3-203(a)] For an instrument to be "delivered," there must be "voluntary transfer of possession." [1-201(14)]

Moreover, this transfer does not have to be for value. Fifteen years after McIlroy Bank, the Arkansas Supreme Court had to decide whether it is necessary to indorse an instrument to give it away. In *Brown v. Bell*, [291 Ark. 116, 118-119, 722 S.W.2d 592, 594 (1987)] the court distinguished between the generic concept of transfer and the specific type of transfer called "negotiation," and held that a donor's rights in an instrument may be transferred without indorsement since indorsement is necessary only for negotiation. But what about the appellant's argument that the gift amounted to an "assignment" and was thus invalid under McIlroy Bank?

The court's response was simply that McIlroy Bank said that a note could be "transferred." However confusing that might have been before the adoption of revised Article 3, the law is easy to understand today. Regardless of whether the transaction is called a "gift," "assignment," "conveyance," "sale," "mortgage," or something else, the succeeding party gets the preceding party's right to enforce the instrument if the transaction meets Article 3's two-fold test for a "transfer." The test is met when (i) possession of the instrument has been voluntarily turned over to the transferee (ii) for the purpose of giving the transferee the right to enforce the instrument.

Transfer of the instrument calls into play the so-called shelter principle of section 3-203, which provides that all of the transferor's rights in connection with enforcing the instrument are vested in the transferee. [3-203(b)] This principle is most dramatic when the transferor (or his transferor, or his transferor's transferor, ad infinitum) was a holder in due course ("HDC" for short). The existence of an HDC anywhere in the chain of transfers means that the last transferee can assert the rights of an HDC without being one in his own right. [3--203(b) & comment 2] As will soon be seen, important rights to enforce the instrument also go with being a holder (even if not "in due course"); these rights, too, can be asserted by a transferee who, although not a holder, can prove that there was a holder in the chain of transfers.

Besides the shelter advantage, section 3-203 states another right of some--but not all--transferees. If the instrument is taken for value, the transferee has "a specifically enforceable right to the unqualified indorsement of the transferor" [3-203(c)] ("unqualified" meaning that the indorser is not permitted to disclaim the liability that goes with the indorsement). [3-203 comment 3] Enforced by a mandatory injunction, this right is asserted when (a) the transferee wants to sue the transferor on his indorsement, (b) the transferee needs to qualify as a holder so that he may negotiate the instrument to another holder, or (c) the transferee needs to qualify as an HDC in his own right and has the "in due course" qualifications but must get the indorsement to be a "holder." [4-205(1)]

In the last situation, since negotiation of the instrument does not occur until the indorsement is made, the Official Comment reminds us that the transferee's effort to become a holder in due course will be frustrated if he receives notice of a defense or claim before the indorsement is actually made by the transferor. [3-203 comment 3]

B. Holders.

Being the specialized type of transferee called "holder" provides advantages not available to a mere transferee. A holder is the person in possession of an instrument if it is payable to that person (or to bearer). [1-201(20)] If the instrument is payable to bearer, it is payable to whoever is in possession; [1-201(5)] if the instrument is payable to an identified person (including an instrument indorsed to an identified person), [3-205(a)] only that person can be the holder. With one exception, [3-103(a)(11) & 3-201] only a holder can negotiate an instrument. Because of the other advantages of being a holder, this ability to negotiate means that the instrument has more commercial value than it would have otherwise.

A second advantage of being a holder is that the law provides procedural advantages when the holder has to sue to collect on the instrument. Unless there is an issue regarding the validity of the signature of the alleged obligor, [3-308(a)] the most significant procedural advantage is the simplicity of making a prima facie case, which consists of nothing more than proof that the claimant is the holder together with proffer of the instrument. [3-308(b) & 3-301] Consequently, except for rarely used defenses (such as validity of signatures or identity of the claimant), the alleged obligor has the burden of proof on every defense and, of course, every claim in recoupment.

There would be much more need to use litigation to collect on instruments if Article 3 did not provide the following advantage to the holder: "the obligation of the party obliged to pay the instrument is discharged even though payment is made with knowledge of a claim to the instrument." [3-602(a)] Except for the occasional situation when an exception to it applies, [3-602(b)] this rule of discharge serves the critical purpose of assuring the obligor that it is safe to pay whoever is the holder, regardless of whether the original payee has notified the obligor that the instrument has been negotiated to someone else. Moreover, each holder is assured that the obligor's payment to the original payee (or to anybody else who was a holder at an earlier point in time) will not discharge the obligation, even if the obligor made the payment without knowing that there was a new holder; the burden is on the obligor to make sure that he pays only the current holder.

Of course, since "H" is a part of "HDC," another advantage of being a holder is that it opens the door to the possibility of being an HDC.

C. Holders in due course.

To have the rights of an HDC is to have the ultimate status of one enforcing an instrument. One may have these rights because his transferee had them, or one may be an HDC in his own right because he has satisfied all of Article 3's requirements for that status. Moreover, one wanting to take an instrument has all the facts he needs to determine whether those requirements are satisfied. Here they are: [3-302] (1) Of course, the writing must be negotiable; the taker must determine from the writing's four corners whether all of Article 3's negotiability requirements have been met. [3-104(a), 3-106 - 3-109] (2) The instrument must be authentic on its face; the taker must determine that it "does not bear such apparent evidence of forgery or alteration or is not otherwise so irregular or incomplete as to call into question its authenticity." [3-302(a)(1)] (3) One must become a holder; the taker must check for any necessary indorsements and take possession of the instrument. (4) The instrument must be taken for "value" as defined in Article 3, which is not the same as "consideration" at common law (or "value" in the rest of the UCC for that matter); the taker must determine whether he is giving one of the five types of Article 3 value. [3-303(a)] (5) The holder must take without notice of any of eight circumstances listed in revised Article 3, [3-302(a)(2)] which we often abbreviate by saying "without notice of a defense." (6) The holder must take "in good faith."

It is in connection with the "good faith" requirement that revised Article 3 has made a change, and only time will tell whether it is a sea change. Former Article 3 (and the Negotiable Instruments Law before that, and the common law before that) defined "good faith" subjectively; the former Article 3 definition was "honesty in fact in the conduct or transaction concerned." That is still the definition for "good faith" in the rest of the UCC, but the Article 3 meaning of "good faith" (and, thus, the requirement for HDC status) now has an objective aspect added to the subjective.

The new definition is "honesty in fact and the observance of reasonable commercial standards of fair dealing." Obviously, "reasonable commercial standards" requires an inquiry into the commercial standards of reasonable people. It is very significant, however, that the drafters of the new definition added the phrase, "of fair dealing." The Official Comment says,

Although fair dealing is a broad term that must be defined in context, it is clear that it is concerned with the fairness of conduct rather than the care with which an act is performed. Failure to exercise ordinary care in conducting a transaction is an entirely different concept than failure to deal fairly in conducting the transaction. Both fair dealing and ordinary care, which is defined in Section 3-103(a)(7), are to be judged in the light of reasonable commercial standards, but those standards in each case are directed to different aspects of commercial conduct. [FN39]

3-103 comment 4. We are thus admonished to distinguish between the "fair dealing" aspect of commercial conduct and the "ordinary care" aspect. The more the difference in these aspects is emphasized, the more likely it is that one can qualify as an HDC even though he has taken the instrument negligently. Of course, this will prove to be the kind of theoretical distinction that only a law professor loves if courts and/or juries decide that there is virtually no conduct lacking ordinary care that can still be considered "fair dealing." In any event, there will surely be cases where the holder will be found to have dealt unfairly even though taking the instrument honestly and without notice of a defense; although an HDC under former Article 3, such a holder no longer qualifies for that status under revised Article 3.

Now to the rights of an HDC. Just as an assignee of a contract takes it subject to the obligor's defenses against the assignor, a mere holder of a negotiable instrument (and, of course, a mere transferee) takes the instrument subject to any defense that an obligor might have against an earlier obligee. The HDC, on the other hand, is not subject to most of the defenses that are raised by obligors; Article 3's list of defenses raisable against an HDC is very short. Garden-variety defenses include the payee's misrepresentation of the property for which the obligor gave the instrument, the payee's failure to deliver the property, and failure of some condition precedent to the obligation to make payment. None of these so-called personal defenses can be asserted against the HDC; there are only two categories of defenses good against the HDC.

The eight so-called real defenses can be raised against the HDC. Six of these are defenses to what would be the obligor's obligation but for the defense: [3-305(a)(1)] (1) infancy of the obligor, but only when such infancy is a defense to a simple contract; (2), (3), & (4) duress, lack of legal capacity, or illegality of the transaction which, under non-UCC law, nullifies the obligation of the obligor; (5) so-called real fraud, [3-305 comment 1] i.e., fraud that induced the obligor to sign the instrument with neither knowledge nor reasonable opportunity to learn of its character or essential terms (garden-variety fraud, sometimes called "fraud in the inducement," not being sufficient for this real defense); and (6) the obligor's discharge in insolvency proceedings. The remaining two real defenses are alteration of the instrument [3-407(c)] and forgery of the alleged obligor's signature; 3-401(a)] these are defenses based on the fact that the party being sued never obligated himself as alleged.

The second category of defenses good against an HDC is any defense that the HDC's own action (or inaction) creates. A good example is when an HDC provides a defense to an obligor by running afoul of an Article 3 requirement for collecting the instrument, such as when an indorser defends against the HDC on the ground that he failed to make a timely presentment of the check. [3-415(e)] (By the way, the time for presentment has been changed by revised Article 3.) [Id.] Although this technical defense could be raised against the HDC in the past, the language in revised Article 3 emphasizes the point by saying that the HDC's right to enforce the instrument "is not subject to [personal] defenses of the obligor ... against a person other than the holder." [3-305(b)] When the obligor attempts to raise a personal defense based upon the action or inaction of an earlier holder (such as the payee), the effort is unsuccessful because the defense is "against a person other than the holder." However, if the current holder (who is obviously the person seeking to enforce the instrument) was the one who failed to make timely presentment, the defense is a winner since it is a defense "against" the holder himself (albeit an HDC).

This is a good time to introduce another refinement of revised Article 3. The possibilities covered by the old word "defenses" have now been split into "defenses" and "claims in recoupment." [3-305] In discussing the difference in the two concepts, the Official Comment says that formerly the "failure of consideration" defense did not distinguish between the case in which a seller (who took an instrument in payment) failed to perform at all and the case in which the buyer makes a claim against the seller because of faulty performance. Under revised Article 3, when the buyer is claiming faulty performance, "use of the term 'claim in recoupment' ... is a more precise statement of the Buyer's right against Holder." [3-305 comment 3] Besides getting used to the new terminology, the thing to remember is that a claim in recoupment against an HDC can be asserted only if it is "against" the HDC himself.

Probably the most common claim in recoupment is that of a buyer who counterclaims for breach of warranty when the seller sues on the promissory note signed by the buyer. As the payee, the seller may well be an HDC since, at the time he sold the goods and took the note, he was in good faith and had no notice that there was anything wrong with the goods. Does the seller's HDC status protect him from the claim in recoupment? No; the Official Comment points out that it "is not relevant whether Seller is or is not a holder in due course of the note or whether Seller knew or had notice that Buyer had the warranty claim" since revised Article 3's language frees the HDC from a claim in recoupment only when it is "against a person other than the holder." [Id.] Thus, the result is the same as that under former Article 3, where the buyer had a good "defense" since he had "dealt" with the HDC. [3-305(2) (1989 Version)]

In addition to claims in recoupment which he did not create, an HDC takes the instrument free of all claims "of a property or possessory right in the instrument or its proceeds." [3-306] The Official Comment says that this language in revised Article 3 includes not only "claims to ownership" but also "the claim to a lien or the claim of a person in rightful possession of an instrument who was wrongfully deprived of possession" and the claim "for rescission of a negotiation of the instrument by the claimant." [3-306 comment]

It is no wonder, then, that every holder would like to have the rights of an HDC, either because he is an HDC or because he has the rights of a transferor who was an HDC. However, a whole class of holders of negotiable instruments who used to be HDC's no longer qualify as such; this is because of the Federal Trade Commission's regulations foreclosing HDC status to the holders of "consumer credit contracts." [16 C.F.R. 433.1 - 433.3] When a consumer credit contract contains the language required by the regulations (and the creditor commits an "unfair or deceptive act or practice" under the Federal Trade Commission Act by not complying), no one who takes that writing can be an HDC. Under former Article 3, this was because the writing was no longer a negotiable instrument; the FTC-required language prevented the obligation from being unconditional, one of the negotiability requirements. [3-104(a)] Under revised Article 3, an instrument is deemed unconditional and is therefore negotiable in spite of the FTC- required language, but "there cannot be a holder in due course of the instrument." [3-106(d)] The result is that all non-HDC rules of Article 3 now apply to these very common instruments; at the same time, the FTC regulations protect consumers by permitting them to raise against all parties enforcing such instruments their personal defenses (and some claims in recoupment). [16 C.F.R. 433.2]

* * *

Conclusion

Revised Articles 3 and 4 contain many significant changes in the law not discussed in this primer. If one despairs of all there is to learn, maybe a little perspective will help. Arkansas had former Articles 3 and 4 on the books for thirty years, and changed them very little through the years. Now, if the General Assembly will just leave us alone for another thirty years....

10. Restrictive indorsements

Walcott v. Manufacturers Hanover Trust

Civil Court of the City of New York, Kings County, 1986
133 Misc.2d 725, 507 N.Y.S.2d 961

Ira B. Harkavy, Judge. * * * Plaintiff, Kenneth Walcott, alleges that on November 1, 1985, he sent his October 19, 1985 paycheck in the sum of $359.05 together with a Crossland Savings Bank money order in the sum of $251.54 to Midatlantic Mortgage Company in payment of his November 1985 mortgage. He claims he signed his name to the back of the check and placed his mortgage number and the Midatlantic mailing sticker on the back of the check. He claims he then deposited the two checks in an envelope directed to Midatlantic Mortgage company and placed the check in a United States Postal Box.

The copy of the check, introduced into evidence, shows Mr. Walcott's indorsement and the mortgage number 603052, but shows no sign of the sticker. It further shows that it was cashed by third party defendant, Bilko Check Cashing Corp. (Bilko) on November 4, 1985 and deposited into the Bilko account at defendant Manufacturers Hanover Trust (Manufacturers Hanover) on November 5, 1985.

In mid-November 1985, Mr. Walcott received a notice from Midatlantic that he was late in the November payment of his mortgage. He inquired and found that his pay check had been cashed on or about November 4, 1985 at Bilko who in turn deposited the check in their account at Manufacturers Hanover. The Crossland money order was never cashed and it was stopped by Mr. Walcott on or about November 22, 1985 and replaced by a new money order at that time.

Plaintiff claimed that an intervening thief stole the check and then cashed it at third party defendant, Bilko who in turn negotiated the check by depositing it in their account at Manufacturers Hanover. The check was finally cleared through Citibank and charged to the account of the original payor, The New York City Transit Authority.

An employee of Manufacturers Hanover testified that third party defendant Bilko had an account at the bank. She further testified that a review of the check showed that Bilko had deposited the check at Manufacturers Hanover in the Bilko account. Additional testimony revealed that once a check is deposited in the Bilko account, the bank waits three to five days for the check to clear and thereafter Bilko may use the proceeds.

The store manager of Bilko had testified previously in a prior trial of this case before this Court which ended in a mistrial. Her testimony from the prior trial was incorporated on consent of all parties into the retrial. She testified that in order for a government check to be cashed, two pieces of identification are required, usually an employee identification card containing an individual's social security number, and a drivers license. She further testified that the person presenting the check in question must have had such identification since the notations as to the calculation of the check cashing fees on the front of the check indicate that identification was shown.

The issue presented to this Court is whether plaintiff's indorsement of his paycheck was such as to be a special or restrictive indorsement, thus limiting the negotiation of the instrument or did it have the effect of creating a bearer instrument.

SPECIAL INDORSEMENT

Uniform Commercial Code §3-204 subdivision (1) defines a special indorsement as being one that "…. specifies the person to whom or to whose order it makes the instrument payable. Any instrument specially indorsed becomes payable to the order of the special indorsee and may be further negotiated only by his indorsement."

Examination of the back of the check, a photocopy of which, as previously stated, was introduced into evidence, reveals that Mr. Walcott did not specify any particular indorsee. In order for the alleged attached sticker to have served that purpose it must have also complied with UCC §3-202 subdivision (2): "An indorsement must be written by or on behalf of the holder and on the instrument or a paper so firmly affixed thereto as to become a part thereof." The back of the check shows no sticker attached at all. Even if it had originally been affixed thereto, as plaintiff claims, it obviously became detached easily, thus failing to meet the indorsement requirements under the UCC to constitute a special indorsement.

RESTRICTIVE INDORSEMENT

As to the numbers written underneath plaintiff's signature, they did not have the effect of restricting plaintiff's indorsement. "An indorsement is restrictive which either (a) is conditional; or (b) purports to prohibit further transfer of the instrument; or (c) includes the words 'for collection,' 'for deposit,' 'pay any bank,' or like terms signifying a purpose of deposit or collection; or (d) otherwise states that it is for the benefit or use of the indorser or of another person." UCC §3-205.

This section of the Uniform Commercial Code is very specific. The series of numbers representing plaintiff's mortgage account was insufficient to restrict negotiation of plaintiff's check.

BLANK INDORSEMENT

Plaintiff's indorsement had the effect of converting the check into a bearer instrument. The series of numbers having no restrictive effect, Mr. Walcott indorsed the check in blank, or otherwise stated, he simply signed his name. A blank indorsement under UCC §3-204 subdivision (2) "... specifies no particular indorsee and may consist of a mere signature." Additionally, "An instrument payable to order and indorsed in blank becomes payable to bearer and may be negotiated by delivery alone...." Consequently, since plaintiff failed to limit his blank indorsement, the check was properly negotiated by delivery to third party defendant Bilko and properly cashed by them.

Judgment for the defendant, Manufacturers Hanover Trust dismissing the complaint. Judgment for third party defendant, Bilko Check Cashing Corp. dismissing the complaint.

Lehigh Presbytery v. Merchants Bancorp, Inc.

Superior Court of Pennsylvania, 1991
410 Pa.Super. 557, 600 A.2d 593

McEwen, Judge: This appeal has been taken from judgment entered following denial of appellant's motion for post-trial relief. The trial court, in reliance upon Section 9 of the Uniform Fiduciaries Act, Act of 1923, May 31, P.L. 468, §9, 7 P.S. §6393, held that the appellee, Merchants Bancorp, Inc. (hereinafter Bank), was not liable to appellant for the value of negotiable instruments credited to the personal account of an employee of appellant. We find that the Uniform Fiduciaries Act is inapplicable to the facts of this case and therefore reverse.

Ms. Mary Ann Hunsberger was hired by the Lehigh Presbytery as a secretary/bookkeeper. In this capacity, Ms. Hunsberger was responsible for opening the Presbytery's mail, affixing a rubber-stamp indorsement to checks received by the Presbytery, and depositing the checks into the Presbytery's account in appellee's bank. It is not disputed that, over a period of more than five years, Ms. Hunsberger deposited into her own account 153 of these checks. The Bank credited the checks to Ms. Hunsberger's account, despite the rubber-stamp restrictive indorsement, * because it relied solely on the account number handwritten on the deposit slips submitted by Ms. Hunsberger with the checks at the time of deposit. Ms. Hunsberger obtained the deposit slips in the lobby of the bank, wrote the proper account title, "Lehigh Presbytery," but inserted her own account number rather than the account number of her employer.

Upon discovery of the diversionary scheme, appellant filed suit against the Bank to recover the funds credited to Ms. Hunsberger's account, alleging breach of express and implied contract. Trial without a jury resulted in a verdict in favor of the appellee. Appellant's motion for post-trial relief was denied and this appeal timely followed.

Appellant's sole argument on appeal is that the Uniform Commercial Code (hereinafter U.C.C.) rather than the Uniform Fiduciaries Act controls disposition of this case. Appellant contends that, pursuant to the relevant sections of the U.C.C., appellee was legally bound to follow the restrictive indorsements on the 153 checks deposited instead to the personal account of appellant's employee.

The U.C.C. §3-205, 13 Pa.C.S. §3205 provides: An indorsement is restrictive which either: (1) is conditional; (2) purports to prohibit further transfer of the instrument; (3) includes the words "for collection," "for deposit," "pay any bank," or like terms signifying a purpose of deposit or collection; or (4) otherwise states that it is for the benefit or use of the indorser or of another person. It is undisputed that the indorsement stamped on each check by Ms. Hunsberger is a restrictive indorsement within the meaning of Section 3205.

Section 3-206 of the U.C.C., 13 Pa.C.S. §3206, addresses the effect of such an indorsement and provides, in pertinent part:

> (c) Conditional or specified purpose indorsement.--Except for an intermediary bank, any transferee under an indorsement which is conditional or includes the words "for collection," "for deposit," "pay any bank," or like terms (section 3205(1) and (3) (relating to restrictive indorsements)) must pay or apply any value given by him for or on the security of the instrument consistently with the indorsement and to the extent that he does so he becomes a holder for value.

Thus, the U.C.C. mandates application of the value of the checks consistently with the indorsement, i.e., for deposit to Lehigh Presbytery's account.

Courts considering the significance of a restrictive indorsement have consistently concluded that the U.C.C. imposes an unwaivable obligation upon the bank to honor the indorsement. The Colorado Supreme Court concluded that "[t]he duty to examine a restrictive indorsement and follow its directions may require a bank to refuse to deposit an item in a particular account if such conduct would be inconsistent with the restrictive indorsement, or to investigate rather than accept an item as a matter of course." La Junta State Bank v. Travis, 727 P.2d 48, 54 (Colo.1986). New York State's highest court has held that "[t]he presence of a restriction imposes upon the depository bank an obligation not to accept that item other than in accord with the restriction. By disregarding the restriction, it not only subjects itself to liability for any losses resulting from its actions, but it also passes up what may be the best opportunity to prevent the fraud." Underpinning & Foundation Constructors, Inc., v. Chase Manhattan, 46 N.Y.2d 459, 469, 386 N.E.2d 1319, 1324, 414 N.Y.S.2d 298, 303 (1979). See also Cairo Co-Op. Exch. v. First National Bank of Cunningham, 228 Kan. 613, 620 P.2d 805 (Kan.1980) (bank liable for failure to honor restrictive indorsements); AmSouth Bank, N.A., v. Reliable Janitorial Service, Inc., 548 So.2d 1365 (Ala.1989) (where bank credited checks to account number on deposit slip and disregarded

---

* Each check was indorsed: "For Deposit Only To The Credit of Presbytery of Lehigh, Ernest Hutcheson, Treas."

restrictive indorsement, bank liable for conversion pursuant to mandate of U.C.C. §§ 3-205 and 3-206).

Appellee argues that the U.C.C. is inapplicable because the Bank acted in accordance with the Uniform Fiduciaries Act, 7 P.S. §6351 et seq., which, they contend, enables them to ignore the restrictive indorsement when the party depositing the check is a fiduciary. Appellee misapprehends the language and purpose of the Uniform Fiduciaries Act.

The Uniform Fiduciaries Act was designed to facilitate banking transactions by relieving the depositary of the responsibility of seeing that an authorized fiduciary uses entrusted funds for proper purposes. Robinson Protective Alarm Co. v. Bolger & Picker, 512 Pa. 116, 124, 516 A.2d 299, 304 (1986). The Act accomplishes this objective by shielding a depositary from liability where it applies funds consistently with the indorsement on a negotiable instrument in reliance upon a fiduciary's authority to so indorse the instrument, without further inquiry into the fiduciary's actual authority to so apply the entrusted funds. The Act is thus in harmony with the clear mandate of the Uniform Commercial Code that a bank must apply funds consistently with restrictive indorsements. The Uniform Fiduciaries Act was not designed to relieve a depositary from liability where, as here, the Bank followed the instructions of a fiduciary which conflicted with the indorsement on the instrument negotiated.

We have reviewed each of the cases offered by appellee in support of its interpretation of the Uniform Fiduciaries Act and find that in none of the relied upon cases did a bank disregard a restrictive indorsement. Rather, in cases in which a bank was relieved of liability by the Act, it was because the bank relied upon the authority of a fiduciary when they applied funds consistently with the indorsement on an instrument.

Appellee cites Jones v. Van Norman, 513 Pa. 572, 522 A.2d 503 (1987), to support its argument that the appellant assumed the risk of its fiduciary's competence and honesty. The fiduciary in Jones was authorized to indorse her principal's name and the bank applied funds consistently with the fiduciary's authorized indorsement without knowledge that the fiduciary was not authorized to cash the indorsed checks. The case is inapposite to the instant case because Ms. Hunsberger was only authorized to stamp a restrictive indorsement on the checks, and because the bank did not apply the funds consistently with the indorsements. Nevertheless, the discussion of our Supreme Court in Jones of the scope of Section 9 of the Act is instructive and consistent with our conclusion that the Uniform Fiduciaries Act will not protect a bank from liability unless it relies on a fiduciary with the authority to indorse checks payable to her principal. The Court stated: "unless the bank has actual knowledge that the fiduciary is committing a breach of his obligation as fiduciary, it is justified, if the fiduciary is empowered to endorse checks payable to his principal, in accepting them as a deposit to his personal account." Jones v. Van Norman, supra, at 581 n. 6, 522 A.2d at 508 n. 6, quoting Bacher v. City National Bank of Philadelphia, 347 Pa. 80, 89, 31 A.2d 725, 727 (1943). See also Levy v. First Pennsylvania Bank N.A., 338 Pa.Super. 73, 487 A.2d 857 (1985) (the Uniform Fiduciaries Act relieves banks of liability only when the fiduciary has the power to indorse). Ms. Hunsberger did not have authority to indorse checks payable to her principal nor did she ever exceed her limited authority to rubber-stamp the restrictive indorsement of the Presbytery's Treasurer.

Our Supreme Court's discussion of irregular conduct on the part of a fiduciary in Robinson Protective Alarm Co. v. Bolger & Picker, 512 Pa. 116, 516 A.2d 299 (1986), is similarly consistent with our ruling in the instant case.* Although Robinson is distinguishable from the instant case on

---

* Appellee incorrectly cites Robinson in support of its contention that it should be relieved of liability because it acted without actual knowledge and in good faith. In Robinson, the bank released funds to a fiduciary on his oral instructions, without obtaining his indorsement, because he was a fiduciary known to bank officials as the person authorized to receive such funds. Interpreting Section 2 of the Uniform Fiduciaries Act, 7 P.S. §6361, the Supreme Court held that

its facts and the law applied thereto, the Supreme Court, addressing the general design of the Uniform Fiduciaries Act, pertinently held that "the UFA does not permit a bank to ignore an irregularity where it is of a nature to place one on notice of improper conduct by the fiduciary." In the instant case, we find that the conflict between the restrictive indorsement on the checks and the account number on the deposit slips is so irregular as to give rise to a duty on the part of the Bank to refuse to deposit the checks without further inquiry.

We therefore conclude that 13 Pa.C.S. §§ 3205 and 3206 are controlling on the facts of this case and that Section 9 of the Uniform Fiduciaries Act is inapplicable.

Judgment reversed. Case remanded. Jurisdiction relinquished.

O'Petro Energy Corp. v. Canadian State Bank
Supreme Court of Oklahoma, 1992
837 P.2d 1391

Lavender, Justice. We are asked to decide in this case of first impression whether a Bank subjects itself to liability by accepting a check bearing a restrictive indorsement, "for deposit only" and depositing it into an account different from the named party on the front of the check. The trial court held the bank liable. We reverse.

FACTS

On June 17, 1982 O'Petro Energy corporation (Appellee), a publicly held corporation with approximately 350 to 400 shareholders, borrowed $165,000.00 from Northwest Bank. The collateral for the loan was a certificate of deposit held by the company at Northwest Bank for $165,000.00. The loan proceeds were in a cashier's check made payable to O'Petro Energy Corporation. Terry Miller, president of O'Petro received the check on June 22, 1982.

Miller took the check to his bank in Yukon, Canadian State Bank (hereinafter Bank), wrote on the back of the check, "for deposit only" and instructed the teller to give the check and his deposit slip to the chief cashier. The cashier deposited the check into Miller's personal account and then at Miller's direction, wired the proceeds to another bank to cover a check for insufficient funds written by Miller a few days before.

O'Petro brought suit alleging Defendant was negligent in accepting the deposit and in allowing a conversion of the funds. Additionally, O'Petro sought punitive damages asserting the Bank's actions were willful, intentional and malicious.

The trial court upon hearing evidence from the Bank's first witness, stopped the trial and withdrew the case from the jury. The judge entered judgment sua sponte for O'Petro. Thereafter, the Bank made an offer of proof which the court rejected and moved for a directed verdict which the court denied. The Court of Appeals affirmed finding no reversible error. We previously granted certiorari.

---

where a depositary acting in good faith pays money to a fiduciary authorized to receive it, the payor bears no liability for a subsequent misappropriation of those funds by the fiduciary. Robinson Protective Alarm Co. v. Bolger & Picker, 512 Pa. 116, 123, 516 A.2d 299, 303 (1986). The Bank's good faith argument fails because Ms. Hunsberger was not authorized to receive the funds, and because good faith would, under no circumstances, excuse the Bank's obligation to follow a restrictive indorsement.

I.

O'Petro claimed the indorsement on the back of the check by Terry Miller stating "for deposit only" was a restrictive indorsement as defined by statute and that Appellant Bank was compelled to deposit the funds into an O'Petro account. In that the Bank failed to follow the restrictive indorsement, it is liable to O'Petro for the full amount of the check.

In 12A O.S.1981 §3-205 the statute states:

[a]n indorsement is restrictive which either (a) is conditional; or (b) purports to prohibit further transfer of the instrument; or (c) includes the words "for collection", "for deposit ", "pay any bank", or like terms signifying a purpose of deposit or collection; or (d) otherwise states that it is for the benefit or use of the indorser or of another person.

Section 3-206 explains the effect of a restrictive indorsement. Relevant portions state:

(1) No restrictive indorsement prevents further transfer or negotiation of the instrument. (3) Except for an intermediary bank, any transferee under an indorsement which is conditional or includes the words "for collection", "for deposit", "pay any bank", or like terms (subparagraphs (a) and (c) of Section 3-205) must pay or apply any value given by him for or on the security of the instrument consistently with the indorsement and to the extent that he does so he becomes a holder for value. In addition such transferee is a holder in due course if he otherwise complies with the requirement of Section 3-202 on what constitutes a holder in due course.

In other words, O'Petro argues the Bank was required to deposit the money into an account for O'Petro Energy Corporation and that its action in depositing the check into Miller's personal account was equal to conversion. The corporation filed suit citing 12A O.S.1981 §3-419(1)(c). That provision provides that "[a]n instrument is converted when ... it is paid on a forged indorsement."

The Bank maintains, however, that Miller's restrictive indorsement was not "forged" in that Miller had authority under the corporate borrowing resolution to indorse the check using the restrictive indorsement and accompanying deposit slip and to deposit the money into his personal account. Further, the Bank alleges that O'Petro should be estopped to claim conversion because the funds eventually benefitted O'Petro and that O'Petro knew this or should have known it.

The Bank urges us to address these issues of first impression which call for us to interpret certain provisions of the UCC. In that the trial court committed reversible error by not allowing the Bank to present relevant evidence in defense of its actions, we reverse.

II.

In Grimshaw Co. v. First Nat. Bank & Tr. Co., [563 P.2d 117 (Okla.1977)] this court stated that "[a]n unauthorized payee indorsement is 'one made without actual, implied or apparent authority and includes a forgery.'" [Id. at 120]

As a general rule, a drawee bank which pays an item containing a payee indorsement not by or on authority of the payee does so with its own funds and may not charge the drawer's account. A drawee bank may, of course, attempt to establish the indorsement as being that of the intended payee or his authorized agent. A payee indorsement is effective when made by an authorized agent or representative, 'and his authority to make it may be established as in other cases of representation.' 12A O.S.1971 §3-403(1) [see now 12A O.S.1991 §3-403].

The policy considerations behind the various UCC defenses intend to foster the commercial reliability of negotiable paper. The general theory being that the loss must fall, as among the innocent parties, on that person nearest to the individual who caused the loss and supposedly, the one who could have prevented it. Consequently, the UCC places the burden on the first bank in the collection chain to insure the indorsement is authentic as it is the bank in the best position to discover the forgery.

Therefore, "barring exceptional circumstances, the general rule is that failure of a bank to inquire when an individual cashes a check made payable to a corporate payee and puts the money in his personal account is an unreasonable commercial banking practice as a matter of law." See Aetna Ca. & Sur. Co. v. Hepler State Bank, 6 Kan.App.2d 543, 630 P.2d 721, 728 (1981) and citations therein. However, in our case, the Bank purportedly called the drawer bank and talked with the loan officer familiar with O'Petro's corporate borrowing resolution. Thereafter, the Bank accepted Miller's authority to so "indorse" the check.

The Bank attempted to present evidence that it was Miller's intent by way of his restrictive indorsement to have the funds deposited into his personal account. The bank maintained Miller had authority to indorse the check under the terms of the corporate borrowing resolution. The corporate borrowing resolution stated in pertinent part: "Be it further resolved that said bank is authorized to follow the instructions of said officers in the disposition of any proceeds of any such loan, credit, discount, or sale, whether for such loan, credit, discount, or sale, whether for payment to or for credit in this or any other bank to the account of this corporation, or such officers individually or in their official capacity, or any third person, or otherwise."

The evidence the Bank wanted to introduce went straight to the issue presented--whether Miller had the authority to sign the check. By definition a forgery includes an "unauthorized signature." A signature that is authorized, however, is not a forgery. If Miller had the right to deposit the check into his personal account, then the bank was not responsible to O'Petro for following Miller's instructions.

Similarly, if Miller had the authority to sign the check then the manner in which the check was indorsed would not create any liability for the Bank if the Bank was complying with Miller's instructions. In that a restrictive indorsement does not prevent further transfer or negotiation of the check, [3-206(1)] even if Miller's indorsement meant, "deposit the check into an O'Petro account," Miller's accompanying deposit slip canceled the indorsement out the same as if Miller had drawn a line through the restriction and further negotiated it with his personal indorsement.

In other words, if Miller had the authority to indorse the check and to put it into any account he wanted, and there was evidence the Bank made inquiry into this authority, then "how" Miller went about doing it was immaterial if the Bank complied with Miller's authorized instructions. If Miller's intent was carried out, then no one else had the right to complain at least as to that banking transaction and the only transaction we are concerned with here. While Miller may have subsequently misused the funds, this fact was irrelevant as to the Bank's liability concerning the deposit.

We are not saying that in all circumstances, a bank that fails to follow a restrictive indorsement is blameless. "Of course if a bank fails to abide by a restrictive endorsement per se, absent a waiver, it does so at its peril." [Rutherford v. Darwin, 95 N.M. 340, 622 P.2d 245 (App.1980).] However, in our case, there was evidence from which it might be found that Miller as President of O'Petro had the right to deposit the check into his personal account. Under these circumstances, the bank was not obligated to go further and question Miller's intended use of the funds.

Whether Miller had the authority and whether the bank acted in a commercially reasonable manner are questions of fact that the jury should have decided. We find the trial judge erred in not allowing the bank to present such evidence to the jury.

III.

Further, we recognize that the UCC has not usurped the common law remedy by which there is "authority supporting protection of the bank that pays without indorsement as long as the actual payee or person authorized by payee receives the money ordered by the drawer to be paid." The bank made an offer of proof that there was evidence the loan proceeds, though deposited into Miller's personal checking account, eventually benefitted O'Petro and that "O'Petro" knew this or should have known this and should be estopped from complaining of it now.

If on remand, the jury should find the Bank acted unreasonably in accepting Miller's deposit with the restrictive indorsement, we hold that additional evidence may be introduced relevant to the Bank's alternate defenses. We, therefore, reverse the case for a new trial consistent with our findings.

§ 11. Restrictions on due-course and like rights

COMMERCIAL CREDIT CO. v. CHILDS, 199 Ark. 1073, 137 S.W.2d 260 (1940). [Appellee bought a used car on credit from Arkansas Motors, Inc. Appellee signed a conditional sales contract and a promissory note, both of which were discounted to Appellant. When Appellee defaulted, Appellant sued to replevy the car, which was collateral for the note. Appellee's defenses were misrepresentation and breach of warranty by Arkansas Motors. Appellant argued, in essence, that it was a holder in due course and thus took free of these defenses. The Arkansas Supreme Court rejected this argument.]

Humphreys, Justice. *** The note and contract are attached and constitute one instrument covering an agreement of the sale and purchase of the automobile in question. The instrument contains many provisions and conditions and there appears on the back of the contract and attached note a printed assignment to the Commercial Credit Co., appellant herein, signed by the seller, the Arkansas Motors, Inc. The note, contract and assignment were all executed and signed the same day. The instrument was prepared and delivered to the Arkansas Motors, Inc., by appellant to be used by it in the sale and purchase of cars. Appellant financed the deal.

We think appellant was so closely connected with the entire transaction or with the deal that it can not be heard to say that it, in good faith, was an innocent purchaser of the instrument for value before maturity. It financed the deal, prepared the instrument, and on the day it was executed took an assignment of it from the Arkansas Motors, Inc. Even before it was executed it prepared the written assignment thereon to itself. Rather than being a purchaser of the instrument after its execution it was to all intents and purposes a party to the agreement and instrument from the beginning. To say the least of it, it put the Arkansas Motors, Inc., in the position to procure appellee's signature to the instrument through fraudulent misrepresentation as to the value and condition of the automobile it was selling to appellee. There is little or no dispute in the testimony that Arkansas Motors, Inc., procured the signature of appellee to the instrument appellant has made the basis of its suit, by falsely and fraudulently representing to appellee that the car it was selling him was worth $578 and in practically perfect condition, whereas it was of little or no value and so defective that it could not be used.

Under the facts detailed above we think it was appellant's duty before taking an assignment of the instrument to inquire whether appellee's signature thereto had been obtained through fraud and misrepresentations.

This court will not disturb, on appeal, the finding of a jury that one is not an innocent purchaser of a note, if the finding is justified or warranted by any substantial evidence. (Citations omitted.)

It is unnecessary to decide whether the instrument in question was negotiable *** for we have concluded under the facts and circumstance detailed above the jury was warranted in finding that appellant was not an innocent purchaser of the note sued on. ***

Courtesy Financial Services, Inc. v. Hughes
Court of Appeal of Louisiana, 1982
424 So.2d 1172

Shortess, Judge. Courtesy Financial Services, Inc. (plaintiff) filed suit against John A. Hughes and Teresa Hughes (defendants) for $1,025.43, the unpaid balance due on a promissory note executed for the purchase price of a used car. Finding that plaintiff was not a holder in due course, and that defendants established a failure of consideration in that the car was defective, the trial judge dismissed plaintiff's suit.

On October 13, 1978, defendants purchased a used 1976 Plymouth Fury Station Wagon from Security Motors. Paul A. Crumrin, Jr., handled the transaction both as salesman for Security Motors and as loan officer for plaintiff. One month after the sale, defendants experienced problems with the brakes and replaced them. During the two years that defendants drove the car, numerous other problems arose: the ceiling liner inside the car fell out and emitted a musty smell; the gas tank rusted and leaked; the water pump went out; the radiator overheated; the electrical system shorted and the brake lights ceased to function; the heater, air conditioner and power steering went out, etc. As the various problems arose, defendants attempted to repair the car themselves. However, they finally "gave up the ghost" in June of 1980. Since that time, the car has been sitting in defendants' front driveway.

Defendants' last payment was made on July 1, 1980. Payments stopped because breakdowns were causing defendants to be late for work, and because defendants felt that they were "getting further and further in the hole trying to keep the car running." Prior to July 1, 1980, defendants continued to make payments even though they were both out of work. Defendants paid approximately $2,502.06, the difference between the amount financed ($3,527.49) and the amount sued upon ($1,025.43) before they ceased making payments. When payments were made, defendants informed plaintiff that they were having problems with the car. In fact, defendants asked plaintiff for a loan of $600.00 so they could get repair work done. In response to plaintiff's suit, defendants raised the affirmative defense of failure of consideration, asserting that the car was defective, rendering it totally unfit for normal use.

Plaintiff says that: (1) the trial judge erred in entering judgment based on the defense of failure of consideration, and (2) the trial judge erred in finding that the plaintiff was not a holder in due course.

In a suit on a promissory note by a payee against the maker, the plaintiff will be given the presumption that the instrument was given for value received unless the maker casts doubt upon the consideration. Once the maker has cast doubt upon the issue of consideration, the burden shifts to the payee to prove consideration by a preponderance of the evidence. Brashears v. Williams, 294 So.2d 246 (La.App. 1st Cir.1974).

Defendants testified as to the various malfunctions in the car and cast doubt on the issue of consideration. Plaintiff did not offer any evidence to rebut the testimony of defendants or to establish that consideration was given. Whether defendants' testimony alone was sufficient to cast doubt on the issue of consideration was a question of fact which the trial judge, by judging the credibility of the witnesses, was most competent to determine. Canter v. Koehring Company, 283 So.2d 716 (La.1973). The trial judge found that:

> Defendants have presented evidence, largely uncontradicted, of an impressive array of defects and malfunctions for even a two-year old used automobile. This court is persuaded that, taken as a whole, they manifest a failure of consideration.

We agree with the conclusion of the trial court that a failure of consideration existed.

Although the original payee on the note, plaintiff claims the status of holder in due course, and thus an exemption from the defense of failure of consideration.

> After it is shown that a defense exists a person claiming the rights of a holder in due course has the burden of establishing that he or some person under whom he claims is in all respects a holder in due course. La.R.S. 10:3-307(3)

Plaintiff says that La.R.S. 10:3-302(2) gives a payee the status of a holder in due course. However, said provision only states that a "payee may be a holder in due course." La.R.S. 10:3-302(2); (emphasis added). Although a payee may be a holder in due course, said status is not automatic. When the payee deals with the maker through an intermediary (remitter) and does not have notice of defenses, such an isolated payee may take as a holder in due course. In most instances, however, a payee will not be a holder in due course because said payee will usually have notice of defenses and claims by virtue of the fact that he has dealt directly with the maker. In order for a payee to be a holder in due course, all of the basic requirements must be met. A holder in due course is a holder who takes the instrument (1) for value, (2) in good faith, and (3) without notice that the instrument is overdue or has been dishonored or of any defense or claim affecting the instrument. La.R.S. 10:3-302. Thus, a payee who is an immediate party to the transaction is not automatically entitled to holder in due course status.

In this case, Security Motors, the vendor, and plaintiff were owned by the same person and occupied the same building. Paul A. Crumrin, Jr., the branch manager for plaintiff, testified that he handled the sale both as salesman for Security Motors and also as loan officer for plaintiff, as he was employed by both corporations. The trial court correctly found that plaintiff, a payee who was an immediate party to the transaction, was not entitled to holder in due course status. Thus, defendants may properly assert the defense of failure of consideration.

Failure of consideration is a defense to an action by one who does not have the rights of a holder in due course. La.R.S. 10:3-306(c), La.R.S. 10:3-408. Since defendants cast doubt upon the issue of consideration, and plaintiff did not meet its burden of proving consideration by a preponderance of the evidence, the trial judge correctly dismissed plaintiff's claim. Brashears v. Williams, supra. Because plaintiff is not entitled to the rights of a holder in due course, the personal defense of failure of consideration can be used to defeat plaintiff's claim. La.R.S. 10:3-306(c); La.R.S. 10:3-408; Fisher v. Childs Inv. Co., Inc., 411 So.2d 1180 (La.App. 4th Cir.1982), writ denied, 416 So.2d 115 (La.1982).

Accordingly, this appeal is affirmed at plaintiff's costs.

Affirmed.

UNIFORM CONSUMER CREDIT CODE
§§3.307; 3.403; 3.404; 3.405 (Official 1974 Text With Comments)

Section 3.307. Certain Negotiable Instruments Prohibited

Section 3.403. Card Issuer Subject to Claims and Defenses

Section 3.404. Assignee Subject to Claims and Defenses

Section 3.405. Lender Subject to Claims and Defenses Arising From Sales and
Leases

*[Reprinted in Selected Commercial Statutes (West Publishing Co. latest ed.) or
comparable work]*

FEDERAL TRADE COMMISSION TRADE REGULATION RULE ON THE PRESERVATION OF CONSUMERS' CLAIMS AND DEFENSES
16 C.F.R. part 433

*[Reprinted in Selected Commercial Statutes (West Publishing Co. latest ed.) or
comparable work]*

Guidelines On Trade Regulation Rule Concerning Preservation Of Consumers' Claims And Defenses
41 Fed.Reg. (no. 95) 20022, 20023-26 (May 14, 1976)

Purpose of The Rule

In adopting this Rule the Commission determined that it constitutes an unfair and deceptive trade practice within the meaning of Section 5 of the Federal Trade Commission Act (15 U.S.C. 45) for a seller, in the course of financing a consumer purchase of goods and services, to employ procedures which make the consumer's duty to pay independent of the seller's duty to fulfill his obligations. ***

Under ordinary contract law, the promises of the parties to a sales transaction are mutually dependent. *** However, it is possible for a seller to arrange credit terms for buyers which separate the consumer's legal duty to pay from the seller's legal duty to keep his promises.

This separation of duties may be accomplished in three ways. First, the seller may execute a credit contract with a buyer which contains a promissory note. In the event that the promissory note is assigned to a credit company, the credit company takes it free of any claim or defense which the buyer would have against the seller. *** Second, *** the seller may incorporate a written provision called a "waiver of defenses" in the text of an installment sales agreement. ***

Finally, a seller may arrange a direct loan for his buyer. Where a seller arranges a loan in this fashion, the lender is legally entitled to payment in full whatever the seller may do or fail to do in the sales transaction which accompanies the loan and for which the loan is obtained. ***

The Commission's Rule is directed at all three of the above situations.

* * *

Mechanism of The Rule

The Rule is designed to insure that consumer credit contracts used in financing the retail purchaser of consumer goods and services specifically preserve the consumer's rights against the seller. It requires sellers to include *** in the text of any consumer credit contract which they execute with a buyer [a Notice that any holder of the credit contract is subject to all claims and defenses which the debtor could assert against the seller of the goods or services]. In addition, if a seller arranges direct loan financing for his customers, the Rule prohibits the seller from accepting the proceeds of the loan [which the Rule labels and defines as a purchase money loan] as payment for a sale, unless any loan contract signed by the buyer and the direct lender contains [the Notice] ***.

For those consumer credit contracts in which the Rule requires insertion of this specific contract provision, or Notice, the Notice will become a part of the agreement between the consumer and the creditor. The required Notice will be treated in the same manner as other written terms and conditions contained in the agreement. ***

While the Rule provides for two different notices, depending on whether or not the consumer credit contract involved is an installment sales agreement or a loan obligation, both Notices mean the same thing. *** The creditor stands in the shoes of the seller.

There is an important limitation on the creditor's liability, however. The wording of the Notice includes the sentence "Recovery hereunder by the debtor shall be limited to amounts paid by the debtor hereunder." This limits the consumer to a refund of monies paid under the contract in the event that an affirmative money recovery is sought. In other words, the consumer may assert, by way of claim or defense, a right not to pay all or part of the outstanding balance owed the creditor under the contract; but the consumer will not be entitled to receive from the creditor an affirmative recovery which exceeds the amounts of money the consumer has paid in.

* * *

It is also important to note that the Rule does not create any new rights or defenses. The words "Claims and Defenses" which must appear in the Notice are not given any special definition by the Commission. The phrase simply incorporates those things which, as a matter of other applicable law, constitute legally sufficient claims and defenses in a sales transaction. Appropriate statutes, decisions, and rules in each jurisdiction will control. ***

For example, where a product is sold "as is" and there can be no warranty claim or defense, the Rule would not create one. ***

The Rule does apply to all claims or defenses connected with the transaction, whether in tort or contract. ***

It is *** possible for a consumer to have a claim or defense against a seller because of a separate transaction. The provision required by the Rule would not allow him to assert such a claim or defense against the holder. The holder's obligations are limited to those arising from the transaction which he finances.

* * *

Credit Contracts Which Must Contain the Notice

The Rule does not apply to all credit instruments. The Notice must appear in written obligations defined as "Consumer Credit Contracts" in the Rule. The definition includes any written instrument which, under the Truth in Lending Act and Regulation Z ***, constitutes a consumer credit contract and which is used to (1) "Finance a Sale" as that term is defined in the Rule or (2) in connection with a "Purchase Money Loan: as that term is defined in the Rule.

Affected Transactions

The initial question is whether a sale constitutes a consumer transaction at all. The Rule defines the term "consumer" to mean a "natural person who seeks or acquires goods or services for personal, family, or household use", and covers sales of all kinds of consumer goods or services for personal, family, or household use. ***

Sales of goods or services for commercial use are not covered by the Rule. This includes the purchase of equipment for agricultural production ... Nor does the Rule apply when a purchase is made by or for an organization rather than a natural person. Finally, only purchases of goods and services are covered by the Rule. Sales of interests in real property are unaffected, as are purchases of commodities and securities. ***

Additional limitations on affected transactions are present because the definitions of "Financing a Sale" and "Purchase Money Loan" expressly refer to the Truth in Lending Act and Regulation Z, and thus incorporate the limitations contained in these laws. As a result, even with respect to transactions involving a sale of consumer goods or services, a purchase involving an expenditure of more than $25,000 is not affected by the rule. Public Utility services are not affected by the Rule. Finally, only those leases which constitute "credit sale" agreements under Regulation Z are affected by the Rule. ***

Financing a Sale

This term is defined to include situations in which a seller within the Commission's jurisdiction extends credit to a buyer and takes a written credit contract from the buyer, in connection with an affected transaction. All such situations are covered by the Rule, and all contracts so executed, except credit card instruments, must contain the required Notice. Credit card instruments are specifically exempted from the Rule.

* * *

Purchase Money Loans

The Rule states that a seller may not accept money which a consumer obtained via a "purchase money loan", as that term is defined in the Rule, unless the consumer credit contract made in connection with the loan contains the required provision preserving the consumer's claims and defenses. Where a "purchase money loan" is used to finance a sale, the seller is obligated to insure that the consumer's loan contract contains the required Notice before he consummates the sale.

* * *

[Purchase money loans are involved] when sellers arrange financing for their customers by means of referrals to direct lenders, or where sellers and direct lenders are affiliated with each other ***.

Part 433 -- Preservation Of Consumers' Claims And Defenses: Statement Of Enforcement Policy
41 Fed.Reg. (no. 159) 34,594, 34,595-97 (August 16, 1976)

[Affiliation And Referral Standards]

(a) *Affiliation.* The Rule requires a seller to insure that the Notice is used in a consumer's loan contract where the seller is "affiliated with the creditor by common control, contract, or business arrangement."

The first type of affiliation is common control. The Commission has concluded that when a creditor and a seller are functionally part of the same business entity, loans made by the lender for the financing of purchases from the seller should be subject to the Rule. For example, common control would be present where two companies are owned by a holding company or by substantially the same individuals; if one is a subsidiary of the other, or if they are under common control relating to retail sales financing.

An affiliation is also created by "contract" and "business arrangement." The Rule defines contract as any oral or written agreement, formal or informal between a creditor and a seller, which contemplates or provides for cooperative or concerted activity in connection with the sale of goods or services to consumers or the financing thereof. A business arrangement includes any understanding, procedure, course of dealing, or arrangement, formal or informal, between a creditor and a seller, in connection with the sale of goods or services to consumers or the financing thereof.

These definitions encompass all situations where a creditor and seller are party to any agreement, arrangement, understanding, or mutually understood procedure which is specifically related to retail sales or retail sales financing. While the business arrangement or contract need not be formal in a legal sense, it must be ongoing and clearly related to sales or sales financing.

Examples of the business arrangements or contracts which are reached by the Rule's definitions would include those contemplating:

> Maintenance of loan application forms in the office of the seller;
> Seller agrees with creditor to prepare loan documents;
> Creditor's referrals of customers to a sales outlet;
> Payment of consideration to a seller for furnishing loan customers or to a creditor for furnishing sales prospects;
> The assignment of indirect paper or the referral of loan customers to a creditor;
> Active creditor participation in a sales program;
> Joint advertising efforts;
> An agreement to purchase paper on an indirect basis.

The Rule is not intended to include the many possible business relationships that do not bear directly on the financing of consumers sales. For example, a commercial checking account is not an affiliation within the meaning of the Rule, nor is a commercial credit agreement between the seller and a credit institution which has no relationship to consumer sales activities or the financing thereof. A commercial lease, the factoring of accounts receivable, a general business loan, the financing of inventory, or other similar commercial arrangements or contracts do not invoke the Rule. The installation in a seller's place of business of a system for approval of personal checks is not a business arrangement within the meaning of the Rule. It should also be noted that an agreement between a credit card issuer and a seller does not constitute a business arrangement or a contract within the meaning of the Rule.

The fact that a creditor and seller must confer over a particular transaction does not in itself create an arrangement. Thus, for example, the mere fact that a creditor issues a joint proceeds check to a seller and a buyer or that seller and lender must confer in order to perfect the security agreement under applicable state law is not a business arrangement or contract.

(b) *Referrals.* The Rule prohibits a seller from accepting the proceeds of a "purchase money loan" unless the credit contract contains the required Notice when the seller "refers consumers to the creditor". The intent of this provision is to reach those situations in which a seller cooperates with a lender to channel consumers to that credit source on a continuing basis. Unlike an "affiliation", which contemplates some preexisting arrangement or agreement, a referral relationship arises from a pattern of cooperative activity directly relating to the arranging of credit.

Several elements are necessary. The seller and creditor must be engaged in cooperative or concerted conduct to channel a consumer to a particular lender. The fact that a seller may suggest credit sources to his customers or otherwise provide information in this regard does not alone invoke the Rule. However, when a seller and a lender work together to arrange financing for seller's customers, the prescribed Notice must be incorporated in the loan contract.

This conduct must occur on a continuing basis. Occasional referrals which are not part of a business routine of the seller do not trigger the Rule. Once a referral relationship is established all credit contracts between that lender and buyers who spend the proceeds at the seller's establishment must contain the Notice.

Finally, it should be emphasized that formal consideration need not pass between the seller and lender. The fact that a seller and lender are cooperatively engaged in an effort which is mutually beneficial to their separate business interests is sufficient.

(c) *Application of the Referral and Affiliation Standards.* The following examples illustrate how the referral and affiliation standards are applied.

1. A seller has an agreement with a creditor to maintain loan application forms in the seller's office. When a buyer requests financing, the seller assists the buyer in filling out the forms. This relationship constitutes an affiliation and the Notice must be included in the consumer credit contract.

2. A seller regularly sends his customers to a particular creditor. The creditor, in turn, agrees to provide a favorable financing arrangement for the seller's inventory or directly or indirectly provides some other consideration. The seller and lender are "affiliated". The Notice must be included in the consumer credit contract.

Comment. -- These circumstances would give rise to a "contact" as defined by §433.1(f).

3. A seller regularly sends his customer to a particular creditor. The creditor agrees that as long as the seller continues to refer his customers, their loan applications will be processed or approved on an expedited basis where the borrower meets certain lending criteria but before a full credit check is completed. The Notice must be in.

Comment. An agreement of this nature would constitute a business arrangement. (Typically in situations such as those in the example, the seller would agree to repurchase any contracts which the lender ultimately did not accept. However, a repurchase agreement of this nature is not essential to bring the above conduct within the Rule.)

4. A seller routinely suggests that customers in need of credit go to a particular source or sources of financing. While the creditor is aware that seller is sending some of his customers, the creditor does not provide any tacit or explicit quid pro quo, and seller and financer have no relationship that would constitute an affiliation and do not otherwise cooperate except insofar as may be necessary to arrange payment, perfect a security interest or otherwise finalize the transaction. The Notice is not required.

Comment. The Rule draws the line between situations in which the seller is acting as an information source or where credit is available and those in which the seller is arranging credit or serving as a conduit for the creditor. For a referral to occur within the meaning of the Rule, there must be something more than a simple suggestion that credit might be available from a particular source. There must be some further affirmative act by the seller to promote the consummation of the loan.

Since a simple suggestion is not a referral, it does not matter how often it is repeated.

This interpretation also answers a question raised by some creditors as to the result if a seller sends customers to them and they do not know the customers are being sent. Such lack of knowledge on the part of the creditor automatically precludes the possibility that a referral has taken place.

5. A buyer asks a seller for credit information. The seller suggests a creditor, calls up the creditor to determine whether the creditor will lend money to the particular buyer, and then sends the buyer to the creditor. Seller and creditor have no agreement, formal or informal, to refer customers. A referral relationship would be created, if the channeling occurs on a continuing basis.

Comment. -- When a seller contacts a lender and arranges credit for his customers on a continuing basis, there is sufficient cooperative activity to constitute a referral relationship. Monetary or other formal consideration need not be involved. A pattern of mutual accommodation in arranging loans is sufficient concerted or cooperative activity to establish a referral relationship. However, contact between the seller and creditor which first occurs after the loan has been secured, for purposes of securing a lien or approving a bank draft is not a referral since there is no cooperative activity in the arranging of credit.

6. A buyer asks a seller for credit sources. Seller provides a list of lenders in the area and provides information on the availability of credit from them as an accommodation to his customers. The seller does not contact a creditor to arrange credit for the customers, nor does he have any other business arrangement or affiliation with the creditors in this respect. The Notice is not required.

Comment. -- When the seller is merely providing buyer with information on the choices available to the buyer, does not channel the buyer by contacting the creditor, and has no agreement to mention a particular creditor, then the buyer is providing information and the Notice is not required.

7. A seller has a referral or affiliation relationship with a creditor. A buyer, on his own, goes to the creditor to obtain a loan to purchase an item from seller. The Notice must be in.

Comment. -- If a seller has an arrangement whereby he refers his customers to a creditor, all loan contracts between that creditor and a borrower who uses the proceeds to purchase goods from that seller must contain the Notice. The Notice must be in whether the particular loan contract was the product of a referral or not.

8. Seller has for years referred his customers to a particular financial institution pursuant to an arrangement with the creditor. He now desires to end the relationship. He stops the referrals and notifies the creditor that he no longer will refer buyers. The referral relationship has been terminated.

Comment. -- A referral relationship is a continuing one. It can be stopped as long as the termination is genuine, and the seller is not attempting to temporarily avoid the Rule for a few transactions. The creditor can also end a referral relationship by notifying seller that he does not wish the relationship to continue and by refusing to place the Notice in his loan contracts with purchasers from that seller.

Determining the Source of the Proceeds

The seller is prohibited from accepting the proceeds of a "purchase money loan" unless the consumer credit contract contains the specified Notice. Since the credit contract is between the borrower and the lender, the seller may not be aware that the money he is receiving is the proceeds of a "purchase money loan." The problem arises when the seller and the creditor are affiliated by common control, contract, or business arrangement or are engaged in a referral relationship and the buyer has unilaterally gone to the creditor for a loan to purchase goods or services from the seller.

The Rule was not intended to subject a seller to liability when he has no reason to believe he is receiving the proceeds of a "purchase money loan." Nor does the Rule require that the seller interrogate the buyer to determine the source of the proceeds. The objective circumstances surrounding the transaction provide the seller with information concerning the source of the proceeds. When these circumstances do not indicate the source of the proceeds or do not provide reason to believe that the proceeds may be from a "purchase money loan", there is no obligation to further investigate the source of the proceeds.

The following examples illustrate how this standard is being applied.

1. A buyer arrives in the seller's showroom with a joint proceeds check or a bank draft drawn on a bank affiliated with the seller. The seller is on notice to inquire as to whether the Notice was included.

Comment. -- A joint proceeds check provides actual knowledge that a purchase money loan is involved. A bank instrument is probably the proceeds of a purchase money loan.

2. A buyer pays for a seller's product or service with cash or a personal check. There is no duty to inquire.

Comment. -- When there are no facts that would place a reasonable man on notice that the money is the proceeds of a "purchase money loan", there is no obligation to interrogate a customer.

3. A buyer pays $5,000 for an automobile with a personal check drawn on the bank that purchases the seller's contracts. The buyer states that he obtained a signature loan from that bank to pay for it. Seller must determine if the Notice was inserted.

4. Seller determines that the money the buyer uses to purchase a product are the proceeds of a "purchase money loan". The seller asks the buyer whether the Notice has been included in the consumer credit contract. The buyer refuses to answer or incorrectly states the Notice was included. The seller must communicate with the creditor.

Comment. -- When the seller has a relationship with a creditor, the best source of information concerning the Notice is the creditor. He cannot escape liability through the ignorance of the buyer.

12. Affirmative liability of persons who lack due-course rights

a. Liability of assignee qua assignee

The rights on an instrument of one not a holder in due course are largely coextensive with the rights of an assignee of a simple contract right. Recently, a debate has developed as to whether an assignee is affirmatively liable for the claims that the obligor has against the assignor. If so, there is not much reason to think that an assignee will be immune from this sort of liability solely because the right she took was in the form of a negotiable instrument.

The traditional, common-law rule of contracts regarding the affirmative liability of an assignee is very clear: an obligor's claim against the assignor can be asserted against the assignee only as a defense or as a matter of recoupment. "The claim is good against the assignee only to the extent that it diminishes his [or her] claim; it cannot be used to impose liability on the assignee unless he [or she] has assumed the assignor's duty of performance." E. Farnsworth, CONTRACTS §11.8 at 781-82 (1982); accord A. Corbin, CORBIN ON CONTRACTS §§896 & 906 (Student ed. 1952); J. Murray, MURRAY ON CONTRACTS §307 at 628 (1974); see also RESTATEMENT (SECOND) OF CONTRACTS §328(1) (1981) (assignment for security ordinarily does not involve delegation or assumption of duties to or by assignee); U.C.C. §2-210(4) (same). The current debate concerns the extent to which modern statutes, regulations, and decisional rules have created, or suggest the need for, exceptions to the common-law doctrine immunizing an assignee from affirmative liability.

Suppose, for example, that S is a Ford dealer who sold a car to B on credit. B made a $1000 down payment and executed an installment sales contract for the balance, which was $10,000. S assigned the contract to Ford Motor Credit Co. (FMCC). B had paid $2000 to FMCC before justifiably revoking her acceptance of the car because of a breach of warranty resulting in personal, property, and economic damages to B. B sues FMCC to recover "so much of the price as has been paid", 2-711(1), and also compensatory and consequential damages. 2-712 & 2-715. What result? See 2-210; 9-317; 9-318(1).

Michelin Tires (Canada) Ltd. v. First National Bank,
United States Court of Appeals, First Circuit, 1981
666 F.2d 673

Mazzone, District Judge. This appeal is from a district court's denial of restitution to the plaintiff, a contractual obligor, of monies mistakenly paid to the defendant, an assignee of contract rights. We begin with a summary of the record.

Michelin Tires (Canada) Ltd. ("Michelin"), a Canadian corporation based in New Glascow, Nova Scotia, and J.C. Corrigan, Inc. ("JCC"), a building contractor, entered into an agreement on June 19, 1970 for the design and installation of a carbon black handling and storage system, which was to form part of a Michelin tire factory under construction in Pictou County, Nova Scotia. Michelin entered into the agreement through its agent, Surveyor, Nenniger & Chenevert ("SNC"), an engineering firm retained by Michelin to procure and supervise the building of the factory.

The construction contract provided that Michelin would make periodic progress payments to JCC in the amount of 90 of each invoice submitted by JCC for work completed. The amounts due were based on a schedule of values of the various parts of the entire project. JCC's invoices were to be submitted first to SNC for its review and certification that the work had been performed and the amount was correct. That certification was contained in an Engineers Progress Certificate ("EPC") and was completed by the SNC project manager. With each invoice, Michelin had the right to require JCC to submit a "Statutory Declaration," or sworn statement, stating the amount JCC owed to subcontractors, supplier, and others in connection with the work and listing any claims that could result in liens on Michelin's property. If JCC failed to make prompt payments to subcontractors and suppliers, SNC could withhold or nullify its certification and Michelin could deduct from its progress payments to JCC the amount necessary to protect its property from liens.

Prior to signing the construction contract with JCC, neither SNC nor Michelin made inquiries concerning JCC's financial situation. Initially, SNC had requested that JCC provide a performance bond to cover its work, and JCC had requested that Michelin provide a letter of credit to cover the payments due for work performed. Michelin, or SNC, dropped its proposal that JCC be required to provide a performance bond in return for JCC's withdrawal of its request for a letter of credit for Michelin.

The First National Bank of Boston ("FNB"), a commercial bank in Boston, Massachusetts, provided financing to JCC under a longstanding agreement dating from 1960. Under that agreement, FNB agreed to loan JCC an amount not greater than 80 of JCC's outstanding invoices. In return, FNB took a security interest in all JCC's accounts receivable and contract rights -- including, of course, JCC's right to receive payments under its contract with Michelin.

On August 14, 1970, two months after the construction contract was executed, JCC assigned its rights under the contract to FNB. The bank notified SNC of the assignment and requested that future JCC invoices be paid directly to FNB. This assignment was acknowledged by SNC on September 3, 1970.

Shortly after JCC's assignment of its contract rights to FNB, Michelin sent FNB the payments it seeks to recover in the instant suit. The first payment was in response to JCC's invoice of August 24, 1970 in the amount of $118,000. JCC presented no EPC and no Statutory Declaration in support of this invoice. SNC prepared an EPC for the invoice and asked JCC to submit a Statutory Declaration with future invoices. Michelin paid 90 of the invoice, to FNB, as provided by the construction contract.

JCC submitted its next invoice on September 23, 1970 in the amount of $187,000. As with the previous invoice, no Statutory Declaration was presented. Michelin withheld payment and asked JCC to submit the Statutory Declaration. JCC did so on October 16, 1970.

JCC then sent Michelin an invoice dated October 22, 1970 in the amount of $313,000, accompanied by a Statutory Declaration and an EPC. Michelin paid 90 of the amounts of the latter two invoices on December 15, 1970, deducting amounts for uncompleted work and for a change order.

Michelin's last payment to FNB was in response to JCC's invoice for $200,000, dated December 21, 1970. JCC sent the corresponding Statutory Declaration to Michelin on January 18, 1971, and Michelin sent its progress payment to FNB on January 20, 1971, including the amount previously withheld for uncompleted work.

It was not until March of 1971 that Michelin learned that JCC had not been paying its subcontractors. Accordingly, the above progress payments were not due under the construction contract, and JCC's Statutory Declarations of October 12, 1970 and January 18, 1971 were fraudulent, JCC made an assignment for the benefit of creditors on April 6, 1971 and was subsequently adjudicated a bankrupt.

The carbon black system was substantially completed by May 1, 1971, and the district court found that JCC performed all the work it could have done prior to May 1, 1971. JCC left, however, a total indebtedness of over $500,000 (Canadian) after its adjudication in bankruptcy.

Throughout this time, FNB maintained its lending relationship with JCC. FNB knew of JCC's financial difficulties. By early 1970, before JCC contracted with Michelin, FNB regarded its loan to JCC as a problem and was concerned about repayment. The bank knew from examining JCC's books that the company's earnings were declining, its trade debt was rising, and its customers were slow to pay. It was further evident from JCC's books that JCC was overstating its income in its reports to the bank. By late August of 1970, the bank was aware that JCC's outstanding indebtedness was greater than the agreed-upon loan ceiling of 80 of JCC's accounts receivable, and a bank officer reminded JCC that loan funds received while JCC was "over-advanced" were to be used only to meet payroll and pay taxes. FNB used the payments it received from Michelin after the assignment to reduce the outstanding amount on its loan to JCC. In October of 1970, FNB sent an inquiry to SNC to verify the accuracy of copies of invoices the bank had received from JCC, used by the bank to calculate the 80 loan ceiling. SNC replied that the invoices were "OK."

The district court specifically found that FNB knew of JCC's contractual obligations to Michelin. Those obligations included prompt payment of subcontractors. FNB, however, did not know that JCC was sending false Statutory Declarations to Michelin, stating under oath that the subcontractors had been paid.

On December 22, 1970, FNB notified JCC that it would extend no further loans to JCC after March 31, 1971 and that JCC should seek financing elsewhere. It was after JCC failed to find a new lender that the company made its assignment for the benefit of creditors on April 6, 1971 and filed a petition in bankruptcy.

After discovering JCC's fraud, Michelin brought this suit to recover the payments it made to FNB, a total of $724,197.60. Michelin asserted it was entitled to restitution under two theories. First, it claimed that since its right to restitution arose from its contract with JCC, the claim could be successfully asserted against FNB, the assignee of contract rights to payment, pursuant to §9-318(1)(a) of the Uniform Commercial Code (UCC), Mass.Gen.Laws Ann. ch. 106,

§9-318(1)(a) Second, Michelin asserted that FNB was liable because it has been unjustly enriched under traditional restitutionary principles.

The district court tried the case without a jury and upon a stipulated record. In a detailed memorandum, the court found that JCC had breached its contract with Michelin by submitting fictitious invoices and fraudulent Statutory Declarations and by failing to pay its subcontractors when payment was due. It further found that Michelin's payments to FNB had been made in reliance on the fraudulent Statutory Declarations. The district court then ruled, first, that §9-318(1)(a) does not create a new affirmative cause of action by an account debtor as against an assignee and, second, that since FNB did not know of the fraudulent Statutory Declarations or of JCC's indebtedness to subcontractors, FNB had not been unjustly enriched at the expense of Michelin. This appeal followed.

We affirm because we believe that (1) §9-318(1)(a) of the UCC was not intended to create a new cause of action by an account debtor against an assignee and (2) the facts the district court found were available to FNB did not put it on notice of JCC's fraud and Michelin's mistake.

I.

Michelin's first argument is that it has an independent cause of action against FNB under §9-318 of the UCC, Mass.Gen.Laws Ann. ch. 106, §9-318 (West Supp.1981). That section reads in pertinent part:

Defenses Against Assignee; Modification of Contract After Notification of Assignment; Term Prohibiting Assignment Ineffective; Identification and Proof of Assignment.

(1) Unless an account debtor has made an enforceable agreement not to assert defenses or claims arising out of a sale as provided in section 9-206 the rights of an assignee are subject to

(a) all the terms of the contract between the account debtor and assignor and any defense or claim arising therefrom.

In essence, Michelin contends that its restitution claim arises from its contract with JCC, and that §9-318(1)(a) accordingly permits Michelin to recover from FNB as JCC's assignee. Although Michelin emphasizes the narrow application of this theory to the instant case, the theory rests upon a construction of §9-318 that would impose full contract liability on assignees of contract rights. Under this view, a bank taking an assignment of contract rights as security for a loan would also receive as "security" a delegation of duties under the contract and the risk of being held liable on the contract in place of its borrower. We do not believe it was the intent of §9-318(1)(a) to create such a result.

The key statutory language is ambiguous. That "the rights of an assignee are subject to *** (a) all the terms of the contract" connotes only that the assignee's rights to recover are limited by the obligor's rights to assert contractual defenses as a set-off, implying that affirmative recovery against the assignee is not intended. See Englestein v. Mintz, 345 Ill. 48, 61, 177 N.E. 746, 752 (1931), quoted in Anderson v. Southwest Savings & Loan Association, 117 Ariz. 246, 248, 571 P.2d 1042, 1044 (1977):

The words "subject to," used in their ordinary sense, mean "subordinate to," "subservient to," or "limited by." There is nothing in the use of the words "subject to," in their ordinary use, which would even hint at the creation of affirmative rights.

On the other hand, the use of the word "claim" raises the possibility that affirmative recovery was indeed contemplated. However, the section's title and the official Comment support the view that the section does not create affirmative rights. The title reads, "Defenses Against Assignee." Official Comment 1 states in pertinent part:

> Subsection (1) makes no substantial change in prior law. An assignee has traditionally been subject to defenses or set-offs existing before an account debtor is notified of the assignment.

Under prior law, an assignee of contract rights was not liable on the contract in the place of his assignor. Wright v. Graustein, 248 Mass. 205, 142 N.E. 797 (1924). Common sense requires that we not twist the "precarious security" of an assignee into potential liability for his assignor's breach.

It is evident that §9-318 has become a red herring in suits against an assignee. We note two cases that have denied account debtors the right to sue. James Talcott, Inc. v. Brewster Sales Corp., 16 UCC Rep.Serv. 1165 (N.Y.Sup.Ct.1975); Meyers v. Postal Finance Co., 287 N.W.2d 614 (Minn.1979). There are also cases that have allowed affirmative claims, at least in limited circumstances. Benton State Bank v. Warren, 263 Ark. 1, 562 S.W.2d 74 (1978); Farmers Acceptance Corp. v. DeLozier, 178 Colo. 291, 496 P.2d 1016 (1972); K Mart Corp. v. First Penn. Bank, 29 UCC Rep.Serv. 701 (Pa.1980).

The decisions permitting an affirmative suit all rely on the pre-UCC case of Firestone Tire and Rubber Co. v. Central Nat. Bank, 159 Ohio St. 423, 112 N.E.2d 636 (1953). There the court required the bank to return payments to an account debtor because, although the bank was innocent of the assignor's fraud, the bank had unwittingly assisted that fraud by independently requesting periodic payment from the account debtor. The bank attached invoices from the assignor to each request thereby impliedly representing that the underlying obligation was valid. The court found that the account debtor relied on the genuineness of the invoices forwarded by the bank. Id., 112 N.E.2d at 639. In the case at hand there was no such reliance. Rather, Michelin established its own system of assuring compliance, including approval of an intermediary, SNC. In addition, they required a Statutory Declaration under oath from JCC. The stipulated record indicates that FNB had no involvement in verifying JCC's performance and was completely unaware of the Statutory Declaration.

Benton State Bank, supra, represented a situation similar to Firestone. In Benton State Bank the bank advanced progress payments to the assignor. Each request for a progress payment was then forwarded by the bank to the general contractor accompanied by the assignor's certification, a representation similar to the Statutory Declaration submitted by JCC in this case. The court permitted the contractor to recover against the bank because the bank "had solid reasons for suspecting the truth of Harp's (the assignors) assertions, which the bank forwarded to the Warrens (the account debtors), that all past-due bills for labor and materials had been paid." Id., 562 S.W.2d at 76. FNB did not assume an active role in sending JCC's statements to Michelin, nor were they even aware of JCC's misrepresentation to Michelin in any way.

The bank in K Mart Corp., supra, was also actively involved in the relationship between the account debtor and the assignor. In K Mart Corp., the court permitted the account debtor, K Mart, to recover from the assignee certain payments made for goods that were later found to be defective. Id. at 707. However, the recovery permitted in K Mart Corp. is best viewed as merely anticipated repayment. For nearly 8 years the bank accepted payment from K Mart equal to the value of the assignor's, PSM, invoices minus an allowance for defective goods received and paid for in the prior month. The assignor's bankruptcy prevented such an adjustment on the final payment so the court allowed recovery. The court noted "that merely because PSM is bankrupt and can no longer be expected to repay K Mart, the bank may not now unilaterally ignore its prior understanding, which was clearly in the contemplation of the parties, and retain funds which should not have been paid to it initially." Id. at 706 (emphasis added). There is no indication that Michelin and FNB agreed to make periodic adjustments depending upon the quality of JCC's performance.

Finally, the Colorado Supreme Court permitted recovery by the account debtor against the assignee in DeLozier, supra. The extent of the involvement by the assignee, Farmers Acceptance Corp. ("FAC"), in the underlying contract is ambiguous in that case. The brief opinion indicates that FAC first used the payment it received from the account debtor to satisfy the personal indebtedness of the assignor and then applied the remainder to the assignor's unpaid account with a materialman. Id., 496 P.2d at 1017. This latter payment to the subcontractor's creditor suggests knowledge and involvement by the assignee that exceeds that of FNB. In the case before us, the stipulated facts indicate that FNB had no involvement in the payments by JCC to its subcontractors. In any event, to the extent that DeLozier can be read to permit an affirmative suit against a lender who is completely unrelated to the underlying contract, we decline to follow this departure from traditional common law principles of restitution. See Massey-Ferguson Credit Corp. v. Brown, 173 Mont. 253, 567 P.2d 440, 443 (1977).

In each of the cases permitting an affirmative suit, with the possible exception of DeLozier, the assignee actively participated in the transactions to a degree not approached here. We are aware of no case that has gone beyond those we have cited and actually permitted an affirmative suit against a nonparticipating assignee like FNB. We do not anticipate that the Supreme Judicial Court would extend the law in this way and we are unwilling to do so ourselves. Given the factual distinctions between the cases discussed above and the transactions at issue here, we do not need to reach the issue of whether Massachusetts law would permit suit against an assignee who became more involved in the course of dealings.

While it is our judgment that analysis of the statutory language, taken in context, indicates that no affirmative right was contemplated and further that those cases that have permitted such a right are factually inapposite, we also believe it would be unwise to permit such suits as a matter of policy. As the dissenting justice in Benton State Bank, 562 S.W.2d 74, noted, allowing affirmative suits would "make every Banker, who has taken an assignment of accounts for security purposes, a deep pocket surety for every bankrupt contractor in the state to whom it had loaned money." Id. at 77 (Byrd, J., dissenting).

We are unwilling to impose such an obligation on the banks of the Commonwealth without some indication that this represents a considered policy choice. By marking the bank a surety, not only will accounts receivable financing be discouraged, but transaction costs will undoubtedly increase for everyone. The case at hand provides a good example. In order to protect themselves, FNB would essentially be forced to undertake the precautionary measures that Michelin attempted to use, independent observation by an intermediary and sworn certifications by the assignor. FNB would have to supervise every construction site where its funds were involved to ensure performance and payment. We simply do not believe that the banks are best suited to monitor contract compliance. The party most interested in adequate performance would be the other contracting party, not the financier. Given this natural interest, it seems likely to us that while the banks will be given additional burdens of supervision, there would be no corresponding reduction in vigilance by the contracting parties, thus creating two inspections where there was formerly one. Costs for everyone thus increase, without any discernible benefit. It is also difficult to predict the full impact a contrary decision would have on the availability of accounts receivable financing in general.

Our holding, of course, is not that §9-318 prohibits claims against the assignee. We hold merely that §9-318 concerns only the preservation of defenses to the assignee's claims and, as such, is wholly inapposite in an affirmative suit against an assignee.

II.

The Restatement of Restitution, §28(d) (1937), states:

§28. Mistake Due to Fraud or Misrepresentation.

A person who has paid money to another because of a mistake of fact and who does not obtain what he expected in return is entitled to restitution from the other if the mistake was induced:

(d) By the fraud or material misrepresentation of a third person, provided that the payee has notice of the fraud or representation before he has given or promised something of value.

For cases where the mistake was not due to fraud, substantially the same rule is stated in §14 of the Restatement:

§14. Discharge for Value.

(1) A creditor of another or one having a lien on another's property who has received from a third person any benefit in discharge of the debt or lien, is under no duty to make restitution therefor, although the discharge was given by mistake of the transferor as to his interests or duties, if the transferee made no misrepresentation and did not have notice of the transferor's mistake.

(2) An assignee of a non-negotiable chose in action who, having paid value therefor, has received payment from the obligor is under no duty to make restitution although the obligor had a defense thereto, if the transferee made no misrepresentation and did not have notice of the defense.

The Supreme Judicial Court of Massachusetts has followed the Restatement in denying restitution against an assignee for value who is without notice of the assignor's fraud. The threshold question, therefore, is whether FNB, by reducing JCC's indebtedness on its outstanding loan, gave value for the funds it received from Michelin. We agree with the district court that value was given. *******

Having decided that FNB gave value, the crucial question becomes whether the defendant, assignee FNB, had notice of the fraudulent conduct of assignor JCC. We have found no Massachusetts cases directly addressing the standard to be applied in determining whether a party has notice of fraud under the law of restitution. Under the analogous rule for voiding of a contract because of fraud, the Supreme Judicial Court held in Rockland Trust that a contract is voidable where a party has "reason to know" of the fraud before giving value or materially changing its position. 366 Mass. at 79, 314 N.E.2d at 441.

The "reason to know" standard has been incorporated into the general definition of notice as it is used in the UCC. Mass.Gen.Laws Ann. ch. 106, §1-201(25) (West 1958) states in pertinent part:

A person has "notice" of a fact when (a) he has actual knowledge of it; or (b) he has received a notice or notification of it; or (c) from all the facts and circumstances known to him at the time in question he has reason to know that it exists. A person "knows" or has "knowledge" of a fact when he has actual knowledge of it.

* * *

Although, as we discuss below, the present issue does not involve the UCC, we look to the statutory definition of notice under the UCC as adopted by the Massachusetts legislature, as well as to analogous case law, for guidance in determining the standard that would be applied by the Supreme Judicial Court of Massachusetts. In the absence of a definitive ruling by the highest state court, a federal court may consider "analogous decisions, considered dicta, scholarly works, and any other reliable data tending convincingly to show how the highest court in the state would decide the issue at hand," taking into account the broad policies and trends so evinced. McKenna v. Ortho Pharmaceutical Corp., 622 F.2d 657, 663 (3d Cir.1980). We believe that, under Massachusetts law, a person has notice of a fact when, from all the information at his disposal, he has reason to know of it. Organizations are chargeable with knowledge of information in their possession when reasonable communications routines would disseminate that information to the appropriate individuals.

Application of this standard requires a heavy reliance on the factual findings of the district court, which we must accept unless clearly erroneous. See Bowling Green, 425 F.2d at 85. We give the same deference to the trial court's findings in a case tried on a stipulation of facts as in any other case. Holmes v. Bateson, 583 F.2d 542, 552 (1st Cir.1978).

The district court found that the bank, FNB, was aware of JCC's financial struggles well before it received the progress payments. The bank had recently informed JCC that loan funds were to be used only for payroll and taxes. Additionally, before it received the last payment, FNB had told JCC that its credit would be terminated in three months. FNB also knew of JCC's contractual duties, including its obligation to pay subcontractors.

Since FNB, the district court found, was unaware of the fraudulent Statutory Declarations that caused Michelin to make the disputed payments, FNB cannot be held to have had notice of JCC's fraud merely from its knowledge of JCC's finances. Although it was JCC's sole major lender, it was not nearly as involved as the bank in Bowling Green, which was also found to have no notice. Recovery under §28 of the Restatement of Restitution is accordingly foreclosed.

Under §14 of the Restatement, FNB would be liable to make restitution if it had notice of Michelin's defense or mistake before giving value for the payments -- i.e., if it had notice that the subcontractors had not been paid. While Michelin does not assert that any of FNB's officers actually knew, or that the bank had actually been informed that JCC was not paying its subcontractors, Michelin argues that FNB had constructive notice of this fact. In support of its argument, Michelin directs us to portions of the Stipulation of Facts purporting to establish that FNB was JCC's only source of funds at the time of the payments and that FNB knew JCC could not have paid its subcontractors because its loan funds had been restricted to use for payroll and taxes. The district court, however, did not find that JCC had no other sources of income, and it specifically found that the bank did nothing to enforce the restrictions on use of loan funds. The record supports these findings and the implication to be drawn from them that FNB did not have reason to know of JCC's failure to pay subcontractors.

If we were to hold FNB chargeable with notice of JCC's nonpayment of subcontractors on this record, we would be imposing an affirmative duty on lenders to look out for the interests of account debtors such as Michelin. In order for FNB to have discovered JCC's failure to pay its subcontractors, FNB would have had to initiate an investigation of JCC's business practices under the Michelin contract, not aimed at determining the company's financial health for purposes of the bank's continued financing, but aimed at verifying JCC's compliance with the Michelin contract. That JCC was in monetary straits could not have indicated that subcontractors had gone unpaid without such an investigation. We are unwilling to impose such a responsibility on lenders.

Here, FNB did attempt to verify the accuracy of the copies of invoices it was receiving from JCC by contacting Michelin. Michelin's agent, SNC, responded that the invoices were "OK." Michelin's losses might have been avoided if it had required JCC to provide a performance bond or if it had availed itself of its right to visit the offices of subcontractors and investigate the progress of the work. It might have demanded more vigilance from its agent, SNC. SNC was on the site and was charged with supervising the job and certifying its progress. The one area where Michelin was most vulnerable to fraud -- the Statutory Declarations -- was the area that it could have checked very easily and where, unfortunately, it failed to check at all. It cannot shift its loss to the bank by arguing now that the bank should have monitored JCC's compliance when it failed to do so.

Affirmed.

Bownes, Circuit Judge (dissenting).

I dissent from the majority's holding that Michelin does not have an independent cause of action against First National Bank of Boston (FNB).

* * *

I believe that the sounder view is that an account debtor may sue the assignee directly under section 9-318(1)(a) for payments received under the assigned contract. This section provides that an assignee's rights are subject to claims and defenses that the account debtor had against the assignor. The Uniform Commercial Code, as enacted in Massachusetts does not define "claim," but the word "claim" is commonly understood to include original cause action. * * *

* * *

This interpretation of section 9-318(1)(a), that the account debtor has rights of action against the assignee, is the fairest way to reconcile the rights of account debtors and secured creditors, particularly where, as here, credit is advanced through a line of credit. This case boils down to the question of whether the secured creditor or the account debtor should bear the cost of not finding out that JCC falsely claimed that it had paid its subcontractors. The secured creditor is in a better position than the account debtor to determine whether the assignor/borrower is complying with the terms of the contract in which the creditor has an interest. The reason is that the secured creditor can employ an effective sanction without having to initiate litigation and without risking any loss itself to ensure compliance; it can threaten to cut off credit unless it is satisfied with the borrower's performance. The other party, the account debtor, has no similar sanction. If he is not satisfied, he must litigate and bear the expense of litigation and the sure delay in completion of the contract. The creditor/assignee is not deterred from enforcing compliance by such costs. Obviously, either the secured creditor or the account debtor can make inquiries regarding compliance with the contract, but at some point both will have to rely on the representations of others, which creates opportunities for fraud, as occurred here. The secured creditor is accustomed to looking over the borrower's shoulder on an ongoing basis and can check compliance. By virtue of his control over credit, the creditor can ensure compliance with the contract. The account debtor can only investigate and if it holds up payments, it puts the contract in jeopardy.

The majority contends that holding for appellants will disrupt the free flow of credit because creditors will have additional duties. This argument goes too far because it counsels against any imposition on creditors. Besides, whatever increased credit costs arise will fall on the class truly at fault in these cases -- the borrower/assignors.

The majority also stresses the concern that actions under section 9-318(1)(a) will make creditors fully liable for the contracts of their borrowers, which would contravene section 9-317. This case does not present this problem, and this result need not occur. I do not argue that the creditor should be the surety for the assignor. The creditor should be exposed only to the extent that he benefits from the assigned contract rights. Tracking the language of section 9-318(1)(a), whatever rights of payment a secured creditor has are subject to the terms of the contract between the account debtor and the borrower/assignor. The account debtor cannot go beyond the benefits the creditor/assignee obtains under the assignment in an action against the creditor. Whether the account debtor asserts the claim as a counterclaim or as an original claim should be irrelevant.

* * *

For the foregoing reasons, I would hold that Michelin has a direct cause of action against FNB for the monies it received from Michelin under its assignment from JCC.

b. Holding Financer Affirmatively Liable on a Common-Law Negligence Theory

In the landmark case *Connor v. Great Western Savings & Loan Ass'n*, 69 Cal.2d 850, 73 Cal.Rptr. 369, 447 P.2d 609 (1968), a lender, Great Western, negotiated with two developers with limited experience in tract construction to secure financing for the purchase of 100 acres of land and the construction thereon of 400 tract homes. The lender was intimately involved at every stage of the subdivision construction project, from financing the development to making mortgage loans to purchasers of the homes.

The arrangement between Great Western and the developers provided that Great Western would first buy the land, and then resell it to the developers at a profit, charging a high interest rate on the loan. The arrangement also provided for encouraging buyers of homes in the development to seek permanent financing from Great Western. A fee was charged for each individual home loan. If a buyer obtained financing elsewhere, the developers were required to pay Great Western the fees obtained by the other lender.

Great Western inspected the development at least once a week, and reserved the right to halt construction funds during the construction period if the work did not conform to plans and specifications. All plans and specifications had been examined and approved by the lender before construction began.

Many of the homes proved defective for the principal reason that the home designs were inadequate for the soil conditions, which caused foundations to crack. Some of the homebuyers brought an action against the developers and Great Western seeking rescission and damages. Because the lender had been an active participant in the enterprise and knew or should have known certain facts concerning the developer and the transaction, the California Supreme Court held that Great Western had a duty to the homebuyers to exercise reasonable care to protect them from damages caused by major structural defects. Great Western breached this duty and thus was affirmatively liable to the homebuyers.

Shortly after the *Connor* case was decided, the California legislature reacted with this statute:

> A lender who makes a loan of money, the proceeds of which are used or may be used by the borrower to finance the design, manufacture, construction, repair, modification or improvement of real or personal property for sale or lease to others, shall not be held liable to third persons for any loss or damage occasioned by any defect in the real or personal property so designed, manufactured, constructed, repaired, modified or improved or for any loss or damage resulting from the failure of the borrower to use due care in the design, manufacture, construction, repair, modification or improvement of such real or personal property, unless such loss or damage is a result of an act of the lender outside the scope of the activities of a

lender of money or unless the lender has been a party to misrepresentations with respect to such real or personal property.

West's Ann.Cal.Civ.Code §3434 (1970). Does this statute overrule, codify, or limit the holding of *Connor*? See Gutierrez, *Liability of a Construction Lender Under Civil Code Section 3434: An Amorphous Epitaph to Connor v. Great Western Savings & Loan Association*, 8 PAC.L.J. 1 (1977).

Homebuyers in other states have relied on Connor as a theory for imposing affirmative liability on financers. In the case *Jeminson v. Montgomery Real Estate and Co.*, 47 Mich.App. 731, 210 N.W.2d 10 (1973), 396 Mich. 106, 240 N.W.2d 205 (1976), a homebuyer sued the vendor and her mortgage company after discovering that the house was uninhabitable. She had been defrauded. The trial court entered summary judgment for the mortgagee on the basis that the plaintiff had failed to state a claim against it. The Court of Appeals of Michigan affirmed because "no established legal principle has been cited by plaintiff or discovered by this Court that would warrant finding that defendant mortgage corporation had a duty to protect the plaintiff from the real estate company's cupidity." 47 Mich.App. at 739, 210 N.W.2d at 14. The court distinguished *Connor* on the basis that the lender in that case had been involved in the overall transaction to a far greater extent than the usual money lender in such transactions. Judge Adams dissented, arguing that the summary judgment for the mortgagee should be reversed because a cause of action existed if the mortgagee and vendor were intimately affiliated and if, as plaintiff alleged, the transaction was unitary rather than binary. 47 Mich.App. at 741, 210 N.W.2d at 15 (Adams, J., dissenting). On further appeal the Supreme Court of Michigan reversed and remanded on the basis of Judge Adams' dissenting opinion. *Jeminson v. Montgomery Real Estate and Co.*, 396 Mich. 106, 240 N.W.2d 205 (1976), rev'ing, 47 Mich.App. 731, 210 N.W.2d 10 (1973).

In a significant number of other cases, purchasers of real estate have relied on *Connor*, or a *Connor*-like theory, to shift to a lender losses resulting from defective housing or a builder's failure otherwise to perform a construction contract. In almost every case, the purchaser has lost. The primary reason is that the courts, including California courts spurred by the legislative reaction to *Connor*, have interpreted Connor to apply only in unusual, extreme circumstances where the lender's activities clearly exceeded its traditional, normal role by the lender having exercised virtually complete control over the construction project. See generally, e.g., *Rudolph v. First Southern Federal Savings & Loan Ass'n*, 414 So.2d 64 (Ala.1982) (summary judgment for lender reversed but court narrowly interprets *Connor*); *Wierzbicki v. Alaska Mutual Savings Bank*, 630 P.2d 998 (Alaska 1981); *Murry v. Western American Mortg. Co.*, 124 Ariz. 387, 604 P.2d 651 (Ariz.App.1979); *Meyers v. Guarantee Savings & Loan Ass'n*, 79 Cal.App.3d 307, 144 Cal.Rptr. 616 (1978); *Kinner v. World Savings & Loan Ass'n*, 57 Cal.App.3d 724, 129 Cal.Rptr. 400 (1976); *Fox & Carskadon Financial Corp. v. San Francisco Federal Savings & Loan Ass'n*, 52 Cal.App.3d 484, 125 Cal.Rptr. 549 (1975); *Bradler v. Craig*, 274 Cal.App.2d 466, 79 Cal.Rptr. 401 (1969); *Butts v. Atlanta Federal Savings & Loan Ass'n*, 152 Ga.App. 40, 262 S.E.2d 230 (1979); *Callaizakis v. Astor Development Co.*, 4 Ill.App.3d 163, 280 N.E.2d 512 (1972); *Allison v. Home*

Savings Ass'n, 643 S.W.2d 847 (Mo.App.1982); but compare *Dunson v. Stockton, Whatley, Davin & Co.*, 346 So.2d 603 (Fla.Dist.Ct.App.1977) (mortgagee accountable for breach of construction contract because mortgagee assumed complete control of developer-borrower's building operations and the separate identities of the mortgagee and developer merged).

In a few cases plaintiffs have relied on *Connor* as the basis for imposing liability on lenders who financed the sale of personal property such as automobiles operated negligently by the borrowers. These efforts to extend *Connor* have failed. See, e.g., *Altman v. Morris Plan Co.*, 58 Cal.App.3d 951, 130 Cal.Rptr. 951 (1976); *Drake v. Morris Plan Co.*, 53 Cal.App.3d 208, 125 Cal.Rptr. 667 (1976).

c. Joint Venture Theory

In the case *Connor v. Great Western Savings & Loan Ass'n*, 69 Cal.2d 850, 73 Cal.Rptr. 369, 447 P.2d 609 (1968), discussed above, the financer's affirmative liability to the plaintiffs-obligors, the homebuyers, was based on the breach of an independent duty the financer itself owed them. Obligors sometimes argue that a financer should be affirmatively liable because of the breach of a duty owed by the seller of the property or services purchased by the obligor. This argument for vicarious liability is often based on the theory that the financer and seller were joint venturers in the transaction involving the obligor.

A joint venture is essentially a partnership for a limited business or commercial purpose. J. Crane & A. Bromberg, Partnership §35 (1968); Mecham, *The Law of Joint Adventures*, 15 Minn.L.Rev. 644 (1931). When the purpose is something other than business, the proper label is joint enterprise. Prosser and Keeton on the Law of Torts §72 (W. Keeton ed. 1984). Joint venturers, like partners, are personally liable for debts of the undertaking. J. Crane & A. Bromberg, Partnership §35 at 193 (1968). The Minnesota Supreme Court has provided a description that is more to the immediate point:

> Joint venture is a remedial status imposed by a court to hold a party responsible for the results of an enterprise over which the party has effective control even though it is not nominally responsible. *** [A] joint adventure is created when two or more persons combine their money, property, time, or skill in a particular business enterprise and agree to share jointly, or in proportion to their respective contributions, in the resulting profits and, usually, in the losses. ***

> [A]n enterprise does not constitute a joint adventure unless each of the following four elements are present, namely:

> (a) *Contribution* -- the parties must combine their money, property, time or skill in some common undertaking, but the contribution of each need not be equal or of the same nature.

(b) *Joint proprietorship and control* -- there must be a proprietary interest and right of mutual control over the subject matter of the property engaged therein.

(c) *Sharing of profits but not necessarily of losses* -- there must be an express or implied agreement for the sharing of profits (aside from profits received in payment of wages as an employee) but not necessarily of the losses.

(d) *Contract* -- there must be a contract, whether express or implied, showing that a joint adventure was in fact entered into.

Meyers v. Postal Fin. Co., 287 N.W.2d 614, 617-18 (Minn.1979).

Under traditional theory, however, as the Minnesota court held in *Meyers*, a financer is not a joint venturer with a seller solely because the financer funds the seller's transactions directly (as by loans to obligors which are used to buy the seller's property or services) or indirectly (as by purchases of seller's rights of action against the obligors for the price of the property or services bought on credit). In addition to *Meyers*, see generally, e.g., *Fuls v. Shastina Properties, Inc.*, 448 F.Supp. 983 (N.D.Cal.1978); *Armetta v. Clevetrust Realty Investors*, 359 So.2d 540 (Fla.Dist.Ct.App.1978); *Christiansen v. Philcent Corp.*, 226 Pa.Super. 157, 313 A.2d 249 (1973); but compare *Central Bank v. Baldwin*, 94 Nev. 581, 583 P.2d 1087 (1978) (substantial evidence supported trial court's finding that bank was joint venturer because in addition to lending money to project the bank owned half of the stock of the developer).

The difficulty of establishing that a financer is a joint venturer is made clear by the *Connor* case, which is discussed in the immediately preceding Note. Remember that in Connor the court found that the financer, Great Western, was so involved in the development of homes purchased by the plaintiffs that the financer owed them an independent duty of care. Yet, the court held in *Connor* that there was no joint adventure between Great Western and the actual developers, Conejo Valley Development Company and related parties, who sold the homes to plaintiffs. Here is the court's reasoning:

Although the evidence establishes that Great Western and Conejo combined their property, skill, and knowledge to carry out the tract development, that each shared in the control of the development, that each anticipated receiving substantial profits therefrom, and that they cooperated with each other in the development, there is no evidence of a community or joint interest in the undertaking. Great Western participated as a buyer and seller of land and lender of funds, and Conejo participated as a builder and seller of homes. Although the profits of each were dependent on the overall success of the development, neither was to share in the profits or the losses that the other might realize or suffer. Although each received substantial payments as seller, lender, or borrower, neither had an interest in the payments received by the other. Under these circumstances, no joint venture existed.

Connor v. Great Western Savings & Loan Ass'n, 69 Cal.2d 850, 863, 73 Cal.Rptr. 369, 375, 447 P.2d 609, 615 (1968).

Think again about the case *Jeminson v. Montgomery Real Estate and Co.*, 396 Mich. 106, 240 N.W.2d 205 (1976), reversing, 47 Mich.App. 731, 210 N.W.2d 10 (1973), which is described above. In his dissenting opinion, which ultimately prevailed, Judge Adams concluded that the defendant-financer was potentially liable to the plaintiff-homebuyer. Is Judge Adams' reasoning necessarily based on the *Connor* case, which is not cited in his dissent and which the majority of his fellow judges found inapposite? Consider the possibility that the basis of his reasoning was a somewhat diluted joint venture theory, which is explainable in terms of a very close connection between the financer and the vendor who sold the house to the plaintiff.

d.   Instrumentality Theory

The instrumentality theory is a distinct, though related, basis for imposing on a creditor affirmative liability for the debtor's obligations. This theory applies "where a creditor's control over a debtor's business and financial affairs is so dominant that either the creditor has become the alter ego of the debtor or the debtor has become the creditor's 'instrument.' " Lundgren, *Liability of a Creditor in a Control Relationship With its Debtor*, 67 Marq.L.Rev. 523, 524 (1984). The creditor's involvement must be such that it is actively managing the debtor's affairs to the extent of assuming total control of the debtor. This theory is most often used when the creditor and debtor are linked by common ownership, overlapping directorates or the like. It is seldom used when the relationship between creditor and debtor is that of lender and borrower. But see *Credit Managers Ass'n v. Superior Court*, 51 Cal.App.3d 352, 124 Cal.Rptr. 242 (1975).

e.   FTC Theory

It is more likely that an obligor can recover something from an assignee or direct financer if the obligor's contract contains the FTC notice preserves whatever claims and defense the obligor might have against her original obligee. Read again, even more carefully than before, Federal Trade Commission Trade Regulation Rule on the Preservation of Consumers' Claims and Defenses, 16 C.F.R. Part 433. Here is what the FTC, or its staff, thought about this issue:

> [The Notice protects] the consumer's right to assert against the creditor any legally sufficient claim or defense against the seller. The creditor stands in the shoes of the seller.
> There is an important limitation on the creditor's liability, however. The wording of the Notice includes the sentence "Recovery hereunder is limited to amounts paid by the debtor hereunder". This limits the consumer to a refund of monies paid under the contract, in the event that an affirmative money recovery is sought. In other words, the consumer may assert, by way of claim or defense, a right not to pay all or part of the outstanding balance owed the creditor under the contract; but the consumer will not be entitled to receive from the creditor an

affirmative recovery which exceeds the amounts of money the consumer has paid in.

Thus, if a seller's conduct gives rise to damages in an amount exceeding the amounts paid under the contract, the consumer may (1) sue to liquidate the unpaid balance owed to the creditor and to recover the amounts paid under the contract and/or (2) defend in a creditor action to collect the unpaid balance. The consumer may not assert [against] the creditor any rights he might have against the seller for additional consequential damages and the like. The same situation would exist where a seller's conduct would, as a matter of law, entitle a buyer to rescission and restitution. The consumer, relying on the required Notice, could initiate proceedings to invalidate the credit contract and receive a return of monies paid on account. If a downpayment were made under the credit contract, the consumer could recover the downpayment as well as other payments. Recovery of a downpayment would be possible under many installment sales contracts. It would not be possible in situations where a direct loan is used, because the downpayment would not have been made pursuant to the loan contract.

The limitation on affirmative recovery does not eliminate any other rights the consumer may have as a matter of local, state, or federal statute. The words "recovery hereunder" which appear in the text of the Notice refer specifically to a recovery under the Notice. If a larger affirmative recovery is available against a creditor as a matter of state law, the consumer would retain this right.

FTC Guidelines on Trade Regulation Rule Concerning Preservation of Consumers' Claims and Defenses, 41 Fed.Reg. (no. 95) 20022, 20023 (May 14, 1976). For cases deciding that an assignee of a contract is affirmatively liable to the obligor because of the FTC Notice in the contract, see, e.g., *Gill v. Caribbean Home Remodeling Co., Inc.*, 73 A.D.2d 609, 610, 422 N.Y.S.2d 448, 449 (1979); *Aillet v. Century Finance Co.*, 391 So.2d 895 (La.Ct.App.1980); *State v. Excel Management Services, Inc.*, 111 Wis.2d 489, 331 N.W.2d 312 (1983); cf. U.C.C.C. §§3.404 comment 2; 3.405 comment 2 (1974) (state law); *Thomas v. Ford Motor Credit Co.*, 48 Md.App. 617, 429 A.2d 277 (1981) (presence of identical notice required by state law subjects assignee to affirmative liability). The FTC Notice suggests that the assignee's affirmative liability is limited to the amount paid her by the debtor. An assignee's affirmative liability might be greater *under state law. See N.Y. -- McKinney's Pers.Prop.Law §403(4) (Consol.1986 Supp.); Hempstead Bank v. Babcock*, 115 Misc.2d 97, 453 N.Y.S.2d 557 (1982) (assignee affirmatively liable to extent of amount owing at time claim is asserted by obligor). Compare Minn.Stat.Ann. §325G.16 (Subd. 3) ("The rights of the consumer under this subdivision can only be asserted as a matter of defense to or set off against a claim by the assignee.").

13. Classifying credit card receivables

Stephen L. Sepinuck, *Classifying Credit Card Receivables Under The U.C.C.: Playing With Instruments?*
32 Ariz. L. Rev. 789 (1990)

* * *

Credit card transactions have, in the past several years, become one of the predominant payment methods for American consumers, generating billions of dollars in outstanding receivables. Some of these receivables are used as collateral for loans to those merchants who accept payment by credit card, while others back certain securities issued by credit card banks.

In spite of their prevalence, neither the cards themselves nor the receivables they help create are expressly mentioned in the Uniform Commercial Code. Although federal law does govern some aspects of credit card transactions, most notably the rights of cardholders, much of the remaining operation of credit cards is left to the auspices of state commercial law, which is generally silent. This silence is particularly troubling in Article Nine, which provides different perfection methods for different types of collateral. Although no court has yet determined the proper Article Nine classification of and perfection method for credit card receivables, the issue is one upon which attorneys and other commercial law experts do differ. Because the issue is also one upon which billions of dollars may be won or lost, the present level of uncertainty is simply too great.

* * *

To illustrate * * * [a] likely scenario, assume that a hypothetical Beacon Airlines ("Beacon") operates a fleet of twenty commuter aircraft with which it transports cargo and passengers between several medium- sized midwestern cities. Like many small businesses, Beacon has numerous creditors. Many of these creditors are suppliers to whom Beacon owes an unsecured debt for fuel, spare parts, and other materials provided on a regular basis. One creditor is a bank (the "Bank") which financed Beacon's initial start-up and subsequent expansion and which, in connection with this financing, took a security interest in Beacon's aircraft, equipment, and accounts. The Bank perfected its security interest in Beacon's airplanes by filing the appropriate documents with the FAA Aircraft Registry in Oklahoma City, and perfected its interest in the remaining collateral by filing a properly executed financing statement in the appropriate state office.

Shortly after its initial start-up, Beacon contracted with another bank (the "Credit Card Bank") to participate in the MasterCard and Visa systems and contracted with American Express to honor that organization's series of cards. Since that time, Beacon has accepted payment from its customers via cash, check, and each of these major credit cards. At a time when some money remains due to Beacon on credit card receivables in its possession and others undergoing processing by American Express and the Credit Card Bank, Beacon's financial situation worsens. In response, Beacon seeks protection from its creditors by filing a petition for relief under Chapter 11 of the United States Bankruptcy Code.

If we assume, as often occurs, that the resale value of the Bank's tangible collateral -- Beacon's aircraft and equipment -- fails to equal the total outstanding indebtedness Beacon owes to the Bank, the Bank will look to its remaining collateral: Beacon's accounts. * * * [O]n any given day, hundreds of millions of dollars in freshly generated credit card receivables are in the hands of merchants, such as Beacon, and these credit card receivables are likely to make up a sizable percentage of these merchants' total receivables. Accordingly, the Bank will likely be very interested in obtaining Beacon's credit card receivables and the Bankruptcy Court may be asked to determine whether the Bank has a perfected security interest in the money owed by Credit Card Bank and American Express to Beacon.

* * *

Under Article Nine of the Uniform Commercial Code, a creditor must perfect a security interest in order to render that interest generally effective against both other creditors of the debtor and subsequent purchasers of the collateral. For most types of collateral, the creditor may perfect by either properly filing a financing statement which adequately describes both the debtor and the collateral or by taking physical possession of the collateral. For certain types of collateral, however, Article Nine restricts perfection to only one of these alternative methods. For example, a creditor may perfect a security interest in accounts or general intangibles only by filing a financing statement. Conversely, a creditor may generally perfect a security interest in instruments only by taking possession. Accordingly, it is essential for a creditor wishing to perfect a security interest in a merchant's credit card receivables to ascertain whether the receivables constitute accounts, general intangibles, or instruments.

* * *

From the outset it is clear that credit card receivables do not qualify as instruments under either of the first two clauses of the instrument definition. They are not negotiable instruments because they lack the "magic words" of negotiability: they fail to state that they are payable to the order of the merchant or to the bearer. They are not certificated securities for similarly obvious reasons. Accordingly, the relevant question becomes whether such a receivable is "any other writing which evidences a right to the payment of money * * * and is of a type which is in ordinary course of business transferred by delivery with any necessary indorsement or assignment."

* * *

It seems apparent that such receivables do evidence a right to the payment of money and therefore satisfy the first half of this definition. Indeed, they appear to evidence no rights other than the right to receive payment in money. The mere fact that payment of such a receivable is likely to be discounted from the face amount would not seem to alter this conclusion.

The difficult question centers on the latter half of the definition: whether such receivables are of a type which is in ordinary course of business transferred by delivery. It remains somewhat unclear whether this phrase requires merely that transfers of writings, however infrequent, customarily be effected through delivery, or whether it alternatively or additionally requires that the writings be of a type which is transferred frequently.

The weight of authority seems to be that transfer by delivery -- not frequency of transfers -- is the main focus of this statutory language. In other words, delivery of the writing must generally be necessary to transfer the right to payment which the writing represents. As one commentator put it, the Article Nine classification should depend on how professionals who deal with such writings handle them. If such professionals attach importance to possession of the writing, then the law should do the same. This is merely a way of restating the traditional maxim that the right to collect must be bound to the writing. If the right to payment exists independent of the writing, it cannot be an instrument, but if possession of the writing alone entitles the holder to receive payment, the writing is an instrument.

When, interpreted in this manner, the rationale for having different perfection mechanisms for accounts and instruments becomes evident. If the transfer of a particular right to money is generally effected through delivery of a writing, a secured creditor must obtain possession of that writing to prevent future -- and possibly fraudulent -- deliveries and transfers of the right. Although filing a financing statement with respect to such collateral might provide notice to the world, it would undermine the ease and operation of the normal transfer-by-delivery process. Moreover, if collection of a right to money requires delivery of a writing to the obligor, possession of the writing by a secured creditor is often essential to prevent the obligor from discharging its obligation by paying the debtor upon presentment.

On the other hand, for rights which are transferred other than by delivery, such as accounts and general intangibles, neither of these concerns applies. While such rights may be referenced in one or more writings, such as a sales or service contract, an order confirmation, a simple bill, or the seller's books and records, they exist independent of such writing and may readily be sued upon separately. Indeed, because such rights may be evidenced in multiple writings, possession of any one writing is not only unnecessary to prevent future, and perhaps fraudulent, transfers, it is insufficient.

Hence, the thrust of section 9-105(1)(i) appears to be that transfer by delivery and collection by presentment is what makes an instrument out of a writing which evidences the right to the payment of money. Even though a specific writing expressly restricts or prohibits transfers to third parties, if it is of a type for which delivery to the obligor is customarily required for collection, possession of the paper is necessary for the secured creditor to be truly secure.

The difficulty with classifying credit card receivables is that they seem to possess some, but not all, of the attributes of instruments. Specifically, while the right to payment on a credit card receivable often requires presentment of a writing -- at least when a writing exists -- presentation of the writing will not alone be sufficient to entitle the holder to payment. To obtain payment, the holder must also have some contractual relationship with one or more members of the credit card system: a member bank for Visa or MasterCard; American Express itself for Optima or the American Express card. Without such a relationship, no one will honor a credit card slip presented for payment. Even when a writing does exist, bank card slips are not always transferred to the issuing bank; the merchant or the merchant bank may retain them and electronically transmit the information necessary to obtain payment and bill the cardholder. This truncation of the collection procedure suggests that the right to collect is not intrinsically bound to the writing. In short, presentment of the writings representing credit card receivables is sometimes required, but is insufficient to obtain payment, and transfer of such writings -- by delivery or otherwise -- is usually not permitted.

Given these facts, the two reasons for classifying a writing as an instrument, and thus requiring possession to perfect a security interest in it, appear not to apply to credit card receivables. First, while possession of an instrument is often necessary to prevent additional and perhaps fraudulent transfers of the writing (and the right to payment which it represents), the receivables are not transferable. Indeed, no one without a contractual relationship with someone in the clearinghouse procedure can hope to collect by mere presentment of the written slip. Second, while the obligor on a receivable may be able to discharge its obligation despite knowing that someone other than the presenter has a claim to it, the mechanism by which payment is made -- at least on bank cards -- undermines the ability of the debtor to use this fact to defraud secured creditors.

Even when merchants do present written bank card slips for payment, the merchant bank makes only a provisional settlement to the merchant's deposit account. Most credit card processing contracts between merchants and merchant banks restrict the merchant's right to withdraw the provisional settlement for quite some time, usually at least 120 days. If a creditor had a security interest in the credit slips redeemed for payment, that interest would extend to the deposit account as proceeds of the credit card slip. The merchant would then have little ability to use the funds for some other purpose. Thus, even assuming that concerns over the obligor's ability to discharge its obligation in circumstances detrimental to the secured creditor is what prompts courts to treat nontransferable writings as instruments, such concerns do not apply to the classification of credit card receivables.

* * *

CONCLUSION

Billions of dollars will be at stake when courts finally determine how credit card receivables and the little slips of paper which evidence them should be classified under Article Nine of the Uniform Commercial Code. Although such writings appear to meet the literal wording of the Code's definition of "instruments," and at least some commentators have suggested that they are instruments, no persuasive reason exists to classify them as such. They are not transferable, they are generally not presented back to the issuer in the collection process, and creditors usually have no access to the clearinghouse procedure through which they are paid. Classifying them as instruments, and thereby requiring secured creditors to take possession of them in order to perfect their interest, would serve no useful purpose.

Moreover, requiring possession to perfect an interest in credit card receivables would undermine the ability of creditors to perfect their security interests and would effectively prevent them from using credit card receivables as collateral. It would also require creditors and debtors to continuously distinguish between credit card receivables created in point-of-sale transactions and those arising from telephone and mail orders, for which no writing exists. The Uniform Commercial Code was not intended to so frustrate commercial transactions.

* * *

14. Modernizing Article 7

Possible Issues to be Addressed in Revision of U.C.C. Article 7

(Memorandum prepared by Professor Linda Rusch, Hamline University School of Law, for the ABA Article 7 Task Force (1993))

I.   Section 7-202 and Section 7-209: Warehouse Receipts and Warehouse Liens
     * * *
     C. Inclusion of All Listed Terms in 7-202(2) to have a Valid Warehouse Receipt and
         Warehouse Lien.

The cases have come to conflicting results in terms of whether a warehouse receipt qualifies as a receipt that can give rise to a warehouse lien if some of the listed terms in 7-202(2) are omitted from the receipt. Those cases holding that the omission of some terms does not affect the validity of the warehouse receipt are: *Michigan Nat. Bank v. Michigan Livestock Exchange*, 432 Mich. 277, 439 N.W.2d 884, 9 UCC Rep.Serv.2d 366 (1989); *Ferrex Intern., Inc. v. M/V Rico Chone*, 718 F.Supp. 451, 10 UCC Rep.Serv.2d 960 (D.Md. 1988).

Cases that hold the omission of 7-202(2) terms does not affect the validity of the warehouse lien are: *In re Julien Co.*, 136 B.R. 755, 16 UCC Rep.Serv.2d 1143 (Bankr.W.D.Tenn. 1991); *Evergreen Intern. Services Corp. v. Wallant Intern. Trade, Inc.*, 228 N.J.Super. 477, 550 A.2d 175, 7 UCC Rep.Serv.2d 1603 (1988); *Kearns v. McNeil Bros. Moving and Storage Co.*, 509 A. 2d 1132, 1 UCC Rep.Serv.2d 856 (D.C. App. 1986).

One case held that the omission of some of the 7-202(2) terms means that the document is not a warehouse receipt. *Nuclear Facilities, Inc. v. Advance Relocation and Storage, Inc.*, 173 A.D.2d 802, 571 N.Y.S.2d 36, 15 UCC Rep.Serv.2d 1290 (N.Y.A.D. 1991).

Cases that go on to hold that the omission of those terms from the receipt means that the warehouse does not have a valid lien under 2-709 are: *In re Siena Publishers Associates,* 149 B.R. 359, 19 UCC Rep.Serv.2d 1139 (Bankr.S.D.N.Y. 1993); *Matter of Celotex Corp.,* 134 B.R. 993, 16 UCC Rep.Serv.2d 482 (Bankr.M.D.Fla. 1991); *In re Charter Co.,* 56 B.R. 91, 42 UCC Rep.Serv. 280 (Bankr.M.D.Fla. 1985).

* * *

G. Priority of Warehouse Lien versus a Secured Party with Perfected Security Interest in Goods and in Negotiable Documents.

Two basic fact scenarios are relevant here. Each will be discussed in turn.

1. The secured party has a properly perfected security interest in goods. The debtor bails the goods with the warehouse. The warehouse asserts a lien against the secured party. The issue is the relative priority of the secured party's perfected security interest in the goods and the warehouse lien.

Article 9 provides in Section 9-201 that except as provided in the Act, the security interest is good as against all third parties. Section 9-310 provides that statutory liens asserted by a person in the ordinary course of their business furnishing services and materials with respect to the goods has priority over a properly protected security interest, unless the statute providing for the statutory lien expressly provides otherwise. The Article 7 warehouse lien is a statutory lien within the meaning of 9-310. The issue is whether anything in Article 7 regarding warehouse liens provides that the warehouse lien is subordinate to the secured party's interest.

Section 7-209(3)(a) provides that the lien is effective against any person who entrusted the bailor, here the debtor, with possession of the goods so that a pledge by the bailor/debtor to a good faith purchaser would have been valid. That subsection also provides that the lien of the warehouse "is not effective against a person as to when the document confers no right in the goods" under Section 7-503. Comment 3 to Section 7-209 provides that this subsection of 2-709 comes within the meaning of the phrase "expressly provides otherwise" in Section 9-310,

The cases construing these provisions have held that the security interest in this situation has priority over the warehouse lien. *In re Siena Publishers Associates,* 149 B.R. 359, 19 UCC Rep.Serv.2d 1139 (Bankr.S.D.N.Y. 1993); *Curry Grain Storage, Inc . v. Hesston Corp.,* 120 Idaho 328, 815 P.2d 1068, 16 UCC Rep.Serv.2d 191 (1991); *K. Furniture Co. v. Sanders Transfer & Storage Co., Inc.,* 532 S.W.2d 910, 17 UCC Rep.Serv. 1092 (Tenn. 1975). The courts used the comment to 2-709 to hold that the implication of 2-709 was that the warehouse lien was subordinate to the second party's interest unless the secured party entrusted the goods to the bailor or acquiesced in procurement of the warehouse receipt. The courts found that the secured party had not entrusted the goods to the bailor or acquiesced in the bailor's procurement of the document of title. The cases are extremely sketchy on the facts regarding entrustment or acquiescence. In *Curry Grain,* the court stated entrustment is not based upon the secured party's consent. Even though the secured party might have consented to storage, the second party did not entrust the goods to the bailor.

2. In the second scenario the secured party takes a perfected security interest in negotiable documents by filing or possession and the warehouse asserts a lien for storage. There are two possible avenues of analysis of the relative priority of the secured party's interest and the warehouse lien.

The same analysis as outlined above using Section 9-310 and Section 7-209 would lead to the same result. The secured party's interest would have priority over the warehouse lien. If the secured party took possession of the negotiable document to perfect the security interest instead of filing to perfect the security interest, it is hard to argue that the secured party is entrusting the bailor with possession of the goods given that the right to possession of the goods is bound up with the negotiable document which is in the hands of the secured party. This result leads to a conflict with Section 7-403(2) which gives the bailee the right to payment of the lien before releasing the goods if someone is using the document to obtain the goods. If the secured party uses the document to claim the goods, even though Section 7-209 has been read to give the secured party priority, the secured party under 7-403 would have to satisfy the lien to have a right to the goods.

On the other hand, when the secured party takes a security interest in the document, the secured party's interest is co-extensive with the bailor/debtor's interest in the property, the bailor/debtor's interest is subject to the warehouse lien under 2-709(1). Under this analysis the security interest would be subordinate to the warehouse lien and no conflict arises with 7-403(2).

Section 7-209 should be materially re-drafted to explicitly set forth when a secured party's interest in goods covered by a document is subordinate to or superior to the warehouse lien.

II. The Rights Of A Qualified Holder: A Holder Of A Negotiable Document Duly Negotiated.

   * * *

B. Rights Of A Qualified Holder

The cases make very clear that the holder of a duly negotiated negotiable document may be either a secured party with the security interest in the document perfected by possession, or a buyer of the document. One case has addressed the issue of whether or not the secured party who was a qualified holder can maintain that status even if it surrenders the document. That case rightly held that the secured party is not still a holder once it surrenders the document. *Scallop Petroleum Co., a Div. of Scallop Corp. v. Banque Trad-Credit Lyonnais France S.A.,* 690 F.Supp. 184, 6 UCC Rep.Serv.2d 1573 (S.D.N.Y. 1988). Thus, if a secured party is going to assert the rights of a holder of a duly negotiated negotiable document, that person must still be in possession of that document.

1. Qualified Holder v. Secured Party With A Security Interest In the Negotiable Document.

The rights of a secured party with a security interest in a negotiable document that is perfected by filing against the rights of a holder of a duly negotiated negotiable document are governed by 9-309. That section explicitly provides that the rights of the holder are paramount to the secured party's security interest. A review of the cases did not find any cases dealing with this situation which leads one to believe that there is no major problem with this concept.

2. Qualified Holder v. A Secured Party With A Security Interest In Goods.

If a secured party attempts to take a security interest in goods while a negotiable document is outstanding, the proper way to take a security interest is to take that interest in the document, not in the goods. 9-304(2). In a priority contest between such a qualified holder of a document and a secured party who has taken a security interest in goods while the document has been issued, 9-309 seems to provide the same result as above. No cases have been decided on this issue and it would seem not to have presented any problem.

What has presented significant problems is if the security interest in the goods was taken before the negotiable document for the goods was issued. Under 9-309, 7-501, 7-502, and 7-503, the rights of the holder of a duly negotiated negotiable document would be inferior to the rights of the secured party unless the secured party entrusted the goods to the bailor/debtor with actual or apparent authority to obtain a document of title or acquiesced in the procurement of a document of title. The major item of contention is what is entrustment or acquiescence so that the secured party would lose to the negotiable document holder. The same concepts of entrustment and consent or waiver are found in other articles of the UCC such as 9-306(2) (authorized dispositions of collateral) and 2-403 (entrustment of goods to a merchant who deals in goods of that kind). In the cases that have construed the concepts of entrustment or acquiescence under Article 7, the courts examine the secured party's particular dealings with the debtor to determine whether or not that party entrusted or acquiesced in the debtor's procurement of a document of title. *In re Jamestown Farmer Elevator, Inc.,* 49 B.R. 661, 41 UCC Rep.Serv. 578 (Bankr. D.N.D. 1985); *U.S. v. Hext,* 444 F.2d 804, 9 UCC Rep.Serv. 321 (5th Cir. 1971); *In re R.V. Segars, Co.,* 54 B.R. 170 (Bankr.D.S.C. 1985). Each of the courts examined the transactions of the debtor and secured party in those cases and basically decided that the creditor knew or should have known that the debtor was engaged in a course of conduct that would result in having negotiable documents of title that could be duly negotiated.

The standard of examining what the secured party knew or should have known under 7-503 seems to be different than the standard under 7-209(3)(a) regarding entrustment which would subordinate the secured party's security interest to the warehouse lien.

An on-going issue in this area is who should bear the burden of putting this negotiable document into the stream of commerce. If the burden of finding entrustment or acquiescence is relatively low, the burden on the secured party to police the debtor's behavior and to attempt to prevent the debtor from getting negotiable documents issued would be high. On the other hand, if the conduct required for finding entrustment or acquiescence is relatively great then the burden on the secured party would be lessened but the burden on the holder of the negotiable document would be increased. Some have suggested that the relevant knowledge to determine acquiescence or entrustment is not the knowledge of the debtor's behavior but a knowledge of the behavior of parties in the industry. That standard would seem to put an impossible burden on a secured party to protect the collateral if a court would find that the industry standard was that people generally obtain negotiable documents for these types of goods and that lender knew or should have known that industry practice, the lender will always lose to the holder of the negotiable document. From a practical perspective, one should note that in the midwestern farm region a significant number of producers of goods that eventually have negotiable documents issued for those goods, self-store the goods before the negotiable documents are issued. It is common practice in farm financing for a secured party to take an interest in those goods stored on the farmer's land in the farmer's own bins. The farmer, of course, cannot issue a negotiable warehouse receipt in this situation to him or herself. Thus the secured party's options if the burden of showing entrustment or acquiescence is relatively low is not to lend to farmers or take security interest in crops and the grain prior to having negotiable documents issued for them or take the risk that the farmer will obtain a negotiable document for the goods and negotiate that document to a duly qualified holder. The burden on the secured party to police the self-stored grain in those instances would be extremely high. On the other hand, given that special situation for self-stored grain, one does not want to burden the entire realm of negotiable documents with the problems of one particular segment of the industry. Perhaps a reasonable balance can be found if the concept of entrustment was more like the concept of authorization to dispose of collateral under 9-306(2). In that respect, one would have to consider the cases that hold the course of dealing between the parties is a waiver of the no-consent clauses in the security agreements. If the secured party has a no-consent clause in the security agreement and the no-consent clause specifically states that the debtor cannot obtain negotiable documents for these goods, and the secured party does not waive that clause by the course of dealing, then it is hard to see how the secured party could do any more to protect itself without taking physical possession of the goods, a totally unworkable concept.

* * *

V. 7-204 Liability

* * *

C. Issues regarding limitation of damages.

* * *

4. Should the limitation clause be conspicuous?

Griffin v. Nationwide Moving and Storage Co., Inc., 187 Conn. 405, 446 A.2d 799, 34 UCC Rep.Serv. 970 (1982) held that because the limitation was not conspicuous, the bailor had not read the limitation, and the limitation was not pointed out to the bailor, the limitation was excluded from the contract. On the other hand, *Strom Intern., Ltd. v. Spar Warehouse and Distributors, Inc.,* 69 Ill.App.3d 696, 388 N.E.2d 108, 26 Ill.Dec. 484, 27 UCC Rep.Serv. 233 (1979), *Sanfisket, Inc. v. Atlantic Cold Storage Corp.,* 347 So.2d 647, 21 UCC Rep.Serv. 1155 (Fla.App. (1977), *Keefe v. Bekins Van & Storage Co.,* 36 Colo. App. 382, 540 P.2d 1132, 17 UCC Rep.Serv. 1286 (1975), held that no requirement exists that the limitation be conspicuous or pointed out to the bailor's attention.

In Article 2, clauses in the contract which limit warranties must be conspicuous. Section 2-316(2). A common rationale for such requirement is that a clause that changes usual expectations of a party should be conspicuous. Perhaps that same rationale should be used in warehouse receipts, if the bailee wants to limit the damages for negligence or other loss.

D. Damage measurement

1. Market value measure.

When the measure of damages is the market value of the goods or a reduction in the value of the goods, issues have arisen about when that market value should be measured. *Lonray, Inc. v. Azucar, Inc.,* 775 F.2d 1521, 42 UCC Rep.Serv. 537 (11th Cir. 1985), stated the New York rule as the market value of the goods on the date missing or if that date is unknown the highest value between the date the bailment started and the date the bailor received notice of the loss. That case went on to hold the Florida rule was the price the bailor would have received if the negligence didn't occur. In that case, that was the date the loss was discovered. *Federal Compress & Warehouse Co. v. Reed,* 339 So.2d 547, 20 UCC Rep.Serv. 722 (Miss. 1976), held that the market value of the goods should be measured as of the date when the bailor knew the goods were destroyed. The cases on market value dealt with goods where the market value fluctuated over time.

2. Should the measurement of damage be other than market value?

Several cases have used other measurements of damages other than market value of the goods lost. One case stated all losses that are the result of the bailee's negligence should be recoverable. *Irving Pulp & Paper, Ltd. v. Dunbar Transfer & Storage Co., Inc.,* 732 F.2d 511, 38 UCC Rep.Serv. 312 (6th Cir. 1984). One case stated that if the goods did not have a market value, such as household goods, the court should use a reasonable value on the basis of the value to the owner. *Keefe v. Bekins Van & Storage Co.,* 36 Colo.App. 382, 540 P.2d 1132, 17 UCC Rep.Serv. 1286 (1975). One court stated that lost profits of the bailor might be recoverable. *Georgia Ports Authority v. Servac Intern.,* 202 Ga.App. 777, 415 S.E.2d 516, 17 UCC Rep.Serv.2d 869 (1992). *Indemnity Marine Assur. Co., Ltd. v. Lipin Robinson Warehouse Corp.,* 99 Mich.App. 6, 297 N.W.2d 846, 30 UCC Rep.Serv. 658 (1980), stated that such lost profits might be recoverable if a bailee knew the goods were for resale and not readily available in the market and such damages were not unduly speculative.

* * *

15. Electronic credits

R. David Whitaker, *Electronic Documentary Credits*
46 Bus. Law. 1781 (August 1991)

A number of ongoing legal reform efforts are creating opportunities for changes in legal standards governing electronic documentary credits. Both Article 5 of the Uniform Commercial Code ("U.C.C.") and International Chamber of Commerce ("ICC") Publication No. 400 are undergoing revision. In addition, the UNCITRAL Working Group on International Contract Practices is working on a possible international convention or model national law on letters of credit and bank guaranties. The Letters of Credit and Related Transactions Working Group ("Working Group") hopes to contribute to these activities by (i) investigating and reporting on developing commercial usage of electronic means to transmit agreements and documents related to documentary credits; and (ii) suggesting methods for addressing and encouraging this developing usage.

The Working Group is accumulating information on current practices. This report contains a discussion of current practices regarding electronic documentary credits, together with an overview of five general categories of concerns which drafters of uniform laws and conventions may wish to address.

CURRENT ELECTRONIC PRACTICES

SWIFT and TELEX are both used domestically to transmit letters of credit from issuing banks to advising banks. A letter of credit transmitted in this fashion is printed in hard copy at the advising bank, stamped "original," and provided to the beneficiary in that form. There is no other original letter of credit provided. The encryption and verification procedures used by SWIFT are considered by many in the banking industry to be commercially sufficient to prevent tampering with either the transmission or reproduction of documents. On the other hand, concern has been expressed over the security of the TELEX system, and the sophistication of its methods for authenticating documents.

The Working Group has also been advised, but has not yet confirmed, that certain large mercantile banks are accepting electronically transmitted bills of lading as part of the process for honoring commercial letters of credit. Electronic bills of lading do not appear to be in general usage in international transactions. Domestically, electronic bills of lading are being used on a limited basis for billing purposes:

(i) Shipment via Rail (Conrail): Conrail transmits bill of lading data directly to a shipper who "automatically" receives data and bills its customer. Hard copies are available at the point of shipment and delivery. The Working Group believes that the information is transmitted via an independent carrier (as opposed to a direct system-to-system link).

(ii) Tank Truck Deliveries: General Electric Company services the oil tank truck community by allowing EDI transmission of bill of lading data via a common link to all participants. This operates like example (i) above. Again, hard copy bills of lading follow.

Looking to the future, certain members of the U.S. banking industry hold the opinion that full electronic transmission, storage, and presentation of both letters of credit and the documents required for payment can be expected. Others disagree. It is interesting to note that the proposed Customs Modernization Act of 1990 provides for electronic submission of shipping documents to U.S. Customs.

It appears, however, that there is also some skepticism in Europe, and specifically at the ICC, with respect to the feasibility and desirability of this trend. The ICC has recently separated the analysis of the use of electronic data interchange ("EDI") in documentary credits into two conceptual frameworks.

The first framework concerns the electronic origination, transmission, and amendment of documentary credits. Certain European banks currently have agreements with large customers that permit those customers to place electronic "orders" for the issuance of commercial credits. If the order "tests" against the authorization procedure, the bank's computer automatically issues a commercial documentary credit to the advising bank via SWIFT. The advising bank will then either print out, or in some cases electronically transmit, the credit to the beneficiary. The ICC takes the position that these arrangements should be left to the private contracting arrangements of the parties, subject, of course, to the system rules imposed by SWIFT. The ICC does not currently, and does not apparently intend, to try to establish standards for such arrangements.

The second framework involves the electronic presentation of documents as part of the demand for payment under the credit. This is not, apparently, a common practice in Europe at the moment. The ICC has not yet indicated an interest in developing a conceptual framework for electronic presentation.

Obviously, there is a great deal of detail to be filled in, both on current banking practices and the future direction of documentary credits. Research on these questions will continue. For the moment, the Working Group has tentatively identified a number of legal issues related to the trends suggested by the practices reviewed above. At the outset, without denying the validity of the distinctions drawn by the ICC, the Working Group is inclined to favor a unified focus on issues raised both by electronic transmission of the credits themselves and by electronic presentation of documents for payment. Many of the same issues arise in both contexts and it is believed drafting will be simplified by evaluating the issues and possible solutions concurrently.

GENERAL OBSERVATIONS

The Working Group has identified five categories of potential concerns which would relate to the drafting of uniform laws and conventions affecting documentary credits:

(i) Definitions of significant terms
(ii) Methods of establishment, transfer or assignment
(iii) Methods of presentation
(iv) Determination of time of establishment
(v) Methods of amendment

DEFINITIONS

Many domestic statutes and standards currently require a "writing" containing a "signature." These writings are sometimes called "documents," and are frequently "negotiable." All of these phrases are problematic when applied to electronic data files. The problem is more significant with domestic law; as exemplified by other UNCITRAL products, the international environment has, for some time, acknowledged the possibility that business communications with legal significance may occur electronically (e.g., the Vienna Sales Convention and the Model Law on International Commercial Arbitration).

One of the primary characteristics of a writing is its immutability. Once a contract is written, changing it without leaving "footprints" is perceived to be very difficult. On the other hand, most electronic data is stored as magnetic patterns on an erasable medium. Generally, the data may be changed or eliminated without traces. As an example of the problem, section 1-201(46) of the U.C.C. defines "writing" to include "printing, typewriting or any other intentional reduction to tangible form." The question of whether magnetic patterns are "tangible" almost rises to the metaphysical. If by "tangible" is meant "permanent" or "unalterable without defacement," then much electronic data storage would not qualify.

Another characteristic of "tangible" records is that they are usually freely movable and, by virtue thereof, transferable. Electronic records do violence to the assumptions underlying such transactions, which include the uniqueness and authenticity of the instrument.

Electronic data files may not, therefore, satisfy the requirements of a "writing" as that term is now understood. The same comments apply to the word "documents."

A signature is intended to serve two functions: (i) to verify the authenticity of an agreement ("this is our final, memorialized agreement") and (ii) to verify that the parties had an opportunity to become familiar with the terms of the agreement ("I must have had the document in front of me, since my signature appears on it"). The process is simple and relatively foolproof. Signatures are not, of course, impossible to duplicate; the process is difficult, however, and often involves recruiting third parties with unusual talents. By contrast, verification of an electronic message, to be effective, may require sophisticated encryption and authentication procedures. Obtaining verification of authenticity and authority, therefore, is a more involved process in the electronic medium, and there is no simple analogue for the "signature" to draw upon.

It has been argued that, by definition, an electronic record cannot be negotiable. The essence of negotiability is the concept that possession of a particular piece of paper imbues the bearer with certain rights. Since magnetic patterns cannot be possessed (or perhaps, more properly, are too easy to possess, being inherently the product of duplication), no electronic document can be "negotiated."

These problems may be best addressed by looking behind the current definitions to the function they fulfill. A writing is intended to provide a record of a transaction that is frozen in time. A signature is an attempt to verify the authenticity of that record. The writing is "negotiated" in order to transfer the underlying rights it records and verifies. Any law seeking to accommodate electronic contracts, or electronic presentation of documents, must focus on these underlying purposes and not their paper-based products.

METHODS OF ESTABLISHMENT, TRANSFER OR ASSIGNMENT

As noted above, the basic concept of "negotiability" is difficult to apply to electronic records. There is no paper to be possessed. Of course, there is nothing particularly revolutionary in the concept of transferring non-negotiable rights, whether in toto or for the purpose of security. Intangible contract rights are transferred constantly. In some instances systems of third-party recordation have been established, as with Article 9 of the U.C.C. or real property title records. For many things, assignment is accomplished by agreement, either oral or written, without any public record at all.

However, given the nature of documentary credits in general, and of commercial credits in particular, transfer and assignment raise difficult problems. Contemporary practice frequently calls for presentation of the "original" credit, with additional signed or indorsed documentation. These conventions make it possible to "track" ownership rights and confirm claims to those rights with relative ease. These concepts have no current electronic equivalent.

METHODS OF PRESENTATION

From a conceptual point of view, there is no problem with electronically presenting a document. If the original is paper-based, it may be scanned and transmitted (via fax or otherwise) to the confirming or issuing bank. If the original is electronic, it may be transmitted in any acceptable electronic protocol. The problem is verifying the authenticity of the document: was it originated by the proper person and, if it is a representation of a paper-based document, is it an accurate representation of the true original? The difficulty here is partly one of degree: paper-based documents may be forged or falsified, but not with such ease or speed.

In some respects, resort may be had in this area to Article 4A of the U.C.C., which addresses a similar problem by focusing on the security of the transmitting system. Article 4A, by imposing certain rules concerning the risk of loss, creates incentives for the institutions who act as intermediaries between the ultimate parties. The intermediate institutions are essentially coerced by the statute to take measures insuring that only authentic electronic records enter the system, and that these records are reliably reproduced upon receipt.

These incentives largely address problems due to interlopers, renegade employees or unintentionally garbled messages, and not deliberate fraud on the part of an authorized party originating a transmission. Therefore, Article 4A does not offer a method for authenticating bills of lading or other documents presented as a condition for payment by a party authorized to use the system.

Another possible solution may lie with the use of third parties as "secure" transmission systems. That is, if one or more common carriers, who can assign a specific "code" to each sender, act as the conduit of information by standardizing the requirements for receipt of electronic data interchange, and who will maintain electronic copies of the records that will be considered the basis for resolving factual issues (e.g., time sent, time received, etc.), then minor modifications to current international and domestic laws which refer to telecommunications might address most problems.

TIME OF ESTABLISHMENT

The problems raised by establishment are not unique to electronic credits. Even with paper credits, there is currently a statutorily-enforced dichotomy in the U.C.C. between the time of issuance, when the credit becomes enforceable between the issuer and applicant, and the time of receipt, when the beneficiary first obtains rights in the credit. With electronic credits, the problem may be magnified because of difficulties with the concepts of "issuance" and "receipt." When is an electronic credit issued, and when is it received? What if it is garbled or altered in transmission? If so, has it been issued at all? If it is established in spite of alteration, is it established according to its original terms or the altered terms? Is it received when it is first recorded by the beneficiary's equipment or when it is first reviewed by the beneficiary? May it be revoked in the interim? If so, how and when must the revocation be transmitted, and when is it received?

METHODS OF AMENDMENT

Amendment raises all of the issues presented by transfer, presentment, and establishment. The authenticity, effective date and time, and ability to track the sequence of amendment are all impaired by the malleability of the electronic medium.

CONCLUSION

As exemplified by the general comments provided above, considerable care must be given in the process of drafting new commercial law standards or guidelines to avoid provisions which inadvertently impair the adoption and expanded use of electronic commercial activity. The Working Group recommends that the objective of accommodating electronic documentation, both with respect to the original credit and with respect to any supporting documentary requirements, be adopted at an early stage in the drafting process.

16. Proposed revision of Article 5

Revised UCC Article 5
(Draft March 31, 1993)

SECTION 5-101. SHORT TITLE. This [Article] may be cited as Uniform Commercial Code--Letters of Credit.

SECTION 5-102. DEFINITIONS.

(a) In this [Article]:

(1) "Adviser" means a person who, at the request of the issuer, confirmer, or other adviser, notifies the beneficiary that a letter of credit has been issued, amended, or transferred.

(2) "Applicant" means a person on whose behalf or for whose account a letter of credit is issued. The term includes a person who requests an issuer to issue a letter of credit on behalf of another or for another's account if the person making the request undertakes the obligations of an applicant by agreement with the issuer.

(3) "Banking day" means a day on which a bank at a particular place is required by law to be open to the public for carrying on substantially all of its banking functions.

(4) "Beneficiary" means a person who under the terms of a letter of credit is entitled to have its complying presentment honored and includes a transferee under a transferable letter of credit.

(5) "Confirmer" means a person who engages, at the request or with the consent of the issuer, to honor a presentment under a letter of credit issued by another.

(6) "Document" means a draft or other demand, document of title, investment security, invoice, certificate, or any other statement required by a letter of credit, whether in writing or consisting of data in another medium which are presented in a form and with the content authorized by the letter of credit or by agreement of the issuer.

(7) "Honor" means to pay, accept and pay, or otherwise incur an unconditional obligation to pay at a future time under a letter of credit and pay. The term in noun form has the corresponding meaning.

Alternative (7) "Honor" means to pay, accept, or otherwise incur an unconditional obligation to pay at a future time under a letter of credit and pay. The term in noun form has the corresponding meaning.

(8) "Issuer" means a bank or other person issuing a letter of credit, but does not include an individual making an engagement for family or household purposes.

Alternative (8) "Issuer means a bank or other merchant issuing a letter of credit."

(9) "Letter of credit" means an engagement that satisfies the requirements of Section 5-104 by an issuer to a beneficiary at the request or for the account of an applicant or for its own account to honor a draft or other demand upon proper presentment of the documents specified in the letter of credit.

(10) "Nominated person" means a person whom the issuer authorizes to pay, accept, negotiate, or otherwise give value under a letter of credit.

(11) "Presenter" means a person presenting a document under a letter of credit to an issuer or nominated person and includes a nominated person that is presenting to an issuer for reimbursement.

(12) "Presentment" means presenting a document to an issuer or nominated person as a part of a demand for honor under a letter of credit.

(13) "Successor of the beneficiary" means:

(i) a corporation with which the beneficiary has been merged or consolidated, or

(ii) a person who succeeds to substantially all of the rights of the beneficiary under a letter of credit by operation of law and includes an administrator, executor, personal representative, trustee in bankruptcy, debtor in possession, liquidator, receiver, and the like.

(b) Definitions in other [Articles] applying to this [Article] and the sections in which they appear are:

"Accept" or "Acceptance"	Section 3-409
Collecting Bank	Section 4-105(5)
"Good Faith"	Section 3-103(a)(4)
"Security"	Section 8-102
"Value"	Sections 3-303, 4-211

(c) [Article] 1 contains additional general definitions and principles of construction and interpretation applicable throughout this [Article].

COMMENTS

1. The terms "issuing bank," "confirming bank," and "advising bank" have been replaced with "issuer," "confirmer," and "adviser" to recognize that letters of credit may be issued by entities other than banks. The addition of the term "substantially all of its functions" in the definition of banking day is intended to make clear, for example, that a bank's operation of automated teller machines on a holiday or the opening of the lobby for some services on a Saturday would not make that day into a banking day.

2. The rights and obligations of a confirmer, nominated person, and an adviser are covered by Section 5-107.

3. The term "customer" has been replaced by the term "applicant" to make the language of [Article] 5 conform to the UCP.

4. In common with many other forms of financial assurance, a letter of credit is part of a matrix of discrete contracts or other arrangements. The function of the letter of credit is to assure performance of the applicant's financial obligation incurred in the underlying transaction, by engaging to make payment to the applicant's obligee in accordance with the terms and conditions stipulated by the issuer in the letter of credit. The issuer makes that engagement at the instance and on behalf of its applicant pursuant to an agreement between the applicant and the issuer.

In the usual three party letter of credit transaction, the issuer is not a party to and has no involvement in the underlying transaction. This is true whether the underlying transaction is the sale of goods or is a non-sales transaction under which default of the applicant or some third party may form the basis for the draw of the beneficiary.

5. The definition of confirmer denies that status to one who "confirms" without the consent of the issuer. These "silent confirmers" do not have the status of confirmer under [Article] 5. All confirmers are nominated persons under 5-102(a)(10).

6. Although all letters of credit should specify the date on which the issuer's engagement expires, the failure to specify an expiration date does not invalidate the letter of credit, or diminish or relieve the obligation of any party with respect to the letter of credit. A letter of credit that does not specify expires one year from issue, see Section 5-106(f).

When a document labelled a letter of credit requires the issuer to pay not upon the presentation of documents, but upon the determination of an extrinsic fact such as applicant's failure to perform a construction contract, and where that condition appears on its face to be fundamental and would, if ignored, leave no obligation to the issuer under the document labelled letter of credit, the issuer's undertaking is not a letter of credit at all. It is probably some form of suretyship or other contractual arrangement and may well be enforceable as such. See Sections 5-102(a)(9) and 5-103(d). Although Section 5-110(d) recognizes that certain non-documentary conditions can be included in a letter of credit without denying the document the status of letter of credit, that section does not reach cases where the non-documentary condition appears on its face to be a fundamental part of the issuer's obligation. The rules in Sections 5-102(a)(9), 5-103(d), and 5-110(d) approve the conclusion in Wichita Eagle & Beacon Publishing Co. v. Pacific Nat. Bank, 493 F.2d 1285 (9th Cir. 1974).

A letter of credit as distinguished from a guarantee or other form of engagement anticipates honor against "documents." An engagement that would require an issuer not merely to pay upon documentary proof of default (but would require, for example, that the issuer investigate to determine whether a default had occurred) would not constitute a letter of credit. Therefore, engagements whose fundamental term requires an issuer to look beyond documents and beyond conventional reference to the clock, calendar, and practices concerning the form of various documents are not governed by [Article] 5.

7. "Document" is far broader under this [Article] than under [Article] 9. (See Section 9-105(1)(e)). The definition has been expanded to include transmission of certain electronic data as documents. Computer technology and electronic transmission of data are having a growing impact upon mercantile practice. As those assume greater importance, formal procedures will have to be developed among the parties in order for electronic messages to become a reliable method of presentment. Under the definition, electronic or electro-optical transmission of data does not constitute presentment of a document and therefore the transmission is not a suitable mode of presentment unless it has both the form and the content authorized by the letter of credit or is otherwise agreed upon. Absent such authorization or agreement, electronic or electro-optical transmission, however honest and accurate, will not constitute the presentment of documents sufficient to entitle the beneficiary to honor under Section 5-110.

Because many electronic transmissions produce a paper copy when they are received by a computer printer, facsimile or telex machine, or the like, one needs to distinguish between such hard copies that otherwise look like paper documents and the transmission of electronic data. For this purpose, transmissions that enter the issuer's premises in electronic form and there cause a paper document to be printed by the issuer's computer printer, telex or a facsimile machine, are the transmission of electronic data, not the presentment of paper documents. One wishing to make presentment by facsimile will have to procure the explicit agreement of the issuer. Failing that, the beneficiary will have to transmit the documents electronically to its own agent who can present them manually.

8. Payment and acceptance are familiar modes of honor. A third mode of honor, incurring an unconditional obligation, has the same legal effect as an acceptance but does not technically constitute an acceptance. In some countries one accepting a draft incurs a tax obligation that can be lawfully avoided if the agreement to pay in the future is not technically an acceptance. Accordingly, in those countries, the practice of "deferred payment undertaking" has grown up. The definition of honor will accommodate that practice.

A letter of credit may be honored only by the issuer or by one authorized by the issuer. Authorized persons include confirmers and other nominated persons. Since a nominated person who gives value must itself again present the documents to the issuer for honor and reimbursement, it is possible for documents to be twice presented and for honor and reimbursement to occur under a single letter of credit. When a person that is not a confirmer or a nominated person receives documents from the beneficiary and gives value against them under a letter of credit, there has not been presentment and its giving of value is not honor, yet the same receipt from a beneficiary and giving of value without disclaimer would constitute presentment and honor if done by a confirmer.

The exclusion for consumers (engagements of individuals in connection with family or household purposes) is to keep creditors from using a letter of credit in consumer transactions in which the consumer might be made the issuer and the creditor would be the beneficiary. If that transaction were recognized under [Article] 5, the effect would be to leave the consumer without defenses against the creditor. That outcome would violate the policy behind the Federal Trade Commission Rule in 16 CFR Part 433. In a consumer transaction, an individual cannot be an issuer where it is the principal debtor, nor could it be an issuer where it is a guarantor.

9. All persons authorized to negotiate or pay under a letter of credit by the terms of the letter of credit or by separate agreement with the issuer are nominated persons. Confirmers are nominated persons. In addition, any bank is a nominated person under a negotiation letter of credit that permits free negotiation. Such a letter might provide: "We hereby engage with the drawer, indorsers, and bona fide holders of drafts drawn under and in compliance with the terms of this credit that the same will be duly honored on due presentment" or "available by negotiation." Other language might make a letter of credit a negotiation letter.

Certain agents who are authorized to make payments related to but not part of the honor of letters of credit are not nominated persons. For example, banks that are identified in international practice as "reimbursing banks" are not normally nominated banks. Reimbursing banks are authorized by the issuer to make payment to confirmers or other nominated persons. Typically reimbursing banks are not called upon to examine documents or otherwise make a determination whether there has been a proper presentment. Once a nominated person has honored or otherwise given value and procures reimbursement from a correspondent or other agent of the issuer, that correspondent or other agent is not acting in the role of a nominated person where it merely pays according to the issuer's instruction. That is so even though it could have acted as a nominated person under a negotiation credit had the beneficiary originally presented documents to it.

The legal significance of the status of a nominated person is severalfold. First, when the issuer nominates a person it is authorizing that person to pay or give value and is authorizing the beneficiary to make presentment to that person. Unless the letter of credit specifies otherwise, the beneficiary need not get the documents to the issuer before the letter of credit expires; it need only present those documents to the nominated person who takes them up. If the nominated person, other than a confirmer, refuses to take up the documents, there has been no presentment and it is the responsibility of the beneficiary to make presentment to the issuer or another nominated person who takes them up. It is sufficient to meet the expiration date that a nominated person takes up the documents even if it does so with recourse or merely as a forwarding agent. Secondly, a nominated person that gives value in good faith has a right to payment from the issuer despite fraud even under a straight letter of credit. Section 5-110(e)(1).

Merely because one is identified as an adviser and in fact advises a letter of credit does not make it a nominated person. If a nominated person (who has not become a confirmer) is unwilling to accept any responsibility for examining the beneficiary's documents or is unwilling to bear the risk that the issuer will dishonor, that person may by disclaimer or agreement limit its duties to those of an agent for forwarding the documents to the issuer.

10. Presentment might be as little as presenting a draft or other demand for payment under a clean letter of credit or as much as presenting an array of documents such as an invoice and packing list in addition to a draft under a conventional commercial letter of credit.

11. Section 5-102(a)(13) defines successor of the beneficiary as one who succeeds to the rights and duties of the beneficiary by the operation of law and not exclusively by the beneficiary's voluntary transfer. In addition to successor corporations, successors include trustees in bankruptcy, debtors in possession, as well as entities such as the Federal Deposit Insurance Corporation in its capacity as a receiver for an insolvent beneficiary bank and assignees from the Federal Deposit Insurance Corporation through a purchase and assignment agreement authorized by federal statute.

SECTION 5-103. SCOPE.

(a) This [Article] applies to letters of credit, as specifically defined in Section 5-102(a)(9), and to confirmations, advices, and similar agreements by nominated persons that are made in connection with letters of credit.

(b) The statement of a rule in this [Article] does not by itself require, imply, or negate application of the same or a different rule to a situation not provided for, or to a person not specified in this [Article].

(c) Except as otherwise provided in Sections 1-102(3), 5-108(a), 5-110(b), 5-111(f), and 5-114(a), the parties may vary their rights and obligations under this [Article] (i) by expressly incorporating rules of practice, such as the Uniform Customs and Practices of the International Chamber of Commerce, (ii) by a term in a letter of credit, confirmation, or advice, or (iii) otherwise by agreement.

(d) The rights and obligations of an issuer under a letter of credit are independent of and are not affected by the performance or non-performance of any contract or arrangement out of which the letter of credit arises or to which it is linked, including contracts or arrangements between the issuer and the applicant and between the applicant and the beneficiary.

SECTION 5-104. FORMAL REQUIREMENTS.

Neither a letter of credit, confirmation, advice, nor a modification or revocation of a letter or credit , confirmation, or advice may be oral. If the letter of credit, confirmation, or advice is entirely in writing, it must be signed by the issuer, confirmer, or adviser. If the letter of credit, confirmation, or advice is entirely or partly in a medium other than writing, the identity of the issuer, confirmer, or adviser must be authenticated by the issuer, confirmer, or adviser in accordance with the agreement of the parties or, in the absence of an agreement, in accordance with applicable system rules, usage of the trade in the banking industry, or other law.

SECTION 5-105. CONSIDERATION.

Consideration is not required to establish or modify a letter of credit, advice, or confirmation.

SECTION 5-106. ESTABLISHMENT, MODIFICATION, AND REVOCATION.

(a) A letter of credit may be revocable or irrevocable. A letter of credit that is silent as to its revocability is irrevocable.

(b) Unless a letter of credit otherwise provides, a letter of credit is established when the issuer sends or otherwise transmits it to the adviser, nominated person, or beneficiary, or when the issuer sends or otherwise transmits a properly authorized statement of its issuance, whichever occurs first.

(c) Unless otherwise agreed, after an irrevocable letter of credit is established, the beneficiary, applicant, or issuer is not bound by an amendment, modification, or cancellation to which that person has not consented, and a nominated person is not bound by an amendment, modification, or cancellation unless it (i) has consented or (ii) has received notice of the amendment, modification, or cancellation before it gives value or otherwise makes an irrevocable commitment based upon the original letter of credit.

(d) Unless otherwise agreed, a revocable letter of credit may be modified or revoked by the issuer without notice to or consent of the applicant or the beneficiary.

(e) If there is no stated expiration date or other provision that determines its period of effectiveness, a letter of credit expires one year after its date of issue as shown on the face of the letter of credit or, if none is shown, after the date on which it is established.

SECTION 5-107. CONFIRMER, NOMINATED PERSON, AND ADVISER.

(a) A confirmer is directly obligated on a letter of credit and has the rights and obligations of an issuer to the extent of its confirmation. Upon proper presentment to the issuer under Section 5-110, the confirmer is entitled to reimbursement by the issuer. By confirming, the confirmer also acquires rights against and assumes duties to the issuer as if the issuer were an applicant and the confirmer had issued the letter of credit at the request of the issuer.

(b) Unless it has otherwise agreed with the beneficiary or issuer, a nominated person that is not a confirmer is not obligated to honor [or otherwise give value] upon a beneficiary's presentment.

(c) By reason of its advice, an adviser does not assume an obligation to honor a draft or demand for payment under a letter of credit. An adviser owes a duty to the issuer and to the beneficiary accurately to advise the terms of the letter of credit which are received by the adviser and a duty to the beneficiary to verify the apparent authenticity of the letter of credit. Even if an adviser inaccurately advises the terms of a letter of credit it has been authorized to advise, the letter of credit is established against the issuer to the extent of its original terms. Unless otherwise specified, an applicant bears all risk of error in transmission, [or] translation [or interpretation] of a message relating to a letter of credit which is not caused by the lack of care of the issuer, confirmer, or adviser.

SECTION 5-108. WARRANTIES.

(a) If its presentment is honored, the beneficiary under a letter of credit warrants to the issuer, any other person to whom presentment is made, and the applicant, that there is no fraud, the documents are what they purport to be, and the statements and representations in the documents are true in all material respects. Those warranties are in addition to warranties arising under [Articles] 3, 4, 7, and 8 because of the presentment of documents covered by any of those [articles]. Except as otherwise provided in subsection (b) and notwithstanding any term in the letter of credit or agreement to the contrary, the beneficiary does not give a warranty of the kind described in the first sentence of this subsection if the beneficiary's presentment is dishonored.

[(b) If a beneficiary's presentment is dishonored by the issuer but the beneficiary has received value from a nominated person upon presentment to that person, the beneficiary under the letter of credit makes the warranties specified in subsection (a) to the nominated person.]

[(c)] Unless otherwise agreed, when presentment is honored, a nominated person or other transferor of documents who is not a beneficiary warrants only the matters warranted by collecting banks under [Article] 4 and a transferor transferring a document covered by [Article] 7 or 8 warrants only the matters warranted by an intermediary under those [Articles].

SECTION 5-109. EXAMINATION, NOTICE, AND PRECLUSION.

(a) Unless a different period is authorized by a letter of credit or by the consent of the beneficiary or presenter and except as otherwise provided in Section 5-113(b), an issuer has a reasonable time, but not beyond the close of the seventh banking day after receipt of documents submitted under the letter of credit to examine documents, procure any necessary waiver, and honor a draft or other demand under a letter of credit. Unless the issuer has either paid, accepted, or made an unconditional commitment to pay within the time permitted by this subsection, it has dishonored.

(b) If an issuer dishonors, it shall give notice to the presenter of all discrepancies in the documents or tender. The notice shall be given by expeditious means and without delay after the earlier of (i) the time of the decision to dishonor, or (ii) the end of the time for honor under subsection (a). Except as otherwise provided in subsection (c), the issuer is precluded from asserting as a basis for dishonor (i) any discrepancy, if no timely notice is given, or (ii) any discrepancy not stated in the notice, if timely notice is given.

(c) Failure to comply with subsection (b) does not preclude the issuer from asserting as a basis for dishonor that the beneficiary has presented documents that the beneficiary knows to be forged or materially fraudulent or that the letter of credit expired before presentment.

(d) Upon dishonor, unless otherwise instructed by the presenter, the issuer shall either return the documents to the presenter or hold them at the disposal of the presenter and send the presenter an advice to that effect.

SECTION 5-110. ISSUER'S RIGHTS AND DUTIES.

(a) Except as otherwise provided in subsections (e) and (f), an issuer shall honor a presentment that appears on its face strictly to comply. If a presentment does not appear so to comply, the issuer shall dishonor the presentment unless otherwise agreed with the applicant.

(b) An issuer shall perform its obligations to a beneficiary, an applicant, and a nominated person in good faith and with reasonable care. An issuer's rights and obligations are not affected by the performance or non-performance of any contract or arrangement out of which the letter of credit arises or to which it is linked. An issuer is not responsible for an act or omission of a person, other than itself or its agent, resulting in loss or destruction of a document in transit or in the possession of others. An issuer is not charged with knowledge of any usage of a particular trade. However, an issuer is charged with knowledge of any general letter of credit usage. The parties may not disclaim by agreement the duties of good faith and reasonable care, but may agree to standards to measure performance of those duties if the standards are not manifestly unreasonable.

(c) Unless other standards are expressly incorporated by reference, sufficiency of compliance of a presentment is measured by commercial banking standards and practices. The determination of the nature and scope of those standards and whether a presentment appears on its face strictly to comply with the terms of the letter of credit are questions of law.

(d) If, despite the presence of non-documentary conditions, an engagement constitutes a letter of credit under Section 5-102(a)(9), an issuer shall disregard the non-documentary conditions and treat them as if they were not stated.

(e) If a presentment is made that appears on its face strictly to comply with the terms of the letter of credit, but the beneficiary has presented documents that the beneficiary knows to be forged or materially fraudulent:

(1) if the honor is demanded by a nominated person that has honored in good faith without notice that the documents are forged or materially fraudulent, the issuer shall honor the draft or demand;

(2) if the conditions in paragraph (1) are not met, the issuer may honor or dishonor.

(f) If the applicant claims that the beneficiary has presented documents that the beneficiary knows to be forged or materially fraudulent, a court of competent jurisdiction may enjoin the issuer from honoring, or grant similar relief, only if the court finds that:

(1) the beneficiary, issuer, and any other person who may be adversely affected are adequately protected by bond or otherwise against loss that may be suffered by those persons if honor is enjoined or otherwise forestalled;

(2) all of the conditions to entitle one to an injunction under the law of the forum State have been met; and

(3) on the basis of information presented, the beneficiary is not entitled to honor under subsection (e)(l), the applicant will suffer irreparable harm if the draft or demand is honored, and the applicant is more likely than not to succeed under its claim of forgery or material fraud against the beneficiary.

(g) An issuer that has duly honored a letter of credit

(1) is entitled to be put in immediately available funds not later than the date of payment,

(2) is barred from the recovery that the issuer might otherwise have against the presenter or beneficiary under Sections [3-414] or [3-415], and

(3) except as otherwise provided in Section 5-108, is barred from recovery against the presenter or beneficiary on the ground of payment by mistake to the extent that any mistake concerns discrepancies in the documents or tender which could have been discovered on presentment.

COMMENTS

1. This section combines the duties previously included in Sections 5-114 and 5-109. Because a confirmer has the rights and duties of an issuer, this section applies equally to a confirmer and an issuer, see Section 5-107(b).

The standard of strict compliance governs the issuer's duty to the beneficiary and to the applicant. By requiring that "presentment" appear strictly to comply, the section requires not only that the documents themselves appear on their face strictly to comply, but also that the other terms of the letter of credit are strictly complied with. Those terms deal with the time and place of presentment and possibly with other terms. Unless the letter of credit specifies otherwise, presentment is timely if it is made to a nominated person prior to the expiration date. A nominated person that has honored a demand or otherwise given value before expiration will have a right to reimbursement from the issuer upon proper presentment even though presentment is made after the expiration of the letter of credit. Where the beneficiary procures payment from or negotiates documents to one who is not a nominated person, the person paying the beneficiary or taking the documents for value must itself make presentment to the nominated person, confirmer, or issuer as the letter of credit requires prior to the expiration date.

Although this section does not impose a bifurcated standard under which the beneficiary would owe a higher obligation to the issuer than the issuer would owe to the applicant, most bank issuers substantially restrict their liability to the applicant. Where that is done, the beneficiary will have a higher duty of compliance to the issuer than the issuer will have to the applicant.

The section adopts the standard of strict compliance, but strict compliance does not mean slavish conformity to the terms of the letter of credit. By adopting commercial banking standards and practices as a way of measuring strict compliance, it indorses the conclusion of the court in New Braunfels Nat. Bank v. Odiorne, 780 S.W.2d 313 (Tex. Ct. App. 1989) (beneficiary could collect when draft requested payment on 'Letter of Credit No. 86-122-5' and letter of credit specified 'Letter of Credit No. 86-122-S' holding strict compliance does not demand oppressive perfectionism).

The section also indorses the result in Tosco Corp. v. Federal Deposit Insurance Corp., 723 F.2d 1242 (6th Cir. 1983). The letter of credit in that case called for "drafts Drawn under Bank of Clarksville Letter of Credit Number 105". The draft presented stated "drawn under Bank of Clarksville, Clarksville, Tennessee letter of Credit No. 105." The court correctly found that despite the change of upper case "L" to a lower case "l" and the use of the word "No." instead of "Number," and despite the addition of the words "Clarksville, Tennessee," the presentment conformed.

The section rejects the standard that commentators have called "substantial compliance," the standard arguably applied in Banco Espanol de Credito v. State Street Bank and Trust Company, 385 F.2d 230 (1st Cir. 1967) and Flagship Cruises Ltd. v. New England Merchants Nat. Bank, 569 F.2d 699 (1st Cir. 1978). The discrepancies in *Banco* and *Flagship* were significant, unlike those in the *New Braunfels* and *Tosco* cases.

The standard adopted is that established by reasonable document checkers in commercial banks. These are diligent and knowledgeable persons who are trained to distinguish between insignificant and important discrepancies. Where such persons could reasonably disagree on the question whether a literal deviation constituted a discrepancy and where there is more than one presentment (as to a confirmer who presents to the issuer), the judgment of the person making the original examination should normally prevail. See, American Bar Association Task Force Report, 45 Bus. Lawyer 1521, at 1609.

Establishing the standards and determining compliance with the standards are questions for the court. As with similar rules in Sections 4A-202(c) and 2-302, it is hoped that there will be more consistency in the outcomes and speedier resolution of disputes if the responsibility for determining the nature and scope of the standards and practices is granted to the court, not to a jury. Granting the court authority to make decisions about standards will also encourage the salutary practice of courts' granting summary judgment in circumstances where there are no significant factual disputes. The statute encourages outcomes such as American Coleman Co. v. Intrawest Bank, 887 F.2d 1382 (10th Cir. 1989), where summary judgment was granted.

2. Parties will soon transmit documents electronically, electro-optically or by yet more exotic media. At present it is appropriate to recognize such transmissions only when the issuer explicitly agrees. The issuer can control its obligation to accept electronic documents by stating in the letter of credit that they are acceptable. Where the letter of credit is silent, such documents are not acceptable. This means that a facsimile document would not be an acceptable method of presentment unless the letter of credit specifically stated that electronic documents could be presented. Before any issuer agrees to accept electronic documents, it will be necessary for it to establish standards between itself and the beneficiary about the mode of transmission and authentication of such documents.

3. Subsection (b) limits the issuer's power to disclaim its responsibility. Sometimes the agreement that an issuer offers to its applicant disclaims liability for "any action taken or omitted by [issuer] or [issuer's] correspondent under or in connection with this letter of credit or its relative drafts, documents, or property, if done in good faith . . . " Neither disclaimers of the sort quoted nor those generally freeing the issuer from liability for lack of ordinary care would absolve an issuer from liability because it paid over defective documents in good faith but without the use of reasonable care.

In some circumstances standards may be established between the issuer and the applicant by agreement or by custom that would free the issuer from liability that it might otherwise have. For example, an applicant could agree that issuer would have no duty whatsoever to examine documents on certain presentments (e.g., those below a certain dollar amount). Where the transaction depended upon the issuer's payment in a very short time period (e.g., on the same day or within a few hours of Presentment), the issuer and the applicant could properly agree to reduce the issuer's responsibility for failure to discover defects. By the same token, an agreement between the applicant and the issuer could permit the issuer to examine documents exclusively by electronic or electro-optical means. Neither those agreements nor others like them knowingly made by issuers and applicants are prohibited by subsection (b).

4. The issuer's duty to honor runs not only to the beneficiary but also to the applicant. It is possible that an applicant who has made a favorable contract with the beneficiary will be injured by the issuer's failure to honor. Except to the extent that the contract between the issuer and the applicant limits that liability, the issuer will have liability to the applicant for wrongful dishonor as a matter of contract law.

The issuer's duty to refuse honor when there is no apparent compliance with the letter of credit runs only to the applicant. No other party to the transaction can complain if the applicant waives compliance with the letter of credit or agrees to a less stringent standard for compliance than that supplied by this [Article].

An applicant's waiver of defects in one presentment does not waive similar defects in a future presentment. Neither the issuer nor the beneficiary can reasonably rely upon honor over past waivers as a basis for concluding that a future defective presentment will justify honor. The reasoning of Courtaulds of North America Inc. v. North Carolina Nat. Bank, 528 F.2d 802 (4th

Cir. 1975) is accepted and that expressed in Schweibish v. Pontchartrain State Bank, 389 So.2d 731 (La.App. 1980) and Titanium Metals Corp. v. Space Metals, Inc., 529 P.2d 431 (Utah 1974) is rejected.

5. The responsibility of the issuer under a letter of credit is to examine documents and to make a prompt decision to honor or dishonor based upon that examination. Non-documentary conditions have no place in this regime and are better accommodated under contract or suretyship law and practice. In requiring that non-documentary conditions in letters of credit be ignored as surplusage, [Article] 5 remains aligned with the UCP (see UCP 500 Article 15d), approves cases like Pringle-Associated Mortgage Corp. v. Southern National Bank, 571 F.2d 871, 874 (5th Cir. 1978), and rejects the reasoning in cases such as Sherwood & Roberts, Inc. v. First Security Bank, 682 P.2d 149 (Mont. 1984).

Subsection (d) recognizes that letters of credit sometimes contain non-documentary terms or conditions. Conditions such as a term prohibiting "shipment on vessels more than 15 years old", are to be disregarded and treated as surplusage. Similarly, a requirement that there be an award by a "duly appointed arbitrator" would not require the issuer to determine whether the arbitrator had been "duly appointed." Likewise a term in a standby letter of credit that provided for differing forms of certification depending upon the particular type of default does not oblige the issuer independently to determine which kind of default has occurred. These conditions may be disregarded by the issuer. Where the non-documentary conditions are central and fundamental to the issuer's obligation (as for example a condition that would require the issuer to determine in fact whether the beneficiary had performed the underlying contract or whether the applicant had defaulted) their inclusion may remove the undertaking from the scope of [Article] 5 entirely. See Section 5-102(a)(9) and Comment 6 to Section 5102.

Subsection (d) of this section would not permit the beneficiary or the issuer to disregard terms in the letter of credit such as place, time, and mode of presentment. The rule in subsection (d) is intended to prevent an issuer from deciding or even investigating extrinsic facts, but not from consulting the clock, the calendar, its own business records, the relevant law and practice, or its own general knowledge of documentation or transactions of the type underlying a particular letter of credit. The term "any usage of a particular trade" in subsection (b) refers to the trade of the applicant, beneficiary, or others who may be involved in the underlying transaction, but the issuer is expected to know usage that is commonly encountered in the course of document inspection. For example, an issuer should know the common usage with respect to documents in the maritime shipping trade.

6. This section omits the term "fraud in the transaction" that appeared in the former Section 5-114. Now any fraud must appear in the form of a forged or fraudulent document to justify an injunction. The change is intended to reduce the cases where an applicant may procure an injunction.

A second change, also designed to restrict the cases where an injunction can be granted, is the requirement that fraud in the documents be "material." Necessarily courts will have to decide the breadth and width of "materiality." The use of the word requires that the fraudulent aspect of the document be significant to the participants in the underlying transaction. Assume, for example, that the beneficiary has a contract to deliver 1,000 barrels of salad oil. Knowing that it has delivered only 998, the beneficiary nevertheless submits an invoice showing 1,000 barrels. If two barrels in a 1,000 barrel shipment would be an insubstantial and immaterial breach of the underlying contract, the beneficiary's act, although fraudulent, is not materially so and would not justify an injunction. Conversely, the knowing submission of those invoices upon delivery of only five barrels would be the submission of materially fraudulent documents. Necessarily, one must examine the underlying transaction when there is an allegation that a document is materially fraudulent, for only by examining that transaction can one determine whether the beneficiary has committed fraud and whether it was material.

Because a document must be forged or materially fraudulent for fraud to exist, the presentment of a draft under a clean letter of credit could never be the basis for an injunction or dishonor. A draft is merely a demand for payment; if it is signed by an authorized representative of the beneficiary, it would not be forged and, being only a demand for money and not a certification that the money is due, could not be fraudulent. Issuers should realize that issuing a clean letter of credit (i.e., one that calls for presentment of only a draft as the basis for payment) is tantamount to issuing a cashier's check.

Fraud by persons other than the beneficiary does not justify an injunction unless such acts result in the beneficiary's knowing presentment of forged or fraudulent documents. See Cromwell v. Commerce & Energy Bank, 464 So.2d 721 (La. 1985). The court denied injunctive relief to limited partners who fraudulently had been induced by the general partner in their partnership to procure letters of credit payable to a beneficiary that was not a party to the fraud.

The standard for injunctive relief is high, and the burden remains on the applicant to show, by evidence and not by mere allegation, that such relief is warranted. Some courts have enjoined payments on letters of credit on insufficient showing by the applicant. For example, in Griffin Cos. v. First Nat. Bank, 374 N.W.2d 768 (Minn. App. 1985), the court enjoined payment under a standby letter of credit, basing its decision on plaintiff's allegation of fraud. The court should have accepted the certification as sufficient unless the applicant could provide competent evidence that it was false. The decision, which was based on a mere allegation of fraud, is rejected by Section 5-110(f)(3). The result in Dynamic Corp. of Am. v. Citizens & S. Nat. Bank, 356 F. Supp. 991 (N.D. Ga. 1973), which involved an analysis similar to that in *Griffin Cos.*, is likewise rejected.

Although the statute deals only with injunctions against honor, the same principles apply when the applicant or issuer attempts to achieve the same legal outcome by injunction against presentment (see Ground Air Transfer Inc. v. Westates Airlines, Inc., 899 F.2d 1269 (1st Cir. 1990)), interpleader, declaratory judgment or attachment. These attempts should face the same obstacles that face efforts to enjoin the issuer from paying. Expanded use of any of these devices could threaten the independence principle just as much as injunctions against honor. For that reason courts should have the same hostility to them and place the same restrictions on their use as would be applied to injunctions against honor. In the words of Henry Harfield, courts should not allow the "sacred cow of equity to trample the tender vines of letter of credit law."

Section 5-110(e) also allocates the risk of fraud in certain transactions between the issuer and a transferee or assignee of the beneficiary's documents. By issuing a letter of credit that nominates a person to negotiate or pay, the issuer (and ultimately the applicant) assumes the risk that a draft drawn under the letter of credit will be transferred to a nominated person with a status like that of a holder in due course who can demand payment despite fraud. The language in Section 5-110(2)(a) of the former Code referring specifically to due negotiatees under Section 7-502, and bona fide purchasers of certificated securities in Section 8-302 has been removed as not necessary. The language in the subsection as it currently reads is designed to identify a generic bona fide purchaser and to grant that person preferred status when it is appropriate. The section contemplates that one might have the "rights" of a holder in due course even in circumstances in which the documents are not negotiable and the holder is not technically a holder in due course or where, for other reasons, the person does not technically comply with the provisions defining a specific kind of bona fide purchaser.

Note that the one seeking the injunction based upon fraudulence of documents will have to do more than merely to allege that a document was fraudulent. That person would be obliged to present competent evidence of falsity and materiality. Although appellate courts have routinely overturned lower court injunctions, vigilance on the part of the appellate courts may not be enough. The letter of credit rests upon its speed and certainty of payment. Where injunctions are granted--even injunctions that are almost certain to be overturned on appeal-the letter of credit becomes more costly, less certain, and slower. In time the prospect of such trial court injunctions could be enough to undermine the entire institution of letters of credit. The "loss" to be protected against by bond or otherwise under subsection (f)(l) includes incidental damages. Among those are legal fees that might be incurred by the beneficiary or issuer in defending against an injunction action.

SECTION 5-111. DAMAGES.

(a) If an issuer wrongfully dishonors a draft or demand for payment presented under a letter of credit, the person entitled to honor may recover from the issuer the face amount of the draft or other demand together with incidental but not consequential damages, together with interest and attorney's fees specified in subsection (d), less any amount realized by any use or disposition of the assets which would have been transferred or exchanged in the underlying transaction. If no disposition or other use is made, the documents, goods, or other subject matter involved in the transaction must be transferred to the issuer upon satisfaction of the judgment.

(b) If an issuer wrongfully dishonors a draft or demand for payment presented under a letter of credit or honors the draft or demand in violation of its obligations under Section 5-110, the applicant may recover damages resulting from the breach, including incidental but not consequential damages together with interest and attorney's fees specified in subsection (d) less any amount saved as a result of the breach.

(c) If a nominated person or adviser breaches its duty under this [Article], a person to whom the duty is owed may recover damages resulting from the breach, including incidental but not consequential damages, together with interest and attorney's fees specified in subsection (d), less any amount saved as a result of the breach.

(d) If an issuer, nominated person, or adviser is found liable under subsections (a), (b), [or] (c) [, or (e)], it shall pay interest on the amount owed from the date of wrongful dishonor, improper honor, or other appropriate date. Reasonable attorney's fees must be awarded to the prevailing party in an action in which a recovery is sought under this section.

(e) If an issuer wrongfully cancels or otherwise repudiates a letter of credit before presentment of a draft or other demand for payment under it, the beneficiary has an immediate right of action for wrongful dishonor if it cannot reasonably avoid procurement of the documents required under the letter of credit after it receives notice of the cancellation or repudiation. If it receives notice of the cancellation or repudiation in time to avoid procurement, the beneficiary may recover damages against the issuer that would be recovered by an obligee whose contract has been repudiated together with interest and attorneys' fees under subsection (d). The beneficiary may not recover a greater amount for cancellation or repudiation of a letter of credit than it could recover for wrongful dishonor of the letter of credit under subsection (a).

(f) Damages that would otherwise be payable by a party for violation of this [Article], may be liquidated by agreement of the relevant parties, but only in an amount or by a formula that is reasonable in light of the then anticipated harm caused by the default or other act or omission.

SECTION 5-112. TRANSFER OF LETTER OF CREDIT.

(a) Except as otherwise provided in Section 5-113, unless a letter of credit is designated as transferable, the right of a beneficiary to draw on or demand payment under a letter of credit may not be transferred.

(b) Even if a letter of credit is designated as transferable, the issuer or nominated person may refuse to recognize or effect a transfer if

    (1) the transfer would violate applicable law, or

    (2) the transferor or transferee has failed to comply with any procedure stated in the letter of credit or any reasonable procedure the issuer or nominated person has otherwise

SECTION 5-113. SUCCESSOR OF THE BENEFICIARY.

(a) A successor of a beneficiary may prepare documents under a letter of credit which would otherwise be prepared by the beneficiary. Upon its presentment of those and other necessary documents, the successor has the same right to honor as if the beneficiary had made presentment of its own documents.

(b) Upon request of a person to whom presentment is made, a successor shall promptly present documents that establish its status as a successor. The request must be made before the expiration of the time specified in Section 5-109(a). If no documents apparently establishing the successor's status are presented within seven banking days after the day of the beneficiary's or presenter's receipt of the request, the person to whom presentment was made may dishonor. The time for honor is extended two banking days beyond the earlier of (i) the day of receipt by the person to whom presentment is made of documents apparently establishing the status of successor, or (ii) the end of seven banking days after the beneficiary's or presenter's receipt of the request. The person to whom presentment is made may honor in reliance upon a document appearing on its face reasonably to establish a successor's status as a successor.

SECTION 5-114. ASSIGNMENT OF PROCEEDS.

(a) Notwithstanding a term in a letter of credit that purports to prohibit assignment, a beneficiary may assign its right to proceeds under a letter of credit. Subject to subsection (b), and upon appropriate presentment by or on behalf of a beneficiary, the assignee has a right to the proceeds assigned.

(b) An issuer or nominated person may honor drafts or demands for payment from the beneficiary drawn under a letter of credit until it receives notification of assignment that complies with its reasonable procedures and contains a request to pay an assignee. The issuer or nominated person may refuse to recognize an assignment of proceeds unless the assignor and assignee have complied with any reasonable procedures that the issuer or nominated person has made known to the assignee. Notification that does not identify the particular letter of credit from which the rights assigned arise is not effective. If requested by the issuer or nominated person, an assignee shall furnish reasonable proof that an assignment has been made and of the terms of the assignment. Until the assignee provides the proof and otherwise complies with reasonable procedures of the issuer or nominated person, the issuer or nominated person may honor conflicting presentments of the original beneficiary or of other assignees. In case of multiple conflicting assignments, the issuer or nominated person may pay in the order of compliance with its reasonable procedures, irrespective of the time of the assignments, time of perfection, or of the relative priority of the various assignees under [Article] 9 or other law.

SECTION 5-115. STATUTE OF LIMITATIONS.

An action to enforce an obligation, duty, or right arising under this [Article] must be commenced within one year after the expiration date of the relevant letter of credit or one year after the [claim for relief] accrues, whichever occurs later. The [claim for relief] accrues when the breach occurs, regardless of the aggrieved party's lack of knowledge of the breach.

SECTION 5-116. CHOICE OF LAW.

(a) The liability of an issuer, nominated person, or adviser for action or omission is governed by the law of the place where the issuer, nominated person or adviser is located.

(b)The liability of an applicant, beneficiary, or presenter for action or omission is governed by the law of the place of performance.

Alternative (b). The liability of an applicant, beneficiary, or presenter for action or omission is governed by the law of the place where applicant, beneficiary, or presenter is located.

Alternative (b) The liability of a beneficiary or presenter for action or omission is governed by the law of the place where the beneficiary or presenter is located if it is located in the United States.

Alternative (b) [omit subsection].

(c) By a term in a letter of credit, confirmation, advice, or by agreement the parties may specify the law of the jurisdiction that governs, whether or not that jurisdiction bears any relationship to the transaction. Unless the parties otherwise agree, an issuer, nominated person, or adviser is considered to be located at the address stated in connection with its name on the letter of credit, confirmation, or advice. If no address is stated in connection with a party's name, the party is considered to be located at the place otherwise indicated in the letter of credit, confirmation, or advice, or, if none is indicated, at the place of its performance.

(d) Except as otherwise provided in subsection (c), in the case of action or omission by or at a branch or separate office of a bank, the bank is considered to be located at the place where the branch or separate office is located.

(e) If there is conflict between this [Article] and [Articles] 2 through 9, this [Article] governs.